FRANCIS PARKMAN

FRANCIS PARKMAN

FRANCE AND ENGLAND IN NORTH AMERICA

VOLUME I

Pioneers of France in the New World
The Jesuits in North America in the Seventeenth Century
La Salle and the Discovery of the Great West
The Old Régime in Canada

THE LIBRARY OF AMERICA

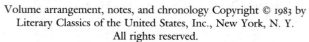

Distributed to the trade by the Viking Press.

Library of Congress Catalog Card Number: 82-18658
For Cataloging in Publication Data, see end of *Notes* section.
ISBN: 0-940450-10-0

First Printing

Manufactured in the United States of America

DAVID LEVIN
WROTE THE NOTES AND CHRONOLOGY
AND SELECTED THE TEXTS
FOR THIS VOLUME

Grateful acknowledgement is made to the National Endowment for the Humanities and the Ford Foundation for their generous financial support of this series.

Contents

PIONEERS OF FRANCE IN
THE
NEW WORLD

MENENDEZ

Prefatory Note
TO THE TWENTY-FIFTH EDITION

SINCE this book first appeared some new documentary evidence touching it has been brought to light, and, during a recent visit to Florida, I have acquired a more exact knowledge of the localities connected with the French occupation of that region. This added information is incorporated in the present edition, which has also received some literary revision.

BOSTON, *September 16, 1885*

Contents

CHAMPLAIN AND HIS ASSOCIATES

CHAPTER XVII   1632–1635
DEATH OF CHAMPLAIN

Introduction

THE springs of American civilization, unlike those of the elder world, lie revealed in the clear light of History. In appearance they are feeble; in reality, copious and full of force. Acting at the sources of life, instruments otherwise weak become mighty for good and evil, and men, lost elsewhere in the crowd, stand forth as agents of Destiny. In their toils, their sufferings, their conflicts, momentous questions were at stake, and issues vital to the future world,—the prevalence of races, the triumph of principles, health or disease, a blessing or a curse. On the obscure strife where men died by tens or by scores hung questions of as deep import for posterity as on those mighty contests of national adolescence where carnage is reckoned by thousands.

The subject to which the proposed series will be devoted is that of "France in the New World,"—the attempt of Feudalism, Monarchy, and Rome to master a continent where, at this hour, half a million of bayonets are vindicating the ascendency of a regulated freedom;—Feudalism still strong in life, though enveloped and overborne by new-born Centralization; Monarchy in the flush of triumphant power; Rome, nerved by disaster, springing with renewed vitality from ashes and corruption, and ranging the earth to reconquer abroad what she had lost at home. These banded powers, pushing into the wilderness their indomitable soldiers and devoted priests, unveiled the secrets of the barbarous continent, pierced the forests, traced and mapped out the streams, planted their emblems, built their forts, and claimed all as their own. New France was all head. Under king, noble, and Jesuit, the lank, lean body would not thrive. Even commerce wore the sword, decked itself with badges of nobility, aspired to forest seigniories and hordes of savage retainers.

Along the borders of the sea an adverse power was strengthening and widening, with slow but steadfast growth, full of blood and muscle,—a body without a head. Each had its strength, each its weakness, each its own modes of vigorous life: but the one was fruitful, the other barren; the one instinct with hope, the other darkening with shadows of despair.

By name, local position, and character, one of these communities of freemen stands forth as the most conspicuous representative of this antagonism;—Liberty and Absolutism, New England and New France. The one was the offspring of a triumphant government; the other, of an oppressed and fugitive people: the one, an unflinching champion of the Roman Catholic reaction; the other, a vanguard of the Reform. Each followed its natural laws of growth, and each came to its natural result. Vitalized by the principles of its foundation, the Puritan commonwealth grew apace. New England was pre-eminently the land of material progress. Here the prize was within every man's reach; patient industry need never doubt its reward; nay, in defiance of the four Gospels, assiduity in pursuit of gain was promoted to the rank of a duty, and thrift and godliness were linked in equivocal wedlock. Politically she was free; socially she suffered from that subtile and searching oppression which the dominant opinion of a free community may exercise over the members who compose it. As a whole, she grew upon the gaze of the world, a signal example of expansive energy; but she has not been fruitful in those salient and striking forms of character which often give a dramatic life to the annals of nations far less prosperous.

We turn to New France, and all is reversed. Here was a bold attempt to crush under the exactions of a grasping hierarchy, to stifle under the curbs and trappings of a feudal monarchy, a people compassed by influences of the wildest freedom,—whose schools were the forest and the sea, whose trade was an armed barter with savages, and whose daily life a lesson of lawless independence. But this fierce spirit had its vent. The story of New France is from the first a story of war: of war—for so her founders believed—with the adversary of mankind himself; war with savage tribes and potent forest commonwealths; war with the encroaching powers of Heresy and of England. Her brave, unthinking people were stamped with the soldier's virtues and the soldier's faults; and in their leaders were displayed, on a grand and novel stage, the energies, aspirations, and passions which belong to hopes vast and vague, ill-restricted powers, and stations of command.

The growth of New England was a result of the aggregate efforts of a busy multitude, each in his narrow circle toiling for himself, to gather competence or wealth. The expansion of New France was the achievement of a gigantic ambition striving to grasp a continent. It was a vain attempt. Long and valiantly her chiefs upheld their cause, leading to battle a vassal population, warlike as themselves. Borne down by numbers from without, wasted by corruption from within, New France fell at last; and out of her fall grew revolutions whose influence to this hour is felt through every nation of the civilized world.

The French dominion is a memory of the past; and when we evoke its departed shades, they rise upon us from their graves in strange, romantic guise. Again their ghostly camp-fires seem to burn, and the fitful light is cast around on lord and vassal and black-robed priest, mingled with wild forms of savage warriors, knit in close fellowship on the same stern errand. A boundless vision grows upon us; an untamed continent; vast wastes of forest verdure; mountains silent in primeval sleep; river, lake, and glimmering pool; wilderness oceans mingling with the sky. Such was the domain which France conquered for Civilization. Plumed helmets gleamed in the shade of its forests, priestly vestments in its dens and fastnesses of ancient barbarism. Men steeped in antique learning, pale with the close breath of the cloister, here spent the noon and evening of their lives, ruled savage hordes with a mild, parental sway, and stood serene before the direst shapes of death. Men of courtly nurture, heirs to the polish of a far-reaching ancestry, here, with their dauntless hardihood, put to shame the boldest sons of toil.

This memorable but half-forgotten chapter in the book of human life can be rightly read only by lights numerous and widely scattered. The earlier period of New France was prolific in a class of publications which are often of much historic value, but of which many are exceedingly rare. The writer, however, has at length gained access to them all. Of the unpublished records of the colonies, the archives of France are of course the grand deposit; but many documents of important bearing on the subject are to be found scattered in public and private libraries, chiefly in France and Canada. The task of collection has proved abundantly irksome and laborious. It has, however, been greatly lightened by the action of the governments of New York, Massachusetts, and Canada, in collecting from Europe copies of documents having more or less relation to their own history. It has been greatly lightened, too, by a most kind co-operation, for which the writer owes obligations too many for recognition at present, but of which he trusts to make fitting acknowledgment hereafter. Yet he cannot forbear to mention the name of Mr. John Gilmary Shea of New York, to whose labors this department of American history has been so deeply indebted, and that of the Hon. Henry Black of Quebec. Nor can he refrain from expressing his obligation to the skilful and friendly criticism of Mr. Charles Folsom.

In this, and still more must it be the case in succeeding volumes, the amount of reading applied to their composition is far greater than the citations represent, much of it being of a collateral and illustrative nature. This was essential to a plan whose aim it was, while scrupulously and rigorously adhering to the truth of facts, to animate them with the life of the past, and, so far as might be, clothe the skeleton with flesh. If, at times it may seem that range has been allowed to fancy, it is so in appearance only; since the minutest details of narrative or description rest on authentic documents or on personal observation.

Faithfulness to the truth of history involves far more than a research, however patient and scrupulous, into special facts. Such facts may be detailed with the most minute exactness, and yet the narrative, taken as a whole, may be unmeaning or untrue. The narrator must seek to imbue himself with the life and spirit of the time. He must study events in their bearings near and remote; in the character, habits, and manners of those who took part in them. He must himself be, as it were, a sharer or a spectator of the action he describes.

With respect to that special research which, if inadequate, is still in the most emphatic sense indispensable, it has been the writer's aim to exhaust the existing material of every subject treated. While it would be folly to claim success in such an attempt, he has reason to hope that, so far at least as relates to the present volume, nothing of much importance has escaped him. With respect to the general preparation just alluded to, he has long been too fond of his theme to neglect any means within his reach of making his conception of it distinct and true.

To those who have aided him with information and documents, the extreme slowness in the progress of the work will naturally have caused surprise. This slowness was unavoidable. During the past eighteen years, the state of his health has exacted throughout an extreme caution in regard to mental application, reducing it at best within narrow and precarious limits, and often precluding it. Indeed, for two periods, each of several years, any attempt at bookish occupation would have been merely suicidal. A condition of sight arising from kindred sources has also retarded the work, since it has never permitted reading or writing continuously for much more than five minutes, and often has not permitted them at all. A previous work, "The Conspiracy of Pontiac," was written in similar circumstances.

The writer means, if possible, to carry the present design to its completion. Such a completion, however, will by no means be essential as regards the individual volumes of the series, since each will form a separate and independent work. The present volume, it will be seen, contains two distinct and completed narratives. Some progress has been made in others.

BOSTON, *January 1, 1865.*

HUGUENOTS IN FLORIDA
with a
Sketch of Huguenot Colonization in Brazil

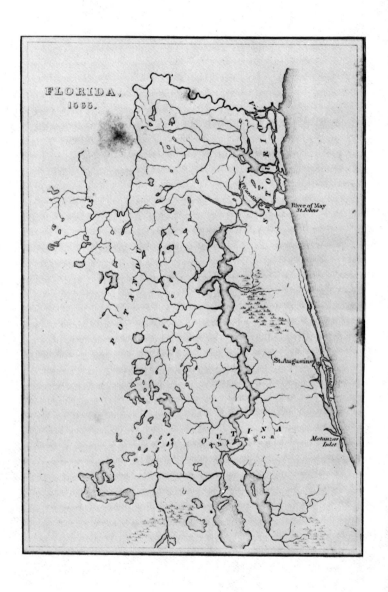

FLORIDA,
1565.

VICTORIA

S. JOHN'S RIVER

River of May
St.Johns

POTAVOU

St.Augustine

OUTINA

Matanzas
Inlet

Huguenots in Florida

THE story of New France opens with a tragedy. The political and religious enmities which were soon to bathe Europe in blood broke out with an intense and concentred fury in the distant wilds of Florida. It was under equivocal auspices that Coligny and his partisans essayed to build up a Calvinist France in America, and the attempt was met by all the forces of national rivalry, personal interest, and religious hate.

This striking passage of our early history is remarkable for the fulness and precision of the authorities that illustrate it. The incidents of the Huguenot occupation of Florida are recorded by eight eyewitnesses. Their evidence is marked by an unusual accord in respect to essential facts, as well as by a minuteness of statement which vividly pictures the events described. The following are the principal authorities consulted for the main body of the narrative.

Ribauld, *The Whole and True Discoverie of Terra Florida*. This is Captain Jean Ribaut's account of his voyage to Florida in 1562. It was "prynted at London," "newly set forthe in Englishe," in 1563, and reprinted by Hakluyt in 1582 in his black-letter tract entitled *Divers Voyages*. It is not known to exist in the original French.

L'Histoire Notable de la Floride, mise en lumière par M. Basanier (Paris, 1586). The most valuable portion of this work consists of the letters of René de Laudonnière, the French commandant in Florida in 1564–65. They are interesting, and, with necessary allowance for the position and prejudices of the writer, trustworthy.

Challeux, *Discours de l'Histoire de la Floride* (Dieppe, 1566). Challeux was a carpenter, who went to Florida in 1565. He was above sixty years of age, a zealous Huguenot, and a philosopher in his way. His story is affecting from its simplicity. Various editions of it appeared under various titles.

Le Moyne, *Brevis Narratio eorum quæ in Florida Americæ Provincia Gallis acciderunt*. Le Moyne was Laudonnière's artist. His narrative forms the Second Part of the *Grands Voyages* of De Bry (Frankfort, 1591). It is illustrated by numerous drawings made by the writer from memory, and accompanied with descriptive letterpress.

Coppie d'une Lettre venant de la Floride (Paris, 1565). This is a letter from one of the adventurers under Laudonnière. It is reprinted in the *Recueil de Pièces sur la Floride* of Ternaux-Compans. Ternaux also prints in the same volume a narrative called *Histoire mémorable du dernier Voyage faict par le Capitaine Jean Ribaut*. It is of no original value, being compiled from Laudonnière and Challeux.

Une Requête au Roy, faite en forme de Complainte (1566). This is a petition for redress to Charles the Ninth from the relatives of the French massacred in Florida by the Spaniards. It recounts many incidents of that tragedy.

La Reprinse de la Floride par le Cappitaine Gourgue. This is a manuscript in the Bibliothèque Nationale, printed in the *Recueil* of Ternaux-Compans. It contains a detailed account of the remarkable expedition of Dominique de Gourgues against the Spaniards in Florida in 1567–68.

Charlevoix, in his *Histoire de la Nouvelle France*, speaks of another narrative of this expedition in manuscript, preserved in the Gourgues family. A copy of it, made in 1831 by the Vicomte de Gourgues, has been placed at the writer's disposal.

Popelinière, De Thou, Wytfleit, D'Aubigné, De Laet, Brantôme, Lescarbot, Champlain, and other writers of the sixteenth and seventeenth centuries, have told or touched upon the story of the Huguenots in Florida; but they all draw their information from one or more of the sources named above.

Lettres et Papiers d' Estat du Sieur de Forquevaulx (Bibliothèque Nationale). These include the correspondence of the French and Spanish courts concerning the massacre of the Huguenots. They are printed by Gaffarel in his *Histoire de la Floride Française*.

The Spanish authorities are the following:—

Barcia, (Cardenas y Cano,) *Ensayo Cronologico para la Historia General de la Florida* (Madrid, 1723). This annalist had access to original documents of great interest. Some of them are used as material for his narrative, others are copied entire. Of these, the most remarkable is that of Solís de las Meras, *Memorial de todas las Jornadas de la Conquista de la Florida*.

Francisco Lopez de Mendoza Grajales, *Relacion de la Jornada de Pedro Menendez de Aviles en la Florida* (*Documentos Inéditos del Archivo de Indias*, III. 441). A French translation of this journal will be found in the *Recueil de Pièces sur la Floride* of Ternaux-Compans. Mendoza was chaplain of the expedition commanded by Menendez de Avilés, and, like Solís, he was an eyewitness of the events which he relates.

Pedro Menendez de Avilés, *Siete Cartas escritas al Rey, Años de 1565 y 1566*, MSS. These are the despatches of the Adelantado Menendez to Philip the Second. They were procured for the writer, together with other documents, from the archives of Seville, and their contents are now for the first time made public. They consist of seventy-two closely written foolscap pages, and are of the highest interest and value as regards the present subject, confirming and amplifying the statements of Solís and Mendoza, and giving new and curious information with respect to the designs of Spain upon the continent of North America.

It is unnecessary to specify the authorities for the introductory and subordinate portions of the narrative.

The writer is indebted to Mr. Buckingham Smith, for procuring copies of documents from the archives of Spain; to Mr. Bancroft, the historian of the United States, for the use of the Vicomte de Gourgues's copy of the journal describing the expedition of his ancestor against the Spaniards; and to Mr. Charles Russell Lowell, of the Boston Athenæum, and Mr. John Langdon Sibley, Librarian of Harvard College, for obliging aid in consulting books and papers.

The portrait at the beginning of this volume is a fac-simile from an old Spanish engraving, of undoubted authenticity. This also was obtained through the kindness of Mr. Buckingham Smith.

Chapter I

EARLY SPANISH ADVENTURE

Spanish Voyagers • Romance and Avarice • Ponce de Leon • The Fountain of Youth and the River Jordan • Florida discovered • Pamphilo de Narvaez • Hernando de Soto • His Career • His Death • Succeeding Voyagers • Spanish Claim to Florida • Spanish Jealousy of France

---

Towards the close of the fifteenth century, Spain achieved her final triumph over the infidels of Granada, and made her name glorious through all generations by the discovery of America. The religious zeal and romantic daring which a long course of Moorish wars had called forth were now exalted to redoubled fervor. Every ship from the New World came freighted with marvels which put the fictions of chivalry to shame; and to the Spaniard of that day America was a region of wonder and mystery, of vague and magnificent promise. Thither adventurers hastened, thirsting for glory and for gold, and often mingling the enthusiasm of the crusader and the valor of the knight-errant with the bigotry of inquisitors and the rapacity of pirates. They roamed over land and sea; they climbed unknown mountains, surveyed unknown oceans, pierced the sultry intricacies of tropical forests; while from year to year and from day to day new wonders were unfolded, new islands and archipelagoes, new regions of gold and pearl, and barbaric empires of more than Oriental wealth. The extravagance of hope and the fever of adventure knew no bounds. Nor is it surprising that amid such waking marvels the imagination should run wild in romantic dreams; that between the possible and the impossible the line of distinction should be but faintly drawn, and that men should be found ready to stake life and honor in pursuit of the most insane fantasies.

Such a man was the veteran cavalier Juan Ponce de Leon. Greedy of honors and of riches, he embarked at Porto Rico with three brigantines, bent on schemes of discovery. But that which gave the chief stimulus to his enterprise was a story, current among the Indians of Cuba and Hispaniola, that on the island of Bimini, said to be one of the Bahamas, there was a fountain of such virtue, that, bathing in its waters, old men resumed their youth.[1] It was said, moreover, that on a neighboring shore might be found a river gifted with the same beneficent property, and believed by some to be no other than the Jordan.[2] Ponce de Leon found the island of Bimini, but not the fountain. Farther westward, in the latitude of thirty degrees and eight minutes, he approached an unknown land, which he named Florida, and, steering southward, explored its coast as far as the extreme point of the peninsula, when, after some farther explorations, he retraced his course to Porto Rico.

Ponce de Leon had not regained his youth, but his active spirit was unsubdued.

Nine years later he attempted to plant a colony in Florida; the Indians attacked him fiercely; he was mortally wounded, and died soon afterwards in Cuba.[3]

The voyages of Garay and Vasquez de Ayllon threw new light on the discoveries of Ponce, and the general outline of the coasts of Florida became known to the Spaniards.[4] Meanwhile, Cortés had conquered Mexico, and the fame of that iniquitous but magnificent exploit rang through all Spain. Many an impatient cavalier burned to achieve a kindred for-

---

[1] Herrera, *Hist. General*, Dec. I. Lib. IX. c. 11; De Laet, *Novus Orbis*, Lib. I. c. 16; Garcilaso, *Hist. de la Florida*, Part I. Lib. I. c. 3; Gomara, *Hist. Gen. des Indes Occidentales*, Lib. II. c. 10. Compare Peter Martyr, *De Rebus Oceanicis*, Dec. VII. c. 7, who says that the fountain was in Florida

The story has an explanation sufficiently characteristic, having been suggested, it is said, by the beauty of the native women, which none could resist, and which kindled the fires of youth in the veins of age.

The terms of Ponce de Leon's bargain with the King are set forth in the MS. *Capitulacion con Juan Ponce sobre Biminy*. He was to have exclusive right to the island, settle it at his own cost, and be called Adelantado of Bimini; but the King was to build and hold forts there, send agents to divide the Indians among the settlers, and receive first a tenth, afterwards a fifth, of the gold.

[2] Fontanedo in Ternaux-Compans, *Recueil sur la Floride*, 18, 19, 42. Compare Herrera, Dec. I. Lib. IX. c. 12. In allusion to this belief, the name Jordan was given eight years afterwards by Ayllon to a river of South Carolina.

[3] Hakluyt, *Voyages*, V. 333; Barcia, *Ensayo Cronologico*, 5.

[4] Peter Martyr in Hakluyt, V. 333; De Laet, Lib. IV. c. 2.

tune. To the excited fancy of the Spaniards the unknown land of Florida seemed the seat of surpassing wealth, and Pamphilo de Narvaez essayed to possess himself of its fancied treasures. Landing on its shores, and proclaiming destruction to the Indians unless they acknowledged the sovereignty of the Pope and the Emperor,[1] he advanced into the forests with three hundred men. Nothing could exceed their sufferings. Nowhere could they find the gold they came to seek. The village of Appalache, where they hoped to gain a rich booty, offered nothing but a few mean wigwams. The horses gave out, and the famished soldiers fed upon their flesh. The men sickened, and the Indians unceasingly harassed their march. At length, after two hundred and eighty leagues[2] of wandering, they found themselves on the northern shore of the Gulf of Mexico, and desperately put to sea in such crazy boats as their skill and means could construct. Cold, disease, famine, thirst, and the fury of the waves, melted them away. Narvaez himself perished, and of his wretched followers no more than four escaped, reaching by land, after years of vicissitude, the Christian settlements of New Spain.[3]

The interior of the vast country then comprehended under the name of Florida still remained unexplored. The Spanish voyager, as his caravel ploughed the adjacent seas, might give full scope to his imagination, and dream that beyond the long, low margin of forest which bounded his horizon lay hid a rich harvest for some future conqueror; perhaps a second Mexico with its royal palace and sacred pyramids, or another Cuzco with its temple of the Sun, encircled with a frieze of

[1] *Sommation aux Habitants de la Floride*, in Ternaux-Compans, I.

[2] Their own exaggerated reckoning. The journey was probably from Tampa Bay to the Appalachicola, by a circuitous route.

[3] Narrative of Alvar Nuñez Cabeça de Vaca, second in command to Narvaez, translated by Buckingham Smith. Cabeça de Vaca was one of the four who escaped, and, after living for years among the tribes of Mississippi, crossed the river Mississippi near Memphis, journeyed westward by the waters of the Arkansas and Red River to New Mexico and Chihuahua, thence to Cinaloa on the Gulf of California, and thence to Mexico. The narrative is one of the most remarkable of the early relations. See also Ramusio, III. 310, and Purchas, IV. 1499, where a portion of Cabeça de Vaca is given. Also, Garcilaso, Part I. Lib. I. c. 3; Gomara, Lib. II. c. 11; De Laet, Lib. IV. c. 3; Barcia, *Ensayo Cronologico*, 19.

gold. Haunted by such visions, the ocean chivalry of Spain could not long stand idle.

Hernando de Soto was the companion of Pizarro in the conquest of Peru. He had come to America a needy adventurer, with no other fortune than his sword and target. But his exploits had given him fame and fortune, and he appeared at court with the retinue of a nobleman.[1] Still, his active energies could not endure repose, and his avarice and ambition goaded him to fresh enterprises. He asked and obtained permission to conquer Florida. While this design was in agitation, Cabeça de Vaca, one of those who had survived the expedition of Narvaez, appeared in Spain, and for purposes of his own spread abroad the mischievous falsehood, that Florida was the richest country yet discovered.[2] De Soto's plans were embraced with enthusiasm. Nobles and gentlemen contended for the privilege of joining his standard; and, setting sail with an ample armament, he landed at the Bay of Espiritu Santo, now Tampa Bay, in Florida, with six hundred and twenty chosen men,[3] a band as gallant and well appointed, as eager in purpose and audacious in hope, as ever trod the shores of the New World. The clangor of trumpets, the neighing of horses, the fluttering of pennons, the glittering of helmet and lance, startled the ancient forest with unwonted greeting. Amid this pomp of chivalry, religion was not forgotten. The sacred vessels and vestments with bread and wine for the Eucharist were carefully provided; and De Soto himself declared that the enterprise was undertaken for God alone, and seemed to be the object of His especial care.[4] These devout marauders could not neglect the spiritual welfare of the Indians whom they had come to plunder; and besides fetters to bind, and bloodhounds to hunt them, they brought priests and monks for the saving of their souls.

The adventurers began their march. Their story has been

[1] *Relation of the Portuguese Gentleman of Elvas*, c. 1. See *Descobrimiente da Florida*, c. 1, and Hakluyt, V. 483.

[2] *Relation of the Gentleman of Elvas*, c. 2.

[3] *Relation of Biedma*, in Ternaux-Compans, 51. The Gentleman of Elvas says in round numbers six hundred. Garcilaso de la Vega, who is unworthy of credit, makes the number much greater.

[4] Letter from De Soto to the Municipality of Santiago, dated at the Harbor of Espiritu Santo, 9 July, 1539. See Ternaux-Compans, *Floride*, 43.

often told. For month after month and year after year, the procession of priests and cavaliers, crossbowmen, arquebus-iers, and Indian captives laden with the baggage, still wan-dered on through wild and boundless wastes, lured hither and thither by the *ignis-fatuus* of their hopes. They traversed great portions of Georgia, Alabama, and Mississippi, everywhere inflicting and enduring misery, but never approaching their phantom El Dorado. At length, in the third year of their jour-neying, they reached the banks of the Mississippi, a hundred and thirty-two years before its second discovery by Mar-quette. One of their number describes the great river as al-most half a league wide, deep, rapid, and constantly rolling down trees and drift-wood on its turbid current.[1]

The Spaniards crossed over at a point above the mouth of the Arkansas. They advanced westward, but found no trea-sures,—nothing indeed but hardships, and an Indian enemy, furious, writes one of their officers, "as mad dogs."[2] They heard of a country towards the north where maize could not be cultivated because the vast herds of wild cattle devoured it.[3] They penetrated so far that they entered the range of the roving prairie tribes; for, one day, as they pushed their way with difficulty across great plains covered with tall, rank grass, they met a band of savages who dwelt in lodges of skins sewed together, subsisting on game alone, and wandering perpetually from place to place.[4] Finding neither gold nor the South Sea, for both of which they had hoped, they returned to the banks of the Mississippi.

De Soto, says one of those who accompanied him, was a "stern man, and of few words." Even in the midst of reverses, his will had been law to his followers, and he had sustained himself through the depths of disappointment with the en-ergy of a stubborn pride. But his hour was come. He fell into deep dejection, followed by an attack of fever, and soon after

---

[1] *Portuguese Relation*, c. 22.

[2] Biedma, 95.

[3] *Portuguese Relation*, c. 24. A still earlier mention of the bison occurs in the journal of Cabeça de Vaca. Thevet, in his *Singularités*, 1558, gives a picture intended to represent a bison-bull. Coronado saw this animal in 1540, but was not, as some assert, its first discoverer.

[4] Biedma, 91.

died miserably. To preserve his body from the Indians, his followers sank it at midnight in the river, and the sullen waters of the Mississippi buried his ambition and his hopes.[1]

The adventurers were now, with few exceptions, disgusted with the enterprise, and longed only to escape from the scene of their miseries. After a vain attempt to reach Mexico by land, they again turned back to the Mississippi, and labored, with all the resources which their desperate necessity could suggest, to construct vessels in which they might make their way to some Christian settlement. Their condition was most forlorn. Few of their horses remained alive; their baggage had been destroyed at the burning of the Indian town of Mavila, and many of the soldiers were without armor and without weapons. In place of the gallant array which, more than three years before, had left the harbor of Espiritu Santo, a company of sickly and starving men were laboring among the swampy forests of the Mississippi, some clad in skins, and some in mats woven from a kind of wild vine.[2]

Seven brigantines were finished and launched; and, trusting their lives on board these frail vessels, they descended the Mississippi, running the gantlet between hostile tribes, who fiercely attacked them. Reaching the Gulf, though not without the loss of eleven of their number, they made sail for the Spanish settlement on the River Panuco, where they arrived safely, and where the inhabitants met them with a cordial welcome. Three hundred and eleven men thus escaped with life, leaving behind them the bones of their comrades strewn broadcast through the wilderness.[3]

De Soto's fate proved an insufficient warning, for those were still found who begged a fresh commission for the conquest of Florida; but the Emperor would not hear them. A more pacific enterprise was undertaken by Cancello, a Dominican monk, who with several brother ecclesiastics undertook to convert the natives to the true faith, but was murdered in the attempt.[4] Nine years later, a plan was formed

[1] *Portuguese Relation*, c. 30.

[2] *Portuguese Relation*, c. 20. See Hakluyt, V. 515.

[3] I have followed the accounts of Biedma and the Portuguese of Elvas, rejecting the romantic narrative of Garcilaso, in which fiction is hopelessly mingled with truth.

[4] *Relation of Beteta*, Ternaux-Compans, 107; *Documentos Inéditos*, XXVI. 340. Comp. Garcilaso, Part I. Lib. I. c. 3.

for the colonization of Florida, and Guido de las Bazares sailed to explore the coasts, and find a spot suitable for the establishment.[1] After his return, a squadron, commanded by Angel de Villafañe, and freighted with supplies and men, put to sea from San Juan d'Ulloa; but the elements were adverse, and the result was a total failure.[2] Not a Spaniard had yet gained foothold in Florida.

That name, as the Spaniards of that day understood it, comprehended the whole country extending from the Atlantic on the east to the longitude of New Mexico on the west, and from the Gulf of Mexico and the River of Palms indefinitely northward towards the polar sea.[3] This vast territory was claimed by Spain in right of the discoveries of Columbus, the grant of the Pope, and the various expeditions mentioned above. England claimed it in right of the discoveries of Cabot; while France could advance no better title than might be derived from the voyage of Verazzano and vague traditions of earlier visits of Breton adventurers.

[1] The spirit of this and other Spanish enterprises may be gathered from the following passage in an address to the King, signed by Dr. Pedro de Santander, and dated 15 July, 1557: —

"It is lawful that your Majesty, like a good shepherd, appointed by the hand of the Eternal Father, should tend and lead out your sheep, since the Holy Spirit has shown spreading pastures whereon are feeding lost sheep which have been snatched away by the dragon, the Demon. These pastures are the New World, wherein is comprised Florida, now in possession of the Demon, and here he makes himself adored and revered. This is the Land of Promise, possessed by idolaters, the Amorite, Amalekite, Moabite, Canaanite. This is the land promised by the Eternal Father to the faithful, since we are commanded by God in the Holy Scriptures to take it from them, being idolaters, and, by reason of their idolatry and sin, to put them all to the knife, leaving no living thing save maidens and children, their cities robbed and sacked, their walls and houses levelled to the earth."

The writer then goes into detail, proposing to occupy Florida at various points with from one thousand to fifteen hundred colonists, found a city to be called Philippina, also another at Tuscaloosa, to be called Cæsarea, another at Tallahassee, and another at Tampa Bay, where he thinks many slaves could be had. *Carta del Doctor Pedro de Santander.*

[2] The papers relating to these abortive expeditions are preserved by Ternaux-Compans.

[3] Garcilaso, Part I. Lib. I. c. 2; Herrera in Purchas, III. 868; De Laet, Lib. IV. c. 13. Barcia, *Ensayo Cronologico*, An. MDCXI., speaks of Quebec as a part of Florida. In a map of the time of Henry II. of France, all North America is named Terra Florida.

With restless jealousy Spain watched the domain which she could not occupy, and on France especially she kept an eye of deep distrust. When, in 1541, Cartier and Roberval essayed to plant a colony in the part of ancient Spanish Florida now called Canada, she sent spies and fitted out caravels to watch that abortive enterprise.[1] Her fears proved just. Canada, indeed, was long to remain a solitude; but, despite the Papal bounty gifting Spain with exclusive ownership of a hemisphere, France and Heresy at length took root in the sultry forests of modern Florida.

[1] See various papers on this subject in the *Coleccion de Varios Documentos* of Buckingham Smith.

Chapter II

VILLEGAGNON

*Spain and France in the Sixteenth Century • Gaspar de Coligny •
Villegagnon • His Early Exploits • His Scheme of a Protestant
Colony • Huguenots at Rio Janeiro • Polemics • Tyranny of
Villegagnon • The Ministers expelled • The Colony ruined*

In the middle of the sixteenth century, Spain was the incubus of Europe. Gloomy and portentous, she chilled the world with her baneful shadow. Her old feudal liberties were gone, absorbed in the despotism of Madrid. A tyranny of monks and inquisitors, with their swarms of spies and informers, their racks, their dungeons, and their fagots, crushed all freedom of thought or speech; and, while the Dominican held his reign of terror and force, the deeper Jesuit guided the mind from infancy into those narrow depths of bigotry from which it was never to escape. Commercial despotism was joined to political and religious despotism. The hands of the government were on every branch of industry. Perverse regulations, uncertain and ruinous taxes, monopolies, encouragements, prohibitions, restrictions, cramped the national energy. Mistress of the Indies, Spain swarmed with beggars. Yet, verging to decay, she had an ominous and appalling strength. Her condition was that of an athletic man penetrated with disease, which had not yet unstrung the thews and sinews formed in his days of vigor. Philip the Second could command the service of warriors and statesmen developed in the years that were past. The gathered energies of ruined feudalism were wielded by a single hand. The mysterious King, in his den in the Escorial, dreary and silent, and bent like a scribe over his papers, was the type and the champion of arbitrary power. More than the Pope himself, he was the head of Catholicity. In doctrine and in deed, the inexorable bigotry of Madrid was ever in advance of Rome.

Not so with France. She was full of life,—a discordant and struggling vitality. Her monks and priests, unlike those of Spain, were rarely either fanatics or bigots; yet not the less did they ply the rack and the fagot, and howl for heretic blood. Their all was at stake: their vast power, their bloated wealth, were wrapped up in the ancient faith. Men were burned, and women buried alive. All was in vain. To the utmost bounds of France, the leaven of the Reform was working. The Huguenots, fugitives from torture and death, found an asylum at Geneva, their city of refuge, gathering around Calvin, their great high-priest. Thence intrepid colporteurs, their lives in their hands, bore the Bible and the psalm-book to city, hamlet, and castle, to feed the rising flame. The scattered churches, pressed by a common danger, began to organize. An ecclesiastical republic spread its ramifications through France, and grew underground to a vigorous life,— pacific at the outset, for the great body of its members were the quiet *bourgeoisie*, by habit, as by faith, averse to violence. Yet a potent fraction of the warlike *noblesse* were also of the new faith; and above them all, pre-eminent in character as in station, stood Gaspar de Coligny, Admiral of France.

The old palace of the Louvre, reared by the "Roi Chevalier" on the site of those dreary feudal towers which of old had guarded the banks of the Seine, held within its sculptured masonry the worthless brood of Valois. Corruption and intrigue ran riot at the court. Factious nobles, bishops, and cardinals, with no God but pleasure and ambition, contended around the throne or the sick-bed of the futile King. Catherine de Medicis, with her stately form, her mean spirit, her bad heart, and her fathomless depths of duplicity, strove by every subtle art to hold the balance of power among them. The bold, pitiless, insatiable Guise, and his brother the Cardinal of Lorraine, the incarnation of falsehood, rested their ambition on the Catholic party. Their army was a legion of priests, and the black swarms of countless monasteries, who by the distribution of alms held in pay the rabble of cities and starving peasants on the lands of impoverished nobles. Montmorency, Condé, and Navarre leaned towards the Reform,— doubtful and inconstant chiefs, whose faith weighed light against their interests. Yet, amid vacillation, selfishness, weakness, treachery, one great man was like a tower of trust, and this was Gaspar de Coligny.

Firm in his convictions, steeled by perils and endurance,

calm, sagacious, resolute, grave even to severity, a valiant and redoubted soldier, Coligny looked abroad on the gathering storm and read its danger in advance. He saw a strange depravity of manners; bribery and violence overriding justice; discontented nobles, and peasants ground down with taxes. In the midst of this rottenness, the Calvinistic churches, patient and stern, were fast gathering to themselves the better life of the nation. Among and around them tossed the surges of clerical hate. Luxurious priests and libertine monks saw their disorders rebuked by the grave virtues of the Protestant zealots. Their broad lands, their rich endowments, their vessels of silver and of gold, their dominion over souls,— in itself a revenue,—were all imperilled by the growing heresy. Nor was the Reform less exacting, less intolerant, or, when its hour came, less aggressive than the ancient faith. The storm was thickening, and it must burst soon.

When the Emperor Charles the Fifth beleaguered Algiers, his camps were deluged by a blinding tempest, and at its height the infidels made a furious sally. A hundred Knights of Malta, on foot, wearing over their armor surcoats of crimson blazoned with the white cross, bore the brunt of the assault. Conspicuous among them was Nicolas Durand de Villegagnon. A Moorish cavalier, rushing upon him, pierced his arm with a lance, and wheeled to repeat the blow; but the knight leaped on the infidel, stabbed him with his dagger, flung him from his horse, and mounted in his place. Again, a Moslem host landed in Malta and beset the *Cité Notable*. The garrison was weak, disheartened, and without a leader. Villegagnon with six followers, all friends of his own, passed under cover of night through the infidel leaguer, climbed the walls by ropes lowered from above, took command, repaired the shattered towers, aiding with his own hands in the work, and animated the garrison to a resistance so stubborn that the besiegers lost heart and betook themselves to their galleys. No less was he an able and accomplished mariner, prominent among that chivalry of the sea who held the perilous verge of Christendom against the Mussulman. He claimed other laurels than those of the sword. He was a scholar, a linguist, a controversialist, potent with the tongue and with the pen, commanding in presence, eloquent and persuasive in discourse. Yet this Crichton of France had proved himself an associate nowise desirable. His sleepless intellect was matched with a spirit as restless, vain, unstable, and ambitious, as it was enterprising and bold. Addicted to dissent, and enamored of polemics, he entered those forbidden fields of inquiry and controversy to which the Reform invited him. Undaunted by his monastic vows, he battled for heresy with tongue and pen, and in the ear of Protestants professed himself a Protestant. As a Commander of his Order, he quarrelled with the Grand Master, a domineering Spaniard; and, as Vice-Admiral of Brittany, he was deep in a feud with the Governor of Brest.[1] Disgusted at home, his fancy crossed the seas. He aspired to build for France and himself an empire amid the tropical splendors of Brazil. Few could match him in the gift of persuasion; and the intrepid seaman whose skill and valor had run the gantlet of the English fleet, and borne Mary Stuart of Scotland in safety to her espousals with the Dauphin,[2] might well be intrusted with a charge of moment so far inferior. Henry the Second was still on the throne. The lance of Montgomery had not yet rid France of that infliction. To win a share in the rich domain of the New World, of which Portuguese and Spanish arrogance claimed the monopoly, was the end held by Villegagnon before the eyes of the King. Of the Huguenots, he said not a word. For Coligny he had another language. He spoke of an asylum for persecuted religion, a Geneva in the wilderness, far from priests and monks and Francis of Guise. The Admiral gave him a ready ear; if, indeed, he himself had not first conceived the plan. Yet to the

[1] Villegagnon himself has left an account in Latin of the expedition against Algiers under the title, *Caroli V. Imperatoris Expeditio in Africam* (Paris, 1542). Also, an account of the war at Malta, *De Bello Melitensi* (Paris, 1553).

He is the subject of a long and erudite treatise in Bayle, *Dictionnaire Historique*. Notices of him are also to be found in Guérin, *Navigateurs Français*, 162; Ib., *Marins Illustres*, 231; Lescarbot, *Hist. de la Nouv. France* (1612), 146–217; La Popelinière, *Les Trois Mondes*, III. 2.

There are extant against him a number of Calvinistic satires, in prose and verse,— *L'Etrille de Nicolas Durand,*— *La Suffisance de Villegaignon,*— *L'Espousette des Armoiries de Villegaignon*, etc.

[2] This was in 1548. The English were on the watch, but Villegagnon, by a union of daring and skill, escaped them, and landed the future Queen of Scots, then six years old, in Brittany, whence she was carried to Paris, and affianced to the future Francis the Second.

King, an active burner of Huguenots, Coligny too urged it as an enterprise, not for the Faith, but for France. In secret, Geneva was made privy to it, and Calvin himself embraced it with zeal. The enterprise, in fact, had a double character, political as well as religious. It was the reply of France, the most emphatic she had yet made, to the Papal bull which gave all the western hemisphere to Portugal and Spain; and, as if to point her answer, she sent, not Frenchmen only, but Protestant Frenchmen, to plant the fleur-de-lis on the shores of the New World.

Two vessels were made ready, in the name of the King. The body of the emigration was Huguenot, mingled with young nobles, restless, idle, and poor, with reckless artisans, and piratical sailors from the Norman and Breton seaports. They put to sea from Havre on the twelfth of July, 1555, and early in November saw the shores of Brazil. Entering the harbor of Rio Janeiro, then called Ganabara, Villegagnon landed men and stores on an island, built huts, and threw up earthworks. In anticipation of future triumphs, the whole continent, by a strange perversion of language, was called Antarctic France, while the fort received the name of Coligny.

Villegagnon signalized his new-born Protestantism by an intolerable solicitude for the manners and morals of his followers. The whip and the pillory requited the least offence. The wild and discordant crew, starved and flogged for a season into submission, conspired at length to rid themselves of him; but while they debated whether to poison him, blow him up, or murder him and his officers in their sleep, three Scotch soldiers, probably Calvinists, revealed the plot, and the vigorous hand of the commandant crushed it in the bud.

But how was the colony to subsist? Their island was too small for culture, while the mainland was infested with hostile tribes, and threatened by the Portuguese, who regarded the French occupancy as a violation of their domain.

Meanwhile, in France, Huguenot influence, aided by ardent letters sent home by Villegagnon in the returning ships, was urging on the work. Nor were the Catholic chiefs averse to an enterprise which, by colonizing heresy, might tend to relieve France of its presence. Another embarkation was prepared, in the name of Henry the Second, under Bois-

Lecomte, a nephew of Villegagnon. Most of the emigrants were Huguenots. Geneva sent a large deputation, and among them several ministers, full of zeal for their land of promise and their new church in the wilderness. There were five young women, also, with a matron to watch over them. Soldiers, emigrants, and sailors, two hundred and ninety in all, were embarked in three vessels; and, to the sound of cannon, drums, fifes, and trumpets, they unfurled their sails at Honfleur. They were no sooner on the high seas than the piratical character of the Norman sailors, in no way exceptional at that day, began to declare itself. They hailed every vessel weaker than themselves, pretended to be short of provisions, and demanded leave to buy them; then, boarding the stranger, plundered her from stem to stern. After a passage of four months, on the ninth of March, 1557, they entered the port of Ganabara, and saw the fleur-de-lis floating above the walls of Fort Coligny. Amid salutes of cannon, the boats, crowded with sea-worn emigrants, moved towards the landing. It was an edifying scene when Villegagnon, in the picturesque attire which marked the warlike nobles of the period, came down to the shore to greet the sombre ministers of Calvin. With hands uplifted and eyes raised to heaven, he bade them welcome to the new asylum of the faithful; then launched into a long harangue full of zeal and unction.[1] His discourse finished, he led the way to the dining-hall. If the redundancy of spiritual ailment had surpassed their expectations, the ministers were little prepared for the meagre provision which

[1] De Léry, *Historia Navigationis in Brasiliam* (1586,) 43. De Léry was one of the ministers. His account is long and very curious. His work was published in French, in 1578 and 1611. The Latin version has appeared under several forms, and is to be found in the Second Part of De Bry, decorated with a profusion of engravings, including portraits of a great variety of devils, with which, it seems, Brazil was overrun, conspicuous among whom is one with the body of a bear and the head of a man. This ungainly fiend is also depicted in the edition of 1586. The conception, a novelty in demonology, was clearly derived from ancient representations of that singular product of Brazil, the sloth. In the curious work of André Thevet, *Les Singularités de la France Antarctique, autrement nommée Amérique*, published in 1558, appears the portraiture of this animal, the body being that "d'un petit ours," and the face that of an intelligent man. Thevet, however, though a firm believer in devils of all kinds, suspects nothing demoniacal in his sloth, which he held for some time in captivity, and describes as "une beste assez estrange."

awaited their temporal cravings; for, with appetites whetted by the sea, they found themselves seated at a board whereof, as one of them complains, the choicest dish was a dried fish, and the only beverage rain-water. They found their consolation in the inward graces of the commandant, whom they likened to the Apostle Paul.

For a time all was ardor and hope. Men of birth and station, and the ministers themselves, labored with pick and shovel to finish the fort. Every day exhortations, sermons, prayers, followed in close succession, and Villegagnon was always present, kneeling on a velvet cushion brought after him by a page. Soon, however, he fell into sharp controversy with the ministers upon points of faith. Among the emigrants was a student of the Sorbonne, one Cointac, between whom and the ministers arose a fierce and unintermitted war of words. Is it lawful to mix water with the wine of the Eucharist? May the sacramental bread be made of meal of Indian corn? These and similar points of dispute filled the fort with wranglings, begetting cliques, factions, and feuds without number. Villegagnon took part with the student, and between them they devised a new doctrine, abhorrent alike to Geneva and to Rome. The advent of this nondescript heresy was the signal of redoubled strife.[1] The dogmatic stiffness of the Geneva ministers chafed Villegagnon to fury. He felt himself, too, in a false position. On one side he depended on the Protestant, Coligny; on the other, he feared the Court. There were Catholics in the colony who might report him as an open heretic. On this point his doubts were set at rest; for a ship from France brought him a letter from the Cardinal of Lorraine, couched, it is said, in terms which restored him forthwith to the bosom of the Church. Villegagnon now affirmed that he had been deceived in Calvin, and pronounced him a "frightful heretic." He became despotic beyond measure, and would bear no opposition. The ministers, reduced nearly to starvation, found themselves under a tyranny worse than that from which they had fled.

At length he drove them from the fort, and forced them to

[1] The history of these theological squabbles is given in detail in the *Histoire des Choses Mémorables advenues en la Terre du Brésil* (Genêve, 1561). The author was an eyewitness. De Léry also enlarges upon them.

bivouac on the mainland, at the risk of being butchered by Indians, until a vessel loading with Brazil-wood in the harbor should be ready to carry them back to France. Having rid himself of the ministers, he caused three of the more zealous Calvinists to be seized, dragged to the edge of a rock, and thrown into the sea.[1] A fourth, equally obnoxious, but who, being a tailor, could ill be spared, was permitted to live on condition of recantation. Then, mustering the colonists, he warned them to shun the heresies of Luther and Calvin; threatened that all who openly professed those detestable doctrines should share the fate of their three comrades; and, his harangue over, feasted the whole assembly, in token, says the narrator, of joy and triumph.[2]

Meanwhile, in their crazy vessel, the banished ministers drifted slowly on their way. Storms fell upon them, their provisions failed, their water-casks were empty, and, tossing in the wilderness of waves, or rocking on the long swells of subsiding gales, they sank almost to despair. In their famine they chewed the Brazil-wood with which the vessel was laden, devoured every scrap of leather, singed and ate the horn of lanterns, hunted rats through the hold, and sold them to each other at enormous prices. At length, stretched on the deck, sick, listless, attenuated, and scarcely able to move a limb, they descried across the waste of sea the faint, cloud-like line that marked the coast of Brittany. Their perils were not past; for, if we may believe one of them, Jean de Léry, they bore a sealed letter from Villegagnon to the magistrates of the first French port at which they might arrive. It denounced them as heretics, worthy to be burned. Happily, the magistrates leaned to the Reform, and the malice of the commandant failed of its victims.

Villegagnon himself soon sailed for France, leaving the wretched colony to its fate. He presently entered the lists against Calvin, and engaged him in a hot controversial war, in which, according to some of his contemporaries, the knight often worsted the theologian at his own weapons. Be-

---

[1] *Histoire des Choses Mémorables*, 44.

[2] *Histoire des Choses Mémorables*, 46. Compare Barré, *Lettres sur la Navigation du Chevalier de Villegagnon* (Paris, 1558). Original documents concerning Villegagnon will be found in Gaffarel, *Brésil Français*, Appendix.

fore the year 1558 was closed, Ganabara fell a prey to the Portuguese. They set upon it in force, battered down the fort, and slew the feeble garrison, or drove them to a miserable refuge among the Indians. Spain and Portugal made good their claim to the vast domain, the mighty vegetation, and undeveloped riches of "Antarctic France."

Chapter III

1562, 1563

JEAN RIBAUT

The Huguenot Party, its motley Character • Ribaut sails for Florida • The River of May • Hopes • Illusions • Port Royal • Charlesfort • Frolic • Improvidence • Famine • Mutiny • Florida abandoned • Desperation • Cannibalism

IN the year 1562 a cloud of black and deadly portent was thickening over France. Surely and swiftly she glided towards the abyss of the religious wars. None could pierce the future, perhaps none dared to contemplate it: the wild rage of fanaticism and hate, friend grappling with friend, brother with brother, father with son; altars profaned, hearthstones made desolate, the robes of Justice herself bedrenched with murder. In the gloom without lay Spain, imminent and terrible. As on the hill by the field of Dreux, her veteran bands of pikemen, dark masses of organized ferocity, stood biding their time while the battle surged below, and then swept downward to the slaughter,—so did Spain watch and wait to trample and crush the hope of humanity.

In these days of fear, a second Huguenot colony sailed for the New World. The calm, stern man who represented and led the Protestantism of France felt to his inmost heart the peril of the time. He would fain build up a city of refuge for the persecuted sect. Yet Gaspar de Coligny, too high in power and rank to be openly assailed, was forced to act with caution. He must act, too, in the name of the Crown, and in virtue of his office of Admiral of France. A nobleman and a soldier,—for the Admiral of France was no seaman,—he shared the ideas and habits of his class; nor is there reason to believe him to have been in advance of his time in a knowledge of the principles of successful colonization. His scheme promised a military colony, not a free commonwealth. The Huguenot party was already a political as well as a religious party. At its foundation lay the religious element, represented by Geneva, the martyrs, and the devoted fugitives who sang the psalms of Marot among rocks and caverns. Joined to these

42

were numbers on whom the faith sat lightly, whose hope was in commotion and change. Of the latter, in great part, was the Huguenot *noblesse*, from Condé, who aspired to the crown,

> "Ce petit homme tant joli,
>   Qui toujours chante, toujours rit,"

to the younger son of the impoverished seigneur whose patrimony was his sword. More than this, the restless, the factious, and the discontented, began to link their fortunes to a party whose triumph would involve confiscation of the wealth of the only rich class in France. An element of the great revolution was already mingling in the strife of religions.

America was still a land of wonder. The ancient spell still hung unbroken over the wild, vast world of mystery beyond the sea,—a land of romance, adventure, and gold.

Fifty-eight years later the Puritans landed on the sands of Massachusetts Bay. The illusion was gone,—the *ignis fatuus* of adventure, the dream of wealth. The rugged wilderness offered only a stern and hard-won independence. In their own hearts, and not in the promptings of a great leader or the patronage of an equivocal government, their enterprise found its birth and its achievement. They were of the boldest and most earnest of their sect. There were such among the French disciples of Calvin; but no Mayflower ever sailed from a port of France. Coligny's colonists were of a different stamp, and widely different was their fate.

An excellent seaman and stanch Protestant, Jean Ribaut of Dieppe, commanded the expedition. Under him, besides sailors, were a band of veteran soldiers, and a few young nobles. Embarked in two of those antiquated craft whose high poops and tub-like proportions are preserved in the old engravings of De Bry, they sailed from Havre on the eighteenth of February, 1562.[1] They crossed the Atlantic, and on the thirtieth of April, in the latitude of twenty-nine and a half degrees, saw the long, low line where the wilderness of waves met the wilderness of woods. It was the coast of Florida. They soon descried a jutting point, which they called French Cape, perhaps

[1] Delaborde, *Gaspard de Coligny*, II. 14, 440.

one of the headlands of Matanzas Inlet. They turned their prows northward, coasting the fringes of that waste of verdure which rolled in shadowy undulation far to the unknown West.

On the next morning, the first of May, they found themselves off the mouth of a great river. Riding at anchor on a sunny sea, they lowered their boats, crossed the bar that obstructed the entrance, and floated on a basin of deep and sheltered water, "boyling and roaring," says Ribaut, "through the multitude of all kind of fish." Indians were running along the beach, and out upon the sand-bars, beckoning them to land. They pushed their boats ashore and disembarked,—sailors, soldiers, and eager young nobles. Corselet and morion, arquebuse and halberd, flashed in the sun that flickered through innumerable leaves, as, kneeling on the ground, they gave thanks to God, who had guided their voyage to an issue full of promise. The Indians, seated gravely under the neighboring trees, looked on in silent respect, thinking that they worshipped the sun. "They be all naked and of a goodly stature, mightie, and as well shapen and proportioned of body as any people in ye world; and the fore part of their body and armes be painted with pretie deuised workes, of Azure, red, and blacke, so well and so properly as the best Painter of Europe could not amende it." With their squaws and children, they presently drew near, and, strewing the earth with laurel boughs, sat down among the Frenchmen. Their visitors were much pleased with them, and Ribaut gave the chief, whom he calls the king, a robe of blue cloth, worked in yellow with the regal fleur-de-lis.

But Ribaut and his followers, just escaped from the dull prison of their ships, were intent on admiring the wild scenes around them. Never had they known a fairer May-day. The quaint old narrative is exuberant with delight. The tranquil air, the warm sun, woods fresh with young verdure, meadows bright with flowers; the palm, the cypress, the pine, the magnolia; the grazing deer; herons, curlews, bitterns, woodcock, and unknown waterfowl that waded in the ripple of the beach; cedars bearded from crown to root with long, gray moss; huge oaks smothering in the folds of enormous grapevines;—such were the objects that greeted them in their roamings, till their new-discovered land seemed "the fairest, fruitfullest, and pleasantest of al the world."

They found a tree covered with caterpillars, and hereupon the ancient black-letter says: "Also there be Silke wormes in meruielous number, a great deale fairer and better than be our silk wormes. To bee short, it is a thing vnspeakable to consider the thinges that bee seene there, and shalbe founde more and more in this incomperable lande."[1]

Above all, it was plain to their excited fancy that the country was rich in gold and silver, turquoises and pearls. One of these last, "as great as an Acorne at ye least," hung from the neck of an Indian who stood near their boats as they re-embarked. They gathered, too, from the signs of their savage visitors, that the wonderful land of Cibola, with its seven cities and its untold riches, was distant but twenty days' journey by water. In truth, it was two thousand miles westward, and its wealth a fable.

They named the river the River of May. It is now the St. John's. "And on the next morning," says Ribault, "we returned to land againe, accompanied with the Captaines, Gentlemen, and Souldiers, and others of our small troope, carrying with us a Pillour or columne of harde stone, our king's armes graved therein, to plant and set the same in the enterie of the Porte; and being come thither we espied on the south syde of the Riuer a place very fitte for that purpose upon a little hill compassed with Cypres, Bayes, Paulmes, and other trees, with sweete smelling and pleasant shrubbes." Here they set the column, and then, again embarking, held their course northward, happy in that benign decree which locks from mortal eyes the secrets of the future.

Next they anchored near Fernandina, and to a neighboring river, probably the St. Mary's, gave the name of the Seine.

---

[1] *The True and Last Discoverie of Florida, made by Captain John Ribault, in the Yeere 1562, dedicated to a great Nobleman in Fraunce, and translated into Englishe by one Thomas Hackit.* This is Ribaut's journal, which seems not to exist in the original. The translation is contained in the rare black-letter tract of Hakluyt called *Divers Voyages*, (London, 1582,) a copy of which is in the library of Harvard College. It has been reprinted by the Hakluyt Society. The journal first appeared in 1563, under the title of *The Whole and True Discoverie of Terra Florida (Englished The Florishing Land)*. This edition is of extreme rarity.

Here, as morning broke on the fresh, moist meadows hung with mists, and on broad reaches of inland waters which seemed like lakes, they were tempted to land again, and soon "espied an innumerable number of footesteps of great Hartes and Hindes of a wonderfull greatnesse, the steppes being all fresh and new, and it seemeth that the people doe nourish them like tame Cattell." By two or three weeks of exploration they seemed to have gained a clear idea of this rich semi-aquatic region. Ribaut describes it as "a countrie full of hauens, riuers, and Ilands, of such fruitfulnes as cannot with tongue be expressed." Slowly moving northward, they named each river, or inlet supposed to be a river, after some stream of France,—the Loire, the Charente, the Garonne, the Gironde. At length, opening betwixt flat and sandy shores, they saw a commodious haven, and named it Port Royal.

On the twenty-seventh of May they crossed the bar where the war-ships of Dupont crossed three hundred years later, passed Hilton Head, and held their course along the peaceful bosom of Broad River.[1] On the left they saw a stream which they named Libourne, probably Skull Creek; on the right, a wide river, probably the Beaufort. When they landed, all was solitude. The frightened Indians had fled, but they lured them back with knives, beads, and looking-glasses, and enticed two of them on board their ships. Here, by feeding, clothing, and caressing them, they tried to wean them from their fears, thinking to carry them to France, in obedience to a command of Catherine de Medicis;[2] but the captive warriors moaned and lamented day and night, and at length made their escape.

Ranging the woods, they found them full of game, wild turkeys and partridges, bears and lynxes. Two deer, of unusual size, leaped from the underbrush. Cross-bow and arquebuse were brought to the level; but the Huguenot captain, "moved with the singular fairness and bigness of them," forbade his men to shoot.

[1] Ribaut thinks that the Broad River of Port Royal is the Jordan of the Spanish navigator Vasquez de Ayllon, who was here in 1520, and gave the name of St. Helena to a neighboring cape (Garcilaso, *Florida del Inca*). The adjacent district, now called St. Helena, is the Chicora of the old Spanish maps.

[2] Laudonnière in Basanier, 14.

Preliminary exploration, not immediate settlement, had been the object of the voyage; but all was still rose-color in the eyes of the voyagers, and many of their number would gladly linger in the New Canaan. Ribaut was more than willing to humor them. He mustered his company on deck, and made them a harangue. He appealed to their courage and their patriotism, told them how, from a mean origin, men rise by enterprise and daring to fame and fortune, and demanded who among them would stay behind and hold Port Royal for the King. The greater part came forward, and "with such a good will and joly corage," writes the commander, "as we had much to do to stay their importunitie." Thirty were chosen, and Albert de Pierria was named to command them.

A fort was begun on a small stream called the Chenonceau, probably Archer's Creek, about six miles from the site of Beaufort.[1] They named it Charlesfort, in honor of the unhappy son of Catherine de Medicis, Charles the Ninth, the future hero of St. Bartholomew. Ammunition and stores were sent on shore, and on the eleventh of June, with his diminished company, Ribaut again embarked and spread his sails for France.

From the beach at Hilton Head, Albert and his companions might watch the receding ships, growing less and less on the vast expanse of blue, dwindling to faint specks, then vanishing on the pale verge of the waters. They were alone in those fearful solitudes. From the north pole to Mexico there was no Christian denizen but they.

The pressing question was how they were to subsist. Their thought was not of subsistence, but of gold. Of the thirty, the greater number were soldiers and sailors, with a few gentlemen; that is to say, men of the sword, born within the pale of nobility, who at home could neither labor nor trade without derogation from their rank. For a time they busied themselves with finishing their fort, and, this done, set forth in quest of adventures.

The Indians had lost fear of them. Ribaut had enjoined upon them to use all kindness and gentleness in their dealing with the men of the woods; and they more than obeyed him.

[1] No trace of this fort has been found. The old fort of which the remains may be seen a little below Beaufort is of later date.

They were soon hand and glove with chiefs, warriors, and squaws; and as with Indians the adage that familiarity breeds contempt holds with peculiar force, they quickly divested themselves of the prestige which had attached at the outset to their supposed character of children of the Sun. Good will, however, remained, and this the colonists abused to the utmost.

Roaming by river, swamp, and forest, they visited in turn the villages of five petty chiefs, whom they called kings, feasting everywhere on hominy, beans, and game, and loaded with gifts. One of these chiefs, named Audusta, invited them to the grand religious festival of his tribe. When they arrived, they found the village alive with preparation, and troops of women busied in sweeping the great circular area where the ceremonies were to take place. But as the noisy and impertinent guests showed a disposition to undue merriment, the chief shut them all in his wigwam, lest their Gentile eyes should profane the mysteries. Here, immured in darkness, they listened to the howls, yelpings, and lugubrious songs that resounded from without. One of them, however, by some artifice, contrived to escape, hid behind a bush, and saw the whole solemnity;—the procession of the medicine-men and the bedaubed and befeathered warriors; the drumming, dancing, and stamping; the wild lamentation of the women as they gashed the arms of the young girls with sharp mussel-shells, and flung the blood into the air with dismal outcries. A scene of ravenous feasting followed, in which the French, released from durance, were summoned to share.

After the carousal they returned to Charlesfort, where they were soon pinched with hunger. The Indians, never niggardly of food, brought them supplies as long as their own lasted; but the harvest was not yet ripe, and their means did not match their good-will. They told the French of two other kings, Ouadé and Couexis, who dwelt towards the south, and were rich beyond belief in maize, beans, and squashes. The mendicant colonists embarked without delay, and, with an Indian guide, steered for the wigwams of these potentates, not by the open sea, but by a perplexing inland navigation, including, as it seems, Calibogue Sound and neighboring waters. Reaching the friendly villages, on or near the Savannah, they were feasted to repletion, and their boat was laden with vegetables and corn. They returned rejoicing; but their joy was short. Their storehouse at Charlesfort, taking fire in the night, burned to the ground, and with it their newly acquired stock. Once more they set out for the realms of King Ouadé, and once more returned laden with supplies. Nay, the generous savage assured them that, so long as his cornfields yielded their harvests, his friends should not want.

How long this friendship would have lasted may well be doubted. With the perception that the dependants on their bounty were no demigods, but a crew of idle and helpless beggars, respect would soon have changed to contempt, and contempt to ill will. But it was not to Indian war-clubs that the infant colony was to owe its ruin. It carried within itself its own destruction. The ill-assorted band of landsmen and sailors, surrounded by that influence of the wilderness which wakens the dormant savage in the breasts of men, soon fell into quarrels. Albert, a rude soldier, with a thousand leagues of ocean betwixt him and responsibility, grew harsh, domineering, and violent beyond endurance. None could question or oppose him without peril of death. He hanged with his own hands a drummer who had fallen under his displeasure, and banished a soldier, named La Chère, to a solitary island, three leagues from the fort, where he left him to starve. For a time his comrades chafed in smothered fury. The crisis came at length. A few of the fiercer spirits leagued together, assailed their tyrant, murdered him, delivered the famished soldier, and called to the command one Nicolas Barré, a man of merit. Barré took the command, and thenceforth there was peace.

Peace, such as it was, with famine, homesickness, and disgust. The rough ramparts and rude buildings of Charlesfort, hatefully familiar to their weary eyes, the sweltering forest, the glassy river, the eternal silence of the lifeless wilds around them, oppressed the senses and the spirits. They dreamed of ease, of home, of pleasures across the sea, of the evening cup on the bench before the cabaret, and dances with kind wenches of Dieppe. But how to escape? A continent was their solitary prison, and the pitiless Atlantic shut them in. Not one of them knew how to build a ship; but Ribaut had left them a forge, with tools and iron, and strong desire supplied the place of skill. Trees were hewn down and the work begun. Had they put forth to maintain themselves at Port Royal the energy and resource which they exerted to escape from it, they might have laid the corner-stone of a solid colony.

All, gentle and simple, labored with equal zeal. They calked the seams with the long moss which hung in profusion from the neighboring trees; the pines supplied them with pitch; the Indians made for them a kind of cordage; and for sails they sewed together their shirts and bedding. At length a brigantine worthy of Robinson Crusoe floated on the waters of the Chenonceau. They laid in what provision they could, gave all that remained of their goods to the Indians, embarked, descended the river, and put to sea. A fair wind filled their patchwork sails and bore them from the hated coast. Day after day they held their course, till at length the breeze died away and a breathless calm fell on the waters. Florida was far behind; France farther yet before. Floating idly on the glassy waste, the craft lay motionless. Their supplies gave out. Twelve kernels of maize a day were each man's portion; then the maize failed, and they ate their shoes and leather jerkins. The water barrels were drained, and they tried to slake their thirst with brine. Several died, and the rest, giddy with exhaustion and crazed with thirst, were forced to ceaseless labor, bailing out the water that gushed through every seam. Headwinds set in, increasing to a gale, and the wretched brigantine, with sails close-reefed, tossed among the savage billows at the mercy of the storm. A heavy sea rolled down upon her, and burst the bulwarks on the windward side. The surges broke over her, and, clinging with desperate gripe to spars and cordage, the drenched voyagers gave up all for lost. At length she righted. The gale subsided, the wind changed, and the crazy, water-logged vessel again bore slowly towards France.

Gnawed with famine, they counted the leagues of barren ocean that still stretched before, and gazed on each other with haggard wolfish eyes, till a whisper passed from man to man, that one, by his death, might ransom all the rest. The lot was cast and it fell on La Chère, the same wretched man whom Albert had doomed to starvation on a lonely island. They killed him, and with ravenous avidity portioned out his flesh. The hideous repast sustained them till the land rose in sight, when, it is said, in a delirium of joy, they could no longer steer their vessel, but let her drift at the will of the tide. A small English bark bore down upon them, took them all on board, and, after landing the feeblest, carried the rest prisoners to Queen Elizabeth.[1]

Thus closed another of those scenes of woe whose lurid clouds are thickly piled around the stormy dawn of American history. It was the opening act of a wild and tragic drama.

[1] For all the latter part of the chapter, the authority is the first of the three long letters of René de Laudonnière, companion of Ribaut and his successor in command. They are contained in the *Histoire Notable de la Floride*, compiled by Basanier, (Paris, 1586,) and are also to be found, quaintly "done into English," in the third volume of Hakluyt's great collection. In the main, they are entitled to much confidence.

Chapter IV

1564

LAUDONNIÈRE

The New Colony • Satouriona • The Promised Land • Miraculous Longevity • Fort Caroline • Native Tribes • Ottigny explores the St. John's • The Thimagoas • Conflicting Alliances • Indian War • Diplomacy of Laudonnière • Vasseur's Expedition

---

O N the twenty-fifth of June, 1564, a French squadron anchored a second time off the mouth of the River of May. There were three vessels, the smallest of sixty tons, the largest of one hundred and twenty, all crowded with men. René de Laudonnière held command. He was of a noble race of Poitou, attached to the house of Châtillon, of which Coligny was the head; pious, we are told, and an excellent marine officer. An engraving, purporting to be his likeness, shows us a slender figure, leaning against the mast, booted to the thigh, with slouched hat and plume, slashed doublet, and short cloak. His thin oval face, with curled moustache and close-trimmed beard, wears a somewhat pensive look, as if already shadowed by the destiny that awaited him.[1]

The intervening year since Ribaut's voyage had been a dark year for France. From the peaceful solitude of the River of May, that voyager returned to a land reeking with slaughter. But the carnival of bigotry and hate had found a pause. The Peace of Amboise had been signed. The fierce monk choked down his venom; the soldier sheathed his sword, the assassin his dagger; rival chiefs grasped hands, and masked their rancor under hollow smiles. The king and the queen-mother, helpless amid the storm of factions which threatened their destruction, smiled now on Condé, now on Guise,—gave ear to the Cardinal of Lorraine, or listened in secret to the emissaries of Theodore Beza. Coligny was again strong at Court. He used his opportunity, and solicited with success the means of renewing his enterprise of colonization.[2]

---

[1] See Guérin, *Navigateurs Français*, 180. The authenticity of the portrait is doubtful.

[2] Delaborde, *Gaspard de Coligny*, II. 443.

Men were mustered for the work. In name, at least, they were all Huguenots; yet now, as before, the staple of the projected colony was unsound: soldiers, paid out of the royal treasury, hired artisans and tradesmen, with a swarm of volunteers from the young Huguenot nobles, whose restless swords had rusted in their scabbards since the peace. The foundation-stone was forgotten. There were no tillers of the soil. Such, indeed, were rare among the Huguenots; for the dull peasants who guided the plough clung with blind tenacity to the ancient faith. Adventurous gentlemen, reckless soldiers, discontented tradesmen, all keen for novelty and heated with dreams of wealth,—these were they who would build for their country and their religion an empire beyond the sea.[1]

On Thursday, the twenty-second of June, Laudonnière saw the low coast line of Florida, and entered the harbor of St. Augustine, which he named the River of Dolphins, "because that at mine arrival I saw there a great number of Dolphins which were playing in the mouth thereof."[2] Then he bore northward, following the coast till, on the twenty-fifth, he reached the mouth of the St. John's or River of May. The vessels anchored, the boats were lowered, and he landed with his principal followers on the south shore, near the present village of Mayport. It was the very spot where he had landed with Ribaut two years before. They were scarcely on shore when they saw an Indian chief, "which having espied us cryed very far off, *Antipola, Antipola*, and being so joyful that he could not containe himselfe, he came to meet us accompanied with two of his sonnes, as faire and mightie persons as might be found in al the world. There was in their trayne a great

---

[1] The principal authorities for this part of the narrative are Laudonnière and his artist, Le Moyne. Laudonnière's letters were published in 1586, under the title *L'Histoire Notable de la Floride, mise en lumière par M. Basanier.* See also Hakluyt's *Voyages,* III. (1812). Le Moyne was employed to make maps and drawings of the country. His maps are curiously inexact. His drawings are spirited, and, with many allowances, give useful hints concerning the habits of the natives. They are engraved in the *Grands Voyages* of De Bry, Part II. (Frankfort, 1591). To each is appended a "declaratio" or explanatory remarks. The same work contains the artist's personal narrative, the *Brevis Narratio.* In the *Recueil de Pièces sur la Floride* of Ternaux-Compans is a letter from one of the adventurers.

[2] Second letter of Laudonnière; contemporary translation in Hakluyt, III.

number of men and women which stil made very much of us, and by signes made us understand how glad they were of our arrivall. This good entertainment past, the Paracoussy [chief] prayed me to goe see the pillar which we had erected in the voyage of John Ribault." The Indians, regarding it with mysterious awe, had crowned it with evergreens, and placed baskets full of maize before it as an offering.

The chief then took Laudonnière by the hand, telling him that he was named Satouriona, and pointed out the extent of his dominions, far up the river and along the adjacent coasts. One of his sons, a man "perfect in beautie, wisedome, and honest sobrietie," then gave the French commander a wedge of silver, and received some trifles in return, after which the voyagers went back to their ships. "I prayse God continually," says Laudonnière, "for the great love I have found in these savages."

In the morning the French landed again, and found their new friends on the same spot, to the number of eighty or more, seated under a shelter of boughs, in festal attire of smoke-tanned deer-skins, painted in many colors. The party then rowed up the river, the Indians following them along the shore. As they advanced, coasting the borders of a great marsh that lay upon their left, the St. John's spread before them in vast sheets of glistening water, almost level with its flat, sedgy shores, the haunt of alligators, and the resort of innumerable birds. Beyond the marsh, some five miles from the mouth of the river, they saw a ridge of high ground abutting on the water, which, flowing beneath in a deep, strong current, had undermined it, and left a steep front of yellowish sand. This was the hill now called St. John's Bluff. Here they landed and entered the woods, where Laudonnière stopped to rest while his lieutenant, Ottigny, with a sergeant and a few soldiers, went to explore the country.

They pushed their way through the thickets till they were stopped by a marsh choked with reeds, at the edge of which, under a great laurel tree, they had seated themselves to rest, overcome with the summer heat, when five Indians suddenly appeared, peering timidly at them from among the bushes. Some of the men went towards them with signs of friendship, on which, taking heart, they drew near, and one of them, who was evidently a chief, made a long speech, inviting the strangers to their dwellings. The way was across the marsh, through which they carried the lieutenant and two or three of the soldiers on their backs, while the rest circled by a narrow path through the woods. When they reached the lodges, a crowd of Indians came out "to receive our men gallantly, and feast them after their manner." One of them brought a large earthen vessel full of spring water, which was served out to each in turn in a wooden cup. But what most astonished the French was a venerable chief, who assured them that he was the father of five successive generations, and that he had lived two hundred and fifty years. Opposite sat a still more ancient veteran, the father of the first, shrunken to a mere anatomy, and "seeming to be rather a dead carkeis than a living body." "Also," pursues the history, "his age was so great that the good man had lost his sight, and could not speak one onely word but with exceeding great paine."[1] In spite of his dismal condition, the visitors were told that he might expect to live, in the course of nature, thirty or forty years more. As the two patriarchs sat face to face, half hidden with their streaming white hair, Ottigny and his credulous soldiers looked from one to the other, lost in speechless admiration.

One of these veterans made a parting present to his guests of two young eagles, and Ottigny and his followers returned to report what they had seen. Laudonnière was waiting for them on the side of the hill, and now, he says, "I went right to the toppe thereof, where we found nothing else but Cedars, Palme, and Baytrees of so sovereigne odour that Baulme smelleth nothing like in comparison." From this high standpoint they surveyed their Canaan. The unruffled river lay before them, with its marshy islands overgrown with sedge and bulrushes, while on the farther side the flat, green meadows spread mile on mile, veined with countless creeks and belts of torpid water, and bounded leagues away by the verge of the dim pine forest. On the right, the sea glistened along the horizon, and on the left, the St. John's stretched westward between verdant shores, a highway to their fancied Eldorado.

[1] Laudonnière in Hakluyt, III. 388; Basanier, fol. 40; *Coppie d'une Lettre venant de la Floride*, in Ternaux-Compans, *Floride*, 233.

"Briefly," writes Laudonnière, "the place is so pleasant that those which are melancholicke would be inforced to change their humour."

On their way back to the ships they stopped for another parley with the chief Satouriona, and Laudonnière eagerly asked where he had got the wedge of silver that he gave him in the morning. The chief told him by signs, that he had taken it in war from a people called Thimagoas, who lived higher up the river, and who were his mortal enemies; on which the French captain had the folly to promise that he would join in an expedition against them. Satouriona was delighted, and declared that, if he kept his word, he should have gold and silver to his heart's content.

Man and nature alike seemed to mark the borders of the River of May as the site of the new colony; for here, around the Indian towns, the harvests of maize, beans, and pumpkins promised abundant food, while the river opened a ready way to the mines of gold and silver and the stores of barbaric wealth which glittered before the dreaming vision of the colonists. Yet, the better to satisfy himself and his men, Laudonnière weighed anchor, and sailed for a time along the neighboring coasts. Returning, confirmed in his first impression, he set out with a party of officers and soldiers to explore the borders of the chosen stream. The day was hot. The sun beat fiercely on the woollen caps and heavy doublets of the men, till at length they gained the shade of one of those deep forests of pine where the dead, hot air is thick with resinous odors, and the earth, carpeted with fallen leaves, gives no sound beneath the foot. Yet, in the stillness, deer leaped up on all sides as they moved along. Then they emerged into sunlight. A meadow was before them, a running brook, and a wall of encircling forests. The men called it the Vale of Laudonnière. The afternoon was spent, and the sun was near its setting, when they reached the bank of the river. They strewed the ground with boughs and leaves, and, stretched on that sylvan couch, slept the sleep of travel-worn and weary men.

They were roused at daybreak by sound of trumpet, and after singing a psalm they set themselves to their task. It was the building of a fort, and the spot they chose was a furlong or more above St. John's Bluff, where close to the water was a wide, flat knoll, raised a few feet above the marsh and the river.[1] Boats came up the stream with laborers, tents, provisions, cannon, and tools. The engineers marked out the work in the form of a triangle; and, from the noble volunteer to the meanest artisan, all lent a hand to complete it. On the river side the defences were a palisade of timber. On the two other sides were a ditch, and a rampart of fascines, earth, and sods. At each angle was a bastion, in one of which was the magazine. Within was a spacious parade, around it were various buildings for lodging and storage, and a large house with covered galleries was built on the side towards the river for Laudonnière and his officers. In honor of Charles the Ninth the fort was named Fort Caroline.

Meanwhile Satouriona, "lord of all that country," as the narratives style him, was seized with misgivings on learning these proceedings. The work was scarcely begun, and all was din and confusion around the incipient fort, when the startled Frenchmen saw the neighboring height of St. John's swarming with naked warriors. Laudonnière set his men in array, and for a season, pick and spade were dropped for arquebuse and pike. The savage chief descended to the camp. The artist Le Moyne, who saw him, drew his likeness from memory, — a tall, athletic figure, tattooed in token of his rank, plumed, bedecked with strings of beads, and girdled with tinkling pieces of metal which hung from the belt which formed his only garment.[2] He came in regal state, a crowd of warriors around him, and, in advance, a troup of young Indians armed with spears. Twenty musicians followed, blowing hideous discord through pipes of reeds,[3] while he seated himself on the ground "like a monkey," as Le Moyne has it in the grave Latin of his *Brevis Narratio*. A council followed, in which broken words were aided by signs and pantomime; and a

---

[1] Above St. John's Bluff the shore curves in a semicircle, along which the water runs in a deep, strong current, which has half cut away the flat knoll above mentioned, and encroached greatly on the bluff itself. The formation of the ground, joined to the indications furnished by Laudonnière and Lemoyne, leave little doubt that the fort was built on the knoll.

[2] Le Moyne, Tabulæ VIII., XI.

[3] Le Moyne, *Brevis Narratio*.

treaty of alliance was made, Laudonnière renewing his rash promise to aid the chief against his enemies. Satouriona, well pleased, ordered his Indians to help the French in their work. They obeyed with alacrity, and in two days the buildings of the fort were all thatched, after the native fashion, with leaves of the palmetto.

These savages belonged to one of the confederacies into which the native tribes of Florida were divided, and with three of which the French came into contact. The first was that of Satouriona, and the second was that of the people called Thimagoas, who, under a chief named Outina, dwelt in forty villages high up the St. John's. The third was that of the chief, cacique, or paracoussy whom the French called King Potanou, and whose dominions lay among the pine barrens, cypress swamps, and fertile hummocks westward and northwestward of this remarkable river. These three confederacies hated each other, and were constantly at war. Their social state was more advanced than that of the wandering hunter tribes. They were an agricultural people, and around all their villages were fields of maize, beans, and pumpkins. The harvest was gathered into a public granary, and they lived on it during three fourths of the year, dispersing in winter to hunt among the forests.

They were exceedingly well formed, the men, or the principal among them, were tattooed on the limbs and body, and in summer were nearly naked. Some wore their straight black hair flowing loose to the waist; others gathered it in a knot at the crown of the head. They danced and sang about the scalps of their enemies, like the tribes of the North, and like them they had their "medicine-men," who combined the functions of physicians, sorcerers, and priests. The most prominent feature of their religion was sun-worship.

Their villages were clusters of large dome-shaped huts, framed with poles and thatched with palmetto leaves. In the midst was the dwelling of the chief, much larger than the rest, and sometimes raised on an artificial mound. They were enclosed with palisades, and, strange to say, some of them were approached by wide avenues, artificially graded, and several hundred yards in length. Traces of these may still be seen, as may also the mounds in which the Floridians, like the Hurons and various other tribes, collected at stated intervals the bones of their dead.

Social distinctions were sharply defined among them. Their chiefs, whose office was hereditary, sometimes exercised a power almost absolute. Each village had its chief, subordinate to the grand chief of the confederacy. In the language of the French narratives, they were all kings or lords, vassals of the great monarch Satouriona, Outina, or Potanou. All these tribes are now extinct, and it is difficult to ascertain with precision their tribal affinities. There can be no doubt that they were the authors of the aboriginal remains at present found in various parts of Florida.

Having nearly finished the fort, Laudonnière declares that he "would not lose the minute of an houre without employing of the same in some vertuous exercise," and he therefore sent his Lieutenant, Ottigny, to spy out the secrets of the interior, and to learn, above all, "what this Thimagoa might be, whereof the Paracoussy Satouriona had spoken to us so often." As Laudonnière stood pledged to attack the Thimagoas, the chief gave Ottigny two Indian guides, who, says the record, were so eager for the fray that they seemed as if bound to a wedding feast.

The lazy waters of the St. John's, tinged to coffee-color by the exudations of the swamps, curled before the prow of Ottigny's sail-boat as he advanced into the prolific wilderness which no European eye had ever yet beheld. By his own reckoning, he sailed thirty leagues up the river, which would have brought him to a point not far below Palatka. Here, more than two centuries later, the Bartrams, father and son, guided their skiff and kindled their nightly bivouac-fire; and here, too, roamed Audubon, with his sketch-book and his gun. It was a paradise for the hunter and the naturalist. Earth, air, and water teemed with life, in endless varieties of beauty and ugliness. A half-tropical forest shadowed the low shores, where the palmetto and the cabbage palm mingled with the oak, the maple, the cypress, the liquid-ambar, the laurel, the myrtle, and the broad glistening leaves of the evergreen magnolia. Here was the haunt of bears, wild-cats, lynxes, cougars, and the numberless deer of which they made their prey. In the sedges and the mud the alligator stretched his brutish length; turtles with outstretched necks basked on half-sunken logs; the rattlesnake sunned himself on the sandy bank, and the yet more dangerous moccason lurked under the water-lilies in inlets and sheltered coves. The air and the water were populous as the earth. The river swarmed with fish, from the fierce and restless gar, cased in his horny armor, to the lazy cat-fish in the muddy depths. There were the golden eagle and the white-headed eagle, the gray pelican and the white pelican, the blue heron and the white heron, the egret, the ibis, ducks of various sorts, the whooping crane, the black vulture, and the cormorant; and when at sunset the voyagers drew their boat upon the strand and built their camp-fire under the arches of the woods, the owls whooped around them all night long, and when morning came the sultry mists that wrapped the river were vocal with the clamor of wild turkeys.

When Ottigny was about twenty leagues from Fort Caroline, his two Indian guides, who were always on the watch, descried three canoes, and in great excitement cried, "Thimagoa! Thimagoa!" As they drew near, one of them snatched up a halberd and the other a sword, and in their fury they seemed ready to jump into the water to get at the enemy. To their great disgust, Ottigny permitted the Thimagoas to run their canoes ashore and escape to the woods. Far from keeping Laudonnière's senseless promise to fight them, he wished to make them friends; to which end he now landed with some of his men, placed a few trinkets in their canoes, and withdrew to a distance to watch the result. The fugitives presently returned, step by step, and allowed the French to approach them; on which Ottigny asked, by signs, if they had gold or silver. They replied that they had none, but that if he would give them one of his men they would show him where it was to be found. One of the soldiers boldly offered himself for the venture, and embarked with them. As, however, he failed to return according to agreement, Ottigny, on the next day, followed ten leagues farther up the stream, and at length had the good luck to see him approaching in a canoe. He brought little or no gold, but reported that he had heard of a certain chief, named Mayrra, marvellously rich, who lived three days' journey up the river; and with these welcome tidings Ottigny went back to Fort Caroline.

A fortnight later, an officer named Vasseur went up the river to pursue the adventure. The fever for gold had seized upon the French. As the villages of the Thimagoas lay between them and the imagined treasures, they shrank from a quarrel, and Laudonnière repented already of his promised alliance with Satouriona.

Vasseur was two days' sail from the fort, when two Indians hailed him from the shore, inviting him to their dwellings. He accepted their guidance, and presently saw before him the cornfields and palisades of an Indian town. He and his followers were led through the wondering crowd to the lodge of Mollua, the chief, seated in the place of honor, and plentifully regaled with fish and bread. The repast over, Mollua made a speech. He told them that he was one of the forty vassal chiefs of the great Outina, lord of all the Thimagoas, whose warriors wore armor of gold and silver plate. He told them, too, of Potanou, his enemy, "a man cruell in warre"; and of the two kings of the distant Appalachian Mountains, Onatheaqua and Houstaqua, "great lords and abounding in riches." While thus, with earnest pantomime and broken words, the chief discoursed with his guests, Vasseur, intent and eager, strove to follow his meaning; and no sooner did he hear of these Appalachian treasures than he promised to join Outina in war against the two potentates of the mountains. Mollua, well pleased, promised that each of Outina's vassal chiefs should requite their French allies with a heap of gold and silver two feet high. Thus, while Laudonnière stood pledged to Satouriona, Vasseur made alliance with his mortal enemy.

On his return, he passed a night in the lodge of one of Satouriona's chiefs, who questioned him touching his dealings with the Thimagoas. Vasseur replied that he had set upon them and put them to utter rout. But as the chief, seeming as yet unsatisfied, continued his inquiries, the sergeant François de la Caille drew his sword, and, like Falstaff, reenacted his deeds of valor, pursuing and thrusting at the imaginary Thimagoas, as they fled before his fury. The chief, at length convinced, led the party to his lodge, and entertained them with a decoction of the herb called Cassina.

Satouriona, elated by Laudonnière's delusive promises of

aid, had summoned his so-called vassals to war. Ten chiefs and some five hundred warriors had mustered at his call, and the forest was alive with their bivouacs. When all was ready, Satouriona reminded the French commander of his pledge, and claimed its fulfilment, but got nothing but evasions in return. He stifled his rage, and prepared to go without his fickle ally.

A fire was kindled near the bank of the river, and two large vessels of water were placed beside it. Here Satouriona took his stand, while his chiefs crouched on the grass around him, and the savage visages of his five hundred warriors filled the outer circle, their long hair garnished with feathers, or covered with the heads and skins of wolves, cougars, bears, or eagles. Satouriona, looking towards the country of his enemy, distorted his features into a wild expression of rage and hate; then muttered to himself; then howled an invocation to his god, the Sun; then besprinkled the assembly with water from one of the vessels, and, turning the other upon the fire, suddenly quenched it. "So," he cried, "may the blood of our enemies be poured out, and their lives extinguished!" and the concourse gave forth an explosion of responsive yells, till the shores resounded with the wolfish din.[1]

The rites over, they set out, and in a few days returned exulting, with thirteen prisoners and a number of scalps. These last were hung on a pole before the royal lodge, and when night came it brought with it a pandemonium of dancing and whooping, drumming and feasting.

A notable scheme entered the brain of Laudonnière. Resolved, cost what it might, to make a friend of Outina, he conceived it to be a stroke of policy to send back to him two of the prisoners. In the morning he sent a soldier to Satouriona to demand them. The astonished chief gave a flat refusal, adding that he owed the French no favors, for they had shamefully broken faith with him. On this, Laudonnière, at the head of twenty soldiers, proceeded to the Indian town, placed a guard at the opening of the great lodge, entered with his arquebusiers, and seated himself without ceremony in the highest place. Here, to show his displeasure, he remained in

[1] Le Moyne makes the scene the subject of one of his pictures.

silence for half an hour. At length he spoke, renewing his demand. For some moments Satouriona made no reply; then he coldly observed that the sight of so many armed men had frightened the prisoners away. Laudonnière grew peremptory, when the chief's son, Athore, went out, and presently returned with the two Indians, whom the French led back to Fort Caroline.[1]

Satouriona, says Laudonnière, "was wonderfully offended with this bravado, and bethought himselfe by all meanes how he might be revenged of us." He dissembled for the time, and presently sent three of his followers to the fort with a gift of pumpkins; though under this show of good-will the outrage rankled in his breast, and he never forgave it. The French had been unfortunate in their dealings with the Indians. They had alienated old friends in vain attempts to make new ones.

Vasseur, with the Swiss ensign Arlac,[2] a sergeant, and ten soldiers, went up the river early in September to carry back the two prisoners to Outina. Laudonnière declares that they sailed eighty leagues, which would have carried them far above Lake Monroe; but it is certain that his reckoning is grossly exaggerated. Their boat crawled up the lazy St. John's, no longer a broad lake-like expanse, but a narrow and tortuous stream, winding between swampy forests, or through the vast savanna, a verdant sea of bulrushes and grass. At length they came to a village called Mayarqua, and thence, with the help of their oars, made their way to another cluster of wigwams, apparently on a branch of the main river. Here they found Outina himself, whom, prepossessed with ideas of feudality, they regarded as the suzerain of a host of subordinate lords and princes, ruling over the surrounding swamps and pine barrens. Outina gratefully received the two prisoners whom Laudonnière had sent to propitiate him, feasted the wonderful strangers, and invited them to join him on a raid against his rival, Potanou. Laudonnière had promised to join Satouriona against Outina, and Vasseur now promised to join Outina against Potanou, the hope of finding gold being in both cases the source of this impolitic compliance. Vasseur

[1] Laudonnière in Hakluyt, III. 396.
[2] So written by Laudonnière. The true name is probably Erlach.

went back to Fort Caroline with five of the men, and left Arlac with the remaining five to fight the battles of Outina.

The warriors mustered to the number of some two hundred, and the combined force of white men and red took up their march. The wilderness through which they passed has not yet quite lost its characteristic features; the bewildering monotony of the pine barrens, with their myriads of bare gray trunks, and their canopy of perennial green, through which a scorching sun throws spots and streaks of yellow light, here on an undergrowth of dwarf palmetto, and there on dry sands half hidden by tufted wire-grass, and dotted with the little mounds that mark the burrows of the gopher; or those oases in the desert, the "hummocks," with their wild, redundant vegetation, their entanglement of trees, bushes, and vines, their scent of flowers and song of birds; or the broad sunshine of the savanna, where they waded to the neck in grass; or the deep swamp, where, out of the black and root-encumbered slough, rise the huge buttressed trunks of the Southern cypress, the gray Spanish moss drooping from every bough and twig, wrapping its victims like a drapery of tattered cobwebs, and slowly draining away their life; for even plants devour each other, and play their silent parts in the universal tragedy of nature.

The allies held their way through forest, savanna, and swamp, with Outina's Indians in the front, till they neared the hostile villages, when the modest warriors fell to the rear, and yielded the post of honor to the Frenchmen.

An open country lay before them, with rough fields of maize, beans, and pumpkins, and the palisades of an Indian town. Their approach was seen, and the warriors of Potanou swarmed out to meet them; but the sight of the bearded strangers, the flash and report of the fire-arms, and the fall of their foremost chief, shot through the brain by Arlac, filled them with consternation, and they fled within their defences. Pursuers and pursued entered pell-mell together. The place was pillaged and burned, its inmates captured or killed, and the victors returned triumphant.

Chapter V

CONSPIRACY

Discontent • Plot of La Roquette • Piratical Excursion • Sedition • Illness of Laudonnière • Outbreak of the Mutiny • Buccaneering • Order restored

IN the little world of Fort Caroline, a miniature France, cliques and parties, conspiracy and sedition, were fast stirring into life. Hopes had been dashed, and wild expectations had come to naught. The adventurers had found, not conquest and gold, but a dull exile in a petty fort by a hot and sickly river, with hard labor, bad fare, prospective famine, and nothing to break the weary sameness but some passing canoe or floating alligator. Gathered in knots, they nursed each other's wrath, and inveighed against the commandant. Why are we put on half-rations, when he told us that provision should be made for a full year? Where are the reinforcements and supplies that he said should follow us from France? And why is he always closeted with Ottigny, Arlac, and this and that favorite, when we, men of blood as good as theirs, cannot gain his ear for a moment?

The young nobles, of whom there were many, were volunteers, who had paid their own expenses in expectation of a golden harvest, and they chafed in impatience and disgust. The religious element in the colony—unlike the former Huguenot emigration to Brazil—was evidently subordinate. The adventurers thought more of their fortunes than of their faith; yet there were not a few earnest enough in the doctrine of Geneva to complain loudly and bitterly that no ministers had been sent with them. The burden of all grievances was thrown upon Laudonnière, whose greatest errors seem to have arisen from weakness and a lack of judgment,—fatal defects in his position.

The growing discontent was brought to a partial head by one La Roquette, who gave out that, high up the river, he had discovered by magic a mine of gold and silver, which would give each of them a share of ten thousand crowns, besides fifteen hundred thousand for the King. But for Laudonnière, he said, their fortunes would all be made. He found an ally in a gentleman named Genre, one of Laudonnière's confidants, who, while still professing fast adherence to his interests, is charged by him with plotting against his life. "This Genre," he says, "secretly enfourmed the Souldiers that were already suborned by La Roquette, that I would deprive them of this great gaine, in that I did set them dayly on worke, not sending them on every side to discover the Countreys; therefore that it were a good deede to dispatch mee out of the way, and to choose another Captaine in my place." The soldiers listened too well. They made a flag of an old shirt, which they carried with them to the rampart when they went to their work, at the same time wearing their arms; and, pursues Laudonnière, "these gentle Souldiers did the same for none other ende but to have killed mee and my Lieutenant also, if by chance I had given them any hard speeches." About this time, overheating himself, he fell ill, and was confined to his quarters. On this, Genre made advances to the apothecary, urging him to put arsenic into his medicine; but the apothecary shrugged his shoulders. They next devised a scheme to blow him up by hiding a keg of gun-powder under his bed; but here, too, they failed. Hints of Genre's machinations reaching the ears of Laudonnière, the culprit fled to the woods, whence he wrote repentant letters, with full confession, to his commander.

Two of the ships meanwhile returned to France,—the third, the Breton, remaining at anchor opposite the fort. The malcontents took the opportunity to send home charges against Laudonnière of peculation, favoritism, and tyranny.[1]

On the fourth of September, Captain Bourdet, apparently a private adventurer, had arrived from France with a small vessel. When he returned, about the tenth of November, Laudonnière persuaded him to carry home seven or eight of the malcontent soldiers. Bourdet left some of his sailors in their place. The exchange proved most disastrous. These pirates joined with others whom they had won over, stole Laudonnière's two pinnaces, and set forth on a plundering excursion

[1] Barcia, *Ensayo Cronologico*, 53; Laudonnière in Hakluyt, III. 400; Basanier, 61.

to the West Indies. They took a small Spanish vessel off the coast of Cuba, but were soon compelled by famine to put into Havana and give themselves up. Here, to make their peace with the authorities, they told all they knew of the position and purposes of their countrymen at Fort Caroline, and thus was forged the thunder-bolt soon to be hurled against the wretched little colony.

On a Sunday morning, François de la Caille[1] came to Laudonnière's quarters, and, in the name of the whole company, requested him to come to the parade-ground. He complied, and issuing forth, his inseparable Ottigny at his side, he saw some thirty of his officers, soldiers, and gentlemen volunteers waiting before the building with fixed and sombre countenances. La Caille, advancing, begged leave to read, in behalf of the rest, a paper which he held in his hand. It opened with protestations of duty and obedience; next came complaints of hard work, starvation, and broken promises, and a request that the petitioners should be allowed to embark in the vessel lying in the river, and cruise along the Spanish Main, in order to procure provisions by purchase "or otherwise."[2] In short, the flower of the company wished to turn buccaneers.

Laudonnière refused, but assured them that, as soon as the defences of the fort should be completed, a search should be begun in earnest for the Appalachian gold mine, and that meanwhile two small vessels then building on the river should be sent along the coast to barter for provisions with the Indians. With this answer they were forced to content themselves; but the fermentation continued, and the plot thickened. Their spokesman, La Caille, however, seeing whither the affair tended, broke with them, and, except Ottigny, Vasseur, and the brave Swiss, Arlac, was the only officer who held to his duty.

A severe illness again seized Laudonnière, and confined him to his bed. Improving their advantage, the malcontents gained over nearly all the best soldiers in the fort. The ring-

---

[1] La Caille, as before mentioned, was Laudonnière's sergeant. The feudal rank of sergeant, it will be remembered, was widely different from the modern grade so named, and was held by men of noble birth. Le Moyne calls La Caille "Captain."

[2] Le Moyne, *Brevis Narratio.*

leader was one Fourneaux, a man of good birth, but whom
Le Moyne calls an avaricious hypocrite. He drew up a paper,
to which sixty-six names were signed. La Caille boldly opposed the conspirators, and they resolved to kill him. His
room-mate, Le Moyne, who had also refused to sign, received
a hint of the design from a friend; upon which he warned La
Caille, who escaped to the woods. It was late in the night.
Fourneaux, with twenty men armed to the teeth, knocked
fiercely at the commandant's door. Forcing an entrance, they
wounded a gentleman who opposed them, and crowded
around the sick man's bed. Fourneaux, armed with steel cap
and cuirass, held his arquebuse to Laudonnière's throat, and
demanded leave to go on a cruise among the Spanish islands.
The latter kept his presence of mind, and remonstrated with
some firmness; on which, with oaths and menaces, they
dragged him from his bed, put him in fetters, carried him out
to the gate of the fort, placed him in a boat, and rowed him
to the ship anchored in the river.

Two other gangs at the same time visited Ottigny and Arlac, whom they disarmed, and ordered to keep their rooms
till the night following, on pain of death. Smaller parties were
busied, meanwhile, in disarming all the loyal soldiers. The
fort was completely in the hands of the conspirators. Fourneaux drew up a commission for his meditated West India
cruise, which he required Laudonnière to sign. The sick commandant, imprisoned in the ship, with one attendant, at first
refused; but, receiving a message from the mutineers, that, if
he did not comply, they would come on board and cut his
throat, he at length yielded.

The buccaneers now bestirred themselves to finish the two
small vessels on which the carpenters had been for some time
at work. In a fortnight they were ready for sea, armed and
provided with the King's cannon, munitions, and stores.
Trenchant, an excellent pilot, was forced to join the party.
Their favorite object was the plunder of a certain church on
one of the Spanish islands, which they proposed to assail during the midnight mass of Christmas, whereby a triple end
would be achieved: first, a rich booty; secondly, the punishment of idolatry; thirdly, vengeance on the arch-enemies of
their party and their faith. They set sail on the eighth of De-

cember, taunting those who remained, calling them green-
horns, and threatening condign punishment if, on their
triumphant return, they should be refused free entrance to the
fort.[1]

They were no sooner gone than the unfortunate Laudonnière was gladdened in his solitude by the approach of his fast
friends Ottigny and Arlac, who conveyed him to the fort and
reinstated him. The entire command was reorganized, and
new officers appointed. The colony was wofully depleted; but
the bad blood had been drawn off, and thenceforth all internal danger was at an end. In finishing the fort, in building
two new vessels to replace those of which they had been
robbed, and in various intercourse with the tribes far and
near, the weeks passed until the twenty-fifth of March, when
an Indian came in with the tidings that a vessel was hovering
off the coast. Laudonnière sent to reconnoitre. The stranger
lay anchored at the mouth of the river. She was a Spanish
brigantine, manned by the returning mutineers, starving,
downcast, and anxious to make terms. Yet, as their posture
seemed not wholly pacific, Laudonnière sent down La Caille,
with thirty soldiers concealed at the bottom of his little vessel.
Seeing only two or three on deck, the pirates allowed her to
come alongside; when, to their amazement, they were
boarded and taken before they could snatch their arms. Discomfited, woe-begone, and drunk, they were landed under a
guard. Their story was soon told. Fortune had flattered them
at the outset, and on the coast of Cuba they took a brigantine
laden with wine and stores. Embarking in her, they next fell
in with a caravel, which also they captured. Landing at a village in Jamaica, they plundered and caroused for a week, and
had hardly re-embarked when they met a small vessel having
on board the governor of the island.[2] She made desperate
fight, but was taken at last, and with her a rich booty. They
thought to put the governor to ransom; but the astute official
deceived them, and, on pretence of negotiating for the sum
demanded,—together with "four or six parrots, and as many

[1] Le Moyne, *Brevis Narratio*. Compare Laudonnière in Basanier, fol. 63–
66.
[2] Laudonnière in Basanier, fol. 66. Le Moyne says that it was the governor
of Havana.

monkeys of the sort called sanguins, which are very beautiful," and for which his captors had also bargained,—contrived to send instructions to his wife. Hence it happened that at daybreak three armed vessels fell upon them, retook the prize, and captured or killed all the pirates but twenty-six, who, cutting the moorings of their brigantine, fled out to sea. Among these was the ringleader, Fourneaux, and also the pilot, Trenchant, who, eager to return to Fort Caroline, whence he had been forcibly taken, succeeded during the night in bringing the vessel to the coast of Florida. Great were the wrath and consternation of the pirates when they saw their dilemma; for, having no provisions, they must either starve or seek succor at the fort. They chose the latter course, and bore away for the St. John's. A few casks of Spanish wine yet remained, and nobles and soldiers, fraternizing in the common peril of a halter, joined in a last carouse. As the wine mounted to their heads, in the mirth of drink and desperation, they enacted their own trial. One personated the judge, another the commandant; witnesses were called, with arguments and speeches on either side.

"Say what you like," said one of them, after hearing the counsel for the defence; "but if Laudonnière does not hang us all, I will never call him an honest man."

They had some hope of getting provisions from the Indians at the mouth of the river, and then putting to sea again; but this was frustrated by La Caille's sudden attack. A court-martial was called near Fort Caroline, and all were found guilty. Fourneaux and three others were sentenced to be hanged.

"Comrades," said one of the condemned, appealing to the soldiers, "will you stand by and see us butchered?"

"These," retorted Laudonnière, "are no comrades of mutineers and rebels."

At the request of his followers, however, he commuted the sentence to shooting.

A file of men, a rattling volley, and the debt of justice was paid. The bodies were hanged on gibbets, at the river's mouth, and order reigned at Fort Caroline.[1]

---

[1] The above is from Le Moyne and Laudonnière, who agree in essential points, but differ in a few details. The artist criticises the commandant freely. Compare Hawkins in Hakluyt, III. 614.

Chapter VI

FAMINE — WAR — SUCCOR

La Roche Ferrière • Pierre Gambie • The King of Calos • Ottigny's Expedition • Starvation • Efforts to escape from Florida • Indians unfriendly • Seizure of Outina • Attempts to extort Ransom • Ambuscade • Battle • Desperation of the French • Sir John Hawkins relieves them • Ribaut brings Reinforcements • Arrival of the Spaniards

WHILE the mutiny was brewing, one La Roche Ferrière had been sent out as an agent or emissary among the more distant tribes. Sagacious, bold, and restless, he pushed his way from town to town, and pretended to have reached the mysterious mountains of Appalache. He sent to the fort mantles woven with feathers, quivers covered with choice furs, arrows tipped with gold, wedges of a green stone like beryl or emerald, and other trophies of his wanderings. A gentleman named Grotaut took up the quest, and penetrated to the dominions of Hostaqua, who, it was pretended, could muster three or four thousand warriors, and who promised, with the aid of a hundred arquebusiers, to conquer all the kings of the adjacent mountains, and subject them and their gold mines to the rule of the French. A humbler adventurer was Pierre Gambie, a robust and daring youth, who had been brought up in the household of Coligny, and was now a soldier under Laudonnière. The latter gave him leave to trade with the Indians, — a privilege which he used so well that he grew rich with his traffic, became prime favorite with the chief of the island of Edelano, married his daughter, and, in his absence, reigned in his stead. But, as his sway verged towards despotism, his subjects took offence, and split his head with a hatchet.

During the winter, Indians from the neighborhood of Cape Canaveral brought to the fort two Spaniards, wrecked fifteen years before on the southwestern extremity of the peninsula. They were clothed like the Indians, — in other words, were not clothed at all, — and their uncut hair streamed loose down their backs. They brought strange tales of those among whom they had dwelt. They told of the King of Calos, on whose domains they had been wrecked, a chief mighty in stature and in power. In one of his villages was a pit, six feet deep and as wide as a hogshead, filled with treasure gathered from Spanish wrecks on adjacent reefs and keys. The monarch was a priest too, and a magician, with power over the elements. Each year he withdrew from the public gaze to hold converse in secret with supernal or infernal powers; and each year he sacrificed to his gods one of the Spaniards whom the fortune of the sea had cast upon his shores. The name of the tribe is preserved in that of the River Caloosa. In close league with him was the mighty Oathcaqua, dwelling near Cape Canaveral, who gave his daughter, a maiden of wondrous beauty, in marriage to his great ally. But as the bride with her bridesmaids was journeying toward Calos, escorted by a chosen band, they were assailed by a wild and warlike race, inhabitants of an island called Sarrope, in the midst of a lake, who put the warriors to flight, bore the maidens captive to their watery fastness, espoused them all, and, we are assured, "loved them above all measure."[1]

Outina, taught by Arlac the efficacy of the French fire-arms, begged for ten arquebusiers to aid him on a new raid among the villages of Potanou, again alluring his greedy allies by the assurance, that, thus reinforced, he would conquer for them a free access to the phantom gold mines of Appalache. Ottigny set forth on this fool's errand with thrice the force demanded. Three hundred Thimagoas and thirty Frenchmen took up their march through the pine barrens. Outina's conjurer was of the number, and had wellnigh ruined the enterprise. Kneeling on Ottigny's shield, that he might not touch the earth, with hideous grimaces, howlings, and contortions, he wrought himself into a prophetic frenzy, and proclaimed to the astounded warriors that to advance farther would be destruction.[2] Outina was for instant retreat, but Ottigny's sarcasms shamed him into a show of courage.

[1] Laudonnière in Hakluyt, III. 406. Brinton, *Floridian Peninsula*, thinks there is truth in the story, and that Lake Weir, in Marion County, is the Lake of Sarrope. I give these romantic tales as I find them.

[2] This scene is the subject of Plate XII. of Le Moyne.

Again they moved forward, and soon encountered Potanou with all his host.[1] The arquebuse did its work; panic, slaughter, and a plentiful harvest of scalps. But no persuasion could induce Outina to follow up his victory. He went home to dance round his trophies, and the French returned disgusted to Fort Caroline.

And now, in ample measure, the French began to reap the harvest of their folly. Conquest, gold, and military occupation had alone been their aims. Not a rood of ground had been stirred with the spade. Their stores were consumed, and the expected supplies had not come. The Indians, too, were hostile. Satouriona hated them as allies of his enemies; and his tribesmen, robbed and maltreated by the lawless soldiers, exulted in their miseries. Yet in these, their dark and subtle neighbors, was their only hope.

May-day came, the third anniversary of the day when Ribaut and his companions, full of delighted anticipation, had first explored the flowery borders of the St. John's. The contrast was deplorable; for within the precinct of Fort Caroline a homesick, squalid band, dejected and worn, dragged their shrunken limbs about the sun-scorched area, or lay stretched in listless wretchedness under the shade of the barracks. Some were digging roots in the forest, or gathering a kind of sorrel upon the meadows. If they had had any skill in hunting and fishing, the river and the woods would have supplied their needs; but in this point, as in others, they were lamentably unfit for the work they had taken in hand. "Our miserie," says Laudonnière, "was so great that one was found that gathered up all the fish bones that he could finde, which he dried and beate into powder to make bread thereof. The effects of this hideous famine appeared incontinently among us, for our bones eftsoones beganne to cleave so neere unto the skinne, that the most part of the souldiers had their skinnes pierced thorow with them in many partes of their bodies." Yet, giddy with weakness, they dragged themselves in turn to the top of

[1] Le Moyne drew a picture of the fight (Plate XIII.). In the foreground Ottigny is engaged in single combat with a gigantic savage, who, with club upheaved, aims a deadly stroke at the plumed helmet of his foe; but the latter, with target raised to guard his head, darts under the arms of the naked Goliath, and transfixes him with his sword.

St. John's Bluff, straining their eyes across the sea to descry the anxiously expected sail.

Had Coligny left them to perish? or had some new tempest of calamity, let loose upon France, drowned the memory of their exile? In vain the watchman on the hill surveyed the solitude of waters. A deep dejection fell upon them,—a dejection that would have sunk to despair could their eyes have pierced the future.

The Indians had left the neighborhood, but from time to time brought in meagre supplies of fish, which they sold to the famished soldiers at exorbitant prices. Lest they should pay the penalty of their extortion, they would not enter the fort, but lay in their canoes in the river, beyond gunshot, waiting for their customers to come out to them. "Oftentimes," says Laudonnière, "our poor soldiers were constrained to give away the very shirts from their backs to get one fish. If at any time they shewed unto the savages the excessive price which they tooke, these villaines would answere them roughly and churlishly: If thou make so great account of thy marchandise, eat it, and we will eat our fish: then fell they out a laughing, and mocked us with open throat."

The spring wore away, and no relief appeared. One thought now engrossed the colonists, that of return to France. Vasseur's ship, the Breton, still remained in the river, and they had also the Spanish brigantine brought by the mutineers. But these vessels were insufficient, and they prepared to build a new one. The energy of reviving hope lent new life to their exhausted frames. Some gathered pitch in the pine forests; some made charcoal; some cut and sawed timber. The maize began to ripen, and this brought some relief; but the Indians, exasperated and greedy, sold it with reluctance, and murdered two half-famished Frenchmen who gathered a handful in the fields.

The colonists applied to Outina, who owed them two victories. The result was a churlish message and a niggardly supply of corn, coupled with an invitation to aid him against an insurgent chief, one Astina, the plunder of whose villages would yield an ample supply. The offer was accepted. Ottigny and Vasseur set out, but were grossly deceived, led against a different enemy, and sent back empty-handed and half-starved.

They returned to the fort, in the words of Laudonnière, "angry and pricked deeply to the quicke for being so mocked," and, joined by all their comrades, fiercely demanded to be led against Outina, to seize him, punish his insolence, and extort from his fears the supplies which could not be looked for from his gratitude. The commandant was forced to comply. Those who could bear the weight of their armor put it on, embarked, to the number of fifty, in two barges, and sailed up the river under Laudonnière himself. Having reached Outina's landing, they marched inland, entered his village, surrounded his mud-plastered palace, seized him amid the yells and howlings of his subjects, and led him prisoner to their boats. Here, anchored in mid-stream, they demanded a supply of corn and beans as the price of his ransom.

The alarm spread. Excited warriors, bedaubed with red, came thronging from all his villages. The forest along the shore was full of them; and the wife of the chief, followed by all the women of the place, uttered moans and outcries from the strand. Yet no ransom was offered, since, reasoning from their own instincts, they never doubted that, after the price was paid, the captive would be put to death.

Laudonnière waited two days, and then descended the river with his prisoner. In a rude chamber of Fort Caroline the sentinel stood his guard, pike in hand, while before him crouched the captive chief, mute, impassive, and brooding on his woes. His old enemy, Satouriona, keen as a hound on the scent of prey, tried, by great offers, to bribe Laudonnière to give Outina into his hands; but the French captain refused, treated his prisoner kindly, and assured him of immediate freedom on payment of the ransom.

Meanwhile his captivity was bringing grievous affliction on his tribesmen; for, despairing of his return, they mustered for the election of a new chief. Party strife ran high. Some were for a boy, his son, and some for an ambitious kinsman. Outina chafed in his prison on learning these dissensions; and, eager to convince his over-hasty subjects that their chief still lived, he was so profuse of promises that he was again embarked and carried up the river.

At no great distance from Lake George, a small affluent of the St. John's gave access by water to a point within six

French leagues of Outina's principal town. The two barges, crowded with soldiers, and bearing also the captive Outina, rowed up this little stream. Indians awaited them at the landing, with gifts of bread, beans, and fish, and piteous prayers for their chief, upon whose liberation they promised an ample supply of corn. As they were deaf to all other terms, Laudonnière yielded, released his prisoner, and received in his place two hostages, who were fast bound in the boats. Ottigny and Arlac, with a strong detachment of arquebusiers, went to receive the promised supplies, for which, from the first, full payment in merchandise had been offered. On their arrival at the village, they filed into the great central lodge, within whose dusky precincts were gathered the magnates of the tribe. Council-chamber, forum, banquet-hall, and dancing-hall all in one, the spacious structure could hold half the population. Here the French made their abode. With armor buckled, and arquebuse matches lighted, they watched with anxious eyes the strange, dim scene, half revealed by the daylight that streamed down through the hole at the apex of the roof. Tall, dark forms stalked to and fro, with quivers at their backs, and bows and arrows in their hands, while groups, crouched in the shadow beyond, eyed the hated guests with inscrutable visages, and malignant, sidelong eyes. Corn came in slowly, but warriors mustered fast. The village without was full of them. The French officers grew anxious, and urged the chiefs to greater alacrity in collecting the promised ransom. The answer boded no good: "Our women are afraid when they see the matches of your guns burning. Put them out, and they will bring the corn faster."

Outina was nowhere to be seen. At length they learned that he was in one of the small huts adjacent. Several of the officers went to him, complaining of the slow payment of his ransom. The kindness of his captors at Fort Caroline seemed to have won his heart. He replied, that such was the rage of his subjects that he could no longer control them; that the French were in danger; and that he had seen arrows stuck in the ground by the side of the path, in token that war was declared. The peril was thickening hourly, and Ottigny resolved to regain the boats while there was yet time.

On the twenty-seventh of July, at nine in the morning, he

set his men in order. Each shouldering a sack of corn, they marched through the rows of huts that surrounded the great lodge, and out betwixt the overlapping extremities of the palisade that encircled the town. Before them stretched a wide avenue, three or four hundred paces long, flanked by a natural growth of trees,—one of those curious monuments of native industry to which allusion has already been made.[1] Here Ottigny halted and formed his line of march. Arlac, with eight matchlock men, was sent in advance, and flanking parties were thrown into the woods on either side. Ottigny told his soldiers that, if the Indians meant to attack them, they were probably in ambush at the other end of the avenue. He was right. As Arlac's party reached the spot, the whole pack gave tongue at once. The war-whoop rose, and a tempest of stone-headed arrows clattered against the breast-plates of the French, or, scorching like fire, tore through their unprotected limbs. They stood firm, and sent back their shot so steadily that several of the assailants were laid dead, and the rest, two or three hundred in number, gave way as Ottigny came up with his men.

They moved on for a quarter of a mile through a country, as it seems, comparatively open, when again the war-cry pealed in front, and three hundred savages bounded to the assault. Their whoops were echoed from the rear. It was the party whom Arlac had just repulsed, and who, leaping and showering their arrows, were rushing on again with a ferocity restrained only by their lack of courage. There was no panic among the French. The men threw down their bags of corn, and took to their weapons. They blew their matches, and, under two excellent officers, stood well to their work. The Indians, on their part, showed good discipline after their fashion, and were perfectly under the control of their chiefs. With cries that imitated the yell of owls, the scream of cougars, and the howl of wolves, they ran up in successive bands, let fly their arrows, and instantly fell back, giving place to others. At the sight of the levelled arquebuse, they dropped flat on the ground. Whenever the French charged upon them, sword in hand, they fled through the woods like foxes; and whenever

[1] See *ante*, p. 58.

the march was resumed, the arrows were showering again upon the flanks and rear of the retiring band. As they fell, the soldiers picked them up and broke them. Thus, beset with swarming savages, the handful of Frenchmen pushed slowly onward, fighting as they went.

The Indians gradually drew off, and the forest was silent again. Two of the French had been killed and twenty-two wounded, several so severely that they were supported to the boats with the utmost difficulty. Of the corn, two bags only had been brought off.

Famine and desperation now reigned at Fort Caroline. The Indians had killed two of the carpenters; hence long delay in the finishing of the new ship. They would not wait, but resolved to put to sea in the Breton and the brigantine. The problem was to find food for the voyage; for now, in their extremity, they roasted and ate snakes, a delicacy in which the neighborhood abounded.

On the third of August, Laudonnière, perturbed and oppressed, was walking on the hill, when, looking seaward, he saw a sight that sent a thrill through his exhausted frame. A great ship was standing towards the river's mouth. Then another came in sight, and another, and another. He despatched a messenger with the tidings to the fort below. The languid forms of his sick and despairing men rose and danced for joy, and voices shrill with weakness joined in wild laughter and acclamation, insomuch, he says, "that one would have thought them to bee out of their wittes."

A doubt soon mingled with their joy. Who were the strangers? Were they the friends so long hoped for in vain? or were they Spaniards, their dreaded enemies? They were neither. The foremost ship was a stately one, of seven hundred tons, a great burden at that day. She was named the Jesus; and with her were three smaller vessels, the Solomon, the Tiger, and the Swallow. Their commander was "a right worshipful and valiant knight,"—for so the record styles him,—a pious man and a prudent, to judge him by the orders he gave his crew when, ten months before, he sailed out of Plymouth: "Serve God daily, love one another, preserve your victuals, beware of fire, and keepe good companie." Nor were the crew unworthy the graces of their chief; for the devout chronicler of the voyage ascribes their deliverance from the perils of the sea to "the Almightie God, who never suffereth his Elect to perish."

Who then were they, this chosen band, serenely conscious of a special Providential care? They were the pioneers of that detested traffic destined to inoculate with its infection nations yet unborn, the parent of discord and death, filling half a continent with the tramp of armies and the clash of fratricidal swords. Their chief was Sir John Hawkins, father of the English slave-trade.

He had been to the coast of Guinea, where he bought and kidnapped a cargo of slaves. These he had sold to the jealous Spaniards of Hispaniola, forcing them, with sword, matchlock, and culverin, to grant him free trade, and then to sign testimonials that he had borne himself as became a peaceful merchant. Prospering greatly by this summary commerce, but distressed by the want of water, he had put into the River of May to obtain a supply.

Among the rugged heroes of the British marine, Sir John stood in the front rank, and along with Drake, his relative, is extolled as "a man borne for the honour of the English name. . . . Neither did the West of England yeeld such an Indian Neptunian paire as were these two Ocean peeres, Hawkins and Drake." So writes the old chronicler, Purchas, and all England was of his thinking. A hardy and skilful seaman, a bold fighter, a loyal friend and a stern enemy, overbearing towards equals, but kind, in his bluff way, to those beneath him, rude in speech, somewhat crafty withal and avaricious, he buffeted his way to riches and fame, and died at last full of years and honor. As for the abject humanity stowed between the reeking decks of the ship Jesus, they were merely in his eyes so many black cattle tethered for the market.[1]

---

[1] For Hawkins, see the three narratives in Hakluyt, III. 594; Purchas, IV. 1177; Stow, *Chron.*, 807; *Biog. Britan.*, Art. *Hawkins*; Anderson, *History of Commerce*, I. 400.

He was not knighted until after the voyage of 1564–65; hence there is an anachronism in the text. As he was held "to have opened a new trade," he was entitled to bear as his crest a "Moor" or negro, bound with a cord. In Fairbairn's *Crests of Great Britain and Ireland*, where it is figured, it is described, not as a negro, but as a "naked man." In Burke's *Landed Gentry*, it

Hawkins came up the river in a pinnace, and landed at Fort Caroline, accompanied, says Laudonnière, "with gentlemen honorably apparelled, yet unarmed." Between the Huguenots and the English Puritans there was a double tie of sympathy. Both hated priests, and both hated Spaniards. Wakening from their apathetic misery, the starveling garrison hailed him as a deliverer. Yet Hawkins secretly rejoiced when he learned their purpose to abandon Florida; for although, not to tempt his cupidity, they hid from him the secret of their Appalachian gold mine, he coveted for his royal mistress the possession of this rich domain. He shook his head, however, when he saw the vessels in which they proposed to embark, and offered them all a free passage to France in his own ships. This, from obvious motives of honor and prudence, Laudonnière declined, upon which Hawkins offered to lend or sell to him one of his smaller vessels.

Laudonnière hesitated, and hereupon arose a great clamor. A mob of soldiers and artisans beset his chamber, threatening loudly to desert him, and take passage with Hawkins, unless the offer were accepted. The commandant accordingly resolved to buy the vessel. The generous slaver, whose reputed avarice nowhere appears in the transaction, desired him to set his own price; and, in place of money, took the cannon of the fort, with other articles now useless to their late owners. He sent them, too, a gift of wine and biscuit, and supplied them with provisions for the voyage, receiving in payment Laudonnière's note; "for which," adds the latter, "untill this present I am indebted to him." With a friendly leave-taking, he returned to his ships and stood out to sea, leaving golden opinions among the grateful inmates of Fort Caroline.

Before the English top-sails had sunk beneath the horizon, the colonists bestirred themselves to depart. In a few days their preparations were made. They waited only for a fair

---

is said that Sir John obtained it in honor of a great victory over the Moors! His only African victories were in kidnapping raids on negro villages. In *Letters on Certain Passages in the Life of Sir John Hawkins*, the coat is engraved in detail. The "demi-Moor" has the thick lips, the flat nose, and the wool of the unequivocal negro.

Sir John became Treasurer of the Royal Navy and Rear-Admiral, and founded a marine hospital at Chatham.

wind. It was long in coming, and meanwhile their troubled fortunes assumed a new phase.

On the twenty-eighth of August, the two captains Vasseur and Verdier came in with tidings of an approaching squadron. Again the fort was wild with excitement. Friends or foes, French or Spaniards, succor or death;—betwixt these were their hopes and fears divided. On the following morning, they saw seven barges rowing up the river, bristling with weapons and crowded with men in armor. The sentries on the bluff challenged, and received no answer. One of them fired at the advancing boats, and still there was no response. Laudonnière was almost defenceless. He had given his heavier cannon to Hawkins, and only two field-pieces were left. They were levelled at the foremost boats, and the word to fire was about to be given, when a voice from among the strangers called out that they were French, commanded by Jean Ribaut.

At the eleventh hour, the long looked for succors were come. Ribaut had been commissioned to sail with seven ships for Florida. A disorderly concourse of disbanded soldiers, mixed with artisans and their families, and young nobles weary of a two years' peace, were mustered at the port of Dieppe, and embarked, to the number of three hundred men, bearing with them all things thought necessary to a prosperous colony.

No longer in dread of the Spaniards, the colonists saluted the new-comers with the cannon by which a moment before they had hoped to blow them out of the water. Laudonnière issued from his stronghold to welcome them, and regaled them with what cheer he could. Ribaut was present, conspicuous by his long beard, an astonishment to the Indians; and here, too, were officers, old friends of Laudonnière. Why, then, had they approached in the attitude of enemies? The mystery was soon explained; for they expressed to the commandant their pleasure at finding that the charges made against him had proved false. He begged to know more; on which Ribaut, taking him aside, told him that the returning ships had brought home letters filled with accusations of arrogance, tyranny, cruelty, and a purpose of establishing an independent command,—accusations which he now saw to be unfounded, but which had been the occasion of his unusual and startling precaution. He gave him, too, a letter from Admiral Coligny. In brief but courteous terms, it required him to resign his command, and requested his return to France to clear his name from the imputations cast upon it.[1] Ribaut warmly urged him to remain; but Laudonnière declined his friendly proposals.

Worn in body and mind, mortified and wounded, he soon fell ill again. A peasant woman attended him, who was brought over, he says, to nurse the sick and take charge of the poultry, and of whom Le Moyne also speaks as a servant, but who had been made the occasion of additional charges against him, most offensive to the austere Admiral.

Stores were landed, tents were pitched, women and children were sent on shore, feathered Indians mingled in the throng, and the borders of the River of May swarmed with busy life. "But, lo, how oftentimes misfortune doth search and pursue us, even then when we thinke to be at rest!" exclaims the unhappy Laudonnière. Amidst the light and cheer of renovated hope, a cloud of blackest omen was gathering in the east.

At half-past eleven on the night of Tuesday, the fourth of September, the crew of Ribaut's flag-ship, anchored on the still sea outside the bar, saw a huge hulk, grim with the throats of cannon, drifting towards them through the gloom; and from its stern rolled on the sluggish air the portentous banner of Spain.

[1] See the letter in Basanier, 102.

Chapter VII

MENENDEZ

Spain • Pedro Menendez de Avilés • His Boyhood • His Early Career • His Petition to the King • Commissioned to conquer Florida • His Powers • His Designs • A New Crusade • Sailing of the Spanish Fleet • A Storm • Porto Rico • Energy of Menendez • He reaches Florida • Attacks Ribaut's Ships • Founds St. Augustine • Alarm of the French • Bold Decision of Ribaut • Defenceless Condition of Fort Caroline • Ribaut thwarted • Tempest • Menendez marches on the French Fort • His Desperate Position • The Fort taken • The Massacre • The Fugitives

---

THE monk, the inquisitor, and the Jesuit were lords of Spain,—sovereigns of her sovereign, for they had formed the dark and narrow mind of that tyrannical recluse. They had formed the minds of her people, quenched in blood every spark of rising heresy, and given over a noble nation to a bigotry blind and inexorable as the doom of fate. Linked with pride, ambition, avarice, every passion of a rich, strong nature, potent for good and ill, it made the Spaniard of that day a scourge as dire as ever fell on man.

Day was breaking on the world. Light, hope, and freedom pierced with vitalizing ray the clouds and the miasma that hung so thick over the prostrate Middle Age, once noble and mighty, now a foul image of decay and death. Kindled with new life, the nations gave birth to a progeny of heroes, and the stormy glories of the sixteenth century rose on awakened Europe. But Spain was the citadel of darkness,—a monastic cell, an inquisitorial dungeon, where no ray could pierce. She was the bulwark of the Church, against whose adamantine wall the waves of innovation beat in vain.[1] In every country of Eu-

---

[1] "Better a ruined kingdom, true to itself and its king, than one left unharmed to the profit of the Devil and the heretics." *Correspondance de Philippe II.*, cited by Prescott, *Philip II.*, Book III. c. 2, note 36.

"A prince can do nothing more shameful, or more hurtful to himself, than to permit his people to live according to their conscience." *The Duke of Alva*, in Davila, Lib. III. p. 341.

rope the party of freedom and reform was the national party, the party of reaction and absolutism was the Spanish party, leaning on Spain, looking to her for help. Above all, it was so in France; and, while within her bounds there was for a time some semblance of peace, the national and religious rage burst forth on a wilder theatre. Thither it is for us to follow it, where, on the shores of Florida, the Spaniard and the Frenchman, the bigot and the Huguenot, met in the grapple of death.

In a corridor of his palace, Philip the Second was met by a man who had long stood waiting his approach, and who with proud reverence placed a petition in the hand of the pale and sombre King. The petitioner was Pedro Menendez de Avilés, one of the ablest and most distinguished officers of the Spanish marine. He was born of an ancient Asturian family. His boyhood had been wayward, ungovernable, and fierce. He ran off at eight years of age, and when, after a search of six months, he was found and brought back, he ran off again. This time he was more successful, escaping on board a fleet bound against the Barbary corsairs, where his precocious appetite for blood and blows had reasonable contentment. A few years later, he found means to build a small vessel, in which he cruised against the corsairs and the French, and, though still hardly more than a boy, displayed a singular address and daring. The wonders of the New World now seized his imagination. He made a voyage thither, and the ships under his charge came back freighted with wealth. The war with France was then at its height. As captain-general of the fleet, he was sent with troops to Flanders; and to their prompt arrival was due, it is said, the victory of St. Quentin. Two years later, he commanded the luckless armada which bore back Philip to his native shore. On the way, the King narrowly escaped drowning in a storm off the port of Laredo. This mischance, or his own violence and insubordination, wrought to the prejudice of Menendez. He complained that his services were ill repaid. Philip lent him a favoring ear, and despatched him to the Indies as general of the fleet and army. Here he found means to amass vast riches; and, in 1561, on his return to Spain, charges were brought against him of a nature which his too friendly biographer does not explain. The Council of the Indies arrested him. He was imprisoned and sentenced to a heavy fine; but, gaining his release, hastened to court to throw himself on the royal clemency.[1] His petition was most graciously received. Philip restored his command, but remitted only half his fine, a strong presumption of his guilt.

Menendez kissed the royal hand; he had another petition in reserve. His son had been wrecked near the Bermudas, and he would fain go thither to find tidings of his fate. The pious King bade him trust in God, and promised that he should be despatched without delay to the Bermudas and to Florida, with a commission to make an exact survey of the neighboring seas for the profit of future voyagers; but Menendez was not content with such an errand. He knew, he said, nothing of greater moment to his Majesty than the conquest and settlement of Florida. The climate was healthful, the soil fertile; and, worldly advantages aside, it was peopled by a race sunk in the thickest shades of infidelity. "Such grief," he pursued, "seizes me, when I behold this multitude of wretched Indians, that I should choose the conquest and settling of Florida above all commands, offices, and dignities which your Majesty might bestow."[2] Those who take this for hypocrisy do not know the Spaniard of the sixteenth century.

The King was edified by his zeal. An enterprise of such spiritual and temporal promise was not to be slighted, and Menendez was empowered to conquer and convert Florida at his own cost. The conquest was to be effected within three years. Menendez was to take with him five hundred men, and supply them with five hundred slaves, besides horses, cattle, sheep, and hogs. Villages were to be built, with forts to defend them; and sixteen ecclesiastics, of whom four should be Jesuits, were to form the nucleus of a Floridan church. The King, on his part, granted Menendez free trade with Hispaniola, Porto Rico, Cuba, and Spain, the office of Adelantado of Florida for life, with the right of naming his successor, and large emoluments to be drawn from the expected conquest.[3]

[1] Barcia, (Cardenas y Cano,) *Ensayo Cronologico*, 57–64.

[2] *Ibid.*, 65.

[3] The above is from Barcia, as the original compact has not been found. For the patent conferring the title of Adelantado, see *Coleccion de Varios Documentos*, I. 13.

The compact struck, Menendez hastened to his native Asturias to raise money among his relatives. Scarcely was he gone, when tidings reached Madrid that Florida was already occupied by a colony of French Protestants, and that a reinforcement, under Ribaut, was on the point of sailing thither. A French historian of high authority declares that these advices came from the Catholic party at the French court, in whom every instinct of patriotism was lost in their hatred of Coligny and the Huguenots. Of this there can be little doubt, though information also came about this time from the buccaneer Frenchmen captured in the West Indies.

Foreigners had invaded the territory of Spain. The trespassers, too, were heretics, foes of God, and liegemen of the Devil. Their doom was fixed. But how would France endure an assault, in time of peace, on subjects who had gone forth on an enterprise sanctioned by the Crown, and undertaken in its name and under its commission?

The throne of France, in which the corruption of the nation seemed gathered to a head, was trembling between the two parties of the Catholics and the Huguenots, whose chiefs aimed at royalty. Flattering both, caressing both, playing one against the other, and betraying both, Catherine de Medicis, by a thousand crafty arts and expedients of the moment, sought to retain the crown on the head of her weak and vicious son. Of late her crooked policy had led her towards the Catholic party, in other words the party of Spain; and she had already given ear to the savage Duke of Alva, urging her to the course which, seven years later, led to the carnage of St. Bartholomew. In short, the Spanish policy was in the ascendant, and no thought of the national interest or honor could restrain that basest of courts from abandoning by hundreds to the national enemy those whom it was itself meditating to immolate by thousands.[1] It might protest for form's sake, or to quiet public clamor; but Philip of Spain well knew that it would end in patient submission.

Menendez was summoned back in haste to the Spanish

---

[1] The French Jesuit Charlevoix says: "On avoit donné à cette expédition tout l'air d'une guerre sainte, entreprise contre les Hérétiques de concert avec le Roy de France." Nor does Charlevoix seem to doubt this complicity of Charles the Ninth in an attack on his own subjects.

court. His force must be strengthened. Three hundred and ninety-four men were added at the royal charge, and a corresponding number of transport and supply ships. It was a holy war, a crusade, and as such was preached by priest and monk along the western coasts of Spain. All the Biscayan ports flamed with zeal, and adventurers crowded to enroll themselves; since to plunder heretics is good for the soul as well as the purse, and broil and massacre have double attraction when promoted into a means of salvation. It was a fervor, deep and hot, but not of celestial kindling; nor yet that buoyant and inspiring zeal which, when the Middle Age was in its youth and prime, glowed in the souls of Tancred, Godfrey, and St. Louis, and which, when its day was long since past, could still find its home in the great heart of Columbus. A darker spirit urged the new crusade,—born not of hope, but of fear, slavish in its nature, the creature and the tool of despotism; for the typical Spaniard of the sixteenth century was not in strictness a fanatic, he was bigotry incarnate.

Heresy was a plague-spot, an ulcer to be eradicated with fire and the knife, and this foul abomination was infecting the shores which the Vicegerent of Christ had given to the King of Spain, and which the Most Catholic King had given to the Adelantado. Thus would countless heathen tribes be doomed to an eternity of flame, and the Prince of Darkness hold his ancient sway unbroken; and for the Adelantado himself, the vast outlays, the vast debts of his bold Floridan venture would be all in vain, and his fortunes be wrecked past redemption through these tools of Satan. As a Catholic, as a Spaniard, and as an adventurer, his course was clear.

The work assigned him was prodigious. He was invested with power almost absolute, not merely over the peninsula which now retains the name of Florida, but over all North America, from Labrador to Mexico; for this was the Florida of the old Spanish geographers, and the Florida designated in the commission of Menendez. It was a continent which he was to conquer and occupy out of his own purse. The impoverished King contracted with his daring and ambitious subject to win and hold for him the territory of the future United States and British Provinces. His plan, as afterwards exposed at length in his letters to Philip the Second, was, first, to plant a garrison at Port Royal, and next to fortify strongly on Chesapeake Bay, called by him St. Mary's. He believed that adjoining this bay was an arm of the sea, running northward and eastward, and communicating with the Gulf of St. Lawrence, thus making New England, with adjacent districts, an island. His proposed fort on the Chesapeake, securing access, by this imaginary passage, to the seas of Newfoundland, would enable the Spaniards to command the fisheries, on which both the French and the English had long encroached, to the great prejudice of Spanish rights. Doubtless, too, these inland waters gave access to the South Sea, and their occupation was necessary to prevent the French from penetrating thither; for that ambitious people, since the time of Cartier, had never abandoned their schemes of seizing this portion of the dominions of the King of Spain. Five hundred soldiers and one hundred sailors must, he urges, take possession, without delay, of Port Royal and the Chesapeake.[1]

Preparation for his enterprise was pushed with furious energy. His whole force, when the several squadrons were united, amounted to two thousand six hundred and forty-six persons, in thirty-four vessels, one of which, the San Pelayo, bearing Menendez himself, was of nine hundred and ninety-six tons' burden, and is described as one of the finest ships afloat.[2] There were twelve Franciscans and eight Jesuits, besides other ecclesiastics; and many knights of Galicia, Biscay, and the Asturias took part in the expedition. With a slight exception, the whole was at the Adelantado's charge. Within the first fourteen months, according to his admirer, Barcia, the adventure cost him a million ducats.[3]

[1] *Cartas escritas al Rey por el General Pero Menendez de Avilés*. These are the official despatches of Menendez, of which the originals are preserved in the archives of Seville. They are very voluminous and minute in detail. Copies of them were obtained by the aid of Buckingham Smith, Esq., to whom the writer is also indebted for various other documents from the same source, throwing new light on the events described. Menendez calls Port Royal "St. Elena," a name afterwards applied to the sound which still retains it. Compare *Historical Magazine*, IV. 320.

[2] This was not so remarkable as it may appear. Charnock, *History of Marine Architecture*, gives the tonnage of the ships of the Invincible Armada. The flag-ship of the Andalusian squadron was of fifteen hundred and fifty tons; several were of about twelve hundred.

[3] Barcia, 69. The following passage in one of the unpublished letters of Menendez seems to indicate that the above is exaggerated: "Your Majesty

Before the close of the year, Sancho de Arciniega was commissioned to join Menendez with an additional force of fifteen hundred men.[1]

Red-hot with a determined purpose, the Adelantado would brook no delay. To him, says the chronicler, every day seemed a year. He was eager to anticipate Ribaut, of whose designs and whose force he seems to have been informed to the minutest particular, but whom he hoped to thwart and ruin by gaining Fort Caroline before him. With eleven ships, therefore, he sailed from Cadiz, on the twenty-ninth of June, 1565, leaving the smaller vessels of his fleet to follow with what speed they might. He touched first at the Canaries, and on the eighth of July left them, steering for Dominica. A minute account of the voyage has come down to us, written by Mendoza, chaplain of the expedition, a somewhat dull and illiterate person, who busily jots down the incidents of each passing day, and is constantly betraying, with a certain awkward simplicity, how the cares of this world and of the next jostle each other in his thoughts.

On Friday, the twentieth of July, a storm fell upon them with appalling fury. The pilots lost their wits, and the sailors gave themselves up to their terrors. Throughout the night, they beset Mendoza for confession and absolution, a boon not easily granted, for the seas swept the crowded decks with cataracts of foam, and the shriekings of the gale in the rigging overpowered the exhortations of the half-drowned priest. Cannon, cables, spars, water-casks, were thrown overboard, and the chests of the sailors would have followed, had not the latter, in spite of their fright, raised such a howl of remonstrance that the order was revoked. At length day dawned. Plunging, reeling, half under water, quivering with the shock

---

may be assured by me, that, had I a million, more or less, I would employ and spend the whole in this undertaking, it being so greatly to [the glory of] God our Lord, and the increase of our Holy Catholic Faith, and the service and authority of your Majesty; and thus I have offered to our Lord whatever He shall give me in this world, [and whatever] I shall possess, gain, or acquire shall be devoted to the planting of the Gospel in this land, and the enlightenment of the natives thereof, and this I do promise to your Majesty." This letter is dated 11 September, 1565.

[1] *Año de 1565. Nombramiento de Capitan-General de la Armada destinada para yr á la Provincia de la Florida al socorro del General Pero Menendez de Avilés, hecho por Su Magestad al Capitan Sancho de Arciniega.*

of the seas, whose mountain ridges rolled down upon her before the gale, the ship lay in deadly peril from Friday till Monday noon. Then the storm abated; the sun broke out; and again she held her course.[1]

They reached Dominica on Sunday, the fifth of August. The chaplain tells us how he went on shore to refresh himself; how, while his Italian servant washed his linen at a brook, he strolled along the beach and picked up shells; and how he was scared, first, by a prodigious turtle, and next by a vision of the cannibal natives, which caused his prompt retreat to the boats.

On the tenth, they anchored in the harbor of Porto Rico, where they found two ships of their squadron, from which they had parted in the storm. One of them was the San Pelayo, with Menendez on board. Mendoza informs us, that in the evening the officers came on board the ship to which he was attached, when he, the chaplain, regaled them with sweetmeats, and that Menendez invited him not only to supper that night, but to dinner the next day, "for the which I thanked him, as reason was," says the gratified churchman.

Here thirty men deserted, and three priests also ran off, of which Mendoza bitterly complains, as increasing his own work. The motives of the clerical truants may perhaps be inferred from a worldly temptation to which the chaplain himself was subjected. "I was offered the service of a chapel where I should have got a *peso* for every mass I said, the whole year round; but I did not accept it, for fear that what I hear said of the other three would be said of me. Besides, it is not a place where one can hope for any great advancement, and I wished to try whether, in refusing a benefice for the love of the Lord, He will not repay me with some other stroke of fortune before the end of the voyage; for it is my aim to serve God and His blessed Mother."[2]

The original design had been to rendezvous at Havana, but with the Adelantado the advantages of despatch outweighed

[1] Francisco Lopez de Mendoza Grajales, *Relacion de la Jornada de Pedro Menendez*, printed in *Coleccion de Documentos Inéditos*, III. 441 (Madrid, 1865). There is a French translation in the *Floride* of Ternaux-Compans. Letter of Menendez to the King, 13 August, 1565.

[2] Mendoza, *Relacion de la Jornada de Pedro Menendez*.

every other consideration. He resolved to push directly for
Florida. Five of his scattered ships had by this time rejoined
company, comprising, exclusive of officers, a force of about
five hundred soldiers, two hundred sailors, and one hundred
colonists.[1] Bearing northward, he advanced by an unknown
and dangerous course along the coast of Hayti and through
the intricate passes of the Bahamas. On the night of the
twenty-sixth, the San Pelayo struck three times on the shoals;
"but," says the chaplain, "inasmuch as our enterprise was undertaken for the sake of Christ and His blessed Mother, two
heavy seas struck her abaft, and set her afloat again."

At length the ships lay becalmed in the Bahama Channel,
slumbering on the glassy sea, torpid with the heats of a West
Indian August. Menendez called a council of the commanders. There was doubt and indecision. Perhaps Ribaut had already reached the French fort, and then to attack the united
force would be an act of desperation. Far better to await their
lagging comrades. But the Adelantado was of another mind;
and, even had his enemy arrived, he was resolved that he
should have no time to fortify himself.

"It is God's will," he said, "that our victory should be due,
not to our numbers, but to His all-powerful aid. Therefore
has He stricken us with tempests, and scattered our ships."[2]
And he gave his voice for instant advance.

There was much dispute; even the chaplain remonstrated;
but nothing could bend the iron will of Menendez. Nor was
a sign of celestial approval wanting. At nine in the evening, a
great meteor burst forth in mid-heaven, and, blazing like the
sun, rolled westward towards the coast of Florida.[3] The fainting spirits of the crusaders were revived. Diligent preparation
was begun. Prayers and masses were said; and, that the temporal arm might not fail, the men were daily practised on
deck in shooting at marks, in order, says the chronicle, that
the recruits might learn not to be afraid of their guns.

The dead calm continued. "We were all very tired," says
the chaplain, "and I above all, with praying to God for a fair

[1] Letter of Menendez to the King, 11 September, 1565.
[2] Barcia, 70.
[3] Mendoza, *Relacion:* "Nos mostró Nuestro Señor un misterio en el cielo,"
etc.

wind. To-day, at about two in the afternoon, He took pity on us, and sent us a breeze."[1] Before night they saw land,— the faint line of forest, traced along the watery horizon, that marked the coast of Florida. But where, in all this vast monotony, was the lurking-place of the French? Menendez anchored, and sent a captain with twenty men ashore, who presently found a band of Indians, and gained from them the needed information. He stood northward, till, on the afternoon of Tuesday, the fourth of September, he descried four ships anchored near the mouth of a river. It was the river St. John's, and the ships were four of Ribaut's squadron. The prey was in sight. The Spaniards prepared for battle, and bore down upon the Lutherans; for, with them, all Protestants alike were branded with the name of the arch-heretic. Slowly, before the faint breeze, the ships glided on their way; but while, excited and impatient, the fierce crews watched the decreasing space, and when they were still three leagues from their prize, the air ceased to stir, the sails flapped against the mast, a black cloud with thunder rose above the coast, and the warm rain of the South descended on the breathless sea. It was dark before the wind stirred again and the ships resumed their course. At half-past eleven they reached the French. The San Pelayo slowly moved to windward of Ribaut's flag-ship, the Trinity, and anchored very near her. The other ships took similar stations. While these preparations were making, a work of two hours, the men labored in silence, and the French, thronging their gangways, looked on in equal silence. "Never, since I came into the world," writes the chaplain, "did I know such a stillness."

It was broken at length by a trumpet from the deck of the San Pelayo. A French trumpet answered. Then Menendez, "with much courtesy," says his Spanish eulogist, inquired, "Gentlemen, whence does this fleet come?"

"From France," was the reply.

"What are you doing here?" pursued the Adelantado.

"Bringing soldiers and supplies for a fort which the King of France has in this country, and for many others which he soon will have."

[1] Mendoza, *Relacion*.

"Are you Catholics or Lutherans?"

Many voices cried out together, "Lutherans, of the new religion." Then, in their turn, they demanded who Menendez was, and whence he came.

He answered: "I am Pedro Menendez, General of the fleet of the King of Spain, Don Philip the Second, who have come to this country to hang and behead all Lutherans whom I shall find by land or sea, according to instructions from my King, so precise that I have power to pardon none; and these commands I shall fulfil, as you will see. At daybreak I shall board your ships, and if I find there any Catholic, he shall be well treated; but every heretic shall die."[1]

The French with one voice raised a cry of wrath and defiance.

"If you are a brave man, don't wait till day. Come on now, and see what you will get!"

And they assailed the Adelantado with a shower of scoffs and insults.

Menendez broke into a rage, and gave the order to board. The men slipped the cables, and the sullen black hulk of the San Pelayo drifted down upon the Trinity. The French did not make good their defiance. Indeed, they were incapable of resistance, Ribaut with his soldiers being ashore at Fort Caroline. They cut their cables, left their anchors, made sail, and fled. The Spaniards fired, the French replied. The other Spanish ships had imitated the movement of the San Pelayo; "but," writes the chaplain, Mendoza, "these devils are such adroit sailors, and manoeuvred so well, that we did not catch

---

[1] "Pedro Menendez os lo pregunta, General de esta Armada del Rei de España Don Felipe Segundo, qui viene à esta Tierra à ahorcar, y degollar todos los Luteranos, que hallare en ella, y en el Mar, segun la Instruccion, que trae de mi Rei, que es tan precisa, que me priva de la facultad de perdonarlos, y la cumplirè en todo, como lo vereis luego que amanezca, que entrarè en vuestros Navios, y si hallare algun Catolico, le harè buen tratamiento; pero el que fuere Herege, morirà." Barcia, 75.

The following is the version, literally given, of Menendez himself: —

"I answered them: 'Pedro Menendez, who was going by your Majesty's command to this coast and country in order to burn and hang the Lutheran French who should be found there, and that in the morning I would board their ships to find out whether any of them belonged to that people, because, in case they did, I could not do otherwise than execute upon them that justice which your Majesty had ordained.'" Letter of Menendez to the King, 11 September, 1565.

one of them."[1] Pursuers and pursued ran out to sea, firing useless volleys at each other.

In the morning Menendez gave over the chase, turned, and, with the San Pelayo alone, ran back for the St. John's. But here a welcome was prepared for him. He saw bands of armed men drawn up on the beach, and the smaller vessels of Ribaut's squadron, which had crossed the bar several days before, anchored behind it to oppose his landing. He would not venture an attack, but, steering southward, sailed along the coast till he came to an inlet which he named San Agustin, the same which Laudonnière had named the River of Dolphins.

Here he found three of his ships already debarking their troops, guns, and stores. Two officers, Patiño and Vicente, had taken possession of the dwelling of the Indian chief Seloy, a huge barn-like structure, strongly framed of entire trunks of trees, and thatched with palmetto leaves.[2] Around it they were throwing up intrenchments of fascines and sand, and gangs of negroes were toiling at the work. Such was the birth of St. Augustine, the oldest town of the United States.

On the eighth, Menendez took formal possession of his domain. Cannon were fired, trumpets sounded, and banners displayed, as he landed in state at the head of his officers and nobles. Mendoza, crucifix in hand, came to meet him, chanting *Te Deum laudamus*, while the Adelantado and all his company, kneeling, kissed the crucifix, and the assembled Indians gazed in silent wonder.[3]

---

[1] Mendoza, *Relacion*.

The above account is that of Barcia, the admirer and advocate of Menendez. A few points have been added from Mendoza, as indicated by the citations. One statement of Barcia is omitted, because there can be little doubt that it is false. He says, that, when the Spanish fleet approached, the French opened a heavy fire on them. Neither the fanatical Mendoza, who was present, nor the French writers, Laudonnière, Le Moyne, and Challeux, mention this circumstance, which, besides, can scarcely be reconciled with the subsequent conduct of either party. Mendoza differs from Barcia also in respect to the time of the attack, which he places "at two hours after sunset." In other points his story tallies as nearly as could be expected with that of Barcia. The same may be said of Challeux and Laudonnière. The latter says, that the Spaniards, before attacking, asked after the French officers by name, whence he infers that they had received very minute information from France.

[2] Compare Hawkins, *Second Voyage*. He visited this or some similar structure, and his journalist minutely describes it.

[3] Mendoza, *Relacion*.

Meanwhile the tenants of Fort Caroline were not idle. Two or three soldiers, strolling along the beach in the afternoon, had first seen the Spanish ships, and hastily summoned Ribaut. He came down to the mouth of the river, followed by an anxious and excited crowd; but, as they strained their eyes through the darkness, they could see nothing but the flashes of the distant guns. At length the returning light showed, far out at sea, the Adelantado in hot chase of their flying comrades. Pursuers and pursued were soon out of sight. The drums beat to arms. After many hours of suspense, the San Pelayo reappeared, hovering about the mouth of the river, then bearing away towards the south. More anxious hours ensued, when three other sail came in sight, and they recognized three of their own returning ships. Communication was opened, a boat's crew landed, and they learned from Cosette, one of the French captains, that, confiding in the speed of his ship, he had followed the Spaniards to St. Augustine, reconnoitred their position, and seen them land their negroes and intrench themselves.[1]

Laudonnière lay sick in bed in his chamber at Fort Caroline when Ribaut entered, and with him La Grange, Sainte Marie, Ottigny, Yonville, and other officers. At the bedside of the displaced commandant, they held their council of war. Three plans were proposed: first, to remain where they were and fortify themselves; next, to push overland for St. Augustine and attack the invaders in their intrenchments; and, finally, to embark and assail them by sea. The first plan would leave their ships a prey to the Spaniards; and so, too, in all likelihood, would the second, besides the uncertainties of an overland march through an unknown wilderness. By sea, the distance was short and the route explored. By a sudden blow they could capture or destroy the Spanish ships, and master the troops on shore before reinforcements could arrive, and before they had time to complete their defences.[2]

---

[1] Laudonnière in Basanier, 105. Le Moyne differs in a few trifling details.

[2] Ribaut showed Laudonnière a letter from Coligny, appended to which were these words: "Captaine *Jean Ribaut*: En fermant ceste lettre i'ay eu certain aduis, comme dom *Petro Melandes* se part d'Espagne, pour aller à la coste de la Nouuelle Frāce: Vous regarderez de n'endurer qu'il n'entrepreine sur nous, non plus qu'il n'veut que nous n'entreprenions sur eux." Ribaut interpreted this into a command to attack the Spaniards. Laudonnière, 106.

Such were the views of Ribaut, with which, not unnaturally, Laudonnière finds fault, and Le Moyne echoes the censures of his chief. And yet the plan seems as well conceived as it was bold, lacking nothing but success. The Spaniards, stricken with terror, owed their safety to the elements, or, as they say, to the special interposition of the Holy Virgin. Menendez was a leader fit to stand with Cortés and Pizarro; but he was matched with a man as cool, skilful, prompt, and daring as himself. The traces that have come down to us indicate in Ribaut one far above the common stamp, — "a distinguished man, of many high qualities," as even the fault-finding Le Moyne calls him; devout after the best spirit of the Reform; and with a human heart under his steel breastplate.

La Grange and other officers took part with Laudonnière, and opposed the plan of an attack by sea; but Ribaut's conviction was unshaken, and the order was given. All his own soldiers fit for duty embarked in haste, and with them went La Caille, Arlac, and, as it seems, Ottigny, with the best of Laudonnière's men. Even Le Moyne, though wounded in the fight with Outina's warriors, went on board to bear his part in the fray, and would have sailed with the rest had not Ottigny, seeing his disabled condition, ordered him back to the fort.

On the tenth, the ships, crowded with troops, set sail. Ribaut was gone, and with him the bone and sinew of the colony. The miserable remnant watched his receding sails with dreary foreboding, — a foreboding which seemed but too just, when, on the next day, a storm, more violent than the Indians had ever known,[1] howled through the forest and lashed the ocean into fury. Most forlorn was the plight of these exiles, left, it might be, the prey of a band of ferocious bigots more terrible than the fiercest hordes of the wilderness; and when night closed on the stormy river and the gloomy waste of pines, what dreams of terror may not have haunted the helpless women who crouched under the hovels of Fort Caroline!

The fort was in a ruinous state, with the palisade on the water side broken down, and three breaches in the rampart. In the driving rain, urged by the sick Laudonnière, the men,

[1] Laudonnière, 107.

bedrenched and disheartened, labored as they could to strengthen their defences. Their muster-roll shows but a beggarly array. "Now," says Laudonnière, "let them which have bene bold to say that I had men ynough left me, so that I had meanes to defend my selfe, give eare a little now vnto mee, and if they have eyes in their heads, let them see what men I had." Of Ribaut's followers left at the fort, only nine or ten had weapons, while only two or three knew how to use them. Four of them were boys, who kept Ribaut's dogs, and another was his cook. Besides these, he had left a brewer, an old crossbow-maker, two shoemakers, a player on the spinet, four valets, a carpenter of threescore,—Challeux, no doubt, who has left us the story of his woes,—with a crowd of women, children, and eighty-six camp-followers.[1] To these were added the remnant of Laudonnière's men, of whom seventeen could bear arms, the rest being sick or disabled by wounds received in the fight with Outina.

Laudonnière divided his force, such as it was, into two watches, over which he placed two officers, Saint Cler and La Vigne, gave them lanterns for going the rounds, and an hourglass for setting the time; while he himself, giddy with weakness and fever, was every night at the guard-room.

It was the night of the nineteenth of September, the season of tempests; floods of rain drenched the sentries on the rampart, and, as day dawned on the dripping barracks and deluged parade, the storm increased in violence. What enemy could venture out on such a night? La Vigne, who had the watch, took pity on the sentries and on himself, dismissed them, and went to his quarters. He little knew what human energies, urged by ambition, avarice, bigotry, and desperation, will dare and do.

To return to the Spaniards at St. Augustine. On the morning of the eleventh, the crew of one of their smaller vessels, lying outside the bar, with Menendez himself on board, saw through the twilight of early dawn two of Ribaut's ships close upon them. Not a breath of air was stirring. There was no escape, and the Spaniards fell on their knees in supplication to Our Lady of Utrera, explaining to her that the heretics

---

[1] The muster-roll is from Laudonnière. Hakluyt's translation is incorrect.

were upon them, and begging her to send them a little wind. "Forthwith," says Mendoza, "one would have said that Our Lady herself came down upon the vessel."[1] A wind sprang up, and the Spaniards found refuge behind the bar. The returning day showed to their astonished eyes all the ships of Ribaut, their decks black with men, hovering off the entrance of the port; but Heaven had them in its charge, and again they experienced its protecting care. The breeze sent by Our Lady of Utrera rose to a gale, then to a furious tempest; and the grateful Adelantado saw through rack and mist the ships of his enemy tossed wildly among the raging waters as they struggled to gain an offing. With exultation in his heart, the skilful seaman read their danger, and saw them in his mind's eye dashed to utter wreck among the sand-bars and breakers of the lee shore.

A bold thought seized him. He would march overland with five hundred men, and attack Fort Caroline while its defenders were absent. First he ordered a mass, and then he called a council. Doubtless it was in that great Indian lodge of Seloy, where he had made his headquarters; and here, in this dim and smoky abode, nobles, officers, and priests gathered at his summons. There were fears and doubts and murmurings, but Menendez was desperate; not with the mad desperation that strikes wildly and at random, but the still white heat that melts and burns and seethes with a steady, unquenchable fierceness. "Comrades," he said, "the time has come to show our courage and our zeal. This is God's war, and we must not flinch. It is a war with Lutherans, and we must wage it with blood and fire."[2]

But his hearers gave no response. They had not a million of ducats at stake, and were not ready for a cast so desperate. A clamor of remonstrance rose from the circle. Many voices, that of Mendoza among the rest, urged waiting till their main forces should arrive. The excitement spread to the men without, and the swarthy, black-bearded crowd broke into tumults mounting almost to mutiny, while an officer was heard to say

---

[1] Mendoza, *Relacion*. Menendez, too, imputes the escape to divine interposition. "Our Lord permitted by a miracle that we should be saved." Letter of Menendez to the King, 15 October, 1565.

[2] "A sangre y fuego." Barcia, 78, where the speech is given at length.

that he would not go on such a hare-brained errand to be butchered like a beast. But nothing could move the Adelantado. His appeals or his threats did their work at last; ·the confusion was quelled, and preparation was made for the march.

On the morning of the seventeenth, five hundred arquebusiers and pikemen were drawn up before the camp. To each was given six pounds of biscuit and a canteen filled with wine. Two Indians and a renegade Frenchman, called François Jean, were to guide them, and twenty Biscayan axemen moved to the front to clear the way. Through floods of driving rain, a hoarse voice shouted the word of command, and the sullen march began.

With dismal misgiving, Mendoza watched the last files as they vanished in the tempestuous forest. Two days of suspense ensued, when a messenger came back with a letter from the Adelantado, announcing that he had nearly reached the French fort, and that on the morrow, September the twentieth, at sunrise, he hoped to assault it. "May the Divine Majesty deign to protect us, for He knows that we have need of it," writes the scared chaplain; "the Adelantado's great zeal and courage make us hope he will succeed, but, for the good of his Majesty's service, he ought to be a little less ardent in pursuing his schemes."

Meanwhile the five hundred pushed their march, now toiling across the inundated savannas, waist-deep in bulrushes and mud; now filing through the open forest to the moan and roar of the storm-racked pines; now hacking their way through palmetto thickets; and now turning from their path to shun some pool, quagmire, cypress swamp, or "hummock," matted with impenetrable bushes, brambles, and vines. As they bent before the tempest, the water trickling from the rusty head-piece crept clammy and cold betwixt the armor and the skin; and when they made their wretched bivouac, their bed was the spongy soil, and the exhaustless clouds their tent.[1]

The night of Wednesday, the nineteenth, found their vanguard in a deep forest of pines, less than a mile from Fort

[1] I have examined the country on the line of march of Menendez. In many places it retains its original features.

Caroline, and near the low hills which extended in its rear, and formed a continuation of St. John's Bluff. All around was one great morass. In pitchy darkness, knee-deep in weeds and water, half starved, worn with toil and lack of sleep, drenched to the skin, their provisions spoiled, their ammunition wet, and their spirit chilled out of them, they stood in shivering groups, cursing the enterprise and the author of it. Menendez heard Fernando Perez, an ensign, say aloud to his comrades: "This Asturian *Corito*, who knows no more of war on shore than an ass, has betrayed us all. By God, if my advice had been followed, he would have had his deserts the day he set out on this cursed journey!"[1]

The Adelantado pretended not to hear.

Two hours before dawn he called his officers about him. All night, he said, he had been praying to God and the Virgin.

"Señores, what shall we resolve on? Our ammunition and provisions are gone. Our case is desperate."[2] And he urged a bold rush on the fort.

But men and officers alike were disheartened and disgusted. They listened coldly and sullenly; many were for returning at every risk; none were in the mood for fight. Menendez put forth all his eloquence, till at length the dashed spirits of his followers were so far revived that they consented to follow him.

All fell on their knees in the marsh; then, rising, they formed their ranks and began to advance, guided by the renegade Frenchman, whose hands, to make sure of him, were tied behind his back. Groping and stumbling in the dark among trees, roots, and underbrush, buffeted by wind and rain, and lashed in the face by the recoiling boughs which they could not see, they soon lost their way, fell into confusion, and came to a stand, in a mood more savagely desponding than before. But soon a glimmer of returning day came

[1] "Como nos trae vendidos este Asturiano Corito, que no sabe de Guerra de Tierra, mas que un Jumento!" etc. Barcia, 79. *Corito* is a nickname given to the inhabitants of Biscay and the Asturias.

[2] "Ved aora, Señores, què determinacion tomarèmos, hallandonos cansados, perdidos, sin Municiones ni Comida, ni esperança de remediarnos?" Barcia, 79.

to their aid, and showed them the dusky sky, and the dark columns of the surrounding pines. Menendez ordered the men forward on pain of death. They obeyed, and presently, emerging from the forest, could dimly discern the ridge of a low hill, behind which, the Frenchman told them, was the fort. Menendez, with a few officers and men, cautiously mounted to the top. Beneath lay Fort Caroline, three bow-shots distant; but the rain, the imperfect light, and a cluster of intervening houses prevented his seeing clearly, and he sent two officers to reconnoitre. As they descended, they met a solitary Frenchman. They knocked him down with a sheathed sword, wounded him, took him prisoner, kept him for a time, and then stabbed him as they returned towards the top of the hill. Here, clutching their weapons, all the gang stood in fierce expectancy.

"Santiago!" cried Menendez. "At them! God is with us! Victory!"[1] And, shouting their hoarse war-cries, the Spaniards rushed down the slope like starved wolves.

Not a sentry was on the rampart. La Vigne, the officer of the guard, had just gone to his quarters; but a trumpeter, who chanced to remain, saw, through sheets of rain, the swarm of assailants sweeping down the hill. He blew the alarm, and at the summons a few half-naked soldiers ran wildly out of the barracks. It was too late. Through the breaches and over the ramparts the Spaniards came pouring in, with shouts of "Santiago! Santiago!"

Sick men leaped from their beds. Women and children, blind with fright, darted shrieking from the houses. A fierce, gaunt visage, the thrust of a pike, or blow of a rusty halberd,—such was the greeting that met all alike. Laudonnière snatched his sword and target, and ran towards the principal breach, calling to his soldiers. A rush of Spaniards met him; his men were cut down around him; and he, with a soldier named Bartholomew, was forced back into the yard of his house. Here stood a tent, and, as the pursuers stumbled among the cords, he escaped behind Ottigny's house, sprang through the breach in the western rampart, and fled for the woods.[2]

[1] Barcia, 80.
[2] Laudonnière, 110; Le Moyne, 24.

Le Moyne had been one of the guard. Scarcely had he thrown himself into a hammock which was slung in his room, when a savage shout, and a wild uproar of shrieks, outcries, and the clash of weapons, brought him to his feet. He rushed by two Spaniards in the door-way, ran behind the guard-house, leaped through an embrasure into the ditch, and escaped to the forest.[1]

Challeux, the carpenter, was going betimes to his work, a chisel in his hand. He was old, but pike and partisan brandished at his back gave wings to his flight. In the ecstasy of his terror, he leaped upward, clutched the top of the palisade, and threw himself over with the agility of a boy. He ran up the hill, no one pursuing, and, as he neared the edge of the forest, turned and looked back. From the high ground where he stood, he could see the butchery, the fury of the conquerors, and the agonizing gestures of the victims. He turned again in horror, and plunged into the woods.[2] As he tore his way through the briers and thickets, he met several fugitives escaped like himself. Others presently came up, haggard and wild, like men broken loose from the jaws of death. They gathered together and consulted. One of them, known as Master Robert, in great repute for his knowledge of the Bible, was for returning and surrendering to the Spaniards. "They are men," he said; "perhaps, when their fury is over, they will spare our lives; and, even if they kill us, it will only be a few moments' pain. Better so, than to starve here in the woods, or be torn to pieces by wild beasts."[3]

The greater part of the naked and despairing company assented, but Challeux was of a different mind. The old Huguenot quoted Scripture, and called the names of prophets and apostles to witness, that, in the direst extremity, God would not abandon those who rested their faith in Him. Six of the fugitives, however, still held to their desperate purpose. Issuing from the woods, they descended towards the fort, and, as with beating hearts their comrades watched the result, a troop of Spaniards rushed out, hewed them down with

[1] Le Moyne, 25.
[2] Challeux in Ternaux-Compans, 272.
[3] Ibid., 275.

swords and halberds, and dragged their bodies to the brink of the river, where the victims of the massacre were already flung in heaps.

Le Moyne, with a soldier named Grandchemin, whom he had met in his flight, toiled all day through the woods and marshes, in the hope of reaching the small vessels anchored behind the bar. Night found them in a morass. No vessel could be seen, and the soldier, in despair, broke into angry upbraidings against his companion,—saying that he would go back and give himself up. Le Moyne at first opposed him, then yielded. But when they drew near the fort, and heard the uproar of savage revelry that rose from within, the artist's heart failed him. He embraced his companion, and the soldier advanced alone. A party of Spaniards came out to meet him. He kneeled, and begged for his life. He was answered by a death-blow; and the horrified Le Moyne, from his hiding-place in the thicket, saw his limbs hacked apart, stuck on pikes, and borne off in triumph.[1]

Meanwhile, Menendez, mustering his followers, had offered thanks to God for their victory; and this pious butcher wept with emotion as he recounted the favors which Heaven had showered upon their enterprise. His admiring historian gives it in proof of his humanity, that, after the rage of the assault was spent, he ordered that women, infants, and boys under fifteen should thenceforth be spared. Of these, by his own account, there were about fifty. Writing in October to the King, he says that they cause him great anxiety, since he fears the anger of God should he now put them to death in cold blood, while, on the other hand, he is in dread lest the venom of their heresy should infect his men.

A hundred and forty-two persons were slain in and around the fort, and their bodies lay heaped together on the bank of the river. Nearly opposite was anchored a small vessel, called the Pearl, commanded by Jacques Ribaut, son of the Admiral. The ferocious soldiery, maddened with victory and drunk with blood, crowded to the water's edge, shouting insults to those on board, mangling the corpses, tearing out their eyes,

[1] Le Moyne, 26.

and throwing them towards the vessel from the points of their daggers.[1] Thus did the Most Catholic Philip champion the cause of Heaven in the New World.

It was currently believed in France, and, though no eyewitness attests it, there is reason to think it true, that among those murdered at Fort Caroline there were some who died a death of peculiar ignominy. Menendez, it is affirmed, hanged his prisoners on trees, and placed over them the inscription, "I do this, not as to Frenchmen, but as to Lutherans."[2]

The Spaniards gained a great booty in armor, clothing, and provisions. "Nevertheless," says the devout Mendoza, after closing his inventory of the plunder, "the greatest profit of this victory is the triumph which our Lord has granted us, whereby His holy Gospel will be introduced into this country, a thing so needful for saving so many souls from perdition." Again he writes in his journal, "We owe to God and His Mother, more than to human strength, this victory over the adversaries of the holy Catholic religion."

To whatever influence, celestial or other, the exploit may best be ascribed, the victors were not yet quite content with their success. Two small French vessels, besides that of Jacques Ribaut, still lay within range of the fort. When the storm had a little abated, the cannon were turned on them. One of them was sunk, but Ribaut, with the others, escaped down the river, at the mouth of which several light craft, including that bought from the English, had been anchored since the arrival of his father's squadron.

While this was passing, the wretched fugitives were flying from the scene of massacre through a tempest, of whose per-

---

[1] ". . . . car, arrachans les yeux des morts, les fichoyent au bout des dagues, et puis auec cris, heurlemens & toute gaudisserie, les iettoyent contre nos François vers l'eau." Challeux, (1566,) 34.

"Ils arrachèrent les yeulx qu'ils avoient meurtris, et les aiant fichez à la poincte de leurs dagues faisoient entre eulx à qui plus loing les jetteroit." Prévost, *Reprinse de la Floride*. This is a contemporary MS. in the Bibliothèque Nationale, printed by Ternaux-Compans in his *Recueil*. It will be often cited hereafter.

[2] Prévost in Ternaux-Compans, 357; Lescarbot, (1612,) I. 127; Charlevoix, *Nouvelle France*, (1744,) I. 81; and nearly all the French secondary writers. Barcia denies the story. How deep the indignation it kindled in France will appear hereafter.

sistent violence all the narratives speak with wonder. Exhausted, starved, half naked,—for most of them had escaped in their shirts,—they pushed their toilsome way amid the ceaseless wrath of the elements. A few sought refuge in Indian villages; but these, it is said, were afterwards killed by the Spaniards. The greater number attempted to reach the vessels at the mouth of the river. Among the latter was Le Moyne, who, notwithstanding his former failure, was toiling through the mazes of tangled forests, when he met a Belgian soldier, with the woman described as Laudonnière's maidservant, who was wounded in the breast; and, urging their flight towards the vessels, they fell in with other fugitives, including Laudonnière himself. As they struggled through the salt marsh, the rank sedge cut their naked limbs, and the tide rose to their waists. Presently they descried others, toiling like themselves through the matted vegetation, and recognized Challeux and his companions, also in quest of the vessels. The old man still, as he tells us, held fast to his chisel, which had done good service in cutting poles to aid the party to cross the deep creeks that channelled the morass. The united band, twenty-six in all, were cheered at length by the sight of a moving sail. It was the vessel of Captain Mallard, who, informed of the massacre, was standing along shore in the hope of picking up some of the fugitives. He saw their signals, and sent boats to their rescue; but such was their exhaustion, that, had not the sailors, wading to their armpits among the rushes, borne them out on their shoulders, few could have escaped. Laudonnière was so feeble that nothing but the support of a soldier, who held him upright in his arms, had saved him from drowning in the marsh.

On gaining the friendly decks, the fugitives counselled together. One and all, they sickened for the sight of France.

After waiting a few days, and saving a few more stragglers from the marsh, they prepared to sail. Young Ribaut, though ignorant of his father's fate, assented with something more than willingness; indeed, his behavior throughout had been stamped with weakness and poltroonery. On the twenty-fifth of September they put to sea in two vessels; and, after a voyage the privations of which were fatal to many of them, they arrived, one party at Rochelle, the other at Swansea, in Wales.

Chapter VIII

1565

MASSACRE OF THE HERETICS

Menendez returns to St. Augustine • Tidings of the French • Ribaut shipwrecked • The March of Menendez • He discovers the French • Interviews • Hopes of Mercy • Surrender of the French • Massacre • Return to St. Augustine • Tidings of Ribaut's Party • His Interview with Menendez • Deceived and betrayed • Murdered • Another Massacre • French Accounts • Schemes of the Spaniards • Survivors of the Carnage

---

IN suspense and fear, hourly looking seaward for the dreaded fleet of Jean Ribaut, the chaplain Mendoza and his brother priests held watch and ward at St. Augustine in the Adelantado's absence. Besides the celestial guardians whom they ceased not to invoke, they had as protectors Bartholomew Menendez, the brother of the Adelantado, and about a hundred soldiers. Day and night they toiled to throw up earthworks and strengthen their position.

A week elapsed, when they saw a man running towards them, shouting as he ran.

Mendoza went to meet him.

"Victory! victory!" gasped the breathless messenger. "The French fort is ours!" And he flung his arms about the chaplain's neck.[1]

"To-day," writes the priest in his journal, "Monday, the twenty-fourth, came our good general himself, with fifty soldiers, very tired, like all those who were with him. As soon as they told me he was coming, I ran to my lodging, took a new cassock, the best I had, put on my surplice, and went out to meet him with a crucifix in my hand; whereupon he, like a gentleman and a good Christian, kneeled down with all his followers, and gave the Lord a thousand thanks for the great favors he had received from Him."

In solemn procession, with four priests in front chanting *Te Deum*, the victors entered St. Augustine in triumph.

[1] Mendoza, *Relacion.*

On the twenty-eighth, when the weary Adelantado was taking his siesta under the sylvan roof of Seloy, a troop of Indians came in with news that quickly roused him from his slumbers. They had seen a French vessel wrecked on the coast towards the south. Those who escaped from her were four or six leagues off, on the banks of a river or arm of the sea, which they could not cross.[1]

Menendez instantly sent forty or fifty men in boats to reconnoitre. Next, he called the chaplain,—for he would fain have him at his elbow to countenance the deeds he meditated,—and, with him, twelve soldiers, and two Indian guides, embarked in another boat. They rowed along the channel between Anastasia Island and the main shore; then they landed, struck across the island on foot, traversed plains and marshes, reached the sea towards night, and searched along shore till ten o'clock to find their comrades who had gone before. At length, with mutual joy, the two parties met, and bivouacked together on the sands. Not far distant they could see lights. These were the camp-fires of the shipwrecked French.

To relate with precision the fortunes of these unhappy men is impossible; for henceforward the French narratives are no longer the narratives of eyewitnesses.

It has been seen how, when on the point of assailing the Spaniards at St. Augustine, Jean Ribaut was thwarted by a gale, which they hailed as a divine interposition. The gale rose to a tempest of strange fury. Within a few days, all the French ships were cast on shore, between Matanzas Inlet and Cape Canaveral. According to a letter of Menendez, many of those on board were lost; but others affirm that all escaped but a captain, La Grange, an officer of high merit, who was washed from a floating mast.[2] One of the ships was wrecked at a point farther northward than the rest, and it was her company whose camp-fires were seen by the Spaniards at their bivouac on the sands of Anastasia Island. They were endeavoring to reach Fort Caroline, of the fate of which they knew nothing, while Ribaut with the remainder was farther southward,

[1] Mendoza, *Relacion*; Solís in Barcia, 85; Letter of Menendez to the King, 18 October, 1565.
[2] Challeux, (1566,) 46.

struggling through the wilderness towards the same goal. What befell the latter will appear hereafter. Of the fate of the former party there is no French record. What we know of it is due to three Spanish eyewitnesses, Mendoza, Doctor Solís de las Meras, and Menendez himself. Solís was a priest, and brother-in-law to Menendez. Like Mendoza, he minutely describes what he saw, and, like him, was a red-hot zealot, lavishing applause on the darkest deeds of his chief. But the principal witness, though not the most minute or most trustworthy, is Menendez, in his long despatches sent from Florida to the King, and now first brought to light from the archives of Seville,—a cool record of unsurpassed atrocities, inscribed on the back with the royal indorsement, "Say to him that he has done well."

When the Adelantado saw the French fires in the distance, he lay close in his bivouac, and sent two soldiers to reconnoitre. At two o'clock in the morning they came back, and reported that it was impossible to get at the enemy, since they were on the farther side of an arm of the sea (Matanzas Inlet). Menendez, however, gave orders to march, and before daybreak reached the hither bank, where he hid his men in a bushy hollow. Thence, as it grew light, they could discern the enemy, many of whom were searching along the sands and shallows for shell-fish, for they were famishing. A thought struck Menendez, an inspiration, says Mendoza, of the Holy Spirit.[1] He put on the clothes of a sailor, entered a boat which had been brought to the spot, and rowed towards the shipwrecked men, the better to learn their condition. A Frenchman swam out to meet him. Menendez demanded what men they were.

"Followers of Ribaut, Viceroy of the King of France," answered the swimmer.

"Are you Catholics or Lutherans?"

"All Lutherans."

A brief dialogue ensued, during which the Adelantado declared his name and character, and the Frenchman gave an account of the designs of Ribaut, and of the disaster that had thwarted them. He then swam back to his companions, but

[1] "Nuestro buen General, alumbrado por el Espíritu Santo, dixo," etc.

soon returned, and asked safe conduct for his captain and four other gentlemen, who wished to hold conference with the Spanish general. Menendez gave his word for their safety, and, returning to the shore, sent his boat to bring them over. On their landing, he met them very courteously. His followers were kept at a distance, so disposed behind hills and among bushes as to give an exaggerated idea of their force,— a precaution the more needful, as they were only about sixty in number, while the French, says Solís, were above two hundred. Menendez, however, declares that they did not exceed a hundred and forty. The French officer told him the story of their shipwreck, and begged him to lend them a boat to aid them in crossing the rivers which lay between them and a fort of their King, whither they were making their way.

Then came again the ominous question,—

"Are you Catholics or Lutherans?"

"We are Lutherans."

"Gentlemen," pursued Menendez, "your fort is taken, and all in it are put to the sword." And, in proof of his declaration, he caused articles plundered from Fort Caroline to be shown to the unhappy petitioners. He then left them, and went to breakfast with his officers, first ordering food to be placed before them. Having breakfasted, he returned to them.

"Are you convinced now," he asked, "that what I have told you is true?"

The French captain assented, and implored him to lend them ships in which to return home. Menendez answered, that he would do so willingly if they were Catholics, and if he had ships to spare, but he had none. The suppliants then expressed the hope, that at least they and their followers would be allowed to remain with the Spaniards till ships could be sent to their relief, since there was peace between the two nations, whose kings were friends and brothers.

"All Catholics," retorted the Spaniard, "I will befriend; but as you are of the New Sect, I hold you as enemies, and wage deadly war against you; and this I will do with all cruelty [*crueldad*] in this country, where I command as Viceroy and Captain-General for my King. I am here to plant the Holy Gospel, that the Indians may be enlightened and come to the knowledge of the Holy Catholic faith of our Lord Jesus

Christ, as the Roman Church teaches it. If you will give up your arms and banners, and place yourselves at my mercy, you may do so, and I will act towards you as God shall give me grace. Do as you will, for other than this you can have neither truce nor friendship with me."[1]

Such were the Adelantado's words, as reported by a by-stander, his admiring brother-in-law; and that they contain an implied assurance of mercy has been held, not only by Protestants, but by Catholics and Spaniards.[2] The report of Menendez himself is more brief, and sufficiently equivocal.

"I answered, that they could give up their arms and place themselves under my mercy,—that I should do with them what our Lord should order; and from that I did not depart, nor would I, unless God our Lord should otherwise inspire."[3]

One of the Frenchmen recrossed to consult with his companions. In two hours he returned, and offered fifty thousand ducats to secure their lives; but Menendez, says his brother-in-law, would give no pledges. On the other hand, expressions in his own despatches point to the inference that a virtual pledge was given, at least to certain individuals.

The starving French saw no resource but to yield themselves to his mercy. The boat was again sent across the river.

[1] ". . . . mas, que por ser ellos de la Nueva Secta, los tenia por Enemigos, è tenia con ellos Guerra, à sangre, è fuego; è que esta la haria con toda crueldad à los que hallase en aquella Mar, è Tierra, donde era Virrei, è Capitan General por su Rei; è que iba à plantar el Santo Evangelio en aquella Tierra, para que fuesen alumbrados los Indios, è viniesen al conocimiento de la Santa Fè Catolica de Jesu Christo N. S. como lo dice, è canta la Iglesia Romana; è que si ellos quieren entregarle las Vanderas, è las Armas, è ponerse en su Misericordia, lo pueden hacer, para que èl haga de ellos lo que Dios le diere de gracia, ò que hogan lo que quisieren, que otras Treguas, ni Amistades no avian de hacer con èl." Solís, 86.

[2] Salazar, *Crisis del Ensayo*, 23; Padre Felipe Briet, *Anales*.

[3] "Respondíles, que las armas me podia rendir y ponerse debaxo de mi gracia para que Yo hiciese dellos aquello que Nuestro Señor me ordenase, y de aquí no me sacó, ní sacára si Dios Nuestro Señor no espirára en mi otra cosa. Y ansi se fué con esta respuesta, y se vinieron y me entregaron las armas, y hiceles amarrar las manos atras y pasarlos à cuchillo. . . . . Parecióme que castigarlos desta manera se servia Dios Nuestro Señor, y V. Mag.d, para que adelante nos dexen mas libres esta mala seta para plantar el evangelio en estas partes." *Carta de Pedro Menendez á su Magestad, Fuerte de S.n Agustin, 15 Octubre, 1565.*

It returned laden with banners, arquebuses, swords, targets, and helmets. The Adelantado ordered twenty soldiers to bring over the prisoners, ten at a time. He then took the French officers aside behind a ridge of sand, two gunshots from the bank. Here, with courtesy on his lips and murder at his heart, he said: —

"Gentlemen, I have but few men, and you are so many that, if you were free, it would be easy for you to take your satisfaction on us for the people we killed when we took your fort. Therefore it is necessary that you should go to my camp, four leagues from this place, with your hands tied."[1]

Accordingly, as each party landed, they were led out of sight behind the sand-hill, and their hands tied behind their backs with the match-cords of the arquebuses, though not before each had been supplied with food. The whole day passed before all were brought together, bound and helpless, under the eye of the inexorable Adelantado. But now Mendoza interposed. "I was a priest," he says, "and had the bowels of a man." He asked that, if there were Christians—that is to say, Catholics—among the prisoners, they should be set apart. Twelve Breton sailors professed themselves to be such; and these, together with four carpenters and calkers, "of whom," writes Menendez, "I was in great need," were put on board the boat and sent to St. Augustine. The rest were ordered to march thither by land.

The Adelantado walked in advance till he came to a lonely spot, not far distant, deep among the bush-covered hills. Here he stopped, and with his cane drew a line in the sand. The sun was set when the captive Huguenots, with their escort, reached the fatal goal thus marked out. And now let the curtain drop; for here, in the name of Heaven, the hounds of hell were turned loose, and the savage soldiery, like wolves in a sheepfold, rioted in slaughter. Of all that wretched company, not one was left alive.

"I had their hands tied behind their backs," writes the chief

[1] "Señores, yo tengo poca Gente, è no mui conocida, è Vosotros sois muchos è andando sueltos, facil cosa os seria satisfaceros de Nosotros, por la Gente que os degollamos quando ganamos el Fuerte; è ansi es menester, que con las manos atràs, amarradas, marcheis de aqui à quatro Leguas, donde yo tengo mi Real." Solís, 87.

criminal, "and themselves put to the knife. It appeared to me that, by thus chastising them, God our Lord and your Majesty were served; whereby in future this evil sect will leave us more free to plant the Gospel in these parts."[1]

Again Menendez returned triumphant to St. Augustine, and behind him marched his band of butchers, steeped in blood to the elbows, but still unsated. Great as had been his success, he still had cause for anxiety. There was ill news of his fleet. Some of the ships were lost, others scattered, or lagging tardily on their way. Of his whole force, less than a half had reached Florida, and of these a large part were still at Fort Caroline. Ribaut could not be far off; and, whatever might be the condition of his shipwrecked company, their numbers would make them formidable, unless taken at advantage. Urged by fear and fortified by fanaticism, Menendez had well begun his work of slaughter; but rest for him there was none; a darker deed was behind.

On the tenth of October, Indians came with the tidings that, at the spot where the first party of the shipwrecked French had been found, there was now another party still larger. This murder-loving race looked with great respect on Menendez for his wholesale butchery of the night before,— an exploit rarely equalled in their own annals of massacre. On his part, he doubted not that Ribaut was at hand. Marching with a hundred and fifty men, he crossed the bush-covered sands of Anastasia Island, followed the strand between the thickets and the sea, reached the inlet at midnight, and again, like a savage, ambushed himself on the bank. Day broke, and he could plainly see the French on the farther side. They had made a raft, which lay in the water ready for crossing. Menendez and his men showed themselves, when, forthwith, the French displayed their banners, sounded drums and trumpets, and set their sick and starving ranks in array of battle. But the Adelantado, regardless of this warlike show, ordered his men to seat themselves at breakfast, while he with three officers walked unconcernedly along the shore. His coolness had its effect. The French blew a trumpet of parley, and showed a white flag. The Spaniards replied. A Frenchman came out

[1] For the original, see *ante*, note 3, p. 110.

upon the raft, and, shouting across the water, asked that a Spanish envoy should be sent over.

"You have a raft," was the reply; "come yourselves."

An Indian canoe lay under the bank on the Spanish side. A French sailor swam to it, paddled back unmolested, and presently returned, bringing with him La Caille, Ribaut's sergeant-major. He told Menendez that the French were three hundred and fifty in all, and were on their way to Fort Caroline; and, like the officers of the former party, he begged for boats to aid them in crossing the river.

"My brother," said Menendez, "go and tell your general, that, if he wishes to speak with me, he may come with four or six companions, and that I pledge my word he shall go back safe."[1]

La Caille returned; and Ribaut, with eight gentlemen, soon came over in the canoe. Menendez met them courteously, caused wine and preserved fruits to be placed before them,— he had come well provisioned on his errand of blood,—and next led Ribaut to the reeking Golgotha, where, in heaps upon the sand, lay the corpses of his slaughtered followers. Ribaut was prepared for the spectacle; La Caille had already seen it; but he would not believe that Fort Caroline was taken till a part of the plunder was shown him. Then, mastering his despair, he turned to the conqueror. "What has befallen us," he said, "may one day befall you." And, urging that the kings of France and Spain were brothers and close friends, he begged, in the name of that friendship, that the Spaniard would aid him in conveying his followers home. Menendez gave him the same equivocal answer that he had given the former party, and Ribaut returned to consult with his officers. After three hours of absence, he came back in the canoe, and told the Adelantado that some of his people were ready to surrender at discretion, but that many refused.

"They can do as they please," was the reply.

In behalf of those who surrendered Ribaut offered a ransom of a hundred thousand ducats.

"It would much grieve me," said Menendez, "not to accept it; for I have great need of it."

[1] Solís, 88.

Ribaut was much encouraged. Menendez could scarcely forego such a prize, and he thought, says the Spanish narrator, that the lives of his followers would now be safe. He asked to be allowed the night for deliberation, and at sunset recrossed the river. In the morning he reappeared among the Spaniards, and reported that two hundred of his men had retreated from the spot, but that the remaining hundred and fifty would surrender.[1] At the same time he gave into the hands of Menendez the royal standard and other flags, with his sword, dagger, helmet, buckler, and the official seal given him by Coligny. Menendez directed an officer to enter the boat and bring over the French by tens. He next led Ribaut among the bushes behind the neighboring sand-hill, and ordered his hands to be bound fast. Then the scales fell from the prisoner's eyes. Face to face his fate rose up before him. He saw his followers and himself entrapped,—the dupes of words artfully framed to lure them to their ruin. The day wore on; and, as band after band of prisoners was brought over, they were led behind the sand-hill out of sight from the farther shore, and bound like their general. At length the transit was finished. With bloodshot eyes and weapons bared, the Spaniards closed around their victims.

"Are you Catholics or Lutherans? and is there any one among you who will go to confession?"

Ribaut answered, "I and all here are of the Reformed Faith."

And he recited the Psalm, *"Domine, memento mei."*[2]

"We are of earth," he continued, "and to earth we must return; twenty years more or less can matter little;"[3] and, turning to the Adelantado, he bade him do his will.

The stony-hearted bigot gave the signal; and those who will may paint to themselves the horrors of the scene.

A few, however, were spared. "I saved," writes Menendez, "the lives of two young gentlemen of about eighteen years of

---

[1] Solís, 89. Menendez speaks only of seventy.

[2] "L'auteur a voulu dire apparemment, *Memento Domine David.* D'ailleurs Ribaut la récita sans doute en Français, à la manière des Protestans." *Hist. Gen. des Voyages,* XIV. 446.

[3] "Dijo; que de Tierra eran, y que en Tierra se avian de bolver; è veinte Años mas, ò menos, todo era una Cuenta." Solís, 89.

age, as well as of three others, the fifer, the drummer, and the trumpeter; and I caused Juan Ribao [Ribaut] with all the rest to be put to the knife, judging this to be necessary for the service of God our Lord and of your Majesty. And I consider it great good fortune that he [Juan Ribao] should be dead, for the King of France could effect more with him and five hundred ducats than with other men and five thousand, and he would do more in one year than another in ten, for he was the most experienced sailor and naval commander known, and of great skill in this navigation of the Indies and the coast of Florida. He was, besides, greatly liked in England, in which kingdom his reputation was such that he was appointed Captain-General of all the English fleet against the French Catholics in the war between England and France some years ago."[1]

Such is the sum of the Spanish accounts,—the self-damning testimony of the author and abettors of the crime; a picture of lurid and awful coloring; and yet there is reason to believe that the truth was darker still. Among those who were spared was one Christophe le Breton, who was carried to Spain, escaped to France, and told his story to Challeux. Among those struck down in the butchery was a sailor of Dieppe, stunned and left for dead under a heap of corpses. In the night he revived, contrived to draw his knife, cut the cords that bound his hands, and made his way to an Indian village. The Indians, not without reluctance, abandoned him to the Spaniards, who sold him as a slave; but, on his way in fetters to Portugal, the ship was taken by the Huguenots, the sailor set free, and his story published in the narrative of Le

---

[1] "Salvé la vida à dos mozos Caballeros de hasta 18 años, y à otros tres, que eran Pifano, Atambor y Trompeta, y à Juan Rivao con todos los demas hice pasar à cuchillo, entendiendo que ansi convenia al servicio de Dios Nuestro Señor, y de V. Mag. y tengo por muy principal suerte que este sea muerto, porque mas hiciera el Rey de Francia con el con 500 ducados, que con otros con 5000, y mas hiciera el en un año que otro en dies, porque era el mas pratico marinero y cosario que se sabia, y muy diestro en esta Navigacion de Indias y costa de la Florida, y tan amigo en Inglaterra que tenia en aquel Reyno tanta reputacion que fué nombrado por Capitan General de toda el Armada Inglesa contra los Catolicos de Francia estos años pasados habiendo guerra entre Inglaterra y Francia." *Carta de Pedro Menendez á su Magestad, Fuerte de S^n Agustin, 15 de Octubre, 1565.*

Moyne. When the massacre was known in France, the friends
and relatives of the victims sent to the King, Charles the
Ninth, a vehement petition for redress; and their memorial
recounts many incidents of the tragedy. From these three
sources is to be drawn the French version of the story. The
following is its substance.

Famished and desperate, the followers of Ribaut were toiling northward to seek refuge at Fort Caroline, when they
found the Spaniards in their path. Some were filled with
dismay; others, in their misery, almost hailed them as deliverers. La Caille, the sergeant-major, crossed the river. Menendez met him with a face of friendship, and protested
that he would spare the lives of the shipwrecked men, seal-
ing the promise with an oath, a kiss, and many signs of
the cross. He even gave it in writing, under seal. Still,
there were many among the French who would not place
themselves in his power. The most credulous crossed the
river in a boat. As each successive party landed, their hands
were bound fast at their backs; and thus, except a few who
were set apart, they were all driven towards the fort, like
cattle to the shambles, with curses and scurrilous abuse.
Then, at sound of drums and trumpets, the Spaniards fell
upon them, striking them down with swords, pikes, and
halberds.[1] Ribaut vainly called on the Adelantado to remember his oath. By his order, a soldier plunged a dagger
into the French commander's heart; and Ottigny, who stood
near, met a similar fate. Ribaut's beard was cut off, and portions of it sent in a letter to Philip the Second. His head was
hewn into four parts, one of which was displayed on the
point of a lance at each corner of Fort St. Augustine. Great

---

[1] Here the French accounts differ. Le Moyne says that only a drummer and
a fifer were spared; Challeux, that carpenters, artillerymen, and others who
might be of use, were also saved,—thirty in all. Le Moyne speaks of the
massacre as taking place, not at St. Augustine, but at Fort Caroline, a blunder
into which, under the circumstances, he might naturally fall.

". . . . ainsi comme on feroit vn trouppeau de bestes lequel on chasseroit
à la boucherie, lors à son de phiffres, tabourins et trompes, la hardiesse de
ces furieux Espagnols se desbende sur ces poures François lesquels estoyent
liez et garottez: là c'estoit à qui donneroit le plus beau cousp de picque, de
hallebarde et d'espée," etc. Challeux, from Christophe le Breton.

fires were kindled, and the bodies of the murdered burned to ashes.[1]

Such is the sum of the French accounts. The charge of breach of faith contained in them was believed by Catholics as well as Protestants, and it was as a defence against this charge that the narrative of the Adelantado's brother-in-law was published. That Ribaut, a man whose good sense and courage were both reputed high, should have submitted himself and his men to Menendez without positive assurance of safety, is scarcely credible; nor is it lack of charity to believe that a bigot so savage in heart and so perverted in conscience would act on the maxim, current among certain casuists of the day, that faith ought not to be kept with heretics.

It was night when the Adelantado again entered St. Augustine. There were some who blamed his cruelty; but many applauded. "Even if the French had been Catholics,"—such was their language,—"he would have done right, for, with the little provision we have, they would all have starved; besides, there were so many of them that they would have cut our throats."

And now Menendez again addressed himself to the despatch, already begun, in which he recounts to the King his labors and his triumphs, a deliberate and business-like document, mingling narratives of butchery with recommendations for promotions, commissary details, and petitions for supplies; enlarging, too, on the vast schemes of encroachment which his successful generalship had brought to naught. The French, he says, had planned a military and naval depot at Los Martires, whence they would make a descent upon Havana, and another at the Bay of Ponce de Leon, whence they

---

[1] *Une Requête au Roy, faite en forme de Complainte par les Femmes veufves, petits Enfans orphelins, et autres leurs Amis, Parents et Alliez de ceux qui ont été cruellement envahis par les Espagnols en la France Antharctique dite la Floride.* This is the petition to Charles the Ninth. There are Latin translations in De Bry and Chauveton. Christophe le Breton told Challeux the same story of the outrages on Ribaut's body. The *Requête au Roy* affirms that the total number of French killed by the Spaniards in Florida in 1565 was more than nine hundred. This is no doubt a gross exaggeration.

Prévost, a contemporary, Lescarbot, and others, affirm that Ribaut's body was flayed, and the skin sent to Spain as a trophy. This is denied by Barcia.

could threaten Vera Cruz. They had long been encroaching on Spanish rights at Newfoundland, from which a great arm of the sea—doubtless meaning the St. Lawrence—would give them access to the Moluccas and other parts of the East Indies. He adds, in a later despatch, that by this passage they may reach the mines of Zacatecas and St. Martin, as well as every part of the South Sea. And, as already mentioned, he urges immediate occupation of Chesapeake Bay, which, by its supposed water communication with the St. Lawrence, would enable Spain to vindicate her rights, control the fisheries of Newfoundland, and thwart her rival in vast designs of commercial and territorial aggrandizement. Thus did France and Spain dispute the possession of North America long before England became a party to the strife.[1]

Some twenty days after Menendez returned to St. Augustine, the Indians, enamored of carnage, and exulting to see their invaders mowed down, came to tell him that on the coast southward, near Cape Canaveral, a great number of Frenchmen were intrenching themselves. They were those of Ribaut's party who had refused to surrender. Having retreated to the spot where their ships had been cast ashore, they were trying to build a vessel from the fragments of the wrecks.

In all haste Menendez despatched messengers to Fort Caroline,—named by him San Mateo,—ordering a reinforcement of a hundred and fifty men. In a few days they came. He added some of his own soldiers, and, with a united force of two hundred and fifty, set out, as he tells us, on the second of November. A part of his force went by sea, while the rest pushed southward along the shore with such merciless energy that several men dropped dead with wading night and day

---

[1] Amid all the confusion of his geographical statements, it seems clear that Menendez believed that Chesapeake Bay communicated with the St. Lawrence, and thence with Newfoundland on the one hand, and the South Sea on the other. The notion that the St. Lawrence would give access to China survived till the time of La Salle, or more than a century. In the map of Gastaldi, made, according to Kohl, about 1550, a belt of water connecting the St. Lawrence and the Atlantic is laid down. So also in the map of Ruscelli, 1561, and that of Martines, 1578, as well as in that of Michael Lok, 1582. In Munster's map, 1545, the St. Lawrence is rudely indicated, with the words; "Per hoc fretū iter ad Molucas."

through the loose sands. When, from behind their frail defences, the French saw the Spanish pikes and partisans glittering into view, they fled in a panic, and took refuge among the hills. Menendez sent a trumpet to summon them, pledging his honor for their safety. The commander and several others told the messenger that they would sooner be eaten by the savages than trust themselves to Spaniards; and, escaping, they fled to the Indian towns. The rest surrendered; and Menendez kept his word. The comparative number of his own men made his prisoners no longer dangerous. They were led back to St. Augustine, where, as the Spanish writer affirms, they were well treated. Those of good birth sat at the Adelantado's table, eating the bread of a homicide crimsoned with the slaughter of their comrades. The priests essayed their pious efforts, and, under the gloomy menace of the Inquisition, some of the heretics renounced their errors. The fate of the captives may be gathered from the indorsement, in the handwriting of the King, on one of the despatches of Menendez.

"Say to him," writes Philip the Second, "that, as to those he has killed, he has done well; and as to those he has saved, they shall be sent to the galleys."[1]

[1] There is an indorsement to this effect on the despatch of Menendez of 12 December, 1565. A marginal note by the copyist states that it is in the well-known handwriting of Philip the Second. Compare the King's letter to Menendez, in Barcia, 116. This letter seems to have been written by a secretary in pursuance of a direction contained in the indorsement, — "Esto serà bien escribir luego à Pero Menendez," — and highly commends him for the "justice he has done upon the Lutheran corsairs."

Chapter IX

CHARLES IX AND PHILIP II

State of International Relations • Complaints of Philip the Second • Reply of Charles the Ninth • News of the Massacre • The French Court demands Redress • The Spanish Court refuses it

THE state of international relations in the sixteenth century is hardly conceivable at this day. The Puritans of England and the Huguenots of France regarded Spain as their natural enemy, and on the high seas and in the British Channel they joined hands with godless freebooters to rifle her ships, kill her sailors, or throw them alive into the sea. Spain on her side seized English Protestant sailors who ventured into her ports, and burned them as heretics, or consigned them to a living death in the dungeons of the Inquisition. Yet in the latter half of the century these mutual outrages went on for years while the nations professed to be at peace. There was complaint, protest, and occasional menace, but no redress, and no declaration of war.

Contemporary writers of good authority have said that, when the news of the massacres in Florida reached the court of France, Charles the Ninth and Catherine de Medicis submitted to the insult in silence; but documents lately brought to light show that a demand for redress was made, though not insisted on. A cry of horror and execration had risen from the Huguenots, and many even of the Catholics had echoed it; yet the perpetrators of the crime, and not its victims, were the first to make complaint. Philip the Second resented the expeditions of Ribaut and Laudonnière as an invasion of the American domains of Spain, and ordered D'Alava, his ambassador at Paris, to denounce them to the French King. Charles, thus put on the defensive, replied, that the country in question belonged to France, having been discovered by Frenchmen a hundred years before, and named by them Terre des Bretons.[1] This alludes to the tradition that the Bretons

---

[1] *Note de Charles IX. en réponse à celle de l'Ambassadeur d'Espagne*, in Gaffarel, *Floride*, 413.

and Basques visited the northern coasts of America before the voyage of Columbus. In several maps of the sixteenth century the region of New England and the neighboring states and provinces is set down as Terre des Bretons, or Tierra de los Bretones,[1] and this name was assumed by Charles to extend to the Gulf of Mexico, as the name of Florida was assumed by the Spaniards to extend to the Gulf of St. Lawrence, and even beyond it.[2] Philip spurned the claim, asserted the Spanish right to all Florida, and asked whether or not the followers of Ribaut and Laudonnière had gone thither by authority of their King. The Queen Mother, Catherine de Medicis, replied in her son's behalf, that certain Frenchmen had gone to a country called Terre aux Bretons, discovered by French subjects, and that in so doing they had been warned not to encroach on lands belonging to the King of Spain. And she added, with some spirit, that the Kings of France were not in the habit of permitting themselves to be threatened.[3]

Philip persisted in his attitude of injured innocence; and Forquevaulx, French ambassador at Madrid, reported that, as a reward for murdering French subjects, Menendez was to receive the title of Marquis of Florida. A demand soon followed from Philip, that Admiral Coligny should be punished for planting a French colony on Spanish ground, and thus causing the disasters that ensued. It was at this time that the first full account of the massacres reached the French court, and the Queen Mother, greatly moved, complained to the Spanish ambassador, saying that she could not persuade herself that his master would refuse reparation. The ambassador replied by again throwing the blame on Coligny and the Huguenots, and Catherine de Medicis returned that, Huguenots or not, the King of Spain had no right to take upon himself the punishment of French subjects. Forquevaulx was in-

[1] See, for example, the map of Ruscelli, 1561.

[2] "Il y a plus de cent ans a esté ledict païs appellé la terre des Bretons en laquelle est comprins l'endroit que les Espaignols s'attribuent, lequel ils ont baptizé du nom qu'ils ont voulu [*Florida*]." *Forquevaulx au Roy, 16 Mars, 1566.* Forquevaulx was French ambassador at Madrid.

"Nous ne pretendons rien que conserver une terre qui a esté descouverte et possédée par des François, comme le nom de la terre aux Bretons le tesmoigne encore." *Catherine de Médicis à Forquevaulx, 30 Dec., 1585.*

[3] *Catherine de Médicis à Forquevaulx, 20 Jan., 1566.*

structed to demand redress at Madrid, but Philip only answered that he was very sorry for what had happened,[1] and again insisted that Coligny should be punished as the true cause of it.

Forquevaulx, an old soldier, remonstrated with firmness, declared that no deed so execrable had ever been committed within his memory, and demanded that Menendez and his followers should be chastised as they deserved. The King said that he was sorry that the sufferers chanced to be Frenchmen, but, as they were pirates also, they ought to be treated as such. The ambassador replied, that they were no pirates, since they bore the commission of the Admiral of France, who in naval affairs represented the King; and Philip closed the conversation by saying that he would speak on the subject with the Duke of Alva. This was equivalent to refusal, for the views of the Duke were well known; "and so, Madame," writes the ambassador to the Queen Mother, "there is no hope that any reparation will be made for the aforesaid massacre."[2]

On this, Charles wrote to Forquevaulx: "It is my will that you renew your complaint, and insist urgently that, for the sake of the union and friendship between the two crowns, reparation be made for the wrong done me and the cruelties committed on my subjects, to which I cannot submit without too great loss of reputation."[3] And, jointly with his mother, he ordered the ambassador to demand once more that Menendez and his men should be punished, adding, that he trusts that Philip will grant justice to the King of France, his brother-in-law and friend, rather than pardon a gang of brigands. "On this demand," concludes Charles, "the Sieur de Forquevaulx will not fail to insist, be the answer what it may, in order that the King of Spain shall understand that his Majesty of France has no less spirit than his predecessors to repel an insult."[4] The ambassador fulfilled his commission, and

---

[1] "Disant avoir santi grand desplaisir du faict advenu; voilà tout, Sire." *Forquevaulx au Roy, 9 Avril, 1566.*

[2] *Forquevaulx à Catherine de Médicis, 9 Avril, 1566.*

[3] *Charles IX. à Forquevaulx, 12 Mai, 1566.*

[4] *Mémoire envoyé par Charles IX. et Catherine de Medicis à Forquevaulx, 12 Mai, 1566.*

Philip replied by referring him to the Duke of Alva. "I have no hope," reports Forquevaulx, "that the Duke will give any satisfaction as to the massacre, for it was he who advised it from the first."[1] A year passed, and then he reported that Menendez had returned from Florida, that the King had given him a warm welcome, and that his fame as a naval commander was such that he was regarded as a sort of Neptune.[2]

In spite of their brave words, Charles and the Queen Mother tamely resigned themselves to the affront, for they would not quarrel with Spain. To have done so would have been to throw themselves into the arms of the Protestant party, adopt the principle of toleration, and save France from the disgrace and blight of her later years. France was not so fortunate. The enterprise of Florida was a national enterprise, undertaken at the national charge, with the royal commission, and under the royal standard; and it had been crushed in time of peace by a power professing the closest friendship. Yet Huguenot influence had prompted and Huguenot hands executed it. That influence had now ebbed low; Coligny's power had waned; Charles, after long vacillation, was leaning more and more towards the Guises and the Catholics, and fast subsiding into the deathly embrace of Spain, for whom, at last, on the bloody eve of St. Bartholomew, he was to become the assassin of his own best subjects.[3]

In vain the relatives of the slain petitioned him for redress; and had the honor of the nation rested in the keeping of its King, the blood of hundreds of murdered Frenchmen would have cried from the ground in vain. But it was not to be so. Injured humanity found an avenger, and outraged France a champion. Her chivalrous annals may be searched in vain for a deed of more romantic daring than the vengeance of Dominique de Gourgues.

[1] *Forquevaulx au Roy, Août* (?), *1566.*

[2] *Forquevaulx au Roy, Juillet, 1567. Ibid., 2 Août, 1567.*

[3] *Lettres et Papiers d'Estat du Sieur de Forquevaulx, Ambassadeur du Roy très-Chrestien Charles Neufviesme*, printed by Gaffarel in his *Histoire de la Floride Française.*

Chapter X

1567–1583

DOMINIQUE DE GOURGUES

His Early Life • His Hatred of Spaniards • Resolves on Vengeance • His Band of Adventurers • His Plan divulged • His Speech • Enthusiasm of his Followers • Condition of the Spaniards • Arrival of Gourgues • Interviews with Indians • The Spaniards attacked • The First Fort carried • Another Victory • The Final Triumph • The Prisoners hanged • The Forts destroyed • Sequel of Gourgues's Career • Menendez • His Death

THERE was a gentleman of Mont-de-Marsan, Dominique de Gourgues, a soldier of ancient birth and high renown. It is not certain that he was a Huguenot. The Spanish annalist calls him a "terrible heretic";[1] but the French Jesuit, Charlevoix, anxious that the faithful should share the glory of his exploits, affirms that, like his ancestors before him, he was a good Catholic.[2] If so, his faith sat lightly upon him; and, Catholic or heretic, he hated the Spaniards with a mortal hate. Fighting in the Italian wars,—for from boyhood he was wedded to the sword,—he had been taken prisoner by them near Siena, where he had signalized himself by a fiery and determined bravery. With brutal insult, they chained him to the oar as a galley slave.[3] After he had long endured this ignominy, the Turks captured the vessel and carried her to Constantinople. It was but a change of tyrants; but, soon after, while she was on a cruise, Gourgues still at the oar, a galley of the knights of Malta hove in sight, bore down on her, recaptured her, and set the prisoner free. For several years after, his restless spirit found employment in voyages to Africa, Brazil, and regions yet more remote. His naval repute rose high, but his grudge against the Spaniards still rankled within him; and when, returned from his rovings, he learned

[1] Barcia, 133.
[2] Charlevoix, *Nouvelle France*, I. 95. Compare Guérin, *Navigateurs Français*, 200. One of De Gourgues's descendants, the Vicomte A. de Gourgues, has recently (1861) written an article to prove the Catholicity of his ancestor.
[3] Lescarbot, *Nouvelle France*, I. 141; Barcia, 133.

the tidings from Florida, his hot Gascon blood boiled with fury.

The honor of France had been foully stained, and there was none to wipe away the shame. The faction-ridden King was dumb. The nobles who surrounded him were in the Spanish interest.[1] Then, since they proved recreant, he, Dominique de Gourgues, a simple gentleman, would take upon him to avenge the wrong, and restore the dimmed lustre of the French name.[2] He sold his inheritance, borrowed money from his brother, who held a high post in Guienne,[3] and equipped three small vessels, navigable by sail or oar. On board he placed a hundred arquebusiers and eighty sailors, prepared to fight on land, if need were.[4] The noted Blaise de Montluc, then lieutenant for the King in Guienne, gave him a commission to make war on the negroes of Benin,—that is, to kidnap them as slaves, an adventure then held honorable.[5]

His true design was locked within his own breast. He mustered his followers,—not a few of whom were of rank equal to his own,—feasted them, and, on the twenty-second of Au-

[1] It was at this time that the Duc de Montpensier was heard to say, that, if his heart was opened, the name of Philip would be found written in it. Ranke, *Civil Wars*, I. 337.

[2] "El, encendido en el Celo de la Honra de su Patria, avia determinado gastar su Hacienda en aquella Empresa, de que no esperaba mas fruto, que vengarse, para eterniçar su Fama." Barcia, 134. This is the statement of an enemy. A contemporary manuscript preserved in the Gourgues family makes a similar statement.

[3] ". . . era Presidente de la Generalidad de Guiena." Barcia, 133. Compare Mezeray, *Hist. of France*, 701. There is repeated mention of him in the Memoirs of Montluc.

[4] De Gourgues MS. Barcia says two hundred; Basanier and Lescarbot, a hundred and fifty.

[5] De Gourgues MS. This is a copy, made in 1831, by the Vicomte de Gourgues, from the original preserved in the Gourgues family, and written either by Dominique de Gourgues himself, or by some person to whom he was intimately known. It is, with but trifling variations, identical with the two narratives entitled *La Reprinse de la Floride*, preserved in the Bibliothèque Impériale. One of these bears the name of Robert Prévost, but whether as author or copyist is not clear. M. Gaillard, who carefully compared them, has written a notice of their contents, with remarks. The Prévost narrative has been printed entire by Ternaux-Compans in his collection. I am indebted to Mr. Bancroft for the use of the Vicomte de Gourgues's copy, and Gaillard's notice.

gust, 1567, sailed from the mouth of the Charente. Off Cape Finisterre, so violent a storm buffeted his ships that his men clamored to return; but Gourgues's spirit prevailed. He bore away for Africa, and, landing at the Rio del Oro, refreshed and cheered them as he best might. Thence he sailed to Cape Blanco, where the jealous Portuguese, who had a fort in the neighborhood, set upon him three negro chiefs. Gourgues beat them off, and remained master of the harbor; whence, however, he soon voyaged onward to Cape Verd, and, steering westward, made for the West Indies. Here, advancing from island to island, he came to Hispaniola, where, between the fury of a hurricane at sea and the jealousy of the Spaniards on shore, he was in no small jeopardy;—"the Spaniards," exclaims the indignant journalist, "who think that this New World was made for nobody but them, and that no other living man has a right to move or breathe here!" Gourgues landed, however, obtained the water of which he was in need, and steered for Cape San Antonio, at the western end of Cuba. There he gathered his followers about him, and addressed them with his fiery Gascon eloquence. For the first time, he told them his true purpose, inveighed against Spanish cruelty, and painted, with angry rhetoric, the butcheries of Fort Caroline and St. Augustine.

"What disgrace," he cried, "if such an insult should pass unpunished! What glory to us if we avenge it! To this I have devoted my fortune. I relied on you. I thought you jealous enough of your country's glory to sacrifice life itself in a cause like this. Was I deceived? I will show you the way; I will be always at your head; I will bear the brunt of the danger. Will you refuse to follow me?"[1]

At first his startled hearers listened in silence; but soon the passions of that adventurous age rose responsive to his words. The combustible French nature burst into flame. The enthusiasm of the soldiers rose to such a pitch, that Gourgues had much ado to make them wait till the moon was full before

[1] The De Gourgues MS., with Prévost and Gaillard, give the speech in substance. Charlevoix professes to give a part in the words of the speaker: "J'ai compté sur vous, je vous ai cru assez jaloux de la gloire de votre Patrie, pour lui sacrifier jusqu'à votre vie en une occasion de cette importance; me suis-je trompé?" etc.

tempting the perils of the Bahama Channel. His time came at length. The moon rode high above the lonely sea, and, silvered in its light, the ships of the avenger held their course.

Meanwhile, it had fared ill with the Spaniards in Florida; the good will of the Indians had vanished. The French had been obtrusive and vexatious guests; but their worst trespasses had been mercy and tenderness compared to the daily outrage of the new-comers. Friendship had changed to aversion, aversion to hatred, and hatred to open war. The forest paths were beset; stragglers were cut off; and woe to the Spaniard who should venture after nightfall beyond call of the outposts.[1]

Menendez, however, had strengthened himself in his new conquest. St. Augustine was well fortified; Fort Caroline, now Fort San Mateo, was repaired; and two redoubts, or small forts, were thrown up to guard the mouth of the River of May,—one of them near the present lighthouse at Mayport, and the other across the river on Fort George Island. Thence, on an afternoon in early spring, the Spaniards saw three sail steering northward. They suspected no enemy, and their batteries boomed a salute. Gourgues's ships replied, then stood out to sea, and were lost in the shades of evening.

They kept their course all night, and, as day broke, anchored at the mouth of a river, the St. Mary's, or the Santilla, by their reckoning fifteen leagues north of the River of May. Here, as it grew light, Gourgues saw the borders of the sea thronged with savages, armed and plumed for war. They, too, had mistaken the strangers for Spaniards, and mustered to meet their tyrants at the landing. But in the French ships there was a trumpeter who had been long in Florida, and knew the Indians well. He went towards them in a boat, with many gestures of friendship; and no sooner was he recognized, than the naked crowd, with yelps of delight, danced for joy along the sands. Why had he ever left them? they asked; and why had he not returned before? The intercourse thus auspiciously begun was actively kept up. Gourgues told the principal chief,—who was no other than Satouriona, once the ally of the French,—that he had come to visit them,

[1] Barcia, 100–130.

make friendship with them, and bring them presents. At this last announcement, so grateful to Indian ears, the dancing was renewed with double zeal. The next morning was named for a grand council, and Satouriona sent runners to summon all Indians within call; while Gourgues, for safety, brought his vessels within the mouth of the river.

Morning came, and the woods were thronged with warriors. Gourgues and his soldiers landed with martial pomp. In token of mutual confidence, the French laid aside their arquebuses, and the Indians their bows and arrows. Satouriona came to meet the strangers, and seated their commander at his side, on a wooden stool, draped and cushioned with the gray Spanish moss. Two old Indians cleared the spot of brambles, weeds, and grass; and, when their task was finished, the tribesmen took their places, ring within ring, standing, sitting, and crouching on the ground,—a dusky concourse, plumed in festal array, waiting with grave visages and intent eyes. Gourgues was about to speak, when the chief, who, says the narrator, had not learned French manners, anticipated him, and broke into a vehement harangue, denouncing the cruelty of the Spaniards.

Since the French fort was taken, he said, the Indians had not had one happy day. The Spaniards drove them from their cabins, stole their corn, ravished their wives and daughters, and killed their children; and all this they had endured because they loved the French. There was a French boy who had escaped from the massacre at the fort; they had found him in the woods; and though the Spaniards, who wished to kill him, demanded that they should give him up, they had kept him for his friends.

"Look!" pursued the chief, "here he is!"—and he brought forward a youth of sixteen, named Pierre Debré, who became at once of the greatest service to the French, his knowledge of the Indian language making him an excellent interpreter.[1]

Delighted as he was at this outburst against the Spaniards, Gourgues did not see fit to display the full extent of his satisfaction. He thanked the Indians for their good-will, exhorted them to continue in it, and pronounced an ill-merited

---

[1] De Gourgues MS.; Gaillard MS; Basanier, 116; Barcia, 134.

eulogy on the greatness and goodness of his King. As for the Spaniards, he said, their day of reckoning was at hand; and, if the Indians had been abused for their love of the French, the French would be their avengers. Here Satouriona forgot his dignity, and leaped up for joy.

"What!" he cried, "will you fight the Spaniards?"[1]

"I came here," replied Gourgues, "only to reconnoitre the country and make friends with you, and then go back to bring more soldiers; but, when I hear what you are suffering from them, I wish to fall upon them this very day, and rescue you from their tyranny." All around the ring a clamor of applauding voices greeted his words.

"But you will do your part," pursued the Frenchman; "you will not leave us all the honor."

"We will go," replied Satouriona, "and die with you, if need be."

"Then, if we fight, we ought to fight at once. How soon can you have your warriors ready to march?"

The chief asked three days for preparation. Gourgues cautioned him to secrecy, lest the Spaniards should take alarm.

"Never fear," was the answer; "we hate them more than you do."[2]

Then came a distribution of gifts,—knives, hatchets, mirrors, bells, and beads,—while the warrior rabble crowded to receive them, with eager faces and outstretched arms. The distribution over, Gourgues asked the chiefs if there was any other matter in which he could serve them. On this, pointing

[1] ". . . si les rois et leurs sujets avoient esté maltraictez en haine des François que aussi seroient-ils vengez par les François-mesmes. Comment? dist Satirona, tressaillant d'aise, vouldriez-vous bien faire la guerre aux Espaignols." *De Gourgues MS.*

[2] The above is a condensation from the original narrative, of the style of which the following may serve as an example: "Le cappitaine Gourgue qui avoit trouvé ce qu'il chercheoit, les loüe et remercie grandement, et pour battre le fer pendant qu'il estoit chault leur dist: Voiremais si nous voullons leur faire la guerre, il fauldroit que ce fust incontinant. Dans combien de temps pourriez-vous bien avoir assemblé voz gens prets à marcher? Dans trois jours dist Satirona, nous et nos subjects pourrons nous rendre icy, pour partir avec vous. Et ce pendant, (dist le cappitaine Gourgue,) vous donnerez bon ordre que le tout soit tenu secret: affin que les Espaignols n'en puissent sentir le vent. Ne vous soulciez, dirent les rois, nous leur voullons plus de mal que vous," etc., etc.

to his shirt, they expressed a peculiar admiration for that garment, and begged each to have one, to be worn at feasts and councils during life, and in their graves after death. Gourgues complied; and his grateful confederates were soon stalking about him, fluttering in the spoils of his wardrobe.

To learn the strength and position of the Spaniards, Gourgues now sent out three scouts; and with them went Olotoraca, Satouriona's nephew, a young brave of great renown.

The chief, eager to prove his good faith, gave as hostages his only surviving son and his favorite wife. They were sent on board the ships, while the Indians dispersed to their encampments, with leaping, stamping, dancing, and whoops of jubilation.

The day appointed came, and with it the savage army, hideous in war-paint, and plumed for battle. The woods rang back their songs and yells, as with frantic gesticulation they brandished their war-clubs and vaunted their deeds of prowess. Then they drank the black drink, endowed with mystic virtues against hardship and danger; and Gourgues himself pretended to swallow the nauseous decoction.[1]

These ceremonies consumed the day. It was evening before the allies filed off into their forests, and took the path for the Spanish forts. The French, on their part, were to repair by sea to the rendezvous. Gourgues mustered and addressed his men. It was needless: their ardor was at fever height. They broke in upon his words, and demanded to be led at once against the enemy. François Bourdelais, with twenty sailors, was left with the ships, and Gourgues affectionately bade him farewell.

"If I am slain in this most just enterprise," he said, "I leave all in your charge, and pray you to carry back my soldiers to France."

[1] The "black drink" was, till a recent period, in use among the Creeks. It is a strong decoction of the plant popularly called cassina, or uupon tea. Major Swan, deputy agent for the Creeks in 1791, thus describes their belief in its properties: "that it purifies them from all sin, and leaves them in a state of perfect innocence; that it inspires them with an invincible prowess in war; and that it is the only solid cement of friendship, benevolence, and hospitality." Swan's account of their mode of drinking and ejecting it corresponds perfectly with Le Moyne's picture in De Bry. See the United States government publication, *History, Condition, and Prospects of Indian Tribes*, V. 266.

There were many embracings among the excited French-men,—many sympathetic tears from those who were to stay behind,—many messages left with them for wives, children, friends, and mistresses; and then this valiant band pushed their boats from shore.[1] It was a hare-brained venture, for, as young Debré had assured them, the Spaniards on the River of May were four hundred in number, secure behind their ramparts.[2]

Hour after hour the sailors pulled at the oar. They glided slowly by the sombre shores in the shimmering moonlight, to the sound of the murmuring surf and the moaning pine trees. In the gray of the morning, they came to the mouth of a river, probably the Nassau; and here a northeast wind set in with a violence that almost wrecked their boats. Their Indian allies were waiting on the bank, but for a while the gale de-layed their crossing. The bolder French would lose no time, rowed through the tossing waves, and, landing safely, left their boats, and pushed into the forest. Gourgues took the lead, in breastplate and back-piece. At his side marched the young chief Olotoraca, with a French pike in his hand; and the files of arquebuse-men and armed sailors followed close behind. They plunged through swamps, hewed their way through brambly thickets and the matted intricacies of the forests, and, at five in the afternoon, almost spent with fatigue and hunger, came to a river or inlet of the sea,[3] not far from the first Spanish fort. Here they found three hundred Indians waiting for them.

Tired as he was, Gourgues would not rest. He wished to attack at daybreak, and with ten arquebusiers and his Indian guide he set out to reconnoitre. Night closed upon him. It was a vain task to struggle on, in pitchy darkness, among trunks of trees, fallen logs, tangled vines, and swollen streams. Gourgues returned, anxious and gloomy. An Indian chief ap-

[1] "Cecy attendrist fort le cueur de tous, et mesmement des mariniers qui demeuroient pour la garde des navires, lesquels ne peurent contenir leurs larmes, et fut ceste départie plaine de compassion d'ouïr tant d'adieux d'une part et d'aultre, et tant de charges et recommendations de la part de ceulx qui s'en alloient à leurs parents et amis, et à leurs femmes et alliez au cas qu'ils ne retournassent." Prévost, 337.

[2] De Gourgues MS.; Basanier, 117; Charlevoix, I. 99.

[3] Talbot Inlet? Compare Sparks, *American Biography*, 2d Ser., VII. 128.

proached him, read through the darkness his perturbed look, and offered to lead him by a better path along the margin of the sea. Gourgues joyfully assented, and ordered all his men to march. The Indians, better skilled in wood-craft, chose the shorter course through the forest.

The French forgot their weariness, and pressed on with speed. At dawn they and their allies met on the bank of a stream, probably Sister Creek, beyond which, and very near, was the fort. But the tide was in, and they tried in vain to cross. Greatly vexed,—for he had hoped to take the enemy asleep,—Gourgues withdrew his soldiers into the forest, where they were no sooner ensconced than a drenching rain fell, and they had much ado to keep their gun-matches burning. The light grew fast. Gourgues plainly saw the fort, the defences of which seemed slight and unfinished. He even saw the Spaniards at work within. A feverish interval elapsed, till at length the tide was out,—so far, at least, that the stream was fordable. A little higher up, a clump of trees lay between it and the fort. Behind this friendly screen the passage was begun. Each man tied his powder-flask to his steel cap, held his arquebuse above his head with one hand, and grasped his sword with the other. The channel was a bed of oysters. The sharp shells cut their feet as they waded through. But the farther bank was gained. They emerged from the water, drenched, lacerated, and bleeding, but with unabated mettle. Gourgues set them in array under cover of the trees. They stood with kindling eyes, and hearts throbbing, but not with fear. Gourgues pointed to the Spanish fort, seen by glimpses through the boughs. "Look!" he said, "there are the robbers who have stolen this land from our King; there are the murderers who have butchered our countrymen!"[1] With voices eager, fierce, but half suppressed, they demanded to be led on.

Gourgues gave the word. Cazenove, his lieutenant, with thirty men, pushed for the fort gate; he himself, with the main body, for the glacis. It was near noon; the Spaniards

[1] " . . . . et, leur monstrant le fort qu'ils pouvoient entreveoir à travers les arbres, voilà (dist il) les volleurs qui ont vollé ceste terre à nostre Roy, voilà les meurtriers qui ont massacré nos françois." *De Gourgues MS.* Compare Charlevoix, I. 100.

had just finished their meal, and, says the narrative, "were still picking their teeth," when a startled cry rang in their ears:—

"To arms! to arms! The French are coming! the French are coming!"

It was the voice of a cannoneer who had that moment mounted the rampart and seen the assailants advancing in unbroken ranks, with heads lowered and weapons at the charge. He fired his cannon among them. He even had time to load and fire again, when the light-limbed Olotoraca bounded forward, ran up the glacis, leaped the unfinished ditch, and drove his pike through the Spaniard from breast to back. Gourgues was now on the glacis, when he heard Cazenove shouting from the gate that the Spaniards were escaping on that side. He turned and led his men thither at a run. In a moment, the fugitives, sixty in all, were enclosed between his party and that of his lieutenant. The Indians, too, came leaping to the spot. Not a Spaniard escaped. All were cut down but a few, reserved by Gourgues for a more inglorious end.[1]

Meanwhile the Spaniards in the other fort, on the opposite shore, cannonaded the victors without ceasing. The latter turned four captured guns against them. One of Gourgues's boats, a very large one, had been brought along-shore, and, entering it with eighty soldiers, he pushed for the farther bank. With loud yells, the Indians leaped into the river, which is here about three fourths of a mile wide. Each held his bow and arrows aloft in one hand, while he swam with the other. A panic seized the garrison as they saw the savage multitude. They broke out of the fort and fled into the forest. But the French had already landed; and, throwing themselves in the path of the fugitives, they greeted them with a storm of lead. The terrified wretches recoiled; but flight was vain. The Indian whoop rang behind them, and war-clubs and arrows finished the work. Gourgues's utmost efforts saved but fifteen, not out of mercy, but from a refinement of vengeance.[2]

[1] Barcia's Spanish account agrees with the De Gourgues MS., except in a statement of the former that the Indians had formed an ambuscade into which the Spaniards fell.

[2] It must be admitted that there is a strong savor of romance in the French narrative. The admissions of the Spanish annalist prove, however, that it has a broad basis of truth.

The next day was Quasimodo Sunday, or the Sunday after Easter. Gourgues and his men remained quiet, making ladders for the assault on Fort San Mateo. Meanwhile the whole forest was in arms, and, far and near, the Indians were wild with excitement. They beset the Spanish fort till not a soldier could venture out. The garrison, aware of their danger, though ignorant of its extent, devised an expedient to gain information; and one of them, painted and feathered like an Indian, ventured within Gourgues's outposts. He himself chanced to be at hand, and by his side walked his constant attendant, Olotoraca. The keen-eyed young savage pierced the cheat at a glance. The spy was seized, and, being examined, declared that there were two hundred and sixty Spaniards in San Mateo, and that they believed the French to be two thousand, and were so frightened that they did not know what they were doing.

Gourgues, well pleased, pushed on to attack them. On Monday evening he sent forward the Indians to ambush themselves on both sides of the fort. In the morning he followed with his Frenchmen; and, as the glittering ranks came into view, defiling between the forest and the river, the Spaniards opened on them with culverins from a projecting bastion. The French took cover in the woods with which the hills below and behind the fort were densely overgrown. Here, himself unseen, Gourgues could survey the whole extent of the defences, and he presently descried a strong party of Spaniards issuing from their works, crossing the ditch, and advancing to reconnoitre. On this, he sent Cazenove, with a detachment, to station himself at a point well hidden by trees on the flank of the Spaniards, who, with strange infatuation, continued their advance. Gourgues and his followers pushed on through the thickets to meet them. As the Spaniards reached the edge of the open ground, a deadly fire blazed in their faces, and, before the smoke cleared, the French were among them, sword in hand. The survivors would have fled; but Cazenove's detachment fell upon their rear, and all were killed or taken.

When their comrades in the fort beheld their fate, a panic seized them. Conscious of their own deeds, perpetrated on this very spot, they could hope no mercy, and their terror multiplied immeasurably the numbers of their enemy. They abandoned the fort in a body, and fled into the woods most remote from the French. But here a deadlier foe awaited them; for a host of Indians leaped up from ambush. Then rose those hideous war-cries which have curdled the boldest blood and blanched the manliest cheek. The forest warriors, with savage ecstasy, wreaked their long arrears of vengeance, while the French hastened to the spot, and lent their swords to the slaughter. A few prisoners were saved alive; the rest were slain; and thus did the Spaniards make bloody atonement for the butchery of Fort Caroline.[1]

But Gourgues's vengeance was not yet appeased. Hard by the fort, the trees were pointed out to him on which Menendez had hanged his captives, and placed over them the inscription, "Not as to Frenchmen, but as to Lutherans."

Gourgues ordered the Spanish prisoners to be led thither.

"Did you think," he sternly said, as the pallid wretches stood ranged before him, "that so vile a treachery, so detestable a cruelty, against a King so potent and a nation so generous, would go unpunished? I, one of the humblest gentlemen among my King's subjects, have charged myself with avenging it. Even if the Most Christian and the Most Catholic Kings had been enemies, at deadly war, such perfidy and extreme cruelty would still have been unpardonable. Now that they are friends and close allies, there is no name vile enough to brand your deeds, no punishment sharp enough to requite them. But though you cannot suffer as you deserve, you shall suffer all that an enemy can honorably inflict, that your example may teach others to observe the peace and alliance which you have so perfidiously violated."[2]

---

[1] This is the French account. The Spaniard Barcia, with greater probability, says that some of the Spaniards escaped to the hills. With this exception, the French and Spanish accounts agree. Barcia ascribes the defeat of his countrymen to an exaggerated idea of the enemy's force. The governor, Gonzalo de Villaroel, was, he says, among those who escaped. I have purposely preserved in the narrative the somewhat exalted tone of the original French account.

[2] ". . . . Mais encores que vous ne puissiez endurer la peine que vous avez méritée, il est besoin que vous enduriez celle que l'ennemy vous peult donner honnestement: affin que par vostre exemple les autres appreignent à garder la paix et alliance que si meschamment et malheureusement vous avez violée. Cela dit, ils sont branchez aux mesmes arbres où ils avoient penduz les François." *De Gourgues MS.*

They were hanged where the French had hung before them; and over them was nailed the inscription, burned with a hot iron on a tablet of pine, "Not as to Spaniards, but as to Traitors, Robbers, and Murderers."[1]

Gourgues's mission was fulfilled. To occupy the country had never been his intention; nor was it possible, for the Spaniards were still in force at St. Augustine. His was a whirlwind visitation,—to ravage, ruin, and vanish. He harangued the Indians, and exhorted them to demolish the fort. They fell to the work with eagerness, and in less than a day not one stone was left on another.[2]

Gourgues returned to the forts at the mouth of the river, destroyed them also, and took up his march for his ships. It was a triumphal procession. The Indians thronged around the victors with gifts of fish and game; and an old woman declared that she was now ready to die, since she had seen the French once more.

The ships were ready for sea. Gourgues bade his disconsolate allies farewell, and nothing would content them but a promise to return soon. Before embarking, he addressed his own men:—

"My friends, let us give thanks to God for the success He has granted us. It is He who saved us from tempests; it is He who inclined the hearts of the Indians towards us; it is He who blinded the understanding of the Spaniards. They were four to one, in forts well armed and provisioned. Our right was our only strength; and yet we have conquered. Not to our own swords, but to God only, we owe our victory. Then let us thank Him, my friends; let us never forget His favors; and let us pray that He may continue them, saving us from dangers, and guiding us safely home. Let us pray, too, that

---

[1] "Je ne faicts cecy comme à Espaignolz, n'y comme à Marannes; mais comme à traistres, volleurs, et meurtriers." *De Gourgues MS*.

Maranne, or *Marane*, was a word of reproach applied to Spaniards. It seems originally to have meant a Moor. Michelet calls Ferdinand of Spain "ce vieux Marane avare." The Spanish Pope, Alexander the Sixth, was always nicknamed *Le Marane* by his enemy and successor, Rovere.

On returning to the forts at the mouth of the river, Gourgues hanged all the prisoners he had left there. One of them, says the narrative, confessed that he had aided in hanging the French.

[2] "Ilz feirent telle diligence qu'en moings d'ung jour ilz ne laissèrent pierre sur pierre." *De Gourgues MS*.

He may so dispose the hearts of men that our perils and toils may find favor in the eyes of our King and of all France, since all we have done was done for the King's service and for the honor of our country."[1]

Thus Spaniards and Frenchmen alike laid their reeking swords on God's altar.

Gourgues sailed on the third of May, and, gazing back along their foaming wake, the adventurers looked their last on the scene of their exploits. Their success had cost its price. A few of their number had fallen, and hardships still awaited the survivors. Gourgues, however, reached Rochelle on the day of Pentecost, and the Huguenot citizens greeted him with all honor. At court it fared worse with him. The King, still obsequious to Spain, looked on him coldly and askance. The Spanish minister demanded his head. It was hinted to him that he was not safe, and he withdrew to Rouen, where he found asylum among his friends. His fortune was gone; debts contracted for his expedition weighed heavily on him; and for years he lived in obscurity, almost in misery.

At length his prospects brightened. Elizabeth of England learned his merits and his misfortunes, and invited him to enter her service. The King, who, says the Jesuit historian, had always at heart been delighted with his achievement,[2] openly restored him to favor; while, some years later, Don Antonio tendered him command of his fleet, to defend his right to the crown of Portugal against Philip the Second. Gourgues, happy once more to cross swords with the Spaniards, gladly embraced this offer; but in 1583, on his way to join the Portuguese prince, he died at Tours of a sudden illness.[3] The French mourned the loss of the man who had wiped a blot from the national scutcheon, and respected his memory as that of one of the best captains of his time. And, in truth, if a zealous patriotism, a fiery valor, and skilful leadership are worthy of honor, then is such a tribute due to Dominique de Gourgues, slave-catcher and half-pirate as he was, like other naval heroes of that wild age.

Romantic as was his exploit, it lacked the fulness of poetic

[1] De Gourgues MS. The speech is a little condensed in the translation.

[2] Charlevoix, *Nouvelle France*, I. 105.

[3] Basanier, 123; Lescarbot, 141; Barcia, 137; Gaillard, *Notice des Manuscrits de la Bibliothèque du Roi*.

justice, since the chief offender escaped him. While Gourgues was sailing towards Florida, Menendez was in Spain, high in favor at court, where he told to approving ears how he had butchered the heretics. Borgia, the sainted General of the Jesuits, was his fast friend; and two years later, when he returned to America, the Pope, Paul the Fifth, regarding him as an instrument for the conversion of the Indians, wrote him a letter with his benediction.[1] He re-established his power in Florida, rebuilt Fort San Mateo, and taught the Indians that death or flight was the only refuge from Spanish tyranny. They murdered his missionaries and spurned their doctrine. "The Devil is the best thing in the world," they cried; "we adore him; he makes men brave." Even the Jesuits despaired, and abandoned Florida in disgust.

Menendez was summoned home, where fresh honors awaited him from the Crown, though, according to the somewhat doubtful assertion of the heretical Grotius, his deeds had left a stain upon his name among the people.[2] He was given command of the armada of three hundred sail and twenty thousand men, which, in 1574, was gathered at Santander against England and Flanders. But now, at the height of his fortunes, his career was abruptly closed. He died suddenly, at the age of fifty-five. Grotius affirms that he killed himself; but, in his eagerness to point the moral of his story, he seems to have overstepped the bounds of historic truth. The Spanish bigot was rarely a suicide; for the rites of Christian burial and repose in consecrated ground were denied to the remains of the self-murderer. There is positive evidence, too, in a codicil to the will of Menendez, dated at Santander on the fifteenth of September, 1574, that he was on that day seriously ill, though, as the instrument declares, "of sound mind." There is reason, then, to believe that this pious cutthroat died a natural death, crowned with honors, and soothed by the consolations of his religion.[3]

[1] "Carta de San Pio V. à Pedro Menendez," Barcia, 139.

[2] Grotius, *Annales*, 63.

[3] For a copy of portions of the will, and other interesting papers concerning Menendez, I am indebted to Buckingham Smith, Esq., whose patient and zealous research in the archives of Spain has thrown new light on Spanish North American history.

There is a brief notice of Menendez in De la Mota's *History of the Order of*

It was he who crushed French Protestantism in America. To plant religious freedom on this western soil was not the mission of France. It was for her to rear in northern forests the banner of absolutism and of Rome; while among the rocks of Massachusetts England and Calvin fronted her in dogged opposition.

Long before the ice-crusted pines of Plymouth had listened to the rugged psalmody of the Puritan, the solitudes of Western New York and the stern wilderness of Lake Huron were trodden by the iron heel of the soldier and the sandalled foot of the Franciscan friar. France was the true pioneer of the Great West. They who bore the fleur-de-lis were always in the van, patient, daring, indomitable. And foremost on this bright roll of forest chivalry stands the half-forgotten name of Samuel de Champlain.

Santiago, (1599,) and also another of later date written to accompany his engraved portrait. Neither of them conveys any hint of suicide.

Menendez was a Commander of the Order of Santiago.

SAMUEL DE CHAMPLAIN

AND

HIS ASSOCIATES

with a

View of Earlier French Adventure in America,
and the
Legends of the Northern Coasts

ROUTE OF
CHAMPLAIN,
1615, 1616.

Champlain and His Associates

S AMUEL DE CHAMPLAIN has been fitly called the Father of New France. In him were embodied her religious zeal and romantic spirit of adventure. Before the close of his career, purged of heresy, she took the posture which she held to the day of her death,—in one hand the crucifix, in the other the sword. His life, full of significance, is the true beginning of her eventful history.

In respect to Champlain, the most satisfactory authorities are his own writings. These consist of the journal of his voyage to the West Indies and Mexico, of which the original is preserved at Dieppe; the account of his first voyage to the St. Lawrence, published at Paris, in 1604, under the title of *Des Sauvages*; a narrative of subsequent adventures and explorations, published at Paris in 1613, 1615, and 1617, under the title of *Voyage de la Nouvelle France*; a narrative of still later discoveries, published at Paris in 1620 and 1627; and, finally, a compendium of all his previous publications, with much additional matter, published in quarto at Paris in 1632, and illustrated by a very curious and interesting map.

Next in value to the writings of Champlain are those of his associate, Lescarbot, whose *Histoire de la Nouvelle France* is of great interest and authority as far as it relates the author's personal experience. The editions here consulted are those of 1612 and 1618. The *Muses de la Nouvelle France*, and other minor works of Lescarbot, have also been examined.

The *Établissement de la Foy* of Le Clerc is of great value in connection with the present subject, containing documents and extracts from documents not elsewhere to be found. It is of extreme rarity, having been suppressed by the French government soon after its appearance in 1691.

The *Histoire du Canada* of Sagard, the *Première Mission des Jésuites* of Carayon, the curious *Relation* of the Jesuit Biard, and those of the Jesuits Charles Lalemant, Le Jeune, and Brébeuf, together with two narratives—one of them perhaps written by Champlain—in the eighteenth and nineteenth volumes of the *Mercure Français*, may also be mentioned as among the leading authorities of the body of this work.

Those of the introductory portion need not be specified at present.

Of manuscripts used, the principal are the *Bref Discours* of Champlain, or the journal of his voyage to the West Indies and Mexico; the *Grand Insulaire et Pilotage d' André Thevet*, an ancient and very curious document, in which the superstitions of Breton and Norman fishermen are recounted by one who shared them; and a variety of official papers, obtained for me through the agency of Mr. B. P. Poore, from the archives of France.

I am indebted to G. B. Faribault, Esq., of Quebec, and to the late Jacques Viger, Esq., of Montreal, for the use of valuable papers and memoranda; to the Rev. John Cordner, of Montreal, for various kind acts of co-operation; to Jared Sparks, LL. D., for the use of a copy of Le Clerc's *Établissement de la Foy*; to Dr. E. B. O'Callaghan, for assistance in examining rare books in the State Library of New York; to John Carter Brown, Esq., and Colonel Thomas Aspinwall, for the use of books from their admirable collections; while to the libraries of Harvard College and of the Boston Athenæum I owe a standing debt of gratitude.

The basis of descriptive passages was supplied through early tastes and habits, which long since made me familiar with most of the localities of the narrative.

Chapter I

1488—1543

EARLY FRENCH ADVENTURE IN NORTH AMERICA

Traditions of French Discovery • Normans, Bretons, Basques • Legends and Superstitions • Verrazzano • Jacques Cartier • Quebec • Hochelaga • Winter Miseries • Roberval • The Isles of Demons • The Colonists of Cap Rouge

---

WHEN America was first made known to Europe, the part assumed by France on the borders of that new world was peculiar, and is little recognized. While the Spaniard roamed sea and land, burning for achievement, red-hot with bigotry and avarice, and while England, with soberer steps and a less dazzling result, followed in the path of discovery and gold-hunting, it was from France that those barbarous shores first learned to serve the ends of peaceful commercial industry.

A French writer, however, advances a more ambitious claim. In the year 1488, four years before the first voyage of Columbus, America, he maintains, was found by Frenchmen. Cousin, a navigator of Dieppe, being at sea off the African coast, was forced westward, it is said, by winds and currents to within sight of an unknown shore, where he presently descried the mouth of a great river. On board his ship was one Pinzon, whose conduct became so mutinous that, on his return to Dieppe, Cousin made complaint to the magistracy, who thereupon dismissed the offender from the maritime service of the town. Pinzon went to Spain, became known to Columbus, told him the discovery, and joined him on his voyage of 1492.[1]

[1] *Mémoires pour servir à l'Histoire de Dieppe*; Vitet, *Histoire de Dieppe*, 226; Gaffarel, *Brésil Français*, 1. *Compte-rendu du Congrès International des Américanistes*, I. 398–414; Guérin, *Navigateurs Français*, 47: Estancelin, *Navigateurs Normands*, 332. This last writer's research to verify the tradition was vain. The bombardment of 1694 nearly destroyed the archives of Dieppe, and nothing could be learned from the Pinzons of Palos. Yet the story may not be quite void of foundation. In 1500, Cabral was blown within sight of Brazil in a similar manner. Herrera (*Hist. General*, Dec. I. Lib. I. c. 3) gives several parallel instances as having reached the ears of Columbus before his first voy-

To leave this cloudland of tradition, and approach the confines of recorded history. The Normans, offspring of an ancestry of conquerors,—the Bretons, that stubborn, hardy,
unchanging race, who, among Druid monuments changeless
as themselves, still cling with Celtic obstinacy to the thoughts
and habits of the past,—the Basques, that primeval people,
older than history,—all frequented from a very early date the
cod-banks of Newfoundland. There is some reason to believe
that this fishery existed before the voyage of Cabot, in 1497;[1]

---

age. Compare the Introduction to Lok's translation of Peter Martyr, and
Eden and Willes, *History of Travayles*, fol. 1; also a story in the *Journal de
l'Amérique* (Troyes, 1709), and Gomara, *Hist. Gen. des Indes Occidentales*, Lib.
I. c. 13. These last, however, are probably inventions.

In the *Description des Costes de la Mer Océane*, a manuscript of the seventeenth century, it is said that a French pilot of St. Jean de Luz first discovered
America: "Il fut le premier jeté en la coste de l'Amérique par une violente
tempeste, laissa son papier journal, communiqua la route qu'il avoit faite à
Coulon, chez qui il mourut." See Monteil, *Traité de Matériaux Manuscrits*, I.
340. The story is scarcely worth the mention. Harrisse (*Les Cortereal*, 27)
thinks there is reason to believe that the Portuguese reached the American
continent as early as 1474, or even ten years earlier.

[1] "Terra hæc ob lucrosissimam piscationis utilitatem summa litterarum me-
moria a Gallis adiri solita, & ante mille sexcentos annos frequentari solita est."
Postel, cited by Lescarbot, I. 237, and by Hornot, 260.

"De toute mémoire, & dès plusieurs siècles noz Diepois, Maloins, Rochelois,
& autres mariniers du Havre de Grace, de Honfleur & autres lieux, font les voyages ordinaires en ces païs-là pour la pècherie des Moruës." Lescarbot, I. 236.

Compare the following extracts:—

"Les Basques et les Bretons sont depuis plusieurs siècles les seuls qui se
soient employés à la pêche de balaines et des molues; et il est fort remarquable que S. Cabot, découvrant la côte de Labrador, y trouva le nom de *Bacal-
los*, qui signifie des Molues en langue des Basques." *MS. in the Royal Library
of Versailles*.

"Quant au nom de *Bacalos*, il est de l'imposition de nos Basques, lesquels
appellent une Moruë, *Bacaillos*, & à leur imitation nos peuples de la Nouvelle
France ont appris à nommer aussi la Moruë *Bacaillos*, quoyqu'en leur langage
le nom propre de la moruë soit *Apegé*." Lescarbot, I. 237.

De Laet also says, incidentally (p. 39), that "Bacalaos" is Basque for a codfish. I
once asked a Basque gentleman the name for a codfish in his language, and he at
once answered *Baccalaos*. The word has been adopted by the Spaniards.

"Sebastian Cabot himself named those lands Baccalaos, because that in the
seas thereabout he found so great multitudes of certain bigge fishes, much
like unto Tunies (which the inhabitants call Baccalaos), that they sometimes
stayed his shippes." Peter Martyr in Hakluyt, III. 30; Eden and Willes, 125.

If, in the original Basque, *Baccalaos* is the word for a codfish, and if Cabot

there is strong evidence that it began as early as the year 1504;[1] and it is well established that, in 1517, fifty Castilian, French, and Portuguese vessels were engaged in it at once; while in 1527, on the third of August, eleven sail of Norman, one of Breton, and two of Portuguese fishermen were to be found in the Bay of St. John.[2]

From this time forth, the Newfoundland fishery was never abandoned. French, English, Spanish, and Portuguese made resort to the Banks, always jealous, often quarrelling, but still drawing up treasure from those exhaustless mines, and bearing home bountiful provision against the season of Lent.

On this dim verge of the known world there were other perils than those of the waves. The rocks and shores of those sequestered seas had, so thought the voyagers, other tenants than the seal, the walrus and the screaming sea-fowl, the bears

---

found it in use among the inhabitants of Newfoundland, it is hard to escape the conclusion that Basques had been there before him.

This name *Baccalaos* is variously used by the old writers. Cabot gave it to the continent, as far as he coasted it. The earliest Spanish writers give it an application almost as comprehensive. On Wytfleit's map (1597) it is confined to Newfoundland and Labrador; on Ramusio's (1556), to the southern parts of Newfoundland; on Lescarbot's (1612), to the island of Cape Breton; on De Laet's (1640), to a small island east of Newfoundland.

[1] *Discorso d' un gran Capitano di Mare Francese*, Ramusio, III. 423. Ramusio does not know the name of the "gran capitano," but Estancelin proves him to have been Jean Parmentier, of Dieppe. From internal evidence, his memoir was written in 1539, and he says that Newfoundland was visited by Bretons and Normans thirty-five years before. "Britones et Normani anno a Christo nato M,CCCC,IIII has terras invenêre." Wytfleit, *Descriptionis Ptolemaicæ Augmentum*, 185. The translation of Wytfleit (Douay, 1611) bears also the name of Antoine Magin. It is cited by Champlain as "Niflet & Antoine Magin." See also Ogilby, *America*, 128; Forster, *Voyages*, 431; Baumgartens, I. 516; Biard, *Relation*, 2; Bergeron, *Traité de la Navigation*, c. 14.

[2] Herrera, Dec. II. Lib. V. c. 3; Letter of John Rut, dated St. John's, 3 August, 1527, in Purchas, III. 809.

The name of Cape Breton, found on the oldest maps, is a memorial of these early French voyages. Cartier, in 1534, found the capes and bays of Newfoundland already named by his countrymen who had preceded him. In 1565, Charles IX. of France informed the Spanish ambassador that the coast of North America had been discovered by French subjects more than a hundred years before, and is therefore called "Terre aux Bretons." *Papiers d'Estat de Forquevaulx*, in Gaffarel, *Floride*, 413.

Navarrete's position, that the fisheries date no farther back than 1540, is wholly untenable.

which stole away their fish before their eyes,[1] and the wild natives dressed in seal-skins. Griffins—so ran the story—infested the mountains of Labrador.[2] Two islands, north of Newfoundland, were given over to the fiends from whom they derived their name, the Isles of Demons. An old map pictures their occupants at length, devils rampant, with wings, horns, and tail.[3] The passing voyager heard the din of their infernal orgies, and woe to the sailor or the fisherman who ventured alone into the haunted woods.[4] "True it is," writes the old cosmographer Thevet, "and I myself have heard it, not from one, but from a great number of the sailors and pilots with whom I have made many voyages, that, when they passed this way, they heard in the air, on the tops and about the masts, a great clamor of men's voices, confused and inarticulate, such as you may hear from the crowd at a fair or market-place; whereupon they well knew that the Isle of Demons was not far off." And he adds, that he himself, when among the Indians, had seen them so tormented by these infernal persecutors, that they would fall into his arms for relief; on which, repeating a passage of the Gospel of St. John, he had driven the imps of darkness to a speedy exodus. They are comely to look upon, he further tells us, yet, by reason of their malice, that island is of late abandoned, and all who dwelt there have fled for refuge to the main.[5]

---

[1] "The Beares also be as bold, which will not spare at midday to take your fish before your face." *Letter of Anthonie Parkhurst*, 1578, in Hakluyt, III. 170.

[2] Wytfleit, 190; Gomara, Lib. I. c. 2.

[3] See Ramusio, III. Compare La Popelinière, *Les Trois Mondes*, II. 25.

[4] *Le Grand Insulaire et Pilotage d'André Thevet, Cosmographe du Roy* (1586). I am indebted to G. B. Faribault, Esq., of Quebec, for a copy of this curious manuscript. The islands are perhaps those of Belle Isle and Quirpon. More probably, however, that most held in dread, "pour autant que les Demons y font terrible tintamarre," is a small island near the northeast extremity of Newfoundland, variously called, by Thevet, Isle de Fiche, Isle de Roberval, and Isle des Démons. It is the same with the Isle Fichet of Sanson, and the Fishot Island of some modern maps. A curious legend connected with it will be given hereafter.

[5] Thevet, *Cosmographie* (1575), II. c. 5. A very rare book. I am indebted to Dr. E. B. O'Callaghan for copies of the passages in it relating to subjects within the scope of the present work. Thevet here contradicts himself in regard to the position of the haunted island, which he places at 60° north latitude.

While French fishermen plied their trade along these gloomy coasts, the French government spent its energies on a different field. The vitality of the kingdom was wasted in Italian wars. Milan and Naples offered a more tempting prize than the wilds of Baccalaos.[1] Eager for glory and for plunder, a swarm of restless nobles followed their knight-errant King, the would-be paladin, who, misshapen in body and fantastic in mind, had yet the power to raise a storm which the lapse of generations could not quell. Under Charles the Eighth and his successor, war and intrigue ruled the day; and in the whirl of Italian politics there was no leisure to think of a new world.

Yet private enterprise was not quite benumbed. In 1506, one Denis of Honfleur explored the Gulf of St. Lawrence;[2] two years later, Aubert of Dieppe followed on his track;[3] and in 1518, the Baron de Léry made an abortive attempt at settlement on Sable Island, where the cattle left by him remained and multiplied.[4]

The crown passed at length to Francis of Angoulême. There were in his nature seeds of nobleness,—seeds destined to bear little fruit. Chivalry and honor were always on his lips; but Francis the First, a forsworn gentleman, a despotic king, vainglorious, selfish, sunk in debaucheries, was but the type of an era which retained the forms of the Middle Age without its soul, and added to a still prevailing barbarism the pestilential vices which hung fog-like around the dawn of civilization. Yet he esteemed arts and letters, and, still more, coveted the *éclat* which they could give. The light which was beginning to pierce the feudal darkness gathered its rays around his throne. Italy was rewarding the robbers who preyed on her with the treasures of her knowledge and her culture; and Italian genius, of whatever stamp, found ready patronage at the hands of Francis. Among artists, philosophers, and men of letters enrolled in his service stands the humbler name of a Florentine navigator, John Verrazzano.

He was born of an ancient family, which could boast names

---

[1] See *ante*, p. 146, note 1.
[2] Parmentier in Ramusio, III. 423; Estancelin, 42–222.
[3] Ibid.
[4] Lescarbot, I. 22; De Laet, *Novus Orbis*, 39; Bergeron, c. 15.

eminent in Florentine history, and of which the last survivor died in 1819. He has been called a pirate, and he was such in the same sense in which Drake, Hawkins, and other valiant sea-rovers of his own and later times, merited the name; that is to say, he would plunder and kill a Spaniard on the high seas without waiting for a declaration of war.

The wealth of the Indies was pouring into the coffers of Charles the Fifth, and the exploits of Cortés had given new lustre to his crown. Francis the First begrudged his hated rival the glories and profits of the New World. He would fain have his share of the prize; and Verrazzano, with four ships, was despatched to seek out a passage westward to the rich kingdom of Cathay.

Some doubt has of late been cast on the reality of this voyage of Verrazzano, and evidence, mainly negative in kind, has been adduced to prove the story of it a fabrication; but the difficulties of incredulity appear greater than those of belief, and no ordinary degree of scepticism is required to reject the evidence that the narrative is essentially true.[1]

Towards the end of the year 1523, his four ships sailed from Dieppe; but a storm fell upon him, and, with two of the vessels, he ran back in distress to a port of Brittany. What became of the other two does not appear. Neither is it clear why, after a preliminary cruise against the Spaniards, he pursued his voyage with one vessel alone, a caravel called the Dauphine. With her he made for Madeira, and, on the seventeenth of January, 1524, set sail from a barren islet in its neighborhood, and bore away for the unknown world. In forty-nine days they neared a low shore, not far from the site of Wilmington in North Carolina, "a newe land," exclaims the voyager, "never before seen of any man, either auncient or moderne."[2] Verrazzano steered southward in search of a harbor, and, finding none, turned northward again. Presently he sent a boat ashore. The inhabitants, who had fled at first, soon came down to the strand in wonder and admiration, pointing out a landing-place, and making gestures of friendship. "These people," says Verrazzano, "goe altogether naked, except only certain skinnes of beastes like unto marterns [mar-

[1] See note, end of chapter.
[2] Hakluyt's translation from Ramusio, in *Divers Voyages* (1582).

tens], which they fasten onto a narrowe girdle made of grasse. They are of colour russet, and not much unlike the Saracens, their hayre blacke, thicke, and not very long, which they tye togeather in a knot behinde, and weare it like a taile."[1]

He describes the shore as consisting of small low hillocks of fine sand, intersected by creeks and inlets, and beyond these a country "full of Palme [pine?] trees, Bay trees, and high Cypresse trees, and many other sortes of trees, vnknowne in Europe, which yeeld most sweete sauours, farre from the shore." Still advancing northward, Verrazzano sent a boat for a supply of water. The surf ran high, and the crew could not land; but an adventurous young sailor jumped overboard and swam shoreward with a gift of beads and trinkets for the Indians, who stood watching him. His heart failed as he drew near; he flung his gift among them, turned, and struck out for the boat. The surf dashed him back, flinging him with violence on the beach among the recipients of his bounty, who seized him by the arms and legs, and, while he called lustily for aid, answered him with outcries designed to allay his terrors. Next they kindled a great fire,—doubtless to roast and devour him before the eyes of his comrades, gazing in horror from their boat. On the contrary, they carefully warmed him, and were trying to dry his clothes, when, recovering from his bewilderment, he betrayed a strong desire to escape to his friends; whereupon, "with great love, clapping him fast about, with many embracings," they led him to the shore, and stood watching till he had reached the boat.

It only remained to requite this kindness, and an opportunity soon occurred; for, coasting the shores of Virginia or Maryland, a party went on shore and found an old woman, a young girl, and several children, hiding with great terror in the grass. Having, by various blandishments, gained their confidence, they carried off one of the children as a curiosity, and, since the girl was comely, would fain have taken her also, but desisted by reason of her continual screaming.

Verrazzano's next resting-place was the Bay of New York. Rowing up in his boat through the Narrows, under the steep heights of Staten Island, he saw the harbor within dotted

[1] Ibid.

with canoes of the feathered natives, coming from the shore to welcome him. But what most engaged the eyes of the white men were the fancied signs of mineral wealth in the neighboring hills.

Following the shores of Long Island, they came to an island, which may have been Block Island, and thence to a harbor, which was probably that of Newport. Here they stayed fifteen days, most courteously received by the inhabitants. Among others appeared two chiefs, gorgeously arrayed in painted deer-skins, — kings, as Verrazzano calls them, with attendant gentlemen; while a party of squaws in a canoe, kept by their jealous lords at a safe distance from the caravel, figure in the narrative as the queen and her maids. The Indian wardrobe had been taxed to its utmost to do the strangers honor; — copper bracelets, lynx-skins, raccoon-skins, and faces bedaubed with gaudy colors.

Again they spread their sails, and on the fifth of May bade farewell to the primitive hospitalities of Newport, steered along the rugged coasts of New England, and surveyed, ill pleased, the surf-beaten rocks, the pine tree and the fir, the shadows and the gloom of mighty forests. Here man and nature alike were savage and repellent. Perhaps some plundering straggler from the fishing-banks, some man-stealer like the Portuguese Cortereal, or some kidnapper of children and ravisher of squaws like themselves, had warned the denizens of the woods to beware of the worshippers of Christ. Their only intercourse was in the way of trade. From the brink of the rocks which overhung the sea the Indians would let down a cord to the boat below, demand fish-hooks, knives, and steel, in barter for their furs, and, their bargain made, salute the voyagers with unseemly gestures of derision and scorn. The French once ventured ashore; but a war-whoop and a shower of arrows sent them back to their boats.

Verrazzano coasted the seaboard of Maine, and sailed northward as far as Newfoundland, whence, provisions failing, he steered for France. He had not found a passage to Cathay, but he had explored the American coast from the thirty-fourth degree to the fiftieth, and at various points had penetrated several leagues into the country. On the eighth of July, he wrote from Dieppe to the King the earliest description known to exist of the shores of the United States.

Great was the joy that hailed his arrival, and great were the hopes of emolument and wealth from the new-found shores.[1] The merchants of Lyons were in a flush of expectation. For himself, he was earnest to return, plant a colony, and bring the heathen tribes within the pale of the Church. But the time was inauspicious. The year of his voyage was to France a year of disasters,—defeat in Italy, the loss of Milan, the death of the heroic Bayard; and, while Verrazzano was writing his narrative at Dieppe, the traitor Bourbon was invading Provence. Preparation, too, was soon on foot for the expedition which, a few months later, ended in the captivity of Francis on the field of Pavia. Without a king, without an army, without money, convulsed within, and threatened from without, France after that humiliation was in no condition to renew her Transatlantic enterprise.

Henceforth few traces remain of the fortunes of Verrazzano. Ramusio affirms, that, on another voyage, he was killed and eaten by savages, in sight of his followers;[2] and a late writer hazards the conjecture that this voyage, if made at all, was made in the service of Henry the Eighth of England.[3] But a Spanish writer affirms that, in 1527, he was hanged at Puerto del Pico as a pirate,[4] and this assertion is fully confirmed by authentic documents recently brought to light.

The fickle-minded King, always ardent at the outset of an enterprise and always flagging before its close, divided, moreover, between the smiles of his mistresses and the assaults of his enemies, might probably have dismissed the New World from his thoughts. But among the favorites of his youth was a high-spirited young noble, Philippe de Brion-Chabot, the partner of his joustings and tennis-playing, his gaming and gallantries.[5] He still stood high in the royal favor, and, after the treacherous escape of Francis from captivity, held the of-

---

[1] *Fernando Carli à suo Padre, 4 Aug., 1524.*

[2] Ramusio, III. 417; Wytfleit, 185. Compare Le Clerc, *Établissement de la Foy*, I. 6.

[3] Biddle, *Memoir of Cabot*, 275.

[4] Barcia, *Ensayo Cronologico*, 8.

[5] Brantôme, II. 277; *Biographie Universelle*, Art. *Chabot*.

fice of Admiral of France. When the kingdom had rallied in some measure from its calamities, he conceived the purpose of following up the path which Verrazzano had opened.

The ancient town of St. Malo, thrust out like a buttress into the sea, strange and grim of aspect, breathing war from its walls and battlements of ragged stone, a stronghold of privateers, the home of a race whose intractable and defiant independence neither time nor change has subdued, has been for centuries a nursery of hardly mariners. Among the earliest and most eminent on its list stands the name of Jacques Cartier. His portrait hangs in the town-hall of St. Malo,—bold, keen features bespeaking a spirit not apt to quail before the wrath of man or of the elements. In him Chabot found a fit agent of his design, if, indeed, its suggestion is not due to the Breton navigator.[1]

Sailing from St. Malo on the twentieth of April, 1534, Cartier steered for Newfoundland, passed through the Straits of Belle Isle, entered the Gulf of Chaleurs, planted a cross at Gaspé, and, never doubting that he was on the high road to Cathay, advanced up the St. Lawrence till he saw the shores of Anticosti. But autumnal storms were gathering. The voyagers took counsel together, turned their prows eastward, and bore away for France, carrying thither, as a sample of the natural products of the New World, two young Indians, lured into their clutches by an act of villanous treachery. The voyage was a mere reconnoissance.[2]

The spirit of discovery was awakened. A passage to India could be found, and a new France built up beyond the Atlantic. Mingled with such views of interest and ambition was another motive scarcely less potent.[3] The heresy of Luther was convulsing Germany, and the deeper heresy of Calvin infecting France. Devout Catholics, kindling with redoubled zeal, would fain requite the Church for her losses in the Old

[1] Cartier was at this time forty years of age, having been born in December, 1494. I examined the St. Malo portrait in 1881. It is a recent work (1839), and its likeness is more than doubtful.

[2] Lescarbot, I. 232 (1612); *Relation originale du Voyage de Jacques Cartier en 1534* (Paris, 1867); Cartier, *Discours du Voyage*, reprinted by the Literary and Historical Society of Quebec. Compare translations in Hakluyt and Ramusio; MS. Map of Cartier's route in *Dépôt des Cartes*, Carton V.

[3] *Lettre de Cartier au Roy très Chrétien.*

World by winning to her fold the infidels of the New. But, in pursuing an end at once so pious and so politic, Francis the First was setting at naught the supreme Pontiff himself, since, by the preposterous bull of Alexander the Sixth, all America had been given to the Spaniards.

In October, 1534, Cartier received from Chabot another commission, and, in spite of secret but bitter opposition from jealous traders of St. Malo, he prepared for a second voyage. Three vessels, the largest not above a hundred and twenty tons, were placed at his disposal, and Claude de Pontbriand, Charles de la Pommeraye, and other gentlemen of birth, enrolled themselves for the adventure. On the sixteenth of May, 1535, officers and sailors assembled in the cathedral of St. Malo, where, after confession and mass, they received the parting blessing of the bishop. Three days later they set sail. The dingy walls of the rude old seaport, and the white rocks that line the neighboring shores of Brittany, faded from their sight, and soon they were tossing in a furious tempest. The scattered ships escaped the danger, and, reuniting at the Straits of Belle Isle, steered westward along the coast of Labrador, till they reached a small bay opposite the island of Anticosti. Cartier called it the Bay of St. Lawrence, a name afterwards extended to the entire gulf, and to the great river above.[1]

[1] Cartier calls the St. Lawrence the "River of Hochelaga," or "the great river of Canada." He confines the name of *Canada* to a district extending from the Isle aux Coudres in the St. Lawrence to a point at some distance above the site of Quebec. The country below, he adds, was called by the Indians *Saguenay*, and that above, *Hochelaga*. In the map of Gérard Mercator (1569) the name Canada is given to a town, with an adjacent district, on the river *Stadin* (St. Charles). Lescarbot, a later writer, insists that the country on both sides of the St. Lawrence, from Hochelaga to its mouth, bore the name of *Canada*.

In the second map of Ortelius, published about the year 1572, New France, Nova Francia, is thus divided: — *Canada*, a district on the St. Lawrence above the River Saguenay; *Chilaga* (Hochelaga), the angle between the Ottawa and the St. Lawrence; *Saguenai*, a district below the river of that name; *Moscosa*, south of the St. Lawrence and east of the River Richelieu; *Avacal*, west and south of Moscosa; *Norumbega*, Maine and New Brunswick; *Apalachen*, Virginia, Pennsylvania, etc.; *Terra Corterealis*, Labrador; *Florida*, Mississippi, Alabama, Florida.

Mercator confines the name of New France to districts bordering on the St. Lawrence. Others give it a much broader application. The use of this

To ascend this great river, and tempt the hazards of its intricate navigation with no better pilots than the two young
Indians kidnapped the year before, was a venture of no light
risk. But skill or fortune prevailed; and, on the first of September, the voyagers reached in safety the gorge of the
gloomy Saguenay, with its towering cliffs and sullen depth of
waters. Passing the Isle aux Coudres, and the lofty promontory of Cape Tourmente, they came to anchor in a quiet channel between the northern shore and the margin of a richly
wooded island, where the trees were so thickly hung with
grapes that Cartier named it the Island of Bacchus.[1]

Indians came swarming from the shores, paddled their canoes about the ships, and clambered to the decks to gaze in
bewilderment at the novel scene, and listen to the story of
their travelled countrymen, marvellous in their ears as a visit
to another planet.[2] Cartier received them kindly, listened to
the long harangue of the great chief Donnacona, regaled him

name, or the nearly allied names of Francisca and La Franciscane, dates back,
to say the least, as far as 1525, and the Dutch geographers are especially free
in their use of it, out of spite to the Spaniards.

The derivation of the name of Canada has been a point of discussion. It
is, without doubt, not Spanish, but Indian. In the vocabulary of the language
of Hochelaga, appended to the journal of Cartier's second voyage, *Canada*
is set down as the word for a town or village. "Ils appellent une ville, Canada." It bears the same meaning in the Mohawk tongue. Both languages are
dialects of the Iroquois. Lescarbot affirms that Canada is simply an Indian
proper name, of which it is vain to seek a meaning. Belleforest also calls it an
Indian word, but translates it "Terre," as does also Thevet.

[1] Now the Island of Orleans.

[2] Doubt has been thrown on this part of Cartier's narrative, on the ground
that these two young Indians, who were captured at Gaspé, could not have
been so intimately acquainted as the journal represents with the savages at
the site of Quebec. From a subsequent part of the journal, however, it appears that they were natives of this place,—"et là est la ville et demeurance
du Seigneur Donnacona, et de nos deux hommes qu'avions pris le premier
voyage." This is curiously confirmed by Thevet, who personally knew Cartier,
and who, in his *Singularités de la France Antarctique*, (p. 147,) says that the
party to which the two Indians captured at Gaspé belonged spoke a language
different from that of the other Indians seen in those parts, and that they had
come on a war expedition from the River Chelogua (Hochelaga). Compare
New Found Worlds (London, 1568), 124. This will also account for Lescarbot's
remark, that the Indians of Gaspé had changed their language since Cartier's
time. The language of Stadaconé, or Quebec, when Cartier visited it, was
apparently a dialect of the Iroquois.

with bread and wine; and, when relieved at length of his guests, set forth in a boat to explore the river above.

As he drew near the opening of the channel, the Hochelaga again spread before him the broad expanse of its waters. A mighty promontory, rugged and bare, thrust its scarped front into the surging current. Here, clothed in the majesty of solitude, breathing the stern poetry of the wilderness, rose the cliffs now rich with heroic memories, where the fiery Count Frontenac cast defiance at his foes, where Wolfe, Montcalm, and Montgomery fell. As yet, all was a nameless barbarism, and a cluster of wigwams held the site of the rock-built city of Quebec.[1] Its name was Stadacone, and it owned the sway of the royal Donnacona.

Cartier set out to visit this greasy potentate, ascended the river St. Charles, by him called the St. Croix,[2] landed, crossed the meadows, climbed the rocks, threaded the forest, and emerged upon a squalid hamlet of bark cabins. When, having satisfied their curiosity, he and his party were rowing for the ships, a friendly interruption met them at the mouth of the St. Charles. An old chief harangued them from the bank, men, boys, and children screeched welcome from the meadow, and a troop of hilarious squaws danced knee-deep in the water. The gift of a few strings of beads completed their delight and redoubled their agility; and, from the distance of a mile, their shrill songs of jubilation still reached the ears of the receding Frenchmen.

The hamlet of Stadacone, with its king, Donnacona, and its naked lords and princes, was not the metropolis of this forest state, since a town far greater—so the Indians averred— stood by the brink of the river, many days' journey above. It was called Hochelaga, and the great river itself, with a wide

[1] On ground now covered by the suburbs of St. Roque and St. John.

[2] Charlevoix denies that the St. Croix and the St. Charles are the same; but he supports his denial by an argument which proves nothing but his own gross carelessness. Champlain, than whom no one was better qualified to form an opinion, distinctly affirms the identity of the two rivers. See his Map of Quebec, and the accompanying key, in the edition of 1613. La Potherie is of the same opinion; as also, among modern writers, Faribault and Fisher. In truth, the description of localities in Cartier's journal cannot, when closely examined, admit a doubt on the subject. See also Berthelot, *Dissertation sur le Canon de Bronze.*

reach of adjacent country, had borrowed its name. Thither, with his two young Indians as guides, Cartier resolved to go; but misgivings seized the guides, as the time drew near, while Donnacona and his tribesmen, jealous of the plan, set themselves to thwart it. The Breton captain turned a deaf ear to their dissuasions; on which, failing to touch his reason, they appealed to his fears.

One morning, as the ships still lay at anchor, the French beheld three Indian devils descending in a canoe towards them, dressed in black and white dog-skins, with faces black as ink, and horns long as a man's arm. Thus arrayed, they drifted by, while the principal fiend, with fixed eyes, as of one piercing the secrets of futurity, uttered in a loud voice a long harangue. Then they paddled for the shore; and no sooner did they reach it than each fell flat like a dead man in the bottom of the canoe. Aid, however, was at hand; for Donnacona and his tribesmen, rushing pell-mell from the adjacent woods, raised the swooning masqueraders, and, with shrill clamors, bore them in their arms within the sheltering thickets. Here, for a full half-hour, the French could hear them haranguing in solemn conclave. Then the two young Indians whom Cartier had brought back from France came out of the bushes, enacting a pantomime of amazement and terror, clasping their hands, and calling on Christ and the Virgin; whereupon Cartier, shouting from the vessel, asked what was the matter. They replied, that the god Coudouagny had sent to warn the French against all attempts to ascend the great river, since, should they persist, snows, tempests, and drifting ice would requite their rashness with inevitable ruin. The French replied that Coudouagny was a fool; that he could not hurt those who believed in Christ; and that they might tell this to his three messengers. The assembled Indians, with little reverence for their deity, pretended great contentment at this assurance, and danced for joy along the beach.[1]

Cartier now made ready to depart. And, first, he caused the two larger vessels to be towed for safe harborage within the

---

[1] M. Berthelot, in his *Dissertation sur le Canon de Bronze*, discovers in this Indian pantomime a typical representation of the supposed shipwreck of Verrazzano in the St. Lawrence. This shipwreck, it is needless to say, is a mere imagination of this ingenious writer.

mouth of the St. Charles. With the smallest, a galleon of forty
tons, and two open boats, carrying in all fifty sailors, besides
Pontbriand, La Pommeraye, and other gentlemen, he set out
for Hochelaga.

Slowly gliding on their way by walls of verdure brightened
in the autumnal sun, they saw forests festooned with grape-
vines, and waters alive with wild-fowl; they heard the song of
the blackbird, the thrush, and, as they fondly thought, the
nightingale. The galleon grounded; they left her, and, advancing with the boats alone, on the second of October neared
the goal of their hopes, the mysterious Hochelaga.

Just below where now are seen the quays and storehouses
of Montreal, a thousand Indians thronged the shore, wild
with delight, dancing, singing, crowding about the strangers,
and showering into the boats their gifts of fish and maize;
and, as it grew dark, fires lighted up the night, while, far and
near, the French could see the excited savages leaping and
rejoicing by the blaze.

At dawn of day, marshalled and accoutred, they marched
for Hochelaga. An Indian path led them through the forest
which covered the site of Montreal. The morning air was chill
and sharp, the leaves were changing hue, and beneath the
oaks the ground was thickly strewn with acorns. They soon
met an Indian chief with a party of tribesmen, or, as the old
narrative has it, "one of the principal lords of the said city,"
attended with a numerous retinue.[1] Greeting them after the
concise courtesy of the forest, he led them to a fire kindled by
the side of the path for their comfort and refreshment, seated
them on the ground, and made them a long harangue, receiving in requital of his eloquence two hatchets, two knives, and
a crucifix, the last of which he was invited to kiss. This done,
they resumed their march, and presently came upon open
fields, covered far and near with the ripened maize, its leaves
rustling, and its yellow grains gleaming between the parting
husks. Before them, wrapped in forests painted by the early
frosts, rose the ridgy back of the Mountain of Montreal, and
below, encompassed with its cornfields, lay the Indian town.
Nothing was visible but its encircling palisades. They were of

[1] ". . . . l'un des principaulx seigneurs de la dicte ville, accompaigné de
plusieurs personnes." Cartier (1545), 23.

trunks of trees, set in a triple row. The outer and inner ranges inclined till they met and crossed near the summit, while the upright row between them, aided by transverse braces, gave to the whole an abundant strength. Within were galleries for the defenders, rude ladders to mount them, and magazines of stones to throw down on the heads of assailants. It was a mode of fortification practised by all the tribes speaking dialects of the Iroquois.[1]

The voyagers entered the narrow portal. Within, they saw some fifty of those large oblong dwellings so familiar in after years to the eyes of the Jesuit apostles in Iroquois and Huron

[1] That the Indians of Hochelaga belonged to the Huron-Iroquois family of tribes is evident from the affinities of their language, (compare Gallatin, *Synopsis of Indian Tribes*,) and from the construction of their houses and defensive works. This was identical with the construction universal, or nearly so, among the Huron-Iroquois tribes. In Ramusio, III. 446, there is a plan of Hochelaga and its defences, marked by errors which seem to show that the maker had not seen the objects represented. Whence the sketch was derived does not appear, as the original edition of Cartier does not contain it. In 1860, a quantity of Indian remains were dug up at Montreal, immediately below Sherbrooke Street, between Mansfield and Metcalfe Streets. (See a paper by Dr. Dawson, in *Canadian Naturalist and Geologist*, V. 430.) They may perhaps indicate the site of Hochelaga. A few, which have a distinctive character, belong not to the Algonquin, but to the Huron-Iroquois type. The short-stemmed pipe of terra-cotta is the exact counterpart of those found in the great Huron deposits of the dead in Canada West, and in Iroquois burial-places of Western New York. So also of the fragments of pottery and the instruments of bone used in ornamenting it.

The assertion of certain Algonquins, who, in 1642, told the missionaries that their ancestors once lived at Montreal, is far from conclusive evidence. It may have referred to an occupancy subsequent to Cartier's visit, or, which is more probable, the Indians, after their favorite practice, may have amused themselves with "hoaxing" their interlocutors.

Cartier calls his vocabulary, *Le Langage des Pays et Royaulmes de Hochelaga et Canada, aultrement appellée par nous la Nouuelle France* (ed. 1545). For this and other reasons it is more than probable that the Indians of Quebec, or Stadaconé, were also of the Huron-Iroquois race, since by *Canada* he means the country about Quebec. Seventy years later, the whole region was occupied by Algonquins, and no trace remained of Hochelaga or Stadaconé.

There was a tradition among the Agniés (Mohawks), one of the five tribes of the Iroquois, that their ancestors were once settled at Quebec. See Lafitau, I. 101. *Canada*, as already mentioned, is a Mohawk word. The tradition recorded by Colden, in his *History of the Five Nations* (Iroquois), that they were formerly settled near Montreal, is of interest here. The tradition declares that they were driven thence by the Adirondacks (Algonquins).

forests. They were about fifty yards in length, and twelve or fifteen wide, framed of sapling poles closely covered with sheets of bark, and each containing several fires and several families. In the midst of the town was an open area, or public square, a stone's throw in width. Here Cartier and his followers stopped, while the surrounding houses of bark disgorged their inmates,—swarms of children, and young women and old, their infants in their arms. They crowded about the visitors, crying for delight, touching their beards, feeling their faces, and holding up the screeching infants to be touched in turn. The marvellous visitors, strange in hue, strange in attire, with moustached lip and bearded chin, with arquebuse, halberd, helmet, and cuirass, seemed rather demigods than men.

Due time having been allowed for this exuberance of feminine rapture, the warriors interposed, banished the women and children to a distance, and squatted on the ground around the French, row within row of swarthy forms and eager faces, "as if," says Cartier, "we were going to act a play."[1] Then appeared a troop of women, each bringing a mat, with which they carpeted the bare earth for the behoof of their guests. The latter being seated, the chief of the nation was borne before them on a deer-skin by a number of his tribesmen, a bedridden old savage, paralyzed and helpless, squalid as the rest in his attire, and distinguished only by a red fillet, inwrought with the dyed quills of the Canada porcupine, encircling his lank black hair. They placed him on the ground at Cartier's feet and made signs of welcome for him, while he pointed feebly to his powerless limbs, and implored the healing touch from the hand of the French chief. Cartier complied, and received in acknowledgment the red fillet of his grateful patient. Then from surrounding dwellings appeared a woful throng, the sick, the lame, the blind, the maimed, the decrepit, brought or led forth and placed on the earth before the perplexed commander, "as if," he says, "a god had come down to cure them." His skill in medicine being far behind the emergency, he pronounced over his petitioners a portion of the Gospel of St. John, made the sign of the cross, and uttered a prayer, not for their bodies only, but for their mis-

[1] ". . . . comme sy eussions voulu iouer vng mystere." Cartier, 25 (1545).

erable souls. Next he read the passion of the Saviour, to which, though comprehending not a word, his audience listened with grave attention. Then came a distribution of presents. The squaws and children were recalled, and, with the warriors, placed in separate groups. Knives and hatchets were given to the men, and beads to the women, while pewter rings and images of the Agnus Dei were flung among the troop of children, whence ensued a vigorous scramble in the square of Hochelaga. Now the French trumpeters pressed their trumpets to their lips, and blew a blast that filled the air with warlike din and the hearts of the hearers with amazement and delight. Bidding their hosts farewell, the visitors formed their ranks and defiled through the gate once more, despite the efforts of a crowd of women, who, with clamorous hospitality, beset them with gifts of fish, beans, corn, and other viands of uninviting aspect, which the Frenchmen courteously declined.

A troop of Indians followed, and guided them to the top of the neighboring mountain. Cartier called it *Mont Royal*, Montreal; and hence the name of the busy city which now holds the site of the vanished Hochelaga. Stadaconé and Hochelaga, Quebec and Montreal, in the sixteenth century as in the nineteenth, were the centres of Canadian population.

From the summit, that noble prospect met his eye which at this day is the delight of tourists, but strangely changed, since, first of white men, the Breton voyager gazed upon it. Tower and dome and spire, congregated roofs, white sail and gliding steamer, animate its vast expanse with varied life. Cartier saw a different scene. East, west, and south, the mantling forest was over all, and the broad blue ribbon of the great river glistened amid a realm of verdure. Beyond, to the bounds of Mexico, stretched a leafy desert, and the vast hive of industry, the mighty battle-ground of later centuries, lay sunk in savage torpor, wrapped in illimitable woods.

The French re-embarked, bade farewell to Hochelaga, retraced their lonely course down the St. Lawrence, and reached Stadaconé in safety. On the bank of the St. Charles, their companions had built in their absence a fort of palisades, and the ships, hauled up the little stream, lay moored before it.[1] Here the self-exiled company were soon besieged by the rigors of the Canadian winter. The rocks, the shores, the pine trees, the solid floor of the frozen river, all alike were blanketed in snow, beneath the keen cold rays of the dazzling sun. The drifts rose above the sides of their ships; masts, spars, and cordage were thick with glittering incrustations and sparkling rows of icicles; a frosty armor, four inches thick, encased the bulwarks. Yet, in the bitterest weather, the neighboring Indians, "hardy," says the journal, "as so many beasts," came daily to the fort, wading, half naked, waist-deep through the snow. At length, their friendship began to abate; their visits grew less frequent, and during December had wholly ceased, when a calamity fell upon the French.

A malignant scurvy broke out among them. Man after man went down before the hideous disease, till twenty-five were dead, and only three or four were left in health. The sound were too few to attend the sick, and the wretched sufferers lay in helpless despair, dreaming of the sun and the vines of France. The ground, hard as flint, defied their feeble efforts, and, unable to bury their dead, they hid them in snow-drifts. Cartier appealed to the saints; but they turned a deaf ear. Then he nailed against a tree an image of the Virgin, and on a Sunday summoned forth his woe-begone followers, who, haggard, reeling, bloated with their maladies, moved in procession to the spot, and, kneeling in the snow, sang litanies and psalms of David. That day died Philippe Rougemont, of Amboise, aged twenty-two years. The Holy Virgin deigned no other response.

There was fear that the Indians, learning their misery, might finish the work that scurvy had begun. None of them, therefore, were allowed to approach the fort; and when a party of savages lingered within hearing, Cartier forced his invalid garrison to beat with sticks and stones against the walls, that their dangerous neighbors, deluded by the clatter, might think them engaged in hard labor. These objects of

[1] In 1608, Champlain found the remains of Cartier's fort. See Champlain (1613), 184–191. Charlevoix is clearly wrong as to the locality. M. Faribault, who has collected the evidence, (see *Voyages de Découverte au Canada*, 109–119,) thinks the fort was near the junction of the little river Lairet with the St. Charles.

their fear proved, however, the instruments of their salvation. Cartier, walking one day near the river, met an Indian, who not long before had been prostrate, like many of his fellows, with the scurvy, but who was now, to all appearance, in high health and spirits. What agency had wrought this marvellous recovery? According to the Indian, it was a certain evergreen, called by him *ameda*,[1] a decoction of the leaves of which was sovereign against the disease. The experiment was tried. The sick men drank copiously of the healing draught,—so copiously indeed that in six days they drank a tree as large as a French oak. Thus vigorously assailed, the distemper relaxed its hold, and health and hope began to revisit the hapless company.

When this winter of misery had worn away, and the ships were thawed from their icy fetters, Cartier prepared to return. He had made notable discoveries; but these were as nothing to the tales of wonder that had reached his ear,—of a land of gold and rubies, of a nation white like the French, of men who lived without food, and of others to whom Nature had granted but one leg. Should he stake his credit on these marvels? It were better that they who had recounted them to him should, with their own lips, recount them also to the King, and to this end he resolved that Donnacona and his chiefs should go with him to court. He lured them therefore to the fort, and led them into an ambuscade of sailors, who, seizing the astonished guests, hurried them on board the ships. Having accomplished this treachery, the voyagers proceeded to plant the emblem of Christianity. The cross was raised, the fleur-de-lis planted near it, and, spreading their sails, they steered for home. It was the sixteenth of July, 1536, when Cartier again cast anchor under the walls of St. Malo.[2]

[1] *Ameda*, in the edition of 1545; *annedda*, in Lescarbot, Ternaux-Compans, and Faribault. The wonderful tree seems to have been a spruce, or, more probably, an arbor-vitæ.

[2] Of the original edition (1545) of the narrative of this voyage only one copy is known,—that in the British Museum. It is styled, *Brief Recit, & succincte narration, de la nauigation faicte es ysles de Canada, Hochelage & Saguenay & autres, auec particulieres meurs, langaige, & ceremonies des habitans d'icelles; fort delectable à veoir*. As may be gathered from the title, the style and orthography are those of the days of Rabelais. It has been reprinted (1863) with valuable notes by M. d'Avezac.

A rigorous climate, a savage people, a fatal disease, and a soil barren of gold were the allurements of New France. Nor were the times auspicious for a renewal of the enterprise. Charles the Fifth, flushed with his African triumphs, challenged the Most Christian King to single combat. The war flamed forth with renewed fury, and ten years elapsed before a hollow truce varnished the hate of the royal rivals with a thin pretence of courtesy. Peace returned; but Francis the First was sinking to his ignominious grave, under the scourge of his favorite goddess, and Chabot, patron of the former voyages, was in disgrace.[1]

Meanwhile the ominous adventure of New France had found a champion in the person of Jean François de la Roque, Sieur de Roberval, a nobleman of Picardy. Though a man of high account in his own province, his past honors paled before the splendor of the titles said to have been now conferred on him,—Lord of Norembega, Viceroy and Lieutenant-General in Canada, Hochelaga, Saguenay, Newfoundland, Belle Isle, Carpunt, Labrador, the Great Bay, and Baccalaos.[2] To this windy gift of ink and parchment was added a solid grant from the royal treasury, with which five vessels were procured and equipped, and to Cartier was given the post of Captain-General. "We have resolved," says Fran-

---

[1] Brantôme, II. 283; Anquetil, V. 397; Sismondi, XVII. 62.

[2] Labrador—*Laboratoris Terra*—is so called from the circumstance that Cortereal in the year 1500 stole thence a cargo of Indians for slaves. Belle Isle and Carpunt,—the strait and islands between Labrador and Newfoundland. The Great Bay,—the Gulf of St. Lawrence. Norembega, or Norumbega, more properly called Arambec (Hakluyt, III. 167), was, in Ramusio's map, the country embraced within Nova Scotia, southern New Brunswick, and a part of Maine. De Laet confines it to a district about the mouth of the Penobscot. Wytfleet and other early writers say that it had a capital city of the same name; and in several old maps this fabulous metropolis is laid down, with towers and churches, on the river Penobscot. The word is of Indian origin.

Before me is the commission of Roberval, *Lettres Patentes accordées à Jehan Françoys de La Roque Sr̃ de Roberval*, copied from the French archives. Here he is simply styled "notre Lieutenant-General, Chef Ducteur et Cappitaine de la d. entreprinse." The patent is in Lescarbot (1618). In the Archives de la Bibliothèque Publique de Rouen, an edict is preserved authorizing Roberval to raise "une armée de volontaires avec victuailles, artillerie, etc. pour aller au pays de Canada." Harrisse has printed curious original documents concerning Roberval in his *Notes sur la Nouvelle France*.

cis, "to send him again to the lands of Canada and Hochelaga, which form the extremity of Asia towards the west."[1]
His commission declares the objects of the enterprise to be
discovery, settlement, and the conversion of the Indians, who
are described as "men without knowledge of God or use of
reason,"[2]—a pious design, held doubtless in full sincerity by
the royal profligate, now, in his decline, a fervent champion
of the Faith and a strenuous tormentor of heretics. The machinery of conversion was of a character somewhat questionable, since Cartier and Roberval were empowered to ransack
the prisons for thieves, robbers, and other malefactors, to
complete their crews and strengthen the colony. "Whereas,"
says the King, "we have undertaken this voyage for the honor
of God our Creator, desiring with all our heart to do that
which shall be agreeable to Him, it is our will to perform a
compassionate and meritorious work towards criminals and
malefactors, to the end that they may acknowledge the Creator, return thanks to Him, and mend their lives. Therefore we
have resolved to cause to be delivered to our aforesaid lieutenant (Roberval), such and so many of the aforesaid criminals
and malefactors detained in our prisons as may seem to him
useful and necessary to be carried to the aforesaid countries."[3]
Of the expected profits of the voyage the adventurers were to
have one third and the King another, while the remainder
was to be reserved towards defraying expenses.

With respect to Donnacona and his tribesmen, basely kidnapped at Stadaconé, their souls had been better cared for
than their bodies; for, having been duly baptized, they all
died within a year or two, to the great detriment, as it
proved, of the expedition.[4]

Meanwhile, from beyond the Pyrenees, the Most Catholic
King, with alarmed and jealous eye, watched the preparations

[1] *De par le Roy*, *17 Oct.*, *1540* (Harrisse).

[2] See the commission in Lescarbot, I. 411; and Hazard, I. 19.

[3] *Pouvoir donné par le Roy au Seigneur de Roberval*, *7 Feb.*, *1540* (Harrisse).

[4] *M. Charles Cunat à M. L. Hovins, Maire de St. Malo.* This is a report of
researches made by M. Cunat in 1844 in the archives of St. Malo.

*Extrait Baptistaire des Sauvages amenés en France par Honneste Homme
Jacques Cartier.*

Thevet says that he knew Donnacona in France, and found him "a good
Christian."

of his Most Christian enemy. America, in his eyes, was one vast province of Spain, to be vigilantly guarded against the intruding foreigner. To what end were men mustered, and ships fitted out in the Breton seaports? Was it for colonization, and if so, where? Was it in Southern Florida, or on the frozen shores of Baccalaos, of which Breton cod-fishers claimed the discovery? Or would the French build forts on the Bahamas, whence they could waylay the gold ships in the Bahama Channel? Or was the expedition destined against the Spanish settlements of the islands or the Main? Reinforcements were despatched in haste, and a spy was sent to France, who, passing from port to port, Quimper, St. Malo, Brest, Morlaix, came back freighted with exaggerated tales of preparation. The Council of the Indies was called. "The French are bound for Baccalaos,"—such was the substance of their report; "your Majesty will do well to send two caravels to watch their movements, and a force to take possession of the said country. And since there is no other money to pay for it, the gold from Peru, now at Panama, might be used to that end." The Cardinal of Seville thought lightly of the danger, and prophesied that the French would reap nothing from their enterprise but disappointment and loss. The king of Portugal, sole acknowledged partner with Spain in the ownership of the New World, was invited by the Spanish ambassador to take part in an expedition against the encroaching French. "They can do no harm at Baccalaos," was the cold reply; "and so," adds the indignant ambassador, "this king would say if they should come and take him here at Lisbon; such is the softness they show here on the one hand, while, on the other, they wish to give law to the whole world."[1]

The five ships, occasions of this turmoil and alarm, had lain at St. Malo waiting for cannon and munitions from Normandy and Champagne. They waited in vain, and as the King's orders were stringent against delay, it was resolved that Cartier should sail at once, leaving Roberval to follow with additional ships when the expected supplies arrived.

On the twenty-third of May, 1541,[2] the Breton captain again

[1] See the documents on this subject in the *Coleccion de Varios Documentos* of Buckingham Smith, I. 107–112.

[2] Hakluyt's date, 1540, is incorrect.

spread his canvas for New France, and, passing in safety the tempestuous Atlantic, the fog-banks of Newfoundland, the island rocks clouded with screaming sea-fowl, and the forests breathing piny odors from the shore, cast anchor again beneath the cliffs of Quebec. Canoes came out from shore filled with feathered savages inquiring for their kidnapped chiefs. "Donnacona," replied Cartier, "is dead"; but he added the politic falsehood, that the others had married in France, and lived in state, like great lords. The Indians pretended to be satisfied; but it was soon apparent that they looked askance on the perfidious strangers.

Cartier pursued his course, sailed three leagues and a half up the St. Lawrence, and anchored off the mouth of the River of Cap Rouge. It was late in August, and the leafy landscape sweltered in the sun. The Frenchmen landed, picked up quartz crystals on the shore and thought them diamonds, climbed the steep promontory, drank at the spring near the top, looked abroad on the wooded slopes beyond the little river, waded through the tall grass of the meadow, found a quarry of slate, and gathered scales of a yellow mineral which glistened like gold, then returned to their boats, crossed to the south shore of the St. Lawrence, and, languid with the heat, rested in the shade of forests laced with an entanglement of grape-vines.

Now their task began, and while some cleared off the woods and sowed turnip-seed, others cut a zigzag road up the height, and others built two forts, one at the summit, and one on the shore below. The forts finished, the Vicomte de Beaupré took command, while Cartier went with two boats to explore the rapids above Hochelaga. When at length he returned, the autumn was far advanced; and with the gloom of a Canadian November came distrust, foreboding, and homesickness. Roberval had not appeared; the Indians kept jealously aloof; the motley colony was sullen as the dull, raw air around it. There was disgust and ire at Charlesbourg-Royal, for so the place was called.[1]

---

[1] The original narrative of this voyage is fragmentary, and exists only in the translation of Hakluyt. Purchas, Belknap, Forster, Chalmers, and the other secondary writers, all draw from this source. The narrative published by the Literary and Historical Society of Quebec is the English version of Hakluyt retranslated into French.

Meanwhile, unexpected delays had detained the impatient Roberval; nor was it until the sixteenth of April, 1542, that, with three ships and two hundred colonists, he set sail from Rochelle. When, on the eighth of June, he entered the harbor of St. John, he found seventeen fishing-vessels lying there at anchor. Soon after, he descried three other sail rounding the entrance of the haven, and, with anger and amazement, recognized the ships of Jacques Cartier. That voyager had broken up his colony and abandoned New France. What motives had prompted a desertion little consonant with the resolute spirit of the man it is impossible to say,—whether sickness within, or Indian enemies without, disgust with an enterprise whose unripened fruits had proved so hard and bitter, or discontent at finding himself reduced to a post of subordination in a country which he had discovered and where he had commanded. The Viceroy ordered him to return; but Cartier escaped with his vessels under cover of night, and made sail for France, carrying with him as trophies a few quartz diamonds from Cap Rouge, and grains of sham gold from the neighboring slate ledges. Thus closed the third Canadian voyage of this notable explorer. His discoveries had gained for him a patent of nobility, and he owned the seigniorial mansion of Limoilou,[1] a rude structure of stone still standing. Here, and in the neighboring town of St. Malo, where also he had a house, he seems to have lived for many years.[2]

Roberval once more set sail, steering northward to the Straits of Belle Isle and the dreaded Isles of Demons. And here an incident befell which the all-believing Thevet records in manifest good faith, and which, stripped of the adorn-

[1] This curious relic, which in 1865 was still entire, in the suburbs of St. Malo, was as rude in construction as an ordinary farmhouse. It had only a kitchen and a hall below, and two rooms above. At the side was a small stable, and, opposite, a barn. These buildings, together with two heavy stone walls, enclosed a square court. Adjacent was a garden and an orchard. The whole indicates a rough and simple way of life. See Ramé, *Note sur le Manoir de Jacques Cartier.*

[2] The above account of the departure of Cartier from Canada is from Hakluyt. Since it was written, M. Gosselin, archivist of the Palais de Justice at Rouen has discovered a paper which shows that Roberval sailed from France, not on the 16th of April, 1542, but on the 22d of August, 1541, thus confusing the narrative of Hakluyt. What remains certain is that Cartier left Canada while Roberval stayed there, and that there were disputes between them. See Ramé, *Documents Inédits* (1865), 22.

ments of superstition and a love of the marvellous, has without doubt a nucleus of truth. I give the tale as I find it.

The Viceroy's company was of a mixed complexion. There
were nobles, officers, soldiers, sailors, adventurers, with
women too, and children. Of the women, some were of birth
and station, and among them a damsel called Marguerite, a
niece of Roberval himself. In the ship was a young gentleman
who had embarked for love of her. His love was too well
requited; and the stern Viceroy, scandalized and enraged at a
passion which scorned concealment and set shame at defiance,
cast anchor by the haunted island, landed his indiscreet relative, gave her four arquebuses for defence, and, with an old
Norman nurse named Bastienne, who had pandered to the
lovers, left her to her fate. Her gallant threw himself into the
surf, and by desperate effort gained the shore, with two more
guns and a supply of ammunition.

The ship weighed anchor, receded, vanished, and they were
left alone. Yet not so, for the demon lords of the island beset
them day and night, raging around their hut with a confused
and hungry clamoring, striving to force the frail barrier. The
lovers had repented of their sin, though not abandoned it,
and Heaven was on their side. The saints vouchsafed their
aid, and the offended Virgin, relenting, held before them her
protecting shield. In the form of beasts or other shapes abom-
inably and unutterably hideous, the brood of hell, howling in
baffled fury, tore at the branches of the sylvan dwelling; but
a celestial hand was ever interposed, and there was a viewless
barrier which they might not pass. Marguerite became pregnant. Here was a double prize, two souls in one, mother and
child. The fiends grew frantic, but all in vain. She stood undaunted amid these horrors; but her lover, dismayed and
heart-broken, sickened and died. Her child soon followed;
then the old Norman nurse found her unhallowed rest in
that accursed soil, and Marguerite was left alone. Neither
her reason nor her courage failed. When the demons assailed her, she shot at them with her gun, but they answered with hellish merriment, and thenceforth she placed
her trust in Heaven alone. There were foes around her of
the upper, no less than of the nether world. Of these, the
bears were the most redoubtable; yet, being vulnerable to

mortal weapons, she killed three of them, all, says the story, "as white as an egg."

It was two years and five months from her landing on the island, when, far out at sea, the crew of a small fishing-craft saw a column of smoke curling upward from the haunted shore. Was it a device of the fiends to lure them to their ruin? They thought so, and kept aloof. But misgiving seized them. They warily drew near, and descried a female figure in wild attire waving signals from the strand. Thus at length was Marguerite rescued and restored to her native France, where, a few years later, the cosmographer Thevet met her at Natron in Perigord, and heard the tale of wonder from her own lips.[1]

Having left his offending niece to the devils and bears of the Isles of Demons, Roberval held his course up the St. Lawrence, and dropped anchor before the heights of Cap Rouge. His company landed; there were bivouacs along the strand, a hubbub of pick and spade, axe, saw, and hammer; and soon in the wilderness uprose a goodly structure, half barrack, half castle, with two towers, two spacious halls, a kitchen, chambers, storerooms, workshops, cellars, garrets, a well, an oven, and two water-mills. Roberval named it France-Roy, and it stood on that bold acclivity where Cartier had before intrenched himself, the St. Lawrence in front, and on the right the River of Cap Rouge. Here all the colony housed under the same roof, like one of the experimental communities of recent days,—officers, soldiers, nobles, artisans, laborers, and convicts, with the women and children in whom lay the future hope of New France.

---

[1] The story is taken from the curious manuscript of 1586. Compare the *Cosmographie* of Thevet, (1575,) II. c. 6. Thevet was the personal friend both of Cartier and of Roberval, the latter of whom he calls "mon familier," and the former, "mon grand et singulier amy." He says that he lived five months with Cartier in his house at St. Malo. He was also a friend of Rabelais, who once, in Italy, rescued him from a serious embarrassment. See the *Notice Biographique* prefixed to the edition of Rabelais of Burgaud des Marets and Rathery. The story of Marguerite is also told in the *Heptameron* of Marguerite de Valois, sister of Francis I. (1559).

In the *Routier* of Jean Alphonse, Roberval's pilot, where the principal points of the voyage are set down, repeated mention is made of "les Isles de la Demoiselle," immediately north of Newfoundland. The inference is obvious that the demoiselle was Marguerite.

Experience and forecast had both been wanting. There were storehouses, but no stores; mills, but no grist; an ample oven, and a dearth of bread. It was only when two of the ships had sailed for France that they took account of their provision and discovered its lamentable shortcoming. Winter and famine followed. They bought fish from the Indians, and dug roots and boiled them in whale-oil. Disease broke out, and, before spring, killed one third of the colony. The rest would have quarrelled, mutinied, and otherwise aggravated their inevitable woes, but disorder was dangerous under the iron rule of the inexorable Roberval. Michel Gaillon was detected in a petty theft, and hanged. Jean de Nantes, for a more venial offence, was kept in irons. The quarrels of men and the scolding of women were alike requited at the whipping-post, "by which means," quaintly says the narrative, "they lived in peace."

Thevet, while calling himself the intimate friend of the Viceroy, gives a darker coloring to his story. He says that, forced to unceasing labor, and chafed by arbitrary rules, some of the soldiers fell under Roberval's displeasure, and six of them, formerly his favorites, were hanged in one day. Others were banished to an island, and there kept in fetters; while, for various light offences, several, both men and women, were shot. Even the Indians were moved to pity, and wept at the sight of their woes.[1]

And here, midway, our guide deserts us; the ancient narrative is broken, and the latter part is lost, leaving us to divine as we may the future of the ill-starred colony. That it did not long survive is certain. The King, in great need of Roberval, sent Cartier to bring him home, and this voyage seems to have taken place in the summer of 1543.[2] It is said that, in after years, the Viceroy essayed to repossess himself of his Transatlantic domain, and lost his life in the attempt.[3] Thevet, on the other hand, with ample means of learning the truth, affirms that Roberval was slain at night, near the Church of the Innocents, in the heart of Paris.

With him closes the prelude of the French-American

---

[1] Thevet MS. (1586).
[2] Lescarbot (1612), I. 416.
[3] Le Clerc, *Établissement de la Foy*, I. 14.

drama. Tempestuous years and a reign of blood and fire were in store for France. The religious wars begot the hapless colony of Florida, but for more than half a century they left New France a desert. Order rose at length out of the sanguinary chaos; the zeal of discovery and the spirit of commercial enterprise once more awoke, while, closely following, more potent than they, moved the black-robed forces of the Roman Catholic reaction.

NOTE.— *The Voyage of Verrazzano*. The narrative of the voyage of Verrazzano is contained in a letter from him, dated at Dieppe, 8 July, 1524. The original letter does not exist. An Italian translation was printed by Ramusio in 1556, and there is another translation in the Magliabecchian Library at Florence. This last is accompanied by a letter concerning the voyage from one Fernando Carli, dated at Lyons, 4 August, 1524. Hieronimo da Verrazzano, brother of the navigator, made in 1529 a large map of the world, which is preserved in the College of the Propaganda at Rome. The discoveries of Verrazzano are laid down upon it, and the North American part bears the inscription, "Verazzana sive nova Gallia quale discoprì 5 anni fa Giovanni da Verazzano fiorentino per ordine e Comandamento del Cristianissimo Re di Francia." A copper globe made by Euphrosynus Ulpius, in 1542, also affirms the discovery of Verrazzano, and gives his name to a part of the continent, while other contemporary maps, notably that of Visconte di Maiollo, 1527, also contain traces of his voyage. Ramusio says that he had conversed with many persons who knew Verrazzano, and he prints a paper called *Discorso d' un gran Capitano di Mare Francese*, in which the voyage of Verrazzano is mentioned by a contemporary navigator of Dieppe.

Various Spanish and Portuguese documents attest the exploits of Verrazzano as a corsair, and a letter of Silveira, Portuguese ambassador to France, shows that in the spring of 1523 he had announced his purpose of a voyage to "Cathay." On the eleventh of May, 1526, he gave a power of attorney to his brother Hieronimo, the maker of the map, and this paper still exists, bearing his autograph. Various other original papers relating to him are extant, one of the most curious being that of the judge of Cadiz, testifying to his capture and his execution at Puerto del Pico. None of the early writers question the reality of the voyage. Among those who affirm it may be mentioned Annibal Caro, 1537; Belleforest, 1570; Herrera, 1601; Wytfleit, 1603; De Laet, 1603; Lescarbot, 1612.

In 1864, Mr. Buckingham Smith questioned the genuineness of the Verrazzano letter in a pamphlet called, *An Inquiry into the Authenticity of Documents concerning a Discovery in North America claimed to have been made by Verrazzano*. Mr. J. Carson Brevoort answered him, in a book entitled *Verrazzano the Navigator*. Mr. Henry C. Murphy followed with another book, *The Voyage of Verrazzano*, in which he endeavored at great length to prove that the evidence concerning the voyage was fabricated. Mr. Henry Harrisse gave a cautious and qualified support to his views in the *Revue Critique*. Mr. Major answered them in the *London Geographical Magazine*, and Mr. De Costa made an elaborate and effective reply in his work called *Verrazzano the Explorer*. An Italian writer, Signor Desimoni, has added some cogent facts in support of the authenticity of the documents. A careful examination of these various writings convinces me that the evidence in favor of the voyage of Verrazzano is far stronger than the evidence against it. Abbé Verreau found a contemporary document in the Bibliothèque Nationale, in which it is mentioned that the "memoirs" of Verrazzano were then in possession of Chatillon (Admiral Coligny). See *Report on Canadian Archives*, 1874, p. 190.

Chapter II

1542—1604

LA ROCHE—CHAMPLAIN—DE MONTS

*French Fishermen and Fur-Traders • La Roche • The Convicts of
Sable Island • Tadoussac • Samuel de Champlain • Visits the
West Indies and Mexico • Explores the St. Lawrence • De Monts •
His Acadian Schemes*

YEARS rolled on. France, long tossed among the surges of
civil commotion, plunged at last into a gulf of fratricidal
war. Blazing hamlets, sacked cities, fields steaming with
slaughter, profaned altars, and ravished maidens, marked the
track of the tornado. There was little room for schemes of
foreign enterprise. Yet, far aloof from siege and battle, the
fishermen of the western ports still plied their craft on the
Banks of Newfoundland. Humanity, morality, decency, might
be forgotten, but codfish must still be had for the use of the
faithful in Lent and on fast days. Still the wandering Esquimaux saw the Norman and Breton sails hovering around
some lonely headland, or anchored in fleets in the harbor of
St. John; and still, through salt spray and driving mist, the
fishermen dragged up the riches of the sea.

In January and February, 1545, about two vessels a day
sailed from French ports for Newfoundland.[1] In 1565, Pedro
Menendez complains that the French "rule despotically" in
those parts. In 1578, there were a hundred and fifty French
fishing-vessels there, besides two hundred of other nations,
Spanish, Portuguese, and English. Added to these were
twenty or thirty Biscayan whalers.[2] In 1607, there was an old
French fisherman at Canseau who had voyaged to these seas
for forty-two successive years.[3]

But if the wilderness of ocean had its treasures, so too had
the wilderness of woods. It needed but a few knives, beads,
and trinkets, and the Indians would throng to the shore bur-

[1] Gosselin, *Documents Authentiques.*

[2] Hakluyt, III. 132. Comp. Pinkerton, *Voyages,* XII. 174, and Thevet MS.
(1586).

[3] Lescarbot, II. 605. Purchas's date is wrong.

dened with the spoils of their winter hunting. Fishermen threw up their old vocation for the more lucrative trade in bear-skins and beaver-skins. They built rude huts along the shores of Anticosti, where, at that day, the bison, it is said, could be seen wallowing in the sands.[1] They outraged the Indians; they quarrelled with each other; and this infancy of the Canadian fur-trade showed rich promise of the disorders which marked its riper growth. Others, meanwhile, were ranging the gulf in search of walrus tusks; and, the year after the battle of Ivry, St. Malo sent out a fleet of small craft in quest of this new prize.

In all the western seaports, merchants and adventurers turned their eyes towards America; not, like the Spaniards, seeking treasures of silver and gold, but the more modest gains of codfish and train-oil, beaver-skins and marine ivory. St. Malo was conspicuous above them all. The rugged Bretons loved the perils of the sea, and saw with a jealous eye every attempt to shackle their activity on this its favorite field. When in 1588 Jacques Noel and Estienne Chaton, the former a nephew of Cartier and the latter pretending to be so, gained a monopoly of the American fur-trade for twelve years, such a clamor arose within the walls of St. Malo that the obnoxious grant was promptly revoked.[2]

But soon a power was in the field against which all St. Malo might clamor in vain. A Catholic nobleman of Brittany, the Marquis de la Roche, bargained with the King to colonize New France. On his part, he was to receive a monopoly of the trade, and a profusion of worthless titles and empty privileges. He was declared Lieutenant-General of Canada, Hochelaga, Newfoundland, Labrador, and the countries adjacent, with sovereign power within his vast and ill-defined domain. He could levy troops, declare war and peace, make laws, pun-

[1] Thevet MS. (1586). Thevet says that he had himself seen them. Perhaps he confounds them with the moose.

In 1565, and for some years previous, bison-skins were brought by the Indians down the Potomac, and thence carried along-shore in canoes to the French about the Gulf of St. Lawrence. During two years, six thousand skins were thus obtained. Letters of Pedro Menendez to Philip II., MS.

On the fur-trade, see Hakluyt, III. 187, 193, 233, 292, etc.

[2] Lescarbot, I. 418. Compare Ramé, *Documents Inédits* (1865). In Hakluyt are two letters of Jacques Noel.

ish or pardon at will, build cities, forts, and castles, and grant out lands in fiefs, seigniories, counties, viscounties, and baronies.[1] Thus was effete and cumbrous feudalism to make a lodgment in the New World. It was a scheme of high-sounding promise, but in performance less than contemptible. La Roche ransacked the prisons, and, gathering thence a gang of thieves and desperadoes, embarked them in a small vessel, and set sail to plant Christianity and civilization in the West. Suns rose and set, and the wretched bark, deep freighted with brutality and vice, held on her course. She was so small, that the convicts, leaning over her side, could wash their hands in the water.[2] At length, on the gray horizon they descried a long, gray line of ridgy sand. It was Sable Island, off the coast of Nova Scotia. A wreck lay stranded on the beach, and the surf broke ominously over the long, submerged arms of sand, stretched far out into the sea on the right hand and on the left.

Here La Roche landed the convicts, forty in number, while, with his more trusty followers, he sailed to explore the neighboring coasts, and choose a site for the capital of his new dominion, to which, in due time, he proposed to remove the prisoners. But suddenly a tempest from the west assailed him. The frail vessel was forced to run before the gale, which, howling on her track, drove her off the coast, and chased her back towards France.

Meanwhile the convicts watched in suspense for the returning sail. Days passed, weeks passed, and still they strained their eyes in vain across the waste of ocean. La Roche had left them to their fate. Rueful and desperate, they wandered among the sand-hills, through the stunted whortleberry bushes, the rank sand-grass, and the tangled cranberry vines which filled the hollows. Not a tree was to be seen; but they built huts of the fragments of the wreck. For food they caught fish in the surrounding sea, and hunted the cattle

---

[1] *Lettres Patentes pour le Sieur de la Roche*, *12 Jan.*, *1598*; Lescarbot, I. 422; *Édits et Ordonnances*, (Quebec, 1804,) II. 4. La Roche had received a similar commission in 1577 and 1578, but seems to have made no use of it. Ramé, *Documents Inédits* (1867). There is evidence that, as early as 1564, the King designed an expedition to colonize Canada. See Gosselin, *Documents Inédits pour servir à l'Histoire de la Marine Normande*.

[2] Lescarbot, I. 421.

which ran wild about the island, sprung, perhaps, from those left here eighty years before by the Baron de Léry.[1] They killed seals, trapped black foxes, and clothed themselves in their skins. Their native instincts clung to them in their exile. As if not content with inevitable miseries, they quarrelled and murdered one another. Season after season dragged on. Five years elapsed, and, of the forty, only twelve were left alive. Sand, sea, and sky,—there was little else around them; though, to break the dead monotony, the walrus would sometimes rear his half-human face and glistening sides on the reefs and sand-bars. At length, on the far verge of the watery desert, they descried a sail. She stood on towards the island; a boat's crew landed on the beach, and the exiles were once more among their countrymen.

When La Roche returned to France, the fate of his followers sat heavy on his mind. But the day of his prosperity was gone. A host of enemies rose against him and his privileges, and it is said that the Duc de Mercœur, seized him and threw him into prison. In time, however, he gained a hearing of the King, and the Norman pilot, Chefdhôtel, was despatched to bring the outcasts home.

He reached Sable Island in September, 1603, and brought back to France eleven survivors, whose names are still preserved.[2] When they arrived, Henry the Fourth summoned them into his presence. They stood before him, says an old writer, like river-gods of yore;[3] for from head to foot they were clothed in shaggy skins, and beards of prodigious length hung from their swarthy faces. They had accumulated, on their island, a quantity of valuable furs. Of these Chefdhôtel had robbed them; but the pilot was forced to disgorge his prey, and, with the aid of a bounty from the King, they were enabled to embark on their own account in the Canadian trade.[4] To their leader, fortune was less kind. Broken by disaster and imprisonment, La Roche died miserably.

[1] Lescarbot, I. 22. Compare De Laet, Lib. II. c. 4. Charlevoix and Champlain say that they escaped from the wreck of a Spanish vessel; Purchas, that they were left by the Portuguese.

[2] Gosselin, *Documents Authentiques* (Rouen, 1876).

[3] Charlevoix, I. 110; Guérin, *Navigateurs Français*, 210.

[4] Purchas, IV. 1807. Before me are several curious papers copied from the archives of the Palais de Justice of Rouen. One of these is entitled *Copie d'un*

In the mean time, on the ruin of his enterprise, a new one had been begun. Pontgravé, a merchant of St. Malo, leagued himself with Chauvin, a captain of the navy, who had influence at court. A patent was granted to them, with the condition that they should colonize the country. But their only thought was to enrich themselves.

At Tadoussac, at the mouth of the Saguenay, under the shadow of savage and inaccessible rocks, feathered with pines, firs, and birch trees, they built a cluster of wooden huts and storehouses. Here they left sixteen men to gather the expected harvest of furs. Before the winter was over, several of them were dead, and the rest scattered through the woods, living on the charity of the Indians.[1]

But a new era had dawned on France. Exhausted with thirty years of conflict, she had sunk at last to a repose, uneasy and disturbed, yet the harbinger of recovery. The rugged soldier whom, for the weal of France and of mankind, Providence had cast to the troubled surface of affairs, was throned in the Louvre, composing the strife of factions and the quarrels of his mistresses. The bear-hunting prince of the Pyrenees wore the crown of France; and to this day, as one gazes on the time-worn front of the Tuileries, above all other memories rises the small, strong figure, the brow wrinkled with cares of love and war, the bristling moustache, the grizzled beard, the bold, vigorous, and withal somewhat odd features of the mountaineer of Béarn. To few has human liberty owed so deep a gratitude or so deep a grudge. He cared little for creeds or dogmas. Impressible, quick in sympathy, his grim lip lighted often with a smile, and his war-worn cheek was no stranger to a tear. He forgave his enemies and forgot his friends. Many loved him; none but fools trusted him. Mingled of mortal good and ill, frailty and force, of all the kings

---

Arrêt rendu contre Chefdhostel, 27 Nov., 1603. It orders him to deliver to the eleven men whom he had just brought home two thirds of their furs. Another, dated 6 March, 1598, relates to the criminals whom La Roche was empowered to take from the prisons. A third, dated 18 May, 1598, orders that one of these criminals, François de Bauldre, convicted of highway robbery, shall not be allowed to go to Canada, but shall be forthwith beheaded. These papers set at rest the disputed question of the date of La Roche's voyage. I owe them to the kindness of M. Gabriel Gravier, of Rouen.

[1] Champlain (1632), 34; Estancelin, 96.

who for two centuries and more sat on the throne of France
Henry the Fourth alone was a man.

Art, industry, and commerce, so long crushed and overborne, were stirring into renewed life, and a crowd of adventurous men, nurtured in war and incapable of repose, must
seek employment for their restless energies in fields of peaceful enterprise.

Two small, quaint vessels, not larger than the fishing-craft
of Gloucester and Marblehead,—one was of twelve, the other
of fifteen tons,—held their way across the Atlantic, passed the
tempestuous headlands of Newfoundland and the St. Lawrence, and, with adventurous knight-errantry, glided deep
into the heart of the Canadian wilderness. On board of one
of them was the Breton merchant, Pontgravé, and with him
a man of spirit widely different, a Catholic of good family,
Samuel de Champlain, born in 1567 at the small seaport of
Brouage on the Bay of Biscay. His father was a captain in
the royal navy, where he himself seems also to have served,
though during the war he had fought for the King in Brittany, under the banners of D'Aumont, St. Luc, and Brissac. His purse was small, his merit great; and Henry the
Fourth out of his own slender revenues had given him a
pension to maintain him near his person. But rest was penance to him. The war in Brittany was over. The rebellious
Duc de Mercœur was reduced to obedience, and the royal
army disbanded. Champlain, his occupation gone, conceived a design consonant with his adventurous nature. He
would visit the West Indies, and bring back to the King a
report of those regions of mystery whence Spanish jealousy
excluded foreigners, and where every intruding Frenchman
was threatened with death. Here much knowledge was to be
won and much peril to be met. The joint attraction was re-
sistless.

The Spaniards, allies of the vanquished Leaguers, were
about to evacuate Blavet, their last stronghold in Brittany.
Thither Champlain repaired: and here he found an uncle,
who had charge of the French fleet destined to take on board
the Spanish garrison. Champlain embarked with them, and,
reaching Cadiz, succeeded, with the aid of his relative, who
had just accepted the post of Pilot-General of the Spanish

marine, in gaining command of one of the ships about to sail for the West Indies under Don Francisco Colombo.

At Dieppe there is a curious old manuscript, in clear, decisive, and somewhat formal handwriting of the sixteenth century, garnished with sixty-one colored pictures, in a style of art which a child of ten might emulate. Here one may see ports, harbors, islands, and rivers, adorned with portraitures of birds, beasts, and fishes thereto pertaining. Here are Indian feasts and dances; Indians flogged by priests for not going to mass; Indians burned alive for heresy, six in one fire; Indians working the silver mines. Here, too, are descriptions of natural objects, each with its illustrative sketch, some drawn from life and some from memory,—as, for example, a chameleon with two legs; others from hearsay, among which is the portrait of the griffin said to haunt certain districts of Mexico, a monster with the wings of a bat, the head of an eagle, and the tail of an alligator.

This is Champlain's journal, written and illustrated by his own hand, in that defiance of perspective and absolute independence of the canons of art which mark the earliest efforts of the pencil.

A true hero, after the chivalrous mediæval type, his character was dashed largely with the spirit of romance. Though earnest, sagacious, and penetrating, he leaned to the marvellous; and the faith which was the life of his hard career was somewhat prone to overstep the bounds of reason and invade the domain of fancy. Hence the erratic character of some of his exploits, and hence his simple faith in the Mexican griffin.

His West-Indian adventure occupied him more than two years. He visited the principal ports of the islands, made plans and sketches of them all, after his fashion, and then, landing at Vera Cruz, journeyed inland to the city of Mexico. On his return he made his way to Panama. Here, more than two centuries and a half ago, his bold and active mind conceived the plan of a ship-canal across the isthmus, "by which," he says, "the voyage to the South Sea would be shortened by more than fifteen hundred leagues."[1]

[1] ". . . . l'on accourciroit par ainsy le chemin de plus de 1500 lieues, et depuis Panama jusques au destroit de Magellan se seroit une isle, et de Panama jusques aux Terres Neufves une autre isle,"—etc. Champlain, *Bref Dis-*

On reaching France he repaired to Court, and it may have been at this time that a royal patent raised him to the rank of the untitled nobility. He soon wearied of the antechambers of the Louvre. It was here, however, that his destiny awaited him, and the work of his life was unfolded. Aymar de Chastes, Commander of the Order of St. John and Governor of Dieppe, a gray-haired veteran of the civil wars, wished to mark his closing days with some notable achievement for France and the Church. To no man was the King more deeply indebted. In his darkest hour, when the hosts of the League were gathering round him, when friends were falling off, and the Parisians, exulting in his certain ruin, were hiring the windows of the Rue St. Antoine to see him led to the Bastille, De Chastes, without condition or reserve, gave up to him the town and castle of Dieppe. Thus he was enabled to fight beneath its walls the battle of Arques, the first in the series of successes which secured his triumph; and he had been heard to say that to this friend in his adversity he owed his own salvation and that of France.

De Chastes was one of those men who, amid the strife of factions and rage of rival fanaticisms, make reason and patriotism their watchwords, and stand on the firm ground of a strong and resolute moderation. He had resisted the madness of Leaguer and Huguenot alike; yet, though a foe of the League, the old soldier was a devout Catholic, and it seemed in his eyes a noble consummation of his life to plant the cross and the fleur-de-lis in the wilderness of New France. Chauvin had just died, after wasting the lives of a score or more of men in a second and a third attempt to establish the fur-trade at Tadoussac. De Chastes came to court to beg a patent of

---

cours. A Biscayan pilot had before suggested the plan to the Spanish government; but Philip the Second, probably in the interest of certain monopolies, forbade the subject to be again brought forward on pain of death.

The journal is entitled, "Bref Discours des Choses plus Remarquables que Samuel Champlain de Brouage a recognues aux Indes Occidentales." The original manuscript, in Champlain's handwriting, is, or was, in the hands of M. Féret of Dieppe, a collateral descendant of the writer's patron, the Commander de Chastes. It consists of a hundred and fifteen small quarto pages. I am indebted to M. Jacques Viger for the use of his copy.

A translation of it was published in 1859 by the Hakluyt Society, with notes and a biographical notice by no means remarkable for accuracy.

Henry the Fourth; "and," says his friend Champlain, "though his head was crowned with gray hairs as with years, he resolved to proceed to New France in person, and dedicate the rest of his days to the service of God and his King."[1]

The patent, costing nothing, was readily granted; and De Chastes, to meet the expenses of the enterprise, and forestall the jealousies which his monopoly would awaken among the keen merchants of the western ports, formed a company with the more prominent of them. Pontgravé, who had some knowledge of the country, was chosen to make a preliminary exploration.

This was the time when Champlain, fresh from the West Indies, appeared at court. De Chastes knew him well. Young, ardent, yet ripe in experience, a skilful seaman and a practised soldier, he above all others was a man for the enterprise. He had many conferences with the veteran, under whom he had served in the royal fleet off the coast of Brittany. De Chastes urged him to accept a post in his new company; and Champlain, nothing loath, consented, provided always that permission should be had from the King, "to whom," he says, "I was bound no less by birth than by the pension with which his Majesty honored me." To the King, therefore, De Chastes repaired. The needful consent was gained, and, armed with a letter to Pontgravé, Champlain set out for Honfleur. Here he found his destined companion, and embarking with him, as we have seen, they spread their sails for the west.

Like specks on the broad bosom of the waters, the two pygmy vessels held their course up the lonely St. Lawrence. They passed abandoned Tadoussac, the channel of Orleans, and the gleaming cataract of Montmorenci; the tenantless rock of Quebec, the wide Lake of St. Peter and its crowded archipelago, till now the mountain reared before them its rounded shoulder above the forest-plain of Montreal. All was solitude. Hochelaga had vanished; and of the savage population that Cartier had found here, sixty-eight years before, no trace remained. In its place were a few wandering Algonquins, of different tongue and lineage. In a skiff, with a few Indians, Champlain essayed to pass the rapids of St. Louis.

[1] On De Chastes, Vitet, *Histoire de Dieppe*, c. 19, 20, 21.

Oars, paddles, and poles alike proved vain against the foaming surges, and he was forced to return. On the deck of his vessel, the Indians drew rude plans of the river above, with its chain of rapids, its lakes and cataracts; and the baffled explorer turned his prow homeward, the objects of his mission accomplished, but his own adventurous curiosity unsated. When the voyagers reached Havre de Grace, a grievous blow awaited them. The Commander de Chastes was dead.[1]

His mantle fell upon Pierre du Guast, Sieur de Monts, gentleman in ordinary of the King's chamber, and Governor of Pons. Undaunted by the fate of La Roche, this nobleman petitioned the king for leave to colonize La Cadie, or Acadie,[2] a region defined as extending from the fortieth to the forty-sixth degree of north latitude, or from Philadelphia to beyond Montreal. The King's minister, Sully, as he himself tells us, opposed the plan, on the ground that the colonization of this northern wilderness would never repay the outlay; but De Monts gained his point. He was made Lieutenant-General in Acadia, with viceregal powers; and withered Feudalism, with her antique forms and tinselled follies, was again to seek a new home among the rocks and pine trees of Nova Scotia. The foundation of the enterprise was a monopoly of the fur-trade, and in its favor all past grants were unceremoniously annulled. St. Malo, Rouen, Dieppe, and Rochelle greeted the announcement with unavailing outcries. Patents granted and

[1] Champlain, *Des Sauvages* (1604). Champlain's Indian informants gave him very confused accounts. They indicated the Falls of Niagara as a mere "rapid." They are laid down, however, in Champlain's great map of 1632 with the following note: "Sault d'eau au bout du Sault [Lac] Sainct Louis fort hault où plusieurs sortes de poissons descendans s'estourdissent."

[2] This name is not found in any earlier public document. It was afterwards restricted to the peninsula of Nova Scotia, but the dispute concerning the limits of Acadia was a proximate cause of the war of 1755.

The word is said to be derived from the Indian *Aquoddiauke*, or *Aquoddie*, supposed to mean the fish called a pollock. The Bay of Passamaquoddy, "Great Pollock Water," if we may accept the same authority, derives its name from the same origin. Potter in *Historical Magazine*, I. 84. This derivation is doubtful. The Micmac word, *Quoddy*, *Kady*, or *Cadie*, means simply a place or region, and is properly used in conjunction with some other noun; as, for example, *Katakady*, the Place of Eels, *Sunakady* (Sunacadie), the Place of Cranberries, *Pestumoquoddy* (Passamaquoddy), the Place of Pollocks. Dawson and Rand, in *Canadian Antiquarian and Numismatic Journal*.

revoked, monopolies decreed and extinguished, had involved the unhappy traders in ceaseless embarrassment. De Monts, however, preserved De Chastes's old company, and enlarged it, thus making the chief malcontents sharers in his exclusive rights, and converting them from enemies into partners.

A clause in his commission empowered him to impress idlers and vagabonds as material for his colony, an ominous provision of which he largely availed himself. His company was strangely incongruous. The best and the meanest of France were crowded together in his two ships. Here were thieves and ruffians dragged on board by force, and here were many volunteers of condition and character, with Baron de Poutrincourt and the indefatigable Champlain. Here, too, were Catholic priests and Huguenot ministers; for, though De Monts was a Calvinist, the Church, as usual, displayed her banner in the van of the enterprise, and he was forced to promise that he would cause the Indians to be instructed in the dogmas of Rome.[1]

[1] *Articles proposez au Roy par le Sieur de Monts; Commissions du Roy et de Monseigneur l'Admiral au Sieur de Monts; Défenses du Roy Premières et Secondes, à tous ses subjects, autres que le Sieur de Monts*, etc., *de traffiquer*, etc.; *Déclaration du Roy; Extraict des Registres de Parlement; Remontrance faict au Roy par le Sieur de Monts;* etc.

Chapter III

1604, 1605

ACADIA OCCUPIED

Catholic and Calvinist • The Lost Priest • St. Croix • Winter Miseries • Champlain on the Coast of New England • Port Royal

---

DE MONTS, with one of his vessels, sailed from Havre de Grace on the seventh of April, 1604. Pontgravé, with stores for the colony, was to follow in a few days.

Scarcely were they at sea, when ministers and priests fell first to discussion, then to quarrelling, then to blows. "I have seen our *curé* and the minister," says Champlain, "fall to with their fists on questions of faith. I cannot say which had the more pluck, or which hit the harder; but I know that the minister sometimes complained to the Sieur de Monts that he had been beaten. This was their way of settling points of controversy. I leave you to judge if it was a pleasant thing to see."[1]

Sagard, the Franciscan friar, relates with horror, that, after their destination was reached, a priest and a minister happening to die at the same time, the crew buried them both in one grave, to see if they would lie peaceably together.[2]

De Monts, who had been to the St. Lawrence with Chauvin, and learned to dread its rigorous winters, steered for a more southern, and, as he flattered himself, a milder region. The first land seen was Cap la Hêve, on the southern coast of Nova Scotia. Four days later, they entered a small bay, where, to their surprise, they saw a vessel lying at anchor. Here was a piece of good luck. The stranger was a fur-trader, pursuing her traffic in defiance, or more probably in ignorance, of De Monts's monopoly. The latter, as empowered by his patent, made prize of ship and cargo, consoling the commander, one Rossignol, by giving his name to the scene of his misfortune. It is now called Liverpool Harbor.

In an adjacent harbor, called by them Port Mouton, be-

[1] Champlain, (1632,) 46.
[2] Sagard, *Histoire du Canada*, 9.

cause a sheep here leaped overboard, they waited nearly a month for Pontgravé's store-ship. At length, to their great relief, she appeared, laden with the spoils of four Basque fur-traders, captured at Canseau. The supplies delivered, Pontgravé sailed for Tadoussac to trade with the Indians, while De Monts, followed by his prize, proceeded on his voyage.

He doubled Cape Sable, and entered St. Mary's Bay, where he lay two weeks, sending boats' crews to explore the adjacent coasts. A party one day went on shore to stroll through the forest, and among them was Nicolas Aubry, a priest from Paris, who, tiring of the scholastic haunts of the Rue de la Sorbonne and the Rue d'Enfer, had persisted, despite the re-monstrance of his friends, in joining the expedition. Thirsty with a long walk, under the sun of June, through the tangled and rock-encumbered woods, he stopped to drink at a brook, laying his sword beside him on the grass. On rejoining his companions, he found that he had forgotten it; and turning back in search of it, more skilled in the devious windings of the Quartier Latin than in the intricacies of the Acadian for-est, he soon lost his way. His comrades, alarmed, waited for a time, and then ranged the woods, shouting his name to the echoing solitudes. Trumpets were sounded, and cannon fired from the ships, but the priest did not appear. All now looked askance on a certain Huguenot, with whom Aubry had often quarrelled on questions of faith, and who was now accused of having killed him. In vain he denied the charge. Aubry was given up for dead, and the ship sailed from St. Mary's Bay; while the wretched priest roamed to and fro, famished and despairing, or, couched on the rocky soil, in the troubled sleep of exhaustion, dreamed, perhaps, as the wind swept moaning through the pines, that he heard once more the or-gan roll through the columned arches of Sainte Geneviève.

The voyagers proceeded to explore the Bay of Fundy, which De Monts called La Baye Françoise. Their first notable discovery was that of Annapolis Harbor. A small inlet invited them. They entered, when suddenly the narrow strait dilated into a broad and tranquil basin, compassed by sunny hills, wrapped in woodland verdure, and alive with waterfalls. Pou-trincourt was delighted with the scene. The fancy seized him of removing thither from France with his family; and, to this end, he asked a grant of the place from De Monts, who by his patent had nearly half the continent in his gift. The grant was made, and Poutrincourt called his new domain Port Royal.

Thence they sailed round the head of the Bay of Fundy, coasted its northern shore, visited and named the river St. John, and anchored at last in Passamaquoddy Bay.

The untiring Champlain, exploring, surveying, sounding, had made charts of all the principal roads and harbors;[1] and now, pursuing his research, he entered a river which he calls La Rivière des Etechemins, from the name of the tribe of whom the present Passamaquoddy Indians are descendants. Near its mouth he found an islet, fenced round with rocks and shoals, and called it St. Croix, a name now borne by the river itself. With singular infelicity this spot was chosen as the site of the new colony. It commanded the river, and was well fitted for defence: these were its only merits; yet cannon were landed on it, a battery was planted on a detached rock at one end, and a fort begun on a rising ground at the other.[2]

At St. Mary's Bay the voyagers thought they had found traces of iron and silver; and Champdoré, the pilot, was now sent back to pursue the search. As he and his men lay at anchor, fishing, not far from land, one of them heard a strange sound, like a weak human voice; and, looking towards the shore, they saw a small black object in motion, apparently a hat waved on the end of a stick. Rowing in haste to the spot, they found the priest Aubry. For sixteen days he had wandered in the woods, sustaining life on berries and wild fruits; and when, haggard and emaciated, a shadow of his former self, Champdoré carried him back to St. Croix, he was greeted as a man risen from the grave.

In 1783 the river St. Croix, by treaty, was made the boundary between Maine and New Brunswick. But which was the true St. Croix? In 1798, the point was settled. De Monts's island was found; and, painfully searching among the sand, the sedge, and the matted whortleberry bushes, the commissioners could trace the foundations of buildings long crum-

[1] See Champlain, *Voyages*, (1613,) where the charts are published.
[2] Lescarbot, *Hist. de la Nouvelle France*, (1612,) II. 461.

bled into dust;[1] for the wilderness had resumed its sway, and silence and solitude brooded once more over this ancient resting place of civilization.

But while the commissioner bends over a moss-grown stone, it is for us to trace back the dim vista of the centuries to the life, the zeal, the energy, of which this stone is the poor memorial. The rock-fenced islet was covered with cedars, and when the tide was out the shoals around were dark with the swash of sea-weed, where, in their leisure moments, the Frenchmen, we are told, amused themselves with detaching the limpets from the stones, as a savory addition to their fare. But there was little leisure at St. Croix. Soldiers, sailors, and artisans betook themselves to their task. Before the winter closed in, the northern end of the island was covered with buildings, surrounding a square, where a solitary tree had been left standing. On the right was a spacious house, well built, and surmounted by one of those enormous roofs characteristic of the time. This was the lodging of De Monts. Behind it, and near the water, was a long, covered gallery, for labor or amusement in foul weather. Champlain and the Sieur d'Orville, aided by the servants of the latter, built a house for themselves nearly opposite that of De Monts; and the remainder of the square was occupied by storehouses, a magazine, workshops, lodgings for gentlemen and artisans, and a barrack for the Swiss soldiers, the whole enclosed with a palisade. Adjacent there was an attempt at a garden, under the auspices of Champlain; but nothing would grow in the sandy soil. There was a cemetery, too, and a small rustic chapel on a projecting point of rock. Such was the "Habitation de l'Isle Saincte-Croix," as set forth by Champlain in quaint plans and drawings, in that musty little quarto of 1613, sold by Jean Berjon, at the sign of the Flying Horse, Rue St. Jean de Beauvais.

Their labors over, Poutrincourt set sail for France, proposing to return and take possession of his domain of Port Royal. Seventy-nine men remained at St. Croix. Here was De Monts, feudal lord of half a continent in virtue of two potent syllables, "Henri," scrawled on parchment by the rugged hand

[1] Holmes, *Annals*, (1829,) I. 122, note 1.

of the Béarnais. Here were gentlemen of birth and breeding, Champlain, D'Orville, Beaumont, Sourin, La Motte, Boulay, and Fougeray; here also were the pugnacious *curé* and his fellow priests, with the Huguenot ministers, objects of their unceasing ire. The rest were laborers, artisans, and soldiers, all in the pay of the company, and some of them forced into its service.

Poutrincourt's receding sails vanished between the water and the sky. The exiles were left to their solitude. From the Spanish settlements northward to the pole, there was no domestic hearth, no lodgment of civilized men, save one weak band of Frenchmen, clinging, as it were for life, to the fringe of the vast and savage continent. The gray and sullen autumn sank upon the waste, and the bleak wind howled down the St. Croix, and swept the forest bare. Then the whirling snow powdered the vast sweep of desolate woodland, and shrouded in white the gloomy green of pine-clad mountains. Ice in sheets, or broken masses, swept by their island with the ebbing and flowing tide, often debarring all access to the main, and cutting off their supplies of wood and water. A belt of cedars, indeed, hedged the island; but De Monts had ordered them to be spared, that the north wind might spend something of its force with whistling through their shaggy boughs. Cider and wine froze in the casks, and were served out by the pound. As they crowded round their half-fed fires, shivering in the icy currents that pierced their rude tenements, many sank into a desperate apathy.

Soon the scurvy broke out, and raged with a fearful malignity. Of the seventy-nine, thirty-five died before spring, and many more were brought to the verge of death. In vain they sought that marvellous tree which had relieved the followers of Cartier. Their little cemetery was peopled with nearly half their number, and the rest, bloated and disfigured with the relentless malady, thought more of escaping from their woes than of building up a Transatlantic empire. Yet among them there was one, at least, who, amid languor and defection, held to his purpose with indomitable tenacity; and where Champlain was present, there was no room for despair.

Spring came at last, and, with the breaking up of the ice, the melting of the snow, and the clamors of the returning wild-fowl, the spirits and the health of the woe-begone company began to revive. But to misery succeeded anxiety and suspense. Where was the succor from France? Were they abandoned to their fate like the wretched exiles of La Roche? In a happy hour, they saw an approaching sail. Pontgravé, with forty men, cast anchor before their island on the sixteenth of June; and they hailed him as the condemned hails the messenger of his pardon.

Weary of St. Croix, De Monts resolved to seek out a more auspicious site, on which to rear the capital of his wilderness dominion. During the preceding September, Champlain had ranged the westward coast in a pinnace, visited and named the island of Mount Desert, and entered the mouth of the river Penobscot, called by him the Pemetigoet, or Pentegoet, and previously known to fur-traders and fishermen as the Norembega, a name which it shared with all the adjacent region.[1] Now, embarking a second time, in a bark of fifteen tons, with De Monts, several gentlemen, twenty sailors, and an Indian with his squaw, he set forth on the eighteenth of June on a second voyage of discovery. They coasted the strangely indented shores of Maine, with its reefs and surf-washed islands, rocky headlands, and deep embosomed bays, passed Mount Desert and the Penobscot, explored the mouths of the Kennebec, crossed Casco Bay, and descried the distant peaks of the White Mountains. The ninth of July brought them to Saco Bay. They were now within the limits of a group of tribes who were called by the French the Armouchiquois, and who included those whom the English afterwards called the Massachusetts. They differed in habits as well as in language from the Etechemins and Micmacs of Acadia, for they were tillers of the soil, and around their wigwams were fields of maize, beans, pumpkins, squashes, tobacco, and the so-called Jerusalem artichoke. Near Prout's Neck, more than eighty of them ran down to the shore to meet the strangers, dancing and yelping to show their joy. They had a fort of palisades on

[1] The earliest maps and narratives indicate a city, also called Norembega, on the banks of the Penobscot. The pilot, Jean Alphonse, of Saintonge, says that this fabulous city is fifteen or twenty leagues from the sea, and that its inhabitants are of small stature and dark complexion. As late as 1607 the fable was repeated in the *Histoire Universelle des Indes Occidentales*.

a rising ground by the Saco, for they were at deadly war with their neighbors towards the east.

On the twelfth, the French resumed their voyage, and, like some adventurous party of pleasure, held their course by the beaches of York and Wells, Portsmouth Harbor, the Isles of Shoals, Rye Beach and Hampton Beach, till, on the fifteenth, they descried the dim outline of Cape Ann. Champlain called it Cap aux Isles, from the three adjacent islands, and in a subsequent voyage he gave the name of Beauport to the neighboring harbor of Gloucester. Thence steering southward and westward, they entered Massachusetts Bay, gave the name of Rivière du Guast to a river flowing into it, probably the Charles; passed the islands of Boston Harbor, which Champlain describes as covered with trees, and were met on the way by great numbers of canoes filled with astonished Indians. On Sunday, the seventeenth, they passed Point Allerton and Nantasket Beach, coasted the shores of Cohasset, Scituate, and Marshfield, and anchored for the night near Brant Point. On the morning of the eighteenth, a head wind forced them to take shelter in Port St. Louis, for so they called the harbor of Plymouth, where the Pilgrims made their memorable landing fifteen years later. Indian wigwams and garden patches lined the shore. A troop of the inhabitants came down to the beach and danced, while others, who had been fishing, approached in their canoes, came on board the vessel, and showed Champlain their fish-hooks, consisting of a barbed bone lashed at an acute angle to a slip of wood.

From Plymouth the party circled round the bay, doubled Cape Cod, called by Champlain Cap Blanc, from its glistening white sands, and steered southward to Nausett Harbor, which, by reason of its shoals and sand-bars, they named Port Mallebarre. Here their prosperity deserted them. A party of sailors went behind the sand-banks to find fresh water at a spring, when an Indian snatched a kettle from one of them, and its owner, pursuing, fell, pierced with arrows by the robber's comrades. The French in the vessel opened fire. Champlain's arquebuse burst, and was near killing him, while the Indians, swift as deer, quickly gained the woods. Several of the tribe chanced to be on board the vessel, but flung themselves with such alacrity into the water that only one was caught. They bound him hand and foot, but soon after humanely set him at liberty.

Champlain, who we are told "delighted marvellously in these enterprises," had busied himself throughout the voyage with taking observations, making charts, and studying the wonders of land and sea. The "horse-foot crab" seems to have awakened his special curiosity, and he describes it with amusing exactness. Of the human tenants of the New England coast he has also left the first precise and trustworthy account. They were clearly more numerous than when the Puritans landed at Plymouth, since in the interval a pestilence made great havoc among them. But Champlain's most conspicuous merit lies in the light that he threw into the dark places of American geography, and the order that he brought out of the chaos of American cartography, for it was a result of this and the rest of his voyages that precision and clearness began at last to supplant the vagueness, confusion, and contradiction of the earlier map-makers.[1]

At Nausett Harbor provisions began to fail, and steering for St. Croix the voyagers reached that ill-starred island on the third of August. De Monts had found no spot to his liking. He now bethought him of that inland harbor of Port Royal which he had granted to Poutrincourt, and thither he resolved to remove. Stores, utensils, even portions of the buildings, were placed on board the vessels, carried across the Bay of Fundy, and landed at the chosen spot. It was on the north side of the basin opposite Goat Island, and a little below the mouth of the river Annapolis, called by the French the Équille, and, afterwards, the Dauphin. The axemen began their task; the dense forest was cleared away, and the buildings of the infant colony soon rose in its place.

[1] President Eliot of Harvard University, and his son, Mr. Charles Eliot, during many yacht voyages along the New England coast, made a study of the points visited by Champlain. I am indebted to them for useful information, as also to Mr. Henry Mitchell of the Coast Survey, who has made careful comparisons of the maps of Champlain with the present features of the places they represent. I am also indebted to the excellent notes of Rev. Edmund F. Slafter in Mr. Otis's translation of Champlain, and to those of Abbé Laverdière in the Quebec edition of the *Voyages*, 1870. In the new light from these sources, I have revised former conclusions touching several localities mentioned in the original narrative.

But while De Monts and his company were struggling against despair at St. Croix, the enemies of his monopoly were busy at Paris; and, by a ship from France, he was warned that prompt measures were needed to thwart their machinations. Therefore he set sail, leaving Pontgravé to command at Port Royal; while Champlain, Champdoré, and others, undaunted by the past, volunteered for a second winter in the wilderness.

Chapter IV

1605—1607

LESCARBOT AND CHAMPLAIN

De Monts at Paris • Marc Lescarbot • Disaster • Embarkation •
Arrival • Disappointment • Winter Life at Port Royal • L'Ordre
de Bon-Temps • Hopes blighted

E VIL reports of a churlish wilderness, a pitiless climate, disease, misery, and death, had heralded the arrival of De Monts. The outlay had been great, the returns small; and when he reached Paris, he found his friends cold, his enemies active and keen. Poutrincourt, however, was still full of zeal; and, though his private affairs urgently called for his presence in France, he resolved, at no small sacrifice, to go in person to Acadia. He had, moreover, a friend who proved an invaluable ally. This was Marc Lescarbot, "avocat en Parlement," who had been roughly handled by fortune, and was in the mood for such a venture, being desirous, as he tells us, "to fly from a corrupt world," in which he had just lost a lawsuit. Unlike De Monts, Poutrincourt, and others of his associates, he was not within the pale of the *noblesse*, belonging to the class of "gens de robe," which stood at the head of the *bourgeoisie*, and which, in its higher grades, formed within itself a virtual nobility. Lescarbot was no common man. Not that his abundant gift of verse-making was likely to avail much in the woods of New France, nor yet his classic lore, dashed with a little harmless pedantry, born not of the man, but of the times. But his zeal, his good sense, the vigor of his understanding, and the breadth of his views, were as conspicuous as his quick wit and his lively fancy. One of the best, as well as earliest, records of the early settlement of North America is due to his pen; and it has been said, with a certain degree of truth, that he was no less able to build up a colony than to write its history. He professed himself a Catholic, but his Catholicity sat lightly on him, and he might have passed for one of those amphibious religionists who in the civil wars were called "Les Politiques."

De Monts and Poutrincourt bestirred themselves to find a

priest, since the foes of the enterprise had been loud in lamentation that the spiritual welfare of the Indians had been slighted. But it was Holy Week. All the priests were, or professed to be, busy with exercises and confessions, and not one could be found to undertake the mission of Acadia. They were more successful in engaging mechanics and laborers for the voyage. These were paid a portion of their wages in advance, and were sent in a body to Rochelle, consigned to two merchants of that port, members of the company. De Monts and Poutrincourt went thither by post. Lescarbot soon followed, and no sooner reached Rochelle than he penned and printed his *Adieu à la France*, a poem which gained for him some credit.

More serious matters awaited him, however, than this dalliance with the Muse. Rochelle was the centre and citadel of Calvinism, a town of austere and grim aspect, divided, like Cisatlantic communities of later growth, betwixt trade and religion, and, in the interest of both, exacting a deportment of discreet and well-ordered sobriety. "One must walk a strait path here," says Lescarbot, "unless he would hear from the mayor or the ministers." But the mechanics sent from Paris, flush of money, and lodged together in the quarter of St. Nicolas, made day and night hideous with riot, and their employers found not a few of them in the hands of the police. Their ship, bearing the inauspicious name of the Jonas, lay anchored in the stream, her cargo on board, when a sudden gale blew her adrift. She struck on a pier, then grounded on the flats, bilged, careened, and settled in the mud. Her captain, who was ashore, with Poutrincourt, Lescarbot, and others, hastened aboard, and the pumps were set in motion; while all Rochelle, we are told, came to gaze from the ramparts, with faces of condolence, but at heart well pleased with the disaster. The ship and her cargo were saved, but she must be emptied, repaired, and reladen. Thus a month was lost; at length, on the thirteenth of May, 1606, the disorderly crew were all brought on board, and the Jonas put to sea. Poutrincourt and Lescarbot had charge of the expedition, De Monts remaining in France.

Lescarbot describes his emotions at finding himself on an element so deficient in solidity, with only a two-inch plank between him and death. Off the Azores, they spoke a supposed pirate. For the rest, they beguiled the voyage by harpooning porpoises, dancing on deck in calm weather, and fishing for cod on the Grand Bank. They were two months on their way, and when, fevered with eagerness to reach land, they listened hourly for the welcome cry, they were involved in impenetrable fogs. Suddenly the mists parted, the sun shone forth, and streamed fair and bright over the fresh hills and forests of the New World, in near view before them. But the black rocks lay between, lashed by the snow-white breakers. "Thus," writes Lescarbot, "doth a man sometimes seek the land as one doth his beloved, who sometimes repulseth her sweetheart very rudely. Finally, upon Saturday, the fifteenth of July, about two o'clock in the afternoon, the sky began to salute us as it were with cannon-shots, shedding tears, as being sorry to have kept us so long in pain; . . . . but, whilst we followed on our course, there came from the land odors incomparable for sweetness, brought with a warm wind so abundantly that all the orient parts could not produce greater abundance. We did stretch out our hands as it were to take them, so palpable were they, which I have admired a thousand times since."[1]

It was noon on the twenty-seventh when the Jonas passed the rocky gateway of Port Royal Basin, and Lescarbot gazed with delight and wonder on the calm expanse of sunny waters, with its amphitheatre of woody hills, wherein he saw the future asylum of distressed merit and impoverished industry. Slowly, before a favoring breeze, they held their course towards the head of the harbor, which narrowed as they advanced; but all was solitude; no moving sail, no sign of human presence. At length, on their left, nestling in deep forests, they saw the wooden walls and roofs of the infant colony. Then appeared a birch canoe, cautiously coming towards them, guided by an old Indian. Then a Frenchman, arquebuse in hand, came down to the shore; and then, from the wooden bastion, sprang the smoke of a saluting shot. The ship replied; the trumpets lent their voices to the din, and the forests and the hills gave back unwonted echoes. The voyagers

[1] The translation is that of Purchas, *Nova Francia*, c. 12.

landed, and found the colony of Port Royal dwindled to two solitary Frenchmen.

These soon told their story. The preceding winter had been one of much suffering, though by no means the counterpart of the woful experience of St. Croix. But when the spring had passed, the summer far advanced, and still no tidings of De Monts had come, Pontgravé grew deeply anxious. To maintain themselves without supplies and succor was impossible. He caused two small vessels to be built, and set out in search of some of the French vessels on the fishing-stations. This was but twelve days before the arrival of the ship Jonas. Two men had bravely offered themselves to stay behind and guard the buildings, guns, and munitions; and an old Indian chief, named Membertou, a fast friend of the French, and still a redoubted warrior, we are told, though reputed to number more than a hundred years, proved a stanch ally. When the ship approached, the two guardians were at dinner in their room at the fort. Membertou, always on the watch, saw the advancing sail, and, shouting from the gate, roused them from their repast. In doubt who the new-comers might be, one ran to the shore with his gun, while the other repaired to the platform where four cannon were mounted, in the valorous resolve to show fight should the strangers prove to be enemies. Happily this redundancy of mettle proved needless. He saw the white flag fluttering at the masthead, and joyfully fired his pieces as a salute.

The voyagers landed, and eagerly surveyed their new home. Some wandered through the buildings; some visited the cluster of Indian wigwams hard by; some roamed in the forest and over the meadows that bordered the neighboring river. The deserted fort now swarmed with life; and, the better to celebrate their prosperous arrival, Poutrincourt placed a hogshead of wine in the courtyard at the discretion of his followers, whose hilarity, in consequence, became exuberant. Nor was it diminished when Pontgravé's vessels were seen entering the harbor. A boat sent by Poutrincourt, more than a week before, to explore the coasts, had met them near Cape Sable, and they joyfully returned to Port Royal.

Pontgravé, however, soon sailed for France in the Jonas, hoping on his way to seize certain contraband fur-traders, re-

ported to be at Canseau and Cape Breton. Poutrincourt and
Champlain, bent on finding a better site for their settlement
in a more southern latitude, set out on a voyage of discovery,
in an ill-built vessel of eighteen tons, while Lescarbot remained in charge of Port Royal. They had little for their pains
but danger, hardship, and mishap. The autumn gales cut
short their exploration; and, after visiting Gloucester Harbor,
doubling Monomoy Point, and advancing as far as the neighborhood of Hyannis, on the southeast coast of Massachusetts,
they turned back, somewhat disgusted with their errand.
Along the eastern verge of Cape Cod they found the shore
thickly studded with the wigwams of a race who were less
hunters than tillers of the soil. At Chatham Harbor—called
by them Port Fortuné—five of the company, who, contrary
to orders, had remained on shore all night, were assailed, as
they slept around their fire, by a shower of arrows from four
hundred Indians. Two were killed outright, while the survivors fled for their boat, bristled like porcupines with the
feathered missiles,—a scene oddly portrayed by the untutored
pencil of Champlain. He and Poutrincourt, with eight men,
hearing the war-whoops and the cries for aid, sprang up from
sleep, snatched their weapons, pulled ashore in their shirts,
and charged the yelling multitude, who fled before their spectral assailants, and vanished in the woods. "Thus," observes
Lescarbot, "did thirty-five thousand Midianites fly before
Gideon and his three hundred." The French buried their dead
comrades; but, as they chanted their funeral hymn, the Indians, at a safe distance on a neighboring hill, were dancing in
glee and triumph, and mocking them with unseemly gestures;
and no sooner had the party re-embarked, than they dug up
the dead bodies, burnt them, and arrayed themselves in their
shirts. Little pleased with the country or its inhabitants, the
voyagers turned their prow towards Port Royal, though not
until, by a treacherous device, they had lured some of their
late assailants within their reach, killed them, and cut off their
heads as trophies. Near Mount Desert, on a stormy night,
their rudder broke, and they had a hair-breadth escape from
destruction. The chief object of their voyage, that of discovering a site for their colony under a more southern sky, had
failed. Pontgravé's son had his hand blown off by the burst-

ing of his gun; several of their number had been killed; others were sick or wounded; and thus, on the fourteenth of November, with somewhat downcast visages, they guided their helpless vessel with a pair of oars to the landing at Port Royal.

"I will not," says Lescarbot, "compare their perils to those of Ulysses, nor yet of Æneas, lest thereby I should sully our holy enterprise with things impure."

He and his followers had been expecting them with great anxiety. His alert and buoyant spirit had conceived a plan for enlivening the courage of the company, a little dashed of late by misgivings and forebodings. Accordingly, as Poutrincourt, Champlain, and their weather-beaten crew approached the wooden gateway of Port Royal, Neptune issued forth, followed by his tritons, who greeted the voyagers in good French verse, written in all haste for the occasion by Lescarbot. And, as they entered, they beheld, blazoned over the arch, the arms of France, circled with laurels, and flanked by the scutcheons of De Monts and Poutrincourt.[1]

The ingenious author of these devices had busied himself, during the absence of his associates, in more serious labors for the welfare of the colony. He explored the low borders of the river Équille, or Annapolis. Here, in the solitude, he saw great meadows, where the moose, with their young, were grazing, and where at times the rank grass was beaten to a pulp by the trampling of their hoofs. He burned the grass, and sowed crops of wheat, rye, and barley in its stead. His appearance gave so little promise of personal vigor, that some of the party assured him that he would never see France again, and warned him to husband his strength; but he knew himself better, and set at naught these comforting monitions. He was the most diligent of workers. He made gardens, near the fort, where, in his zeal, he plied the hoe with his own hands late into the moonlight evenings. The priests, of whom at the outset there had been no lack, had all succumbed to the scurvy at St. Croix; and Lescarbot, so far as a layman might, essayed to supply their place, reading on Sundays from the Scriptures, and adding expositions of his own after a fash-

---

[1] Lescarbot, *Muses de la Nouvelle France*, where the programme is given, and the speeches of Neptune and the tritons in full.

ion not remarkable for rigorous Catholicity. Of an evening, when not engrossed with his garden, he was reading or writing in his room, perhaps preparing the material of that *History of New France* in which, despite the versatility of his busy brain, his good sense and capacity are clearly made manifest.

Now, however, when the whole company were reassembled, Lescarbot found associates more congenial than the rude soldiers, mechanics, and laborers who gathered at night around the blazing logs in their rude hall. Port Royal was a quadrangle of wooden buildings, enclosing a spacious court. At the southeast corner was the arched gateway, whence a path, a few paces in length, led to the water. It was flanked by a sort of bastion of palisades, while at the southwest corner was another bastion, on which four cannon were mounted. On the east side of the quadrangle was a range of magazines and storehouses; on the west were quarters for the men; on the north, a dining-hall and lodgings for the principal persons of the company; while on the south, or water side, were the kitchen, the forge, and the oven. Except the garden-patches and the cemetery, the adjacent ground was thickly studded with the stumps of the newly felled trees.

Most bountiful provision had been made for the temporal wants of the colonists, and Lescarbot is profuse in praise of the liberality of De Monts and two merchants of Rochelle, who had freighted the ship Jonas. Of wine, in particular, the supply was so generous, that every man in Port Royal was served with three pints daily.

The principal persons of the colony sat, fifteen in number, at Poutrincourt's table, which, by an ingenious device of Champlain, was always well furnished. He formed the fifteen into a new order, christened "L'Ordre de Bon-Temps." Each was Grand Master in turn, holding office for one day. It was his function to cater for the company; and, as it became a point of honor to fill the post with credit, the prospective Grand Master was usually busy, for several days before coming to his dignity, in hunting, fishing, or bartering provisions with the Indians. Thus did Poutrincourt's table groan beneath all the luxuries of the winter forest: flesh of moose, caribou, and deer, beaver, otter, and hare, bears and wildcats; with ducks, geese, grouse, and plover; sturgeon, too, and trout, and fish innumerable, speared through the ice of the Équille, or drawn from the depths of the neighboring bay. "And," says Lescarbot, in closing his bill of fare, "whatever our gourmands at home may think, we found as good cheer at Port Royal as they at their Rue aux Ours[1] in Paris, and that, too, at a cheaper rate." For the preparation of this manifold provision, the Grand Master was also answerable; since, during his day of office, he was autocrat of the kitchen.

Nor did this bounteous repast lack a solemn and befitting ceremonial. When the hour had struck,—after the manner of our fathers they dined at noon,—the Grand Master entered the hall, a napkin on his shoulder, his staff of office in his hand, and the collar of the Order—valued by Lescarbot at four crowns—about his neck. The brotherhood followed, each bearing a dish. The invited guests were Indian chiefs, of whom old Membertou was daily present, seated at table with the French, who took pleasure in this red-skin companionship. Those of humbler degree, warriors, squaws, and children, sat on the floor, or crouched together in the corners of the hall, eagerly waiting their portion of biscuit or of bread, a novel and much coveted luxury. Being always treated with kindness, they became fond of the French, who often followed them on their moose-hunts, and shared their winter bivouac.

At the evening meal there was less of form and circumstance; and when the winter night closed in, when the flame crackled and the sparks streamed up the wide-throated chimney, and the founders of New France with their tawny allies were gathered around the blaze, then did the Grand Master resign the collar and the staff to the successor of his honors, and, with jovial courtesy, pledge him in a cup of wine.[2] Thus these ingenious Frenchmen beguiled the winter of their exile.

It was an unusually mild winter. Until January, they wore no warmer garment than their doublets. They made hunting and fishing parties, in which the Indians, whose lodges were always to be seen under the friendly shelter of the buildings, failed not to bear part. "I remember," says Lescarbot, "that

---

[1] A short street between Rue St. Martin and Rue St. Denis, once renowned for its restaurants.

[2] Lescarbot, (1612,) II. 581.

on the fourteenth of January, of a Sunday afternoon, we amused ourselves with singing and music on the river Équille, and that in the same month we went to see the wheat-fields two leagues from the fort, and dined merrily in the sunshine."

Good spirits and good cheer saved them in great measure from the scurvy, and though towards the end of winter severe cold set in, yet only four men died. The snow thawed at last, and as patches of the black and oozy soil began to appear, they saw the grain of their last autumn's sowing already piercing the mould. The forced inaction of the winter was over. The carpenters built a water-mill on the stream now called Allen's River; others enclosed fields and laid out gardens; others, again, with scoop-nets and baskets, caught the herrings and alewives as they ran up the innumerable rivulets. The leaders of the colony set a contagious example of activity. Poutrincourt forgot the prejudices of his noble birth, and went himself into the woods to gather turpentine from the pines, which he converted into tar by a process of his own invention; while Lescarbot, eager to test the qualities of the soil, was again, hoe in hand, at work all day in his garden.

All seemed full of promise; but alas for the bright hope that kindled the manly heart of Champlain and the earnest spirit of the vivacious advocate! A sudden blight fell on them, and their rising prosperity withered to the ground. On a morning, late in spring, as the French were at breakfast, the ever watchful Membertou came in with news of an approaching sail. They hastened to the shore; but the vision of the centenarian sagamore put them all to shame. They could see nothing. At length their doubts were resolved. A small vessel stood on towards them, and anchored before the fort. She was commanded by one Chevalier, a young man from St. Malo, and was freighted with disastrous tidings. De Monts's monopoly was rescinded. The life of the enterprise was stopped, and the establishment at Port Royal could no longer be supported; for its expense was great, the body of the colony being laborers in the pay of the company. Nor was the annulling of the patent the full extent of the disaster; for, during the last summer, the Dutch had found their way to the St. Lawrence, and carried away a rich harvest of furs, while other interloping traders had plied a busy traffic along the coasts, and, in the excess of their avidity, dug up the bodies of buried Indians to rob them of their funeral robes.

It was to the merchants and fishermen of the Norman, Breton, and Biscayan ports, exasperated at their exclusion from a lucrative trade, and at the confiscations which had sometimes followed their attempts to engage in it, that this sudden blow was due. Money had been used freely at court, and the monopoly, unjustly granted, had been more unjustly withdrawn. De Monts and his company, who had spent a hundred thousand livres, were allowed six thousand in requital, to be collected, if possible, from the fur-traders in the form of a tax.

Chevalier, captain of the ill-omened bark, was entertained with a hospitality little deserved, since, having been entrusted with sundry hams, fruits, spices, sweetmeats, jellies, and other dainties, sent by the generous De Monts to his friends of New France, he with his crew had devoured them on the voyage, alleging that, in their belief, the inmates of Port Royal would all be dead before their arrival.

Choice there was none, and Port Royal must be abandoned. Built on a false basis, sustained only by the fleeting favor of a government, the generous enterprise had come to naught. Yet Poutrincourt, who in virtue of his grant from De Monts owned the place, bravely resolved that, come what might, he would see the adventure to an end, even should it involve emigration with his family to the wilderness. Meanwhile, he began the dreary task of abandonment, sending boat-loads of men and stores to Canseau, where lay the ship Jonas, eking out her diminished profits by fishing for cod.

Membertou was full of grief at the departure of his friends. He had built a palisaded village not far from Port Royal, and here were mustered some four hundred of his warriors for a foray into the country of the Armouchiquois, dwellers along the coasts of Massachusetts, New Hampshire, and Western Maine. One of his tribesmen had been killed by a chief from the Saco, and he was bent on revenge. He proved himself a sturdy beggar, pursuing Poutrincourt with daily petitions, now for a bushel of beans, now for a basket of bread, and now for a barrel of wine to regale his greasy crew. Membertou's long life had not been one of repose. In deeds of blood and treachery he had no rival in the Acadian forest; and, as his old age was beset with enemies, his alliance with the French had a foundation of policy no less than of affection. In right of his rank of Sagamore, he claimed perfect equality both with Poutrincourt and with the King, laying his shrivelled forefingers together in token of friendship between peers. Calumny did not spare him; and a rival chief intimated to the French, that, under cover of a war with the Armouchiquois, the crafty veteran meant to seize and plunder Port Royal. Precautions, therefore, were taken; but they were seemingly needless; for, their feasts and dances over, the warriors launched their birchen flotilla and set out. After an absence of six weeks they reappeared with howls of victory, and their exploits were commemorated in French verse by the muse of the indefatigable Lescarbot.[1]

With a heavy heart the advocate bade farewell to the dwellings, the cornfields, the gardens, and all the dawning prosperity of Port Royal, and sailed for Canseau in a small vessel on the thirtieth of July. Poutrincourt and Champlain remained behind, for the former was resolved to learn before his departure the results of his agricultural labors. Reaching a harbor on the southern coast of Nova Scotia, six leagues west of Canseau, Lescarbot found a fishing-vessel commanded and owned by an old Basque, named Savalet, who for forty-two successive years had carried to France his annual cargo of codfish. He was in great glee at the success of his present venture, reckoning his profits at ten thousand francs. The Indians, however, annoyed him beyond measure, boarding him from their canoes as his fishing-boats came alongside, and helping themselves at will to his halibut and cod. At Canseau—a harbor near the strait now bearing the name—the ship Jonas still lay, her hold well stored with fish; and here, on the twenty-seventh of August, Lescarbot was rejoined by Poutrincourt and Champlain, who had come from Port Royal in an open boat. For a few days, they amused themselves with gathering raspberries on the islands; then they spread their sails for France, and early in October, 1607, anchored in the harbor of St. Malo.

First of Europeans, they had essayed to found an agricul-

[1] See *Muses de la Nouvelle France.*

tural colony in the New World. The leaders of the enterprise had acted less as merchants than as citizens; and the fur-trading monopoly, odious in itself, had been used as the instrument of a large and generous design. There was a radical defect, however, in their scheme of settlement. Excepting a few of the leaders, those engaged in it had not chosen a home in the wilderness of New France, but were mere hirelings, without wives or families, and careless of the welfare of the colony. The life which should have pervaded all the members was confined to the heads alone. In one respect, however, the enterprise of De Monts was truer in principle than the Roman Catholic colonization of Canada, on the one hand, or the Puritan colonization of Massachusetts, on the other, for it did not attempt to enforce religious exclusion.

Towards the fickle and bloodthirsty race who claimed the lordship of the forests, these colonists, excepting only in the treacherous slaughter at Port Fortuné, bore themselves in a spirit of kindness contrasting brightly with the rapacious cruelty of the Spaniards and the harshness of the English settlers. When the last boat-load left Port Royal, the shore resounded with lamentation; and nothing could console the afflicted savages but reiterated promises of a speedy return.

Chapter V

THE JESUITS AND THEIR PATRONESS

Poutrincourt and the Jesuits • He sails for Acadia • Sudden Conversions • Biencourt • Death of the King • Madame de Guercheville • Biard and Masse • The Jesuits Triumphant

POUTRINCOURT, we have seen, owned Port Royal in virtue of a grant from De Monts. The ardent and adventurous baron was in evil case, involved in litigation and low in purse; but nothing could damp his zeal. Acadia must become a new France, and he, Poutrincourt, must be its father. He gained from the King a confirmation of his grant, and, to supply the lack of his own weakened resources, associated with himself one Robin, a man of family and wealth. This did not save him from a host of delays and vexations; and it was not until the spring of 1610 that he found himself in a condition to embark on his new and doubtful venture.

Meanwhile an influence, of sinister omen as he thought, had begun to act upon his schemes. The Jesuits were strong at court. One of their number, the famous Father Coton, was confessor to Henry the Fourth, and, on matters of this world as of the next, was ever whispering at the facile ear of the renegade King. New France offered a fresh field of action to the indefatigable Society of Jesus, and Coton urged upon the royal convert, that, for the saving of souls, some of its members should be attached to the proposed enterprise. The King, profoundly indifferent in matters of religion, saw no evil in a proposal which at least promised to place the Atlantic betwixt him and some of those busy friends whom at heart he deeply mistrusted.[1] Other influences, too, seconded the confessor. Devout ladies of the court, and the Queen herself, supplying the lack of virtue with an overflowing piety, burned, we are assured, with a holy zeal for snatching the tribes of the West from the bondage of Satan. Therefore it was insisted that the

[1] The missionary Biard makes the characteristic assertion, that the King initiated the Jesuit project, and that Father Coton merely obeyed his orders. Biard, *Relation*, c. II.

projected colony should combine the spiritual with the temporal character, or, in other words, that Poutrincourt should take Jesuits with him. Pierre Biard, Professor of Theology at Lyons, was named for the mission, and repaired in haste to Bordeaux, the port of embarkation, where he found no vessel, and no sign of preparation; and here, in wrath and discomfiture, he remained for a whole year.

That Poutrincourt was a good Catholic appears from a letter to the Pope, written for him in Latin by Lescarbot, asking a blessing on his enterprise, and assuring his Holiness that one of his grand objects was the saving of souls.[1] But, like other good citizens, he belonged to the national party in the Church, those liberal Catholics, who, side by side with the Huguenots, had made head against the League, with its Spanish allies, and placed Henry the Fourth upon the throne. The Jesuits, an order Spanish in origin and policy, determined champions of ultramontane principles, the sword and shield of the Papacy in its broadest pretensions to spiritual and temporal sway, were to him, as to others of his party, objects of deep dislike and distrust. He feared them in his colony, evaded what he dared not refuse, left Biard waiting in solitude at Bordeaux, and sought to postpone the evil day by assuring Father Coton that, though Port Royal was at present in no state to receive the missionaries, preparation should be made to entertain them the next year after a befitting fashion.

Poutrincourt owned the barony of St. Just in Champagne, inherited a few years before from his mother. Hence, early in February, 1610, he set out in a boat loaded to the gunwales with provisions, furniture, goods, and munitions for Port Royal, descended the rivers Aube and Seine, and reached Dieppe safely with his charge.[2] Here his ship was awaiting him; and on the twenty-sixth of February he set sail, giving the slip to the indignant Jesuit at Bordeaux.

The tedium of a long passage was unpleasantly broken by a mutiny among the crew. It was suppressed, however, and Poutrincourt entered at length the familiar basin of Port

---

[1] See Lescarbot, (1618,) 605.
[2] Lescarbot, *Relation Dernière*, 6. This is a pamphlet of thirty-nine pages, containing matters not included in the larger work.

Royal. The buildings were still standing, whole and sound save a partial falling in of the roofs. Even furniture was found untouched in the deserted chambers. The centenarian Membertou was still alive, his leathern, wrinkled visage beaming with welcome.

Poutrincourt set himself without delay to the task of Christianizing New France, in an access of zeal which his desire of proving that Jesuit aid was superfluous may be supposed largely to have reinforced. He had a priest with him, one La Flèche, whom he urged to the pious work. No time was lost. Membertou first was catechised, confessed his sins, and renounced the Devil, whom we are told he had faithfully served during a hundred and ten years. His squaws, his children, his grandchildren, and his entire clan, were next won over. It was in June, the day of St. John the Baptist, when the naked proselytes, twenty-one in number, were gathered on the shore at Port Royal. Here was the priest in the vestments of his office; here were gentlemen in gay attire, soldiers, laborers, lackeys, all the infant colony. The converts kneeled; the sacred rite was finished, *Te Deum* was sung, and the roar of cannon proclaimed this triumph over the powers of darkness.[1] Membertou was named Henri, after the King; his principal squaw, Marie, after the Queen. One of his sons received the name of the Pope, another that of the Dauphin; his daughter was called Marguerite, after the divorced Marguerite de Valois, and, in like manner, the rest of the squalid company exchanged their barbaric appellatives for the names of princes, nobles, and ladies of rank.[2]

The fame of this *chef-d'œuvre* of Christian piety, as Lescarbot gravely calls it, spread far and wide through the forest, whose denizens, partly out of a notion that the rite would bring good luck, partly to please the French, and partly to share in the good cheer with which the apostolic efforts of Father La Flèche had been sagaciously seconded, came flocking to enroll themselves under the banners of the Faith. Their zeal ran high. They would take no refusal. Membertou was for war on all who would not turn Christian. A living skeleton was seen crawling from hut to hut in search of the priest

[1] Lescarbot, *Relation Dernière*, II.
[2] *Régitre de Baptême de l'Église du Port Royal en la Nouvelle France.*

and his saving waters; while another neophyte, at the point of death, asked anxiously whether, in the realms of bliss to which he was bound, pies were to be had comparable to those with which the French regaled him.

A formal register of baptisms was drawn up to be carried to France in the returning ship, of which Poutrincourt's son, Biencourt, a spirited youth of eighteen, was to take charge. He sailed in July, his father keeping him company as far as Port la Hêve, whence, bidding the young man farewell, he attempted to return in an open boat to Port Royal. A north wind blew him out to sea; and for six days he was out of sight of land, subsisting on rain-water wrung from the boat's sail, and on a few wild-fowl which he had shot on an island. Five weeks passed before he could rejoin his colonists, who, despairing of his safety, were about to choose a new chief.

Meanwhile young Biencourt, speeding on his way, heard dire news from a fisherman on the Grand Bank. The knife of Ravaillac had done its work. Henry the Fourth was dead.

There is an ancient street in Paris, where a great thorough-fare contracts to a narrow pass, the Rue de la Ferronnerie. Tall buildings overshadow it, packed from pavement to tiles with human life, and from the dingy front of one of them the sculptured head of a man looks down on the throng that ceaselessly defiles beneath. On the fourteenth of May, 1610, a ponderous coach, studded with fleurs-de-lis and rich with gilding, rolled along this street. In it was a small man, well advanced in life, whose profile once seen could not be forgot-ten: a hooked nose, a protruding chin, a brow full of wrin-kles, grizzled hair, a short, grizzled beard, and stiff, gray moustaches, bristling like a cat's. One would have thought him some whiskered satyr, grim from the rack of tumultuous years; but his alert, upright port bespoke unshaken vigor, and his clear eye was full of buoyant life. Following on the foot-way strode a tall, strong, and somewhat corpulent man, with sinister, deep-set eyes and a red beard, his arm and shoulder covered with his cloak. In the throat of the thoroughfare, where the sculptured image of Henry the Fourth still guards the spot, a collision of two carts stopped the coach. Ravaillac quickened his pace. In an instant he was at the door. With his cloak dropped from his shoulders, and a long knife in his hand, he set his foot upon a guardstone, thrust his head and shoulders into the coach, and with frantic force stabbed thrice at the King's heart. A broken exclamation, a gasping convulsion; and then the grim visage dropped on the bleeding breast. Henry breathed his last, and the hope of Europe died with him.

The omens were sinister for Old France and for New. Marie de Medicis, "cette grosse banquière," coarse scion of a bad stock, false wife and faithless queen, paramour of an intriguing foreigner, tool of the Jesuits and of Spain, was Regent in the minority of her imbecile son. The Huguenots drooped, the national party collapsed, the vigorous hand of Sully was felt no more, and the treasure gathered for a vast and beneficent enterprise became the instrument of despotism and the prey of corruption. Under such dark auspices, young Biencourt entered the thronged chambers of the Louvre.

He gained audience of the Queen, and displayed his list of baptisms; while the ever present Jesuits failed not to seize him by the button,[1] assuring him, not only that the late King had deeply at heart the establishment of their Society in Acadia, but that to this end he had made them a grant of two thousand livres a year. The Jesuits had found an ally and the intended mission a friend at court, whose story and whose character are too striking to pass unnoticed.

This was a lady of honor to the Queen, Antoinette de Pons, Marquise de Guercheville, once renowned for grace and beauty, and not less conspicuous for qualities rare in the unbridled court of Henry's predecessor, where her youth had been passed. When the civil war was at its height, the royal heart, leaping with insatiable restlessness from battle to battle, from mistress to mistress, had found a brief repose in the affections of his Corisande, famed in tradition and romance; but Corisande was suddenly abandoned, and the young widow, Madame de Guercheville, became the loadstar of his erratic fancy. It was an evil hour for the Béarnais. Henry sheathed in rusty steel, battling for his crown and his life, and Henry robed in royalty and throned triumphant in the Louvre, alike urged their suit in vain. Unused to defeat, the

[1] Lescarbot, (1618,) 662: ". . . . ne manquerent de l'empoigner par les cheveux."

King's passion rose higher for the obstacle that barred it. On one occasion he was met with an answer not unworthy of record:—

"Sire, my rank, perhaps, is not high enough to permit me to be your wife, but my heart is too high to permit me to be your mistress."[1]

She left the court and retired to her chateau of La Roche-Guyon, on the Seine, ten leagues below Paris, where, fond of magnificence, she is said to have lived in much expense and splendor. The indefatigable King, haunted by her memory, made a hunting-party in the neighboring forests; and, as evening drew near, separating himself from his courtiers, he sent a gentleman of his train to ask of Madame de Guercheville the shelter of her roof. The reply conveyed a dutiful acknowledgment of the honor, and an offer of the best entertainment within her power. It was night when Henry, with his little band of horsemen, approached the chateau, where lights were burning in every window, after a fashion of the day on occasions of welcome to an honored guest. Pages stood in the gateway, each with a blazing torch; and here, too, were gentlemen of the neighborhood, gathered to greet their sovereign. Madame de Guercheville came forth, followed by the women of her household; and when the King, unprepared for so benign a welcome, giddy with love and hope, saw her radiant in pearls and more radiant yet in a beauty enhanced by the wavy torchlight and the surrounding shadows, he scarcely dared trust his senses:—

"Que vois-je, madame; est-ce bien vous, et suis-je ce roi méprisé?"

He gave her his hand, and she led him within the chateau, where, at the door of the apartment destined for him, she left him, with a graceful reverence. The King, nowise disconcerted, did not doubt that she had gone to give orders for his entertainment, when an attendant came to tell him that she had descended to the courtyard and called for her coach. Thither he hastened in alarm:—

[1] A similar reply is attributed to Catherine de Rohan, Duchesse de Deux-Ponts: "Je suis trop pauvre pour être votre femme, et de trop bonne maison pour être votre maîtresse." Her suitor also was Henry the Fourth. *Dictionnaire de Bayle*, III. 2182.

"What! am I driving you from your house?"

"Sire," replied Madame de Guercheville, "where a king is, he should be the sole master; but, for my part, I like to preserve some little authority wherever I may be."

With another deep reverence, she entered her coach and disappeared, seeking shelter under the roof of a friend, some two leagues off, and leaving the baffled King to such consolation as he might find in a magnificent repast, bereft of the presence of the hostess.[1]

[1] *Mémoires de l'Abbé de Choisy*, Liv. XII. The elaborate notices of Madame de Guercheville in the *Biographie Générale* and the *Biographie Universelle* are from this source. She figures under the name of Scilinde in *Les Amours du Grand Alcandre* (Henry IV.). See *Collection Petitot*, LXIII. 515, note, where the passage is extracted.

The Abbé de Choisy says that when the King was enamored of her she was married to M. de Liancourt. This, it seems, is a mistake, this second marriage not taking place till 1594. Madame de Guercheville refused to take the name of Liancourt, because it had once been borne by the Duchesse de Beaufort, who had done it no honor,—a scruple very reasonably characterized by her biographer as "trop affecté."

The following is De Choisy's account:—

"Enfin ce prince s'avisa un jour, pour dernière ressource, de faire une partie de chasse du côté de La Roche-Guyon; et, sur la fin de la journée, s'étant séparé de la plupart de ses courtisans, il envoya un gentilhomme à La Roche-Guyon demander le couvert pour une nuit. Madame de Guercheville, sans s'embarrasser, répondit au gentilhomme, que le Roi lui feroit beaucoup d'honneur, et qu'elle le recevroit de son mieux. En effet, elle donna ordre à un magnifique souper; on éclaira toutes les fenêtres du château avec des torches (c'étoit la mode en ce temps-là); elle se para de ses plus beaux habits, se couvrit de perles (c'étoit aussi la mode); et lorsque le Roi arriva à l'entrée de la nuit, elle alla le recevoir à la porte de sa maison, accompagnée de toutes ses femmes, et de quelques gentilhommes du voisinage. Des pages portoient les torches devant elle. Le Roi, transporté de joie, la trouva plus belle que jamais: les ombres de la nuit, la lumière des flambeaux, les diamans, la surprise d'un accueil si favorable et si peu accoutumé, tout contribuait à renouveler ses anciennes blessures. 'Que vois-je, madame?' lui dit ce monarque tremblant; 'est-ce bien vous, et suis-je ce roi méprisé?' Madame de Guercheville l'interrompit, en le priant de monter dans son appartement pour se reposer. Il lui donna la main. Elle le conduisit jusqu'à la porte de sa chambre, lui fit une grande révérence, et se retira. Le Roi ne s'en étonna pas; il crut qu'elle vouloit aller donner ordre à la fête qu'elle lui préparoit. Mais il fut bien surpris quand on lui vint dire qu'elle étoit déscendue dans sa cour, et qu'elle avoit crié tout haut: *Qu'on attelle* mon coche! comme pour aller coucher hors de chez elle. Il descendit aussitôt, et tout éperdu lui dit: 'Quoi! madame, je vous chasserai de votre maison?' 'Sire,' lui répondit-elle d'un ton ferme, 'un roi doit être le maître partout où il est; et pour moi, je suis bien

Henry could admire the virtue which he could not van-
quish; and, long after, on his marriage, he acknowledged his
sense of her worth by begging her to accept an honorable
post near the person of the Queen.

"Madame," he said, presenting her to Marie de Medicis, "I
give you a lady of honor who is a lady of honor indeed."

Some twenty years had passed since the adventure of La
Roche-Guyon. Madame de Guercheville had outlived the
charms which had attracted her royal suitor, but the virtue
which repelled him was reinforced by a devotion no less uncompromising. A rosary in her hand and a Jesuit at her side,
she realized the utmost wishes of the subtle fathers who had
moulded and who guided her. She readily took fire when they
told her of the benighted souls of New France, and the
wrongs of Father Biard kindled her utmost indignation. She
declared herself the protectress of the American missions; and
the only difficulty, as a Jesuit writer tells us, was to restrain
her zeal within reasonable bounds.[1]

She had two illustrious coadjutors. The first was the jealous
Queen, whose unbridled rage and vulgar clamor had made
the Louvre a hell. The second was Henriette d'Entragues,
Marquise de Verneuil, the crafty and capricious siren who
had awakened these conjugal tempests. To this singular coali-
tion were joined many other ladies of the court; for the pious
flame, fanned by the Jesuits, spread through hall and boudoir,
and fair votaries of the Loves and Graces found it a more
grateful task to win heaven for the heathen than to merit it
for themselves.

Young Biencourt saw it vain to resist. Biard must go with
him in the returning ship, and also another Jesuit, Enemond
Masse. The two fathers repaired to Dieppe, wafted on the
wind of court favor, which they never doubted would bear
them to their journey's end. Not so, however. Poutrincourt
and his associates, in the dearth of their own resources, had
bargained with two Huguenot merchants of Dieppe, Du Jar-

---

aise d'avoir quelque pouvoir dans les lieux où je me trouve.' Et, sans vouloir
l'écouter davantage, elle monta dans son coche, et alla coucher à deux lieues
de là chez une de ses amies."

[1] Charlevoix, I. 122.

din and Du Quesne, to equip and load the vessel, in consideration of their becoming partners in the expected profits. Their indignation was extreme when they saw the intended passengers. They declared, that they would not aid in building up a colony for the profit of the king of Spain, nor risk their money in a venture where Jesuits were allowed to intermeddle; and they closed with a flat refusal to receive them on board, unless, they added with patriotic sarcasm, the Queen would direct them to transport the whole order beyond sea.[1] Biard and Masse insisted, on which the merchants demanded reimbursement for their outlay, as they would have no further concern in the business.

Biard communicated with Father Coton, Father Coton with Madame de Guercheville. No more was needed. The zealous lady of honor, "indignant," says Biard, "to see the efforts of hell prevail," and resolved "that Satan should not remain master of the field," set on foot a subscription, and raised an ample fund within the precincts of the court. Biard, in the name of the "Province of France of the Order of Jesus," bought out the interest of the two merchants for thirty-eight hundred livres, thus constituting the Jesuits equal partners in business with their enemies. Nor was this all; for, out of the ample proceeds of the subscription, he lent to the needy associates a further sum of seven hundred and thirty-seven livres, and advanced twelve hundred and twenty-five more to complete the outfit of the ship. Well pleased, the triumphant priests now embarked, and friend and foe set sail together on the twenty-sixth of January, 1611.[2]

[1] Lescarbot, (1618,) 664.

[2] *Contract d'Association des Jésuites au Trafique du Canada, 20 Jan. 1611*; a certified copy of the original parchment. It is noteworthy that the first contract of the French Jesuits in America relates to a partnership to carry on the fur-trade. Compare Lescarbot, (1618,) 665; Biard, *Relation*, c. 12; Champlain, (1632,) 100; Charlevoix, I. 123; De Laet, Lib. II. c. 21; *Lettre du P. Pierre Biard au T. R. P. Claude Aquaviva, Général de la Compagnie de Jésus à Rome, Dieppe, 21 Jan., 1611*; *Lettre du P. Biard au R. P. Christophe Balthazar, Provincial de France à Paris, Port Royal, 10 Juin, 1611*; *Lettre du P. Biard au T. R. P. Claude Aquaviva, Port Royal, 31 Jan., 1612*. These letters form part of an interesting collection recently published by R. P. Auguste Carayon, S.J., under the title, *Première Mission des Jésuites au Canada* (Paris, 1864). They are taken from the Jesuit archives at Rome.

Chapter VI

JESUITS IN ACADIA

The Jesuits arrive • Collision of Powers Temporal and Spiritual • Excursion of Biencourt • Biard's Indian Studies • Misery at Port Royal • Grant to Madame de Guercheville • Gilbert du Thet • Quarrels • Anathemas • Truce

THE voyage was one of inordinate length,—beset, too, with icebergs, larger and taller, according to the Jesuit voyagers, than the Church of Notre Dame; but on the day of Pentecost their ship, "The Grace of God," anchored before Port Royal. Then first were seen in the wilderness of New France the close black cap, the close black robe, of the Jesuit father, and the features seamed with study and thought and discipline. Then first did this mighty Proteus, this many-colored Society of Jesus, enter upon that rude field of toil and woe, where, in after years, the devoted zeal of its apostles was to lend dignity to their order and do honor to humanity.

Few were the regions of the known world to which the potent brotherhood had not stretched the vast network of its influence. Jesuits had disputed in theology with the bonzes of Japan, and taught astronomy to the mandarins of China; had wrought prodigies of sudden conversion among the followers of Brahma, preached the papal supremacy to Abyssinian schismatics, carried the cross among the savages of Caffraria, wrought reputed miracles in Brazil, and gathered the tribes of Paraguay beneath their paternal sway. And now, with the aid of the Virgin and her votary at court, they would build another empire among the tribes of New France. The omens were sinister and the outset was unpropitious. The Society was destined to reap few laurels from the brief apostleship of Biard and Masse.

When the voyagers landed, they found at Port Royal a band of half-famished men, eagerly expecting their succor. The voyage of four months had, however, nearly exhausted their own very moderate stock of provisions, and the mutual congratulations of the old colonists and the new were damped by a vision of starvation. A friction, too, speedily declared itself between the spiritual and the temporal powers. Pontgravé's son, then trading on the coast, had exasperated the Indians by an outrage on one of their women, and, dreading the wrath of Poutrincourt, had fled to the woods. Biard saw fit to take his part, remonstrated for him with vehemence, gained his pardon, received his confession, and absolved him. The Jesuit says, that he was treated with great consideration by Poutrincourt, and that he should be forever beholden to him. The latter, however, chafed at Biard's interference.

"Father," he said, "I know my duty, and I beg you will leave me to do it. I, with my sword, have hopes of paradise, as well as you with your breviary. Show me my path to heaven. I will show you yours on earth."[1]

He soon set sail for France, leaving his son Biencourt in charge. This hardy young sailor, of ability and character beyond his years, had, on his visit to court, received the post of Vice-Admiral in the seas of New France, and in this capacity had a certain authority over the trading-vessels of St. Malo and Rochelle, several of which were upon the coast. To compel the recognition of this authority, and also to purchase provisions, he set out along with Biard in a boat filled with armed followers. His first collision was with young Pontgravé, who with a few men had built a trading-hut on the St. John, where he proposed to winter. Meeting with resistance, Biencourt took the whole party prisoners, in spite of the remonstrances of Biard. Next, proceeding along the coast, he levied tribute on four or five traders wintering at St. Croix, and, continuing his course to the Kennebec, found the Indians of that region greatly enraged at the conduct of certain English adventurers, who, three or four years before, had, as they said, set dogs upon them and otherwise maltreated them. These were the colonists under Popham and Gilbert, who in 1607 and 1608 made an abortive attempt to settle near the mouth of the river. Nothing now was left of them but their deserted fort. The neighboring Indians were Abenakis, one of the tribes included by the French under the general name of Armouchiquois. Their disposition was doubtful, and it

[1] Lescarbot, (1618,) 669. Compare Biard, *Relation*, c. 14; and Biard, *Lettre au R. P. Christophe Balthazar*, in Carayon, 9.

needed all the coolness of young Biencourt to avoid a fatal collision. On one occasion a curious incident took place. The French met six canoes full of warriors descending the Kennebec, and, as neither party trusted the other, the two encamped on opposite banks of the river. In the evening the Indians began to sing and dance. Biard suspected these proceedings to be an invocation of the Devil, and "in order," he says, "to thwart this accursed tyrant, I made our people sing a few church hymns, such as the *Salve*, the *Ave Maris Stella*, and others. But being once in train, and getting to the end of their spiritual songs, they fell to singing such others as they knew, and when these gave out they took to mimicking the dancing and singing of the Armouchiquois on the other side of the water; and as Frenchmen are naturally good mimics, they did it so well that the Armouchiquois stopped to listen; at which our people stopped too; and then the Indians began again. You would have laughed to hear them, for they were like two choirs answering each other in concert, and you would hardly have known the real Armouchiquois from the sham ones."

Before the capture of young Pontgravé, Biard made him a visit at his camp, six leagues up the St. John. Pontgravé's men were sailors from St. Malo, between whom and the other Frenchmen there was much ill blood. Biard had hardly entered the river when he saw the evening sky crimsoned with the dancing fires of a superb aurora borealis, and he and his attendants marvelled what evil thing the prodigy might portend. Their Indian companions said that it was a sign of war. In fact, the night after they had joined Pontgravé a furious quarrel broke out in the camp, with abundant shouting, gesticulating, and swearing; and, says the father, "I do not doubt that an accursed band of furious and sanguinary spirits were hovering about us all night, expecting every moment to see a horrible massacre of the few Christians in those parts; but the goodness of God bridled their malice. No blood was shed, and on the next day the squall ended in a fine calm."

He did not like the Indians, whom he describes as "lazy, gluttonous, irreligious, treacherous, cruel, and licentious." He makes an exception in favor of Membertou, whom he calls "the greatest, most renowned, and most redoubted savage that ever lived in the memory of man," and especially commends him for contenting himself with but one wife, hardly a superlative merit in a centenarian. Biard taught him to say the Lord's Prayer, though at the petition, "Give us this day our daily bread," the chief remonstrated, saying, "If I ask for nothing but bread, I shall get no fish or moose-meat." His protracted career was now drawing to a close, and, being brought to the settlement in a dying state, he was placed in Biard's bed and attended by the two Jesuits. He was as remarkable in person as in character, for he was bearded like a Frenchman. Though, alone among La Flèche's converts, the Faith seemed to have left some impression upon him, he insisted on being buried with his heathen forefathers, but was persuaded to forego a wish fatal to his salvation, and slept at last in consecrated ground.

Another of the scanty fruits of the mission was a little girl on the point of death, whom Biard had asked her parents to give him for baptism. "Take her and keep her, if you like," was the reply, "for she is no better than a dead dog." "We accepted the offer," says Biard, "in order to show them the difference between Christianity and their impiety; and after giving her what care we could, together with some instruction, we baptized her. We named her after Madame the Marquise de Guercheville, in gratitude for the benefits we have received from that lady, who can now rejoice that her name is already in heaven; for, a few days after baptism, the chosen soul flew to that place of glory."

Biard's greatest difficulty was with the Micmac language. Young Biencourt was his best interpreter, and on common occasions served him well; but the moment that religion was in question he was, as it were, stricken dumb, the reason being that the language was totally without abstract terms. Biard resolutely set himself to the study of it, a hard and thorny path, on which he made small progress, and often went astray. Seated, pencil in hand, before some Indian squatting on the floor, whom with the bribe of a mouldy biscuit he had lured into the hut, he plied him with questions which he often neither would nor could answer. What was the Indian word for *Faith*, *Hope*, *Charity*, *Sacrament*, *Baptism*, *Eucharist*, *Trinity*, *Incarnation*? The perplexed savage, willing to amuse himself, and impelled, as Biard thinks, by the Devil, gave him scurrilous and unseemly phrases as the equivalent of things holy, which, studiously incorporated into the father's Indian catechism, produced on his pupils an effect the reverse of that intended. Biard's colleague, Masse, was equally zealous, and still less fortunate. He tried a forest life among the Indians with signal ill success. Hard fare, smoke, filth, the scolding of squaws, and the cries of children, reduced him to a forlorn condition of body and mind, wore him to a skeleton, and sent him back to Port Royal without a single convert.

The dark months wore slowly on. A band of half-famished men gathered about the huge fires of their barn-like hall, moody, sullen, and quarrelsome. Discord was here in the black robe of the Jesuit and the brown capote of the rival trader. The position of the wretched little colony may well provoke reflection. Here lay the shaggy continent, from Florida to the Pole, outstretched in savage slumber along the sea, the stern domain of Nature, or, to adopt the ready solution of the Jesuits, a realm of the powers of night, blasted beneath the sceptre of hell. On the banks of James River was a nest of woe-begone Englishmen, a handful of Dutch fur-traders at the mouth of the Hudson,[1] and a few shivering Frenchmen among the snow-drifts of Acadia; while deep within the wild monotony of desolation, on the icy verge of the great northern river, the hand of Champlain upheld the fleur-de-lis on the rock of Quebec. These were the advance guard; the forlorn hope of civilization, messengers of promise to a desert continent. Yet, unconscious of their high function, not content with inevitable woes, they were rent by petty jealousies and miserable feuds, while each of these detached fragments of rival nationalities, scarcely able to maintain its own wretched existence on a few square miles, begrudged to the others the smallest share in a domain which all the nations of Europe could hardly have sufficed to fill.

One evening, as the forlorn tenants of Port Royal sat together disconsolate, Biard was seized with a spirit of

---

[1] It is not certain that the Dutch had any permanent trading-post here before 1613, when they had four houses at Manhattan. O'Callaghan, *Hist. New Netherland*, I. 69.

prophecy. He called upon Biencourt to serve out the little of wine that remained,—a proposal which met with high favor from the company present, though apparently with none from the youthful Vice-Admiral. The wine was ordered, however, and, as an unwonted cheer ran around the circle, the Jesuit announced that an inward voice told him how, within a month, they should see a ship from France. In truth, they saw one within a week. On the twenty-third of January, 1612, arrived a small vessel laden with a moderate store of provisions and abundant seeds of future strife.

This was the expected succor sent by Poutrincourt. A series of ruinous voyages had exhausted his resources; but he had staked all on the success of the colony, had even brought his family to Acadia, and he would not leave them and his companions to perish.[1] His credit was gone; his hopes were dashed; yet assistance was proffered, and, in his extremity, he was forced to accept it. It came from Madame de Guercheville and her Jesuit advisers. She offered to buy the interest of a thousand crowns in the enterprise. The ill-omened succor could not be refused; but this was not all. The zealous protectress of the missions obtained from De Monts, whose fortunes, like those of Poutrincourt, had ebbed low, a transfer of all his claims to the lands of Acadia; while the young King, Louis the Thirteenth, was persuaded to give her, in addition, a new grant of all the territory of North America, from the St. Lawrence to Florida. Thus did Madame de Guercheville, or in other words, the Jesuits who used her name as a cover, become proprietors of the greater part of the future United States and British Provinces. The English colony of Virginia and the Dutch trading-houses of New York were included within the limits of this destined Northern Paraguay, while Port Royal, the seigniory of the unfortunate Poutrincourt, was encompassed, like a petty island, by the vast domain of the Society of Jesus. They could not deprive him of it, since his title had been confirmed by the late King, but they flattered themselves, to borrow their own language, that he would be "confined as in a prison."[2] His grant, however, had

---

[1] Biard, *Epistola ex Portu-regali in Acadia*, 1612. Biard says that there was no other family in the colony.

[2] Biard, *Relation*, c. 19.

been vaguely worded, and, while they held him restricted to an insignificant patch of ground, he claimed lordship over a wide and indefinite territory. Here was argument for endless strife. Other interests, too, were adverse. Poutrincourt, in his discouragement, had abandoned his plan of liberal colonization, and now thought of nothing but beaver-skins. He wished to make a trading-post; the Jesuits wished to make a mission.

When the vessel anchored before Port Royal, Biencourt, with disgust and anger, saw another Jesuit landed at the pier. This was Gilbert du Thet, a lay brother, versed in affairs of this world, who had come out as representative and administrator of Madame de Guercheville. Poutrincourt, also, had his agent on board; and, without the loss of a day, the two began to quarrel. A truce ensued; then a smothered feud, pervading the whole colony, and ending in a notable explosion. The Jesuits, chafing under the sway of Biencourt, had withdrawn without ceremony, and betaken themselves to the vessel, intending to sail for France. Biencourt, exasperated at such a breach of discipline, and fearing their representations at court, ordered them to return, adding that, since the Queen had commended them to his especial care, he could not, in conscience, lose sight of them. The indignant fathers excommunicated him. On this, the sagamore Louis, son of the grisly convert Membertou, begged leave to kill them; but Biencourt would not countenance this summary mode of relieving his embarrassment. He again, in the King's name, ordered the clerical mutineers to return to the fort. Biard declared that he would not, threatened to excommunicate any who should lay hand on him, and called the Vice-Admiral a robber. His wrath, however, soon cooled; he yielded to necessity, and came quietly ashore, where, for the next three months, neither he nor his colleagues would say mass, or perform any office of religion.[1] At length a change came over him; he made advances of peace, prayed that the past might be forgotten, said mass again, and closed with a

---

[1] Lescarbot, (1618,) 676. Biard passes over the affair in silence. In his letters (see Carayon) prior to this time, he speaks favorably both of Biencourt and Poutrincourt.

petition that Brother du Thet might be allowed to go to France in a trading vessel then on the coast. His petition being granted, he wrote to Poutrincourt a letter overflowing with praises of his son; and, charged with this missive, Du Thet set sail.

Chapter VII

1613

LA SAUSSAYE—ARGALL

Voyage of La Saussaye • *Mount Desert* • *Argall attacks the French* • *Death of Du Thet* • *St. Sauveur destroyed*

PENDING these squabbles, the Jesuits at home were far from idle. Bent on ridding themselves of Poutrincourt, they seized, in satisfaction of debts due them, all the cargo of his returning vessel, and involved him in a network of litigation. If we accept his own statements in a letter to his friend Lescarbot, he was outrageously misused, and indeed defrauded, by his clerical copartners, who at length had him thrown into prison.[1] Here, exasperated, weary, sick of Acadia, and anxious for the wretched exiles who looked to him for succor, the unfortunate man fell ill. Regaining his liberty, he again addressed himself with what strength remained to the forlorn task of sending relief to his son and his comrades.

Scarcely had Brother Gilbert du Thet arrived in France, when Madame de Guercheville and her Jesuits, strong in court favor and in the charity of wealthy penitents, prepared to take possession of their empire beyond sea. Contributions were asked, and not in vain; for the sagacious fathers, mindful of every spring of influence, had deeply studied the mazes of feminine psychology, and then, as now, were favorite confessors of the fair. It was on the twelfth of March, 1613, that the "Mayflower" of the Jesuits sailed from Honfleur for the shores of New England. She was the "Jonas," formerly in the service of De Monts, a small craft bearing forty-eight sailors and colonists, including two Jesuits, Father Quentin and Brother Du Thet. She carried horses, too, and goats, and was abundantly stored with all things needful by the pious munificence of her patrons. A courtier named La Saussaye was chief of the colony, Captain Charles Fleury commanded the ship,[2]

[1] See the letter, in Lescarbot, (1618,) 678.

[2] *Rapport fait à l'Amirauté de Rouen par Charles Fleury, Capitaine du Jonas, le 27 Aoust, 1614.* I am indebted to M. Gabriel Gravier of Rouen for a copy of this document.

and, as she winged her way across the Atlantic, benedictions hovered over her from lordly halls and perfumed chambers.

On the sixteenth of May, La Saussaye touched at La Hêve, where he heard mass, planted a cross, and displayed the scutcheon of Madame de Guercheville. Thence, passing on to Port Royal, he found Biard, Masse, their servant-boy, an apothecary, and one man beside. Biencourt and his followers were scattered about the woods and shores, digging the tuberous roots called ground-nuts, catching alewives in the brooks, and by similar expedients sustaining their miserable existence. Taking the two Jesuits on board, the voyagers steered for the Penobscot. A fog rose upon the sea. They sailed to and fro, groping their way in blindness, straining their eyes through the mist, and trembling each instant lest they should descry the black outline of some deadly reef and the ghostly death-dance of the breakers. But Heaven heard their prayers. At night they could see the stars.[1] The sun rose resplendent on a laughing sea, and his morning beams streamed fair and full on the wild heights of the island of Mount Desert. They entered a bay that stretched inland between iron-bound shores, and gave it the name of St. Sauveur. It is now called Frenchman's Bay. They saw a coast-line of weather-beaten crags set thick with spruce and fir, the surf-washed cliffs of Great Head and Schooner Head, the rocky front of Newport Mountain, patched with ragged woods, the arid domes of Dry Mountain and Green Mountain, the round bristly backs of the Porcupine Islands, and the waving outline of the Gouldsborough Hills.

La Saussaye cast anchor not far from Schooner Head, and here he lay till evening. The jet-black shade betwixt crags and sea, the pines along the cliff, pencilled against the fiery sunset, the dreamy slumber of distant mountains bathed in shadowy purple,—such is the scene that in this our day greets the wandering artist, the roving collegian bivouacked on the shore, or

---

[1] "Suruint en mer vne si espaisse brume, que nous n'y voyons pas plus de iour que de nuict. Nous apprehendions grandement ce danger, parce qu'en cét endroict, il y a beaucoup de brisans et rochers. . . . . De sa bonté, Dieu nous exauça, car le soir mesme nous commençasmes à voir les estoiles, et le matin les brouées se dissiperent; nous nous reconnusmes estre au deuant des Monts deserts." Biard, *Relation*, c. 23.

the pilgrim from stifled cities renewing his jaded strength in the mighty life of nature. Perhaps they then greeted the adventurous Frenchmen. There was peace on the wilderness and peace on the sea; but none in this missionary bark, pioneer of Christianity and civilization. A rabble of angry sailors clamored on her deck, ready to mutiny over the terms of their engagement. Should the time of their stay be reckoned from their landing at La Hêve, or from their anchoring at Mount Desert? Fleury, the naval commander, took their part. Sailor, courtier, and priest gave tongue together in vociferous debate. Poutrincourt was far away, a ruined man; and the intractable Vice-Admiral had ceased from troubling; yet not the less were the omens of the pious enterprise sinister and dark. The company, however, went ashore, raised a cross, and heard mass.

At a distance in the woods they saw the signal smoke of Indians, whom Biard lost no time in visiting. Some of them were from a village on the shore, three leagues westward. They urged the French to go with them to their wigwams. The astute savages had learned already how to deal with a Jesuit.

"Our great chief, Asticou, is there. He wishes for baptism. He is very sick. He will die unbaptized. He will burn in hell, and it will be all your fault."

This was enough. Biard embarked in a canoe, and they paddled him to the spot, where he found the great chief, Asticou, in his wigwam, with a heavy cold in the head. Disappointed of his charitable purpose, the priest consoled himself with observing the beauties of the neighboring shore, which seemed to him better fitted than St. Sauveur for the intended settlement. It was a gentle slope, descending to the water, covered with tall grass, and backed by rocky hills. It looked southeast upon a harbor where a fleet might ride at anchor, sheltered from the gales by a cluster of islands.[1]

[1] Biard says that the place was only three leagues from St. Sauveur, and that he could go and return in an afternoon. He adds that it was "séparé de la grande Isle des Monts Déserts." He was evidently mistaken in this. St. Sauveur being on the east side of Mount Desert, there is no place separated from it, and answering to his description, which he could have reached within the time mentioned. He no doubt crossed Mount Desert Sound, which, with Soames's Sound, nearly severs the island. The settlement must have been on

The ship was brought to the spot, and the colonists disembarked. First they planted a cross; then they began their labors, and, with their labors, their quarrels. La Saussaye, zealous for agriculture, wished to break ground and raise crops immediately; the rest opposed him, wishing first to be housed and fortified. Fleury demanded that the ship should be unladen, and La Saussaye would not consent.[1] Debate ran high, when suddenly all was harmony, and the disputants were friends once more in the pacification of a common danger.

Far out at sea, beyond the islands that sheltered their harbor, they saw an approaching sail; and, as she drew near, straining their anxious eyes, they could descry the red flags that streamed from her masthead and her stern; then the black muzzles of her cannon,—they counted seven on a side; then the throng of men upon her decks. The wind was brisk and fair; all her sails were set; she came on, writes a spectator, more swiftly than an arrow.[2]

Six years before, in 1607, the ships of Captain Newport had conveyed to the banks of James River the first vital germ of English colonization on the continent. Noble and wealthy speculators, with Hispaniola, Mexico, and Peru for their inspiration, had combined to gather the fancied golden harvest of Virginia, received a charter from the Crown, and taken possession of their El Dorado. From tavern, gaming-house, and brothel was drawn the staple of the colony,—ruined gentlemen, prodigal sons, disreputable retainers, debauched tradesmen. Yet it would be foul slander to affirm that the

---

the western side of Soames's Sound. Here, about a mile from the open sea, on the farm of Mr. Fernald, is a spot perfectly answering to the minute description of Biard: "Le terroir noir, gras, et fertile, ... la jolie colline esleuée doucement sur la mer, et baignée à ses costez de deux fontaines; . . . . les petites islettes qui rompent les flots et les vents." The situation is highly picturesque. On the opposite or eastern shore of the sound are found heaps of clam-shells and other indications of an Indian village, probably that of Asticou. I am indebted to E. L. Hamlin, Esq., of Bangor, for pointing out this locality.

[1] *Rapport de Fleury à l'Amirauté de Rouen.*

[2] "La nauire Anglois venoit plus viste qu'un dard, ayant le vent à souhait, tout pauis de rouge, les pauillons d'Angleterre flottans, et trois trompettes et deux tambours faisans rage de sonner." Biard, *Relation*, c. 25.

founders of Virginia were all of this stamp; for among the
riotous crew were men of worth, and, above them all, a hero
disguised by the homeliest of names. Again and again, in direst woe and jeopardy, the infant settlement owed its life to
the heart and hand of John Smith.

Several years had elapsed since Newport's voyage; and the
colony, depleted by famine, disease, and an Indian war, had
been recruited by fresh emigration, when one Samuel Argall
arrived at Jamestown, captain of an illicit trading-vessel. He
was a man of ability and force,—one of those compounds of
craft and daring in which the age was fruitful; for the rest,
unscrupulous and grasping. In the spring of 1613 he achieved
a characteristic exploit, the abduction of Pocahontas, that
most interesting of young squaws, or, to borrow the style of
the day, of Indian princesses. Sailing up the Potomac, he
lured her on board his ship, and then carried off the benefactress of the colony a prisoner to Jamestown. Here a young
man of family, Rolfe, became enamored of her, married her
with more than ordinary ceremony, and thus secured a firm
alliance between her tribesmen and the English.

Meanwhile Argall had set forth on another enterprise. With
a ship of one hundred and thirty tons, carrying fourteen guns
and sixty men, he sailed in May for islands off the coast of
Maine to fish, as he says, for cod.[1] He had a more important
errand, for Sir Thomas Dale, Governor of Virginia, had commissioned him to expel the French from any settlement they
might have made within the limits of King James's patents.[2]
Thick fogs involved him; and, when the weather cleared, he
found himself not far from the Bay of Penobscot. Canoes
came out from shore; the Indians climbed the ship's side, and,
as they gained the deck, greeted the astonished English with
an odd pantomime of bows and flourishes, which, in the belief of the latter, could have been learned from none but
Frenchmen.[3] By signs, too, and by often repeating the word
Norman,—by which they always designated the French,—

[1] Letter of Argall to Nicholas Hawes, June, 1613, in Purchas, IV. 1764.

[2] *Collections Mass. Hist. Soc.*, Fourth Series, IX. 41, 489.

[3] ". . . . et aux cérémonies que les sauvages faisoient pour leur complaire,
ils recognoissoient que c'étoient cérémonies de courtoisie et ciuilitez françoises." Biard, *Relation*, c. 25.

they betrayed the presence of the latter. Argall questioned them as well as his total ignorance of their language would permit, and learned, by signs, the position and numbers of the colonists. Clearly they were no match for him. Assuring the Indians that the Normans were his friends, and that he longed to see them, he retained one of the visitors as a guide, dismissed the rest with presents, and shaped his course for Mount Desert.[1]

Now the wild heights rose in view; now the English could see the masts of a small ship anchored in the sound; and now, as they rounded the islands, four white tents were visible on the grassy slope between the water and the woods. They were a gift from the Queen to Madame de Guercheville and her missionaries. Argall's men prepared for fight, while their Indian guide, amazed, broke into a howl of lamentation.

On shore all was confusion. Bailleul, the pilot, went to reconnoitre, and ended by hiding among the islands. La Saussaye lost presence of mind, and did nothing for defence. La Motte, his lieutenant, with Captain Fleury, an ensign, a sergeant, the Jesuit Du Thet, and a few of the bravest men, hastened on board the vessel, but had no time to cast loose her cables. Argall bore down on them, with a furious din of drums and trumpets, showed his broadside, and replied to their hail with a volley of cannon and musket shot. "Fire! Fire!" screamed Fleury. But there was no gunner to obey, till Du Thet seized and applied the match. "The cannon made as much noise as the enemy's," writes Biard; but, as the inexperienced artillerist forgot to aim the piece, no other result ensued. Another storm of musketry, and Brother Gilbert du Thet rolled helpless on the deck. The French ship was mute. The English plied her for a time with shot, then lowered a boat and boarded. Under the awnings which covered her, dead and wounded men lay strewn about her deck, and among them the brave lay brother, smothering in his blood. He had his wish; for, on leaving France, he had prayed with uplifted hands that he might not return, but perish in that holy enterprise. Like the Order of which he was a humble

[1] Holmes, *American Annals*, by a misapprehension of Champlain's narrative, represents Argall as having a squadron of eleven ships. He certainly had but one.

member, he was a compound of qualities in appearance contradictory. La Motte, sword in hand, showed fight to the last,
and won the esteem of his captors.[1]

The English landed without meeting any show of resistance, and ranged at will among the tents, the piles of baggage and stores, and the buildings and defences newly begun.
Argall asked for the commander, but La Saussaye had fled to
the woods. The crafty Englishman seized his chests, caused
the locks to be picked, searched till he found the royal letters
and commissions, withdrew them, replaced everything else as
he had found it, and again closed the lids. In the morning,
La Saussaye, between the English and starvation, preferred
the former, and issued from his hiding-place. Argall received
him with studious courtesy. That country, he said, belonged
to his master, King James. Doubtless they had authority from
their own sovereign for thus encroaching upon it; and, for
his part, he was prepared to yield all respect to the commissions of the king of France, that the peace between the two
nations might not be disturbed. Therefore he prayed that the
commissions might be shown to him. La Saussaye opened his
chests. The royal signature was nowhere to be found. At this,
Argall's courtesy was changed to wrath. He denounced the
Frenchmen as robbers and pirates who deserved the gallows,
removed their property on board his ship, and spent the afternoon in dividing it among his followers. The disconsolate
French remained on the scene of their woes, where the greedy
sailors as they came ashore would snatch from them, now a
cloak, now a hat, and now a doublet, till the unfortunate colonists were left half naked. In other respects the English
treated their captives well,—except two of them, whom they
flogged; and Argall, whom Biard, after recounting his knav-
ery, calls "a gentleman of noble courage," having gained his
point, returned to his former courtesy.

But how to dispose of the prisoners? Fifteen of them, including La Saussaye and the Jesuit Massé, were turned adrift

---

[1] Fleury, who was wounded, greatly blames the flight of La Saussaye: "Si
luy et ses dicts compagnons eussent donné combat et se fussent defendus, le
dict navire n'eust esté prins." In a reply to complaints of the French ambassador, it was said that the French fired the first shot. See *Coll. Mass. Hist.
Soc.*, Fourth Series, IX. 489.

in an open boat, at the mercy of the wilderness and the sea. Nearly all were landsmen; but while their unpractised hands were struggling with the oars, they were joined among the islands by the fugitive pilot and his boat's crew. Worn and half starved, the united bands made their perilous way eastward, stopping from time to time to hear mass, make a procession, or catch codfish. Thus sustained in the spirit and in the flesh, cheered too by the Indians, who proved fast friends in need, they crossed the Bay of Fundy, doubled Cape Sable, and followed the southern coast of Nova Scotia, till they happily fell in with two French trading-vessels, which bore them in safety to St. Malo.

Chapter VIII

1613-1615

RUIN OF FRENCH ACADIA

The Jesuits at Jamestown • Wrath of Sir Thomas Dale • A New Expedition • Port Royal demolished • Equivocal Posture of the Jesuits • Their Adventures • The French will not abandon Acadia

---

P RAISED be God, behold two thirds of our company safe in France, telling their strange adventures to their relatives and friends. And now you will wish to know what befell the rest of us."[1] Thus writes Father Biard, who, with his companions in misfortune, fourteen in all, prisoners on board Argall's ship and the prize, were borne captive to Virginia. Old Point Comfort was reached at length, the site of Fortress Monroe; Hampton Roads, renowned in our day for the seafight of the Titans; Sewell's Point; the Rip Raps; Newport News;—all household words in the ears of this generation. Now, far on their right, buried in the damp shade of immemorial verdure, lay, untrodden and voiceless, the fields where stretched the leaguering lines of Washington, where the lilies of France floated beside the banners of the new-born republic, and where, in later years, embattled treason confronted the manhood of an outraged nation.[2] And now before them they could descry the masts of small craft at anchor, a cluster of rude dwellings fresh from the axe, scattered tenements, and fields green with tobacco.

Throughout the voyage the prisoners had been soothed with flattering tales of the benignity of the Governor of Virginia, Sir Thomas Dale, his love of the French, and his respect for the memory of Henry the Fourth, to whom, they were told, he was much beholden for countenance and favor. On their landing at Jamestown, this consoling picture was reversed. The Governor fumed and blustered, talked of halter

---

[1] "Dieu soit beny. Voyla ja les deux tiers de nostre troupe reconduicts en France sains et sauues parmy leurs parents et amis, qui les oyent conter leurs grandes aventures. Ores consequemment vous desirez sçauoir ce qui deniendra l'autre tiers." Biard, *Relation*, c. 28.

[2] Written immediately after the War of Secession.

and gallows, and declared that he would hang them all. In vain Argall remonstrated, urging that he had pledged his word for their lives. Dale, outraged by their invasion of British territory, was deaf to all appeals; till Argall, driven to extremity, displayed the stolen commissions, and proclaimed his stratagem, of which the French themselves had to that moment been ignorant. As they were accredited by their government, their lives at least were safe. Yet the wrath of Sir Thomas Dale still burned high. He summoned his council, and they resolved promptly to wipe off all stain of French intrusion from shores which King James claimed as his own.

Their action was utterly unauthorized. The two kingdoms were at peace. James the First, by the patents of 1606, had granted all North America, from the thirty-fourth to the forty-fifth degree of latitude, to the two companies of London and Plymouth, Virginia being assigned to the former, while to the latter were given Maine and Acadia, with adjacent regions. Over these, though as yet the claimants had not taken possession of them, the authorities of Virginia had no color of jurisdiction. England claimed all North America, in virtue of the discovery of Cabot; and Sir Thomas Dale became the self-constituted champion of British rights, not the less zealous that his championship promised a harvest of booty.

Argall's ship, the captured ship of La Saussaye, and another smaller vessel, were at once equipped and despatched on their errand of havoc. Argall commanded; and Biard, with Quentin and several others of the prisoners, were embarked with him.[1] They shaped their course first for Mount Desert. Here they landed, levelled La Saussaye's unfinished defences, cut down the French cross, and planted one of their own in its place. Next they sought out the island of St. Croix, seized a quantity of salt, and razed to the ground all that remained of the dilapidated buildings of De Monts. They crossed the Bay of Fundy to Port Royal, guided, says Biard, by an Indian chief,—an

[1] In his *Relation*, Biard does not explain the reason of his accompanying the expedition. In his letter to the General of the Jesuits, dated Amiens, 26 May, 1614, (Carayon,) he says that it was "dans le dessein de profiter de la première occasion qui se rencontrerait, pour nous renvoyer dans notre patrie."

improbable assertion, since the natives of these coasts hated the English as much as they loved the French, and now well knew the designs of the former. The unfortunate settlement was tenantless. Biencourt, with some of his men, was on a visit to neighboring bands of Indians, while the rest were reaping in the fields on the river, two leagues above the fort. Succor from Poutrincourt had arrived during the summer. The magazines were by no means empty, and there were cattle, horses, and hogs in adjacent fields and enclosures. Exulting at their good fortune, Argall's men butchered or carried off the animals, ransacked the buildings, plundered them even to the locks and bolts of the doors, and then laid the whole in ashes; "and may it please the Lord," adds the pious Biard, "that the sins therein committed may likewise have been consumed in that burning."

Having demolished Port Royal, the marauders went in boats up the river to the fields where the reapers were at work. These fled, and took refuge behind the ridge of a hill, whence they gazed helplessly on the destruction of their harvest. Biard approached them, and, according to the declaration of Poutrincourt made and attested before the Admiralty of Guienne, tried to persuade them to desert his son, Biencourt, and take service with Argall. The reply of one of the men gave little encouragement for further parley: —

"Begone, or I will split your head with this hatchet."

There is flat contradiction here between the narrative of the Jesuit and the accounts of Poutrincourt and contemporary English writers, who agree in affirming that Biard, "out of indigestible malice that he had conceived against Biencourt,"[1] encouraged the attack on the settlements of St. Croix and Port Royal, and guided the English thither. The priest himself admits that both French and English regarded him as a traitor, and that his life was in danger. While Argall's ship was at anchor, a Frenchman shouted to the English from a distance that they would do well to kill him. The master of the ship, a Puritan, in his abomination of priests, and above

---

[1] *Briefe Intelligence from Virginia by Letters.* See Purchas, IV. 1808. Compare Poutrincourt's letter to Lescarbot, in Lescarbot, (1618,) 684. Also, *Plainte du Sieur de Poutrincourt devant le Juge de l'Admirauté de Guyenne*, Lescarbot, 687.

all of Jesuits, was at the same time urging his commander to set Biard ashore and leave him to the mercy of his country-men. In this pass, he was saved, to adopt his own account, by what he calls his simplicity; for he tells us, that, while—insti-gated, like the rest of his enemies, by the Devil—the robber and the robbed were joining hands to ruin him, he was on his knees before Argall, begging him to take pity on the French, and leave them a boat, together with provisions to sustain their miserable lives through the winter. This spectacle of charity, he further says, so moved the noble heart of the commander, that he closed his ears to all the promptings of foreign and domestic malice.[1]

The English had scarcely re-embarked, when Biencourt ar-rived with his followers, and beheld the scene of destruction. Hopelessly outnumbered, he tried to lure Argall and some of his officers into an ambuscade, but they would not be en-trapped. Biencourt now asked for an interview. The word of honor was mutually given, and the two chiefs met in a meadow not far from the demolished dwellings. An anony-mous English writer says that Biencourt offered to transfer his allegiance to King James, on condition of being permitted to remain at Port Royal and carry on the fur-trade under a guaranty of English protection; but that Argall would not lis-ten to his overtures.[2] The interview proved a stormy one. Biard says that the Frenchman vomited against him every spe-cies of malignant abuse. "In the mean time," he adds, "you

[1] "Ie ne sçay qui secourut tant à propos le Iesuite en ce danger que sa simplicité. Car tout de mesme que s'il eust esté bien fauorisé et qu'il eust peu beaucoup enuers ledit Anglois, il se mit à genoux deuant le Capitaine par deux diuerses fois et a deux diuerses occasions, à celle fin de le flechir à mis-ericorde enuers les François du dit Port Royal esgarés par les bois, et pour luy persuader de leur laisser quelques viures, leur chaloupe et quelqu'autre moyen de passer l'hyuer. Et voyez combien differentes petitions on faisoit audit Capitaine: car au mesme temps que le P. Biard le supplioit ainsi pour les François, vn François crioit de loin, avec outrages et iniures, qu'il le falloit massacrer.

"Or Argal, qui est d'vn cœur noble, voyant ceste tant sincere affection du Iesuite, et de l'autre costé tant bestiale et enragée inhumanité de ce François, laquelle ne recognoissoit ny sa propre nation, ny bien-faicts, ny religion, ny estoit dompté par l'affliction et verges de Dieu, estima," etc. Biard, *Relation*, c. 29. He writes throughout in the third person.
[2] *Briefe Intelligence*, Purchas, IV. 1808.

will considerately observe to what madness the evil spirit ex-
citeth those who sell themselves to him."[1]

According to Poutrincourt,[2] Argall admitted that the priest
had urged him to attack Port Royal. Certain it is, that Biencourt demanded his surrender, frankly declaring that he
meant to hang him. "Whilest they were discoursing together," says the old English writer above mentioned, "one
of the savages, rushing suddenly forth from the Woods, and
licentiated to come neere, did after his manner, with such
broken *French* as he had, earnestly mediate a peace, wondring
why they that seemed to be of one Country should vse others
with such hostilitie, and that with such a forme of habit and
gesture as made them both to laugh."[3]

His work done, and, as he thought, the French settlements
of Acadia effectually blotted out, Argall set sail for Virginia
on the thirteenth of November. Scarcely was he at sea when
a storm scattered the vessels. Of the smallest of the three
nothing was ever heard. Argall, severely buffeted, reached his
port in safety, having first, it is said, compelled the Dutch at
Manhattan to acknowledge for a time the sovereignty of King
James.[4] The captured ship of La Saussaye, with Biard and his
colleague Quentin on board, was forced to yield to the fury
of the western gales, and bear away for the Azores. To Biard
the change of destination was not unwelcome. He stood in
fear of the truculent Governor of Virginia, and his tempest-
rocked slumbers were haunted with unpleasant visions of a
rope's end.[5] It seems that some of the French at Port Royal,
disappointed in their hope of hanging him, had commended
him to Sir Thomas Dale as a proper subject for the gallows,
drawing up a paper, signed by six of them, and containing

[1] Biard, c. 29: "Cependant vous remarquerez sagement iusques à quelle rage
le malin esprit agite ceux qui se vendent à luy."

[2] *Plainte du Sieur de Poutrincourt*, Lescarbot, (1618,) 689.

[3] Purchas, IV. 1808.

[4] *Description of the Province of New Albion*, in *New York Historical Collections*,
Second Series, I. 335. The statement is doubtful. It is supported, however, by
the excellent authority of Dr. O'Callaghan, *History of New Netherland*, I. 69.

[5] "Le Mareschal Thomas Deel (que vous avez ouy estre fort aspre en ses
humeurs) . . . . attendoit en bon deuotion le Pere Biard pour luy tost ac-
courcir les voyages, luy faisant trouuer au milieu d'une eschelle le bout du
monde." Biard, *Relation*, c. 30, 33.

allegations of a nature well fitted to kindle the wrath of that vehement official. The vessel was commanded by Turnel, Argall's lieutenant, apparently an officer of merit, a scholar and linguist. He had treated his prisoner with great kindness, because, says the latter, "he esteemed and loved him for his naïve simplicity and ingenuous candor."[1] But of late, thinking his kindness misplaced, he had changed it for an extreme coldness, preferring, in the words of Biard himself, "to think that the Jesuit had lied, rather than so many who accused him."[2]

Water ran low, provisions began to fail, and they eked out their meagre supply by butchering the horses taken at Port Royal. At length they came within sight of Fayal, when a new terror seized the minds of the two Jesuits. Might not the Englishmen fear that their prisoners would denounce them to the fervent Catholics of that island as pirates and sacrilegious kidnappers of priests? From such hazard the escape was obvious. What more simple than to drop the priests into the sea?[3] In truth, the English had no little dread of the results of conference between the Jesuits and the Portuguese authorities of Fayal; but the conscience or humanity of Turnel revolted at the expedient which awakened such apprehension in the troubled mind of Biard. He contented himself with requiring that the two priests should remain hidden while the ship lay off the port. Biard does not say that he enforced the demand either by threats or by the imposition of oaths. He and his companion, however, rigidly complied with it, lying close in the hold or under the boats, while suspicious officials searched the ship,—a proof, he triumphantly declares, of the audacious malice which has asserted it as a tenet of Rome that no faith need be kept with heretics.

Once more at sea, Turnel shaped his course for home, having, with some difficulty, gained a supply of water and pro-

[1] ". . . . il avoit faict estat de le priser et l'aymer pour sa naïfue simplicité et ouuerte candeur." *Ibid.*, c. 30.

[2] ". . . . il aimoit mieux croire que le Iesuite fust menteur que non pas tant d'autres qui l'accusoyent." *Ibid.*

[3] "Ce souci nous inquiétait fort. Qu'allaient-ils faire? Nous jetteraient-ils à l'eau?" *Lettre du P. Biard au T.R.P. Claude Aquaviva, Amiens, 26 Mai, 1614*, in Carayon, 106. Like all Biard's letters to Aquaviva, this is translated from the original Latin.

visions at Fayal. All was now harmony between him and his prisoners. When he reached Pembroke, in Wales, the appearance of the vessel—a French craft in English hands—again drew upon him the suspicion of piracy. The Jesuits, dangerous witnesses among the Catholics of Fayal, could at the worst do little harm with the Vice-Admiral at Pembroke. To him, therefore, he led the prisoners, in the sable garb of their order, now much the worse for wear, and commended them as persons without reproach, "wherein," adds the modest father, "he spoke the truth."[1] The result of their evidence was, we are told, that Turnel was henceforth treated, not as a pirate, but, according to his deserts, as an honorable gentleman. This interview led to a meeting with certain dignitaries of the Anglican Church, who, much interested in an encounter with Jesuits in their robes, were filled, says Biard, with wonder and admiration at what they were told of their conduct.[2] He explains that these churchmen differ widely in form and doctrine from the English Calvinists, who, he says, are called Puritans; and he adds, that they are superior in every respect to these, whom they detest as an execrable pest.[3]

Biard was sent to Dover and thence to Calais, returning, perhaps, to the tranquil honors of his chair of theology at Lyons. La Saussaye, La Motte, Fleury, and other prisoners, were, at various times, sent from Virginia to England, and ultimately to France. Madame de Guercheville, her pious designs crushed in the bud, seems to have gained no further satisfaction than the restoration of the vessel. The French ambassador complained of the outrage, but answer was postponed; and, in the troubled state of France, the matter appears to have been dropped.[4]

Argall, whose violent and crafty character was offset by a gallant bearing and various traits of martial virtue, became Deputy-Governor of Virginia, and, under a military code,

---

[1] ". . . . gens irreprochables, ce disoit-il, et disoit vray." Biard, *Relation*, c. 32.

[2] ". . . . et les ministres en demonstroyent grands signes estonnement et d'admiration." *Ibid.*, c. 31.

[3] ". . . . et les detestent comme peste execrable." *Ibid.*, c. 32.

[4] *Order of Council respecting certain claims against Capt. Argall*, etc. *Answer to the preceding Order*. See *Colonial Documents of New York*, III. 1, 2.

ruled the colony with a rod of iron. He enforced the observance of Sunday with an edifying rigor. Those who absented themselves from church were, for the first offence, imprisoned for the night, and reduced to slavery for a week; for the second offence, enslaved a month; and for the third, a year. Nor was he less strenuous in his devotion to mammon. He enriched himself by extortion and wholesale peculation, and his audacious dexterity, aided by the countenance of the Earl of Warwick, who is said to have had a trading connection with him, thwarted all the efforts of the company to bring him to account. In 1623, he was knighted by the hand of King James.[1]

Early in the spring following the English attack, Poutrincourt came to Port Royal. He found the place in ashes, and his unfortunate son, with the men under his command, wandering houseless in the forests. They had passed a winter of extreme misery, sustaining their wretched existence with roots, the buds of trees, and lichens peeled from the rocks.

Despairing of his enterprise, Poutrincourt returned to France. In the next year, 1615, during the civil disturbances which followed the marriage of the King, command was given him of the royal forces destined for the attack on Méry; and here, happier in his death than in his life, he fell, sword in hand.[2]

In spite of their reverses, the French kept hold on Acadia.[3] Biencourt, partially at least, rebuilt Port Royal; while winter after winter the smoke of fur-traders' huts curled into the still, sharp air of these frosty wilds, till at length, with happier auspices, plans of settlement were resumed.[4]

---

[1] Argall's history may be gleaned from Purchas, Smith, Stith, Gorges, Beverly, etc. An excellent summary will be found in Belknap's *American Biography*, and a briefer one in Allen's.

[2] *Nobilissimi Herois Potrincurtii Epitaphium*, Lescarbot, (1618,) 694. He took the town, but was killed immediately after by a treacherous shot, in the fifty-eighth year of his age. He was buried on his barony of St. Just.

[3] According to Biard, more than five hundred French vessels sailed annually, at this time, to America, for the whale and cod fishery and the fur-trade.

[4] There is an autograph letter in the Archives de la Marine from Biencourt,—who had succeeded to his father's designation,—written at Port Royal in September, 1618, and addressed "aux Autorités de la Ville de Paris," in which he urges upon them the advantages of establishing fortified posts in

Rude hands strangled the "Northern Paraguay" in its birth. Its beginnings had been feeble, but behind were the forces of a mighty organization, at once devoted and ambitious, enthusiastic and calculating. Seven years later the Mayflower landed her emigrants at Plymouth. What would have been the issues had the zeal of the pious lady of honor preoccupied New England with a Jesuit colony?

In an obscure stroke of lawless violence began the strife of France and England, Protestantism and Rome, which for a century and a half shook the struggling communities of North America, and closed at last in the memorable triumph on the Plains of Abraham.

Acadia, thus defending it against incursions of the English, who had lately seized a French trader from Dieppe, and insuring the continuance and increase of the traffic in furs, from which the city of Paris derived such advantages. Moreover, he adds, it will serve as an asylum for the indigent and suffering of the city, to their own great benefit and the advantage of the municipality, who will be relieved of the burden of their maintenance. It does not appear that the city responded to his appeal.

Chapter IX

1608, 1609

CHAMPLAIN AT QUEBEC

A New Enterprise • The St. Lawrence • Conflict with Basques • Tadoussac • Quebec founded • Conspiracy • Winter • The Montagnais • Spring • Projects of Exploration

---

A LONELY ship sailed up the St. Lawrence. The white whales floundering in the Bay of Tadoussac, and the wild duck diving as the foaming prow drew near,—there was no life but these in all that watery solitude, twenty miles from shore to shore. The ship was from Honfleur, and was commanded by Samuel de Champlain. He was the Æneas of a destined people, and in her womb lay the embryo life of Canada.

De Monts, after his exclusive privilege of trade was revoked, and his Acadian enterprise ruined, had, as we have seen, abandoned it to Poutrincourt. Perhaps would it have been well for him had he abandoned with it all Transatlantic enterprises; but the passion for discovery and the noble ambition of founding colonies had taken possession of his mind. These, rather than a mere hope of gain, seem to have been his controlling motives; yet the profits of the fur-trade were vital to the new designs he was meditating, to meet the heavy outlay they demanded; and he solicited and obtained a fresh monopoly of the traffic for one year.[1]

Champlain was, at the time, in Paris; but his unquiet thoughts turned westward. He was enamored of the New World, whose rugged charms had seized his fancy and his heart; and as explorers of Arctic seas have pined in their repose for polar ice and snow, so did his restless thoughts revert to the fog-wrapped coasts, the piny odors of forests, the noise of waters, the sharp and piercing sunlight, so dear to his remembrance. He longed to unveil the mystery of that boundless wilderness, and plant the Catholic faith and the power of France amid its ancient barbarism.

[1] See the patent in Champlain, (1613,) 163.

Five years before, he had explored the St. Lawrence as far as the rapids above Montreal. On its banks, as he thought, was the true site for a settlement,—a fortified post, whence, as from a secure basis, the waters of the vast interior might be traced back towards their sources, and a western route discovered to China and Japan. For the fur-trade, too, the innumerable streams that descended to the great river might all be closed against foreign intrusion by a single fort at some commanding point, and made tributary to a rich and permanent commerce; while—and this was nearer to his heart, for he had often been heard to say that the saving of a soul was worth more than the conquest of an empire—countless savage tribes, in the bondage of Satan, might by the same avenues be reached and redeemed.

De Monts embraced his views; and, fitting out two ships, gave command of one to the elder Pontgravé, of the other to Champlain. The former was to trade with the Indians and bring back the cargo of furs which, it was hoped, would meet the expense of the voyage. To Champlain fell the harder task of settlement and exploration.

Pontgravé, laden with goods for the Indian trade of Tadoussac, sailed from Honfleur on the fifth of April, 1608. Champlain, with men, arms, and stores for the colony, followed, eight days later. On the fifteenth of May he was on the Grand Bank; on the thirtieth he passed Gaspé, and on the third of June neared Tadoussac. No living thing was to be seen. He anchored, lowered a boat, and rowed into the port, round the rocky point at the southeast, then, from the fury of its winds and currents, called La Pointe de Tous les Diables.[1] There was life enough within, and more than he cared to find. In the still anchorage under the cliffs lay Pontgravé's vessel, and at her side another ship, which proved to be a Basque fur-trader.

Pontgravé, arriving a few days before, had found himself anticipated by the Basques, who were busied in a brisk trade with bands of Indians cabined along the borders of the cove. He displayed the royal letters, and commanded a cessation of the prohibited traffic; but the Basques proved refractory, de-

[1] Champlain, (1613,) 166. Also called La Pointe aux Rochers. Ibid., (1632,) 119.

clared that they would trade in spite of the King, fired on Pontgravé with cannon and musketry, wounded him and two of his men, and killed a third. They then boarded his vessel, and carried away all his cannon, small arms, and ammunition, saying that they would restore them when they had finished their trade and were ready to return home.

Champlain found his comrade on shore, in a disabled condition. The Basques, though still strong enough to make fight, were alarmed for the consequences of their conduct, and anxious to come to terms. A peace, therefore, was signed on board their vessel; all differences were referred to the judgment of the French courts, harmony was restored, and the choleric strangers betook themselves to catching whales.

This port of Tadoussac was long the centre of the Canadian fur-trade. A desolation of barren mountains closes round it, betwixt whose ribs of rugged granite, bristling with savins, birches, and firs, the Saguenay rolls its gloomy waters from the northern wilderness. Centuries of civilization have not tamed the wildness of the place; and still, in grim repose, the mountains hold their guard around the waveless lake that glistens in their shadow, and doubles, in its sullen mirror, crag, precipice, and forest.

Near the brink of the cove or harbor where the vessels lay, and a little below the mouth of a brook which formed one of the outlets of this small lake, stood the remains of the wooden barrack built by Chauvin eight years before. Above the brook were the lodges of an Indian camp,[1] — stacks of poles covered with birch-bark. They belonged to an Algonquin horde, called *Montagnais*, denizens of surrounding wilds, and gatherers of their only harvest, — skins of the moose, caribou, and bear; fur of the beaver, marten, otter, fox, wild-cat, and lynx. Nor was this all, for they were intermediate traders betwixt the French and the shivering bands who roamed the weary stretch of stunted forest between the head-waters of the Saguenay and Hudson's Bay. Indefatigable canoe-men, in their birchen vessels, light as egg-shells, they threaded the devious tracks of countless rippling streams, shady by-ways of the forest, where the wild duck scarcely finds depth to swim; then

[1] *Plan du Port de Tadoussac*, Champlain, (1613,) 172.

descended to their mart along those scenes of picturesque yet dreary grandeur which steam has made familiar to modern tourists. With slowly moving paddles, they glided beneath the cliff whose shaggy brows frown across the zenith, and whose base the deep waves wash with a hoarse and hollow cadence; and they passed the sepulchral Bay of the Trinity, dark as the tide of Acheron,—a sanctuary of solitude and silence: depths which, as the fable runs, no sounding line can fathom, and heights at whose dizzy verge the wheeling eagle seems a speck.[1]

Peace being established with the Basques, and the wounded Pontgravé busied, as far as might be, in transferring to the hold of his ship the rich lading of the Indian canoes, Champlain spread his sails, and again held his course up the St. Lawrence. Far to the south, in sun and shadow, slumbered the woody mountains whence fell the countless springs of the St. John, behind tenantless shores, now white with glimmering villages,—La Chenaie, Granville, Kamouraska, St. Roche, St. Jean, Vincelot, Berthier. But on the north the jealous wilderness still asserts its sway, crowding to the river's verge its walls, domes, and towers of granite; and to this hour, its solitude is scarcely broken.

Above the point of the Island of Orleans, a constriction of the vast channel narrows it to less than a mile, with the green heights of Point Levi on one side, and on the other the cliffs of Quebec.[2] Here, a small stream, the St. Charles, enters the

---

[1] Bouchette estimates the height of these cliffs at eighteen hundred feet. They overhang the river and bay. The scene is one of the most remarkable on the continent.

[2] The origin of this name has been disputed, but there is no good ground to doubt its Indian origin, which is distinctly affirmed by Champlain and Lescarbot. Charlevoix, *Fastes Chronologiques* (1608), derives it from the Algonquin word *Quebeio*, or *Quelibec*, signifying a *narrowing* or *contracting* (*rétrécissement*). A half-breed Algonquin told Garneau that the word *Quebec*, or *Oaubec*, means a *strait*. The same writer was told by M. Malo, a missionary among the Micmacs, a branch of the Algonquins, that in their dialect the word *Kibec* had the same meaning. Martin says, "Les Algonquins l'appellent *Ouabec*, et les Micmacs *Kebèque*, c'est à dire, 'là où la rivière est fermée.'" Martin's *Bressani*, App., 326. The derivations given by La Potherie, Le Beau, and others, are purely fanciful. The circumstance of the word *Quebec* being found engraved on the ancient seal of Lord Suffolk (see Hawkins, *Picture of Quebec*) can only be regarded as a curious coincidence. In Cartier's times the

St. Lawrence, and in the angle betwixt them rises the promontory, on two sides a natural fortress. Between the cliffs and
the river lay a strand covered with walnuts and other trees.
From this strand, by a rough passage gullied downward from
the place where Prescott Gate now guards the way, one might
climb the heights to the broken plateau above, now burdened
with its ponderous load of churches, convents, dwellings,
ramparts, and batteries. Thence, by a gradual ascent, the rock
sloped upward to its highest summit, Cape Diamond,[1] looking down on the St. Lawrence from a height of three
hundred and fifty feet. Here the citadel now stands; then the
fierce sun fell on the bald, baking rock, with its crisped
mosses and parched lichens. Two centuries and a half have
quickened the solitude with swarming life, covered the deep
bosom of the river with barge and steamer and gliding sail,
and reared cities and villages on the site of forests; but nothing can destroy the surpassing grandeur of the scene.

On the strand between the water and the cliffs Champlain's
axemen fell to their work. They were pioneers of an advancing
host,—advancing, it is true, with feeble and uncertain progress:
priests, soldiers, peasants, feudal scutcheons, royal insignia. Not
the Middle Age, but engendered of it by the stronger life of
modern centralization; sharply stamped with a parental likeness; heir to parental weakness and parental force.

In a few weeks a pile of wooden buildings rose on the
brink of the St. Lawrence, on or near the site of the market-
place of the Lower Town of Quebec.[2] The pencil of Champlain, always regardless of proportion and perspective, has
preserved its likeness. A strong wooden wall, surmounted by
a gallery loopholed for musketry, enclosed three buildings,
containing quarters for himself and his men, together with a
courtyard, from one side of which rose a tall dove-cot, like a

---

site of Quebec was occupied by a tribe of the Iroquois race, who called their
village *Stadaconé*. The Hurons called it, says Sagard, *Atou-ta-requee*. In the
modern Huron dialect, *Tiatou-ta-riti* means *the narrows*.

[1] Champlain calls Cape Diamond Mont du Gas (Guast), from the family
name of De Monts. He gives the name of Cape Diamond to Pointe à Puiseaux. See Map of Quebec (1613).

[2] Compare Faribault, *Voyages de Découverte au Canada*, 105.

belfry. A moat surrounded the whole, and two or three small
cannon were planted on salient platforms towards the river.
There was a large storehouse near at hand, and a part of the
adjacent ground was laid out as a garden.

In this garden Champlain was one morning directing his
laborers, when Têtu, his pilot, approached him with an anxious countenance, and muttered a request to speak with
him in private. Champlain assenting, they withdrew to the
neighboring woods, when the pilot disburdened himself of
his secret. One Antoine Natel, a locksmith, smitten by conscience or fear, had revealed to him a conspiracy to murder
his commander and deliver Quebec into the hands of the
Basques and Spaniards then at Tadoussac. Another locksmith, named Duval, was author of the plot, and, with the
aid of three accomplices, had befooled or frightened nearly
all the company into taking part in it. Each was assured
that he should make his fortune, and all were mutually
pledged to poniard the first betrayer of the secret. The critical point of their enterprise was the killing of Champlain.
Some were for strangling him, some for raising a false
alarm in the night and shooting him as he came out from his
quarters.

Having heard the pilot's story, Champlain, remaining in
the woods, desired his informant to find Antoine Natel, and
bring him to the spot. Natel soon appeared, trembling with
excitement and fear, and a close examination left no doubt of
the truth of his statement. A small vessel, built by Pontgravé
at Tadoussac, had lately arrived, and orders were now given
that it should anchor close at hand. On board was a young
man in whom confidence could be placed. Champlain sent
him two bottles of wine, with a direction to tell the four ringleaders that they had been given him by his Basque friends at
Tadoussac, and to invite them to share the good cheer. They
came aboard in the evening, and were seized and secured.
"Voyla donc mes galants bien estonnez," writes Champlain.

It was ten o'clock, and most of the men on shore were
asleep. They were wakened suddenly, and told of the discovery of the plot and the arrest of the ringleaders. Pardon was
then promised them, and they were dismissed again to their
beds, greatly relieved, for they had lived in trepidation, each

fearing the other. Duval's body, swinging from a gibbet, gave wholesome warning to those he had seduced; and his head was displayed on a pike, from the highest roof of the buildings, food for birds, and a lesson to sedition. His three accomplices were carried by Pontgravé to France, where they made their atonement in the galleys.[1]

It was on the eighteenth of September that Pontgravé set sail, leaving Champlain with twenty-eight men to hold Quebec through the winter. Three weeks later, and shores and hills glowed with gay prognostics of approaching desolation,—the yellow and scarlet of the maples, the deep purple of the ash, the garnet hue of young oaks, the crimson of the tupelo at the water's edge, and the golden plumage of birch saplings in the fissures of the cliff. It was a short-lived beauty. The forest dropped its festal robes. Shrivelled and faded, they rustled to the earth. The crystal air and laughing sun of October passed away, and November sank upon the shivering waste, chill and sombre as the tomb.

A roving band of Montagnais had built their huts near the buildings, and were busying themselves with their autumn eel-fishery, on which they greatly relied to sustain their miserable lives through the winter. Their slimy harvest being gathered, and duly smoked and dried, they gave it for safe-keeping to Champlain, and set out to hunt beavers. It was deep in the winter before they came back, reclaimed their eels, built their birch cabins again, and disposed themselves for a life of ease, until famine or their enemies should put an end to their enjoyments. These were by no means without alloy. While, gorged with food, they lay dozing on piles of branches in their smoky huts, where, through the crevices of the thin birch-bark, streamed in a cold capable at times of congealing mercury, their slumbers were beset with nightmare visions of Iroquois forays, scalpings, butcherings, and burnings. As dreams were their oracles, the camp was wild with fright. They sent out no scouts and placed no guard; but, with each repetition of these nocturnal terrors, they came flocking in a body to beg admission within the fort. The women and children were allowed to enter the yard and remain during the

[1] Lescarbot, (1612), 623; Purchas, IV. 1642.

night, while anxious fathers and jealous husbands shivered in the darkness without.

On one occasion, a group of wretched beings was seen on the farther bank of the St. Lawrence, like wild animals driven by famine to the borders of the settler's clearing. The river was full of drifting ice, and there was no crossing without risk of life. The Indians, in their desperation, made the attempt; and midway their canoes were ground to atoms among the tossing masses. Agile as wild-cats, they all leaped upon a huge raft of ice, the squaws carrying their children on their shoulders, a feat at which Champlain marvelled when he saw their starved and emaciated condition. Here they began a wail of despair; when happily the pressure of other masses thrust the sheet of ice against the northern shore. They landed and soon made their appearance at the fort, worn to skeletons and horrible to look upon. The French gave them food, which they devoured with a frenzied avidity, and, unappeased, fell upon a dead dog left on the snow by Champlain for two months past as a bait for foxes. They broke this carrion into fragments, and thawed and devoured it, to the disgust of the spectators, who tried vainly to prevent them.

This was but a severe access of the periodical famine which, during winter, was a normal condition of the Algonquin tribes of Acadia and the Lower St. Lawrence, who, unlike the cognate tribes of New England, never tilled the soil, or made any reasonable provision against the time of need.

One would gladly know how the founders of Quebec spent the long hours of their first winter; but on this point the only man among them, perhaps, who could write, has not thought it necessary to enlarge. He himself beguiled his leisure with trapping foxes, or hanging a dead dog from a tree and watching the hungry martens in their efforts to reach it. Towards the close of winter, all found abundant employment in nursing themselves or their neighbors, for the inevitable scurvy broke out with virulence. At the middle of May, only eight men of the twenty-eight were alive, and of these half were suffering from disease.[1]

[1] Champlain, (1613,) 205.

This wintry purgatory wore away; the icy stalactites that hung from the cliffs fell crashing to the earth; the clamor of the wild geese was heard; the bluebirds appeared in the naked woods; the water-willows were covered with their soft caterpillar-like blossoms; the twigs of the swamp-maple were flushed with ruddy bloom; the ash hung out its black tufts; the shad-bush seemed a wreath of snow; the white stars of the bloodroot gleamed among dank, fallen leaves; and in the young grass of the wet meadows, the marsh-marigolds shone like spots of gold.

Great was the joy of Champlain when, on the fifth of June, he saw a sailboat rounding the Point of Orleans, betokening that the spring had brought with it the longed for succors. A son-in-law of Pontgravé, named Marais, was on board, and he reported that Pontgravé was then at Tadoussac, where he had lately arrived. Thither Champlain hastened, to take counsel with his comrade. His constitution or his courage had defied the scurvy. They met, and it was determined betwixt them, that, while Pontgravé remained in charge of Quebec, Champlain should enter at once on his long-meditated explorations, by which, like La Salle seventy years later, he had good hope of finding a way to China.

But there was a lion in the path. The Indian tribes, to whom peace was unknown, infested with their scalping parties the streams and pathways of the forest, and increased tenfold its inseparable risks. The after career of Champlain gives abundant proof that he was more than indifferent to all such chances; yet now an expedient for evading them offered itself, so consonant with his instincts that he was glad to accept it.

During the last autumn, a young chief from the banks of the then unknown Ottawa had been at Quebec; and, amazed at what he saw, he had begged Champlain to join him in the spring against his enemies. These enemies were a formidable race of savages, the Iroquois, or Five Confederate Nations, who dwelt in fortified villages within limits now embraced by the State of New York, and who were a terror to all the surrounding forests. They were deadly foes of their kindred, the Hurons, who dwelt on the lake which bears their name, and were allies of Algonquin bands on the Ottawa. All alike were

tillers of the soil, living at ease when compared with the famished Algonquins of the Lower St. Lawrence.[1]

By joining these Hurons and Algonquins against their Iroquois enemies, Champlain might make himself the indispensable ally and leader of the tribes of Canada, and at the same
time fight his way to discovery in regions which otherwise
were barred against him. From first to last, it was the policy
of France in America to mingle in Indian politics, hold the
balance of power between adverse tribes, and envelop in the
network of her power and diplomacy the remotest hordes of
the wilderness. Of this policy the Father of New France may
perhaps be held to have set a rash and premature example.
Yet, while he was apparently following the dictates of his own
adventurous spirit, it became evident, a few years later, that
under his thirst for discovery and spirit of knight-errantry lay
a consistent and deliberate purpose. That it had already assumed a definite shape is not likely; but his after course makes
it plain that, in embroiling himself and his colony with the
most formidable savages on the continent, he was by no
means acting so recklessly as at first sight would appear.

[1] The tribes east of the Mississippi, between the latitudes of Lake Superior
and of the Ohio, were divided, with slight exceptions, into two groups or
families, distinguished by a radical difference of language. One of these families of tribes is called *Algonquin*, from the name of a small Indian community
on the Ottawa. The other is called the *Huron-Iroquois*, from the names of its
two principal members.

Chapter X

1609

LAKE CHAMPLAIN

Champlain joins a War Party • Preparation • Departure • The River Richelieu • The Spirits consulted • Discovery of Lake Champlain • Battle with the Iroquois • Fate of Prisoners • Panic of the Victors

---

IT was past the middle of June, and the expected warriors from the upper country had not come: a delay which seems to have given Champlain little concern, for, without waiting longer, he set out with no better allies than a band of Montagnais. But, as he moved up the St. Lawrence, he saw, thickly clustered in the bordering forest, the lodges of an Indian camp, and, landing, found his Huron and Algonquin allies. Few of them had ever seen a white man, and they surrounded the steel-clad strangers in speechless wonder. Champlain asked for their chief, and the staring throng moved with him towards a lodge where sat, not one chief, but two, for each band had its own. There were feasting, smoking, and speeches; and, the needful ceremony over, all descended together to Quebec; for the strangers were bent on seeing those wonders of architecture, the fame of which had pierced the recesses of their forests.

On their arrival, they feasted their eyes and glutted their appetites; yelped consternation at the sharp explosions of the arquebuse and the roar of the cannon; pitched their camps, and bedecked themselves for their war-dance. In the still night, their fire glared against the black and jagged cliff, and the fierce red light fell on tawny limbs convulsed with frenzied gestures and ferocious stampings; on contorted visages, hideous with paint; on brandished weapons, stone war-clubs, stone hatchets, and stone-pointed lances; while the drum kept up its hollow boom, and the air was split with mingled yells.

The war-feast followed, and then all embarked together. Champlain was in a small shallop, carrying besides himself, eleven men of Pontgravé's party, including his son-in-law, Marais, and the pilot La Routte. They were armed with the arquebuse, a matchlock or firelock somewhat like the modern carbine, and from its shortness not ill suited for use in the forest. On the twenty-eighth of June[1] they spread their sails and held their course against the current, while around them the river was alive with canoes, and hundreds of naked arms plied the paddle with a steady, measured sweep. They crossed the Lake of St. Peter, threaded the devious channels among its many islands, and reached at last the mouth of the Rivière des Iroquois, since called the Richelieu, or the St. John.[2] Here, probably on the site of the town of Sorel, the leisurely warriors encamped for two days, hunted, fished, and took their ease, regaling their allies with venison and wild-fowl. They quarrelled, too; three fourths of their number seceded, took to their canoes in dudgeon, and paddled towards their homes, while the rest pursued their course up the broad and placid stream.

Walls of verdure stretched on left and right. Now, aloft in the lonely air rose the cliffs of Belœil, and now, before them, framed in circling forests, the Basin of Chambly spread its tranquil mirror, glittering in the sun. The shallop outsailed the canoes. Champlain, leaving his allies behind, crossed the basin and tried to pursue his course; but, as he listened in the stillness, the unwelcome noise of rapids reached his ear, and, by glimpses through the dark foliage of the Islets of St. John, he could see the gleam of snowy foam and the flash of hurrying waters. Leaving the boat by the shore in charge of four men, he went with Marais, La Routte, and five others, to explore the wild before him. They pushed their way through the damps and shadows of the wood, through thickets and tangled vines, over mossy rocks and mouldering logs. Still the hoarse surging of the rapids followed them; and when, parting the screen of foliage, they looked out upon the river, they saw it thick set with rocks, where, plunging over ledges, gurgling under drift-logs, darting along clefts, and boiling in chasms, the angry waters filled the solitude with monotonous ravings.[3]

Champlain retraced his steps. He had learned the value of

[1] Champlain's dates, in this part of his narrative, are exceedingly careless and confused, May and June being mixed indiscriminately.

[2] Also called the Chambly, the St. Louis, and the Sorel.

[3] In spite of the changes of civilization, the tourist, with Champlain's journal in his hand, can easily trace each stage of his progress.

an Indian's word. His allies had promised him that his boat could pass unobstructed throughout the whole journey. "It afflicted me," he says, "and troubled me exceedingly to be obliged to return without having seen so great a lake, full of fair islands and bordered with the fine countries which they had described to me."

When he reached the boat, he found the whole savage crew gathered at the spot. He mildly rebuked their bad faith, but added, that, though they had deceived him, he, as far as might be, would fulfil his pledge. To this end, he directed Marais, with the boat and the greater part of the men, to return to Quebec, while he, with two who offered to follow him, should proceed in the Indian canoes.

The warriors lifted their canoes from the water, and bore them on their shoulders half a league through the forest to the smoother stream above. Here the chiefs made a muster of their forces, counting twenty-four canoes and sixty warriors. All embarked again, and advanced once more, by marsh, meadow, forest, and scattered islands, then full of game, for it was an uninhabited land, the war-path and battle-ground of hostile tribes. The warriors observed a certain system in their advance. Some were in front as a vanguard; others formed the main body; while an equal number were in the forests on the flanks and rear, hunting for the subsistence of the whole; for, though they had a provision of parched maize pounded into meal, they kept it for use when, from the vicinity of the enemy, hunting should become impossible.

Late in the day they landed and drew up their canoes, ranging them closely, side by side. Some stripped sheets of bark, to cover their camp sheds; others gathered wood, the forest being full of dead, dry trees; others felled the living trees, for a barricade. They seem to have had steel axes, obtained by barter from the French; for in less than two hours they had made a strong defensive work, in the form of a half-circle, open on the river side, where their canoes lay on the strand, and large enough to enclose all their huts and sheds.[1] Some of their number had gone forward as

---

[1] Such extempore works of defence are still used among some tribes of the remote West. The author has twice seen them, made of trees piled together

scouts, and, returning, reported no signs of an enemy. This was the extent of their precaution, for they placed no guard, but all, in full security, stretched themselves to sleep,—a vicious custom from which the lazy warrior of the forest rarely departs.

They had not forgotten, however, to consult their oracle. The medicine-man pitched his magic lodge in the woods, formed of a small stack of poles, planted in a circle and brought together at the tops like stacked muskets. Over these he placed the filthy deer-skins which served him for a robe, and, creeping in at a narrow opening, hid himself from view. Crouched in a ball upon the earth, he invoked the spirits in mumbling inarticulate tones; while his naked auditory, squatted on the ground like apes, listened in wonder and awe. Suddenly, the lodge moved, rocking with violence to and fro, by the power of the spirits, as the Indians thought, while Champlain could plainly see the tawny fist of the medicine-man shaking the poles. They begged him to keep a watchful eye on the peak of the lodge, whence fire and smoke would presently issue; but with the best efforts of his vision, he discovered none. Meanwhile the medicine-man was seized with such convulsions, that, when his divination was over, his naked body streamed with perspiration. In loud, clear tones, and in an unknown tongue, he invoked the spirit, who was understood to be present in the form of a stone, and whose feeble and squeaking accents were heard at intervals, like the wail of a young puppy.[1]

In this manner they consulted the spirit—as Champlain thinks, the Devil—at all their camps. His replies, for the most

---

as described by Champlain, probably by war parties of the Crow or Snake Indians.

Champlain, usually too concise, is very minute in his description of the march and encampment.

[1] This mode of divination was universal among the Algonquin tribes, and is not extinct to this day among their roving Northern bands. Le Jeune, Lafitau, and other early Jesuit writers, describe it with great minuteness. The former (*Relation*, 1634) speaks of an audacious conjurer, who, having invoked the Manitou, or spirit, killed him with a hatchet. To all appearance he was a stone, which, however, when struck with the hatchet, proved to be full of flesh and blood. A kindred superstition prevails among the Crow Indians.

part, seem to have given them great content; yet they took other measures, of which the military advantages were less questionable. The principal chief gathered bundles of sticks, and, without wasting his breath, stuck them in the earth in a certain order, calling each by the name of some warrior, a few taller than the rest representing the subordinate chiefs. Thus was indicated the position which each was to hold in the expected battle. All gathered round and attentively studied the sticks, ranged like a child's wooden soldiers, or the pieces on a chessboard; then, with no further instruction, they formed their ranks, broke them, and reformed them again and again with excellent alacrity and skill.

Again the canoes advanced, the river widening as they went. Great islands appeared, leagues in extent,—Isle à la Motte, Long Island, Grande Isle. Channels where ships might float and broad reaches of water stretched between them, and Champlain entered the lake which preserves his name to posterity. Cumberland Head was passed, and from the opening of the great channel between Grande Isle and the main he could look forth on the wilderness sea. Edged with woods, the tranquil flood spread southward beyond the sight. Far on the left rose the forest ridges of the Green Mountains, and on the right the Adirondacks, haunts in these later years of amateur sportsmen from counting-rooms or college halls. Then the Iroquois made them their hunting-ground; and beyond, in the valleys of the Mohawk, the Onondaga, and the Genesee, stretched the long line of their five cantons and palisaded towns.

At night they encamped again. The scene is a familiar one to many a tourist; and perhaps, standing at sunset on the peaceful strand, Champlain saw what a roving student of this generation has seen on those same shores, at that same hour: the glow of the vanished sun behind the western mountains, darkly piled in mist and shadow along the sky; near at hand, the dead pine, mighty in decay, stretching its ragged arms athwart the burning heaven, the crow perched on its top like an image carved in jet; and aloft, the nighthawk, circling in his flight, and, with a strange whirring sound, diving through the air each moment for the insects he makes his prey.

The progress of the party was becoming dangerous. They

changed their mode of advance, and moved only in the night. All day, they lay close in the depth of the forest, sleeping, lounging, smoking tobacco of their own raising, and beguiling the hours, no doubt, with the shallow banter and obscene jesting with which knots of Indians are wont to amuse their leisure. At twilight they embarked again, paddling their cautious way till the eastern sky began to redden. Their goal was the rocky promontory where Fort Ticonderoga was long afterward built. Thence, they would pass the outlet of Lake George, and launch their canoes again on that Como of the wilderness, whose waters, limpid as a fountain-head, stretched far southward between their flanking mountains. Landing at the future site of Fort William Henry, they would carry their canoes through the forest to the river Hudson, and, descending it, attack perhaps some outlying town of the Mohawks. In the next century this chain of lakes and rivers became the grand highway of savage and civilized war, linked to memories of momentous conflicts.

The allies were spared so long a progress. On the morning of the twenty-ninth of July, after paddling all night, they hid as usual in the forest on the western shore, apparently between Crown Point and Ticonderoga. The warriors stretched themselves to their slumbers, and Champlain, after walking till nine or ten o'clock through the surrounding woods, returned to take his repose on a pile of spruce-boughs. Sleeping, he dreamed a dream, wherein he beheld the Iroquois drowning in the lake; and, trying to rescue them, he was told by his Algonquin friends that they were good for nothing, and had better be left to their fate. For some time past he had been beset every morning by his superstitious allies, eager to learn about his dreams; and, to this moment, his unbroken slumbers had failed to furnish the desired prognostics. The announcement of this auspicious vision filled the crowd with joy, and at nightfall they embarked, flushed with anticipated victories.[1]

[1] The power of dreams among Indians in their primitive condition can scarcely be over-estimated. Among the ancient Hurons and cognate tribes, they were the universal authority and oracle; but while a dreamer of reputation had unlimited power, the dream of a *vaurien* was held in no account. There were professed interpreters of dreams. Brébeuf, *Rel. des Hurons*, 117. A

It was ten o'clock in the evening, when, near a projecting point of land, which was probably Ticonderoga, they descried dark objects in motion on the lake before them. These were a flotilla of Iroquois canoes, heavier and slower than theirs, for they were made of oak bark.[1] Each party saw the other, and the mingled war-cries pealed over the darkened water. The Iroquois, who were near the shore, having no stomach for an aquatic battle, landed, and, making night hideous with their clamors, began to barricade themselves. Champlain could see them in the woods, laboring like beavers, hacking down trees with iron axes taken from the Canadian tribes in war, and with stone hatchets of their own making. The allies remained on the lake, a bowshot from the hostile barricade, their canoes made fast together by poles lashed across. All night they danced with as much vigor as the frailty of their vessels would permit, their throats making amends for the enforced restraint of their limbs. It was agreed on both sides that the fight should be deferred till daybreak; but meanwhile a commerce of abuse, sarcasm, menace, and boasting gave unceasing exercise to the lungs and fancy of the combatants,—"much," says Champlain, "like the besiegers and besieged in a beleaguered town."

As day approached, he and his two followers put on the light armor of the time. Champlain wore the doublet and long hose then in vogue. Over the doublet he buckled on a breastplate, and probably a back-piece, while his thighs were protected by cuisses of steel, and his head by a plumed casque. Across his shoulder hung the strap of his bandoleer, or ammunition-box; at his side was his sword, and in his

---

man, dreaming that he had killed his wife, made it an excuse for killing her in fact. All these tribes, including the Iroquois, had a stated game called *Ononhara*, or the dreaming game, in which dreams were made the pretext for the wildest extravagances. See Lafitau, Charlevoix, Sagard, Brébeuf, etc.

[1] Champlain, (1613,) 232. Probably a mistake; the Iroquois canoes were usually of elm bark. The paper-birch was used wherever it could be had, being incomparably the best material. All the tribes, from the mouth of the Saco northward and eastward, and along the entire northern portion of the valley of the St. Lawrence and the Great Lakes, used the birch. The best substitutes were elm and spruce. The birch bark, from its laminated texture, could be peeled at any time; the others only when the sap was in motion.

hand his arquebuse.[1] Such was the equipment of this ancient Indian-fighter, whose exploits date eleven years before the landing of the Puritans at Plymouth, and sixty-six years before King Philip's War.

Each of the three Frenchmen was in a separate canoe, and, as it grew light, they kept themselves hidden, either by lying at the bottom, or covering themselves with an Indian robe. The canoes approached the shore, and all landed without opposition at some distance from the Iroquois, whom they presently could see filing out of their barricade, tall, strong men, some two hundred in number, the boldest and fiercest warriors of North America. They advanced through the forest with a steadiness which excited the admiration of Champlain. Among them could be seen three chiefs, made conspicuous by their tall plumes. Some bore shields of wood and hide, and some were covered with a kind of armor made of tough twigs interlaced with a vegetable fibre supposed by Champlain to be cotton.[2]

The allies, growing anxious, called with loud cries for their champion, and opened their ranks that he might pass to the front. He did so, and, advancing before his red companions in arms, stood revealed to the gaze of the Iroquois, who, beholding the warlike apparition in their path, stared in mute amazement. "I looked at them," says Champlain, "and they looked at me. When I saw them getting ready to shoot their arrows at us, I levelled my arquebuse, which I had loaded with four balls, and aimed straight at one of the three chiefs. The shot brought down two, and wounded another. On this, our Indians set up such a yelling that one could not have heard a thunder-clap, and all the while the arrows flew thick

[1] Champlain, in his rude drawing of the battle, (ed. 1613,) portrays himself and his equipment with sufficient distinctness. Compare plates of the weapons and armor of the period in Meyrick, *Ancient Armor*, and Susane, *Histoire de l'Ancienne Infanterie Française*.

[2] According to Lafitau, both bucklers and breastplates were in frequent use among the Iroquois. The former were very large and made of cedar wood covered with interwoven thongs of hide. The kindred nation of the Hurons, says Sagard (*Voyage des Hurons*, 126–206), carried large shields, and wore greaves for the legs and cuirasses made of twigs interwoven with cords. His account corresponds with that of Champlain, who gives a wood-cut of a warrior thus armed.

on both sides. The Iroquois were greatly astonished and frightened to see two of their men killed so quickly, in spite of their arrow-proof armor. As I was reloading, one of my companions fired a shot from the woods, which so increased their astonishment that, seeing their chiefs dead, they abandoned the field and fled into the depth of the forest." The allies dashed after them. Some of the Iroquois were killed, and more were taken. Camp, canoes, provisions, all were abandoned, and many weapons flung down in the panic flight. The victory was complete.

At night, the victors led out one of the prisoners, told him that he was to die by fire, and ordered him to sing his death-song, if he dared. Then they began the torture, and presently scalped their victim alive,[1] when Champlain, sickening at the sight, begged leave to shoot him. They refused, and he turned away in anger and disgust; on which they called him back and told him to do as he pleased. He turned again and a shot from his arquebuse put the wretch out of misery.

The scene filled him with horror; but, a few months later, on the Place de la Grève at Paris, he might have witnessed tortures equally revolting and equally vindictive, inflicted on the regicide Ravaillac by the sentence of grave and learned judges.

The allies made a prompt retreat from the scene of their triumph. Three or four days brought them to the mouth of the Richelieu. Here they separated; the Hurons and Algonquins made for the Ottawa, their homeward route, each with a share of prisoners for future torments. At parting they invited Champlain to visit their towns, and aid them again in their wars, an invitation which this paladin of the woods failed not to accept.

The companions now remaining to him were the Monta-

---

[1] It has been erroneously asserted that the practice of scalping did not prevail among the Indians before the advent of Europeans. In 1535, Cartier saw five scalps at Quebec, dried and stretched on hoops. In 1564, Laudonnière saw them among the Indians of Florida. The Algonquins of New England and Nova Scotia were accustomed to cut off and carry away the head, which they afterwards scalped. Those of Canada, it seems, sometimes scalped dead bodies on the field. The Algonquin practice of carrying off heads as trophies is mentioned by Lalemant, Roger Williams, Lescarbot, and Champlain. Compare *Historical Magazine*, First Series, V. 253.

gnais. In their camp on the Richelieu, one of them dreamed
that a war party of Iroquois was close upon them; on which,
in a torrent of rain, they left their huts, paddled in dismay to
the islands above the Lake of St. Peter, and hid themselves all
night in the rushes. In the morning, they took heart, emerged
from their hiding-places, descended to Quebec, and went
thence to Tadoussac, whither Champlain accompanied them.
Here the squaws, stark naked, swam out to the canoes to receive the heads of the dead Iroquois, and, hanging them from
their necks, danced in triumph along the shore. One of the
heads and a pair of arms were then bestowed on Champlain,—touching memorials of gratitude, which, however, he
was by no means to keep for himself, but to present to the
King.

Thus did New France rush into collision with the redoubted warriors of the Five Nations. Here was the beginning, and in some measure doubtless the cause, of a long suite
of murderous conflicts, bearing havoc and flame to generations yet unborn. Champlain had invaded the tiger's den; and
now, in smothered fury, the patient savage would lie biding
his day of blood.

Chapter XI

WAR — TRADE — DISCOVERY

Champlain at Fontainebleau • Champlain on the St. Lawrence •
Alarm • Battle • War Parties • Icebergs • Adventurers • Cham-
plain at Montreal • Return to France • The Comte de Soissons •
The Prince de Condé

CHAMPLAIN and Pontgravé returned to France, while Pierre Chauvin of Dieppe held Quebec in their absence. The King was at Fontainebleau, — it was a few months before his assassination, — and here Champlain recounted his adventures, to the great satisfaction of the lively monarch. He gave him also, not the head of the dead Iroquois, but a belt wrought in embroidery of dyed quills of the Canada porcupine, together with two small birds of scarlet plumage, and the skull of a garfish.

De Monts was at court, striving for a renewal of his monopoly. His efforts failed; on which, with great spirit but little discretion, he resolved to push his enterprise without it. Early in the spring of 1610, the ship was ready, and Champlain and Pontgravé were on board, when a violent illness seized the former, reducing him to the most miserable of all conflicts, the battle of the eager spirit against the treacherous and failing flesh. Having partially recovered, he put to sea, giddy and weak, in wretched plight for the hard career of toil and battle which the New World offered him. The voyage was prosperous, no other mishap occurring than that of an ardent youth of St. Malo, who drank the health of Pontgravé with such persistent enthusiasm that he fell overboard and was drowned.

There were ships at Tadoussac, fast loading with furs; and boats, too, higher up the river, anticipating the trade, and draining De Monts's resources in advance. Champlain, who was left free to fight and explore wherever he should see fit, had provided, to use his own phrase, "two strings to his bow." On the one hand, the Montagnais had promised to guide him northward to Hudson's Bay; on the other, the Hurons were to show him the Great Lakes, with the mines of copper on their shores; and to each the same reward was promised,—to join them against the common foe, the Iroquois. The rendezvous was at the mouth of the River Richelieu. Thither the Hurons were to descend in force, together with Algonquins of the Ottawa; and thither Champlain now repaired, while around his boat swarmed a multitude of Montagnais canoes, filled with warriors whose lank hair streamed loose in the wind.

There is an island in the St. Lawrence near the mouth of the Richelieu. On the nineteenth of June, it was swarming with busy and clamorous savages, Champlain's Montagnais allies, cutting down the trees and clearing the ground for a dance and a feast; for they were hourly expecting the Algonquin warriors, and were eager to welcome them with befitting honors. But suddenly, far out on the river, they saw an advancing canoe. Now on this side, now on that, the flashing paddles urged it forward as if death were on its track; and as it drew near, the Indians on board cried out that the Algonquins were in the forest, a league distant, engaged with a hundred warriors of the Iroquois, who, outnumbered, were fighting savagely within a barricade of trees.

The air was split with shrill outcries. The Montagnais snatched their weapons,—shields, bows, arrows, war-clubs, sword-blades made fast to poles,—and ran headlong to their canoes, impeding each other in their haste, screeching to Champlain to follow, and invoking with no less vehemence the aid of certain fur-traders, just arrived in four boats from below. These, as it was not their cue to fight, lent them a deaf ear; on which, in disgust and scorn, they paddled off, calling to the recusants that they were women, fit for nothing but to make war on beaver-skins.

Champlain and four of his men were in the canoes. They shot across the intervening water, and, as their prows grated on the pebbles, each warrior flung down his paddle, snatched his weapons, and ran into the woods. The five Frenchmen followed, striving vainly to keep pace with the naked, light-limbed rabble, bounding like shadows through the forest. They quickly disappeared. Even their shrill cries grew faint, till Champlain and his men, discomforted and vexed, found themselves deserted in the midst of a swamp. The day was sultry, the forest air heavy, close, and filled with hosts of mosquitoes, "so thick," says the chief sufferer, "that we could scarcely draw breath, and it was wonderful how cruelly they persecuted us."[1] Through black mud, spongy moss, water knee-deep, over fallen trees, among slimy logs and entangling roots, tripped by vines, lashed by recoiling boughs, panting under their steel head-pieces and heavy corselets, the Frenchmen struggled on, bewildered and indignant. At length they descried two Indians running in the distance, and shouted to them in desperation, that, if they wanted their aid, they must guide them to the enemy.

At length they could hear the yells of the combatants; there was light in the forest before them, and they issued into a partial clearing made by the Iroquois axemen near the river. Champlain saw their barricade. Trees were piled into a circular breastwork, trunks, boughs, and matted foliage forming a strong defence, within which the Iroquois stood savagely at bay. Around them flocked the allies, half hidden in the edges of the forest, like hounds around a wild boar, eager, clamorous, yet afraid to rush in. They had attacked, and had met a bloody rebuff. All their hope was now in the French; and when they saw them, a yell arose from hundreds of throats that outdid the wilderness voices whence its tones were borrowed,—the whoop of the horned owl, the scream of the cougar, the howl of starved wolves on a winter night. A fierce response pealed from the desperate band within; and amid a storm of arrows from both sides, the Frenchmen threw themselves into the fray, firing at random through the fence of trunks, boughs, and drooping leaves, with which the Iroquois had encircled themselves. Champlain felt a stone-headed arrow splitting his ear and tearing through the muscles of his neck. He drew it out, and, the moment after, did a similar office for one of his men. But the Iroquois had not recovered from their first terror at the arquebuse; and when the mysterious and terrible assailants, clad in steel and armed with

[1]". . . . quantité de mousquites, qui estoient si espoisses qu'elles ne nous permettoient point presque de reprendre nostre halaine, tant elles nous persécutoient, et si cruellement que c'estoit chose estrange." Champlain, (1613,) 250.

thunder-bolts, ran up to the barricade, thrust their pieces through the openings, and shot death among the crowd within, they could not control their fright, but with every report threw themselves flat on the ground. Animated with unwonted valor, the allies, covered by their large shields, began to drag out the felled trees of the barricade, while others, under Champlain's direction, gathered at the edge of the forest, preparing to close the affair with a final rush. New actors soon appeared on the scene. These were a boat's crew of the fur-traders under a young man of St. Malo, one Des Prairies, who, when he heard the firing, could not resist the impulse to join the fight. On seeing them, Champlain checked the assault, in order, as he says, that the new-comers might have their share in the sport. The traders opened fire, with great zest and no less execution; while the Iroquois, now wild with terror, leaped and writhed to dodge the shot which tore through their frail armor of twigs. Champlain gave the signal; the crowd ran to the barricade, dragged down the boughs or clambered over them, and bore themselves, in his own words, "so well and manfully," that, though scratched and torn by the sharp points, they quickly forced an entrance. The French ceased their fire, and, followed by a smaller body of Indians, scaled the barricade on the farther side. Now, amid howlings, shouts, and screeches, the work was finished. Some of the Iroquois were cut down as they stood, hewing with their war-clubs, and foaming like slaughtered tigers; some climbed the barrier and were killed by the furious crowd without; some were drowned in the river; while fifteen, the only survivors, were made prisoners. "By the grace of God," writes Champlain, "behold the battle won!" Drunk with ferocious ecstasy, the conquerors scalped the dead and gathered fagots for the living, while some of the fur-traders, too late to bear part in the fight, robbed the carcasses of their blood-bedrenched robes of beaver-skin, amid the derision of the surrounding Indians.[1]

That night, the torture fires blazed along the shore. Champlain saved one prisoner from their clutches, but nothing

[1] Champlain, (1613,) 254. This narrative, like most others, is much abridged in the edition of 1632.

could save the rest. One body was quartered and eaten.[1] "As for the rest of the prisoners," says Champlain, "they were kept to be put to death by the women and girls, who in this respect are no less inhuman than the men, and, indeed, much more so; for by their subtlety they invent more cruel tortures, and take pleasure in it."

On the next day, a large band of Hurons appeared at the rendezvous, greatly vexed that they had come too late. The shores were thickly studded with Indian huts, and the woods were full of them. Here were warriors of three designations, including many subordinate tribes, and representing three grades of savage society: the Hurons, the Algonquins of the Ottawa, and the Montagnais; afterwards styled by a Franciscan friar, than whom few men better knew them, the nobles, the burghers, and the peasantry and paupers of the forest.[2] Many of them, from the remote interior, had never before seen a white man; and, wrapped like statues in their robes, they stood gazing on the French with a fixed stare of wild and wondering eyes.

Judged by the standard of Indian war, a heavy blow had been struck on the common enemy. Here were hundreds of assembled warriors; yet none thought of following up their success. Elated with unexpected fortune, they danced and sang; then loaded their canoes, hung their scalps on poles, broke up their camps, and set out triumphant for their homes. Champlain had fought their battles, and now might claim, on their part, guidance and escort to the distant interior. Why he did not do so is scarcely apparent. There were cares, it seems, connected with the very life of his puny colony, which demanded his return to France. Nor were his anx-

[1] Traces of cannibalism may be found among most of the North American tribes, though they are rarely very conspicuous. Sometimes the practice arose, as in the present instance, from revenge or ferocity; sometimes it bore a religious character, as with the Miamis, among whom there existed a secret religious fraternity of man-eaters; sometimes the heart of a brave enemy was devoured in the idea that it made the eater brave. This last practice was common. The ferocious threat, used in speaking of an enemy, "I will eat his heart," is by no means a mere figure of speech. The roving hunter-tribes, in their winter wanderings, were not infrequently impelled to cannibalism by famine.

[2] Sagard, *Voyage des Hurons*, 184.

ieties lessened by the arrival of a ship from his native town of Brouage, with tidings of the King's assassination. Here was a death-blow to all that had remained of De Monts's credit at court; while that unfortunate nobleman, like his old associate, Poutrincourt, was moving with swift strides toward financial ruin. With the revocation of his monopoly, fur-traders had swarmed to the St. Lawrence. Tadoussac was full of them, and for that year the trade was spoiled. Far from aiding to support a burdensome enterprise of colonization, it was in itself an occasion of heavy loss.

Champlain bade farewell to his garden at Quebec, where maize, wheat, rye, and barley, with vegetables of all kinds, and a small vineyard of native grapes,—for he was a zealous horticulturist,[1]—held forth a promise which he was not to see fulfilled. He left one Du Parc in command, with sixteen men, and, sailing on the eighth of August, arrived at Honfleur with no worse accident than that of running over a sleeping whale near the Grand Bank.

With the opening spring he was afloat again. Perils awaited him worse than those of Iroquois tomahawks; for, approaching Newfoundland, the ship was entangled for days among drifting fields and bergs of ice. Escaping at length, she arrived at Tadoussac on the thirteenth of May, 1611. She had anticipated the spring. Forests and mountains, far and near, all were white with snow. A principal object with Champlain was to establish such relations with the great Indian communities of the interior as to secure to De Monts and his associates the advantage of trade with them; and to this end he now repaired to Montreal, a position in the gateway, as it were, of their yearly descents of trade or war. On arriving, he began to survey the ground for the site of a permanent post.

A few days convinced him, that, under the present system, all his efforts would be vain. Wild reports of the wonders of New France had gone abroad, and a crowd of hungry adventurers had hastened to the land of promise, eager to grow rich, they scarcely knew how, and soon to return disgusted. A fleet of boats and small vessels followed in Champlain's wake. Within a few days, thirteen of them arrived at Mon-

---

[1] During the next year, he planted roses around Quebec. Champlain, (1613,) 313.

treal, and more soon appeared. He was to break the ground; others would reap the harvest. Travel, discovery, and battle, all must inure to the profit, not of the colony, but of a crew of greedy traders.

Champlain, however, chose the site and cleared the ground for his intended post. It was immediately above a small stream, now running under arches of masonry, and entering the St. Lawrence at Point Callières, within the modern city. He called it Place Royale;[1] and here, on the margin of the river, he built a wall of bricks made on the spot, in order to measure the destructive effects of the "ice-shove" in the spring.

Now, down the surges of St. Louis, where the mighty floods of the St. Lawrence, contracted to a narrow throat, roll in fury among their sunken rocks,—here, through foam and spray and the roar of the angry torrent, a fleet of birch canoes came dancing like dry leaves on the froth of some riotous brook. They bore a band of Hurons, first at the rendezvous. As they drew near the landing, all the fur-traders' boats blazed out a clattering fusillade, which was designed to bid them welcome, but in fact terrified many of them to such a degree that they scarcely dared to come ashore. Nor were they reassured by the bearing of the disorderly crowd, who, in jealous competition for their beaver-skins, left them not a moment's peace, and outraged all their notions of decorum. More soon appeared, till hundreds of warriors were encamped along the shore, all restless, suspicious, and alarmed. Late one night, they awakened Champlain. On going with them to their camp, he found chiefs and warriors in solemn conclave around the glimmering firelight. Though they were fearful of the rest, their trust in him was boundless. "Come to our country, buy our beaver, build a fort, teach us the true faith, do what you will, but do not bring this crowd with you." The idea had seized them that these lawless bands of rival traders, all well armed, meant to plunder, and kill them. Champlain assured them of safety, and the whole night was consumed in friendly colloquy. Soon afterward, however, the camp broke up, and the uneasy warriors removed to the bor-

[1] The mountain being Mont Royal (Montreal). The Hospital of the Gray Nuns was built on a portion of Champlain's Place Royale.

ders of the Lake of St. Louis, placing the rapids betwixt themselves and the objects of their alarm. Here Champlain visited them, and hence these intrepid canoe-men, kneeling in their birchen egg-shells, carried him homeward down the rapids, somewhat, as he admits, to the discomposure of his nerves.[1]

The great gathering dispersed: the traders descended to Tadoussac, and Champlain to Quebec; while the Indians went, some to their homes, some to fight the Iroquois. A few months later, Champlain was in close conference with De Monts, at Pons, a place near Rochelle, of which the latter was governor. The last two years had made it apparent that, to keep the colony alive and maintain a basis for those discoveries on which his heart was bent, was impossible without a change of system. De Monts, engrossed with the cares of his government, placed all in the hands of his associate, and Champlain, fully empowered to act as he should judge expedient, set out for Paris. On the way, Fortune, at one stroke, wellnigh crushed him and New France together; for his horse fell on him, and he narrowly escaped with life. When he was partially recovered, he resumed his journey, pondering on means of rescue for the fading colony. A powerful protector must be had,—a great name to shield the enterprise from assaults and intrigues of jealous rival interests. On reaching Paris he addressed himself to a prince of the blood, Charles de Bourbon, Comte de Soissons; described New France, its resources, and its boundless extent, urged the need of unfolding a mystery pregnant perhaps with results of the deepest moment, laid before him maps and memoirs, and begged him to become the guardian of this new world. The royal consent being obtained, the Comte de Soissons became Lieutenant-General for the King in New France, with vice-regal powers. These, in turn, he conferred upon Champlain, making him his lieutenant, with full control over the trade in furs at and

[1] The first white man to descend the rapids of St. Louis was a youth named Louis, who, on the 10th of June, 1611, went with two Indians to shoot herons on an island, and was drowned on the way down; the second was a young man who in the summer before had gone with the Hurons to their country, and who returned with them on the 13th of June; the third was Champlain himself.

above Quebec, and with power to associate with himself such persons as he saw fit, to aid in the exploration and settlement of the country.[1]

Scarcely was the commission drawn when the Comte de Soissons, attacked with fever, died, to the joy of the Breton and Norman traders, whose jubilation, however, found a speedy end. Henri de Bourbon, Prince de Condé, first prince of the blood, assumed the vacant protectorship. He was grandson of the gay and gallant Condé of the civil wars, was father of the great Condé, the youthful victor of Rocroy, and was husband of Charlotte de Montmorenci, whose blonde beauties had fired the inflammable heart of Henry the Fourth. To the unspeakable wrath of that keen lover, the prudent Condé fled with his bride, first to Brussels, and then to Italy; nor did he return to France till the regicide's knife had put his jealous fears to rest.[2] After his return, he began to intrigue against the court. He was a man of common abilities, greedy of money and power, and scarcely seeking even the decency of a pretext to cover his mean ambition.[3] His chief honor— an honor somewhat equivocal—is, as Voltaire observes, to have been father of the great Condé. Busy with his intrigues, he cared little for colonies and discoveries; and his rank and power were his sole qualifications for his new post.

In Champlain alone was the life of New France. By instinct and temperament he was more impelled to the adventurous toils of exploration than to the duller task of building colonies. The profits of trade had value in his eyes only as means to these ends, and settlements were important chiefly as a base of discovery. Two great objects eclipsed all others,—to find a route to the Indies, and to bring the heathen tribes into the embraces of the Church, since, while he cared little for their bodies, his solicitude for their souls knew no bounds.

It was no part of his plan to establish an odious monopoly.

[1] *Commission de Monseigneur le Comte de Soissons donnée au Sieur de Champlein, 15 Oct., 1612.* See Champlain, (1632,) 231, and *Mémoires des Commissaires,* II. 451.

[2] The anecdote, as told by the Princess herself to her wandering court during the romantic campaigning of the Fronde, will be found in the curious *Mémoires de Lenet.*

[3] *Mémoires de Madame de Motteville, passim*; Sismondi, *Histoire des Français,* XXIV., XXV., *passim.*

He sought rather to enlist the rival traders in his cause; and he now, in concurrence with De Monts, invited them to become sharers in the traffic, under certain regulations, and on condition of aiding in the establishment and support of the colony. The merchants of St. Malo and Rouen accepted the terms, and became members of the new company; but the intractable heretics of Rochelle, refractory in commerce as in religion, kept aloof, and preferred the chances of an illicit trade. The prospects of New France were far from flattering; for little could be hoped from this unwilling league of selfish traders, each jealous of the rest. They gave the Prince of Condé large gratuities to secure his countenance and support. The hungry viceroy took them, and with these emoluments his interest in the colony ended.

Chapter XII

THE IMPOSTER VIGNAU

Illusions • A Path to the North Sea • The Ottawa • Forest Travellers • Indian Feast • The Impostor exposed • Return to Montreal

---

THE arrangements just indicated were a work of time. In the summer of 1612, Champlain was forced to forego his yearly voyage to New France; nor, even in the following spring, were his labors finished and the rival interests brought to harmony. Meanwhile, incidents occurred destined to have no small influence on his movements. Three years before, after his second fight with the Iroquois, a young man of his company had boldly volunteered to join the Indians on their homeward journey, and winter among them. Champlain gladly assented, and in the following summer the adventurer returned. Another young man, one Nicolas de Vignau, next offered himself; and he also, embarking in the Algonquin canoes, passed up the Ottawa, and was seen no more for a twelvemonth. In 1612 he reappeared in Paris, bringing a tale of wonders; for, says Champlain, "he was the most impudent liar that has been seen for many a day." He averred that at the sources of the Ottawa he had found a great lake; that he had crossed it, and discovered a river flowing northward; that he had descended this river, and reached the shores of the sea; that here he had seen the wreck of an English ship, whose crew, escaping to land, had been killed by the Indians; and that this sea was distant from Montreal only seventeen days by canoe. The clearness, consistency, and apparent simplicity of his story deceived Champlain, who had heard of a voyage of the English to the northern seas, coupled with rumors of wreck and disaster,[1] and was thus confirmed in his belief of Vignau's honesty. The Maréchal de Brissac, the President Jeannin, and other persons of eminence about the court,

---

[1] Evidently the voyage of Henry Hudson in 1610–12, when that navigator, after discovering Hudson's Strait, lost his life through a mutiny. Compare Jérémie, *Relation*, in *Recueil de Voyages au Nord*, VI.

greatly interested by these dexterous fabrications, urged Champlain to follow up without delay a discovery which promised results so important; while he, with the Pacific, Japan, China, the Spice Islands, and India stretching in flattering vista before his fancy, entered with eagerness on the chase of this illusion. Early in the spring of 1613 the unwearied voyager crossed the Atlantic, and sailed up the St. Lawrence. On Monday, the twenty-seventh of May, he left the island of St. Helen, opposite Montreal, with four Frenchmen, one of whom was Nicolas de Vignau, and one Indian, in two small canoes. They passed the swift current at St. Ann's, crossed the Lake of Two Mountains, and advanced up the Ottawa till the rapids of Carillon and the Long Saut checked their course. So dense and tangled was the forest, that they were forced to remain in the bed of the river, trailing their canoes along the bank with cords, or pushing them by main force up the current. Champlain's foot slipped; he fell in the rapids, two boulders, against which he braced himself, saving him from being swept down, while the cord of the canoe, twisted round his hand, nearly severed it. At length they reached smoother water, and presently met fifteen canoes of friendly Indians. Champlain gave them the most awkward of his Frenchmen, and took one of their number in return,—an exchange greatly to his profit.

All day they plied their paddles, and when night came they made their camp-fire in the forest. He who now, when two centuries and a half are passed, would see the evening bivouac of Champlain, has but to encamp, with Indian guides, on the upper waters of this same Ottawa, or on the borders of some lonely river of New Brunswick or of Maine.

Day dawned. The east glowed with tranquil fire, that pierced, with eyes of flame, the fir trees whose jagged tops stood drawn in black against the burning heaven. Beneath, the glossy river slept in shadow, or spread far and wide in sheets of burnished bronze; and the white moon, paling in the face of day, hung like a disk of silver in the western sky. Now, a fervid light touched the dead top of the hemlock, and, creeping downward, bathed the mossy beard of the patriarchal cedar, unstirred in the breathless air. Now, a fiercer spark beamed from the east; and now, half risen on the sight, a dome of crimson fire, the sun blazed with floods of radiance across the awakened wilderness.

The canoes were launched again, and the voyagers held their course. Soon the still surface was flecked with spots of foam; islets of froth floated by, tokens of some great convulsion. Then, on their left, the falling curtain of the Rideau shone like silver betwixt its bordering woods, and in front, white as a snow-drift, the cataracts of the Chaudière barred their way. They saw the unbridled river careering down its sheeted rocks, foaming in unfathomed chasms, wearying the solitude with the hoarse outcry of its agony and rage.

On the brink of the rocky basin where the plunging torrent boiled like a caldron, and puffs of spray sprang out from its concussion like smoke from the throat of a cannon, Champlain's two Indians took their stand, and, with a loud invocation, threw tobacco into the foam, an offering to the local spirit, the Manitou of the cataract.[1]

They shouldered their canoes over the rocks, and through the woods; then launched them again, and, with toil and struggle, made their amphibious way, pushing, dragging, lifting, paddling, shoving with poles; till, when the evening sun poured its level rays across the quiet Lake of the Chaudière, they landed, and made their camp on the verge of a woody island.

Day by day brought a renewal of their toils. Hour by hour, they moved prosperously up the long windings of the solitary stream; then, in quick succession, rapid followed rapid, till the bed of the Ottawa seemed a slope of foam. Now, like a wall bristling at the top with woody islets, the Falls of the Chats faced them with the sheer plunge of their sixteen cataracts. Now they glided beneath overhanging cliffs, where, seeing but unseen, the crouched wild-cat eyed them from the thicket; now through the maze of water-girded rocks, which

[1] An invariable custom with the upper Indians on passing this place. When many were present, it was attended with solemn dances and speeches, a contribution of tobacco being first taken on a dish. It was thought to insure a safe voyage; but was often an occasion of disaster, since hostile war parties, lying in ambush at the spot, would surprise and kill the votaries of the Manitou in the very presence of their guardian. It is on the return voyage that Champlain particularly describes the sacrifice.

the white cedar and the spruce clasped with serpent-like roots, or among islands where old hemlocks darkened the water with deep green shadow. Here, too, the rock-maple reared its verdant masses, the beech its glistening leaves and clean, smooth stem, and behind, stiff and sombre, rose the balsam-fir. Here, in the tortuous channels, the muskrat swam and plunged, and the splashing wild duck dived beneath the alders or among the red and matted roots of thirsty water-willows. Aloft, the white pine towered above a sea of verdure; old fir trees, hoary and grim, shaggy with pendent mosses, leaned above the stream, and beneath, dead and submerged, some fallen oak thrust from the current its bare, bleached limbs, like the skeleton of a drowned giant. In the weedy cove stood the moose, neck-deep in water to escape the flies, wading shore-ward, with glistening sides, as the canoes drew near, shaking his broad antlers and writhing his hideous nostril, as with clumsy trot he vanished in the woods.

In these ancient wilds, to whose ever verdant antiquity the pyramids are young and Nineveh a mushroom of yesterday; where the sage wanderer of the Odyssey, could he have urged his pilgrimage so far, would have surveyed the same grand and stern monotony, the same dark sweep of melancholy woods;—here, while New England was a solitude, and the settlers of Virginia scarcely dared venture inland beyond the sound of a cannon-shot, Champlain was planting on shores and islands the emblems of his faith. Of the pioneers of the North American forests, his name stands foremost on the list. It was he who struck the deepest and boldest strokes into the heart of their pristine barbarism. At Chantilly, at Fontaine-bleau, at Paris, in the cabinets of princes and of royalty itself, mingling with the proud vanities of the court; then lost from sight in the depths of Canada, the companion of savages, sharer of their toils, privations, and battles, more hardy, pa-tient, and bold than they;—such, for successive years, were the alternations of this man's life.

To follow on his trail once more. His Indians said that the rapids of the river above were impassable. Nicolas de Vignau affirmed the contrary; but, from the first, Vignau had been found always in the wrong. His aim seems to have been to involve his leader in difficulties, and disgust him with a journey which must soon result in exposing the imposture which had occasioned it. Champlain took counsel of the Indians. The party left the river, and entered the forest.

"We had a hard march," says Champlain. "I carried for my share of the luggage three arquebuses, three paddles, my overcoat, and a few *bagatelles*. My men carried a little more than I did, and suffered more from the mosquitoes than from their loads. After we had passed four small ponds and advanced two leagues and a half, we were so tired that we could go no farther, having eaten nothing but a little roasted fish for nearly twenty-four hours. So we stopped in a pleasant place enough by the edge of a pond, and lighted a fire to drive off the mosquitoes, which plagued us beyond all description; and at the same time we set our nets to catch a few fish."

On the next day they fared still worse, for their way was through a pine forest where a tornado had passed, tearing up the trees and piling them one upon another in a vast "windfall," where boughs, roots, and trunks were mixed in confusion. Sometimes they climbed over and sometimes crawled through these formidable barricades, till, after an exhausting march, they reached the banks of Muskrat Lake, by the edge of which was an Indian settlement.[1]

This neighborhood was the seat of the principal Indian population of the river,[2] and, as the canoes advanced, un-

---

[1] In 1867 a man in the employ of Captain Overman found, on the line of march followed by Champlain from the pond where he passed the night to Muskrat Lake, a brass astrolabe bearing the date 1603. As the astrolabe, an antiquated instrument for taking latitudes, was not many years after Champlain's day superseded by the quadrant, at least so far as French usage is concerned, the conjecture is admissible that this one was dropped by him. See a pamphlet by A. J. Russell, *Champlain's Astrolabe* (Montreal, 1879), and another by O. H. Marshall, *Discovery of an Astrolabe supposed to have been lost by Champlain* (New York, 1879).

[2] Usually called Algoumequins, or Algonquins, by Champlain and other early writers,—a name now always used in a generic sense to designate a large family of cognate tribes, speaking languages radically similar, and covering a vast extent of country.

The Algonquins of the Isle des Allumettes and its neighborhood are most frequently mentioned by the early writers as *la Nation de l'Isle*. Lalemant (*Relation des Hurons, 1639*) calls them *Ehonkeronons*. Vimont (*Relation, 1640*) calls them *Kichesipirini*. The name *Algonquin* was used generically as early as

wonted signs of human life could be seen on the borders of the lake. Here was a rough clearing. The trees had been burned; there was a rude and desolate gap in the sombre green of the pine forest. Dead trunks, blasted and black with fire, stood grimly upright amid the charred stumps and prostrate bodies of comrades half consumed. In the intervening spaces, the soil had been feebly scratched with hoes of wood or bone, and a crop of maize was growing, now some four inches high.[1] The dwellings of these slovenly farmers, framed of poles covered with sheets of bark, were scattered here and there, singly or in groups, while their tenants were running to the shore in amazement. The chief, Nibachis, offered the calumet, then harangued the crowd: "These white men must have fallen from the clouds. How else could they have reached us through the woods and rapids which even we find it hard to pass? The French chief can do anything. All that we have heard of him must be true." And they hastened to regale the hungry visitors with a repast of fish.

Champlain asked for guidance to the settlements above. It was readily granted. Escorted by his friendly hosts, he advanced beyond the foot of Muskrat Lake, and, landing, saw the unaccustomed sight of pathways through the forest. They led to the clearings and cabins of a chief named Tessouat, who, amazed at the apparition of the white strangers, exclaimed that he must be in a dream.[2] Next, the voyagers

---

the time of Sagard, whose *Histoire du Canada* appeared in 1636. Champlain always limits it to the tribes of the Ottawa.

Isle des Allumettes was called also Isle du Borgne, from a renowned one-eyed chief who made his abode here, and who, after greatly exasperating the Jesuits by his evil courses, at last became a convert and died in the faith. They regarded the people of this island as the haughtiest of all the tribes. Le Jeune, *Relation* (1636), 230.

[1] Champlain, *Quatriesme Voyage*, 29. This is a pamphlet of fifty-two pages, containing the journal of his voyage of 1613, and apparently published at the close of that year.

[2] Tessouat's village seems to have been on the lower Lac des Allumettes, a wide expansion of that arm of the Ottawa which flows along the southern side of Isle des Allumettes. Champlain, perhaps from the loss of his astrolabe, is wrong, by one degree, in his reckoning of the latitude, 47° for 46°. Tessouat was father, or predecessor, of the chief Le Borgne, whose Indian name was the same. See note, *ante*.

crossed to the neighboring island, then deeply wooded with pine, elm, and oak. Here were more desolate clearings, more rude cornfields and bark-built cabins. Here, too, was a cemetery, which excited the wonder of Champlain, for the dead were better cared for than the living. Each grave was covered with a double row of pieces of wood, inclined like a roof till they crossed at the ridge, along which was laid a thick tablet of wood, meant apparently either to bind the whole together or protect it from rain. At one end stood an upright tablet, or flattened post, rudely carved with an intended representation of the features of the deceased. If a chief, the head was adorned with a plume. If a warrior, there were figures near it of a shield, a lance, a war-club, and a bow and arrows; if a boy, of a small bow and one arrow; and if a woman or a girl, of a kettle, an earthen pot, a wooden spoon, and a paddle. The whole was decorated with red and yellow paint; and beneath slept the departed, wrapped in a robe of skins, his earthly treasures about him, ready for use in the land of souls.

Tessouat was to give a *tabagie*, or solemn feast, in honor of Champlain, and the chiefs and elders of the island were invited. Runners were sent to summon the guests from neighboring hamlets; and, on the morrow, Tessouat's squaws swept his cabin for the festivity. Then Champlain and his Frenchmen were seated on skins in the place of honor, and the naked guests appeared in quick succession, each with his wooden dish and spoon, and each ejaculating his guttural salute as he stooped at the low door. The spacious cabin was full. The congregated wisdom and prowess of the nation sat expectant on the bare earth. Each long, bare arm thrust forth its dish in turn as the host served out the banquet, in which, as courtesy enjoined, he himself was to have no share. First, a mess of pounded maize, in which were boiled, without salt, morsels of fish and dark scraps of meat; then, fish and flesh broiled on the embers, with a kettle of cold water from the river. Champlain, in wise distrust of Ottawa cookery, confined himself to the simpler and less doubtful viands. A few minutes, and all alike had vanished. The kettles were empty. Then pipes were filled and touched with fire brought in by the squaws, while the young men who had stood thronged about the entrance now modestly withdrew, and the door was closed for counsel.[1]

First, the pipes were passed to Champlain. Then, for full half an hour, the assembly smoked in silence. At length, when the fitting time was come, he addressed them in a speech in which he declared, that, moved by affection for them, he visited their country to see its richness and its beauty, and to aid them in their wars; and he now begged them to furnish him with four canoes and eight men, to convey him to the country of the Nipissings, a tribe dwelling northward on the lake which bears their name.[2]

His audience looked grave, for they were but cold and jealous friends of the Nipissings. For a time they discoursed in murmuring tones among themselves, all smoking meanwhile with redoubled vigor. Then Tessouat, chief of these forest republicans, rose and spoke in behalf of all.

"We always knew you for our best friend among the Frenchmen. We love you like our own children. But why did you break your word with us last year when we all went down to meet you at Montreal, to give you presents and go with you to war? You were not there, but other Frenchmen were there who abused us. We will never go again. As for the four canoes, you shall have them if you insist upon it; but it grieves us to think of the hardships you must endure. The Nipissings have weak hearts. They are good for nothing in war, but they kill us with charms, and they poison us. Therefore we are on bad terms with them. They will kill you, too."

[1] Champlain's account of this feast (*Quatriesme Voyage*, 32) is unusually minute and graphic. In every particular—excepting the pounded maize—it might, as the writer can attest from personal experience, be taken as the description of a similar feast among some of the tribes of the Far West at the present day, as, for example, one of the remoter bands of the Dacotah, a race radically distinct from the Algonquin.

[2] The *Nebecerini* of Champlain, called also *Nipissingues, Nipissiriniens, Nibissiriniens, Bissiriniens, Epiciriniens*, by various early French writers. They are the *Askikouanheronons* of Lalemant, who borrowed the name from the Huron tongue, and were also called *Sorciers* from their ill repute as magicians. They belonged, like the Ottawas, to the great Algonquin family, and are considered by Charlevoix (*Journal Historique*, 186) as alone preserving the original type of that race and language. They had, however, borrowed certain usages from their Huron neighbors.

Such was the pith of Tessouat's discourse, and at each clause the conclave responded in unison with an approving grunt.

Champlain urged his petition; sought to relieve their tender scruples in his behalf; assured them that he was charmproof, and that he feared no hardships. At length he gained his point. The canoes and the men were promised, and, seeing himself as he thought on the highway to his phantom Northern Sea, he left his entertainers to their pipes, and with a light heart issued from the close and smoky den to breathe the fresh air of the afternoon. He visited the Indian fields, with their young crops of pumpkins, beans, and French peas,—the last a novelty obtained from the traders.[1] Here, Thomas, the interpreter, soon joined him with a countenance of ill news. In the absence of Champlain, the assembly had reconsidered their assent. The canoes were denied.

With a troubled mind he hastened again to the hall of council, and addressed the naked senate in terms better suited to his exigencies than to their dignity.

"I thought you were men; I thought you would hold fast to your word: but I find you children, without truth. You call yourselves my friends, yet you break faith with me. Still I would not incommode you; and if you cannot give me four canoes, two will serve."[2]

The burden of the reply was, rapids, rocks, cataracts, and the wickedness of the Nipissings. "We will not give you the canoes, because we are afraid of losing you," they said.

"This young man," rejoined Champlain, pointing to Vignau, who sat by his side, "has been to their country, and did not find the road or the people so bad as you have said."

"Nicolas," demanded Tessouat, "did you say that you had been to the Nipissings?"

The imposter sat mute for a time, and then replied, "Yes, I have been there."

---

[1] "Pour passer le reste du jour, je fus me pourmener par les jardins, qui n'estoient remplis que de quelques citrouilles, phasioles, et de nos pois, qu'ils commencent à cultiver, où Thomas, mon truchement, qui entendoit fort bien la langue, me vint trouver," etc. Champlain, (1632,) Lib. IV. c 2.

[2] " . . . . et leur dis, que je les avois jusques à ce jour estimez hommes, et veritables, et que maintenant ils se monstroient enfants et mensongers," etc. *Ibid.*

Hereupon an outcry broke from the assembly, and they turned their eyes on him askance, "as if," says Champlain, "they would have torn and eaten him."

"You are a liar," returned the unceremonious host; "you know very well that you slept here among my children every night, and got up again every morning; and if you ever went to the Nipissings, it must have been when you were asleep. How can you be so impudent as to lie to your chief, and so wicked as to risk his life among so many dangers? He ought to kill you with tortures worse than those with which we kill our enemies."[1]

Champlain urged him to reply, but he sat motionless and dumb. Then he led him from the cabin, and conjured him to declare if in truth he had seen this sea of the north. Vignau, with oaths, affirmed that all he had said was true. Returning to the council, Champlain repeated the impostor's story: how he had seen the sea, the wreck of an English ship, the heads of eighty Englishmen, and an English boy, prisoner among the Indians.

At this, an outcry rose louder than before, and the Indians turned in ire upon Vignau.

"You are a liar." "Which way did you go?" "By what rivers?" "By what lakes?" "Who went with you?"

Vignau had made a map of his travels, which Champlain now produced, desiring him to explain it to his questioners; but his assurance failed him, and he could not utter a word.

Champlain was greatly agitated. His heart was in the enterprise; his reputation was in a measure at stake; and now, when he thought his triumph so near, he shrank from believing himself the sport of an impudent impostor. The council broke up; the Indians displeased and moody, and he, on his part, full of anxieties and doubts.

"I called Vignau to me in presence of his companions," he

[1] "Alors Tessouat . . . . luy dit en son langage: Nicolas, est-il vray que tu as dit avoir esté aux Nebecerini? Il fut longtemps sans parler, puis il leur dit en leur langue, qu'il parloit aucunement: Ouy j'y ay esté. Aussitost ils le regardèrent de travers, et se jettant sur luy, comme s'ils l'eussent voulu manger ou deschirer, firent de grands cris, et Tessouat luy dit: Tu es un asseuré menteur: tu sçais bien que tous les soirs tu couchois à mes costez avec mes enfants, et tous les matins tu t'y levois: si tu as esté vers ces peuples, ç'a esté en dormant," etc. Champlain, (1632,) Lib. IV. c. 2.

says. "I told him that the time for deceiving me was ended; that he must tell me whether or not he had really seen the things he had told of; that I had forgotten the past, but that, if he continued to mislead me, I would have him hanged without mercy."

Vignau pondered for a moment; then fell on his knees, owned his treachery, and begged forgiveness. Champlain broke into a rage, and, unable, as he says, to endure the sight of him, ordered him from his presence, and sent the interpreter after him to make further examination. Vanity, the love of notoriety, and the hope of reward, seem to have been his inducements; for he had in fact spent a quiet winter in Tessouat's cabin, his nearest approach to the northern sea; and he had flattered himself that he might escape the necessity of guiding his commander to this pretended discovery. The Indians were somewhat exultant. "Why did you not listen to chiefs and warriors, instead of believing the lies of this fellow?" And they counselled Champlain to have him killed at once, adding, "Give him to us, and we promise you that he shall never lie again."

No motive remaining for farther advance, the party set out on their return, attended by a fleet of forty canoes bound to Montreal[1] for trade. They passed the perilous rapids of the Calumet, and were one night encamped on an island, when an Indian, slumbering in an uneasy posture, was visited with a nightmare. He leaped up with a yell, screamed that somebody was killing him, and ran for refuge into the river. Instantly all his companions sprang to their feet, and, hearing in fancy the Iroquois war-whoop, took to the water, splashing, diving, and wading up to their necks, in the blindness of their fright. Champlain and his Frenchmen, roused at the noise, snatched their weapons and looked in vain for an enemy. The panic-stricken warriors, reassured at length, waded crestfallen ashore, and the whole ended in a laugh.

At the Chaudière, a contribution of tobacco was collected on a wooden platter, and, after a solemn harangue, was thrown to the guardian Manitou. On the seventeenth of June they approached Montreal, where the assembled traders

---

[1] The name is used here for distinctness. The locality is indicated by Champlain as *Le Saut*, from the Saut St. Louis, immediately above.

greeted them with discharges of small arms and cannon. Here, among the rest, was Champlain's lieutenant, Du Parc, with his men, who had amused their leisure with hunting, and were revelling in a sylvan abundance, while their baffled chief, with worry of mind, fatigue of body, and a Lenten diet of half-cooked fish, was grievously fallen away in flesh and strength. He kept his word with De Vignau, left the scoundrel unpunished, bade farewell to the Indians, and, promising to rejoin them the next year, embarked in one of the trading-ships for France.

Chapter XIII

1615

DISCOVERY OF LAKE HURON

Religious Zeal of Champlain • Récollet Friars • St. Francis • Exploration and War • Le Caron on the Ottawa • Champlain reaches Lake Huron • The Huron Towns • Mass in the Wilderness

IN New France, spiritual and temporal interests were inseparably blended, and, as will hereafter appear, the conversion of the Indians was used as a means of commercial and political growth. But, with the single-hearted founder of the colony, considerations of material advantage, though clearly recognized, were no less clearly subordinate. He would fain rescue from perdition a people living, as he says, "like brute beasts, without faith, without law, without religion, without God." While the want of funds and the indifference of his merchant associates, who as yet did not fully see that their trade would find in the missions its surest ally, were threatening to wreck his benevolent schemes, he found a kindred spirit in his friend Houël, secretary to the King, and comptroller-general of the salt-works of Brouage. Near this town was a convent of Récollet friars, some of whom were well known to Houël. To them he addressed himself; and several of the brotherhood, "inflamed," we are told, "with charity," were eager to undertake the mission. But the Récollets, mendicants by profession, were as weak in resources as Champlain himself. He repaired to Paris, then filled with bishops, cardinals, and nobles, assembled for the States-General. Responding to his appeal, they subscribed fifteen hundred livres for the purchase of vestments, candles, and ornaments for altars. The King gave letters patent in favor of the mission, and the Pope gave it his formal authorization. By this instrument the papacy in the person of Paul the Fifth virtually repudiated the action of the papacy in the person of Alexander the Sixth, who had proclaimed all America the exclusive property of Spain.[1]

[1] The papal brief and the royal letter are in Sagard, *Histoire de la Nouvelle France*, and Le Clerc, *Établissement de la Foy.*

The Récollets form a branch of the great Franciscan order, founded early in the thirteenth century by St. Francis of Assisi. Saint, hero, or madman, according to the point of view from which he is regarded, he belonged to an era of the Church when the tumult of invading heresies awakened in her defence a band of impassioned champions, widely different from the placid saints of an earlier age. He was very young when dreams and voices began to reveal to him his vocation, and kindle his high-wrought nature to sevenfold heat. Self-respect, natural affection, decency, became in his eyes but stumbling-blocks and snares. He robbed his father to build a church; and, like so many of the Roman Catholic saints, confounded filth with humility, exchanged clothes with beggars, and walked the streets of Assisi in rags amid the hootings of his townsmen. He vowed perpetual poverty and perpetual beggary, and, in token of his renunciation of the world, stripped himself naked before the Bishop of Assisi, and then begged of him in charity a peasant's mantle. Crowds gathered to his fervid and dramatic eloquence. His handful of disciples multiplied, till Europe became thickly dotted with their convents. At the end of the eighteenth century, the three Orders of St. Francis numbered a hundred and fifteen thousand friars and twenty-eight thousand nuns. Four popes, forty-five cardinals, and forty-six canonized martyrs were enrolled on their record, besides about two thousand more who had shed their blood for the faith.[1] Their missions embraced nearly all the known world; and, in 1621, there were in Spanish America alone five hundred Franciscan convents.[2]

In process of time the Franciscans had relaxed their ancient rigor; but much of their pristine spirit still subsisted in the Récollets, a reformed branch of the Order, sometimes known as Franciscans of the Strict Observance.

Four of their number were named for the mission of New France,—Denis Jamay, Jean Dolbeau, Joseph le Caron, and the lay brother Pacifique du Plessis. "They packed their church ornaments," says Champlain, "and we, our luggage."

---

[1] Helyot, *Histoire des Ordres Religieux et Militaires*, devotes his seventh volume (ed. 1792) to the Franciscans and Jesuits. He draws largely from the great work of Wadding on the Franciscans.

[2] Le Clerc, *Établissement de la Foy*, I. 33–52.

All alike confessed their sins, and, embarking at Honfleur, reached Quebec at the end of May, 1615. Great was the perplexity of the Indians as the apostolic mendicants landed beneath the rock. Their garb was a form of that common to the brotherhood of St. Francis, consisting of a rude garment of coarse gray cloth, girt at the waist with the knotted cord of the Order, and furnished with a peaked hood, to be drawn over the head. Their naked feet were shod with wooden sandals, more than an inch thick.[1]

Their first care was to choose a site for their convent, near the fortified dwellings and storehouses built by Champlain. This done, they made an altar, and celebrated the first mass ever said in Canada. Dolbeau was the officiating priest; all New France kneeled on the bare earth around him, and cannon from the ship and the ramparts hailed the mystic rite.[2] Then, in imitation of the Apostles, they took counsel together, and assigned to each his province in the vast field of their mission: to Le Caron, the Hurons, and to Dolbeau, the Montagnais; while Jamay and Du Plessis were to remain for the present near Quebec.

Dolbeau, full of zeal, set out for his post, and, in the next winter, tried to follow the roving hordes of Tadoussac to their frozen hunting-grounds. He was not robust, and his eyes were weak. Lodged in a hut of birch bark, full of abominations, dogs, fleas, stench, and all uncleanness, he succumbed at length to the smoke, which had wellnigh blinded him, forcing him to remain for several days with his eyes closed.[3] After debating within himself whether God required of him the sacrifice of his sight, he solved his doubts with a negative, and returned to Quebec, only to depart again with opening spring on a tour so extensive, that it brought him in contact with outlying bands of the Esquimaux.[4] Meanwhile Le Caron had long been absent on a more noteworthy mission.

While his brethren were building their convent and gar-

---

[1] An engraving of their habit will be found in Helyot (1792).

[2] *Lettre du P. Jean Dolbeau au P. Didace David, son ami; de Quebec le 20 Juillet, 1615.* See Le Clerc, *Établissement de la Foy,* I. 62.

[3] Sagard, *Hist. de la Nouvelle France,* 26.

[4] Le Clerc, *Établissement de la Foy,* I. 71.

nishing their altar at Quebec, the ardent friar had hastened to the site of Montreal, then thronged with a savage concourse, come down for the yearly trade. He mingled with them, studied their manners, tried to learn their languages, and, when Champlain and Pontgravé arrived, declared his purpose of wintering in their villages. Dissuasion availed nothing. "What," he demanded, "are privations to him whose life is devoted to perpetual poverty, and who has no ambition but to serve God?"

The assembled Indians were more eager for temporal than for spiritual succor, and beset Champlain with clamors for aid against the Iroquois. He and Pontgravé were of one mind. The aid demanded must be given, and that from no motive of the hour, but in pursuance of a deliberate policy. It was evident that the innumerable tribes of New France, otherwise divided, were united in a common fear and hate of these formidable bands, who, in the strength of their fivefold league, spread havoc and desolation through all the surrounding wilds. It was the aim of Champlain, as of his successors, to persuade the threatened and endangered hordes to live at peace with each other, and to form against the common foe a virtual league, of which the French colony would be the heart and the head, and which would continually widen with the widening area of discovery. With French soldiers to fight their battles, French priests to baptize them, and French traders to supply their increasing wants, their dependence would be complete. They would become assured tributaries to the growth of New France. It was a triple alliance of soldier, priest, and trader. The soldier might be a roving knight, and the priest a martyr and a saint; but both alike were subserving the interests of that commerce which formed the only solid basis of the colony. The scheme of English colonization made no account of the Indian tribes. In the scheme of French colonization they were all in all.

In one point the plan was fatally defective, since it involved the deadly enmity of a race whose character and whose power were as yet but ill understood,—the fiercest, boldest, most politic, and most ambitious savages to whom the American forest has ever given birth.

The chiefs and warriors met in council,—Algonquins of

the Ottawa, and Hurons from the borders of the great Fresh-Water Sea. Champlain promised to join them with all the men at his command, while they, on their part, were to muster without delay twenty-five hundred warriors for an inroad into the country of the Iroquois. He descended at once to Quebec for needful preparation; but when, after a short delay, he returned to Montreal, he found, to his chagrin, a solitude. The wild concourse had vanished; nothing remained but the skeleton poles of their huts, the smoke of their fires, and the refuse of their encampments. Impatient at his delay, they had set out for their villages, and with them had gone Father Joseph le Caron.

Twelve Frenchmen, well armed, had attended him. Summer was at its height, and as his canoe stole along the bosom of the glassy river, and he gazed about him on the tawny multitude whose fragile craft covered the water like swarms of gliding insects, he thought, perhaps, of his white-washed cell in the convent of Brouage, of his book, his table, his rosary, and all the narrow routine of that familiar life from which he had awakened to contrasts so startling. That his progress up the Ottawa was far from being an excursion of pleasure is attested by his letters, fragments of which have come down to us.

"It would be hard to tell you," he writes to a friend, "how tired I was with paddling all day, with all my strength, among the Indians; wading the rivers a hundred times and more, through the mud and over the sharp rocks that cut my feet; carrying the canoe and luggage through the woods to avoid the rapids and frightful cataracts; and half starved all the while, for we had nothing to eat but a little *sagamite*, a sort of porridge of water and pounded maize, of which they gave us a very small allowance every morning and night. But I must needs tell you what abundant consolation I found under all my troubles; for when one sees so many infidels needing nothing but a drop of water to make them children of God, one feels an inexpressible ardor to labor for their conversion, and sacrifice to it one's repose and life."[1]

[1] ". . . . Car helas quand on voit un si grand nombre d'Infidels, et qu'il ne tient qu'à une goutte d'eau pour les rendre enfans de Dieu, on ressent je ne sçay quelle ardeur de travailler à leur conversion et d'y sacrifier son repos et

Another Récollet, Gabriel Sagard, followed the same route in similar company a few years later, and has left an account of his experience, of which Le Caron's was the counterpart. Sagard reckons from eighty to a hundred waterfalls and rapids in the course of the journey, and the task of avoiding them by pushing through the woods was the harder for him because he saw fit to go barefoot, "in imitation of our seraphic father, Saint Francis." "We often came upon rocks, mudholes, and fallen trees, which we had to scramble over, and sometimes we must force our way with head and hands through dense woods and thickets, without road or path. When the time came, my Indians looked for a good place to pass the night. Some went for dry wood; others for poles to make a shed; others kindled a fire, and hung the kettle to a stick stuck aslant in the ground; and others looked for two flat stones to bruise the Indian corn, of which they make sagamite."

This sagamite was an extremely thin porridge; and, though scraps of fish were now and then boiled in it, the friar pined away daily on this weak and scanty fare, which was, moreover, made repulsive to him by the exceeding filthiness of the cookery. Nevertheless, he was forced to disguise his feelings. "One must always keep a smiling, modest, contented face, and now and then sing a hymn, both for his own consolation and to please and edify the savages, who take a singular pleasure in hearing us sing the praises of our God." Among all his trials, none afflicted him so much as the flies and mosquitoes. "If I had not kept my face wrapped in a cloth, I am almost sure they would have blinded me, so pestiferous and poisonous are the bites of these little demons. They make one look like a leper, hideous to the sight. I confess that this is the worst martyrdom I suffered in this country; hunger, thirst, weariness, and fever are nothing to it. These little beasts not only persecute you all day, but at night they get

sa vie." Le Caron, in Le Clerc, I. 74. Le Clerc, usually exact, affixes a wrong date to Le Caron's departure, which took place, not in the autumn, but about the first of July, Champlain following on the ninth. Of Champlain the editions consulted have been those of 1620 and 1627, the narrative being abridged in the edition of 1632. Compare Sagard, *Histoire de la Nouvelle France*.

into your eyes and mouth, crawl under your clothes, or stick their long stings through them, and make such a noise that it distracts your attention, and prevents you from saying your prayers." He reckons three or four kinds of them, and adds, that in the Montagnais country there is still another kind, so small that they can hardly be seen, but which "bite like devils' imps." The sportsman who has bivouacked in the woods of Maine will at once recognize the minute tormentors there known as "no-see-'ems."

While through tribulations like these Le Caron made his way towards the scene of his apostleship, Champlain was following on his track. With two canoes, ten Indians, Étienne Brulé his interpreter, and another Frenchman, he pushed up the Ottawa till he reached the Algonquin villages which had formed the term of his former journeying. He passed the two lakes of the Allumettes; and now, for twenty miles, the river stretched before him, straight as the bee can fly, deep, narrow, and black, between its mountain shores. He passed the rapids of the Joachims and the Caribou, the Rocher Capitaine, and the Deux Rivières, and reached at length the tributary waters of the Mattawan. He turned to the left, ascended this little stream forty miles or more, and, crossing a portage track, well trodden, reached the margin of Lake Nipissing. The canoes were launched again, and glided by leafy shores and verdant islands till at length appeared signs of human life and clusters of bark lodges, half hidden in the vastness of the woods. It was the village of an Algonquin band, called the Nipissings,—a race so beset with spirits, infested by demons, and abounding in magicians, that the Jesuits afterwards stigmatized them as "the Sorcerers." In this questionable company Champlain spent two days, feasted on fish, deer, and bears. Then, descending to the outlet of the lake, he steered his canoes westward down the current of French River.

Days passed, and no sign of man enlivened the rocky desolation. Hunger was pressing them hard, for the ten gluttonous Indians had devoured already nearly all their provision for the voyage, and they were forced to subsist on the blueberries and wild raspberries that grew abundantly in the meagre soil, when suddenly they encountered a troop of three hundred savages, whom, from their strange and startling mode of wearing their hair, Champlain named the *Cheveux Relevés.* "Not one of our courtiers," he says, "takes so much pains in dressing his locks." Here, however, their care of the toilet ended; for, though tattooed on various parts of the body, painted, and armed with bows, arrows, and shields of bison-hide, they wore no clothing whatever. Savage as was their aspect, they were busied in the pacific task of gathering blue-berries for their winter store. Their demeanor was friendly; and from them the voyager learned that the great lake of the Hurons was close at hand.[1]

Now, far along the western sky was traced the watery line of that inland ocean, and, first of white men except the Friar Le Caron, Champlain beheld the "Mer Douce," the Fresh-Water Sea of the Hurons. Before him, too far for sight, lay the spirit-haunted Manitoualins, and, southward, spread the vast bosom of the Georgian Bay. For more than a hundred miles, his course was along its eastern shores, among islets countless as the sea-sands,—an archipelago of rocks worn for ages by the wash of waves. He crossed Byng Inlet, Franklin Inlet, Parry Sound, and the wider bay of Matchedash, and seems to have landed at the inlet now called Thunder Bay, at the entrance of the Bay of Matchedash, and a little west of the Harbor of Penetanguishine.

An Indian trail led inland, through woods and thickets, across broad meadows, over brooks, and along the skirts of green acclivities. To the eye of Champlain, accustomed to the desolation he had left behind, it seemed a land of beauty and abundance. He reached at last a broad opening in the forest, with fields of maize, pumpkins ripening in the sun, patches of sunflowers, from the seeds of which the Indians made hair-

[1] These savages belonged to a numerous Algonquin tribe who occupied a district west and southwest of the Nottawassaga Bay of Lake Huron, within the modern counties of Bruce and Grey, Canada West. Sagard speaks of meeting a party of them near the place where they were met by Champlain. Sagard, *Grand Voyage du Pays des Hurons,* 77. The Hurons called them On-dataouaouat, or Ondatahouat, whence the name Outaouat (Ottawa), which is now commonly used to designate a particular tribe, or group of tribes, but which the French often employed as a generic term for all the Algonquin tribes of the Upper Lakes. It is written in various forms by French and English writers, as *Outouais, Outaouaks, Tawaas, Oadauwaus, Outauies, Outa-ouacs, Utawas, Ottawwawwug, Outtoaets, Outtawaats, Attawawas.*

oil, and, in the midst, the Huron town of Otouacha. In all essential points, it resembled that which Cartier, eighty years before, had seen at Montreal: the same triple palisade of crossed and intersecting trunks, and the same long lodges of bark, each containing several families. Here, within an area of thirty or forty miles, was the seat of one of the most remarkable savage communities on the continent. By the Indian standard, it was a mighty nation; yet the entire Huron population did not exceed that of a third or fourth class American city.[1]

To the south and southeast lay other tribes of kindred race and tongue, all stationary, all tillers of the soil, and all in a state of social advancement when compared with the roving bands of Eastern Canada: the Neutral Nation[2] west of the Niagara, and the Eries and Andastes in Western New York and Pennsylvania; while from the Genesee eastward to the Hudson lay the banded tribes of the Iroquois, leading members of this potent family, deadly foes of their kindred, and at last their destroyers.

In Champlain the Hurons saw the champion who was to lead them to victory. There was bountiful feasting in his honor in the great lodge at Otouacha; and other welcome, too, was tendered, of which the Hurons were ever liberal, but which, with all courtesy, was declined by the virtuous Champlain. Next, he went to Carmaron, a league distant, and then to Touaguainchain and Tequenonquihaye; till at length he reached Carhagouha, with its triple palisade thirty-five feet high. Here he found Le Caron. The Indians, eager to do him honor, were building for him a bark lodge in the neighboring forest, fashioned like their own, but much smaller. In it the friar made an altar, garnished with those indispensable decorations which he had brought with him through all the vicissitudes of his painful journeying; and hither, night and day,

[1] Champlain estimates the number of Huron villages at seventeen or eighteen. Le Jeune, Sagard, and Lalemant afterwards reckoned them at from twenty to thirty-two. Le Clerc, following Le Caron, makes the population about ten thousand souls; but several later observers, as well as Champlain himself, set it at above thirty thousand.

[2] A warlike people, called Neutral from their neutrality between the Hurons and the Iroquois, which did not save them from sharing the destruction which overwhelmed the former.

came a curious multitude to listen to his annunciation of the new doctrine. It was a joyful hour when he saw Champlain approach his hermitage; and the two men embraced like brothers long sundered.

The twelfth of August was a day evermore marked with white in the friar's calendar. Arrayed in priestly vestments, he stood before his simple altar; behind him his little band of Christians,—the twelve Frenchmen who had attended him, and the two who had followed Champlain. Here stood their devout and valiant chief, and, at his side, that pioneer of pioneers, Étienne Brulé, the interpreter. The Host was raised aloft; the worshippers kneeled. Then their rough voices joined in the hymn of praise, *Te Deum laudamus*; and then a volley of their guns proclaimed the triumph of the faith to the *okies*, the *manitous*, and all the brood of anomalous devils who had reigned with undisputed sway in these wild realms of darkness. The brave friar, a true soldier of the Church, had led her forlorn hope into the fastnesses of hell; and now, with contented heart, he might depart in peace, for he had said the first mass in the country of the Hurons.

Chapter XIV

1615, 1616

THE GREAT WAR PARTY

Muster of Warriors • Departure • The River Trent • Lake Ontario • The Iroquois Town • Attack • Repulse • Champlain wounded • Retreat • Adventures of Étienne Brulé • Winter Hunt • Champlain lost in the Forest • Made Umpire of Indian Quarrels

THE lot of the favored guest of an Indian camp or village is idleness without repose, for he is never left alone, and the repletion of incessant and inevitable feasts. Tired of this inane routine, Champlain, with some of his Frenchmen, set forth on a tour of observation. Journeying at their ease by the Indian trails, they visited, in three days, five palisaded villages. The country delighted them, with its meadows, its deep woods, its pine and cedar thickets, full of hares and partridges, its wild grapes and plums, cherries, crab-apples, nuts, and raspberries. It was the seventeenth of August when they reached the Huron metropolis, Cahiagué, in the modern township of Orillia, three leagues west of the river Severn, by which Lake Simcoe pours its waters into the bay of Matchedash. A shrill clamor of rejoicing, the fixed stare of wondering squaws, and the screaming flight of terrified children, hailed the arrival of Champlain. By his estimate, the place contained two hundred lodges; but they must have been relatively small, since, had they been of the enormous capacity sometimes found in these structures, Cahiagué alone would have held the whole Huron population. Here was the chief rendezvous, and the town swarmed with gathering warriors. There was cheering news; for an allied nation, called Carantouans, probably identical with the Andastes, had promised to join the Hurons in the enemy's country, with five hundred men.[1] Feasts and the war-dance consumed the days, till at length the

[1] Champlain, (1627,) 31. While the French were aiding the Hurons against the Iroquois, the Dutch on the Hudson aided the Iroquois against this nation of allies, who captured three Dutchmen, but are said to have set them free in the belief that they were French. Ibid.

tardy bands had all arrived; and, shouldering their canoes and scanty baggage, the naked host set forth.

At the outlet of Lake Simcoe they all stopped to fish,— their simple substitute for a commissariat. Hence, too, the intrepid Étienne Brulé, at his own request, was sent with twelve Indians to hasten forward the five hundred allied warriors, a dangerous venture, since his course must lie through the borders of the Iroquois.

He set out on the eighth of September, and on the morning of the tenth, Champlain, shivering in his blanket, awoke to see the meadows sparkling with an early frost, soon to vanish under the bright autumnal sun. The Huron fleet pursued its course along Lake Simcoe, across the portage to Balsam or Sturgeon Lake, and down the chain of lakes which form the sources of the river Trent. As the long line of canoes moved on its way, no human life was seen, no sign of friend or foe; yet, at times, to the fancy of Champlain, the borders of the stream seemed decked with groves and shrubbery by the hands of man, and the walnut trees, laced with grape-vines, seemed decorations of a pleasure-ground.

They stopped and encamped for a deer hunt. Five hundred Indians, in line, like the skirmishers of an army advancing to battle, drove the game to the end of a woody point; and the canoe-men killed them with spears and arrows as they took to the river. Champlain and his men keenly relished the sport, but paid a heavy price for their pleasure. A Frenchman, firing at a buck, brought down an Indian, and there was need of liberal gifts to console the sufferer and his friends.

The canoes now issued from the mouth of the Trent. Like a flock of venturous wild-fowl, they put boldly out upon Lake Ontario, crossed it in safety, and landed within the borders of New York, on or near the point of land west of Hungry Bay. After hiding their light craft in the woods, the warriors took up their swift and wary march, filing in silence between the woods and the lake, for four leagues along the strand. Then they struck inland, threaded the forest, crossed the outlet of Lake Oneida, and after a march of four days, were deep within the limits of the Iroquois. On the ninth of October some of their scouts met a fishing-party of this people, and captured them, eleven in number, men, women, and children.

They were brought to the camp of the exultant Hurons. As a beginning of the jubilation, a chief cut off a finger of one of the women; but desisted from further torturing on the angry protest of Champlain, reserving that pleasure for a more convenient season.

On the next day they reached an open space in the forest. The hostile town was close at hand, surrounded by rugged fields with a slovenly and savage cultivation. The young Hurons in advance saw the Iroquois at work among the pumpkins and maize, gathering their rustling harvest. Nothing could restrain the hare-brained and ungoverned crew. They screamed their war-cry and rushed in; but the Iroquois snatched their weapons, killed and wounded five or six of the assailants, and drove back the rest discomfited. Champlain and his Frenchmen were forced to interpose; and the report of their pieces from the border of the woods stopped the pursuing enemy, who withdrew to their defences, bearing with them their dead and wounded.[1]

It appears to have been a fortified town of the Onondagas, the central tribe of the Iroquois confederacy, standing, there is some reason to believe, within the limits of Madison County, a few miles south of Lake Oneida.[2] Champlain describes its defensive works as much stronger than those of the Huron villages. They consisted of four concentric rows of palisades, formed of trunks of trees, thirty feet high, set aslant in the earth, and intersecting each other near the top, where they supported a kind of gallery, well defended by shot-proof

[1] Le Clerc (I. 79–87) gives a few particulars not mentioned by Champlain, whose account will be found in the editions of 1620, 1627, and 1632.

[2] Champlain calls the tribe Antouoronons, Antouhonorons, or Entouhonorons. I at first supposed them to be the Senecas, but further inquiry leads me to believe that they were the Onondagas. Mr. O. H. Marshall thinks that the town was on Lake Onondaga, and supports his opinion in an excellent article in the *Magazine of American History*. General John S. Clark has, however, shown that the site of an ancient Indian fort on Nichols Pond, in the town of Fenner, Madison County, fulfils the conditions sufficiently to give some countenance to the supposition of its identity with that described by Champlain. A plan of the locality was kindly sent me by Mr. L. W. Ledyard, and another by Rev. W. M. Beauchamp, whose careful examination of the spot confirms but partially the conclusions of General Clark. Champlain's drawing of the fort was clearly made from memory, and contains obvious inaccuracies.

timber, and furnished with wooden gutters for quenching fire. A pond or lake, which washed one side of the palisade, and was led by sluices within the town, gave an ample supply of water, while the galleries were well provided with magazines of stones.

Champlain was greatly exasperated at the desultory and futile procedure of his Huron allies. Against his advice, they now withdrew to the distance of a cannon-shot from the fort, and encamped in the forest, out of sight of the enemy. "I was moved," he says, "to speak to them roughly and harshly enough, in order to incite them to do their duty, for I foresaw that, if things went according to their fancy, nothing but harm could come of it, to their loss and ruin." He proceeded, therefore, to instruct them in the art of war.

In the morning, aided doubtless by his ten or twelve Frenchmen, they set themselves with alacrity to their prescribed task. A wooden tower was made, high enough to overlook the palisade, and large enough to shelter four or five marksmen. Huge wooden shields, or movable parapets, like the mantelets of the Middle Ages, were also constructed. Four hours sufficed to finish the work, and then the assault began. Two hundred of the strongest warriors dragged the tower forward, and planted it within a pike's length of the palisade. Three arquebusiers mounted to the top, where, themselves well sheltered, they opened a raking fire along the galleries, now thronged with wild and naked defenders. But nothing could restrain the ungovernable Hurons. They abandoned their mantelets, and, deaf to every command, swarmed out like bees upon the open field, leaped, shouted, shrieked their war-cries, and shot off their arrows; while the Iroquois, yelling defiance from their ramparts, sent back a shower of stones and arrows in reply. A Huron, bolder than the rest, ran forward with firebrands to burn the palisade, and others followed with wood to feed the flame. But it was stupidly kindled on the leeward side, without the protecting shields designed to cover it; and torrents of water, poured down from the gutters above, quickly extinguished it. The confusion was redoubled. Champlain strove in vain to restore order. Each warrior was yelling at the top of his throat, and his voice was drowned in the outrageous din. Thinking, as he says, that his head would split with shouting, he gave over the attempt, and busied himself and his men with picking off the Iroquois along their ramparts.

The attack lasted three hours, when the assailants fell back to their fortified camp, with seventeen warriors wounded. Champlain, too, had received an arrow in the knee, and another in the leg, which, for the time, disabled him. He was urgent, however, to renew the attack; while the Hurons, crestfallen and disheartened, refused to move from their camp unless the five hundred allies, for some time expected, should appear. They waited five days in vain, beguiling the interval with frequent skirmishes, in which they were always worsted; then began hastily to retreat, carrying their wounded in the centre, while the Iroquois, sallying from their stronghold, showered arrows on their flanks and rear. The wounded, Champlain among the rest, after being packed in baskets made on the spot, were carried each on the back of a strong warrior, "bundled in a heap," says Champlain, "doubled and strapped together after such a fashion that one could move no more than an infant in swaddling-clothes. The pain is extreme, as I can truly say from experience, having been carried several days in this way, since I could not stand, chiefly on account of the arrow-wound I had got in the knee. I never was in such torment in my life, for the pain of the wound was nothing to that of being bound and pinioned on the back of one of our savages. I lost patience, and as soon as I could bear my weight I got out of this prison, or rather out of hell."[1]

At length the dismal march was ended. They reached the spot where their canoes were hidden, found them untouched, embarked, and recrossed to the northern shore of Lake Ontario. The Hurons had promised Champlain an escort to Quebec; but as the chiefs had little power, in peace or war, beyond that of persuasion, each warrior found good reasons for refusing to lend his canoe. Champlain, too, had lost prestige. The "man with the iron breast" had proved not inseparably wedded to victory; and though the fault was their own, yet not the less was the lustre of their hero tarnished. There

[1] Champlain, (1627,) 46. In the edition of 1632 there are some omissions and verbal changes in this part of the narrative.

was no alternative. He must winter with the Hurons. The great war party broke into fragments, each band betaking itself to its hunting-ground. A chief named Durantal, or Darontal,[1] offered Champlain the shelter of his lodge, and he was glad to accept it.

Meanwhile, Étienne Brulé had found cause to rue the hour when he undertook his hazardous mission to the Carantouan allies. Three years passed before Champlain saw him. It was in the summer of 1618, that, reaching the Saut St. Louis, he there found the interpreter, his hands and his swarthy face marked with traces of the ordeal he had passed. Brulé then told him his story.

He had gone, as already mentioned, with twelve Indians, to hasten the march of the allies, who were to join the Hurons before the hostile town. Crossing Lake Ontario, the party pushed onward with all speed, avoiding trails, threading the thickest forests and darkest swamps, for it was the land of the fierce and watchful Iroquois. They were well advanced on their way when they saw a small party of them crossing a meadow, set upon them, surprised them, killed four, and took two prisoners, whom they led to Carantouan, a palisaded town with a population of eight hundred warriors, or about four thousand souls. The dwellings and defences were like those of the Hurons, and the town seems to have stood on or near the upper waters of the Susquehanna. They were welcomed with feasts, dances, and an uproar of rejoicing. The five hundred warriors prepared to depart, but, engrossed by the general festivity, they prepared so slowly, that, though the hostile town was but three days distant, they found on reaching it that the besiegers were gone. Brulé now returned with them to Carantouan, and, with enterprise worthy of his commander, spent the winter in a tour of exploration. Descending a river, evidently the Susquehanna, he followed it to its junction with the sea, through territories of populous tribes, at war the one with the other. When, in the spring, he returned to Carantouan, five or six of the Indians offered to guide him towards his countrymen. Less fortunate than before, he encountered on the way a band of Iroquois, who, rushing upon

[1] Champlain, with his usual carelessness, calls him by either name indifferently.

the party, scattered them through the woods. Brulé ran like the rest. The cries of pursuers and pursued died away in the distance. The forest was silent around him. He was lost in the shady labyrinth. For three or four days he wandered, helpless and famished, till at length he found an Indian foot-path, and, choosing between starvation and the Iroquois, desperately followed it to throw himself on their mercy. He soon saw three Indians in the distance, laden with fish newly caught, and called to them in the Huron tongue, which was radically similar to that of the Iroquois. They stood amazed, then turned to fly; but Brulé, gaunt with famine, flung down his weapons in token of friendship. They now drew near, listened to the story of his distress, lighted their pipes, and smoked with him; then guided him to their village, and gave him food.

A crowd gathered about him. "Whence do you come? Are you not one of the Frenchmen, the men of iron, who make war on us?"

Brulé answered that he was of a nation better than the French, and fast friends of the Iroquois.

His incredulous captors tied him to a tree, tore out his beard by handfuls, and burned him with firebrands, while their chief vainly interposed in his behalf. He was a good Catholic, and wore an *Agnus Dei* at his breast. One of his torturers asked what it was, and thrust out his hand to take it.

"If you touch it," exclaimed Brulé, "you and all your race will die."

The Indian persisted. The day was hot, and one of those thunder-gusts which often succeed the fierce heats of an American midsummer was rising against the sky. Brulé pointed to the inky clouds as tokens of the anger of his God. The storm broke, and, as the celestial artillery boomed over their darkening forests, the Iroquois were stricken with a superstitious terror. They all fled from the spot, leaving their victim still bound fast, until the chief who had endeavored to protect him returned, cut the cords, led him to his lodge, and dressed his wounds. Thenceforth there was neither dance nor feast to which Brulé was not invited; and when he wished to return to his countrymen, a party of Iroquois guided him four days on his way. He reached the friendly Hurons in safety, and joined them on their yearly descent to meet the French traders at Montreal.[1]

Brulé's adventures find in some points their counterpart in those of his commander on the winter hunting-grounds of his Huron allies. As we turn the ancient, worm-eaten page which preserves the simple record of his fortunes, a wild and dreary scene rises before the mind,—a chill November air, a murky sky, a cold lake, bare and shivering forests, the earth strewn with crisp brown leaves, and, by the water-side, the bark sheds and smoking camp-fires of a band of Indian hunters. Champlain was of the party. There was ample occupation for his gun, for the morning was vocal with the clamor of wild-fowl, and his evening meal was enlivened by the rueful music of the wolves. It was a lake north or northwest of the site of Kingston. On the borders of a neighboring river, twenty-five of the Indians had been busied ten days in preparing for their annual deer-hunt. They planted posts interlaced with boughs in two straight converging lines, each extending more than half a mile through forests and swamps. At the angle where they met was made a strong enclosure like a pound. At dawn of day the hunters spread themselves through the woods, and advanced with shouts, clattering of sticks, and howlings like those of wolves, driving the deer before them into the enclosure, where others lay in wait to despatch them with arrows and spears.

Champlain was in the woods with the rest, when he saw a bird whose novel appearance excited his attention; and, gun in hand, he went in pursuit. The bird, flitting from tree to

[1] The story of Étienne Brulé, whose name may possibly allude to the fiery ordeal through which he had passed, is in Champlain's narrative of his voyage of 1618. It will be found in the edition of 1627, but is omitted in the condensed edition of 1632. It is also told by Sagard.

Brulé met a lamentable fate. In 1632 he was treacherously murdered by Hurons at one of their villages near Penetanguishine. Several years after, when the Huron country was ravaged and half depopulated by an epidemic, the Indians believed that it was caused by the French in revenge for his death, and a renowned sorcerer averred that he had seen a sister of the murdered man flying over their country, breathing forth pestilence and death. Le Jeune, *Relation, 1633*, 34; Brébeuf, *Relation des Hurons, 1635*, 28; *1637*, 160, 167 (Quebec, 1858).

tree, lured him deeper and deeper into the forest; then took wing and vanished. The disappointed sportsman tried to retrace his steps. But the day was clouded, and he had left his pocket-compass at the camp. The forest closed around him, trees mingled with trees in endless confusion. Bewildered and lost, he wandered all day, and at night slept fasting at the foot of a tree. Awaking, he wandered on till afternoon, when he reached a pond slumbering in the shadow of the woods. There were water-fowl along its brink, some of which he shot, and for the first time found food to allay his hunger. He kindled a fire, cooked his game, and, exhausted, blanketless, drenched by a cold rain, made his prayer to Heaven, and again lay down to sleep. Another day of blind and weary wandering succeeded, and another night of exhaustion. He had found paths in the wilderness, but they were not made by human feet. Once more roused from his shivering repose, he journeyed on till he heard the tinkling of a little brook, and bethought him of following its guidance, in the hope that it might lead him to the river where the hunters were now encamped. With toilsome steps he followed the infant stream, now lost beneath the decaying masses of fallen trunks or the impervious intricacies of matted "windfalls," now stealing through swampy thickets or gurgling in the shade of rocks, till it entered at length, not into the river, but into a small lake. Circling around the brink, he found the point where the brook ran out and resumed its course. Listening in the dead stillness of the woods, a dull, hoarse sound rose upon his ear. He went forward, listened again, and could plainly hear the plunge of waters. There was light in the forest before him, and, thrusting himself through the entanglement of bushes he stood on the edge of a meadow. Wild animals were here of various kinds; some skulking in the bordering thickets, some browsing on the dry and matted grass. On his right rolled the river, wide and turbulent, and along its bank he saw the portage path by which the Indians passed the neighboring rapids. He gazed about him. The rocky hills seemed familiar to his eye. A clue was found at last; and, kindling his evening fire, with grateful heart he broke a long fast on the game he had killed. With the break of day he descended at his ease along the bank, and soon descried the smoke of the Indian fires

curling in the heavy morning air against the gray borders of
the forest. The joy was great on both sides. The Indians had
searched for him without ceasing; and from that day forth his
host, Durantal, would never let him go into the forest alone.

They were thirty-eight days encamped on this nameless
river, and killed in that time a hundred and twenty deer. Hard
frosts were needful to give them passage over the land of lakes
and marshes that lay between them and the Huron towns.
Therefore they lay waiting till the fourth of December; when
the frost came, bridged the lakes and streams, and made the
oozy marsh as firm as granite. Snow followed, powdering the
broad wastes with dreary white. Then they broke up their
camp, packed their game on sledges or on their shoulders,
tied on their snow-shoes, and began their march. Champlain
could scarcely endure his load, though some of the Indians
carried a weight fivefold greater. At night, they heard the
cleaving ice uttering its strange groans of torment, and on the
morrow there came a thaw. For four days they waded
through slush and water up to their knees; then came the
shivering north-west wind, and all was hard again. In nineteen days they reached the town of Cahiagué, and, lounging
around their smoky lodge-fires, the hunters forgot the hardships of the past.

For Champlain there was no rest. A double motive urged
him,—discovery, and the strengthening of his colony by widening its circle of trade. First, he repaired to Carhagouha; and
here he found the friar, in his hermitage, still praying, preaching, making catechisms, and struggling with the manifold difficulties of the Huron tongue. After spending several weeks
together, they began their journeyings, and in three days
reached the chief village of the Nation of Tobacco, a powerful
tribe akin to the Hurons, and soon to be incorporated with
them.[1] The travellers visited seven of their towns, and then
passed westward to those of the people whom Champlain
calls the *Cheveux Relevés*, and whom he commends for neat-
ness and ingenuity no less than he condemns them for the
nullity of their summer attire.[2] As the strangers passed from

[1] The Dionondadies, Petuneux, or Nation of Tobacco, had till recently,
according to Lalemant, been at war with the Hurons.

[2] See *ante*, p. 290.

town to town, their arrival was everywhere the signal of festivity. Champlain exchanged pledges of amity with his hosts, and urged them to come down with the Hurons to the yearly trade at Montreal.

Spring was now advancing, and, anxious for his colony, he turned homeward, following that long circuit of Lake Huron and the Ottawa which Iroquois hostility made the only practicable route. Scarcely had he reached the Nipissings, and gained from them a pledge to guide him to that delusive northern sea which never ceased to possess his thoughts, when evil news called him back in haste to the Huron towns. A band of those Algonquins who dwelt on the great island in the Ottawa had spent the winter encamped near Cahiagué, whose inhabitants made them a present of an Iroquois prisoner, with the friendly intention that they should enjoy the pleasure of torturing him. The Algonquins, on the contrary, fed, clothed, and adopted him. On this, the donors, in a rage, sent a warrior to kill the Iroquois. He stabbed him, accordingly, in the midst of the Algonquin chiefs, who in requital killed the murderer. Here was a *casus belli* involving most serious issues for the French, since the Algonquins, by their position on the Ottawa, could cut off the Hurons and all their allies from coming down to trade. Already a fight had taken place at Cahiagué; the principal Algonquin chief had been wounded, and his band forced to purchase safety by a heavy tribute of wampum[1] and a gift of two female prisoners.

All eyes turned to Champlain as umpire of the quarrel. The great council-house was filled with Huron and Algonquin chiefs, smoking with that immobility of feature beneath which their race often hide a more than tiger-like ferocity. The umpire addressed the assembly, enlarged on the folly of falling to blows between themselves when the common enemy stood ready to devour them both, extolled the advantages of the French trade and alliance, and, with zeal not

[1] Wampum was a sort of beads, of several colors, made originally by the Indians from the inner portion of certain shells, and afterwards by the French of porcelain and glass. It served a treble purpose,—that of currency, decoration, and record. Wrought into belts of various devices, each having its significance, it preserved the substance of treaties and compacts from generation to generation.

wholly disinterested, urged them to shake hands like brothers. The friendly counsel was accepted, the pipe of peace was smoked, the storm dispelled, and the commerce of New France rescued from a serious peril.[1]

Once more Champlain turned homeward, and with him went his Huron host, Durantal. Le Caron had preceded him; and, on the eleventh of July, the fellow travellers met again in the infant capital of Canada. The Indians had reported that Champlain was dead, and he was welcomed as one risen from the grave. The friars, who were all here, chanted lauds in their chapel, with a solemn mass and thanksgiving. To the two travellers, fresh from the hardships of the wilderness, the hospitable board of Quebec, the kindly society of countrymen and friends, the adjacent gardens,—always to Champlain an object of especial interest,—seemed like the comforts and repose of home.

The chief Durantal found entertainment worthy of his high estate. The fort, the ship, the armor, the plumes, the cannon, the marvellous architecture of the houses and barracks, the splendors of the chapel, and above all the good cheer, outran the boldest excursion of his fancy; and he paddled back at last to his lodge in the woods, bewildered with astonishment and admiration.

[1] Champlain, (1627,) 63–72.

Chapter XV

HOSTILE SECTS—RIVAL INTERESTS

Quebec • Tadoussac • Embarrassments of Champlain • Montmo-
rency • Madame de Champlain • Disorder and Danger • The
Duc de Ventadour • The Jesuits • Catholics and Heretics •
Richelieu • The Hundred Associates

AT Quebec the signs of growth were faint and few. By the water-side, under the cliff, the so-called "habitation," built in haste eight years before, was already tottering, and Champlain was forced to rebuild it. On the verge of the rock above, where now are seen the buttresses of the demolished castle of St. Louis, he began, in 1620, a fort, behind which were fields and a few buildings. A mile or more distant, by the bank of the St. Charles, where the General Hospital now stands, the Récollets, in the same year, built for themselves a small stone house, with ditches and outworks for defence; and here they began a farm, the stock consisting of several hogs, a pair of asses, a pair of geese, seven pairs of fowls, and four pairs of ducks.[1] The only other agriculturist in the colony was Louis Hébert, who had come to Canada in 1617 with a wife and three children, and who made a house for himself on the rock, at a little distance from Champlain's fort.

Besides Quebec, there were the three trading-stations of Montreal, Three Rivers, and Tadoussac, occupied during a part of the year. Of these, Tadoussac was still the most important. Landing here from France in 1617, the Récollet Paul Huet said mass for the first time in a chapel built of branches, while two sailors standing beside him waved green boughs to drive off the mosquitoes. Thither afterward came Brother Gervais Mohier, newly arrived in Canada; and meeting a crowd of Indians in festal attire, he was frightened at first, suspecting that they might be demons. Being invited by them to a feast, and told that he must not decline, he took his place among a party of two hundred, squatted about four large ket-

---

[1] *Lettre du P. Denis Jamet, 15 Aout, 1620,* in Sagard, *Histoire du Canada,* 58.

tles full of fish, bear's meat, pease, and plums, mixed with figs, raisins, and biscuit procured at great cost from the traders, the whole boiled together and well stirred with a canoe-paddle. As the guest did no honor to the portion set before him, his entertainers tried to tempt his appetite with a large lump of bear's fat, a supreme luxury in their eyes. This only increased his embarrassment, and he took a hasty leave, uttering the ejaculation, "Ho, ho, ho!" which, as he had been correctly informed, was the proper mode of acknowledgment to the master of the feast.

A change had now begun in the life of Champlain. His forest rovings were over. To battle with savages and the elements was more congenial with his nature than to nurse a puny colony into growth and strength; yet to each task he gave himself with the same strong devotion.

His difficulties were great. Quebec was half trading-factory, half mission. Its permanent inmates did not exceed fifty or sixty persons, — fur-traders, friars, and two or three wretched families, who had no inducement, and little wish, to labor. The fort is facetiously represented as having two old women for garrison, and a brace of hens for sentinels.[1] All was discord and disorder. Champlain was the nominal commander; but the actual authority was with the merchants, who held, excepting the friars, nearly everybody in their pay. Each was jealous of the other, but all were united in a common jealousy of Champlain. The few families whom they brought over were forbidden to trade with the Indians, and compelled to sell the fruits of their labor to the agents of the company at a low, fixed price, receiving goods in return at an inordinate valuation. Some of the merchants were of Rouen, some of St. Malo; some were Catholics, some were Huguenots. Hence unceasing bickerings. All exercise of the Reformed religion, on land or water, was prohibited within the limits of New France; but the Huguenots set the prohibition at naught, roaring their heretical psalmody with such vigor from their ships in the river, that the unhallowed strains polluted the ears of the Indians on shore. The merchants of Rochelle, who had refused to join the company, carried on a bold illicit

[1] *Advis au Roy sur les Affaires de la Nouvelle France*, 7.

traffic along the borders of the St. Lawrence, endangering the colony by selling fire-arms to the Indians, eluding pursuit, or, if hard pressed, showing fight; and this was a source of·perpetual irritation to the incensed monopolists.[1]

The colony could not increase. The company of merchants, though pledged to promote its growth, did what they could to prevent it. They were fur-traders, and the interests of the fur-trade are always opposed to those of settlement and population. They feared, too, and with reason, that their monopoly might be suddenly revoked, like that of De Monts, and they thought only of making profit from it while it lasted. They had no permanent stake in the country; nor had the men in their employ, who formed nearly all the scanty population of Canada. Few, if any, of these had brought wives to the colony, and none of them thought of cultivating the soil. They formed a floating population, kept from starving by yearly supplies from France.

Champlain, in his singularly trying position, displayed a mingled zeal and fortitude. He went every year to France, laboring for the interests of the colony. To throw open the trade to all competitors was a measure beyond the wisdom of the times; and he hoped only to bind and regulate the monopoly so as to make it subserve the generous purpose to which he had given himself. The imprisonment of Condé was a source of fresh embarrassment; but the young Duc de Montmorenci assumed his place, purchasing from him the profitable lieutenancy of New France for eleven thousand crowns, and continuing Champlain in command. Champlain had succeeded in binding the company of merchants with new and more stringent engagements; and, in the vain belief that these might not be wholly broken, he began to conceive fresh hopes for the colony. In this faith he embarked with his wife for Quebec in the spring of 1620; and, as the boat drew near the landing, the cannon welcomed her to the rock of her banishment. The buildings were falling to ruin; rain entered on all sides; the courtyard, says Champlain, was as squalid

---

[1] Champlain, 1627 and 1632, *passim*; Sagard, *Hist. du Canada, passim*; Le Clerc, *Établissement de la Foy*, cc. 4–7; *Advis au Roy sur les Affaires de la Nouvelle France; Décret de Prise de Corps d'Hébert; Plainte de la Nouvelle France à la France sa Germaine, passim.*

and dilapidated as a grange pillaged by soldiers. Madame de Champlain was still very young. If the Ursuline tradition is to be trusted, the Indians, amazed at her beauty and touched by her gentleness, would have worshipped her as a divinity. Her husband had married her at the age of twelve;[1] when, to his horror, he presently discovered that she was infected with the heresies of her father, a disguised Huguenot. He addressed himself at once to her conversion, and his pious efforts were something more than successful. During the four years which she passed in Canada, her zeal, it is true, was chiefly exercised in admonishing Indian squaws and catechising their children; but, on her return to France, nothing would content her but to become a nun. Champlain refused; but, as she was child-less, he at length consented to a virtual, though not formal separation. After his death she gained her wish, became an Ursuline nun, founded a convent of that order at Meaux, and died with a reputation almost saintly.[2]

At Quebec, matters grew from bad to worse. The few em-igrants, with no inducement to labor, fell into a lazy apathy, lounging about the trading-houses, gaming, drinking when drink could be had, or roving into the woods on vagabond hunting excursions. The Indians could not be trusted. In the year 1617 they had murdered two men near the end of the Island of Orleans. Frightened at what they had done, and in-cited perhaps by other causes, the Montagnais and their kindred bands mustered at Three Rivers to the number of eight hundred, resolved to destroy the French. The secret was betrayed; and the childish multitude, naked and famishing, became suppliants to their intended victims for the means of life. The French, themselves at the point of starvation, could give little or nothing. An enemy far more formidable awaited them; and now were seen the fruits of Champlain's intermed-dling in Indian wars. In the summer of 1622, the Iroquois descended upon the settlement. A strong party of their war-riors hovered about Quebec, but, still fearful of the arque-buse, forbore to attack it, and assailed the Récollet convent

---

[1] *Contrat de Mariage de Samuel de Champlain, 27 Dec., 1610.* Charavay, *Doc-uments Inédits sur Samuel de Champlain.*

[1] *Extraits des Chroniques de l'Ordre des Ursulines, Journal de Quebec, 10 Mars, 1855.*

on the St. Charles. The prudent friars had fortified themselves. While some prayed in the chapel, the rest, with their Indian converts, manned the walls. The Iroquois respected their palisades and demi-lunes, and withdrew, after burning two Huron prisoners.

Yielding at length to reiterated complaints, the Viceroy Montmorency suppressed the company of St. Malo and Rouen, and conferred the trade of New France, burdened with similar conditions, destined to be similarly broken, on two Huguenots, William and Émery de Caen.[1] The change was a signal for fresh disorders. The enraged monopolists refused to yield. The rival traders filled Quebec with their quarrels; and Champlain, seeing his authority set at naught, was forced to occupy his newly built fort with a band of armed followers. The evil rose to such a pitch, that he joined with the Récollets and the better-disposed among the colonists in sending one of the friars to lay their grievances before the King. The dispute was compromised by a temporary union of the two companies, together with a variety of *arrêts* and regulations, suited, it was thought, to restore tranquillity.[2]

A new change was at hand. Montmorency, tired of his viceroyalty, which gave him ceaseless annoyance, sold it to his nephew, Henri de Lévis, Duc de Ventadour. It was no worldly motive which prompted this young nobleman to assume the burden of fostering the infancy of New France. He had retired from the court, and entered into holy orders. For trade and colonization he cared nothing. The conversion of infidels was his sole care. The Jesuits had the keeping of his conscience, and in his eyes they were the most fitting instruments for his purpose. The Récollets, it is true, had labored with an unflagging devotion. The six friars of their Order— for this was the number which the Calvinist Caen had bound himself to support—had established five distinct missions, extending from Acadia to the borders of Lake Huron; but the field was too vast for their powers. Ostensibly by a sponta-

---

[1] *Lettre de Montmorency à Champlain, 2 Février, 1621*; Paris Documents in archives of Massachusetts, I. 493.

[2] *Le Roy à Champlain, 20 Mars, 1622*; Champlain, (1632, Seconde Partie,) Livre I.; Le Clerc, *Établissement de la Foy*, c. 6; Sagard, *Histoire du Canada*, Livre I. c. 7.

neous movement of their own, but in reality, it is probable, under influences brought to bear on them from without, the Récollets applied for the assistance of the Jesuits, who, strong in resources as in energy, would not be compelled to rest on the reluctant support of Huguenots. Three of their brotherhood, Charles Lalemant, Enemond Masse, and Jean de Brébeuf, accordingly embarked; and, fourteen years after Biard and Masse had landed in Acadia, Canada beheld for the first time those whose names stand so prominent in her annals,— the mysterious followers of Loyola. Their reception was most inauspicious. Champlain was absent. Caen would not lodge them in the fort; the traders would not admit them to their houses. Nothing seemed left for them but to return as they came; when a boat, bearing several Récollets, approached the ship to proffer them the hospitalities of the convent on the St. Charles.[1] They accepted the proffer, and became guests of the charitable friars, who nevertheless entertained a lurking jealousy of these formidable co-workers.

The Jesuits soon unearthed and publicly burnt a libel against their Order belonging to some of the traders. Their strength was soon increased. The Fathers Noirot and De la Noüe landed, with twenty laborers, and the Jesuits were no longer houseless.[2] Brébeuf set forth for the arduous mission of the Hurons; but, on arriving at Trois Rivières, he learned that one of his Franciscan predecessors, Nicolas Viel, had recently been drowned by Indians of that tribe, in the rapid behind Montreal, known to this day as the Saut au Récollet. Less ambitious for martyrdom than he afterwards approved himself, he postponed his voyage to a more auspicious season. In the following spring he renewed the attempt, in company with De la Noüe and one of the friars. The Indians, however, refused to receive him into their canoes, alleging that his tall and portly frame would overset them; and it was only by dint of many presents that their pretended scruples

[1] Le Clerc, *Établissement de la Foy*, I. 310; *Lalemant à Champlain, 28 Juillet, 1625*, in Le Clerc, I. 313; Lalemant, *Relation, 1625*, in *Mercure Français*, XIII.

[2] Lalemant, in a letter dated 1 August, 1626, says that at that time there were only forty-three Frenchmen at Quebec. The Jesuits employed themselves in confessing them, preaching two sermons a month, studying the Indian languages, and cultivating the ground, as a preparation for more arduous work. See Carayon, *Première Mission*, 117.

could be conquered. Brébeuf embarked with his companions, and, after months of toil, reached the barbarous scene of his labors, his sufferings, and his death.

Meanwhile the Viceroy had been deeply scandalized by the contumacious heresy of Émery de Caen, who not only assembled his Huguenot sailors at prayers, but forced Catholics to join them. He was ordered thenceforth to prohibit his crews from all praying and psalm-singing on the river St. Lawrence. The crews revolted, and a compromise was made. It was agreed, that, for the present, they might pray, but not sing.[1] "A bad bargain," says the pious Champlain, "but we made the best of it we could." Caen, enraged at the Viceroy's reproofs, lost no opportunity to vent his spleen against the Jesuits, whom he cordially hated.

Eighteen years had passed since the founding of Quebec, and still the colony could scarcely be said to exist but in the founder's brain. Those who should have been its support were engrossed by trade or propagandism. Champlain might look back on fruitless toils, hopes deferred, a life spent seemingly in vain. The population of Quebec had risen to a hundred and five persons, men, women, and children. Of these, one or two families only had learned to support themselves from the products of the soil. All withered under the monopoly of the Caens.[2] Champlain had long desired to rebuild the fort, which was weak and ruinous; but the merchants would not grant the men and means which, by their charter, they were bound to furnish. At length, however, his urgency in part prevailed, and the work began to advance. Meanwhile the Caens and their associates had greatly prospered, paying, it is said, an annual dividend of forty per cent. In a single year they brought from Canada twenty-two thousand beaver-skins, though the usual number did not exceed twelve or fifteen thousand.[3]

While infant Canada was thus struggling into a half-stifled

[1] ". . . . en fin, fut accordé qu'ils ne chanteroient point les Pseaumes, mais qu'ils s'assembleroient pour faire leur prières." Champlain, (1632, Seconde Partie,) 108.

[2] *Advis au Roy, passim; Plainte de la Nouvelle France.*

[3] Lalemant, *Relation*, 1625, in *Mercure Français*, XIII. The skins sold at a pistole each. The Caens employed forty men and upwards in Canada, besides a hundred and fifty in their ships.

being, the foundation of a commonwealth destined to a marvellous vigor of development had been laid on the Rock of Plymouth. In their character, as in their destiny, the rivals were widely different; yet, at the outset, New England was unfaithful to the principle of freedom. New England Protestantism appealed to Liberty, then closed the door against her; for all Protestantism is an appeal from priestly authority to the right of private judgment, and the New England Puritan, after claiming this right for himself, denied it to all who differed with him. On a stock of freedom he grafted a scion of despotism;[1] yet the vital juices of the root penetrated at last to the uttermost branches, and nourished them to an irrepressible strength and expansion. With New France it was otherwise. She was consistent to the last. Root, stem, and branch, she was the nursling of authority. Deadly absolutism blighted her early and her later growth. Friars and Jesuits, a Ventadour and a Richelieu, shaped her destinies. All that conflicted against advancing liberty—the centralized power of the crown and the tiara, the ultramontane in religion, the despotic in policy—found their fullest expression and most fatal exercise. Her records shine with glorious deeds, the self-devotion of heroes and of martyrs; and the result of all is disorder, imbecility, ruin.

[1] In Massachusetts, none but church-members could vote or hold office. In other words, the deputies to the General Court were deputies of churches, and the Governor and magistrates were church-members, elected by church-members. Church and State were not united: they were identified. A majority of the people, including men of wealth, ability, and character, were deprived of the rights of freemen because they were not church-members. When some of them petitioned the General Court for redress, they were imprisoned and heavily fined as guilty of sedition. Their sedition consisted in their proposing to appeal to Parliament, though it was then composed of Puritans. See Palfrey, *History of New England*, Vol. II. Ch. IV.

The New England Puritans were foes, not only of episcopacy, but of presbytery. But under their system of separate and independent churches, it was impossible to enforce the desired uniformity of doctrine. Therefore, while inveighing against English and Scottish presbytery, they established a virtual presbytery of their own. A distinction was made. The New England Synod could not *coerce* an erring church; it could only *advise* and *exhort*. This was clearly insufficient, and, accordingly, in cases of heresy and schism, the *civil power was invoked*. That is to say, the churches in their ecclesiastical capacity consigned doctrinal offenders for punishment to the same churches acting in

The great champion of absolutism, Richelieu, was now supreme in France. His thin frame, pale cheek, and cold, calm
eye, concealed an inexorable will, and a mind of vast capacity,
armed with all the resources of boldness and of craft. Under
his potent agency, the royal power, in the weak hands of
Louis the Thirteenth, waxed and strengthened daily, triumph-
ing over the factions of the court, the turbulence of the Huguenots, the ambitious independence of the nobles, and all
the elements of anarchy which, since the death of Henry the
Fourth, had risen into fresh life. With no friends and a thousand enemies, disliked and feared by the pitiful King whom
he served, making his tool by turns of every party and of
every principle, he advanced by countless crooked paths towards his object,—the greatness of France under a concentred and undivided authority.

In the midst of more urgent cares, he addressed himself to
fostering the commercial and naval power. Montmorency
then held the ancient charge of Admiral of France. Richelieu
bought it, suppressed it, and, in its stead, constituted himself
Grand Master and Superintendent of Navigation and Commerce. In this new capacity, the mismanaged affairs of New
France were not long concealed from him; and he applied a
prompt and powerful remedy. The privileges of the Caens
were annulled. A company was formed, to consist of a
hundred associates, and to be called the Company of New
France. Richelieu himself was the head, and the Maréchal
Deffiat and other men of rank, besides many merchants and
burghers of condition, were members.[1] The whole of New
France, from Florida to the Arctic Circle, and from Newfoundland to the sources of the St. Lawrence and its tributary
waters, was conferred on them forever, with the attributes of
sovereign power. A perpetual monopoly of the fur-trade was
granted them, with a monopoly of all other commerce within

---

a civil capacity, while they professed an abomination of presbytery because it
endangered liberty of conscience. See *A Platform of Church Discipline, gather'd
out of the Word of God and agreed upon by the Elders and Messengers of the
Churches assembled in the Synod at Cambridge, in New England*, Ch. XVII.
§§ 8, 9.

[1] *Noms, Surnoms, et Qualitez des Associez de la Compagnie de la Nouvelle
France.*

the limits of their government for fifteen years.[1] The trade of
the colony was declared free, for the same period, from all
duties and imposts. Nobles, officers, and ecclesiastics, members of the Company, might engage in commercial pursuits
without derogating from the privileges of their order. And,
in evidence of his good will, the King gave them two ships
of war, armed and equipped.

On their part, the Company were bound to convey to New
France during the next year, 1628, two or three hundred men
of all trades, and before the year 1643 to increase the number
to four thousand persons,[2] of both sexes; to lodge and support them for three years; and, this time expired, to give them
cleared lands for their maintenance. Every settler must be a
Frenchman and a Catholic; and for every new settlement at
least three ecclesiastics must be provided. Thus was New
France to be forever free from the taint of heresy. The stain
of her infancy was to be wiped away. Against the foreigner
and the Huguenot the door was closed and barred. England
threw open her colonies to all who wished to enter,—to the
suffering and oppressed, the bold, active, and enterprising.
France shut out those who wished to come, and admitted
only those who did not,—the favored class who clung to
the old faith and had no motive or disposition to leave
their homes. English colonization obeyed a natural law,
and sailed with wind and tide; French colonization spent
its whole struggling existence in futile efforts to make head
against them. The English colonist developed inherited
freedom on a virgin soil; the French colonist was pursued
across the Atlantic by a paternal despotism better in intention and more withering in effect than that which he left
behind. If, instead of excluding Huguenots, France had
given them an asylum in the west, and left them there to
work out their own destinies, Canada would never have
been a British province, and the United States would have

---

[1] The whale and the cod fishery were, however, to remain open to all.

[2] Charlevoix erroneously says sixteen thousand. Compare *Acte pour l'Établissement de la Compagnie des Cent Associés*, in *Mercure Français*, XIV. Partie
II. 232; *Édits et Ordonnances*, I. 5. The act of establishment was originally
published in a small duodecimo volume, which differs, though not very essentially, from the copy in the *Mercure*.

shared their vast domain with a vigorous population of self-governing Frenchmen.

A trading company was now feudal proprietor of all domains in North America within the claim of France. Fealty and homage on its part, and on the part of the Crown the appointment of supreme judicial officers, and the confirmation of the titles of dukes, marquises, counts, and barons, were the only reservations. The King heaped favors on the new corporation. Twelve of the *bourgeois* members were ennobled; while artisans and even manufacturers were tempted, by extraordinary privileges, to emigrate to the New World. The associates, of whom Champlain was one, entered upon their functions with a capital of three hundred thousand livres.[1]

[1] *Articles et Conventions de Société et Compagnie*, in *Mercure Français*, XIV. Partie II. 250.

Chapter XVI

1628, 1629

THE ENGLISH AT QUEBEC

Revolt of Rochelle • War with England • The English on the St. Lawrence • Bold Attitude of Champlain • The French Squadron destroyed • Famine • Return of the English • Quebec surrendered • Another Naval Battle • Michel • Champlain at London.

THE first care of the new Company was to succor Quebec, whose inmates were on the verge of starvation. Four armed vessels, with a fleet of transports commanded by Roquemont, one of the associates, sailed from Dieppe with colonists and supplies in April, 1628; but nearly at the same time another squadron, destined also for Quebec, was sailing from an English port. War had at length broken out in France. The Huguenot revolt had come to a head. Rochelle was in arms against the King; and Richelieu, with his royal ward, was beleaguering it with the whole strength of the kingdom. Charles the First of England, urged by the heated passions of Buckingham, had declared himself for the rebels, and sent a fleet to their aid. At home, Charles detested the followers of Calvin as dangerous to his own authority; abroad, he befriended them as dangerous to the authority of a rival. In France, Richelieu crushed protestantism as a curb to the house of Bourbon; in Germany, he nursed and strengthened it as a curb to the house of Austria.

The attempts of Sir William Alexander to colonize Acadia had of late turned attention in England towards the New World; and, on the breaking out of the war, an expedition was set on foot, under the auspices of that singular personage, to seize on the French possessions in North America. It was a private enterprise, undertaken by London merchants, prominent among whom was Gervase Kirke, an Englishman of Derbyshire, who had long lived at Dieppe, and had there married a Frenchwoman.[1] Gervase Kirke and his associates

---

[1] Henry Kirke, *First English Conquest of Canada*, (1871,) 27, 28, 206–208. David Kirke was knighted in Scotland. Hence he is said to have been Scotch by descent.

fitted out three small armed ships, commanded respectively by his sons David, Lewis, and Thomas. Letters of marque were obtained from the King, and the adventurers were authorized to drive out the French from Acadia and Canada. Many Huguenot refugees were among the crews. Having been expelled from New France as settlers, the persecuted sect were returning as enemies. One Captain Michel, who had been in the service of the Caens, "a furious Calvinist,"[1] is said to have instigated the attempt, acting, it is affirmed, under the influence of one of his former employers.

Meanwhile the famished tenants of Quebec were eagerly waiting the expected succor. Daily they gazed beyond Point Levi and along the channels of Orleans, in the vain hope of seeing the approaching sails. At length, on the ninth of July, two men, worn with struggling through forests and over torrents, crossed the St. Charles and mounted the rock. They were from Cape Tourmente, where Champlain had some time before established an outpost, and they brought news that, according to the report of Indians, six large vessels lay in the harbor of Tadoussac.[2] The friar Le Caron was at Quebec, and, with a brother Récollet, he went in a canoe to gain further intelligence. As the missionary scouts were paddling along the borders of the Island of Orleans, they met two canoes advancing in hot haste, manned by Indians, who with shouts and gestures warned them to turn back.

The friars, however, waited till the canoes came up, when they saw a man lying disabled at the bottom of one of them, his moustaches burned by the flash of the musket which had wounded him. He proved to be Foucher, who commanded at Cape Tourmente. On that morning,—such was the story of the fugitives,—twenty men had landed at that post from a small fishing-vessel. Being to all appearance French, they were hospitably received; but no sooner had they entered the houses than they began to pillage and burn all before them, killing the cattle, wounding the commandant, and making several prisoners.[3]

The character of the fleet at Tadoussac was now sufficiently

[1] Charlevoix, I. 171.
[2] Champlain, (1632, Seconde Partie,) 152.
[3] Sagard, 919.

clear. Quebec was incapable of defence. Only fifty pounds of gunpowder were left in the magazine; and the fort, owing to the neglect and ill-will of the Caens, was so wretchedly constructed, that, a few days before, two towers of the main building had fallen. Champlain, however, assigned to each man his post, and waited the result.[1] On the next afternoon, a boat was seen issuing from behind the Point of Orleans and hovering hesitatingly about the mouth of the St. Charles. On being challenged, the men on board proved to be Basque fishermen, lately captured by the English, and now sent by Kirke unwilling messengers to Champlain. Climbing the steep pathway to the fort, they delivered their letter,—a summons, couched in terms of great courtesy, to surrender Quebec. There was no hope but in courage. A bold front must supply the lack of batteries and ramparts; and Champlain dismissed the Basques with a reply, in which, with equal courtesy, he expressed his determination to hold his position to the last.[2]

All now stood on the watch, hourly expecting the enemy; when, instead of the hostile squadron, a small boat crept into sight, and one Desdames, with ten Frenchmen, landed at the storehouses. He brought stirring news. The French commander, Roquemont, had despatched him to tell Champlain that the ships of the Hundred Associates were ascending the St. Lawrence, with reinforcements and supplies of all kinds. But on his way Desdames had seen an ominous sight,—the English squadron standing under full sail out of Tadoussac, and steering downwards as if to intercept the advancing succor. He had only escaped them by dragging his boat up the beach and hiding it; and scarcely were they out of sight when the booming of cannon told him that the fight was begun.

Racked with suspense, the starving tenants of Quebec waited the result; but they waited in vain. No white sail moved athwart the green solitudes of Orleans. Neither friend nor foe appeared; and it was not till long afterward that Indians brought them the tidings that Roquemont's crowded transports had been overpowered, and all the supplies destined to relieve their miseries sunk in the St. Lawrence or seized by the victorious English. Kirke, however, deceived by

[1] 10 July, 1628.
[2] Sagard, 922; Champlain, (1632, Seconde Partie,) 157.

the bold attitude of Champlain, had been too discreet to attack Quebec, and after his victory employed himself in cruising for French fishing-vessels along the borders of the Gulf.

Meanwhile, the suffering at Quebec increased daily. Somewhat less than a hundred men, women, and children were cooped up in the fort, subsisting on a meagre pittance of pease and Indian corn. The garden of the Héberts, the only thrifty settlers, was ransacked for every root or seed that could afford nutriment. Months wore on, and, in the spring, the distress had risen to such a pitch that Champlain had wellnigh resolved to leave to the women, children, and sick the little food that remained, and with the able-bodied men invade the Iroquois, seize one of their villages, fortify himself in it, and sustain his followers on the buried stores of maize with which the strongholds of these provident savages were always furnished.

Seven ounces of pounded pease were now the daily food of each; and, at the end of May, even this failed. Men, women, and children betook themselves to the woods, gathering acorns and grubbing up roots. Those of the plant called Solomon's seal were most in request.[1] Some joined the Hurons or the Algonquins; some wandered towards the Abenakis of Maine; some descended in a boat to Gaspé, trusting to meet a French fishing-vessel. There was scarcely one who would not have hailed the English as deliverers. But the English had sailed home with their booty, and the season was so late that there was little prospect of their return. Forgotten alike by friends and foes, Quebec was on the verge of extinction.

On the morning of the nineteenth of July, an Indian, renowned as a fisher of eels, who had built his hut on the St. Charles, hard by the new dwelling of the Jesuits, came, with his usual imperturbability of visage, to Champlain. He had just discovered three ships sailing up the south channel of Orleans. Champlain was alone. All his followers were absent, fishing or searching for roots. At about ten o'clock his servant appeared with four small bags of roots, and the tidings that he had seen the three ships a league off, behind Point Levi. As man after man hastened in, Champlain ordered the starved

[1] Sagard, 977.

and ragged band, sixteen in all,[1] to their posts, whence, with
hungry eyes, they watched the English vessels anchoring in
the basin below, and a boat with a white flag moving towards
the shore. A young officer landed with a summons to surrender. The terms of capitulation were at length settled. The
French were to be conveyed to their own country, and each
soldier was allowed to take with him his clothes, and, in addition, a coat of beaver-skin.[2] On this some murmuring rose,
several of those who had gone to the Hurons having lately
returned with peltry of no small value. Their complaints were
vain; and on the twentieth of July, amid the roar of cannon
from the ships, Lewis Kirke, the Admiral's brother, landed at
the head of his soldiers, and planted the cross of St. George
where the followers of Wolfe again planted it a hundred and
thirty years later. After inspecting the worthless fort, he repaired to the houses of the Récollets and Jesuits on the St.
Charles. He treated the former with great courtesy, but displayed against the latter a violent aversion, expressing his regret that he could not have begun his operations by battering
their house about their ears. The inhabitants had no cause to
complain of him. He urged the widow and family of the settler Hébert, the patriarch, as he has been styled, of New
France, to remain and enjoy the fruits of their industry under
English allegiance; and, as beggary in France was the alternative, his offer was accepted.

Champlain, bereft of his command, grew restless, and
begged to be sent to Tadoussac, where the Admiral, David
Kirke, lay with his main squadron, having sent his brothers
Lewis and Thomas to seize Quebec. Accordingly, Champlain,
with the Jesuits, embarking with Thomas Kirke, descended
the river. Off Mal Bay a strange sail was seen. As she approached, she proved to be a French ship. In fact, she was on
her way to Quebec with supplies, which, if earlier sent, would
have saved the place. She had passed the Admiral's squadron
in a fog; but here her good fortune ceased. Thomas Kirke
bore down on her, and the cannonade began. The fight was
hot and doubtful; but at length the French struck, and Kirke

[1] Champlain, (1632, Seconde Partie,) 267.
[2] *Articles granted to the Sieurs Champlain and Le Pont by Thomas Kearke*, 19
July, 1629.

sailed into Tadoussac with his prize. Here lay his brother, the Admiral, with five armed ships.

The Admiral's two voyages to Canada were private ventures; and, though he had captured nineteen fishing-vessels, besides Roquemont's eighteen transports and other prizes, the result had not answered his hopes. His mood, therefore, was far from benign, especially as he feared, that, owing to the declaration of peace, he would be forced to disgorge a part of his booty; yet, excepting the Jesuits, he treated his captives with courtesy, and often amused himself with shooting larks on shore in company with Champlain. The Huguenots, however, of whom there were many in his ships, showed an exceeding bitterness against the Catholics. Chief among them was Michel, who had instigated and conducted the enterprise, the merchant admiral being but an indifferent seaman. Michel, whose skill was great, held a high command and the title of Rear-Admiral. He was a man of a sensitive temperament, easily piqued on the point of honor. His morbid and irritable nerves were wrought to the pitch of frenzy by the reproaches of treachery and perfidy with which the French prisoners assailed him, while, on the other hand, he was in a state of continual rage at the fancied neglect and contumely of his English associates. He raved against Kirke, who, as he declared, treated him with an insupportable arrogance. "I have left my country," he exclaimed, "for the service of foreigners; and they give me nothing but ingratitude and scorn." His fevered mind, acting on his diseased body, often excited him to transports of fury, in which he cursed indiscriminately the people of St. Malo, against whom he had a grudge, and the Jesuits, whom he detested. On one occasion, Kirke was conversing with some of the latter.

"Gentlemen," he said, "your business in Canada was to enjoy what belonged to M. de Caen, whom you dispossessed."

"Pardon me, sir," answered Brébeuf, "we came purely for the glory of God, and exposed ourselves to every kind of danger to convert the Indians."

Here Michel broke in: "Ay, ay, convert the Indians! You mean, convert the beaver!"

"That is false!" retorted Brébeuf.

Michel raised his fist, exclaiming, "But for the respect I owe the General, I would strike you for giving me the lie."

Brébeuf, a man of powerful frame and vehement passions, nevertheless regained his practised self-command, and replied: "You must excuse me. I did not mean to give you the lie. I should be very sorry to do so. The words I used are those we use in the schools when a doubtful question is advanced, and they mean no offence. Therefore I ask you to pardon me."

Despite the apology, Michel's frenzied brain harped on the presumed insult, and he raved about it without ceasing.

"*Bon Dieu!*" said Champlain, "you swear well for a Reformer!"

"I know it," returned Michel; "I should be content if I had but struck that Jesuit who gave me the lie before my general."

At length, one of his transports of rage ended in a lethargy from which he never awoke. His funeral was conducted with a pomp suited to his rank; and, amid discharges of cannon whose dreary roar was echoed from the yawning gulf of the Saguenay, his body was borne to its rest under the rocks of Tadoussac. Good Catholics and good Frenchmen saw in his fate the immediate finger of Providence. "I do not doubt that his soul is in perdition," remarks Champlain, who, however, had endeavored to befriend the unfortunate man during the access of his frenzy.[1]

Having finished their carousings, which were profuse, and their trade with the Indians, which was not lucrative, the English steered down the St. Lawrence. Kirke feared greatly a meeting with Razilly, a naval officer of distinction,[2] who was to have sailed from France with a strong force to succor Quebec; but, peace having been proclaimed, the expedition had been limited to two ships under Captain Daniel. Thus Kirke, wilfully ignoring the treaty of peace, was left to pursue his depredations unmolested. Daniel, however, though too weak to cope with him, achieved a signal exploit. On the island of Cape Breton, near the site of Louisburg, he found an English

---

[1] Champlain, (1632, Seconde Partie) 256: "Je ne doute point qu'elle ne soit aux enfers." The dialogue above is literally translated. The Jesuits Le Jeune and Charlevoix tell the story with evident satisfaction.

[2] Claude de Razilly was one of three brothers, all distinguished in the marine service.

fort, built two months before, under the auspices, doubtless, of Sir William Alexander. Daniel, regarding it as a bold encroachment on French territory, stormed it at the head of his pikemen, entered sword in hand, and took it with all its defenders.[1]

Meanwhile, Kirke with his prisoners was crossing the Atlantic. His squadron at length reached Plymouth, whence Champlain set out for London. Here he had an interview with the French ambassador, who, at his instance, gained from the King a promise, that, in pursuance of the terms of the treaty concluded in the previous April, New France should be restored to the French Crown.

It long remained a mystery why Charles consented to a stipulation which pledged him to resign so important a conquest. The mystery is explained by the recent discovery of a letter from the King to Sir Isaac Wake, his ambassador at Paris. The promised dowry of Queen Henrietta Maria, amounting to eight hundred thousand crowns, had been but half paid by the French government, and Charles, then at issue with his Parliament and in desperate need of money, instructs his ambassador, that, when he receives the balance due, and not before, he is to give up to the French both Quebec and Port Royal, which had also been captured by Kirke. The letter was accompanied by "solemn instruments under our hand and seal" to make good the transfer on fulfilment of the condition. It was for a sum equal to about two hundred and forty thousand dollars that Charles entailed on Great Britain and her colonies a century of bloody wars. The Kirkes and their associates, who had made the conquest at their own cost, under the royal authority, were never reimbursed, though David Kirke received the honor of knighthood, which cost the King nothing.[2]

[1] *Relation du Voyage fait par le Capitaine Daniel*; Champlain, (1632, Seconde Partie,) 271. Captain Farrar, who commanded the fort, declares, however, that they were "treacherously surprised." *Petition of Captain Constance Farrar*, Dec., 1629.

[2] *Charles I. to Sir Isaac Wake*, 12 June, 1631, printed in Brymner, *Report on Canadian Archives*, 1884, p. lx.

Before me is a copy of the original agreement for the restitution of Quebec and Port Royal, together with ships and goods taken after the peace. It is indorsed, *Articles arrestés entre les Deputés des Deux Couronnes pour la Restitu-*

tion des Choses qui ont été prinses depuis le Traicté de Paix fait entre elles; 24 Avril, 1629. It was not till two years later that King Charles carried it into effect, on receiving the portion of the Queen. See also *Lettres de Chateauneuf, Ambassadeur de France, au Cardinal de Richelieu,* Nov., Dec., 1629, and *Memorial of the French Ambassador to King Charles,* Feb., 1630; *Lord Dorchester to Sir Isaac Wake,* 15 April, 1630; *Examination of Capt. David Kirke before Sir Henry Marten,* 27 May (?), 1631; *The King to Sir William Alexander,* 12 June, 1632; *Extrait concernant ce qui s'est passé dans l'Acadie et le Canada en 1627 et 1628 tiré d'un Requête du Chevalier Louis Kirk,* in *Mémoires des Commissaires,* II. 275; *Literæ continentes Promissionem Regis ad tradendum,* etc., in Hazard, I. 314; *Traité de Paix fait à Suze,* Ibid. 319; *Règlemens entre les Roys de France et d'Angleterre,* in *Mercure Français,* XVIII. 39; Rushworth, II. 24; *Traité entre le Roi Louis XIII. et Charles I., Roi d'Angleterre, pour la Restitution de la Nouvelle France, l'Acadie, et Canada, 29 Mars, 1632.*

In the Archives des Affaires Étrangères is a letter, not signed, but evidently written by Champlain, apparently on the 16th of October, the day of his arrival in England. It gives a few details not in his printed narrative. It states that Lewis Kirke took two silver chalices from a chest of the Jesuits, on which the Jesuit Masse said, "Do not profane them, for they are sacred." "Profane them!" returned Kirke; "since you tell me that, I will keep them, which I would not have done otherwise. I take them because you believe in them, for I will have no idolatry."

Chapter XVII

DEATH OF CHAMPLAIN

*New France restored to the French Crown • Zeal of Champlain •
The English leave Quebec • Return of Jesuits • Arrival of Cham-
plain • Daily Life at Quebec • Propagandism • Policy and
Religion • Death of Champlain*

O N Monday, the fifth of July, 1632, Émery de Caen anchored before Quebec. He was commissioned by the
French Crown to reclaim the place from the English; to hold,
for one year, a monopoly of the fur-trade, as an indemnity for
his losses in the war; and, when this time had expired, to give
place to the Hundred Associates of New France.[1]

By the convention of Suza, New France was to be restored
to the French Crown; yet it had been matter of debate
whether a fulfilment of this engagement was worth the demanding. That wilderness of woods and savages had been
ruinous to nearly all connected with it. The Caens, successful
at first, had suffered heavily in the end. The Associates were
on the verge of bankruptcy. These deserts were useless unless
peopled; and to people them would depopulate France. Thus
argued the inexperienced reasoners of the time, judging from
the wretched precedents of Spanish and Portuguese colonization. The world had not as yet the example of an island
kingdom, which, vitalized by a stable and regulated liberty,
has peopled a continent and spread colonies over all the earth,
gaining constantly new vigor with the matchless growth of its
offspring.

On the other hand, honor, it was urged, demanded that
France should be reinstated in the land which she had discovered and explored. Should she, the centre of civilization, remain cooped up within her own narrow limits, while rivals
and enemies were sharing the vast regions of the West? The
commerce and fisheries of New France would in time become
a school for French sailors. Mines even now might be discov-

[1] *Articles accordés au Sr. de Caen; Acte de Protestation du Sr. de Caen.*

ered; and the fur-trade, well conducted, could not but be a source of wealth. Disbanded soldiers and women from the streets might be shipped to Canada. Thus New France would be peopled and old France purified. A power more potent than reason reinforced such arguments. Richelieu seems to have regarded it as an act of personal encroachment that the subjects of a foreign crown should seize on the domain of a company of which he was the head; and it could not be supposed, that, with power to eject them, the arrogant minister would suffer them to remain in undisturbed possession.

A spirit far purer and more generous was active in the same behalf. The character of Champlain belonged rather to the Middle Age than to the seventeenth century. Long toil and endurance had calmed the adventurous enthusiasm of his youth into a steadfast earnestness of purpose; and he gave himself with a loyal zeal and devotedness to the profoundly mistaken principles which he had espoused. In his mind, patriotism and religion were inseparably linked. France was the champion of Christianity, and her honor, her greatness, were involved in her fidelity to this high function. Should she abandon to perdition the darkened nations among whom she had cast the first faint rays of hope? Among the members of the Company were those who shared his zeal; and though its capital was exhausted, and many of the merchants were withdrawing in despair, these enthusiasts formed a subordinate association, raised a new fund, and embarked on the venture afresh.[1]

England, then, resigned her prize, and Caen was despatched to reclaim Quebec from the reluctant hands of Thomas Kirke. The latter, obedient to an order from the King of England, struck his flag, embarked his followers, and abandoned the scene of his conquest. Caen landed with the Jesuits, Paul le Jeune and Anne de la Nouë. They climbed the steep stairway which led up the rock, and, as they reached the top, the dilapidated fort lay on their left, while farther on was the stone cottage of the Héberts, surrounded with its vegetable gardens,—the only thrifty spot amid a scene of neglect. But few Indians could be seen. True to their native instincts,

---

[1] *État de la dépense de la Compagnie de la Nouvelle France.*

they had, at first, left the defeated French and welcomed the conquerors. Their English partialities were, however, but short-lived. Their intrusion into houses and storerooms, the stench of their tobacco, and their importunate begging, though before borne patiently, were rewarded by the new-comers with oaths, and sometimes with blows. The Indians soon shunned Quebec, seldom approaching it except when drawn by necessity or a craving for brandy. This was now the case; and several Algonquin families, maddened with drink, were howling, screeching, and fighting within their bark lodges. The women were frenzied like the men. It was dangerous to approach the place unarmed.[1]

In the following spring, 1633, on the twenty-third of May, Champlain, commissioned anew by Richelieu, resumed command at Quebec in behalf of the Company.[2] Father le Jeune, Superior of the mission, was wakened from his morning sleep by the boom of the saluting cannon. Before he could sally forth, the convent door was darkened by the stately form of his brother Jesuit, Brébeuf, newly arrived; and the Indians who stood by uttered ejaculations of astonishment at the raptures of their greeting. The father hastened to the fort, and arrived in time to see a file of musketeers and pikemen mounting the pathway of the cliff below, and the heretic Caen resigning the keys of the citadel into the Catholic hands of Champlain. Le Jeune's delight exudes in praises of one not always a theme of Jesuit eulogy, but on whom, in the hope of a continuance of his favors, no praise could now be ill bestowed. "I sometimes think that this great man [Richelieu], who by his admirable wisdom and matchless conduct of affairs is so renowned on earth, is preparing for himself a dazzling crown of glory in heaven by the care he evinces for the conversion of so many lost infidel souls in this savage land. I pray affectionately for him every day," etc.[3]

For Champlain, too, he has praises which, if more measured, are at least as sincere. Indeed, the Father Superior had the best reason to be pleased with the temporal head of the

[1] *Relation du Voyage fait à Canada pour la Prise de Possession du Fort de Quebec par les François*, in *Mercure Français*, XVIII.

[2] *Voyage de Champlain*, in *Mercure Français*, XIX.; *Lettre de Caen à* . . . .

[3] Le Jeune, *Relation, 1633*, 26 (Quebec, 1858).

colony. In his youth, Champlain had fought on the side of that more liberal and national form of Romanism of which the Jesuits were the most emphatic antagonists. Now, as Le Jeune tells us, with evident contentment, he chose him, the Jesuit, as director of his conscience. In truth, there were none but Jesuits to confess and absolve him; for the Récollets, prevented, to their deep chagrin, from returning to the missions they had founded, were seen no more in Canada, and the followers of Loyola were sole masters of the field.[1] The manly heart of the commandant, earnest, zealous, and direct, was seldom chary of its confidence, or apt to stand too warily on its guard in presence of a profound art mingled with a no less profound sincerity.

A stranger visiting the fort of Quebec would have been astonished at its air of conventual decorum. Black Jesuits and scarfed officers mingled at Champlain's table. There was little conversation, but, in its place, histories and the lives of saints were read aloud, as in a monastic refectory.[2] Prayers, masses, and confessions followed one another with an edifying regularity, and the bell of the adjacent chapel, built by Champlain, rang morning, noon, and night. Godless soldiers caught the infection, and whipped themselves in penance for their sins. Debauched artisans outdid each other in the fury of their contrition. Quebec was become a mission. Indians gathered thither as of old, not from the baneful lure of brandy, for the traffic in it was no longer tolerated, but from the less pernicious attractions of gifts, kind words, and politic blandishments. To the vital principle of propagandism both the commercial and the military character were subordinated; or, to speak more justly, trade, policy, and military power leaned on the missions as their main support, the grand instrument of their extension. The missions were to explore the interior; the missions were to win over the savage hordes at once to Heaven and to France. Peaceful, benign, beneficent, were the weapons of this conquest. France aimed to subdue, not by

---

[1] *Mémoire faict en 1637 pour l'Affaire des Pères Récollects . . . . touchant le Droit qu'ils ont depuis l'An 1615 d'aller en Quanada. Mémoire instructif contenant la Conduite des Pères Récollects de Paris en leur Mission de Canada.*

[2] Le Jeune, *Relation, 1634,* 2 (Quebec, 1858). Compare Du Creux, *Historia Canadensis,* 156.

the sword, but by the cross; not to overwhelm and crush the nations she invaded, but to convert, civilize, and embrace them among her children.

And who were the instruments and the promoters of this proselytism, at once so devout and so politic? Who can answer? who can trace out the crossing and mingling currents of wisdom and folly, ignorance and knowledge, truth and falsehood, weakness and force, the noble and the base,—can analyze a systematized contradiction, and follow through its secret wheels, springs, and levers a phenomenon of moral mechanism? Who can define the Jesuits? The story of their missions is marvellous as a tale of chivalry, or legends of the lives of saints. For many years, it was the history of New France and of the wild communities of her desert empire.

Two years passed. The mission of the Hurons was established, and here the indomitable Brébeuf, with a band worthy of him, toiled amid miseries and perils as fearful as ever shook the constancy of man; while Champlain at Quebec, in a life uneventful, yet harassing and laborious, was busied in the round of cares which his post involved.

Christmas day, 1635, was a dark day in the annals of New France. In a chamber of the fort, breathless and cold, lay the hardy frame which war, the wilderness, and the sea had buffeted so long in vain. After two months and a half of illness, Champlain, stricken with paralysis, at the age of sixty-eight, was dead. His last cares were for his colony and the succor of its suffering families. Jesuits, officers, soldiers, traders, and the few settlers of Quebec, followed his remains to the church; Le Jeune pronounced his eulogy,[1] and the feeble community built a tomb to his honor.[2]

The colony could ill spare him. For twenty-seven years he had labored hard and ceaselessly for its welfare, sacrificing fortune, repose, and domestic peace to a cause embraced with enthusiasm and pursued with intrepid persistency. His char-

---

[1] Le Jeune, *Relation, 1636*, 56 (Quebec, 1858).

[2] Vimont, *Relation, 1643*, 3 (Quebec, 1858). A supposed discovery, in 1865, of the burial-place of Champlain, produced a sharp controversy at Quebec. Champlain made a will, leaving 4,000 livres, with other property, to the Jesuits. The will was successfully contested before the Parliament of Paris, and was annulled on the ground of informality.

acter belonged partly to the past, partly to the present. The *preux chevalier*, the crusader, the romance-loving explorer, the curious, knowledge-seeking traveller, the practical navigator, all claimed their share in him. His views, though far beyond those of the mean spirits around him, belonged to his age and his creed. He was less statesman than soldier. He leaned to the most direct and boldest policy, and one of his last acts was to petition Richelieu for men and munitions for repressing that standing menace to the colony, the Iroquois.[1] His dauntless courage was matched by an unwearied patience, proved by life-long vexations, and not wholly subdued even by the saintly follies of his wife. He is charged with credulity, from which few of his age were free, and which in all ages has been the foible of earnest and generous natures, too ardent to criticise, and too honorable to doubt the honor of others. Perhaps the heretic might have liked him more if the Jesuit had liked him less. The adventurous explorer of Lake Huron, the bold invader of the Iroquois, befits but indifferently the monastic sobrieties of the fort of Quebec, and his sombre environment of priests. Yet Champlain was no formalist, nor was his an empty zeal. A soldier from his youth, in an age of unbridled license, his life had answered to his maxims; and when a generation had passed after his visit to the Hurons, their elders remembered with astonishment the continence of the great French war-chief.

His books mark the man, — all for his theme and his purpose, nothing for himself. Crude in style, full of the superficial errors of carelessness and haste, rarely diffuse, often brief to a fault, they bear on every page the palpable impress of truth.

With the life of the faithful soldier closes the opening period of New France. Heroes of another stamp succeed; and it remains to tell the story of their devoted lives, their faults, follies, and virtues.

[1] *Lettre de Champlain au Ministre*, 15 *Aout*, 1635.

THE JESUITS
IN NORTH AMERICA
IN THE
SEVENTEENTH CENTURY

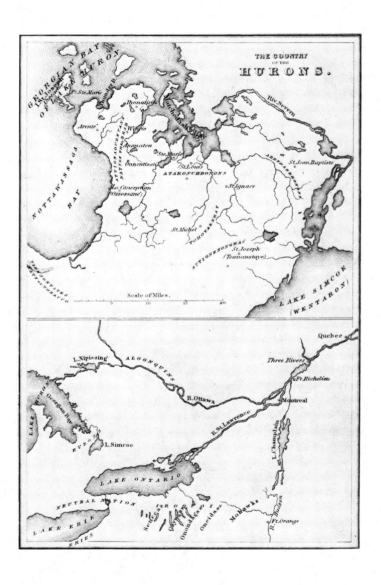

Contents

Preface

Few passages of history are more striking than those which record the efforts of the earlier French Jesuits to convert the Indians. Full as they are of dramatic and philosophic interest, bearing strongly on the political destinies of America, and closely involved with the history of its native population, it is wonderful that they have been left so long in obscurity. While the infant colonies of England still clung feebly to the shores of the Atlantic, events deeply ominous to their future were in progress, unknown to them, in the very heart of the continent. It will be seen, in the sequel of this volume, that civil and religious liberty found strange allies in this Western World.

The sources of information concerning the early Jesuits of New France are very copious. During a period of forty years, the Superior of the Mission sent, every summer, long and detailed reports, embodying or accompanied by the reports of his subordinates, to the Provincial of the Order at Paris, where they were annually published, in duodecimo volumes, forming the remarkable series known as the Jesuit *Relations*. Though the productions of men of scholastic training, they are simple and often crude in style, as might be expected of narratives hastily written in Indian lodges or rude mission-houses in the forest, amid annoyances and interruptions of all kinds. In respect to the value of their contents, they are exceedingly unequal. Modest records of marvellous adventures and sacrifices, and vivid pictures of forest-life, alternate with prolix and monotonous details of the conversion of individual savages, and the praiseworthy deportment of some exemplary neophyte. With regard to the condition and character of the primitive inhabitants of North America, it is impossible to exaggerate their value as an authority. I should add, that the closest examination has left me no doubt that these missionaries wrote in perfect good faith, and that the *Relations* hold a high place as authentic and trustworthy historical documents. They are very scarce, and no complete collection of them exists in America. The entire series was, however, republished, in 1858, by the Canadian government, in three large octavo volumes.[1]

These form but a part of the surviving writings of the French-American Jesuits. Many additional reports, memoirs, journals, and letters, official and private, have come down to us; some of which have recently been printed, while others remain in manuscript. Nearly every prominent actor in the scenes to be described has left his own record of events in which he bore part, in the shape of reports to his Superiors or letters to his friends. I have studied and compared these authorities, as well as a great mass of collateral evidence, with more than usual care, striving to secure the greatest possible accuracy of statement, and to reproduce an image of the past with photographic clearness and truth.

The introductory chapter of the volume is independent of the rest; but a knowledge of the facts set forth in it is essential to the full understanding of the narrative which follows.

In the collection of material, I have received valuable aid from Mr. J. G. Shea, Rev. Felix Martin, S.J., the Abbés Laverdière and H. R. Casgrain, Dr. J. C. Taché, and the late Jacques Viger, Esq.

I propose to devote the next volume of this series to the discovery and occupation by the French of the Valley of the Mississippi.

BOSTON, *1st May, 1867*

---

[1] Both editions—the old and the new—are cited in the following pages. Where the reference is to the old edition, it is indicated by the name of the publisher (Cramoisy), appended to the citation, in brackets.

In extracts given in the notes, the antiquated orthography and accentuation are preserved.

Introduction

NATIVE TRIBES

Divisions • The Algonquins • The Hurons • Their Houses • Fortifications • Habits • Arts • Women • Trade • Festivities • Medicine • The Tobacco Nation • The Neutrals • The Eries • The Andastes • The Iroquois • Social and Political Organization • Iroquois Institutions, Customs, and Character • Indian Religion and Superstitions • The Indian Mind

---

AMERICA, when it became known to Europeans, was, as it had long been, a scene of wide-spread revolution. North and South, tribe was giving place to tribe, language to language; for the Indian, hopelessly unchanging in respect to individual and social development, was, as regarded tribal relations and local haunts, mutable as the wind. In Canada and the northern section of the United States, the elements of change were especially active. The Indian population which, in 1535, Cartier found at Montreal and Quebec, had disappeared at the opening of the next century, and another race had succeeded, in language and customs widely different; while, in the region now forming the State of New York, a power was rising to a ferocious vitality, which, but for the presence of Europeans, would probably have subjected, absorbed, or exterminated every other Indian community east of the Mississippi and north of the Ohio.

The vast tract of wilderness from the Mississippi to the Atlantic, and from the Carolinas to Hudson's Bay, was divided between two great families of tribes, distinguished by a radical difference of language. A part of Virginia and of Pennsylvania, New Jersey, Southeastern New York, New England, New Brunswick, Nova Scotia, and Lower Canada were occupied, so far as occupied at all, by tribes speaking various Algonquin languages and dialects. They extended, moreover, along the shores of the Upper Lakes, and into the dreary Northern wastes beyond. They held Wisconsin, Michigan,

Illinois, and Indiana, and detached bands ranged the lonely hunting-ground of Kentucky.[1]

Like a great island in the midst of the Algonquins lay the country of tribes speaking the generic tongue of the Iroquois. The true Iroquois, or Five Nations, extended through Central New York, from the Hudson to the Genesee. Southward lay the Andastes, on and near the Susquehanna; westward, the Eries, along the southern shore of Lake Erie, and the Neutral Nation, along its northern shore from Niagara towards the Detroit; while the towns of the Hurons lay near the lake to which they have left their name.[2]

Of the Algonquin populations, the densest, despite a recent epidemic which had swept them off by thousands, was in New England. Here were Mohicans, Pequots, Narragansetts, Wampanoags, Massachusetts, Penacooks, thorns in the side of the Puritan. On the whole, these savages were favorable specimens of the Algonquin stock, belonging to that section of it which tilled the soil, and was thus in some measure spared the extremes of misery and degradation to which the wandering hunter tribes were often reduced. They owed much, also, to the bounty of the sea, and hence they tended towards the coast; which, before the epidemic, Champlain and Smith had seen at many points studded with wigwams and waving with harvests of maize. Fear, too, drove them eastward; for the Iroquois pursued them with an inveterate enmity. Some paid yearly tribute to their tyrants, while others were still subject

[1] The word *Algonquin* is here used in its broadest signification. It was originally applied to a group of tribes north of the River St. Lawrence. The difference of language between the original Algonquins and the Abenaquis of New England, the Ojibwas of the Great Lakes, or the Illinois of the West, corresponded to the difference between French and Italian, or Italian and Spanish. Each of these languages, again, had its dialects, like those of different provinces of France.

[2] To the above general statements there was, in the first half of the seventeenth century, but one exception worth notice. A detached branch of the Dahcotah stock, the Winnebago, was established south of Green Bay, on Lake Michigan, in the midst of Algonquins; and small Dahcotah bands had also planted themselves on the eastern side of the Mississippi, nearly in the same latitude.

There was another branch of the Iroquois in the Carolinas, consisting of the Tuscaroras and kindred bands. In 1715 they were joined to the Five Nations.

to their inroads, flying in terror at the sound of the Mohawk war-cry. Westward, the population thinned rapidly; northward, it soon disappeared. Northern New Hampshire, the whole of Vermont, and Western Massachusetts had no human tenants but the roving hunter or prowling warrior.

We have said that this group of tribes was relatively very populous; yet it is more than doubtful whether all of them united, had union been possible, could have mustered eight thousand fighting men. To speak further of them is needless, for they were not within the scope of the Jesuit labors. The heresy of heresies had planted itself among them; and it was for the apostle Eliot, not the Jesuit, to essay their conversion.[1]

Landing at Boston, three years before a solitude, let the traveller push northward, pass the River Piscataqua and the Penacooks, and cross the River Saco. Here, a change of dialect would indicate a different tribe, or group of tribes. These were the Abenaquis, found chiefly along the course of the Kennebec and other rivers, on whose banks they raised their rude harvests, and whose streams they ascended to hunt the moose and bear in the forest desert of Northern Maine, or descended to fish in the neighboring sea.[2]

Crossing the Penobscot, one found a visible descent in the scale of humanity. Eastern Maine and the whole of New Brunswick were occupied by a race called Etchemins, to whom agriculture was unknown, though the sea, prolific of fish, lobsters, and seals, greatly lightened their miseries. The

[1] These Indians, the Armouchiquois of the old French writers, were in a state of chronic war with the tribes of New Brunswick and Nova Scotia. Champlain, on his voyage of 1603, heard strange accounts of them. The following is literally rendered from the first narrative of that heroic, but credulous explorer.

"They are savages of shape altogether monstrous: for their heads are small, their bodies short, and their arms thin as a skeleton, as are also their thighs; but their legs are stout and long, and all of one size, and, when they are seated on their heels, their knees rise more than half a foot above their heads, which seems a thing strange and against Nature. Nevertheless, they are active and bold, and they have the best country on all the coast towards Acadia."— *Des Sauvages*, f. 34.

This story may match that of the great city of Norembega, on the Penobscot, with its population of dwarfs, as related by Jean Alphonse.

[2] The Tarratines of New-England writers were the Abenaquis, or a portion of them.

Souriquois, or Micmacs, of Nova Scotia, closely resembled them in habits and condition. From Nova Scotia to the St. Lawrence, there was no population worthy of the name. From the Gulf of St. Lawrence to Lake Ontario, the southern border of the great river had no tenants but hunters. Northward, between the St. Lawrence and Hudson's Bay, roamed the scattered hordes of the Papinachois, Bersiamites, and others, included by the French under the general name of Montagnais. When, in spring, the French trading-ships arrived and anchored in the port of Tadoussac, they gathered from far and near, toiling painfully through the desolation of forests, mustering by hundreds at the point of traffic, and setting up their bark wigwams along the strand of that wild harbor. They were of the lowest Algonquin type. Their ordinary sustenance was derived from the chase; though often, goaded by deadly famine, they would subsist on roots, the bark and buds of trees, or the foulest offal; and in extremity, even cannibalism was not rare among them.

Ascending the St. Lawrence, it was seldom that the sight of a human form gave relief to the loneliness, until, at Quebec, the roar of Champlain's cannon from the verge of the cliff announced that the savage prologue of the American drama was drawing to a close, and that the civilization of Europe was advancing on the scene. Ascending farther, all was solitude, except at Three Rivers, a noted place of trade, where a few Algonquins of the tribe called Atticamegues might possibly be seen. The fear of the Iroquois was everywhere; and as the voyager passed some wooded point, or thicket-covered island, the whistling of a stone-headed arrow proclaimed, perhaps, the presence of these fierce marauders. At Montreal there was no human life, save during a brief space in early summer, when the shore swarmed with savages, who had come to the yearly trade from the great communities of the interior. To-day there were dances, songs, and feastings; to-morrow all again was solitude, and the Ottawa was covered with the canoes of the returning warriors.

Along this stream, a main route of traffic, the silence of the wilderness was broken only by the splash of the passing paddle. To the north of the river there was indeed a small Algonquin band, called *La Petite Nation*, together with one or two other feeble communities; but they dwelt far from the banks, through fear of the ubiquitous Iroquois. It was nearly three hundred miles, by the windings of the stream, before one reached that Algonquin tribe, *La Nation de l'Isle*, who occupied the great island of the Allumettes. Then, after many a day of lonely travel, the voyager found a savage welcome among the Nipissings, on the lake which bears their name; and then circling west and south for a hundred and fifty miles of solitude, he reached for the first time a people speaking a dialect of the Iroquois tongue. Here all was changed. Populous towns, rude fortifications, and an extensive, though barbarous tillage, indicated a people far in advance of the famished wanderers of the Saguenay, or their less abject kindred of New England. These were the Hurons, of whom the modern Wyandots are a remnant. Both in themselves and as a type of their generic stock they demand more than a passing notice.[1]

THE HURONS

More than two centuries have elapsed since the Hurons vanished from their ancient seats, and the settlers of this rude solitude stand perplexed and wondering over the relics of a lost people. In the damp shadow of what seems a virgin forest, the axe and plough bring strange secrets to light: huge pits, close packed with skeletons and disjointed bones, mixed with weapons, copper kettles, beads, and trinkets. Not even the straggling Algonquins, who linger about the scene of Huron prosperity, can tell their origin. Yet, on ancient wormeaten pages, between covers of begrimed parchment, the daily life of this ruined community, its firesides, its festivals, its funeral rites, are painted with a minute and vivid fidelity.

The ancient country of the Hurons is now the northern and eastern portion of Simcoe County, Canada West, and is

[1] The usual confusion of Indian tribal names prevails in the case of the Hurons. The following are their synonymes: —

Hurons (of French origin); Ochateguins (Champlain); Attigouantans (the name of one of their tribes, used by Champlain for the whole nation); Ouendat (their true name, according to Lalemant); Yendat, Wyandot, Guyandot (corruptions of the preceding); Ouaouakecinatouek (Potier); Quatogies (Colden).

embraced within the peninsula formed by the Nottawassaga and Matchedash Bays of Lake Huron, the River Severn, and Lake Simcoe. Its area was small,—its population comparatively large. In the year 1639 the Jesuits made an enumeration of all its villages, dwellings, and families. The result showed thirty-two villages and hamlets, with seven hundred dwellings, about four thousand families, and twelve thousand adult persons, or a total population of at least twenty thousand.[1]

The region whose boundaries we have given was an alternation of meadows and deep forests, interlaced with footpaths leading from town to town. Of these towns, some were fortified, but the greater number were open and defenceless. They were of a construction common to all tribes of Iroquois lineage, and peculiar to them. Nothing similar exists at the present day.[2] They covered a space of from one to ten acres, the dwellings clustering together with little or no pretension to order. In general, these singular structures were about thirty or thirty-five feet in length, breadth, and height; but many were much larger, and a few were of prodigious length. In some of the villages there were dwellings two hundred and

[1] Lalemant, *Relation des Hurons, 1640*, 38 (Cramoisy). His words are, "de feux enuiron deux mille, et enuiron douze mille personnes." There were two families to every fire. That by "personnes" adults only are meant cannot be doubted, as the *Relations* abound in incidental evidence of a total population far exceeding twelve thousand. A Huron family usually numbered from five to eight persons. The number of the Huron towns changed from year to year. Champlain and Le Caron, in 1615, reckoned them at seventeen or eighteen, with a population of about ten thousand, meaning, no doubt, adults. Brébeuf, in 1635, found twenty villages, and, as he thinks, thirty thousand souls. Both Le Mercier and De Quen, as well Dollier de Casson and the anonymous author of the *Relation* of 1660, state the population at from thirty to thirty-five thousand. Since the time of Champlain's visit, various kindred tribes or fragments of tribes had been incorporated with the Hurons, thus more than balancing the ravages of a pestilence which had decimated them.

[2] The permanent bark villages of the Dahcotah of the St. Peter's are the nearest modern approach to the Huron towns. The whole Huron country abounds with evidences of having been occupied by a numerous population. "On a close inspection of the forest," Dr. Taché writes to me, "the greatest part of it seems to have been cleared at former periods, and almost the only places bearing the character of the primitive forest are the low grounds."

forty feet long, though in breadth and height they did not much exceed the others.[1] In shape they were much like an arbor overarching a garden-walk. Their frame was of tall and strong saplings, planted in a double row to form the two sides of the house, bent till they met, and lashed together at the top. To these other poles were bound transversely, and the whole was covered with large sheets of the bark of the oak, elm, spruce, or white cedar, overlapping like the shingles of a roof, upon which, for their better security, split poles were made fast with cords of linden bark. At the crown of the arch, along the entire length of the house, an opening a foot wide was left for the admission of light and the escape of smoke. At each end was a close porch of similar construction; and here were stowed casks of bark, filled with smoked fish, Indian corn, and other stores not liable to injury from frost. Within, on both sides, were wide scaffolds, four feet from the floor, and extending the entire length of the house, like the seats of a colossal omnibus.[2] These were formed of thick sheets of bark, supported by posts and transverse poles, and covered with mats and skins. Here, in summer, was the sleeping-place of the inmates, and the space beneath served for storage of their firewood. The fires were on the ground, in a line down the middle of the house. Each sufficed for two families, who, in winter, slept closely packed around them. Above, just under the vaulted roof, were a great number of poles, like the perches of a hen-roost, and here were suspended weapons, clothing, skins, and ornaments. Here, too, in harvest time, the squaws hung the ears of unshelled corn, till the rude abode, through all its length, seemed decked with a golden

---

[1] Brébeuf, *Relation des Hurons, 1635*, 31. Champlain says that he saw them, in 1615, more than thirty fathoms long; while Vanderdonck reports the length, from actual measurement, of an Iroquois house, at a hundred and eighty yards, or five hundred and forty feet!

[2] Often, especially among the Iroquois, the internal arrangement was different. The scaffolds or platforms were raised only a foot from the earthen floor, and were only twelve or thirteen feet long, with intervening spaces, where the occupants stored their family provisions and other articles. Five or six feet above was another platform, often occupied by children. One pair of platforms sufficed for a family, and here during summer they slept pellmell, in the clothes they wore by day, and without pillows.

tapestry. In general, however, its only lining was a thick coating of soot from the smoke of fires with neither draught, chimney, nor window. So pungent was the smoke, that it produced inflammation of the eyes, attended in old age with frequent blindness. Another annoyance was the fleas; and a third, the unbridled and unruly children. Privacy there was none. The house was one chamber, sometimes lodging more than twenty families.[1]

He who entered on a winter night beheld a strange spectacle: the vista of fires lighting the smoky concave; the bronzed groups encircling each,—cooking, eating, gambling, or amusing themselves with idle badinage; shrivelled squaws, hideous with threescore years of hardship; grisly old warriors, scarred with Iroquois war-clubs; young aspirants, whose honors were yet to be won; damsels gay with ochre and wam-

---

[1] One of the best descriptions of the Huron and Iroquois houses is that of Sagard, *Voyage des Hurons*, 118. See also Champlain (1627), 78; Brébeuf, *Relation des Hurons, 1635*, 31; Vanderdonck, *New Netherlands*, in N. Y. Hist. *Coll.*, *Second Ser.*, I. 196; Lafitau, *Mœurs des Sauvages*, II. 10. The account given by Cartier of the houses he saw at Montreal corresponds with the above. He describes them as about fifty yards long. In this case, there were partial partitions for the several families, and a sort of loft above. Many of the Iroquois and Huron houses were of similar construction, the partitions being at the sides only, leaving a wide passage down the middle of the house. Bartram, *Observations on a Journey from Pennsylvania to Canada*, gives a description and plan of the Iroquois Council-House in 1751, which was of this construction. Indeed, the Iroquois preserved this mode of building, in all essential points, down to a recent period. They usually framed the sides of their houses on rows of upright posts, arched with separate poles for the roof. The Hurons, no doubt, did the same in their larger structures. For a door, there was a sheet of bark hung on wooden hinges, or suspended by cords from above.

On the site of Huron towns which were destroyed by fire, the size, shape, and arrangement of the houses can still, in some instances, be traced by remains in the form of charcoal, as well as by the charred bones and fragments of pottery found among the ashes.

Dr. Taché, after a zealous and minute examination of the Huron country, extended through five years, writes to me as follows. "From the remains I have found, I can vouch for the scrupulous correctness of our ancient writers. With the aid of their indications and descriptions, I have been able to detect the sites of villages in the midst of the forest, and by the study, *in situ*, of archæological monuments, small as they are, to understand and confirm their many interesting details of the habits, and especially the funeral rites, of these extraordinary tribes."

pum; restless children pellmell with restless dogs. Now a tongue of resinous flame painted each wild feature in vivid light; now the fitful gleam expired, and the group vanished from sight, as their nation has vanished from history.

The fortified towns of the Hurons were all on the side exposed to Iroquois incursions. The fortifications of all this family of tribes were, like their dwellings, in essential points alike. A situation was chosen favorable to defence,—the bank of a lake, the crown of a difficult hill, or a high point of land in the fork of confluent rivers. A ditch, several feet deep, was dug around the village, and the earth thrown up on the inside. Trees were then felled by an alternate process of burning and hacking the burnt part with stone hatchets, and by similar means were cut into lengths to form palisades. These were planted on the embankment, in one, two, three, or four concentric rows,—those of each row inclining towards those of the other rows until they intersected. The whole was lined within, to the height of a man, with heavy sheets of bark; and at the top, where the palisades crossed, was a gallery of timber for the defenders, together with wooden gutters, by which streams of water could be poured down on fires kindled by the enemy. Magazines of stones, and rude ladders for mounting the rampart, completed the provision for defence. The forts of the Iroquois were stronger and more elaborate than those of the Hurons; and to this day large districts in New York are marked with frequent remains of their ditches and embankments.[1]

[1]There is no mathematical regularity in these works. In their form, the builders were guided merely by the nature of the ground. Frequently a precipice or river sufficed for partial defence, and the line of embankment occurs only on one or two sides. In one instance, distinct traces of a double line of palisades are visible along the embankment. (See Squier, *Aboriginal Monuments of New York*, 38.) It is probable that the palisade was planted first, and the earth heaped around it. Indeed, this is stated by the Tuscarora Indian, Cusick, in his curious *History of the Six Nations* (Iroquois). Brébeuf says, that as early as 1636 the Jesuits taught the Hurons to build rectangular palisaded works, with bastions. The Iroquois adopted the same practice at an early period, omitting the ditch and embankment; and it is probable, that, even in their primitive defences, the palisades, where the ground was of a nature to yield easily to their rude implements, were planted simply in holes dug for the purpose. Such seems to have been the Iroquois fortress attacked by Champlain in 1615.

Among these tribes there was no individual ownership of land, but each family had for the time exclusive right to as much as it saw fit to cultivate. The clearing process—a most toilsome one—consisted in hacking off branches, piling them together with brushwood around the foot of the standing trunks, and setting fire to the whole. The squaws, working with their hoes of wood and bone among the charred stumps, sowed their corn, beans, pumpkins, tobacco, sunflowers, and Huron hemp. No manure was used; but, at intervals of from ten to thirty years, when the soil was exhausted, and firewood distant, the village was abandoned and a new one built.

There was little game in the Huron country; and here, as among the Iroquois, the staple of food was Indian corn, cooked without salt in a variety of forms, each more odious than the last. Venison was a luxury found only at feasts; dog-flesh was in high esteem; and, in some of the towns captive bears were fattened for festive occasions. These tribes were far less improvident than the roving Algonquins, and stores of provision were laid up against a season of want. Their main stock of corn was buried in *caches*, or deep holes in the earth, either within or without the houses.

In respect to the arts of life, all these stationary tribes were in advance of the wandering hunters of the North. The women made a species of earthen pot for cooking, but these were supplanted by the copper kettles of the French traders. They wove rush mats with no little skill. They spun twine from hemp, by the primitive process of rolling it on their thighs; and of this twine they made nets. They extracted oil from fish and from the seeds of the sunflower,—the latter, apparently, only for the purposes of the toilet. They pounded their maize in huge mortars of wood, hollowed by alternate burnings and scrapings. Their stone axes, spear and arrow heads, and bone fish-hooks, were fast giving place to the iron of the French; but they had not laid aside their shields of raw bison-hide, or of wood overlaid with plaited and twisted

---

The Muscogees, with other Southern tribes, and occasionally the Algonquins, had palisaded towns; but the palisades were usually but a single row, planted upright. The tribes of Virginia occasionally surrounded their dwellings with a triple palisade.—Beverly, *History of Virginia*, 149.

thongs of skin. They still used, too, their primitive breast-plates and greaves of twigs interwoven with cordage.[1] The masterpiece of Huron handiwork, however, was the birch canoe, in the construction of which the Algonquins were no less skilful. The Iroquois, in the absence of the birch, were forced to use the bark of the elm, which was greatly inferior both in lightness and strength. Of pipes, than which nothing was more important in their eyes, the Hurons made a great variety, some of baked clay, others of various kinds of stone, carved by the men, during their long periods of monotonous leisure, often with great skill and ingenuity. But their most mysterious fabric was wampum. This was at once their cur-rency, their ornament, their pen, ink, and parchment; and its use was by no means confined to tribes of the Iroquois stock. It consisted of elongated beads, white and purple, made from the inner part of certain shells. It is not easy to conceive how, with their rude implements, the Indians contrived to shape and perforate this intractable material. The art soon fell into disuse, however; for wampum better than their own was brought them by the traders, besides abundant imitations in glass and porcelain. Strung into necklaces, or wrought into collars, belts, and bracelets, it was the favorite decoration of the Indian girls at festivals and dances. It served also a graver purpose. No compact, no speech, or clause of a speech, to the representative of another nation, had any force, unless con-firmed by the delivery of a string or belt of wampum.[2] The belts, on occasions of importance, were wrought into signifi-cant devices, suggestive of the substance of the compact or speech, and designed as aids to memory. To one or more old men of the nation was assigned the honorable, but very oner-ous, charge of keepers of the wampum,—in other words, of the national records; and it was for them to remember and interpret the meaning of the belts. The figures on wampum-belts were, for the most part, simply mnemonic. So also were those carved on wooden tablets, or painted on bark and

[1] Some of the northern tribes of California, at the present day, wear a sort of breastplate "composed of thin parallel battens of very tough wood, woven together with a small cord."

[2] Beaver-skins and other valuable furs were sometimes, on such occasions, used as a substitute.

skin, to preserve in memory the songs of war, hunting, or magic.[1] The Hurons had, however, in common with other tribes, a system of rude pictures and arbitrary signs, by which they could convey to each other, with tolerable precision, information touching the ordinary subjects of Indian interest.

Their dress was chiefly of skins, cured with smoke after the well-known Indian mode. That of the women, according to the Jesuits, was more modest than that "of our most pious ladies of France." The young girls on festal occasions must be excepted from this commendation, as they wore merely a kilt from the waist to the knee, besides the wampum decorations of the breast and arms. Their long black hair, gathered behind the neck, was decorated with disks of native copper, or gay pendants made in France, and now occasionally unearthed in numbers from their graves. The men, in summer, were nearly naked,—those of a kindred tribe wholly so, with the sole exception of their moccasins. In winter they were clad in tunics and leggins of skin, and at all seasons, on occasions of ceremony, were wrapped from head to foot in robes of beaver or otter furs, sometimes of the greatest value. On the inner side, these robes were decorated with painted figures and devices, or embroidered with the dyed quills of the Canada hedgehog. In this art of embroidery, however, the Hurons were equalled or surpassed by some of the Algonquin tribes. They wore their hair after a variety of grotesque and startling fashions. With some, it was loose on one side, and tight braided on the other; with others, close shaved, leaving one or more long and cherished locks; while, with others again, it bristled in a ridge across the crown, like the back of a hyena.[2] When in full dress, they were painted with ochre, white clay, soot, and the red juice of certain berries. They practised tattooing, sometimes covering the whole body with indelible devices.[3] When of such extent, the process was very severe; and though

[1] Engravings of many specimens of these figured songs are given in the voluminous reports on the condition of the Indians, published by Government, under the editorship of Mr. Schoolcraft. The specimens are chiefly Algonquin.

[2] See Le Jeune, *Relation, 1633,* 35.—"Quelles hures!" exclaimed some astonished Frenchman. Hence the name, *Hurons.*

[3] Bressani, *Relation Abrégée,* 72.—Champlain has a picture of a warrior thus tattooed.

no murmur escaped the sufferer, he sometimes died from its effects.

Female life among the Hurons had no bright side. It was a youth of license, an age of drudgery. Despite an organization which, while it perhaps made them less sensible of pain, certainly made them less susceptible of passion, than the higher races of men, the Hurons were notoriously dissolute, far exceeding in this respect the wandering and starving Algonquins.[1] Marriage existed among them, and polygamy was exceptional; but divorce took place at the will or caprice of either party. A practice also prevailed of temporary or experimental marriage, lasting a day, a week, or more. The seal of the compact was merely the acceptance of a gift of wampum made by the suitor to the object of his desire or his whim. These gifts were never returned on the dissolution of the connection; and as an attractive and enterprising damsel might, and often did, make twenty such marriages before her final establishment, she thus collected a wealth of wampum with

[1] Among the Iroquois there were more favorable features in the condition of women. The matrons had often a considerable influence on the decisions of the councils. Lafitau, whose book appeared in 1724, says that the nation was corrupt in his time, but that this was a degeneracy from their ancient manners. La Potherie and Charlevoix make a similar statement. Megapolensis, however, in 1644, says that they were then exceedingly debauched; and Greenhalgh, in 1677, gives ample evidence of a shameless license. One of their most earnest advocates of the present day admits that the passion of love among them had no other than an animal existence. (Morgan, *League of the Iroquois*, 322.) There is clear proof that the tribes of the South were equally corrupt. (See Lawson, *Carolina*, 34, and other early writers.) On the other hand, chastity in women was recognized as a virtue by many tribes. This was peculiarly the case among the Algonquins of Gaspé, where a lapse in this regard was counted a disgrace. (See Le Clerc, *Nouvelle Relation de la Gaspésie*, 417, where a contrast is drawn between the modesty of the girls of this region and the open prostitution practised among those of other tribes.) Among the Sioux, adultery on the part of a woman is punished by mutilation.

The remarkable forebearance observed by Eastern and Northern tribes towards female captives was probably the result of a superstition. Notwithstanding the prevailing license, the Iroquois and other tribes had among themselves certain conventional rules which excited the admiration of the Jesuit celibates. Some of these had a superstitious origin; others were in accordance with the iron requirements of their savage etiquette. To make the Indian a hero of romance is mere nonsense.

which to adorn herself for the village dances.[1] This provisional matrimony was no bar to a license boundless and apparently universal, unattended with loss of reputation on either side. Every instinct of native delicacy quickly vanished under the influence of Huron domestic life; eight or ten families, and often more, crowded into one undivided house, where privacy was impossible, and where strangers were free to enter at all hours of the day or night.

Once a mother, and married with a reasonable permanency, the Huron woman from a wanton became a drudge. In March and April she gathered the year's supply of firewood. Then came sowing, tilling, and harvesting, smoking fish, dressing skins, making cordage and clothing, preparing food. On the march it was she who bore the burden; for, in the words of Champlain, "their women were their mules." The natural effect followed. In every Huron town were shrivelled hags, hideous and despised, who, in vindictiveness, ferocity, and cruelty, far exceeded the men.

To the men fell the task of building the houses, and making weapons, pipes, and canoes. For the rest, their home-life was a life of leisure and amusement. The summer and autumn were their seasons of serious employment,—of war, hunting, fishing, and trade. There was an established system of traffic between the Hurons and the Algonquins of the Ottawa and Lake Nipissing: the Hurons exchanging wampum, fishing-nets, and corn for fish and furs.[2] From various relics found in their graves, it may be inferred that they also traded with tribes of the Upper Lakes, as well as with tribes far southward, towards the Gulf of Mexico. Each branch of traffic was

[1]"Il s'en trouue telle qui passe ainsi sa ieunesse, qui aura eu plus de vingt maris, lesquels vingt maris ne sont pas seuls en la jouyssance de la beste, quelques mariez qu'ils soient: car la nuict venuë, les ieunes femmes courent d'une cabane en une autre, come font les ieunes hommes de leur costé, qui en prennent par ou bon leur semble, toutesfois sans violence aucune, et n'en reçoiuent aucune infamie, ny injure, la coustume du pays estant telle."— Champlain (1627), 90. Compare Sagard, *Voyage des Hurons*, 176. Both were personal observers.

The ceremony, even of the most serious marriage, consisted merely in the bride's bringing a dish of boiled maize to the bridegroom, together with an armful of fuel. There was often a feast of the relatives, or of the whole village.

[2]Champlain (1627), 84.

the monopoly of the family or clan by whom it was opened. They might, if they could, punish interlopers, by stripping them of all they possessed, unless the latter had succeeded in reaching home with the fruits of their trade,—in which case the outraged monopolists had no further right of redress, and could not attempt it without a breaking of the public peace, and exposure to the authorized vengeance of the other party.[1] Their fisheries, too, were regulated by customs having the force of laws. These pursuits, with their hunting,—in which they were aided by a wolfish breed of dogs unable to bark,— consumed the autumn and early winter; but before the new year the greater part of the men were gathered in their villages.

Now followed their festal season; for it was the season of idleness for the men, and of leisure for the women. Feasts, gambling, smoking, and dancing filled the vacant hours. Like other Indians, the Hurons were desperate gamblers, staking their all,—ornaments, clothing, canoes, pipes, weapons, and wives. One of their principal games was played with plum-stones, or wooden lozenges, black on one side and white on the other. These were tossed up in a wooden bowl, by striking it sharply upon the ground, and the players betted on the black or white. Sometimes a village challenged a neighboring village. The game was played in one of the houses. Strong poles were extended from side to side, and on these sat or perched the company, party facing party, while two players struck the bowl on the ground between. Bets ran high; and Brébeuf relates, that once, in midwinter, with the snow nearly three feet deep, the men of his village returned from a gambling visit, bereft of their leggins, and barefoot, yet in excellent humor.[2] Ludicrous as it may appear, these games were often medical prescriptions, and designed as a cure of the sick.

Their feasts and dances were of various character, social, medical, and mystical or religious. Some of their feasts were

[1] Brébeuf, *Relation des Hurons, 1636*, 156 (Cramoisy).

[2] Brébeuf, *Relation des Hurons, 1636*, 113.—This game is still a favorite among the Iroquois, some of whom hold to the belief that they will play it after death in the realms of bliss. In all their important games of chance, they employed charms, incantations, and all the resources of their magical art, to gain good luck.

on a scale of extravagant profusion. A vain or ambitious host threw all his substance into one entertainment, inviting the whole village, and perhaps several neighboring villages also. In the winter of 1635 there was a feast at the village of Contarrea, where thirty kettles were on the fires, and twenty deer and four bears were served up.[1] The invitation was simple. The messenger addressed the desired guest with the concise summons, "Come and eat"; and to refuse was a grave offence. He took his dish and spoon, and repaired to the scene of festivity. Each, as he entered, greeted his host with the guttural ejaculation, *Ho!* and ranged himself with the rest, squatted on the earthen floor or on the platform along the sides of the house. The kettles were slung over the fires in the midst. First, there was a long prelude of lugubrious singing. Then the host, who took no share in the feast, proclaimed in a loud voice the contents of each kettle in turn, and at each announcement the company responded in unison, *Ho!* The attendant squaws filled with their ladles the bowls of all the guests. There was talking, laughing, jesting, singing, and smoking; and at times the entertainment was protracted through the day.

When the feast had a medical or mystic character, it was indispensable that each guest should devour the whole of the portion given him, however enormous. Should he fail, the host would be outraged, the community shocked, and the spirits roused to vengeance. Disaster would befall the nation,—death, perhaps, the individual. In some cases, the imagined efficacy of the feast was proportioned to the rapidity with which the viands were despatched. Prizes of tobacco were offered to the most rapid feeder; and the spectacle then became truly porcine.[2] These *festins à manger tout* were much dreaded by many of the Hurons, who, however, were never known to decline them.

Invitation to a dance was no less concise than to a feast.

[1] Brébeuf, *Relation des Hurons, 1636*, III.

[2] This superstition was not confined to the Hurons, but extended to many other tribes, including, probably, all the Algonquins, with some of which it holds in full force to this day. A feaster, unable to do his full part, might, if he could, hire another to aid him; otherwise, he must remain in his place till the work was done.

Sometimes a crier proclaimed the approaching festivity through the village. The house was crowded. Old men, old women, and children thronged the platforms, or clung to the poles which supported the sides and roof. Fires were raked out, and the earthen floor cleared. Two chiefs sang at the top of their voices, keeping time to their song with tortoise-shell rattles.[1] The men danced with great violence and gesticulation; the women, with a much more measured action. The former were nearly divested of clothing, — in mystical dances, sometimes wholly so; and, from a superstitious motive, this was now and then the case with the women. Both, however, were abundantly decorated with paint, oil, beads, wampum, trinkets, and feathers.

Religious festivals, councils, the entertainment of an envoy, the inauguration of a chief, were all occasions of festivity, in which social pleasure was joined with matter of grave import, and which at times gathered nearly all the nation into one great and harmonious concourse. Warlike expeditions, too, were always preceded by feasting, at which the warriors vaunted the fame of their ancestors, and their own past and prospective exploits. A hideous scene of feasting followed the torture of a prisoner. Like the torture itself, it was, among the Hurons, partly an act of vengeance, and partly a religious rite. If the victim had shown courage, the heart was first roasted, cut into small pieces, and given to the young men and boys, who devoured it to increase their own courage. The body was then divided, thrown into the kettles, and eaten by the assembly, the head being the portion of the chief. Many of the Hurons joined in the feast with reluctance and horror, while

---

[1] Sagard gives specimens of their songs. In both dances and feasts there was no little variety. These were sometimes combined. It is impossible, in brief space, to indicate more than their general features. In the famous "wardance," — which was frequently danced, as it still is, for amusement, — speeches, exhortations, jests, personal satire, and repartee were commonly introduced as a part of the performance, sometimes by way of patriotic stimulus, sometimes for amusement. The music in this case was the drum and the war-song. Some of the other dances were also interspersed with speeches and sharp witticisms, always taken in good part, though Lafitau says that he has seen the victim so pitilessly bantered that he was forced to hide his head in his blanket.

others took pleasure in it.[1] This was the only form of cannibalism among them, since, unlike the wandering Algonquins, they were rarely under the desperation of extreme famine.

A great knowledge of simples for the cure of disease is popularly ascribed to the Indian. Here, however, as elsewhere, his knowledge is in fact scanty. He rarely reasons from cause to effect, or from effect to cause. Disease, in his belief, is the result of sorcery, the agency of spirits or supernatural influences, undefined and indefinable. The Indian doctor was a conjurer, and his remedies were to the last degree preposterous, ridiculous, or revolting. The well-known Indian sweating-bath is the most prominent of the few means of cure based on agencies simply physical; and this, with all the other natural remedies, was applied, not by the professed doctor, but by the sufferer himself, or his friends.[2]

The Indian doctor beat, shook, and pinched his patient, howled, whooped, rattled a tortoise-shell at his ear to expel the evil spirit, bit him till blood flowed, and then displayed in triumph a small piece of wood, bone, or iron, which he had hidden in his mouth, and which he affirmed was the source of the disease, now happily removed.[3] Sometimes he

---

[1] "Il y en a qui en mangent auec plaisir."—Brébeuf, *Relation des Hurons, 1636,* 121.—Le Mercier gives a description of one of these scenes, at which he was present. (*Ibid., 1637,* 118.) The same horrible practice prevailed to a greater extent among the Iroquois. One of the most remarkable instances of Indian cannibalism is that furnished by a Western tribe, the Miamis, among whom there was a clan, or family, whose hereditary duty and privilege it was to devour the bodies of prisoners burned to death. The act had somewhat of a religious character, was attended with ceremonial observances, and was restricted to the family in question.—See Hon. Lewis Cass, in the appendix to Colonel Whiting's poem, "Ontwa."

[2] The Indians had many simple applications for wounds, said to have been very efficacious; but the purity of their blood, owing to the absence from their diet of condiments and stimulants, as well as to their active habits, aided the remedy. In general, they were remarkably exempt from disease or deformity, though often seriously injured by alternations of hunger and excess. The Hurons sometimes died from the effects of their *festins à manger tout.*

[3] The Hurons believed that the chief cause of disease and death was a monstrous serpent, that lived under the earth. By touching a tuft of hair, a feather, or a fragment of bone, with a portion of his flesh or fat, the sorcerer imparted power to it of entering the body of his victim, and gradually killing him. It was an important part of the doctor's function to extract these charms from the vitals of his patient.—Ragueneau, *Relation des Hurons, 1648,* 75.

prescribed a dance, feast, or game; and the whole village bestirred themselves to fulfil the injunction to the letter. They
gambled away their all; they gorged themselves like vultures;
they danced or played ball naked among the snow-drifts from
morning till night. At a medical feast, some strange or unusual act was commonly enjoined as vital to the patient's cure:
as, for example, the departing guest, in place of the customary
monosyllable of thanks, was required to greet his host with
an ugly grimace. Sometimes, by prescription, half the village
would throng into the house where the patient lay, led by old
women disguised with the heads and skins of bears, and beating with sticks on sheets of dry bark. Here the assembly
danced and whooped for hours together, with a din to which
a civilized patient would promptly have succumbed. Sometimes the doctor wrought himself into a prophetic fury, raving through the length and breadth of the dwelling, snatching
firebrands and flinging them about him, to the terror of the
squaws, with whom, in their combustible tenements, fire was
a constant bugbear.

Among the Hurons and kindred tribes, disease was frequently ascribed to some hidden wish ungratified. Hence the
patient was overwhelmed with gifts, in the hope, that, in their
multiplicity, the desideratum might be supplied. Kettles,
skins, awls, pipes, wampum, fish-hooks, weapons, objects of
every conceivable variety, were piled before him by a host of
charitable contributors; and if, as often happened, a dream,
the Indian oracle, had revealed to the sick man the secret of
his cure, his demands were never refused, however extravagant, idle, nauseous, or abominable.[1] Hence it is no matter

---

[1] "Dans le pays de nos Hurons, il se faict aussi des assemblées de toutes les
filles d'vn bourg auprés d'vne malade, tant à sa priere, suyuant la resuerie ou
le songe qu'elle en aura euë, que par l'ordonnance de Loki (*the doctor*), pour
sa santé et guerison. Les filles ainsi assemblées, on leur demande à toutes, les
vnes apres les autres, celuy qu'elles veulent des ieunes hommes du bourg pour
dormir auec elles la nuict prochaine: elles en nomment chacune vn, qui sont
aussi-tost aduertis par les Maistres de la ceremonie, lesquels viennent tous au
soir en la presence de la malade dormir chacun auec celle qui l'a choysi, d'vn
bout à l'autre de la Cabane, et passent ainsi toute la nuict, pendant que deux
Capitaines aux deux bouts du logis chantent et sonnent de leur Tortuë du
soir au lendemain matin, que la ceremonie cesse. Dieu vueille abolir vne si
damnable et malheureuse ceremonie."—Sagard, *Voyage des Hurons*, 158.—

of wonder that sudden illness and sudden cures were frequent among the Hurons. The patient reaped profit, and the doctor both profit and honor.

THE HURON-IROQUOIS FAMILY

And now, before entering upon the very curious subject of Indian social and tribal organization, it may be well briefly to observe the position and prominent distinctive features of the various communities speaking dialects of the generic tongue of the Iroquois. In this remarkable family of tribes occur the fullest developments of Indian character, and the most conspicuous examples of Indian intelligence. If the higher traits popularly ascribed to the race are not to be found here, they are to be found nowhere. A palpable proof of the superiority of this stock is afforded in the size of the Iroquois and Huron brains. In average internal capacity of the cranium, they surpass, with few and doubtful exceptions, all other aborigines of North and South America, not excepting the civilized races of Mexico and Peru.[1]

In the woody valleys of the Blue Mountains, south of the Nottawassaga Bay of Lake Huron, and two days' journey west of the frontier Huron towns, lay the nine villages of the

---

This unique mode of cure, which was called *Andacwandet*, is also described by Lalemant, who saw it. (*Relation des Hurons, 1639*, 84.) It was one of the recognized remedies.

For the medical practices of the Hurons, see also Champlain, Brébeuf, Lafitau, Charlevoix, and other early writers. Those of the Algonquins were in some points different. The doctor often consulted the spirits, to learn the cause and cure of the disease, by a method peculiar to that family of tribes. He shut himself in a small conical lodge, and the spirits here visited him, manifesting their presence by a violent shaking of the whole structure. This superstition will be described in another connection.

[1] "On comparing five Iroquois heads, I find that they give an average internal capacity of eighty-eight cubic inches, which is within two inches of the Caucasian mean."—Morton, *Crania Americana*, 195.—It is remarkable that the internal capacity of the skulls of the barbarous American tribes is greater than that of either the Mexicans or the Peruvians. "The difference in volume is chiefly confined to the occipital and basal portions,"—in other words, to the region of the animal propensities; and hence, it is argued, the ferocious, brutal, and uncivilizable character of the wild tribes.—See J. S. Phillips, *Admeasurements of Crania of the Principal Groups of Indians in the United States*.

Tobacco Nation, or Tionnontates.[1] In manners, as in language, they closely resembled the Hurons. Of old they were
their enemies, but were now at peace with them, and about
the year 1640 became their close confederates. Indeed, in the
ruin which befell that hapless people, the Tionnontates alone
retained a tribal organization; and their descendants, with a
trifling exception, are to this day the sole inheritors of the
Huron or Wyandot name. Expatriated and wandering, they
held for generations a paramount influence among the Western tribes.[2] In their original seats among the Blue Mountains,
they offered an example extremely rare among Indians, of a
tribe raising a crop for the market; for they traded in tobacco
largely with other tribes. Their Huron confederates, keen
traders, would not suffer them to pass through their country
to traffic with the French, preferring to secure for themselves
the advantage of bartering with them in French goods at an
enormous profit.[3]

Journeying southward five days from the Tionnontate
towns, the forest traveller reached the border villages of the
Attiwandarons, or Neutral Nation.[4] As early as 1626, they
were visited by the Franciscan friar, La Roche Dallion, who
reports a numerous population in twenty-eight towns, besides
many small hamlets. Their country, about forty leagues in extent, embraced wide and fertile districts on the north shore of
Lake Erie, and their frontier extended eastward across the Niagara, where they had three or four outlying towns.[5] Their
name of Neutrals was due to their neutrality in the war between the Hurons and the Iroquois proper. The hostile war-

---

[1] *Synonymes:* Tionnontates, Etionontates, Tuinontatek, Dionondadies,
Khionontaterrhonons, Petuneux or Nation du Petun (Tobacco).

[2] "L'ame de tous les Conseils."—Charlevoix, *Voyage*, 199.—In 1763 they
were Pontiac's best warriors.

[3] On the Tionnontates, see Le Mercier, *Relation, 1637*, 163; Lalemant, *Relation, 1641*, 69; Ragueneau, *Relation, 1648*, 61. An excellent summary of their
character and history, by Mr. Shea, will be found in *Hist. Mag.*, V. 262.

[4] Attiwandarons, Attiwendaronk, Atirhagenrenrets, Rhagenratka (*Jesuit Relations*), Attionidarons (*Sagard*). They, and not the Eries, were the *Kahkwas*
of Seneca tradition.

[5] Lalemant, *Relation des Hurons, 1641*, 71.—The Niagara was then called the
River of the Neutrals, or the Onguiaahra. Lalemant estimates the Neutral
population, in 1640, at twelve thousand, in forty villages.

riors, meeting in a Neutral cabin, were forced to keep the peace, though, once in the open air, the truce was at an end. Yet this people were abundantly ferocious, and, while holding a pacific attitude betwixt their warring kindred, waged deadly strife with the Mascoutins, an Algonquin horde beyond Lake Michigan. Indeed, it was but recently that they had been at blows with seventeen Algonquin tribes.[1] They burned female prisoners, a practice unknown to the Hurons.[2] Their country was full of game, and they were bold and active hunters. In form and stature they surpassed even the Hurons, whom they resembled in their mode of life, and from whose language their own, though radically similar, was dialectically distinct. Their licentiousness was even more open and shameless; and they stood alone in the extravagance of some of their usages. They kept their dead in their houses till they became insupportable; then scraped the flesh from the bones, and displayed them in rows along the walls, there to remain till the periodical Feast of the Dead, or general burial. In summer, the men wore no clothing whatever, but were usually tattooed from head to foot with powdered charcoal.

The sagacious Hurons refused them a passage through their country to the French; and the Neutrals apparently had not sense or reflection enough to take the easy and direct route of Lake Ontario, which was probably open to them, though closed against the Hurons by Iroquois enmity. Thus the former made excellent profit by exchanging French goods at high rates for the valuable furs of the Neutrals.[3]

Southward and eastward of Lake Erie dwelt a kindred peo-

---

[1] *Lettre du Père La Roche Dallion, 8 Juillet, 1627*, in Le Clerc, *Établissement de la Foy*, I. 346.

[2] Women were often burned by the Iroquois: witness the case of Catherine Mercier in 1651, and many cases of Indian women mentioned by the early writers.

[3] The Hurons became very jealous, when La Roche Dallion visited the Neutrals, lest a direct trade should be opened between the latter and the French, against whom they at once put in circulation a variety of slanders: that they were a people who lived on snakes and venom; that they were furnished with tails; and that French women, though having but one breast, bore six children at a birth. The missionary nearly lost his life in consequence, the Neutrals conceiving the idea that he would infect their country with a pestilence.—La Roche Dallion, in Le Clerc, I. 346.

ple, the Eries, or Nation of the Cat. Little besides their existence is known of them. They seem to have occupied Southwestern New York, as far east as the Genesee, the frontier of the Senecas, and in habits and language to have resembled the Hurons.[1] They were noted warriors, fought with poisoned arrows, and were long a terror to the neighboring Iroquois.[2]

On the Lower Susquehanna dwelt the formidable tribe called by the French Andastes. Little is known of them, beyond their general resemblance to their kindred, in language, habits, and character. Fierce and resolute warriors, they long made head against the Iroquois of New York, and were vanquished at last more by disease than by the tomahawk.[3]

In Central New York, stretching east and west from the Hudson to the Genesee, lay that redoubted people who have lent their name to the tribal family of the Iroquois, and stamped it indelibly on the early pages of American history. Among all the barbarous nations of the continent, the Iroquois of New York stand paramount. Elements which among other tribes were crude, confused, and embryotic, were among them systematized and concreted into an established polity. The Iroquois was the Indian of Indians. A thorough savage, yet a finished and developed savage, he is perhaps an example of the highest elevation which man can reach without emerging from his primitive condition of the hunter. A geographical position, commanding on one hand the portal

---

[1] Ragueneau, *Relation des Hurons, 1648*, 46.

[2] Le Mercier, *Relation, 1654*, 10.—"Nous les appellons la Nation Chat, à cause qu'il y a dans leur pais vne quantité prodigieuse de Chats sauuages."— *Ibid.*—The Iroquois are said to have given the same name, *Jegosasa, Cat Nation*, to the Neutrals.—Morgan, *League of the Iroquois*, 41.

Synonymes: Eriés, Erigas, Eriehronon, Riguehronon. The Jesuits never had a mission among them, though they seem to have been visited by Champlain's adventurous interpreter, Étienne Brulé, in the summer of 1615.—They are probably the Carantoüans of Champlain.

[3] Gallatin erroneously places the Andastes on the Alleghany, Bancroft and others adopting the error. The research of Mr. Shea has shown their identity with the *Susquehannocks* of the English, and the *Minquas* of the Dutch.— See *Hist. Mag.*, II. 294.

Synonymes: Andastes, Andastracronnons, Andastaeronnons, Andastaguez, Antastoui (French), Susquehannocks (English), Mengwe, Minquas (Dutch), Conestogas, Conessetagoes (English).

of the Great Lakes, and on the other the sources of the streams flowing both to the Atlantic and the Mississippi, gave the ambitious and aggressive confederates advantages which they perfectly understood, and by which they profited to the utmost. Patient and politic as they were ferocious, they were not only conquerors of their own race, but the powerful allies and the dreaded foes of the French and English colonies, flattered and caressed by both, yet too sagacious to give themselves without reserve to either. Their organization and their history evince their intrinsic superiority. Even their traditionary lore, amid its wild puerilities, shows at times the stamp of an energy and force in striking contrast with the flimsy creations of Algonquin fancy. That the Iroquois, left under their institutions to work out their destiny undisturbed, would ever have developed a civilization of their own, I do not believe. These institutions, however, are sufficiently characteristic and curious, and we shall soon have occasion to observe them.[1]

SOCIAL AND POLITICAL ORGANIZATION

In Indian social organization, a problem at once suggests

[1] The name *Iroquois* is French. Charlevoix says: "Il a été formé du terme *Hiro*, ou *Hero*, qui signifie *J'ai dit*, et par lequel ces sauvages finissent tous leur discours, comme les Latins faisoient autrefois par leur *Dixi*; et de *Koué*, qui est un cri tantôt de tristesse, lorsqu'on le prononce en traînant, et tantôt de joye, quand on le prononce plus court."—*Hist. de la N. F.*, I. 271.—Their true name is *Hodenosaunee*, or People of the Long House, because their confederacy of five distinct nations, ranged in a line along Central New York, was likened to one of the long bark houses already described, with five fires and five families. The name *Agonnonsionni*, or *Aquanuscioni*, ascribed to them by Lafitau and Charlevoix, who translated it "House-Makers," *Faiseurs de Cabannes*, may be a conversion of the true name with an erroneous rendering. The following are the true names of the five nations severally, with their French and English synonymes. For other synonymes, see "History of the Conspiracy of Pontiac," 8, *note*.

	ENGLISH	FRENCH
Ganeagaono,	Mohawk,	Agnier.
Onayotekaono,	Oneida,	Onneyut.
Onundagaono,	Onondaga,	Onnontagué.
Gweugwehono,	Cayuga,	Goyogouin.
Nundawaono,	Seneca,	Tsonnontouans.

The Iroquois termination in *ono*—or *onon*, as the French write it—simply means *people*.

itself. In these communities, comparatively populous, how could spirits so fierce, and in many respects so ungoverned, live together in peace, without law and without enforced authority? Yet there were towns where savages lived together in thousands with a harmony which civilization might envy. This was in good measure due to peculiarities of Indian character and habits. This intractable race were, in certain external respects, the most pliant and complaisant of mankind. The early missionaries were charmed by the docile acquiescence with which their dogmas were received; but they soon discovered that their facile auditors neither believed nor understood that to which they had so promptly assented. They assented from a kind of courtesy, which, while it vexed the priests, tended greatly to keep the Indians in mutual accord. That well-known self-control, which, originating in a form of pride, covered the savage nature of the man with a veil, opaque, though thin, contributed not a little to the same end. Though vain, arrogant, boastful, and vindictive, the Indian bore abuse and sarcasm with an astonishing patience. Though greedy and grasping, he was lavish without stint, and would give away his all to soothe the manes of a departed relative, gain influence and applause, or ingratiate himself with his neighbors. In his dread of public opinion, he rivalled some of his civilized successors.

All Indians, and especially these populous and stationary tribes, had their code of courtesy, whose requirements were rigid and exact; nor might any infringe it without the ban of public censure. Indian nature, inflexible and unmalleable, was peculiarly under the control of custom. Established usage took the place of law,—was, in fact, a sort of common law, with no tribunal to expound or enforce it. In these wild democracies,—democracies in spirit, though not in form,—a respect for native superiority, and a willingness to yield to it, were always conspicuous. All were prompt to aid each other in distress, and a neighborly spirit was often exhibited among them. When a young woman was permanently married, the other women of the village supplied her with firewood for the year, each contributing an armful. When one or more families were without shelter, the men of the village joined in building them a house. In return, the recipients of the favor gave a feast, if they could; if not, their thanks were sufficient.[1] Among the Iroquois and Hurons—and doubtless among the kindred tribes—there were marked distinctions of noble and base, prosperous and poor; yet, while there was food in the village, the meanest and the poorest need not suffer want. He had but to enter the nearest house, and seat himself by the fire, when, without a word on either side, food was placed before him by the women.[2]

Contrary to the received opinion, these Indians, like others of their race, when living in communities, were of a very social disposition. Besides their incessant dances and feasts, great and small, they were continually visiting, spending most of their time in their neighbors' houses, chatting, joking, bantering one another with witticisms, sharp, broad, and in no sense delicate, yet always taken in good part. Every village had its adepts in these wordy tournaments, while the shrill laugh of young squaws, untaught to blush, echoed each hardy jest or rough sarcasm.

In the organization of the savage communities of the continent, one feature, more or less conspicuous, continually appears. Each nation or tribe—to adopt the names by which these communities are usually known—is subdivided into several clans. These clans are not locally separate, but are mingled throughout the nation. All the members of each clan are, or are assumed to be, intimately joined in consanguinity.

---

[1] The following testimony concerning Indian charity and hospitality is from Ragueneau: "As often as we have seen tribes broken up, towns destroyed, and their people driven to flight, we have seen them, to the number of seven or eight hundred persons, received with open arms by charitable hosts, who gladly gave them aid, and even distributed among them a part of the lands already planted, that they might have the means of living."—*Relation, 1650,* 28.

[2] The Jesuit Brébeuf, than whom no one knew the Hurons better, is very emphatic in praise of their harmony and social spirit. Speaking of one of the four nations of which the Hurons were composed, he says: "Ils ont vne douceur et vne affabilité quasi incroyable pour des Sauuages; ils ne se picquent pas aisément. . . . Ils se maintiennent dans cette si parfaite intelligence par les frequentes visites, les secours qu'ils se donnent mutuellement dans leurs maladies, par les festins et les alliances. . . . Ils sont moins en leurs Cabanes que chez leurs amis. . . . S'ils ont vn bon morceau, ils en font festin à leurs amis, et ne le mangent quasi iamais en leur particulier," etc.—*Relation des Hurons, 1636,* 118.

Hence it is held an abomination for two persons of the same clan to intermarry; and hence, again, it follows that every family must contain members of at least two clans. Each·clan has its name, as the clan of the Hawk, of the Wolf, or of the Tortoise; and each has for its emblem the figure of the beast, bird, reptile, plant, or other object, from which its name is derived. This emblem, called *totem* by the Algonquins, is often tattooed on the clansman's body, or rudely painted over the entrance of his lodge. The child belongs to the clan, not of the father, but of the mother. In other words, descent, not of the totem alone, but of all rank, titles, and possessions, is through the female. The son of a chief can never be a chief by hereditary title, though he may become so by force of personal influence or achievement. Neither can he inherit from his father so much as a tobacco-pipe. All possessions alike pass of right to the brothers of the chief, or to the sons of his sisters, since these are all sprung from a common mother. This rule of descent was noticed by Champlain among the Hurons in 1615. That excellent observer refers it to an origin which is doubtless its true one. The child may not be the son of his reputed father, but must be the son of his mother,—a consideration of more than ordinary force in an Indian community.[1]

This system of clanship, with the rule of descent inseparable from it, was of very wide prevalence. Indeed, it is more than probable that close observation would have detected it in every tribe east of the Mississippi; while there is positive evidence of its existence in by far the greater number. It is found also among the Dahcotah and other tribes west of the Mississippi; and there is reason to believe it universally prevalent as far as the Rocky Mountains, and even beyond them. The fact that with most of these hordes there is little property worth transmission, and that the most influential becomes

[1] "Les enfans ne succedent iamais aux biens et dignitez de leurs peres, doubtant comme i'ay dit de leur geniteur, mais bien font-ils leurs successeurs et heritiers, les enfans de leurs sœurs, et desquels ils sont asseurez d'estre yssus et sortis."—Champlain (1627), 91.

Captain John Smith had observed the same, several years before, among the tribes of Virginia: "For the Crowne, their heyres inherite not, but the first heyres of the Sisters."— *True Relation*, 43 (ed. Deane).

chief, with little regard to inheritance, has blinded casual observers to the existence of this curious system.

It was found in full development among the Creeks, Choctaws, Cherokees, and other Southern tribes, including that remarkable people, the Natchez, who, judged by their religious and political institutions, seem a detached offshoot of the Toltec family. It is no less conspicuous among the roving Algonquins of the extreme North, where the number of totems is almost countless. Everywhere it formed the foundation of the polity of all the tribes, where a polity could be said to exist.

The Franciscans and Jesuits, close students of the languages and superstitions of the Indians, were by no means so zealous to analyze their organization and government. In the middle of the seventeenth century the Hurons as a nation had ceased to exist, and their political portraiture, as handed down to us, is careless and unfinished. Yet some decisive features are plainly shown. The Huron nation was a confederacy of four distinct contiguous nations, afterwards increased to five by the addition of the Tionnontates;—it was divided into clans;—it was governed by chiefs, whose office was hereditary through the female;—the power of these chiefs, though great, was wholly of a persuasive or advisory character;— there were two principal chiefs, one for peace, the other for war;—there were chiefs assigned to special national functions, as the charge of the great Feast of the Dead, the direction of trading voyages to other nations, etc.;—there were numerous other chiefs, equal in rank, but very unequal in influence, since the measure of their influence depended on the measure of their personal ability;—each nation of the confederacy had a separate organization, but at certain periods grand councils of the united nations were held, at which were present, not chiefs only, but also a great concourse of the people; and at these and other councils the chiefs and principal men voted on proposed measures by means of small sticks or reeds, the opinion of the plurality ruling.[1]

---

[1] These facts are gathered here and there from Champlain, Sagard, Bressani, and the Jesuit *Relations* prior to 1650. Of the Jesuits, Brébeuf is the most full and satisfactory. Lafitau and Charlevoix knew the Huron institutions only through others.

THE IROQUOIS

The Iroquois were a people far more conspicuous in history, and their institutions are not yet extinct. In early and recent times, they have been closely studied, and no little light has been cast upon a subject as difficult and obscure as it is curious. By comparing the statements of observers, old and new, the character of their singular organization becomes sufficiently clear.[1]

Both reason and tradition point to the conclusion, that the Iroquois formed originally one undivided people. Sundered, like countless other tribes, by dissension, caprice, or the necessities of the hunter life, they separated into five distinct nations, cantoned from east to west along the centre of New York, in the following order: Mohawks, Oneidas, Onondagas, Cayugas, Senecas. There was discord among them; wars followed, and they lived in mutual fear, each ensconced in its palisaded villages. At length, says tradition, a celestial being, incarnate on earth, counselled them to compose their strife and unite in a league of defence and aggression. Another per-

---

The names of the four confederate Huron nations were the Ataronchronons, Attignenonghac, Attignaouentans, and Ahrendarrhonons. There was also a subordinate "nation" called Tohotaenrat, which had but one town. (See the map of the Huron Country.) They all bore the name of some animal or other object: thus the Attignaouentans were the Nation of the Bear. As the clans are usually named after animals, this makes confusion, and may easily lead to error. The Bear Nation was the principal member of the league.

[1] Among modern students of Iroquois institutions, a place far in advance of all others is due to Lewis H. Morgan, himself an Iroquois by adoption, and intimate with the race from boyhood. His work, *The League of the Iroquois*, is a production of most thorough and able research, conducted under peculiar advantages, and with the aid of an efficient co-laborer, Hasanoanda (Ely S. Parker), an educated and highly intelligent Iroquois of the Seneca nation. Though often differing widely from Mr. Morgan's conclusions, I cannot bear a too emphatic testimony to the value of his researches. The *Notes on the Iroquois* of Mr. H. R. Schoolcraft also contain some interesting facts; but here, as in all Mr. Schoolcraft's productions, the reader must scrupulously reserve his right of private judgment. None of the old writers are so satisfactory as Lafitau. His work, *Mœurs des Sauvages Ameriquains comparées aux Mœurs des Premiers Temps*, relates chiefly to the Iroquois and Hurons: the basis for his account of the former being his own observations and those of Father Julien Garnier, who was a missionary among them more than sixty years, from his novitiate to his death.

sonage, wholly mortal, yet wonderfully endowed, a renowned warrior and a mighty magician, stands, with his hair of writhing snakes, grotesquely conspicuous through the dim light of tradition at this birth of Iroquois nationality. This was Atotarho, a chief of the Onondagas; and from this honored source has sprung a long line of chieftains, heirs not to the blood alone, but to the name of their great predecessor. A few years since, there lived in Onondaga Hollow a handsome Indian boy on whom the dwindled remnant of the nation looked with pride as their destined Atotarho. With earthly and celestial aid the league was consummated, and through all the land the forests trembled at the name of the Iroquois.

The Iroquois people was divided into eight clans. When the original stock was sundered into five parts, each of these clans was also sundered into five parts; and as, by the principle already indicated, the clans were intimately mingled in every village, hamlet, and cabin, each one of the five nations had its portion of each of the eight clans.[1] When the league

---

[1] With a view to clearness, the above statement is made categorical. It requires, however, to be qualified. It is not quite certain, that, at the formation of the confederacy, there were eight clans, though there is positive proof of the existence of seven. Neither is it certain, that, at the separation, every clan was represented in every nation. Among the Mohawks and Oneidas there is no positive proof of the existence of more than three clans, — the Wolf, Bear, and Tortoise; though there is presumptive evidence of the existence of several others. — See Morgan, 81, note.

The eight clans of the Iroquois were as follows: Wolf, Bear, Beaver, Tortoise, Deer, Snipe, Heron, Hawk. (Morgan, 79.) The clans of the Snipe and the Heron are the same designated in an early French document as *La famille du Petit Pluvier* and *La famille du Grand Pluvier*. (*New York Colonial Documents*, IX. 47.) The anonymous author of this document adds a ninth clan, that of the Potato, meaning the wild Indian potato, *Glycine apios*. This clan, if it existed, was very inconspicuous, and of little importance.

Remarkable analogies exist between Iroquois clanship and that of other tribes. The eight clans of the Iroquois were separated into two divisions, four in each. Originally, marriage was interdicted between all the members of the same division, but in time the interdict was limited to the members of the individual clans. Another tribe, the Choctaws, remote from the Iroquois, and radically different in language, had also eight clans, similarly divided, with a similar interdict of marriage. — Gallatin, *Synopsis*, 109.

The Creeks, according to the account given by their old chief, Sekopechi, to Mr. D. W. Eakins, were divided into nine clans, named in most cases from animals: clanship being transmitted, as usual, through the female.

was formed, these separate portions readily resumed their ancient tie of fraternity. Thus, of the Turtle clan, all the members became brothers again, nominal members of one family, whether Mohawks, Oneidas, Onondagas, Cayugas, or Senecas; and so, too, of the remaining clans. All the Iroquois, irrespective of nationality, were therefore divided into eight families, each tracing its descent to a common mother, and each designated by its distinctive emblem or *totem*. This connection of clan or family was exceedingly strong, and by it the five nations of the league were linked together as by an eightfold chain.

The clans were by no means equal in numbers, influence, or honor. So marked were the distinctions among them, that some of the early writers recognize only the three most conspicuous,—those of the Tortoise, the Bear, and the Wolf. To some of the clans, in each nation, belonged the right of giving a chief to the nation and to the league. Others had the right of giving three, or, in one case, four chiefs; while others could give none. As Indian clanship was but an extension of the family relation, these chiefs were, in a certain sense, hereditary; but the law of inheritance, though binding, was extremely elastic, and capable of stretching to the farthest limits of the clan. The chief was almost invariably succeeded by a near relative, always through the female, as a brother by the same mother, or a nephew by the sister's side. But if these were manifestly unfit, they were passed over, and a chief was chosen at a council of the clan from among remoter kindred. In these cases, the successor is said to have been nominated by the matron of the late chief's household.[1] Be this as it may, the choice was never adverse to the popular inclination. The new chief was "raised up," or installed, by a formal council of the sachems of the league; and on entering upon his office, he dropped his own name, and assumed that which, since the formation of the league, had belonged to this especial chieftainship.

The number of these principal chiefs, or, as they have been called by way of distinction, sachems, varied in the several nations from eight to fourteen. The sachems of the five na-

---

[1] Lafitau, I. 471.

tions, fifty in all, assembled in council, formed the government of the confederacy. All met as equals, but a peculiar dignity was ever attached to the Atotarho of the Onondagas.

There was a class of subordinate chiefs, in no sense hereditary, but rising to office by address, ability, or valor. Yet the rank was clearly defined, and the new chief installed at a formal council. This class embodied, as might be supposed, the best talent of the nation, and the most prominent warriors and orators of the Iroquois have belonged to it. In its character and functions, however, it was purely civil. Like the sachems, these chiefs held their councils, and exercised an influence proportionate to their number and abilities.

There was another council, between which and that of the subordinate chiefs the line of demarcation seems not to have been very definite. The Jesuit Lafitau calls it "the senate." Familiar with the Iroquois at the height of their prosperity, he describes it as the central and controlling power, so far, at least, as the separate nations were concerned. In its character it was essentially popular, but popular in the best sense, and one which can find its application only in a small community. Any man took part in it whose age and experience qualified him to do so. It was merely the gathered wisdom of the nation. Lafitau compares it to the Roman Senate, in the early and rude age of the Republic, and affirms that it loses nothing by the comparison. He thus describes it: "It is a greasy assemblage, sitting *sur leur derrière*, crouched like apes, their knees as high as their ears, or lying, some on their bellies, some on their backs, each with a pipe in his mouth, discussing affairs of state with as much coolness and gravity as the Spanish Junta or the Grand Council of Venice."[1]

The young warriors had also their councils; so, too, had the women; and the opinions and wishes of each were represented by means of deputies before the "senate," or council of the old men, as well as before the grand confederate council of the sachems.

The government of this unique republic resided wholly in councils. By councils all questions were settled, all regulations established,—social, political, military, and religious. The war-path, the chase, the council-fire,—in these was the life of

[1] Lafitau, I. 478.

the Iroquois; and it is hard to say to which of the three he was most devoted.

The great council of the fifty sachems formed, as we have seen, the government of the league. Whenever a subject arose before any of the nations, of importance enough to demand its assembling, the sachems of that nation might summon their colleagues by means of runners, bearing messages and belts of wampum. The usual place of meeting was the valley of Onondaga, the political as well as geographical centre of the confederacy. Thither, if the matter were one of deep and general interest, not the sachems alone, but the greater part of the population, gathered from east and west, swarming in the hospitable lodges of the town, or bivouacked by thousands in the surrounding fields and forests. While the sachems deliberated in the council-house, the chiefs and old men, the warriors, and often the women, were holding their respective councils apart; and their opinions, laid by their deputies before the council of sachems, were never without influence on its decisions.

The utmost order and deliberation reigned in the council, with rigorous adherence to the Indian notions of parliamentary propriety. The conference opened with an address to the spirits, or the chief of all the spirits. There was no heat in debate. No speaker interrupted another. Each gave his opinion in turn, supporting it with what reason or rhetoric he could command,—but not until he had stated the subject of discussion in full, to prove that he understood it, repeating also the arguments, *pro* and *con*, of previous speakers. Thus their debates were excessively prolix; and the consumption of tobacco was immoderate. The result, however, was a thorough sifting of the matter in hand; while the practised astuteness of these savage politicians was a marvel to their civilized contemporaries. "It is by a most subtle policy," says Lafitau, "that they have taken the ascendant over the other nations, divided and overcome the most warlike, made themselves a terror to the most remote, and now hold a peaceful neutrality between the French and English, courted and feared by both."[1]

[1] Lafitau, I. 480.—Many other French writers speak to the same effect. The following are the words of the soldier historian, La Potherie, after describing

Unlike the Hurons, they required an entire unanimity in their decisions. The ease and frequency with which a requisition seemingly so difficult was fulfilled afford a striking illustration of Indian nature,—on one side, so stubborn, tenacious, and impracticable; on the other, so pliant and acquiescent. An explanation of this harmony is to be found also in an intense spirit of nationality: for never since the days of Sparta were individual life and national life more completely fused into one.

The sachems of the league were likewise, as we have seen, sachems of their respective nations; yet they rarely spoke in the councils of the subordinate chiefs and old men, except to present subjects of discussion.[1] Their influence in these councils was, however, great, and even paramount; for they commonly succeeded in securing to their interest some of the most dexterous and influential of the conclave, through whom, while they themselves remained in the background, they managed the debates.[2]

There was a class of men among the Iroquois always put

-----

the organization of the league: "C'est donc là cette politique qui les unit si bien, à peu près comme tous les ressorts d'une horloge, qui par une liaison admirable de toutes les parties qui les composent, contribuent toutes unanimement au merveilleux effet qui en resulte."—*Hist. de l'Amérique Septentrionale*, III. 32.—He adds: "Les François ont avoüé eux-mêmes qu'ils étoient nez pour la guerre, & quelques maux qu'ils nous ayent faits nous les avons toujours estimez."—*Ibid.*, 2.—La Potherie's book was published in 1722,

[1] Lafitau, I. 479.

[2] The following from Lafitau is very characteristic: "Ce que je dis de leur zèle pour le bien public n'est cependant pas si universel, que plusieurs ne pensent à leur interêts particuliers, & que les Chefs (*sachems*) principalement ne fassent joüer plusieurs ressorts secrets pour venir à bout de leurs intrigues. Il y en a tel, dont l'adresse joüe si bien à coup sûr, qu'il fait déliberer le Conseil plusieurs jours de suite, sur une matière dont la détermination est arrêtée entre lui & les principales têtes avant d'avoir été mise sur le tapis. Cependant comme les Chefs s'entre-regardent, & qu'aucun ne veut paroître se donner une superiorité qui puisse piquer la jalousie, ils se ménagent dans les Conseils plus que les autres; & quoiqu'ils en soient l'ame, leur politique les oblige à y parler peu, & à écouter plûtôt le sentiment d'autrui, qu'à y dire le leur; mais chacun a un homme à sa main, qui est comme une espèce de Brûlot, & qui étant sans consequence pour sa personne hazarde en pleine liberté tout ce qu'il juge à propos, selon qu'il l'a concerté avec le Chef même pour qui il agit."—*Mœurs des Sauvages*, I. 481.

forward on public occasions to speak the mind of the nation or defend its interests. Nearly all of them were of the number of the subordinate chiefs. Nature and training had fitted them for public speaking, and they were deeply versed in the history and traditions of the league. They were in fact professed orators, high in honor and influence among the people. To a huge stock of conventional metaphors, the use of which required nothing but practice, they often added an astute intellect, an astonishing memory, and an eloquence which deserved the name.

In one particular, the training of these savage politicians was never surpassed. They had no art of writing to record events, or preserve the stipulations of treaties. Memory, therefore, was tasked to the utmost, and developed to an extraordinary degree. They had various devices for aiding it, such as bundles of sticks, and that system of signs, emblems, and rude pictures, which they shared with other tribes. Their famous wampum-belts were so many mnemonic signs, each standing for some act, speech, treaty, or clause of a treaty. These represented the public archives, and were divided among various custodians, each charged with the memory and interpretation of those assigned to him. The meaning of the belts was from time to time expounded in their councils. In conferences with them, nothing more astonished the French, Dutch, and English officials than the precision with which, before replying to their addresses, the Indian orators repeated them point by point.

It was only in rare cases that crime among the Iroquois or Hurons was punished by public authority. Murder, the most heinous offence, except witchcraft, recognized among them, was rare. If the slayer and the slain were of the same household or clan, the affair was regarded as a family quarrel, to be settled by the immediate kin on both sides. This, under the pressure of public opinion, was commonly effected without bloodshed, by presents given in atonement. But if the murderer and his victim were of different clans or different nations, still more, if the slain was a foreigner, the whole community became interested to prevent the discord or the war which might arise. All directed their efforts, not to bring the murderer to punishment, but to satisfy the injured parties

by a vicarious atonement.[1] To this end, contributions were
made and presents collected. Their number and value were
determined by established usage. Among the Hurons, thirty
presents of very considerable value were the price of a man's
life. That of a woman's was fixed at forty, by reason of her
weakness, and because on her depended the continuance and
increase of the population. This was when the slain belonged
to the nation. If of a foreign tribe, his death demanded a
higher compensation, since it involved the danger of war.[2]
These presents were offered in solemn council, with prescribed formalities. The relatives of the slain might refuse
them, if they chose, and in this case the murderer was given
them as a slave; but they might by no means kill him, since,
in so doing, they would incur public censure, and be compelled in their turn to make atonement. Besides the principal
gifts, there was a great number of less value, all symbolical,
and each delivered with a set form of words: as, "By this we
wash out the blood of the slain: By this we cleanse his
wound: By this we clothe his corpse with a new shirt: By this
we place food on his grave": and so, in endless prolixity,
through particulars without number.[3]

The Hurons were notorious thieves; and perhaps the Iroquois were not much better, though the contrary has been
asserted. Among both, the robbed was permitted not only to
retake his property by force, if he could, but to strip the robber of all he had. This apparently acted as a restraint in favor
only of the strong, leaving the weak a prey to the plunderer;
but here the tie of family and clan intervened to aid him.
Relatives and clansmen espoused the quarrel of him who
could not right himself.[4]

---

[1] Lalemant, while inveighing against a practice which made the public, and
not the criminal, answerable for an offence, admits that heinous crimes were
more rare than in France, where the guilty party himself was punished.—
Lettre au P. Provincial, 15 May, 1645.

[2] Ragueneau, *Relation des Hurons, 1648*, 80.

[3] Ragueneau, *Relation des Hurons, 1648*, gives a description of one of these
ceremonies at length. Those of the Iroquois on such occasions were similar.
Many other tribes had the same custom, but attended with much less form
and ceremony. Compare Perrot, 73–76.

[4] The proceedings for detecting thieves were regular and methodical, after
established customs. According to Bressani, no thief ever inculpated the innocent.

Witches, with whom the Hurons and Iroquois were grievously infested, were objects of utter abomination to both, and
any one might kill them at any time. If any person was guilty
of treason, or by his character and conduct made himself dangerous or obnoxious to the public, the council of chiefs and
old men held a secret session on his case, condemned him to
death, and appointed some young man to kill him. The executioner, watching his opportunity, brained or stabbed him
unawares, usually in the dark porch of one of the houses.
Acting by authority, he could not be held answerable; and
the relatives of the slain had no redress, even if they desired
it. The council, however, commonly obviated all difficulty in
advance, by charging the culprit with witchcraft, thus alienating his best friends.

The military organization of the Iroquois was exceedingly
imperfect and derived all its efficiency from their civil union
and their personal prowess. There were two hereditary war-
chiefs, both belonging to the Senecas; but, except on occasions of unusual importance, it does not appear that they took
a very active part in the conduct of wars. The Iroquois lived
in a state of chronic warfare with nearly all the surrounding
tribes, except a few from whom they exacted tribute. Any
man of sufficient personal credit might raise a war-party when
he chose. He proclaimed his purpose through the village,
sang his war-songs, struck his hatchet into the war-post, and
danced the war-dance. Any who chose joined him; and the
party usually took up their march at once, with a little
parched-corn-meal and maple-sugar as their sole provision.
On great occasions, there was concert of action,—the various
parties meeting at a rendezvous, and pursuing the march together. The leaders of war-parties, like the orators, belonged,
in nearly all cases, to the class of subordinate chiefs. The Iroquois had a discipline suited to the dark and tangled forests
where they fought. Here they were a terrible foe: in an open
country, against a trained European force, they were, despite
their ferocious valor, far less formidable.

In observing this singular organization, one is struck by the
incongruity of its spirit and its form. A body of hereditary
oligarchs was the head of the nation, yet the nation was essentially democratic. Not that the Iroquois were levellers.
None were more prompt to acknowledge superiority and

defer to it, whether established by usage and prescription, or the result of personal endowment. Yet each man, whether of high or low degree, had a voice in the conduct of affairs, and was never for a moment divorced from his wild spirit of independence. Where there was no property worthy the name, authority had no fulcrum and no hold. The constant aim of sachems and chiefs was to exercise it without seeming to do so. They had no insignia of office. They were no richer than others; indeed, they were often poorer, spending their substance in largesses and bribes to strengthen their influence. They hunted and fished for subsistence; they were as foul, greasy, and unsavory as the rest; yet in them, withal, was often seen a native dignity of bearing, which ochre and bear's grease could not hide, and which comported well with their strong, symmetrical, and sometimes majestic proportions.

To the institutions, traditions, rites, usages, and festivals of the league the Iroquois was inseparably wedded. He clung to them with Indian tenacity; and he clings to them still. His political fabric was one of ancient ideas and practices, crystallized into regular and enduring forms. In its component parts it has nothing peculiar to itself. All its elements are found in other tribes: most of them belong to the whole Indian race. Undoubtedly there was a distinct and definite effort of legislation; but Iroquois legislation invented nothing. Like all sound legislation, it built of materials already prepared. It organized the chaotic past, and gave concrete forms to Indian nature itself. The people have dwindled and decayed; but, banded by its ties of clan and kin, the league, in feeble miniature, still subsists, and the degenerate Iroquois looks back with a mournful pride to the glory of the past.

Would the Iroquois, left undisturbed to work out their own destiny, ever have emerged from the savage state? Advanced as they were beyond most other American tribes, there is no indication whatever of a tendency to overpass the confines of a wild hunter and warrior life. They were inveterately attached to it, impracticable conservatists of barbarism, and in ferocity and cruelty they matched the worst of their race. Nor did the power of expansion apparently belonging to their system ever produce much result. Between the years 1712 and 1715, the Tuscaroras, a kindred people, were admitted into the league as a sixth nation; but they were never admitted on equal terms. Long after, in the period of their decline, several other tribes were announced as new members of the league; but these admissions never took effect. The Iroquois were always reluctant to receive other tribes, or parts of tribes, collectively, into the precincts of the "Long House." Yet they constantly practised a system of adoptions, from which, though cruel and savage, they drew great advantages. Their prisoners of war, when they had burned and butchered as many of them as would serve to sate their own ire and that of their women, were divided, man by man, woman by woman, and child by child, adopted into different families and clans, and thus incorporated into the nation. It was by this means, and this alone, that they could offset the losses of their incessant wars. Early in the eighteenth century, and even long before, a vast proportion of their population consisted of adopted prisoners.[1]

It remains to speak of the religious and superstitious ideas which so deeply influenced Indian life.

RELIGION AND SUPERSTITIONS

The religious belief of the North-American Indians seems, on a first view, anomalous and contradictory. It certainly is so, if we adopt the popular impression. Romance, Poetry, and Rhetoric point, on the one hand, to the august conception of a one all-ruling Deity, a Great Spirit, omniscient and omnipresent; and we are called to admire the untutored intellect which could conceive a thought too vast for Socrates and

---

[1] *Relation, 1660*, 7 (anonymous). The Iroquois were at the height of their prosperity about the year 1650. Morgan reckons their number at this time at 25,000 souls; but this is far too high an estimate. The author of the *Relation* of 1660 makes their whole number of warriors 2,200. Le Mercier, in the *Relation* of 1665, says 2,350. In the Journal of Greenhalgh, an Englishman who visited them in 1677, their warriors are set down at 2,150. Du Chesneau, in 1681, estimates them at 2,000; De la Barre, in 1684, at 2,600, they having been strengthened by adoptions. A memoir addressed to the Marquis de Seignelay, in 1687, again makes them 2,000. (See *N. Y. Col. Docs.*, IX. 162, 196, 321.) These estimates imply a total population of ten or twelve thousand.

The anonymous writer of the *Relation* of 1660 may well remark: "It is marvellous that so few should make so great a havoc, and strike such terror into so many tribes."

Plato. On the other hand, we find a chaos of degrading, ridiculous, and incoherent superstitions. A closer examination will show that the contradiction is more apparent than real. We will begin with the lowest forms of Indian belief, and thence trace it upward to the highest conceptions to which the unassisted mind of the savage attained.

To the Indian, the material world is sentient and intelligent. Birds, beasts, and reptiles have ears for human prayers, and are endowed with an influence on human destiny. A mysterious and inexplicable power resides in inanimate things. They, too, can listen to the voice of man, and influence his life for evil or for good. Lakes, rivers, and waterfalls are sometimes the dwelling-place of spirits; but more frequently they are themselves living beings, to be propitiated by prayers and offerings. The lake has a soul; and so has the river, and the cataract. Each can hear the words of men, and each can be pleased or offended. In the silence of a forest, the gloom of a deep ravine, resides a living mystery, indefinite, but redoubtable. Through all the works of Nature or of man, nothing exists, however seemingly trivial, that may not be endowed with a secret power for blessing or for bane.

Men and animals are closely akin. Each species of animal has its great archetype, its progenitor or king, who is supposed to exist somewhere, prodigious in size, though in shape and nature like his subjects. A belief prevails, vague, but perfectly apparent, that men themselves owe their first parentage to beasts, birds, or reptiles, as bears, wolves, tortoises, or cranes; and the names of the totemic clans, borrowed in nearly every case from animals, are the reflection of this idea.[1]

An Indian hunter was always anxious to propitiate the an-

[1] This belief occasionally takes a perfectly definite shape. There was a tradition among Northern and Western tribes, that men were created from the carcasses of beasts, birds, and fishes, by Manabozho, a mythical personage, to be described hereafter. The Amikouas, or People of the Beaver, an Algonquin tribe of Lake Huron, claimed descent from the carcass of the great original beaver, or father of the beavers. They believed that the rapids and cataracts on the French River and the Upper Ottawa were caused by dams made by their amphibious ancestor. (See the tradition in Perrot, *Mémoire sur les Mœurs, Coustumes et Relligion des Sauvages de l'Amérique Septentrionale*, p. 20.) Charlevoix tells the same story. Each Indian was supposed to inherit something of the nature of the animal whence he sprung.

imals he sought to kill. He has often been known to address a wounded bear in a long harangue of apology.[1] The bones of the beaver were treated with especial tenderness, and carefully kept from the dogs, lest the spirit of the dead beaver, or his surviving brethren, should take offence.[2] This solicitude was not confined to animals, but extended to inanimate things. A remarkable example occurred among the Hurons, a people comparatively advanced, who, to propitiate their fishing-nets, and persuade them to do their office with effect, married them every year to two young girls of the tribe, with a ceremony far more formal than that observed in the case of mere human wedlock.[3] The fish, too, no less than the nets, must be propitiated; and to this end they were addressed every evening from the fishing-camp by one of the party chosen for that function, who exhorted them to take courage and be caught, assuring them that the utmost respect should be shown to their bones. The harangue, which took place after the evening meal, was made in solemn form; and while it lasted, the whole party, except the speaker, were required to lie on their backs, silent and motionless, around the fire.[4]

Besides ascribing life and intelligence to the material world, animate and inanimate, the Indian believes in supernatural existences, known among the Algonquins as *Manitous*, and

[1] McKinney, *Tour to the Lakes*, 284, mentions the discomposure of a party of Indians when shown a stuffed moose. Thinking that its spirit would be offended at the indignity shown to its remains, they surrounded it, making apologetic speeches, and blowing tobacco-smoke at it as a propitiatory offering.

[2] This superstition was very prevalent, and numerous examples of it occur in old and recent writers, from Father Le Jeune to Captain Carver.

[3] There are frequent allusions to this ceremony in the early writers. The Algonquins of the Ottawa practised it, as well as the Hurons. Lalemant, in his chapter "Du Regne de Satan en ces Contrées" (*Relation des Hurons, 1639*), says that it took place yearly, in the middle of March. As it was indispensable that the brides should be virgins, mere children were chosen. The net was held between them; and its spirit, or *oki*, was harangued by one of the chiefs, who exhorted him to do his part in furnishing the tribe with food. Lalemant was told that the spirit of the net had once appeared in human form to the Algonquins, complaining that he had lost his wife, and warning them, that, unless they could find him another equally immaculate, they would catch no more fish.

[4] Sagard, *Le Grand Voyage du Pays des Hurons*, 257. Other old writers make a similar statement.

among the Iroquois and Hurons as *Okies* or *Otkons*. These words comprehend all forms of supernatural being, from the highest to the lowest, with the exception, possibly, of certain diminutive fairies or hobgoblins, and certain giants and anomalous monsters, which appear under various forms, grotesque and horrible, in the Indian fireside legends.[1] There are local manitous of streams, rocks, mountains, cataracts, and forests. The conception of these beings betrays, for the most part, a striking poverty of imagination. In nearly every case, when they reveal themselves to mortal sight, they bear the semblance of beasts, reptiles, or birds, in shapes unusual or distorted.[2] There are other manitous without local habitation, some good, some evil, countless in number and indefinite in attributes. They fill the world, and control the destinies of men,—that is to say, of Indians: for the primitive Indian holds that the white man lives under a spiritual rule distinct from that which governs his own fate. These beings, also, appear for the most part in the shape of animals. Sometimes, however, they assume human proportions; but more frequently they take the form of stones, which, being broken, are found full of living blood and flesh.

Each primitive Indian has his guardian manitou, to whom he looks for counsel, guidance, and protection. These spiritual allies are gained by the following process. At the age of fourteen or fifteen, the Indian boy blackens his face, retires to some solitary place, and remains for days without food. Superstitious expectancy and the exhaustion of abstinence rarely fail of their results. His sleep is haunted by visions, and the form which first or most often appears is that of his guardian manitou,—a beast, a bird, a fish, a serpent, or some other object, animate or inanimate. An eagle or a bear is the vision of a destined warrior; a wolf, of a successful hunter; while a

---

[1] Many tribes have tales of diminutive beings, which, in the absence of a better word, may be called fairies. In the *Travels of Lewis and Clarke*, there is mention of a hill on the Missouri, supposed to be haunted by them. These Western fairies correspond to the *Puck Wudj Ininee* of Ojibwa tradition. As an example of the monsters alluded to, see the Saginaw story of the *Weendigoes*, in Schoolcraft, *Algic Researches*, II. 105.

[2] The figure of a large bird is perhaps the most common,—as, for example, the good spirit of Rock Island: "He was white, with wings like a swan, but ten times larger."—*Autobiography of Blackhawk*, 70.

serpent foreshadows the future medicine-man, or, according
to others, portends disaster.[1] The young Indian thenceforth
wears about his person the object revealed in his dream, or
some portion of it,—as a bone, a feather, a snake-skin, or a
tuft of hair. This, in the modern language of the forest and
prairie, is known as his "medicine." The Indian yields to it a
sort of worship, propitiates it with offerings of tobacco,
thanks it in prosperity, and upbraids it in disaster.[2] If his
medicine fails to bring the desired success, he will sometimes
discard it and adopt another. The superstition now becomes
mere fetich-worship, since the Indian regards the mysterious
object which he carries about him rather as an embodiment
than as a representative of a supernatural power.

Indian belief recognizes also another and very different
class of beings. Besides the giants and monsters of legendary
lore, other conceptions may be discerned, more or less distinct, and of a character partly mythical. Of these the most
conspicuous is that remarkable personage of Algonquin tradition, called Manabozho, Messou, Michabou, Nanabush, or
the Great Hare. As each species of animal has its archetype or
king, so, among the Algonquins, Manabozho is king of all
these animal kings. Tradition is diverse as to his origin. According to the most current belief, his father was the West-

[1] Compare Cass, in *North-American Review*, Second Series, XIII. 100. A
turkey-buzzard, according to him, is the vision of a medicine-man. I once
knew an old Dahcotah chief, who was greatly respected, but had never been
to war, though belonging to a family of peculiarly warlike propensities. The
reason was, that, in his initiatory fast, he had dreamed of an antelope,—the
peace-spirit of his people.

Women fast, as well as men,—always at the time of transition from childhood to maturity. In the *Narrative* of John Tanner, there is an account of an
old woman who had fasted, in her youth, for ten days, and throughout her
life placed the firmest faith in the visions which had appeared to her at that
time. Among the Northern Algonquins, the practice, down to a recent day,
was almost universal.

[2] The author has seen a Dahcotah warrior open his medicine-bag, talk with
an air of affectionate respect to the bone, feather, or horn within, and blow
tobacco-smoke upon it as an offering. "Medicines" are acquired not only by
fasting, but by casual dreams, and otherwise. They are sometimes even
bought and sold. For a curious account of medicine-bags and fetich-worship
among the Algonquins of Gaspé, see Le Clerc, *Nouvelle Relation de la Gaspésie*, Chap. XIII.

Wind, and his mother a great-granddaughter of the Moon.
His character is worthy of such a parentage. Sometimes he is
a wolf, a bird, or a gigantic hare, surrounded by a court of
quadrupeds; sometimes he appears in human shape, majestic
in stature and wondrous in endowment, a mighty magician,
a destroyer of serpents and evil manitous; sometimes he is a
vain and treacherous imp, full of childish whims and petty
trickery, the butt and victim of men, beasts, and spirits. His
powers of transformation are without limit; his curiosity and
malice are insatiable; and of the numberless legends of which
he is the hero, the greater part are as trivial as they are incoherent.[1] It does not appear that Manabozho was ever an object of worship; yet, despite his absurdity, tradition declares
him to be chief among the manitous, in short, the "Great
Spirit."[2] It was he who restored the world, submerged by a
deluge. He was hunting in company with a certain wolf, who
was his brother, or, by other accounts, his grandson, when
his quadruped relative fell through the ice of a frozen lake,
and was at once devoured by certain serpents lurking in the
depths of the waters. Manabozho, intent on revenge, transformed himself into the stump of a tree, and by this artifice
surprised and slew the king of the serpents, as he basked with
his followers in the noontide sun. The serpents, who were all
manitous, caused, in their rage, the waters of the lake to deluge the earth. Manabozho climbed a tree, which, in answer
to his entreaties, grew as the flood rose around it, and thus
saved him from the vengeance of the evil spirits. Submerged
to the neck, he looked abroad on the waste of waters, and at
length descried the bird known as the loon, to whom he appealed for aid in the task of restoring the world. The loon
dived in search of a little mud, as material for reconstruction,

[1] Mr. Schoolcraft has collected many of these tales. See his *Algic Researches*,
Vol. I. Compare the stories of Messou, given by Le Jeune (*Relations, 1633,
1634*), and the account of Nanabush, by Edwin James, in his notes to Tanner's
*Narrative of Captivity and Adventures during a Thirty-Years' Residence among
the Indians*; also the account of the Great Hare, in the *Mémoire* of Nicolas
Perrot, Chaps. I., II.

[2] "Presque toutes les Nations Algonquines ont donné le nom de *Grand
Lièvre* au Premier Esprit, quelques-uns l'appellent *Michabou* (Manabozho)."—Charlevoix, *Journal Historique*, 344.

but could not reach the bottom. A musk-rat made the same attempt, but soon reappeared floating on his back, and apparently dead. Manabozho, however, on searching his paws, discovered in one of them a particle of the desired mud, and of this, together with the body of the loon, created the world anew.[1]

There are various forms of this tradition, in some of which Manabozho appears, not as the restorer, but as the creator of the world, forming mankind from the carcasses of beasts, birds, and fishes.[2] Other stories represent him as marrying a female musk-rat, by whom he became the progenitor of the human race.[3]

Searching for some higher conception of supernatural existence, we find, among a portion of the primitive Algonquins, traces of a vague belief in a spirit dimly shadowed forth under the name of Atahocan, to whom it does not appear that any attributes were ascribed or any worship offered, and of whom the Indians professed to know nothing whatever;[4] but there is no evidence that this belief extended beyond certain tribes of the Lower St. Lawrence. Others saw a supreme manitou

[1] This is a form of the story still current among the remoter Algonquins. Compare the story of Messou, in Le Jeune, *Relation, 1633*, 16. It is substantially the same.

[2] In the beginning of all things, Manabozho, in the form of the Great Hare, was on a raft, surrounded by animals who acknowledged him as their chief. No land could be seen. Anxious to create the world, the Great Hare persuaded the beaver to dive for mud; but the adventurous diver floated to the surface senseless. The otter next tried, and failed like his predecessor. The musk-rat now offered himself for the desperate task. He plunged, and, after remaining a day and night beneath the surface, reappeared, floating on his back beside the raft, apparently dead, and with all his paws fast closed. On opening them, the other animals found in one of them a grain of sand, and of this the Great Hare created the world.—Perrot, *Mémoire*, Chap. I.

[3] Le Jeune, *Relation, 1633*, 16.—The musk-rat is always a conspicuous figure in Algonquin cosmogony.

It is said that Messou, or Manabozho, once gave to an Indian the gift of immortality, tied in a bundle, enjoining him never to open it. The Indian's wife, however, impelled by curiosity, one day cut the string, the precious gift flew out, and Indians have ever since been subject to death.—Le Jeune, *Relation, 1634*, 13.

[4] Le Jeune, *Relation, 1633*, 16; *Relation, 1634*, 13.

in the Sun.[1] The Algonquins believed also in a malignant manitou, in whom the early missionaries failed not to recognize the Devil, but who was far less dreaded than his wife. She wore a robe made of the hair of her victims, for she was the cause of death; and she it was whom, by yelling, drumming, and stamping, they sought to drive away from the sick. Sometimes, at night, she was seen by some terrified squaw in the forest, in shape like a flame of fire; and when the vision was announced to the circle crouched around the lodge-fire, they burned a fragment of meat to appease the female fiend.

The East, the West, the North, and the South were vaguely personified as spirits or manitous. Some of the winds, too, were personal existences. The West-Wind, as we have seen, was father of Manabozho. There was a Summer-Maker and a Winter-Maker; and the Indians tried to keep the latter at bay by throwing firebrands into the air.

When we turn from the Algonquin family of tribes to that of the Iroquois, we find another cosmogony, and other conceptions of spiritual existence. While the earth was as yet a waste of waters, there was, according to Iroquois and Huron traditions, a heaven with lakes, streams, plains, and forests, inhabited by animals, by spirits, and, as some affirm, by human beings. Here a certain female spirit, named Ataentsic, was once chasing a bear, which, slipping through a hole, fell down to the earth. Ataentsic's dog followed, when she herself, struck with despair, jumped after them. Others declare that she was kicked out of heaven by the spirit, her husband, for an amour with a man; while others, again, hold the belief that she fell in the attempt to gather for her husband the medicinal leaves of a certain tree. Be this as it may, the animals swimming in the watery waste below saw her falling, and hastily met in council to determine what should be done. The

[1] Biard, *Relation, 1611*, Chap. VIII.—This belief was very prevalent. The Ottawas, according to Ragueneau (*Relation des Hurons, 1648*, 77), were accustomed to invoke the "Maker of Heaven" at their feasts; but they recognized as distinct persons the Maker of the Earth, the Maker of Winter, the God of the Waters, and the Seven Spirits of the Wind. He says, at the same time, "The people of these countries have received from their ancestors no knowledge of a God"; and he adds, that there is no sentiment of religion in this invocation.

case was referred to the beaver. The beaver commended it to the judgment of the tortoise, who thereupon called on the other animals to dive, bring up mud, and place it on his back. Thus was formed a floating island, on which Ataentsic fell; and here, being pregnant, she was soon delivered of a daughter, who in turn bore two boys, whose paternity is unexplained. They were called Taouscaron and Jouskeha, and presently fell to blows, Jouskeha killing his brother with the horn of a stag. The back of the tortoise grew into a world full of verdure and life; and Jouskeha, with his grandmother, Ataentsic, ruled over its destinies.[1]

He is the Sun; she is the Moon. He is beneficent; but she is malignant, like the female demon of the Algonquins. They have a bark house, made like those of the Iroquois, at the end of the earth, and they often come to feasts and dances in the Indian villages. Jouskeha raises corn for himself, and makes plentiful harvests for mankind. Sometimes he is seen, thin as a skeleton, with a spike of shrivelled corn in his hand, or greedily gnawing a human limb; and then the Indians know that a grievous famine awaits them. He constantly interposes between mankind and the malice of his wicked grandmother, whom, at times, he soundly cudgels. It was he who made lakes and streams: for once the earth was parched and barren, all the water being gathered under the armpit of a colossal frog; but Jouskeha pierced the armpit, and let out the water.

[1] The above is the version of the story given by Brébeuf, *Relation des Hurons*, *1636*, 86 (Cramoisy). No two Indians told it precisely alike, though nearly all the Hurons and Iroquois agreed as to its essential points. Compare Vanderdonck, Cusick, Sagard, and other writers. According to Vanderdonck, Ataentsic became mother of a deer, a bear, and a wolf, by whom she afterwards bore all the other animals, mankind included. Brébeuf found also among the Hurons a tradition inconsistent with that of Ataentsic, and bearing a trace of Algonquin origin. It declares, that, in the beginning, a man, a fox, and a skunk found themselves together on an island, and that the man made the world out of mud brought him by the skunk.

The Delawares, an Algonquin tribe, seem to have borrowed somewhat of the Iroquois cosmogony, since they believed that the earth was formed on the back of a tortoise.

According to some, Jouskeha became the father of the human race; but, in the third generation, a deluge destroyed his posterity, so that it was necessary to transform animals into men.—Charlevoix, III. 345.

No prayers were offered to him, his benevolent nature rendering them superfluous.[1]

The early writers call Jouskeha the creator of the world, and speak of him as corresponding to the vague Algonquin deity, Atahocan. Another deity appears in Iroquois mythology, with equal claims to be regarded as supreme. He is called Areskoui, or Agreskoui, and his most prominent attributes are those of a god of war. He was often invoked, and the flesh of animals and of captive enemies was burned in his honor.[2] Like Jouskeha, he was identified with the sun; and he is perhaps to be regarded as the same being, under different attributes. Among the Iroquois proper, or Five Nations, there was also a divinity called Tarenyowagon, or Teharonhiawagon,[3] whose place and character it is very difficult to determine. In some traditions he appears as the son of Jouskeha. He had a prodigious influence; for it was he who spoke to men in dreams. The Five Nations recognized still another superhuman personage,—plainly a deified chief or hero. This was Taounyawatha, or Hiawatha, said to be a divinely appointed messenger, who made his abode on earth for the political and social instruction of the chosen race, and whose counterpart is to be found in the traditions of the Peruvians, Mexicans, and other primitive nations.[4]

[1] Compare Brébeuf, as before cited, and Sagard, *Voyage des Hurons*, p. 228.

[2] Father Jogues saw a female prisoner burned to Areskoui, and two bears offered to him to atone for the sin of not burning more captives.— *Lettre de Jogues, 5 Aug., 1643.*

[3] Le Mercier, *Relation, 1670*, 66; Dablon, *Relation, 1671*, 17. Compare Cusick, Megapolensis, and Vanderdonck. Some writers identify Tarenyowagon and Hiawatha. Vanderdonck assumes that Areskoui is the Devil, and Tarenyowagon is God. Thus Indian notions are often interpreted by the light of preconceived ideas.

[4] For the tradition of Hiawatha, see Clark, *History of Onondaga*, I. 21. It will also be found in Schoolcraft's *Notes on the Iroquois*, and in his *History, Condition, and Prospects of Indian Tribes*.

The Iroquois name for God is Hawenniio, sometimes written Owayneo; but this use of the word is wholly due to the missionaries. Hawenniio is an Iroquois verb, and means, *he rules, he is master*. There is no Iroquois word which, in its primitive meaning, can be interpreted, the Great Spirit, or God. On this subject, see *Études Philologiques sur quelques Langues Sauvages* (Montreal, 1866), where will also be found a curious exposure of a few of Schoolcraft's ridiculous blunders in this connection.

Close examination makes it evident that the primitive Indian's idea of a Supreme Being was a conception no higher than might have been expected. The moment he began to contemplate this object of his faith, and sought to clothe it with attributes, it became finite, and commonly ridiculous. The Creator of the World stood on the level of a barbarous and degraded humanity, while a natural tendency became apparent to look beyond him to other powers sharing his dominion. The Indian belief, if developed, would have developed into a system of polytheism.[1]

In the primitive Indian's conception of a God the idea of moral good has no part. His deity does not dispense justice for this world or the next, but leaves mankind under the power of subordinate spirits, who fill and control the universe. Nor is the good and evil of these inferior beings a moral good and evil. The good spirit is the spirit that gives good luck, and ministers to the necessities and desires of mankind: the evil spirit is simply a malicious agent of disease, death, and mischance.

In no Indian language could the early missionaries find a word to express the idea of God. *Manitou* and *Oki* meant anything endowed with supernatural powers, from a snakeskin, or a greasy Indian conjurer, up to Manabozho and Jouskeha. The priests were forced to use a circumlocution,—"The Great Chief of Men," or "He who lives in the Sky."[2] Yet it should seem that the idea of a supreme controlling spirit might naturally arise from the peculiar character of Indian belief. The idea that each race of animals has its archetype or chief would easily suggest the existence of a supreme chief of the spirits or of the human race,—a conception imperfectly shadowed forth in Manabozho. The Jesuit missionaries seized this advantage. "If each sort of animal has its king," they urged, "so, too, have men; and as man is above all the ani-

[1] Some of the early writers could discover no trace of belief in a supreme spirit of any kind. Perrot, after a life spent among the Indians, ignores such an idea. Allouez emphatically denies that it existed among the tribes of Lake Superior. (*Relation, 1667*, 11.) He adds, however, that the Sacs and Foxes believed in a great *génie*, who lived not far from the French settlements.—*Ibid.*, 21.

[2] See "Divers Sentimens," appended to the *Relation* of 1635, § 27; and also many other passages of early missionaries.

mals, so is the spirit that rules over men the master of all the other spirits." The Indian mind readily accepted the idea, and tribes in no sense Christian quickly rose to the belief in one controlling spirit. The Great Spirit became a distinct existence, a pervading power in the universe, and a dispenser of justice. Many tribes now pray to him, though still clinging obstinately to their ancient superstitions; and with some, as the heathen portion of the modern Iroquois, he is clothed with attributes of moral good.[1]

The primitive Indian believed in the immortality of the soul,[2] but he did not always believe in a state of future reward and punishment. Nor, when such a belief existed, was the good to be rewarded a moral good, or the evil to be punished a moral evil. Skilful hunters, brave warriors, men of influence and consideration, went, after death, to the happy hunting-ground; while the slothful, the cowardly, and the weak were doomed to eat serpents and ashes in dreary regions of mist

[1] In studying the writers of the last and of the present century, it is to be remembered that their observations were made upon savages who had been for generations in contact, immediate or otherwise, with the doctrines of Christianity. Many observers have interpreted the religious ideas of the Indians after preconceived ideas of their own; and it may safely be affirmed that an Indian will respond with a grunt of acquiescence to any question whatever touching his spiritual state. Loskiel and the simple-minded Heckewelder write from a missionary point of view; Adair, to support a theory of descent from the Jews; the worthy theologian, Jarvis, to maintain his dogma, that all religious ideas of the heathen world are perversions of revelation; and so, in a greater or less degree, of many others. By far the most close and accurate observers of Indian superstition were the French and Italian Jesuits of the first half of the seventeenth century. Their opportunities were unrivalled; and they used them in a spirit of faithful inquiry, accumulating facts, and leaving theory to their successors. Of recent American writers, no one has given so much attention to the subject as Mr. Schoolcraft; but, in view of his opportunities and his zeal, his results are most unsatisfactory. The work in six large quarto volumes, *History, Condition, and Prospects of Indian Tribes*, published by Government under his editorship, includes the substance of most of his previous writings. It is a singularly crude and illiterate production, stuffed with blunders and contradictions, giving evidence on every page of a striking unfitness either for historical or philosophical inquiry, and taxing to the utmost the patience of those who would extract what is valuable in it from its oceans of pedantic verbiage.

[2] The exceptions are exceedingly rare. Father Gravier says that a Peoria Indian once told him that there was no future life. It would be difficult to find another instance of the kind.

and darkness. In the general belief, however, there was but one land of shades for all alike. The spirits, in form and feature as they had been in life, wended their way through dark forests to the villages of the dead, subsisting on bark and rotten wood. On arriving, they sat all day in the crouching posture of the sick, and, when night came, hunted the shades of animals, with the shades of bows and arrows, among the shades of trees and rocks: for all things, animate and inanimate, were alike immortal, and all passed together to the gloomy country of the dead.

The belief respecting the land of souls varied greatly in different tribes and different individuals. Among the Hurons there were those who held that departed spirits pursued their journey through the sky, along the Milky Way, while the souls of dogs took another route, by certain constellations, known as the "Way of the Dogs."[1]

At intervals of ten or twelve years, the Hurons, the Neutrals, and other kindred tribes, were accustomed to collect the bones of their dead, and deposit them, with great ceremony, in a common place of burial. The whole nation was sometimes assembled at this solemnity; and hundreds of corpses, brought from their temporary resting-places, were inhumed in one capacious pit. From this hour the immortality of their souls began. They took wing, as some affirmed, in the shape of pigeons; while the greater number declared that they journeyed on foot, and in their own likeness, to the land of shades, bearing with them the ghosts of the wampum-belts, beaver-skins, bows, arrows, pipes, kettles, beads, and rings buried with them in the common grave.[2] But as the spirits of the old and of children are too feeble for the march, they are forced to stay behind, lingering near their earthly villages, where the living often hear the shutting of their invisible cabin-doors, and the weak voices of the disembodied children

[1] Sagard, *Voyage des Hurons*, 233.

[2] The practice of burying treasures with the dead is not peculiar to the North American aborigines. Thus, the London *Times* of Oct. 28, 1865, describing the funeral rites of Lord Palmerston, says: "And as the words, 'Dust to dust, ashes to ashes,' were pronounced, the chief mourner, as a last precious offering to the dead, threw into the grave several diamond and gold rings."

driving birds from their corn-fields.[1] An endless variety of incoherent fancies is connected with the Indian idea of a future
life. They commonly owe their origin to dreams, often to the
dreams of those in extreme sickness, who, on awaking, supposed that they had visited the other world, and related to
the wondering bystanders what they had seen.

The Indian land of souls is not always a region of shadows
and gloom. The Hurons sometimes represented the souls of
their dead—those of their dogs included—as dancing joy-
ously in the presence of Ataentsic and Jouskeha. According
to some Algonquin traditions, heaven was a scene of endless
festivity, the ghosts dancing to the sound of the rattle and the
drum, and greeting with hospitable welcome the occasional
visitor from the living world: for the spirit-land was not far
off, and roving hunters sometimes passed its confines unawares.

Most of the traditions agree, however, that the spirits, on
their journey heavenward, were beset with difficulties and
perils. There was a swift river which must be crossed on a log
that shook beneath their feet, while a ferocious dog opposed
their passage, and drove many into the abyss. This river was
full of sturgeon and other fish, which the ghosts speared for
their subsistence. Beyond was a narrow path between moving
rocks, which each instant crashed together, grinding to atoms
the less nimble of the pilgrims who essayed to pass. The Hurons believed that a personage named Oscotarach, or the
Head-Piercer, dwelt in a bark house beside the path, and that
it was his office to remove the brains from the heads of all
who went by, as a necessary preparation for immortality. This
singular idea is found also in some Algonquin traditions, according to which, however, the brain is afterwards restored
to its owner.[2]

[1] Brébeuf, *Relation des Hurons, 1636*, 99 (Cramoisy).

[2] On Indian ideas of another life, compare Sagard, the Jesuit *Relations*, Perrot, Charlevoix, and Lafitau, with Tanner, James, Schoolcraft, and the Appendix to Morse's Indian Report.

Le Clerc recounts a singular story, current in his time among the Algonquins of Gaspé and Northern New Brunswick. The favorite son of an old
Indian died; whereupon the father, with a party of friends, set out for the
land of souls to recover him. It was only necessary to wade through a shallow
lake, several days' journey in extent. This they did, sleeping at night on plat-

Dreams were to the Indian a universal oracle. They revealed to him his guardian spirit, taught him the cure of his diseases, warned him of the devices of sorcerers, guided him to the lurking-places of his enemy or the haunts of game, and unfolded the secrets of good and evil destiny. The dream was a mysterious and inexorable power, whose least behests must be obeyed to the letter,—a source, in every Indian town, of endless mischief and abomination. There were professed dreamers, and professed interpreters of dreams. One of the most noted festivals among the Hurons and Iroquois was the Dream Feast, a scene of frenzy, where the actors counterfeited madness, and the town was like a bedlam turned loose. Each pretended to have dreamed of something necessary to his welfare, and rushed from house to house, demanding of all he met to guess his secret requirement and satisfy it.

Believing that the whole material world was instinct with powers to influence and control his fate, that good and evil spirits, and existences nameless and indefinable, filled all Nature, that a pervading sorcery was above, below, and around him, and that issues of life and death might be controlled by instruments the most unnoticeable and seemingly the most feeble, the Indian lived in perpetual fear. The turning of a leaf, the crawling of an insect, the cry of a bird, the creaking of a bough, might be to him the mystic signal of weal or woe.

An Indian community swarmed with sorcerers, medicine-

---

forms of poles which supported them above the water. At length they arrived, and were met by Papkootparout, the Indian Pluto, who rushed on them in a rage, with his war-club upraised; but, presently relenting, changed his mind, and challenged them to a game of ball. They proved the victors, and won the stakes, consisting of corn, tobacco, and certain fruits, which thus became known to mankind. The bereaved father now begged hard for his son's soul, and Papkootparout at last gave it to him, in the form and size of a nut, which, by pressing it hard between his hands, he forced into a small leather bag. The delighted parent carried it back to earth, with instructions to insert it in the body of his son, who would thereupon return to life. When the adventurers reached home, and reported the happy issue of their journey, there was a dance of rejoicing; and the father, wishing to take part in it, gave his son's soul to the keeping of a squaw who stood by. Being curious to see it, she opened the bag; on which it escaped at once, and took flight for the realms of Papkootparout, preferring them to the abodes of the living.—Le Clerc, *Nouvelle Relation de la Gaspésie*, 310–328.

men, and diviners, whose functions were often united in the same person. The sorcerer, by charms, magic songs, magic feasts, and the beating of his drum, had power over the spirits and those occult influences inherent in animals and inanimate things. He could call to him the souls of his enemies. They appeared before him in the form of stones. He chopped and bruised them with his hatchet; blood and flesh issued forth; and the intended victim, however distant, languished and died. Like the sorcerer of the Middle Ages, he made images of those he wished to destroy, and, muttering incantations, punctured them with an awl, whereupon the persons represented sickened and pined away.

The Indian doctor relied far more on magic than on natural remedies. Dreams, beating of the drum, songs, magic feasts and dances, and howling to frighten the female demon from his patient, were his ordinary methods of cure.

The prophet, or diviner, had various means of reading the secrets of futurity, such as the flight of birds, and the movements of water and fire. There was a peculiar practice of divination very general in the Algonquin family of tribes, among some of whom it still subsists. A small, conical lodge was made by planting poles in a circle, lashing the tops together at the height of about seven feet from the ground, and closely covering them with hides. The prophet crawled in, and closed the aperture after him. He then beat his drum and sang his magic songs to summon the spirits, whose weak, shrill voices were soon heard, mingled with his lugubrious chanting, while at intervals the juggler paused to interpret their communications to the attentive crowd seated on the ground without. During the whole scene, the lodge swayed to and fro with a violence which has astonished many a civilized beholder, and which some of the Jesuits explain by the ready solution of a genuine diabolic intervention.[1]

The sorcerers, medicine-men, and diviners did not usually exercise the function of priests. Each man sacrificed for himself to the powers he wished to propitiate, whether his guard-

[1] This practice was first observed by Champlain. (See "Pioneers of France in the New World.") From his time to the present, numerous writers have remarked upon it. Le Jeune, in the *Relation* of 1637, treats it at some length. The lodge was sometimes of a cylindrical, instead of a conical form.

ian spirit, the spirits of animals, or the other beings of his belief. The most common offering was tobacco, thrown into the fire or water; scraps of meat were sometimes burned to the manitous; and, on a few rare occasions of public solemnity, a white dog, the mystic animal of many tribes, was tied to the end of an upright pole, as a sacrifice to some superior spirit, or to the sun, with which the superior spirits were constantly confounded by the primitive Indian. In recent times, when Judaism and Christianity have modified his religious ideas, it has been, and still is, the practice to sacrifice dogs to the Great Spirit. On these public occasions, the sacrificial function is discharged by chiefs, or by warriors appointed for the purpose.[1]

Among the Hurons and Iroquois, and indeed all the stationary tribes, there was an incredible number of mystic ceremonies, extravagant, puerile, and often disgusting, designed for the cure of the sick or for the general weal of the community. Most of their observances seem originally to have been dictated by dreams, and transmitted as a sacred heritage from generation to generation. They consisted in an endless variety of dances, masqueradings, and nondescript orgies; and a scrupulous adherence to all the traditional forms was held to be of the last moment, as the slightest failure in this respect might entail serious calamities. If children were seen in their play imitating any of these mysteries, they were grimly rebuked and punished. In many tribes secret magical societies existed, and still exist, into which members are initiated with

[1] Many of the Indian feasts were feasts of sacrifice, — sometimes to the guardian spirit of the host, sometimes to an animal of which he has dreamed, sometimes to a local or other spirit. The food was first offered in a loud voice to the being to be propitiated, after which the guests proceeded to devour it for him. This unique method of sacrifice was practised at war-feasts and similar solemnities. For an excellent account of Indian religious feasts, see Perrot, Chap. V.

One of the most remarkable of Indian sacrifices was that practised by the Hurons in the case of a person drowned or frozen to death. The flesh of the deceased was cut off, and thrown into a fire made for the purpose, as an offering of propitiation to the spirits of the air or water. What remained of the body was then buried near the fire. — Brébeuf, *Relation des Hurons, 1636,* 108.

The tribes of Virginia, as described by Beverly and others, not only had priests who offered sacrifice, but idols and houses of worship.

peculiar ceremonies. These associations are greatly respected and feared. They have charms for love, war, and private revenge, and exert a great, and often a very mischievous influence. The societies of the Metai and the Wabeno, among the Northern Algonquins, are conspicuous examples; while other societies of similar character have, for a century, been known to exist among the Dahcotah.[1]

A notice of the superstitious ideas of the Indians would be imperfect without a reference to the traditionary tales through which these ideas are handed down from father to son. Some of these tales can be traced back to the period of the earliest intercourse with Europeans. One at least of those recorded by the first missionaries, on the Lower St. Lawrence, is still current among the tribes of the Upper Lakes. Many of them are curious combinations of beliefs seriously entertained with strokes intended for humor and drollery, which never fail to awaken peals of laughter in the lodge-circle. Giants, dwarfs, cannibals, spirits, beasts, birds, and anomalous monsters, transformations, tricks, and sorcery, form the staple of the story. Some of the Iroquois tales embody conceptions which, however preposterous, are of a bold and striking character; but those of the Algonquins are, to an incredible degree, flimsy, silly, and meaningless; nor are those of the Dahcotah tribes much better. In respect to this wigwam lore, there is a curious superstition of very wide prevalence. The tales must not be told in summer; since at that season, when all Nature is full of life, the spirits are awake, and, hearing what is said of them, may take offence; whereas in winter they are fast sealed up in snow and ice, and no longer capable of listening.[2]

[1] The Friendly Society of the Spirit, of which the initiatory ceremonies were seen and described by Carver (*Travels*, 271), preserves to this day its existence and its rites.

[2] The prevalence of this fancy among the Algonquins in the remote parts of Canada is well established. The writer found it also among the extreme western bands of the Dahcotah. He tried, in the month of July, to persuade an old chief, a noted story-teller, to tell him some of the tales; but, though abundantly loquacious in respect to his own adventures, and even his dreams, the Indian obstinately refused, saying that winter was the time for the tales, and that it was bad to tell them in summer.

Mr. Schoolcraft has published a collection of Algonquin tales, under the title of *Algic Researches*. Most of them were translated by his wife, an educated Ojibwa half-breed. This book is perhaps the best of Mr. Schoolcraft's works, though its value is much impaired by the want of a literal rendering,

It is obvious that the Indian mind has never seriously occupied itself with any of the higher themes of thought. The beings of its belief are not impersonations of the forces of Nature, the courses of human destiny, or the movements of human intellect, will, and passion. In the midst of Nature, the Indian knew nothing of her laws. His perpetual reference of her phenomena to occult agencies forestalled inquiry and precluded inductive reasoning. If the wind blew with violence, it was because the water-lizard, which makes the wind, had crawled out of his pool; if the lightning was sharp and frequent, it was because the young of the thunder-bird were restless in their nest; if a blight fell upon the corn, it was because the Corn Spirit was angry; and if the beavers were shy and difficult to catch, it was because they had taken offence at seeing the bones of one of their race thrown to a dog. Well, and even highly developed, in a few instances,—I allude especially to the Iroquois,—with respect to certain points of material concernment, the mind of the Indian in other respects was and is almost hopelessly stagnant. The very traits that raise him above the servile races are hostile to the kind and degree of civilization which those races so easily attain. His intractable spirit of independence, and the pride which forbids him to be an imitator, reinforce but too strongly that savage lethargy of mind from which it is so hard to rouse him. No race, perhaps, ever offered greater difficulties to those laboring for its improvement.

To sum up the results of this examination, the primitive Indian was as savage in his religion as in his life. He was divided between fetich-worship and that next degree of religious development which consists in the worship of deities embodied in the human form. His conception of their attributes was such as might have been expected. His gods were

---

and the introduction of decorations which savor more of a popular monthly magazine than of an Indian wigwam. Mrs. Eastman's interesting *Legends of the Sioux* (Dahcotah) is not free from the same defect. Other tales are scattered throughout the works of Mr. Schoolcraft and various modern writers. Some are to be found in the works of Lafitau and the other Jesuits. But few of the Iroquois legends have been printed, though a considerable number have been written down. The singular *History of the Five Nations*, by the old Tuscarora Indian, Cusick, gives the substance of some of them. Others will be found in Clark's *History of Onondaga*.

no whit better than himself. Even when he borrows from Christianity the idea of a Supreme and Universal Spirit, his tendency is to reduce Him to a local habitation and a bodily shape; and this tendency disappears only in tribes that have been long in contact with civilized white men. The primitive Indian, yielding his untutored homage to One All-pervading and Omnipotent Spirit, is a dream of poets, rhetoricians, and sentimentalists.

Chapter I

1634

NOTRE-DAME DES ANGES

Quebec in 1634 • Father Le Jeune • The Mission-House • Its Domestic Economy • The Jesuits and their Designs

---

OPPOSITE Quebec lies the tongue of land called Point Levi. One who, in the summer of the year 1634, stood on its margin and looked northward, across the St. Lawrence, would have seen, at the distance of a mile or more, a range of lofty cliffs, rising on the left into the bold heights of Cape Diamond, and on the right sinking abruptly to the bed of the tributary river St. Charles. Beneath these cliffs, at the brink of the St. Lawrence, he would have described a cluster of warehouses, sheds, and wooden tenements. Immediately above, along the verge of the precipice, he could have traced the outlines of a fortified work, with a flagstaff, and a few small cannon to command the river; while, at the only point where Nature had made the heights accessible, a zigzag path connected the warehouses and the fort.

Now, embarked in the canoe of some Montagnais Indian, let him cross the St. Lawrence, land at the pier, and, passing the cluster of buildings, climb the pathway up the cliff. Pausing for rest and breath, he might see, ascending and descending, the tenants of this outpost of the wilderness: a soldier of the fort, or an officer in slouched hat and plume; a factor of the fur company, owner and sovereign lord of all Canada; a party of Indians; a trader from the upper country, one of the precursors of that hardy race of *coureurs de bois*, destined to form a conspicuous and striking feature of the Canadian population: next, perhaps, would appear a figure widely different. The close, black cassock, the rosary hanging from the waist, and the wide, black hat, looped up at the sides, proclaimed the Jesuit,—Father Le Jeune, Superior of the Residence of Quebec.

And now, that we may better know the aspect and condition of the infant colony and incipient mission, we will follow the priest on his way. Mounting the steep path, he reached the top of the cliff, some two hundred feet above the river and the warehouses. On the left lay the fort built by Champlain, covering a part of the ground now forming Durham Terrace and the Place d'Armes. Its ramparts were of logs and earth, and within was a turreted building of stone, used as a barrack, as officers' quarters, and for other purposes.[1] Near the fort stood a small chapel, newly built. The surrounding country was cleared and partially cultivated; yet only one dwelling-house worthy the name appeared. It was a substantial cottage, where lived Madame Hébert, widow of the first settler of Canada, with her daughter, her son-in-law Couillard, and their children, good Catholics all, who, two years before, when Quebec was evacuated by the English,[2] wept for joy at beholding Le Jeune, and his brother Jesuit, De Noüe, crossing their threshold to offer beneath their roof the long-forbidden sacrifice of the Mass. There were inclosures with cattle near at hand; and the house, with its surroundings, betokened industry and thrift.

Thence Le Jeune walked on, across the site of the modern market-place, and still onward, near the line of the cliffs which sank abruptly on his right. Beneath lay the mouth of the St. Charles; and, beyond, the wilderness shore of Beauport swept in a wide curve eastward, to where, far in the distance, the Gulf of Montmorenci yawned on the great river.[3] The priest soon passed the clearings, and entered the woods which covered the site of the present suburb of St. John. Thence he descended to a lower plateau, where now lies the suburb of St. Roch, and, still advancing, reached a pleasant spot at the extremity of the Pointe-aux-Lièvres, a tract of meadow land nearly inclosed by a sudden bend of the St. Charles. Here lay a canoe or skiff; and, paddling across the narrow stream, Le Jeune saw on the meadow, two

[1] Compare the various notices in Champlain (1632) with that of Du Creux, *Historia Canadensis*, 204.

[2] See "Pioneers of France in the New World." Hébert's cottage seems to have stood between Ste.-Famille and Couillard Streets, as appears by a contract of 1634, cited by M. Ferland.

[3] The settlement of Beauport was begun this year, or the year following, by the Sieur Giffard, to whom a large tract had been granted here.—Langevin, *Notes sur les Archives de N. D. de Beauport*, 5.

hundred yards from the bank, a square inclosure formed of palisades, like a modern picket fort of the Indian frontier.[1] Within this inclosure were two buildings, one of which had been half burned by the English, and was not yet repaired. It served as storehouse, stable, workshop, and bakery. Opposite stood the principal building, a structure of planks, plastered with mud, and thatched with long grass from the meadows. It consisted of one story, a garret, and a cellar, and contained four principal rooms, of which one served as chapel, another as refectory, another as kitchen, and the fourth as a lodging for workmen. The furniture of all was plain in the extreme. Until the preceding year, the chapel had had no other ornament than a sheet on which were glued two coarse engravings; but the priests had now decorated their altar with an image of a dove representing the Holy Ghost, an image of Loyola, another of Xavier, and three images of the Virgin. Four cells opened from the refectory, the largest of which was eight feet square. In these lodged six priests, while two lay brothers found shelter in the garret. The house had been hastily built, eight years before, and now leaked in all parts. Such was the Residence of Notre-Dame des Anges. Here was nourished the germ of a vast enterprise, and this was the cradle of the great mission of New France.[2]

Of the six Jesuits gathered in the refectory for the evening meal, one was conspicuous among the rest,—a tall, strong man, with features that seemed carved by Nature for a soldier, but which the mental habits of years had stamped with the

[1] This must have been very near the point where the streamlet called the River Lairet enters the St. Charles. The place has a triple historic interest. The wintering-place of Cartier in 1535–6 (see "Pioneers of France") seems to have been here. Here, too, in 1759, Montcalm's bridge of boats crossed the St. Charles; and in a large intrenchment, which probably included the site of the Jesuit mission-house, the remnants of his shattered army rallied, after their defeat on the Plains of Abraham.—See the very curious *Narrative of the Chevalier Johnstone*, published by the Historical Society of Quebec.

[2] The above particulars are gathered from the *Relations* of 1626 (Lalemant), and 1632, 1633, 1634, 1635 (Le Jeune), but chiefly from a long letter of the Father Superior to the Provincial of the Jesuits at Paris, containing a curiously minute report of the state of the mission. It was sent from Quebec by the returning ships in the summer of 1634, and will be found in Carayon, *Première Mission des Jésuites au Canada*, 122. The original is in the archives of the Order at Rome.

visible impress of the priesthood. This was Jean de Brébeuf, descendant of a noble family of Normandy, and one of the ablest and most devoted zealots whose names stand on the missionary rolls of his Order. His companions were Masse, Daniel, Davost, De Noue, and the Father Superior, Le Jeune. Masse was the same priest who had been the companion of Father Biard in the abortive mission of Acadia.[1] By reason of his useful qualities, Le Jeune nicknamed him "le Père Utile." At present, his special function was the care of the pigs and cows, which he kept in the inclosure around the buildings, lest they should ravage the neighboring fields of rye, barley, wheat, and maize.[2] De Noue had charge of the eight or ten workmen employed by the mission, who gave him at times no little trouble by their repinings and complaints.[3] They were forced to hear mass every morning and prayers every evening, besides an exhortation on Sunday. Some of them were for returning home, while two or three, of a different complexion, wished to be Jesuits themselves. The Fathers, in their intervals of leisure, worked with their men, spade in hand. For the rest, they were busied in preaching, singing vespers, saying mass and hearing confessions at the fort of Quebec, catechizing a few Indians, and striving to master the enormous difficulties of the Huron and Algonquin languages.

Well might Father Le Jeune write to his Superior, "The harvest is plentiful, and the laborers few." These men aimed at the conversion of a continent. From their hovel on the St. Charles, they surveyed a field of labor whose vastness might tire the wings of thought itself; a scene repellent and appalling, darkened with omens of peril and woe. They were an advance-guard of the great army of Loyola, strong in a disci-

---

[1] See "Pioneers of France in the New World."

[2] "Le P. Masse, que je nomme quelquefois en riant le Père *Utile*, est bien cognu de V. R. Il a soin des choses domestiques et du bestail que nous avons, en quoy il a très-bien reussy."—*Lettre du P. Paul le Jeune au R. P. Provincial*, in Carayon, 122.—Le Jeune does not fail to send an inventory of the "bestail" to his Superior, namely: "Deux grosses truies qui nourissent chacune quatre petits cochons, deux vaches, deux petites genisses, et un petit taureau."

[3] The methodical Le Jeune sets down the causes of their discontent under six different heads, each duly numbered. Thus:—

"1°. C'est le naturel des artisans de se plaindre et de gronder."

"2°. La diversité des gages les fait murmurer," etc.

pline that controlled not alone the body and the will, but the intellect, the heart, the soul, and the inmost consciousness. The lives of these early Canadian Jesuits attest the earnestness of their faith and the intensity of their zeal; but it was a zeal bridled, curbed, and ruled by a guiding hand. Their marvellous training in equal measure kindled enthusiasm and controlled it, roused into action a mighty power, and made it as subservient as those great material forces which modern science has learned to awaken and to govern. They were drilled to a factitious humility, prone to find utterance in expressions of self-depreciation and self-scorn, which one may often judge unwisely, when he condemns them as insincere. They were devoted believers, not only in the fundamental dogmas of Rome, but in those lesser matters of faith which heresy despises as idle and puerile superstitions. One great aim engrossed their lives. "For the greater glory of God"— *ad majorem Dei gloriam*—they would act or wait, dare, suffer, or die, yet all in unquestioning subjection to the authority of the Superiors, in whom they recognized the agents of Divine authority itself.

Chapter II

LOYOLA AND THE JESUITS

Conversion of Loyola • Foundation of the Society of Jesus • Preparation of the Novice • Characteristics of the Order • The Canadian Jesuits

---

IT was an evil day for new-born Protestantism, when a French artilleryman fired the shot that struck down Ignatius Loyola in the breach of Pampeluna. A proud noble, an aspiring soldier, a graceful courtier, an ardent and daring gallant was metamorphosed by that stroke into the zealot whose brain engendered and brought forth the mighty Society of Jesus. His story is a familiar one: how, in the solitude of his sick-room, a change came over him, upheaving, like an earthquake, all the forces of his nature; how, in the cave of Manresa, the mysteries of Heaven were revealed to him; how he passed from agonies to transports, from transports to the calm of a determined purpose. The soldier gave himself to a new warfare. In the forge of his great intellect, heated, but not disturbed by the intense fires of his zeal, was wrought the prodigious enginery whose power has been felt to the uttermost confines of the world.

Loyola's training had been in courts and camps: of books he knew little or nothing. He had lived in the unquestioning faith of one born and bred in the very focus of Romanism; and thus, at the age of about thirty, his conversion found him. It was a change of life and purpose, not of belief. He presumed not to inquire into the doctrines of the Church. It was for him to enforce those doctrines; and to this end he turned all the faculties of his potent intellect, and all his deep knowledge of mankind. He did not aim to build up barren communities of secluded monks, aspiring to heaven through prayer, penance, and meditation, but to subdue the world to the dominion of the dogmas which had subdued him; to organize and discipline a mighty host, controlled by one purpose and one mind, fired by a quenchless zeal or nerved by a fixed resolve, yet impelled, restrained, and directed by a single master hand. The Jesuit is no dreamer: he is emphatically a man of action; action is the end of his existence.

It was an arduous problem which Loyola undertook to solve,—to rob a man of volition, yet to preserve in him, nay, to stimulate, those energies which would make him the most efficient instrument of a great design. To this end the Jesuit novitiate and the constitutions of the Order are directed. The enthusiasm of the novice is urged to its intensest pitch; then, in the name of religion, he is summoned to the utter abnegation of intellect and will in favor of the Superior, in whom he is commanded to recognize the representative of God on earth. Thus the young zealot makes no slavish sacrifice of intellect and will; at least, so he is taught: for he sacrifices them, not to man, but to his Maker. No limit is set to his submission: if the Superior pronounces black to be white, he is bound in conscience to acquiesce.[1]

Loyola's book of *Spiritual Exercises* is well known. In these exercises lies the hard and narrow path which is the only entrance to the Society of Jesus. The book is, to all appearance, a dry and superstitious formulary; but, in the hands of a skilful director of consciences, it has proved of terrible efficacy. The novice, in solitude and darkness, day after day and night after night, ponders its images of perdition and despair. He is taught to hear, in imagination, the howlings of the damned, to see their convulsive agonies, to feel the flames that burn without consuming, to smell the corruption of the tomb and the fumes of the infernal pit. He must picture to himself an array of adverse armies, one commanded by Satan on the plains of Babylon, one encamped under Christ about the walls of Jerusalem; and the perturbed mind, humbled by long contemplation of its own vileness, is ordered to enroll itself under one or the other banner. Then, the choice made, it is led to a region of serenity and celestial peace, and soothed with images of divine benignity and grace. These meditations last, without intermission, about a month, and, under an astute and experienced directorship, they have been found of such power, that the *Manual of Spiritual Exercises*

---

[1] Those who wish to know the nature of the Jesuit virtue of obedience will find it set forth in the famous *Letter on Obedience* of Loyola.

boasts to have saved souls more in number than the letters it contains.

To this succeed two years of discipline and preparation, directed, above all things else, to perfecting the virtues of humility and obedience. The novice is obliged to perform the lowest menial offices, and the most repulsive duties of the sick-room and the hospital; and he is sent forth, for weeks together, to beg his bread like a common mendicant. He is required to reveal to his confessor, not only his sins, but all those hidden tendencies, instincts, and impulses which form the distinctive traits of character. He is set to watch his comrades, and his comrades are set to watch him. Each must report what he observes of the acts and dispositions of the others; and this mutual espionage does not end with the novitiate, but extends to the close of life. The characteristics of every member of the Order are minutely analyzed, and methodically put on record.

This horrible violence to the noblest qualities of manhood, joined to that equivocal system of morality which eminent casuists of the Order have inculcated, must, it may be thought, produce deplorable effects upon the characters of those under its influence. Whether this has been actually the case, the reader of history may determine. It is certain, however, that the Society of Jesus has numbered among its members men whose fervent and exalted natures have been intensified, without being abased, by the pressure to which they have been subjected.

It is not for nothing that the Society studies the character of its members so intently, and by methods so startling. It not only uses its knowledge to thrust into obscurity or cast out altogether those whom it discovers to be dull, feeble, or unwilling instruments of its purposes, but it assigns to every one the task to which his talents or his disposition may best adapt him: to one, the care of a royal conscience, whereby, unseen, his whispered word may guide the destiny of nations; to another, the instruction of children; to another, a career of letters or science; and to the fervent and the self-sacrificing, sometimes also to the restless and uncompliant, the distant missions to the heathen.

The Jesuit was, and is, everywhere,—in the school-room,

in the library, in the cabinets of princes and ministers, in the huts of savages, in the tropics, in the frozen North, in India, in China, in Japan, in Africa, in America; now as a Christian priest, now as a soldier, a mathematician, an astrologer, a Brahmin, a mandarin, under countless disguises, by a thousand arts, luring, persuading, or compelling souls into the fold of Rome.

Of this vast mechanism for guiding and governing the minds of men, this mighty enginery for subduing the earth to the dominion of an idea, this harmony of contradictions, this moral Proteus, the faintest sketch must now suffice. A disquisition on the Society of Jesus would be without end. No religious order has ever united in itself so much to be admired and so much to be detested. Unmixed praise has been poured on its Canadian members. It is not for me to eulogize them, but to portray them as they were.

Chapter III

1632, 1633

PAUL LE JEUNE

*Le Jeune's Voyage • His First Pupils • His Studies • His Indian
Teacher • Winter at the Mission-house • Le Jeune's School •
Reinforcements*

IN another narrative, we have seen how the Jesuits, sup-
planting the Récollet friars, their predecessors, had
adopted as their own the rugged task of Christianizing New
France. We have seen, too, how a descent of the English, or
rather of Huguenots fighting under English colors, had overthrown for a time the miserable little colony, with the mission
to which it was wedded; and how Quebec was at length restored to France, and the broken thread of the Jesuit enterprise resumed.[1]

It was then that Le Jeune had embarked for the New
World. He was in his convent at Dieppe when he received
the order to depart; and he set forth in haste for Havre, filled,
he assures us, with inexpressible joy at the prospect of a living
or a dying martyrdom. At Rouen he was joined by De Noüe,
with a lay brother named Gilbert; and the three sailed together on the eighteenth of April, 1632. The sea treated them
roughly; Le Jeune was wretchedly sea-sick; and the ship
nearly foundered in a gale. At length they came in sight of
"that miserable country," as the missionary calls the scene of
his future labors. It was in the harbor of Tadoussac that he
first encountered the objects of his apostolic cares; for, as he
sat in the ship's cabin with the master, it was suddenly invaded by ten or twelve Indians, whom he compares to a party
of maskers at the Carnival. Some had their cheeks painted
black, their noses blue, and the rest of their faces red. Others
were decorated with a broad band of black across the eyes;
and others, again, with diverging rays of black, red, and blue
on both cheeks. Their attire was no less uncouth. Some of

[1] "Pioneers of France."

them wore shaggy bear-skins, reminding the priest of the pictures of St. John the Baptist.

After a vain attempt to save a number of Iroquois prisoners whom they were preparing to burn alive on shore, Le Jeune and his companions again set sail, and reached Quebec on the fifth of July. Having said mass, as already mentioned, under the roof of Madame Hébert and her delighted family, the Jesuits made their way to the two hovels built by their predecessors on the St. Charles, which had suffered woful dilapidation at the hands of the English. Here they made their abode, and applied themselves, with such skill as they could command, to repair the shattered tenements and cultivate the waste meadows around.

The beginning of Le Jeune's missionary labors was neither imposing nor promising. He describes himself seated with a small Indian boy on one side and a small negro on the other, the latter of whom had been left by the English as a gift to Madame Hébert. As neither of the three understood the language of the others, the pupils made little progress in spiritual knowledge. The missionaries, it was clear, must learn Algonquin at any cost; and, to this end, Le Jeune resolved to visit the Indian encampments. Hearing that a band of Montagnais were fishing for eels on the St. Lawrence, between Cape Diamond and the cove which now bears the name of Wolfe, he set forth for the spot on a morning in October. As, with toil and trepidation, he scrambled around the foot of the cape,— whose precipices, with a chaos of loose rocks, thrust themselves at that day into the deep tidewater,— he dragged down upon himself the trunk of a fallen tree, which, in its descent, well nigh swept him into the river. The peril past, he presently reached his destination. Here, among the lodges of bark, were stretched innumerable strings of hide, from which hung to dry an incredible multitude of eels. A boy invited him into the lodge of a withered squaw, his grandmother, who hastened to offer him four smoked eels on a piece of birch bark, while other squaws of the household instructed him how to roast them on a forked stick over the embers. All shared the feast together, his entertainers using as napkins their own hair or that of their dogs; while Le Jeune, intent on increasing his knowledge of Algonquin, maintained an active discourse of broken words and panto-mime.[1]

The lesson, however, was too laborious, and of too little profit, to be often repeated, and the missionary sought anx-iously for more stable instruction. To find such was not easy. The interpreters—Frenchmen, who, in the interest of the fur company, had spent years among the Indians—were averse to Jesuits, and refused their aid. There was one resource, however, of which Le Jeune would fain avail himself. An In-dian, called Pierre by the French, had been carried to France by the Récollet friars, instructed, converted, and baptized. He had lately returned to Canada, where, to the scandal of the Jesuits, he had relapsed into his old ways, retaining of his French education little besides a few new vices. He still haunted the fort at Quebec, lured by the hope of an occa-sional gift of wine or tobacco, but shunned the Jesuits, of whose rigid way of life he stood in horror. As he spoke good French and good Indian, he would have been invaluable to the embarrassed priests at the mission. Le Jeune invoked the aid of the Saints. The effect of his prayers soon appeared, he tells us, in a direct interposition of Providence, which so dis-posed the heart of Pierre that he quarrelled with the French commandant, who thereupon closed the fort against him. He then repaired to his friends and relatives in the woods, but only to encounter a rebuff from a young squaw to whom he made his addresses. On this, he turned his steps towards the mission-house, and, being unfitted by his French education for supporting himself by hunting, begged food and shelter from the priests. Le Jeune gratefully accepted him as a gift vouchsafed by Heaven to his prayers, persuaded a lackey at the fort to give him a cast-off suit of clothes, promised him maintenance, and installed him as his teacher.

Seated on wooden stools by the rough table in the refec-tory, the priest and the Indian pursued their studies. "How thankful I am," writes Le Jeune, "to those who gave me to-bacco last year! At every difficulty I give my master a piece of it, to make him more attentive."[2]

[1] Le Jeune, *Relation*, 1633, 2.

[2] *Relation*, 1633, 7. He continues: "Ie ne sçaurois assez rendre graces à Nostre Seigneur de cet heureux rencontre. . . . Que Dieu soit beny pour vn iamais, sa prouidence est adorable, et sa bonté n'a point de limites."

Meanwhile, winter closed in with a severity rare even in Canada. The St. Lawrence and the St. Charles were hard frozen; rivers, forests, and rocks were mantled alike in dazzling sheets of snow. The humble mission-house of Notre-Dame des Anges was half buried in the drifts, which, heaped up in front where a path had been dug through them, rose two feet above the low eaves. The priests, sitting at night before the blazing logs of their wide-throated chimney, heard the trees in the neighboring forest cracking with frost, with a sound like the report of a pistol. Le Jeune's ink froze, and his fingers were benumbed, as he toiled at his declensions and conjugations, or translated the Pater Noster into blundering Algonquin. The water in the cask beside the fire froze nightly, and the ice was broken every morning with hatchets. The blankets of the two priests were fringed with the icicles of their congealed breath, and the frost lay in a thick coating on the lozenge-shaped glass of their cells.[1]

By day, Le Jeune and his companion practised with snowshoes, with all the mishaps which attend beginners, — the trippings, the falls, and headlong dives into the soft drifts, amid the laughter of the Indians. Their seclusion was by no means a solitude. Bands of Montagnais, with their sledges and dogs, often passed the mission-house on their way to hunt the moose. They once invited De Noüe to go with them; and he, scarcely less eager than Le Jeune to learn their language, readily consented. In two or three weeks he appeared, sick, famished, and half dead with exhaustion. "Not ten priests in a hundred," writes Le Jeune to his Superior, "could bear this winter life with the savages." But what of that? It was not for them to falter. They were but instruments in the hands of God, to be used, broken, and thrown aside, if such should be His will.[2]

An Indian made Le Jeune a present of two small children, greatly to the delight of the missionary, who at once set him-

[1] Le Jeune, *Relation, 1633,* 14, 15.

[2] "Voila, mon Reuerend Pere, vn eschantillon de ce qu'il faut souffrir courant apres les Sauuages. . . . Il faut prendre sa vie, et tout ce qu'on a, et le ietter à l'abandon, pour ainsi dire, se contentant d'vne croix bien grosse et bien pesante pour toute richesse. Il est bien vray que Dieu ne se laisse point vaincre, et que plus on quitte, plus on trouue: plus on perd, plus on gaigne: mais Dieu se cache par fois, et alors le Calice est bien amer."—Le Jeune, *Relation, 1633,* 19.

self to teaching them to pray in Latin. As the season grew milder, the number of his scholars increased; for, when parties of Indians encamped in the neighborhood, he would take his stand at the door, and, like Xavier at Goa, ring a bell. At this, a score of children would gather around him; and he, leading them into the refectory, which served as his schoolroom, taught them to repeat after him the Pater, Ave, and Credo, expounded the mystery of the Trinity, showed them the sign of the cross, and made them repeat an Indian prayer, the joint composition of Pierre and himself; then followed the catechism, the lesson closing with singing the Pater Noster, translated by the missionary into Algonquin rhymes; and when all was over, he rewarded each of his pupils with a porringer of peas, to insure their attendance at his next bell-ringing.[1]

It was the end of May, when the priests one morning heard the sound of cannon from the fort, and were gladdened by the tidings that Samuel de Champlain had arrived to resume command at Quebec, bringing with him four more Jesuits,— Brébeuf, Masse, Daniel, and Davost.[2] Brébeuf, from the first, turned his eyes towards the distant land of the Hurons,—a field of labor full of peril, but rich in hope and promise. Le Jeune's duties as Superior restrained him from wanderings so remote. His apostleship must be limited, for a time, to the vagabond hordes of Algonquins, who roamed the forests of the lower St. Lawrence, and of whose language he had been so sedulous a student. His difficulties had of late been increased by the absence of Pierre, who had run off as Lent drew near, standing in dread of that season of fasting. Masse brought tidings of him from Tadoussac, whither he had gone, and where a party of English had given him liquor, destroying the last trace of Le Jeune's late exhortations. "God forgive those," writes the Father, "who introduced heresy into this

---

[1] "I'ay commencé à appeller quelques enfans auec vne petite clochette. La premiere fois i'en auois six, puis douze, puis quinze, puis vingt et davantage; ie leur fais dire le *Pater, Aue, et Credo,* etc. . . . . Nous finissons par le *Pater Noster,* que i'ay composé quasi en rimes en leur langue, que ie leur fais chanter: et pour derniere conclusion, ie leur fais donner chacun vne escuellée de pois, qu'ils mangent de bon appetit," etc.—Le Jeune, *Relation, 1633,* 23.

[2] See "Pioneers of France."

country! If this savage, corrupted as he is by these miserable
heretics, had any wit, he would be a great hindrance to the
spread of the Faith. It is plain that he was given us, not for
the good of his soul, but only that we might extract from him
the principles of his language."[1]

Pierre had two brothers. One, well known as a hunter, was
named Mestigoit; the other was the most noted "medicine-
man," or, as the Jesuits called him, sorcerer, in the tribe of
the Montagnais. Like the rest of their people, they were accustomed to set out for their winter hunt in the autumn, after
the close of their eel-fishery. Le Jeune, despite the experience
of De Noüe, had long had a mind to accompany one of these
roving bands, partly in the hope, that, in some hour of distress, he might touch their hearts, or, by a timely drop of
baptismal water, dismiss some dying child to paradise, but
chiefly with the object of mastering their language. Pierre had
rejoined his brothers; and, as the hunting season drew near,
they all begged the missionary to make one of their party,—
not, as he thought, out of any love for him, but solely with a
view to the provisions with which they doubted not he would
be well supplied. Le Jeune, distrustful of the sorcerer, demurred, but at length resolved to go.

[1] *Relation, 1633,* 29.

Chapter IV

1633, 1634

LE JEUNE AND THE HUNTERS

Le Jeune joins the Indians • The First Encampment • The Apostate • Forest Life in Winter • The Indian Hut • The Sorcerer • His Persecution of the Priest • Evil Company • Magic • Incantations • Christmas • Starvation • Hopes of Conversion • Backsliding • Peril and Escape of Le Jeune • His Return

O N a morning in the latter part of October, Le Jeune embarked with the Indians, twenty in all, men, women, and children. No other Frenchman was of the party. Champlain bade him an anxious farewell, and commended him to the care of his red associates, who had taken charge of his store of biscuit, flour, corn, prunes, and turnips, to which, in an evil hour, his friends had persuaded him to add a small keg of wine. The canoes glided along the wooded shore of the Island of Orleans, and the party landed, towards evening, on the small island immediately below. Le Jeune was delighted with the spot, and the wild beauties of the autumnal sunset.

His reflections, however, were soon interrupted. While the squaws were setting up their bark lodges, and Mestigoit was shooting wild-fowl for supper, Pierre returned to the canoes, tapped the keg of wine, and soon fell into the mud, helplessly drunk. Revived by the immersion, he next appeared at the camp, foaming at the mouth, threw down the lodges, overset the kettle, and chased the shrieking squaws into the woods. His brother Mestigoit rekindled the fire, and slung the kettle anew; when Pierre, who meanwhile had been raving like a madman along the shore, reeled in a fury to the spot to repeat his former exploit. Mestigoit anticipated him, snatched the kettle from the fire, and threw the scalding contents in his face. "He was never so well washed before in his life," says Le Jeune; "he lost all the skin of his face and breast. Would to God his heart had changed also!"[1] He roared in his frenzy

---

[1] "Iamais il ne fut si bien laué, il changea de peau en la face et en tout l'estomach: pleust à Dieu que son ame eust changé aussi bien que son corps!"—*Relation, 1634,* 59.

for a hatchet to kill the missionary, who therefore thought it prudent to spend the night in the neighboring woods. Here he stretched himself on the earth, while a charitable squaw covered him with a sheet of birch-bark. "Though my bed," he writes, "had not been made up since the creation of the world, it was not hard enough to prevent me from sleeping."

Such was his initiation into Indian winter life. Passing over numerous adventures by water and land, we find the party, on the twelfth of November, leaving their canoes on an island, and wading ashore at low tide over the flats to the southern bank of the St. Lawrence. As two other bands had joined them, their number was increased to forty-five persons. Now, leaving the river behind, they entered those savage highlands whence issue the springs of the St. John,—a wilderness of rugged mountain-ranges, clad in dense, continuous forests, with no human tenant but this troop of miserable rovers, and here and there some kindred band, as miserable as they. Winter had set in, and already dead Nature was sheeted in funereal white. Lakes and ponds were frozen, rivulets sealed up, torrents encased with stalactites of ice; the black rocks and the black trunks of the pine-trees were beplastered with snow, and its heavy masses crushed the dull green boughs into the drifts beneath. The forest was silent as the grave.

Through this desolation the long file of Indians made its way, all on snow-shoes, each man, woman, and child bending under a heavy load, or dragging a sledge, narrow, but of prodigious length. They carried their whole wealth with them, on their backs or on their sledges,—kettles, axes, bales of meat, if such they had, and huge rolls of birch-bark for covering their wigwams. The Jesuit was loaded like the rest. The dogs alone floundered through the drifts unburdened. There was neither path nor level ground. Descending, climbing, stooping beneath half-fallen trees, clambering over piles of prostrate trunks, struggling through matted cedar-swamps, threading chill ravines, and crossing streams no longer visible, they toiled on till the day began to decline, then stopped to encamp.[1] Burdens were thrown down, and sledges unladen.

[1] "S'il arriuoit quelque dégel, ô Dieu quelle peine! Il me sembloit que ie marchois sur vn chemin de verre qui se cassoit à tous coups soubs mes pieds:

The squaws, with knives and hatchets, cut long poles of birch and spruce saplings; while the men, with snow-shoes for shovels, cleared a round or square space in the snow, which formed an upright wall three or four feet high, inclosing the area of the wigwam. On one side, a passage was cut for an entrance, and the poles were planted around the top of the wall of snow, sloping and converging. On these poles were spread the sheets of birch-bark; a bear-skin was hung in the passage-way for a door; the bare ground within and the surrounding snow were covered with spruce boughs; and the work was done.

This usually occupied about three hours, during which Le Jeune, spent with travel, and weakened by precarious and unaccustomed fare, had the choice of shivering in idleness, or taking part in a labor which fatigued, without warming, his exhausted frame. The sorcerer's wife was in far worse case. Though in the extremity of a mortal sickness, they left her lying in the snow till the wigwam was made,—without a word, on her part, of remonstrance or complaint. Le Jeune, to the great ire of her husband, sometimes spent the interval in trying to convert her; but she proved intractable, and soon died unbaptized.

Thus lodged, they remained so long as game could be found within a circuit of ten or twelve miles, and then, subsistence failing, removed to another spot. Early in the winter, they hunted the beaver and the Canada porcupine; and, later, in the season of deep snows, chased the moose and the caribou.

Put aside the bear-skin, and enter the hut. Here, in a space some thirteen feet square, were packed nineteen savages, men,

---

la neige congelée venant à s'amollir, tomboit et s'enfonçoit par esquarres ou grandes pieces, et nous en auions bien souuent iusques aux genoux, quelquefois iusqu'à la ceinture. Que s'il y auoit de la peine à tomber, il y en auoit encor plus à se retirer: car nos raquettes se chargeoient de neiges et se rendoient si pesantes, que quand vous veniez à les retirer il vous sembloit qu'on vous tiroit les iambes pour vous démembrer. l'en ay veu qui glissoient tellement soubs des souches enseuelies soubs la neige, qu'ils ne pouuoient tirer ny iambes ny raquettes sans secours: or figurez vous maintenant vne personne chargée comme vn mulet, et iugez si la vie des Sauuages est douce."—*Relation, 1634,* 67.

women, and children, with their dogs, crouched, squatted, coiled like hedgehogs, or lying on their backs, with knees drawn up perpendicularly to keep their feet out of the fire. Le Jeune, always methodical, arranges the grievances inseparable from these rough quarters under four chief heads,—Cold, Heat, Smoke, and Dogs. The bark covering was full of crevices, through which the icy blasts streamed in upon him from all sides; and the hole above, at once window and chimney, was so large, that, as he lay, he could watch the stars as well as in the open air. While the fire in the midst, fed with fat pine-knots, scorched him on one side, on the other he had much ado to keep himself from freezing. At times, however, the crowded hut seemed heated to the temperature of an oven. But these evils were light, when compared to the intolerable plague of smoke. During a snow-storm, and often at other times, the wigwam was filled with fumes so dense, stifling, and acrid, that all its inmates were forced to lie flat on their faces, breathing through mouths in contact with the cold earth. Their throats and nostrils felt as if on fire; their scorched eyes streamed with tears; and when Le Jeune tried to read, the letters of his breviary seemed printed in blood. The dogs were not an unmixed evil, for, by sleeping on and around him, they kept him warm at night; but, as an offset to this good service, they walked, ran, and jumped over him as he lay, snatched the food from his birchen dish, or, in a mad rush at some bone or discarded morsel, now and then overset both dish and missionary.

Sometimes of an evening he would leave the filthy den, to read his breviary in peace by the light of the moon. In the forest around sounded the sharp crack of frost-riven trees; and from the horizon to the zenith shot up the silent meteors of the northern lights, in whose fitful flashings the awe-struck Indians beheld the dancing of the spirits of the dead. The cold gnawed him to the bone; and, his devotions over, he turned back shivering. The illumined hut, from many a chink and crevice, shot forth into the gloom long streams of light athwart the twisted boughs. He stooped and entered. All within glowed red and fiery around the blazing pine-knots, where, like brutes in their kennel, were gathered the savage crew. He stepped to his place, over recumbent bodies and

leggined and moccasined limbs, and seated himself on the carpet of spruce boughs. Here a tribulation awaited him, the
crowning misery of his winter-quarters,—worse, as he declares, than cold, heat, and dogs.

Of the three brothers who had invited him to join the
party, one, we have seen, was the hunter, Mestigoit; another,
the sorcerer; and the third, Pierre, whom, by reason of his
failing away from the Faith, Le Jeune always mentions as the
Apostate. He was a weak-minded young Indian, wholly under the influence of his brother, the sorcerer, who, if not
more vicious, was far more resolute and wily. From the antagonism of their respective professions, the sorcerer hated
the priest, who lost no opportunity of denouncing his incantations, and who ridiculed his perpetual singing and drumming as puerility and folly. The former, being an indifferent
hunter, and disabled by a disease which he had contracted,
depended for subsistence on his credit as a magician; and, in
undermining it, Le Jeune not only outraged his pride, but
threatened his daily bread.[1] He used every device to retort
ridicule on his rival. At the outset, he had proffered his aid to
Le Jeune in his study of the Algonquin; and, like the Indian
practical jokers of Acadia in the case of Father Biard,[2] palmed
off upon him the foulest words in the language as the equivalent of things spiritual. Thus it happened, that, while the
missionary sought to explain to the assembled wigwam some
point of Christian doctrine, he was interrupted by peals of
laughter from men, children, and squaws. And now, as Le
Jeune took his place in the circle, the sorcerer bent upon him
his malignant eyes, and began that course of rude bantering
which filled to overflowing the cup of the Jesuit's woes. All
took their cue from him, and made their afflicted guest the
butt of their inane witticisms. "Look at him! His face is like
a dog's!"—"His head is like a pumpkin!"—"He has a beard

---

[1] "Ie ne laissois perdre aucune occasion de le conuaincre de niaiserie et de
puerilité, mettant au iour l'impertinence de ses superstitions: or c'estoit luy
arracher l'ame du corps par violence: car comme il ne sçauroit plus chasser, il
fait plus que iamais du Prophete et du Magicien pour conseruer son credit,
et pour auoir les bons morceaux; si bien qu'esbranlant son authorité qui se
va perdant tous les iours, ie le touchois à la prunelle de l'œil."—*Relation,
1634*, 56.

[2] See "Pioneers of France," 219–20.

like a rabbit's!" The missionary bore in silence these and countless similar attacks; indeed, so sorely was he harassed, that, lest he should exasperate his tormentor, he sometimes passed whole days without uttering a word.[1]

Le Jeune, a man of excellent observation, already knew his red associates well enough to understand that their rudeness did not of necessity imply ill-will. The rest of the party, in their turn, fared no better. They rallied and bantered each other incessantly, with as little forbearance, and as little malice, as a troop of unbridled schoolboys.[2] No one took offence. To have done so would have been to bring upon one's self genuine contumely. This motley household was a model of harmony. True, they showed no tenderness or consideration towards the sick and disabled; but for the rest, each shared with all in weal or woe: the famine of one was the famine of the whole, and the smallest portion of food was distributed in fair and equal partition. Upbraidings and complaints were unheard; they bore each other's foibles with wondrous equanimity; and while persecuting Le Jeune with constant importunity for tobacco, and for everything else he had, they never begged among themselves.

When the fire burned well and food was abundant, their conversation, such as it was, was incessant. They used no

---

[1] *Relation, 1634*, 207 (Cramoisy). "Ils me chargeoient incessament de mille brocards & de mille injures; je me suis veu en tel estat, que pour ne les aigrir, je passois les jours entiers sans ouvrir la bouche." Here follows the abuse, in the original Indian, with French translations. Le Jeune's account of his experiences is singularly graphic. The following is his summary of his annoyances: —

"Or ce miserable homme" (the sorcerer), "& la fumée m'ont esté les deux plus grands tourmens que i'aye enduré parmy ces Barbares: ny le froid, ny le chaud, ny l'incommodité des chiens, ny coucher à l'air, ny dormir sur un lict de terre, ny la posture qu'il faut tousiours tenir dans leurs cabanes, se ramassans en peloton, ou se couchans, ou s'asseans sans siege & sans mattelas, ny la faim, ny la soif, ny la pauureté & saleté de leur boucan, ny la maladie, tout cela ne m'a semblé que ieu à comparaison de la fumeé & de la malice du Sorcier."— *Relation, 1634*, 201 (Cramoisy).

[2] "Leur vie se passe à manger, à rire, et à railler les vns des autres, et de tous les peuples qu'ils cognoissent; ils n'ont rien de serieux, sinon par fois l'exterieur, faisans parmy nous les graues et les retenus, mais entr'eux sont de vrais badins, de vrais enfans, qui ne demandent qu'à rire."— *Relation, 1634*, 30.

oaths, for their language supplied none,—doubtless because their mythology had no beings sufficiently distinct to swear by. Their expletives were foul words, of which they had a superabundance, and which men, women, and children alike used with a frequency and hardihood that amazed and scandalized the priest.[1] Nor was he better pleased with their postures, in which they consulted nothing but their ease. Thus, of an evening when the wigwam was heated to suffocation, the sorcerer, in the closest possible approach to nudity, lay on his back, with his right knee planted upright and his left leg crossed on it, discoursing volubly to the company, who, on their part, listened in postures scarcely less remote from decency.

There was one point touching which Le Jeune and his Jesuit brethren had as yet been unable to solve their doubts. Were the Indian sorcerers mere impostors, or were they in actual league with the Devil? That the fiends who possess this land of darkness make their power felt by action direct and potential upon the persons of its wretched inhabitants there is, argues Le Jeune, good reason to conclude; since it is a matter of grave notoriety, that the fiends who infest Brazil are accustomed cruelly to beat and otherwise torment the natives of that country, as many travellers attest. "A Frenchman worthy of credit," pursues the Father, "has told me that he has heard with his own ears the voice of the Demon and the sound of the blows which he discharges upon these his miserable slaves; and in reference to this a very remarkable fact has been reported to me, namely, that, when a Catholic approaches, the Devil takes flight and beats these wretches no longer, but that in presence of a Huguenot he does not stop beating them."[2]

---

[1] "Aussi leur disois-je par fois, que si les pourceaux et les chiens sçauoient parler, ils tiendroient leur langage. . . . Les filles et les ieunes femmes sont à l'exterieur tres honnestement couuertes, mais entre elles leurs discours sont puants, comme des cloaques."—*Relation, 1634*, 32.—The social manners of remote tribes of the present time correspond perfectly with Le Jeune's account of those of the Montagnais.

[2] "Surquoy on me rapporte vne chose tres remarquable, c'est que le Diable s'enfuit, et ne frappe point ou cesse de frapper ces miserables, quand vn Catholique entre en leur compagnie, et qu'il ne laise point de les battre en la presence d'vn Huguenot: d'où vient qu'vn iour se voyans battus en la compagnie d'vn certain François, ils luy dirent: Nous nous estonnons que le diable nous batte, toy estant auec nous, veu qu'il n'oseroit le faire quand tes

Thus prone to believe in the immediate presence of the nether powers, Le Jeune watched the sorcerer with an eye prepared to discover in his conjurations the signs of a genuine diabolic agency. His observations, however, led him to a different result; and he could detect in his rival nothing but a vile compound of impostor and dupe. The sorcerer believed in the efficacy of his own magic, and was continually singing and beating his drum to cure the disease from which he was suffering. Towards the close of the winter, Le Jeune fell sick, and, in his pain and weakness, nearly succumbed under the nocturnal uproar of the sorcerer, who, hour after hour, sang and drummed without mercy,—sometimes yelling at the top of his throat, then hissing like a serpent, then striking his drum on the ground as if in a frenzy, then leaping up, raving about the wigwam, and calling on the women and children to join him in singing. Now ensued a hideous din; for every throat was strained to the utmost, and all were beating with sticks or fists on the bark of the hut to increase the noise, with the charitable object of aiding the sorcerer to conjure down his malady, or drive away the evil spirit that caused it.

He had an enemy, a rival sorcerer, whom he charged with having caused by charms the disease that afflicted him. He therefore announced that he should kill him. As the rival dwelt at Gaspé, a hundred leagues off, the present execution of the threat might appear difficult; but distance was no bar to the vengeance of the sorcerer. Ordering all the children and all but one of the women to leave the wigwam, he seated himself, with the woman who remained, on the ground in the centre, while the men of the party, together with those from other wigwams in the neighborhood, sat in a ring around. Mestigoit, the sorcerer's brother, then brought in the charm, consisting of a few small pieces of wood, some arrowheads, a broken knife, and an iron hook, which he wrapped

compagnons sont presents. Luy se douta incontinent que cela pouuoit prouenir de sa religion (car il estoit Caluiniste); s'addressant donc à Dieu, il luy promit de se faire Catholique si le diable cessoit de battre ces pauures peuples en sa presence. Le vœu fait, iamais plus aucun Demon ne molesta Ameriquain en sa compagnie, d'où vient qu'il se fit Catholique, selon la promesse qu'il en auoit faicte. Mais retournons à nostre discours."—*Relation, 1634*, 22.

in a piece of hide. The woman next rose, and walked around the hut, behind the company. Mestigoit and the sorcerer now dug a large hole with two pointed stakes, the whole assembly singing, drumming, and howling meanwhile with a deafening uproar. The hole made, the charm, wrapped in the hide, was thrown into it. Pierre, the Apostate, then brought a sword and a knife to the sorcerer, who, seizing them, leaped into the hole, and, with furious gesticulation, hacked and stabbed at the charm, yelling with the whole force of his lungs. At length he ceased, displayed the knife and sword stained with blood, proclaimed that he had mortally wounded his enemy, and demanded if none present had heard his death-cry. The assembly, more occupied in making noises than in listening for them, gave no reply, till at length two young men declared that they had heard a faint scream, as if from a great distance; whereat a shout of gratulation and triumph rose from all the company.[1]

There was a young prophet, or diviner, in one of the neighboring huts, of whom the sorcerer took counsel as to the prospect of his restoration to health. The divining-lodge was formed, in this instance, of five or six upright posts planted in a circle and covered with a blanket. The prophet ensconced himself within; and after a long interval of singing, the spirits declared their presence by their usual squeaking utterances from the recesses of the mystic tabernacle. Their responses were not unfavorable; and the sorcerer drew much consolation from the invocations of his brother impostor.[2]

Besides his incessant endeavors to annoy Le Jeune, the sor-

---

[1] "Le magicien tout glorieux dit que son homme est frappé, qu'il mourra bien tost, demande si on n'a point entendu ses cris: tout le monde dit que non, horsmis deux ieunes hommes ses parens, qui disent auoir ouy des plaintes fort sourdes, et comme de loing. O qu'ils le firent aise! Se tournant vers moy, il se mit à rire, disant: Voyez cette robe noire, qui nous vient dire qu'il ne faut tuer personne. Comme ie regardois attentiuement l'espée et le poignard, il me les fit presenter: Regarde, dit-il, qu'est cela? C'est du sang, repartis-ie. De qui? De quelque Orignac ou d'autre animal. Ils se mocquerent de moy, disants que c'estoit du sang de ce Sorcier de Gaspé. Comment, dis-je, il est à plus de cent lieuës d'icy? Il est vray, font-ils, mais c'est le Manitou, c'est à dire le Diable, qui apporte son sang pardessous la terre."—*Relation*, *1634*, 21.

[2] See Introduction. Also, "Pioneers of France," 254.

cerer now and then tried to frighten him. On one occasion, when a period of starvation had been followed by a successful hunt, the whole party assembled for one of the gluttonous feasts usual with them at such times. While the guests sat expectant, and the squaws were about to ladle out the banquet, the sorcerer suddenly leaped up, exclaiming, that he had lost his senses, and that knives and hatchets must be kept out of his way, as he had a mind to kill somebody. Then, rolling his eyes towards Le Jeune, he began a series of frantic gestures and outcries,—then stopped abruptly and stared into vacancy, silent and motionless,—then resumed his former clamor, raged in and out of the hut, and, seizing some of its supporting poles, broke them, as if in an uncontrollable frenzy. The missionary, though alarmed, sat reading his breviary as before. When, however, on the next morning, the sorcerer began again to play the maniac, the thought occurred to him, that some stroke of fever might in truth have touched his brain. Accordingly, he approached him and felt his pulse, which he found, in his own words, "as cool as a fish." The pretended madman looked at him with astonishment, and, giving over the attempt to frighten him, presently returned to his senses.[1]

Le Jeune, robbed of his sleep by the ceaseless thumping of the sorcerer's drum and the monotonous cadence of his medicine-songs, improved the time in attempts to convert him. "I began," he says, "by evincing a great love for him, and by praises, which I threw to him as a bait whereby I might catch him in the net of truth."[2] But the Indian, though pleased with the Father's flatteries, was neither caught nor conciliated.

Nowhere was his magic in more requisition than in procuring a successful chase to the hunters,—a point of vital interest, since on it hung the lives of the whole party. They often,

[1] The Indians, it is well known, ascribe mysterious and supernatural powers to the insane, and respect them accordingly. The Neutral Nation (see Introduction, p. 365) was full of pretended madmen, who raved about the villages, throwing firebrands, and making other displays of frenzy.

[2] "Ie commençay par vn témoignage de grand amour en son endroit, et par des loüanges que ie luy iettay comme vne amorce pour le prendre dans les filets de la verité. Ie luy fis entendre que si vn esprit, capable des choses grandes comme le sien, cognoissoit Dieu, que tous les Sauuages induis par son exemple le voudroient aussi cognoistre."—*Relation, 1634*, 71.

however, returned empty-handed; and, for one, two, or three successive days, no other food could be had than the bark of trees or scraps of leather. So long as tobacco lasted, they found solace in their pipes, which seldom left their lips. "Unhappy infidels," writes Le Jeune, "who spend their lives in smoke, and their eternity in flames!"

As Christmas approached, their condition grew desperate. Beavers and porcupines were scarce, and the snow was not deep enough for hunting the moose. Night and day the medicine-drums and medicine-songs resounded from the wigwams, mingled with the wail of starving children. The hunters grew weak and emaciated; and, as after a forlorn march the wanderers encamped once more in the lifeless forest, the priest remembered that it was the eve of Christmas. "The Lord gave us for our supper a porcupine, large as a sucking pig, and also a rabbit. It was not much, it is true, for eighteen or nineteen persons; but the Holy Virgin and St. Joseph, her glorious spouse, were not so well treated, on this very day, in the stable of Bethlehem."[1]

On Christmas Day, the despairing hunters, again unsuccessful, came to pray succor from Le Jeune. Even the Apostate had become tractable, and the famished sorcerer was ready to try the efficacy of an appeal to the deity of his rival. A bright hope possessed the missionary. He composed two prayers, which, with the aid of the repentant Pierre, he translated into Algonquin. Then he hung against the side of the hut a napkin which he had brought with him, and against the napkin a crucifix and a reliquary, and, this done, caused all the Indians to kneel before them, with hands raised and clasped. He now read one of the prayers, and required the Indians to repeat the other after him, promising to renounce their superstitions, and obey Christ, whose image they saw before them, if he would give them food and save them from perishing. The pledge given, he dismissed the hunters with a benediction. At night they returned with game enough to re-

[1] "Pour nostre souper, N. S. nous donna vn Porc-espic gros comme vn cochon de lait, et vn liéure; c'estoit peu pour dix-huit ou vingt personnes que nous estions, il est vray, mais la saincte Vierge et son glorieux Espoux sainct Ioseph ne furent pas si bien traictez à mesme iour dans l'estable de Bethleem."—*Relation, 1634*, 74.

lieve the immediate necessity. All was hilarity. The kettles were slung, and the feasters assembled. Le Jeune rose to speak, when Pierre, who, having killed nothing, was in ill humor, said, with a laugh, that the crucifix and the prayer had nothing to do with their good luck; while the sorcerer, his jealousy reviving as he saw his hunger about to be appeased, called out to the missionary, "Hold your tongue! You have no sense!" As usual, all took their cue from him. They fell to their repast with ravenous jubilation, and the disappointed priest sat dejected and silent.

Repeatedly, before the spring, they were thus threatened with starvation. Nor was their case exceptional. It was the ordinary winter life of all those Northern tribes who did not till the soil, but lived by hunting and fishing alone. The desertion or the killing of the aged, sick, and disabled, occasional cannibalism, and frequent death from famine, were natural incidents of an existence which, during half the year, was but a desperate pursuit of the mere necessaries of life under the worst conditions of hardship, suffering, and debasement.

At the beginning of April, after roaming for five months among forests and mountains, the party made their last march, regained the bank of the St. Lawrence, and waded to the island where they had hidden their canoes. Le Jeune was exhausted and sick, and Mestigoit offered to carry him in his canoe to Quebec. This Indian was by far the best of the three brothers, and both Pierre and the sorcerer looked to him for support. He was strong, active, and daring, a skilful hunter, and a dexterous canoeman. Le Jeune gladly accepted his offer; embarked with him and Pierre on the dreary and tempestuous river; and, after a voyage full of hardship, during which the canoe narrowly escaped being ground to atoms among the floating ice, landed on the Island of Orleans, six miles from Quebec. The afternoon was stormy and dark, and the river was covered with ice, sweeping by with the tide. They were forced to encamp. At midnight, the moon had risen, the river was comparatively unencumbered, and they embarked once more. The wind increased, and the waves tossed furiously. Nothing saved them but the skill and courage of Mestigoit. At length they could see the rock of Quebec towering through the gloom, but piles of ice lined the shore, while floating masses were drifting down on the angry current. The Indian watched his moment, shot his canoe through them, gained the fixed ice, leaped out, and shouted to his companions to follow. Pierre scrambled up, but the ice was six feet out of the water, and Le Jeune's agility failed him. He saved himself by clutching the ankle of Mestigoit, by whose aid he gained a firm foothold at the top, and, for a moment, the three voyagers, aghast at the narrowness of their escape, stood gazing at each other in silence.

It was three o'clock in the morning when Le Jeune knocked at the door of his rude little convent on the St. Charles; and the Fathers, springing in joyful haste from their slumbers, embraced their long absent Superior with ejaculations of praise and benediction.

Chapter V

1633, 1634

THE HURON MISSION

Plans of Conversion • Aims and Motives • Indian Diplomacy •
Hurons at Quebec • Councils • The Jesuit Chapel • Le Borgne •
The Jesuits Thwarted • Their Perseverance • The Journey to the
Hurons • Jean de Brébeuf • The Mission Begun

LE JEUNE had learned the difficulties of the Algonquin mission. To imagine that he recoiled or faltered would be
an injustice to his Order; but on two points he had gained
convictions: first, that little progress could be made in converting these wandering hordes till they could be settled in
fixed abodes; and, secondly, that their scanty numbers, their
geographical position, and their slight influence in the politics
of the wilderness offered no flattering promise that their conversion would be fruitful in further triumphs of the Faith. It
was to another quarter that the Jesuits looked most earnestly.
By the vast lakes of the West dwelt numerous stationary populations, and particularly the Hurons, on the lake which bears
their name. Here was a hopeful basis of indefinite conquests;
for, the Hurons won over, the Faith would spread in wider
and wider circles, embracing, one by one, the kindred
tribes,—the Tobacco Nation, the Neutrals, the Eries, and the
Andastes. Nay, in His own time, God might lead into His
fold even the potent and ferocious Iroquois.

The way was pathless and long, by rock and torrent and
the gloom of savage forests. The goal was more dreary yet.
Toil, hardship, famine, filth, sickness, solitude, insult,—all
that is most revolting to men nurtured among arts and letters,
all that is most terrific to monastic credulity: such were the
promise and the reality of the Huron mission. In the eyes of
the Jesuits, the Huron country was the innermost stronghold
of Satan, his castle and his donjon-keep.[1] All the weapons of
his malice were prepared against the bold invader who should

---

[1]"Une des principales forteresses & comme un donjon des Demons."—
Lalemant, *Relation des Hurons, 1639*, 100 (Cramoisy).

assail him in this, the heart of his ancient domain. Far from shrinking, the priest's zeal rose to tenfold ardor. He signed the cross, invoked St. Ignatius, St. Francis Xavier, or St. Francis Borgia, kissed his reliquary, said nine masses to the Virgin, and stood prompt to battle with all the hosts of Hell.

A life sequestered from social intercourse, and remote from every prize which ambition holds worth the pursuit, or a lonely death, under forms, perhaps, the most appalling,— these were the missionaries' alternatives. Their maligners may taunt them, if they will, with credulity, superstition, or a blind enthusiasm; but slander itself cannot accuse them of hypocrisy or ambition. Doubtless, in their propagandism, they were acting in concurrence with a mundane policy; but, for the present at least, this policy was rational and humane. They were promoting the ends of commerce and national expansion. The foundations of French dominion were to be laid deep in the heart and conscience of the savage. His stubborn neck was to be subdued to the "yoke of the Faith." The power of the priest established, that of the temporal ruler was secure. These sanguinary hordes, weaned from intestine strife, were to unite in a common allegiance to God and the King. Mingled with French traders and French settlers, softened by French manners, guided by French priests, ruled by French officers, their now divided bands would become the constituents of a vast wilderness empire, which in time might span the continent. Spanish civilization crushed the Indian; English civilization scorned and neglected him; French civilization embraced and cherished him.

Policy and commerce, then, built their hopes on the priests. These commissioned interpreters of the Divine Will, accredited with letters patent from Heaven, and affiliated to God's anointed on earth, would have pushed to its most unqualified application the Scripture metaphor of the shepherd and the sheep. They would have tamed the wild man of the woods to a condition of obedience, unquestioning, passive, and absolute,—repugnant to manhood, and adverse to the invigorating and expansive spirit of modern civilization. Yet, full of error and full of danger as was their system, they embraced its serene and smiling falsehoods with the sincerity of martyrs and the self-devotion of saints.

We have spoken already of the Hurons, of their populous villages on the borders of the great "Fresh Sea," their trade, their rude agriculture, their social life, their wild and incongruous superstitions, and the sorcerers, diviners, and medicine-men who lived on their credulity.[1] Iroquois hostility left open but one avenue to their country, the long and circuitous route which, eighteen years before, had been explored by Champlain,[2]—up the river Ottawa, across Lake Nipissing, down French River, and along the shores of the great Georgian Bay of Lake Huron,—a route as difficult as it was tedious. Midway, on Allumette Island, in the Ottawa, dwelt the Algonquin tribe visited by Champlain in 1613, and who, amazed at the apparition of the white stranger, thought that he had fallen from the clouds.[3] Like other tribes of this region, they were keen traders, and would gladly have secured for themselves the benefits of an intermediate traffic between the Hurons and the French, receiving the furs of the former in barter at a low rate, and exchanging them with the latter at their full value. From their position, they could at any time close the passage of the Ottawa; but, as this would have been a perilous exercise of their rights,[4] they were forced to act with discretion. An opportunity for the practice of their diplomacy had lately occurred. On or near the Ottawa, at some distance below them, dwelt a small Algonquin tribe, called *La Petite Nation*. One of this people had lately killed a French-

---

[1] See Introduction.

[2] "Pioneers of France," 288.

[3] *Ibid.*, 276.

[4] Nevertheless, the Hurons always passed this way as a matter of favor, and gave yearly presents to the Algonquins of the island, in acknowledgment of the privilege.—Le Jeune, *Relation, 1636*, 70.—By the unwritten laws of the Hurons and Algonquins, every tribe had the right, even in full peace, of prohibiting the passage of every other tribe across its territory. In ordinary cases, such prohibitions were quietly submitted to.

"Ces Insulaires voudraient bien que les Hurons ne vinssent point aux François & que les François n'allassent point aux Hurons, afin d'emporter eux seuls tout le trafic," etc.—*Relation, 1633*, 205 (Cramoisy),—"desirans eux-mesmes aller recueiller les marchandises des peuples circonvoisins pour les apporter aux François." This "Nation de l'Isle" has been erroneously located at Montreal. Its true position is indicated on the map of Du Creux, and on an ancient MS. map in the *Dépôt des Cartes*, of which a fac-simile is before me. See also "Pioneers of France," 275.

man, and the murderer was now in the hands of Champlain, a prisoner at the fort of Quebec. The savage politicians of Allumette Island contrived, as will soon be seen, to turn this incident to profit.

In the July that preceded Le Jeune's wintering with the Montagnais, a Huron Indian, well known to the French, came to Quebec with the tidings, that the annual canoe-fleet of his countrymen was descending the St. Lawrence. On the twenty-eighth, the river was alive with them. A hundred and forty canoes, with six or seven hundred savages, landed at the warehouses beneath the fortified rock of Quebec, and set up their huts and camp-sheds on the strand now covered by the lower town. The greater number brought furs and tobacco for the trade; others came as sight-seers; others to gamble, and others to steal,[1] — accomplishments in which the Hurons were proficient: their gambling skill being exercised chiefly against each other, and their thieving talents against those of other nations.

The routine of these annual visits was nearly uniform. On the first day, the Indians built their huts; on the second, they held their council with the French officers at the fort; on the third and fourth, they bartered their furs and tobacco for kettles, hatchets, knives, cloth, beads, iron arrow-heads, coats, shirts, and other commodities; on the fifth, they were feasted by the French; and at daybreak of the next morning, they embarked and vanished like a flight of birds.[2]

On the second day, then, the long file of chiefs and warriors mounted the pathway to the fort, — tall, well-moulded figures, robed in the skins of the beaver and the bear, each wild visage glowing with paint and glistening with the oil which the Hurons extracted from the seeds of the sunflower. The lank black hair of one streamed loose upon his shoulders; that of another was close shaven, except an upright ridge, which, bristling like the crest of a dragoon's helmet, crossed the crown from the forehead to the neck; while that of a third

---

[1] "Quelques vns d'entre eux ne viennent à la traite auec les François que pour iouër, d'autres pour voir, quelques vns pour dérober, et les plus sages et les plus riches pour trafiquer."—Le Jeune, *Relation, 1633*, 34.

[2] "Comme une volée d'oiseaux."—Le Jeune, *Relation, 1633*, 190 (Cramoisy).—The tobacco brought to the French by the Hurons may have been raised by the adjacent tribe of the Tionnontates, who cultivated it largely for sale. See Introduction.

hung, long and flowing from one side, but on the other was cut short. Sixty chiefs and principal men, with a crowd of younger warriors, formed their council-circle in the fort, those of each village grouped together, and all seated on the ground with a gravity of bearing sufficiently curious to those who had seen the same men in the domestic circle of their lodge-fires. Here, too, were the Jesuits, robed in black, anxious and intent; and here was Champlain, who, as he surveyed the throng, recognized among the elder warriors not a few of those who, eighteen years before, had been his companions in arms on his hapless foray against the Iroquois.[1]

Their harangues of compliment being made and answered, and the inevitable presents given and received, Champlain introduced to the silent conclave the three missionaries, Brébeuf, Daniel, and Davost. To their lot had fallen the honors, dangers, and woes of the Huron mission. "These are our fathers," he said. "We love them more than we love ourselves. The whole French nation honors them. They do not go among you for your furs. They have left their friends and their country to show you the way to heaven. If you love the French, as you say you love them, then love and honor these our fathers."[2]

Two chiefs rose to reply, and each lavished all his rhetoric in praises of Champlain and of the French. Brébeuf rose next, and spoke in broken Huron,—the assembly jerking in unison, from the bottom of their throats, repeated ejaculations of applause. Then they surrounded him, and vied with each other for the honor of carrying him in their canoes. In short, the mission was accepted; and the chiefs of the different villages disputed among themselves the privilege of receiving and entertaining the three priests.

On the last of July, the day of the feast of St. Ignatius, Champlain and several masters of trading vessels went to the house of the Jesuits in quest of indulgences; and here they were soon beset by a crowd of curious Indians, who had finished their traffic, and were making a tour of observation. Being excluded from the house, they looked in at the windows of the room which served as a chapel; and Champlain, amused at their exclamations of wonder, gave one of them a

[1] See "Pioneers of France," 293.
[2] Le Jeune, *Relation, 1633*, 274 (Cramoisy); *Mercure Français*, 1634, 845.

piece of citron. The Huron tasted it, and, enraptured, demanded what it was. Champlain replied, laughing, that it was
a rind of a French pumpkin. The fame of this delectable production was instantly spread abroad; and, at every window,
eager voices and outstretched hands petitioned for a share of
the marvellous vegetable. They were at length allowed to enter the chapel, which had lately been decorated with a few
hangings, images, and pieces of plate. These unwonted splendors filled them with admiration. They asked if the dove over
the altar was the bird that makes the thunder; and, pointing
to the images of Loyola and Xavier, inquired if they were
okies, or spirits: nor was their perplexity much diminished by
Brébeuf's explanation of their true character. Three images of
the Virgin next engaged their attention; and, in answer to
their questions, they were told that they were the mother of
Him who made the world. This greatly amused them, and
they demanded if he had three mothers. "Oh!" exclaims the
Father Superior, "had we but images of all the holy mysteries
of our faith! They are a great assistance, for they speak their
own lesson."[1] The mission was not doomed long to suffer
from a dearth of these inestimable auxiliaries.

The eve of departure came. The three priests packed their
baggage, and Champlain paid their passage, or, in other
words, made presents to the Indians who were to carry them
in their canoes. They lodged that night in the storehouse of
the fur company, around which the Hurons were encamped;
and Le Jeune and De Noüe stayed with them to bid them
farewell in the morning. At eleven at night, they were roused
by a loud voice in the Indian camp, and saw Le Borgne, the
one-eyed chief of Allumette Island, walking round among
the huts, haranguing as he went. Brébeuf, listening, caught
the import of his words. "We have begged the French captain
to spare the life of the Algonquin of the Petite Nation whom
he keeps in prison; but he will not listen to us. The prisoner
will die. Then his people will revenge him. They will try to
kill the three black-robes whom you are about to carry to
your country. If you do not defend them, the French will be
angry, and charge you with their death. But if you do, then
the Algonquins will make war on you, and the river will be

[1] *Relation, 1633,* 38.

closed. If the French captain will not let the prisoner go, then leave the three black-robes where they are; for, if you take them with you, they will bring you to trouble."

Such was the substance of Le Borgne's harangue. The anxious priests hastened up to the fort, gained admittance, and roused Champlain from his slumbers. He sent his interpreter with a message to the Hurons, that he wished to speak to them before their departure; and, accordingly, in the morning an Indian crier proclaimed through their camp that none should embark till the next day. Champlain convoked the chiefs, and tried persuasion, promises, and threats; but Le Borgne had been busy among them with his intrigues, and now he declared in the council, that, unless the prisoner were released, the missionaries would be murdered on their way, and war would ensue. The politic savage had two objects in view. On the one hand, he wished to interrupt the direct intercourse between the French and the Hurons; and, on the other, he thought to gain credit and influence with the nation of the prisoner by effecting his release. His first point was won. Champlain would not give up the murderer, knowing those with whom he was dealing too well to take a course which would have proclaimed the killing of a Frenchman a venial offence. The Hurons thereupon refused to carry the missionaries to their country; coupling the refusal with many regrets and many protestations of love, partly, no doubt, sincere,—for the Jesuits had contrived to gain no little favor in their eyes. The council broke up, the Hurons embarked, and the priests returned to their convent.

Here, under the guidance of Brébeuf, they employed themselves, amid their other avocations, in studying the Huron tongue. A year passed, and again the Indian traders descended from their villages. In the meanwhile, grievous calamities had befallen the nation. They had suffered deplorable reverses at the hands of the Iroquois; while a pestilence, similar to that which a few years before had swept off the native populations of New England, had begun its ravages among them. They appeared at Three Rivers—this year the place of trade—in small numbers, and in a miserable state of dejection and alarm. Du Plessis Bochart, commander of the French fleet, called them to a council, harangued them, feasted them, and made them presents; but they refused to take the Jesuits. In private, however, some of them were gained over; then again refused; then, at the eleventh hour, a second time consented. On the eve of embarkation, they once more wavered. All was confusion, doubt, and uncertainty, when Brébeuf bethought him of a vow to St. Joseph. The vow was made. At once, he says, the Indians became tractable; the Fathers embarked, and, amid salvos of cannon from the ships, set forth for the wild scene of their apostleship.

They reckoned the distance at nine hundred miles; but distance was the least repellent feature of this most arduous journey. Barefoot, lest their shoes should injure the frail vessel, each crouched in his canoe, toiling with unpractised hands to propel it. Before him, week after week, he saw the same lank, unkempt hair, the same tawny shoulders, and long, naked arms ceaselessly plying the paddle. The canoes were soon separated; and, for more than a month, the Frenchmen rarely or never met. Brébeuf spoke a little Huron, and could converse with his escort; but Daniel and Davost were doomed to a silence unbroken save by the occasional unintelligible complaints and menaces of the Indians, of whom many were sick with the epidemic, and all were terrified, desponding, and sullen. Their only food was a pittance of Indian corn, crushed between two stones and mixed with water. The toil was extreme. Brébeuf counted thirty-five portages, where the canoes were lifted from the water, and carried on the shoulders of the voyagers around rapids or cataracts. More than fifty times, besides, they were forced to wade in the raging current, pushing up their empty barks, or dragging them with ropes. Brébeuf tried to do his part; but the boulders and sharp rocks wounded his naked feet, and compelled him to desist. He and his companions bore their share of the baggage across the portages, sometimes a distance of several miles. Four trips, at the least, were required to convey the whole. The way was through the dense forest, incumbered with rocks and logs, tangled with roots and underbrush, damp with perpetual shade, and redolent of decayed leaves and mouldering wood.[1] The Indians themselves were often spent with fatigue. Bré-

[1]"Adioustez à ces difficultez, qu'il faut coucher sur la terre nuë, ou sur quelque dure roche, faute de trouuer dix ou douze pieds de terre en quarré

beuf, a man of iron frame and a nature unconquerably resolute, doubted if his strength would sustain him to the
journey's end. He complains that he had no moment to read
his breviary, except by the moonlight or the fire, when
stretched out to sleep on a bare rock by some savage cataract
of the Ottawa, or in a damp nook of the adjacent forest.

All the Jesuits, as well as several of their countrymen who
accompanied them, suffered more or less at the hands of their
ill-humored conductors.[1] Davost's Indian robbed him of a
part of his baggage, threw a part into the river, including
most of the books and writing-materials of the three priests,

---

pour placer vne chetiue cabane; qu'il faut sentir incessamment la puanteur
des Sauuages recreus, marcher dans les eaux, dans les fanges, dans l'obscurité
et l'embarras des forest, où les piqueures d'vne multitude infinie de mous-
quilles et cousins vous importunent fort."—Brébeuf, *Relation des Hurons*,
1635, 25, 26.

[1] "En ce voyage, il nous a fallu tous commencer par ces experiences à porter
la Croix que Nostre Seigneur nous presente pour son honneur, et pour le
salut de ces pauures Barbares. Certes ie me suis trouué quelquesfois si las,
que le corps n'en pouuoit plus. Mais d'ailleurs mon âme ressentoit de tres-
grands contentemens, considerant que ie souffrois pour Dieu: nul ne le sçait,
s'il ne l'experimente. Tous n'en ont pas esté quittes à si bon marché."—Brébeuf, *Relation des Hurons, 1635*, 26.

Three years afterwards, a paper was printed by the Jesuits of Paris, called
Instruction pour les Pères de nostre Compagnie qui seront enuoiez aux Hurons,
and containing directions for their conduct on this route by the Ottawa. It
is highly characteristic, both of the missionaries and of the Indians. Some of
the points are, in substance, as follows.—You should love the Indians like
brothers, with whom you are to spend the rest of your life.—Never make
them wait for you in embarking.—Take a flint and steel to light their pipes
and kindle their fire at night; for these little services win their hearts.—Try
to eat their sagamite as they cook it, bad and dirty as it is.—Fasten up the
skirts of your cassock, that you may not carry water or sand into the canoe.—
Wear no shoes or stockings in the canoe; but you may put them on in crossing the portages.—Do not make yourself troublesome, even to a single Indian.—Do not ask them too many questions.—Bear their faults in silence,
and appear always cheerful.—Buy fish for them from the tribes you will pass;
and for this purpose take with you some awls, beads, knives, and fish-
hooks.—Be not ceremonious with the Indians; take at once what they offer
you: ceremony offends them.—Be very careful, when in the canoe, that the
brim of your hat does not annoy them. Perhaps it would be better to wear
your night-cap. There is no such thing as impropriety among Indians.—
Remember that it is Christ and his cross that you are seeking; and if you aim
at anything else, you will get nothing but affliction for body and mind.

and then left him behind, among the Algonquins of Allumette Island. He found means to continue the journey, and
at length reached the Huron towns in a lamentable state of
bodily prostration. Daniel, too, was deserted, but fortunately
found another party who received him into their canoe. A
young Frenchman, named Martin, was abandoned among the
Nipissings; another, named Baron, on reaching the Huron
country, was robbed by his conductors of all he had, except
the weapons in his hands. Of these he made good use, compelling the robbers to restore a part of their plunder.

Descending French River, and following the lonely shores
of the great Georgian Bay, the canoe which carried Brébeuf
at length neared its destination, thirty days after leaving Three
Rivers. Before him, stretched in savage slumber, lay the forest
shore of the Hurons. Did his spirit sink as he approached his
dreary home, oppressed with a dark foreboding of what the
future should bring forth? There is some reason to think so.
Yet it was but the shadow of a moment; for his masculine
heart had lost the sense of fear, and his intrepid nature was
fired with a zeal before which doubts and uncertainties fled
like the mists of the morning. Not the grim enthusiasm of
negation, tearing up the weeds of rooted falsehood, or with
bold hand felling to the earth the baneful growth of overshad-
owing abuses: his was the ancient faith uncurtailed, redeemed
from the decay of centuries, kindled with a new life, and stimulated to a preternatural growth and fruitfulness.

Brébeuf and his Huron companions having landed, the Indians, throwing the missionary's baggage on the ground, left
him to his own resources; and, without heeding his remonstrances, set forth for their respective villages, some twenty miles
distant. Thus abandoned, the priest kneeled, not to implore succor in his perplexity, but to offer thanks to the Providence which
had shielded him thus far. Then, rising, he pondered as to what
course he should take. He knew the spot well. It was on the borders of the small inlet called Thunder Bay. In the neighboring
Huron town of Toanché he had lived three years, preaching and
baptizing;[1] but Toanché had now ceased to exist. Here, Étienne
Brulé, Champlain's adventurous interpreter, had recently been

[1] From 1626 to 1629. There is no record of the events of this first mission,
which was ended with the English occupation of Quebec. Brébeuf had pre-

murdered by the inhabitants, who, in excitement and alarm, dreading the consequences of their deed, had deserted the spot, and built, at the distance of a few miles, a new town, called Ihonatiria.[1] Brébeuf hid his baggage in the woods, including the vessels for the Mass, more precious than all the rest, and began his search for this new abode. He passed the burnt remains of Toanché, saw the charred poles that had formed the frame of his little chapel of bark, and found, as he thought, the spot where Brulé had fallen.[2] Evening was near, when, after following, bewildered and anxious, a gloomy forest path, he issued upon a wild clearing, and saw before him the bark roofs of Ihonatiria.

A crowd ran out to meet him. "Echom has come again! Echom has come again!" they cried, recognizing in the distance the stately figure, robed in black, that advanced from the border of the forest. They led him to the town, and the whole population swarmed about him. After a short rest, he set out with a number of young Indians in quest of his baggage, returning with it at one o'clock in the morning. There was a certain Awandoay in the village, noted as one of the richest and most hospitable of the Hurons,—a distinction not easily won where hospitality was universal. His house was large, and amply stored with beans and corn; and though his prosperity had excited the jealousy of the villagers, he had recovered their good-will by his generosity. With him Brébeuf made his abode, anxiously waiting, week after week, the arrival of his companions. One by one, they appeared: Daniel, weary and worn; Davost, half dead with famine and fatigue; and their French attendants, each with his tale of hardship and indignity. At length, all were assembled under the roof of the hospitable Indian, and once more the Huron mission was begun.

---

viously spent the winter of 1625–26 among the Algonquins, like Le Jeune in 1633–34.— *Lettre du P. Charles Lalemant au T. R. P. Mutio Vitelleschi, 1 Aug., 1626*, in Carayon.

[1]Concerning Brulé, see "Pioneers of France," 298–300.

[2]"Ie vis pareillement l'endroit où le pauure Estienne Brulé auoit esté barbarement et traîtreusement assommé; ce qui me fit penser que quelque iour on nous pourroit bien traitter de la sorte, et desirer au moins que ce fust en pourchassant la gloire de N. Seigneur."—Brébeuf, *Relation des Hurons, 1635*, 28, 29.—The missionary's prognostics were but too well founded.

Chapter VI

1634, 1635

BRÉBEUF AND HIS ASSOCIATES

The Huron Mission-House • Its Inmates • Its Furniture • Its Guests • The Jesuit as a Teacher • As an Engineer • Baptisms • Huron Village Life • Festivities and Sorceries • The Dream Feast • The Priests accused of Magic • The Drought and the Red Cross

WHERE should the Fathers make their abode? Their first thought had been to establish themselves at a place called by the French *Rochelle*, the largest and most important town of the Huron confederacy; but Brébeuf now resolved to remain at Ihonatiria. Here he was well known; and here, too, he flattered himself, seeds of the Faith had been planted, which, with good nurture, would in time yield fruit.

By the ancient Huron custom, when a man or a family wanted a house, the whole village joined in building one. In the present case, not Ihonatiria only, but the neighboring town of Wenrio also, took part in the work,—though not without the expectation of such gifts as the priests had to bestow. Before October, the task was finished. The house was constructed after the Huron model.[1] It was thirty-six feet long and about twenty feet wide, framed with strong sapling poles planted in the earth to form the sides, with the ends bent into an arch for the roof,—the whole lashed firmly together, braced with cross-poles, and closely covered with overlapping sheets of bark. Without, the structure was strictly Indian; but within, the priests, with the aid of their tools, made innovations which were the astonishment of all the country. They divided their dwelling by transverse partitions into three apartments, each with its wooden door,—a wondrous novelty in the eyes of their visitors. The first served as a hall, an anteroom, and a place of storage for corn, beans, and dried fish. The second—the largest of the three—was at once kitchen, workshop, dining-room, drawing-room, school-room, and bed-chamber. The third was the chapel. Here they

[1] See Introduction.

made their altar, and here were their images, pictures, and
sacred vessels. Their fire was on the ground, in the middle of
the second apartment, the smoke escaping by a hole in the
roof. At the sides were placed two wide platforms, after the
Huron fashion, four feet from the earthen floor. On these
were chests in which they kept their clothing and vestments,
and beneath them they slept, reclining on sheets of bark, and
covered with skins and the garments they wore by day. Rude
stools, a hand-mill, a large Indian mortar of wood for crushing corn, and a clock, completed the furniture of the room.

There was no lack of visitors, for the house of the black-
robes contained marvels[1] the fame of which was noised
abroad to the uttermost confines of the Huron nation. Chief
among them was the clock. The guests would sit in expectant
silence by the hour, squatted on the ground, waiting to hear
it strike. They thought it was alive, and asked what it ate. As
the last stroke sounded, one of the Frenchmen would cry
"Stop!"—and, to the admiration of the company, the obedient clock was silent. The mill was another wonder, and they
were never tired of turning it. Besides these, there was a
prism and a magnet; also a magnifying-glass, wherein a flea
was transformed to a frightful monster, and a multiplying
lens, which showed them the same object eleven times repeated. "All this," says Brébeuf, "serves to gain their affection,
and make them more docile in respect to the admirable and
incomprehensible mysteries of our Faith; for the opinion they
have of our genius and capacity makes them believe whatever
we tell them."[2]

"What does the Captain say?" was the frequent question;
for by this title of honor they designated the clock.

"When he strikes twelve times, he says, 'Hang on the kettle';
and when he strikes four times, he says, 'Get up, and go home.' "

Both interpretations were well remembered. At noon, visi-

---

[1] "Ils ont pensé qu'elle entendoit, principalement quand, pour rire, quelqu'vn de nos François s'escrioit au dernier coup de marteau, c'est assez sonné,
et que tout aussi tost elle se taisoit. Ils l'appellent le Capitaine du iour. Quand
elle sonne, ils disent qu'elle parle, et demandent, quand ils nous viennent
veoir, combien de fois le Capitaine a desia parlé. Ils nous interrogent de son
manger. Ils demeurent les heures entieres, et quelquefois plusieurs, afin de
la pouuoir ouyr parler."—Brébeuf, *Relation des Hurons, 1635*, 33.

[2] *Ibid.*

tors were never wanting, to share the Fathers' sagamite; but at the stroke of four, all rose and departed, leaving the missionaries for a time in peace. Now the door was barred, and, gathering around the fire, they discussed the prospects of the mission, compared their several experiences, and took counsel for the future. But the standing topic of their evening talk was the Huron language. Concerning this each had some new discovery to relate, some new suggestion to offer; and in the task of analyzing its construction and deducing its hidden laws, these intelligent and highly cultivated minds found a congenial employment.[1]

But while zealously laboring to perfect their knowledge of the language, they spared no pains to turn their present acquirements to account. Was man, woman, or child sick or suffering, they were always at hand with assistance and relief, — adding, as they saw opportunity, explanations of Christian doctrine, pictures of Heaven and Hell, and exhortations to embrace the Faith. Their friendly offices did not cease here, but included matters widely different. The Hurons lived in constant fear of the Iroquois. At times the whole village population would fly to the woods for concealment, or take refuge in one of the neighboring fortified towns, on the rumor of an approaching war-party. The Jesuits promised them the aid of the four Frenchmen armed with arquebuses, who had come with them from Three Rivers. They advised the Hurons to make their palisade forts, not, as hitherto, in a circular form, but rectangular, with small flanking towers at the corners for the arquebuse-men. The Indians at once saw the value of the advice, and soon after began to act on it in the case of their great town of Ossossané, or Rochelle.[2]

At every opportunity, the missionaries gathered together the children of the village at their house. On these occasions, Brébeuf, for greater solemnity, put on a surplice, and the close, angular cap worn by Jesuits in their convents. First he chanted the *Pater Noster*, translated by Father Daniel into Huron rhymes, — the children chanting in their turn. Next he taught them the sign of the cross; made them repeat the *Ave*, the *Credo*, and the Commandments; questioned them as to

[1] Lalemant, *Relation des Hurons, 1639*, 17 (Cramoisy).
[2] Brébeuf, *Relation des Hurons, 1636*, 86.

past instructions; gave them briefly a few new ones; and dismissed them with a present of two or three beads, raisins, or prunes. A great emulation was kindled among this small fry of heathendom. The priests, with amusement and delight, saw them gathered in groups about the village, vying with each other in making the sign of the cross, or in repeating the rhymes they had learned.

At times, the elders of the people, the repositories of its ancient traditions, were induced to assemble at the house of the Jesuits, who explained to them the principal points of their doctrine, and invited them to a discussion. The auditors proved pliant to a fault, responding, "Good," or "That is true," to every proposition; but, when urged to adopt the faith which so readily met their approval, they had always the same reply: "It is good for the French; but we are another people, with different customs." On one occasion, Brébeuf appeared before the chiefs and elders at a solemn national council, described Heaven and Hell with images suited to their comprehension, asked to which they preferred to go after death, and then, in accordance with the invariable Huron custom in affairs of importance, presented a large and valuable belt of wampum, as an invitation to take the path to Paradise.[1]

Notwithstanding all their exhortations, the Jesuits, for the present, baptized but few. Indeed, during the first year or more, they baptized no adults except those apparently at the point of death; for, with excellent reason, they feared backsliding and recantation. They found especial pleasure in the baptism of dying infants, rescuing them from the flames of perdition, and changing them, to borrow Le Jeune's phrase, "from little Indians into little angels."[2]

The Fathers' slumbers were brief and broken. Winter was

---

[1] Brébeuf, *Relation des Hurons, 1636*, 81. For the use of wampum belts, see Introduction.

[2] "Le seiziesme du mesme mois, deux petits Sauvages furent changez en deux petits Anges." — *Relation, 1636*, 89 (Cramoisy).

"O mon cher frère, vous pourrois-je expliquer quelle consolation ce m'etoit quand je voyois un pauure baptisé mourir deux heures, une demi journée, une ou deux journées, après son baptesme, particulièrement quand c'etoit un petit enfant!" — *Lettre du Père Garnier à son Frère, MS.* — This form of benevolence is beyond heretic appreciation.

the season of Huron festivity; and, as they lay stretched on their hard couch, suffocating with smoke and tormented by an inevitable multitude of fleas, the thumping of the drum resounded all night long from a neighboring house, mingled with the sound of the tortoise-shell rattle, the stamping of moccasined feet, and the cadence of voices keeping time with the dancers. Again, some ambitious villager would give a feast, and invite all the warriors of the neighboring towns; or some grand wager of gambling, with its attendant drumming, singing, and outcries, filled the night with discord.

But these were light annoyances, compared with the insane rites to cure the sick, prescribed by the "medicine-men," or ordained by the eccentric inspiration of dreams. In one case, a young sorcerer, by alternate gorging and fasting,—both in the interest of his profession,—joined with excessive exertion in singing to the spirits, contracted a disorder of the brain, which caused him, in mid-winter, to run naked about the village, howling like a wolf. The whole population bestirred itself to effect a cure. The patient had, or pretended to have, a dream, in which the conditions of his recovery were revealed to him. These were equally ridiculous and difficult; but the elders met in council, and all the villagers lent their aid, till every requisition was fulfilled, and the incongruous mass of gifts which the madman's dream had demanded were all bestowed upon him. This cure failing, a "medicine-feast" was tried; then several dances in succession. As the patient remained as crazy as before, preparations were begun for a grand dance, more potent than all the rest. Brébeuf says, that, except the masquerades of the Carnival among Christians, he never saw a folly equal to it. "Some," he adds, "had sacks over their heads, with two holes for the eyes. Some were as naked as your hand, with horns or feathers on their heads, their bodies painted white, and their faces black as devils. Others were daubed with red, black, and white. In short, every one decked himself as extravagantly as he could, to dance in this

---

"La joye qu'on a quand on a baptisé un Sauvage qui se meurt peu apres, & qui s'envole droit au Ciel, pour devenir un Ange, certainement c'est un joye qui surpasse tout ce qu'on se peut imaginer."—Le Jeune, *Relation, 1635,* 221 (Cramoisy).

ballet, and contribute something towards the health of the sick man."[1] This remedy also failing, a crowning effort of the medical art was essayed. Brébeuf does not describe it, for fear, as he says, of being tedious; but, for the time, the village was a pandemonium.[2] This, with other ceremonies, was supposed to be ordered by a certain image like a doll, which a sorcerer placed in his tobacco-pouch, whence it uttered its oracles, at the same time moving as if alive. "Truly," writes Brébeuf, "here is nonsense enough: but I greatly fear there is something more dark and mysterious in it."

But all these ceremonies were outdone by the grand festival of the *Ononhara*, or Dream Feast,—esteemed the most powerful remedy in cases of sickness, or when a village was infested with evil spirits. The time and manner of holding it were determined at a solemn council. This scene of madness began at night. Men, women, and children, all pretending to have lost their senses, rushed shrieking and howling from house to house, upsetting everything in their way, throwing firebrands, beating those they met or drenching them with water, and availing themselves of this time of license to take a safe revenge on any who had ever offended them. This scene of frenzy continued till daybreak. No corner of the village was secure from the maniac crew. In the morning there was a change. They ran from house to house, accosting the inmates by name, and demanding of each the satisfaction of some secret want, revealed to the pretended madman in a dream, but of the nature of which he gave no hint whatever. The person addressed thereupon threw to him at random any article at hand, as a hatchet, a kettle, or a pipe; and the applicant continued his rounds till the desired gift was hit upon, when he gave an outcry of delight, echoed by gratulatory cries from all present. If, after all his efforts, he failed in ob-

---

[1] *Relation des Hurons, 1636*, 116.

[2] "Suffit pour le present de dire en general, que iamais les Bacchantes forcenées du temps passé ne firent rien de plus furieux en leurs orgyes. C'est icy à s'entretuer, disent-ils, par des sorts qu'ils s'entreiettent, dont la composition est d'ongles d'Ours, de dents de Loup, d'ergots d'Aigles, de certaines pierres et de nerfs de Chien; c'est à rendre du sang par la bouche et par les narines, ou plustost d'vne poudre rouge qu'ils prennent subtilement, estans tombez sous le sort, et blessez; et dix mille autres sottises que ie laisse volontiers."— Brébeuf, *Relation des Hurons, 1636*, 117.

taining the object of his dream, he fell into a deep dejection, convinced that some disaster was in store for him.[1]

The approach of summer brought with it a comparative peace. Many of the villagers dispersed,—some to their fishing, some to expeditions of trade, and some to distant lodges by their detached corn-fields. The priests availed themselves of the respite to engage in those exercises of private devotion which the rule of St. Ignatius enjoins. About midsummer, however, their quiet was suddenly broken. The crops were withering under a severe drought, a calamity which the sandy nature of the soil made doubly serious. The sorcerers put forth their utmost power, and, from the tops of the houses, yelled incessant invocations to the spirits. All was in vain; the pitiless sky was cloudless. There was thunder in the east and thunder in the west; but over Ihonatiria all was serene. A renowned "rain-maker," seeing his reputation tottering under his repeated failures, bethought him of accusing the Jesuits, and gave out that the red color of the cross which stood before their house scared the bird of thunder, and caused him to fly another way.[2] On this a clamor arose. The popular ire turned against the priests, and the obnoxious cross was condemned to be hewn down. Aghast at the threatened sacrilege, they attempted to reason away the storm, assuring the

[1] Brébeuf's account of the Dream Feast is brief. The above particulars are drawn chiefly from Charlevoix, *Journal Historique*, 356, and Sagard, *Voyage du Pays des Hurons*, 280. See also Lafitau, and other early writers. This ceremony was not confined to the Hurons, but prevailed also among the Iroquois, and doubtless other kindred tribes. The Jesuit Dablon saw it in perfection at Onondaga. It usually took place in February, occupying about three days, and was often attended with great indecencies. The word *ononhara* means *turning of the brain*.

[2] The following is the account of the nature of thunder, given to Brébeuf on a former occasion by another sorcerer.

"It is a man in the form of a turkey-cock. The sky is his palace, and he remains in it when the air is clear. When the clouds begin to grumble, he descends to the earth to gather up snakes, and other objects which the Indians call *okies*. The lightning flashes whenever he opens or closes his wings. If the storm is more violent than usual, it is because his young are with him, and aiding in the noise as well as they can."—*Relation des Hurons, 1636*, 114.

The word *oki* is here used to denote any object endued with supernatural power. A belief similar to the above exists to this day among the Dacotahs. Some of the Hurons and Iroquois, however, held that the thunder was a giant in human form. According to one story, he vomited from time to time a number of snakes, which, falling to the earth, caused the appearance of lightning.

crowd that the lightning was not a bird, but certain hot and fiery exhalations, which, being imprisoned, darted this way and that, trying to escape. As this philosophy failed to convince the hearers, the missionaries changed their line of defence.

"You say that the red color of the cross frightens the bird of thunder. Then paint the cross white, and see if the thunder will come."

This was accordingly done; but the clouds still kept aloof. The Jesuits followed up their advantage.

"Your spirits cannot help you, and your sorcerers have deceived you with lies. Now ask the aid of Him who made the world, and perhaps He will listen to your prayers." And they added, that, if the Indians would renounce their sins and obey the true God, they would make a procession daily to implore His favor towards them.

There was no want of promises. The processions were begun, as were also nine masses to St. Joseph; and, as heavy rains occurred soon after, the Indians conceived a high idea of the efficacy of the French "medicine."[1]

In spite of the hostility of the sorcerers, and the transient commotion raised by the red cross, the Jesuits had gained the confidence and good-will of the Huron population. Their patience, their kindness, their intrepidity, their manifest disinterestedness, the blamelessness of their lives, and the tact which, in the utmost fervors of their zeal, never failed them, had won the hearts of these wayward savages; and chiefs of distant villages came to urge that they would make their abode with them.[2] As yet, the results of the mission had been faint and few; but the priests toiled on courageously, high in hope that an abundant harvest of souls would one day reward their labors.

[1]"Nous deuons aussi beaucoup au glorieux sainct Ioseph, espoux de Nostre Dame, et protecteur des Hurons, dont nous auons touché au doigt l'assistance plusieurs fois. Ce fut vne chose remarquable, que le iour de sa feste et durant l'Octaue, les commoditez nous venoient de toutes parts."—Brébeuf, *Relation des Hurons, 1635*, 41.

The above extract is given as one out of many illustrations of the confidence with which the priests rested on the actual and direct aid of their celestial guardians. To St. Joseph, in particular, they find no words for their gratitude.

[2]Brébeuf preserves a speech made to him by one of these chiefs, as a specimen of Huron eloquence.—*Ibid., 1636*, 123.

Chapter VII

1636, 1637

THE FEAST OF THE DEAD

Huron Graves • Preparation for the Ceremony • Disinterment • The Mourning • The Funeral March • The Great Sepulchre • Funeral Games • Encampment of the Mourners • Gifts • Harangues • Frenzy of the Crowd • The Closing Scene • Another Rite • The Captive Iroquois • The Sacrifice

---

MENTION has been made of those great depositories of human bones found at the present day in the ancient country of the Hurons.[1] They have been a theme of abundant speculation;[2] yet their origin is a subject, not of conjecture, but of historic certainty. The peculiar rites to which they owe their existence were first described at length by Brébeuf, who, in the summer of the year 1636, saw them at the town of Ossossané.

The Jesuits had long been familiar with the ordinary rites of sepulture among the Hurons: the corpse placed in a crouching posture in the midst of the circle of friends and relatives; the long, measured wail of the mourners; the speeches in praise of the dead, and consolation to the living; the funeral feast; the gifts at the place of burial; the funeral games, where the young men of the village contended for prizes; and the long period of mourning to those next of kin. The body was usually laid on a scaffold, or, more rarely, in the earth. This, however, was not its final resting-place. At intervals of ten or twelve years, each of the four nations which composed the Huron Confederacy gathered together its dead, and conveyed them all to a common place of sepulture. Here was celebrated the great "Feast of the Dead,"—in the eyes of the Hurons, their most solemn and important ceremonial.

In the spring of 1636, the chiefs and elders of the Nation of the Bear—the principal nation of the Confederacy, and that

[1] See Introduction.

[2] Among those who have wondered and speculated over these remains is Mr. Schoolcraft. A slight acquaintance with the early writers would have solved his doubts.

to which Ihonatiria belonged—assembled in a general council, to prepare for the great solemnity. There was an unwonted spirit of dissension. Some causes of jealousy had
arisen, and three or four of the Bear villages announced their
intention of holding their Feast of the Dead apart from the
rest. As such a procedure was thought abhorrent to every
sense of propriety and duty, the announcement excited an intense feeling; yet Brébeuf, who was present, describes the debate which ensued as perfectly calm, and wholly free from
personal abuse or recrimination. The secession, however, took
place, and each party withdrew to its villages to gather and
prepare its dead.

The corpses were lowered from their scaffolds, and lifted
from their graves. Their coverings were removed by certain
functionaries appointed for the office, and the hideous relics
arranged in a row, surrounded by the weeping, shrieking,
howling concourse. The spectacle was frightful. Here were all
the village dead of the last twelve years. The priests, connois-
seurs in such matters, regarded it as a display of mortality so
edifying, that they hastened to summon their French attendants to contemplate and profit by it. Each family reclaimed
its own, and immediately addressed itself to removing what
remained of flesh from the bones. These, after being tenderly
caressed, with tears and lamentations, were wrapped in skins
and adorned with pendent robes of fur. In the belief of the
mourners, they were sentient and conscious. A soul was
thought still to reside in them;[1] and to this notion, very general among Indians, is in no small degree due that extravagant
attachment to the remains of their dead, which may be said
to mark the race.

These relics of mortality, together with the recent
corpses,—which were allowed to remain entire, but which
were also wrapped carefully in furs,—were now carried to
one of the largest houses, and hung to the numerous cross-
poles, which, like rafters, supported the roof. Here the concourse of mourners seated themselves at a funeral feast; and,
as the squaws of the household distributed the food, a chief

---

[1] In the general belief, the soul took flight after the great ceremony was
ended. Many thought that there were two souls, one remaining with the
bones, while the other went to the land of spirits.

harangued the assembly, lamenting the loss of the deceased, and extolling their virtues. This solemnity over, the mourners began their march for Ossossané, the scene of the final rite. The bodies remaining entire were borne on a kind of litter, while the bundles of bones were slung at the shoulders of the relatives, like fagots. Thus the procession slowly defiled along the forest pathways, with which the country of the Hurons was everywhere intersected; and as they passed beneath the dull shadow of the pines, they uttered at intervals, in unison, a dreary, wailing cry, designed to imitate the voices of disembodied souls winging their way to the land of spirits, and believed to have an effect peculiarly soothing to the conscious relics which each man bore. When, at night, they stopped to rest at some village on the way, the inhabitants came forth to welcome them with a grave and mournful hospitality.

From every town of the Nation of the Bear,—except the rebellious few that had seceded,—processions like this were converging towards Ossossané. This chief town of the Hurons stood on the eastern margin of Nottawassaga Bay, encompassed with a gloomy wilderness of fir and pine. Thither, on the urgent invitation of the chiefs, the Jesuits repaired. The capacious bark houses were filled to overflowing, and the surrounding woods gleamed with camp-fires: for the processions of mourners were fast arriving, and the throng was swelled by invited guests of other tribes. Funeral games were in progress, the young men and women practising archery and other exercises, for prizes offered by the mourners in the name of their dead relatives.[1] Some of the chiefs conducted Brébeuf and his companions to the place prepared for the ceremony. It was a cleared area in the forest, many acres in extent. In the midst was a pit, about ten feet deep and thirty feet wide. Around it was reared a high and strong scaffolding; and on this were planted numerous upright poles, with cross-poles extended between, for hanging the funeral gifts and the remains of the dead.

Meanwhile there was a long delay. The Jesuits were lodged

[1] Funeral games were not confined to the Hurons and Iroquois: Perrot mentions having seen them among the Ottawas. An illustrated description of them will be found in Lafitau.

in a house where more than a hundred of these bundles of mortality were hanging from the rafters. Some were mere shapeless rolls; others were made up into clumsy effigies, adorned with feathers, beads, and belts of dyed porcupine-quills. Amidst this throng of the living and the dead, the priests spent a night which the imagination and the senses conspired to render almost insupportable.

At length the officiating chiefs gave the word to prepare for the ceremony. The relics were taken down, opened for the last time, and the bones caressed and fondled by the women amid paroxysms of lamentation.[1] Then all the processions were formed anew, and, each bearing its dead, moved towards the area prepared for the last solemn rites. As they reached the ground, they defiled in order, each to a spot assigned to it, on the outer limits of the clearing. Here the bearers of the dead laid their bundles on the ground, while those who carried the funeral gifts outspread and displayed them for the admiration of the beholders. Their number was immense, and their value relatively very great. Among them were many robes of beaver and other rich furs, collected and preserved for years, with a view to this festival. Fires were now lighted, kettles slung, and, around the entire circle of the clearing, the scene was like a fair or caravansary. This continued till three o'clock in the afternoon, when the gifts were repacked, and the bones shouldered afresh. Suddenly, at a signal from the chiefs, the crowd ran forward from every side towards the scaffold, like soldiers to the assault of a town, scaled it by rude ladders with which it was furnished, and hung their relics and their gifts to the forest of poles which surmounted it. Then the ladders were removed; and a number of chiefs, standing on the scaffold, harangued the crowd below, praising the dead, and extolling the gifts, which the

---

[1] "J'admiray la tendresse d'vne femme enuers son pere et ses enfans; elle est fille d'vn Capitaine, qui est mort fort âgé, et a esté autrefois fort considerable dans le Païs: elle luy peignoit sa cheuelure, elle manioit ses os les vns apres les autres, auec la mesme affection que si elle luy eust voulu rendre la vie; elle luy mit aupres de luy son Atsatone8ai, c'est à dire son pacquet de buchettes de Conseil, qui sont tous les liures et papiers du Païs. Pour ses petits enfans, elle leur mit des brasselets de Pourcelaine et de rassade aux bras, et baigna leurs os de ses larmes; on ne l'en pouuoit quasi separer, mais on pressoit, et il fallut incontinent partir."—Brébeuf, *Relation des Hurons, 1636*, 134.

relatives of the departed now bestowed, in their names, upon their surviving friends.

During these harangues, other functionaries were lining the grave throughout with rich robes of beaver-skin. Three large copper kettles were next placed in the middle,[1] and then ensued a scene of hideous confusion. The bodies which had been left entire were brought to the edge of the grave, flung in, and arranged in order at the bottom by ten or twelve Indians stationed there for the purpose, amid the wildest excitement and the uproar of many hundred mingled voices.[2] When this part of the work was done, night was fast closing in. The concourse bivouacked around the clearing, and lighted their camp-fires under the brows of the forest which hedged in the scene of the dismal solemnity. Brébeuf and his companions withdrew to the village, where, an hour before dawn, they were roused by a clamor which might have wakened the dead. One of the bundles of bones, tied to a pole on the scaffold, had chanced to fall into the grave. This accident had precipitated the closing act, and perhaps increased its frenzy. Guided by the unearthly din, and the broad glare of flames fed with heaps of fat pine logs, the priests soon reached the spot, and saw what seemed, in their eyes, an image of Hell. All around blazed countless fires, and the air resounded with discordant outcries.[3] The naked multitude, on, under, and around the scaffold, were flinging the remains of their dead, discharged from their envelopments of skins, pell-mell into the pit, where Brébeuf discerned men who, as the ghastly shower fell around them, arranged the bones in their places with long poles. All was soon over; earth, logs, and stones were cast upon the

---

[1] In some of these graves, recently discovered, five or six large copper kettles have been found, in a position corresponding with the account of Brébeuf. In one, there were no less than twenty-six kettles.

[2] "Iamais rien ne m'a mieux figuré la confusion qui est parmy les damnez. Vous eussiez veu décharger de tous costez des corps à demy pourris, et de tous costez on entendoit vn horrible tintamarre de voix confuses de personnes qui parloient et ne s'entendoient pas."—Brébeuf, *Relation des Hurons, 1636*, 135.

[3] "Approchans, nous vismes tout à fait une image de l'Enfer: cette grande place estoit toute remplie de feux & de flammes, & l'air retentissoit de toutes parts des voix confuses de ces Barbares," etc.—Brébeuf, *Relation des Hurons, 1636*, 209 (Cramoisy).

grave, and the clamor subsided into a funereal chant,—so dreary and lugubrious, that it seemed to the Jesuits the wail of despairing souls from the abyss of perdition.[1]

Such was the origin of one of those strange sepulchres

[1] "Se mirent à chanter, mais d'un ton si lamentable & si lugubre, qu'il nous representoit l'horrible tristesse & l'abysme du desespoir dans lequel sont plongées pour iamais ces âmes malheureuses."—*Ibid.*, 210.

For other descriptions of these rites, see Charlevoix, Bressani, Du Creux, and especially Lafitau, in whose work they are illustrated with engravings. In one form or another, they were widely prevalent. Bartram found them among the Floridian tribes. Traces of a similar practice have been observed in recent times among the Dacotahs. Remains of places of sepulture, evidently of kindred origin, have been found in Tennessee, Missouri, Kentucky, and Ohio. Many have been discovered in several parts of New York, especially near the River Niagara. (See Squier, *Aboriginal Monuments of New York.*) This was the eastern extremity of the ancient territory of the Neuters. One of these deposits is said to have contained the bones of several thousand individuals. There is a large mound on Tonawanda Island, said by the modern Senecas to be a Neuter burial-place. (See Marshall, *Historical Sketches of the Niagara Frontier,* 8.) In Canada West, they are found throughout the region once occupied by the Neuters, and are frequent in the Huron district.

Dr. Taché writes to me,—"I have inspected sixteen *bone-pits,*" (in the Huron country,) "the situation of which is indicated on the little pencil map I send you. They contain from six hundred to twelve hundred skeletons each, of both sexes and all ages, all mixed together *purposely.* With one exception, these pits also contain pipes of stone or clay, small earthen pots, shells, and wampum wrought of these shells, copper ornaments, beads of glass, and other trinkets. Some pits contained articles of copper of *aboriginal Mexican fabric.*"

This remarkable fact, together with the frequent occurrence in these graves of large conch-shells, of which wampum was made, and which could have been procured only from the Gulf of Mexico, or some part of the southern coast of the United States, proves the extent of the relations of traffic by which certain articles were passed from tribe to tribe over a vast region. The transmission of pipes from the famous Red Pipe-Stone Quarry of the St. Peter's to tribes more than a thousand miles distant is an analogous modern instance, though much less remarkable.

The Taché Museum, at the Laval University of Quebec, contains a large collection of remains from these graves. In one instance, the human bones are of a size that may be called gigantic.

In nearly every case, the Huron graves contain articles of use or ornament of European workmanship. From this it may be inferred, that the nation itself, or its practice of inhumation, does not date back to a period long before the arrival of the French.

The Northern Algonquins had also a solemn Feast of the Dead; but it was widely different from that of the Hurons.—See the very curious account of it by Lalemant, *Relation des Hurons, 1642,* 94, 95.

which are the wonder and perplexity of the modern settler in the abandoned forests of the Hurons.

The priests were soon to witness another and a more terrible rite, yet one in which they found a consolation, since it signalized the saving of a soul,—the snatching from perdition of one of that dreaded race, into whose very midst they hoped, with devoted daring, to bear hereafter the cross of salvation. A band of Huron warriors had surprised a small party of Iroquois, killed several, and captured the rest. One of the prisoners was led in triumph to a village where the priests then were. He had suffered greatly; his hands, especially, were frightfully lacerated. Now, however, he was received with every mark of kindness. "Take courage," said a chief, addressing him; "you are among friends." The best food was prepared for him, and his captors vied with each other in offices of good-will.[1] He had been given, according to Indian custom, to a warrior who had lost a near relative in battle, and the captive was supposed to be adopted in place of the slain. His actual doom was, however, not for a moment in doubt. The Huron received him affectionately, and, having seated him in his lodge, addressed him in a tone of extreme kindness. "My nephew, when I heard that you were coming, I was very glad, thinking that you would remain with me to take the place of him I have lost. But now that I see your condition, and your hands crushed and torn so that you will never use them, I change my mind. Therefore take courage, and prepare to die tonight like a brave man."

The prisoner coolly asked what should be the manner of his death.

"By fire," was the reply.

"It is well," returned the Iroquois.

Meanwhile, the sister of the slain Huron, in whose place the prisoner was to have been adopted, brought him a dish of food, and, her eyes flowing with tears, placed it before him with an air of the utmost tenderness; while, at the same time, the warrior brought him a pipe, wiped the sweat from his brow, and fanned him with a fan of feathers.

About noon he gave his farewell feast, after the custom of

[1] This pretended kindness in the treatment of a prisoner destined to the torture was not exceptional. The Hurons sometimes even supplied their intended victim with a temporary wife.

those who knew themselves to be at the point of death. All were welcome to this strange banquet; and when the company were gathered, the host addressed them in a loud, firm voice: "My brothers, I am about to die. Do your worst to me. I do not fear torture or death." Some of those present seemed to have visitings of real compassion; and a woman asked the priests if it would be wrong to kill him, and thus save him from the fire.

The Jesuits had from the first lost no opportunity of accosting him; while he, grateful for a genuine kindness amid the cruel hypocrisy that surrounded him, gave them an attentive ear, till at length, satisfied with his answers, they baptized him. His eternal bliss secure, all else was as nothing; and they awaited the issue with some degree of composure.

A crowd had gathered from all the surrounding towns, and after nightfall the presiding chief harangued them, exhorting them to act their parts well in the approaching sacrifice, since they would be looked upon by the Sun and the God of War.[1] It is needless to dwell on the scene that ensued. It took place in the lodge of the great war-chief, Atsan. Eleven fires blazed on the ground, along the middle of this capacious dwelling. The platforms on each side were closely packed with spectators; and, betwixt these and the fires, the younger warriors stood in lines, each bearing lighted pine-knots or rolls of birch-bark. The heat, the smoke, the glare of flames, the wild yells, contorted visages, and furious gestures of these human devils, as their victim, goaded by their torches, bounded through the fires again and again, from end to end of the house, transfixed the priests with horror. But when, as day dawned, the last spark of life had fled, they consoled themselves with the faith that the tortured wretch had found his rest at last in Paradise.[2]

[1] Areskoui (see Introduction). He was often regarded as identical with the Sun. The semi-sacrificial character of the torture in this case is also shown by the injunction, "que pour ceste nuict on n'allast point folastrer dans les bois."—Le Mercier, *Relation des Hurons, 1637*, 114.

[2] Le Mercier's long and minute account of the torture of this prisoner is too revolting to be dwelt upon. One of the most atrocious features of the scene was the alternation of raillery and ironical compliment which attended it throughout, as well as the pains taken to preserve life and consciousness in the victim as long as possible. Portions of his flesh were afterwards devoured.

Chapter VIII

1636, 1637

THE HURON AND THE JESUIT

Enthusiasm for the Mission • Sickness of the Priests • The Pest among the Hurons • The Jesuit on his Rounds • Efforts at Conversion • Priests and Sorcerers • The Man-Devil • The Magician's Prescription • Indian Doctors and Patients • Covert Baptisms • Self-Devotion of the Jesuits

---

MEANWHILE from Old France to New came succors and reinforcements to the missions of the forest. More Jesuits crossed the sea to urge on the work of conversion. These were no stern exiles, seeking on barbarous shores an asylum for a persecuted faith. Rank, wealth, power, and royalty itself, smiled on their enterprise, and bade them God-speed. Yet, withal, a fervor more intense, a self-abnegation more complete, a self-devotion more constant and enduring, will scarcely find its record on the page of human history.

Holy Mother Church, linked in sordid wedlock to governments and thrones, numbered among her servants a host of the worldly and the proud, whose service of God was but the service of themselves,—and many, too, who, in the sophistry of the human heart, thought themselves true soldiers of Heaven, while earthly pride, interest, and passion were the life-springs of their zeal. This mighty Church of Rome, in her imposing march along the high road of history, heralded as infallible and divine, astounds the gazing world with prodigies of contradiction: now the protector of the oppressed, now the right arm of tyrants; now breathing charity and love, now dark with the passions of Hell; now beaming with celestial truth, now masked in hypocrisy and lies; now a virgin, now a harlot; an imperial queen, and a tinselled actress. Clearly, she is of earth, not of heaven; and her transcendently dramatic life is a type of the good and ill, the baseness and nobleness, the foulness and purity, the love and hate, the pride, passion, truth, falsehood, fierceness, and tenderness, that battle in the restless heart of man.

It was her nobler and purer part that gave life to the early missions of New France. That gloomy wilderness, those hordes of savages, had nothing to tempt the ambitious, the proud, the grasping, or the indolent. Obscure toil, solitude, privation, hardship, and death were to be the missionary's portion. He who set sail for the country of the Hurons left behind him the world and all its prizes. True, he acted under orders,—obedient, like a soldier, to the word of command: but the astute Society of Jesus knew its members, weighed each in the balance, gave each his fitting task; and when the word was passed to embark for New France, it was but the response to a secret longing of the fervent heart. The letters of these priests, departing for the scene of their labors, breathe a spirit of enthusiastic exaltation, which, to a colder nature and a colder faith, may sometimes seem overstrained, but which is in no way disproportionate to the vastness of the effort and the sacrifice demanded of them.[1]

All turned with longing eyes towards the mission of the Hurons; for here the largest harvest promised to repay their labor, and here hardships and dangers most abounded. Two Jesuits, Pijart and Le Mercier, had been sent thither in 1635;

[1] The following are passages from letters of missionaries at this time. See "Divers Sentimens," appended to the *Relation* of 1635.

"On dit que les premiers qui fondent les Eglises d'ordinaire sont saincts: cette pensée m'attendrit si fort le cœur, que quoy que ie me voye icy fort inutile dans ceste fortunée Nouuelle France, si faut-il que i'auoüe que ie ne me sçaurois defendre d'vne pensée qui me presse le cœur: *Cupio impendi, et superimpendi pro vobis*, Pauure Nouuelle France, ie desire me sacrifier pour ton bien, et quand il me deuroit couster mille vies, moyennant que ie puisse aider à sauuer vne seule âme, ie seray trop heureux, et ma vie tres bien employée."

"Ma consolation parmy les Hurons, c'est que tous les iours ie me confesse, et puis ie dis la Messe, comme si ie deuois prendre le Viatique et mourir ce iour là, et ie ne crois pas qu'on puisse mieux viure, ny auec plus de satisfaction et de courage, et mesme de merites, que viure en un lieu, où on pense pouuoir mourir tous les iours, et auoir la deuise de S. Paul, *Quotidie morior, fratres*, etc. mes freres, je fais estat de mourir tous les iours."

"Qui ne void la Nouuelle France que par les yeux de chair et de nature, il n'y void que des bois et des croix; mais qui les considere auec les yeux de la grace et d'vne bonne vocation, il n'y void que Dieu, les vertus et les graces, et on y trouue tant et de si solides consolations, que si ie pouuois acheter la Nouuelle France, en donnant tout le Paradis Terrestre, certainement ie l'acheterois. Mon Dieu, qu'il fait bon estre au lieu où Dieu nous a mis de sa grace! veritablement i'ay trouué icy ce que i'auois esperé, vn cœur selon le cœur de Dieu, qui ne cherche que Dieu."

and in midsummer of the next year three more arrived,—
Jogues, Chatelain, and Garnier. When, after their long and
lonely journey, they reached Ihonatiria one by one, they were
received by their brethren with scanty fare indeed, but with a
fervor of affectionate welcome which more than made
amends; for among these priests, united in a community of
faith and enthusiasm, there was far more than the genial com-
radeship of men joined in a common enterprise of self-devotion and peril.[1] On their way, they had met Daniel and
Davost descending to Quebec, to establish there a seminary
of Huron children,—a project long cherished by Brébeuf and
his companions.

Scarcely had the new-comers arrived, when they were attacked by a contagious fever, which turned their mission-
house into a hospital. Jogues, Garnier, and Chatelain fell ill
in turn; and two of their domestics also were soon prostrated,
though the only one of the number who could hunt fortunately escaped. Those who remained in health attended the
sick, and the sufferers vied with each other in efforts often
beyond their strength to relieve their companions in misfortune.[2] The disease in no case proved fatal; but scarcely had
health begun to return to their household, when an unfore-
seen calamity demanded the exertion of all their energies.

The pestilence, which for two years past had from time to
time visited the Huron towns, now returned with tenfold
violence, and with it soon appeared a new and fearful
scourge,—the small-pox. Terror was universal. The contagion increased as autumn advanced; and when winter came,
far from ceasing, as the priests had hoped, its ravages were
appalling. The season of Huron festivity was turned to a season of mourning; and such was the despondency and dismay,
that suicide became frequent. The Jesuits, singly or in pairs,

[1] "Ie luy preparay de ce que nous auions, pour le receuoir, mais quel festin!
vne poignée de petit poisson sec auec vn peu de farine; i'enuoyay chercher
quelques nouueaux espics, que nous luy fismes rostir à la façon du pays; mais
il est vray que dans son cœur et à l'entendre, il ne fit iamais meilleure chere.
La ioye qui se ressent à ces entreueuës semble estre quelque image du con-
tentement des bien-heureux à leur arriuée dans le Ciel, tant elle est pleine de
suauité."—Le Mercier, *Relation des Hurons, 1637*, 106.

[2] *Lettre de Brébeuf au T. R. P. Mutio Vitelleschi, 20 Mai, 1637*, in Carayon,
157. Le Mercier, *Relation des Hurons, 1637*, 120, 123.

journeyed in the depth of winter from village to village, ministering to the sick, and seeking to commend their religious teachings by their efforts to relieve bodily distress. Happily, perhaps, for their patients, they had no medicine but a little senna. A few raisins were left, however; and one or two of these, with a spoonful of sweetened water, were always eagerly accepted by the sufferers, who thought them endowed with some mysterious and sovereign efficacy. No house was left unvisited. As the missionary, physician at once to body and soul, entered one of these smoky dens, he saw the inmates, their heads muffled in their robes of skins, seated around the fires in silent dejection. Everywhere was heard the wail of sick and dying children; and on or under the platforms at the sides of the house crouched squalid men and women, in all the stages of the distemper. The Father approached, made inquiries, spoke words of kindness, administered his harmless remedies, or offered a bowl of broth made from game brought in by the Frenchman who hunted for the mission.[1] The body cared for, he next addressed himself to the soul. "This life is short, and very miserable. It matters little whether we live or die." The patient remained silent, or grumbled his dissent. The Jesuit, after enlarging for a time, in broken Huron, on the brevity and nothingness of mortal weal or woe, passed next to the joys of Heaven and the pains of Hell, which he set forth with his best rhetoric. His pictures of infernal fires and torturing devils were readily comprehended, if the listener had consciousness enough to comprehend anything; but with respect to the advantages of the French Paradise, he was slow of conviction. "I wish to go where my relations and ancestors have gone," was a common reply. "Heaven is a good place for Frenchmen," said another; "but I wish to be among Indians, for the French will give me nothing to eat when I get there."[2] Often the patient was stol-

[1] Game was so scarce in the Huron country, that it was greatly prized as a luxury. Le Mercier speaks of an Indian, sixty years of age, who walked twelve miles to taste the wild-fowl killed by the French hunter. The ordinary food was corn, beans, pumpkins, and fish.

[2] It was scarcely possible to convince the Indians, that there was but one God for themselves and the whites. The proposition was met by such arguments as this: "If we had been of one father, we should know how to make knives and coats as well as you."—Le Mercier, *Relation des Hurons, 1637*, 147.

idly silent; sometimes he was hopelessly perverse and contradictory. Again, Nature triumphed over Grace. "Which will
you choose," demanded the priest of a dying woman,
"Heaven or Hell?" "Hell, if my children are there, as you
say," returned the mother. "Do they hunt in Heaven, or make
war, or go to feasts?" asked an anxious inquirer. "Oh, no!"
replied the Father. "Then," returned the querist, "I will not
go. It is not good to be lazy." But above all other obstacles
was the dread of starvation in the regions of the blest. Nor,
when the dying Indian had been induced at last to express a
desire for Paradise, was it an easy matter to bring him to a
due contrition for his sins; for he would deny with indignation that he had ever committed any. When at length, as
sometimes happened, all these difficulties gave way, and the
patient had been brought to what seemed to his instructor a
fitting frame for baptism, the priest, with contentment at his
heart, brought water in a cup or in the hollow of his hand,
touched his forehead with the mystic drop, and snatched him
from an eternity of woe. But the convert, even after his baptism, did not always manifest a satisfactory spiritual condition. "Why did you baptize that Iroquois?" asked one of the
dying neophytes, speaking of the prisoner recently tortured;
"he will get to Heaven before us, and, when he sees us coming, he will drive us out."[1]

Thus did these worthy priests, too conscientious to let
these unfortunates die in peace, follow them with benevolent
persecutions to the hour of their death.

It was clear to the Fathers, that their ministrations were
valued solely because their religion was supposed by many to
be a "medicine," or charm, efficacious against famine, disease,
and death. They themselves, indeed, firmly believed that
saints and angels were always at hand with temporal succors
for the faithful. At their intercession, St. Joseph had interposed to procure a happy delivery to a squaw in protracted
pains of childbirth;[2] and they never doubted, that, in the hour
of need, the celestial powers would confound the unbeliever

[1] Most of the above traits are drawn from Le Mercier's report of 1637. The
rest are from Brébeuf.

[2] Brébeuf, *Relation des Hurons, 1636*, 89. Another woman was delivered on
touching a relic of St. Ignatius. *Ibid.*, 90.

with intervention direct and manifest. At the town of Wenrio, the people, after trying in vain all the feasts, dances, and preposterous ceremonies by which their medicine-men sought to stop the pest, resolved to essay the "medicine" of the French, and, to that end, called the priests to a council. "What must we do, that your God may take pity on us?" Brébeuf's answer was uncompromising:—

"Believe in Him; keep His commandments; abjure your faith in dreams; take but one wife, and be true to her; give up your superstitious feasts; renounce your assemblies of debauchery; eat no human flesh; never give feasts to demons; and make a vow, that, if God will deliver you from this pest, you will build a chapel to offer Him thanksgiving and praise."[1]

The terms were too hard. They would fain bargain to be let off with building the chapel alone; but Brébeuf would bate them nothing, and the council broke up in despair.

At Ossossané, a few miles distant, the people, in a frenzy of terror, accepted the conditions, and promised to renounce their superstitions and reform their manners. It was a labor of Hercules, a cleansing of Augean stables; but the scared savages were ready to make any promise that might stay the pestilence. One of their principal sorcerers proclaimed in a loud voice through the streets of the town, that the God of the French was their master, and that thenceforth all must live according to His will. "What consolation," exclaims Le Mercier, "to see God glorified by the lips of an imp of Satan!"[2]

Their joy was short. The proclamation was on the twelfth of December. On the twenty-first, a noted sorcerer came to Ossossané. He was of a dwarfish, hump-backed figure,— most rare among this symmetrical people,—with a vicious face, and a dress consisting of a torn and shabby robe of beaver-skin. Scarcely had he arrived, when, with ten or twelve other savages, he ensconced himself in a kennel of bark made for the occasion. In the midst were placed several stones, heated red-hot. On these the sorcerer threw tobacco, producing a stifling fumigation; in the midst of which, for a full half-hour, he sang, at the top of his throat, those boastful, yet

[1] Le Mercier, *Relation des Hurons, 1637*, 114, 116 (Cramoisy).
[2] *Ibid.*, 127, 128 (Cramoisy).

meaningless, rhapsodies of which Indian magical songs are composed. Then came a grand "medicine-feast"; and the disappointed Jesuits saw plainly that the objects of their spiritual care, unwilling to throw away any chance of cure, were bent on invoking aid from God and the Devil at once.

The hump-backed sorcerer became a thorn in the side of the Fathers, who more than half believed his own account of his origin. He was, he said, not a man, but an *oki*,—a spirit, or, as the priests rendered it, a demon,—and had dwelt with other *okies* under the earth, when the whim seized him to become a man. Therefore he ascended to the upper world, in company with a female spirit. They hid beside a path, and, when they saw a woman passing, they entered her womb. After a time they were born, but not until the male *oki* had quarrelled with and strangled his female companion, who came dead into the world.[1] The character of the sorcerer seems to have comported reasonably well with this story of his origin. He pretended to have an absolute control over the pestilence, and his prescriptions were scrupulously followed.

He had several conspicuous rivals, besides a host of humbler competitors. One of these magician-doctors, who was nearly blind, made for himself a kennel at the end of his house, where he fasted for seven days.[2] On the sixth day the spirits appeared, and, among other revelations, told him that the disease could be frightened away by means of images of straw, like scarecrows, placed on the tops of the houses. Within forty-eight hours after this announcement, the roofs of Onnentisati and the neighboring villages were covered with an army of these effigies. The Indians tried to persuade the Jesuits to put them on the mission-house; but the priests replied, that the cross before their door was a better protector; and, for further security, they set another on their roof, declaring that they would rely on it to save them from infection.[3] The Indians, on their part, anxious that their scare-

---

[1] Le Mercier, *Relation des Hurons*, 1637, 72 (Cramoisy). This "petit sorcier" is often mentioned elsewhere.

[2] See Introduction.

[3] "Qu'en vertu de ce signe nous ne redoutions point les demons, et esperions que Dieu preserueroit nostre petite maison de cette maladie contagieuse."—Le Mercier, *Relation des Hurons, 1637*, 150.

crows should do their office well, addressed them in loud harangues and burned offerings of tobacco to them.[1]

There was another sorcerer, whose medical practice was so extensive, that, unable to attend to all his patients, he sent substitutes to the surrounding towns, first imparting to them his own mysterious power. One of these deputies came to Ossossané while the priests were there. The principal house was thronged with expectant savages, anxiously waiting his arrival. A chief carried before him a kettle of mystic water, with which the envoy sprinkled the company,[2] at the same time fanning them with the wing of a wild turkey. Then came a grand medicine-feast, followed by a medicine-dance of women.

Opinion was divided as to the nature of the pest; but the greater number were agreed that it was a malignant *oki*, who came from Lake Huron.[3] As it was of the last moment to conciliate or frighten him, no means to these ends were neglected. Feasts were held for him, at which, to do him honor, each guest gorged himself like a vulture. A mystic fraternity danced with firebrands in their mouths; while other dancers wore masks, and pretended to be hump-backed. Tobacco was burned to the Demon of the Pest, no less than to the scarecrows which were to frighten him. A chief climbed to the roof of a house, and shouted to the invisible monster, "If you want flesh, go to our enemies, go to the Iroquois!"—while, to add terror to persuasion, the crowd in the dwelling below yelled with all the force of their lungs, and beat furiously with sticks on the walls of bark.

[1] *Ibid.*, 157.

[2] The idea seems to have been taken from the holy water of the French. Le Mercier says that a Huron who had been to Quebec once asked him the use of the vase of water at the door of the chapel. The priest told him that it was "to frighten away the devils." On this, he begged earnestly to have some of it.

[3] Many believed that the country was bewitched by wicked sorcerers, one of whom, it was said, had been seen at night roaming around the villages, vomiting fire. (Le Mercier, *Relation des Hurons, 1637*, 134.) This superstition of sorcerers vomiting fire was common among the Iroquois of New York.—Others held that a sister of Étienne Brulé caused the evil, in revenge for the death of her brother, murdered some years before. She was said to have been seen flying over the country, breathing forth pestilence.

Besides these public efforts to stay the pestilence, the sufferers, each for himself, had their own methods of cure, dictated by dreams or prescribed by established usage. Thus two of the priests, entering a house, saw a sick man crouched in a corner, while near him sat three friends. Before each of these was placed a huge portion of food,—enough, the witness declares, for four,—and though all were gorged to suffocation, with starting eyeballs and distended veins, they still held staunchly to their task, resolved at all costs to devour the whole, in order to cure the patient, who meanwhile ceased not, in feeble tones, to praise their exertions, and implore them to persevere.[1]

Turning from these eccentricities of the "noble savage"[2] to the zealots who were toiling, according to their light, to snatch him from the clutch of Satan, we see the irrepressible Jesuits roaming from town to town in restless quest of subjects for baptism. In the case of adults, they thought some little preparation essential; but their efforts to this end, even with the aid of St. Joseph, whom they constantly invoked,[3] were not always successful; and, cheaply as they offered salvation, they sometimes failed to find a purchaser. With infants, however, a simple drop of water sufficed for the transfer from a prospective Hell to an assured Paradise. The Indians,

---

[1] "En fin il leur fallut rendre gorge, ce qu'ils firent à diuerses reprises, ne laissants pas pour cela de continuer à vuider leur plat."—Le Mercier, *Relation des Hurons, 1637,* 142.—This beastly superstition exists in some tribes at the present day. A kindred superstition once fell under the writer's notice, in the case of a wounded Indian, who begged of every one he met to drink a large bowl of water, in order that he, the Indian, might be cured.

[2] In the midst of these absurdities we find recorded one of the best traits of the Indian character. At Ihonatiria, a house occupied by a family of orphan children was burned to the ground, leaving the inmates destitute. The villagers united to aid them. Each contributed something, and they were soon better provided for than before.

[3] "C'est nostre refuge ordinaire en semblables necessitez, et d'ordinaire auec tels succez, que nous auons sujet d'en benir Dieu à iamais, qui nous fait cognoistre en cette barbarie le credit de ce S. Patriarche aupres de son infinie misericorde."—*Ibid.,* 153.—In the case of a woman at Onnentisati, "Dieu nous inspira de luy voüer quelques Messes en l'honneur de S. Joseph." The effect was prompt. In half an hour the woman was ready for baptism. On the same page we have another subject secured to Heaven, "sans doute par les merites du glorieux Patriarche S. Joseph."

who at first had sought baptism as a cure, now began to regard it as a cause of death; and when the priest entered a lodge where a sick child lay in extremity, the scowling parents watched him with jealous distrust, lest unawares the deadly drop should be applied. The Jesuits were equal to the emergency. Father Le Mercier will best tell his own story.

"On the third of May, Father Pierre Pijart baptized at Anonatea a little child two months old, in manifest danger of death, without being seen by the parents, who would not give their consent. This is the device which he used. Our sugar does wonders for us. He pretended to make the child drink a little sugared water, and at the same time dipped a finger in it. As the father of the infant began to suspect something, and called out to him not to baptize it, he gave the spoon to a woman who was near, and said to her, 'Give it to him yourself.' She approached and found the child asleep; and at the same time Father Pijart, under pretence of seeing if he was really asleep, touched his face with his wet finger, and baptized him. At the end of forty-eight hours he went to Heaven.

"Some days before, the missionary had used the same device (*industrie*) for baptizing a little boy six or seven years old. His father, who was very sick, had several times refused to receive baptism; and when asked if he would not be glad to have his son baptized, he had answered, *No*. 'At least,' said Father Pijart, 'you will not object to my giving him a little sugar.' 'No; but you must not baptize him.' The missionary gave it to him once; then again; and at the third spoonful, before he had put the sugar into the water, he let a drop of it fall on the child, at the same time pronouncing the sacramental words. A little girl, who was looking at him, cried out, 'Father, he is baptizing him!' The child's father was much disturbed; but the missionary said to him, 'Did you not see that I was giving him sugar?' The child died soon after; but God showed His grace to the father, who is now in perfect health."[1]

That equivocal morality, lashed by the withering satire of Pascal,—a morality built on the doctrine that all means are

[1] Le Mercier, *Relation des Hurons, 1637*, 165. Various other cases of the kind are mentioned in the *Relations*.

permissible for saving souls from perdition, and that sin itself is no sin when its object is the "greater glory of God,"—found far less scope in the rude wilderness of the Hurons than among the interests, ambitions, and passions of civilized life. Nor were these men, chosen from the purest of their Order, personally well fitted to illustrate the capabilities of this elastic system. Yet now and then, by the light of their own writings, we may observe that the teachings of the school of Loyola had not been wholly without effect in the formation of their ethics.

But when we see them, in the gloomy February of 1637, and the gloomier months that followed, toiling on foot from one infected town to another, wading through the sodden snow, under the bare and dripping forests, drenched with incessant rains, till they descried at length through the storm the clustered dwellings of some barbarous hamlet,—when we see them entering, one after another, these wretched abodes of misery and darkness, and all for one sole end, the baptism of the sick and dying, we may smile at the futility of the object, but we must needs admire the self-sacrificing zeal with which it was pursued.

Chapter IX

1637

CHARACTER OF THE CANADIAN JESUITS

Jean de Brébeuf • Charles Garnier • Joseph Marie Chaumonot •
Noël Chabanel • Isaac Jogues • Other Jesuits • Nature of their
Faith • Supernaturalism • Visions • Miracles

BEFORE pursuing farther these obscure, but noteworthy, scenes in the drama of human history, it will be well to indicate, so far as there are means of doing so, the distinctive traits of some of the chief actors. Mention has often been made of Brébeuf,—that masculine apostle of the Faith,—the Ajax of the mission. Nature had given him all the passions of a vigorous manhood, and religion had crushed them, curbed them, or tamed them to do her work,—like a dammed-up torrent, sluiced and guided to grind and saw and weave for the good of man. Beside him, in strange contrast, stands his co-laborer, Charles Garnier. Both were of noble birth and gentle nurture; but here the parallel ends. Garnier's face was beardless, though he was above thirty years old. For this he was laughed at by his friends in Paris, but admired by the Indians, who thought him handsome.[1] His constitution, bodily or mental, was by no means robust. From boyhood, he had shown a delicate and sensitive nature, a tender conscience, and a proneness to religious emotion. He had never gone with his schoolmates to inns and other places of amusement, but kept his pocket-money to give to beggars. One of his brothers relates of him, that, seeing an obscene book, he bought and destroyed it, lest other boys should be injured by it. He had always wished to be a Jesuit, and, after a novitiate which is described as most edifying, he became a professed member of the Order. The Church, indeed, absorbed the greater part, if not the whole, of this pious family,—one brother being a Carmelite, another a Capuchin, and a third a Jesuit, while there seems also to have been a fourth under

---

[1] "C'est pourquoi j'ai bien gagne à quitter la France, où vous me fesiez la guerre de n'avoir point de barbe; car c'est ce qui me fait estimer beau des Sauvages."— *Lettres de Garnier*, MSS.

vows. Of Charles Garnier there remain twenty-four letters, written at various times to his father and two of his brothers, chiefly during his missionary life among the Hurons. They breathe the deepest and most intense Roman Catholic piety, and a spirit enthusiastic, yet sad, as of one renouncing all the hopes and prizes of the world, and living for Heaven alone. The affections of his sensitive nature, severed from earthly objects, found relief in an ardent adoration of the Virgin Mary. With none of the bone and sinew of rugged manhood, he entered, not only without hesitation, but with eagerness, on a life which would have tried the boldest; and, sustained by the spirit within him, he was more than equal to it. His fellow-missionaries thought him a saint; and had he lived a century or two earlier, he would perhaps have been canonized: yet, while all his life was a willing martyrdom, one can discern, amid his admirable virtues, some slight lingerings of mortal vanity. Thus, in three several letters, he speaks of his great success in baptizing, and plainly intimates that he had sent more souls to Heaven than the other Jesuits.[1]

Next appears a young man of about twenty-seven years, Joseph Marie Chaumonot. Unlike Brébeuf and Garnier, he was of humble origin,—his father being a vine-dresser, and his mother the daughter of a poor village schoolmaster. At an early age they sent him to Châtillon on the Seine, where he lived with his uncle, a priest, who taught him to speak Latin, and awakened his religious susceptibilities, which were naturally strong. This did not prevent him from yielding to the persuasions of one of his companions to run off to Beaune, a town of Burgundy, where the fugitives proposed to study music under the Fathers of the Oratory. To provide funds for

[1] The above sketch of Garnier is drawn from various sources. *Observations du P. Henri de St. Joseph, Carme, sur son Frère le P. Charles Garnier*, MS.— *Abrégé de la Vie du R. Père Charles Garnier*, MS. This unpublished sketch bears the signature of the Jesuit Ragueneau, with the date 1652. For the opportunity of consulting it I am indebted to Rev. Felix Martin, S. J.—*Lettres du P. Charles Garnier*, MSS. These embrace his correspondence from the Huron country, and are exceedingly characteristic and striking. There is another letter in Carayon, *Première Mission*.—Garnier's family was wealthy, as well as noble. Its members seem to have been strongly attached to each other, and the young priest's father was greatly distressed at his departure for Canada.

the journey, he stole a sum of about the value of a dollar from his uncle, the priest. This act, which seems to have been a mere peccadillo of boyish levity, determined his future career. Finding himself in total destitution at Beaune, he wrote to his mother for money, and received in reply an order from his father to come home. Stung with the thought of being posted as a thief in his native village, he resolved not to do so, but to set out forthwith on a pilgrimage to Rome; and accordingly, tattered and penniless, he took the road for the sacred city. Soon a conflict began within him between his misery and the pride which forbade him to beg. The pride was forced to succumb. He begged from door to door; slept under sheds by the wayside, or in haystacks; and now and then found lodging and a meal at a convent. Thus, sometimes alone, sometimes with vagabonds whom he met on the road, he made his way through Savoy and Lombardy in a pitiable condition of destitution, filth, and disease. At length he reached Ancona, when the thought occurred to him of visiting the Holy House of Loretto, and imploring the succor of the Virgin Mary. Nor were his hopes disappointed. He had reached that renowned shrine, knelt, paid his devotions, and offered his prayer, when, as he issued from the door of the chapel, he was accosted by a young man, whom he conjectures to have been an angel descended to his relief, and who was probably some penitent or devotee bent on works of charity or self-mortification. With a voice of the greatest kindness, he proffered his aid to the wretched boy, whose appearance was alike fitted to awaken pity and disgust. The conquering of a natural repugnance to filth, in the interest of charity and humility, is a conspicuous virtue in most of the Roman Catholic saints; and whatever merit may attach to it was acquired in an extraordinary degree by the young man in question. Apparently, he was a physician; for he not only restored the miserable wanderer to a condition of comparative decency, but cured him of a grievous malady, the result of neglect. Chaumonot went on his way, thankful to his benefactor, and overflowing with an enthusiasm of gratitude to Our Lady of Loretto.[1]

[1] "Si la moindre dame m'avoit fait rendre ce service par le dernier de ses valets, n'aurois-je pas dus lui en rendre toutes les reconnoissances possibles?

As he journeyed towards Rome, an old burgher, at whose door he had begged, employed him as a servant. He soon became known to a Jesuit, to whom he had confessed himself in Latin; and as his acquirements were considerable for his years, he was eventually employed as teacher of a low class in one of the Jesuit schools. Nature had inclined him to a life of devotion. He would fain be a hermit, and, to that end, practised eating green ears of wheat; but, finding he could not swallow them, conceived that he had mistaken his vocation. Then a strong desire grew up within him to become a Récollet, a Capuchin, or, above all, a Jesuit; and at length the wish of his heart was answered. At the age of twenty-one, he was admitted to the Jesuit novitiate.[1] Soon after its close, a small duodecimo volume was placed in his hands. It was a *Relation* of the Canadian mission, and contained one of those narratives of Brébeuf which have been often cited in the preceding

---

Et si après une telle charité elle s'étoit offerte à me servir toujours de mesme, comment aurois-je dû l'honorer, lui obéir, l'aimer toute ma vie! Pardon, Reine des Anges et des hommes! pardon de ce qu'après avoir reçu de vous tant de marques, par lesquelles vous m'avez convaincu que vous m'avez adopté pour votre fils, j'ai eu l'ingratitude pendant des années entières de me comporter encore plutôt en esclave de Satan qu'en enfant d'une Mère Vierge. O que vous êtes bonne et charitable! puisque quelques obstacles que mes péchés ayent pu mettre à vos graces, vous n'avez jamais cessé de m'attirer au bien; jusque là que vous m'avez fait admettre dans la Sainte Compagnie de Jésus, votre fils."—Chaumonot, *Vie*, 20. The above is from the very curious autobiography written by Chaumonot, at the command of his Superior, in 1688. The original manuscript is at the Hôtel Dieu of Quebec. Mr. Shea has printed it.

[1] His age, when he left his uncle, the priest, is not mentioned. But he must have been a mere child; for, at the end of his novitiate, he had forgotten his native language, and was forced to learn it a second time.

"Jamais y eut-il homme sur terre plus obligé que moi à la Sainte Famille de Jésus, de Marie et de Joseph! Marie en me guérissant de ma vilaine galle ou teigne, me délivra d'une infinité de peines et d'incommodités corporelles, que cette hideuse maladie qui me rongeoit m'avoit causé. Joseph m'ayant obtenu la grace d'être incorporé à un corps aussi saint qu'est celui des Jésuites, m'a preservé d'une infinité de misères spirituelles, de tentations très dangereuses et de péchés très énormes. Jésus n'ayant pas permis que j'entrasse dans aucun autre ordre qu'en celui qu'il honore tout à la fois de son beau nom, de sa douce présence et de sa protection spéciale. O Jésus! O Marie! O Joseph! qui méritoit moins que moi vos divines faveurs, et envers qui avez vous été plus prodigue?"—Chaumonot, *Vie*, 37.

pages. Its effect was immediate. Burning to share those glorious toils, the young priest asked to be sent to Canada; and
his request was granted.

Before embarking, he set out with the Jesuit Poncet, who
was also destined for Canada, on a pilgrimage from Rome to
the shrine of Our Lady of Loretto. They journeyed on
foot, begging alms by the way. Chaumonot was soon
seized with a pain in the knee, so violent that it seemed
impossible to proceed. At San Severino, where they lodged
with the Barnabites, he bethought him of asking the intercession of a certain poor woman of that place, who had
died some time before with the reputation of sanctity. Accordingly he addressed to her his prayer, promising to
publish her fame on every possible occasion, if she would
obtain his cure from God.[1] The intercession was accepted;
the offending limb became sound again, and the two pilgrims pursued their journey. They reached Loretto, and,
kneeling before the Queen of Heaven, implored her favor and
aid; while Chaumonot, overflowing with devotion to this celestial mistress of his heart, conceived the purpose of building
in Canada a chapel to her honor, after the exact model of the
Holy House of Loretto. They soon afterwards embarked together, and arrived among the Hurons early in the autumn of
1639.

Noël Chabanel came later to the mission; for he did not
reach the Huron country until 1643. He detested the Indian
life,—the smoke, the vermin, the filthy food, the impossibility of privacy. He could not study by the smoky lodge-fire,
among the noisy crowd of men and squaws, with their dogs,
and their restless, screeching children. He had a natural inap-
titude to learning the language, and labored at it for five years
with scarcely a sign of progress. The Devil whispered a suggestion into his ear: Let him procure his release from these
barren and revolting toils, and return to France, where congenial and useful employments awaited him. Chabanel refused to listen; and when the temptation still beset him, he

[1] "Je me recommandai à elle en lui promettant de la faire connoître dans
toutes les occasions que j'en aurois jamais, si elle m'obtenoit de Dieu ma
guérison."—Chaumonot, *Vie*, 46.

bound himself by a solemn vow to remain in Canada to the day of his death.[1]

Isaac Jogues was of a character not unlike Garnier. Nature had given him no especial force of intellect or constitutional energy, yet the man was indomitable and irrepressible, as his history will show. We have but few means of characterizing the remaining priests of the mission otherwise than as their traits appear on the field of their labors. Theirs was no faith of abstractions and generalities. For them, heaven was very near to earth, touching and mingling with it at many points. On high, God the Father sat enthroned; and, nearer to human sympathies, Divinity incarnate in the Son, with the benign form of his immaculate mother, and her spouse, St. Joseph, the chosen patron of New France. Interceding saints and departed friends bore to the throne of grace the petitions of those yet lingering in mortal bondage, and formed an ascending chain from earth to heaven.

These priests lived in an atmosphere of supernaturalism. Every day had its miracle. Divine power declared itself in action immediate and direct, controlling, guiding, or reversing the laws of Nature. The missionaries did not reject the ordinary cures for disease or wounds; but they relied far more on a prayer to the Virgin, a vow to St. Joseph, or the promise of a *neuvaine*, or nine days' devotion, to some other celestial personage; while the touch of a fragment of a tooth or bone of some departed saint was of sovereign efficacy to cure sickness, solace pain, or relieve a suffering squaw in the throes of childbirth. Once, Chaumonot, having a headache, remembered to have heard of a sick man who regained his health by commending his case to St. Ignatius, and at the same time putting a medal stamped with his image into his mouth. Accordingly he tried a similar experiment, putting into his mouth a medal bearing a representation of the Holy Family, which was the object of his especial devotion. The next morning found him cured.[2]

The relation between this world and the next was some-

[1] *Abrégé de la Vie du Père Noël Chabanel*, MS. This anonymous paper bears the signature of Ragueneau, in attestation of its truth. See also Ragueneau, *Relation, 1650,* 17, 18. Chabanel's vow is here given *verbatim*.

[2] Chaumonot, *Vie,* 73.

times of a nature curiously intimate. Thus, when Chaumonot heard of Garnier's death, he immediately addressed his departed colleague, and promised him the benefit of all the good works which he, Chaumonot, might perform during the next week, provided the defunct missionary would make him heir to his knowledge of the Huron tongue.[1] And he ascribed to the deceased Garnier's influence the mastery of that language which he afterwards acquired.

The efforts of the missionaries for the conversion of the savages were powerfully seconded from the other world, and the refractory subject who was deaf to human persuasions softened before the superhuman agencies which the priest invoked to his aid.[2]

It is scarcely necessary to add, that signs and voices from another world, visitations from Hell and visions from Heaven, were incidents of no rare occurrence in the lives of these ardent apostles. To Brébeuf, whose deep nature, like a furnace white hot, glowed with the still intensity of his enthusiasm, they were especially frequent. Demons in troops appeared before him, sometimes in the guise of men, sometimes as bears, wolves, or wild-cats. He called on God, and the apparitions vanished. Death, like a skeleton, sometimes menaced him, and once, as he faced it with an unquailing eye, it fell powerless at his feet. A demon, in the form of a woman, assailed him with the temptation which beset St. Benedict among the rocks of Subiaco; but Brébeuf signed the cross, and the infernal siren melted into air. He saw the vision of a vast and gorgeous palace; and a miraculous voice assured him

[1] "Je n'eus pas plutôt appris sa glorieuse mort, que je lui promis tout ce que je ferois de bien pendant huit jours, à condition qu'il me feroit son héritier dans la connoissance parfaite qu'il avoit du Huron."—Chaumonot, *Vie*, 61.

[2] As these may be supposed to be exploded ideas of the past, the writer may recall an incident of his youth, while spending a few days in the convent of the Passionists, near the Coliseum at Rome. These worthy monks, after using a variety of arguments for his conversion, expressed the hope that a miraculous interposition would be vouchsafed to that end, and that the Virgin would manifest herself to him in a nocturnal vision. To this end they gave him a small brass medal, stamped with her image, to be worn at his neck, while they were to repeat a certain number of *Aves* and *Paters*, in which he was urgently invited to join; as the result of which, it was hoped the Virgin would appear on the same night. No vision, however, occurred.

that such was to be the reward of those who dwelt in savage hovels for the cause of God. Angels appeared to him; and, more than once, St. Joseph and the Virgin were visibly present before his sight. Once, when he was among the Neutral Nation, in the winter of 1640, he beheld the ominous apparition of a great cross slowly approaching from the quarter where lay the country of the Iroquois. He told the vision to his comrades. "What was it like? How large was it?" they eagerly demanded. "Large enough," replied the priest, "to crucify us all."[1] To explain such phenomena is the province of psychology, and not of history. Their occurrence is no matter of surprise, and it would be superfluous to doubt that they were recounted in good faith, and with a full belief in their reality.

In these enthusiasts we shall find striking examples of one of the morbid forces of human nature; yet in candor let us do honor to what was genuine in them,—that principle of self-abnegation which is the life of true religion, and which is vital no less to the highest forms of heroism.

[1] *Quelques Remarques sur la Vie du Père Jean de Brébeuf*, MS. On the margin of this paper, opposite several of the statements repeated above, are the words, signed by Ragueneau, *"Ex ipsius autographo,"* indicating that the statements were made in writing by Brébeuf himself.

Still other visions are recorded by Chaumonot as occurring to Brébeuf, when they were together in the Neutral country. See also the long notice of Brébeuf, written by his colleague, Ragueneau, in the *Relation* of 1649; and Tanner, *Societas Jesu Militans*, 533.

Chapter X

PERSECUTION

Ossossané • The New Chapel • A Triumph of the Faith • The Nether Powers • Signs of a Tempest • Slanders • Rage against the Jesuits • Their Boldness and Persistency • Nocturnal Council • Danger of the Priests • Brébeuf's Letter • Narrow Escapes • Woes and Consolations

THE town of Ossossané, or Rochelle, stood, as we have seen, on the borders of Lake Huron, at the skirts of a gloomy wilderness of pine. Thither, in May, 1637, repaired Father Pijart, to found, in this, one of the largest of the Huron towns, the new mission of the Immaculate Conception.[1] The Indians had promised Brébeuf to build a house for the black-robes, and Pijart found the work in progress. There were at this time about fifty dwellings in the town, each containing eight or ten families. The quadrangular fort already alluded to had now been completed by the Indians, under the instruction of the priests.[2]

The new mission-house was about seventy feet in length. No sooner had the savage workmen secured the bark covering on its top and sides than the priests took possession, and began their preparations for a notable ceremony. At the farther end they made an altar, and hung such decorations as they had on the rough walls of bark throughout half the length of the structure. This formed their chapel. On the altar was a crucifix, with vessels and ornaments of shining metal; while above hung several pictures,—among them a painting of Christ, and another of the Virgin, both of life-size. There was also a representation of the Last Judgment, wherein dragons and serpents might be seen feasting on the entrails of the wicked, while demons scourged them into the flames of Hell.

---

[1] The doctrine of the immaculate conception of the Virgin, recently sanctioned by the Pope, has long been a favorite tenet of the Jesuits.

[2] *Lettres de Garnier*, MSS. It was of upright pickets, ten feet high, with flanking towers at two angles.

The entrance was adorned with a quantity of tinsel, together with green boughs skilfully disposed.[1]

Never before were such splendors seen in the land of the Hurons. Crowds gathered from afar, and gazed in awe and admiration at the marvels of the sanctuary. A woman came from a distant town to behold it, and, tremulous between curiosity and fear, thrust her head into the mysterious recess, declaring that she would see it, though the look should cost her life.[2]

One is forced to wonder at, if not to admire, the energy with which these priests and their scarcely less zealous attendants[3] toiled to carry their pictures and ornaments through the most arduous of journeys, where the traveller was often famished from the sheer difficulty of transporting provisions.

A great event had called forth all this preparation. Of the many baptisms achieved by the Fathers in the course of their indefatigable ministry, the subjects had all been infants, or adults at the point of death; but at length a Huron, in full health and manhood, respected and influential in his tribe, had been won over to the Faith, and was now to be baptized with solemn ceremonial, in the chapel thus gorgeously adorned. It was a strange scene. Indians were there in throngs, and the house was closely packed: warriors, old and young, glistening in grease and sunflower-oil, with uncouth locks, a trifle less coarse than a horse's mane, and faces perhaps smeared with paint in honor of the occasion; wenches in gay attire; hags muffled in a filthy discarded deer-skin, their

---

[1] "Nostre Chapelle estoit extraordinairement bien ornée, . . . nous auions dressé vn portique entortillé de feüillage, meslé d'oripeau, en vn mot nous auions estallé tout ce que vostre R. nous a enuoié de beau," etc., etc.—Le Mercier, *Relation des Hurons, 1637*, 175, 176.—In his *Relation* of the next year he recurs to the subject, and describes the pictures displayed on this memorable occasion.—*Relation des Hurons, 1638*, 33.

[2] *Ibid., 1637*, 176.

[3] The Jesuits on these distant missions were usually attended by followers who had taken no vows, and could leave their service at will, but whose motives were religious, and not mercenary. Probably this was the character of their attendants in the present case. They were known as *donnés*, or "given men." It appears from a letter of the Jesuit Du Peron, that twelve hired laborers were soon after sent up to the mission.

leathery visages corrugated with age and malice, and their hard, glittering eyes riveted on the spectacle before them. The priests, no longer in their daily garb of black, but radiant in their surplices, the genuflections, the tinkling of the bell, the swinging of the censer, the sweet odors so unlike the fumes of the smoky lodge-fires, the mysterious elevation of the Host, (for a mass followed the baptism,) and the agitation of the neophyte, whose Indian imperturbability fairly deserted him,—all these combined to produce on the minds of the savage beholders an impression that seemed to promise a rich harvest for the Faith. To the Jesuits it was a day of triumph and of hope. The ice had been broken; the wedge had entered; light had dawned at last on the long night of heathendom. But there was one feature of the situation which in their rejoicing they overlooked.

The Devil had taken alarm. He had borne with reasonable composure the loss of individual souls snatched from him by former baptisms; but here was a convert whose example and influence threatened to shake his Huron empire to its very foundation. In fury and fear, he rose to the conflict, and put forth all his malice and all his hellish ingenuity. Such, at least, is the explanation given by the Jesuits of the scenes that followed.[1] Whether accepting it or not, let us examine the circumstances which gave rise to it.

The mysterious strangers, garbed in black, who of late years had made their abode among them, from motives past finding out, marvellous in knowledge, careless of life, had awakened in the breasts of the Hurons mingled emotions of wonder, perplexity, fear, respect, and awe. From the first, they had held them answerable for the changes of the weather, commending them when the crops were abundant, and upbraiding them in times of scarcity. They thought them mighty

---

[1] Several of the Jesuits allude to this supposed excitement among the tenants of the nether world. Thus, Le Mercier says, "Le Diable se sentoit pressé de prés, il ne pouuoit supporter le Baptesme solennel de quelques Sauuages des plus signalez."—*Relation des Hurons, 1638*, 33.—Several other baptisms of less note followed that above described. Garnier, writing to his brother, repeatedly alludes to the alarm excited in Hell by the recent successes of the mission, and adds,—"Vous pouvez juger quelle consolation nous étoit-ce de voir le diable s'armer contre nous et se servir de ses esclaves pour nous attaquer et tâcher de nous perdre en haine de J. C."

magicians, masters of life and death; and they came to them for spells, sometimes to destroy their enemies, and sometimes to kill grasshoppers. And now it was whispered abroad that it was they who had bewitched the nation, and caused the pest which threatened to exterminate it.

It was Isaac Jogues who first heard this ominous rumor, at the town of Onnentisati, and it proceeded from the dwarfish sorcerer already mentioned, who boasted himself a devil incarnate. The slander spread fast and far. Their friends looked at them askance; their enemies clamored for their lives. Some said that they concealed in their houses a corpse, which infected the country,—a perverted notion, derived from some half-instructed neophyte, concerning the body of Christ in the Eucharist. Others ascribed the evil to a serpent, others to a spotted frog, others to a demon which the priests were supposed to carry in the barrel of a gun. Others again gave out that they had pricked an infant to death with awls in the forest, in order to kill the Huron children by magic. "Perhaps," observes Father Le Mercier, "the Devil was enraged because we had placed a great many of these little innocents in Heaven."[1]

The picture of the Last Judgment became an object of the utmost terror. It was regarded as a charm. The dragons and serpents were supposed to be the demons of the pest, and the sinners whom they were so busily devouring to represent its victims. On the top of a spruce-tree, near their house at Ihonatiria, the priests had fastened a small streamer, to show the direction of the wind. This, too, was taken for a charm, throwing off disease and death to all quarters. The clock, once an object of harmless wonder, now excited the wildest alarm; and the Jesuits were forced to stop it, since, when it struck, it was supposed to sound the signal of death. At sunset, one would have seen knots of Indians, their faces dark with dejection and terror, listening to the measured sounds which issued from within the neighboring house of the mission, where, with bolted doors, the priests were singing litanies, mistaken for incantations by the awe-struck savages.

Had the objects of these charges been Indians, their term

---

[1] "Le diable enrageoit peutestre de ce que nous avions placé dans le ciel quantité de ces petits innocens."—Le Mercier, *Relation des Hurons, 1638*, 12 (Cramoisy).

of life would have been very short. The blow of a hatchet, stealthily struck in the dusky entrance of a lodge, would have promptly avenged the victims of their sorcery, and delivered the country from peril. But the priests inspired a strange awe. Nocturnal councils were held; their death was decreed; and, as they walked their rounds, whispering groups of children gazed after them as men doomed to die. But who should be the executioner? They were reviled and upbraided. The Indian boys threw sticks at them as they passed, and then ran behind the houses. When they entered one of these pestiferous dens, this impish crew clambered on the roof, to pelt them with snowballs through the smoke-holes. The old squaw who crouched by the fire scowled on them with mingled anger and fear, and cried out, "Begone! there are no sick ones here." The invalids wrapped their heads in their blankets; and when the priest accosted some dejected warrior, the savage looked gloomily on the ground, and answered not a word.

Yet nothing could divert the Jesuits from their ceaseless quest of dying subjects for baptism, and above all of dying children. They penetrated every house in turn. When, through the thin walls of bark, they heard the wail of a sick infant, no menace and no insult could repel them from the threshold. They pushed boldly in, asked to buy some trifle, spoke of late news of Iroquois forays,—of anything, in short, except the pestilence and the sick child; conversed for a while till suspicion was partially lulled to sleep, and then, pretending to observe the sufferer for the first time, approached it, felt its pulse, and asked of its health. Now, while apparently fanning the heated brow, the dexterous visitor touched it with a corner of his handkerchief, which he had previously dipped in water, murmured the baptismal words with motionless lips, and snatched another soul from the fangs of the "Infernal Wolf."[1] Thus, with the patience of saints, the cour-

---

[1] *Ce loup infernal* is a title often bestowed in the *Relations* on the Devil. The above details are gathered from the narratives of Brébeuf, Le Mercier, and Lalemant, and letters, published and unpublished, of several other Jesuits.

In another case, an Indian girl was carrying on her back a sick child, two months old. Two Jesuits approached, and while one of them amused the girl with his rosary, "l'autre le baptise lestement; le pauure petit n'attendoit que ceste faueur du Ciel pour s'y enuoler."

age of heroes, and an intent truly charitable, did the Fathers put forth a nimble-fingered adroitness that would have done credit to the profession of which the function is less to dispense the treasures of another world than to grasp those which pertain to this.

The Huron chiefs were summoned to a great council, to discuss the state of the nation. The crisis demanded all their wisdom; for, while the continued ravages of disease threatened them with annihilation, the Iroquois scalping-parties infested the outskirts of their towns, and murdered them in their fields and forests. The assembly met in August, 1637; and the Jesuits, knowing their deep stake in its deliberations, failed not to be present, with a liberal gift of wampum, to show their sympathy in the public calamities. In private, they sought to gain the good-will of the deputies, one by one; but though they were successful in some cases, the result on the whole was far from hopeful.

In the intervals of the council, Brébeuf discoursed to the crowd of chiefs on the wonders of the visible heavens,—the sun, the moon, the stars, and the planets. They were inclined to believe what he told them; for he had lately, to their great amazement, accurately predicted an eclipse. From the fires above he passed to the fires beneath, till the listeners stood aghast at his hideous pictures of the flames of perdition,—the only species of Christian instruction which produced any perceptible effect on this unpromising auditory.

The council opened on the evening of the fourth of August, with all the usual ceremonies; and the night was spent in discussing questions of treaties and alliances, with a deliberation and good sense which the Jesuits could not help admiring.[1] A few days after, the assembly took up the more exciting question of the epidemic and its causes. Deputies from three of the four Huron nations were present, each deputation sitting apart. The Jesuits were seated with the Nation of the Bear, in whose towns their missions were established. Like all important councils, the session was held at night. It was a strange scene. The light of the fires flickered aloft into the smoky vault and among the soot-begrimed raf-

[1] Le Mercier, *Relation des Hurons, 1638,* 38.

ters of the great council-house,[1] and cast an uncertain gleam on the wild and dejected throng that filled the platforms and the floor. "I think I never saw anything more lugubrious," writes Le Mercier: "they looked at each other like so many corpses, or like men who already feel the terror of death. When they spoke, it was only with sighs, each reckoning up the sick and dead of his own family. All this was to excite each other to vomit poison against us."

A grisly old chief, named Ontitarac, withered with age and stone-blind, but renowned in past years for eloquence and counsel, opened the debate in a loud, though tremulous voice. First he saluted each of the three nations present, then each of the chiefs in turn,—congratulated them that all were there assembled to deliberate on a subject of the last importance to the public welfare, and exhorted them to give it a mature and calm consideration. Next rose the chief whose office it was to preside over the Feast of the Dead. He painted in dismal colors the woful condition of the country, and ended with charging it all upon the sorceries of the Jesuits. Another old chief followed him. "My brothers," he said, "you know well that I am a war-chief, and very rarely speak except in councils of war; but I am compelled to speak now, since nearly all the other chiefs are dead, and I must utter what is in my heart before I follow them to the grave. Only two of my family are left alive, and perhaps even these will not long escape the fury of the pest. I have seen other diseases ravaging the country, but nothing that could compare with this. In two or three moons we saw their end: but now we have suffered for a year and more, and yet the evil does not abate. And what is worst of all, we have not yet discovered its source." Then, with words of studied moderation, alternating with bursts of angry invective, he proceeded to accuse the Jesuits of causing, by their sorceries, the unparalleled calamities that afflicted them; and in support of his charge he adduced a prodigious mass of evidence. When he had spent his eloquence, Brébeuf rose to reply, and in a few words exposed the absurdities of his statements; whereupon another accuser brought a new array of charges. A clamor soon arose from

[1] It must have been the house of a chief. The Hurons, unlike some other tribes, had no houses set apart for public occasions.

the whole assembly, and they called upon Brébeuf with one voice to give up a certain charmed cloth which was the cause of their miseries. In vain the missionary protested that he had no such cloth. The clamor increased.

"If you will not believe me," said Brébeuf, "go to our house; search everywhere; and if you are not sure which is the charm, take all our clothing and all our cloth, and throw them into the lake."

"Sorcerers always talk in that way," was the reply.

"Then what will you have me say?" demanded Brébeuf.

"Tell us the cause of the pest."

Brébeuf replied to the best of his power, mingling his explanations with instructions in Christian doctrine and exhortations to embrace the Faith. He was continually interrupted; and the old chief, Ontitarac, still called upon him to produce the charmed cloth. Thus the debate continued till after midnight, when several of the assembly, seeing no prospect of a termination, fell asleep, and others went away. One old chief, as he passed out, said to Brébeuf, "If some young man should split your head, we should have nothing to say." The priest still continued to harangue the diminished conclave on the necessity of obeying God and the danger of offending Him, when the chief of Ossossané called out impatiently, "What sort of men are these? They are always saying the same thing, and repeating the same words a hundred times. They are never done with telling us about their *Oki*, and what he demands and what he forbids, and Paradise and Hell."[1]

"Here was the end of this miserable council," writes Le Mercier; . . . "and if less evil came of it than was designed, we owe it, after God, to the Most Holy Virgin, to whom we had made a vow of nine masses in honor of her immaculate conception."

The Fathers had escaped for the time; but they were still in deadly peril. They had taken pains to secure friends in private, and there were those who were attached to their interests; yet none dared openly take their part. The few converts they had lately made came to them in secret, and warned them that their death was determined upon. Their house was set on fire;

[1] The above account of the council is drawn from Le Mercier, *Relation des Hurons, 1638*, Chap. II. See also Bressani, *Relation Abrégée*, 163.

in public, every face was averted from them; and a new council was called to pronounce the decree of death. They appeared before it with a front of such unflinching assurance, that their judges, Indian-like, postponed the sentence. Yet it seemed impossible that they should much longer escape. Brébeuf, therefore, wrote a letter of farewell to his Superior, Le Jeune, at Quebec, and confided it to some converts whom he could trust, to be carried by them to its destination.

"We are perhaps," he says, "about to give our blood and our lives in the cause of our Master, Jesus Christ. It seems that His goodness will accept this sacrifice, as regards me, in expiation of my great and numberless sins, and that He will thus crown the past services and ardent desires of all our Fathers here. . . . Blessed be His name forever, that He has chosen us, among so many better than we, to aid Him to bear His cross in this land! In all things, His holy will be done!" He then acquaints Le Jeune that he has directed the sacred vessels, and all else belonging to the service of the altar, to be placed, in case of his death, in the hands of Pierre, the convert whose baptism has been described, and that especial care will be taken to preserve the dictionary and other writings on the Huron language. The letter closes with a request for masses and prayers.[1]

The imperilled Jesuits now took a singular, but certainly a very wise step. They gave one of those farewell feasts—*festins*

---

[1] The following is the conclusion of the letter. (Le Mercier, *Relation des Hurons, 1638,* 43.)

"En tout, sa sainte volonté soit faite; s'il veut que dés ceste heure nous mourions, ô la bonne heure pour nous! s'il veut nous reseruer à d'autres trauaux, qu'il soit beny; si vous entendez que Dieu ait couronné nos petits trauaux, ou plustost nos desirs, benissez-le: car c'est pour luy que nous desirons viure et mourir, et c'est luy qui nous en donne la grace. Au reste si quelques-vns suruiuent, i'ay donné ordre de tout ce qu'ils doiuent faire. I'ay esté d'aduis que nos Peres et nos domestiques se retirent chez ceux qu'ils croyront estre leurs meilleurs amis; i'ay donné charge qu'on porte chez Pierre nostre premier Chrestien tout ce qui est de la Sacristie, sur tout qu'on ait vn soin particulier de mettre en lieu d'asseurance le Dictionnaire et tout ce que nous auons de la langue. Pour moy, si Dieu me fait la grace d'aller au Ciel, ie prieray Dieu pour eux, pour les pauures Hurons, et n'oublieray pas Vostre Reuerence.

"Apres tout, nous supplions V. R. et tous nos Peres de ne nous oublier en leurs saincts Sacrifices et prieres, afin qu'en la vie et apres la mort, il nous

d'adieu—which Huron custom enjoined on those about to die, whether in the course of Nature or by public execution. Being interpreted, it was a declaration that the priests knew their danger, and did not shrink from it. It might have the effect of changing overawed friends into open advocates, and even of awakening a certain sympathy in the breasts of an assembly on whom a bold bearing could rarely fail of influence. The house was packed with feasters, and Brébeuf addressed them as usual on his unfailing themes of God, Paradise, and Hell. The throng listened in gloomy silence; and each, when he had emptied his bowl, rose and departed, leaving his entertainers in utter doubt as to his feelings and intentions. From this time forth, however, the clouds that overhung the Fathers became less dark and threatening. Voices were heard in their defence, and looks were less constantly averted. They ascribed the change to the intercession of St. Joseph, to whom they had vowed a nine days' devotion. By whatever cause produced, the lapse of a week wrought a hopeful improvement in their prospects; and when they went out of doors in the morning, it was no longer with the expectation of having a hatchet struck into their brains as they crossed the threshold.[1]

The persecution of the Jesuits as sorcerers continued, in an intermittent form, for years; and several of them escaped very

fasse misericorde; nous sommes tous en la vie et à l'Eternité,

"De vostre Reuerence tres-humbles et tres-affectionnez seruiteurs en Nostre Seigneur,

> "IEAN DE BREBEVF.
> FRANÇOIS IOSEPH LE MERCIER.
> PIERRE CHASTELLAIN.
> CHARLES GARNIER.
> PAVL RAGVENEAV.

"En la Residence de la Conception, à Ossossané,
ce 28 Octobre.

"J'ay laissé en la Residence de sainct Ioseph les Peres Pierre Piiart, et Isaac Iogves, dans les mesmes sentimens."

[1] "Tant y a que depuis le 6. de Nouembre que nous acheuasmes nos Messes votiues à son honneur, nous auons iouy d'vn repos incroyable, nous nous en emerueillons nous-mesmes de iour en iour, quand nous considerons en quel estat estoient nos affaires il n'y a que huict iours."—Le Mercier, *Relation des Hurons, 1638*, 44.

narrowly. In a house at Ossossané, a young Indian rushed
suddenly upon François Du Peron, and lifted his tomahawk
to brain him, when a squaw caught his hand. Paul Ragueneau
wore a crucifix, from which hung the image of a skull. An
Indian, thinking it a charm, snatched it from him. The priest
tried to recover it, when the savage, his eyes glittering with
murder, brandished his hatchet to strike. Ragueneau stood
motionless, waiting the blow. His assailant forbore, and withdrew, muttering. Pierre Chaumonot was emerging from a
house at the Huron town called by the Jesuits St. Michel,
where he had just baptized a dying girl, when her brother,
standing hidden in the doorway, struck him on the head with
a stone. Chaumonot, severely wounded, staggered without
falling, when the Indian sprang upon him with his tomahawk. The bystanders arrested the blow. François Le Mercier,
in the midst of a crowd of Indians in a house at the town
called St. Louis, was assailed by a noted chief, who rushed in,
raving like a madman, and, in a torrent of words, charged
upon him all the miseries of the nation. Then, snatching a
brand from the fire, he shook it in the Jesuit's face, and told
him that he should be burned alive. Le Mercier met him with
looks as determined as his own, till, abashed at his undaunted
front and bold denunciations, the Indian stood confounded.[1]

The belief that their persecutions were owing to the fury of
the Devil, driven to desperation by the home-thrusts he had
received at their hands, was an unfailing consolation to the
priests. "Truly," writes Le Mercier, "it is an unspeakable happiness for us, in the midst of this barbarism, to hear the roaring of the demons, and to see Earth and Hell raging against
a handful of men who will not even defend themselves."[2] In
all the copious records of this dark period, not a line gives
occasion to suspect that one of this loyal band flinched or

---

[1] The above incidents are from Le Mercier, Lalemant, Bressani, the autobiography of Chaumonot, the unpublished writings of Garnier, and the ancient manuscript volume of memoirs of the early Canadian missionaries, at
St. Mary's College, Montreal.

[2] "C'est veritablement un bonheur indicible pour nous, au milieu de cette
barbarie, d'entendre les rugissemens des demons, & de voir tout l'Enfer &
quasi tous les hommes animez & remplis de fureur contre une petite poignée
de gens qui ne voudroient pas se defendre."—*Relation des Hurons, 1640*, 31
(Cramoisy).

hesitated. The iron Brébeuf, the gentle Garnier, the all-enduring Jogues, the enthusiastic Chaumonot, Lalemant, Le Mercier, Chatelain, Daniel, Pijart, Ragueneau, Du Peron, Poncet,
Le Moyne,—one and all bore themselves with a tranquil
boldness, which amazed the Indians and enforced their respect.

Father Jerome Lalemant, in his journal of 1639, is disposed
to draw an evil augury for the mission from the fact that as
yet no priest had been put to death, inasmuch as it is a received maxim that the blood of the martyrs is the seed of the
Church.[1] He consoles himself with the hope that the daily
life of the missionaries may be accepted as a living martyrdom; since abuse and threats without end, the smoke, fleas,
filth, and dogs of the Indian lodges,—which are, he says, little images of Hell,—cold, hunger, and ceaseless anxiety, and
all these continued for years, are a portion to which many
might prefer the stroke of a tomahawk. Reasonable as the
Father's hope may be, its expression proved needless in the
sequel; for the Huron church was not destined to suffer from
a lack of martyrdom in any form.

[1]"Nous auons quelque fois douté, sçauoir si on pouuoit esperer la conuer-
sion de ce païs sans qu'il y eust effusion de sang: le principe reçeu ce semble
dans l'Eglise de Dieu, que le sang des Martyrs est la semence des Chrestiens,
me faisoit conclure pour lors, que cela n'estoit pas à esperer, voire mesme
qu'il n'étoit pas à souhaiter, consideré la gloire qui reuient à Dieu de la constance des Martyrs, du sang desquels tout le reste de la terre ayant tantost
esté abreuué, ce seroit vne espece de malediction, que ce quartier du monde
ne participast point au bonheur d'auoir contribué à l'esclat de ceste gloire."—
Lalemant, *Relation des Hurons, 1639,* 56, 57.

Chapter XI

1638–1640

PRIEST AND PAGAN

*Du Peron's Journey • Daily Life of the Jesuits • Their Missionary
Excursions • Converts at Ossossané • Machinery of Conversion •
Conditions of Baptism • Backsliders • The Converts and their
Countrymen • The Cannibals at St. Joseph*

WE have already touched on the domestic life of the Jesuits. That we may the better know them, we will follow one of their number on his journey towards the scene of his labors, and observe what awaited him on his arrival.

Father François Du Peron came up the Ottawa in a Huron canoe in September, 1638, and was well treated by the Indian owner of the vessel. Lalemant and Le Moyne, who had set out from Three Rivers before him, did not fare so well. The former was assailed by an Algonquin of Allumette Island, who tried to strangle him in revenge for the death of a child, which a Frenchman in the employ of the Jesuits had lately bled, but had failed to restore to health by the operation. Le Moyne was abandoned by his Huron conductors, and remained for a fortnight by the bank of the river, with a French attendant who supported him by hunting. Another Huron, belonging to the flotilla that carried Du Peron, then took him into his canoe; but, becoming tired of him, was about to leave him on a rock in the river, when his brother priest bribed the savage with a blanket to carry him to his journey's end.

It was midnight, on the twenty-ninth of September, when Du Peron landed on the shore of Thunder Bay, after paddling without rest since one o'clock of the preceding morning. The night was rainy, and Ossossané was about fifteen miles distant. His Indian companions were impatient to reach their towns; the rain prevented the kindling of a fire; while the priest, who for a long time had not heard mass, was eager to renew his communion as soon as possible. Hence, tired and hungry as he was, he shouldered his sack, and took the path for Ossossané without breaking his fast. He toiled on, half-spent, amid the ceaseless pattering, trickling, and whispering of innumerable drops among innumerable leaves, till, as day dawned, he reached a clearing, and descried through the mists a cluster of Huron houses. Faint and bedrenched, he entered the principal one, and was greeted with the monosyllable *"Shay!"*—"Welcome!" A squaw spread a mat for him by the fire, roasted four ears of Indian corn before the coals, baked two squashes in the embers, ladled from her kettle a dish of sagamite, and offered them to her famished guest. Missionaries seem to have been a novelty at this place; for, while the Father breakfasted, a crowd, chiefly of children, gathered about him, and stared at him in silence. One examined the texture of his cassock; another put on his hat; a third took the shoes from his feet, and tried them on her own. Du Peron requited his entertainers with a few trinkets, and begged, by signs, a guide to Ossossané. An Indian accordingly set out with him, and conducted him to the mission-house, which he reached at six o'clock in the evening.

Here he found a warm welcome, and little other refreshment. In respect to the commodities of life, the Jesuits were but a step in advance of the Indians. Their house, though well ventilated by numberless crevices in its bark walls, always smelt of smoke, and, when the wind was in certain quarters, was filled with it to suffocation. At their meals, the Fathers sat on logs around the fire, over which their kettle was slung in the Indian fashion. Each had his wooden platter, which, from the difficulty of transportation, was valued, in the Huron country, at the price of a robe of beaver-skin, or a hundred francs.[1] Their food consisted of sagamite, or "mush," made of pounded Indian-corn, boiled with scraps of smoked fish. Chaumonot compares it to the paste used for papering the walls of houses. The repast was occasionally varied by a pumpkin or squash baked in the ashes, or, in the season, by Indian corn roasted in the ear. They used no salt whatever. They could bring their cumbrous pictures, ornaments, and vestments through the savage journey of the Ottawa; but they

---

[1] "Nos plats, quoyque de bois, nous coûtent plus cher que les vôtres; ils sont de la valeur d'une robe de castor, c'est à dire cent francs."—*Lettre du P. Du Peron à son Frère, 27 Avril, 1639.*—The Father's appraisement seems a little questionable.

could not bring the common necessaries of life. By day, they read and studied by the light that streamed in through the large smoke-holes in the roof,—at night, by the blaze of the fire. Their only candles were a few of wax, for the altar. They cultivated a patch of ground, but raised nothing on it except wheat for making the sacramental bread. Their food was supplied by the Indians, to whom they gave, in return, cloth, knives, awls, needles, and various trinkets. Their supply of wine for the Eucharist was so scanty, that they limited themselves to four or five drops for each mass.[1]

Their life was regulated with a conventual strictness. At four in the morning, a bell roused them from the sheets of bark on which they slept. Masses, private devotions, reading religious books, and breakfasting, filled the time until eight, when they opened their door and admitted the Indians. As many of these proved intolerable nuisances, they took what Lalemant calls the *honnête* liberty of turning out the most intrusive and impracticable,—an act performed with all tact and courtesy, and rarely taken in dudgeon. Having thus winnowed their company, they catechized those that remained, as opportunity offered. In the intervals, the guests squatted by the fire and smoked their pipes.

As among the Spartan virtues of the Hurons that of thieving was especially conspicuous, it was necessary that one or more of the Fathers should remain on guard at the house all day. The rest went forth on their missionary labors, baptizing and instructing, as we have seen. To each priest who could speak Huron[2] was assigned a certain number of houses,—in some instances, as many as forty; and as these often had five or six fires, with two families to each, his spiritual flock was

---

[1] The above particulars are drawn from a long letter of François Du Peron to his brother, Joseph-Imbert Du Peron, dated at *La Conception* (Ossossané), April 27, 1639, and from a letter, equally long, of Chaumonot to Father Philippe Nappi, dated *Du Pays des Hurons, May 26, 1640*. Both are in Carayon. These private letters of the Jesuits, of which many are extant, in some cases written on birch-bark, are invaluable as illustrations of the subject.

The Jesuits soon learned to make wine from wild grapes. Those in Maine and Acadia, at a later period, made good candles from the waxy fruit of the shrub known locally as the "bayberry."

[2] At the end of the year 1638, there were seven priests who spoke Huron, and three who had begun to learn it.

as numerous as it was intractable. It was his care to see that none of the number died without baptism, and by every means in his power to commend the doctrines of his faith to the acceptance of those in health.

At dinner, which was at two o'clock, grace was said in Huron,—for the benefit of the Indians present,—and a chapter of the Bible was read aloud during the meal. At four or five, according to the season, the Indians were dismissed, the door closed, and the evening spent in writing, reading, studying the language, devotion, and conversation on the affairs of the mission.

The local missions here referred to embraced Ossossané and the villages of the neighborhood; but the priests by no means confined themselves within these limits. They made distant excursions, two in company, until every house in every Huron town had heard the annunciation of the new doctrine. On these journeys, they carried blankets or large mantles at their backs, for sleeping in at night, besides a supply of needles, awls, beads, and other small articles, to pay for their lodging and entertainment: for the Hurons, hospitable without stint to each other, expected full compensation from the Jesuits.

At Ossossané, the house of the Jesuits no longer served the double purpose of dwelling and chapel. In 1638, they had in their pay twelve artisans and laborers, sent up from Quebec,[1] who had built, before the close of the year, a chapel of wood.[2] Hither they removed their pictures and ornaments; and here, in winter, several fires were kept burning, for the comfort of the half-naked converts.[3] Of these they now had at Ossossané about sixty,—a large, though evidently not a very solid nucleus for the Huron church,—and they labored hard and anxiously to confirm and multiply them. Of a Sunday morning in winter, one could have seen them coming to mass, often from a considerable distance, "as naked," says Lalemant, "as your hand, except a skin over their backs like a mantle, and,

---

[1] Du Peron in Carayon, 173.

[2] "La chapelle est faite d'une charpente bien jolie, semblable presque, en façon et grandeur, à notre chapelle de St. Julien."—*Ibid.*, 183.

[3] Lalemant, *Relation des Hurons, 1639,* 62.

in the coldest weather, a few skins around their feet and legs."
They knelt, mingled with the French mechanics, before the
altar,—very awkwardly at first, for the posture was new to
them,—and all received the sacrament together: a spectacle
which, as the missionary chronicler declares, repaid a hundred
times all the labor of their conversion.[1]

Some of the principal methods of conversion are curiously
illustrated in a letter written by Garnier to a friend in France.
"Send me," he says, "a picture of Christ without a beard."
Several Virgins are also requested, together with a variety of
souls in perdition— *âmes damnées*—most of them to be
mounted in a portable form. Particular directions are given
with respect to the demons, dragons, flames, and other essentials of these works of art. Of souls in bliss— *âmes bienheu-
reuses*—he thinks that one will be enough. All the pictures
must be in full face, not in profile; and they must look directly
at the beholder, with open eyes. The colors should be bright;
and there must be no flowers or animals, as these distract the
attention of the Indians.[2]

The first point with the priests was of course to bring the
objects of their zeal to an acceptance of the fundamental doctrines of the Roman Church; but, as the mind of the savage
was by no means that beautiful blank which some have represented it, there was much to be erased as well as to be written. They must renounce a host of superstitions, to which
they were attached with a strange tenacity, or which may
rather be said to have been ingrained in their very natures.
Certain points of Christian morality were also strongly urged
by the missionaries, who insisted that the convert should take
but one wife, and not cast her off without grave cause, and
that he should renounce the gross license almost universal
among the Hurons. Murder, cannibalism, and several other
offences, were also forbidden. Yet, while laboring at the work
of conversion with an energy never surpassed, and battling

---

[1] Lalemant, *Relation des Hurons, 1639*, 62.

[2] Garnier, *Lettre 17ᵐᵉ*, MS. These directions show an excellent knowledge of
Indian peculiarities. The Indian dislike of a beard is well known. Catlin, the
painter, once caused a fatal quarrel among a party of Sioux, by representing
one of them in profile, whereupon he was jibed by a rival as being but *half
a man.*

against the powers of darkness with the mettle of paladins, the Jesuits never had the folly to assume towards the Indians a dictatorial or overbearing tone. Gentleness, kindness, and patience were the rule of their intercourse.[1] They studied the nature of the savage, and conformed themselves to it with an admirable tact. Far from treating the Indian as an alien and barbarian, they would fain have adopted him as a country-man; and they proposed to the Hurons that a number of young Frenchmen should settle among them, and marry their daughters in solemn form. The listeners were gratified at an overture so flattering. "But what is the use," they demanded, "of so much ceremony? If the Frenchmen want our women, they are welcome to come and take them whenever they please, as they always used to do."[2]

The Fathers are well agreed that their difficulties did not arise from any natural defect of understanding on the part of the Indians, who, according to Chaumonot, were more intel-ligent than the French peasantry, and who, in some instances, showed in their way a marked capacity. It was the inert mass of pride, sensuality, indolence, and superstition that opposed the march of the Faith, and in which the Devil lay intrenched as behind impregnable breastworks.[3]

[1] The following passage from the "Divers Sentimens," before cited, will il-lustrate this point. "Pour conuertir les Sauuages, il n'y faut pas tant de science que de bonté et vertu bien solide. Les quatre Elemens d'vn homme Aposto-lique en la Nouuelle France sont l'Affabilité, l'Humilité, la Patience et vne Charité genereuse. Le zele trop ardent brusle plus qu'il n'eschauffe, et gaste tout; il faut vne grande magnanimité et condescendance, pour attirer peu à peu ces Sauuages. Ils n'entendent pas bien nostre Theologie, mais ils entendent parfaictement bien nostre humilité et nostre affabilité, et se laissent gaigner."

So too Brébeuf, in a letter to Vitelleschi, General of the Jesuits (see Cara-yon, 163): "Ce qu'il faut demander, avant tout, des ouvriers destinés à cette mission, c'est une douceur inaltérable et une patience à toute épreuve."

[2] Le Mercier, *Relation des Hurons, 1637*, 160.

[3] In this connection, the following specimen of Indian reasoning is worth noting. At the height of the pestilence, a Huron said to one of the priests, "I see plainly that your God is angry with us because we will not believe and obey him. Ihonatiria, where you first taught his word, is entirely ruined. Then you came here to Ossossané, and we would not listen; so Ossossané is ruined too. This year you have been all through our country, and found scarcely any who would do what God commands; therefore the pestilence is everywhere." After premises so hopeful, the Fathers looked for a satisfactory conclusion; but the Indian proceeded,—"My opinion is, that we ought to

It soon became evident that it was easier to make a convert than to keep him. Many of the Indians clung to the idea that baptism was a safeguard against pestilence and misfortune; and when the fallacy of this notion was made apparent, their zeal cooled. Their only amusements consisted of feasts, dances, and games, many of which were, to a greater or less degree, of a superstitious character; and as the Fathers could rarely prove to their own satisfaction the absence of the diabolic element in any one of them, they proscribed the whole indiscriminately, to the extreme disgust of the neophyte. His countrymen, too, beset him with dismal prognostics: as, "You will kill no more game,"—"All your hair will come out before spring," and so forth. Various doubts also assailed him with regard to the substantial advantages of his new profession; and several converts were filled with anxiety in view of the probable want of tobacco in Heaven, saying that they could not do without it.[1] Nor was it pleasant to these incipient Christians, as they sat in class listening to the instructions of their teacher, to find themselves and him suddenly made the targets of a shower of sticks, snowballs, corn-cobs, and other rubbish, flung at them by a screeching rabble of vagabond boys.[2]

Yet, while most of the neophytes demanded an anxious and diligent cultivation, there were a few of excellent promise; and of one or two especially, the Fathers, in the fulness of their satisfaction, assure us again and again "that they were savage only in name."[3]

---

shut you out from all the houses, and stop our ears when you speak of God, so that we cannot hear. Then we shall not be so guilty of rejecting the truth, and he will not punish us so cruelly."—Lalemant, *Relation des Hurons, 1640*, 80.

[1] *Ibid., 1639*, 80.

[2] *Ibid.*, 78.

[3] From June, 1639, to June, 1640, about a thousand persons were baptized. Of these, two hundred and sixty were infants, and many more were children. Very many died soon after baptism. Of the whole number, less than twenty were baptized in health,—a number much below that of the preceding year.

The following is a curious case of precocious piety. It is that of a child at St. Joseph. "Elle n'a que deux ans, et fait joliment le signe de la croix, et prend elle-même de l'eau bénite; et une fois se mit à crier, sortant de la Chapelle, à cause que sa mère qui la portoit ne lui avoit donné le loisir d'en prendre. Il l'a fallu reporter en prendre."—*Lettres de Garnier*, MSS.

As the town of Ihonatiria, where the Jesuits had made their first abode, was ruined by the pestilence, the mission established there, and known by the name of St. Joseph, was removed, in the summer of 1638, to Teanaustayé, a large town at the foot of a range of hills near the southern borders of the Huron territory. The Hurons, this year, had had unwonted successes in their war with the Iroquois, and had taken, at various times, nearly a hundred prisoners. Many of these were brought to the seat of the new mission of St. Joseph, and put to death with frightful tortures, though not before several had been converted and baptized. The torture was followed, in spite of the remonstrances of the priests, by those cannibal feasts customary with the Hurons on such occasions. Once, when the Fathers had been strenuous in their denunciations, a hand of the victim, duly prepared, was flung in at their door, as an invitation to join in the festivity. As the owner of the severed member had been baptized, they dug a hole in their chapel, and buried it with solemn rites of sepulture.[1]

[1] Lalemant, *Relation des Hurons, 1639*, 70.

Chapter XII

1639, 1640

THE TOBACCO NATION—THE NEUTRALS

*A Change of Plan • Sainte Marie • Mission of the Tobacco Nation
• Winter Journeying • Reception of the Missionaries • Superstitious
Terrors • Peril of Garnier and Jogues • Mission of the Neutrals •
Huron Intrigues • Miracles • Fury of the Indians • Intervention
of Saint Michael • Return to Sainte Marie • Intrepidity of the
Priests • Their Mental Exaltation*

IT had been the first purpose of the Jesuits to form permanent missions in each of the principal Huron towns; but,
before the close of the year 1639, the difficulties and risks of
this scheme had become fully apparent. They resolved, therefore, to establish one central station, to be a base of operations, and, as it were, a focus, whence the light of the Faith
should radiate through all the wilderness around. It was to
serve at once as residence, fort, magazine, hospital, and convent. Hence the priests would set forth on missionary expeditions far and near; and hither they might retire, as to an
asylum, in times of sickness or extreme peril. Here the neophytes could be gathered together, safe from perverting influences; and here in time a Christian settlement, Hurons
mingled with Frenchmen, might spring up and thrive under
the shadow of the cross.

The site of the new station was admirably chosen. The little
river Wye flows from the southward into the Matchedash Bay of
Lake Huron, and, at about a mile from its mouth, passes
through a small lake. The Jesuits made choice of the right bank
of the Wye, where it issues from this lake,—gained permission
to build from the Indians, though not without difficulty,—and
began their labors with an abundant energy, and a very deficient
supply of workmen and tools. The new establishment was called
Sainte Marie. The house at Teanaustayé, and the house and
chapel at Ossossané, were abandoned, and all was concentrated
at this spot. On one hand, it had a short water communication
with Lake Huron; and on the other, its central position gave the
readiest access to every part of the Huron territory.

During the summer before, the priests had made a survey of their field of action, visited all the Huron towns, and christened each of them with the name of a saint. This heavy draft on the calendar was followed by another, for the designation of the nine towns of the neighboring and kindred people of the Tobacco Nation.[1] The Huron towns were portioned into four districts, while those of the Tobacco Nation formed a fifth, and each district was assigned to the charge of two or more priests. In November and December, they began their missionary excursions,—for the Indians were now gathered in their settlements,—and journeyed on foot through the denuded forests, in mud and snow, bearing on their backs the vessels and utensils necessary for the service of the altar.

The new and perilous mission of the Tobacco Nation fell to Garnier and Jogues. They were well chosen; and yet neither of them was robust by nature, in body or mind, though Jogues was noted for personal activity. The Tobacco Nation lay at the distance of a two days' journey from the Huron towns, among the mountains at the head of Nottawassaga Bay. The two missionaries tried to find a guide at Ossossané; but none would go with them, and they set forth on their wild and unknown pilgrimage alone.

The forests were full of snow; and the soft, moist flakes were still falling thickly, obscuring the air, beplastering the gray trunks, weighing to the earth the boughs of spruce and pine, and hiding every footprint of the narrow path. The Fathers missed their way, and toiled on till night, shaking down at every step from the burdened branches a shower of fleecy white on their black cassocks. Night overtook them in a spruce swamp. Here they made a fire with great difficulty, cut the evergreen boughs, piled them for a bed, and lay down. The storm presently ceased; and, "praised be God," writes one of the travellers, "we passed a very good night."[2]

In the morning they breakfasted on a morsel of corn bread, and, resuming their journey, fell in with a small party of Indians, whom they followed all day without food. At eight in the evening they reached the first Tobacco town, a miserable cluster of bark cabins, hidden among forests and half buried

[1] See Introduction.

[2] Jogues and Garnier in Lalemant, *Relation des Hurons, 1640*, 95.

in snow-drifts, where the savage children, seeing the two black apparitions, screamed that Famine and the Pest were coming. Their evil fame had gone before them. They were unwelcome guests; nevertheless, shivering and famished as they were, in the cold and darkness, they boldly pushed their way into one of these dens of barbarism. It was precisely like a Huron house. Five or six fires blazed on the earthen floor, and around them were huddled twice that number of families, sitting, crouching, standing, or flat on the ground; old and young, women and men, children and dogs, mingled pell-mell. The scene would have been a strange one by daylight: it was doubly strange by the flicker and glare of the lodge-fires. Scowling brows, sidelong looks of distrust and fear, the screams of scared children, the scolding of squaws, the growl-ing of wolfish dogs,—this was the greeting of the strangers. The chief man of the household treated them at first with the decencies of Indian hospitality; but when he saw them kneel-ing in the litter and ashes at their devotions, his suppressed fears found vent, and he began a loud harangue, addressed half to them and half to the Indians. "Now, what are these *okies* doing? They are making charms to kill us, and destroy all that the pest has spared in this house. I heard that they were sorcerers; and now, when it is too late, I believe it."[1] It is wonderful that the priests escaped the tomahawk. Nowhere is the power of courage, faith, and an unflinching purpose more strikingly displayed than in the record of these missions.

In other Tobacco towns their reception was much the same; but at the largest, called by them St. Peter and St. Paul, they fared worse. They reached it on a winter afternoon. Every door of its capacious bark houses was closed against them; and they heard the squaws within calling on the young men to go out and split their heads, while children screamed abuse at the black-robed sorcerers. As night approached, they left the town, when a band of young men followed them, hatchet in hand, to put them to death. Darkness, the forest, and the mountain favored them; and, eluding their pursuers, they escaped. Thus began the mission of the Tobacco Nation.

In the following November, a yet more distant and perilous

---

[1] Lalemant, *Relation des Hurons, 1640,* 96.

mission was begun. Brébeuf and Chaumonot set out for the Neutral Nation. This fierce people, as we have already seen, occupied that part of Canada which lies immediately north of Lake Erie, while a wing of their territory extended across the Niagara into Western New York.[1] In their athletic proportions, the ferocity of their manners, and the extravagance of their superstitions, no American tribe has ever exceeded them. They carried to a preposterous excess the Indian notion, that insanity is endowed with a mysterious and superhuman power. Their country was full of pretended maniacs, who, to propitiate their guardian spirits, or *okies*, and acquire the mystic virtue which pertained to madness, raved stark naked through the villages, scattering the brands of the lodge-fires, and upsetting everything in their way.

The two priests left Sainte Marie on the second of November, found a Huron guide at St. Joseph, and, after a dreary march of five days through the forest, reached the first Neutral town. Advancing thence, they visited in turn eighteen others; and their progress was a storm of maledictions. Brébeuf especially was accounted the most pestilent of sorcerers. The Hurons, restrained by a superstitious awe, and unwilling to kill the priests, lest they should embroil themselves with the French at Quebec, conceived that their object might be safely gained by stirring up the Neutrals to become their ex-

---

[1] Introduction.—The river Niagara was at this time, 1640, well known to the Jesuits, though none of them had visited it. Lalemant speaks of it as the "famous river of this nation" (the Neutrals). The following translation, from his *Relation* of 1641, shows that both Lake Ontario and Lake Erie had already taken their present names.

"This river" (the Niagara) "is the same by which our great lake of the Hurons, or Fresh Sea, discharges itself, in the first place, into Lake Erie (*le lac d'Erié*), or the Lake of the Cat Nation. Then it enters the territories of the Neutral Nation, and takes the name of Onguiaahra (Niagara), until it discharges itself into Ontario, or the Lake of St. Louis; whence at last issues the river which passes before Quebec, and is called the St. Lawrence." He makes no allusion to the cataract, which is first mentioned as follows by Ragueneau, in the *Relation* of 1648.

"Nearly south of this same Neutral Nation there is a great lake, about two hundred leagues in circuit, named Erie (Erié), which is formed by the discharge of the Fresh Sea, and which precipitates itself by a cataract of frightful height into a third lake, named Ontario, which we call Lake St. Louis."— *Relation des Hurons, 1648*, 46.

ecutioners. To that end, they sent two emissaries to the Neutral towns, who, calling the chiefs and young warriors to a council, denounced the Jesuits as destroyers of the human race, and made their auditors a gift of nine French hatchets on condition that they would put them to death. It was now that Brébeuf, fully conscious of the danger, half starved and half frozen, driven with revilings from every door, struck and spit upon by pretended maniacs, beheld in a vision that great cross, which, as we have seen, moved onward through the air, above the wintry forests that stretched towards the land of the Iroquois.[1]

Chaumonot records yet another miracle. "One evening, when all the chief men of the town were deliberating in council whether to put us to death, Father Brébeuf, while making his examination of conscience, as we were together at prayers, saw the vision of a spectre, full of fury, menacing us both with three javelins which he held in his hands. Then he hurled one of them at us; but a more powerful hand caught it as it flew: and this took place a second and a third time, as he hurled his two remaining javelins. . . . Late at night our host came back from the council, where the two Huron emissaries had made their gift of hatchets to have us killed. He wakened us to say that three times we had been at the point of death; for the young men had offered three times to strike the blow, and three times the old men had dissuaded them. This explained the meaning of Father Brébeuf's vision."[2]

They had escaped for the time; but the Indians agreed among themselves, that thenceforth no one should give them shelter. At night, pierced with cold and faint with hunger, they found every door closed against them. They stood and watched, saw an Indian issue from a house, and, by a quick movement, pushed through the half-open door into this abode of smoke and filth. The inmates, aghast at their boldness, stared in silence. Then a messenger ran out to carry the tidings, and an angry crowd collected.

"Go out, and leave our country," said an old chief, "or we will put you into the kettle, and make a feast of you."

"I have had enough of the dark-colored flesh of our ene-

[1] See *ante*, p. 476.
[2] Chaumonot, *Vie*, 55.

mies," said a young brave; "I wish to know the taste of white meat, and I will eat yours."

A warrior rushed in like a madman, drew his bow, and aimed the arrow at Chaumonot. "I looked at him fixedly," writes the Jesuit, "and commended myself in full confidence to St. Michael. Without doubt, this great archangel saved us; for almost immediately the fury of the warrior was appeased, and the rest of our enemies soon began to listen to the explanation we gave them of our visit to their country."[1]

The mission was barren of any other fruit than hardship and danger, and after a stay of four months the two priests resolved to return. On the way, they met a genuine act of kindness. A heavy snow-storm arresting their progress, a Neutral woman took them into her lodge, entertained them for two weeks with her best fare, persuaded her father and relatives to befriend them, and aided them to make a vocabulary of the dialect. Bidding their generous hostess farewell, they journeyed northward, through the melting snows of spring, and reached Sainte Marie in safety.[2]

The Jesuits had borne all that the human frame seems capable of bearing. They had escaped as by miracle from torture and death. Did their zeal flag or their courage fail? A fervor intense and unquenchable urged them on to more distant and more deadly ventures. The beings, so near to mortal sympathies, so human, yet so divine, in whom their faith impersonated and dramatized the great principles of Christian truth,— virgins, saints, and angels,—hovered over them, and held before their raptured sight crowns of glory and garlands of immortal bliss. They burned to do, to suffer, and to die; and now, from out a living martyrdom, they turned their heroic gaze towards an horizon dark with perils yet more appalling,

---

[1] *Ibid.*, 57.

[2] Lalemant, in his *Relation* of 1641, gives the narrative of this mission at length. His account coincides perfectly with the briefer notice of Chaumonot in his Autobiography. Chaumonot describes the difficulties of the journey very graphically in a letter to his friend, Father Nappi, dated Aug. 3, 1640, preserved in Carayon. See also the next letter, *Brébeuf au T. R. P. Mutio Vitelleschi, 20 Août, 1641.*

The Récollet La Roche Dallion had visited the Neutrals fourteen years before, (see Introduction, *note*,) and, like his two successors, had been seriously endangered by Huron intrigues.

and saw in hope the day when they should bear the cross into the blood-stained dens of the Iroquois.[1]

But, in this exaltation and tension of the powers, was there no moment when the recoil of Nature claimed a temporary sway? When, an exile from his kind, alone, beneath the desolate rock and the gloomy pine-trees, the priest gazed forth on the pitiless wilderness and the hovels of its dark and ruthless tenants, his thoughts, it may be, flew longingly beyond those wastes of forest and sea that lay between him and the home of his boyhood: or rather, led by a deeper attraction, they revisited the ancient centre of his faith, and he seemed to stand once more in that gorgeous temple, where, shrined in lazuli and gold, rest the hallowed bones of Loyola. Column and arch and dome rise upon his vision, radiant in painted light, and trembling with celestial music. Again he kneels before the altar, from whose tablature beams upon him that loveliest of shapes in which the imagination of man has embodied the spirit of Christianity. The illusion overpowers him. A thrill shakes his frame, and he bows in reverential rapture. No longer a memory, no longer a dream, but a visioned presence, distinct and luminous in the forest shades, the Virgin stands before him. Prostrate on the rocky earth, he adores the benign angel of his ecstatic faith, then turns with rekindled fervors to his stern apostleship.

Now, by the shores of Thunder Bay, the Huron traders freight their birch vessels for their yearly voyage; and, embarked with them, let us, too, revisit the rock of Quebec.

[1] This zeal was in no degree due to success; for in 1641, after seven years of toil, the mission counted only about fifty living converts,—a falling off from former years.

Chapter XIII

1636–1646

QUEBEC AND ITS TENANTS

The New Governor • Edifying Examples • Le Jeune's Correspondents • Rank and Devotion • Nuns • Priestly Authority • Condition of Quebec • The Hundred Associates • Church Discipline • Plays • Fireworks • Processions • Catechizing • Terrorism • Pictures • The Converts • The Society of Jesus • The Foresters

---

I HAVE traced, in another volume, the life and death of the noble founder of New France, Samuel de Champlain. It was on Christmas Day, 1635, that his heroic spirit bade farewell to the frame it had animated, and to the rugged cliff where he had toiled so long to lay the corner-stone of a Christian empire.

Quebec was without a governor. Who should succeed Champlain? and would his successor be found equally zealous for the Faith, and friendly to the mission? These doubts, as he himself tells us, agitated the mind of the Father Superior, Le Jeune; but they were happily set at rest, when, on a morning in June, he saw a ship anchoring in the basin below, and, hastening with his brethren to the landing-place, was there met by Charles Huault de Montmagny, a Knight of Malta, followed by a train of officers and gentlemen. As they all climbed the rock together, Montmagny saw a crucifix planted by the path. He instantly fell on his knees before it; and nobles, soldiers, sailors, and priests imitated his example. The Jesuits sang Te Deum at the church, and the cannon roared from the adjacent fort. Here the new governor was scarcely installed, when a Jesuit came in to ask if he would be godfather to an Indian about to be baptized. "Most gladly," replied the pious Montmagny. He repaired on the instant to the convert's hut, with a company of gayly apparelled gentlemen; and while the inmates stared in amazement at the scarlet and embroidery, he bestowed on the dying savage the name of Joseph, in honor of the spouse of the Virgin and the patron of New France.[1] Three days after, he was told that a dead proselyte was to be buried; on which, leaving the lines of the new fortification he was tracing, he took in hand a torch, De Lisle, his lieutenant, took another, Repentigny and St. Jean, gentlemen of his suite, with a band of soldiers followed, two priests bore the corpse, and thus all moved together in procession to the place of burial. The Jesuits were comforted. Champlain himself had not displayed a zeal so edifying.[2]

A considerable reinforcement came out with Montmagny, and among the rest several men of birth and substance, with their families and dependants. "It was a sight to thank God for," exclaims Father Le Jeune, "to behold these delicate young ladies and these tender infants issuing from their wooden prison, like day from the shades of night." The Father, it will be remembered, had for some years past seen nothing but squaws, with papooses swathed like mummies and strapped to a board.

He was even more pleased with the contents of a huge packet of letters that was placed in his hands, bearing the signatures of nuns, priests, soldiers, courtiers, and princesses. A great interest in the mission had been kindled in France. Le Jeune's printed *Relations* had been read with avidity; and his Jesuit brethren, who, as teachers, preachers, and confessors, had spread themselves through the nation, had successfully fanned the rising flame. The Father Superior finds no words for his joy. "Heaven," he exclaims, "is the conductor of this enterprise. Nature's arms are not long enough to touch so many hearts."[3] He reads how in a single convent, thirteen nuns have devoted themselves by a vow to the work of converting the Indian women and children; how, in the church of Montmartre, a nun lies prostrate day and night before the altar, praying for the mission;[4] how "the Carmelites are all on

---

[1] Le Jeune, *Relation, 1636*, 5 (Cramoisy). "Monsieur le Gouverneur se transporte aux Cabanes de ces pauures barbares, suiuy d'une leste Noblesse. Je vous laisse à penser quel estonnement à ces Peuples de voir tant d'écarlate, tant de personnes bien faites sous leurs toits d'écorce!"

[2] *Ibid.*, 83 (Cramoisy).

[3] "C'est Dieu qui conduit cette entreprise. La Nature n'a pas les bras assez longs," etc. — *Relation, 1636*, 3.

[4] Brébeuf, *Relation des Hurons, 1636*, 76.

fire, the Ursulines full of zeal, the sisters of the Visitation have no words to speak their ardor";[1] how some person unknown, but blessed of Heaven, means to found a school for Huron children; how the Duchesse d'Aiguillon has sent out six workmen to build a hospital for the Indians; how, in every house of the Jesuits, young priests turn eager eyes towards Canada; and how, on the voyage thither, the devils raised a tempest, endeavoring, in vain fury, to drown the invaders of their American domain.[2]

Great was Le Jeune's delight at the exalted rank of some of those who gave their patronage to the mission; and again and again his satisfaction flows from his pen in mysterious allusions to these eminent persons.[3] In his eyes, the vicious imbecile who sat on the throne of France was the anointed champion of the Faith, and the cruel and ambitious priest who ruled king and nation alike was the chosen instrument of Heaven. Church and State, linked in alliance close and potential, played faithfully into each other's hands; and that enthusiasm, in which the Jesuit saw the direct inspiration of God, was fostered by all the prestige of royalty and all the patronage of power. And, as often happens where the interests of a hierarchy are identified with the interests of a ruling class, religion was become a fashion, as graceful and as comforting as the courtier's embroidered mantle or the court lady's robe of fur.

Such, we may well believe, was the complexion of the enthusiasm which animated some of Le Jeune's noble and princely correspondents. But there were deeper fervors, glowing in the still depths of convent cells, and kindling the breasts of their inmates with quenchless longings. Yet we hear of no zeal for the mission among religious communities of

[1] Le Jeune, *Relation, 1636,* 6. Compare "Divers Sentimens," appended to the *Relation* of 1635.

[2] "L'Enfer enrageant de nous veoir aller en la Nouuelle France pour conuertir les infidelles et diminuer sa puissance, par dépit il sousleuoit tous les Elemens contre nous, et vouloit abysmer la flotte." — *Divers Sentimens.*

[3] Among his correspondents was the young Duc d'Enghien, afterwards the Great Condé, at this time fifteen years old. "Dieu soit loüé! tout le ciel de nostre chere Patrie nous promet de fauorables influences, iusques à ce nouuel astre, qui commence à paroistre parmy ceux de la premiere grandeur." — Le Jeune, *Relation, 1636,* 3, 4.

men. The Jesuits regarded the field as their own, and desired no rivals. They looked forward to the day when Canada should be another Paraguay.[1] It was to the combustible hearts of female recluses that the torch was most busily applied; and here, accordingly, blazed forth a prodigious and amazing flame. "If all had their pious will," writes Le Jeune, "Quebec would soon be flooded with nuns."[2]

Both Montmagny and De Lisle were half churchmen, for both were Knights of Malta. More and more the powers spiritual engrossed the colony. As nearly as might be, the sword itself was in priestly hands. The Jesuits were all in all. Authority, absolute and without appeal, was vested in a council composed of the governor, Le Jeune, and the syndic, an official supposed to represent the interests of the inhabitants.[3] There was no tribunal of justice, and the governor pronounced summarily on all complaints. The church adjoined the fort; and before it was planted a stake bearing a placard with a prohibition against blasphemy, drunkenness, or neglect of mass and other religious rites. To the stake was also attached a chain and iron collar; and hard by was a wooden horse, whereon a culprit was now and then mounted by way of example and warning.[4] In a community so absolutely priest-governed, overt offences were, however, rare; and, except on the annual arrival of the ships from France, when the rock swarmed with godless sailors, Quebec was a model of decorum, and wore, as its chroniclers tell us, an aspect unspeakably edifying.

In the year 1640, various new establishments of religion and charity might have been seen at Quebec. There was the beginning of a college and a seminary for Huron children, an embryo Ursuline convent, an incipient hospital, and a new Algonquin mission at a place called Sillery, four miles distant. Champlain's fort had been enlarged and partly rebuilt in stone by Montmagny, who had also laid out streets on the site of

[1]"Que si celuy qui a escrit cette lettre a leu la Relation de ce qui se passe au Paraguais, qu'il a veu ce qui se fera un jour en la Nouuelle France."—Le Jeune, *Relation, 1637*, 304 (Cramoisy).

[2]Chaulmer, *Le Nouveau Monde Chrestien*, 41, is eloquent on this theme.

[3]Le Clerc, *Etablissement de la Foy*, Chap. XV.

[4]Le Jeune, *Relation, 1636*, 153, 154 (Cramoisy).

the future city, though as yet the streets had no houses. Behind the fort, and very near it, stood the church and a house for the Jesuits. Both were of pine wood; and this year, 1640, both were burned to the ground, to be afterwards rebuilt in stone. The Jesuits, however, continued to occupy their rude mission-house of Notre-Dame des Anges, on the St. Charles, where we first found them.

The country around Quebec was still an unbroken wilderness, with the exception of a small clearing made by the Sieur Giffard on his seigniory of Beauport, another made by M. de Puiseaux between Quebec and Sillery, and possibly one or two feeble attempts in other quarters.[1] The total population did not much exceed two hundred, including women and children. Of this number, by far the greater part were agents of the fur company known as the Hundred Associates, and men in their employ. Some of these had brought over their families. The remaining inhabitants were priests, nuns, and a very few colonists.

The Company of the Hundred Associates was bound by its charter to send to Canada four thousand colonists before the year 1643.[2] It had neither the means nor the will to fulfil this engagement. Some of its members were willing to make personal sacrifices for promoting the missions, and building up a colony purely Catholic. Others thought only of the profits of trade; and the practical affairs of the company had passed entirely into the hands of this portion of its members. They sought to evade obligations the fulfilment of which would have ruined them. Instead of sending out colonists, they granted lands with the condition that the grantees should furnish a certain number of settlers to clear and till them, and these were to be credited to the Company.[3] The grantees took

---

[1] For Giffard, Puiseaux, and other colonists, compare Langevin, *Notes sur les Archives de Notre-Dame de Beauport*, 5, 6, 7; Ferland, *Notes sur les Archives de N. D. de Québec*, 22, 24 (1863); Ibid., *Cours d'Histoire du Canada*, I. 266; Le Jeune, *Relation, 1636*, 45; Faillon, *Histoire de la Colonie Française*, I. c. iv., v.

[2] See "Pioneers of France," 314.

[3] This appears in many early grants of the Company. Thus, in a grant to Simon Le Maître, Jan. 15, 1636, "que les hommes que le dit . . . fera passer en la N. F. tourneront à la décharge de la dite Compagnie," etc., etc. — See *Pièces sur la Tenure Seigneuriale*, published by the Canadian government, *passim*.

the land, but rarely fulfilled the condition. Some of these grants were corrupt and iniquitous. Thus, a son of Lauson, president of the Company, received, in the name of a third person, a tract of land on the south side of the St. Lawrence of sixty leagues front. To this were added all the islands in that river, excepting those of Montreal and Orleans, together with the exclusive right of fishing in it through its whole extent.[1] Lauson sent out not a single colonist to these vast concessions.

There was no real motive for emigration. No persecution expelled the colonist from his home; for none but good Catholics were tolerated in New France. The settler could not trade with the Indians, except on condition of selling again to the Company at a fixed price. He might hunt, but he could not fish; and he was forced to beg or buy food for years before he could obtain it from that rude soil in sufficient quantity for the wants of his family. The Company imported provisions every year for those in its employ; and of these supplies a portion was needed for the relief of starving settlers. Giffard and his seven men on his seigniory of Beauport were for some time the only settlers—excepting, perhaps, the Hébert family—who could support themselves throughout the year. The rigor of the climate repelled the emigrant; nor were the attractions which Father Le Jeune held forth— "piety, freedom, and independence"—of a nature to entice him across the sea, when it is remembered that this freedom consisted in subjection to the arbitrary will of a priest and a soldier, and in the liability, should he forget to go to mass, of being made fast to a post with a collar and chain, like a dog.

Aside from the fur trade of the Company, the whole life of the colony was in missions, convents, religious schools, and hospitals. Here on the rock of Quebec were the appendages, useful and otherwise, of an old-established civilization. While as yet there were no inhabitants, and no immediate hope of any, there were institutions for the care of children, the sick, and the decrepit. All these were supported by a charity in most cases precarious. The Jesuits relied chiefly on the Company, who, by the terms of their patent, were obliged to

[1] *Archives du Séminaire de Villemarie*, cited by Faillon, I. 350. Lauson's father owned Montreal. The son's grant extended from the River St. Francis to a point far above Montreal.—La Fontaine, *Mémoire sur la Famille de Lauson*.

maintain religious worship.[1] Of the origin of the convent, hospital, and seminary I shall soon have occasion to speak.

Quebec wore an aspect half military, half monastic. At sunrise and sunset, a squad of soldiers in the pay of the Company paraded in the fort; and, as in Champlain's time, the bells of the church rang morning, noon, and night. Confessions, masses, and penances were punctiliously observed; and, from the governor to the meanest laborer, the Jesuit watched and guided all. The social atmosphere of New England itself was not more suffocating. By day and by night, at home, at church, or at his daily work, the colonist lived under the eyes of busy and over-zealous priests. At times, the denizens of Quebec grew restless. In 1639, deputies were covertly sent to beg relief in France, and "to represent the hell in which the consciences of the colony were kept by the union of the temporal and spiritual authority in the same hands."[2] In 1642, partial and ineffective measures were taken, with the countenance of Richelieu, for introducing into New France an Order less greedy of seigniories and endowments than the Jesuits, and less prone to political encroachment.[3] No favorable result followed; and the colony remained as before, in a pitiful state of cramping and dwarfing vassalage.

This is the view of a heretic. It was the aim of the founders of New France to build on a foundation purely and supremely Catholic. What this involved is plain; for no degree

---

[1] It is a principle of the Jesuits, that each of its establishments shall find a support of its own, and not be a burden on the general funds of the Society. The *Relations* are full of appeals to the charity of devout persons in behalf of the missions.

"Of what use to the country at this period could have been two communities of cloistered nuns?" asks the modern historian of the Ursulines of Quebec. And he answers by citing the words of Pope Gregory the Great, who, when Rome was ravaged by famine, pestilence, and the barbarians, declared that his only hope was in the prayers of the three thousand nuns then assembled in the holy city.— *Les Ursulines de Québec. Introd.*, XI.

[2] "Pour leur representer la gehenne où estoient les consciences de la Colonie, de se voir gouverné par les mesmes personnes pour le spirituel et pour le temporel."—Le Clerc, I. 478.

[3] *Declaration de Pierre Breant, par devant les Notaires du Roy*, MS. The Order was that of the Capuchins, who, like the Récollets, are a branch of the Franciscans. Their introduction into Canada was prevented; but they established themselves in Maine.

of personal virtue is a guaranty against the evils which attach to the temporal rule of ecclesiastics. Burning with love and devotion to Christ and his immaculate Mother, the fervent and conscientious priest regards with mixed pity and indignation those who fail in this supreme allegiance. Piety and charity alike demand that he should bring back the rash wanderer to the fold of his divine Master, and snatch him from the perdition into which his guilt must otherwise plunge him. And while he, the priest, himself yields reverence and obedience to the Superior, in whom he sees the representative of Deity, it behooves him, in his degree, to require obedience from those whom he imagines that God has confided to his guidance. His conscience, then, acts in perfect accord with the love of power innate in the human heart. These allied forces mingle with a perplexing subtlety; pride, disguised even from itself, walks in the likeness of love and duty; and a thousand times on the pages of history we find Hell beguiling the virtues of Heaven to do its work. The instinct of domination is a weed that grows rank in the shadow of the temple, climbs over it, possesses it, covers its ruin, and feeds on its decay. The unchecked sway of priests has always been the most mischievous of tyrannies; and even were they all well-meaning and sincere, it would be so still.

To the Jesuits, the atmosphere of Quebec was well-nigh celestial. "In the climate of New France," they write, "one learns perfectly to seek only God, to have no desire but God, no purpose but for God." And again: "To live in New France is in truth to live in the bosom of God." "If," adds Le Jeune, "any one of those who die in this country goes to perdition, I think he will be doubly guilty."[1]

The very amusements of this pious community were acts of religion. Thus, on the fête-day of St. Joseph, the patron of New France, there was a show of fireworks to do him honor. In the forty volumes of the Jesuit *Relations* there is but one

[1] "La Nouuelle France est vn vray climat où on apprend parfaictement bien à ne chercher que Dieu, ne desirer que Dieu seul, auoir l'intention purement à Dieu, etc. . . . Viure en la Nouuelle France, c'est à vray dire viure dans le sein de Dieu, et ne respirer que l'air de sa Diuine conduite."—*Divers Sentimens*. "Si quelqu'un de ceux qui meurent en ces contrées se damne, je croy qu'il sera doublement coupable."—*Relation, 1640*, 5 (Cramoisy).

pictorial illustration; and this represents the pyrotechnic con-
trivance in question, together with a figure of the Governor
in the act of touching it off.[1] But, what is more curious, a
Catholic writer of the present day, the Abbé Faillon, in an
elaborate and learned work, dilates at length on the details of
the display; and this, too, with a gravity which evinces his
conviction that squibs, rockets, blue-lights, and serpents are
important instruments for the saving of souls.[2] On May-Day
of the same year, 1637, Montmagny planted before the church
a May-pole surmounted by a triple crown, beneath which
were three symbolical circles decorated with wreaths, and
bearing severally the names, *Iesus*, *Maria*, *Ioseph*; the soldiers drew up before it, and saluted it with a volley of musketry.[3]

On the anniversary of the Dauphin's birth there was a dramatic performance, in which an unbeliever, speaking Algonquin for the profit of the Indians present, was hunted into
Hell by fiends.[4] Religious processions were frequent. In one
of them, the Governor in a court dress and a baptized Indian
in beaver-skins were joint supporters of the canopy which
covered the Host.[5] In another, six Indians led the van, arrayed each in a velvet coat of scarlet and gold sent them by
the King. Then came other Indian converts, two and two;
then the foundress of the Ursuline convent, with Indian children in French gowns; then all the Indian girls and women,
dressed after their own way; then the priests; then the Governor; and finally the whole French population, male and female, except the artillery-men at the fort, who saluted with
their cannon the cross and banner borne at the head of the
procession. When all was over, the Governor and the Jesuits
rewarded the Indians with a feast.[6]

Now let the stranger enter the church of Notre-Dame de
la Recouvrance, after vespers. It is full, to the very porch:

[1] *Relation*, *1637*, 8. The *Relations*, as originally published, comprised about
forty volumes.
[2] *Histoire de la Colonie Française*, I. 291, 292.
[3] *Relation*, *1637*, 82.
[4] Vimont, *Relation*, *1640*, 6.
[5] Le Jeune, *Relation*, *1638*, 6.
[6] *Ibid.*, *1639*, 3.

officers in slouched hats and plumes, musketeers, pikemen, mechanics, and laborers. Here is Montmagny himself; Repentigny and Poterie, gentlemen of good birth; damsels of nurture ill fitted to the Canadian woods; and, mingled with these, the motionless Indians, wrapped to the throat in embroidered moose-hides. Le Jeune, not in priestly vestments, but in the common black dress of his Order, is before the altar; and on either side is a row of small red-skinned children listening with exemplary decorum, while, with a cheerful, smiling face, he teaches them to kneel, clasp their hands, and sign the cross. All the principal members of this zealous community are present, at once amused and edified at the grave deportment, and the prompt, shrill replies of the infant catechumens; while their parents in the crowd grin delight at the gifts of beads and trinkets with which Le Jeune rewards his most proficient pupils.[1]

We have seen the methods of conversion practised among the Hurons. They were much the same at Quebec. The principal appeal was to fear.[2] "You do good to your friends," said Le Jeune to an Algonquin chief, "and you burn your enemies. God does the same." And he painted Hell to the startled neophyte as a place where, when he was hungry, he would get nothing to eat but frogs and snakes, and, when thirsty, nothing to drink but flames.[3] Pictures were found invaluable. "These holy representations," pursues the Father Superior, "are half the instruction that can be given to the Indians. I wanted some pictures of Hell and souls in perdition, and a few were sent us on paper; but they are too confused. The devils and the men are so mixed up, that one can make out nothing without particular attention. If three, four, or five devils were painted tormenting a soul with different punishments,—one applying fire, another serpents, another tearing him with pincers, and another holding him fast with a chain,—this would have a good effect, especially if everything were made distinct,

<hr/>

[1] Le Jeune, *Relation, 1637*, 122 (Cramoisy).

[2] *Ibid., 1636*, 119, and *1637*, 32 (Cramoisy). "La crainte est l'auan couriere de la foy dans ces esprits barbares."

[3] *Ibid., Relation, 1637*, 80–82 (Cramoisy). "Avoir faim et ne manger que des serpens et des crapaux, avoir soif et ne boire que des flammes."

and misery, rage, and desperation appeared plainly in his face."[1]

The preparation of the convert for baptism was often very slight. A dying Algonquin, who, though meagre as a skeleton, had thrown himself, with a last effort of expiring ferocity, on an Iroquois prisoner, and torn off his ear with his teeth, was baptized almost immediately.[2] In the case of converts in health there was far more preparation; yet these often apostatized. The various objects of instruction may all be included in one comprehensive word, submission,— an abdication of will and judgment in favor of the spiritual director, who was the interpreter and vicegerent of God. The director's function consisted in the enforcement of dogmas by which he had himself been subdued, in which he believed profoundly, and to which he often clung with an absorbing enthusiasm. The Jesuits, an Order thoroughly and vehemently reactive, had revived in Europe the mediæval type of Christianity, with all its attendant superstitions. Of these the Canadian missions bear abundant marks. Yet, on the whole, the labors of the missionaries tended greatly to the benefit of the Indians. Reclaimed, as the Jesuits tried to reclaim them, from their wan-

[1] "Les heretiques sont grandement blasmables, de condamner et de briser les images qui ont de si bons effets. Ces sainctes figures sont la moitié de l'instruction qu'on peut donner aux Sauuages. l'auois desiré quelques portraits de l'enfer et de l'âme damnée; on nous en a enuoyé quelques vns en papier, mais cela est trop confus. Les diables sont tellement meslez auec les hommes, qu'on n'y peut rien recognoistre, qu'auec vne particuliere attention. Qui depeindroit trois ou quatre ou cinq demons, tourmentans vne âme de diuers supplices, l'vn luy appliquant des feux, l'autre des serpens, l'autre la tenaillant, l'autre la tenant liée auec des chaisnes, cela auroit vn bon effet, notamment si tout estoit bien distingué, et que la rage et la tristesse parussent bien en la face de cette âme desesperée."— Relation, 1637, 32 (Cramoisy).

[2] "Ce seroit vne estrange cruauté de voir descendre vne âme toute viuante dans les enfers, par le refus d'vn bien que Iesus Christ luy a acquis au prix de son sang."— Ibid., 66.

"Considerez d'autre coté la grande appréhension que nous avions sujet de redouter la guérison; pour autant que bien souvent étant guéris il ne leur reste du St. Baptême que le caractère."— Lettres de Garnier, MSS.

It was not very easy to make an Indian comprehend the nature of baptism. An Iroquois at Montreal, hearing a missionary speaking of the water which cleansed the soul from sin, said that he was well acquainted with it, as the Dutch had once given him so much that they were forced to tie him, hand and foot, to prevent him from doing mischief.— Faillon, II. 43.

dering life, settled in habits of peaceful industry, and reduced to a passive and childlike obedience, they would have gained more than enough to compensate them for the loss of their ferocious and miserable independence. At least, they would have escaped annihilation. The Society of Jesus aspired to the mastery of all New France; but the methods of its ambition were consistent with a Christian benevolence. Had this been otherwise, it would have employed other instruments. It would not have chosen a Jogues or a Garnier. The Society had men for every work, and it used them wisely. It utilized the apostolic virtues of its Canadian missionaries, fanned their enthusiasm, and decorated itself with their martyr crowns. With joy and gratulation, it saw them rival in another hemisphere the noble memory of its saint and hero, Francis Xavier.[1]

I have spoken of the colonists as living in a state of temporal and spiritual vassalage. To this there was one exception,—a small class of men whose home was the forest, and their companions savages. They followed the Indians in their roamings, lived with them, grew familiar with their language, allied themselves with their women, and often became oracles in the camp and leaders on the war-path. Champlain's bold interpreter, Étienne Brulé, whose adventures I have recounted elsewhere,[2] may be taken as a type of this class. Of the rest, the most conspicuous were Jean Nicollet, Jacques Hertel, François Marguerie, and Nicolas Marsolet.[3] Doubtless, when they returned from their rovings, they often had pressing need of penance and absolution; yet, for the most part, they were good Catholics, and some of them were zealous for the missions. Nicollet and others were at times settled as interpreters at Three Rivers and Quebec. Several of them were men of great intelligence and an invincible courage. From

---

[1] Enemies of the Jesuits, while denouncing them in unmeasured terms, speak in strong eulogy of many of the Canadian missionaries. See, for example, Steinmetz, *History of the Jesuits*, II. 415.

[2] "Pioneers of France," 298.

[3] See Ferland, *Notes sur les Registres de N. D. de Québec*, 30.

Nicollet, especially, was a remarkable man. As early as 1639, he ascended the Green Bay of Lake Michigan, and crossed to the waters of the Mississippi. This was first shown by the researches of Mr. Shea. See his *Discovery and Exploration of the Mississippi Valley*, XX.

hatred of restraint, and love of a wild and adventurous independence, they encountered privations and dangers scarcely
less than those to which the Jesuit exposed himself from motives widely different,—he from religious zeal, charity, and
the hope of Paradise; they simply because they liked it. Some
of the best families of Canada claim descent from this vigorous and hardy stock.

Chapter XIV

1636–1652

DEVOTEES AND NUNS

The Huron Seminary • Madame de la Peltrie • Her Pious Schemes • Her Sham Marriage • She visits the Ursulines of Tours • Marie de Saint Bernard • Marie de l'Incarnation • Her Enthusiasm • Her Mystical Marriage • Her Dejection • Her Mental Conflicts • Her Vision • Made Superior of the Ursulines • The Hôtel-Dieu • The Voyage to Canada • Sillery • Labors and Sufferings of the Nuns • Character of Marie de l'Incarnation • Of Madame de la Peltrie

QUEBEC, as we have seen, had a seminary, a hospital, and a convent, before it had a population. It will be well to observe the origin of these institutions.

The Jesuits from the first had cherished the plan of a seminary for Huron boys at Quebec. The Governor and the Company favored the design; since not only would it be an efficient means of spreading the Faith and attaching the tribe to the French interest, but the children would be pledges for the good behavior of the parents, and hostages for the safety of missionaries and traders in the Indian towns.[1] In the summer of 1636, Father Daniel, descending from the Huron country, worn, emaciated, his cassock patched and tattered, and his shirt in rags, brought with him a boy, to whom two others were soon added; and through the influence of the interpreter, Nicollet, the number was afterwards increased by several more. One of them ran away, two ate themselves to death, a fourth was carried home by his father, while three of those remaining stole a canoe, loaded it with all they could lay their hands upon, and escaped in triumph with their plunder.[2]

The beginning was not hopeful; but the Jesuits persevered, and at length established their seminary on a firm basis. The

[1]"M. de Montmagny cognoit bien l'importance de ce Seminaire pour la gloire de Nostre Seigneur, et pour le Commerce de ces Messieurs."—*Relation, 1637*, 209 (Cramoisy).

[2]Le Jeune, *Relation, 1637*, 55–59. Ibid., *Relation, 1638*, 23.

Marquis de Gamache had given the Society six thousand crowns for founding a college at Quebec. In 1637, a year before the building of Harvard College, the Jesuits began a wooden structure in the rear of the fort; and here, within one inclosure, was the Huron seminary and the college for French boys.

Meanwhile the female children of both races were without instructors; but a remedy was at hand. At Alençon, in 1603, was born Marie Madeleine de Chauvigny, a scion of the *haute noblesse* of Normandy. Seventeen years later she was a young lady, abundantly wilful and superabundantly enthusiastic, — one who, in other circumstances, might perhaps have made a romantic elopement and a *mésalliance*.[1] But her impressible and ardent nature was absorbed in other objects. Religion and its ministers possessed her wholly, and all her enthusiasm was spent on works of charity and devotion. Her father, passionately fond of her, resisted her inclination for the cloister, and sought to wean her back to the world; but she escaped from the chateau to a neighboring convent, where she resolved to remain. Her father followed, carried her home, and engaged her in a round of fêtes and hunting parties, in the midst of which she found herself surprised into a betrothal to M. de la Peltrie, a young gentleman of rank and character. The marriage proved a happy one, and Madame de la Peltrie, with an excellent grace, bore her part in the world she had wished to renounce. After a union of five years, her husband died, and she was left a widow and childless at the age of twenty-two. She returned to the religious ardors of her girlhood, again gave all her thoughts to devotion and charity, and again resolved to be a nun. She had heard of Canada; and when Le Jeune's first *Relations* appeared, she read them with avidity. "Alas!" wrote the Father, "is there no charitable and virtuous lady who will come to this country to gather up the blood of Christ, by teaching His word to the little Indian girls?" His appeal found a prompt and vehement response

---

[1] There is a portrait of her, taken at a later period, of which a photograph is before me. She has a semi-religious dress, hands clasped in prayer, large dark eyes, a smiling and mischievous mouth, and a face somewhat pretty and very coquettish. An engraving from the portrait is prefixed to the "Notice Biographique de Madame de la Peltrie" in *Les Ursulines de Québec*, I. 348.

from the breast of Madame de la Peltrie. Thenceforth she thought of nothing but Canada. In the midst of her zeal, a fever seized her. The physicians despaired; but, at the height of the disease, the patient made a vow to St. Joseph, that, should God restore her to health, she would build a house in honor of Him in Canada, and give her life and her wealth to the instruction of Indian girls. On the following morning, say her biographers, the fever had left her.

Meanwhile her relatives, or those of her husband, had confirmed her pious purposes by attempting to thwart them. They pronounced her a romantic visionary, incompetent to the charge of her property. Her father, too, whose fondness for her increased with his advancing age, entreated her to remain with him while he lived, and to defer the execution of her plans till he should be laid in his grave. From entreaties he passed to commands, and at length threatened to disinherit her, if she persisted. The virtue of obedience, for which she is extolled by her clerical biographers, however abundantly exhibited in respect to those who held charge of her conscience, was singularly wanting towards the parent who, in the way of Nature, had the best claim to its exercise; and Madame de la Peltrie was more than ever resolved to go to Canada. Her father, on his part, was urgent that she should marry again. On this she took counsel of a Jesuit,[1] who, "having seriously reflected before God," suggested a device, which to the heretical mind is a little startling, but which commended itself to Madame de la Peltrie as fitted at once to soothe the troubled spirit of her father, and to save her from the sin involved in the abandonment of her pious designs.

Among her acquaintance was M. de Bernières, a gentleman of high rank, great wealth, and zealous devotion. She wrote to him, explained the situation, and requested him to feign a marriage with her. His sense of honor recoiled: moreover, in the fulness of his zeal, he had made a vow of chastity, and an

---

[1] "Partagée ainsi entre l'amour filial et la religion, en proie aux plus poignantes angoisses, elle s'adressa à un religieux de la Compagnie de Jésus, dont elle connaissait la prudence consommée, et le supplia de l'éclairer de ses lumières. Ce religieux, après y avoir sérieusement réfléchi devant Dieu, lui répondit qu'il croyait avoir trouvé un moyen de tout concilier."—Casgrain, *Vie de Marie de l'Incarnation*, 243.

apparent breach of it would cause scandal. He consulted his spiritual director and a few intimate friends. All agreed that the glory of God was concerned, and that it behooved him to accept the somewhat singular overtures of the young widow,[1] and request her hand from her father. M. de Chauvigny, who greatly esteemed Bernières, was delighted; and his delight was raised to transport at the dutiful and modest acquiescence of his daughter.[2] A betrothal took place; all was harmony, and for a time no more was said of disinheriting Madame de la Peltrie, or putting her in wardship.

Bernières's scruples returned. Divided between honor and conscience, he postponed the marriage, until at length M. de Chauvigny conceived misgivings, and again began to speak of disinheriting his daughter, unless the engagement was fulfilled.[3] Bernières yielded, and went with Madame de la Peltrie to consult "the most eminent divines."[4] A sham marriage took place, and she and her accomplice appeared in public as man and wife. Her relatives, however, had already renewed their attempts to deprive her of the control of her property. A suit, of what nature does not appear, had been decided against her at Caen, and she had appealed to the Parliament of Normandy. Her lawyers were in despair; but, as her biographer justly observes, "the saints have resources which others

[1] "Enfin après avoir longtemps imploré les lumières du ciel, il remit toute l'affaire entre les mains de son directeur et de quelques amis intimes. Tous, d'un commun accord, lui déclarèrent que la gloire de Dieu y était interessée, et qu'il devait accepter."— *Ibid.*, 244.

[2] "The prudent young widow answered him with much respect and modesty, that, as she knew M. de Bernières to be a favorite with him, *she* also preferred him to all others."

The above is from a letter of Marie de l'Incarnation, translated by Mother St. Thomas, of the Ursuline convent of Quebec, in her *Life of Madame de la Peltrie*, 41. Compare *Les Ursulines de Québec*, 10, and the "Notice Biographique" in the same volume.

[3] "Our virtuous widow did not lose courage. As she had given her confidence to M. de Bernières, she informed him of all that passed, while she flattered her father each day, telling him that this nobleman was too honorable to fail in keeping his word."— St. Thomas, *Life of Madame de la Peltrie*, 42.

[4] "He" (Bernières) "went to stay at the house of a mutual friend, where they had frequent opportunities of seeing each other, and consulting the most eminent divines on the means of effecting this pretended marriage."— *Ibid.*, 43.

have not." A vow to St. Joseph secured his intercession and gained her case. Another thought now filled her with agitation. Her plans were laid, and the time of action drew near. How could she endure the distress of her father, when he learned that she had deluded him with a false marriage, and that she and all that was hers were bound for the wilderness of Canada? Happily for him, he fell ill, and died in ignorance of the deceit that had been practised upon him.[1]

Whatever may be thought of the quality of Madame de la Peltrie's devotion, there can be no reasonable doubt of its sincerity or its ardor; and yet one can hardly fail to see in her the signs of that restless longing for *éclat*, which, with some women, is a ruling passion. When, in company with Bernières, she passed from Alençon to Tours, and from Tours to Paris, an object of attention to nuns, priests, and prelates,— when the Queen herself summoned her to an interview,— it may be that the profound contentment of soul ascribed to her had its origin in sources not exclusively of the spirit. At Tours, she repaired to the Ursuline convent. The Superior and all the nuns met her at the entrance of the cloister, and, separating into two rows as she appeared, sang the *Veni Creator*, while the bell of the monastery sounded its loudest peal. Then they led her in triumph to their church, sang *Te Deum*, and, while the honored guest knelt before the altar, all the

---

[1] It will be of interest to observe the view taken of this pretended marriage by Madame de la Peltrie's Catholic biographers. Charlevoix tells the story without comment, but with apparent approval. Sainte-Foi, in his *Premières Ursulines de France*, says, that, as God had taken her under His guidance, we should not venture to criticize her. Casgrain, in his *Vie de Marie de l'Incarnation*, remarks:—

"Une telle conduite peut encore aujourd'hui paraître étrange à bien des personnes; mais outre que l'avenir fit bien voir que c'était une inspiration du ciel, nous pouvons répondre, avec un savant et pieux auteur, que nous ne devons point juger ceux que Dieu se charge lui-même de conduire."—p. 247.

Mother St. Thomas highly approves the proceeding, and says:—

"Thus ended the pretended engagement of this virtuous lady and gentleman, which caused, at the time, so much inquiry and excitement among the nobility in France, and which, after a lapse of two hundred years, cannot fail exciting feelings of admiration in the heart of every virtuous woman!"

Surprising as it may appear, the book from which the above is taken was written a few years since, in so-called English, for the instruction of the pupils in the Ursuline Convent at Quebec.

sisterhood knelt around her in a semicircle. Their hearts beat high within them. That day they were to know who of their number were chosen for the new convent of Quebec, of which Madame de la Peltrie was to be the foundress; and when their devotions were over, they flung themselves at her feet, each begging with tears that the lot might fall on her. Aloof from this throng of enthusiastic suppliants stood a young nun, Marie de St. Bernard, too timid and too modest to ask the boon for which her fervent heart was longing. It was granted without asking. This delicate girl was chosen, and chosen wisely.[1]

There was another nun who stood apart, silent and motion-less,—a stately figure, with features strongly marked and per-haps somewhat masculine;[2] but, if so, they belied her, for Marie de l'Incarnation was a woman to the core. For her there was no need of entreaties; for she knew that the Jesuits had made her their choice, as Superior of the new convent. She was born, forty years before, at Tours, of a good *bour-geois* family. As she grew up towards maturity, her qualities soon declared themselves. She had uncommon talents and strong religious susceptibilities, joined to a vivid imagina-tion,—an alliance not always desirable under a form of faith where both are excited by stimulants so many and so power-ful. Like Madame de la Peltrie, she married, at the desire of her parents, in her eighteenth year. The marriage was not happy. Her biographers say that there was no fault on either side. Apparently, it was a severe case of "incompatibility." She sought her consolation in the churches; and, kneeling in dim chapels, held communings with Christ and the angels. At the end of two years her husband died, leaving her with an infant son. She gave him to the charge of her sister, abandoned her-self to solitude and meditation, and became a mystic of the intense and passional school. Yet a strong maternal instinct

[1] Casgrain, *Vie de Marie de l'Incarnation*, 271–273. There is a long account of Marie de St. Bernard, by Ragueneau, in the *Relation* of 1652. Here it is said that she showed an unaccountable indifference as to whether she went to Canada or not, which, however, was followed by an ardent desire to go.

[2] There is an engraved portrait of her, taken some years later, of which a photograph is before me. When she was "in the world," her stately propor-tions are said to have attracted general attention. Her family name was Marie Guyard. She was born on the eighteenth of October, 1599.

battled painfully in her breast with a sense of religious vocation. Dreams, visions, interior voices, ecstasies, revulsions, periods of rapture and periods of deep dejection, made up the agitated tissue of her life. She fasted, wore hair-cloth, scourged herself, washed dishes among the servants, and did their most menial work. She heard, in a trance, a miraculous voice. It was that of Christ, promising to become her spouse. Months and years passed, full of troubled hopes and fears, when again the voice sounded in her ear, with assurance that the promise was fulfilled, and that she was indeed his bride. Now ensued phenomena which are not infrequent among Roman Catholic female devotees, when unmarried, or married unhappily, and which have their source in the necessities of a woman's nature. To her excited thought, her divine spouse became a living presence; and her language to him, as recorded by herself, is that of the most intense passion. She went to prayer, agitated and tremulous, as if to a meeting with an earthly lover. "O my Love!" she exclaimed, "when shall I embrace you? Have you no pity on me in the torments that I suffer? Alas! alas! my Love, my Beauty, my Life! instead of healing my pain, you take pleasure in it. Come, let me embrace you, and die in your sacred arms!" And again she writes: "Then, as I was spent with fatigue, I was forced to say, 'My divine Love, since you wish me to live, I pray you let me rest a little, that I may the better serve you'; and I promised him that afterward I would suffer myself to consume in his chaste and divine embraces."[1]

[1] "Allant à l'oraison, je tressaillois en moi-même, et disois: Allons dans la solitude, mon cher amour, afin que je vous embrasse à mon aise, et que, respirant mon âme en vous, elle ne soit plus que vous-même par union d'amour. . . . Puis, mon corps étant brisé de fatigues, j'étois contrainte de dire: Mon divin amour, je vous prie de me laisser prendre un peu de repos, afin que je puisse mieux vous servir, puisque vous voulez que je vive. . . . Je le priois de me laisser agir; lui promettant de me laisser après cela consumer dans ses chastes et divins embrassemens. . . . O amour! quand vous embrasserai-je? N'avez-vous point pitié de moi dans le tourment que je souffre? helas! helas! mon amour, ma beauté, ma vie! au lieu de me guérir, vous vous plaisez à mes maux. Venez donc que je vous embrasse, et que je meure entre vos bras sacréz!"

The above passages, from various pages of her journal, will suffice, though they give but an inadequate idea of these strange extravagances. What is most astonishing is, that a man of sense like Charlevoix, in his Life of Marie de

Clearly, here is a case for the physiologist as well as the theologian; and the "holy widow," as her biographers call her, becomes an example, and a lamentable one, of the tendency of the erotic principle to ally itself with high religious excitement.

But the wings of imagination will tire and droop, the brightest dream-land of contemplative fancy grow dim, and an abnormal tension of the faculties find its inevitable reaction at last. From a condition of highest exaltation, a mystical heaven of light and glory, the unhappy dreamer fell back to a dreary earth, or rather to an abyss of darkness and misery. Her biographers tell us that she became a prey to dejection, and thoughts of infidelity, despair, estrangement from God, aversion to mankind, pride, vanity, impurity, and a supreme disgust at the rites of religion. Exhaustion produced common-sense, and the dreams which had been her life now seemed a tissue of illusions. Her confessor became a weariness to her, and his words fell dead on her ear. Indeed, she conceived a repugnance to the holy man. Her old and favorite confessor, her oracle, guide, and comforter, had lately been taken from her by promotion in the Church,—which may serve to explain her dejection; and the new one, jealous of his predecessor, told her that all his counsels had been visionary and dangerous to her soul. Having overwhelmed her with this announcement, he left her, apparently out of patience with her refractory and gloomy mood; and she remained for several months deprived of spiritual guidance.[1] Two years elapsed before her mind recovered its tone, when she soared once more in the seventh heaven of imaginative devotion.

---

l'Incarnation, should extract them in full, as matter of edification and evidence of saintship. Her recent biographer, the Abbé Casgrain, refrains from quoting them, though he mentions them approvingly as evincing fervor. The Abbé Racine, in his *Discours à l'Occasion du 192ème Anniversaire de l'heureuse Mort de la Vén. Mère de l'Incarnation*, delivered at Quebec in 1864, speaks of them as transcendent proofs of the supreme favor of Heaven.—Some of the pupils of Marie de l'Incarnation also had mystical marriages with Christ; and the impassioned rhapsodies of one of them being overheard, she nearly lost her character, as it was thought that she was apostrophizing an earthly lover.

[1] Casgrain, 195–197.

Marie de l'Incarnation, we have seen, was unrelenting in every practice of humiliation; dressed in mean attire, did the servants' work, nursed sick beggars, and, in her meditations, taxed her brain with metaphysical processes of self-annihilation. And yet, when one reads her "Spiritual Letters," the conviction of an enormous spiritual pride in the writer can hardly be repressed. She aspired to that inner circle of the faithful, that aristocracy of devotion, which, while the common herd of Christians are busied with the duties of life, eschews the visible and the present, and claims to live only for God. In her strong maternal affection she saw a lure to divert her from the path of perfect saintship. Love for her child long withheld her from becoming a nun; but at last, fortified by her confessor, she left him to his fate, took the vows, and immured herself with the Ursulines of Tours. The boy, frenzied by his desertion, and urged on by indignant relatives, watched his opportunity, and made his way into the refectory of the convent, screaming to the horrified nuns to give him back his mother. As he grew older, her anxiety increased; and at length she heard in her seclusion that he had fallen into bad company, had left the relative who had sheltered him, and run off, no one knew whither. The wretched mother, torn with anguish, hastened for consolation to her confessor, who met her with stern upbraidings. Yet, even in this her intensest ordeal, her enthusiasm and her native fortitude enabled her to maintain a semblance of calmness, till she learned that the boy had been found and brought back.

Strange as it may seem, this woman, whose habitual state was one of mystical abstraction, was gifted to a rare degree with the faculties most useful in the practical affairs of life. She had spent several years in the house of her brother-in-law. Here, on the one hand, her vigils, visions, and penances set utterly at nought the order of a well-governed family; while, on the other, she made amends to her impatient relative by able and efficient aid in the conduct of his public and private affairs. Her biographers say, and doubtless with truth, that her heart was far away from these mundane interests; yet her talent for business was not the less displayed. Her spiritual guides were aware of it, and saw clearly that gifts so useful to the world might be made equally useful to the Church.

Hence it was that she was chosen Superior of the convent which Madame de la Peltrie was about to endow at Quebec.[1]

Yet it was from heaven itself that Marie de l'Incarnation received her first "vocation" to Canada. The miracle was in this wise.

In a dream she beheld a lady unknown to her. She took her hand; and the two journeyed together westward, towards the sea. They soon met one of the Apostles, clothed all in white, who, with a wave of his hand, directed them on their way. They now entered on a scene of surpassing magnificence. Beneath their feet was a pavement of squares of white marble, spotted with vermilion, and intersected with lines of vivid scarlet; and all around stood monasteries of matchless architecture. But the two travellers, without stopping to admire, moved swiftly on till they beheld the Virgin seated with her Infant Son on a small temple of white marble, which served her as a throne. She seemed about fifteen years of age, and was of a "ravishing beauty." Her head was turned aside; she was gazing fixedly on a wild waste of mountains and valleys, half concealed in mist. Marie de l'Incarnation approached with outstretched arms, adoring. The vision bent towards her, and, smiling, kissed her three times; whereupon, in a rapture, the dreamer awoke.[2]

She told the vision to Father Dinet, a Jesuit of Tours. He was at no loss for an interpretation. The land of mists and mountains was Canada, and thither the Virgin called her. Yet one mystery remained unsolved. Who was the unknown companion of her dream? Several years had passed, and signs from heaven and inward voices had raised to an intense fervor her zeal for her new vocation, when, for the first time, she saw Madame de la Peltrie on her visit to the convent at Tours, and recognized, on the instant, the lady of her nocturnal vision. No one can be surprised at this who has considered with the slightest attention the phenomena of religious enthusiasm.

---

[1] The combination of religious enthusiasm, however extravagant and visionary, with a talent for business, is not very rare. Nearly all the founders of monastic Orders are examples of it.

[2] Marie de l'Incarnation recounts this dream at great length in her letters; and Casgrain copies the whole, *verbatim*, as a revelation from God.

On the fourth of May, 1639, Madame de la Peltrie, Marie de l'Incarnation, Marie de St. Bernard, and another Ursuline, embarked at Dieppe for Canada. In the ship were also three young hospital nuns, sent out to found at Quebec a Hôtel-Dieu, endowed by the famous niece of Richelieu, the Duchesse d'Aiguillon.[1] Here, too, were the Jesuits Chaumonot and Poncet, on the way to their mission, together with Father Vimont, who was to succeed Le Jeune in his post of Superior. To the nuns, pale from their cloistered seclusion, there was a strange and startling novelty in this new world of life and action,—the ship, the sailors, the shouts of command, the flapping of sails, the salt wind, and the boisterous sea. The voyage was long and tedious. Sometimes they lay in their berths, seasick and woe-begone; sometimes they sang in choir on deck, or heard mass in the cabin. Once, on a misty morning, a wild cry of alarm startled crew and passengers alike. A huge iceberg was drifting close upon them. The peril was extreme. Madame de la Peltrie clung to Marie de l'Incarnation, who stood perfectly calm, and gathered her gown about her feet that she might drown with decency. It is scarcely necessary to say that they were saved by a vow to the Virgin and St. Joseph. Vimont offered it in behalf of all the company, and the ship glided into the open sea unharmed.

They arrived at Tadoussac on the fifteenth of July; and the nuns ascended to Quebec in a small craft deeply laden with salted codfish, on which, uncooked, they subsisted until the first of August, when they reached their destination. Cannon roared welcome from the fort and batteries; all labor ceased; the storehouses were closed; and the zealous Montmagny, with a train of priests and soldiers, met the new-comers at the landing. All the nuns fell prostrate, and kissed the sacred soil of Canada.[2] They heard mass at the church, dined at the fort, and presently set forth to visit the new settlement of Sillery, four miles above Quebec.

Noel Brulart de Sillery, a Knight of Malta, who had once

[1] Juchereau, *Histoire de l'Hôtel-Dieu de Québec*, 4.

[2] Juchereau, 14; Le Clerc, II. 33; Ragueneau, *Vie de Catherine de St. Augustin*, "Epistre dédicatoire;" Le Jeune, *Relation, 1639*, Chap. II.; Charlevoix, *Vie de Marie de l'Incarnation*, 264; "Acte de Reception," in *Les Ursulines de Québec*, I. 21.

filled the highest offices under the Queen Marie de Médicis, had now severed his connection with his Order, renounced the world, and become a priest. He devoted his vast revenues—for a dispensation of the Pope had freed him from his vow of poverty—to the founding of religious establishments.[1] Among other endowments, he had placed an ample fund in the hands of the Jesuits for the formation of a settlement of Christian Indians at the spot which still bears his name. On the strand of Sillery, between the river and the woody heights behind, were clustered the small log-cabins of a number of Algonquin converts, together with a church, a mission-house, and an infirmary,—the whole surrounded by a palisade. It was to this place that the six nuns were now conducted by the Jesuits. The scene delighted and edified them; and, in the transports of their zeal, they seized and kissed every female Indian child on whom they could lay hands, "without minding," says Father Le Jeune, "whether they were dirty or not." "Love and charity," he adds, "triumphed over every human consideration."[2]

The nuns of the Hôtel-Dieu soon after took up their abode at Sillery, whence they removed to a house built for them at Quebec by their foundress, the Duchesse d'Aiguillon. The Ursulines, in the absence of better quarters, were lodged at first in a small wooden tenement under the rock of Quebec, at the brink of the river. Here they were soon beset with such a host of children, that the floor of their wretched tenement was covered with beds, and their toil had no respite. Then came the small-pox, carrying death and terror among the neighboring Indians. These thronged to Quebec in misery and desperation, begging succor from the French. The labors both of the Ursulines and of the hospital nuns were prodigious. In the infected air of their miserable hovels, where sick and dying savages covered the floor, and were packed one above another in berths,—amid all that is most distressing

---

[1] See *Vie de l'Illustre Serviteur de Dieu Noel Brulart de Sillery*; also *Études et Recherches Biographiques sur le Chevalier Noel Brulart de Sillery*; and several documents in Martin's translation of Bressani, Appendix IV.

[2] " . . . sans prendre garde si ces petits enfans sauvages estoient sales ou non; . . . la loy d'amour et de charité l'emportoit par dessus toutes les considerations humaines."—*Relation, 1639*, 26 (Cramoisy).

and most revolting, with little food and less sleep, these women passed the rough beginning of their new life. Several of them fell ill. But the excess of the evil at length brought relief; for so many of the Indians died in these pest-houses that the survivors shunned them in horror.

But how did these women bear themselves amid toils so arduous? A pleasant record has come down to us of one of them,—that fair and delicate girl, Marie de St. Bernard, called, in the convent, Sister St. Joseph, who had been chosen at Tours as the companion of Marie de l'Incarnation. Another Ursuline, writing at a period when the severity of their labors was somewhat relaxed, says, "Her disposition is charming. In our times of recreation, she often makes us cry with laughing: it would be hard to be melancholy when she is near."[1]

It was three years later before the Ursulines and their pupils took possession of a massive convent of stone, built for them on the site which they still occupy. Money had failed before the work was done, and the interior was as unfinished as a barn.[2] Beside the cloister stood a large ash-tree; and it stands there still. Beneath its shade, says the convent tradition, Marie de l'Incarnation and her nuns instructed the Indian children in the truths of salvation; but it might seem rash to affirm that their teachings were always either wise or useful, since Father Vimont tells us approvingly, that they reared their pupils in so chaste a horror of the other sex, that a little girl, whom a man had playfully taken by the hand, ran crying to a bowl of water to wash off the unhallowed influence.[3]

Now and henceforward one figure stands nobly conspicuous in this devoted sisterhood. Marie de l'Incarnation, no longer lost in the vagaries of an insane mysticism, but engaged in the duties of Christian charity and the responsibilities of an arduous post, displays an ability, a fortitude, and an earnestness which command respect and admiration. Her

[1] *Lettre de la Mère Ste Claire à une de ses Sœurs Ursulines de Paris. Québec, 2 Sept., 1640.*—See *Les Ursulines de Québec,* I. 38.

[2] The interior was finished after a year or two, with cells as usual. There were four chimneys, with fireplaces burning a hundred and seventy-five cords of wood in a winter; and though the nuns were boxed up in beds which closed like chests, Marie de l'Incarnation complains bitterly of the cold. See her letter of Aug. 26, 1644.

[3] Vimont, *Relation, 1642,* 112 (Cramoisy).

mental intoxication had ceased, or recurred only at intervals; and false excitements no longer sustained her. She was racked with constant anxieties about her son, and was often in a condition described by her biographers as a "deprivation of all spiritual consolations." Her position was a very difficult one. She herself speaks of her life as a succession of crosses and humiliations. Some of these were due to Madame de la Peltrie, who, in a freak of enthusiasm, abandoned her Ursulines for a time, as we shall presently see, leaving them in the utmost destitution. There were dissensions to be healed among them; and money, everything, in short, to be provided. Marie de l'Incarnation, in her saddest moments, neither failed in judgment nor slackened in effort. She carried on a vast correspondence, embracing every one in France who could aid her infant community with money or influence; she harmonized and regulated it with excellent skill; and, in the midst of relentless austerities, she was loved as a mother by her pupils and dependants. Catholic writers extol her as a saint.[1] Protestants may see in her a Christian heroine, admirable, with all her follies and her faults.

The traditions of the Ursulines are full of the virtues of Madame de la Peltrie,—her humility, her charity, her penances, and her acts of mortification. No doubt, with some little allowance, these traditions are true; but there is more of reason than of uncharitableness in the belief, that her zeal would have been less ardent and sustained, if it had had fewer spectators. She was now fairly committed to the conventual life, her enthusiasm was kept within prescribed bounds, and she was no longer mistress of her own movements. On the one hand, she was anxious to accumulate merits against the Day of Judgment; and, on the other, she had a keen appreciation of the applause which the sacrifice of her fortune and her acts of piety had gained for her. Mortal vanity takes many

---

[1] There is a letter extant from Sister Anne de Ste Claire, an Ursuline who came to Quebec in 1640, written soon after her arrival, and containing curious evidence that a reputation of saintship already attached to Marie de l'Incarnation. "When I spoke to her," writes Sister Anne, speaking of her first interview, "I perceived in the air a certain odor of sanctity, which gave me the sensation of an agreeable perfume." See the letter in a recent Catholic work, *Les Ursulines de Québec*, I. 38, where the passage is printed in Italics, as worthy the especial attention of the pious reader.

shapes. Sometimes it arrays itself in silk and jewels; sometimes it walks in sackcloth, and speaks the language of self-abasement. In the convent, as in the world, the fair devotee thirsted for admiration. The halo of saintship glittered in her eyes like a diamond crown, and she aspired to outshine her sisters in humility. She was as sincere as Simeon Stylites on his column; and, like him, found encouragement and comfort in the gazing and wondering eyes below.[1]

[1] Madame de la Peltrie died in her convent in 1671. Marie de l'Incarnation died the following year. She had the consolation of knowing that her son had fulfilled her ardent wishes, and become a priest.

Chapter XV

VILLEMARIE DE MONTREAL

Dauversière and the Voice from Heaven • Abbé Olier • Their Schemes • The Society of Notre-Dame de Montreal • Maisonneuve • Devout Ladies • Mademoiselle Mance • Marguerite Bourgeois • The Montrealists at Quebec • Jealousy • Quarrels • Romance and Devotion • Embarkation • Foundation of Montreal

WE come now to an enterprise as singular in its character as it proved important in its results.

At La Flèche, in Anjou, dwelt one Jérôme le Royer de la Dauversière, receiver of taxes. His portrait shows us a round, *bourgeois* face, somewhat heavy perhaps, decorated with a slight moustache, and redeemed by bright and earnest eyes. On his head he wears a black skull-cap; and over his ample shoulders spreads a stiff white collar, of wide expanse and studious plainness. Though he belonged to the *noblesse*, his look is that of a grave burgher, of good renown and sage deportment. Dauversière was, however, an enthusiastic devotee, of mystical tendencies, who whipped himself with a scourge of small chains till his shoulders were one wound, wore a belt with more than twelve hundred sharp points, and invented for himself other torments, which filled his confessor with admiration.[1] One day, while at his devotions, he heard an inward voice commanding him to become the founder of a new Order of hospital nuns; and he was further ordered to establish, on the island called Montreal, in Canada, a hospital, or Hôtel-Dieu, to be conducted by these nuns. But Montreal was a wilderness, and the hospital would have no patients. Therefore, in order to supply them, the island must first be colonized. Dauversière was greatly perplexed. On the one hand, the voice of Heaven must be obeyed; on the other, he had a wife, six children, and a very moderate fortune.[2]

[1] Fancamp in Faillon, *Vie de Mlle Mance. Introduction.*

[2] Faillon, *Vie de Mlle Mance, Introduction*; Dollier de Casson, *Hist. de Montreal*, MS.; *Les Véritables Motifs des Messieurs et Dames de Montreal*, 25; Juchereau, 33.

Again: there was at Paris a young priest, about twenty-eight years of age,—Jean Jacques Olier, afterwards widely known as founder of the Seminary of St. Sulpice. Judged by his engraved portrait, his countenance, though marked both with energy and intellect, was anything but prepossessing. Every lineament proclaims the priest. Yet the Abbé Olier has high titles to esteem. He signalized his piety, it is true, by the most disgusting exploits of self-mortification; but, at the same time, he was strenuous in his efforts to reform the people and the clergy. So zealous was he for good morals, that he drew upon himself the imputation of a leaning to the heresy of the Jansenists,—a suspicion strengthened by his opposition to certain priests, who, to secure the faithful in their allegiance, justified them in lives of licentiousness.[1] Yet Olier's catholicity was past attaintment, and in his horror of Jansenists he yielded to the Jesuits alone.

He was praying in the ancient church of St. Germain des Prés, when, like Dauversière, he thought he heard a voice from Heaven, saying that he was destined to be a light to the Gentiles. It is recorded as a mystic coincidence attending this miracle, that the choir was at that very time chanting the words, *Lumen ad revelationem Gentium;*[2] and it seems to have occurred neither to Olier nor to his biographer, that, falling on the ear of the rapt worshipper, they might have unconsciously suggested the supposed revelation. But there was a further miracle. An inward voice told Olier that he was to form a society of priests, and establish them on the island called Montreal, in Canada, for the propagation of the True Faith; and writers old and recent assert, that, while both he and Dauversière were totally ignorant of Canadian geography, they suddenly found themselves in possession, they knew not how, of the most exact details concerning Montreal, its size, shape, situation, soil, climate, and productions.

The annual volumes of the Jesuit *Relations*, issuing from the renowned press of Cramoisy, were at this time spread broadcast throughout France; and, in the circles of *haute dévotion*, Canada and its missions were everywhere the themes

[1] Faillon, *Vie de M. Olier*, II. 188.

[2] *Mémoires Autographes de M. Olier*, cited by Faillon, in *Histoire de la Colonie Française*, I. 384.

of enthusiastic discussion; while Champlain, in his published works, had long before pointed out Montreal as the proper site for a settlement. But we are entering a region of miracle, and it is superfluous to look far for explanations. The illusion, in these cases, is a part of the history.

Dauversière pondered the revelation he had received; and the more he pondered, the more was he convinced that it came from God. He therefore set out for Paris, to find some means of accomplishing the task assigned him. Here, as he prayed before an image of the Virgin in the church of Notre-Dame, he fell into an ecstasy, and beheld a vision. "I should be false to the integrity of history," writes his biographer, "if I did not relate it here." And he adds, that the reality of this celestial favor is past doubting, inasmuch as Dauversière himself told it to his daughters. Christ, the Virgin, and St. Joseph appeared before him. He saw them distinctly. Then he heard Christ ask three times of his Virgin Mother, *Where can I find a faithful servant?* On which, the Virgin, taking him (Dauversière) by the hand, replied, *See, Lord, here is that faithful servant!*—and Christ, with a benignant smile, received him into his service, promising to bestow on him wisdom and strength to do his work.[1] From Paris he went to the neighboring chateau of Meudon, which overlooks the valley of the Seine, not far from St. Cloud. Entering the gallery of the old castle, he saw a priest approaching him. It was Olier. Now we are told that neither of these men had ever seen or heard of the other; and yet, says the pious historian, "impelled by a kind of inspiration, they knew each other at once, even to the depths of their hearts; saluted each other by name, as we read of St. Paul, the Hermit, and St. Anthony, and of St. Dominic and St. Francis; and ran to embrace each other, like two friends who had met after a long separation."[2]

"Monsieur," exclaimed Olier, "I know your design, and I go to commend it to God at the holy altar."

And he went at once to say mass in the chapel. Dauversière received the communion at his hands; and then they walked for three hours in the park, discussing their plans. They were

---

[1] Faillon, *Vie de Mlle Mance, Introduction*, xxviii., The Abbé Ferland, in his *Histoire du Canada*, passes over the miracles in silence.

[2] Ibid., *La Colonie Française*, I. 390.

of one mind, in respect both to objects and means; and when they parted, Olier gave Dauversière a hundred louis, saying, "This is to begin the work of God."

They proposed to found at Montreal three religious communities,— *three* being the mystic number,— one of secular priests to direct the colonists and convert the Indians, one of nuns to nurse the sick, and one of nuns to teach the Faith to the children, white and red. To borrow their own phrases, they would plant the banner of Christ in an abode of desolation and a haunt of demons; and to this end a band of priests and women were to invade the wilderness, and take post between the fangs of the Iroquois. But first they must make a colony, and to do so must raise money. Olier had pious and wealthy penitents; Dauversière had a friend, the Baron de Fancamp, devout as himself and far richer. Anxious for his soul, and satisfied that the enterprise was an inspiration of God, he was eager to bear part in it. Olier soon found three others; and the six together formed the germ of the Society of Notre-Dame de Montreal. Among them they raised the sum of seventy-five thousand livres, equivalent to about as many dollars at the present day.[1]

Now to look for a moment at their plan. Their eulogists say, and with perfect truth, that, from a worldly point of

[1] Dollier de Casson, *Histoire de Montreal*, MS.; also Belmont, *Histoire du Canada*, 2. Juchereau doubles the sum. Faillon agrees with Dollier.

On all that relates to the early annals of Montreal a flood of new light has been thrown by the Abbé Faillon. As a priest of St. Sulpice, he had ready access to the archives of the Seminaries of Montreal and Paris, and to numerous other ecclesiastical depositories, which would have been closed hopelessly against a layman and a heretic. It is impossible to commend too highly the zeal, diligence, exactness, and extent of his conscientious researches. His credulity is enormous, and he is completely in sympathy with the supernaturalists of whom he writes: in other words, he identifies himself with his theme, and is indeed a fragment of the seventeenth century, still extant in the nineteenth. He is minute to prolixity, and abounds in extracts and citations from the ancient manuscripts which his labors have unearthed. In short, the Abbé is a prodigy of patience and industry; and if he taxes the patience of his readers, he also rewards it abundantly. Such of his original authorities as have proved accessible are before me, including a considerable number of manuscripts. Among these, that of Dollier de Casson, *Histoire de Montreal*, as cited above, is the most important. The copy in my possession was made from the original in the Mazarin Library.

view, it was mere folly. The partners mutually bound themselves to seek no return for the money expended. Their profit was to be reaped in the skies: and, indeed, there was none to be reaped on earth. The feeble settlement at Quebec was at this time in danger of utter ruin; for the Iroquois, enraged at the attacks made on them by Champlain, had begun a fearful course of retaliation, and the very existence of the colony trembled in the balance. But if Quebec was exposed to their ferocious inroads, Montreal was incomparably more so. A settlement here would be a perilous outpost,—a hand thrust into the jaws of the tiger. It would provoke attack, and lie almost in the path of the war-parties. The associates could gain nothing by the fur-trade; for they would not be allowed to share in it. On the other hand, danger apart, the place was an excellent one for a mission; for here met two great rivers: the St. Lawrence, with its countless tributaries, flowed in from the west, while the Ottawa descended from the north; and Montreal, embraced by their uniting waters, was the key to a vast inland navigation. Thither the Indians would naturally resort; and thence the missionaries could make their way into the heart of a boundless heathendom. None of the ordinary motives of colonization had part in this design. It owed its conception and its birth to religious zeal alone.

The island of Montreal belonged to Lauson, former president of the great company of the Hundred Associates; and, as we have seen, his son had a monopoly of fishing in the St. Lawrence. Dauversière and Fancamp, after much diplomacy, succeeded in persuading the elder Lauson to transfer his title to them; and, as there was a defect in it, they also obtained a grant of the island from the Hundred Associates, its original owners, who, however, reserved to themselves its western extremity as a site for a fort and storehouses.[1] At the same time,

[1] *Donation et Transport de la Concession de l'Isle de Montreal par M. Jean de Lauzon aux Sieurs Chevrier de Fouancant* (Fancamp) *et le Royer de la Doversière*, MS.

Concession d'une Partie de l'Isle de Montreal accordée par la Compagnie de la Nouvelle France aux Sieurs Chevrier et le Royer, MS.

Lettres de Ratification, MS.

Acte qui prouve que les Sieurs Chevrier de Fancamps et Royer de la Dauversière n'ont stipulé qu'au nom de la Compagnie de Montreal, MS.

From copies of other documents before me, it appears that in 1659 the

the younger Lauson granted them a right of fishery within two leagues of the shores of the island, for which they were to make a yearly acknowledgment of ten pounds of fish. A confirmation of these grants was obtained from the King. Dauversière and his companions were now *seigneurs* of Montreal. They were empowered to appoint a governor, and to establish courts, from which there was to be an appeal to the Supreme Court of Quebec, supposing such to exist. They were excluded from the fur-trade, and forbidden to build castles or forts other than such as were necessary for defence against the Indians.

Their title assured, they matured their plan. First they would send out forty men to take possession of Montreal, intrench themselves, and raise crops. Then they would build a house for the priests, and two convents for the nuns. Meanwhile, Olier was toiling at Vaugirard, on the outskirts of Paris, to inaugurate the seminary of priests, and Dauversière at La Flèche, to form the community of hospital nuns. How the school nuns were provided for we shall see hereafter. The colony, it will be observed, was for the convents, not the convents for the colony.

The Associates needed a soldier-governor to take charge of their forty men; and, directed as they supposed by Providence, they found one wholly to their mind. This was Paul de Chomedey, Sieur de Maisonneuve, a devout and valiant gentleman, who in long service among the heretics of Holland had kept his faith intact, and had held himself resolutely aloof from the license that surrounded him. He loved his profession of arms, and wished to consecrate his sword to the Church. Past all comparison, he is the manliest figure that appears in this group of zealots. The piety of the design, the miracles that inspired it, the adventure and the peril, all combined to charm him; and he eagerly embraced the enterprise. His father opposed his purpose; but he met him with a text of St. Mark, "There is no man that hath left house or brethren or sisters or father for my sake, but he shall receive an hundred-fold." On this the elder Maisonneuve, deceived by his own worldliness, imagined that the plan covered some

reserved portion of the island was also ceded to the Company of Montreal.
See also *Edits, Ordonnances Royaux*, etc., I. 20–26 (Quebec, 1854).

hidden speculation, from which enormous profits were expected, and therefore withdrew his opposition.[1]

Their scheme was ripening fast, when both Olier and Dauversière were assailed by one of those revulsions of spirit, to
which saints of the ecstatic school are naturally liable. Dauversière, in particular, was a prey to the extremity of dejection, uncertainty, and misgiving. What had he, a family man,
to do with ventures beyond sea? Was it not his first duty to
support his wife and children? Could he not fulfil all his obligations as a Christian by reclaiming the wicked and relieving
the poor at La Flèche? Plainly, he had doubts that his vocation was genuine. If we could raise the curtain of his domestic
life, perhaps we should find him beset by wife and daughters,
tearful and wrathful, inveighing against his folly, and imploring him to provide a support for them before squandering his
money to plant a convent of nuns in a wilderness. How long
his fit of dejection lasted does not appear; but at length[2] he
set himself again to his appointed work. Olier, too, emerging
from the clouds and darkness, found faith once more, and
again placed himself at the head of the great enterprise.[3]

There was imperative need of more money; and Dauversière, under judicious guidance, was active in obtaining it.
This miserable victim of illusions had a squat, uncourtly figure, and was no proficient in the graces either of manners or
of speech: hence his success in commending his objects to
persons of rank and wealth is set down as one of the many
miracles which attended the birth of Montreal. But zeal and
earnestness are in themselves a power; and the ground had
been well marked out and ploughed for him in advance. That
attractive, though intricate, subject of study, the female mind,
has always engaged the attention of priests, more especially in
countries where, as in France, women exert a strong social
and political influence. The art of kindling the flames of zeal,
and the more difficult art of directing and controlling them,
have been themes of reflection the most diligent and profound. Accordingly we find that a large proportion of the

[1] Faillon, *La Colonie Française*, I. 409.

[2] Faillon, *Vie de M*[lle] *Mance, Introduction*, xxxv.

[3] Faillon (*Vie de M. Olier*) devotes twenty-one pages to the history of his
fit of nervous depression.

money raised for this enterprise was contributed by devout ladies. Many of them became members of the Association of Montreal, which was eventually increased to about forty-five persons, chosen for their devotion and their wealth.

Olier and his associates had resolved, though not from any collapse of zeal, to postpone the establishment of the seminary and the college until after a settlement should be formed. The hospital, however, might, they thought, be begun at once; for blood and blows would be the assured portion of the first settlers. At least, a discreet woman ought to embark with the first colonists as their nurse and housekeeper. Scarcely was the need recognized when it was supplied.

Mademoiselle Jeanne Mance was born of an honorable family of Nogent-le-Roi, and in 1640 was thirty-four years of age. These Canadian heroines began their religious experiences early. Of Marie de l'Incarnation we read, that at the age of seven Christ appeared to her in a vision;[1] and the biographer of Mademoiselle Mance assures us, with admiring gravity, that, at the same tender age, she bound herself to God by a vow of perpetual chastity.[2] This singular infant in due time became a woman, of a delicate constitution, and manners graceful, yet dignified. Though an earnest devotee, she felt no vocation for the cloister; yet, while still "in the world," she led the life of a nun. The Jesuit *Relations*, and the example of Madame de la Peltrie, of whom she had heard, inoculated her with the Canadian enthusiasm, then so prevalent; and, under the pretence of visiting relatives, she made a journey to Paris, to take counsel of certain priests. Of one thing she was assured: the Divine will called her to Canada, but to what end she neither knew nor asked to know; for she abandoned herself as an atom to be borne to unknown destinies on the breath of God. At Paris, Father St. Jure, a Jesuit, assured her that her vocation to Canada was, past doubt, a call from Heaven; while Father Rapin, a Récollet, spread abroad the fame of her virtues, and introduced her to many ladies of rank, wealth, and zeal. Then, well supplied with money for any pious work to which she might be summoned, she journeyed to Rochelle, whence ships were to sail for New France.

[1] Casgrain, *Vie de Marie de l'Incarnation*, 78.
[2] Faillon, *Vie de Mlle Mance*, I. 3.

Thus far she had been kept in ignorance of the plan with regard to Montreal; but now Father La Place, a Jesuit, revealed it to her. On the day after her arrival at Rochelle, as she entered the Church of the Jesuits, she met Dauversière coming out. "Then," says her biographer, "these two persons, who had never seen nor heard of each other, were enlightened supernaturally, whereby their most hidden thoughts were mutually made known, as had happened already with M. Olier and this same M. de la Dauversière."[1] A long conversation ensued between them; and the delights of this interview were never effaced from the mind of Mademoiselle Mance. "She used to speak of it like a seraph," writes one of her nuns, "and far better than many a learned doctor could have done."[2]

She had found her destiny. The ocean, the wilderness, the solitude, the Iroquois,—nothing daunted her. She would go to Montreal with Maisonneuve and his forty men. Yet, when the vessel was about to sail, a new and sharp misgiving seized her. How could she, a woman, not yet bereft of youth or charms, live alone in the forest, among a troop of soldiers? Her scruples were relieved by two of the men, who, at the last moment, refused to embark without their wives,—and by a young woman, who, impelled by enthusiasm, escaped from her friends, and took passage, in spite of them, in one of the vessels.

All was ready; the ships set sail; but Olier, Dauversière, and Fancamp remained at home, as did also the other Associates, with the exception of Maisonneuve and Mademoiselle Mance. In the following February, an impressive scene took place in the Church of Notre Dame, at Paris. The Associates, at this time numbering about forty-five,[3] with Olier at their head, assembled before the altar of the Virgin, and, by a solemn ceremonial, consecrated Montreal to the Holy Family. Henceforth it was to be called *Villemarie de Montreal*,[4]—a sacred

---

[1] Faillon, *Vie de Mlle Mance*, I. 18. Here again the Abbé Ferland, with his usual good sense, tacitly rejects the supernaturalism.

[2] La Sœur Morin, *Annales des Hospitalières de Villemarie*, MS., cited by Faillon.

[3] Dollier de Casson, A.D. 1641–42, MS. Vimont says thirty five.

[4] Vimont, *Relation, 1642*, 37. Compare Le Clerc, *Établissement de la Foy*, II. 49.

town, reared to the honor and under the patronage of Christ, St. Joseph, and the Virgin, to be typified by three persons on earth, founders respectively of the three destined communities,—Olier, Dauversière, and a maiden of Troyes, Marguerite Bourgeoys: the seminary to be consecrated to Christ, the Hôtel-Dieu to St. Joseph, and the college to the Virgin.

But we are anticipating a little; for it was several years as yet before Marguerite Bourgeoys took an active part in the work of Montreal. She was the daughter of a respectable tradesman, and was now twenty-two years of age. Her portrait has come down to us; and her face is a mirror of frankness, loyalty, and womanly tenderness. Her qualities were those of good sense, conscientiousness, and a warm heart. She had known no miracles, ecstasies, or trances; and though afterwards, when her religious susceptibilities had reached a fuller development, a few such are recorded of her, yet even the Abbé Faillon, with the best intentions, can credit her with but a meagre allowance of these celestial favors. Though in the midst of visionaries, she distrusted the supernatural, and avowed her belief, that, in His government of the world, God does not often set aside its ordinary laws. Her religion was of the affections, and was manifested in an absorbing devotion to duty. She had felt no vocation to the cloister, but had taken the vow of chastity, and was attached, as an *externe*, to the Sisters of the Congregation of Troyes, who were fevered with eagerness to go to Canada. Marguerite, however, was content to wait until there was a prospect that she could do good by going; and it was not till the year 1653, that, renouncing an inheritance, and giving all she had to the poor, she embarked for the savage scene of her labors. To this day, in crowded school-rooms of Montreal and Quebec, fit monuments of her unobtrusive virtue, her successors instruct the children of the poor, and embalm the pleasant memory of Marguerite Bourgeoys. In the martial figure of Maisonneuve, and the fair form of this gentle nun, we find the true heroes of Montreal.[1]

Maisonneuve, with his forty men and four women, reached Quebec too late to ascend to Montreal that season. They en-

[1] For Marguerite Bourgeoys, see her life by Faillon.

countered distrust, jealousy, and opposition. The agents of the Company of the Hundred Associates looked on them askance; and the Governor of Quebec, Montmagny, saw a rival governor in Maisonneuve. Every means was used to persuade the adventurers to abandon their project, and settle at Quebec. Montmagny called a council of the principal persons of his colony, who gave it as their opinion that the new-comers had better exchange Montreal for the Island of Orleans, where they would be in a position to give and receive succor; while, by persisting in their first design, they would expose themselves to destruction, and be of use to nobody.[1] Maisonneuve, who was present, expressed his surprise that they should assume to direct his affairs. "I have not come here," he said, "to deliberate, but to act. It is my duty and my honor to found a colony at Montreal; and I would go, if every tree were an Iroquois!"[2]

At Quebec there was little ability and no inclination to shelter the new colonists for the winter; and they would have fared ill, but for the generosity of M. Puiseaux, who lived not far distant, at a place called St. Michel. This devout and most hospitable person made room for them all in his rough, but capacious dwelling. Their neighbors were the hospital nuns, then living at the mission of Sillery, in a substantial, but comfortless house of stone; where, amidst destitution, sickness, and irrepressible disgust at the filth of the savages whom they had in charge, they were laboring day and night with devoted assiduity. Among the minor ills which beset them were the eccentricities of one of their lay sisters, crazed with religious enthusiasm, who had the care of their poultry and domestic animals, of which she was accustomed to inquire, one by one, if they loved God; when, not receiving an immediate answer in the affirmative, she would instantly put them to death, telling them that their impiety deserved no better fate.[3]

At St. Michel, Maisonneuve employed his men in building

---

[1] Juchereau, 32; Faillon, *Colonie Française*, I. 423.

[2] La Tour, *Mémoire de Laval*, Liv. VIII; Belmont, *Histoire du Canada*, 3.

[3] Juchereau, 45. A great mortification to these excellent nuns was the impossibility of keeping their white dresses clean among their Indian patients, so that they were forced to dye them with butternut juice. They were the *Hospitalières* who had come over in 1639.

boats to ascend to Montreal, and in various other labors for the behoof of the future colony. Thus the winter wore away; but, as celestial minds are not exempt from ire, Montmagny and Maisonneuve fell into a quarrel. The twenty-fifth of January was Maisonneuve's *fête* day; and, as he was greatly beloved by his followers, they resolved to celebrate the occasion. Accordingly, an hour and a half before daylight, they made a general discharge of their muskets and cannon. The sound reached Quebec, two or three miles distant, startling the Governor from his morning slumbers; and his indignation was redoubled when he heard it again at night: for Maisonneuve, pleased at the attachment of his men, had feasted them and warmed their hearts with a distribution of wine. Montmagny, jealous of his authority, resented these demonstrations as an infraction of it, affirming that they had no right to fire their pieces without his consent; and, arresting the principal offender, one Jean Gory, he put him in irons. On being released, a few days after, his companions welcomed him with great rejoicing, and Maisonneuve gave them all a feast. He himself came in during the festivity, drank the health of the company, shook hands with the late prisoner, placed him at the head of the table, and addressed him as follows: —

"Jean Gory, you have been put in irons for me: you had the pain, and I the affront. For that, I add ten crowns to your wages." Then, turning to the others: "My boys," he said, "though Jean Gory has been misused, you must not lose heart for that, but drink, all of you, to the health of the man in irons. When we are once at Montreal, we shall be our own masters, and can fire our cannon when we please."[1]

Montmagny was wroth when this was reported to him; and, on the ground that what had passed was "contrary to the service of the King and the authority of the Governor," he summoned Gory and six others before him, and put them separately under oath. Their evidence failed to establish a case against their commander; but thenceforth there was great coldness between the powers of Quebec and Montreal.

Early in May, Maisonneuve and his followers embarked.

---

[1] *Documents Divers*, MSS., now or lately in possession of G. B. Faribault, Esq.; Ferland, *Notes sur les Registres de N. D. de Québec*, 25; Faillon, *La Colonie Française*, I. 433.

They had gained an unexpected recruit during the winter, in the person of Madame de la Peltrie. The piety, the novelty, and the romance of their enterprise, all had their charms for the fair enthusiast; and an irresistible impulse—imputed by a slandering historian to the levity of her sex[1]—urged her to share their fortunes. Her zeal was more admired by the Montrealists whom she joined than by the Ursulines whom she abandoned. She carried off all the furniture she had lent them, and left them in the utmost destitution.[2] Nor did she remain quiet after reaching Montreal, but was presently seized with a longing to visit the Hurons, and preach the Faith in person to those benighted heathen. It needed all the eloquence of a Jesuit, lately returned from that most arduous mission, to convince her that the attempt would be as useless as rash.[3]

It was the eighth of May when Maisonneuve and his followers embarked at St. Michel; and as the boats, deep-laden with men, arms, and stores, moved slowly on their way, the forest, with leaves just opening in the warmth of spring, lay on their right hand and on their left, in a flattering semblance of tranquillity and peace. But behind woody islets, in tangled thickets and damp ravines, and in the shade and stillness of the columned woods, lurked everywhere a danger and a terror.

What shall we say of these adventurers of Montreal,—of these who bestowed their wealth, and, far more, of these who sacrificed their peace and risked their lives, on an enterprise at once so romantic and so devout? Surrounded as they were with illusions, false lights, and false shadows,—breathing an atmosphere of miracle,—compassed about with angels and devils,—urged with stimulants most powerful, though unreal,—their minds drugged, as it were, to preternatural excitement,—it is very difficult to judge of them. High merit, without doubt, there was in some of their number; but one may beg to be spared the attempt to measure or define it. To estimate a virtue involved in conditions so anomalous demands, perhaps, a judgment more than human.

---

[1] La Tour, *Mémoire de Laval*, Liv. VIII.

[2] Charlevoix, *Vie de Marie de l'Incarnation*, 279; Casgrain, *Vie de Marie de l'Incarnation*, 333.

[3] St. Thomas, *Life of Madame de la Peltrie*, 98.

The Roman Church, sunk in disease and corruption when the Reformation began, was roused by that fierce trumpet-blast to purge and brace herself anew. Unable to advance, she drew back to the fresher and comparatively purer life of the past; and the fervors of mediæval Christianity were renewed in the sixteenth century. In many of its aspects, this enterprise of Montreal belonged to the time of the first Crusades. The spirit of Godfrey de Bouillon lived again in Chomedey de Maisonneuve; and in Marguerite Bourgeoys was realized that fair ideal of Christian womanhood, a flower of Earth expanding in the rays of Heaven, which soothed with gentle influence the wildness of a barbarous age.

On the seventeenth of May, 1642, Maisonneuve's little flotilla—a pinnace, a flat-bottomed craft moved by sails, and two row-boats[1]—approached Montreal; and all on board raised in unison a hymn of praise. Montmagny was with them, to deliver the island, in behalf of the Company of the Hundred Associates, to Maisonneuve, representative of the Associates of Montreal.[2] And here, too, was Father Vimont, Superior of the missions; for the Jesuits had been prudently invited to accept the spiritual charge of the young colony. On the following day, they glided along the green and solitary shores now thronged with the life of a busy city, and landed on the spot which Champlain, thirty-one years before, had chosen as the fit site of a settlement.[3] It was a tongue or triangle of land, formed by the junction of a rivulet with the St. Lawrence, and known afterwards as Point Callière. The rivulet was bordered by a meadow, and beyond rose the forest with its vanguard of scattered trees. Early spring flowers were blooming in the young grass, and birds of varied plumage flitted among the boughs.[4]

Maisonneuve sprang ashore, and fell on his knees. His followers imitated his example; and all joined their voices in enthusiastic songs of thanksgiving. Tents, baggage, arms, and stores were landed. An altar was raised on a pleasant spot near at hand; and Mademoiselle Mance, with Madame de la Pel-

[1] Dollier de Casson, A.D. 1641–42, MS.
[2] Le Clerc, II. 50, 51.
[3] "Pioneers of France," 267. It was the *Place Royale* of Champlain.
[4] Dollier de Casson, A.D. 1641–42, MS.

trie, aided by her servant, Charlotte Barré, decorated it with a taste which was the admiration of the beholders.[1] Now all the company gathered before the shrine. Here stood Vimont, in the rich vestments of his office. Here were the two ladies, with their servant; Montmagny, no very willing spectator; and Maisonneuve, a warlike figure, erect and tall, his men clustering around him,—soldiers, sailors, artisans, and labor-ers,—all alike soldiers at need. They kneeled in reverent si-lence as the Host was raised aloft; and when the rite was over, the priest turned and addressed them:—

"You are a grain of mustard-seed, that shall rise and grow till its branches overshadow the earth. You are few, but your work is the work of God. His smile is on you, and your chil-dren shall fill the land."[2]

The afternoon waned; the sun sank behind the western for-est, and twilight came on. Fireflies were twinkling over the darkened meadow. They caught them, tied them with threads into shining festoons, and hung them before the altar, where the Host remained exposed. Then they pitched their tents, lighted their bivouac fires, stationed their guards, and lay down to rest. Such was the birth-night of Montreal.[3]

---

[1] Morin, *Annales*, MS., cited by Faillon, *La Colonie Française*, I. 440; also Dollier de Casson, A.D. 1641–42, MS.

[2] Dollier de Casson, MS., *as above*. Vimont, in the *Relation* of 1642, p. 37, briefly mentions the ceremony.

[3] The Associates of Montreal published, in 1643, a thick pamphlet in quarto, entitled *Les Véritables Motifs de Messieurs et Dames de la Société de Notre-Dame de Montréal, pour la Conversion des Sauvages de la Nouvelle France*. It was writ-ten as an answer to aspersions cast upon them, apparently by persons at-tached to the great Company of New France known as the "Hundred Associates," and affords a curious exposition of the spirit of their enterprise. It is excessively rare; but copies of the essential portions are before me. The following is a characteristic extract:—

"Vous dites que l'entreprise de Montréal est d'une dépense infinie, plus convenable à un roi qu'à quelques particuliers, trop faibles pour la soutenir; & vous alléguez encore les périls de la navigation & les naufrages qui peuvent la ruiner. Vous avez mieux reoontré ce que vous ne pensiez, en disant que c'est une œuvre de roi, puisque le Roi des rois s'en mêle, lui à qui obéissent la mer & les vents. Nous ne craignons donc pas les naufrages; il n'en suscitera que lorsque nous en aurons besoin, & qu'il sera plus expédient pour sa gloire, que nous cherchons uniquement. Comment avez-vous pu mettre dans votre esprit qu'appuyés de nos propres forces, nous eussions présumé de penser à un si glorieux dessein? Si Dieu n'est point dans l'affaire de Montréal, si c'est

Is this true history, or a romance of Christian chivalry? It is both.

---

une invention humaine, ne vous en mettez point en peine, elle ne durera guère. Ce que vous prédisez arrivera, & quelque chose de pire encore; mais si Dieu l'a ainsi voulu, qui êtes-vous pour lui contredire? C'était la reflexion que le docteur Gamaliel faisait aux Juifs, en faveur des Apôtres; pour vous, qui ne pouvez ni croire, ni faire, laissez les autres en liberté de faire ce qu'ils croient que Dieu demande d'eux. Vous assurez qu'il ne se fait plus de miracles; mais qui vous l'a dit? où cela est-il écrit? Jésus-Christ assure, au contraire, *que ceux qui auront autant de Foi qu'un grain de senevé, feront, en son nom, des miracles plus grands que ceux qu'il a faits lui-même.* Depuis quand êtes-vous les directeurs des operations divines, pour les réduire à certains temps & dans la conduite ordinaire? Tant de saints mouvements, d'inspirations & de vues intérieures, qu'il lui plaît de donner à quelques âmes dont il se sert pour l'avancement de cette œuvre, sont des marques de son bon plaisir. Jusqu'-ici, il a pourvu au nécessaire; nous ne voulons point d'abondance, & nous espérons que sa Providence continuera."

Chapter XVI

1641–1644

ISAAC JOGUES

*The Iroquois War • Jogues • His Capture • His Journey to the
Mohawks • Lake George • The Mohawk Towns • The Missionary
Tortured • Death of Goupil • Misery of Jogues • The Mohawk
"Babylon" • Fort Orange • Escape of Jogues • Manhattan • The
Voyage to France • Jogues among his Brethren • He returns
to Canada*

T HE waters of the St. Lawrence rolled through a virgin
wilderness, where, in the vastness of the lonely wood-
lands, civilized man found a precarious harborage at three
points only,—at Quebec, at Montreal, and at Three Rivers.
Here and in the scattered missions was the whole of New
France,—a population of some three hundred souls in all.
And now, over these miserable settlements, rose a war-cloud
of frightful portent.

It was thirty-two years since Champlain had first attacked
the Iroquois.[1] They had nursed their wrath for more than a
generation, and at length their hour was come. The Dutch
traders at Fort Orange, now Albany, had supplied them with
fire-arms. The Mohawks, the most easterly of the Iroquois
nations, had, among their seven or eight hundred warriors,
no less than three hundred armed with the arquebuse, a
weapon somewhat like the modern carbine.[2] They were masters of the thunderbolts which, in the hands of Champlain,
had struck terror into their hearts.

We have surveyed in the introductory chapter the character
and organization of this ferocious people; their confederacy
of five nations, bound together by a peculiar tie of clanship;

---

[1] See "Pioneers of France," 256.

[2] Vimont, *Relation, 1643*, 62. The Mohawks were the Agniés, or Agnero-
nons, of the old French writers.

According to the *Journal of New Netherland*, a contemporary Dutch document, (see *Colonial Documents of New York*, I. 179,) the Dutch at Fort Orange
had supplied the Mohawks with four hundred guns; the profits of the trade,
which was free to the settlers, blinding them to the danger.

their chiefs, half hereditary, half elective; their government, an oligarchy in form and a democracy in spirit; their minds, thoroughly savage, yet marked here and there with traits of a vigorous development. The war which they had long waged with the Hurons was carried on by the Senecas and the other Western nations of their league; while the conduct of hostilities against the French and their Indian allies in Lower Canada was left to the Mohawks. In parties of from ten to a hundred or more, they would leave their towns on the River Mohawk, descend Lake Champlain and the River Richelieu, lie in ambush on the banks of the St. Lawrence, and attack the passing boats or canoes. Sometimes they hovered about the fortifications of Quebec and Three Rivers, killing stragglers, or luring armed parties into ambuscades. They followed like hounds on the trail of travellers and hunters; broke in upon unguarded camps at midnight; and lay in wait, for days and weeks, to intercept the Huron traders on their yearly descent to Quebec. Had they joined to their ferocious courage the discipline and the military knowledge that belong to civilization, they could easily have blotted out New France from the map, and made the banks of the St. Lawrence once more a solitude; but, though the most formidable of savages, they were savages only.

In the early morning of the second of August, 1642,[1] twelve Huron canoes were moving slowly along the northern shore of the expansion of the St. Lawrence known as the Lake of St. Peter. There were on board about forty persons, including four Frenchmen, one of them being the Jesuit, Isaac Jogues, whom we have already followed on his missionary journey to the towns of the Tobacco Nation. In the interval he had not been idle. During the last autumn, (1641,) he, with Father Charles Raymbault, had passed along the shore of Lake Huron northward, entered the strait through which Lake Superior discharges itself, pushed on as far as the Sault Sainte Marie, and preached the Faith to two thousand Ojibwas, and other Algonquins there assembled.[2] He was now on his return from a far more perilous errand. The Huron mission was in a state of destitution. There was need of clothing for the

[1] For the date, see Lalemant, *Relation des Hurons, 1647*, 18.
[2] Lalemant, *Relation des Hurons, 1642*, 97.

priests, of vessels for the altars, of bread and wine for the eucharist, of writing materials,—in short, of everything; and, early in the summer of the present year, Jogues had descended to Three Rivers and Quebec with the Huron traders, to procure the necessary supplies. He had accomplished his task, and was on his way back to the mission. With him were a few Huron converts, and among them a noted Christian chief, Eustache Ahatsistari. Others of the party were in course of instruction for baptism; but the greater part were heathen, whose canoes were deeply laden with the proceeds of their bargains with the French fur-traders.

Jogues sat in one of the leading canoes. He was born at Orleans in 1607, and was thirty-five years of age. His oval face and the delicate mould of his features indicated a modest, thoughtful, and refined nature. He was constitutionally timid, with a sensitive conscience and great religious susceptibilities. He was a finished scholar, and might have gained a literary reputation; but he had chosen another career, and one for which he seemed but ill fitted. Physically, however, he was well matched with his work; for, though his frame was slight, he was so active, that none of the Indians could surpass him in running.[1]

With him were two young men, René Goupil and Guillaume Couture, *donnés* of the mission,—that is to say, laymen who, from a religious motive and without pay, had attached themselves to the service of the Jesuits. Goupil had formerly entered upon the Jesuit novitiate at Paris, but failing health had obliged him to leave it. As soon as he was able, he came to Canada, offered his services to the Superior of the mission, was employed for a time in the humblest offices, and afterwards became an attendant at the hospital. At length, to his delight, he received permission to go up to the Hurons, where the surgical skill which he had acquired was greatly needed; and he was now on his way thither.[2] His companion, Couture, was a man of intelligence and vigor, and of a char-

---

[1] Buteux, *Narré de la Prise du Père Jogues*, MS.; *Mémoire touchant le Père Jogues*, MS.

There is a portrait of him prefixed to Mr. Shea's admirable edition in quarto of Jogues's *Novum Belgium*.

[2] Jogues, *Notice sur René Goupil*.

acter equally disinterested.[1] Both were, like Jogues, in the foremost canoes; while the fourth Frenchman was with the unconverted Hurons, in the rear.

The twelve canoes had reached the western end of the Lake of St. Peter, where it is filled with innumerable islands.[2] The forest was close on their right, they kept near the shore to avoid the current, and the shallow water before them was covered with a dense growth of tall bulrushes. Suddenly the silence was frightfully broken. The war-whoop rose from among the rushes, mingled with the reports of guns and the whistling of bullets; and several Iroquois canoes, filled with warriors, pushed out from their concealment, and bore down upon Jogues and his companions. The Hurons in the rear were seized with a shameful panic. They leaped ashore; left canoes, baggage, and weapons; and fled into the woods. The French and the Christian Hurons made fight for a time; but when they saw another fleet of canoes approaching from the opposite shores or islands, they lost heart, and those escaped who could. Goupil was seized amid triumphant yells, as were also several of the Huron converts. Jogues sprang into the bulrushes, and might have escaped; but when he saw Goupil and the neophytes in the clutches of the Iroquois, he had no heart to abandon them, but came out from his hiding-place, and gave himself up to the astonished victors. A few of them had remained to guard the prisoners; the rest were chasing the fugitives. Jogues mastered his agony, and began to baptize those of the captive converts who needed baptism.

Couture had eluded pursuit; but when he thought of Jogues and of what perhaps awaited him, he resolved to share his fate, and, turning, retraced his steps. As he approached, five Iroquois ran forward to meet him; and one of them snapped his gun at his breast, but it missed fire. In his confusion and excitement, Couture fired his own piece, and laid the savage dead. The remaining four sprang upon him, stripped off all his clothing, tore away his finger-nails with their teeth, gnawed his fingers with the fury of famished

---

[1] For an account of him, see Ferland, *Notes sur les Registres de N. D. de Québec*, 83 (1863).

[2] Buteux, *Narré de la Prise du Père Jogues*, MS. This document leaves no doubt as to the locality.

dogs, and thrust a sword through one of his hands. Jogues broke from his guards, and, rushing to his friend, threw his arms about his neck. The Iroquois dragged him away, beat him with their fists and war-clubs till he was senseless, and, when he revived, lacerated his fingers with their teeth, as they had done those of Couture. Then they turned upon Goupil, and treated him with the same ferocity. The Huron prisoners were left for the present unharmed. More of them were brought in every moment, till at length the number of captives amounted in all to twenty-two, while three Hurons had been killed in the fight and pursuit. The Iroquois, about seventy in number, now embarked with their prey; but not until they had knocked on the head an old Huron, whom Jogues, with his mangled hands, had just baptized, and who refused to leave the place. Then, under a burning sun, they crossed to the spot on which the town of Sorel now stands, at the mouth of the river Richelieu, where they encamped.[1]

Their course was southward, up the River Richelieu and Lake Champlain; thence, by way of Lake George, to the Mohawk towns. The pain and fever of their wounds, and the clouds of mosquitoes, which they could not drive off, left the prisoners no peace by day nor sleep by night. On the eighth day, they learned that a large Iroquois war-party, on their way to Canada, were near at hand; and they soon approached their camp, on a small island near the southern end of Lake Champlain. The warriors, two hundred in number, saluted their victorious countrymen with volleys from their guns; then, armed with clubs and thorny sticks, ranged themselves

[1] The above, with much of what follows, rests on three documents. The first is a long letter, written in Latin, by Jogues, to the Father Provincial at Paris. It is dated at Rensselaerswyck (Albany), Aug. 5, 1643, and is preserved in the *Societas Jesu Militans* of Tanner, and in the *Mortes Illustres et Gesta eorum de Societate Jesu*, etc., of Alegambe. There is a French translation in Martin's Bressani, and an English translation, by Mr. Shea, in the *New York Hist. Coll.* of 1857. The second document is an old manuscript, entitled *Narré de la Prise du Père Jogues*. It was written by the Jesuit Buteux, from the lips of Jogues. Father Martin, S. J., in whose custody it was, kindly permitted me to have a copy made from it. Besides these, there is a long account in the *Relation des Hurons* of 1647, and a briefer one in that of 1644. All these narratives show the strongest internal evidence of truth, and are perfectly concurrent. They are also supported by statements of escaped Huron prisoners, and by several letters and memoirs of the Dutch at Rensselaerswyck.

in two lines, between which the captives were compelled to pass up the side of a rocky hill. On the way, they were beaten with such fury, that Jogues, who was last in the line, fell powerless, drenched in blood and half dead. As the chief man among the French captives, he fared the worst. His hands were again mangled, and fire applied to his body; while the Huron chief, Eustache, was subjected to tortures even more atrocious. When, at night, the exhausted sufferers tried to rest, the young warriors came to lacerate their wounds and pull out their hair and beards.

In the morning they resumed their journey. And now the lake narrowed to the semblance of a tranquil river. Before them was a woody mountain, close on their right a rocky promontory, and between these flowed a stream, the outlet of Lake George. On those rocks, more than a hundred years after, rose the ramparts of Ticonderoga. They landed, shouldered their canoes and baggage, took their way through the woods, passed the spot where the fierce Highlanders and the dauntless regiments of England breasted in vain the storm of lead and fire, and soon reached the shore where Abercrombie landed and Lord Howe fell. First of white men, Jogues and his companions gazed on the romantic lake that bears the name, not of its gentle discoverer, but of the dull Hanoverian king. Like a fair Naiad of the wilderness, it slumbered between the guardian mountains that breathe from crag and forest the stern poetry of war. But all then was solitude; and the clang of trumpets, the roar of cannon, and the deadly crack of the rifle had never as yet awakened their angry echoes.[1]

[1] Lake George, according to Jogues, was called by the Mohawks "Andiatarocte," or *Place where the Lake closes*. "Andiataraque" is found on a map of Sanson. Spofford, *Gazetteer of New York*, article "Lake George," says that it was called "Canideri-oit," or *Tail of the Lake*. Father Martin, in his notes on Bressani, prefixes to this name that of "Horicon," but gives no original authority.

I have seen an old Latin map on which the name "Horiconi" is set down as belonging to a neighboring tribe. This seems to be only a misprint for "Horicoui," that is, "Irocoui," or "Iroquois." In an old English map, prefixed to the rare tract, *A Treatise of New England*, the "Lake of Hierocoyes" is laid down. The name "Horicon," as used by Cooper in his *Last of the Mohicans*, seems to have no sufficient historical foundation. In 1646, the lake, as we shall see, was named "Lac St. Sacrement."

Again the canoes were launched, and the wild flotilla glided on its way,—now in the shadow of the heights, now on the broad expanse, now among the devious channels of the narrows, beset with woody islets, where the hot air was redolent of the pine, the spruce, and the cedar,—till they neared that tragic shore, where, in the following century, New-England rustics baffled the soldiers of Dieskau, where Montcalm planted his batteries, where the red cross waved so long amid the smoke, and where at length the summer night was hideous with carnage, and an honored name was stained with a memory of blood.[1]

The Iroquois landed at or near the future site of Fort William Henry, left their canoes, and, with their prisoners, began their march for the nearest Mohawk town. Each bore his share of the plunder. Even Jogues, though his lacerated hands were in a frightful condition and his body covered with bruises, was forced to stagger on with the rest under a heavy load. He with his fellow-prisoners, and indeed the whole party, were half starved, subsisting chiefly on wild berries. They crossed the upper Hudson, and, in thirteen days after leaving the St. Lawrence, neared the wretched goal of their pilgrimage, a palisaded town, standing on a hill by the banks of the River Mohawk.

The whoops of the victors announced their approach, and the savage hive sent forth its swarms. They thronged the side of the hill, the old and the young, each with a stick, or a slender iron rod, bought from the Dutchmen on the Hudson. They ranged themselves in a double line, reaching upward to the entrance of the town; and through this "narrow road of Paradise," as Jogues calls it, the captives were led in single file, Couture in front, after him a half-score of Hurons, then Goupil, then the remaining Hurons, and at last Jogues. As they passed, they were saluted with yells, screeches, and a tempest of blows. One, heavier than the others, knocked

---

[1] The allusion is, of course, to the siege of Fort William Henry in 1757, and the ensuing massacre by Montcalm's Indians. Charlevoix, with his usual carelessness, says that Jogues's captors took a circuitous route to avoid enemies. In truth, however, they were not in the slightest danger of meeting any; and they followed the route which, before the present century, was the great highway between Canada and New Holland, or New York.

Jogues's breath from his body, and stretched him on the ground; but it was death to lie there, and, regaining his feet, he staggered on with the rest.[1] When they reached the town, the blows ceased, and they were all placed on a scaffold, or high platform, in the middle of the place. The three Frenchmen had fared the worst, and were frightfully disfigured. Goupil, especially, was streaming with blood, and livid with bruises from head to foot.

They were allowed a few minutes to recover their breath, undisturbed, except by the hootings and gibes of the mob below. Then a chief called out, "Come, let us caress these Frenchmen!"—and the crowd, knife in hand, began to mount the scaffold. They ordered a Christian Algonquin woman, a prisoner among them, to cut off Jogues's left thumb, which she did; and a thumb of Goupil was also severed, a clam-shell being used as the instrument, in order to increase the pain. It is needless to specify further the tortures to which they were subjected, all designed to cause the greatest possible suffering without endangering life. At night, they were removed from the scaffold, and placed in one of the houses, each stretched on his back, with his limbs extended, and his ankles and wrists bound fast to stakes driven into the earthen floor. The children now profited by the examples of their parents, and amused themselves by placing live coals and red-hot ashes on the naked bodies of the prisoners, who, bound fast, and covered with wounds and bruises which made every movement a torture, were sometimes unable to shake them off.

In the morning, they were again placed on the scaffold, where, during this and the two following days, they remained exposed to the taunts of the crowd. Then they were led in triumph to the second Mohawk town, and afterwards to the third,[2] suffering at each a repetition of cruelties, the detail of which would be as monotonous as revolting.

[1] This practice of forcing prisoners to "run the gauntlet" was by no means peculiar to the Iroquois, but was common to many tribes.

[2] The Mohawks had but three towns. The first, and the lowest on the river, was Osseruenon; the second, two miles above, was Andagaron; and the third, Teonontogen: or, as Megapolensis, in his *Sketch of the Mohawks*, writes the names, Asserué, Banagiro, and Thenondiogo. They all seem to have been fortified in the Iroquois manner, and their united population was thirty-five

In a house in the town of Teonontogen, Jogues was hung by the wrists between two of the upright poles which supported the structure, in such a manner that his feet could not touch the ground; and thus he remained for some fifteen minutes, in extreme torture, until, as he was on the point of swooning, an Indian, with an impulse of pity, cut the cords and released him. While they were in this town, four fresh Huron prisoners, just taken, were brought in, and placed on the scaffold with the rest. Jogues, in the midst of his pain and exhaustion, took the opportunity to convert them. An ear of green corn was thrown to him for food, and he discovered a few rain-drops clinging to the husks. With these he baptized two of the Hurons. The remaining two received baptism soon after from a brook which the prisoners crossed on the way to another town.

Couture, though he had incensed the Indians by killing one of their warriors, had gained their admiration by his bravery; and, after torturing him most savagely, they adopted him into one of their families, in place of a dead relative. Thenceforth he was comparatively safe. Jogues and Goupil were less fortunate. Three of the Hurons had been burned to death, and they expected to share their fate. A council was held to pronounce their doom; but dissensions arose, and no result was reached. They were led back to the first village, where they remained, racked with suspense and half dead with exhaustion. Jogues, however, lost no opportunity to baptize dying infants, while Goupil taught children to make the sign of the cross. On one occasion, he made the sign on the forehead of a child, grandson of an Indian in whose lodge they lived. The superstition of the old savage was aroused. Some Dutchmen had told him that the sign of the cross came from the Devil, and would cause mischief. He thought that Goupil was bewitching the child; and, resolving to rid himself of so dangerous a guest, applied for aid to two young braves. Jogues and Goupil, clad in their squalid garb of tattered skins, were soon after walking together in the forest that adjoined the town,

---

hundred, or somewhat more. At a later period, 1720, there were still three towns, named respectively Teahtontaioga, Ganowauga, and Ganeganaga. See the map in Morgan, *League of the Iroquois*.

consoling themselves with prayer, and mutually exhorting each other to suffer patiently for the sake of Christ and the Virgin, when, as they were returning, reciting their rosaries, they met the two young Indians, and read in their sullen visages an augury of ill. The Indians joined them, and accompanied them to the entrance of the town, where one of the two, suddenly drawing a hatchet from beneath his blanket, struck it into the head of Goupil, who fell, murmuring the name of Christ. Jogues dropped on his knees, and, bowing his head in prayer, awaited the blow, when the murderer ordered him to get up and go home. He obeyed, but not until he had given absolution to his still breathing friend, and presently saw the lifeless body dragged through the town amid hootings and rejoicings.

Jogues passed a night of anguish and desolation, and in the morning, reckless of life, set forth in search of Goupil's remains. "Where are you going so fast?" demanded the old Indian, his master. "Do you not see those fierce young braves, who are watching to kill you?" Jogues persisted, and the old man asked another Indian to go with him as a protector. The corpse had been flung into a neighboring ravine, at the bottom of which ran a torrent; and here, with the Indian's help, Jogues found it, stripped naked, and gnawed by dogs. He dragged it into the water, and covered it with stones to save it from further mutilation, resolving to return alone on the following day and secretly bury it. But with the night there came a storm; and when, in the gray of the morning, Jogues descended to the brink of the stream, he found it a rolling, turbid flood, and the body was nowhere to be seen. Had the Indians or the torrent borne it away? Jogues waded into the cold current; it was the first of October; he sounded it with his feet and with his stick; he searched the rocks, the thicket, the forest; but all in vain. Then, crouched by the pitiless stream, he mingled his tears with its waters, and, in a voice broken with groans, chanted the service of the dead.[1]

The Indians, it proved, and not the flood, had robbed him of the remains of his friend. Early in the spring, when the

[1] Jogues in Tanner, *Societas Militans*, 519; Bressani, 216; Lalemant, *Relation, 1647*, 25, 26; Buteux, *Narré*, MS.; Jogues, *Notice sur René Goupil*.

snows were melting in the woods, he was told by Mohawk children that the body was lying, where it had been flung, in a lonely spot lower down the stream. He went to seek it; found the scattered bones, stripped by the foxes and the birds; and, tenderly gathering them up, hid them in a hollow tree, hoping that a day might come when he could give them a Christian burial in consecrated ground.

After the murder of Goupil, Jogues's life hung by a hair. He lived in hourly expectation of the tomahawk, and would have welcomed it as a boon. By signs and words, he was warned that his hour was near; but, as he never shunned his fate, it fled from him, and each day, with renewed astonishment, he found himself still among the living.

Late in the autumn, a party of the Indians set forth on their yearly deer-hunt, and Jogues was ordered to go with them. Shivering and half famished, he followed them through the chill November forest, and shared their wild bivouac in the depths of the wintry desolation. The game they took was devoted to Areskoui, their god, and eaten in his honor. Jogues would not taste the meat offered to a demon; and thus he starved in the midst of plenty. At night, when the kettle was slung, and the savage crew made merry around their fire, he crouched in a corner of the hut, gnawed by hunger, and pierced to the bone with cold. They thought his presence unpropitious to their hunting, and the women especially hated him. His demeanor at once astonished and incensed his masters. He brought them fire-wood, like a squaw; he did their bidding without a murmur, and patiently bore their abuse; but when they mocked at his God, and laughed at his devotions, their slave assumed an air and tone of authority, and sternly rebuked them.[1]

He would sometimes escape from "this Babylon," as he calls the hut, and wander in the forest, telling his beads and repeating passages of Scripture. In a remote and lonely spot, he cut the bark in the form of a cross from the trunk of a great tree; and here he made his prayers. This living martyr, half clad in shaggy furs, kneeling on the snow among the icicled rocks and beneath the gloomy pines, bowing in ado-

[1] Lalemant, *Relation, 1647,* 41.

ration before the emblem of the faith in which was his only
consolation and his only hope, is alike a theme for the pen
and a subject for the pencil.

The Indians at last grew tired of him, and sent him back to
the village. Here he remained till the middle of March, baptizing infants and trying to convert adults. He told them of
the sun, moon, planets, and stars. They listened with interest;
but when from astronomy he passed to theology, he spent his
breath in vain. In March, the old man with whom he lived
set forth for his spring fishing, taking with him his squaw,
and several children. Jogues also was of the party. They repaired to a lake, perhaps Lake Saratoga, four days distant.
Here they subsisted for some time on frogs, the entrails of
fish, and other garbage. Jogues passed his days in the forest,
repeating his prayers, and carving the name of Jesus on trees,
as a terror to the demons of the wilderness. A messenger at
length arrived from the town; and on the following day, under the pretence that signs of an enemy had been seen, the
party broke up their camp, and returned home in hot haste.
The messenger had brought tidings that a war-party, which
had gone out against the French, had been defeated and destroyed, and that the whole population were clamoring to appease their grief by torturing Jogues to death. This was the
true cause of the sudden and mysterious return; but when
they reached the town, other tidings had arrived. The missing
warriors were safe, and on their way home in triumph with a
large number of prisoners. Again Jogues's life was spared; but
he was forced to witness the torture and butchery of the converts and allies of the French. Existence became unendurable
to him, and he longed to die. War-parties were continually
going out. Should they be defeated and cut off, he would pay
the forfeit at the stake; and if they came back, as they usually
did, with booty and prisoners, he was doomed to see his
countrymen and their Indian friends mangled, burned, and
devoured.

Jogues had shown no disposition to escape, and great liberty was therefore allowed him. He went from town to town,
giving absolution to the Christian captives, and converting
and baptizing the heathen. On one occasion, he baptized a
woman in the midst of the fire, under pretence of lifting a

cup of water to her parched lips. There was no lack of objects for his zeal. A single war-party returned from the Huron country with nearly a hundred prisoners, who were distributed among the Iroquois towns, and the greater part burned.[1] Of the children of the Mohawks and their neighbors, he had baptized, before August, about seventy; insomuch that he began to regard his captivity as a Providential interposition for the saving of souls.

At the end of July, he went with a party of Indians to a fishing-place on the Hudson, about twenty miles below Fort Orange. While here, he learned that another war-party had lately returned with prisoners, two of whom had been burned to death at Osseruenon. On this, his conscience smote him that he had not remained in the town to give the sufferers absolution or baptism; and he begged leave of the old woman who had him in charge to return at the first opportunity. A canoe soon after went up the river with some of the Iroquois, and he was allowed to go in it. When they reached Rensselaerswyck, the Indians landed to trade with the Dutch, and took Jogues with them.

The center of this rude little settlement was Fort Orange, a miserable structure of logs, standing on a spot now within the limits of the city of Albany.[2] It contained several houses and other buildings; and behind it was a small church, recently erected, and serving as the abode of the pastor, Dominie Megapolensis, known in our day as the writer of an interesting, though short, account of the Mohawks. Some twenty-five or thirty houses, roughly built of boards and roofed with thatch, were scattered at intervals on or near the borders of the Hudson, above and below the fort. Their inhabitants, about a hundred in number, were for the most part rude Dutch farmers, tenants of Van Rensselaer, the patroon,

[1] The Dutch clergyman, Megapolensis, at this time living at Fort Orange, bears the strongest testimony to the ferocity with which his friends, the Mohawks, treated their prisoners. He mentions the same modes of torture which Jogues describes, and is very explicit as to cannibalism. "The common people," he says, "eat the arms, buttocks, and trunk; but the chiefs eat the head and the heart." (*Short Sketch of the Mohawk Indians.*) This feast was of a religious character.

[2] The site of the Phœnix Hotel.—*Note by Mr. Shea to Jogues's Novum Belgium.*

or lord of the manor. They raised wheat, of which they made beer, and oats, with which they fed their numerous horses. They traded, too, with the Indians, who profited greatly by the competition among them, receiving guns, knives, axes, kettles, cloth, and beads, at moderate rates, in exchange for their furs.[1] The Dutch were on excellent terms with their red neighbors, met them in the forest without the least fear, and sometimes intermarried with them. They had known of Jogues's captivity, and, to their great honor, had made efforts for his release, offering for that purpose goods to a considerable value, but without effect.[2]

At Fort Orange Jogues heard startling news. The Indians of the village where he lived were, he was told, enraged against him, and determined to burn him. About the first of July, a war-party had set out for Canada, and one of the warriors had offered to Jogues to be the bearer of a letter from him to the French commander at Three Rivers, thinking probably to gain some advantage under cover of a parley. Jogues knew that the French would be on their guard; and he felt it his duty to lose no opportunity of informing them as to the state of affairs among the Iroquois. A Dutchman gave him a piece of paper; and he wrote a letter, in a jargon of Latin, French, and Huron, warning his countrymen to be on their guard, as war-parties were constantly going out, and they could hope for no respite from attack until late in the autumn.[3] When the Iroquois reached the mouth of the River Richelieu, where a small fort had been built by the French the preceding summer, the messenger asked for a parley, and gave Jogues's letter to the commander of the post, who, after reading it, turned his cannon on the savages. They fled in

[1] Jogues, *Novum Belgium*; Barnes, *Settlement of Albany*, 50–55; O'Callaghan, *New Netherland*, Chap. VI.

On the relations of the Mohawks and Dutch, see Megapolensis, *Short Sketch of the Mohawk Indians*, and portions of the letter of Jogues to his Superior, dated Rensselaerswyck, Aug. 30, 1643.

[2] See a long letter of Arendt Van Curler (Corlaer) to Van Rensselaer, June 16, 1643, in O'Callaghan's *New Netherland*, Appendix L. "We persuaded them so far," writes Van Curler, "that they promised not to kill them. . . . The French captives ran screaming after us, and besought us to do all in our power to release them out of the hands of the barbarians."

[3] See a French rendering of the letter in Vimont, *Relation, 1643*, p. 75.

dismay, leaving behind them their baggage and some of their guns; and, returning home in a fury, charged Jogues with having caused their discomfiture. Jogues had expected this result, and was prepared to meet it; but several of the principal Dutch settlers, and among them Van Curler, who had made the previous attempt to rescue him, urged that his death was certain, if he returned to the Indian town, and advised him to make his escape. In the Hudson, opposite the settlement, lay a small Dutch vessel nearly ready to sail. Van Curler offered him a passage in her to Bordeaux or Rochelle,—representing that the opportunity was too good to be lost, and making light of the prisoner's objection, that a connivance in his escape on the part of the Dutch would excite the resentment of the Indians against them. Jogues thanked him warmly; but, to his amazement, asked for a night to consider the matter, and take counsel of God in prayer.

He spent the night in great agitation, tossed by doubt, and full of anxiety lest his self-love should beguile him from his duty.[1] Was it not possible that the Indians might spare his life, and that, by a timely drop of water, he might still rescue souls from torturing devils, and eternal fires of perdition? On the other hand, would he not, by remaining to meet a fate almost inevitable, incur the guilt of suicide? And even should he escape torture and death, could he hope that the Indians would again permit him to instruct and baptize their prisoners? Of his French companions, one, Goupil, was dead; while Courture had urged Jogues to flight, saying that he would then follow his example, but that, so long as the Father remained a prisoner, he, Couture, would share his fate. Before morning, Jogues had made his decision. God, he thought, would be better pleased should he embrace the opportunity given him. He went to find his Dutch friends, and, with a profusion of thanks, accepted their offer. They told him that a boat should be left for him on the shore, and that he must watch his time, and escape in it to the vessel, where he would be safe.

He and his Indian masters were lodged together in a large building, like a barn, belonging to a Dutch farmer. It was a

[1] Buteux, *Narré*, MS.

hundred feet long, and had no partition of any kind. At one end the farmer kept his cattle; at the other he slept with his wife, a Mohawk squaw, and his children, while his Indian guests lay on the floor in the middle.[1] As he is described as one of the principal persons of the colony, it is clear that the civilization of Rensselaerswyck was not high.

In the evening, Jogues, in such a manner as not to excite the suspicion of the Indians, went out to reconnoitre. There was a fence around the house, and, as he was passing it, a large dog belonging to the farmer flew at him, and bit him very severely in the leg. The Dutchman, hearing the noise, came out with a light, led Jogues back into the building, and bandaged his wound. He seemed to have some suspicion of the prisoner's design; for, fearful perhaps that his escape might exasperate the Indians, he made fast the door in such a manner that it could not readily be opened. Jogues now lay down among the Indians, who, rolled in their blankets, were stretched around him. He was fevered with excitement; and the agitation of his mind, joined to the pain of his wound, kept him awake all night. About dawn, while the Indians were still asleep, a laborer in the employ of the farmer came in with a lantern, and Jogues, who spoke no Dutch, gave him to understand by signs that he needed his help and guidance. The man was disposed to aid him, silently led the way out, quieted the dogs, and showed him the path to the river. It was more than half a mile distant, and the way was rough and broken. Jogues was greatly exhausted, and his wounded limb gave him such pain that he walked with the utmost difficulty. When he reached the shore, the day was breaking, and he found, to his dismay, that the ebb of the tide had left the boat high and dry. He shouted to the vessel, but no one heard him. His desperation gave him strength; and, by working the boat to and fro, he pushed it at length, little by little, into the water, entered it, and rowed to the vessel. The Dutch sailors received him kindly, and hid him in the bottom of the hold, placing a large box over the hatchway.

He remained two days, half stifled, in this foul lurking-place, while the Indians, furious at his escape, ransacked the

[1] *Ibid.*

settlement in vain to find him. They came off to the vessel, and so terrified the officers, that Jogues was sent on shore at night, and led to the fort. Here he was hidden in the garret of a house occupied by a miserly old man, to whose charge he was consigned. Food was sent to him; but, as his host appropriated the larger part to himself, Jogues was nearly starved. There was a compartment of his garret, separated from the rest by a partition of boards. Here the old Dutch-man, who, like many others of the settlers, carried on a trade with the Mohawks, kept a quantity of goods for that purpose; and hither he often brought his customers. The boards of the partition had shrunk, leaving wide crevices; and Jogues could plainly see the Indians, as they passed between him and the light. They, on their part, might as easily have seen him, if he had not, when he heard them entering the house, hidden himself behind some barrels in the corner, where he would sometimes remain crouched for hours, in a constrained and painful posture, half suffocated with heat, and afraid to move a limb. His wounded leg began to show dangerous symp-toms; but he was relieved by the care of a Dutch surgeon of the fort. The minister, Megapolensis, also visited him, and did all in his power for the comfort of his Catholic brother, with whom he seems to have been well pleased, and whom he calls "a very learned scholar."[1]

When Jogues had remained for six weeks in this hiding-place, his Dutch friends succeeded in satisfying his Indian masters by the payment of a large ransom.[2] A vessel from Manhattan, now New York, soon after brought up an order from the Director-General, Kieft, that he should be sent to him. Accordingly he was placed in a small vessel, which car-ried him down the Hudson. The Dutch on board treated him with great kindness; and, to do him honor, named after him one of the islands in the river. At Manhattan he found a di-lapidated fort, garrisoned by sixty soldiers, and containing a stone church and the Director-General's house, together with storehouses and barracks. Near it were ranges of small houses, occupied chiefly by mechanics and laborers; while the dwell-

---

[1] Megapolensis, *A Short Sketch of the Mohawk Indians.*

[2] *Lettre de Jogues à Lalemant, Rennes, Jan. 6, 1644.* — See *Relation, 1643*, p. 79. — Goods were given the Indians to the value of three hundred livres.

ings of the remaining colonists, numbering in all four or five hundred, were scattered here and there on the island and the neighboring shores. The settlers were of different sects and nations, but chiefly Dutch Calvinists. Kieft told his guest that eighteen different languages were spoken at Manhattan.[1] The colonists were in the midst of a bloody Indian war, brought on by their own besotted cruelty; and while Jogues was at the fort, some forty of the Dutchmen were killed on the neighboring farms, and many barns and houses burned.[2]

The Director-General, with a humanity that was far from usual with him, exchanged Jogues's squalid and savage dress for a suit of Dutch cloth, and gave him passage in a small vessel which was then about to sail. The voyage was rough and tedious; and the passenger slept on deck or on a coil of ropes, suffering greatly from cold, and often drenched by the waves that broke over the vessel's side. At length she reached Falmouth, on the southern coast of England, when all the crew went ashore for a carouse, leaving Jogues alone on board. A boat presently came alongside with a gang of desperadoes, who boarded her, and rifled her of everything valuable, threatened Jogues with a pistol, and robbed him of his hat and coat. He obtained some assistance from the crew of a French ship in the harbor, and, on the day before Christmas, took passage in a small coal vessel for the neighboring coast of Brittany. In the following afternoon he was set on shore a little to the north of Brest, and, seeing a peasant's cottage not far off, he approached it, and asked the way to the nearest church. The peasant and his wife, as the narrative gravely tells us, mistook him, by reason of his modest deportment, for some poor, but pious Irishman, and asked him to share their supper, after finishing his devotions, an invitation which Jogues, half famished as he was, gladly accepted. He reached the church in time for the evening mass, and with an unutterable joy knelt before the altar, and renewed the communion of which he had been deprived so long. When he returned to the cottage, the attention of his hosts was at once attracted to his mutilated and distorted hands. They asked with amaze-

[1] Jogues, *Novum Belgium.*
[2] This war was with Algonquin tribes of the neighborhood. — See O'Callaghan, *New Netherland,* I., Chap. III.

ment how he could have received such injuries; and when they heard the story of his tortures, their surprise and veneration knew no bounds. Two young girls, their daughters, begged him to accept all they had to give,—a handful of sous; while the peasant made known the character of his new guest to his neighbors. A trader from Rennes brought a horse to the door, and offered the use of it to Jogues, to carry him to the Jesuit college in that town. He gratefully accepted it; and, on the morning of the fifth of January, 1644, reached his destination.

He dismounted, and knocked at the door of the college. The porter opened it, and saw a man wearing on his head an old woollen nightcap, and in an attire little better than that of a beggar. Jogues asked to see the Rector; but the porter answered, coldly, that the Rector was busied in the Sacristy. Jogues begged him to say that a man was at the door with news from Canada. The missions of Canada were at this time an object of primal interest to the Jesuits, and above all to the Jesuits of France. A letter from Jogues, written during his captivity, had already reached France, as had also the Jesuit *Relation* of 1643, which contained a long account of his capture; and he had no doubt been an engrossing theme of conversation in every house of the French Jesuits. The Father Rector was putting on his vestments to say mass; but when he heard that a poor man from Canada had asked for him at the door, he postponed the service, and went to meet him. Jogues, without discovering himself, gave him a letter from the Dutch Director-General attesting his character. The Rector, without reading it, began to question him as to the affairs of Canada, and at length asked him if he knew Father Jogues.

"I knew him very well," was the reply.

"The Iroquois have taken him," pursued the Rector. "Is he dead? Have they murdered him?

"No," answered Jogues; "he is alive and at liberty, and I am he." And he fell on his knees to ask his Superior's blessing.

That night was a night of jubilation and thanksgiving in the college of Rennes.[1]

---

[1] For Jogues's arrival in Brittany, see *Lettre de Jogues à Lalemant, Rennes, Jan. 6, 1644; Lettre de Jogues à ——, Rennes, Jan. 5, 1644,* (in *Relation, 1643,*) and the long account in the *Relation* of 1647.

Jogues became a centre of curiosity and reverence. He was summoned to Paris. The Queen, Anne of Austria, wished to see him; and when the persecuted slave of the Mohawks was conducted into her presence, she kissed his mutilated hands, while the ladies of the Court thronged around to do him homage. We are told, and no doubt with truth, that these honors were unwelcome to the modest and single-hearted missionary, who thought only of returning to his work of converting the Indians. A priest with any deformity of body is debarred from saying mass. The teeth and knives of the Iroquois had inflicted an injury worse than the torturers imagined, for they had robbed Jogues of the privilege which was the chief consolation of his life; but the Pope, by a special dispensation, restored it to him, and with the opening spring he sailed again for Canada.

Chapter XVII
1641–1646
THE IROQUOIS—BRESSANI—DE NOUË

War • Distress and Terror • Richelieu • Battle • Ruin of Indian Tribes • Mutual Destruction • Iroquois and Algonquin • Atrocities • Frightful Position of the French • Joseph Bressani • His Capture • His Treatment • His Escape • Anne de Nouë • His Nocturnal Journey • His Death

Two forces were battling for the mastery of Canada: on the one side, Christ, the Virgin, and the Angels, with their agents, the priests; on the other, the Devil, and his tools, the Iroquois. Such at least was the view of the case held in full faith, not by the Jesuit Fathers alone, but by most of the colonists. Never before had the fiend put forth such rage, and in the Iroquois he found instruments of a nature not uncongenial with his own.

At Quebec, Three Rivers, Montreal, and the little fort of Richelieu, that is to say, in all Canada, no man could hunt, fish, till the fields, or cut a tree in the forest, without peril to his scalp. The Iroquois were everywhere, and nowhere. A yell, a volley of bullets, a rush of screeching savages, and all was over. The soldiers hastened to the spot to find silence, solitude, and a mangled corpse.

"I had as lief," writes Father Vimont, "be beset by goblins as by the Iroquois. The one are about as invisible as the other. Our people on the Richelieu and at Montreal are kept in a closer confinement than ever were monks or nuns in our smallest convents in France."

The Confederates at this time were in a flush of unparalleled audacity. They despised white men as base poltroons, and esteemed themselves warriors and heroes, destined to conquer all mankind.[1] The fire-arms with which the Dutch

---

[1] Bressani, when a prisoner among them, writes to this effect in a letter to his Superior.—See *Relation Abrégée*, 131.

The anonymous author of the *Relation* of 1660 says, that, in their belief, if their nation were destroyed, a general confusion and overthrow of mankind must needs be the consequence.—*Relation, 1660*, 6.

had rashly supplied them, joined to their united councils, their courage, and ferocity, gave them an advantage over the surrounding tribes which they fully understood. Their passions rose with their sense of power. They boasted that they would wipe the Hurons, the Algonquins, and the French from the face of the earth, and carry the "white girls," meaning the nuns, to their villages. This last event, indeed, seemed more than probable; and the Hospital nuns left their exposed station at Sillery, and withdrew to the ramparts and palisades of Quebec. The St. Lawrence and the Ottawa were so infested, that communication with the Huron country was cut off; and three times the annual packet of letters sent thither to the missionaries fell into the hands of the Iroquois.

It was towards the close of the year 1640 that the scourge of Iroquois war had begun to fall heavily on the French. At that time, a party of their warriors waylaid and captured Thomas Godefroy and François Marguerie, the latter a young man of great energy and daring, familiar with the woods, a master of the Algonquin language, and a scholar of no mean acquirements.[1] To the great joy of the colonists, he and his companion were brought back to Three Rivers by their captors, and given up, in the vain hope that the French would respond with a gift of fire-arms. Their demand for them being declined, they broke off the parley in a rage, fortified themselves, fired on the French, and withdrew under cover of night.

Open war now ensued, and for a time all was bewilderment and terror. How to check the inroads of an enemy so stealthy and so keen for blood was the problem that taxed the brain of Montmagny, the Governor. He thought he had found a solution, when he conceived the plan of building a fort at the mouth of the River Richelieu, by which the Iroquois always made their descents to the St. Lawrence. Happily for the perishing colony, the Cardinal de Richelieu, in 1642, sent out thirty or forty soldiers for its defence.[2] Ten times the number would have been scarcely sufficient; but even this slight succor was hailed with delight, and Montmagny was enabled to

---

[1] During his captivity, he wrote, on a beaver-skin, a letter to the Dutch in French, Latin, and English.

[2] Faillon, *Colonie Française*, II. 2; Vimont, *Relation, 1642*, 2, 44.

carry into effect his plan of the fort, for which hitherto he had had neither builders nor garrison. He took with him, besides the new-comers, a body of soldiers and armed laborers from Quebec, and, with a force of about a hundred men in all,[1] sailed for the Richelieu, in a brigantine and two or three open boats.

On the thirteenth of August he reached his destination, and landed where the town of Sorel now stands. It was but eleven days before that Jogues and his companions had been captured, and Montmagny's followers found ghastly tokens of the disaster. The heads of the slain were stuck on poles by the side of the river; and several trees, from which portions of the bark had been peeled, were daubed with the rude picture-writing in which the victors recorded their exploit.[2] Among the rest, a representation of Jogues himself was clearly distinguishable. The heads were removed, the trees cut down, and a large cross planted on the spot. An altar was raised, and all heard mass; then a volley of musketry was fired; and then they fell to their work. They hewed an opening into the forest, dug up the roots, cleared the ground, and cut, shaped, and planted palisades. Thus a week passed, and their defences were nearly completed, when suddenly the war-whoop rang in their ears, and two hundred Iroquois rushed upon them from the borders of the clearing.[3]

It was the party of warriors that Jogues had met on an island in Lake Champlain. But for the courage of Du Rocher, a corporal, who was on guard, they would have carried all before them. They were rushing through an opening in the palisade, when he, with a few soldiers, met them with such vigor and resolution, that they were held in check long enough for the rest to snatch their arms. Montmagny, who

[1] Marie de l'Incarnation, *Lettre, Sept. 29, 1642.*

[2] Vimont, *Relation, 1642,* 52.

This practice was common to many tribes, and is not yet extinct. The writer has seen similar records, made by recent war-parties of Crows or Blackfeet, in the remote West. In this case, the bark was removed from the trunks of large cotton-wood trees, and the pictures traced with charcoal and vermilion. There were marks for scalps, for prisoners, and for the conquerors themselves.

[3] The *Relation* of 1642 says three hundred. Jogues, who had been among them to his cost, is the better authority.

was on the river in his brigantine, hastened on shore, and the soldiers, encouraged by his arrival, fought with great determination.

The Iroquois, on their part, swarmed up to the palisade, thrust their guns through the loop-holes, and fired on those within; nor was it till several of them had been killed and others wounded that they learned to keep a more prudent distance. A tall savage, wearing a crest of the hair of some animal, dyed scarlet and bound with a fillet of wampum, leaped forward to the attack, and was shot dead. Another shared his fate, with seven buck-shot in his shield, and as many in his body. The French, with shouts, redoubled their fire, and the Indians at length lost heart and fell back. The wounded dropped guns, shields, and war-clubs, and the whole band withdrew to the shelter of a fort which they had built in the forest, three miles above. On the part of the French, one man was killed and four wounded. They had narrowly escaped a disaster which might have proved the ruin of the colony; and they now gained time so far to strengthen their defences as to make them reasonably secure against any attack of savages.[1] The new fort, however, did not effectually answer its purpose of stopping the inroads of the Iroquois. They would land a mile or more above it, carry their canoes through the forest across an intervening tongue of land, and then launch them in the St. Lawrence, while the garrison remained in total ignorance of their movements.

While the French were thus beset, their Indian allies fared still worse. The effect of Iroquois hostilities on all the Algonquin tribes of Canada, from the Saguenay to the Lake of the Nipissings, had become frightfully apparent. Famine and pestilence had aided the ravages of war, till these wretched bands seemed in the course of rapid extermination. Their spirit was broken. They became humble and docile in the hands of the

[1] Vimont, *Relation, 1642*, 50, 51.

Assaults by Indians on fortified places are rare. The Iroquois are known, however, to have made them with success in several cases, some of the most remarkable of which will appear hereafter. The courage of Indians is uncertain and spasmodic. They are capable, at times, of a furious temerity, approaching desperation; but this is liable to sudden and extreme reaction. Their courage, too, is much oftener displayed in covert than in open attacks.

missionaries, ceased their railings against the new doctrine, and leaned on the French as their only hope in this extremity of woe. Sometimes they would appear in troops at Sillery or Three Rivers, scared out of their forests by the sight of an Iroquois footprint; then some new terror would seize them, and drive them back to seek a hiding-place in the deepest thickets of the wilderness. Their best hunting-grounds were beset by the enemy. They starved for weeks together, subsisting on the bark of trees or the thongs of raw hide which formed the net-work of their snow-shoes. The mortality among them was prodigious. "Where, eight years ago," writes Father Vimont, "one would see a hundred wigwams, one now sees scarcely five or six. A chief who once had eight hundred warriors has now but thirty or forty; and in place of fleets of three or four hundred canoes, we see less than a tenth of that number."[1]

These Canadian tribes were undergoing that process of extermination, absorption, or expatriation, which, as there is reason to believe, had for many generations formed the gloomy and meaningless history of the greater part of this continent. Three or four hundred Dutch guns, in the hands of the conquerors, gave an unwonted quickness and decision to the work, but in no way changed its essential character. The horrible nature of this warfare can be known only through examples; and of these one or two will suffice.

A band of Algonquins, late in the autumn of 1641, set forth from Three Rivers on their winter hunt, and, fearful of the Iroquois, made their way far northward, into the depths of the forests that border the Ottawa. Here they thought themselves safe, built their lodges, and began to hunt the moose and beaver. But a large party of their enemies, with a persistent ferocity that is truly astonishing, had penetrated even here, found the traces of the snow-shoes, followed up their human prey, and hid at nightfall among the rocks and thickets around the encampment. At midnight, their yells and the blows of their war-clubs awakened their sleeping victims. In a few minutes all were in their power. They bound the prisoners hand and foot, rekindled the fire, slung

[1] *Relation, 1644*, 3.

the kettles, cut the bodies of the slain to pieces, and boiled and devoured them before the eyes of the wretched survivors. "In a word," says the narrator, "they ate men with as much appetite and more pleasure than hunters eat a boar or a stag."[1]

Meanwhile they amused themselves with bantering their prisoners. "Uncle," said one of them to an old Algonquin, "you are a dead man. You are going to the land of souls. Tell them to take heart: they will have good company soon, for we are going to send all the rest of your nation to join them. This will be good news for them."[2]

This old man, who is described as no less malicious than his captors, and even more crafty, soon after escaped, and brought tidings of the disaster to the French. In the following spring, two women of the party also escaped; and, after suffering almost incredible hardships, reached Three Rivers, torn with briers, nearly naked, and in a deplorable state of bodily and mental exhaustion. One of them told her story to Father Buteux, who translated it into French, and gave it to Vimont to be printed in the *Relation* of 1642. Revolting as it is, it is necessary to recount it. Suffice it to say, that it is sustained by the whole body of contemporary evidence in regard to the practices of the Iroquois and some of the neighboring tribes.

The conquerors feasted in the lodge till nearly daybreak, and then, after a short rest, began their march homeward with their prisoners. Among these were three women, of whom the narrator was one, who had each a child of a few weeks or months old. At the first halt, their captors took the infants from them, tied them to wooden spits, placed them to die slowly before a fire, and feasted on them before the eyes of the agonized mothers, whose shrieks, supplications, and frantic efforts to break the cords that bound them were met with mockery and laughter. "They are not men, they are wolves!" sobbed the wretched woman, as she told what had befallen her to the pitying Jesuit.[3] At the Fall of the Chaudière, another of the women ended her woes by leaping into

[1] Vimont, *Relation, 1642*, 46.
[2] *Ibid.*, 45.
[3] *Ibid.*, 46.

the cataract. When they approached the first Iroquois town, they were met, at the distance of several leagues, by a crowd of the inhabitants, and among them a troop of women, bringing food to regale the triumphant warriors. Here they halted, and passed the night in songs of victory, mingled with the dismal chant of the prisoners, who were forced to dance for their entertainment.

On the morrow, they entered the town, leading the captive Algonquins, fast bound, and surrounded by a crowd of men, women, and children, all singing at the top of their throats. The largest lodge was ready to receive them; and as they entered, the victims read their doom in the fires that blazed on the earthen floor, and in the aspect of the attendant savages, whom the Jesuit Father calls attendant demons, that waited their coming. The torture which ensued was but preliminary, designed to cause all possible suffering without touching life. It consisted in blows with sticks and cudgels, gashing their limbs with knives, cutting off their fingers with clam-shells, scorching them with firebrands, and other indescribable torments.[1] The women were stripped naked, and forced to dance to the singing of the male prisoners, amid the applause and laughter of the crowd. They then gave them food, to strengthen them for further suffering.

On the following morning, they were placed on a large scaffold, in sight of the whole population. It was a gala-day. Young and old were gathered from far and near. Some mounted the scaffold, and scorched them with torches and firebrands; while the children, standing beneath the bark platform, applied fire to the feet of the prisoners between the crevices. The Algonquin women were told to burn their husbands and companions; and one of them obeyed, vainly thinking to appease her tormentors. The stoicism of one of the warriors enraged his captors beyond measure. "Scream! why don't you scream?" they cried, thrusting their burning brands at his naked body. "Look at me," he answered; "you

---

[1] "Cette pauure creature qui s'est sauuée, a les deux pouces couppez, ou plus tost hachez. Quand ils me les eurent couppez, disoit-elle, ils me les voulurent faire manger; mais ie les mis sur mon giron, et leur dis qu'ils me taussent s'ils vouloient, que ie ne leur pouuois obeir."—Buteux, in *Relation*, *1642*, 47.

cannot make me wince. If you were in my place, you would screech like babies." At this they fell upon him with redoubled fury, till their knives and firebrands left in him no semblance of humanity. He was defiant to the last, and when death came to his relief, they tore out his heart and devoured it; then hacked him in pieces, and made their feast of triumph on his mangled limbs.[1]

All the men and all the old women of the party were put to death in a similar manner, though but few displayed the same amazing fortitude. The younger women, of whom there were about thirty, after passing their ordeal of torture, were permitted to live; and, disfigured as they were, were distributed among the several villages, as concubines or slaves to the Iroquois warriors. Of this number were the narrator and her companion, who, being ordered to accompany a war-party and carry their provisions, escaped at night into the forest, and reached Three Rivers, as we have seen.

While the Indian allies of the French were wasting away beneath this atrocious warfare, the French themselves, and especially the travelling Jesuits, had their full share of the infliction. In truth, the puny and sickly colony seemed in the gasps of dissolution. The beginning of spring, particularly, was a season of terror and suspense; for with the breaking up of the ice, sure as a destiny, came the Iroquois. As soon as a canoe could float, they were on the war-path; and with the cry of the returning wild-fowl mingled the yell of these human tigers. They did not always wait for the breaking ice, but set forth on foot, and, when they came to open water, made canoes and embarked.

Well might Father Vimont call the Iroquois "the scourge of this infant church." They burned, hacked, and devoured the neophytes; exterminated whole villages at once; destroyed

---

[1] The diabolical practices described above were not peculiar to the Iroquois. The Neutrals and other kindred tribes were no whit less cruel. It is a remark of Mr. Gallatin, and I think a just one, that the Indians west of the Mississippi are less ferocious than those east of it. The burning of prisoners is rare among the prairie tribes, but is not unknown. An Ogillallah chief, in whose lodge I lived for several weeks in 1846, described to me, with most expressive pantomime, how he had captured and burned a warrior of the Snake Tribe, in a valley of the Medicine Bow Mountains, near which we were then encamped.

the nations whom the Fathers hoped to convert; and ruined that sure ally of the missions, the fur-trade. Not the most hideous nightmare of a fevered brain could transcend in horror the real and waking perils with which they beset the path of these intrepid priests.

In the spring of 1644, Joseph Bressani, an Italian Jesuit, born in Rome, and now for two years past a missionary in Canada, was ordered by his Superior to go up to the Hurons. It was so early in the season that there seemed hope that he might pass in safety; and as the Fathers in that wild mission had received no succor for three years, Bressani was charged with letters to them, and such necessaries for their use as he was able to carry. With him were six young Hurons, lately converted, and a French boy in his service. The party were in three small canoes. Before setting out, they all confessed and prepared for death.

They left Three Rivers on the twenty-seventh of April, and found ice still floating in the river, and patches of snow lying in the naked forests. On the first day, one of the canoes overset, nearly drowning Bressani, who could not swim. On the third day, a snow-storm began, and greatly retarded their progress. The young Indians foolishly fired their guns at the wild-fowl on the river, and the sound reached the ears of a war-party of Iroquois, one of ten that had already set forth for the St. Lawrence, the Ottawa, and the Huron towns.[1] Hence it befell, that, as they crossed the mouth of a small stream entering the St. Lawrence, twenty-seven Iroquois suddenly issued from behind a point, and attacked them in canoes. One of the Hurons was killed, and all the rest of the party captured without resistance.

On the fifteenth of July following, Bressani wrote from the Iroquois country to the General of the Jesuits at Rome:—"I do not know if your Paternity will recognize the handwriting of one whom you once knew very well. The letter is soiled and ill-written; because the writer has only one finger of his right hand left entire, and cannot prevent the blood from his wounds, which are still open, from staining the paper. His

[1] Vimont, *Relation, 1644*, 41.

ink is gunpowder mixed with water, and his table is the earth."[1]

Then follows a modest narrative of what he endured at the hands of his captors. First they thanked the Sun for their victory; then plundered the canoes; then cut up, roasted, and devoured the slain Huron before the eyes of the prisoners. On the next day they crossed to the southern shore, and ascended the River Richelieu as far as the rapids of Chambly, whence they pursued their march on foot among the brambles, rocks, and swamps of the trackless forest. When they reached Lake Champlain, they made new canoes and re-embarked, landed at its southern extremity six days afterwards, and thence made for the Upper Hudson. Here they found a fishing camp of four hundred Iroquois, and now Bressani's torments began in earnest. They split his hand with a knife, between the little finger and the ring finger; then beat him with sticks, till he was covered with blood; and afterwards placed him on one of their torture-scaffolds of bark, as a spectacle to the crowd. Here they stripped him, and while he shivered with cold from head to foot, they forced him to sing. After about two hours they gave him up to the children, who ordered him to dance, at the same time thrusting sharpened sticks into his flesh, and pulling out his hair and beard. "Sing!" cried one; "Hold your tongue!" screamed another; and if he obeyed the first, the second burned him. "We will burn you to death; we will eat you." "I will eat one of your hands." "And I will eat one of your feet."[2] These scenes were renewed every night for a week. Every evening a chief cried aloud through the camp, "Come, my children, come and caress our prisoners!"—and the savage crew thronged jubilant to a large hut, where the captives lay. They stripped off the

[1] This letter is printed anonymously in the Second Part, Chap. II., of Bressani's *Relation Abrégée*. A comparison with Vimont's account, in the *Relation* of 1644, makes its authorship apparent. Vimont's narrative agrees in all essential points. His informant was "vne personne digne de foy, qui a esté tesmoin oculaire de tout ce qu'il a souffert pendant sa captiuité."—Vimont, *Relation, 1644*, 43.

[2] "Ils me répétaient sans cesse: Nous te brûlerons; nous te mangerons;—je te mangerai un pied;—et moi, une main," etc.—Bressani, in *Relation Abrégée*, 137.

torn fragment of a cassock, which was the priest's only garment; burned him with live coals and red-hot stones; forced him to walk on hot cinders; burned off now a finger-nail and now the joint of a finger,—rarely more than one at a time, however, for they economized their pleasures, and reserved the rest for another day. This torture was protracted till one or two o'clock, after which they left him on the ground, fast bound to four stakes, and covered only with a scanty fragment of deer-skin.[1] The other prisoners had their share of torture; but the worst fell upon the Jesuit, as the chief man of the party. The unhappy boy who attended him, though only twelve or thirteen years old, was tormented before his eyes with a pitiless ferocity.

At length they left this encampment, and, after a march of several days,—during which Bressani, in wading a rocky stream, fell from exhaustion and was nearly drowned,—they reached an Iroquois town. It is needless to follow the revolting details of the new torments that succeeded. They hung him by the feet with chains; placed food for their dogs on his naked body, that they might lacerate him as they ate; and at last had reduced his emaciated frame to such a condition, that even they themselves stood in horror of him. "I could not have believed," he writes to his Superior, "that a man was so hard to kill." He found among them those who, from compassion, or from a refinement of cruelty, fed him, for he could not feed himself. They told him jestingly that they wished to fatten him before putting him to death.

[1] "Chaque nuit après m'avoir fait chanter, et m'avoir tourmenté comme ie l'ai dit, ils passaient environ un quart d'heure à me brûler un ongle ou un doigt. Il ne m'en reste maintenant qu'un seul entier, et encore ils en ont arraché l'ongle avec les dents. Un soir ils m'enlevaient un ongle, le lendemain la première phalange, le jour suivant la seconde. En six fois, ils en brûlèrent presque six. Aux mains seules, ils m'ont appliqué le feu et le fer plus de 18 fois, et i'étais obligé de chanter pendant ce supplice. Ils ne cessaient de me tourmenter qu'à une ou deux heures de la nuit."—Bressani, *Relation Abrégée*, 122.

Bressani speaks in another passage of tortures of a nature yet more excruciating. They were similar to those alluded to by the anonymous author of the *Relation* of 1660: "Ie ferois rougir ce papier, et les oreilles frémiroient, si ie rapportois les horribles traitemens que les Agnieronnons" (*the Mohawk nation of the Iroquois*) "ont faits sur quelques captifs." He adds, that past ages have never heard of such.—*Relation*, *1660*, 7, 8.

The council that was to decide his fate met on the nine-teenth of June, when, to the prisoner's amazement, and, as it seemed, to their own surprise, they resolved to spare his life. He was given, with due ceremony, to an old woman, to take the place of a deceased relative; but, since he was as repulsive, in his mangled condition, as, by the Indian standard, he was useless, she sent her son with him to Fort Orange, to sell him to the Dutch. With the same humanity which they had shown in the case of Jogues, they gave a generous ransom for him, supplied him with clothing, kept him till his strength was in some degree recruited, and then placed him on board a vessel bound for Rochelle. Here he arrived on the fifteenth of No-vember; and in the following spring, maimed and disfigured, but with health restored, embarked to dare again the knives and firebrands of the Iroquois.[1]

It should be noticed, in justice to the Iroquois, that, fero-cious and cruel as past all denial they were, they were not so bereft of the instincts of humanity as at first sight might ap-pear. An inexorable severity towards enemies was a very es-sential element, in their savage conception, of the character of the warrior. Pity was a cowardly weakness, at which their pride revolted. This, joined to their thirst for applause and their dread of ridicule, made them smother every movement of compassion,[2] and conspired with their native fierceness to form a character of unrelenting cruelty rarely equalled.

The perils which beset the missionaries did not spring from the fury of the Iroquois alone, for Nature herself was armed with terror in this stern wilderness of New France. On the

---

[1] Immediately on his return to Canada he was ordered to set out again for the Hurons. More fortunate than on his first attempt, he arrived safely, early in the autumn of 1645.—Ragueneau, *Relation des Hurons, 1646*, 73.

On Bressani, besides the authorities cited, see Du Creux, *Historia Cana-densis*, 399–403; Juchereau, *Histoire de l'Hôtel-Dieu*, 53; and Martin, *Biogra-phie du P. François-Joseph Bressani*, prefixed to the *Relation Abrégée*.

He made no converts while a prisoner, but he baptized a Huron catechu-men at the stake, to the great fury of the surrounding Iroquois. He has left, besides his letters, some interesting notes on his captivity, preserved in the *Relation Abrégée*.

[2] Thus, when Bressani, tortured by the tightness of the cords that bound him, asked an Indian to loosen them, he would reply by mockery, if others were present; but if no one saw him, he usually complied.

thirtieth of January, 1646, Father Anne de Noüe set out from Three Rivers to go to the fort built by the French at the mouth of the River Richelieu, where he was to say mass and hear confessions. De Noüe was sixty-three years old, and had come to Canada in 1625.[1] As an indifferent memory disabled him from mastering the Indian languages, he devoted himself to the spiritual charge of the French, and of the Indians about the forts, within reach of an interpreter. For the rest, he attended the sick, and, in times of scarcity, fished in the river or dug roots in the woods for the subsistence of his flock. In short, though sprung from a noble family of Champagne, he shrank from no toil, however humble, to which his idea of duty or his vow of obedience called him.[2]

The old missionary had for companions two soldiers and a Huron Indian. They were all on snow-shoes, and the soldiers dragged their baggage on small sledges. Their highway was the St. Lawrence, transformed to solid ice, and buried, like all the country, beneath two or three feet of snow, which, far and near, glared dazzling white under the clear winter sun. Before night they had walked eighteen miles, and the soldiers, unused to snow-shoes, were greatly fatigued. They made their camp in the forest, on the shore of the great expansion of the St. Lawrence called the Lake of St. Peter,—dug away the snow, heaped it around the spot as a barrier against the wind, made their fire on the frozen earth in the midst, and lay down to sleep. At two o'clock in the morning De Noüe awoke. The moon shone like daylight over the vast white desert of the frozen lake, with its bordering fir-trees bowed to the ground with snow; and the kindly thought struck the Father, that he might ease his companions by going in advance to Fort Richelieu, and sending back men to aid them in dragging their sledges. He knew the way well. He directed them to follow the tracks of his snow-shoes in the morning; and, not doubting to reach the fort before night, left behind his blanket and his flint and steel. For provisions, he put a morsel of bread

---

[1] See "Pioneers of France," 310.

[2] He was peculiarly sensitive as regarded the cardinal Jesuit virtue of obedience; and both Lalemant and Bressani say, that, at the age of sixty and upwards, he was sometimes seen in tears, when he imagined that he had not fulfilled to the utmost the commands of his Superior.

and five or six prunes in his pocket, told his rosary, and set forth.

Before dawn the the weather changed. The air thickened, clouds hid the moon, and a snow-storm set in. The traveller was in utter darkness. He lost the points of the compass, wandered far out on the lake, and when day appeared could see nothing but the snow beneath his feet, and the myriads of falling flakes that encompassed him like a curtain, impervious to the sight. Still he toiled on, winding hither and thither, and at times unwittingly circling back on his own footsteps. At night he dug a hole in the snow under the shore of an island, and lay down, without fire, food, or blanket.

Meanwhile the two soldiers and the Indian, unable to trace his footprints, which the snow had hidden, pursued their way for the fort; but the Indian was ignorant of the country, and the Frenchmen were unskilled. They wandered from their course, and at evening encamped on the shore of the island of St. Ignace, at no great distance from De Nouë. Here the Indian, trusting to his instinct, left them and set forth alone in search of their destination, which he soon succeeded in finding. The palisades of the feeble little fort, and the rude buildings within, were whitened with snow, and half buried in it. Here, amid the desolation, a handful of men kept watch and ward against the Iroquois. Seated by the blazing logs, the Indian asked for De Nouë, and, to his astonishment, the soldiers of the garrison told him that he had not been seen. The captain of the post was called; all was anxiety; but nothing could be done that night.

At daybreak parties went out to search. The two soldiers were readily found; but they looked in vain for the missionary. All day they were ranging the ice, firing their guns and shouting; but to no avail, and they returned disconsolate. There was a converted Indian, whom the French called Charles, at the fort, one of four who were spending the winter there. On the next morning, the second of February, he and one of his companions, together with Baron, a French soldier, resumed the search; and, guided by the slight depressions in the snow which had fallen on the wanderer's footprints, the quick-eyed savages traced him through all his windings, found his camp by the shore of the island, and thence followed him beyond the fort. He had passed near without discovering it,—perhaps weakness had dimmed his sight,—stopped to rest at a point a league above, and thence made his way about three leagues farther. Here they found him. He had dug a circular excavation in the snow, and was kneeling in it on the earth. His head was bare, his eyes open and turned upwards, and his hands clasped on his breast. His hat and his snow-shoes lay at his side. The body was leaning slightly forward, resting against the bank of snow before it, and frozen to the hardness of marble.

Thus, in an act of kindness and charity, died the first martyr of the Canadian mission.[1]

[1] Lalemant, *Relation*, *1646*, 9; Marie de l'Incarnation, *Lettre*, *10 Sept.*, *1646;* Bressani, *Relation Abrégée*, 175.

One of the Indians who found the body of De Noüe was killed by the Iroquois at Ossossané, in the Huron country, three years after. He received the death-blow in a posture like that in which he had seen the dead missionary. His body was found with the hands still clasped on the breast.—*Lettre de Chaumonot à Lalemant*, *1 Juin*, *1649*.

The next death among the Jesuits was that of Masse, who died at Sillery, on the twelfth of May of this year, 1646, at the age of seventy-two. He had come with Biard to Acadia as early as 1611. (See "Pioneers of France," 220.) Lalemant, in the *Relation* of 1646, gives an account of him, and speaks of penances which he imposed on himself, some of which are to the last degree disgusting.

Chapter XVIII
1642—1644
VILLEMARIE

Infancy of Montreal • *The Flood* • *Vow of Maisonneuve* • *Pilgrimage* • *D'Ailleboust* • *The Hôtel-Dieu* • *Piety* • *Propagandism* • *War* • *Hurons and Iroquois* • *Dogs* • *Sally of the French* • *Battle* • *Exploit of Maisonneuve*

L ET us now ascend to the island of Montreal. Here, as we have seen, an association of devout and zealous persons had essayed to found a mission-colony under the protection of the Holy Virgin; and we left the adventurers, after their landing, bivouacked on the shore, on an evening in May. There was an altar in the open air, decorated with a taste that betokened no less of good nurture than of piety; and around it clustered the tents that sheltered the commandant, Maisonneuve, the two ladies, Madame de la Peltrie and Mademoiselle Mance, and the soldiers and laborers of the expedition.

In the morning they all fell to their work, Maisonneuve hewing down the first tree,—and labored with such goodwill, that their tents were soon inclosed with a strong palisade, and their altar covered by a provisional chapel, built, in the Huron mode, of bark. Soon afterward, their canvas habitations were supplanted by solid structures of wood, and the feeble germ of a future city began to take root.

The Iroquois had not yet found them out; nor did they discover them till they had had ample time to fortify themselves. Meanwhile, on a Sunday, they would stroll at their leisure over the adjacent meadow and in the shade of the bordering forest, where, as the old chronicler tells us, the grass was gay with wild-flowers, and the branches with the flutter and song of many strange birds.[1]

The day of the Assumption of the Virgin was celebrated with befitting solemnity. There was mass in their bark chapel; then a Te Deum; then public instruction of certain Indians who chanced to be at Montreal; then a procession of all the

[1] Dollier de Casson, MS.

colonists after vespers, to the admiration of the redskinned beholders. Cannon, too, were fired, in honor of their celestial patroness. "Their thunder made all the island echo," writes Father Vimont; "and the demons, though used to thunder-bolts, were scared at a noise which told them of the love we bear our great Mistress; and I have scarcely any doubt that the tutelary angels of the savages of New France have marked this day in the calendar of Paradise."[1]

The summer passed prosperously, but with the winter their faith was put to a rude test. In December, there was a rise of the St. Lawrence, threatening to sweep away in a night the results of all their labor. They fell to their prayers; and Mai-sonneuve planted a wooden cross in face of the advancing deluge, first making a vow, that, should the peril be averted, he, Maisonneuve, would bear another cross on his shoulders up the neighboring mountain, and place it on the summit. The vow seemed in vain. The flood still rose, filled the fort ditch, swept the foot of the palisade, and threatened to sap the magazine; but here it stopped, and presently began to recede, till at length it had withdrawn within its lawful chan-nel, and Villemarie was safe.[2]

Now it remained to fulfil the promise from which such happy results had proceeded. Maisonneuve set his men at work to clear a path through the forest to the top of the mountain. A large cross was made, and solemnly blessed by the priest; then, on the sixth of January, the Jesuit Du Peron led the way, followed in procession by Madame de la Peltrie, the artisans, and soldiers, to the destined spot. The comman-dant, who with all the ceremonies of the Church had been declared First Soldier of the Cross, walked behind the rest, bearing on his shoulder a cross so heavy that it needed his utmost strength to climb the steep and rugged path. They planted it on the highest crest, and all knelt in adoration be-fore it. Du Peron said mass; and Madame de la Peltrie, always romantic and always devout, received the sacrament on the

[1] Vimont, *Relation, 1642*, 38. Compare Le Clerc, *Premier Etablissement de la Foy*, II. 51.
[2] A little MS. map in M. Jacques Viger's copy of *Le Petit Registre de la Cure de Montreal*, lays down the position and shape of the fort at this time, and shows the spot where Maisonneuve planted the cross.

mountain-top, a spectacle to the virgin world outstretched below. Sundry relics of saints had been set in the wood of the
cross, which remained an object of pilgrimage to the pious
colonists of Villemarie.[1]

Peace and harmony reigned within the little fort; and so
edifying was the demeanor of the colonists, so faithful were
they to the confessional, and so constant at mass, that a
chronicler of the day exclaims, in a burst of enthusiasm, that
the deserts lately a resort of demons were now the abode of
angels.[2] The two Jesuits who for the time were their pastors
had them well in hand. They dwelt under the same roof with
most of their flock, who lived in community, in one large
house, and vied with each other in zeal for the honor of the
Virgin and the conversion of the Indians.

At the end of August, 1643, a vessel arrived at Villemarie
with a reinforcement commanded by Louis d'Ailleboust de
Coulonges, a pious gentleman of Champagne, and one of the
Associates of Montreal.[3] Some years before, he had asked in
wedlock the hand of Barbe de Boulogne; but the young lady
had, when a child, in the ardor of her piety, taken a vow of
perpetual chastity. By the advice of her Jesuit confessor, she
accepted his suit, on condition that she should preserve, to
the hour of her death, the state to which Holy Church has
always ascribed a peculiar merit.[4] D'Ailleboust married her;
and when, soon after, he conceived the purpose of devoting
his life to the work of the Faith in Canada, he invited his
maiden spouse to go with him. She refused, and forbade him
to mention the subject again. Her health was indifferent, and
about this time she fell ill. As a last resort, she made a promise
to God, that, if He would restore her, she would go to Canada with her husband; and forthwith her maladies ceased.
Still her reluctance continued; she hesitated, and then refused
again, when an inward light revealed to her that it was her
duty to cast her lot in the wilderness. She accordingly em-

[1] Vimont, *Relation, 1643*, 52, 53.

[2] *Véritables Motifs*, cited by Faillon, I. 453, 454.

[3] Chaulmer, 101; Juchereau, 91.

[4] Juchereau, *Histoire de l'Hôtel-Dieu de Québec*, 276. The confessor told
D'Ailleboust, that, if he persuaded his wife to break her vow of continence,
"God would chastise him terribly." The nun historian adds, that, undeterred
by the menace, he tried and failed.

barked with d'Ailleboust, accompanied by her sister, Mademoiselle Philippine de Boulogne, who had caught the contagion of her zeal. The presence of these damsels would, to all appearance, be rather a burden than a profit to the colonists, beset as they then were by Indians, and often in peril of starvation; but the spectacle of their ardor, as disinterested as it was extravagant, would serve to exalt the religious enthusiasm in which alone was the life of Villemarie.

Their vessel passed in safety the Iroquois who watched the St. Lawrence, and its arrival filled the colonists with joy. D'Ailleboust was a skilful soldier, specially versed in the arts of fortification; and, under his direction, the frail palisades which formed their sole defence were replaced by solid ramparts and bastions of earth. He brought news that the "unknown benefactress," as a certain generous member of the Association of Montreal was called, in ignorance of her name, had given funds, to the amount, as afterwards appeared, of forty-two thousand livres, for the building of a hospital at Villemarie.[1] The source of the gift was kept secret, from a religious motive; but it soon became known that it proceeded from Madame de Bullion, a lady whose rank and wealth were exceeded only by her devotion. It is true that the hospital was not wanted, as no one was sick at Villemarie, and one or two chambers would have sufficed for every prospective necessity; but it will be remembered that the colony had been established in order that a hospital might be built, and Madame de Bullion would not hear to any other application of her money.[2] Instead, therefore, of tilling the land to supply their own pressing needs, all the laborers of the settlement were set at this pious, though superfluous, task.[3] There was no room

[1] *Archives du Séminaire de Villemarie*, cited by Faillon, I. 466. The amount of the gift was not declared until the next year.

[2] Mademoiselle Mance wrote to her, to urge that the money should be devoted to the Huron mission; but she absolutely refused.—Dollier de Casson, MS.

[3] *Journal des Supérieurs des Jésuites*, MS.

The hospital was sixty feet long and twenty-four feet wide, with a kitchen, a chamber for Mademoiselle Mance, others for servants, and two large apartments for the patients. It was amply provided with furniture, linen, medicines, and all necessaries; and had also two oxen, three cows, and twenty sheep. A small oratory of stone was built adjoining it. The inclosure was four *arpents* in extent.—*Archives du Séminaire de Villemarie*, cited by Faillon.

in the fort, which, moreover, was in danger of inundation; and the hospital was accordingly built on higher ground adjacent. To leave it unprotected would be to abandon its inmates to the Iroquois; it was therefore surrounded by a strong palisade, and, in time of danger, a part of the garrison was detailed to defend it. Here Mademoiselle Mance took up her abode, and waited the day when wounds or disease should bring patients to her empty wards.

Dauversière, who had first conceived this plan of a hospital in the wilderness, was a senseless enthusiast, who rejected as a sin every protest of reason against the dreams which governed him; yet one rational and practical element entered into the motives of those who carried the plan into execution. The hospital was intended not only to nurse sick Frenchmen, but to nurse and convert sick Indians; in other words, it was an engine of the mission.

From Maisonneuve to the humblest laborer, these zealous colonists were bent on the work of conversion. To that end, the ladies made pilgrimages to the cross on the mountain, sometimes for nine days in succession, to pray God to gather the heathen into His fold. The fatigue was great; nor was the danger less; and armed men always escorted them, as a precaution against the Iroquois.[1] The male colonists were equally fervent; and sometimes as many as fifteen or sixteen persons would kneel at once before the cross, with the same charitable petition.[2] The ardor of their zeal may be inferred from the fact, that these pious expeditions consumed the greater part of the day, when time and labor were of a value past reckoning to the little colony. Besides their pilgrimages, they used other means, and very efficient ones, to attract and gain over the Indians. They housed, fed, and clothed them at every opportunity; and though they were subsisting chiefly on provisions brought at great cost from France, there was always a portion for the hungry savages who from time to time encamped near their fort. If they could persuade any of them to be nursed, they were consigned to the tender care of Mademoiselle Mance; and if a party went to war, their women and children were taken in charge till their return. As this attention to their bodies had for its object the profit of their souls,

---

[1] Morin, *Annales de l'Hôtel-Dieu de St. Joseph*, MS., cited by Faillon, I. 457.
[2] Marguerite Bourgeoys, *Écrits Autographes*, MS., extracts in Faillon, I. 458.

it was accompanied with incessant catechizing. This, with the other influences of the place, had its effect; and some notable conversions were made. Among them was that of the renowned chief, Tessouat, or Le Borgne, as the French called him,—a crafty and intractable savage, whom, to their own surprise, they succeeded in taming and winning to the Faith.[1] He was christened with the name of Paul, and his squaw with that of Madeleine. Maisonneuve rewarded him with a gun, and celebrated the day by a feast to all the Indians present.[2]

The French hoped to form an agricultural settlement of Indians in the neighborhood of Villemarie; and they spared no exertion to this end, giving them tools, and aiding them to till the fields. They might have succeeded, but for that pest of the wilderness, the Iroquois, who hovered about them, harassed them with petty attacks, and again and again drove the Algonquins in terror from their camps. Some time had elapsed, as we have seen, before the Iroquois discovered Villemarie; but at length ten fugitive Algonquins, chased by a party of them, made for the friendly settlement as a safe asylum; and thus their astonished pursuers became aware of its existence. They reconnoitred the place, and went back to their towns with the news.[3] From that time forth the colonists had no peace; no more excursions for fishing and hunting; no more Sunday strolls in woods and meadows. The men went armed to their work, and returned at the sound of a bell, marching in a compact body, prepared for an attack.

Early in June, 1643, sixty Hurons came down in canoes for traffic, and, on reaching the place now called Lachine, at the head of the rapids of St. Louis, and a few miles above Villemarie, they were amazed at finding a large Iroquois war-party in a fort hastily built of the trunks and boughs of trees. Surprise and fright seem to have infatuated them. They neither

---

[1] Vimont, *Relation, 1643*, 54, 55. Tessouat was chief of Allumette Island, in the Ottawa. His predecessor, of the same name, was Champlain's host in 1613.—See "Pioneers of France," Chap. XII.

[2] It was the usual practice to give guns to converts, "pour attirer leur compatriotes à la Foy." They were never given to heathen Indians. "It seems," observes Vimont, "that our Lord wishes to make use of this method in order that Christianity may become acceptable in this country."—*Relation, 1643*, 71.

[3] Dollier de Casson, MS.

fought nor fled, but greeted their inveterate foes as if they were friends and allies, and, to gain their good graces, told them all they knew of the French settlement, urging them to attack it, and promising an easy victory. Accordingly, the Iroquois detached forty of their warriors, who surprised six Frenchmen at work hewing timber within a gunshot of the fort, killed three of them, took the remaining three prisoners, and returned in triumph. The captives were bound with the usual rigor; and the Hurons taunted and insulted them, to please their dangerous companions. Their baseness availed them little; for at night, after a feast of victory, when the Hurons were asleep or off their guard, their entertainers fell upon them, and killed or captured the greater part. The rest ran for Villemarie, where, as their treachery was as yet unknown, they were received with great kindness.[1]

The next morning the Iroquois decamped, carrying with them their prisoners, and the furs plundered from the Huron canoes. They had taken also, and probably destroyed, all the letters from the missionaries in the Huron country, as well as a copy of their *Relation* of the preceding year. Of the three French prisoners, one escaped and reached Montreal; the remaining two were burned alive.

At Villemarie it was usually dangerous to pass beyond the ditch of the fort or the palisades of the hospital. Sometimes a solitary warrior would lie hidden for days, without sleep and almost without food, behind a log in the forest, or in a dense thicket, watching like a lynx for some rash straggler. Sometimes parties of a hundred or more made ambuscades near by, and sent a few of their number to lure out the soldiers by a petty attack and a flight. The danger was much diminished, however, when the colonists received from France a number of dogs, which proved most efficient sentinels and scouts. Of the instinct of these animals the writers of the time speak with

[1] I have followed Dollier de Casson. Vimont's account is different. He says that the Iroquois fell upon the Hurons at the outset, and took twenty-three prisoners, killing many others; after which they made the attack at Villemarie. — *Relation, 1643,* 62.

Faillon thinks that Vimont was unwilling to publish the treachery of the Hurons, lest the interests of the Huron mission should suffer in consequence.

Belmont, *Histoire du Canada,* 1643, confirms the account of the Huron treachery.

astonishment. Chief among them was a bitch named Pilot, who every morning made the rounds of the forests and fields about the fort, followed by a troop of her offspring. If one of them lagged behind, she bit him to remind him of his duty; and if any skulked and ran home, she punished them severely in the same manner on her return. When she discovered the Iroquois, which she was sure to do by the scent, if any were near, she barked furiously, and ran at once straight to the fort, followed by the rest. The Jesuit chronicler adds, with an amusing *naïveté*, that, while this was her duty, "her natural inclination was for hunting squirrels."[1]

Maisonneuve was as brave a knight of the cross as ever fought in Palestine for the sepulchre of Christ; but he could temper his valor with discretion. He knew that he and his soldiers were but indifferent woodsmen; that their crafty foe had no equal in ambuscades and surprises; and that, while a defeat might ruin the French, it would only exasperate an enemy whose resources in men were incomparably greater. Therefore, when the dogs sounded the alarm, he kept his followers close, and stood patiently on the defensive. They chafed under this Fabian policy, and at length imputed it to cowardice. Their murmurings grew louder, till they reached the ear of Maisonneuve. The religion which animated him had not destroyed the soldierly pride which takes root so readily and so strongly in a manly nature; and an imputation of cowardice from his own soldiers stung him to the quick. He saw, too, that such an opinion of him must needs weaken his authority, and impair the discipline essential to the safety of the colony.

On the morning of the thirtieth of March, Pilot was heard barking with unusual fury in the forest eastward from the fort; and in a few moments they saw her running over the clearing, where the snow was still deep, followed by her brood, all giving tongue together. The excited Frenchmen flocked about their commander.

[1] Lalemant, *Relation, 1647*, 74, 75. "Son attrait naturel estoit la chasse aux écurieux." Dollier de Casson also speaks admiringly of her and her instinct. Faillon sees in it a manifest proof of the protecting care of God over Ville-marie.

"*Monsieur, les ennemis sont dans le bois; ne les irons-nous jamais voir?*" [1]

Maisonneuve, habitually composed and calm, answered sharply,—

"Yes, you shall see the enemy. Get yourselves ready at once, and take care that you are as brave as you profess to be. I shall lead you myself."

All was bustle in the fort. Guns were loaded, pouches filled, and snow-shoes tied on by those who had them and knew how to use them. There were not enough, however, and many were forced to go without them. When all was ready, Maisonneuve sallied forth at the head of thirty men, leaving d'Ailleboust, with the remainder, to hold the fort. They crossed the snowy clearing and entered the forest, where all was silent as the grave. They pushed on, wading through the deep snow, with the countless pitfalls hidden beneath it, when suddenly they were greeted with the screeches of eighty Iroquois,[2] who sprang up from their lurking-places, and showered bullets and arrows upon the advancing French. The emergency called, not for chivalry, but for woodcraft; and Maisonneuve ordered his men to take shelter, like their assailants, behind trees. They stood their ground resolutely for a long time; but the Iroquois pressed them close, three of their number were killed, others were wounded, and their ammunition began to fail. Their only alternatives were destruction or retreat; and to retreat was not easy. The order was given. Though steady at first, the men soon became confused, and over-eager to escape the galling fire which the Iroquois sent after them. Maisonneuve directed them towards a sledge-track which had been used in dragging timber for building the hospital, and where the snow was firm beneath the foot. He himself remained to the last, encouraging his followers and aiding the wounded to escape. The French, as they struggled through the snow, faced about from time to time, and fired back to check the pursuit; but no sooner had they reached the

[1] Dollier de Casson, MS.

[2] Vimont, *Relation, 1644*, 42. Dollier de Casson says two hundred; but it is usually safe in these cases to accept the smaller number, and Vimont founds his statement on the information of an escaped prisoner.

sledge-track than they gave way to their terror, and ran in a body for the fort. Those within, seeing this confused rush of men from the distance, mistook them for the enemy; and an over-zealous soldier touched the match to a cannon which had been pointed to rake the sledge-track. Had not the piece missed fire, from dampness of the priming, he would have done more execution at one shot than the Iroquois in all the fight of that morning.

Maisonneuve was left alone, retreating backwards down the track, and holding his pursuers in check, with a pistol in each hand. They might easily have shot him; but, recognizing him as the commander of the French, they were bent on taking him alive. Their chief coveted this honor for himself, and his followers held aloof to give him the opportunity. He pressed close upon Maisonneuve, who snapped a pistol at him, which missed fire. The Iroquois, who had ducked to avoid the shot, rose erect, and sprang forward to seize him, when Maisonneuve, with his remaining pistol, shot him dead. Then ensued a curious spectacle, not infrequent in Indian battles. The Iroquois seemed to forget their enemy, in their anxiety to secure and carry off the body of their chief; and the French commander continued his retreat unmolested, till he was safe under the cannon of the fort. From that day, he was a hero in the eyes of his men.[1]

Quebec and Montreal are happy in their founders. Samuel de Champlain and Chomedey de Maisonneuve are among the names that shine with a fair and honest lustre on the infancy of nations.

[1] Dollier de Casson, MS. Vimont's mention of the affair is brief. He says that two Frenchmen were made prisoners, and burned. Belmont, *Histoire du Canada*, 1645, gives a succinct account of the fight, and indicates the scene of it. It seems to have been a little below the site of the Place d'Armes, on which stands the great Parish Church of Villemarie, commonly known to tourists as the "Cathedral." Faillon thinks that Maisonneuve's exploit was achieved on this very spot.

Marguerite Bourgeoys also describes the affair in her unpublished writings.

Chapter XIX

1644, 1645

PEACE

*Iroquois Prisoners • Piskaret • His Exploits • More Prisoners •
Iroquois Embassy • The Orator • The Great Council • Speeches of
Kiotsaton • Muster of Savages • Peace Confirmed*

IN the damp and freshness of a midsummer morning, when
the sun had not yet risen, but when the river and the sky
were red with the glory of approaching day, the inmates of
the fort at Three Rivers were roused by a tumult of joyous
and exultant voices. They thronged to the shore,—priests,
soldiers, traders, and officers, mingled with warriors and
shrill-voiced squaws from Huron and Algonquin camps in the
neighboring forest. Close at hand they saw twelve or fifteen
canoes slowly drifting down the current of the St. Lawrence,
manned by eighty young Indians, all singing their songs of
victory, and striking their paddles against the edges of their
bark vessels in cadence with their voices. Among them three
Iroquois prisoners stood upright, singing loud and defiantly,
as men not fearing torture or death.

A few days before, these young warriors, in part Huron and in
part Algonquin, had gone out on the war-path to the River
Richelieu, where they had presently found themselves entangled among several bands of Iroquois. They withdrew in the
night, after a battle in the dark with an Iroquois canoe, and, as
they approached Fort Richelieu, had the good fortune to discover ten of their enemy ambuscaded in a clump of bushes and
fallen trees, watching to waylay some of the soldiers on their
morning visit to the fishing-nets in the river hard by. They captured three of them, and carried them back in triumph.

The victors landed amid screams of exultation. Two of the
prisoners were assigned to the Hurons, and the third to the
Algonquins, who immediately took him to their lodges near
the fort at Three Rivers, and began the usual "caress," by
burning his feet with red-hot stones, and cutting off his fingers. Champfleur, the commandant, went out to them with
urgent remonstrances, and at length prevailed on them to

leave their victim without further injury, until Montmagny, the Governor, should arrive. He came with all dispatch,—not wholly from a motive of humanity, but partly in the hope that the three captives might be made instrumental in concluding a peace with their countrymen.

A council was held in the fort at Three Rivers. Montmagny made valuable presents to the Algonquins and the Hurons, to induce them to place the prisoners in his hands. The Algonquins complied; and the unfortunate Iroquois, gashed, maimed, and scorched, was given up to the French, who treated him with the greatest kindness. But neither the Governor's gifts nor his eloquence could persuade the Hurons to follow the example of their allies; and they departed for their own country with their two captives,—promising, however, not to burn them, but to use them for negotiations of peace. With this pledge, scarcely worth the breath that uttered it, Montmagny was forced to content himself.[1]

Thus it appeared that the fortune of war did not always smile even on the Iroquois. Indeed, if there is faith in Indian tradition, there had been a time, scarcely half a century past, when the Mohawks, perhaps the fiercest and haughtiest of the confederate nations, had been nearly destroyed by the Algonquins, whom they now held in contempt.[2] This people, whose inferiority arose chiefly from the want of that compact organization in which lay the strength of the Iroquois, had not lost their ancient warlike spirit; and they had one champion of whom even the audacious confederates stood in awe. His name was Piskaret; and he dwelt on that great island in the Ottawa of which Le Borgne was chief. He had lately turned Christian, in the hope of French favor and countenance,—always useful to an ambitious Indian,—and perhaps, too, with an eye to the gun and powder-horn which formed

[1] Vimont, *Relation, 1644*, 45–49.

[2] *Relation, 1660*, 6 (anonymous).

Both Perrot and La Potherie recount traditions of the ancient superiority of the Algonquins over the Iroquois, who formerly, it is said, dwelt near Montreal and Three Rivers, whence the Algonquins expelled them. They withdrew, first to the neighborhood of Lake Erie, then to that of Lake Ontario, their historic seat. There is much to support the conjecture that the Indians found by Cartier at Montreal in 1535 were Iroquois. (See "Pioneers of France," 159–60.) That they belonged to the same family of tribes is certain. For the traditions alluded to, see Perrot, 9, 12, 79, and La Potherie, I. 288–295.

the earthly reward of the convert.[1] Tradition tells marvellous
stories of his exploits. Once, it is said, he entered an Iroquois
town on a dark night. His first care was to seek out a hiding-
place, and he soon found one in the midst of a large wood-
pile.[2] Next he crept into a lodge, and, finding the inmates
asleep, killed them with his war-club, took their scalps, and
quietly withdrew to the retreat he had prepared. In the morning a howl of lamentation and fury rose from the astonished
villagers. They ranged the fields and forests in vain pursuit of
the mysterious enemy, who remained all day in the wood-
pile, whence, at midnight, he came forth and repeated his
former exploit. On the third night, every family placed its
sentinels; and Piskaret, stealthily creeping from lodge to
lodge, and reconnoitring each through crevices in the bark,
saw watchers everywhere. At length he descried a sentinel
who had fallen asleep near the entrance of a lodge, though
his companion at the other end was still awake and vigilant.
He pushed aside the sheet of bark that served as a door,
struck the sleeper a deadly blow, yelled his war-cry, and fled
like the wind. All the village swarmed out in furious chase;
but Piskaret was the swiftest runner of his time, and easily
kept in advance of his pursuers. When daylight came, he
showed himself from time to time to lure them on, then
yelled defiance, and distanced them again. At night, all but six
had given over the chase; and even these, exhausted as they
were, had begun to despair. Piskaret, seeing a hollow tree,
crept into it like a bear, and hid himself; while the Iroquois,
losing his traces in the dark, lay down to sleep near by. At
midnight he emerged from his retreat, stealthily approached
his slumbering enemies, nimbly brained them all with his
war-club, and then, burdened with a goodly bundle of scalps,
journeyed homeward in triumph.[3]

This is but one of several stories that tradition has preserved

[1] "Simon Pieskaret . . . n'estoit Chrestien qu'en apparence et par police."—Lalemant, *Relation, 1647*, 68.—He afterwards became a convert in earnest.

[2] Both the Iroquois and the Hurons collected great quantities of wood in
their villages in the autumn.

[3] This story is told by La Potherie, I. 299, and, more briefly, by Perrot, 107.
La Potherie, writing more than half a century after the time in question,
represents the Iroquois as habitually in awe of the Algonquins. In this all the
contemporary writers contradict him.

of his exploits; and, with all reasonable allowances, it is certain that the crafty and valiant Algonquin was the model of an Indian warrior. That which follows rests on a far safer basis.

Early in the spring of 1645, Piskaret, with six other converted Indians, some of them better Christians than he, set out on a war-party, and, after dragging their canoes over the frozen St. Lawrence, launched them on the open stream of the Richelieu. They ascended to Lake Champlain, and hid themselves in the leafless forests of a large island, watching patiently for their human prey. One day they heard a distant shot. "Come, friends," said Piskaret, "let us get our dinner: perhaps it will be the last, for we must die before we run." Having dined to their contentment, the philosophic warriors prepared for action. One of them went to reconnoitre, and soon reported that two canoes full of Iroquois were approaching the island. Piskaret and his followers crouched in the bushes at the point for which the canoes were making, and, as the foremost drew near, each chose his mark, and fired with such good effect, that, of seven warriors, all but one were killed. The survivor jumped overboard, and swam for the other canoe, where he was taken in. It now contained eight Iroquois, who, far from attempting to escape, paddled in haste for a distant part of the shore, in order to land, give battle, and avenge their slain comrades. But the Algonquins, running through the woods, reached the landing before them, and, as one of them rose to fire, they shot him. In his fall he overset the canoe. The water was shallow, and the submerged warriors, presently finding foothold, waded towards the shore, and made desperate fight. The Algonquins had the advantage of position, and used it so well, that they killed all but three of their enemies, and captured two of the survivors. Next they sought out the bodies, carefully scalped them, and set out in triumph on their return. To the credit of their Jesuit teachers, they treated their prisoners with a forbearance hitherto without example. One of them, who was defiant and abusive, received a blow to silence him; but no further indignity was offered to either.[1]

---

[1] According to Marie de l'Incarnation, *Lettre, 14 Sept., 1645,* Piskaret was for torturing the captives; but a convert, named Bernard by the French, protested against it.

As the successful warriors approached the little mission settlement of Sillery, immediately above Quebec, they raised
their song of triumph, and beat time with their paddles on
the edges of their canoes; while, from eleven poles raised
aloft, eleven fresh scalps fluttered in the wind. The Father
Jesuit and all his flock were gathered on the strand to welcome them. The Indians fired their guns, and screeched in
jubilation; one Jean Baptiste, a Christian chief of Sillery,
made a speech from the shore; Piskaret replied, standing upright in his canoe; and, to crown the occasion, a squad of
soldiers, marching in haste from Quebec, fired a salute of
musketry, to the boundless delight of the Indians. Much to
the surprise of the two captives, there was no running of the
gantlet, no gnawing off of finger-nails or cutting off of fingers; but the scalps were hung, like little flags, over the en-
trances of the lodges, and all Sillery betook itself to feasting
and rejoicing.[1] One old woman, indeed, came to the Jesuit
with a pathetic appeal: "Oh, my Father! let me caress these
prisoners a little: they have killed, burned, and eaten my father, my husband, and my children." But the missionary answered with a lecture on the duty of forgiveness.[2]

On the next day, Montmagny came to Sillery, and there
was a grand council in the house of the Jesuits. Piskaret, in a
solemn harangue, delivered his captives to the Governor, who
replied with a speech of compliment and an ample gift. The
two Iroquois were present, seated with a seeming imperturbability, but great anxiety of heart; and when at length they
comprehended that their lives were safe, one of them, a man
of great size and symmetry, rose and addressed Montmagny: —

"Onontio,[3] I am saved from the fire; my body is delivered
from death. Onontio, you have given me my life. I thank you
for it. I will never forget it. All my country will be grateful to

---

[1] Vimont, *Relation, 1645*, 19–21.

[2] *Ibid.*, 21, 22.

[3] *Onontio, Great Mountain*, a translation of Montmagny's name. It was the
Iroquois name ever after for the Governor of Canada. In the same manner,
Onas, Feather or *Quill*, became the official name of William Penn, and all
succeeding Governors of Pennsylvania. We have seen that the Iroquois hereditary chiefs had official names, which are the same to-day that they were
at the period of this narrative.

you. The earth will be bright; the river calm and smooth; there will be peace and friendship between us. The shadow is before my eyes no longer. The spirits of my ancestors slain by the Algonquins have disappeared. Onontio, you are good: we are bad. But our anger is gone; I have no heart but for peace and rejoicing." As he said this, he began to dance, holding his hands upraised, as if apostrophizing the sky. Suddenly he snatched a hatchet, brandished it for a moment like a madman, and then flung it into the fire, saying, as he did so, "Thus I throw down my anger! thus I cast away the weapons of blood! Farewell, war! Now I am your friend forever!"[1]

The two prisoners were allowed to roam at will about the settlement, withheld from escaping by an Indian point of honor. Montmagny soon after sent them to Three Rivers, where the Iroquois taken during the last summer had remained all winter. Champfleur, the commandant, now received orders to clothe, equip, and send him home, with a message to his nation that Onontio made them a present of his life, and that he had still two prisoners in his hands, whom he would also give them, if they saw fit to embrace this opportunity of making peace with the French and their Indian allies.

This was at the end of May. On the fifth of July following, the liberated Iroquois reappeared at Three Rivers, bringing with him two men of renown, ambassadors of the Mohawk nation. There was a fourth man of the party, and, as they approached, the Frenchmen on the shore recognized, to their great delight, Guillaume Couture, the young man captured three years before with Father Jogues, and long since given up as dead. In dress and appearance he was an Iroquois. He had gained a great influence over his captors, and this embassy of peace was due in good measure to his persuasions.[2]

The chief of the Iroquois, Kiotsaton, a tall savage, covered from head to foot with belts of wampum, stood erect in the prow of the sail-boat which had brought him and his companions from Richelieu, and in a loud voice announced himself as the accredited envoy of his nation. The boat fired a

---

[1] Vimont, *Relation, 1645*, 22, 23. He adds, that, "if these people are barbarous in deed, they have thoughts worthy of Greeks and Romans."

[2] Marie de l'Incarnation, *Lettre, 14 Sept., 1645*.

swivel, the fort replied with a cannon-shot, and the envoys landed in state. Kiotsaton and his colleague were conducted to the room of the commandant, where, seated on the floor, they were regaled sumptuously, and presented in due course with pipes of tobacco. They had never before seen anything so civilized, and were delighted with their entertainment. "We are glad to see you," said Champfleur to Kiotsaton; "you may be sure that you are safe here. It is as if you were among your own people, and in your own house."

"Tell your chief that he lies," replied the honored guest, addressing the interpreter.

Champfleur, though he probably knew that this was but an Indian mode of expressing dissent, showed some little surprise; when Kiotsaton, after tranquilly smoking for a moment, proceeded: —

"Your chief says it is as if I were in my own country. This is not true; for there I am not so honored and caressed. He says it is as if I were in my own house; but in my own house I am sometimes very ill served, and here you feast me with all manner of good cheer." From this and many other replies, the French conceived that they had to do with a man of *esprit*.[1]

He undoubtedly belonged to that class of professed orators who, though rarely or never claiming the honors of hereditary chieftainship, had great influence among the Iroquois, and were employed in all affairs of embassy and negotiation. They had memories trained to an astonishing tenacity, were perfect in all the conventional metaphors in which the language of Indian diplomacy and rhetoric mainly consisted, knew by heart the traditions of the nation, and were adepts in the parliamentary usages, which, among the Iroquois, were held little less than sacred.

The ambassadors were feasted for a week, not only by the French, but also by the Hurons and Algonquins; and then the grand peace council took place. Montmagny had come up from Quebec, and with him the chief men of the colony. It was a bright midsummer day; and the sun beat hot upon the parched area of the fort, where awnings were spread to shelter

[1] Vimont, *Relation, 1645,* 24.

the assembly. On one side sat Montmagny, with officers and others who attended him. Near him was Vimont, Superior of the Mission, and other Jesuits,—Jogues among the rest. Immediately before them sat the Iroquois, on sheets of spruce-bark spread on the ground like mats: for they had insisted on being near the French, as a sign of the extreme love they had of late conceived towards them. On the opposite side of the area were the Algonquins, in their several divisions of the Algonquins proper, the Montagnais, and the Atticamegues,[1] sitting, lying, or squatting on the ground. On the right hand and on the left were Hurons mingled with Frenchmen. In the midst was a large open space like the arena of a prize-ring; and here were planted two poles with a line stretched from one to the other, on which, in due time, were to be hung the wampum belts that represented the words of the orator. For the present, these belts were in part hung about the persons of the two ambassadors, and in part stored in a bag carried by one of them.

When all was ready, Kiotsaton arose, strode into the open space, and, raising his tall figure erect, stood looking for a moment at the sun. Then he gazed around on the assembly, took a wampum belt in his hand, and began:—

"Onontio, give ear. I am the mouth of all my nation. When you listen to me, you listen to all the Iroquois. There is no evil in my heart. My song is a song of peace. We have many war-songs in our country; but we have thrown them all away, and now we sing of nothing but gladness and rejoicing."

Hereupon he began to sing, his countrymen joining with him. He walked to and fro, gesticulated towards the sky, and seemed to apostrophize the sun; then, turning towards the Governor, resumed his harangue. First he thanked him for the life of the Iroquois prisoner released in the spring, but blamed him for sending him home without company or escort. Then he led forth the young Frenchman, Guillaume Couture, and tied a wampum belt to his arm.

"With this," he said, "I give you back this prisoner. I did not say to him, 'Nephew, take a canoe and go home to Quebec.' I should have been without sense, had I done so. I

[1] The Atticamegues, or tribe of the White Fish, dwelt in the forests north of Three Rivers. They much resembled their Montagnais kindred.

should have been troubled in my heart, lest some evil might befall him. The prisoner whom you sent back to us suffered every kind of danger and hardship on the way." Here he proceeded to represent the difficulties of the journey in pantomime, "so natural," says Father Vimont, "that no actor in France could equal it." He counterfeited the lonely traveller toiling up some rocky portage track, with a load of baggage on his head, now stopping as if half spent, and now tripping against a stone. Next he was in his canoe, vainly trying to urge it against the swift current, looking around in despair on the foaming rapids, then recovering courage, and paddling desperately for his life. "What did you mean," demanded the orator, resuming his harangue, "by sending a man alone among these dangers? I have not done so. 'Come, nephew,' I said to the prisoner there before you,"—pointing to Couture,—" 'follow me: I will see you home at the risk of my life.' " And to confirm his words, he hung another belt on the line.

The third belt was to declare that the nation of the speaker had sent presents to the other nations to recall their war-parties, in view of the approaching peace. The fourth was an assurance that the memory of the slain Iroquois no longer stirred the living to vengeance. "I passed near the place where Piskaret and the Algonquins slew our warriors in the spring. I saw the scene of the fight where the two prisoners here were taken. I passed quickly; I would not look on the blood of my people. Their bodies lie there still; I turned away my eyes, that I might not be angry." Then, stooping, he struck the ground and seemed to listen. "I heard the voice of my ancestors, slain by the Algonquins, crying to me in a tone of affection, 'My grandson, my grandson, restrain your anger: think no more of us, for you cannot deliver us from death; think of the living; rescue them from the knife and the fire.' When I heard these voices, I went on my way, and journeyed hither to deliver those whom you still hold in captivity."

The fifth, sixth, and seventh belts were to open the passage by water from the French to the Iroquois, to chase hostile canoes from the river, smooth away the rapids and cataracts, and calm the waves of the lake. The eighth cleared the path by land. "You would have said," writes Vimont, "that he was cutting down trees, hacking off branches, dragging away bushes, and filling up holes."—"Look!" exclaimed the orator, when he had ended this pantomime, "the road is open, smooth, and straight"; and he bent towards the earth, as if to see that no impediment remained. "There is no thorn, or stone, or log in the way. Now you may see the smoke of our villages from Quebec to the heart of our country."

Another belt, of unusual size and beauty, was to bind the Iroquois, the French, and their Indian allies together as one man. As he presented it, the orator led forth a Frenchman and an Algonquin from among his auditors, and, linking his arms with theirs, pressed them closely to his sides, in token of indissoluble union.

The next belt invited the French to feast with the Iroquois. "Our country is full of fish, venison, moose, beaver, and game of every kind. Leave these filthy swine that run about among your houses, feeding on garbage, and come and eat good food with us. The road is open; there is no danger."

There was another belt to scatter the clouds, that the sun might shine on the hearts of the Indians and the French, and reveal their sincerity and truth to all; then others still, to confirm the Hurons in thoughts of peace. By the fifteenth belt, Kiotsaton declared that the Iroquois had always wished to send home Jogues and Bressani to their friends, and had meant to do so; but that Jogues was stolen from them by the Dutch, and they had given Bressani to them because he desired it. "If he had but been patient," added the ambassador, "I would have brought him back myself. Now I know not what has befallen him. Perhaps he is drowned. Perhaps he is dead." Here Jogues said, with a smile, to the Jesuits near him, "They had the pile laid to burn me. They would have killed me a hundred times, if God had not saved my life."

Two or three more belts were hung on the line, each with its appropriate speech; and then the speaker closed his harangue: "I go to spend what remains of the summer in my own country, in games and dances and rejoicing for the blessing of peace." He had interspersed his discourse throughout with now a song and now a dance; and the council ended in a general dancing, in which Iroquois, Hurons, Algonquins,

Montagnais, Atticamegues, and French, all took part, after their respective fashions.

In spite of one or two palpable falsehoods that embellished his oratory, the Jesuits were delighted with him. "Every one admitted," says Vimont, "that he was eloquent and pathetic. In short, he showed himself an excellent actor, for one who has had no instructor but Nature. I gathered only a few fragments of his speech from the mouth of the interpreter, who gave us but broken portions of it, and did not translate consecutively."[1]

Two days after, another council was called, when the Governor gave his answer, accepting the proffered peace, and confirming his acceptance by gifts of considerable value. He demanded as a condition, that the Indian allies of the French should be left unmolested, until their principal chiefs, who were not then present, should make a formal treaty with the Iroquois in behalf of their several nations. Piskaret then made a present to wipe away the remembrance of the Iroquois he had slaughtered, and the assembly was dissolved.

In the evening, Vimont invited the ambassadors to the mission-house, and gave each of them a sack of tobacco and a pipe. In return, Kiotsaton made him a speech: "When I left my country, I gave up my life; I went to meet death, and I owe it to you that I am yet alive. I thank you that I still see the sun; I thank you for all your words and acts of kindness; I thank you for your gifts. You have covered me with them from head to foot. You left nothing free but my mouth; and now you have stopped that with a handsome pipe, and regaled it with the taste of the herb we love. I bid you farewell,—not for a long time, for you will hear from us soon. Even if we should be drowned on our way home, the winds and the waves will bear witness to our countrymen of your favors; and I am sure that some good spirit has gone before us to tell them of the good news that we are about to bring."[2]

On the next day, he and his companion set forth on their return. Kiotsaton, when he saw his party embarked, turned

---

[1] Vimont describes the council at length in the *Relation* of 1645. Marie de l'Incarnation also describes it in a letter to her son, of Sept. 14, 1645. She evidently gained her information from Vimont and the other Jesuits present.

[2] Vimont, *Relation, 1645*, 28.

to the French and Indians who lined the shore, and said with a loud voice, "Farewell, brothers! I am one of your relations now." Then turning to the Governor,—"Onontio, your name will be great over all the earth. When I came hither, I never thought to carry back my head, I never thought to come out of your doors alive; and now I return loaded with honors, gifts, and kindness." "Brothers,"—to the Indians,—"obey Onontio and the French. Their hearts and their thoughts are good. Be friends with them, and do as they do. You shall hear from us soon."

The Indians whooped and fired their guns; there was a cannon-shot from the fort; and the sail-boat that bore the distinguished visitors moved on its way towards the Richelieu.

But the work was not done. There must be more councils, speeches, wampum-belts, and gifts of all kinds,—more feasts, dances, songs, and uproar. The Indians gathered at Three Rivers were not sufficient in numbers or in influence to represent their several tribes; and more were on their way. The principal men of the Hurons were to come down this year, with Algonquins of many tribes, from the North and the Northwest; and Kiotsaton had promised that Iroquois ambassadors, duly empowered, should meet them at Three Rivers, and make a solemn peace with them all, under the eye of Onontio. But what hope was there that this swarm of fickle and wayward savages could be gathered together at one time and at one place,—or that, being there, they could be restrained from cutting each other's throats? Yet so it was; and in this happy event the Jesuits saw the interposition of God, wrought upon by the prayers of those pious souls in France who daily and nightly besieged Heaven with supplications for the welfare of the Canadian missions.[1]

First came a band of Montagnais; next followed Nipissings, Atticamegues, and Algonquins of the Ottawa, their canoes deep-laden with furs. Then, on the tenth of September, appeared the great fleet of the Hurons, sixty canoes, bearing a host of warriors, among whom the French recognized the tattered black cassock of Father Jerome Lalemant. There were twenty French soldiers, too, returning from the Huron

[1] Vimont, *Relation, 1645,* 29.

country, whither they had been sent the year before, to guard the Fathers and their flock.

Three Rivers swarmed like an ant-hill with savages. The shore was lined with canoes; the forests and the fields were alive with busy camps. The trade was brisk; and in its attendant speeches, feasts, and dances, there was no respite.

But where were the Iroquois? Montmagny and the Jesuits grew very anxious. In a few days more the concourse would begin to disperse, and the golden moment be lost. It was a great relief when a canoe appeared with tidings that the promised embassy was on its way; and yet more, when, on the seventeenth, four Iroquois approached the shore, and, in a loud voice, announced themselves as envoys of their nation. The tumult was prodigious. Montmagny's soldiers formed a double rank, and the savage rabble, with wild eyes and faces smeared with grease and paint, stared over the shoulders and between the gun-barrels of the musketeers, as the ambassadors of their deadliest foe stalked, with unmoved visages, towards the fort.

Now council followed council, with an insufferable prolixity of speech-making. There were belts to wipe out the memory of the slain; belts to clear the sky, smooth the rivers, and calm the lakes; a belt to take the hatchet from the hands of the Iroquois; another to take away their guns; another to take away their shields; another to wash the war-paint from their faces; and another to break the kettle in which they boiled their prisoners.[1] In short, there were belts past numbering, each with its meaning, sometimes literal, sometimes figurative, but all bearing upon the great work of peace. At length all was ended. The dances ceased, the songs and the whoops died away, and the great muster dispersed,—some to their smoky lodges on the distant shores of Lake Huron, and some to frozen hunting-grounds in northern forests.

There was peace in this dark and blood-stained wilderness. The lynx, the panther, and the wolf had made a covenant of love; but who should be their surety? A doubt and a fear mingled with the joy of the Jesuit Fathers; and to their thanksgivings to God they joined a prayer, that the hand which had given might still be stretched forth to preserve.

[1] *Ibid.*, 34.

Chapter XX

THE PEACE BROKEN

*Uncertainties • The Mission of Jogues • He reaches the Mohawks •
His Reception • His Return • His Second Mission • Warnings of
Danger • Rage of the Mohawks • Murder of Jogues*

THERE is little doubt that the Iroquois negotiators acted,
for the moment, in sincerity. Guillaume Couture, who
returned with them and spent the winter in their towns, saw
sufficient proof that they sincerely desired peace. And yet the
treaty had a double defect. First, the wayward, capricious, and
ungoverned nature of the Indian parties to it, on both sides,
made a speedy rupture more than likely. Secondly, in spite of
their own assertion to the contrary, the Iroquois envoys represented, not the confederacy of the five nations, but only one
of these nations, the Mohawks: for each of the members of
this singular league could, and often did, make peace and war
independently of the rest.

It was the Mohawks who had made war on the French and
their Indian allies on the lower St. Lawrence. They claimed,
as against the other Iroquois, a certain right of domain to all
this region; and though the warriors of the four upper nations had sometimes poached on the Mohawk preserve, by
murdering both French and Indians at Montreal, they employed their energies for the most part in attacks on the Hurons, the Upper Algonquins, and other tribes of the interior.
These attacks still continued, unaffected by the peace with the
Mohawks. Imperfect, however, as the treaty was, it was invaluable, could it but be kept inviolate; and to this end Montmagny, the Jesuits, and all the colony, anxiously turned their
thoughts.[1]

It was to hold the Mohawks to their faith that Couture had

---

[1] The Mohawks were at this time more numerous, as compared with the
other four nations of the Iroquois, than they were a few years later. They
seem to have suffered more reverses in war than any of the others. At this
time they may be reckoned at six or seven hundred warriors. A war with the

bravely gone back to winter among them; but an agent of
more acknowledged weight was needed, and Father Isaac
Jogues was chosen. No white man, Couture excepted, knew
their language and their character so well. His errand was half
political, half religious; for not only was he to be the bearer
of gifts, wampum-belts, and messages from the Governor, but
he was also to found a new mission, christened in advance
with a prophetic name,— *the Mission of the Martyrs*.

For two years past, Jogues had been at Montreal; and it
was here that he received the order of his Superior to proceed
to the Mohawk towns. At first, nature asserted itself, and he
recoiled involuntarily at the thought of the horrors of which
his scarred body and his mutilated hands were a living memento.[1] It was a transient weakness; and he prepared to depart with more than willingness, giving thanks to Heaven
that he had been found worthy to suffer and to die for the
saving of souls and the greater glory of God.

He felt a presentiment that his death was near, and wrote
to a friend, "I shall go, and shall not return."[2] An Algonquin
convert gave him sage advice. "Say nothing about the Faith
at first, for there is nothing so repulsive, in the beginning, as
our doctrine, which seems to destroy everything that men
hold dear; and as your long cassock preaches, as well as your
lips, you had better put on a short coat." Jogues, therefore,
exchanged the uniform of Loyola for a civilian's doublet and
hose; "for," observes his Superior, "one should be all things

---

Mohegans, and another with the Andastes, besides their war with the Algonquins and the French of Canada soon after, told severely on their strength.
The following are estimates of the numbers of the Iroquois warriors made in
1660 by the author of the *Relation* of that year, and by Wentworth Greenhalgh in 1677, from personal inspection:—

	1660	1677
Mohawks	500	300
Oneidas	100	200
Onondagas	300	350
Cayugas	300	300
Senecas	1,000	1,000
	2,200	2,150

[1] *Lettre du P. Isaac Jogues au R.P. Jérosme L'Allemant. Montreal, 2 Mai,
1646*. MS.

[2] "Ibo et non redibo." *Lettre du P. Jogues au R.P. No date.*

to all men, that he may gain them all to Jesus Christ."[1] It would be well, if the application of the maxim had always been as harmless.

Jogues left Three Rivers about the middle of May, with the Sieur Bourdon, engineer to the Governor, two Algonquins with gifts to confirm the peace, and four Mohawks as guides and escort. He passed the Richelieu and Lake Champlain, well-remembered scenes of former miseries, and reached the foot of Lake George on the eve of Corpus Christi. Hence he called the lake Lac St. Sacrement; and this name it preserved, until, a century after, an ambitious Irishman, in compliment to the sovereign from whom he sought advancement, gave it the name it bears.[2]

From Lake George they crossed on foot to the Hudson, where, being greatly fatigued by their heavy loads of gifts, they borrowed canoes at an Iroquois fishing station, and descended to Fort Orange. Here Jogues met the Dutch friends to whom he owed his life, and who now kindly welcomed and entertained him. After a few days he left them, and ascended the River Mohawk to the first Mohawk town. Crowds gathered from the neighboring towns to gaze on the man whom they had known as a scorned and abused slave, and who now appeared among them as the ambassador of a power which hitherto, indeed, they had despised, but which in their present mood they were willing to propitiate.

There was a council in one of the lodges; and while his crowded auditory smoked their pipes, Jogues stood in the midst, and harangued them. He offered in due form the gifts of the Governor, with the wampum belts and their messages of peace, while at every pause his words were echoed by a unanimous grunt of applause from the attentive concourse. Peace speeches were made in return; and all was harmony. When, however, the Algonquin deputies stood before the council, they and their gifts were coldly received. The old hate, maintained by traditions of mutual atrocity, burned fiercely under a thin semblance of peace; and though no outbreak took place, the prospect of the future was very ominous.

[1] Lalemant, *Relation*, *1646*, 15.

[2] Mr. Shea very reasonably suggests, that a change from *Lake George* to *Lake Jogues* would be equally easy and appropriate.

The business of the embassy was scarcely finished, when the Mohawks counselled Jogues and his companions to go home with all despatch, saying, that, if they waited longer, they might meet on the way warriors of the four upper nations, who would inevitably kill the two Algonquin deputies, if not the French also. Jogues, therefore, set out on his return; but not until, despite the advice of the Indian convert, he had made the round of the houses, confessed and instructed a few Christian prisoners still remaining here, and baptized several dying Mohawks. Then he and his party crossed through the forest to the southern extremity of Lake George, made bark canoes, and descended to Fort Richelieu, where they arrived on the twenty-seventh of June.[1]

His political errand was accomplished. Now, should he return to the Mohawks, or should the Mission of the Martyrs be for a time abandoned? Lalemant, who had succeeded Vimont as Superior of the missions, held a council at Quebec with three other Jesuits, of whom Jogues was one, and it was determined, that, unless some new contingency should arise, he should remain for the winter at Montreal.[2] This was in July. Soon after, the plan was changed, for reasons which do not appear, and Jogues received orders to repair to his dangerous post. He set out on the twenty-fourth of August, accompanied by a young Frenchman named Lalande, and three or four Hurons.[3] On the way they met Indians who warned them of a change of feeling in the Mohawk towns, and the Hurons, alarmed, refused to go farther. Jogues, naturally perhaps the most timid man of the party, had no thought of drawing back, and pursued his journey with his young companion, who, like other *donnés* of the missions, was scarcely behind the Jesuits themselves in devoted enthusiasm.

The reported change of feeling had indeed taken place; and the occasion of it was characteristic. On his previous visit to the Mohawks, Jogues, meaning to return, had left in their charge a small chest or box. From the first they were distrustful, suspecting that it contained some secret mischief. He therefore opened it, and showed them the contents, which

[1] Lalemant, *Relation, 1646*, 17.
[2] *Journal des Supérieurs des Jésuites*. MS.
[3] *Ibid.*

were a few personal necessaries; and having thus, as he thought, reassured them, locked the box, and left it in their keeping. The Huron prisoners in the town attempted to make favor with their Iroquois enemies by abusing their French friends,—declaring them to be sorcerers, who had bewitched, by their charms and mummeries, the whole Huron nation, and caused drought, famine, pestilence, and a host of insupportable miseries. Thereupon, the suspicions of the Mohawks against the box revived with double force, and they were convinced that famine, the pest, or some malignant spirit was shut up in it, waiting the moment to issue forth and destroy them. There was sickness in the town, and caterpillars were eating their corn: this was ascribed to the sorceries of the Jesuit.[1] Still they were divided in opinion. Some stood firm for the French; others were furious against them. Among the Mohawks, three clans or families were predominant, if indeed they did not compose the entire nation,—the clans of the Bear, the Tortoise, and the Wolf.[2] Though, by the nature of their constitution, it was scarcely possible that these clans should come to blows, so intimately were they bound together by ties of blood, yet they were often divided on points of interest or policy; and on this occasion the Bear raged against the French, and howled for war, while the Tortoise and the Wolf still clung to the treaty. Among savages, with no government except the intermittent one of councils, the party of action and violence must always prevail. The Bear chiefs sang their war-songs, and, followed by the young men of their own clan, and by such others as they had infected with their frenzy, set forth, in two bands, on the war-path.

The warriors of one of these bands were making their way through the forests between the Mohawk and Lake George, when they met Jogues and Lalande. They seized them, stripped them, and led them in triumph to their town. Here a savage crowd surrounded them, beating them with sticks and with their fists. One of them cut thin strips of flesh from the back and arms of Jogues, saying, as he did so, "Let us see if this white flesh is the flesh of an oki."—"I am a man like yourselves," replied Jogues; "but I do not fear death or tor-

[1] *Lettre de Marie de l'Incarnation à son Fils. Québec, . . . 1647.*
[2] See Introduction.

ture. I do not know why you would kill me. I come here to confirm the peace and show you the way to heaven, and you treat me like a dog."[1] — "You shall die to-morrow," cried the rabble. "Take courage, we shall not burn you. We shall strike you both with a hatchet, and place your heads on the palisade, that your brothers may see you when we take them prisoners."[2] The clans of the Wolf and the Tortoise still raised their voices in behalf of the captive Frenchmen; but the fury of the minority swept all before it.

In the evening,— it was the eighteenth of October,— Jogues, smarting with his wounds and bruises, was sitting in one of the lodges, when an Indian entered, and asked him to a feast. To refuse would have been an offence. He arose and followed the savage, who led him to the lodge of the Bear chief. Jogues bent his head to enter, when another Indian, standing concealed within, at the side of the doorway, struck at him with a hatchet. An Iroquois, called by the French Le Berger,[3] who seems to have followed in order to defend him, bravely held out his arm to ward off the blow; but the hatchet cut through it, and sank into the missionary's brain. He fell at the feet of his murderer, who at once finished the work by hacking off his head. Lalande was left in suspense all night, and in the morning was killed in a similar manner. The bodies of the two Frenchmen were then thrown into the Mohawk, and their heads displayed on the points of the palisade which inclosed the town.[4]

Thus died Isaac Jogues, one of the purest examples of Roman Catholic virtue which this Western continent has seen.

[1] *Lettre du P. De Quen au R. P. Lallemant; no date.* MS.

[2] *Lettre de J. Labatie à M. La Montagne, Fort d'Orange, 30 Oct., 1646.*

[3] It has been erroneously stated that this brave attempt to save Jogues was made by the orator Kiotsaton. Le Berger was one of those who had been made prisoners by Piskaret, and treated kindly by the French. In 1648, he voluntarily came to Three Rivers, and gave himself up to a party of Frenchmen. He was converted, baptized, and carried to France, where his behavior is reported to have been very edifying, but where he soon died. "Perhaps he had eaten his share of more than fifty men," is the reflection of Father Ragueneau, after recounting his exemplary conduct. — *Relation, 1650*, 43–48.

[4] In respect to the death of Jogues, the best authority is the letter of Labatie, before cited. He was the French interpreter at Fort Orange, and, being near the scene of the murder, took pains to learn the facts. The letter was inclosed in another written to Montmagny by the Dutch Governor, Kieft,

The priests, his associates, praise his humility, and tell us that it reached the point of self-contempt,—a crowning virtue in their eyes; that he regarded himself as nothing, and lived solely to do the will of God as uttered by the lips of his Superiors. They add, that, when left to the guidance of his own judgment, his self-distrust made him very slow of decision, but that, when acting under orders, he knew neither hesitation nor fear. With all his gentleness, he had a certain warmth or vivacity of temperament; and we have seen how, during his first captivity, while humbly submitting to every caprice of his tyrants and appearing to rejoice in abasement, a derisive word against his faith would change the lamb into the lion, and the lips that seemed so tame would speak in sharp, bold tones of menace and reproof.

which is also before me, together with a MS. account, written from hearsay, by Father Buteux, and a letter of De Quen, cited above. Compare the *Relations* of 1647 and 1650.

Chapter XXI
1646, 1647
ANOTHER WAR

Mohawk Inroads • The Hunters of Men • The Captive Converts •
The Escape of Marie • Her Story • The Algonquin Prisoner's Re-
venge • Her Flight • Terror of the Colonists • Jesuit Intrepidity

THE peace was broken, and the hounds of war turned
loose. The contagion spread through all the Mohawk nation, the war-songs were sung, and the warriors took the path
for Canada. The miserable colonists and their more miserable
allies woke from their dream of peace to a reality of fear and
horror. Again Montreal and Three Rivers were beset with
murdering savages, skulking in thickets and prowling under
cover of night, yet, when it came to blows, displaying a courage almost equal to the ferocity that inspired it. They plundered and burned Fort Richelieu, which its small garrison had
abandoned, thus leaving the colony without even the semblance of protection. Before the spring opened, all the fighting men of the Mohawks took the war-path; but it is clear
that many of them still had little heart for their bloody and
perfidious work; for, of these hardy and all-enduring warriors, two-thirds gave out on the way, and returned, complaining that the season was too severe.[1] Two hundred or
more kept on, divided into several bands.

On Ash-Wednesday, the French at Three Rivers were at
mass in the chapel, when the Iroquois, quietly approaching,
plundered two houses close to the fort, containing all the
property of the neighboring inhabitants, which had been
brought hither as to a place of security. They hid their booty,
and then went in quest of two large parties of Christian Algonquins engaged in their winter hunt. Two Indians of the
same nation, whom they captured, basely set them on the
trail; and they took up the chase like hounds on the scent of
game. Wrapped in furs or blanket-coats, some with gun in
hand, some with bows and quivers, and all with hatchets,

[1] *Lettre du P. Buteux au R. P. Lalemant.* MS.

war-clubs, knives, or swords,—striding on snow-shoes, with bodies half bent, through the gray forests and the frozen pine-swamps, among wet, black trunks, along dark ravines and under savage hill-sides, their small, fierce eyes darting quick glances that pierced the farthest recesses of the naked woods,—the hunters of men followed the track of their human prey. At length they descried the bark wigwams of the Algonquin camp. The warriors were absent; none were here but women and children. The Iroquois surrounded the huts, and captured all the shrieking inmates. Then ten of them set out to find the traces of the absent hunters. They soon met the renowned Piskaret returning alone. As they recognized him and knew his mettle, they thought treachery better than an open attack. They therefore approached him in the attitude of friends; while he, ignorant of the rupture of the treaty, began to sing his peace-song. Scarcely had they joined him, when one of them ran a sword through his body; and, having scalped him, they returned in triumph to their companions.[1] All the hunters were soon after waylaid, overpowered by numbers, and killed or taken prisoners.

Another band of the Mohawks had meanwhile pursued the other party of Algonquins, and overtaken them on the march, as, incumbered with their sledges and baggage, they were moving from one hunting-camp to another. Though taken by surprise, they made fight, and killed several of their assailants; but in a few moments their resistance was overcome, and those who survived the fray were helpless in the clutches of the enraged victors. Then began a massacre of the old, the disabled, and the infants, with the usual beating, gashing, and severing of fingers to the rest. The next day, the two bands of Mohawks, each with its troop of captives fast bound, met at an appointed spot on the Lake of St. Peter, and greeted each other with yells of exultation, with which mingled a wail of anguish, as the prisoners of either party recognized their companions in misery. They all kneeled in the midst of their savage conquerors, and one of the men, a noted convert, after

---

[1] Lalemant, *Relation, 1647*, 4. Marie de l'Incarnation, *Lettre à son Fils. Québec, . . . 1647*. Perrot's account, drawn from tradition, is different, though not essentially so.

a few words of exhortation, repeated in a loud voice a prayer, to which the rest responded. Then they sang an Algonquin hymn, while the Iroquois, who at first had stared in wonder, broke into laughter and derision, and at length fell upon them with renewed fury. One was burned alive on the spot. Another tried to escape, and they burned the soles of his feet that he might not repeat the attempt. Many others were maimed and mangled; and some of the women who afterwards escaped affirmed, that, in ridicule of the converts, they crucified a small child by nailing it with wooden spikes against a thick sheet of bark.

The prisoners were led to the Mohawk towns; and it is needless to repeat the monotonous and revolting tale of torture and death. The men, as usual, were burned; but the lives of the women and children were spared, in order to strengthen the conquerors by their adoption,—not, however, until both, but especially the women, had been made to endure the extremes of suffering and indignity. Several of them from time to time escaped, and reached Canada with the story of their woes. Among these was Marie, the wife of Jean Baptiste, one of the principal Algonquin converts, captured and burned with the rest. Early in June, she appeared in a canoe at Montreal, where Madame d'Ailleboust, to whom she was well known, received her with great kindness, and led her to her room in the fort. Here Marie was overcome with emotion. Madame d'Ailleboust spoke Algonquin with ease; and her words of sympathy, joined to the associations of a place where the unhappy fugitive, with her murdered husband and child, had often found a friendly welcome, so wrought upon her, that her voice was smothered with sobs.

She had once before been a prisoner of the Iroquois, at the town of Onondaga. When she and her companions in misfortune had reached the Mohawk towns, she was recognized by several Onondagas who chanced to be there, and who, partly by threats and partly by promises, induced her to return with them to the scene of her former captivity, where they assured her of good treatment. With their aid, she escaped from the Mohawks, and set out with them for Onondaga. On their way, they passed the great town of the Oneidas; and her conductors, fearing that certain Mohawks who were there would lay claim to her, found a hiding-place for her in the forest, where they gave her food, and told her to wait their return. She lay concealed all day, and at night approached the town, under cover of darkness. A dull red glare of flames rose above the jagged tops of the palisade that encompassed it; and, from the pandemonium within, an uproar of screams, yells, and bursts of laughter told her that they were burning one of her captive countrymen. She gazed and listened, shivering with cold and aghast with horror. The thought possessed her that she would soon share his fate, and she resolved to fly. The ground was still covered with snow, and her footprints would infallibly have betrayed her, if she had not, instead of turning towards home, followed the beaten Indian path westward. She journeyed on, confused and irresolute, and tortured between terror and hunger. At length she approached Onondaga, a few miles from the present city of Syracuse, and hid herself in a dense thicket of spruce or cedar, whence she crept forth at night, to grope in the half-melted snow for a few ears of corn, left from the last year's harvest. She saw many Indians from her lurking-place, and once a tall savage, with an axe on his shoulder, advanced directly towards the spot where she lay: but, in the extremity of her fright, she murmured a prayer, on which he turned and changed his course. The fate that awaited her, if she remained,— for a fugitive could not hope for mercy,— and the scarcely less terrible dangers of the pitiless wilderness between her and Canada, filled her with despair, for she was half dead already with hunger and cold. She tied her girdle to the bough of a tree, and hung herself from it by the neck. The cord broke. She repeated the attempt with the same result, and then the thought came to her that God meant to save her life. The snow by this time had melted in the forests, and she began her journey for home, with a few handfuls of corn as her only provision. She directed her course by the sun, and for food dug roots, peeled the soft inner bark of trees, and sometimes caught tortoises in the muddy brooks. She had the good fortune to find a hatchet in a deserted camp, and with it made one of those wooden implements which the Indians used for kindling fire by friction. This saved her from her worst suffering; for she had no covering but a thin tunic, which left her legs and arms bare, and

exposed her at night to tortures of cold. She built her fire in
some deep nook of the forest, warmed herself, cooked what
food she had found, told her rosary on her fingers, and slept
till daylight, when she always threw water on the embers, lest
the rising smoke should attract attention. Once she discovered a party of Iroquois hunters; but she lay concealed, and
they passed without seeing her. She followed their trail back,
and found their bark canoe, which they had hidden near the
bank of a river. It was too large for her use; but, as she was
a practised canoe-maker, she reduced it to a convenient size,
embarked in it, and descended the stream. At length she
reached the St. Lawrence, and paddled with the current towards Montreal. On islands and rocky shores she found eggs
of water-fowl in abundance; and she speared fish with a
sharpened pole, hardened at the point with fire. She even
killed deer, by driving them into the water, chasing them in
her canoe, and striking them on the head with her hatchet.
When she landed at Montreal, her canoe had still a good store
of eggs and dried venison.[1]

Her journey from Onondaga had occupied about two
months, under hardships which no woman but a squaw could
have survived. Escapes not less remarkable of several other
women are chronicled in the records of this year; and one of
them, with a notable feat of arms which attended it, calls for
a brief notice.

Eight Algonquins, in one of those fits of desperate valor
which sometimes occur in Indians, entered at midnight a
camp where thirty or forty Iroquois warriors were buried in
sleep, and with quick, sharp blows of their tomahawks began
to brain them as they lay. They killed ten of them on the spot,
and wounded many more. The rest, panic-stricken and bewildered by the surprise and the thick darkness, fled into the
forest, leaving all they had in the hands of the victors, including a number of Algonquin captives, of whom one had been
unwittingly killed by his countrymen in the confusion. Another captive, a woman, had escaped on a previous night.

[1] This story is taken from the *Relation* of 1647, and the letter of Marie de
l'Incarnation to her son, before cited. The woman must have descended the
great rapids of Lachine in her canoe: a feat demanding no ordinary nerve
and skill.

They had stretched her on her back, with limbs extended, and bound her wrists and ankles to four stakes firmly driven into the earth,—their ordinary mode of securing prisoners. Then, as usual, they all fell asleep. She presently became aware that the cord that bound one of her wrists was somewhat loose, and, by long and painful efforts, she freed her hand. To release the other hand and her feet was then comparatively easy. She cautiously rose. Around her, breathing in deep sleep, lay stretched the dark forms of the unconscious warriors, scarcely visible in the gloom. She stepped over them to the entrance of the hut; and here, as she was passing out, she descried a hatchet on the ground. The temptation was too strong for her Indian nature. She seized it, and struck again and again, with all her force, on the skull of the Iroquois who lay at the entrance. The sound of the blows, and the convulsive struggles of the victim, roused the sleepers. They sprang up, groping in the dark, and demanding of each other what was the matter. At length they lighted a roll of birch-bark, found their prisoner gone and their comrade dead, and rushed out in a rage in search of the fugitive. She, meanwhile, instead of running away, had hid herself in the hollow of a tree, which she had observed the evening before. Her pursuers ran through the dark woods, shouting and whooping to each other; and when all had passed, she crept from her hiding-place, and fled in an opposite direction. In the morning they found her tracks and followed them. On the second day they had overtaken and surrounded her, when, hearing their cries on all sides, she gave up all hope. But near at hand, in the thickest depths of the forest, the beavers had dammed a brook and formed a pond, full of gnawed stumps, dead fallen trees, rank weeds, and tangled bushes. She plunged in, and, swimming and wading, found a hiding-place, where her body was concealed by the water, and her head by the masses of dead and living vegetation. Her pursuers were at fault, and, after a long search, gave up the chase in despair. Shivering, naked, and half-starved, she crawled out from her wild asylum, and resumed her flight. By day, the briers and bushes tore her unprotected limbs; by night, she shivered with cold, and the mosquitoes and small black gnats of the forest persecuted her with torments which the modern sportsman will appreciate.

She subsisted on such roots, bark, reptiles, or other small animals, as her Indian habits enabled her to gather on her way. She crossed streams by swimming, or on rafts of driftwood, lashed together with strips of linden-bark; and at length reached the St. Lawrence, where, with the aid of her hatchet, she made a canoe. Her home was on the Ottawa, and she was ignorant of the great river, or, at least, of this part of it. She had scarcely even seen a Frenchman, but had heard of the French as friends, and knew that their dwellings were on the banks of the St. Lawrence. This was her only guide; and she drifted on her way, doubtful whether the vast current would bear her to the abodes of the living or to the land of souls. She passed the watery wilderness of the Lake of St. Peter, and presently descried a Huron canoe. Fearing that it was an enemy, she hid herself, and resumed her voyage in the evening, when she soon came in sight of the wooden buildings and palisades of Three Rivers. Several Hurons saw her at the same moment, and made towards her; on which she leaped ashore and hid in the bushes, whence, being entirely without clothing, she would not come out till one of them threw her his coat. Having wrapped herself in it, she went with them to the fort and the house of the Jesuits, in a wretched state of emaciation, but in high spirits at the happy issue of her voyage.[1]

Such stories might be multiplied; but these will suffice. Nor is it necessary to dwell further on the bloody record of inroads, butcheries, and tortures. We have seen enough to show the nature of the scourge that now fell without mercy on the Indians and the French of Canada. There was no safety but in the imprisonment of palisades and ramparts. A deep dejection sank on the white and red men alike; but the Jesuits would not despair.

"Do not imagine," writes the Father Superior, "that the rage of the Iroquois, and the loss of many Christians and many catechumens, can bring to nought the mystery of the cross of Jesus Christ, and the efficacy of his blood. We shall die; we shall be captured, burned, butchered: be it so. Those who die in their beds do not always die the best death. I see none of our

[1] Lalemant, *Relation, 1647*, 15, 16.

company cast down. On the contrary, they ask leave to go up to the Hurons, and some of them protest that the fires of the Iroquois are one of their motives for the journey."[1]

[1] *Ibid.*, 8.

Chapter XXII

1645–1651

PRIEST AND PURITAN

Miscou • Tadoussac • Journeys of De Quen • Druilletes • His Winter with the Montagnais • Influence of the Missions • The Abenaquis • Druilletes on the Kennebec • His Embassy to Boston • Gibbons • Dudley • Bradford • Eliot • Endicott • French and Puritan Colonization • Failure of Druilletes's Embassy • New Regulations • New-Year's Day at Quebec

BEFORE passing to the closing scenes of this wilderness drama, we will touch briefly on a few points aside from its main action, yet essential to an understanding of the scope of the mission. Besides their establishments at Quebec, Sillery, Three Rivers, and the neighborhood of Lake Huron, the Jesuits had an outlying post at the island of Miscou, on the Gulf of St. Lawrence, near the entrance of the Bay of Chaleurs, where they instructed the wandering savages of those shores, and confessed the French fishermen. The island was unhealthy in the extreme. Several of the priests sickened and died; and scarcely one convert repaid their toils. There was a more successful mission at Tadoussac, or Sadilege, as the neighboring Indians called it. In winter, this place was a solitude; but in summer, when the Montagnais gathered from their hunting-grounds to meet the French traders, Jesuits came yearly from Quebec to instruct them in the Faith. Sometimes they followed them northward, into wilds where, at this day, a white man rarely penetrates. Thus, in 1646, De Quen ascended the Saguenay, and, by a series of rivers, torrents, lakes, and rapids, reached a Montagnais horde called the Nation of the Porcupine, where he found that the teachings at Tadoussac had borne fruit, and that the converts had planted a cross on the borders of the savage lake where they dwelt. There was a kindred band, the Nation of the White Fish, among the rocks and forests north of Three Rivers. They proved tractable beyond all others, threw away their "medicines" or fetiches, burned their magic drums, renounced their medicine-songs, and accepted instead rosaries, crucifixes, and versions of Catholic hymns.

In a former chapter, we followed Father Paul Le Jeune on his winter roamings, with a band of Montagnais, among the forests on the northern boundary of Maine. Now Father Gabriel Druilletes sets forth on a similar excursion, but with one essential difference. Le Jeune's companions were heathen, who persecuted him day and night with their gibes and sarcasms. Those of Druilletes were all converts, who looked on him as a friend and a father. There were prayers, confessions, masses, and invocations of St. Joseph. They built their bark chapel at every camp, and no festival of the Church passed unobserved. On Good Friday they laid their best robe of beaver-skin on the snow, placed on it a crucifix, and knelt around it in prayer. What was their prayer? It was a petition for the forgiveness and the conversion of their enemies, the Iroquois.[1] Those who know the intensity and tenacity of an Indian's hatred will see in this something more than a change from one superstition to another. An idea had been presented to the mind of the savage, to which he had previously been an utter stranger. This is the most remarkable record of success in the whole body of the Jesuit *Relations*; but it is very far from being the only evidence, that, in teaching the dogmas and observances of the Roman Church, the missionaries taught also the morals of Christianity. When we look for the results of these missions, we soon become aware that the influence of the French and the Jesuits extended far beyond the circle of converts. It eventually modified and softened the manners of many unconverted tribes. In the wars of the next century we do not often find those examples of diabolic atrocity with which the earlier annals are crowded. The savage burned his enemies alive, it is true, but he rarely ate them; neither did he torment them with the same deliberation and persistency. He was a savage still, but not so often a devil. The improvement was not great, but it was distinct; and it seems to have taken place wherever Indian tribes were in close relations with any respectable community of white men. Thus Philip's war in New England, cruel as it was, was less fero-

[1] Vimont, *Relation, 1645,* 16.

cious, judging from Canadian experience, than it would have been, if a generation of civilized intercourse had not worn down the sharpest asperities of barbarism. Yet it was to French priests and colonists, mingled as they were soon to be among the tribes of the vast interior, that the change is chiefly to be ascribed. In this softening of manners, such as it was, and in the obedient Catholicity of a few hundred tamed savages gathered at stationary missions in various parts of Canada, we find, after a century had elapsed, all the results of the heroic toil of the Jesuits. The missions had failed, because the Indians had ceased to exist. Of the great tribes on whom rested the hopes of the early Canadian Fathers, nearly all were virtually extinct. The missionaries built laboriously and well, but they were doomed to build on a failing foundation. The Indians melted away, not because civilization destroyed them, but because their own ferocity and intractable indolence made it impossible that they should exist in its presence. Either the plastic energies of a higher race or the servile pliancy of a lower one would, each in its way, have preserved them: as it was, their extinction was a foregone conclusion. As for the religion which the Jesuits taught them, however Protestants may carp at it, it was the only form of Christianity likely to take root in their crude and barbarous nature.

To return to Druilletes. The smoke of the wigwam blinded him; and it is no matter of surprise to hear that he was cured by a miracle. He returned from his winter roving to Quebec in high health, and soon set forth on a new mission. On the River Kennebec, in the present State of Maine, dwelt the Abenaquis, an Algonquin people, destined hereafter to become a thorn in the sides of the New-England colonists. Some of them had visited their friends, the Christian Indians of Sillery. Here they became converted, went home, and preached the Faith to their countrymen, and this to such purpose that the Abenaquis sent to Quebec to ask for a missionary. Apart from the saving of souls, there were solid reasons for acceding to their request. The Abenaquis were near the colonies of New England,—indeed, the Plymouth colony, under its charter, claimed jurisdiction over them; and in case of rupture, they would prove serviceable friends or dangerous enemies to New France.[1] Their messengers were favorably received; and Druilletes was ordered to proceed upon the new mission.

He left Sillery, with a party of Indians, on the twenty-ninth of August, 1646,[2] and following, as it seems, the route by which, a hundred and twenty-nine years later, the soldiers of Arnold made their way to Quebec, he reached the waters of the Kennebec and descended to the Abenaqui villages. Here he nursed the sick, baptized the dying, and gave such instruction as, in his ignorance of the language, he was able. Apparently he had been ordered to reconnoitre; for he presently descended the river from Norridgewock to the first English trading-post, where Augusta now stands. Thence he continued his journey to the sea, and followed the coast in a canoe to the Penobscot, visiting seven or eight English posts on the way, where, to his surprise, he was very well received. At the Penobscot he found several Capuchin friars, under their Superior, Father Ignace, who welcomed him with the utmost cordiality. Returning, he again ascended the Kennebec to the English post at Augusta. At a spot three miles above the Indians had gathered in considerable numbers, and here they built him a chapel after their fashion. He remained till midwinter, catechizing and baptizing, and waging war so successfully against the Indian sorcerers, that medicine-bags were thrown away, and charms and incantations were supplanted by prayers. In January the whole troop set off on their grand hunt, Druilletes following them,—"with toil," says the chronicler, "too great to buy the kingdoms of this world, but very small as a price for the Kingdom of Heaven."[3] They encamped on Moosehead Lake, where new disputes with the "medicine-men" ensued, and the Father again remained master of the field. When, after a prosperous hunt, the party returned to the English trading-house, John Winslow, the agent in charge, again received the missionary with a kindness which showed no trace of jealousy or religious prejudice.[4]

[1] Charlevoix, I. 280, gives this as a motive of the mission.

[2] Lalemant, *Relation, 1647*, 51.

[3] Lalemant, *Relation, 1647*, 54. For an account of this mission, see also Maurault, *Histoire des Abenakis*, 116–156.

[4] Winslow would scarcely have recognized his own name in the Jesuit spelling,—"Le Sieur de *Houinslaud*." In his journal of 1650 Druilletes is more successful in his orthography, and spells it *Winslau*.

Early in the summer Druilletes went to Quebec; and during the two following years, the Abenaquis, for reasons which are not clear, were left without a missionary. He spent another winter of extreme hardship with the Algonquins on their winter rovings, and during summer instructed the wandering savages of Tadoussac. It was not until the autumn of 1650 that he again descended the Kennebec. This time he went as an envoy charged with the negotiation of a treaty. His journey is worthy of notice, since, with the unimportant exception of Jogues's embassy to the Mohawks, it is the first occasion on which the Canadian Jesuits appear in a character distinctly political. Afterwards, when the fervor and freshness of the missions had passed away, they frequently did the work of political agents among the Indians: but the Jesuit of the earlier period was, with rare exceptions, a missionary only; and though he was expected to exert a powerful influence in gaining subjects and allies for France, he was to do so by gathering them under the wings of the Church.

The Colony of Massachusetts had applied to the French officials at Quebec, with a view to a reciprocity of trade. The Iroquois had brought Canada to extremity, and the French Governor conceived the hope of gaining the powerful support of New England by granting the desired privileges on condition of military aid. But, as the Puritans would scarcely see it for their interest to provoke a dangerous enemy, who had thus far never molested them, it was resolved to urge the proposed alliance as a point of duty. The Abenaquis had suffered from Mohawk inroads; and the French, assuming for the occasion that they were under the jurisdiction of the English colonies, argued that they were bound to protect them. Druilletes went in a double character,—as an envoy of the government at Quebec, and as an agent of his Abenaqui flock, who had been advised to petition for English assistance. The time seemed inauspicious for a Jesuit visit to Boston; for not only had it been announced as foremost among the objects in colonizing New England, "to raise a bulwark against the kingdom of Antichrist, which the Jesuits labor to rear up in all places of the world,"[1] but, three years before, the Legisla-

---

[1] *Considerations for the Plantation in New England.* — See Hutchinson, *Collection*, 27. Mr. Savage thinks that this paper was by Winthrop. See Savage's Winthrop. I. 360, *note*.

ture of Massachusetts had enacted, that Jesuits entering the colony should be expelled, and, if they returned, hanged.[1]

Nevertheless, on the first of September, Druilletes set forth from Quebec with a Christian chief of Sillery, crossed forests, mountains, and torrents, and reached Norridgewock, the highest Abenaqui settlement on the Kennebec. Thence he descended to the English trading-house at Augusta, where his fast friend, the Puritan Winslow, gave him a warm welcome, entertained him hospitably, and promised to forward the object of his mission. He went with him, at great personal inconvenience, to Merrymeeting Bay, where Druilletes embarked in an English vessel for Boston. The passage was stormy, and the wind ahead. He was forced to land at Cape Ann, or, as he calls it, *Kepane*, whence, partly on foot, partly in boats along the shore, he made his way to Boston. The three-hilled city of the Puritans lay chill and dreary under a December sky, as the priest crossed in a boat from the neighboring peninsula of Charlestown.

Winslow was agent for the merchant, Edward Gibbons, a personage of note, whose life presents curious phases,—a reveller of Merry Mount, a bold sailor, a member of the church, an adventurous trader, an associate of buccaneers, a magistrate of the commonwealth, and a major-general.[2] The Jesuit, with credentials from the Governor of Canada and letters from Winslow, met a reception widely different from that which the law enjoined against persons of his profession.[3] Gibbons welcomed him heartily, prayed him to accept no other lodging than his house while he remained in Boston, and gave him the key of a chamber, in order that he might pray after his own fashion, without fear of disturbance. An accurate Catholic writer thinks it likely that he brought with him the means of celebrating the Mass.[4] If so, the house of the Puritan was, no doubt, desecrated by that Popish abomi-

[1] See the Act, in Hazard, 550.

[2] An account of him will be found in Palfrey, *Hist. of New England*, II. 225, *note*.

[3] In the Act, an exception, however, was made in favor of Jesuits coming as ambassadors or envoys from their government, who were declared not liable to the penalty of hanging.

[4] J. G. Shea, in *Boston Pilot*.

nation; but be this as it may, Massachusetts, in the person of her magistrate, became the gracious host of one of those whom, next to the Devil and an Anglican bishop, she most abhorred.

On the next day, Gibbons took his guest to Roxbury,— called *Rogsbray* by Druilletes,—to see the Governor, the harsh and narrow Dudley, grown gray in repellent virtue and grim honesty. Some half a century before, he had served in France, under Henry the Fourth; ·but he had forgotten his French, and called for an interpreter to explain the visitor's credentials. He received Druilletes with courtesy, and promised to call the magistrates together on the following Tuesday to hear his proposals. They met accordingly, and Druilletes was asked to dine with them. The old Governor sat at the head of the table, and after dinner invited the guest to open the business of his embassy. They listened to him, desired him to withdraw, and, after consulting among themselves, sent for him to join them again at supper, when they made him an answer, of which the record is lost, but which evidently was not definitive.

As the Abenaqui Indians were within the jurisdiction of Plymouth,[1] Druilletes proceeded thither in his character of their agent. Here, again, he was received with courtesy and kindness. Governor Bradford invited him to dine, and, as it was Friday, considerately gave him a dinner of fish. Druilletes conceived great hope that the colony could be wrought upon to give the desired assistance; for some of the chief inhabitants had an interest in the trade with the Abenaquis.[2] He came back by land to Boston, stopping again at Roxbury on the way. It was night when he arrived; and, after the usual custom, he took lodging with the minister. Here were several young Indians, pupils of his host: for he was no other than the celebrated Eliot, who, during the past summer, had estab-

---

[1] For the documents on the title of Plymouth to lands on the Kennebec, see Drake's additions to Baylies's *History of New Plymouth*, 36, where they are illustrated by an ancient map. The patent was obtained as early as 1628, and a trading-house soon after established.

[2] *The Record of the Colony of Plymouth*, June 5, 1651, contains, however, the entry, "The Court declare themselves not to be willing to aid them (*the French*) in their design, or to grant them liberty to go through their jurisdiction for the aforesaid purpose" (*to attack the Mohawks*).

lished his mission at Natick,[1] and was now laboring, in the fulness of his zeal, in the work of civilization and conversion. There was great sympathy between the two missionaries; and Eliot prayed his guest to spend the winter with him.

At Salem, which Druilletes also visited, in company with the minister of Marblehead, he had an interview with the stern, but manly, Endicott, who, he says, spoke French, and expressed both interest and good-will towards the objects of the expedition. As the envoy had no money left, Endicott paid his charges, and asked him to dine with the magistrates.[2]

Druilletes was evidently struck with the thrift and vigor of these sturdy young colonies, and the strength of their population. He says that Boston, meaning Massachusetts, could alone furnish four thousand fighting men, and that the four united colonies could count forty thousand souls.[3] These numbers may be challenged; but, at all events, the contrast was striking with the attenuated and suffering bands of priests, nuns, and fur-traders on the St. Lawrence. About twenty-one thousand persons had come from Old to New England, with the resolve of making it their home; and though this immigration had virtually ceased, the natural increase had been great. The necessity, or the strong desire, of escaping from persecution had given the impulse to Puritan colonization; while, on the other hand, none but good Catholics, the favored class of France, were tolerated in Canada. These had no motive for exchanging the comforts of home and the smiles of Fortune for a starving wilderness and the scalping-knives of the Iroquois. The Huguenots would have emigrated in swarms; but they were rigidly forbidden. The zeal of propagandism and the fur-trade were, as we have seen, the vital forces of New France. Of her feeble population, the best part was bound to perpetual chastity; while the fur-traders and those in their service rarely brought their wives to the

[1] See Palfrey, *New England*, II. 336.

[2] On Druilletes's visit to New England, see his journal, entitled *Narré du Voyage faict pour la Mission des Abenaquois, et des Connoissances tiréz de la Nouvelle Angleterre et des Dispositions des Magistrats de cette Republique pour le Secours contre les Iroquois*. See also Druilletes, *Rapport sur le Résultat de ses Négotiations*, in Ferland, *Notes sur les Registres*, 95.

[3] Druilletes, *Reflexions touchant ce qu'on peut esperer de la Nouvelle Angleterre contre l'Irocquois* (sic), appended to his journal.

wilderness. The fur-trader, moreover, is always the worst of colonists; since the increase of population, by diminishing the numbers of the fur-bearing animals, is adverse to his interest. But behind all this there was in the religious ideal of the rival colonies an influence which alone would have gone far to produce the contrast in material growth.

To the mind of the Puritan, heaven was God's throne; but no less was the earth His footstool: and each in its degree and its kind had its demands on man. He held it a duty to labor and to multiply; and, building on the Old Testament quite as much as on the New, thought that a reward on earth as well as in heaven awaited those who were faithful to the law. Doubtless, such a belief is widely open to abuse, and it would be folly to pretend that it escaped abuse in New England; but there was in it an element manly, healthful, and invigorating. On the other hand, those who shaped the character, and in great measure the destiny, of New France had always on their lips the nothingness and the vanity of life. For them, time was nothing but a preparation for eternity, and the highest virtue consisted in a renunciation of all the cares, toils, and interests of earth. That such a doctrine has often been joined to an intense worldliness, all history proclaims; but with this we have at present nothing to do. If all mankind acted on it in good faith, the world would sink into decrepitude. It is the monastic idea carried into the wide field of active life, and is like the error of those who, in their zeal to cultivate their higher nature, suffer the neglected body to dwindle and pine, till body and mind alike lapse into feebleness and disease.

Druilletes returned to the Abenaquis, and thence to Quebec, full of hope that the object of his mission was in a fair way of accomplishment. The Governor, d'Ailleboust,[1] who had succeeded Montmagny, called his council, and Druilletes was again dispatched to New England, together with one of the principal inhabitants of Quebec, Jean Paul Godefroy.[2] They repaired to New Haven, and appeared before the Commissioners of the Four Colonies, then in session there; but

[1] The same who, with his wife, had joined the colonists of Montreal. See *ante*, p. 585.

[2] He was one of the Governor's council.—Ferland, *Notes sur les Registres*, 67.

their errand proved bootless. The Commissioners refused either to declare war or to permit volunteers to be raised in New England against the Iroquois. The Puritan, like his descendant, would not fight without a reason. The bait of free-trade with Canada failed to tempt him; and the envoys retraced their steps, with a flat, though courteous refusal.[1]

Now let us stop for a moment at Quebec, and observe some notable changes that had taken place in the affairs of the colony. The Company of the Hundred Associates, whose outlay had been great and their profit small, transferred to the inhabitants of the colony their monopoly of the fur-trade, and with it their debts. The inhabitants also assumed their obligations to furnish arms, munitions, soldiers, and works of defence, to pay the Governor and other officials, introduce emigrants, and contribute to support the missions. The Company was to receive, besides, an annual acknowledgement of a thousand pounds of beaver, and was to retain all seigniorial rights. The inhabitants were to form a corporation, of which any one of them might be a member; and no individual could trade on his own account, except on condition of selling at a fixed price to the magazine of this new company.[2]

This change took place in 1645. It was followed, in 1647, by the establishment of a Council, composed of the Governor-General, the Superior of the Jesuits, and the Governor of Montreal, who were invested with absolute powers, legislative, judicial, and executive. The Governor-General had an appointment of twenty-five thousand livres, besides the privilege of bringing over seventy tons of freight, yearly, in the Company's ships. Out of this he was required to pay the soldiers, repair the forts, and supply arms and munitions. Ten thousand livres and thirty tons of freight, with similar conditions,

[1] On Druilletes's second embassy, see *Lettre écrite par le Conseil de Quebec aux Commissionaires de la Nouvelle Angleterre*, in Charlevoix, I. 287; *Extrait des Registres de l'Ancien Conseil de Quebec*, Ibid., I. 288; *Copy of a Letter from the Commissioners of the United Colonies to the Governor of Canada*, in Hazard, II. 183; *Answare to the Propositions presented by the honored French Agents*, Ibid., II. 184; and Hutchinson, *Collection of Papers*, 166. Also, *Records of the Commissioners of the United Colonies, Sept. 5, 1651;* and *Commission of Druilletes and Godefroy, in N.Y. Col. Docs.*, IX. 6.

[2] *Articles accordés entre les Directeurs et Associés de la Compagnie de la N^{elle} France et les Députés des Habitans du dit Pays, 6 Mars, 1645.* MS.

were assigned to the Governor of Montreal. Under these circumstances, one cannot wonder that the colony was but indifferently defended against the Iroquois, and that the King had to send soldiers to save it from destruction. In the next year, at the instance of Maisonneuve, another change was made. A specified sum was set apart for purposes of defence, and the salaries of the Governors were proportionably reduced. The Governor-General, Montmagny, though he seems to have done better than could reasonably have been expected, was removed; and, as Maisonneuve declined the office, d'Ailleboust, another Montrealist, was appointed to it. This movement, indeed, had been accomplished by the interest of the Montreal party; for already there was no slight jealousy between Quebec and her rival.

The Council was reorganized, and now consisted of the Governor, the Superior of the Jesuits, and three of the principal inhabitants.[1] These last were to be chosen every three years by the Council itself, in conjunction with the Syndics of Quebec, Montreal, and Three Rivers. The Syndic was an officer elected by the inhabitants of the community to which he belonged, to manage its affairs. Hence a slight ingredient of liberty was introduced into the new organization.

The colony, since the transfer of the fur-trade, had become a resident corporation of merchants, with the Governor and Council at its head. They were at once the directors of a trading company, a legislative assembly, a court of justice, and an executive body: more even than this, for they regulated the private affairs of families and individuals. The appointment and payment of clerks and the examining of accounts mingled with high functions of government; and the new corporation of the inhabitants seems to have been managed with very little consultation of its members. How the Father Superior acquitted himself in his capacity of director of a fur-company is nowhere recorded.[2]

As for Montreal, though it had given a Governor to the colony, its prospects were far from hopeful. The ridiculous

[1] The Governors of Montreal and Three Rivers, when present, had also seats in the Council.

[2] Those curious in regard to these new regulations will find an account of them, at greater length, in Ferland and Faillon.

Dauversière, its chief founder, was sick and bankrupt; and the Associates of Montreal, once so full of zeal and so abounding in wealth, were reduced to nine persons. What it had left of vitality was in the enthusiastic Mademoiselle Mance, the earnest and disinterested soldier, Maisonneuve, and the priest, Olier, with his new Seminary of St. Sulpice.

Let us visit Quebec in midwinter. We pass the warehouses and dwellings of the lower town, and as we climb the zigzag way now called Mountain Street, the frozen river, the roofs, the summits of the cliff, and all the broad landscape below and around us glare in the sharp sunlight with a dazzling whiteness. At the top, scarcely a private house is to be seen; but, instead, a fort, a church, a hospital, a cemetery, a house of the Jesuits, and an Ursuline convent. Yet, regardless of the keen air, soldiers, Jesuits, servants, officials, women, all of the little community who are not cloistered, are abroad and astir. Despite the gloom of the times, an unwonted cheer enlivens this rocky perch of France and the Faith; for it is New-Year's Day, and there is an active interchange of greetings and presents. Thanks to the nimble pen of the Father Superior, we know what each gave and what each received. He thus writes in his private journal: —

"The soldiers went with their guns to salute Monsieur the Governor; and so did also the inhabitants in a body. He was beforehand with us, and came here at seven o'clock to wish us a happy New-Year, each in turn, one after another. I went to see him after mass. Another time we must be beforehand with him. M. Giffard also came to see us. The Hospital nuns sent us letters of compliment very early in the morning; and the Ursulines sent us some beautiful presents, with candles, rosaries, a crucifix, etc., and, at dinner-time, two excellent pies. I sent them two images, in enamel, of St. Ignatius and St. Francis Xavier. We gave to M. Giffard Father Bonnet's book on the life of Our Lord; to M. des Châtelets, a little volume on Eternity; to M. Bourdon, a telescope and compass; and to others, reliquaries, rosaries, medals, images, etc. I went to see M. Giffard, M. Couillard, and Mademoiselle de Repentigny. The Ursulines sent to beg that I would come and see them before the end of the day. I went, and paid my compliments also to Madame de la Peltrie, who sent us some presents. I was near leaving this out, which would have been a sad oversight. We gave a crucifix to the woman who washes the church-linen, a bottle of *eau-de-vie* to Abraham, four handkerchiefs to his wife, some books of devotion to others, and two handkerchiefs to Robert Hache. He asked for two more, and we gave them to him."[1]

[1] *Journal des Supérieurs des Jésuites*, MS. Only fragments of this curious record are extant. It was begun by Lalemant in 1645. For the privilege of having what remains of it copied I am indebted to M. Jacques Viger. The entry translated above is of Jan. 1, 1646. Of the persons named in it, Giffard was seigneur of Beauport, and a member of the Council; Des Châtelets was one of the earliest settlers, and connected by marriage with Giffard; Couillard was son-in-law of the first settler, Hébert; Mademoiselle de Repentigny was daughter of Le Gardeur de Repentigny, commander of the fleet; Madame de la Peltrie has been described already; Bourdon was chief engineer of the colony; Abraham was Abraham Martin, pilot for the King on the St. Lawrence, from whom the historic Plains of Abraham received their name. (See Ferland, *Notes sur Registres*, 16.) The rest were servants, or persons of humble station.

Chapter XXIII

1645–1648

A DOOMED NATION

*Indian Infatuation • Iroquois and Huron • Huron Triumphs •
The Captive Iroquois • His Ferocity and Fortitude • Partisan
Exploits • Diplomacy • The Andastes • The Huron Embassy
• New Negotiations • The Iroquois Ambassador • His
Suicide • Iroquois Honor*

IT was a strange and miserable spectacle to behold the savages of this continent at the time when the knell of their
common ruin had already sounded. Civilization had gained a
foothold on their borders. The long and gloomy reign of barbarism was drawing near its close, and their united efforts
could scarcely have availed to sustain it. Yet, in this crisis of
their destiny, these doomed tribes were tearing each other's
throats in a wolfish fury, joined to an intelligence that served
little purpose but mutual destruction.

How the quarrel began between the Iroquois and their Huron kindred no man can tell, and it is not worth while to
conjecture. At this time, the ruling passion of the savage Confederates was the annihilation of this rival people and of their
Algonquin allies,—if the understanding between the Hurons
and these incoherent hordes can be called an alliance. United,
they far outnumbered the Iroquois. Indeed, the Hurons alone
were not much inferior in force; for, by the largest estimates,
the strength of the five Iroquois nations must now have been
considerably less than three thousand warriors. Their true superiority was a moral one. They were in one of those transports of pride, self-confidence, and rage for ascendency,
which, in a savage people, marks an era of conquest. With all
the defects of their organization, it was far better than that of
their neighbors. There were bickerings, jealousies, plottings
and counter-plottings, separate wars and separate treaties,
among the five members of the league; yet nothing could sun-
der them. The bonds that united them were like cords of
India-rubber: they would stretch, and the parts would be
seemingly disjoined, only to return to their old union with

the recoil. Such was the elastic strength of those relations of clanship which were the life of the league.[1]

The first meeting of white men with the Hurons found them at blows with the Iroquois; and from that time forward, the war raged with increasing fury. Small scalping-parties infested the Huron forests, killing squaws in the cornfields, or entering villages at midnight to tomahawk their sleeping inhabitants. Often, too, invasions were made in force. Sometimes towns were set upon and burned, and sometimes there were deadly conflicts in the depths of the forests and the passes of the hills. The invaders were not always successful. A bloody rebuff and a sharp retaliation now and then requited them. Thus, in 1638, a war-party of a hundred Iroquois met in the forest a band of three hundred Huron and Algonquin warriors. They might have retreated, and the greater number were for doing so; but Ononkwaya, an Oneida chief, refused. "Look!" he said, "the sky is clear; the Sun beholds us. If there were clouds to hide our shame from his sight, we might fly; but, as it is, we must fight while we can." They stood their ground for a time, but were soon overborne. Four or five escaped; but the rest were surrounded, and killed or taken. This year, Fortune smiled on the Hurons; and they took, in all, more than a hundred prisoners, who were distributed among their various towns, to be burned. These scenes, with them, occurred always in the night; and it was held to be of the last importance that the torture should be protracted from sunset till dawn. The too valiant Ononkwaya was among the victims. Even in death he took his revenge; for it was thought an augury of disaster to the victors, if no cry of pain could be extorted from the sufferer, and, on the present occasion, he displayed an unflinching courage, rare even among Indian warriors. His execution took place at the town of Teanaustayé, called St. Joseph by the Jesuits. The Fathers could not save his life, but, what was more to the purpose, they baptized him. On the scaffold where he was burned, he wrought himself into a fury which seemed to render him insensible to pain. Thinking him nearly spent, his tormentors scalped him, when, to their amazement, he leaped up, snatched the brands

[1] See *ante*, Introduction.

that had been the instruments of his torture, drove the screeching crowd from the scaffold, and held them all at bay, while they pelted him from below with sticks, stones, and showers of live coals. At length he made a false step and fell to the ground, when they seized him and threw him into the fire. He instantly leaped out, covered with blood, cinders, and ashes, and rushed upon them, with a blazing brand in each hand. The crowd gave way before him, and he ran towards the town, as if to set it on fire. They threw a pole across his way, which tripped him and flung him headlong to the earth, on which they all fell upon him, cut off his hands and feet, and again threw him into the fire. He rolled himself out, and crawled forward on his elbows and knees, glaring upon them with such unutterable ferocity that they recoiled once more, till, seeing that he was helpless, they threw themselves upon him, and cut off his head.[1]

When the Iroquois could not win by force, they were sometimes more successful with treachery. In the summer of 1645, two war-parties of the hostile nations met in the forest. The Hurons bore themselves so well that they had nearly gained the day, when the Iroquois called for a parley, displayed a great number of wampum-belts, and said that they wished to treat for peace. The Hurons had the folly to consent. The chiefs on both sides sat down to a council, during which the Iroquois, seizing a favorable moment, fell upon their dupes and routed them completely, killing and capturing a considerable number.[2]

The large frontier town of St. Joseph was well fortified with palisades, on which, at intervals, were wooden watch-towers. On an evening of this same summer of 1645, the Iroquois approached the place in force; and the young Huron warriors, mounting their palisades, sang their war-songs all night, with the utmost power of their lungs, in order that the enemy, knowing them to be on their guard, might be deterred from an attack. The night was dark, and the hideous dissonance resounded far and wide; yet, regardless of the din, two Iroquois crept close to the palisade, where they lay mo-

---

[1] Lalemant, *Relation des Hurons, 1639*, 68. It was this chief whose severed hand was thrown to the Jesuits. See *ante*, p. 496.

[2] Ragueneau, *Relation des Hurons, 1646*, 55.

tionless till near dawn. By this time the last song had died away, and the tired singers had left their posts or fallen asleep. One of the Iroquois, with the silence and agility of a wild-cat, climbed to the top of a watch-tower, where he found two slumbering Hurons, brained one of them with his hatchet, and threw the other down to his comrade, who quickly despoiled him of his life and his scalp. Then, with the reeking trophies of their exploit, the adventurers rejoined their countrymen in the forest.

The Hurons planned a counter-stroke; and three of them, after a journey of twenty days, reached the great town of the Senecas. They entered it at midnight, and found, as usual, no guard; but the doors of the houses were made fast. They cut a hole in the bark side of one of them, crept in, stirred the fading embers to give them light, chose each his man, tomahawked him, scalped him, and escaped in the confusion.[1]

Despite such petty triumphs, the Hurons felt themselves on the verge of ruin. Pestilence and war had wasted them away, and left but a skeleton of their former strength. In their distress, they cast about them for succor, and, remembering an ancient friendship with a kindred nation, the Andastes, they sent an embassy to ask of them aid in war or intervention to obtain peace. This powerful people dwelt, as has been shown, on the River Susquehanna.[2] The way was long, even in a direct line; but the Iroquois lay between, and a wide circuit was necessary to avoid them. A Christian chief, whom the Jesuits had named Charles, together with four Christian and four heathen Hurons, bearing wampum-belts and gifts from the council, departed on this embassy on the thirteenth of April, 1647, and reached the great town of the Andastes early in June. It contained, as the Jesuits were told, no less than

---

[1] Ragueneau, *Relation des Hurons, 1646*, 55, 56.

[2] See Introduction. The Susquehannocks of Smith, clearly the same people, are placed, in his map, on the east side of the Susquehanna, some twenty miles from its mouth. He speaks of them as great enemies of the Massawomekes (Mohawks). No other savage people so boldly resisted the Iroquois; but the story in Hazard's *Annals of Pennsylvania*, that a hundred of them beat off sixteen hundred Senecas, is disproved by the fact, that the Senecas, in their best estate, never had so many warriors. The miserable remnant of the Andastes, called Conestogas, were massacred by the Paxton Boys, in 1763. See "Conspiracy of Pontiac," 414. Compare *Historical Magazine*, II. 294.

thirteen hundred warriors. The council assembled, and the chief ambassador addressed them: —

"We come from the Land of Souls, where all is gloom, dismay, and desolation. Our fields are covered with blood; our houses are filled only with the dead; and we ourselves have but life enough to beg our friends to take pity on a people who are drawing near their end."[1] Then he presented the wampum-belts and other gifts, saying that they were the voice of a dying country.

The Andastes, who had a mortal quarrel with the Mohawks, and who had before promised to aid the Hurons in case of need, returned a favorable answer, but were disposed to try the virtue of diplomacy rather than the tomahawk. After a series of councils, they determined to send ambassadors, not to their old enemies, the Mohawks, but to the Onondagas, Oneidas, and Cayugas,[2] who were geographically the central nations of the Iroquois league, while the Mohawks and the Senecas were respectively at its eastern and western extremities. By inducing the three central nations, and, if possible, the Senecas also, to conclude a treaty with the Hurons, these last would be enabled to concentrate their force against the Mohawks, whom the Andastes would attack at the same time, unless they humbled themselves and made peace. This scheme, it will be seen, was based on the assumption, that the dreaded league of the Iroquois was far from being a unit in action or counsel.

Charles, with some of his colleagues, now set out for home, to report the result of their mission; but the Senecas were lying in wait for them, and they were forced to make a wide sweep through the Alleghanies, Western Pennsylvania, and

[1] "Il leur dit qu'il venoit du pays des Ames, où la guerre et la terreur des ennemis auoit tout desolé, où les campagnes n'estoient couuertes que de sang, où les cabanes n'estoient remplies que de cadaures, et qu'il ne leur restoit à eux-mesmes de vie, sinon autant qu'il en auoient eu besoin pour venir dire à leurs amis, qu'ils eussent pitié d'vn pays qui tiroit à sa fin." — Ragueneau, *Relation des Hurons, 1648*, 58.

[2] Examination leaves no doubt that the *Ouiouenronnons* of Ragueneau (*Relation des Hurons, 1648*, 46, 59) were the Oiogouins or *Goyogouins*, that is to say, the Cayugas. They must not be confounded with the Ouenrohronnons, a small tribe hostile to the Iroquois, who took refuge among the Hurons in 1638.

apparently Ohio, to avoid these vigilant foes. It was October before they reached the Huron towns, and meanwhile hopes of peace had arisen from another quarter.[1]

Early in the spring, a band of Onondagas had made an inroad, but were roughly handled by the Hurons, who killed several of them, captured others, and put the rest to flight. The prisoners were burned, with the exception of one who committed suicide to escape the torture, and one other, the chief man of the party, whose name was Annenrais. Some of the Hurons were dissatisfied at the mercy shown him, and gave out that they would kill him; on which the chiefs, who never placed themselves in open opposition to the popular will, secretly fitted him out, made him presents, and aided him to escape at night, with an understanding that he should use his influence at Onondaga in favor of peace. After crossing Lake Ontario, he met nearly all the Onondaga warriors on the march to avenge his supposed death; for he was a man of high account. They greeted him as one risen from the grave; and, on his part, he persuaded them to renounce their warlike purpose and return home. On their arrival, the chiefs and old men were called to council, and the matter was debated with the usual deliberation.

About this time the ambassador of the Andastes appeared with his wampum-belts. Both this nation and the Onondagas had secret motives which were perfectly in accordance. The Andastes hated the Mohawks as enemies, and the Onondagas were jealous of them as confederates; for, since they had armed themselves with Dutch guns, their arrogance and boastings had given umbrage to their brethren of the league; and a peace with the Hurons would leave the latter free to turn their undivided strength against the Mohawks, and curb their insolence. The Oneidas and the Cayugas were of one mind with the Onondagas. Three nations of the league, to satisfy their spite against a fourth, would strike hands with the common enemy of all. It was resolved to send an embassy to the Hurons. Yet it may be, that, after all, the Onondagas had but half a mind for peace. At least, they were unfortunate in their choice of an ambassador. He was by birth a Huron,

[1] On this mission of the Hurons to the Andastes, see Ragueneau, *Relation des Hurons, 1648*, 58–60.

who, having been captured when a boy, adopted and naturalized, had become more an Iroquois than the Iroquois themselves; and scarcely one of the fierce confederates had shed so
much Huron blood. When he reached the town of St. Ignace,
which he did about mid-summer, and delivered his messages
and wampum-belts, there was a great division of opinion
among the Hurons. The Bear Nation—the member of their
confederacy which was farthest from the Iroquois, and least
exposed to danger—was for rejecting overtures made by so
offensive an agency; but those of the Hurons who had suffered most were eager for peace at any price, and, after solemn deliberation, it was resolved to send an embassy in
return. At its head was placed a Christian chief named Jean
Baptiste Atironta; and on the first of August he and four others departed for Onondaga, carrying a profusion of presents,
and accompanied by the apostate envoy of the Iroquois. As
the ambassadors had to hunt on the way for subsistence, besides making canoes to cross Lake Ontario, it was twenty days
before they reached their destination. When they arrived,
there was great jubilation, and, for a full month, nothing but
councils. Having thus sifted the matter to the bottom, the
Onondagas determined at last to send another embassy with
Jean Baptiste on his return, and with them fifteen Huron prisoners, as an earnest of their good intentions, retaining, on
their part, one of Baptiste's colleagues as a hostage. This time
they chose for their envoy a chief of their own nation, named
Scandawati, a man of renown, sixty years of age, joining with
him two colleagues. The old Onondaga entered on his mission with a troubled mind. His anxiety was not so much for
his life as for his honor and dignity; for, while the Oneidas
and the Cayugas were acting in concurrence with the Onondagas, the Senecas had refused any part in the embassy, and
still breathed nothing but war. Would they, or still more the
Mohawks, so far forget the consideration due to one whose
name had been great in the councils of the League as to assault the Hurons while he was among them in the character
of an ambassador of his nation, whereby his honor would be
compromised and his life endangered? His mind brooded on
this idea, and he told one of his colleagues, that, if such a
slight were put upon him, he should die of mortification. "I

am not a dead dog," he said, "to be despised and forgotten. I am worthy that all men should turn their eyes on me while I am among enemies, and do nothing that may involve me in danger."

What with hunting, fishing, canoe-making, and bad weather, the progress of the august travellers was so slow, that they did not reach the Huron towns till the twenty-third of October. Scandawati presented seven large belts of wampum, each composed of three or four thousand beads, which the Jesuits call the pearls and diamonds of the country. He delivered, too, the fifteen captives, and promised a hundred more on the final conclusion of peace. The three Onondagas remained, as surety for the good faith of those who sent them, until the beginning of January, when the Hurons on their part sent six ambassadors to conclude the treaty, one of the Onondagas accompanying them. Soon there came dire tidings. The prophetic heart of the old chief had not deceived him. The Senecas and Mohawks, disregarding negotiations in which they had no part, and resolved to bring them to an end, were invading the country in force. It might be thought that the Hurons would take their revenge on the Onondaga envoys, now hostages among them; but they did not do so, for the character of an ambassador was, for the most part, held in respect. One morning, however, Scandawati had disappeared. They were full of excitement; for they thought that he had escaped to the enemy. They ranged the woods in search of him, and at length found him in a thicket near the town. He lay dead, on a bed of spruce-boughs which he had made, his throat deeply gashed with a knife. He had died by his own hand, a victim of mortified pride. "See," writes Father Ragueneau, "how much our Indians stand on the point of honor!"[1]

We have seen that one of his two colleagues had set out for Onondaga with a deputation of six Hurons. This party was met by a hundred Mohawks, who captured them all and killed the six Hurons, but spared the Onondaga, and compelled him to join them. Soon after, they made a sudden onset on about three hundred Hurons journeying through the

[1]This remarkable story is told by Ragueneau, *Relation des Hurons, 1648*, 56–58. He was present at the time, and knew all the circumstances.

forest from the town of St. Ignace; and, as many of them were women, they routed the whole, and took forty prisoners. The Onondaga bore part in the fray, and captured a Christian Huron girl; but the next day he insisted on returning to the Huron town. "Kill me, if you will," he said to the Mohawks, "but I cannot follow you; for then I should be ashamed to appear among my countrymen, who sent me on a message of peace to the Hurons; and I must die with them, sooner than seem to act as their enemy." On this, the Mohawks not only permitted him to go, but gave him the Huron girl whom he had taken; and the Onondaga led her back in safety to her countrymen.[1] Here, then, is a ray of light out of Egyptian darkness. The principle of honor was not extinct in these wild hearts.

We hear no more of the negotiations between the Onondagas and the Hurons. They and their results were swept away in the storm of events soon to be related.

[1] "Celuy qui l'auoit prise estoit Onnontaeronnon, qui estant icy en os tage à cause de la paix qui se traite auec les Onnontaeronnons, et s'estant trouué auec nos Hurons à cette chasse, y fut pris tout des premiers par les Sonnontoueronnons (*Annieronnons?*), qui l'ayans reconnu ne luy firent aucun mal, et mesme l'obligerent de les suiure et prendre part à leur victoire; et ainsi en ce rencontre cét Onnontaeronnon auoit fait sa prise, tellement neantmoins qu'il desira s'en retourner le lendemain, disant aux Sonnontoueronnons qu'ils le tuassent s'ils vouloient, mais qu'il ne pouuoit se resoudre à les suiure, et qu'il auroit honte de reparoistre en son pays, les affaires qui l'auoient amené aux Hurons pour la paix ne permettant pas qu'il fist autre chose que de mourir auec eux plus tost que de paroistre s'estre comporté en ennemy. Ainsi les Sonnontoueronnons luy permirent de s'en retourner et de ramener cette bonne Chrestienne, qui estoit sa captiue, laquelle nous a consolé par le recit des entretiens de ces pauures gens dans leur affliction."—Ragueneau, *Relation des Hurons, 1648,* 65.

Apparently the word *Sonnontoueronnons* (Senecas), in the above, should read *Annieronnons* (Mohawks); for, on pp. 50, 57, the writer twice speaks of the party as Mohawks.

Chapter XXIV

THE HURON CHURCH

*Hopes of the Mission • Christian and Heathen • Body and Soul •
Position of Proselytes • The Huron Girl's Visit to Heaven • A Crisis
• Huron Justice • Murder and Atonement • Hopes and Fears*

How did it fare with the missions in these days of woe
and terror? They had thriven beyond hope. The Hurons, in their time of trouble, had become tractable. They
humbled themselves, and, in their desolation and despair,
came for succor to the priests. There was a harvest of converts, not only exceeding in numbers that of all former years,
but giving in many cases undeniable proofs of sincerity and
fervor. In some towns the Christians outnumbered the
heathen, and in nearly all they formed a strong party. The
mission of La Conception, or Ossossané, was the most successful. Here there were now a church and one or more resident Jesuits,—as also at St. Joseph, St. Ignace, St. Michel,
and St. Jean Baptiste:[1] for we have seen that the Huron
towns were christened with names of saints. Each church had
its bell, which was sometimes hung in a neighboring tree.[2]
Every morning it rang its summons to mass; and, issuing
from their dwellings of bark, the converts gathered within the
sacred precinct, where the bare, rude walls, fresh from the axe
and saw, contrasted with the sheen of tinsel and gilding, and
the hues of gay draperies and gaudy pictures. At evening they
met again at prayers; and on Sunday, masses, confession, catechism, sermons, and repeating the rosary consumed the
whole day.[3]

These converts rarely took part in the burning of prisoners.

[1] Ragueneau, *Relation des Hurons, 1646,* 56.

[2] A fragment of one of these bells, found on the site of a Huron town, is
preserved in the museum of Huron relics at the Laval University, Quebec.
The bell was not large, but was of very elaborate workmanship. Before 1644
the Jesuits had used old copper kettles as a substitute.—*Lettre de Lalemant,
31 March, 1644.*

[3] Ragueneau, *Relation des Hurons, 1646,* 56.

On the contrary, they sometimes set their faces against the practice; and on one occasion, a certain Étienne Totiri, while his heathen countrymen were tormenting a captive Iroquois at St. Ignace, boldly denounced them, and promised them an eternity of flames and demons, unless they desisted. Not content with this, he addressed an exhortation to the sufferer in one of the intervals of his torture. The dying wretch demanded baptism, which Étienne took it upon himself to administer, amid the hootings of the crowd, who, as he ran with a cup of water from a neighboring house, pushed him to and fro to make him spill it, crying out, "Let him alone! Let the devils burn him after we have done!"[1]

In regard to these atrocious scenes, which formed the favorite Huron recreation of a summer night, the Jesuits, it must be confessed, did not quite come up to the requirements of modern sensibility. They were offended at them, it is true, and prevented them when they could; but they were wholly given to the saving of souls, and held the body in scorn, as the vile source of incalculable mischief, worthy the worst inflictions that could be put upon it. What were a few hours of suffering to an eternity of bliss or woe? If the victim were heathen, these brief pangs were but the faint prelude of an undying flame; and if a Christian, they were the fiery portal of Heaven. They might, indeed, be a blessing; since, accepted in atonement for sin, they would shorten the torments of Purgatory. Yet, while schooling themselves to despise the body, and all the pain or pleasure that pertained to it, the Fathers were emphatic on one point. It must not be eaten. In the matter of cannibalism, they were loud and vehement in invective.[2]

---

[1] *Ibid.*, 58. The Hurons often resisted the baptism of their prisoners, on the ground that Hell, and not Heaven, was the place to which they would have them go.—See Lalemant, *Relation des Hurons, 1642*, 60, Ragueneau, *Ibid.*, *1648*, 53, and several other passages.

[2] The following curious case of conversion at the stake, gravely related by Lalemant, is worth preserving.

"An Iroquois was to be burned at a town some way off. What consolation to set forth, in the hottest summer weather, to deliver this poor victim from the hell prepared for him! The Father approaches him, and instructs him even in the midst of his torments. Forthwith the Faith finds a place in his heart. He recognizes and adores, as the author of his life, Him whose name he had never heard till the hour of his death. He receives the grace of baptism, and

Undeniably, the Faith was making progress; yet it is not to be supposed that its path was a smooth one. The old opposition and the old calumnies were still alive and active. "It is *la prière* that kills us. Your books and your strings of beads have bewitched the country. Before you came, we were happy and prosperous. You are magicians. Your charms kill our corn, and bring sickness and the Iroquois. Echon (Brébeuf) is a traitor among us, in league with our enemies." Such discourse was still rife, openly and secretly.

The Huron who embraced the Faith renounced thenceforth, as we have seen, the feasts, dances, and games in which was his delight, since all these savored of diabolism. And if, being in health, he could not enjoy himself, so also, being sick, he could not be cured; for his physician was a sorcerer, whose medicines were charms and incantations. If the convert was a chief, his case was far worse; since, writes Father Lalemant, "to be a chief and a Christian is to combine water and fire; for the business of the chiefs is mainly to do the Devil's bidding, preside over ceremonies of hell, and excite the young Indians to dances, feasts, and shameless indecencies."[1]

It is not surprising, then, that proselytes were difficult to make, or that, being made, they often relapsed. The Jesuits complain that they had no means of controlling their converts, and coercing backsliders to stand fast; and they add, that the Iroquois, by destroying the fur-trade, had broken the principal bond between the Hurons and the French, and greatly weakened the influence of the mission.[2]

Among the slanders devised by the heathen party against

---

breathes nothing but heaven. . . . This newly made, but generous Christian, mounted on the scaffold which is the place of his torture, in the sight of a thousand spectators, who are at once his enemies, his judges, and his executioners, raises his eyes and his voice heavenward, and cries aloud, 'Sun, who art witness of my torments, hear my words! I am about to die; but, after my death, I shall go to dwell in heaven.' "—*Relation des Hurons, 1641*, 67.

The Sun, it will be remembered, was the god of the heathen Iroquois. The convert appealed to his old deity to rejoice with him in his happy future.

[1] *Relation des Hurons, 1642*, 89. The indecencies alluded to were chiefly naked dances, of a superstitious character, and the mystical cure called *Andacwandet*, before mentioned.

[2] *Lettre du P. Hierosme Lalemant*, appended to the *Relation* of 1645.

the teachers of the obnoxious doctrine was one which found wide credence, even among the converts, and produced a great effect. They gave out that a baptized Huron girl, who had lately died, and was buried in the cemetery at Sainte Marie, had returned to life, and given a deplorable account of the heaven of the French. No sooner had she entered,—such was the story,—than they seized her, chained her to a stake, and tormented her all day with inconceivable cruelty. They did the same to all the other converted Hurons; for this was the recreation of the French, and especially of the Jesuits, in their celestial abode. They baptized Indians with no other object than that they might have them to torment in heaven; to which end they were willing to meet hardships and dangers in this life, just as a war-party invades the enemy's country at great risk that it may bring home prisoners to burn. After her painful experience, an unknown friend secretly showed the girl a path down to the earth; and she hastened thither to warn her countrymen against the wiles of the missionaries.[1]

In the spring of 1648 the excitement of the heathen party reached a crisis. A young Frenchman, named Jacques Douart, in the service of the mission, going out at evening a short distance from the Jesuit house of Sainte Marie, was tomahawked by unknown Indians,[2] who proved to be two brothers, instigated by the heathen chiefs. A great commotion followed, and for a few days it seemed that the adverse parties would fall to blows, at a time when the common enemy threatened to destroy them both. But sager counsels prevailed. In view of the manifest strength of the Christians, the pagans lowered their tone; and it soon became apparent that it was the part of the Jesuits to insist boldly on satisfaction for the outrage. They made no demand that the murderers should be punished or surrendered, but, with their usual good sense in such matters, conformed to Indian usage, and required that the nation at large should make atonement for the crime by presents.[3] The number of these, their value, and

[1] Ragueneau, *Relation des Hurons, 1646*, 65.

[2] *Ibid.*, *1648*, 77. Compare *Lettre du P. Jean de Brébeuf au T.R.P. Vincent Carafa, Général de la Compagnie de Jésus, Sainte Marie, 2 Juin, 1648,* in Carayon.

[3] See Introduction.

the mode of delivering them were all fixed by ancient custom; and some of the converts, acting as counsel, advised the Fathers of every step it behooved them to take in a case of such importance. As this is the best illustration of Huron justice on record, it may be well to observe the method of procedure,—recollecting that the public, and not the criminal, was to pay the forfeit of the crime.

First of all, the Huron chiefs summoned the Jesuits to meet them at a grand council of the nation, when an old orator, chosen by the rest, rose and addressed Ragueneau, as chief of the French, in the following harangue. Ragueneau, who reports it, declares that he has added nothing to it, and the translation is as literal as possible.

"My Brother," began the speaker, "behold all the tribes of our league assembled!"—and he named them one by one. "We are but a handful; you are the prop and stay of this nation. A thunderbolt has fallen from the sky, and rent a chasm in the earth. We shall fall into it, if you do not support us. Take pity on us. We are here, not so much to speak as to weep over our loss and yours. Our country is but a skeleton, without flesh, veins, sinews, or arteries; and its bones hang together by a thread. This thread is broken by the blow that has fallen on the head of your nephew,[1] for whom we weep. It was a demon of Hell who placed the hatchet in the murderer's hand. Was it you, Sun, whose beams shine on us, who led him to do this deed? Why did you not darken your light, that he might be stricken with horror at his crime? Were you his accomplice? No; for he walked in darkness, and did not see where he struck. He thought, this wretched murderer, that he aimed at the head of a young Frenchman; but the blow fell upon his country, and gave it a death-wound. The earth opens to receive the blood of the innocent victim, and we shall be swallowed up in the chasm; for we are all guilty. The Iroquois rejoice at his death, and celebrate it as a triumph; for they see that our weapons are turned against each other, and know well that our nation is near its end.

"Brother, take pity on this nation. You alone can restore it

[1] The usual Indian figure in such cases, and not meant to express an actual relationship;—"Uncle" for a superior, "Brother" for an equal, "Nephew" for an inferior.

to life. It is for you to gather up all these scattered bones, and close this chasm that opens to ingulf us. Take pity on your country. I call it yours, for you are the master of it; and we came here like criminals to receive your sentence, if you will not show us mercy. Pity those who condemn themselves and come to ask forgiveness. It is you who have given strength to the nation by dwelling with it; and if you leave us, we shall be like a wisp of straw torn from the ground to be the sport of the wind. This country is an island drifting on the waves, for the first storm to overwhelm and sink. Make it fast again to its foundation, and posterity will never forget to praise you. When we first heard of this murder, we could do nothing but weep; and we are ready to receive your orders and comply with your demands. Speak, then, and ask what satisfaction you will, for our lives and our possessions are yours; and even if we rob our children to satisfy you, we will tell them that it is not of you that they have to complain, but of him whose crime has made us all guilty. Our anger is against him; but for you we feel nothing but love. He destroyed our lives; and you will restore them, if you will but speak and tell us what you will have us do."

Ragueneau, who remarks that this harangue is a proof that eloquence is the gift of Nature rather than of Art, made a reply, which he has not recorded, and then gave the speaker a bundle of small sticks, indicating the number of presents which he required in satisfaction for the murder. These sticks were distributed among the various tribes in the council, in order that each might contribute its share towards the indemnity. The council dissolved, and the chiefs went home, each with his allotment of sticks, to collect in his village a corresponding number of presents. There was no constraint; those gave who chose to do so; but, as all were ambitious to show their public spirit, the contributions were ample. No one thought of molesting the murderers. Their punishment was their shame at the sacrifices which the public were making in their behalf.

The presents being ready, a day was set for the ceremony of their delivery; and crowds gathered from all parts to witness it. The assembly was convened in the open air, in a field beside the mission-house of Sainte Marie; and, in the midst, the chiefs held solemn council. Towards evening, they deputed four of their number, two Christians and two heathen, to carry their address to the Father Superior. They came, loaded with presents; but these were merely preliminary. One was to open the door, another for leave to enter; and as Sainte Marie was a large house, with several interior doors, at each one of which it behooved them to repeat this formality, their stock of gifts became seriously reduced before they reached the room where Father Ragueneau awaited them. On arriving, they made him a speech, every clause of which was confirmed by a present. The first was to wipe away his tears; the second, to restore his voice, which his grief was supposed to have impaired; the third, to calm the agitation of his mind; and the fourth, to allay the just anger of his heart.[1] These gifts consisted of wampum and the large shells of which it was made, together with other articles, worthless in any eyes but those of an Indian. Nine additional presents followed: four for the four posts of the sepulchre or scaffold of the murdered man; four for the cross-pieces which connected the posts; and one for a pillow to support his head. Then came eight more, corresponding to the eight largest bones of the victim's body, and also to the eight clans of the Hurons.[2] Ragueneau, as required by established custom, now made them a present in his turn. It consisted of three thousand beads of wampum, and was designed to soften the earth, in order that they might not be hurt, when falling upon it, overpowered by his reproaches for the enormity of their crime. This closed the interview, and the deputation withdrew.

The grand ceremony took place on the next day. A kind of arena had been prepared, and here were hung the fifty presents in which the atonement essentially consisted,—the rest, amounting to as many more, being only accessory.[3] The Jesuits had the right of examining them all, rejecting any that

---

[1] Ragueneau himself describes the scene. *Relation des Hurons, 1648*, 80.

[2] Ragueneau says, "les huit nations"; but, as the Hurons consisted of only four, or at most five, nations, he probably means the clans. For the nature of these divisions, see Introduction.

[3] The number was unusually large,—partly because the affair was thought very important, and partly because the murdered man belonged to another nation. See Introduction.

did not satisfy them, and demanding others in place of them. The naked crowd sat silent and attentive, while the orator in the midst delivered the fifty presents in a series of harangues, which the tired listener has not thought it necessary to preserve. Then came the minor gifts, each with its signification explained in turn by the speaker. First, as a sepulchre had been provided the day before for the dead man, it was now necessary to clothe and equip him for his journey to the next world; and to this end three presents were made. They represented a hat, a coat, a shirt, breeches, stockings, shoes, a gun, powder, and bullets; but they were in fact something quite different, as wampum, beaver-skins, and the like. Next came several gifts to close up the wounds of the slain. Then followed three more. The first closed the chasm in the earth, which had burst through horror of the crime. The next trod the ground firm, that it might not open again; and here the whole assembly rose and danced, as custom required. The last placed a large stone over the closed gulf, to make it doubly secure.

Now came another series of presents, seven in number,— to restore the voices of all the missionaries,—to invite the men in their service to forget the murder,—to appease the Governor when he should hear of it,—to light the fire at Sainte Marie,—to open the gate,—to launch the ferry-boat in which the Huron visitors crossed the river,—and to give back the paddle to the boy who had charge of the boat. The Fathers, it seems, had the right of exacting two more presents, to rebuild their house and church,—supposed to have been shaken to the earth by the late calamity; but they forbore to urge the claim. Last of all were three gifts to confirm all the rest, and to entreat the Jesuits to cherish an undying love for the Hurons.

The priests on their part gave presents, as tokens of goodwill; and with that the assembly dispersed. The mission had gained a triumph, and its influence was greatly strengthened. The future would have been full of hope, but for the portentous cloud of war that rose, black and wrathful, from where lay the dens of the Iroquois.

Chapter XXV

1648, 1649

SAINTE MARIE

The Centre of the Missions • Fort • Convent • Hospital •
Caravansary • Church • The Inmates of Sainte Marie •
Domestic Economy • Missions • A Meeting of Jesuits • The
Dead Missionary

THE River Wye enters the Bay of Glocester, an inlet of the
Bay of Matchedash, itself an inlet of the vast Georgian
Bay of Lake Huron. Retrace the track of two centuries and
more, and ascend this little stream in the summer of the year
1648. Your vessel is a birch canoe, and your conductor a Huron Indian. On the right hand and on the left, gloomy and
silent, rise the primeval woods; but you have advanced
scarcely half a league when the scene is changed, and cultivated fields, planted chiefly with maize, extend far along the
bank, and back to the distant verge of the forest. Before you
opens the small lake from which the stream issues; and on
your left, a stone's throw from the shore, rises a range of
palisades and bastioned walls, inclosing a number of buildings. Your canoe enters a canal or ditch immediately above
them, and you land at the Mission, or Residence, or Fort of
Sainte Marie.

Here was the centre and base of the Huron missions; and
now, for once, one must wish that Jesuit pens had been more
fluent. They have told us but little of Sainte Marie, and even
this is to be gathered chiefly from incidental allusions. In the
forest, which long since has resumed its reign over this memorable spot, the walls and ditches of the fortifications may still
be plainly traced; and the deductions from these remains are
in perfect accord with what we can gather from the *Relations*
and letters of the priests.[1] The fortified work which inclosed
the buildings was in the form of a parallelogram, about a
hundred and seventy-five feet long, and from eighty to ninety
wide. It lay parallel with the river, and somewhat more than

[1] Before me is an elaborate plan of the remains, taken on the spot.

a hundred feet distant from it. On two sides it was a continuous wall of masonry,[1] flanked with square bastions, adapted
to musketry, and probably used as magazines, storehouses, or
lodgings. The sides towards the river and the lake had no
other defences than a ditch and palisade, flanked, like the others, by bastions, over each of which was displayed a large
cross.[2] The buildings within were, no doubt, of wood; and
they included a church, a kitchen, a refectory, places of retreat
for religious instruction and meditation,[3] and lodgings for at
least sixty persons. Near the church, but outside the fortification, was a cemetery. Beyond the ditch or canal which opened
on the river was a large area, still traceable, in the form of an
irregular triangle, surrounded by a ditch, and apparently by
palisades. It seems to have been meant for the protection of
the Indian visitors who came in throngs to Sainte Marie, and
who were lodged in a large house of bark, after the Huron
manner.[4] Here, perhaps, was also the hospital, which was
placed without the walls, in order that Indian women, as well
as men, might be admitted into it.[5]

No doubt the buildings of Sainte Marie were of the roughest,—rude walls of boards, windows without glass, vast
chimneys of unhewn stone. All its riches were centred in the
church, which, as Lalemant tells us, was regarded by the Indians as one of the wonders of the world, but which, he adds,
would have made but a beggarly show in France. Yet one
wonders, at first thought, how so much labor could have been

---

[1] It seems probable that the walls, of which the remains may still be traced,
were foundations supporting a wooden superstructure. Ragueneau, in a letter
to the General of the Jesuits, dated March 13, 1650, alludes to the defences of
Saint Marie as "*une simple palissade.*"

[2] "Quatre grandes Croix qui sont aux quatre coins de nostre enclos."—
Ragueneau, *Relation des Hurons, 1648*, 81.

[3] It seems that these places, besides those for the priests, were of two
kinds,—"vne retraite pour les pelerins (*Indians*), enfin vn lieu plus separé, où
les infideles, qui n'y sont admis que de iour au passage, y puissent tousiours
receuoir quelque bon mot pour leur salut."—Lalemant, *Relation des Hurons,
1644*, 74.

[4] At least it was so in 1642. "Nous leur auons dressé vn Hospice ou Cabane
d'écorce."—*Ibid., 1642*, 57.

[5] "Cet hospital est tellement separé de nostre demeure, que non seulement
les hommes et enfans, mais les femmes y peuuent estre admises."—*Ibid., 1644*,
74.

accomplished here. Of late years, however, the number of men at the command of the mission had been considerable. Soldiers had been sent up from time to time, to escort the Fathers on their way, and defend them on their arrival. Thus, in 1644, Montmagny ordered twenty men of a reinforcement just arrived from France to escort Brébeuf, Garreau, and Chabanel to the Hurons, and remain there during the winter.[1] These soldiers lodged with the Jesuits, and lived at their table.[2] It was not, however, on detachments of troops that they mainly relied for labor or defence. Any inhabitant of Canada who chose to undertake so hard and dangerous a service was allowed to do so, receiving only his maintenance from the mission, without pay. In return, he was allowed to trade with the Indians, and sell the furs thus obtained at the magazine of the Company, at a fixed price.[3] Many availed themselves of this permission; and all whose services were accepted by the Jesuits seem to have been men to whom they had communicated no small portion of their own zeal, and who were enthusiastically attached to their Order and their cause. There is abundant evidence that a large proportion of them acted from motives wholly disinterested. They were, in fact, *donnés* of the mission,[4] — given, heart and hand, to its service. There is probability in the conjecture, that the profits of their trade with the Indians were reaped, not for their own behoof, but for that of the mission.[5] It is difficult otherwise to explain the

[1] Vimont, *Relation, 1644*, 49. He adds, that some of these soldiers, though they had once been "assez mauvais garçons," had shown great zeal and devotion in behalf of the mission.

[2] *Journal des Supérieurs des Jésuites*, MS. In 1648, a small cannon was sent to Sainte Marie in the Huron canoes. — *Ibid.*

[3] *Registres des Arrêts du Conseil*, extract in Faillon, II. 94.

[4] See *ante*, p. 550. Garnier calls them "séculiers d'habit, mais religieux de cœur." — *Lettres*, MSS.

[5] The Jesuits, even at this early period, were often and loudly charged with sharing in the fur-trade. It is certain that this charge was not wholly without foundation. Le Jeune, in the *Relation* of 1657, speaking of the wampum, guns, powder, lead, hatchets, kettles, and other articles which the missionaries were obliged to give to the Indians, at councils and elsewhere, says that these must be bought from the traders with beaver-skins, which are the money of the country; and he adds, "Que si vn Iesuite en reçoit ou en recueille quelques-vns pour ayder aux frais immenses qu'il faut faire dans ces Missions si éloignées, et pour gagner ces peuples à Iesus-Christ et les porter à la paix, il seroit

confidence with which the Father Superior, in a letter to the
General of the Jesuits at Rome, speaks of its resources. He
says, "Though our number is greatly increased, and though
we still hope for more men, and especially for more priests of
our Society, it is not necessary to increase the pecuniary aid
given us."[1]

Much of this prosperity was no doubt due to the excellent
management of their resources, and a very successful agriculture. While the Indians around them were starving, they
raised maize in such quantities, that, in the spring of 1649, the
Father Superior thought that their stock of provisions might
suffice for three years. "Hunting and fishing," he says, "are
better than heretofore"; and he adds, that they had fowls,
swine, and even cattle.[2] How they could have brought these
last to Sainte Marie it is difficult to conceive. The feat, under
the circumstances, is truly astonishing. Everything indicates a
fixed resolve on the part of the Fathers to build up a solid
and permanent establishment.

It is by no means to be inferred that the household fared
sumptuously. Their ordinary food was maize, pounded and

à souhaiter que ceux-là mesme qui deuroient faire ces despenses pour la con-
seruation du pays, ne fussent pas du moins les premiers à condamner le zele
de ces Peres, et à les rendre par leurs discours plus noirs que leurs robes."—
Relation, 1657, 16.

In the same year, Chaumonot, addressing a council of the Iroquois during
a period of truce, said, "Keep your beaver-skins, if you choose, for the Dutch.
Even such of them as may fall into our possession will be employed for your
service."—*Ibid.*, 17.

In 1636, Le Jeune thought it necessary to write a long letter of defence
against the charge; and in 1643, a declaration, appended to the *Relation* of
that year, and certifying that the Jesuits took no part in the fur-trade, was
drawn up and signed by twelve members of the Company of New France.
Its only meaning is, that the Jesuits were neither partners nor rivals of the
Company's monopoly. They certainly bought supplies from its magazines
with furs which they obtained from the Indians.

Their object evidently was to make the mission partially self-supporting.
To impute mercenary motives to Garnier, Jogues, and their co-laborers, is
manifestly idle; but, even in the highest flights of his enthusiasm, the Jesuit
never forgot his worldly wisdom.

[1] *Lettre du P. Paul Ragueneau au T.R.P. Vincent Carafa, Général de la
Compagnie de Jésus à Rome, Sainte Marie aux Hurons, 1 Mars, 1649* (Carayon).
[2] *Ibid.*

boiled, and seasoned, in the absence of salt, which was regarded as a luxury, with morsels of smoked fish.[1]

In March, 1649, there were in the Huron country and its
neighborhood eighteen Jesuit priests, four lay brothers,
twenty-three men serving without pay, seven hired men, four
boys, and eight soldiers.[2] Of this number, fifteen priests were
engaged in the various missions, while all the rest were retained permanently at Sainte Marie. All was method, discipline, and subordination. Some of the men were assigned to
household work, and some to the hospital; while the rest labored at the fortifications, tilled the fields, and stood ready,
in case of need, to fight the Iroquois. The Father Superior,
with two other priests as assistants, controlled and guided all.
The remaining Jesuits, undisturbed by temporal cares, were
devoted exclusively to the charge of their respective missions.
Two or three times in the year, they all, or nearly all, assembled at Sainte Marie, to take counsel together and determine
their future action. Hither, also, they came at intervals for a
period of meditation and prayer, to nerve themselves and gain
new inspiration for their stern task.

Besides being the citadel and the magazine of the mission,
Sainte Marie was the scene of a bountiful hospitality. On
every alternate Saturday, as well as on feast-days, the converts
came in crowds from the farthest villages. They were entertained during Saturday, Sunday, and a part of Monday; and
the rites of the Church were celebrated before them with all
possible solemnity and pomp. They were welcomed also at
other times, and entertained, usually with three meals to each.
In these latter years the prevailing famine drove them to
Sainte Marie in swarms. In the course of 1647 three thousand
were lodged and fed here; and in the following year the number was doubled.[3] Heathen Indians were also received and
supplied with food, but were not permitted to remain at

---

[1] Ragueneau, *Relation des Hurons, 1648*, 48.

[2] See the report of the Father Superior to the General, above cited. The
number was greatly increased within the year. In April, 1648, Ragueneau
reports but forty-two French in all, including priests. Before the end of the
summer a large reinforcement came up in the Huron canoes.

[3] Compare Ragueneau in *Relation des Hurons, 1648*, 48, and in his report to
the General in 1649.

night. There was provision for the soul as well as the body; and, Christian or heathen, few left Sainte Marie without a word of instruction or exhortation. Charity was an instrument of conversion.

Such, so far as we can reconstruct it from the scattered hints remaining, was this singular establishment, at once military, monastic, and patriarchal. The missions of which it was the basis were now eleven in number. To those among the Hurons already mentioned another had lately been added,—that of Sainte Madeleine; and two others, called St. Jean and St. Matthias, had been established in the neighboring Tobacco Nation.[1] The three remaining missions were all among tribes speaking the Algonquin languages. Every winter, bands of these savages, driven by famine and fear of the Iroquois, sought harborage in the Huron country, and the mission of Sainte Elisabeth was established for their benefit. The next Algonquin mission was that of Saint Esprit, embracing the Nipissings and other tribes east and north-east of Lake Huron; and, lastly, the mission of St. Pierre included the tribes at the outlet of Lake Superior, and throughout a vast extent of surrounding wilderness.[2]

These missions were more laborious, though not more perilous, than those among the Hurons. The Algonquin hordes were never long at rest; and, summer and winter, the priest must follow them by lake, forest, and stream: in summer plying the paddle all day, or toiling through pathless thickets, bending under the weight of a birch canoe or a load of baggage,—at night, his bed the rugged earth, or some bare rock,

[1] The mission of the Neutral Nation had been abandoned for the time, from the want of missionaries. The Jesuits had resolved on concentration, and on the thorough conversion of the Hurons, as a preliminary to more extended efforts.

[2] Besides these tribes, the Jesuits had become more or less acquainted with many others, also Algonquin, on the west and south of Lake Huron; as well as with the Puans, or Winnebagoes, a Dacotah tribe between Lake Michigan and the Mississippi.

The Mission of Sault Sainte Marie, at the outlet of Lake Superior, was established at a later period. Modern writers have confounded it with Sainte Marie of the Hurons.

By the *Relation* of 1649 it appears that another mission had lately been begun at the Grand Manitoulin Island, which the Jesuits also christened Isle Sainte Marie.

lashed by the restless waves of Lake Huron; while famine, the
snow-storms, the cold, the treacherous ice of the Great Lakes,
smoke, filth, and, not rarely, threats and persecution, were the
lot of his winter wanderings. It seemed an earthly paradise,
when, at long intervals, he found a respite from his toils
among his brother Jesuits under the roof of Sainte Marie.

Hither, while the Fathers are gathered from their scattered
stations at one of their periodical meetings, — a little before
the season of Lent, 1649,[1] — let us, too, repair, and join them.
We enter at the eastern gate of the fortification, midway in
the wall between its northern and southern bastions, and pass
to the hall, where, at a rude table, spread with ruder fare, all
the household are assembled, — laborers, domestics, soldiers,
and priests.

It was a scene that might recall a remote half feudal, half
patriarchal age, when, under the smoky rafters of his antique
hall, some warlike thane sat, with kinsmen and dependants
ranged down the long board, each in his degree. Here,
doubtless, Ragueneau, the Father Superior, held the place of
honor; and, for chieftains scarred with Danish battle-axes,
was seen a band of thoughtful men, clad in a threadbare garb
of black, their brows swarthy from exposure, yet marked with
the lines of intellect and a fixed enthusiasm of purpose. Here
was Bressani, scarred with firebrand and knife; Chabanel,
once a professor of rhetoric in France, now a missionary,
bound by a self-imposed vow to a life from which his nature
recoiled; the fanatical Chaumonot, whose character savored
of his peasant birth, — for the grossest fungus of superstition
that ever grew under the shadow of Rome was not too much
for his omnivorous credulity, and miracles and mysteries were
his daily food; yet, such as his faith was, he was ready to die
for it. Garnier, beardless like a woman, was of a far finer nature. His religion was of the affections and the sentiments;
and his imagination, warmed with the ardor of his faith,
shaped the ideal forms of his worship into visible realities.
Brébeuf sat conspicuous among his brethren, portly and tall,
his short moustache and beard grizzled with time, — for he
was fifty-six years old. If he seemed impassive, it was because

---

[1] The date of this meeting is a supposition merely. It is adopted with reference to events which preceded and followed.

one overmastering principle had merged and absorbed all the impulses of his nature and all the faculties of his mind. The enthusiasm which with many is fitful and spasmodic was with him the current of his life,—solemn and deep as the tide of destiny. The Divine Trinity, the Virgin, the Saints, Heaven and Hell, Angels and Fiends,—to him, these alone were real, and all things else were nought. Gabriel Lalemant, nephew of Jerome Lalemant, Superior at Quebec, was Brébeuf's colleague at the mission of St. Ignace. His slender frame and delicate features gave him an appearance of youth, though he had reached middle life; and, as in the case of Garnier, the fervor of his mind sustained him through exertions of which he seemed physically incapable. Of the rest of that company little has come down to us but the bare record of their missionary toils; and we may ask in vain what youthful enthusiasm, what broken hope or faded dream, turned the current of their lives, and sent them from the heart of civilization to this savage outpost of the world.

No element was wanting in them for the achievement of such a success as that to which they aspired,—neither a transcendent zeal, nor a matchless discipline, nor a practical sagacity very seldom surpassed in the pursuits where men strive for wealth and place; and if they were destined to disappointment, it was the result of external causes, against which no power of theirs could have insured them.

There was a gap in their number. The place of Antoine Daniel was empty, and never more to be filled by him,—never at least in the flesh: for Chaumonot averred, that not long since, when the Fathers were met in council, he had seen their dead companion seated in their midst, as of old, with a countenance radiant and majestic.[1] They believed his story,—

---

[1] "Ce bon Pere s'apparut aprés sa mort à vn des nostres par deux diuerses fois. En l'vne il se fit voir en estat de gloire, portant le visage d'vn homme d'enuiron trente ans, quoy qu'il soit mort en l'âge de quarante-huict. . . . Vne autre fois il fut veu assister à vne assemblée que nous tenions," etc.—Ragueneau, *Relation des Hurons, 1649,* 5.

"Le P. Chaumonot vit au milieu de l'assemblée le P. Daniel qui aidait les Pères de ses conseils, et les remplissait d'une force surnaturelle; son visage était plein de majesté et d'éclat."—Ibid., *Lettre au Général de la Compagnie de Jésus* (Carayon, 243).

"Le P. Chaumonot nous a quelque fois raconté, à la gloire de cet illustre

no doubt he believed it himself; and they consoled one another with the thought, that, in losing their colleague on
earth, they had gained him as a powerful intercessor in
heaven. Daniel's station had been at St. Joseph; but the mission and the missionary had alike ceased to exist.

confesseur de J.C. (*Daniel*) qu'il s'étoit fait voir à lui dans la gloire, à l'âge
d'environ 30 ans, quoiqu'il en eut près de 50, et avec les autres circonstances
qui se trouuent là (*in the Historia Canadensis of Du Creux*). Il ajoutait seulement qu'à la vue de ce bien-heureux tant de choses lui vinrent à l'esprit pour
les lui demander, qu'il ne savoit pas où commencer son entretien avec ce cher
défunt. Enfin, lui dit-il: 'Apprenez moi, mon Père, ce que ie dois faire pour
être bien agréable à Dieu.'—'Jamais,' répondit le martyr, 'ne perdez le sou-
venir de vos péchés.' "—*Suite de la Vie de Chaumonot*, II.

Chapter XXVI

1648

ANTOINE DANIEL

*Huron Traders • Battle at Three Rivers • St. Joseph • Onset of
the Iroquois • Death of Daniel • The Town Destroyed*

I N the summer of 1647 the Hurons dared not go down to
the French settlements, but in the following year they took
heart, and resolved at all risks to make the attempt; for the
kettles, hatchets, and knives of the traders had become necessaries of life. Two hundred and fifty of their best warriors
therefore embarked, under five valiant chiefs. They made the
voyage in safety, approached Three Rivers on the seventeenth
of July, and, running their canoes ashore among the bulrushes, began to grease their hair, paint their faces, and otherwise adorn themselves, that they might appear after a
befitting fashion at the fort. While they were thus engaged,
the alarm was sounded. Some of their warriors had discovered a large body of Iroquois, who for several days had been
lurking in the forest, unknown to the French garrison, watching their opportunity to strike a blow. The Hurons snatched
their arms, and, half-greased and painted, ran to meet them.
The Iroquois received them with a volley. They fell flat to
avoid the shot, then leaped up with a furious yell, and sent
back a shower of arrows and bullets. The Iroquois, who were
outnumbered, gave way and fled, excepting a few who for a
time made fight with their knives. The Hurons pursued.
Many prisoners were taken, and many dead left on the field.[1]
The rout of the enemy was complete; and when their trade
was ended, the Hurons returned home in triumph, decorated
with the laurels and the scalps of victory. As it proved, it
would have been well, had they remained there to defend
their families and firesides.

The oft-mentioned town of Teanaustayé, or St. Joseph, lay
on the south-eastern frontier of the Huron country, near the

---

[1]Lalemant, *Relation, 1648*, 11. The Jesuit Bressani had come down with the
Hurons, and was with them in the fight.

foot of a range of forest-covered hills, and about fifteen miles from Sainte Marie. It had been the chief town of the nation, and its population, by the Indian standard, was still large; for it had four hundred families, and at least two thousand inhabitants. It was well fortified with palisades, after the Huron manner, and was esteemed the chief bulwark of the country. Here countless Iroquois had been burned and devoured. Its people had been truculent and intractable heathen, but many of them had surrendered to the Faith, and for four years past Father Daniel had preached among them with excellent results.

On the morning of the fourth of July, when the forest around basked lazily in the early sun, you might have mounted the rising ground on which the town stood, and passed unchallenged through the opening in the palisade. Within, you would have seen the crowded dwellings of bark, shaped like the arched coverings of huge baggage-wagons, and decorated with the *totems* or armorial devices of their owners daubed on the outside with paint. Here some squalid wolfish dog lay sleeping in the sun, a group of Huron girls chatted together in the shade, old squaws pounded corn in large wooden mortars, idle youths gambled with cherry-stones on a wooden platter, and naked infants crawled in the dust. Scarcely a warrior was to be seen. Some were absent in quest of game or of Iroquois scalps, and some had gone with the trading-party to the French settlements. You followed the foul passage-ways among the houses, and at length came to the church. It was full to the door. Daniel had just finished the mass, and his flock still knelt at their devotions. It was but the day before that he had returned to them, warmed with new fervor, from his meditations in retreat at Sainte Marie. Suddenly an uproar of voices, shrill with terror, burst upon the languid silence of the town. "The Iroquois! the Iroquois!" A crowd of hostile warriors had issued from the forest, and were rushing across the clearing, towards the opening in the palisade. Daniel ran out of the church, and hurried to the point of danger. Some snatched weapons; some rushed to and fro in the madness of a blind panic. The priest rallied the defenders; promised Heaven to those who died for their homes and their faith; then hastened from house to house, calling on unbelievers to repent and receive baptism, to snatch them from the Hell that yawned to ingulf them. They crowded around him, imploring to be saved; and, immersing his handkerchief in a bowl of water, he shook it over them, and baptized them by aspersion. They pursued him, as he ran again to the church, where he found a throng of women, children, and old men, gathered as in a sanctuary. Some cried for baptism, some held out their children to receive it, some begged for absolution, and some wailed in terror and despair. "Brothers," he exclaimed again and again, as he shook the baptismal drops from his handkerchief,—"brothers, to-day we shall be in Heaven."

The fierce yell of the war-whoop now rose close at hand. The palisade was forced, and the enemy was in the town. The air quivered with the infernal din. "Fly!" screamed the priest, driving his flock before him. "I will stay here. We shall meet again in Heaven." Many of them escaped through an opening in the palisade opposite to that by which the Iroquois had entered; but Daniel would not follow, for there still might be souls to rescue from perdition. The hour had come for which he had long prepared himself. In a moment he saw the Iroquois, and came forth from the church to meet them. When they saw him in turn, radiant in the vestments of his office, confronting them with a look kindled with the inspiration of martyrdom, they stopped and stared in amazement; then recovering themselves, bent their bows, and showered him with a volley of arrows, that tore through his robes and his flesh. A gunshot followed; the ball pierced his heart, and he fell dead, gasping the name of Jesus. They rushed upon him with yells of triumph, stripped him naked, gashed and hacked his lifeless body, and, scooping his blood in their hands, bathed their faces in it to make them brave. The town was in a blaze; when the flames reached the church, they flung the priest into it, and both were consumed together.[1]

Teanaustayé was a heap of ashes, and the victors took up

---

[1] Ragueneau, *Relation des Hurons, 1649*, 3–5; Bressani, *Relation Abrégée*, 247; Du Creux, *Historia Canadensis*, 524; Tanner, *Societas Jesu Militans*, 531; Marie de l'Incarnation, *Lettre aux Ursulines de Tours, Quebec, 1649*.

Daniel was born at Dieppe, and was forty-eight years old at the time of his death. He had been a Jesuit from the age of twenty.

their march with a train of nearly seven hundred prisoners, many of whom they killed on the way. Many more had been slain in the town and the neighboring forest, where the pursuers hunted them down, and where women, crouching for refuge among thickets, were betrayed by the cries and wailing of their infants.

The triumph of the Iroquois did not end here; for a neighboring fortified town, included within the circle of Daniel's mission, shared the fate of Teanaustayé. Never had the Huron nation received such a blow.

RUIN OF THE HURONS

St. Louis on Fire • Invasion • St. Ignace captured • Brébeuf and Lalemant • Battle at St. Louis • Sainte Marie threatened • Renewed Fighting • Desperate Conflict • A Night of Suspense • Panic among the Victors • Burning of St. Ignace • Retreat of the Iroquois

MORE than eight months had passed since the catastrophe of St. Joseph. The winter was over, and that dreariest of seasons had come, the churlish forerunner of spring. Around Sainte Marie the forests were gray and bare, and, in the cornfields, the oozy, half-thawed soil, studded with the sodden stalks of the last autumn's harvest, showed itself in patches through the melting snow.

At nine o'clock on the morning of the sixteenth of March, the priests saw a heavy smoke rising over the naked forest towards the south-east, about three miles distant. They looked at each other in dismay. "The Iroquois! They are burning St. Louis!" Flames mingled with the smoke; and, as they stood gazing, two Christian Hurons came, breathless and aghast, from the burning town. Their worst fear was realized. The Iroquois were there; but where were the priests of the mission, Brébeuf and Lalemant?

Late in the autumn, a thousand Iroquois, chiefly Senecas and Mohawks, had taken the war-path for the Hurons. They had been all winter in the forests, hunting for subsistence, and moving at their leisure towards their prey. The destruction of the two towns of the mission of St. Joseph had left a wide gap, and in the middle of March they entered the heart of the Huron country, undiscovered. Common vigilance and common sense would have averted the calamities that followed; but the Hurons were like a doomed people, stupefied, sunk in dejection, fearing everything, yet taking no measures for defence. They could easily have met the invaders with double their force, but the besotted warriors lay idle in their towns, or hunted at leisure in distant forests; nor could the Jesuits, by counsel or exhortation, rouse them to face the danger.

Before daylight of the sixteenth, the invaders approached St. Ignace, which, with St. Louis and three other towns, formed the mission of the same name. They reconnoitred the place in the darkness. It was defended on three sides by a deep ravine, and further strengthened by palisades fifteen or sixteen feet high, planted under the direction of the Jesuits. On the fourth side it was protected by palisades alone; and these were left, as usual, unguarded. This was not from a sense of security; for the greater part of the population had abandoned the town, thinking it too much exposed to the enemy, and there remained only about four hundred, chiefly women, children, and old men, whose infatuated defenders were absent hunting, or on futile scalping-parties against the Iroquois. It was just before dawn, when a yell, as of a legion of devils, startled the wretched inhabitants from their sleep; and the Iroquois, bursting in upon them, cut them down with knives and hatchets, killing many, and reserving the rest for a worse fate. They had entered by the weakest side; on the other sides there was no exit, and only three Hurons escaped. The whole was the work of a few minutes. The Iroquois left a guard to hold the town, and secure the retreat of the main body in case of a reverse; then, smearing their faces with blood, after their ghastly custom, they rushed, in the dim light of the early dawn, towards St. Louis, about a league distant.

The three fugitives had fled, half naked, through the forest, for the same point, which they reached about sunrise, yelling the alarm. The number of inhabitants here was less, at this time, than seven hundred; and, of these, all who had strength to escape, excepting about eighty warriors, made in wild terror for a place of safety. Many of the old, sick, and decrepit were left perforce in the lodges. The warriors, ignorant of the strength of the assailants, sang their war-songs, and resolved to hold the place to the last. It had not the natural strength of St. Ignace; but, like it, was surrounded by palisades.

Here were the two Jesuits, Brébeuf and Lalemant. Brébeuf's converts entreated him to escape with them; but the Norman zealot, bold scion of a warlike stock, had no thought of flight. His post was in the teeth of danger, to cheer on those who fought, and open Heaven to those who fell. His colleague, slight of frame and frail of constitution, trembled despite himself; but deep enthusiasm mastered the weakness of Nature, and he, too, refused to fly.

Scarcely had the sun risen, and scarcely were the fugitives gone, when, like a troop of tigers, the Iroquois rushed to the assault. Yell echoed yell, and shot answered shot. The Hurons, brought to bay, fought with the utmost desperation, and with arrows, stones, and the few guns they had, killed thirty of their assailants, and wounded many more. Twice the Iroquois recoiled, and twice renewed the attack with unabated ferocity. They swarmed at the foot of the palisades, and hacked at them with their hatchets, till they had cut them through at several different points. For a time there was a deadly fight at these breaches. Here were the two priests, promising Heaven to those who died for their faith,—one giving baptism, and the other absolution. At length the Iroquois broke in, and captured all the surviving defenders, the Jesuits among the rest. They set the town on fire; and the helpless wretches who had remained, unable to fly, were consumed in their burning dwellings. Next they fell upon Brébeuf and Lalemant, stripped them, bound them fast, and led them with the other prisoners back to St. Ignace, where all turned out to wreak their fury on the two priests, beating them savagely with sticks and clubs as they drove them into the town. At present, there was no time for further torture, for there was work in hand.

The victors divided themselves into several bands, to burn the neighboring villages and hunt their flying inhabitants. In the flush of their triumph, they meditated a bolder enterprise; and, in the afternoon, their chiefs sent small parties to reconnoitre Sainte Marie, with a view to attacking it on the next day.

Meanwhile the fugitives of St. Louis, joined by other bands as terrified and as helpless as they, were struggling through the soft snow which clogged the forests towards Lake Huron, where the treacherous ice of spring was still unmelted. One fear expelled another. They ventured upon it, and pushed forward all that day and all the following night, shivering and famished, to find refuge in the towns of the Tobacco Nation. Here, when they arrived, they spread a universal panic.

Ragueneau, Bressani, and their companions waited in suspense at Sainte Marie. On the one hand, they trembled for Brébeuf and Lalemant; on the other, they looked hourly for an attack: and when at evening they saw the Iroquois scouts prowling along the edge of the bordering forest, their fears were confirmed. They had with them about forty Frenchmen, well armed; but their palisades and wooden buildings were not fire-proof, and they had learned from fugitives the number and ferocity of the invaders. They stood guard all night, praying to the Saints, and above all to their great patron, Saint Joseph, whose festival was close at hand.

In the morning they were somewhat relieved by the arrival of about three hundred Huron warriors, chiefly converts from La Conception and Sainte Madeleine, tolerably well armed, and full of fight. They were expecting others to join them; and meanwhile, dividing into several bands, they took post by the passes of the neighboring forest, hoping to waylay parties of the enemy. Their expectation was fulfilled; for, at this time, two hundred of the Iroquois were making their way from St. Ignace, in advance of the main body, to begin the attack on Sainte Marie. They fell in with a band of the Hurons, set upon them, killed many, drove the rest to headlong flight, and, as they plunged in terror through the snow, chased them within sight of Sainte Marie. The other Hurons, hearing the yells and firing, ran to the rescue, and attacked so fiercely, that the Iroquois in turn were routed, and ran for shelter to St. Louis, followed closely by the victors. The houses of the town had been burned, but the palisade around them was still standing, though breached and broken. The Iroquois rushed in; but the Hurons were at their heels. Many of the fugitives were captured, the rest killed or put to utter rout, and the triumphant Hurons remained masters of the place.

The Iroquois who escaped fled to St. Ignace. Here, or on the way thither, they found the main body of the invaders; and when they heard of the disaster, the whole swarm, beside themselves with rage, turned towards St. Louis to take their revenge. Now ensued one of the most furious Indian battles on record. The Hurons within the palisade did not much exceed a hundred and fifty; for many had been killed or disabled, and many, perhaps, had straggled away. Most of their enemies had guns, while they had but few. Their weapons were bows and arrows, war-clubs, hatchets, and knives; and of these they made good use, sallying repeatedly, fighting like devils, and driving back their assailants again and again. There are times when the Indian warrior forgets his cautious maxims, and throws himself into battle with a mad and reckless ferocity. The desperation of one party, and the fierce courage of both, kept up the fight after the day had closed; and the scout from Sainte Marie, as he bent listening under the gloom of the pines, heard, far into the night, the howl of battle rising from the darkened forest. The principal chief of the Iroquois was severely wounded, and nearly a hundred of their warriors were killed on the spot. When, at length, their numbers and persistent fury prevailed, their only prize was some twenty Huron warriors, spent with fatigue and faint with loss of blood. The rest lay dead around the shattered palisades which they had so valiantly defended. Fatuity, not cowardice, was the ruin of the Huron nation.

The lamps burned all night at Sainte Marie, and its defenders stood watching till daylight, musket in hand. The Jesuits prayed without ceasing, and Saint Joseph was besieged with invocations. "Those of us who were priests," writes Ragueneau, "each made a vow to say a mass in his honor every month, for the space of a year; and all the rest bound themselves by vows to divers penances." The expected onslaught did not take place. Not an Iroquois appeared. Their victory had been bought too dear, and they had no stomach for more fighting. All the next day, the eighteenth, a stillness, like the dead lull of a tempest, followed the turmoil of yesterday,—as if, says the Father Superior, "the country were waiting, palsied with fright, for some new disaster."

On the following day,—the journalist fails not to mention that it was the festival of Saint Joseph,—Indians came in with tidings that a panic had seized the Iroquois camp, that the chiefs could not control it, and that the whole body of invaders was retreating in disorder, possessed with a vague terror that the Hurons were upon them in force. They had found time, however, for an act of atrocious cruelty. They planted stakes in the bark houses of St. Ignace, and bound to them those of their prisoners whom they meant to sacrifice, male and female, from old age to infancy, husbands, mothers, and children, side by side. Then, as they retreated, they set the town on fire, and laughed with savage glee at the shrieks of anguish that rose from the blazing dwellings.[1]

They loaded the rest of their prisoners with their baggage and plunder, and drove them through the forest southward, braining with their hatchets any who gave out on the march. An old woman, who had escaped out of the midst of the flames of St. Ignace, made her way to St. Michel, a large town not far from the desolate site of St. Joseph. Here she found about seven hundred Huron warriors, hastily mustered. She set them on the track of the retreating Iroquois, and they took up the chase,—but evidently with no great eagerness to overtake their dangerous enemy, well armed as he was with Dutch guns, while they had little beside their bows and arrows. They found, as they advanced, the dead bodies of prisoners tomahawked on the march, and others bound fast to trees and half burned by the fagots piled hastily around them. The Iroquois pushed forward with such headlong speed, that the pursuers could not, or would not, overtake them; and, after two days, they gave over the attempt.

[1] The site of St. Ignace still bears evidence of the catastrophe, in the ashes and charcoal that indicate the position of the houses, and the fragments of broken pottery and half-consumed bone, together with trinkets of stone, metal, or glass, which have survived the lapse of two centuries and more. The place has been minutely examined by Dr. Taché.

Chapter XXVIII

1649

THE MARTYRS

The Ruins of St. Ignace • The Relics found • Brébeuf at the Stake • His unconquerable Fortitude • Lalemant • Renegade Hurons • Iroquois Atrocities • Death of Brébeuf • His Character • Death of Lalemant

O N the morning of the twentieth, the Jesuits at Sainte Marie received full confirmation of the reported retreat of the invaders; and one of them, with seven armed Frenchmen, set out for the scene of havoc. They passed St. Louis, where the bloody ground was strown thick with cropses, and, two or three miles farther on, reached St. Ignace. Here they saw a spectacle of horror; for among the ashes of the burnt town were scattered in profusion the half-consumed bodies of those who had perished in the flames. Apart from the rest, they saw a sight that banished all else from their thoughts; for they found what they had come to seek,—the scorched and mangled relics of Brébeuf and Lalemant.[1]

They had learned their fate already from Huron prisoners, many of whom had made their escape in the panic and confusion of the Iroquois retreat. They described what they had seen, and the condition in which the bodies were found confirmed their story.

On the afternoon of the sixteenth,—the day when the two priests were captured,—Brébeuf was led apart, and bound to a stake. He seemed more concerned for his captive converts than for himself, and addressed them in a loud voice, exhorting them to suffer patiently, and promising Heaven as their reward. The Iroquois, incensed, scorched him from head to foot, to silence him; whereupon, in the tone of a master, he threatened them with everlasting flames, for persecuting the worshippers of God. As he continued to speak, with voice and countenance unchanged, they cut away his lower lip and

[1]"Ils y trouuerent vn spectacle d'horreur, les restes de la cruauté mesme, ou plus tost les restes de l'amour de Dieu, qui seul triomphe dans la mort des Martyrs."—Ragueneau, *Relation des Hurons, 1649*, 13.

thrust a red-hot iron down his throat. He still held his tall form erect and defiant, with no sign or sound of pain; and they tried another means to overcome him. They led out Lalemant, that Brébeuf might see him tortured. They had tied strips of bark, smeared with pitch, about his naked body. When he saw the condition of his Superior, he could not hide his agitation, and called out to him, with a broken voice, in the words of Saint Paul, "We are made a spectacle to the world, to angels, and to men." Then he threw himself at Brébeuf's feet; upon which the Iroquois seized him, made him fast to a stake, and set fire to the bark that enveloped him. As the flame rose, he threw his arms upward, with a shriek of supplication to Heaven. Next they hung around Brébeuf's neck a collar made of hatchets heated red-hot; but the indomitable priest stood like a rock. A Huron in the crowd, who had been a convert of the mission, but was now an Iroquois by adoption, called out, with the malice of a renegade, to pour hot water on their heads, since they had poured so much cold water on those of others. The kettle was accordingly slung, and the water boiled and poured slowly on the heads of the two missionaries. "We baptize you," they cried, "that you may be happy in Heaven; for nobody can be saved without a good baptism." Brébeuf would not flinch; and, in a rage, they cut strips of flesh from his limbs, and devoured them before his eyes. Other renegade Hurons called out to him, "You told us, that, the more one suffers on earth, the happier he is in Heaven. We wish to make you happy; we torment you because we love you; and you ought to thank us for it." After a succession of other revolting tortures, they scalped him; when, seeing him nearly dead, they laid open his breast, and came in a crowd to drink the blood of so valiant an enemy, thinking to imbibe with it some portion of his courage. A chief then tore out his heart, and devoured it.

Thus died Jean de Brébeuf, the founder of the Huron mission, its truest hero, and its greatest martyr. He came of a noble race,—the same, it is said, from which sprang the English Earls of Arundel; but never had the mailed barons of his line confronted a fate so appalling, with so prodigious a constancy. To the last he refused to flinch, and "his death was the astonishment of his murderers."[1] In him an enthusiastic devotion was grafted on an heroic nature. His bodily endowments were as remarkable as the temper of his mind. His manly proportions, his strength, and his endurance, which incessant fasts and penances could not undermine, had always won for him the respect of the Indians, no less than a courage unconscious of fear, and yet redeemed from rashness by a cool and vigorous judgment; for, extravagant as were the chimeras which fed the fires of his zeal, they were consistent with the soberest good sense on matters of practical bearing.

Lalemant, physically weak from childhood, and slender almost to emaciation, was constitutionally unequal to a display of fortitude like that of his colleague. When Brébeuf died, he was led back to the house whence he had been taken, and tortured there all night, until, in the morning, one of the Iroquois, growing tired of the protracted entertainment, killed him with a hatchet.[2] It was said, that, at times, he seemed beside himself; then, rallying, with hands uplifted, he offered his sufferings to Heaven as a sacrifice. His robust companion had lived less than four hours under the torture, while he survived it for nearly seventeen. Perhaps the Titanic effort of will with which Brébeuf repressed all show of suffering conspired with the Iroquois knives and firebrands to exhaust his vitality; perhaps his tormentors, enraged at his fortitude, forgot their subtlety, and struck too near the life.

The bodies of the two missionaries were carried to Sainte Marie, and buried in the cemetery there; but the skull of Brébeuf was preserved as a relic. His family sent from France a silver bust of their martyred kinsman, in the base of which was a recess to contain the skull; and, to this day, the bust

[1] Charlevoix, I. 294. Alegambe uses a similar expression.

[2] "We saw no part of his body," says Ragueneau, "from head to foot, which was not burned, even to his eyes, in the sockets of which these wretches had placed live coals."—*Relation des Hurons, 1649*, 15.

Lalemant was a Parisian, and his family belonged to the class of *gens de robe*, or hereditary practitioners of the law. He was thirty-nine years of age. His physical weakness is spoken of by several of those who knew him. Marie de l'Incarnation says, "C'était l'homme le plus faible et le plus délicat qu'on eût pu voir." Both Bressani and Ragueneau are equally emphatic on this point.

and the relic within are preserved with pious care by the nuns of the Hôtel-Dieu at Quebec.[1]

[1] Photographs of the bust are before me. Various relics of the two missionaries were preserved; and some of them may still be seen in Canadian monastic establishments. The following extract from a letter of Marie de l'Incarnation to her son, written from Quebec in October of this year, 1649, is curious.

"Madame our foundress (*Madame de la Peltrie*) sends you relics of our holy martyrs; but she does it secretly, since the reverend Fathers would not give us any, for fear that we should send them to France: but, as she is not bound by vows, and as the very persons who went for the bodies have given relics of them to her in secret, I begged her to send you some of them, which she has done very gladly, from the respect she has for you." She adds, in the same letter, "Our Lord having revealed to him (*Brébeuf*) the time of his martyrdom three days before it happened, he went, full of joy, to find the other Fathers; who, seeing him in extraordinary spirits, caused him, by an inspiration of God, to be bled; after which the surgeon dried his blood, through a presentiment of what was to take place, lest he should be treated like Father Daniel, who, eight months before, had been so reduced to ashes that no remains of his body could be found."

Brébeuf had once been ordered by the Father Superior to write down the visions, revelations, and inward experiences with which he was favored, — "at least," says Ragueneau, "those which he could easily remember, for their multitude was too great for the whole to be recalled."—"I find nothing," he adds, "more frequent in this memoir than the expression of his desire to die for Jesus Christ: '*Sentio me vehementer impelli ad moriendum pro Christo.*' . . . In fine, wishing to make himself a holocaust and a victim consecrated to death, and holily to anticipate the happiness of martyrdom which awaited him, he bound himself by a vow to Christ, which he conceived in these terms"; and Ragueneau gives the vow in the original Latin. It binds him never to refuse "the grace of martyrdom, if, at any day, Thou shouldst, in Thy infinite pity, offer it to me, Thy unworthy servant;" . . . "and when I shall have received the stroke of death, I bind myself to accept it at Thy hand, with all the contentment and joy of my heart."

Some of his innumerable visions have been already mentioned. (See *ante*, p. 475.) Tanner, *Societas Militans*, gives various others, — as, for example, that he once beheld a mountain covered thick with saints, but above all with virgins, while the Queen of Virgins sat at the top in a blaze of glory. In 1637, when the whole country was enraged against the Jesuits, and above all against Brébeuf, as sorcerers who had caused the pest, Ragueneau tells us that "a troop of demons appeared before him divers times, — sometimes like men in a fury, sometimes like frightful monsters, bears, lions, or wild horses, trying to rush upon him. These spectres excited in him neither horror nor fear. He said to them, 'Do to me whatever God permits you; for without His will not one hair will fall from my head.' And at these words all the demons vanished in a moment." — *Relation des Hurons, 1649*, 20. Compare the long notice in Alegambe, *Mortes Illustres*, 644.

In Ragueneau's notice of Brébeuf, as in all other notices of deceased missionaries in the *Relations*, the saintly qualities alone are brought forward, as obedience, humility, etc.; but wherever Brébeuf himself appears in the course of those voluminous records, he always brings with him an impression of power.

We are told that, punning on his own name, he used to say that he was an ox, fit only to bear burdens. This sort of humility may pass for what it is worth; but it must be remembered, that there is a kind of acting in which the actor firmly believes in the part he is playing. As for the obedience, it was as genuine as that of a well-disciplined soldier, and incomparably more profound. In the case of the Canadian Jesuits, posterity owes to this, their favorite virtue, the record of numerous visions, inward voices, and the like miracles, which the object of these favors set down on paper, at the command of his Superior; while, otherwise, humility would have concealed them forever. The truth is, that, with some of these missionaries, one may throw off trash and nonsense by the cart-load, and find under it all a solid nucleus of saint and hero.

Chapter XXIX

1649, 1650

THE SANCTUARY

Dispersion of the Hurons • Sainte Marie abandoned • Isle St. Joseph • Removal of the Mission • The New Fort • Misery of the Hurons • Famine • Epidemic • Employments of the Jesuits

---

ALL was over with the Hurons. The death-knell of their nation had struck. Without a leader, without organization, without union, crazed with fright and paralyzed with misery, they yielded to their doom without a blow. Their only thought was flight. Within two weeks after the disasters of St. Ignace and St. Louis, fifteen Huron towns were abandoned, and the greater number burned, lest they should give shelter to the Iroquois. The last year's harvest had been scanty; the fugitives had no food, and they left behind them the fields in which was their only hope of obtaining it. In bands, large or small, some roamed northward and eastward, through the half-thawed wilderness; some hid themselves on the rocks or islands of Lake Huron; some sought an asylum among the Tobacco Nation; a few joined the Neutrals on the north of Lake Erie. The Hurons, as a nation, ceased to exist.[1]

Hitherto Sainte Marie had been covered by large fortified towns which lay between it and the Iroquois; but these were all destroyed, some by the enemy and some by their own people, and the Jesuits were left alone to bear the brunt of the next attack. There was, moreover, no reason for their remaining. Sainte Marie had been built as a basis for the missions; but its occupation was gone: the flock had fled from the shepherds, and its existence had no longer an object. If the priests stayed to be butchered, they would perish, not as martyrs, but as fools. The necessity was as clear as it was bitter. All their toil must come to nought. Sainte Marie must be abandoned. They confess the pang which the resolution cost them; but,

[1] Chaumonot, who was at Ossossané at the time of the Iroquois invasion, gives a vivid picture of the panic and lamentation which followed the news of the destruction of the Huron warriors at St. Louis, and of the flight of the inhabitants to the country of the Tobacco Nation. — *Vie*, 62.

pursues the Father Superior, "since the birth of Christianity, the Faith has nowhere been planted except in the midst of sufferings and crosses. Thus this desolation consoles us; and in the midst of persecution, in the extremity of the evils which assail us and the greater evils which threaten us, we are all filled with joy: for our hearts tell us that God has never had a more tender love for us than now."[1]

Several of the priests set out to follow and console the scattered bands of fugitive Hurons. One embarked in a canoe, and coasted the dreary shores of Lake Huron northward, among the wild labyrinth of rocks and islets, whither his scared flock had fled for refuge; another betook himself to the forest with a band of half-famished proselytes, and shared their miserable rovings through the thickets and among the mountains. Those who remained took counsel together at Sainte Marie. Whither should they go, and where should be the new seat of the mission? They made choice of the Grand Manitoulin Island, called by them Isle Sainte Marie, and by the Hurons Ekaentoton. It lay near the northern shores of Lake Huron, and by its position would give a ready access to numberless Algonquin tribes along the borders of all these inland seas. Moreover, it would bring the priests and their flock nearer to the French settlements, by the route of the Ottawa, whenever the Iroquois should cease to infest that river. The fishing, too, was good; and some of the priests, who knew the island well, made a favorable report of the soil. Thither, therefore, they had resolved to transplant the mission, when twelve Huron chiefs arrived, and asked for an interview with the Father Superior and his fellow Jesuits. The conference lasted three hours. The deputies declared that many of the scattered Hurons had determined to reunite, and form a settlement on a neighboring island of the lake, called by the Jesuits Isle St. Joseph; that they needed the aid of the Fathers; that without them they were helpless, but with them they could hold their ground and repel the attacks of the Iroquois. They urged their plea in language which Ragueneau describes as pathetic and eloquent; and, to confirm their words, they gave him ten large collars of wampum, saying

[1] Ragueneau, *Relation des Hurons, 1649,* 26.

that these were the voices of their wives and children. They gained their point. The Jesuits abandoned their former plan, and promised to join the Hurons on Isle St. Joseph.

They had built a boat, or small vessel, and in this they embarked such of their stores as it would hold. The greater part were placed on a large raft made for the purpose, like one of the rafts of timber which every summer float down the St. Lawrence and the Ottawa. Here was their stock of corn,—in part the produce of their own fields, and in part bought from the Hurons in former years of plenty,—pictures, vestments, sacred vessels and images, weapons, ammunition, tools, goods for barter with the Indians, cattle, swine, and poultry.[1] Sainte Marie was stripped of everything that could be moved. Then, lest it should harbor the Iroquois, they set it on fire, and saw consumed in an hour the results of nine or ten years of toil. It was near sunset, on the fourteenth of June.[2] The houseless band descended to the mouth of the Wye, went on board their raft, pushed it from the shore, and, with sweeps and oars, urged it on its way all night. The lake was calm and the weather fair; but it crept so slowly over the water that

[1] Some of these were killed for food after reaching the island. In March following, they had ten fowls, a pair of swine, two bulls and two cows, kept for breeding.— *Lettre de Ragueneau au Général de la Compagnie de Jésus, St. Joseph, 13 Mars, 1650.*

[2] Ragueneau, *Relation des Hurons, 1650,* 3. In the *Relation* of the preceding year he gives the fifteenth of May as the date,—evidently an error.

"Nous sortismes de ces terres de Promission qui estoient nostre Paradis, et où la mort nous eust esté mille fois plus douce que ne sera la vie en quelque lieu que nous puissions estre. Mais il faut suiure Dieu, et il faut aimer ses conduites, quelque opposées qu'elles paroissent à nos desirs, à nos plus saintes esperances et aux plus tendres amours de nostre cœur.— *Lettre de Ragueneau au P. Provincial à Paris,* in *Relation des Hurons, 1650,* 1.

"Mais il fallut, à tous tant que nous estions, quitter cette ancienne demeure de saincte Marie; ces edifices, qui quoy que pauures, paroissoient des chefs-d'œuure de l'art aux yeux de nos pauures Sauuages; ces terres cultiuées, qui nous promettoient vne riche moisson. Il nous fallut abandonner ce lieu, que ie puis appeler nostre seconde Patrie et nos delices innocentes, puis qu'il auoit esté le berceau de ce Christianisme, qu'il estoit le temple de Dieu et la maison des seruiteurs de Iesus-Christ; et crainte que nos ennemis trop impies, ne profanassent ce lieu de saincteté et n'en prissent leur auantage, nous y mismes le feu nous mesmes, et nous vismes brusler à nos yeux, en moins d'vne heure, nos trauaux de neuf et de dix ans."—Ragueneau, *Relation des Hurons, 1650,* 2, 3.

several days elapsed before they reached their destination, about twenty miles distant.

Near the entrance of Matchedash Bay lie the three islands now known as Faith, Hope, and Charity. Of these, Charity or Christian Island, called Ahoendoé by the Hurons and St. Joseph by the Jesuits, is by far the largest. It is six or eight miles wide; and when the Hurons sought refuge here, it was densely covered with the primeval forest. The priests landed with their men, some forty soldiers, laborers, and others, and found about three hundred Huron families bivouacked in the woods. Here were wigwams and sheds of bark, and smoky kettles slung over fires, each on its tripod of poles, while around lay groups of famished wretches, with dark, haggard visages and uncombed hair, in every posture of despondency and woe. They had not been wholly idle; for they had made some rough clearings, and planted a little corn. The arrival of the Jesuits gave them new hope; and, weakened as they were with famine, they set themselves to the task of hewing and burning down the forest, making bark houses, and planting palisades. The priests, on their part, chose a favorable spot, and began to clear the ground and mark out the lines of a fort. Their men—the greater part serving without pay—labored with admirable spirit, and before winter had built a square, bastioned fort of solid masonry, with a deep ditch, and walls about twelve feet high. Within were a small chapel, houses for lodging, and a well, which, with the ruins of the walls, may still be seen on the south-eastern shore of the island, a hundred feet from the water.[1] Detached redoubts were also built near at hand, where French musketeers could aid in defending the adjacent Huron village.[2] Though the island was called St. Joseph, the fort, like that on the Wye, received the name of Sainte Marie. Jesuit devotion scattered these names broadcast over all the field of their labors.

[1] The measurement between the angles of the two southern bastions is 123 feet, and that of the curtain wall connecting these bastions is 78 feet. Some curious relics have been found in the fort,—among others, a steel mill for making wafers for the Host. It was found in 1848, in a remarkable state of preservation, and is now in an English museum, having been bought on the spot by an amateur. As at Sainte Marie on the Wye, the remains are in perfect conformity with the narratives and letters of the priests.

[2] Compare Martin, Introduction to Bressani, *Relation Abrégée*, 38.

The island, thanks to the vigilance of the French, escaped attack throughout the summer; but Iroquois scalping-parties ranged the neighboring shores, killing stragglers and keeping the Hurons in perpetual alarm. As winter drew near, great numbers, who, trembling and by stealth, had gathered a miserable subsistence among the northern forests and islands, rejoined their countrymen at St. Joseph, until six or eight thousand expatriated wretches were gathered here under the protection of the French fort. They were housed in a hundred or more bark dwellings, each containing eight or ten families.[1] Here were widows without children, and children without parents; for famine and the Iroquois had proved more deadly enemies than the pestilence which a few years before had wasted their towns.[2] Of this multitude but few had strength enough to labor, scarcely any had made provision for the winter, and numbers were already perishing from want, dragging themselves from house to house, like living skeletons. The priests had spared no effort to meet the demands upon their charity. They sent men during the autumn to buy smoked fish from the Northern Algonquins, and employed Indians to gather acorns in the woods. Of this miserable food they succeeded in collecting five or six hundred bushels. To

---

[1] Ragueneau, *Relation des Hurons, 1650*, 3, 4. He reckons eight persons to a family.

[2] "Ie voudrois pouuoir representer à toutes les personnes affectionnées à nos Hurons, l'état pitoyable auquel ils sont reduits; . . . comment seroit-il possible que ces imitateurs de Iésus Christ ne fussent émeus à pitié à la veuë des centaines et centaines de veuues dont non seulement les enfans, mais quasi les parens ont esté outrageusement ou tuez, ou emmenez captifs, et puis inhumainement bruslez, cuits, déchirez et deuorez des ennemis."—*Lettre de Chaumonot à Lalemant, Supérieur à Quebec, Isle de St. Joseph, 1 Juin, 1649.*

"Vne mère s'est veuë, n'ayant que ses deux mamelles, mais sans suc et sans laict, qui toutefois estoit l'vnique chose qu'elle eust peu presenter à trois ou quatre enfans qui pleuroient y estans attachez. Elle les voyoit mourir entre ses bras, les vns apres les autres, et n'auoit pas mesme les forces de les pousser dans le tombeau. Elle mouroit sous cette charge, et en mourant elle disoit: Ouy, Mon Dieu, vous estes le maistre de nos vies; nous mourrons puisque vous le voulez; voila qui est bien que nous mourrions Chrestiens. l'estois damnée, et mes enfans auec moy, si nous ne fussions morts miserables; ils ont receu le sainct Baptesme, et ie croy fermement que mourans tous de compagnie, nous ressusciterons tous ensemble."—Ragueneau, *Relation des Hurons, 1650*, 5.

diminish its bitterness, the Indians boiled it with ashes, or the priests served it out to them pounded, and mixed with corn.[1]

As winter advanced, the Huron houses became a frightful spectacle. Their inmates were dying by scores daily. The priests and their men buried the bodies, and the Indians dug them from the earth or the snow and fed on them, sometimes in secret and sometimes openly; although, notwithstanding their superstitious feasts on the bodies of their enemies, their repugnance and horror were extreme at the thought of devouring those of relatives and friends.[2] An epidemic presently appeared, to aid the work of famine. Before spring, about half of their number were dead.

Meanwhile, though the cold was intense and the snow several feet deep, yet not an hour was free from the danger of the Iroquois; and, from sunset to daybreak, under the cold moon or in the driving snow-storm, the French sentries walked their rounds along the ramparts.

The priests rose before dawn, and spent the time till sunrise in their private devotions. Then the bell of their chapel rang, and the Indians came in crowds at the call; for misery had softened their hearts, and nearly all on the island were now Christian. There was a mass, followed by a prayer and a few words of exhortation; then the hearers dispersed to make room for others. Thus the little chapel was filled ten or twelve times, until all had had their turn. Meanwhile other priests

---

[1] Eight hundred sacks of this mixture were given to the Hurons during the winter.—Bressani, *Relation Abrégée*, 283.

[2] "Ce fut alors que nous fusmes contraints de voir des squeletes mourantes, qui soustenoient vne vie miserable, mangeant iusqu'aux ordures et les rebuts de la nature. Le gland estoit à la pluspart, ce que seroient en France les mets les plus exquis. Les charognes mesme deterrées, les restes des Renards et des Chiens ne faisoient point horreur, et se mangeoient, quoy qu'en cachete: car quoy que les Hurons, auant que la foy leur eust donné plus de lumiere qu'ils n'en auoient dans l'infidelité, ne creussent pas commettre aucun peché de manger leurs ennemis, aussi peu qu'il y en a de les tuer, toutefois ie puis dire auec verité, qu'ils n'ont pas moins d'horreur de manger de leurs compatriotes, qu'on peut auoir en France de manger de la chair humaine. Mais la necessité n'a plus de loy, et des dents fameliques ne discernent plus ce qu'elles mangent. Les mères se sont repeuës de leurs enfans, des freres de leurs freres, et des enfans ne reconnoissoient plus en vn cadaure mort, celuy lequel lors qu'il viuoit, ils appelloient leur Pere."—Ragueneau, *Relation des Hurons, 1650*, 4. Compare Bressani, *Relation Abrégée*, 283.

were hearing confessions and giving advice and encouragement in private, according to the needs of each applicant. This lasted till nine o'clock, when all the Indians returned to their village, and the priests presently followed, to give what assistance they could. Their cassocks were worn out, and they were dressed chiefly in skins.[1] They visited the Indian houses, and gave to those whose necessities were most urgent small scraps of hide, severally stamped with a particular mark, and entitling the recipients, on presenting them at the fort, to a few acorns, a small quantity of boiled maize, or a fragment of smoked fish, according to the stamp on the leather ticket of each. Two hours before sunset the bell of the chapel again rang, and the religious exercises of the morning were repeated.[2]

Thus this miserable winter wore away, till the opening spring brought new fears and new necessities.[3]

[1] *Lettre de Ragueneau au Général de la Compagnie de Jésus, Isle St. Joseph, 13 Mars, 1650.*

[2] Ragueneau, *Relation des Hurons, 1650,* 6, 7.

[3] Concerning the retreat of the Hurons to Isle St. Joseph, the principal authorities are the *Relations* of 1649 and 1650, which are ample in detail, and written with an excellent simplicity and modesty; the *Relation Abrégée* of Bressani; the reports of the Father Superior to the General of the Jesuits at Rome; the manuscript of 1652, entitled *Mémoires touchant la Mort et les Vertus des Pères, etc.*; the unpublished letters of Garnier; and a letter of Chaumonot, written on the spot, and preserved in the *Relations.*

Chapter XXX
1649
GARNIER — CHABANEL

The Tobacco Missions • St. Jean attacked • Death of Garnier •
The Journey of Chabanel • His Death • Garreau and Grelon

LATE in the preceding autumn the Iroquois had taken the war-path in force. At the end of November, two escaped prisoners came to Isle St. Joseph with the news that a band of three hundred warriors was hovering in the Huron forests, doubtful whether to invade the island or to attack the towns of the Tobacco Nation in the valleys of the Blue Mountains. The Father Superior, Ragueneau, sent a runner thither in all haste, to warn the inhabitants of their danger.

There were at this time two missions in the Tobacco Nation, St. Jean and St. Matthias,[1] — the latter under the charge of the Jesuits Garreau and Grelon, and the former under that of Garnier and Chabanel. St. Jean, the principal seat of the mission of the same name, was a town of five or six hundred families. Its population was, moreover, greatly augmented by the bands of fugitive Hurons who had taken refuge there. When the warriors were warned by Ragueneau's messenger of a probable attack from the Iroquois, they were far from being daunted, but, confiding in their numbers, awaited the enemy in one of those fits of valor which characterize the unstable courage of the savage. At St. Jean all was paint, feathers, and uproar, — singing, dancing, howling, and stamping. Quivers were filled, knives whetted, and tomahawks sharpened; but when, after two days of eager expectancy, the enemy did not appear, the warriors lost patience. Thinking, and probably with reason, that the Iroquois were afraid of them, they resolved to sally forth, and take the offensive. With yelps and whoops they defiled into the forest, where the branches were gray and bare, and the ground thickly covered with snow. They pushed on rapidly till the following day, but

---

[1] The Indian name of St. Jean was Etarita; and that of St. Matthias, Ekarenniondi.

could not discover their wary enemy, who had made a wide circuit, and was approaching the town from another quarter. By ill luck, the Iroquois captured a Tobacco Indian and his squaw, straggling in the forest not far from St. Jean; and the two prisoners, to propitiate them, told them the defenceless condition of the place, where none remained but women, children, and old men. The delighted Iroquois no longer hesitated, but silently and swiftly pushed on towards the town.

It was two o'clock in the afternoon of the seventh of December.[1] Chabanel had left the place a day or two before, in obedience to a message from Ragueneau, and Garnier was here alone. He was making his rounds among the houses, visiting the sick and instructing his converts, when the horrible din of the war-whoop rose from the borders of the clearing, and, on the instant, the town was mad with terror. Children and girls rushed to and fro, blind with fright; women snatched their infants, and fled they knew not whither. Garnier ran to his chapel, where a few of his converts had sought asylum. He gave them his benediction, exhorted them to hold fast to the Faith, and bade them fly while there was yet time. For himself, he hastened back to the houses, running from one to another, and giving absolution or baptism to all whom he found. An Iroquois met him, shot him with three balls through the body and thigh, tore off his cassock, and rushed on in pursuit of the fugitives. Garnier lay for a moment on the ground, as if stunned; then, recovering his senses, he was seen to rise into a kneeling posture. At a little distance from him lay a Huron, mortally wounded, but still showing signs of life. With the Heaven that awaited him glowing before his fading vision, the priest dragged himself towards the dying Indian, to give him absolution; but his strength failed, and he fell again to the earth. He rose once more, and again crept forward, when a party of Iroquois rushed upon him, split his head with two blows of a hatchet, stripped him, and left his body on the ground.[2] At this time

[1] Bressani, *Relation Abrégée*, 264.

[2] The above particulars of Garnier's death rest on the evidence of a Christian Huron woman, named Marthe, who saw him shot down, and also saw

the whole town was on fire. The invaders, fearing that the absent warriors might return and take their revenge, hastened to finish their work, scattered firebrands everywhere, and threw children alive into the burning houses. They killed many of the fugitives, captured many more, and then made a hasty retreat through the forest with their prisoners, butchering such of them as lagged on the way. St. Jean lay a waste of smoking ruins thickly strewn with blackened corpses of the slain.

Towards evening, parties of fugitives reached St. Matthias, with tidings of the catastrophe. The town was wild with alarm, and all stood on the watch, in expectation of an attack; but when, in the morning, scouts came in and reported the retreat of the Iroquois, Garreau and Grelon set out with a party of converts to visit the scene of havoc. For a long time they looked in vain for the body of Garnier; but at length they found him lying where he had fallen,—so scorched and disfigured, that he was recognized with difficulty. The two priests wrapped his body in a part of their own clothing; the Indian converts dug a grave on the spot where his church had stood; and here they buried him. Thus, at the age of forty-four, died Charles Garnier, the favorite child of wealthy and noble parents, nursed in Parisian luxury and ease, then living and dying, a more than willing exile, amid the hardships and horrors of the Huron wilderness. His life and his death are his best eulogy. Brébeuf was the lion of the Huron mission, and Garnier was the lamb; but the lamb was as fearless as the lion.[1]

---

his attempt to reach the dying Indian. She was herself struck down immediately after with a war-club, but remained alive, and escaped in the confusion. She died three months later, at Isle St. Joseph, from the effects of the injuries she had received, after reaffirming the truth of her story to Ragueneau, who was with her, and who questioned her on the subject. (*Mémoires touchant la Mort et les Vertus des Pères Garnier, etc.*, MS.). Ragueneau also speaks of her in *Relation des Hurons, 1650*, 9.—The priests Grelon and Garreau found the body stripped naked, with three gunshot wounds in the abdomen and thigh, and two deep hatchet wounds in the head.

[1] Garnier's devotion to the mission was absolute. He took little or no interest in the news from France, which, at intervals of from one to three years, found its way to the Huron towns. His companion Bressani says, that he would walk thirty or forty miles in the hottest summer day, to baptize some

When, on the following morning, the warriors of St. Jean returned from their rash and bootless sally, and saw the ashes of their desolated homes and the ghastly relics of their murdered families, they seated themselves amid the ruin, silent and motionless as statues of bronze, with heads bowed down and eyes fixed on the ground. Thus they remained through half the day. Tears and wailing were for women; this was the mourning of warriors.

Garnier's colleague, Chabanel, had been recalled from St. Jean by an order from the Father Superior, who thought it needless to expose the life of more than one priest in a position of so much danger. He stopped on his way at St. Matthias, and on the morning of the seventh of December, the day of the attack, left that town with seven or eight Christian Hurons. The journey was rough and difficult. They proceeded through the forest about eighteen miles, and then encamped in the snow. The Indians fell asleep; but Chabanel, from an apprehension of danger, or some other cause, remained awake. About midnight he heard a strange sound in the distance,—a confusion of fierce voices, mingled with songs and outcries. It was the Iroquois on their retreat with

---

dying Indian, when the country was infested by the enemy. On similar errands, he would sometimes pass the night alone in the forest in the depth of winter. He was anxious to fall into the hands of the Iroquois, that he might preach the Faith to them even out of the midst of the fire. In one of his unpublished letters he writes, "Praised be our Lord, who punishes me for my sins by depriving me of this crown" (the crown of martyrdom). After the death of Brébeuf and Lalemant, he writes to his brother:—

"Hélas! Mon cher frère, si ma conscience ne me convainquait et ne me confondait de mon infidélité au service de notre bon mâitre, je pourrais espérer quelque faveur approchante de celles qu'il a faites aux bienheureux martyrs avec qui j'avais le bien de converser souvent, étant dans les mêmes occasions et dangers qu'ils étaient, mais sa justice me fait craindre que je ne demeure toujours indigne d'une telle couronne."

He contented himself with the most wretched fare during the last years of famine, living in good measure on roots and acorns; "although," says Ragueneau, "he had been the cherished son of a rich and noble house, on whom all the affection of his father had centred, and who had been nourished on food very different from that of swine."—*Relation des Hurons, 1650,* 12.

For his character, see Ragueneau, Bressani, Tanner, and Alegambe, who devotes many pages to the description of his religious traits; but the complexion of his mind is best reflected in his private letters.

their prisoners, some of whom were defiantly singing their war-songs, after the Indian custom. Chabanel waked his companions, who instantly took flight. He tried to follow, but could not keep pace with the light-footed savages, who returned to St. Matthias, and told what had occurred. They said, however, that Chabanel had left them and taken an opposite direction, in order to reach Isle St. Joseph. His brother priests were for some time ignorant of what had befallen him. At length a Huron Indian, who had been converted, but afterward apostatized, gave out that he had met him in the forest, and aided him with his canoe to cross a river which lay in his path. Some supposed that he had lost his way, and died of cold and hunger; but others were of a different opinion. Their suspicion was confirmed some time afterwards by the renegadé Huron, who confessed that he had killed Chabanel and thrown his body into the river, after robbing him of his clothes, his hat, the blanket or mantle which was strapped to his shoulders, and the bag in which he carried his books and papers. He declared that his motive was hatred of the Faith, which had caused the ruin of the Hurons.[1] The priest had prepared himself for a worse fate. Before leaving Sainte Marie on the Wye, to go to his post in the Tobacco Nation, he had written to his brother to regard him as a victim destined to the fires of the Iroquois.[2] He added, that, though he was naturally timid, he was now wholly indifferent to danger; and he expressed the belief that only a superhuman power could have wrought such a change in him.[3]

[1] *Mémoires touchant la Mort et les Vertus des Pères, etc.* MS.

[2] *Abrégé de la Vie du P. Noël Chabanel.* MS

[3] "Ie suis fort apprehensif de mon naturel; toutefois, maintenant que ie vay au plus grand danger et qu'il me semble que la mort n'est pas esloignée, ie ne sens plus de crainte. Cette disposition ne vient pas de moy."—*Relation des Hurons, 1650,* 18.

The following is the vow made by Chabanel, at a time when his disgust at the Indian mode of life beset him with temptations to ask to be recalled from the mission. It is translated from the Latin original:—

"My Lord Jesus Christ, who, in the admirable disposition of thy paternal providence, hast willed that I, although most unworthy, should be a colaborer with the holy Apostles in this vineyard of the Hurons,—I, Noël Chabanel, impelled by the desire of fulfilling thy holy will in advancing the conversion of the savages of this land to thy faith, do vow, in the presence of the most holy sacrament of thy precious body and blood, which is God's

Garreau and Grelon, in their mission of St. Matthias, were exposed to other dangers than those of the Iroquois. A report was spread, not only that they were magicians, but that they had a secret understanding with the enemy. A nocturnal council was called, and their death was decreed. In the morning, a furious crowd gathered before a lodge which they were about to enter, screeching and yelling after the manner of Indians when they compel a prisoner to run the gantlet. The two priests, giving no sign of fear, passed through the crowd and entered the lodge unharmed. Hatchets were brandished over them, but no one would be the first to strike. Their converts were amazed at their escape, and they themselves ascribed it to the interposition of a protecting Providence. The Huron missionaries were doubly in danger,—not more from the Iroquois than from the blind rage of those who should have been their friends.[1]

---

tabernacle among men, to remain perpetually attached to this mission of the Hurons, understanding all things according to the interpretation and disposal of the Superiors of the Society of Jesus. Therefore I entreat thee to receive me as the perpetual servant of this mission, and to render me worthy of so sublime a ministry. Amen. This twentieth day of June, 1647."

[1] Ragueneau, *Relation des Hurons, 1650*, 20.

One of these two missionaries, Garreau, was afterwards killed by the Iroquois, who shot him through the spine, in 1656, near Montreal.—De Quen, *Relation, 1656*, 41.

Chapter XXXI
1650–1652
THE HURON MISSION ABANDONED

Famine and the Tomahawk • A New Asylum • Voyage of the Refugees to Quebec • Meeting with Bressani • Desperate Courage of the Iroquois • Inroads and Battles • Death of Buteux

---

As spring approached, the starving multitude on Isle St. Joseph grew reckless with hunger. Along the main shore, in spots where the sun lay warm, the spring fisheries had already begun, and the melting snow was uncovering the acorns in the woods. There was danger everywhere, for bands of Iroquois were again on the track of their prey.[1] The miserable Hurons, gnawed with inexorable famine, stood in the dilemma of a deadly peril and an assured death. They chose the former; and, early in March, began to leave their island and cross to the main-land, to gather what sustenance they could. The ice was still thick, but the advancing season had softened it; and, as a body of them were crossing, it broke under their feet. Some were drowned; while others dragged themselves out, drenched and pierced with cold, to die miserably on the frozen lake, before they could reach a shelter. Other parties, more fortunate, gained the shore safely, and began their fishing, divided into companies of from eight or ten to a hundred persons. But the Iroquois were in wait for them. A large band of warriors had already made their way, through ice and snow, from their towns in Central New York. They surprised the Huron fishermen, surrounded them, and cut them in pieces without resistance, — tracking out the various parties of their victims, and hunting down fugitives

---

[1] "Mais le Printemps estant venu, les Iroquois nous furent encore plus cruels; et ce sont eux qui vrayement ont ruiné toutes nos esperances, et qui ont fait vn lieu d'horreur, vne terre de sang et de carnage, vn theatre de cruauté et vn sepulchre de carcasses décharnées par les langueurs d'vne longue famine, d'vn païs de benediction, d'vne terre de Sainteté et d'vn lieu qui n'auoit plus rien de barbare, depuis que le sang respandu pour son amour auoit rendu tout son peuple Chrestien." — Ragueneau, *Relation des Hurons*, *1650*, 23.

with such persistency and skill, that, of all who had gone over to the main, the Jesuits knew of but one who escaped.[1]

"My pen," writes Ragueneau, "has no ink black enough to describe the fury of the Iroquois." Still the goadings of famine were relentless and irresistible. "It is said," adds the Father Superior, "that hunger will drive wolves from the forest. So, too, our starving Hurons were driven out of a town which had become an abode of horror. It was the end of Lent. Alas, if these poor Christians could have had but acorns and water to keep their fast upon! On Easter Day we caused them to make a general confession. On the following morning they went away, leaving us all their little possessions; and most of them declared publicly that they made us their heirs, knowing well that they were near their end. And, in fact, only a few days passed before we heard of the disaster which we had foreseen. These poor people fell into ambuscades of our Iroquois enemies. Some were killed on the spot; some were dragged into captivity; women and children were burned. A few made their escape, and spread dismay and panic everywhere. A week after, another band was overtaken by the same fate. Go where they would, they met with slaughter on all sides. Famine pursued them, or they encountered an enemy more cruel than cruelty itself; and, to crown their misery, they heard that two great armies of Iroquois were on the way to exterminate them. . . . Despair was universal."[2]

The Jesuits at St. Joseph knew not what course to take. The doom of their flock seemed inevitable. When dismay and de-

---

[1]"Le iour de l'Annonciation, vingt-cinquiesme de Mars, vne armée d'Iroquois ayans marché prez de deux cents lieuës de païs, à trauers les glaces et les neges, trauersans les montagnes et les forests pleines d'horreur, surprirent au commencement de la nuit le camp de nos Chrestiens, et en firent vne cruelle boucherie. Il sembloit que le Ciel conduisit toutes leurs demarches et qu'ils eurent vn Ange pour guide: car ils diuiserent leurs troupes auec tant de bon-heur, qu'ils trouuerent en moins de deux iours, toutes les bandes de nos Chrestiens qui estoient dispersées ça et là, esloignées les vnes des autres de six, sept et huit lieuës, cent personnes en vn lieu, en vn autre cinquante; et mesme il y auoit quelques familles solitaires, qui s'estoient escartées en des lieux moins connus et hors de tout chemin. Chose estrange! de tout ce monde dissipé, vn seul homme s'eschappa, qui vint nous en apporter les nouuelles."—Ragueneau, *Relation des Hurons, 1650,* 23, 24.

[2]*Ibid.,* 24.

spondency were at their height, two of the principal Huron
chiefs came to the fort, and asked an interview with Ragueneau and his companions. They told them that the Indians
had held a council the night before, and resolved to abandon
the island. Some would disperse in the most remote and inaccessible forests; others would take refuge in a distant spot,
apparently the Grand Manitoulin Island; others would try to
reach the Andastes; and others would seek safety in adoption
and incorporation with the Iroquois themselves.

"Take courage, brother," continued one of the chiefs, addressing Ragueneau. "You can save us, if you will but resolve
on a bold step. Choose a place where you can gather us together, and prevent this dispersion of our people. Turn your
eyes towards Quebec, and transport thither what is left of this
ruined country. Do not wait till war and famine have destroyed us to the last man. We are in your hands. Death has
taken from you more than ten thousand of us. If you wait
longer, not one will remain alive; and then you will be sorry
that you did not save those whom you might have snatched
from danger, and who showed you the means of doing so. If
you do as we wish, we will form a church under the protection of the fort at Quebec. Our faith will not be extinguished.
The examples of the French and the Algonquins will encourage us in our duty, and their charity will relieve some of our
misery. At least, we shall sometimes find a morsel of bread
for our children, who so long have had nothing but bitter
roots and acorns to keep them alive."[1]

The Jesuits were deeply moved. They consulted together
again and again, and prayed in turn during forty hours without ceasing, that their minds might be enlightened. At length
they resolved to grant the petition of the two chiefs, and save
the poor remnant of the Hurons, by leading them to an asylum where there was at least a hope of safety. Their resolution
once taken, they pushed their preparations with all speed, lest
the Iroquois might learn their purpose, and lie in wait to cut
them off. Canoes were made ready, and on the tenth of June

[1] Ragueneau, *Relation des Hurons, 1650,* 25. It appears from the MS. *Journal
des Supérieurs des Jésuites,* that a plan of bringing the remnant of the Hurons
to Quebec was discussed and approved by Lalemant and his associates, in a
council held by them at that place in April.

they began the voyage, with all their French followers and about three hundred Hurons. The Huron mission was abandoned.

"It was not without tears," writes the Father Superior, "that we left the country of our hopes and our hearts, where our brethren had gloriously shed their blood."[1] The fleet of canoes held its melancholy way along the shores where two years before had been the seat of one of the chief savage communities of the continent, and where now all was a waste of death and desolation. Then they steered northward, along the eastern coast of the Georgian Bay, with its countless rocky islets; and everywhere they saw the traces of the Iroquois. When they reached Lake Nipissing, they found it deserted,— nothing remaining of the Algonquins who dwelt on its shore, except the ashes of their burnt wigwams. A little farther on, there was a fort built of trees, where the Iroquois who made this desolation had spent the winter; and a league or two below, there was another similar fort. The River Ottawa was a solitude. The Algonquins of Allumette Island and the shores adjacent had all been killed or driven away, never again to return. "When I came up this great river, only thirteen years ago," writes Ragueneau, "I found it bordered with Algonquin tribes, who knew no God, and, in their infidelity, thought themselves gods on earth; for they had all that they desired, abundance of fish and game, and a prosperous trade with allied nations: besides, they were the terror of their enemies. But since they have embraced the Faith and adored the cross of Christ, He has given them a heavy share in this cross, and made them a prey to misery, torture, and a cruel death. In a word, they are a people swept from the face of the earth. Our only consolation is, that, as they died Christians, they have a part in the inheritance of the true children of God, who scourgeth every one whom He receiveth."[2]

As the voyagers descended the river, they had a serious alarm. Their scouts came in, and reported that they had found fresh footprints of men in the forest. These proved, however,

[1] Compare Bressani, *Relation Abrégée*, 288.

[2] Ragueneau, *Relation des Hurons, 1650*, 27. These Algonquins of the Ottawa, though broken and dispersed, were not destroyed, as Ragueneau supposes.

to be the tracks, not of enemies, but of friends. In the preceding autumn Bressani had gone down to the French settlements with about twenty Hurons, and was now returning with them, and twice their number of armed Frenchmen, for the defence of the mission. His scouts had also been alarmed by discovering the footprints of Ragueneau's Indians; and for some time the two parties stood on their guard, each taking the other for an enemy. When at length they discovered their mistake, they met with embraces and rejoicing. Bressani and his Frenchmen had come too late. All was over with the Hurons and the Huron mission; and, as it was useless to go farther, they joined Ragueneau's party, and retraced their course for the settlements.

A day or two before, they had had a sharp taste of the mettle of the enemy. Ten Iroquois warriors had spent the winter in a little fort of felled trees on the borders of the Ottawa, hunting for subsistence, and waiting to waylay some passing canoe of Hurons, Algonquins, or Frenchmen. Bressani's party outnumbered them six to one; but they resolved that it should not pass without a token of their presence. Late on a dark night, the French and Hurons lay encamped in the forest, sleeping about their fires. They had set guards: but these, it seems, were drowsy or negligent; for the ten Iroquois, watching their time, approached with the stealth of lynxes, and glided like shadows into the midst of the camp, where, by the dull glow of the smouldering fires, they could distinguish the recumbent figures of their victims. Suddenly they screeched the war-whoop, and struck like lightning with their hatchets among the sleepers. Seven were killed before the rest could spring to their weapons. Bressani leaped up, and received on the instant three arrow-wounds in the head. The Iroquois were surrounded, and a desperate fight ensued in the dark. Six of them were killed on the spot, and two made prisoners; while the remaining two, breaking through the crowd, bounded out of the camp and escaped in the forest.

The united parties soon after reached Montreal; but the Hurons refused to remain in a spot so exposed to the Iroquois. Accordingly, they all descended the St. Lawrence, and at length, on the twenty-eighth of July, reached Quebec. Here the Ursulines, the hospital nuns, and the inhabitants taxed their resources to the utmost to provide food and shelter for the exiled Hurons. Their good-will exceeded their power; for food was scarce at Quebec, and the Jesuits themselves had to bear the chief burden of keeping the sufferers alive.[1]

But, if famine was an evil, the Iroquois were a far greater one; for, while the western nations of their confederacy were engrossed with the destruction of the Hurons, the Mohawks kept up incessant attacks on the Algonquins and the French. A party of Christian Indians, chiefly from Sillery, planned a stroke of retaliation, and set out for the Mohawk country, marching cautiously and sending forward scouts to scour the forest. One of these, a Huron, suddenly fell in with a large Iroquois war-party, and, seeing that he could not escape, formed on the instant a villanous plan to save himself. He ran towards the enemy, crying out, that he had long been looking for them and was delighted to see them; that his nation, the Hurons, had come to an end; and that henceforth his country was the country of the Iroquois, where so many of his kinsmen and friends had been adopted. He had come, he declared, with no other thought than that of joining them, and turning Iroquois, as they had done. The Iroquois demanded if he had come alone. He answered, "No," and said, that, in order to accomplish his purpose, he had joined an Algonquin war-party who were in the woods not far off. The Iroquois, in great delight, demanded to be shown where they were. This Judas, as the Jesuits call him, at once complied; and the Algonquins were surprised by a sudden onset, and routed with severe loss. The treacherous Huron was well treated by the Iroquois, who adopted him into their nation. Not long after, he came to Canada, and, with a view, as it was thought, to some further treachery, rejoined the French. A sharp cross-questioning put him to confusion, and he presently confessed his guilt. He was sentenced to death; and the sentence was executed by one of his own countrymen, who split his head with a hatchet.[2]

In the course of the summer, the French at Three Rivers became aware that a band of Iroquois was prowling in the

[1] Compare Juchereau, *Histoire de l'Hôtel-Dieu*, 79, 80.
[2] Ragueneau, *Relation, 1650*, 30.

neighborhood, and sixty men went out to meet them. Far from retreating, the Iroquois, who were about twenty-five in number, got out of their canoes, and took post, waist-deep in mud and water, among the tall rushes at the margin of the river. Here they fought stubbornly, and kept all the Frenchmen at bay. At length, finding themselves hard pressed, they entered their canoes again, and paddled off. The French rowed after them, and soon became separated in the chase; whereupon the Iroquois turned, and made desperate fight with the foremost, retreating again as soon as the others came up. This they repeated several times, and then made their escape, after killing a number of the best French soldiers. Their leader in this affair was a famous half-breed, known as the Flemish Bastard, who is styled by Ragueneau "an abomination of sin, and a monster produced between a heretic Dutch father and a pagan mother."

In the forests far north of Three Rivers dwelt the tribe called the Atticamegues, or Nation of the White Fish. From their remote position, and the difficult nature of the intervening country, they thought themselves safe; but a band of Iroquois, marching on snow-shoes a distance of twenty days' journey northward from the St. Lawrence, fell upon one of their camps in the winter, and made a general butchery of the inmates. The tribe, however, still held its ground for a time, and, being all good Catholics, gave their missionary, Father Buteux, an urgent invitation to visit them in their own country. Buteux, who had long been stationed at Three Rivers, was in ill health, and for years had rarely been free from some form of bodily suffering. Nevertheless, he acceded to their request, and, before the opening of spring, made a remarkable journey on snow-shoes into the depths of this frozen wilderness.[1] In the year following, he repeated the undertaking. With him were a large party of Atticamegues, and several Frenchmen. Game was exceedingly scarce, and they were forced by hunger to separate, a Huron convert and a Frenchman named Fontarabie remaining with the missionary. The snows had melted, and all the streams were swollen. The three travellers, in a small birch canoe, pushed their way up a

[1] *Iournal du Pere Iacques Buteux du Voyage qu'il a fait pour la Mission des Attikamegues*. See *Relation, 1651*, 15.

turbulent river, where falls and rapids were so numerous, that many times daily they were forced to carry their bark vessel and their baggage through forests and thickets and over rocks and precipices. On the tenth of May, they made two such portages, and, soon after, reaching a third fall, again lifted their canoe from the water. They toiled through the naked forest, among the wet, black trees, over tangled roots, green, spongy mosses, mouldering leaves, and rotten, prostrate trunks, while the cataract foamed amidst the rocks hard by. The Indian led the way with the canoe on his head, while Buteux and the other Frenchman followed with the baggage. Suddenly they were set upon by a troop of Iroquois, who had crouched behind thickets, rocks, and fallen trees, to waylay them. The Huron was captured before he had time to fly. Buteux and the Frenchman tried to escape, but were instantly shot down, the Jesuit receiving two balls in the breast. The Iroquois rushed upon them, mangled their bodies with tomahawks and swords, stripped them, and then flung them into the torrent.[1]

[1] Ragueneau, *Relation*, *1652*, 2, 3.

Chapter XXXII

THE LAST OF THE HURONS

*Fate of the Vanquished • The Refugees of St. Jean Baptiste and St.
Michel • The Tobacco Nation and its Wanderings • The Modern
Wyandots • The Biter Bit • The Hurons at Quebec •
Notre-Dame de Lorette*

IROQUOIS bullets and tomahawks had killed the Hurons by
hundreds, but famine and disease had killed incomparably
more. The miseries of the starving crowd on Isle St. Joseph
had been shared in an equal degree by smaller bands, who
had wintered in remote and secret retreats of the wilderness.
Of those who survived that season of death, many were so
weakened that they could not endure the hardships of a wandering life, which was new to them. The Hurons lived by
agriculture: their fields and crops were destroyed, and they
were so hunted from place to place that they could rarely till
the soil. Game was very scarce; and, without agriculture, the
country could support only a scanty and scattered population
like that which maintained a struggling existence in the wilderness of the lower St. Lawrence. The mortality among the
exiles was prodigious.

It is a matter of some interest to trace the fortunes of the
shattered fragments of a nation once prosperous, and, in its
own eyes and those of its neighbors, powerful and great.
None were left alive within their ancient domain. Some had
sought refuge among the Neutrals and the Eries, and shared
the disasters which soon overwhelmed those tribes; others
succeeded in reaching the Andastes; while the inhabitants of
two towns, St. Michel and St. Jean Baptiste, had recourse to
an expedient which seems equally strange and desperate, but
which was in accordance with Indian practices. They contrived to open a communication with the Seneca Nation of
the Iroquois, and promised to change their nationality and
turn Senecas as the price of their lives. The victors accepted
the proposal; and the inhabitants of these two towns, joined
by a few other Hurons, migrated in a body to the Seneca

country. They were not distributed among different villages, but were allowed to form a town by themselves, where they were afterwards joined by some prisoners of the Neutral Nation. They identified themselves with the Iroquois in all but religion,—holding so fast to their faith, that, eighteen years after, a Jesuit missionary found that many of them were still good Catholics.[1]

The division of the Hurons called the Tobacco Nation, favored by their isolated position among mountains, had held their ground longer than the rest; but at length they, too, were compelled to fly, together with such other Hurons as had taken refuge with them. They made their way northward, and settled on the Island of Michilimackinac, where they were joined by the Ottawas, who, with other Algonquins, had been driven by fear of the Iroquois from the western shores of Lake Huron and the banks of the River Ottawa. At Michilimackinac the Hurons and their allies were again attacked by the Iroquois, and, after remaining several years, they made another remove, and took possession of the islands at the mouth of the Green Bay of Lake Michigan. Even here their old enemy did not leave them in peace; whereupon they fortified themselves on the main-land, and afterwards migrated southward and westward. This brought them in contact with the Illinois, an Algonquin people, at that time very numerous, but who, like many other tribes at this epoch, were doomed to a rapid diminution from wars with other savage nations. Continuing their migration westward, the Hurons and Ottawas reached the Mississippi, where they fell in with the Sioux. They soon quarrelled with those fierce children of the prairie, who drove them from their country. They retreated to the south-western extremity of Lake Superior, and settled on Point Saint Esprit, or Shagwamigon Point, near the Islands of the Twelve Apostles. As the Sioux continued to harass them, they left this place about the year 1671, and returned to Michilimackinac, where they settled, not on the island, but on the neighboring Point St. Ignace, at the northern extremity of the great peninsula of Michigan. The greater part of

[1] Compare *Relation, 1651*, 4; *1660*, 14, 28; and *1670*, 69. The Huron town among the Senecas was called Gandougaraé. Father Fremin was here in 1668, and gives an account of his visit in the *Relation* of 1670.

them afterwards removed thence to Detroit and Sandusky, where they lived under the name of Wyandots until within the present century, maintaining a marked influence over the surrounding Algonquins. They bore an active part, on the side of the French, in the war which ended in the reduction of Canada; and they were the most formidable enemies of the English in the Indian war under Pontiac.[1] The government of the United States at length removed them to reserves on the western frontier, where a remnant of them may still be found. Thus it appears that the Wyandots, whose name is so conspicuous in the history of our border wars, are descendants of the ancient Hurons, and chiefly of that portion of them called the Tobacco Nation.[2]

When Ragueneau and his party left Isle St. Joseph for Quebec, the greater number of the Hurons chose to remain. They took possession of the stone fort which the French had abandoned, and where, with reasonable vigilance, they could maintain themselves against attack. In the succeeding autumn a small Iroquois war-party had the audacity to cross over to the island, and build a fort of felled trees in the woods. The Hurons attacked them; but the invaders made so fierce a defence, that they kept their assailants at bay, and at length retreated with little or no loss. Soon after, a much larger band of Onondaga Iroquois, approaching undiscovered, built a fort on the main-land, opposite the island, but concealed from sight in the forest. Here they waited to waylay any party of Hurons who might venture ashore. A Huron war-chief, named Étienne Annaotaha, whose life is described as a succession of conflicts and adventures, and who is said to have been always in luck, landed with a few companions, and fell into an ambuscade of the Iroquois. He prepared to defend himself, when they called out to him, that they came not as ene-

---

[1] See "History of the Conspiracy of Pontiac."

[2] The migrations of this band of the Hurons may be traced by detached passages and incidental remarks in the *Relations* of 1654, 1660, 1667, 1670, 1671, and 1672. Nicolas Perrot, in his chapter, *Deffaitte et Füitte des Hurons chassés de leur Pays*, and in the chapter following, gives a long and rather confused account of their movements and adventures. See also La Poterie, *Histoire de l'Amérique Septentrionale*, II. 51–56. According to the *Relation* of 1670, the Hurons, when living at Shagwamigon Point, numbered about fifteen hundred souls.

mies, but as friends, and that they brought wampum-belts and presents to persuade the Hurons to forget the past, go back with them to their country, become their adopted countrymen, and live with them as one nation. Étienne suspected treachery, but concealed his distrust, and advanced towards the Iroquois with an air of the utmost confidence. They received him with open arms, and pressed him to accept their invitation; but he replied, that there were older and wiser men among the Hurons, whose counsels all the people followed, and that they ought to lay the proposal before them. He proceeded to advise them to keep him as a hostage, and send over his companions, with some of their chiefs, to open the negotiation. His apparent frankness completely deceived them; and they insisted that he himself should go to the Huron village, while his companions remained as hostages. He set out accordingly with three of the principal Iroquois.

When he reached the village, he gave the whoop of one who brings good tidings, and proclaimed with a loud voice that the hearts of their enemies had changed, that the Iroquois would become their countrymen and brothers, and that they should exchange their miseries for a life of peace and plenty in a fertile and prosperous land. The whole Huron population, full of joyful excitement, crowded about him and the three envoys, who were conducted to the principal lodge, and feasted on the best that the village could supply. Étienne seized the opportunity to take aside four or five of the principal chiefs, and secretly tell them his suspicions that the Iroquois were plotting to compass their destruction under cover of overtures of peace; and he proposed that they should meet treachery with treachery. He then explained his plan, which was highly approved by his auditors, who begged him to charge himself with the execution of it. Étienne now caused criers to proclaim through the village that every one should get ready to emigrate in a few days to the country of their new friends. The squaws began their preparations at once, and all was bustle and alacrity; for the Hurons themselves were no less deceived than were the Iroquois envoys.

During one or two succeeding days, many messages and visits passed between the Hurons and the Iroquois, whose confidence was such, that thirty-seven of their best warriors at length came over in a body to the Huron village. Étienne's time had come. He and the chiefs who were in the secret gave the word to the Huron warriors, who, at a signal, raised the war-whoop, rushed upon their visitors, and cut them to pieces. One of them, who lingered for a time, owned before he died that Étienne's suspicions were just, and that they had designed nothing less than the massacre or capture of all the Hurons. Three of the Iroquois, immediately before the slaughter began, had received from Étienne a warning of their danger in time to make their escape. The year before, he had been captured, with Brébeuf and Lalemant, at the town of St. Louis, and had owed his life to these three warriors, to whom he now paid back the debt of gratitude. They carried tidings of what had befallen to their countrymen on the main-land, who, aghast at the catastrophe, fled homeward in a panic.[1]

Here was a sweet morsel of vengeance. The miseries of the Hurons were lighted up with a brief gleam of joy; but it behooved them to make a timely retreat from their island before the Iroquois came to exact a bloody retribution. Towards spring, while the lake was still frozen, many of them escaped on the ice, while another party afterwards followed in canoes. A few, who had neither strength to walk nor canoes to transport them, perforce remained behind, and were soon massacred by the Iroquois. The fugitives directed their course to the Grand Manitoulin Island, where they remained for a short time, and then, to the number of about four hundred, descended the Ottawa, and rejoined their countrymen who had gone to Quebec the year before.

These united parties, joined from time to time by a few other fugitives, formed a settlement on land belonging to the Jesuits, near the south-western extremity of the Isle of Orleans, immediately below Quebec. Here the Jesuits built a fort, like that on Isle St. Joseph, with a chapel, and a small house for the missionaries, while the bark dwellings of the Hurons were clustered around the protecting ram-

---

[1] Ragueneau, *Relation des Hurons, 1651*, 5, 6. Le Mercier, in the *Relation* of 1654, preserves the speech of a Huron chief, in which he speaks of this affair, and adds some particulars not mentioned by Ragueneau. He gives thirty-four as the number killed.

parts.[1] Tools and seeds were given them, and they were encouraged to cultivate the soil. Gradually they rallied from their dejection, and the mission settlement was beginning to wear an appearance of thrift, when, in 1656, the Iroquois made a descent upon them, and carried off a large number of captives, under the very cannon of Quebec; the French not daring to fire upon the invaders, lest they should take revenge upon the Jesuits who were at that time in their country. This calamity was, four years after, followed by another, when the best of the Huron warriors, including their leader, the crafty and valiant Étienne Annaotaha, were slain, fighting side by side with the French, in the desperate conflict of the Long Sault.[2]

The attenuated colony, replenished by some straggling bands of the same nation, and still numbering several hundred persons, was removed to Quebec after the inroad in 1656, and lodged in a square inclosure of palisades close to the fort.[3] Here they remained about ten years, when, the danger of the times having diminished, they were again removed to a place called Notre-Dame de Foy, now St. Foi, three or four miles west of Quebec. Six years after, when the soil was impoverished and the wood in the neighborhood exhausted, they again changed their abode, and, under the auspices of the Jesuits, who owned the land, settled at Old Lorette, nine miles from Quebec.

Chaumonot was at this time their missionary. It may be remembered that he had professed special devotion to Our Lady of Loretto, who, in his boyhood, had cured him, as he believed, of a distressing malady.[4] He had always cherished the idea of building a chapel in honor of her in Canada, after the model of the Holy House of Loretto,—which, as all the world

---

[1] The site of the fort was the estate now known as "La Terre du Fort," near the landing of the steam ferry. In 1856, Mr. N. H. Bowen, a resident near the spot, in making some excavations, found a solid stone wall five feet thick, which, there can be little doubt, was that of the work in question. This wall was originally crowned with palisades. See Bowen, *Historical Sketch of the Isle of Orleans*, 25.

[2] *Relation, 1660* (anonymous), 14.

[3] In a plan of Quebec of 1660, the "Fort des Hurons" is laid down on a spot adjoining the north side of the present Place d'Armes.

[4] See *ante*, p. 471.

knows, is the house wherein Saint Joseph dwelt with his virgin spouse, and which angels bore through the air from the Holy Land to Italy, where it remains an object of pilgrimage to this day. Chaumonot opened his plan to his brother Jesuits, who were delighted with it, and the chapel was begun at once, not without the intervention of miracle to aid in raising the necessary funds. It was built of brick, like its original, of which it was an exact facsimile; and it stood in the centre of a quadrangle, the four sides of which were formed by the bark dwellings of the Hurons, ranged with perfect order in straight lines. Hither came many pilgrims from Quebec and more distant settlements, and here Our Lady granted to her suppliants, says Chaumonot, many miraculous favors, insomuch that "it would require an entire book to describe them all."[1]

But the Hurons were not destined to remain permanently even here; for, before the end of the century, they removed to a place four miles distant, now called New Lorette, or Indian Lorette. It was a wild spot, covered with the primitive forest, and seamed by a deep and tortuous ravine, where the St. Charles foams, white as a snow-drift, over the black ledges, and where the sunlight struggles through matted boughs of the pine and fir, to bask for brief moments on the mossy rocks or flash on the hurrying waters. On a plateau beside the torrent, another chapel was built to Our Lady, and another Huron town sprang up; and here, to this day, the tourist finds the remnant of a lost people, harmless weavers of baskets and sewers of moccasins, the Huron blood fast bleaching out of them, as, with every generation, they mingle and fade away in the French population around.[2]

---

[1] "Les grâces qu'on y obtient par l'entremise de la Mère de Dieu vont jusqu'au miracle. Comme il faudroit composer un livre entier pour décrire toutes ces faveurs extraordinaires, je n'en rapporterai que deux, ayant été témoin oculaire de l'une et propre sujet de l'autre."— *Vie*, 95.

The removal from Notre-Dame de Foy took place at the end of 1673, and the chapel was finished in the following year. Compare *Vie de Chaumonot* with Dablon, *Relation, 1672–73*, p. 21; and Ibid., *Relation, 1673–79*, p. 259.

[2] An interesting account of a visit to Indian Lorette in 1721 will be found in the *Journal Historique* of Charlevoix. Kalm, in his *Travels in North America*, describes its condition in 1749. See also Le Beau, *Aventures*, I. 103; who, however, can hardly be regarded as an authority.

Chapter XXXIII

1650–1670

THE DESTROYERS

Iroquois Ambition • Its Victims • The Fate of the Neutrals • The Fate of the Eries • The War with the Andastes • Supremacy of the Iroquois

---

IT was well for the European colonies, above all for those of England, that the wisdom of the Iroquois was but the wisdom of savages. Their sagacity is past denying; it showed itself in many ways; but it was not equal to a comprehension of their own situation and that of their race. Could they have read their destiny, and curbed their mad ambition, they might have leagued with themselves four great communities of kindred lineage, to resist the encroachments of civilization, and oppose a barrier of fire to the spread of the young colonies of the East. But their organization and their intelligence were merely the instruments of a blind frenzy, which impelled them to destroy those whom they might have made their allies in a common cause.

Of the four kindred communities, two at least, the Hurons and the Neutrals, were probably superior in numbers to the Iroquois. Either one of these, with union and leadership, could have held its ground against them, and the two united could easily have crippled them beyond the power of doing mischief. But these so-called nations were mere aggregations of villages and families, with nothing that deserved to be called a government. They were very liable to panics, because the part attacked by an enemy could never rely with confidence on prompt succor from the rest; and when once broken, they could not be rallied, because they had no centre around which to gather. The Iroquois, on the other hand, had an organization with which the ideas and habits of several generations were interwoven, and they had also sagacious leaders for peace and war. They discussed all questions of policy with the coolest deliberation, and knew how to turn to profit even imperfections in their plan of government which seemed to promise only weakness and discord. Thus, any nation, or any large town, of their confederacy, could make a separate war or a separate peace with a foreign nation, or any part of it. Some member of the league, as, for example, the Cayugas, would make a covenant of friendship with the enemy, and, while the infatuated victims were thus lulled into a delusive security, the war-parties of the other nations, often joined by the Cayuga warriors, would overwhelm them by a sudden onset. But it was not by their craft, nor by their organization,—which for military purposes was wretchedly feeble,— that this handful of savages gained a bloody supremacy. They carried all before them, because they were animated throughout, as one man, by the same audacious pride and insatiable rage for conquest. Like other Indians, they waged war on a plan altogether democratic,—that is, each man fought or not, as he saw fit; and they owed their unity and vigor of action to the homicidal frenzy that urged them all alike.

The Neutral Nation had taken no part, on either side, in the war of extermination against the Hurons; and their towns were sanctuaries where either of the contending parties might take asylum. On the other hand, they made fierce war on their western neighbors, and, a few years before, destroyed, with atrocious cruelties, a large fortified town of the Nation of Fire.[1] Their turn was now come, and their victims found fit avengers; for no sooner were the Hurons broken up and dis-

---

[1] "Last summer," writes Lalemant in 1643, "two thousand warriors of the Neutral Nation attacked a town of the Nation of Fire, well fortified with a palisade, and defended by nine hundred warriors. They took it after a siege of ten days; killed many on the spot; and made eight hundred prisoners, men, women, and children. After burning seventy of the best warriors, they put out the eyes of the old men, and cut away their lips, and then left them to drag out a miserable existence. Behold the scourge that is depopulating all this country!"— *Relation des Hurons, 1644*, 98.

The Assistaeronnons, Atsistaehonnons, Mascoutins, or Nation of Fire (more correctly, perhaps, Nation of the Prairie), were a very numerous Algonquin people of the West, speaking the same language as the Sacs and Foxes. In the map of Sanson, they are placed in the southern part of Michigan; and according to the *Relation* of 1658, they had thirty towns. They were a stationary, and in some measure an agricultural people. They fled before their enemies to the neighborhood of Fox River in Wisconsin, where they long remained. Frequent mention of them will be found in the later *Relations*, and in contemporary documents. They are now extinct as a tribe.

persed, than the Iroquois, without waiting to take breath, turned their fury on the Neutrals. At the end of the autumn of 1650, they assaulted and took one of their chief towns, said to have contained at the time more than sixteen hundred men, besides women and children; and early in the following spring, they took another town. The slaughter was prodigious, and the victors drove back troops of captives for butchery or adoption. It was the death-blow of the Neutrals. They abandoned their corn-fields and villages in the wildest terror, and dispersed themselves abroad in forests, which could not yield sustenance to such a multitude. They perished by thousands, and from that time forth the nation ceased to exist.[1]

During two or three succeeding years, the Iroquois contented themselves with harassing the French and Algonquins; but in 1653 they made treaties of peace, each of the five nations for itself, and the colonists and their red allies had an interval of rest. In the following May, an Onondaga orator, on a peace visit to Montreal, said, in a speech to the Governor, "Our young men will no more fight the French; but they are too warlike to stay at home, and this summer we shall invade the country of the Eries. The earth trembles and quakes in that quarter; but here all remains calm."[2] Early in the autumn, Father Le Moyne, who had taken advantage of the peace to go on a mission to the Onondagas, returned with the tidings that the Iroquois were all on fire with this new enterprise, and were about to march against the Eries with eighteen hundred warriors.[3]

The occasion of this new war is said to have been as

[1] Ragueneau, *Relation, 1651*, 4. In the unpublished journal kept by the Superior of the Jesuits at Quebec, it is said, under date of April, 1651, that news had just come from Montreal, that, in the preceding autumn, fifteen hundred Iroquois had taken a Neutral town; that the Neutrals had afterwards attacked them, and killed two hundred of their warriors; and that twelve hundred Iroquois had again invaded the Neutral country to take their revenge. Lafitau, *Mœurs des Sauvages*, II. 176, gives, on the authority of Father Julien Garnier, a singular and improbable account of the origin of the war.

An old chief, named Kenjockety, who claimed descent from an adopted prisoner of the Neutral Nation, was recently living among the Senecas of Western New York.

[2] Le Mercier, *Relation, 1654*, 9.

[3] *Ibid.*, 10. Le Moyne, in his interesting journal of his mission, repeatedly alludes to their preparations.

follows. The Eries, who it will be remembered dwelt on the south of the lake named after them, had made a treaty of peace with the Senecas, and in the preceding year had sent a deputation of thirty of their principal men to confirm it. While they were in the great Seneca town, it happened that one of that nation was killed in a casual quarrel with an Erie; whereupon his countrymen rose in a fury, and murdered the thirty deputies. Then ensued a brisk war of reprisals, in which not only the Senecas, but the other Iroquois nations, took part. The Eries captured a famous Onondaga chief, and were about to burn him, when he succeeded in convincing them of the wisdom of a course of conciliation; and they resolved to give him to the sister of one of the murdered deputies, to take the place of her lost brother. The sister, by Indian law, had it in her choice to receive him with a fraternal embrace or to burn him; but, though she was absent at the time, no one doubted that she would choose the gentler alternative. Accordingly, he was clothed in gay attire, and all the town fell to feasting in honor of his adoption. In the midst of the festivity, the sister returned. To the amazement of the Erie chiefs, she rejected with indignation their proffer of a new brother, declared that she would be revenged for her loss, and insisted that the prisoner should forthwith be burned. The chiefs remonstrated in vain, representing the danger in which such a procedure would involve the nation: the female fury was inexorable; and the unfortunate prisoner, stripped of his festal robes, was bound to the stake, and put to death.[1] He warned his tormentors with his last breath, that they were burning not only him, but the whole Erie nation; since his countrymen would take a fiery vengeance for his fate. His words proved true; for no sooner was his story spread abroad among the Iroquois, than the confederacy resounded with war-songs from end to end, and the warriors took the field under their two great war-chiefs. Notwithstanding Le Moyne's report, their number, according to the Iroquois account, did not exceed twelve hundred.[2]

[1] De Quen, *Relation, 1656,* 30.

[2] This was their statement to Chaumonot and Dablon, at Onondaga, in November of this year. They added, that the number of the Eries was between three and four thousand. (*Journal des PP. Chaumonot et Dablon,* in

They embarked in canoes on the lake. At their approach the Eries fell back, withdrawing into the forests towards the west, till they were gathered into one body, when, fortifying themselves with palisades and felled trees, they awaited the approach of the invaders. By the lowest estimate, the Eries numbered two thousand warriors, besides women and children. But this is the report of the Iroquois, who were naturally disposed to exaggerate the force of their enemies.

They approached the Erie fort, and two of their chiefs, dressed like Frenchmen, advanced and called on those within to surrender. One of them had lately been baptized by Le Moyne; and he shouted to the Eries, that, if they did not yield in time, they were all dead men, for the Master of Life was on the side of the Iroquois. The Eries answered with yells of derision. "Who is this master of your lives?" they cried; "our hatchets and our right arms are the masters of ours." The Iroquois rushed to the assault, but were met with a shower of poisoned arrows, which killed and wounded many of them, and drove the rest back. They waited awhile, and then attacked again with unabated mettle. This time, they carried their bark canoes over their heads like huge shields, to protect them from the storm of arrows; then planting them upright, and mounting them by the cross-bars like ladders, scaled the barricade with such impetuous fury that the Eries were thrown into a panic. Those escaped who could; but the butchery was frightful, and from that day the Eries as a nation were no more. The victors paid dear for their conquest. Their losses were so heavy that they were forced to remain for two months in the Erie country, to bury their dead and nurse their wounded.[1]

Relation, 1656, 18.) In the narrative of De Quen (*Ibid.,* 30, 31), based, of course, on Iroquois reports, the Iroquois force is also set down at twelve hundred, but that of the Eries is reduced to between two and three thousand warriors. Even this may safely be taken as an exaggeration.

Though the Eries had no fire-arms, they used poisoned arrows with great effect, discharging them, it is said, with surprising rapidity.

[1] De Quen, *Ibid.,* 31. The Iroquois, it seems, afterwards made other expeditions, to finish their work. At least, they told Chaumonot and Dablon, in the autumn of this year, that they meant to do so in the following spring.

It seems, that, before attacking the great fort of the Eries, the Iroquois had made a promise to worship the new God of the French, if He would give

One enemy of their own race remained,—the Andastes. This nation appears to have been inferior in numbers to either the Hurons, the Neutrals, or the Eries; but they cost their assailants more trouble than all these united. The Mohawks seem at first to have borne the brunt of the Andaste war; and, between the years 1650 and 1660, they were so roughly handled by these stubborn adversaries, that they were reduced from the height of audacious insolence to the depths of dejection.[1] The remaining four nations of the Iroquois league now took up the quarrel, and fared scarcely better than the Mohawks. In the spring of 1662, eight hundred of their warriors set out for the Andaste country, to strike a decisive blow; but when they reached the great town of their enemies, they saw that they had received both aid and counsel from the neighboring Swedish colonists. The town was fortified by a double palisade, flanked by two bastions, on which, it is said, several small pieces of cannon were mounted. Clearly, it was not to be carried by assault, as the invaders had promised themselves. Their only hope was in treachery; and, accordingly, twenty-five of their warriors gained entrance, on pretence of settling the terms of a peace. Here, again, ensued a grievous disappointment; for the Andastes seized them all, built high scaffolds visible from without, and tortured them to death in sight of their countrymen, who thereupon decamped in miserable discomfiture.[2]

The Senecas, by far the most numerous of the five Iroquois nations, now found themselves attacked in turn,—and this,

---

them the victory. This promise, and the success which followed, proved of great advantage to the mission.

Various traditions are extant among the modern remnant of the Iroquois concerning the war with the Eries. They agree in little beyond the fact of the existence and destruction of that people. Indeed, Indian traditions are very rarely of any value as historical evidence. One of these stories, told me some years ago by a very intelligent Iroquois of the Cayuga Nation, is a striking illustration of Iroquois ferocity. It represents, that, the night after the great battle, the forest was lighted up with more than a thousand fires, at each of which an Erie was burning alive. It differs from the historical accounts in making the Eries the aggressors.

[1] *Relation, 1660*, 6 (anonymous).

The Mohawks also suffered great reverses about this time at the hands of their Algonquin neighbors, the Mohicans.

[2] Lalemant, *Relation, 1663*, 10.

too, at a time when they were full of despondency at the ravages of the small-pox. The French reaped a profit from their
misfortunes; for the disheartened savages made them overtures of peace, and begged that they would settle in their
country, teach them to fortify their towns, supply them with
arms and ammunition, and bring "black-robes" to show them
the road to Heaven.[1]

The Andaste war became a war of inroads and skirmishes,
under which the weaker party gradually wasted away, though
it sometimes won laurels at the expense of its adversary. Thus,
in 1672, a party of twenty Senecas and forty Cayugas went
against the Andastes. They were at a considerable distance the
one from the other, the Cayugas being in advance, when the
Senecas were set upon by about sixty young Andastes, of the
class known as "Burnt-Knives," or "Soft-Metals," because as
yet they had taken no scalps. Indeed, they are described as
mere boys, fifteen or sixteen years old. They killed one of the
Senecas, captured another, and put the rest to flight; after
which, flushed with their victory, they attacked the Cayugas
with the utmost fury, and routed them completely, killing
eight of them, and wounding twice that number, who, as is
reported by the Jesuit then in the Cayuga towns, came home
half dead with gashes of knives and hatchets.[2] "May God preserve the Andastes," exclaims the Father, "and prosper their
arms, that the Iroquois may be humbled, and we and our
missions left in peace!" "None but they," he elsewhere adds,
"can curb the pride of the Iroquois." The only strength of the
Andastes, however, was in their courage: for at this time they
were reduced to three hundred fighting men; and about the
year 1675 they were finally overborne by the Senecas.[3] Yet
they were not wholly destroyed; for a remnant of this valiant
people continued to subsist, under the name of Conestogas,
for nearly a century, until, in 1763, they were butchered, as
already mentioned, by the white ruffians known as the "Paxton Boys."[4]

[1] *Ibid.*, *1664*, 33.

[2] Dablon, *Relation, 1672*, 24.

[3] *État Présent des Missions*, in *Relations Inédites*, II. 44. *Relation, 1676*, 2. This
is one of the *Relations* printed by Mr. Lenox.

[4] "History of the Conspiracy of Pontiac," Chap. XXIV. Compare Shea, in
Historical Magazine, II. 297.

The bloody triumphs of the Iroquois were complete. They had "made a solitude, and called it peace." All the surrounding nations of their own lineage were conquered and broken up, while neighboring Algonquin tribes were suffered to exist only on condition of paying a yearly tribute of wampum. The confederacy remained a wedge thrust between the growing colonies of France and England.

But what was the state of the conquerors? Their triumphs had cost them dear. As early as the year 1660, a writer, evidently well-informed, reports that their entire force had been reduced to twenty-two hundred warriors, while of these not more than twelve hundred were of the true Iroquois stock. The rest was a medley of adopted prisoners,—Hurons, Neutrals, Eries, and Indians of various Algonquin tribes.[1] Still their aggressive spirit was unsubdued. These incorrigible warriors pushed their murderous raids to Hudson's Bay, Lake Superior, the Mississippi, and the Tennessee; they were the tyrants of all the intervening wilderness; and they remained, for more than half a century, a terror and a scourge to the afflicted colonists of New France.

[1] *Relation, 1660,* 6, 7 (anonymous). Le Jeune says, "Their victories have so depopulated their towns, that there are more foreigners in them than natives. At Onondaga there are Indians of seven different nations permanently established; and, among the Senecas, of no less than eleven." (*Relation, 1657,* 34.) These were either adopted prisoners, or Indians who had voluntarily joined the Iroquois to save themselves from their hostility. They took no part in councils, but were expected to join war-parties, though they were usually excused from fighting against their former countrymen. The condition of female prisoners was little better than that of slaves, and those to whom they were assigned often killed them on the slightest pique.

Chapter XXXIV

THE END

Failure of the Jesuits • What their Success would have involved •
Future of the Mission

WITH the fall of the Hurons, fell the best hope of the Canadian mission. They, and the stable and populous communities around them, had been the rude material from which the Jesuit would have formed his Christian empire in the wilderness; but, one by one, these kindred peoples were uprooted and swept away, while the neighboring Algonquins, to whom they had been a bulwark, were involved with them in a common ruin. The land of promise was turned to a solitude and a desolation. There was still work in hand, it is true,—vast regions to explore, and countless heathens to snatch from perdition; but these, for the most part, were remote and scattered hordes, from whose conversion it was vain to look for the same solid and decisive results.

In a measure, the occupation of the Jesuits was gone. Some of them went home, "well resolved," writes the Father Superior, "to return to the combat at the first sound of the trumpet;"[1] while of those who remained, about twenty in number, several soon fell victims to famine, hardship, and the Iroquois. A few years more, and Canada ceased to be a mission; political and commercial interests gradually became ascendant, and the story of Jesuit propagandism was interwoven with her civil and military annals.

Here, then, closes this wild and bloody act of the great drama of New France; and now let the curtain fall, while we ponder its meaning.

The cause of the failure of the Jesuits is obvious. The guns and tomahawks of the Iroquois were the ruin of their hopes. Could they have curbed or converted those ferocious bands, it is little less than certain that their dream would have become a reality. Savages tamed—not civilized, for that was scarcely possible—would have been distributed in communities through the valleys of the Great Lakes and the Mississippi,

[1] *Lettre de Lalemant au R.P. Provincial* (*Relation, 1650*, 48).

ruled by priests in the interest of Catholicity and of France. Their habits of agriculture would have been developed, and their instincts of mutual slaughter repressed. The swift decline of the Indian population would have been arrested; and it would have been made, through the fur-trade, a source of prosperity to New France. Unmolested by Indian enemies, and fed by a rich commerce, she would have put forth a vigorous growth. True to her far-reaching and adventurous genius, she would have occupied the West with traders, settlers, and garrisons, and cut up the virgin wilderness into fiefs, while as yet the colonies of England were but a weak and broken line along the shore of the Atlantic; and when at last the great conflict came, England and Liberty would have been confronted, not by a depleted antagonist, still feeble from the exhaustion of a starved and persecuted infancy, but by an athletic champion of the principles of Richelieu and of Loyola.

Liberty may thank the Iroquois, that, by their insensate fury, the plans of her adversary were brought to nought, and a peril and a woe averted from her future. They ruined the trade which was the life-blood of New France; they stopped the current of her arteries, and made all her early years a misery and a terror. Not that they changed her destinies. The contest on this continent between Liberty and Absolutism was never doubtful; but the triumph of the one would have been dearly bought, and the downfall of the other incomplete. Populations formed in the ideas and habits of a feudal monarchy, and controlled by a hierarchy profoundly hostile to freedom of thought, would have remained a hindrance and a stumbling-block in the way of that majestic experiment of which America is the field.

The Jesuits saw their hopes struck down; and their faith, though not shaken, was sorely tried. The Providence of God seemed in their eyes dark and inexplicable; but, from the stand-point of Liberty, that Providence is clear as the sun at noon. Meanwhile let those who have prevailed yield due honor to the defeated. Their virtues shine amidst the rubbish of error, like diamonds and gold in the gravel of the torrent.

But now new scenes succeed, and other actors enter on the stage, a hardy and valiant band, moulded to endure and dare,—the Discoverers of the Great West.

LA SALLE AND THE
DISCOVERY
OF THE GREAT WEST

Contents

Preface of the Eleventh Edition

WHEN the earlier editions of this book were published, I was aware of the existence of a collection of documents relating to La Salle, and containing important material to which I had not succeeded in gaining access. This collection was in possession of M. Pierre Margry, director of the Archives of the Marine and Colonies at Paris, and was the result of more than thirty years of research. With rare assiduity and zeal, M. Margry had explored not only the vast depository with which he has been officially connected from youth, and of which he is now the chief, but also the other public archives of France, and many private collections in Paris and the provinces. The object of his search was to throw light on the career and achievements of French explorers, and, above all, of La Salle. A collection of extraordinary richness grew gradually upon his hands. In the course of my own inquiries, I owed much to his friendly aid; but his collections, as a whole, remained inaccessible, since he naturally wished to be the first to make known the results of his labors. An attempt to induce Congress to furnish him with the means of printing documents so interesting to American history was made in 1870 and 1871, by Henry Harrisse, Esq., aided by the American Minister at Paris; but it unfortunately failed.

In the summer and autumn of 1872, I had numerous interviews with M. Margry, and at his desire undertook to try to induce some American bookseller to publish the collection. On returning to the United States, I accordingly made an arrangement with Messrs. Little, Brown, & Co., of Boston, by which they agreed to print the papers, if a certain number of subscriptions should first be obtained. The condition proved very difficult; and it became clear that the best hope of success lay in another appeal to Congress. This was made in the following winter, in conjunction with Hon. E. B. Washburne, Colonel Charles Whittlesey, of Cleveland, O. H. Marshall, Esq., of Buffalo, and other gentlemen interested in early American history. The attempt succeeded. Congress made an appropriation for the purchase of five hundred copies of the work, to be printed at Paris, under direction of M. Margry; and the three volumes devoted to La Salle are at length before the public.

Of the papers contained in them which I had not before examined, the most interesting are the letters of La Salle, found in the original by M. Margry, among the immense accumulations of the Archives of the Marine and Colonies and the Bibliothèque Nationale. The narrative of La Salle's companion, Joutel, far more copious than the abstract printed in 1713, under the title of *Journal Historique*, also deserves special mention. These, with other fresh material in these three volumes, while they add new facts and throw new light on the character of La Salle, confirm nearly every statement made in the first edition of the Discovery of the Great West. The only exception of consequence relates to the causes of La Salle's failure to find the mouth of the Mississippi in 1684, and to the conduct, on that occasion, of the naval commander, Beaujeu.

This edition is revised throughout, and in part rewritten with large additions. A map of the country traversed by the explorers is also added. The name of La Salle is placed on the title-page, as seems to be demanded by his increased prominence in the narrative of which he is the central figure.

BOSTON, *10 December, 1878*.

NOTE.—The title of M. Margry's printed collection is "Découvertes et Établissements des Français dans l'Ouest et dans le Sud de l'Amérique Septentrionale (1614–1754), Mémoires et Documents originaux." I., II., III. Besides the three volumes relating to La Salle, there will be two others, relating to other explorers. In accordance with the agreement with Congress, an independent edition will appear in France, with an introduction setting forth the circumstances of the publication.

Preface of the First Edition

THE discovery of the "Great West," or the valleys of the Mississippi and the Lakes, is a portion of our history hitherto very obscure. Those magnificent regions were revealed to the world through a series of daring enterprises, of which the motives and even the incidents have been but partially and superficially known. The chief actor in them wrote much, but printed nothing; and the published writings of his associates stand wofully in need of interpretation from the unpublished documents which exist, but which have not heretofore been used as material for history.

This volume attempts to supply the defect. Of the large amount of wholly new material employed in it, by far the greater part is drawn from the various public archives of France, and the rest from private sources. The discovery of many of these documents is due to the indefatigable research of M. Pierre Margry, assistant director of the Archives of the Marine and Colonies at Paris, whose labors as an investigator of the maritime and colonial history of France can be appreciated only by those who have seen their results. In the department of American colonial history, these results have been invaluable; for, besides several private collections made by him, he rendered important service in the collection of the French portion of the Brodhead documents, selected and arranged the two great series of colonial papers ordered by the Canadian government, and prepared with vast labor analytical indexes of these and of supplementary documents in the French archives, as well as a copious index of the mass of papers relating to Louisiana. It is to be hoped that the valuable publications on the maritime history of France which have appeared from his pen are an earnest of more extended contributions in future.

The late President Sparks, some time after the publication of his Life of La Salle, caused a collection to be made of documents relating to that explorer, with the intention of incorporating them in a future edition. This intention was never carried into effect, and the documents were never used. With the liberality which always distinguished him, he placed them at my disposal, and this privilege has been kindly continued by Mrs. Sparks.

Abbé Faillon, the learned author of "La Colonie Française en Canada," has sent me copies of various documents found by him, including family papers of La Salle. Among others who in various ways have aided my inquiries are Dr. John Paul, of Ottawa, Ill.; Count Adolphe de Circourt, and M. Jules Marcou, of Paris; M. A. Gérin Lajoie, Assistant Librarian of the Canadian Parliament; M. J. M. Le Moine, of Quebec; General Dix, Minister of the United States at the Court of France; O. H. Marshall, of Buffalo; J. G. Shea, of New York; Buckingham Smith, of St. Augustine; and Colonel Thomas Aspinwall, of Boston.

The smaller map contained in the book is a portion of the manuscript map of Franquelin, of which an account will be found in the Appendix.

The next volume of the series will be devoted to the efforts of Monarchy and Feudalism under Louis XIV. to establish a permanent power on this continent, and to the stormy career of Louis de Buade, Count of Frontenac.

BOSTON, *16 September, 1869.*

Introduction

THE Spaniards discovered the Mississippi. De Soto was buried beneath its waters; and it was down its muddy current that his followers fled from the Eldorado of their dreams, transformed to a wilderness of misery and death. The discovery was never used, and was well-nigh forgotten. On early Spanish maps, the Mississippi is often indistinguishable from other affluents of the Gulf. A century passed after De Soto's journeyings in the South, before a French explorer reached a northern tributary of the great river.

This was Jean Nicollet, interpreter at Three Rivers on the St. Lawrence. He had been some twenty years in Canada, had lived among the savage Algonquins of Allumette Island, and spent eight or nine years among the Nipissings, on the lake which bears their name. Here he became an Indian in all his habits, but remained, nevertheless, a zealous Catholic, and returned to civilization at last, because he could not live without the sacraments. Strange stories were current among the Nipissings, of a people without hair or beard, who came from the West, to trade with a tribe beyond the Great Lakes. Who could doubt that these strangers were Chinese or Japanese? Such tales may well have excited Nicollet's curiosity; and when, in 1635, or possibly in 1638, he was sent as an ambassador to the tribe in question, he would not have been surprised if on arriving he had found a party of mandarins among them. Perhaps it was with a view to such a contingency that he provided himself, as a dress of ceremony, with a robe of Chinese damask embroidered with birds and flowers. The tribe to which he was sent was that of the Winnebagoes, living near the head of the Green Bay of Lake Michigan. They had come to blows with the Hurons, allies of the French; and Nicollet was charged to negotiate a peace. When he approached the Winnebago town, he sent one of his Indian attendants to announce his coming, put on his robe of damask, and advanced to meet the expectant crowd with a pistol in each hand. The squaws and children fled, screaming that it was a manito, or spirit, armed with thunder and lightning; but the chiefs and warriors regaled him with so bountiful a hospitality that a hundred and twenty beavers were devoured at a single feast. From the Winnebagoes, he passed westward, ascended Fox River, crossed to the Wisconsin, and descended it so far that, as he reported on his return, in three days more he would have reached the sea. The truth seems to be, that he mistook the meaning of his Indian guides, and that the "great water" to which he was so near was not the sea, but the Mississippi.

It has been affirmed that one Colonel Wood, of Virginia, reached a branch of the Mississippi as early as the year 1654, and that about 1670 a certain Captain Bolton penetrated to the river itself. Neither statement is sustained by sufficient evidence. It is further affirmed that, in 1678, a party from New England crossed the Mississippi, reached New Mexico, and, returning, reported their discoveries to the authorities of Boston: a story without proof or probability. Meanwhile, French Jesuits and fur-traders pushed deeper and deeper into the wilderness of the northern lakes. In 1641, Jogues and Raymbault preached the Faith to a concourse of Indians at the outlet of Lake Superior. Then came the havoc and desolation of the Iroquois war, and for years farther exploration was arrested. At length, in 1658, two daring traders penetrated to Lake Superior, wintered there, and brought back tales of the ferocious Sioux, and of a great western river on which they dwelt. Two years later, the aged Jesuit Ménard attempted to plant a mission on the southern shore of the lake, but perished in the forest, by famine or the tomahawk. Allouez succeeded him, explored a part of Lake Superior, and heard, in his turn, of the Sioux and their great river, the "Messipi." More and more, the thoughts of the Jesuits—and not of the Jesuits alone—dwelt on this mysterious stream. Through what regions did it flow; and whither would it lead them,—to the South Sea or the "Sea of Virginia," to Mexico, Japan, or China? The problem was soon to be solved, and the mystery revealed.

Chapter I

1643—1669

CAVELIER DE LA SALLE

The Youth of La Salle • His Connection with the Jesuits • He goes to Canada • His Character • His Schemes • His Seigniory at La Chine • His Expedition in Search of a Western Passage to India

---

Among the burghers of Rouen was the old and rich family of the Caveliers. Though citizens and not nobles, some of their connections held high diplomatic posts and honorable employments at Court. They were destined to find a better claim to distinction. In 1643 was born at Rouen Robert Cavelier, better known by the designation of La Salle.[1] His father Jean and his uncle Henri were wealthy merchants, living more like nobles than like burghers; and the boy received an education answering to the marked traits of intellect and character which he soon began to display. He showed an inclination for the exact sciences, and especially for the mathematics, in which he made great proficiency. At an early age, it is said, he became connected with the Jesuits; and, though doubt has been expressed of the statement, it is probably true.[2]

La Salle was always an earnest Catholic; and yet, judging by the qualities which his after life evinced, he was not very

[1] The following is the *acte de naissance*, discovered by Margry in the *registres de l'état civil*, Paroisse St. Herbland, Rouen: "Le vingt-deuxième jour de novembre, 1643, a été baptisé Robert Cavelier, fils de honorable homme Jean Cavelier et de Catherine Geest; ses parrain et marraine honorables personnes Nicolas Geest et Marguerite Morice."

La Salle's name in full was Réné-Robert Cavelier, Sieur de la Salle. La Salle was the name of an estate near Rouen, belonging to the Caveliers. The wealthy French burghers often distinguished the various members of their families by designations borrowed from landed estates. Thus, François Marie Arouet, son of an ex-notary, received the name of Voltaire, which he made famous.

[2] Margry, after investigations at Rouen, is satisfied of its truth. *Journal Général de l'Instruction Publique*, xxxi. 571. Family papers of the Caveliers, examined by the Abbé Faillon, and copies of some of which he has sent to me, lead to the same conclusion. We shall find several allusions hereafter to La Salle's having in his youth taught in a school, which, in his position, could only have been in connection with some religious community. The doubts

liable to religious enthusiasm. It is nevertheless clear that the Society of Jesus may have had a powerful attraction for his youthful imagination. This great organization, so complicated yet so harmonious, a mighty machine moved from the centre by a single hand, was an image of regulated power, full of fascination for a mind like his. But, if it was likely that he would be drawn into it, it was no less likely that he would soon wish to escape. To find himself not at the centre of power, but at the circumference; not the mover, but the moved; the passive instrument of another's will, taught to walk in prescribed paths, to renounce his individuality and become a component atom of a vast whole,—would have been intolerable to him. Nature had shaped him for other uses than to teach a class of boys on the benches of a Jesuit school. Nor, on his part, was he likely to please his directors; for, self-controlled and self-contained as he was, he was far too intractable a subject to serve their turn. A youth whose calm exterior hid an inexhaustible fund of pride; whose inflexible purposes, nursed in secret, the confessional and the "manifestation of conscience" could hardly drag to the light; whose strong personality would not yield to the shaping hand; and who, by a necessity of his nature, could obey no initiative but his own,—was not after the model that Loyola had commended to his followers.

La Salle left the Jesuits, parting with them, it is said, on good terms, and with a reputation of excellent acquirements and unimpeachable morals. This last is very credible. The cravings of a deep ambition, the hunger of an insatiable intellect, the intense longing for action and achievement, subdued in him all other passions; and in his faults the love of pleasure had no part. He had an elder brother in Canada, the Abbé Jean Cavelier, a priest of St. Sulpice. Apparently, it was this that shaped his destinies. His connection with the Jesuits had deprived him, under the French law, of the inheritance of his father, who had died not long before. An allowance was made

---

alluded to have proceeded from the failure of Father Felix Martin, S.J., to find the name of *La Salle* on the list of novices. If he had looked for the name of *Robert Cavelier*, he would probably have found it. The companion of La Salle, Hennepin, is very explicit with regard to this connection with the Jesuits, a point on which he had no motive for falsehood.

to him of three or, as is elsewhere stated, four hundred livres a year, the capital of which was paid over to him; and with this pittance he sailed for Canada, to seek his fortune, in the spring of 1666.[1]

Next, we find him at Montreal. In another volume, we have seen how an association of enthusiastic devotees had made a settlement at this place.[2] Having in some measure accomplished its work, it was now dissolved; and the corporation of priests, styled the Seminary of St. Sulpice, which had taken a prominent part in the enterprise, and, indeed, had been created with a view to it, was now the proprietor and the feudal lord of Montreal. It was destined to retain its seigniorial rights until the abolition of the feudal tenures of Canada in our own day, and it still holds vast possessions in the city and island. These worthy ecclesiastics, models of a discreet and sober conservatism, were holding a post with which a band of veteran soldiers or warlike frontiersmen would have been better matched. Montreal was perhaps the most dangerous place in Canada. In time of war, which might have been called the normal condition of the colony, it was exposed by its position to incessant inroads of the Iroquois, or Five Nations, of New York; and no man could venture into the forests or the fields without bearing his life in his hand. The savage confederates had just received a sharp chastisement at the hands of Courcelle, the governor; and the result was a treaty of peace, which might at any moment be broken, but which was an inexpressible relief while it lasted.

The priests of St. Sulpice were granting out their lands, on very easy terms, to settlers. They wished to extend a thin line of settlements along the front of their island, to form a sort of outpost, from which an alarm could be given on any descent of the Iroquois. La Salle was the man for such a purpose. Had the priests understood him,—which they evidently did not, for some of them suspected him of levity, the last

[1] It does not appear what vows La Salle had taken. By a recent ordinance, 1666, persons entering religious orders could not take the final vows before the age of twenty-five. By the family papers above mentioned, it appears, however, that he had brought himself under the operation of the law, which debarred those who, having entered religious orders, afterwards withdrew, from claiming the inheritance of relatives who had died after their entrance.

[2] The Jesuits in North America, c. xv.

foible with which he could be charged,—had they understood him, they would have seen in him a young man in whom the fire of youth glowed not the less ardently for the veil of reserve that covered it; who would shrink from no danger, but would not court it in bravado; and who would cling with an invincible tenacity of gripe to any purpose which he might espouse. There is good reason to think that he had come to Canada with purposes already conceived, and that he was ready to avail himself of any stepping-stone which might help to realize them. Queylus, Superior of the Seminary, made him a generous offer; and he accepted it. This was the gratuitous grant of a large tract of land at the place now called La Chine, above the great rapids of the same name, and eight or nine miles from Montreal. On one hand, the place was greatly exposed to attack; and, on the other, it was favorably situated for the fur-trade. La Salle and his successors became its feudal proprietors, on the sole condition of delivering to the Seminary, on every change of ownership, a medal of fine silver, weighing one mark.[1] He entered on the improvement of his new domain with what means he could command, and began to grant out his land to such settlers as would join him.

Approaching the shore where the city of Montreal now stands, one would have seen a row of small compact dwellings, extending along a narrow street, parallel to the river, and then, as now, called St. Paul Street. On a hill at the right stood the windmill of the seigniors, built of stone, and pierced with loopholes to serve, in time of need, as a place of defence. On the left, in an angle formed by the junction of a rivulet with the St. Lawrence, was a square bastioned fort of stone. Here lived the military governor, appointed by the Seminary, and commanding a few soldiers of the regiment of Carignan. In front, on the line of the street, were the enclosure and buildings of the Seminary, and, nearly adjoining them, those of the Hôtel-Dieu, or Hospital, both provided for defence in case of an Indian attack. In the hospital enclo-

---

[1] *Transport de la Seigneurie de St. Sulpice*, cited by Faillon. La Salle called his new domain as above. Two or three years later, it received the name of La Chine, for a reason which will appear.

sure was a small church, opening on the street, and, in the absence of any other, serving for the whole settlement.[1]

Landing, passing the fort, and walking southward along the shore, one would soon have left the rough clearings, and entered the primeval forest. Here, mile after mile, he would have journeyed on in solitude, when the hoarse roar of the rapids, foaming in fury on his left, would have reached his listening ear; and at length, after a walk of some three hours, he would have found the rude beginnings of a settlement. It was where the St. Lawrence widens into the broad expanse called the Lake of St. Louis. Here, La Salle had traced out the circuit of a palisaded village, and assigned to each settler half an arpent, or about the third of an acre, within the enclosure, for which he was to render to the young seignior a yearly acknowledgment of three capons, besides six deniers— that is, half a sou—in money. To each was assigned, moreover, sixty arpents of land beyond the limits of the village, with the perpetual rent of half a sou for each arpent. He also set apart a common, two hundred arpents in extent, for the use of the settlers, on condition of the payment by each of five sous a year. He reserved four hundred and twenty arpents for his own personal domain, and on this he began to clear the ground and erect buildings. Similar to this were the beginnings of all the Canadian seigniories formed at this troubled period.[2]

That La Salle came to Canada with objects distinctly in view, is probable from the fact that he at once began to study the Indian languages, and with such success that he is said, within two or three years, to have mastered the Iroquois and seven or eight other languages and dialects.[3] From the shore of his seigniory, he could gaze westward over the broad

[1] A detailed plan of Montreal at this time is preserved in the Archives de l'Empire, and has been reproduced by Faillon. There is another, a few years later, and still more minute, of which a fac-simile will be found in the Library of the Canadian Parliament.

[2] The above particulars have been unearthed by the indefatigable Abbé Faillon. Some of La Salle's grants are still preserved in the ancient records of Montreal.

[3] *Papiers de Famille.* He is said to have made several journeys into the forests, towards the North, in the years 1667 and 1668, and to have satisfied himself that little could be hoped from explorations in that direction.

breast of the Lake of St. Louis, bounded by the dim forests
of Chateauguay and Beauharnois; but his thoughts flew far
beyond, across the wild and lonely world that stretched towards the sunset. Like Champlain, and all the early explorers,
he dreamed of a passage to the South Sea, and a new road
for commerce to the riches of China and Japan. Indians often
came to his secluded settlement; and, on one occasion, he was
visited by a band of the Seneca Iroquois, not long before the
scourge of the colony, but now, in virtue of the treaty, wearing the semblance of friendship. The visitors spent the winter
with him, and told him of a river called the Ohio, rising in
their country, and flowing into the sea, but at such a distance
that its mouth could only be reached after a journey of eight
or nine months. Evidently, the Ohio and the Mississippi are
here merged into one.[1] In accordance with geographical
views then prevalent, he conceived that this great river must
needs flow into the "Vermilion Sea;" that is, the Gulf of California. If so, it would give him what he sought, a western
passage to China; while, in any case, the populous Indian
tribes said to inhabit its banks might be made a source of
great commercial profit.

   La Salle's imagination took fire. His resolution was soon
formed; and he descended the St. Lawrence to Quebec, to
gain the countenance of the governor for his intended exploration. Few men were more skilled than he in the art of clear
and plausible statement. Both the governor, Courcelle, and
the intendant, Talon, were readily won over to his plan; for
which, however, they seem to have given him no more substantial aid than that of the governor's letters patent authorizing the enterprise.[2] The cost was to be his own; and he
had no money, having spent it all on his seigniory. He therefore proposed that the Seminary, which had given it to him,
should buy it back again, with such improvements as he had
made. Queylus, the Superior, being favorably disposed towards him, consented, and bought of him the greater part;
while La Salle sold the remainder, including the clearings, to

---

[1] According to Dollier de Casson, who had good opportunities of knowing, the Iroquois always called the Mississippi the Ohio, while the Algonquins gave it its present name.

[2] *Patoulet à Colbert*, 11 Nov., 1669.

one Jean Milot, an ironmonger, for twenty-eight hundred livres.[1] With this he bought four canoes, with the necessary supplies, and hired fourteen men.

Meanwhile, the Seminary itself was preparing a similar enterprise. The Jesuits at this time not only held an ascendency over the other ecclesiastics in Canada, but exercised an inordinate influence on the civil government. The Seminary priests of Montreal were jealous of these powerful rivals, and eager to emulate their zeal in the saving of souls, and the conquering of new domains for the Faith. Under this impulse, they had, three years before, established a mission at Quinté, on the north shore of Lake Ontario, in charge of two of their number, one of whom was the Abbé Fénelon, elder brother of the celebrated Archbishop of Cambray. Another of them, Dollier de Casson, had spent the winter in a hunting-camp of the Nipissings, where an Indian prisoner, captured in the North-west, told him of populous tribes of that quarter, living in heathenish darkness. On this, the Seminary priests resolved to essay their conversion; and an expedition, to be directed by Dollier, was fitted out to this end.

He was not ill suited to the purpose. He had been a soldier in his youth, and had fought valiantly as an officer of cavalry under Turenne. He was a man of great courage; of a tall, commanding person; and of uncommon bodily strength, which he had notably proved in the campaign of Courcelle against the Iroquois, three years before.[2] On going to Quebec to procure the necessary outfit, he was urged by Courcelle to modify his plans so far as to act in concert with La Salle in exploring the mystery of the great unknown river of the West. Dollier and his brother priests consented. One of them, Galinée, was joined with him as a colleague, because he was skilled in surveying, and could make a map of their route. Three canoes were procured, and seven hired men completed the party. It was determined that La Salle's expedition and that of the Seminary should be combined in one; an arrangement ill suited to the character of the young explorer, who

[1] *Cession de la Seigneurie*; *Contrat de Vente* (Margry, I. 103, 104).

[2] He was the author of the very curious and valuable *Histoire de Montréal*, preserved in the Bibliothèque Mazarine, of which a copy is in my possession. The Historical Society of Montreal has recently resolved to print it.

was unfit for any enterprise of which he was not the undisputed chief. •

Midsummer was near, and there was no time to lose. Yet the moment was most unpropitious, for a Seneca chief had lately been murdered by three scoundrel soldiers of the fort of Montreal; and, while they were undergoing their trial, it became known that three other Frenchmen had treacherously put to death several Iroquois of the Oneida tribe, in order to get possession of their furs. The whole colony trembled in expectation of a new outbreak of the war. Happily, the event proved otherwise. The authors of the last murder escaped; but the three soldiers were shot at Montreal, in presence of a considerable number of the Iroquois, who declared themselves satisfied with the atonement; and on this same day, the sixth of July, the adventurers began their voyage.

Chapter II

LA SALLE AND THE SULPITIANS

The French in Western New York • Louis Joliet • The Sulpitians on Lake Erie • At Detroit • At Saut Ste. Marie • The Mystery of La Salle • He discovers the Ohio • He descends the Illinois • Did he reach the Mississippi?

L A CHINE was the starting-point, and the combined parties, in all twenty-four men with seven canoes, embarked on the Lake of St. Louis. With them were two other canoes, bearing the party of Senecas who had wintered at La Salle's settlement, and who were now to act as guides. Father Galinée recounts the journey. He was no woodsman: the river, the forests, the rapids, were all new to him, and he dilates on them with the minuteness of a novice. Above all, he admired the Indian birch canoes. "If God," he says, "grants me the grace of returning to France, I shall try to carry one with me." Then he describes the bivouac. "Your lodging is as extraordinary as your vessels; for, after paddling or carrying the canoes all day, you find mother earth ready to receive your wearied body. If the weather is fair, you make a fire and lie down to sleep without farther trouble; but, if it rains, you must peel bark from the trees, and make a shed by laying it on a frame of sticks. As for your food, it is enough to make you burn all the cookery books that ever were written; for in the woods of Canada one finds means to live well without bread, wine, salt, pepper, or spice. The ordinary food is Indian corn, or Turkey wheat as they call it in France, which is crushed between two stones and boiled, seasoning it with meat or fish, when you can get them. This sort of life seemed so strange to us, that we all felt the effects of it; and, before we were a hundred leagues from Montreal, not one of us was free from some malady or other. At last, after all our misery, on the second of August we discovered Lake Ontario, like a great sea with no land beyond it."

Thirty-five days after leaving La Chine, they reached Irondequoit Bay, on the south side of the lake. Here they were met by a number of Seneca Indians, who professed friendship and invited them to their villages, fifteen or twenty miles distant. As this was on their way to the upper waters of the Ohio, and as they hoped to find guides at the villages to conduct them, they accepted the invitation. Dollier, with most of the men, remained to guard the canoes; while La Salle, with Galinée and eight other Frenchmen, accompanied by a troop of Indians, set out on the morning of the twelfth, and reached the principal village before evening. It stood on a hill, in the midst of a clearing nearly two leagues in compass.[1] A rude stockade surrounded it, and as the visitors drew near they saw a band of old men seated on the grass, waiting to receive them. One of these veterans, so feeble with age that he could hardly stand, made them an harangue, in which he declared that the Senecas were their brothers, and invited them to enter the village. They did so, surrounded by a crowd of savages, and presently found themselves in the midst of a disorderly cluster of large but filthy abodes of bark, about a hundred and fifty in number, the most capacious of which was assigned to their use. Here they made their quarters, and were soon overwhelmed by Seneca hospitality. Children brought them pumpkins and berries from the woods, and boy messengers came to summon them to endless feasts, where they were regaled with the flesh of dogs and with boiled maize seasoned with oil pressed from nuts and the seeds of sunflowers.

La Salle had flattered himself that he knew enough Iroquois to hold communication with the Senecas; but he failed completely in the attempt. The priests had a Dutch interpreter, who spoke Iroquois fluently, but knew so little French, and was withal so obstinate, that he proved useless; so that it was necessary to employ a man in the service of the Jesuit Fremin, whose mission was at this village. What the party needed was a guide to conduct them to the Ohio; and soon after their arrival a party of warriors appeared, with a young prisoner belonging to one of the tribes of that region. Galinée wanted to beg or buy him from his captors; but the Senecas had other intentions. "I saw," writes the priest, "the

---

[1] This village seems to have been that attacked by Denonville in 1687. It stood on Boughton Hill, near the present town of Victor.

most miserable spectacle I ever beheld in my life." It was the prisoner tied to a stake and tortured for six hours with diabolical ingenuity, while the crowd danced and yelled with delight, and the chiefs and elders sat in a row smoking their pipes and watching the contortions of the victim with an air of serene enjoyment. The body was at last cut up and eaten, and in the evening the whole population occupied themselves in scaring away the angry ghost by beating with sticks against the bark sides of the lodges.

La Salle and his companions began to fear for their own safety. Some of their hosts wished to kill them in revenge for the chief murdered near Montreal; and, as these and others were at times in a frenzy of drunkenness, the position of the French became critical. They suspected that means had been used to prejudice the Senecas against them. Not only could they get no guides, but they were told that if they went to the Ohio the tribes of those parts would infallibly kill them. Their Dutch interpreter became disheartened and unmanageable, and, after staying a month at the village, the hope of getting farther on their way seemed less than ever. Their plan, it was clear, must be changed; and an Indian from Otinawatawa, a kind of Iroquois colony at the head of Lake Ontario, offered to guide them to his village and show them a better way to the Ohio. They left the Senecas, coasted the south shore of the lake, passed the mouth of the Niagara, where they heard the distant roar of the cataract, and on the twenty-fourth of September reached Otinawatawa, which was a few miles north of the present town of Hamilton. The inhabitants proved friendly, and La Salle received the welcome present of a Shawanoe prisoner, who told them that the Ohio could be reached in six weeks, and that he would guide them to it. Delighted at this good fortune, they were about to set out; when they heard, to their astonishment, of the arrival of two other Frenchmen at a neighboring village. One of the strangers was destined to hold a conspicuous place in the history of western discovery. This was Louis Joliet, a young man of about the age of La Salle. Like him, he had studied for the priesthood; but the world and the wilderness had conquered his early inclinations, and changed him to an active and adventurous fur-trader. Talon had sent him to discover and explore the copper-mines of Lake Superior. He had failed in the attempt, and was now returning. His Indian guide, afraid of passing the Niagara portage lest he should meet enemies, had led him from Lake Erie, by way of Grand River, towards the head of Lake Ontario; and thus it was that he met La Salle and the Sulpitians.

This meeting caused a change of plan. Joliet showed the priests a map which he had made, of such parts of the Upper Lakes as he had visited, and gave them a copy of it; telling them, at the same time, of the Pottawattamies, and other tribes of that region in grievous need of spiritual succor. The result was a determination on their part to follow the route which he suggested, notwithstanding the remonstrances of La Salle, who in vain reminded them that the Jesuits had pre-occupied the field, and would regard them as intruders. They resolved that the Pottawattamies should no longer sit in darkness; while, as for the Mississippi, it could be reached, as they conceived, with less risk by this northern route than by that of the south.

La Salle was of a different mind. His goal was the Ohio, and not the northern lakes. A few days before, while hunting, he had been attacked by a fever, sarcastically ascribed by Ga-linée to his having seen three large rattlesnakes crawling up a rock. He now told his two colleagues that he was in no condition to go forward, and should be forced to part with them. The staple of La Salle's character, as his life will attest, was an invincible determination of purpose, which set at naught all risks and all sufferings. He had cast himself with all his resources into this enterprise, and, while his faculties remained, he was not a man to recoil from it. On the other hand, the masculine fibre of which he was made did not always withhold him from the practice of the arts of address, and the use of what Dollier de Casson styles *belles paroles*. He respected the priesthood, with the exception, it seems, of the Jesuits; and he was under obligations to the Sulpitians of Montreal. Hence there can be no doubt that he used his illness as a pretext for escaping from their company without ungraciousness, and following his own path in his own way.

On the last day of September, the priests made an altar, supported by the paddles of the canoes laid on forked sticks.

Dollier said mass; La Salle and his followers received the sacrament, as did also those of his late colleagues; and thus they parted, the Sulpitians and their party descending the Grand River towards Lake Erie, while La Salle, as they supposed, began his return to Montreal. What course he actually took we shall soon inquire; and meanwhile, for a few moments, we will follow the priests. When they reached Lake Erie, they saw it tossing like an angry ocean. They had no mind to tempt the dangerous and unknown navigation, and encamped for the winter in the forest near the peninsula called the Long Point. Here they gathered a good store of chestnuts, hickory-nuts, plums, and grapes; and built themselves a log cabin, with a recess at the end for an altar. They passed the winter unmolested, shooting game in abundance, and saying mass three times a week. Early in spring, they planted a large cross, attached to it the arms of France, and took formal possession of the country in the name of Louis XIV. This done, they resumed their voyage, and, after many troubles, landed one evening in a state of exhaustion on or near Point Pelée, towards the western extremity of Lake Erie. A storm rose as they lay asleep, and swept off a great part of their baggage, which, in their fatigue, they had left at the edge of the water. Their altar-service was lost with the rest, a misfortune which they ascribed to the jealousy and malice of the Devil. Debarred henceforth from saying Mass, they resolved to return to Montreal and leave the Pottawattamies uninstructed. They presently entered the strait by which Lake Huron joins Lake Erie; and, landing near where Detroit now stands, found a large stone, somewhat suggestive of the human figure, which the Indians had bedaubed with paint, and which they worshipped as a manito. In view of their late misfortune, this device of the arch-enemy excited their utmost resentment. "After the loss of our altar-service," writes Galinée, "and the hunger we had suffered, there was not a man of us who was not filled with hatred against this false deity. I devoted one of my axes to breaking him in pieces; and then, having fastened our canoes side by side, we carried the largest piece to the middle of the river, and threw it, with all the rest, into the water, that he might never be heard of again. God rewarded us immediately for this good action, for we killed a deer and a bear that same day."

This is the first recorded passage of white men through the Strait of Detroit; though Joliet had, no doubt, passed this way on his return from the Upper Lakes.[1] The two missionaries took this course, with the intention of proceeding to the Saut Sainte Marie, and there joining the Ottawas, and other tribes of that region, in their yearly descent to Montreal. They issued upon Lake Huron; followed its eastern shores till they reached the Georgian Bay, near the head of which the Jesuits had established their great mission of the Hurons, destroyed, twenty years before, by the Iroquois;[2] and, ignoring or slighting the labors of the rival missionaries, held their way northward along the rocky archipelago that edged those lonely coasts. They passed the Manatoulins, and, ascending the strait by which Lake Superior discharges its waters, arrived on the twenty-fifth of May at Ste. Marie du Saut. Here they found the two Jesuits, Dablon and Marquette, in a square fort of cedar pickets, built by their men within the past year, and enclosing a chapel and a house. Near by, they had cleared a large tract of land, and sown it with wheat, Indian corn, peas, and other crops. The new-comers were graciously received, and invited to vespers in the chapel; but they very soon found La Salle's prediction made good, and saw that the Jesuit fathers wanted no help from St. Sulpice. Galinée, on his part, takes occasion to remark that, though the Jesuits had baptized a few Indians at the Saut, not one of them was a good enough Christian to receive the Eucharist; and he intimates that the case, by their own showing, was still worse at their mission of St. Esprit. The two Sulpitians did not care to prolong their stay; and, three days after their arrival, they left the Saut: not, as they expected, with the Indians, but with a French guide, furnished by the Jesuits. Ascending French River to Lake Nipissing, they crossed to the waters of the Ottawa, and descended to Montreal, which they reached on the eighteenth of June. They had made no discoveries and no con-

[1] The Jesuits and fur-traders, on their way to the Upper Lakes, had followed the route of the Ottawa, or, more recently, that of Toronto and the Georgian Bay. Iroquois hostility had long closed the Niagara portage and Lake Erie against them.

[2] The Jesuits in North America.

verts; but Galinée, after his arrival, made the earliest map of the Upper Lakes known to exist.[1]

We return now to La Salle, only to find ourselves involved in mist and obscurity. What did he do after he left the two priests? Unfortunately, a definite answer is not possible; and the next two years of his life remain in some measure an enigma. That he was busied in active exploration, and that he made important discoveries, is certain; but the extent and character of these discoveries remain wrapped in doubt. He is known to have kept journals and made maps; and these were in existence, and in possession of his niece, Madeleine Cavelier, then in advanced age, as late as the year 1756; beyond which time the most diligent inquiry has failed to trace them. Abbé Faillon affirms that some of La Salle's men, refusing to follow him, returned to La Chine, and that the place then received its name, in derision of the young adventurer's dream of a westward passage to China.[2] As for himself, the only distinct record of his movements is that contained in a paper, entitled "Histoire de Monsieur de la Salle." It is an account of his explorations, and of the state of parties in Canada previous to the year 1678; taken from the lips of La Salle himself, by a person whose name does not appear, but who declares that he had ten or twelve conversations with him at Paris, whither he had come with a petition to the Court. The writer himself had never been in America, and was ignorant of its geography; hence blunders on his part might reasonably be expected. His statements, however, are in some measure intelligible; and the following is the substance of them. After leaving the priests, La Salle went to Onondaga, where we are left to infer that he succeeded better in getting a guide than he had before done among the Senecas. Thence he made his way to a point six or seven leagues distant from Lake Erie, where he reached a branch of the Ohio; and, descending it, followed the river as far as the rapids at Louisville, or, as has been maintained, beyond its confluence with the Mississippi.

[1] See Appendix. The above narrative is from *Récit de ce qui s'est passe de plus remarquable dans le Voyage de MM. Dollier et Galinée.* (Bibliothèque Nationale.)

[2] Dollier de Casson alludes to this as "cette transmigration célèbre qui se fit de la Chine dans ces quartiers."

His men now refused to go farther, and abandoned him, escaping to the English and the Dutch; whereupon he retraced his steps alone.[1] This must have been in the winter of 1669–70, or in the following spring; unless there is an error of date in the statement of Nicolas Perrot, the famous *voyageur*, who says that he met him in the summer of 1670, hunting on the Ottawa with a party of Iroquois.[2]

But how was La Salle employed in the following year? The same memoir has its solution to the problem. By this it appears that the indefatigable explorer embarked on Lake Erie, ascended the Detroit to Lake Huron, coasted the unknown shores of Michigan, passed the Straits of Michillimackinac, and, leaving Green Bay behind him, entered what is described as an incomparably larger bay, but which was evidently the southern portion of Lake Michigan. Thence he crossed to a river flowing westward,—evidently the Illinois,—and followed it until it was joined by another river flowing from the north-west to the south-east. By this, the Mississippi only can be meant; and he is reported to have said that he descended it to the thirty-sixth degree of latitude; where he stopped, assured that it discharged itself not into the Gulf of California, but into the Gulf of Mexico; and resolved to follow it

[1] The following is the passage relating to this journey, in the remarkable paper above mentioned. After recounting La Salle's visit with the Sulpitians to the Seneca village, and stating that the intrigues of the Jesuit missionary prevented them from obtaining a guide, it speaks of the separation of the travellers and the journey of Galinée and his party to the Saut Ste. Marie, where "les Jésuites les congédièrent." It then proceeds as follows: "Cependant Mr. de la Salle continua son chemin par une rivière qui va de l'est à l'ouest; et passe à Onontaqué [*Onondaga*], puis à six ou sept lieues au-dessous du Lac Erié; et estant parvenu jusqu'au 280me ou 83me degré de longitude, et jusqu'au 41me degré de latitude, trouva un sault qui tombe vers l'ouest dans un pays bas, marescageux, tout couvert de vielles souches, dont il y en a quelques-unes qui sont encore sur pied. Il fut donc contraint de prendre terre, et suivant une hauteur qui le pouvoit mener loin, il trouva quelques sauvages qui luy dirent que fort loin de là le mesme fleuve qui se perdoit dans cette terre basse et vaste se réunnissoit en un lit. Il continua donc son chemin, mais comme la fatigue estoit grande, 23 ou 24 hommes qu'il avoit menez jusques là le quittèrent tous en une nuit, regagnèrent le fleuve, et se sauvèrent, les uns à la Nouvelle Hollande et les autres à la Nouvelle Angleterre. Il se vit donc seul à 400 lieues de chez luy, où il ne laisse pas de revenir, remontant la rivière et vivant de chasse, d'herbes, et de ce que luy donnèrent les sauvages qu'il rencontra en son chemin."

[2] Perrot, *Mémoires*, 119, 120.

thither at a future day, when better provided with men and supplies.[1]

The first of these statements,—that relating to the Ohio,—confused, vague, and in great part incorrect, as it certainly is, is nevertheless well sustained as regards one essential point. La Salle himself, in a memorial addressed to Count Frontenac in 1677, affirms that he discovered the Ohio, and descended it as far as to a fall which obstructed it.[2] Again, his rival, Louis Joliet, whose testimony on this point cannot be suspected, made two maps of the region of the Mississippi and the Great Lakes. The Ohio is laid down on both of them, with an inscription to the effect that it had been explored by La Salle.[3]

[1] The memoir—after stating, as above, that he entered Lake Huron, doubled the peninsula of Michigan, and passed La Baye des Puants (*Green Bay*)—says: "Il reconnut une baye incomparablement plus large; au fond de laquelle vers l'ouest il trouva un très-beau havre et au fond de ce havre un fleuve qui va de l'est à l'ouest. Il suivit ce fleuve, et estant parvenu jusqu'environ le 280me degré de longitude et le 39me de latitude, il trouva un autre fleuve qui se joignant au premier coulait du nordouest au sudest, et il suivit ce fleuve jusqu'au 36me degré de latitude."

The "très-beau havre" may have been the entrance of the river Chicago, whence, by an easy portage, he might have reached the Des Plaines branch of the Illinois. We shall see that he took this course in his famous exploration of 1682.

The intendant, Talon, announces, in his despatches of this year, that he had sent La Salle southward and westward to explore.

[2] The following are his words (he speaks of himself in the third person): "L'année 1667, et les suivantes, il fit divers voyages avec beaucoup de dépenses, dans lesquels il découvrit le premier beaucoup de pays au sud des grands lacs, et *entre autres la grande rivière d'Ohio*; il la suivit jusqu'à un endroit où elle tombe de fort haut dans de vastes marais, à la hauteur de 37 degrés, après avoir été grossie par une autre rivière fort large qui vient du nord; et toutes ces eaux se déchargent selon toutes les apparences dans le Golfe du Mexique."

This "autre rivière," which, it seems, was above the fall, may have been the Miami or the Scioto. There is but one fall on the river, that of Louisville, which is not so high as to deserve to be described as "fort haut," being only a strong rapid. The latitude, as will be seen, is different in the two accounts, and incorrect in both.

[3] One of these maps is entitled *Carte de la découverte du Sieur Joliet, 1674.* Over the lines representing the Ohio are the words, "Route du sieur de la Salle pour aller dans le Mexique." The other map of Joliet bears, also written over the Ohio, the words, "Rivière par où descendit le sieur de la Salle au sortir du lac Erié pour aller dans le Mexique." I have also another manuscript map, made before the voyage of Joliet and Marquette, and apparently in the year 1673, on which the Ohio is represented as far as to a point a little below Louisville, and over it is written, "Rivière Ohio, ainsy appellée par les Iro-

That he discovered the Ohio may then be regarded as established. That he descended it to the Mississippi, he himself does not pretend; nor is there reason to believe that he did so.

With regard to his alleged voyage down the Illinois, the case is different. Here, he is reported to have made a statement which admits but one interpretation,—that of the discovery by him of the Mississippi prior to its discovery by Joliet and Marquette. This statement is attributed to a man not prone to vaunt his own exploits, who never proclaimed them in print, and whose testimony, even in his own case, must therefore have weight. But it comes to us through the medium of a person strongly biassed in favor of La Salle, and against Marquette and the Jesuits.

Seven years had passed since the alleged discovery, and La Salle had not before laid claim to it; although it was matter of notoriety that during five years it had been claimed by Joliet, and that his claim was generally admitted. The correspondence of the governor and the intendant is silent as to La Salle's having penetrated to the Mississippi; though the attempt was made under the auspices of the latter, as his own letters declare; while both had the discovery of the great river earnestly at heart. The governor, Frontenac, La Salle's ardent supporter and ally, believed in 1672, as his letters show, that the Mississippi flowed into the Gulf of California; and, two years later, he announces to the minister Colbert its discovery by Joliet.[1] After La Salle's death, his brother, his nephew, and his niece addressed a memorial to the king, petitioning for certain grants in consideration of the discoveries of their relative, which they specify at some length; but they do not pretend that he reached the Mississippi before his expeditions of

---

quois à cause de sa beauté, par où le sieur de la Salle est descendu." The Mississippi is not represented on this map; but—and this is very significant, as indicating the extent of La Salle's exploration of the following year—a small part of the upper Illinois is laid down.

[1] *Lettre de Frontenac au Ministre, 14 Nov., 1674.* He here speaks of "la grande rivière qu'il [*Joliet*] a trouvée, qui va du nord au sud, et qui est aussi large que celle du Saint-Laurent vis-à-vis de Québec." Four years later, Frontenac speaks slightingly of Joliet, but neither denies his discovery of the Mississippi nor claims it for La Salle, in whose interest he writes.

1679 to 1682.[1] This silence is the more significant, as it is this very niece who had possession of the papers in which La Salle recounts the journeys of which the issues are in question.[2] Had they led him to the Mississippi, it is reasonably certain that she would have made it known in her memorial. La Salle discovered the Ohio, and in all probability the Illinois also; but that he discovered the Mississippi has not been proved, nor, in the light of the evidence we have, is it likely.

[1] *Papiers de Famille*; *Mémoire présenté au Roi*. The following is an extract: "Il parvient . . . jusqu'à la rivière des Illinois. Il y construisit un fort situé à 350 lieues au-delà du fort de Frontenac, et suivant ensuite le cours de cette rivière, il trouva qu'elle se jettoit dans un grand fleuve appellé par ceux du pays Missisippi, c'est à dire *grande eau*, environ cent lieues au-dessous du fort qu'il venoit de construire." This fort was Fort Crèvecœur, built in 1680, near the site of Peoria. The memoir goes on to relate the descent of La Salle to the Gulf, which concluded this expedition of 1679–82.

[2] The following is an extract, given by Margry, from a letter of the aged Madeleine Cavelier, dated 21 Février, 1756, and addressed to her nephew, M. Le Baillif, who had applied for the papers in behalf of the minister, Silhouette: "J'ay cherché une occasion sûre pour vous anvoyé les papiers de M. de la Salle. Il y a des cartes que j'ay jointe à ces papiers, qui doivent prouver que, en 1675, M. de Lasalle avet déja fet deux voyages en ces decouverte, puisqu'il y avet une carte, que je vous envoye, par laquelle il est fait mention de l'androit auquel M. de Lasalle aborda près le fleuve de Mississippi: un autre androit qu'il nomme le fleuve Colbert; en un autre il prans possession de ce pais au nom du roy et fait planter une crois."

The words of the aged and illiterate writer are obscure, but her expression *aborda près* seems to indicate that La Salle had not reached the Mississippi prior to 1675, but only approached it.

Finally, a memorial presented to Seignelay, along with the official narrative of 1679–81, by a friend of La Salle, whose object was to place the discoverer and his achievements in the most favorable light, contains the following: "Il [*La Salle*] a esté le premier à former le dessein de ces descouvertes, qu'il communiqua, il y a plus de quinze ans, à M. de Courcelles, gouverneur, et à M. Talon, intendant du Canada, qui l'approuvèrent. Il a fait ensuite plusieurs voyages de ce costé-là, et un entr'autres en 1669 avec MM. Dolier et Galinée, prestres du Séminaire de St. Sulpice. *Il est vray que le sieur Jolliet, pour le prévenir, fit un voyage in 1673, à la rivière Colbert*; mais ce fut uniquement pour y faire commerce." See Margry, II. 285. This passage is a virtual admission that Joliet reached the Mississippi (*Colbert*) before La Salle.

Margry, in a series of papers in the *Journal Général de l'Instruction Publique* for 1862, first took the position that La Salle reached the Mississippi in 1670 and 1671, and has brought forward in defence of it all the documents which his unwearied research enabled him to discover. Father Tailhan, S.J., has replied at length, in the copious notes to his edition of Nicolas Perrot, but without having seen the principal document cited by Margry, and of which extracts have been given in the notes to this chapter.

Chapter III

1670 — 1672

THE JESUITS ON THE LAKES

The Old Missions and the New • A Change of Spirit • Lake Superior and the Copper-mines • Ste. Marie • La Pointe • Michillimackinac • Jesuits on Lake Michigan • Allouez and Dablon • The Jesuit Fur-trade

---

W HAT were the Jesuits doing? Since the ruin of their great mission of the Hurons, a perceptible change had taken place in them. They had put forth exertions almost superhuman, set at naught famine, disease, and death, lived with the self-abnegation of saints and died with the devotion of martyrs; and the result of all had been a disastrous failure. From no short-coming on their part, but from the force of events beyond the sphere of their influence, a very demon of havoc had crushed their incipient churches, slaughtered their converts, uprooted the populous communities on which their hopes had rested, and scattered them in bands of wretched fugitives far and wide through the wilderness.[1] They had devoted themselves in the fulness of faith to the building up of a Christian and Jesuit empire on the conversion of the great stationary tribes of the lakes; and of these none remained but the Iroquois, the destroyers of the rest, among whom, indeed, was a field which might stimulate their zeal by an abundant promise of sufferings and martyrdoms, but which, from its geographical position, was too much exposed to Dutch and English influence to promise great and decisive results. Their best hopes were now in the North and the West; and thither, in great part, they had turned their energies.

We find them on Lake Huron, Lake Superior, and Lake Michigan, laboring vigorously as of old, but in a spirit not quite the same. Now, as before, two objects inspired their zeal, the "greater glory of God," and the influence and credit of the Order of Jesus. If the one motive had some-

[1] See The Jesuits in North America.

what lost in power, the other had gained. The epoch of the saints and martyrs was passing away; and henceforth we find the Canadian Jesuit less and less an apostle, more and more an explorer, a man of science, and a politician. The yearly reports of the missions are still, for the edification of the pious reader, filled with intolerably tedious stories of baptisms, conversions, and the exemplary deportment of neophytes; for these have become a part of the formula; but they are relieved abundantly by more mundane topics. One finds observations on the winds, currents, and tides of the Great Lakes; speculations on a subterranean outlet of Lake Superior; accounts of its copper-mines, and how we, the Jesuit fathers, are laboring to explore them for the profit of the colony; surmises touching the North Sea, the South Sea, the Sea of China, which we hope ere long to discover; and reports of that great mysterious river of which the Indians tell us,—flowing southward, perhaps to the Gulf of Mexico, perhaps to the Vermilion Sea,—and the secrets whereof, with the help of the Virgin, we will soon reveal to the world.

The Jesuit was as often a fanatic for his Order as for his faith; and oftener yet the two fanaticisms mingled in him inextricably. Ardently as he burned for the saving of souls, he would have none saved on the Upper Lakes except by his brethren and himself. He claimed a monopoly of conversion, with its attendant monopoly of toil, hardship, and martyrdom. Often disinterested for himself, he was inordinately ambitious for the great corporate power in which he had merged his own personality; and here lies one cause, among many, of the seeming contradictions which abound in the annals of the Order.

Prefixed to the *Relation* of 1671 is that monument of Jesuit hardihood and enterprise, the map of Lake Superior; a work of which, however, the exactness has been exaggerated, as compared with other Canadian maps of the day. While making surveys, the priests were diligently looking for copper. Father Dablon reports that they had found it in greatest abundance on Isle Minong, now Isle Royale. "A day's journey from the head of the lake, on the south side, there is," he says, "a rock of copper weighing from six hundred to eight hundred pounds, lying on the shore where any who pass may see it;" and he farther speaks of great copper boulders in the bed of the river Ontonagan.[1]

There were two principal missions on the Upper Lakes, which were, in a certain sense, the parents of the rest. One of these was Ste. Marie du Saut,—the same visited by Dollier and Galinée,—at the outlet of Lake Superior. This was a noted fishing-place; for the rapids were full of white-fish, and Indians came thither in crowds. The permanent residents were an Ojibwa band, whom the French called Sauteurs, and whose bark lodges were clustered at the foot of the rapids, near the fort of the Jesuits. Besides these, a host of Algonquins, of various tribes, resorted thither in the spring and summer; living in abundance on the fishery, and dispersing in winter to wander and starve in scattered hunting-parties far and wide through the forests.

The other chief mission was that of St. Esprit, at La Pointe, near the western extremity of Lake Superior. Here were the Hurons, fugitives twenty years before from the slaughter of their countrymen; and the Ottawas, who, like them, had sought an asylum from the rage of the Iroquois. Many other tribes—Illinois, Pottawattamies, Foxes, Menomonies, Sioux, Assiniboins, Knisteneaux, and a multitude besides—came hither yearly to trade with the French. Here was a young

---

[1] He complains that the Indians were very averse to giving information on the subject, so that the Jesuits had not as yet discovered the metal *in situ*, though they hoped soon to do so. The Indians told him that the copper had first been found by four hunters, who had landed on a certain island, near the north shore of the lake. Wishing to boil their food in a vessel of bark, they gathered stones on the shore, heated them red hot, and threw them in, but presently discovered them to be pure copper. Their repast over, they hastened to re-embark, being afraid of the lynxes and the hares, which, on this island, were as large as dogs, and which would have devoured their provisions, and perhaps their canoe. They took with them some of the wonderful stones; but scarcely had they left the island, when a deep voice, like thunder, sounded in their ears, "Who are these thieves who steal the toys of my children?" It was the God of the Waters, or some other powerful manito. The four adventurers retreated in great terror; but three of them soon died, and the fourth survived only long enough to reach his village, and tell the story. The island has no foundation, but floats with the movement of the wind; and no Indian dares land on its shores, dreading the wrath of the manito. Dablon, *Relation, 1670,* 84.

Jesuit, Jacques Marquette, lately arrived from the Saut Ste. Marie. His savage flock disheartened him by its backslidings; and the best that he could report of the Hurons, after all the toil and all the blood lavished in their conversion, was, that they "still retain a little Christianity;" while the Ottawas are "far removed from the kingdom of God, and addicted beyond all other tribes to foulness, incantations, and sacrifices to evil spirits."[1]

Marquette heard from the Illinois—yearly visitors at La Pointe—of the great river which they had crossed on their way,[2] and which, as he conjectured, flowed into the Gulf of California. He heard marvels of it also from the Sioux, who lived on its banks; and a strong desire possessed him to explore the mystery of its course. A sudden calamity dashed his hopes. The Sioux—the Iroquois of the West, as the Jesuits call them—had hitherto kept the peace with the expatriated tribes of La Pointe; but now, from some cause not worth inquiry, they broke into open war, and so terrified the Hurons and Ottawas that they abandoned their settlements and fled. Marquette followed his panic-stricken flock, who, passing the Saut Ste. Marie, and descending to Lake Huron, stopped at length, the Hurons at Michillimackinac, and the Ottawas at the Great Manatoulin Island. Two missions were now necessary to minister to the divided bands. That of Michillimackinac was assigned to Marquette, and that of the Manatoulin Island to Louis André. The former took post at Point St. Ignace, on the north shore of the Straits of Michillimackinac, while the latter began the mission of St. Simon at the new abode of the Ottawas. When winter came, scattering his flock to their hunting-grounds, André made a missionary tour among the Nipissings and other neighboring tribes. The shores of Lake Huron had long been an utter solitude, swept

---

[1] *Lettre du Père Jacques Marquette au R.P. Supérieur des Missions*; in *Relation, 1670*, 87.

[2] The Illinois lived at this time beyond the Mississippi, thirty days' journey from La Pointe; whither they had been driven by the Iroquois, from their former abode near Lake Michigan. Dablon (*Relation, 1671*, 24, 25) says that they lived seven days' journey beyond the Mississippi, in eight villages. A few years later, most of them returned to the east side, and made their abode on the river Illinois.

of their denizens by the terror of the all-conquering Iroquois; but now that these tigers had felt the power of the French, and learned for a time to leave their Indian allies in peace, the fugitive hordes were returning to their ancient abodes. André's experience among them was of the roughest. The staple of his diet was acorns and *tripe de roche*, a species of lichen, which, being boiled, resolved itself into a black glue, nauseous, but not void of nourishment. At times, he was reduced to moss, the bark of trees, or moccasins and old moose-skins cut into strips and boiled. His hosts treated him very ill, and the worst of their fare was always his portion. When spring came to his relief, he returned to his post of St. Simon, with impaired digestion and unabated zeal.

Besides the Saut Ste. Marie and Michillimackinac, both noted fishing-places, there was another spot, no less famous for game and fish, and therefore a favorite resort of Indians. This was the head of the Green Bay of Lake Michigan.[1] Here and in adjacent districts several distinct tribes had made their abode. The Menomonies were on the river which bears their name; the Pottawattamies and Winnebagoes were near the borders of the bay; the Sacs, on Fox River; the Mascoutins, Miamis, and Kickapoos, on the same river, above Lake Winnebago; and the Outagamies, or Foxes, on a tributary of it flowing from the north. Green Bay was manifestly suited for a mission; and, as early as the autumn of 1669, Father Claude Allouez was sent thither to found one. After nearly perishing by the way, he set out to explore the destined field of his labors, and went as far as the town of the Mascoutins. Early in the autumn of 1670, having been joined by Dablon, Superior of the missions on the Upper Lakes, he made another journey, but not until the two fathers had held a council with the congregated tribes at St. François Xavier; for so they named their mission of Green Bay. Here, as they harangued

---

[1] The Baye des Puans of the early writers; or, more correctly, La Baye des Eaux Puantes. The Winnebago Indians, living near it, were called Les Puans, apparently for no other reason than because some portion of the bay was said to have an odor like the sea.

Lake Michigan, the Lac des Illinois of the French, was, according to a letter of Father Allouez, called Machihiganing by the Indians. Dablon writes the name Mitchiganon.

their naked audience, their gravity was put to the proof; for a band of warriors, anxious to do them honor, walked incessantly up and down, aping the movements of the soldiers on guard before the governor's tent at Montreal. "We could hardly keep from laughing," writes Dablon, "though we were discoursing on very important subjects; namely, the mysteries of our religion, and the things necessary to escaping from eternal fire."[1]

The fathers were delighted with the country, which Dablon calls an earthly paradise; but he adds that the way to it is as hard as the path to heaven. He alludes especially to the rapids of Fox River, which gave the two travellers great trouble. Having safely passed them, they saw an Indian idol on the bank, similar to that which Dollier and Galinée found at Detroit; being merely a rock, bearing some resemblance to a man, and hideously painted. With the help of their attendants, they threw it into the river. Dablon expatiates on the buffalo, which he describes apparently on the report of others, as his description is not very accurate. Crossing Winnebago Lake, the two priests followed the river leading to the town of the Mascoutins and Miamis, which they reached on the fifteenth of September.[2] These two tribes lived together within the compass of the same enclosure of palisades; to the number, it is said, of more than three thousand souls. The missionaries, who had brought a highly-colored picture of the Last Judgment, called the Indians to council and displayed it before them; while Allouez, who spoke Algonquin, harangued them on hell, demons, and eternal flames. They listened with open ears, beset him night and day with questions, and invited him and his companion to unceasing feasts. They were welcomed in every lodge, and followed everywhere with eyes of curiosity, wonder, and awe. Dablon overflows with praises of the Miami chief, who was honored by his subjects like a king, and whose demeanor towards his guests had no savor of the savage.

[1] *Relation, 1671,* 43.
[2] This town was on the Neenah or Fox River, above Lake Winnebago. The Mascoutins, Fire Nation, or Nation of the Prairie, are extinct or merged in other tribes. See The Jesuits in North America. The Miamis soon removed to the banks of the river St. Joseph, near Lake Michigan.

Their hosts told them of the great river Mississippi, rising far in the north and flowing southward,—they knew not whither,—and of many tribes that dwelt along its banks. When at length they took their departure, they left behind them a reputation as medicine-men of transcendent power.

In the winter following, Allouez visited the Foxes, whom he found in extreme ill-humor. They were incensed against the French by the ill-usage which some of their tribe had lately met when on a trading visit to Montreal; and they received the Faith with shouts of derision. The priest was horror-stricken at what he saw. Their lodges, each containing from five to ten families, seemed in his eyes like seraglios; for some of the chiefs had eight wives. He armed himself with patience, and at length gained a hearing. Nay, he succeeded so well, that when he showed them his crucifix they would throw tobacco on it as an offering; and, on another visit which he made them soon after, he taught the whole village to make the sign of the cross. A war-party was going out against their enemies, and he bethought him of telling them the story of the Cross and the Emperor Constantine. This so wrought upon them that they all daubed the figure of a cross on their shields of bull-hide, set out for the war, and came back victorious, extolling the sacred symbol as a great war-medicine.

"Thus it is," writes Dablon, who chronicles the incident, "that our holy faith is established among these people; and we have good hope that we shall soon carry it to the famous river called the Mississippi, and perhaps even to the South Sea."[1] Most things human have their phases of the ludicrous; and the heroism of these untiring priests is no exception to the rule.

The various missionary stations were much alike. They consisted of a chapel (commonly of logs) and one or more houses, with perhaps a storehouse and a workshop; the whole fenced with palisades, and forming, in fact, a stockade fort, surrounded with clearings and cultivated fields. It is evident that the priests had need of other hands than their own and

[1] *Relation, 1672,* 42.

those of the few lay brothers attached to the mission. They required men inured to labor, accustomed to the forest life, able to guide canoes and handle tools and weapons. In the earlier epoch of the missions, when enthusiasm was at its height, they were served in great measure by volunteers, who joined them through devotion or penitence, and who were known as *donnés*, or "given men." Of late, the number of these had much diminished; and they now relied chiefly on hired men, or *engagés*. These were employed in building, hunting, fishing, clearing and tilling the ground, guiding canoes, and, if faith is to be placed in reports current throughout the colony, in trading with the Indians for the profit of the missions. This charge of trading—which, if the results were applied exclusively to the support of the missions, does not of necessity involve much censure—is vehemently reiterated in many quarters, including the official despatches of the governor of Canada; while, so far as I can discover, the Jesuits never distinctly denied it; and, on several occasions, they partially admitted its truth.[1]

[1]This charge was made from the first establishment of the missions. For remarks on it, see The Jesuits in North America and The Old Régime in Canada.

Chapter IV

1667–1672

FRANCE TAKES POSSESSION
OF THE WEST

Talon • *Saint-Lusson* • *Perrot* • *The Ceremony at Saut Ste. Marie* • *The Speech of Allouez* • *Count Frontenac*

JEAN TALON, intendant of Canada, was full of projects for the good of the colony. On the one hand, he set himself to the development of its industries, and, on the other, to the extension of its domain. He meant to occupy the interior of the continent, control the rivers, which were its only highways, and hold it for France against every other nation. On the east, England was to be hemmed within a narrow strip of seaboard; while, on the south, Talon aimed at securing a port on the Gulf of Mexico, to keep the Spaniards in check, and dispute with them the possession of the vast regions which they claimed as their own. But the interior of the continent was still an unknown world. It behooved him to explore it; and to that end he availed himself of Jesuits, officers, fur-traders, and enterprising schemers like La Salle. His efforts at discovery seem to have been conducted with a singular economy of the king's purse. La Salle paid all the expenses of his first expedition made under Talon's auspices; and apparently of the second also, though the intendant announces it in his despatches as an expedition sent out by himself.[1] When, in 1670, he ordered Daumont de Saint-Lusson to search for copper mines on Lake Superior, and at the same time to take formal possession of the whole interior for the king, it was

---

[1] At least, La Salle was in great need of money, about the time of his second journey. On the sixth of August, 1671, he had received on credit, "dans son grand besoin et nécessité," from Branssac, fiscal attorney of the Seminary, merchandise to the amount of four hundred and fifty livres; and, on the eighteenth of December of the following year, he gave his promise to pay the same sum, in money or furs, in the August following. Faillon found the papers in the ancient records of Montreal.

arranged that he should pay the costs of the journey by trading with the Indians.[1]

Saint-Lusson set out with a small party of men, and Nicolas
Perrot as his interpreter. Among Canadian *voyageurs*, few
names are so conspicuous as that of Perrot; not because there
were not others who matched him in achievement, but because he could write, and left behind him a tolerable account
of what he had seen.[2] He was at this time twenty-six years
old, and had formerly been an *engagé* of the Jesuits. He was
a man of enterprise, courage, and address; the last being especially shown in his dealings with Indians, over whom he
had great influence. He spoke Algonquin fluently, and was
favorably known to many tribes of that family. Saint-Lusson
wintered at the Manatoulin Islands; while Perrot, having first
sent messages to the tribes of the north, inviting them to
meet the deputy of the governor at the Saut Ste. Marie in the
following spring, proceeded to Green Bay, to urge the same
invitation upon the tribes of that quarter. They knew him
well, and greeted him with clamors of welcome. The Miamis,
it is said, received him with a sham battle, which was designed to do him honor, but by which nerves more susceptible would have been severely shaken.[3] They entertained him
also with a grand game of *la crosse*, the Indian ball-play. Perrot gives a marvellous account of the authority and state of
the Miami chief, who, he says, was attended day and night by
a guard of warriors; an assertion which would be incredible,
were it not sustained by the account of the same chief given
by the Jesuit Dablon. Of the tribes of the Bay, the greater
part promised to send delegates to the Saut; but the Pottawattamies dissuaded the Miami potentate from attempting so

[1] In his despatch of 2d Nov., 1671, Talon writes to the king that "Saint-
Lusson's expedition will cost nothing, as he has received beaver enough from
the Indians to pay him."

[2] *Mœurs, Coustumes, et Relligion des Sauvages de l'Amérique Septentrionale.*
This work of Perrot, hitherto unpublished, appeared in 1864, under the
editorship of Father Tailhan, S.J. A great part of it is incorporated in La
Potherie.

[3] See La Potherie, II. 125. Perrot himself does not mention it. Charlevoix
erroneously places this interview at Chicago. Perrot's narrative shows that he
did not go farther than the tribes of Green Bay; and the Miamis were then,
as we have seen, on the upper part of Fox River.

long a journey, lest the fatigue incident to it might injure his health; and he therefore deputed them to represent him and his tribesmen at the great meeting. Their principal chiefs, with those of the Sacs, Winnebagoes, and Menomonies, embarked, and paddled for the place of rendezvous, where they and Perrot arrived on the fifth of May.[1]

Saint-Lusson was here with his men, fifteen in number, among whom was Louis Joliet;[2] and Indians were fast thronging in from their wintering grounds, attracted, as usual, by the fishery of the rapids or moved by the messages sent by Perrot,—Crees, Monsonis, Amikoués, Nipissings, and many more. When fourteen tribes, or their representatives, had arrived, Saint-Lusson prepared to execute the commission with which he was charged.

At the foot of the rapids was the village of the Sauteurs, above the village was a hill, and hard by stood the fort of the Jesuits. On the morning of the fourteenth of June, Saint-Lusson led his followers to the top of the hill, all fully equipped and under arms. Here, too, in the vestments of their priestly office, were four Jesuits,—Claude Dablon, Superior of the Missions of the Lakes, Gabriel Druilletes, Claude Allouez, and Louis André.[3] All around, the great throng of Indians stood, or crouched, or reclined at length, with eyes and ears intent. A large cross of wood had been made ready. Dablon, in solemn form, pronounced his blessing on it; and then it was reared and planted in the ground, while the Frenchmen, uncovered, sang the *Vexilla Regis*. Then a post of cedar was planted beside it, with a metal plate attached, engraven with the royal arms; while Saint-Lusson's followers sang the *Exaudiat*, and one of the Jesuits uttered a prayer for the king. Saint-Lusson now advanced, and, holding his sword in one hand, and raising with the other a sod of earth, proclaimed in a loud voice,—

"In the name of the Most High, Mighty, and Redoubted Monarch, Louis, Fourteenth of that name, Most Christian

---

[1] Perrot, *Mémoires*, 127.

[2] *Procès Verbal de la Prise de Possession*, etc., *14 Juin, 1671*. The names are attached to this instrument.

[3] Marquette is said to have been present; but the official act, just cited, proves the contrary. He was still at St. Esprit.

King of France and of Navarre, I take possession of this place, Sainte Marie du Saut, as also of Lakes Huron and Superior, the Island of Manatoulin, and all countries, rivers, lakes, and streams contiguous and adjacent thereunto: both those which have been discovered and those which may be discovered hereafter, in all their length and breadth, bounded on the one side by the seas of the North and of the West, and on the other by the South Sea: declaring to the nations thereof that from this time forth they are vassals of his Majesty, bound to obey his laws and follow his customs; promising them on his part all succor and protection against the incursions and invasions of their enemies: declaring to all other potentates, princes, sovereigns, states, and republics,—to them and to their subjects,—that they cannot and are not to seize or settle upon any parts of the aforesaid countries, save only under the good pleasure of His Most Christian Majesty, and of him who will govern in his behalf; and this on pain of incurring his resentment and the efforts of his arms. *Vive le Roi.*"[1]

The Frenchmen fired their guns and shouted "*Vive le Roi*," and the yelps of the astonished Indians mingled with the din.

What now remains of the sovereignty thus pompously proclaimed? Now and then, the accents of France on the lips of some straggling boatman or vagabond half-breed,—this, and nothing more.

When the uproar was over, Father Allouez addressed the Indians in a solemn harangue; and these were his words: "It is a good work, my brothers, an important work, a great work, that brings us together in council to-day. Look up at the cross which rises so high above your heads. It was there that Jesus Christ, the Son of God, after making himself a man for the love of men, was nailed and died, to satisfy his Eternal Father for our sins. He is the master of our lives; the ruler of Heaven, Earth, and Hell. It is he of whom I am continually speaking to you, and whose name and word I have borne through all your country. But look at this post to which are fixed the arms of the great chief of France, whom we call King. He lives across the sea. He is the chief of the greatest

---

[1] *Procès Verbal de la Prise de Possession.*

chiefs, and has no equal on earth. All the chiefs whom you have ever seen are but children beside him. He is like a great tree, and they are but the little herbs that one walks over and tramples under foot. You know Onontio,[1] that famous chief at Quebec; you know and you have seen that he is the terror of the Iroquois, and that his very name makes them tremble, since he has laid their country waste and burned their towns with fire. Across the sea there are ten thousand Onontios like him, who are but the warriors of our great King, of whom I have told you. When he says, 'I am going to war,' everybody obeys his orders; and each of these ten thousand chiefs raises a troop of a hundred warriors, some on sea and some on land. Some embark in great ships, such as you have seen at Quebec. Your canoes carry only four or five men, or, at the most, ten or twelve; but our ships carry four or five hundred, and sometimes a thousand. Others go to war by land, and in such numbers that if they stood in a double file they would reach from here to Mississaquenk, which is more than twenty leagues off. When our King attacks his enemies, he is more terrible than the thunder: the earth trembles; the air and the sea are all on fire with the blaze of his cannon: he is seen in the midst of his warriors, covered over with the blood of his enemies, whom he kills in such numbers that he does not reckon them by the scalps, but by the streams of blood which he causes to flow. He takes so many prisoners that he holds them in no account, but lets them go where they will, to show that he is not afraid of them. But now nobody dares make war on him. All the nations beyond the sea have submitted to him and begged humbly for peace. Men come from every quarter of the earth to listen to him and admire him. All that is done in the world is decided by him alone.

"But what shall I say of his riches? You think yourselves rich when you have ten or twelve sacks of corn, a few hatchets, beads, kettles, and other things of that sort. He has cities of his own, more than there are of men in all this country for five hundred leagues around. In each city there are storehouses where there are hatchets enough to cut down all your forests, kettles enough to cook all your moose, and beads

---

[1] The Indian name of the governor of Canada.

enough to fill all your lodges. His house is longer than from here to the top of the Saut,—that is to say, more than half a league,—and higher than your tallest trees; and it holds more families than the largest of your towns."[1] The father added more in a similar strain; but the peroration of his harangue is not on record.

Whatever impression this curious effort of Jesuit rhetoric may have produced upon the hearers, it did not prevent them from stripping the royal arms from the post to which they were nailed, as soon as Saint-Lusson and his men had left the Saut; probably, not because they understood the import of the symbol, but because they feared it as a charm. Saint-Lusson proceeded to Lake Superior, where, however, he accomplished nothing, except, perhaps, a traffic with the Indians on his own account; and he soon after returned to Quebec. Talon was resolved to find the Mississippi, the most interesting object of search, and seemingly the most attainable, in the wild and vague domain which he had just claimed for the king. The Indians had described it; the Jesuits were eager to discover it; and La Salle, if he had not reached it, had explored two several avenues by which it might be approached. Talon looked about him for a fit agent of the enterprise, and made choice of Louis Joliet, who had returned from Lake Superior.[2] But the intendant was not to see the fulfilment of his design. His busy and useful career in Canada was drawing to an end. A misunderstanding had arisen between him and the governor, Courcelle. Both were faithful servants of the king; but the relations between the two chiefs of the colony were of a nature necessarily so critical, that a conflict of authority was scarcely to be avoided. Each thought his functions encroached upon, and both asked for recall. Another governor succeeded; one who was to stamp his mark, broad, bold, and ineffaceable, on the most memorable page of French-American History, Louis de Buade, Count of Palluau and Frontenac.

[1] A close translation of Dablon's report of the speech. See *Relation, 1671*, 27.

[2] *Lettre de Frontenac au Ministre, 2 Nov., 1672.* In the Brodhead Collection, by a copyist's error, the name of the Chevalier de Grandfontaine is substituted for that of Talon.

Chapter V

THE DISCOVERY OF THE MISSISSIPPI

Joliet sent to find the Mississippi • Jacques Marquette • Departure • Green Bay • The Wisconsin • The Mississippi • Indians • Man-itous • The Arkansas • The Illinois • Joliet's Misfortune • Marquette at Chicago • His Illness • His Death

---

IF Talon had remained in the colony, Frontenac would infallibly have quarrelled with him; but he was too clear-sighted not to approve his plans for the discovery and occu-pation of the interior. Before sailing for France, Talon rec-ommended Joliet as a suitable agent for the discovery of the Mississippi, and the governor accepted his counsel.[1]

Louis Joliet was the son of a wagon-maker in the service of the Company of the Hundred Associates,[2] then owners of Canada. He was born at Quebec in 1645, and was educated by the Jesuits. When still very young, he resolved to be a priest. He received the tonsure and the minor orders at the age of seventeen. Four years after, he is mentioned with especial honor for the part he bore in the disputes in philosophy, at which the dignitaries of the colony were present, and in which the intendant himself took part.[3] Not long after, he renounced his clerical vocation, and turned fur-trader. Talon sent him, with one Péré, to explore the copper-mines of Lake Superior; and it was on his return from this expedition that he met La Salle and the Sulpitians near the head of Lake Ontario.[4]

[1] *Lettre de Frontenac au Ministre, 2 Nov., 1672; Ibid. 14 Nov., 1674.*

[2] See The Jesuits in North America.

[3] "Le 2 Juillet (1666) les premières disputes de philosophie se font dans la congrégation avec succès. Toutes les puissances s'y trouvent; M. l'Intendant entr'autres y a argumenté très-bien. M. Jolliet et Pierre Francheville y ont très-bien répondu de toute la logique."—*Journal des Jésuites.*

[4] Nothing was known of Joliet till Shea investigated his history. Ferland, in his *Notes sur les Registres de Notre-Dame de Québec*; Faillon, in his *Colonie Française en Canada*; and Margry, in a series of papers in the *Journal Général de l'Instruction Publique*,—have thrown much new light on his life. From journals of a voyage made by him at a later period to the coast of Labrador, given in substance by Margry, he seems to have been a man of close and

In what we know of Joliet, there is nothing that reveals any salient or distinctive trait of character, any especial breadth of view or boldness of design. He appears to have been simply a merchant, intelligent, well educated, courageous, hardy, and enterprising. Though he had renounced the priesthood, he retained his partiality for the Jesuits; and it is more than probable that their influence had aided not a little to determine Talon's choice. One of their number, Jacques Marquette, was chosen to accompany him.

He passed up the lakes to Michillimackinac, and found his destined companion at Point St. Ignace, on the north side of the strait, where, in his palisaded mission-house and chapel, he had labored for two years past to instruct the Huron refugees from St. Esprit, and a band of Ottawas who had joined them. Marquette was born in 1637, of an old and honorable family at Laon, in the north of France, and was now thirty-five years of age. When about seventeen, he had joined the Jesuits, evidently from motives purely religious; and in 1666 he was sent to the missions of Canada. At first, he was destined to the station of Tadoussac; and, to prepare himself for it, he studied the Montagnais language under Gabriel Druilletes. But his destination was changed, and he was sent to the Upper Lakes in 1668, where he had since remained. His talents as a linguist must have been great; for, within a few years, he learned to speak with ease six Indian languages. The traits of his character are unmistakable. He was of the brotherhood of the early Canadian missionaries, and the true counterpart of Garnier or Jogues. He was a devout votary of the Virgin Mary, who, imaged to his mind in shapes of the most transcendent loveliness with which the pencil of human genius has ever informed the canvas, was to him the object of an adoration not unmingled with a sentiment of chivalrous devotion. The longings of a sensitive heart, divorced from earth, sought solace in the skies. A subtile element of romance was blended with the fervor of his worship, and hung like an illumined cloud over the harsh and hard realities of his daily lot. Kindled by the smile of his celestial mistress, his gentle

---

intelligent observation. His mathematical acquirements appear to have been very considerable.

and noble nature knew no fear. For her he burned to dare and to suffer, discover new lands and conquer new realms to her sway.

He begins the journal of his voyage thus: "The day of the Immaculate Conception of the Holy Virgin; whom I had continually invoked, since I came to this country of the Ottawas, to obtain from God the favor of being enabled to visit the nations on the river Mississippi,—this very day was precisely that on which M. Joliet arrived with orders from Count Frontenac, our governor, and from M. Talon, our intendant, to go with me on this discovery. I was all the more delighted at this good news, because I saw my plans about to be accomplished, and found myself in the happy necessity of exposing my life for the salvation of all these tribes; and especially of the Illinois, who, when I was at Point St. Esprit, had begged me very earnestly to bring the word of God among them."

The outfit of the travellers was very simple. They provided themselves with two birch canoes, and a supply of smoked meat and Indian corn; embarked with five men; and began their voyage on the seventeenth of May. They had obtained all possible information from the Indians, and had made, by means of it, a species of map of their intended route. "Above all," writes Marquette, "I placed our voyage under the protection of the Holy Virgin Immaculate, promising that, if she granted us the favor of discovering the great river, I would give it the name of the Conception."[1] Their course was westward; and, plying their paddles, they passed the Straits of Michillimackinac, and coasted the northern shores of Lake Michigan; landing at evening to build their camp-fire at the edge of the forest, and draw up their canoes on the strand. They soon reached the river Menomonie, and ascended it to the village of the Menomonies, or Wild-rice Indians.[2] When they told them the object of their voyage, they were filled

[1] The doctrine of the Immaculate Conception, sanctioned in our own time by the Pope, was always a favorite tenet of the Jesuits; and Marquette was especially devoted to it.

[2] The Malhoumines, Malouminek, Oumalouminek, or Nation des Folles-Avoines, of early French writers. The *folle-avoine*, wild oats or "wild rice," *Zizania aquatica*, was their ordinary food, as also of other tribes of this region.

with astonishment, and used their best ingenuity to dissuade them. The banks of the Mississippi, they said, were inhabited by ferocious tribes, who put every stranger to death, toma-hawking all new-comers without cause or provocation. They added that there was a demon in a certain part of the river, whose roar could be heard at a great distance, and who would engulf them in the abyss where he dwelt; that its waters were full of frightful monsters, who would devour them and their canoe; and, finally, that the heat was so great that they would perish inevitably. Marquette set their counsel at naught, gave them a few words of instruction in the mysteries of the Faith, taught them a prayer, and bade them farewell.

The travellers next reached the mission at the head of Green Bay; entered Fox River; with difficulty and labor dragged their canoes up the long and tumultuous rapids; crossed Lake Winnebago; and followed the quiet windings of the river beyond, where they glided through an endless growth of wild rice, and scared the innumerable birds that fed upon it. On either hand rolled the prairie, dotted with groves and trees, browsing elk and deer.[1] On the seventh of June, they reached the Mascoutins and Miamis, who, since the visit of Dablon and Allouez, had been joined by the Kickapoos. Marquette, who had an eye for natural beauty, was delighted with the situation of the town, which he de-scribes as standing on the crown of a hill; while, all around, the prairie stretched beyond the sight, interspersed with groves and belts of tall forest. But he was still more delighted when he saw a cross planted in the midst of the place. The Indians had decorated it with a number of dressed deer-skins, red girdles, and bows and arrows, which they had hung upon it as an offering to the Great Manitou of the French; a sight by which Marquette says he was "extremely consoled."

The travellers had no sooner reached the town than they called the chiefs and elders to a council. Joliet told them that the governor of Canada had sent him to discover new coun-tries, and that God had sent his companion to teach the true

[1]Dablon, on his journey with Allouez in 1670, was delighted with the as-pect of the country and the abundance of game along this river. Carver, a century later, speaks to the same effect, saying that the birds rose up in clouds from the wild-rice marshes.

faith to the inhabitants; and he prayed for guides to show them the way to the waters of the Wisconsin. The council readily consented; and on the tenth of June the Frenchmen embarked again, with two Indians to conduct them. All the town came down to the shore to see their departure. Here were the Miamis, with long locks of hair dangling over each ear, after a fashion which Marquette thought very becoming; and here, too, the Mascoutins and the Kickapoos, whom he describes as mere boors in comparison with their Miami townsmen. All stared alike at the seven adventurers, marvelling that men could be found to risk an enterprise so hazardous.

The river twisted among lakes and marshes choked with wild rice; and, but for their guides, they could scarcely have followed the perplexed and narrow channel. It brought them at last to the portage, where, after carrying their canoes a mile and a half over the prairie and through the marsh, they launched them on the Wisconsin, bade farewell to the waters that flowed to the St. Lawrence, and committed themselves to the current that was to bear them they knew not whither,—perhaps to the Gulf of Mexico, perhaps to the South Sea or the Gulf of California. They glided calmly down the tranquil stream, by islands choked with trees and matted with entangling grape-vines; by forests, groves, and prairies, the parks and pleasure-grounds of a prodigal nature; by thickets and marshes and broad bare sand-bars; under the shadowing trees, between whose tops looked down from afar the bold brow of some woody bluff. At night, the bivouac,—the canoes inverted on the bank, the flickering fire, the meal of bison-flesh or venison, the evening pipes, and slumber beneath the stars; and when in the morning they embarked again, the mist hung on the river like a bridal veil; then melted before the sun, till the glassy water and the languid woods basked breathless in the sultry glare.[1]

On the 17th of June, they saw on their right the broad meadows, bounded in the distance by rugged hills, where now stand the town and fort of Prairie du Chien. Before them a wide and rapid current coursed athwart their way, by the foot of lofty heights wrapped thick in forests. They had

[1] The above traits of the scenery of the Wisconsin are taken from personal observation of the river during midsummer.

found what they sought, and "with a joy," writes Marquette, "which I cannot express," they steered forth their canoes on the eddies of the Mississippi.

Turning southward, they paddled down the stream, through a solitude unrelieved by the faintest trace of man. A large fish, apparently one of the huge cat-fish of the Mississippi, blundered against Marquette's canoe, with a force which seems to have startled him; and once, as they drew in their net, they caught a "spade-fish," whose eccentric appearance greatly astonished them. At length, the buffalo began to appear, grazing in herds on the great prairies which then bordered the river; and Marquette describes the fierce and stupid look of the old bulls, as they stared at the intruders through the tangled mane which nearly blinded them.

They advanced with extreme caution, landed at night, and made a fire to cook their evening meal; then extinguished it, embarked again, paddled some way farther, and anchored in the stream, keeping a man on the watch till morning. They had journeyed more than a fortnight without meeting a human being, when, on the twenty-fifth, they discovered footprints of men in the mud of the western bank, and a well-trodden path that led to the adjacent prairie. Joliet and Marquette resolved to follow it; and, leaving the canoes in charge of their men, they set out on their hazardous adventure. The day was fair, and they walked two leagues in silence, following the path through the forest and across the sunny prairie, till they discovered an Indian village on the banks of a river, and two others on a hill half a league distant.[1] Now, with beating hearts, they invoked the aid of Heaven, and, again advancing, came so near, without being seen, that they could hear the voices of the Indians among the wigwams. Then they stood forth in full view, and shouted to attract attention. There was great commotion in the village. The inmates swarmed out of their huts, and four of their chief men presently came forward to meet the strangers, advancing very deliberately, and holding up toward the sun two calumets, or

---

[1] The Indian villages, under the names of Peouaria (*Peoria*) and Moingouena, are represented in Marquette's map upon a river corresponding in position with the Des Moines; though the distance from the Wisconsin, as given by him, would indicate a river farther north.

peace-pipes, decorated with feathers. They stopped abruptly before the two Frenchmen, and stood gazing at them without speaking a word. Marquette was much relieved on seeing that they wore French cloth, whence he judged that they must be friends and allies. He broke the silence, and asked them who they were; whereupon they answered that they were Illinois, and offered the pipe; which having been duly smoked, they all went together to the village. Here the chief received the travellers after a singular fashion, meant to do them honor. He stood stark naked at the door of a large wigwam, holding up both hands as if to shield his eyes. "Frenchmen, how bright the sun shines when you come to visit us! All our village awaits you; and you shall enter our wigwams in peace." So saying, he led them into his own, which was crowded to suffocation with savages, staring at their guests in silence. Having smoked with the chiefs and old men, they were invited to visit the great chief of all the Illinois, at one of the villages they had seen in the distance; and thither they proceeded, followed by a throng of warriors, squaws, and children. On arriving, they were forced to smoke again, and listen to a speech of welcome from the great chief, who delivered it standing between two old men, naked like himself. His lodge was crowded with the dignitaries of the tribe, whom Marquette addressed in Algonquin, announcing himself as a messenger sent by the God who had made them, and whom it behooves them to recognize and obey. He added a few words touching the power and glory of Count Frontenac, and concluded by asking information concerning the Mississippi, and the tribes along its banks, whom he was on his way to visit. The chief replied with a speech of compliment; assuring his guests that their presence added flavor to his tobacco, made the river more calm, the sky more serene, and the earth more beautiful. In conclusion, he gave them a young slave and a calumet, begging them at the same time to abandon their purpose of descending the Mississippi.

A feast of four courses now followed. First, a wooden bowl full of a porridge of Indian meal boiled with grease was set before the guests; and the master of ceremonies fed them in turn, like infants, with a large spoon. Then appeared a platter of fish; and the same functionary, carefully removing the bones with his fingers, and blowing on the morsels to cool them, placed them in the mouths of the two Frenchmen. A large dog, killed and cooked for the occasion, was next placed before them; but, failing to tempt their fastidious appetites, was supplanted by a dish of fat buffalo-meat, which concluded the entertainment. The crowd having dispersed, buffalo-robes were spread on the ground, and Marquette and Joliet spent the night on the scene of the late festivity. In the morning, the chief, with some six hundred of his tribesmen, escorted them to their canoes, and bade them, after their stolid fashion, a friendly farewell.

Again they were on their way, slowly drifting down the great river. They passed the mouth of the Illinois, and glided beneath that line of rocks on the eastern side, cut into fantastic forms by the elements, and marked as "The Ruined Castles" on some of the early French maps. Presently they beheld a sight which reminded them that the Devil was still lord paramount of this wilderness. On the flat face of a high rock were painted, in red, black, and green, a pair of monsters, each "as large as a calf, with horns like a deer, red eyes, a beard like a tiger, and a frightful expression of countenance. The face is something like that of a man, the body covered with scales; and the tail so long that it passes entirely round the body, over the head and between the legs, ending like that of a fish." Such is the account which the worthy Jesuit gives of these manitous, or Indian gods.[1] He confesses that at first

[1] The rock where these figures were painted is immediately above the city of Alton. The tradition of their existence remains, though they are entirely effaced by time. In 1867, when I passed the place, a part of the rock had been quarried away, and, instead of Marquette's monsters, it bore a huge advertisement of "Plantation Bitters." Some years ago, certain persons, with more zeal than knowledge, proposed to restore the figures, after conceptions of their own; but the idea was abandoned.

Marquette made a drawing of the two monsters, but it is lost. I have, however, a fac-simile of a map made a few years later, by order of the Intendant Duchesneau, which is decorated with the portrait of one of them, answering to Marquette's description, and probably copied from his drawing. St. Cosme, who saw them in 1699, says that they were even then almost effaced. Douay and Joutel also speak of them; the former, bitterly hostile to his Jesuit contemporaries, charging Marquette with exaggeration in his account of them. Joutel could see nothing terrifying in their appearance; but he says that his Indians made sacrifices to them as they passed.

they frightened him; and his imagination and that of his credulous companions were so wrought upon by these unhallowed efforts of Indian art, that they continued for a long
time to talk of them as they plied their paddles. They were
thus engaged, when they were suddenly aroused by a real
danger. A torrent of yellow mud rushed furiously athwart the
calm blue current of the Mississippi; boiling and surging, and
sweeping in its course logs, branches, and uprooted trees.
They had reached the mouth of the Missouri, where that savage river, descending from its mad career through a vast unknown of barbarism, poured its turbid floods into the bosom
of its gentler sister. Their light canoes whirled on the miry
vortex like dry leaves on an angry brook. "I never," writes
Marquette, "saw any thing more terrific;" but they escaped
with their fright, and held their way down the turbulent and
swollen current of the now united rivers.[1] They passed the
lonely forest that covered the site of the destined city of St.
Louis, and, a few days later, saw on their left the mouth of
the stream to which the Iroquois had given the well-merited
name of Ohio, or the Beautiful River.[2] Soon they began to
see the marshy shores buried in a dense growth of the cane,
with its tall straight stems and feathery light-green foliage.
The sun glowed through the hazy air with a languid stifling
heat, and by day and night mosquitoes in myriads left them
no peace. They floated slowly down the current, crouched in
the shade of the sails which they had spread as awnings, when
suddenly they saw Indians on the east bank. The surprise was
mutual, and each party was as much frightened as the other.
Marquette hastened to display the calumet which the Illinois
had given him by way of passport; and the Indians, recognizing the pacific symbol, replied with an invitation to land. Evidently, they were in communication with Europeans, for
they were armed with guns, knives, and hatchets, wore gar-

[1] The Missouri is called Pekitanouï by Marquette. It also bears, on early
French maps, the names of Rivière des Osages, and Rivière des Emissourites,
or Oumessourits. On Marquette's map, a tribe of this name is placed near its
banks, just above the Osages. Judging by the course of the Mississippi that
it discharged into the Gulf of Mexico, he conceived the hope of one day
reaching the South Sea by way of the Missouri.

[2] Called, on Marquette's map, Ouabouskiaou. On some of the earliest
maps, it is called Ouabache (Wabash).

ments of cloth, and carried their gunpowder in small bottles of thick glass. They feasted the Frenchmen with buffalo-meat, bear's oil, and white plums; and gave them a variety of doubtful information, including the agreeable but delusive assurance that they would reach the mouth of the river in ten days. It was, in fact, more than a thousand miles distant.

They resumed their course, and again floated down the interminable monotony of river, marsh, and forest. Day after day passed on in solitude, and they had paddled some three hundred miles since their meeting with the Indians, when, as they neared the mouth of the Arkansas, they saw a cluster of wigwams on the west bank. Their inmates were all astir, yelling the war-whoop, snatching their weapons, and running to the shore to meet the strangers, who, on their part, called for succor to the Virgin. In truth, they had need of her aid; for several large wooden canoes, filled with savages, were putting out from the shore, above and below them, to cut off their retreat, while a swarm of headlong young warriors waded into the water to attack them. The current proved too strong; and, failing to reach the canoes of the Frenchmen, one of them threw his war-club, which flew over the heads of the startled travellers. Meanwhile, Marquette had not ceased to hold up his calumet, to which the excited crowd gave no heed, but strung their bows and notched their arrows for immediate action; when at length the elders of the village arrived, saw the peace-pipe, restrained the ardor of the youth, and urged the Frenchmen to come ashore. Marquette and his companions complied, trembling, and found a better reception than they had reason to expect. One of the Indians spoke a little Illinois, and served as interpreter; a friendly conference was followed by a feast of sagamite and fish; and the travellers, not without sore misgivings, spent the night in the lodges of their entertainers.[1]

Early in the morning, they embarked again, and proceeded to a village of the Arkansas tribe, about eight leagues below. Notice of their coming was sent before them by their late hosts; and, as they drew near, they were met by a canoe, in the prow of which stood a naked personage, holding a calu-

[1] This village, called Mitchigamea, is represented on several contemporary maps.

met, singing, and making gestures of friendship. On reaching the village, which was on the east side,[1] opposite the mouth of the river Arkansas, they were conducted to a sort of scaffold, before the lodge of the war-chief. The space beneath had been prepared for their reception, the ground being neatly covered with rush mats. On these they were seated; the warriors sat around them in a semicircle; then the elders of the tribe; and then the promiscuous crowd of villagers, standing, and staring over the heads of the more dignified members of the assembly. All the men were naked; but, to compensate for the lack of clothing, they wore strings of beads in their noses and ears. The women were clothed in shabby skins, and wore their hair clumped in a mass behind each ear. By good luck, there was a young Indian in the village, who had an excellent knowledge of Illinois; and through him Marquette endeavored to explain the mysteries of Christianity, and to gain information concerning the river below. To this end he gave his auditors the presents indispensable on such occasions, but received very little in return. They told him that the Mississippi was infested by hostile Indians, armed with guns procured from white men; and that they, the Arkansas, stood in such fear of them that they dared not hunt the buffalo, but were forced to live on Indian corn, of which they raised three crops a year.

During the speeches on either side, food was brought in without ceasing: sometimes a platter of sagamite or mush; sometimes of corn boiled whole; sometimes a roasted dog. The villagers had large earthen pots and platters, made by themselves with tolerable skill, as well as hatchets, knives, and beads, gained by traffic with the Illinois and other tribes in contact with the French or Spaniards. All day there was feasting without respite, after the merciless practice of Indian hospitality; but at night some of their entertainers proposed to kill and plunder them, a scheme which was defeated by the vigilance of the chief, who visited their quarters, and danced the calumet dance to reassure his guests.

The travellers now held counsel as to what course they should take. They had gone far enough, as they thought, to establish one important point: that the Mississippi discharged its waters, not into the Atlantic or sea of Virginia, nor into

[1] A few years later, the Arkansas were all on the west side.

the Gulf of California or Vermilion Sea, but into the Gulf of Mexico. They thought themselves nearer to its mouth than they actually were, the distance being still about seven hundred miles; and they feared that, if they went farther, they might be killed by Indians or captured by Spaniards, whereby the results of their discovery would be lost. Therefore they resolved to return to Canada, and report what they had seen.

They left the Arkansas village, and began their homeward voyage on the seventeenth of July. It was no easy task to urge their way upward, in the heat of midsummer, against the current of the dark and gloomy stream, toiling all day under the parching sun, and sleeping at night in the exhalations of the unwholesome shore, or in the narrow confines of their birchen vessels, anchored on the river. Marquette was attacked with dysentery. Languid and well-nigh spent, he invoked his celestial mistress, as day after day, and week after week, they won their slow way northward. At length, they reached the Illinois, and, entering its mouth, followed its course, charmed, as they went, with its placid waters, its shady forests, and its rich plains, grazed by the bison and the deer. They stopped at a spot soon to be made famous in the annals of western discovery. This was a village of the Illinois, then called Kaskaskia; a name afterwards transferred to another locality.[1] A chief, with a band of young warriors, offered to guide them to the Lake of the Illinois; that is to say, Lake Michigan. Thither they repaired; and, coasting its shores, reached Green Bay at the end of September, after an absence of about four months, during which they had paddled their canoes somewhat more than two thousand five hundred miles.[2]

---

[1] Marquette says that it consisted at this time of seventy-four lodges. These, like the Huron and Iroquois lodges, contained each several fires and several families. This village was about seven miles below the site of the present town of Ottawa.

[2] The journal of Marquette, first published in an imperfect form by Thevenot, in 1681, has been reprinted by Mr. Lenox, under the direction of Mr. Shea, from the manuscript preserved in the archives of the Canadian Jesuits. It will also be found in Shea's *Discovery and Exploration of the Mississippi Valley*, and the *Relations Inédites* of Martin. The true map of Marquette accompanies all these publications. The map published by Thevenot and reproduced by Bancroft is not Marquette's. The original of this, of which I

Marquette remained to recruit his exhausted strength; but Joliet descended to Quebec, to bear the report of his discovery to Count Frontenac. Fortune had wonderfully favored him on his long and perilous journey; but now she abandoned him on the very threshold of home. At the foot of the rapids of La Chine, and immediately above Montreal, his canoe was overset, two of his men and an Indian boy were drowned, all his papers were lost, and he himself narrowly escaped.[1] In a letter to Frontenac, he speaks of the accident as follows: "I had escaped every peril from the Indians; I had passed forty-two rapids; and was on the point of disembarking, full of joy at the success of so long and difficult an enterprise, when my canoe capsized, after all the danger seemed over. I lost two men, and my box of papers, within sight of the first French settlements, which I had left almost two years before. Nothing remains to me but my life, and the ardent desire to employ it on any service which you may please to direct."[2]

---

have a fac-simile, bears the title *Carte de la Nouvelle Découverte que les Pères Jésuites ont faite en l'année 1672, et continuée par le Père Jacques Marquette, etc.* The return route of the expedition is incorrectly laid down on it. A manuscript map of the Jesuit Raffeix, preserved in the Bibliothèque Impériale, is more accurate in this particular. I have also another contemporary manuscript map, indicating the various Jesuit stations in the West at this time, and representing the Mississippi, as discovered by Marquette. For these and other maps, see Appendix.

[1] *Lettre de Frontenac au Ministre, Québec, 14 Nov., 1674.*

[2] This letter is appended to Joliet's smaller map of his discoveries. See Appendix. Compare *Détails sur le Voyage de Louis Joliet* and *Relation de la Decouverte de plusieurs Pays situez au midi de la Nouvelle France, faite en 1673* (Margry, I. 259). These are oral accounts given by Joliet after the loss of his papers. Also, *Lettre de Joliet, Oct. 10, 1674* (Harrisse). On the seventh of October, 1675, Joliet married Claire Bissot, daughter of a wealthy Canadian merchant, engaged in trade with the northern Indians. This drew Joliet's attention to Hudson's Bay; and he made a journey thither in 1679, by way of the Saguenay. He found three English forts on the bay, occupied by about sixty men, who had also an armed vessel of twelve guns and several small trading-craft. The English held out great inducements to Joliet to join them; but he declined, and returned to Quebec, where he reported that, unless these formidable rivals were dispossessed, the trade of Canada would be ruined. In consequence of this report, some of the principal merchants of the colony formed a company to compete with the English in the trade of Hudson's Bay. In the year of this journey, Joliet received a grant of the islands of Mignan; and in the following year, 1680, he received another grant, of the

Marquette spent the winter and the following summer at the mission of Green Bay, still suffering from his malady. In the autumn, however, it abated; and he was permitted by his Superior to attempt the execution of a plan to which he was devotedly attached,—the founding, at the principal town of the Illinois, of a mission to be called the Immaculate Conception, a name which he had already given to the river Mississippi. He set out on this errand on the twenty-fifth of October, accompanied by two men, named Pierre and Jacques, one of whom had been with him on his great journey of discovery. A band of Pottawattamies and another band of Illinois also joined him. The united parties—ten canoes in all—followed the east shore of Green Bay as far as the inlet then called Sturgeon Cove, from the head of which they crossed by a difficult portage through the forest to the shore of Lake Michigan. November had come. The bright hues of the autumn foliage were changed to rusty brown. The shore was desolate, and the lake was stormy. They were more than a month in coasting its western border, when at length they reached the river Chicago, entered it, and ascended about two leagues. Marquette's disease had lately returned, and hemorrhage now ensued. He told his two companions that this journey would be his last. In the condition in which he was, it was impossible to go farther. The two men built a log hut by the river, and here they prepared to spend the winter; while Marquette, feeble as he was, began the spiritual exercises of Saint Ignatius, and confessed his two companions twice a week.

Meadow, marsh, and forest were sheeted with snow, but game was abundant. Pierre and Jacques killed buffalo and

---

great island of Anticosti in the lower St. Lawrence. In 1681, he was established here, with his wife and six servants. He was engaged in fisheries; and, being a skilful navigator and surveyor, he made about this time a chart of the St. Lawrence. In 1690, Sir William Phips, on his way with an English fleet to attack Quebec, made a descent on Joliet's establishment, burnt his buildings, and took prisoners his wife and his mother-in-law. In 1694, Joliet explored the coasts of Labrador, under the auspices of a company formed for the whale and seal fishery. On his return, Frontenac made him royal pilot for the St. Lawrence; and at about the same time he received the appointment of hydrographer at Quebec. He died, apparently poor, in 1699 or 1700, and was buried on one of the islands of Mignan. The discovery of the above facts is due in great part to the researches of Margry.

deer and shot wild turkeys close to their hut. There was an
encampment of Illinois within two days' journey; and other
Indians, passing by this well-known thoroughfare, occasionally visited them, treating the exiles kindly, and sometimes
bringing them game and Indian corn. Eighteen leagues distant was the camp of two adventurous French traders: one of
them, a noted *coureur de bois*, nicknamed La Taupine;[1] and
the other, a self-styled surgeon. They also visited Marquette,
and befriended him to the best of their power.

Urged by a burning desire to lay, before he died, the foundation of his new mission of the Immaculate Conception,
Marquette begged his two followers to join him in a *novena*,
or nine days' devotion to the Virgin. In consequence of this,
as he believed, his disease relented; he began to regain
strength, and in March was able to resume the journey. On
the thirtieth of the month, they left their hut, which had been
inundated by a sudden rise of the river, and carried their
canoe through mud and water over the portage which led to
the Des Plaines. Marquette knew the way, for he had passed
by this route on his return from the Mississippi. Amid the
rains of opening spring, they floated down the swollen current of the Des Plaines, by naked woods and spongy, saturated prairies, till they reached its junction with the main
stream of the Illinois, which they descended to their destination, the Indian town which Marquette calls Kaskaskia. Here,
as we are told, he was received "like an angel from Heaven."
He passed from wigwam to wigwam, telling the listening
crowds of God and the Virgin, Paradise and Hell, angels and
demons; and, when he thought their minds prepared, he
summoned them all to a grand council.

It took place near the town, on the great meadow which
lies between the river and the modern village of Utica. Here
five hundred chiefs and old men were seated in a ring; behind
stood fifteen hundred youths and warriors, and behind these
again all the women and children of the village. Marquette,
standing in the midst, displayed four large pictures of the Virgin; harangued the assembly on the mysteries of the Faith,

---

[1] Pierre Moreau, *alias* La Taupine, was afterwards bitterly complained of
by the Intendant Duchesneau, for acting as the governor's agent in illicit
trade with the Indians.

and exhorted them to adopt it. The temper of his auditory met his utmost wishes. They begged him to stay among them and continue his instructions; but his life was fast ebbing away, and it behooved him to depart.

A few days after Easter he left the village, escorted by a crowd of Indians, who followed him as far as Lake Michigan. Here he embarked with his two companions. Their destination was Michillimackinac, and their course lay along the eastern borders of the lake. As, in the freshness of advancing spring, Pierre and Jacques urged their canoe along that lonely and savage shore, the priest lay with dimmed sight and prostrated strength, communing with the Virgin and the angels. On the nineteenth of May, he felt that his hour was near; and, as they passed the mouth of a small river, he requested his companions to land. They complied, built a shed of bark on a rising ground near the bank, and carried thither the dying Jesuit. With perfect cheerfulness and composure, he gave directions for his burial, asked their forgiveness for the trouble he had caused them, administered to them the sacrament of penitence, and thanked God that he was permitted to die in the wilderness, a missionary of the Faith and a member of the Jesuit brotherhood. At night, seeing that they were fatigued, he told them to take rest, saying that he would call them when he felt his time approaching. Two or three hours after, they heard a feeble voice, and, hastening to his side, found him at the point of death. He expired calmly, murmuring the names of Jesus and Mary, with his eyes fixed on the crucifix which one of his followers held before him. They dug a grave beside the hut, and here they buried him according to the directions which he had given them; then, re-embarking, they made their way to Michillimackinac, to bear the tidings to the priests at the mission of St. Ignace.[1]

In the winter of 1676, a party of Kiskakon Ottawas were hunting on Lake Michigan; and when, in the following spring, they prepared to return home, they bethought them, in accordance with an Indian custom, of taking with them the

---

[1] The contemporary *Relation* tells us that a miracle took place at the burial of Marquette. One of the two Frenchmen, overcome with grief and colic, bethought him of applying a little earth from the grave to the seat of pain. This at once restored him to health and cheerfulness.

bones of Marquette, who had been their instructor at the mission of St. Esprit. They repaired to the spot, found the grave, opened it, washed and dried the bones and placed them carefully in a box of birch-bark. Then, in a procession of thirty canoes, they bore it, singing their funeral songs, to St. Ignace of Michillimackinac. As they approached, priests, Indians, and traders all thronged to the shore. The relics of Marquette were received with solemn ceremony, and buried beneath the floor of the little chapel of the mission.[1]

[1] For Marquette's death, see the contemporary *Relation*, published by Shea, Lenox, and Martin, with the accompanying *Lettre et Journal*. The river where he died is a small stream in the west of Michigan, some distance south of the promontory called the "Sleeping Bear." It long bore his name, which is now borne by a larger neighboring stream. Charlevoix's account of Marquette's death is derived from tradition, and is not supported by the contemporary narrative. In 1877, human bones, with fragments of birch bark, were found buried on the supposed site of the Jesuit chapel at Point St. Ignace.

In 1847, the missionary of the Algonquins at the Lake of Two Mountains, above Montreal, wrote down a tradition of the death of Marquette, from the lips of an old Indian woman, born in 1777, at Michillimackinac. Her ancestress had been baptized by the subject of the story. The tradition has a resemblance to that related as fact by Charlevoix. The old squaw said that the Jesuit was returning, very ill, to Michillimackinac, when a storm forced him and his two men to land near a little river. Here he told them that he should die, and directed them to ring a bell over his grave and plant a cross. They all remained four days at the spot; and, though without food, the men felt no hunger. On the night of the fourth day he died, and the men buried him as he had directed. On waking in the morning, they saw a sack of Indian corn, a quantity of bacon, and some biscuit, miraculously sent to them, in accordance with the promise of Marquette, who had told them that they should have food enough for their journey to Michillimackinac. At the same instant, the stream began to rise, and in a few moments encircled the grave of the Jesuit, which formed, thenceforth, an islet in the waters. The tradition adds, that an Indian battle afterwards took place on the banks of this stream, between Christians and infidels; and that the former gained the victory, in consequence of invoking the name of Marquette. This story bears the attestation of the priest of the Two Mountains that it is a literal translation of the tradition, as recounted by the old woman.

It has been asserted that the Illinois country was visited by two priests, some time before the visit of Marquette. This assertion was first made by M. Noiseux, late Grand Vicar of Quebec, who gives no authority for it. Not the slightest indication of any such visit appears in any contemporary document or map, thus far discovered. The contemporary writers, down to the time of Marquette and La Salle, all speak of the Illinois as an unknown country. The entire groundlessness of Noiseux's assertion is shown by Shea in a paper in the "Weekly Herald," of New York, April 21, 1855.

Chapter VI

1673–1678

LA SALLE AND FRONTENAC

*Objects of La Salle • Frontenac favors him • Projects of Frontenac
• Cataraqui • Frontenac on Lake Ontario • Fort Frontenac • La
Salle and Fénelon • Success of La Salle • His Enemies*

WE turn from the humble Marquette, thanking God with his last breath that he died for his Order and his Faith; and by our side stands the masculine form of Cavelier de la Salle. Prodigious was the contrast between the two discoverers: the one, with clasped hands and upturned eyes, seems a figure evoked from some dim legend of mediæval saintship; the other, with feet firm planted on the hard earth, breathes the self-relying energies of modern practical enterprise. Nevertheless, La Salle's enemies called him a visionary. His projects perplexed and startled them. At first, they ridiculed him; and then, as step by step he advanced towards his purpose, they denounced and maligned him. What was this purpose? It was not of sudden growth, but developed as years went on. La Salle at La Chine dreamed of a western passage to China, and nursed vague schemes of western discovery. Then, when his earlier journeyings revealed to him the valley of the Ohio and the fertile plains of Illinois, his imagination took wing over the boundless prairies and forests drained by the great river of the West. His ambition had found its field. He would leave barren and frozen Canada behind, and lead France and civilization into the valley of the Mississippi. Neither the English nor the Jesuits should conquer that rich domain: the one must rest content with the country east of the Alleghanies, and the other with the forests, savages, and beaver-skins of the northern lakes. It was for him to call into light the latent riches of the great West. But the way to his land of promise was rough and long: it lay through Canada, filled with hostile traders and hostile priests, and barred by ice for half the year. The difficulty was soon solved. La Salle became convinced that the Mississippi flowed, not into the Pacific or the Gulf of California, but into the Gulf of Mexico. By a fortified post at its mouth, he could guard it against both English and Spaniards, and secure for the trade of the interior an access and an outlet under his own control, and open at every season. Of this trade, the hides of the buffalo would at first form the staple; and, along with furs, would reward the enterprise till other resources should be developed.

Such were the vast projects that unfolded themselves in the mind of La Salle. Canada must needs be, at the outset, his base of action, and without the support of its authorities he could do nothing. This support he found. From the moment when Count Frontenac assumed the government of the colony, he seems to have looked with favor on the young discoverer. There were points of likeness between the two men. Both were ardent, bold, and enterprising. The irascible and fiery pride of the noble found its match in the reserved and seemingly cold pride of the ambitious burgher. Each could comprehend the other; and they had, moreover, strong prejudices and dislikes in common. An understanding, not to say an alliance, soon grew up between them.

Frontenac had come to Canada a ruined man. He was ostentatious, lavish, and in no way disposed to let slip an opportunity of mending his fortune. He presently thought that he had found a plan by which he could serve both the colony and himself. His predecessor, Courcelle, had urged upon the king the expediency of building a fort on Lake Ontario, in order to hold the Iroquois in check and intercept the trade which the tribes of the Upper Lakes had begun to carry on with the Dutch and English of New York. Thus, a stream of wealth would be turned into Canada, which would otherwise enrich her enemies. Here, to all appearance, was a great public good, and from the military point of view it was so in fact; but it was clear that the trade thus secured might be made to profit, not the colony at large, but those alone who had control of the fort, which would then become the instrument of a monopoly. This the governor understood; and, without doubt, he meant that the projected establishment should pay him tribute. How far he and La Salle were acting in concurrence at this time, it is not easy to say; but Frontenac often took counsel of the explorer, who, on his part, saw in the design a possible first step towards the accomplishment of his own far-reaching schemes.

Such of the Canadian merchants as were not in the governor's confidence looked on his plan with extreme distrust. Frontenac, therefore, thought it expedient "to make use," as he expresses it, "of address." He gave out merely that he intended to make a tour through the upper parts of the colony with an armed force, in order to inspire the Indians with respect, and secure a solid peace. He had neither troops, money, munitions, nor means of transportation; yet there was no time to lose, for, should he delay the execution of his plan, it might be countermanded by the king. His only resource, therefore, was in a prompt and hardy exertion of the royal authority; and he issued an order requiring the inhabitants of Quebec, Montreal, Three Rivers, and other settlements, to furnish him, at their own cost, as soon as the spring sowing should be over, with a certain number of armed men, besides the requisite canoes. At the same time, he invited the officers settled in the country to join the expedition; an invitation which, anxious as they were to gain his good graces, few of them cared to decline. Regardless of murmurs and discontent, he pushed his preparation vigorously, and on the third of June left Quebec with his guard, his staff, a part of the garrison of the Castle of St. Louis, and a number of volunteers. He had already sent to La Salle, who was then at Montreal, directing him to repair to Onondaga, the political centre of the Iroquois, and invite their sachems to meet the governor in council at the Bay of Quinté on the north of Lake Ontario. La Salle had set out on his mission, but first sent Frontenac a map, which convinced him that the best site for his proposed fort was the mouth of the Cataraqui, where Kingston now stands. Another messenger was accordingly despatched, to change the rendezvous to this point.

Meanwhile, the governor proceeded, at his leisure, towards Montreal, stopping by the way to visit the officers settled along the bank, who, eager to pay their homage to the newly risen sun, received him with a hospitality which, under the roof of a log hut, was sometimes graced by the polished courtesies of the salon and the boudoir. Reaching Montreal, which he had never before seen, he gazed, we may suppose, with some interest at the long row of humble dwellings which lined the bank, the massive buildings of the Seminary, and the spire of the church predominant over all. It was a rude scene, but the greeting that awaited him savored nothing of the rough simplicity of the wilderness. Perrot, the local governor, was on the shore with his soldiers and the inhabitants, drawn up under arms, and firing a salute, to welcome the representative of the king. Frontenac was compelled to listen to a long harangue from the judge of the place, followed by another from the syndic. Then there was a solemn procession to the church, where he was forced to undergo a third effort of oratory from one of the priests. *Te Deum* followed, in thanks for his arrival; and then he took refuge in the fort. Here he remained thirteen days, busied with his preparations, organizing the militia, soothing their mutual jealousies, and settling knotty questions of rank and precedence. During this time, every means, as he declares, was used to prevent him from proceeding; and among other devices a rumor was set on foot that a Dutch fleet, having just captured Boston, was on its way to attack Quebec.[1]

Having sent men, canoes, and baggage, by land, to La Salle's old settlement of La Chine, Frontenac himself followed on the twenty-eighth of June. Including Indians from the missions, he now had with him about four hundred men, and a hundred and twenty canoes, besides two large flat-boats, which he caused to be painted in red and blue, with strange devices, intended to dazzle the Iroquois by a display of unwonted splendor. Now their hard task began. Shouldering canoes through the forest, dragging the flat-boats along the shore, working like beavers, sometimes in water to the knees, sometimes to the armpits, their feet cut by the sharp stones, and they themselves well-nigh swept down by the furious current, they fought their way upward against the chain of mighty rapids that break the navigation of the St. Lawrence. The Indians were of the greatest service. Frontenac, like La Salle, showed from the first a special faculty of managing

---

[1] *Lettre de Frontenac à Colbert, 13 Nov., 1673.* This rumor, it appears, originated with the Jesuit Dablon. *Journal du Voyage du Comte de Frontenac au Lac Ontario.* The Jesuits were greatly opposed to the establishment of forts and trading-posts in the upper country, for reasons that will appear hereafter.

them; for his keen, incisive spirit was exactly to their liking, and they worked for him as they would have worked for no man else. As they approached the Long Saut, rain fell in torrents; and the governor, without his cloak, and drenched to the skin, directed in person the amphibious toil of his followers. Once, it is said, he lay awake all night, in his anxiety lest the biscuit should be wet, which would have ruined the expedition. No such mischance took place, and at length the last rapid was passed, and smooth water awaited them to their journey's end. Soon they reached the Thousand Islands, and their light flotilla glided in long file among those watery labyrinths, by rocky islets, where some lonely pine towered like a mast against the sky; by sun-scorched crags, where the brown lichens crisped in the parching glare; by deep dells, shady and cool, rich in rank ferns, and spongy, dark green mosses; by still coves, where the water-lilies lay like snowflakes on their broad, flat leaves; till at length they neared their goal, and the glistening bosom of Lake Ontario opened on their sight.

Frontenac, to impose respect on the Iroquois, now set his canoes in order of battle. Four divisions formed the first line, then came the two flat-boats; he himself, with his guards, his staff, and the gentlemen volunteers, followed, with the canoes of Three Rivers on his right, and those of the Indians on his left, while two remaining divisions formed a rear line. Thus, with measured paddles, they advanced over the still lake, till they saw a canoe approaching to meet them. It bore several Iroquois chiefs, who told them that the dignitaries of their nation awaited them at Cataraqui, and offered to guide them to the spot. They entered the wide mouth of the river, and passed along the shore, now covered by the quiet little city of Kingston, till they reached the point at present occupied by the barracks, at the western end of Cataraqui bridge. Here they stranded their canoes and disembarked. Baggage was landed, fires lighted, tents pitched, and guards set. Close at hand, under the lee of the forest, were the camping sheds of the Iroquois, who had come to the rendezvous in considerable numbers.

At daybreak of the next morning, the thirteenth of July, the drums beat, and the whole party were drawn up under arms.

A double line of men extended from the front of Frontenac's tent to the Indian camp; and, through the lane thus formed, the savage deputies, sixty in number, advanced to the place of council. They could not hide their admiration at the martial array of the French, many of whom were old soldiers of the regiment of Carignan; and, when they reached the tent, they ejaculated their astonishment at the uniforms of the governor's guard who surrounded it. Here the ground had been carpeted with the sails of the flat-boats, on which the deputies squatted themselves in a ring and smoked their pipes for a time with their usual air of deliberate gravity, while Frontenac, who sat surrounded by his officers, had full leisure to contemplate the formidable adversaries whose mettle was hereafter to put his own to so severe a test. A chief named Garakontié, a noted friend of the French, at length opened the council, in behalf of all the five Iroquois nations, with expressions of great respect and deference towards "Onontio;" that is to say, the governor of Canada. Whereupon Frontenac, whose native arrogance where Indians were concerned always took a form which imposed respect without exciting anger, replied in the following strain: —

"Children! Mohawks, Oneidas, Onondagas, Cayugas, and Senecas. I am glad to see you here, where I have had a fire lighted for you to smoke by, and for me to talk to you. You have done well, my children, to obey the command of your Father. Take courage: you will hear his word, which is full of peace and tenderness. For do not think that I have come for war. My mind is full of peace, and she walks by my side. Courage, then, children, and take rest."

With that, he gave them six fathoms of tobacco, reiterated his assurances of friendship, promised that he would be a kind father so long as they should be obedient children, regretted that he was forced to speak through an interpreter, and ended with a gift of guns to the men, and prunes and raisins to their wives and children. Here closed this preliminary meeting, the great council being postponed to another day.

During the meeting, Raudin, Frontenac's engineer, was tracing out the lines of a fort, after a predetermined plan; and the whole party, under the direction of their officers, now set

themselves to construct it. Some cut down trees, some dug
the trenches, some hewed the palisades; and with such order
and alacrity was the work urged on, that the Indians were lost
in astonishment. Meanwhile, Frontenac spared no pains to
make friends of the chiefs, some of whom he had constantly
at his table. He fondled the Iroquois children, and gave them
bread and sweetmeats, and in the evening feasted the squaws,
to make them dance. The Indians were delighted with these
attentions, and conceived a high opinion of the new Onontio.

On the seventeenth, when the construction of the fort was
well advanced, Frontenac called the chiefs to a grand council,
which was held with all possible state and ceremony. His
dealing with the Indians on this and other occasions was truly
admirable. Unacquainted as he was with them, he seems to
have had an instinctive perception of the treatment they required. His predecessors had never ventured to address the
Iroquois as "Children," but had always styled them "Brothers;" and yet the assumption of paternal authority on the part
of Frontenac was not only taken in good part, but was received with apparent gratitude. The martial nature of the man,
his clear decisive speech, and his frank and downright manner, backed as they were by a display of force which in their
eyes was formidable, struck them with admiration, and gave
tenfold effect to his words of kindness. They thanked him
for that which from another they would not have endured.

Frontenac began by again expressing his satisfaction that
they had obeyed the commands of their Father, and come to
Cataraqui to hear what he had to say. Then he exhorted them
to embrace Christianity; and on this theme he dwelt at
length, in words excellently adapted to produce the desired
effect; words which it would be most superfluous to tax as
insincere, though doubtless they lost nothing in emphasis because in this instance conscience and policy aimed alike. Then,
changing his tone, he pointed to his officers, his guard, the
long files of the militia, and the two flat-boats, mounted with
cannon, which lay in the river near by. "If," he said, "your
Father can come so far, with so great a force, through such
dangerous rapids, merely to make you a visit of pleasure and
friendship, what would he do, if you should awaken his anger, and make it necessary for him to punish his disobedient

children? He is the arbiter of peace and war. Beware how you offend him." And he warned them not to molest the Indian allies of the French, telling them, sharply, that he would chastise them for the least infraction of the peace.

From threats he passed to blandishments, and urged them to confide in his paternal kindness, saying that, in proof of his affection, he was building a storehouse at Cataraqui, where they could be supplied with all the goods they needed, without the necessity of a long and dangerous journey. He warned them against listening to bad men, who might seek to delude them by misrepresentations and falsehoods; and he urged them to give heed to none but "men of character, like the Sieur de la Salle." He expressed a hope that they would suffer their children to learn French from the missionaries, in order that they and his nephews—meaning the French colonists—might become one people; and he concluded by requesting them to give him a number of their children to be educated in the French manner, at Quebec.

This speech, every clause of which was reinforced by abundant presents, was extremely well received; though one speaker reminded him that he had forgotten one important point, inasmuch as he had not told them at what prices they could obtain goods at Cataraqui. Frontenac evaded a precise answer, but promised them that the goods should be as cheap as possible, in view of the great difficulty of transportation. As to the request concerning their children, they said that they could not accede to it till they had talked the matter over in their villages; but it is a striking proof of the influence which Frontenac had gained over them, that, in the following year, they actually sent several of their children to Quebec to be educated, the girls among the Ursulines, and the boys in the household of the governor.

Three days after the council, the Iroquois set out on their return; and, as the palisades of the fort were now finished, and the barracks nearly so, Frontenac began to send his party homeward by detachments. He himself was detained for a time by the arrival of another band of Iroquois, from the villages on the north side of Lake Ontario. He repeated to them the speech he had made to the others; and, this final meeting over, embarked with his guard, leaving a sufficient number to hold the fort, which was to be provisioned for a year by means of a convoy, then on its way up the river. Passing the rapids safely, he reached Montreal on the first of August.

His enterprise had been a complete success. He had gained every point, and, in spite of the dangerous navigation, had not lost a single canoe. Thanks to the enforced and gratuitous assistance of the inhabitants, the whole had cost the king only about ten thousand francs, which Frontenac had advanced on his own credit. Though, in a commercial point of view, the new establishment was of very questionable benefit to the colony at large, the governor had, nevertheless, conferred an inestimable blessing on all Canada, by the assurance he had gained of a long respite from the fearful scourge of Iroquois hostility. "Assuredly," he writes, "I may boast of having impressed them at once with respect, fear, and good-will."[1] He adds that the fort at Cataraqui, with the aid of a vessel now building, will command Lake Ontario, keep the peace with the Iroquois, and cut off the trade with the English. And he proceeds to say that, by another fort at the mouth of the Niagara, and another vessel on Lake Erie, we, the French, can command all the upper lakes. This plan was an essential link in the schemes of La Salle; and we shall soon find him employed in executing it.

A curious incident occurred soon after the building of the fort on Lake Ontario. Frontenac, on his way back, quarrelled with Perrot, the governor of Montreal, whom, in view of his speculations in the fur-trade, he seems to have regarded as a rival in business; but who, by his folly and arrogance, would have justified any reasonable measure of severity. Frontenac, however, was not reasonable. He arrested Perrot, threw him into prison, and set up a man of his own as governor in his place; and, as the judge of Montreal was not in his interest, he removed him, and substituted another, on whom he could rely. Thus for a time he had Montreal well in hand.

The priests of the Seminary, seigniors of the island, regarded these arbitrary proceedings with extreme uneasiness. They claimed the right of nominating their own governor; and Perrot, though he held a commission from the king,

<hr />

[1] *Lettre de Frontenac au Ministre, 13 Nov., 1678.*

owed his place to their appointment. True, he had set them at nought, and proved a veritable King Stork, yet nevertheless they regarded his removal as an infringement of their rights.

During the quarrel with Perrot, La Salle chanced to be at Montreal, lodged in the house of Jacques Le Ber, who, though one of the principal merchants and most influential inhabitants of the settlement, was accustomed to sell goods across his counter in person to white men and Indians, his wife taking his place when he was absent. Such were the primitive manners of the secluded little colony. Le Ber, at this time, was in the interest of Frontenac and La Salle; though he afterwards became one of their most determined opponents. Amid the excitement and discussion occasioned by Perrot's arrest, La Salle declared himself an adherent of the governor, and warned all persons against speaking ill of him in his hearing.

The Abbé Fénelon, already mentioned as half-brother to the famous Archbishop, had attempted to mediate between Frontenac and Perrot, and to this end had made a journey to Quebec on the ice, in midwinter. Being of an ardent temperament, and more courageous than prudent, he had spoken somewhat indiscreetly, and had been very roughly treated by the stormy and imperious Count. He returned to Montreal greatly excited, and not without cause. It fell to his lot to preach the Easter sermon. The service was held in the little church of the Hôtel-Dieu, which was crowded to the porch, all the chief persons of the settlement being present. The curé of the parish, whose name also was Perrot, said High Mass, assisted by La Salle's brother, Cavelier, and two other priests. Then Fénelon mounted the pulpit. Certain passages of his sermon were obviously levelled against Frontenac. Speaking of the duties of those clothed with temporal authority, he said that the magistrate, inspired with the spirit of Christ, was as ready to pardon offences against himself as to punish those against his prince; that he was full of respect for the ministers of the altar, and never maltreated them when they attempted to reconcile enemies and restore peace; that he never made favorites of those who flattered him, nor under specious pretexts oppressed other persons in authority who opposed his enterprises; that he used his power to serve his king, and not to his own advantage; that he remained content with his salary, without disturbing the commerce of the country, or abusing those who refused him a share in their profits; and that he never troubled the people by inordinate and unjust levies of men and material, using the name of his prince as a cover to his own designs.[1]

La Salle sat near the door; but, as the preacher proceeded, he suddenly rose to his feet in such a manner as to attract the notice of the congregation. As they turned their heads, he signed to the principal persons among them, and by his angry looks and gesticulation called their attention to the words of Fénelon. Then meeting the eye of the curé, who sat beside the altar, he made the same signs to him, to which the curé replied by a deprecating shrug of the shoulders. Fénelon changed color, but continued his sermon.[2]

This indecent proceeding of La Salle, and the zeal with which throughout the quarrel he took the part of the governor, did not go unrewarded. Henceforth, Frontenac was more than ever his friend; and this plainly appeared in the disposition made, through his influence, of the new fort on Lake Ontario. Attempts had been made to induce the king to have it demolished; but it was resolved at last that, being built, it should be allowed to stand; and, after long delay, a final arrangement was made for its maintenance, in the manner following: In the autumn of 1674, La Salle went to France, with letters of strong recommendation from Frontenac.[3] He was well received at Court; and he made two petitions to the king: the one for a patent of nobility, in

[1] Faillon, *Colonie Française*, III. 497, and manuscript authorities there cited. I have examined the principal of these. Faillon himself is a priest of St. Sulpice. Compare H. Verreau, *Les Deux Abbés de Fénelon*, chap. vii.

[2] *Information faicte par nous, Charles Le Tardieu, Sieur de Tilly, et Nicolas Dupont, etc., etc., contre le S.ʳ Abbé de Fénelon*. Tilly and Dupont were sent by Frontenac to inquire into the affair. Among the deponents is La Salle himself.

[3] In his despatch to the minister Colbert, of the fourteenth of November, 1674, Frontenac speaks of La Salle as follows: "I cannot help, Monseigneur, recommending to you the Sieur de la Salle, who is about to go to France, and who is a man of intelligence and ability, more capable than anybody else I know here to accomplish every kind of enterprise and discovery which may be entrusted to him, as he has the most perfect knowledge of the state of the country, as you will see, if you are disposed to give him a few moments of audience."

consideration of his services as an explorer; and the other for a grant in seigniory of Fort Frontenac, for so he called the new post, in honor of his patron. On his part, he offered to pay back the ten thousand francs which the fort had cost the king; to maintain it at his own charge, with a garrison equal to that of Montreal, besides fifteen or twenty laborers; to form a French colony around it; to build a church, whenever the number of inhabitants should reach one hundred; and, meanwhile, to support one or more Récollet friars; and, finally, to form a settlement of domesticated Indians in the neighborhood. His offers were accepted. He was raised to the rank of the untitled nobles; received a grant of the fort, and lands adjacent, to the extent of four leagues in front and half a league in depth, besides the neighboring islands; and was invested with the government of the fort and settlement, subject to the orders of the governor-general.[1]

La Salle returned to Canada, proprietor of a seigniory, which, all things considered, was one of the most valuable in the colony. His friends and his family, rejoicing in his good fortune, and not unwilling to share it, made him large advances of money, enabling him to pay the stipulated sum to the king, to rebuild the fort in stone, maintain soldiers and laborers, and procure in part, at least, the necessary outfit. Had La Salle been a mere merchant, he was in a fair way to make a fortune, for he was in a position to control the better part of the Canadian fur-trade. But he was not a mere merchant; and no commercial profit could content his ambition.

Those may believe, who will, that Frontenac did not expect a share in the profits of the new post. That he did expect it, there is positive evidence; for a deposition is extant, taken at the instance of his enemy, the Intendant Duchesneau, in which three witnesses attest that the governor, La Salle, his lieutenant La Forest, and one Boisseau, had formed a partnership to carry on the trade of Fort Frontenac.

---

[1] *Mémoire pour l'entretien du Fort Frontenac, par le S* de la Salle, 1674. Pétition du S* de la Salle au Roi. Lettres patentes de concession, du Fort de Frontenac et terres adjacentes au profit du S* de la Salle; données à Compiègne le 13 Mai, 1675. Arrêt qui accepte les offres faites par Robert Cavalier S* de la Salle; à Compiègne le 13 Mai, 1675. Lettres de noblesse pour le S* Cavelier de la Salle; données à Compiègne le 13 Mai, 1675. Papiers de Famille; Mémoire au Roi.*

No sooner was La Salle installed in his new post than the merchants of Canada joined hands to oppose him. Le Ber, once his friend, became his bitter enemy; for he himself had hoped to share the monopoly of Fort Frontenac, of which he and one Bazire had at first been placed provisionally in control, and from which he now saw himself ejected. La Chesnaye, Le Moyne, and others of more or less influence, took part in the league, which, in fact, embraced all the traders in the colony except the few joined with Frontenac and La Salle. Duchesneau, intendant of the colony, aided the malcontents. As time went on, their bitterness grew more bitter; and when at last it was seen that, not satisfied with the monopoly of Fort Frontenac, La Salle aimed at the control of the valleys of the Ohio and the Mississippi, and the usufruct of half a continent, the ire of his opponents redoubled, and Canada became for him a nest of hornets, buzzing in wrath, and watching the moment to sting. But there was another element of opposition, less noisy, but not less formidable; and this arose from the Jesuits. Frontenac hated them; and they, under befitting forms of duty and courtesy, paid him back in the same coin. Having no love for the governor, they would naturally have little for his partisan and *protégé*; but their opposition had another and a deeper root, for the plans of the daring young schemer jarred with their own.

We have seen the Canadian Jesuits in the early apostolic days of their mission, when the flame of their zeal, fed by an ardent hope, burned bright and high. This hope was doomed to disappointment. Their avowed purpose of building another Paraguay on the borders of the Great Lakes[1] was never accomplished, and their missions and their converts were swept away in an avalanche of ruin. Still, they would not despair. From the lakes, they turned their eyes to the Valley of the Mississippi, in the hope to see it one day the seat of their new empire of the Faith. But what did this new Paraguay mean? It meant a little nation of converted and domesticated savages, docile as children, under the paternal and absolute rule of Jesuit fathers, and trained by them in industrial pursuits, the results of which were to inure, not to the profit of

[1] This purpose is several times indicated in the *Relations*. For an instance, see The Jesuits in North America, pp. 506–07.

the producers, but to the building of churches, the founding of colleges, the establishment of warehouses and magazines, and the construction of works of defence,—all controlled by Jesuits, and forming a part of the vast possessions of the Order. Such was the old Paraguay;[1] and such, we may suppose, would have been the new, had the plans of those who designed it been realized.

I have said that since the middle of the century the religious exaltation of the early missions had sensibly declined. In the nature of things, that grand enthusiasm was too intense and fervent to be long sustained. But the vital force of Jesuitism had suffered no diminution. That marvelous *esprit de corps*, that extinction of self, and absorption of the individual in the Order, which has marked the Jesuits from their first existence as a body, was no whit changed or lessened; a principle, which, though different, was no less strong than the self-devoted patriotism of Sparta or the early Roman Republic.

The Jesuits were no longer supreme in Canada, or, in other words, Canada was no longer simply a mission. It had become a colony. Temporal interests and the civil power were constantly gaining ground; and the disciples of Loyola felt that relatively, if not absolutely, they were losing it. They struggled vigorously to maintain the ascendency of their Order, or, as they would have expressed it, the ascendency of religion; but in the older and more settled parts of the colony it was clear that the day of their undivided rule was past. Therefore, they looked with redoubled solicitude to their missions in the West. They had been among its first explorers; and they hoped that here the Catholic Faith, as represented by Jesuits, might reign with undisputed sway. In Paraguay, it was their constant aim to exclude white men from their missions. It was the same in North America. They dreaded fur-traders, partly because they interfered with their teachings and perverted their converts, and partly for other reasons. But La Salle was a fur-trader, and far worse than a fur-trader: he aimed at occupation, fortification, and settlement. The scope and vigor of his enterprises, and the powerful influence that aided them, made him a stumbling-block in their path. He

[1] Compare Charlevoix, *Histoire de Paraguay*, with Robertson, *Letters on Paraguay*.

was their most dangerous rival for the control of the West, and from first to last they set themselves against him.

What manner of man was he who could conceive designs so vast and defy enmities so many and so powerful? And in what spirit did he embrace these designs? We will look hereafter for an answer.

Chapter VII

1678

PARTY STRIFE

La Salle and his Reporter • Jesuit Ascendency • The Missions and the Fur-trade • Female Inquisitors • Plots against La Salle • His Brother the Priest • Intrigues of the Jesuits • La Salle poisoned • He exculpates the Jesuits • Renewed Intrigues

---

ONE of the most curious monuments of La Salle's time is a long memoir, written by a person who made his acquaintance at Paris, in the summer of 1678, when, as we shall soon see, he had returned to France, in prosecution of his plans. The writer knew the Sulpitian Galinée,[1] who, as he says, had a very high opinion of La Salle; and he was also in close relations with the discoverer's patron, the Prince de Conti.[2] He says that he had ten or twelve interviews with La Salle, and, becoming interested in him and in that which he communicated, he wrote down the substance of his conversation. The paper is divided into two parts: the first, called "Mémoire sur Mr. de la Salle," is devoted to the state of affairs in Canada, and chiefly to the Jesuits; the second, entitled "Histoire de Mr. de la Salle," is an account of the discoverer's life, or as much of it as the writer had learned from him.[3] Both parts bear throughout the internal evidence of being what they profess to be; but they embody the statements of a man of intense partisan feeling, transmitted through the mind of another person in sympathy with him, and evidently sharing his prepossessions. In one respect, however, the paper is of unquestionable historical value; for it gives us a vivid and not an exaggerated picture of the bitter strife of parties which then raged in Canada, and which was destined to tax to the utmost the vast energy and fortitude of La Salle. At times, the memoir is fully sustained by contemporary evidence; but of-

[1] *Ante*, p. 733.
[2] Louis-Armand de Bourbon, second Prince de Conti. The author of the memoir seems to have been Abbé Renaudot, a learned churchman.
[3] Extracts from this have already been given in connection with La Salle's supposed discovery of the Mississippi. *Ante*, p. 741.

ten, again, it rests on its own unsupported authority. I give an abstract of its statements as I find them.

The following is the writer's account of La Salle: "All those among my friends who have seen him find him a man of great intelligence and sense. He rarely speaks of any subject except when questioned about it, and his words are very few and very precise. He distinguishes perfectly between that which he knows with certainty and that which he knows with some mingling of doubt. When he does not know, he does not hesitate to avow it; and though I have heard him say the same thing more than five or six times, when persons were present who had not heard it before, he always said it in the same manner. In short, I never heard anybody speak whose words carried with them more marks of truth."[1]

After mentioning that he is thirty-three or thirty-four years old, and that he has been twelve years in America, the memoir declares that he made the following statements: that the Jesuits are masters at Quebec; that the bishop is their creature, and does nothing but in concert with them;[2] that he is not well inclined towards the Récollets,[3] who have little credit, but who are protected by Frontenac; that in Canada the Jesuits think everybody an enemy to religion who is an

---

[1] "Tous ceux de mes amis qui l'ont vu luy trouve beaucoup d'esprit et un très grand sens; il ne parle guères que des choses sur lesquelles on l'interroge; il les dit en très-peu de mots et très-bien circonstanciées; il distingue parfaitement ce qu'il scait avec certitude, de ce qu'il scait avec quelque mélange de doute. Il avoue sans aucune façon ne pas savoir ce qu'il ne scait pas, et quoyque je luy aye ouy dire plus de cinq ou six fois les mesme choses à l'occasion de quelques personnes qui ne les avaient point encore entendues, je les luy ay toujours ouy dire de la mesme manière. En un mot je n'ay jamais ouy parler personne dont les paroles portassent plus de marques de vérité."

[2] "Il y a une autre chose qui me déplait, qui est l'entière dépendance dans laquelle les Prêtres du Séminaire de Québec et le Grand Vicaire de l'Evêque sont pour les Pères Jésuites, car il ne fait pas la moindre chose sans leur ordre; ce qui fait qu'indirectement ils sont les maîtres de ce qui regarde le spirituel, qui, comme vous savez, est une grande machine pour remuer tout le reste."— *Lettre de Frontenac à Colbert, 2 Nov., 1672.*

[3] "Ces réligieux [*les Récollets*] sont fort protégés partout par le comte de Frontenac, gouverneur du pays, et à cause de cela assez maltraités par l'évesque, parceque la doctrine de l'évesque et des Jésuites est que les affaires de la Réligion chrestienne n'iront point bien dans ce pays-là que quand le gouverneur sera créature des Jésuites, ou que l'évesque sera gouverneur."— *Mémoire sur M*ʳ *de la Salle.*

enemy to them; that, though they refused absolution to all who sold brandy to the Indians, they sold it themselves, and that he, La Salle, had himself detected them in it;[1] that the bishop laughs at the orders of the king when they do not agree with the wishes of the Jesuits; that the Jesuits dismissed one of their servants named Robert, because he told of their trade in brandy; that Albanel,[2] in particular, carried on a great fur-trade, and that the Jesuits have built their college in part from the profits of this kind of traffic; that they admitted that they carried on a trade, but denied that they gained so much by it as was commonly supposed.[3]

The memoir proceeds to affirm that they trade largely with the Sioux, at Ste. Marie, and with other tribes at Michillimackinac, and that they are masters of the trade of that region, where the forts are in their possession.[4] An Indian said, in full council, at Quebec, that he had prayed and been a Christian as long as the Jesuits would stay and teach him, but

---

[1] "Ils [les Jésuites] réfusent l'absolution á ceux qui ne veulent pas promettre de n'en plus vendre [de l'eau-de-vie], et s'ils meurent en cet état, ils les privent de la sépulture ecclésiastique; au contraire ils se permettent à eux-mêmes sans aucune difficulté ce mesme trafic quoique toute sorte de trafic soit interdite à tous les ecclésiastiques par les ordonnances du Roy, et par une bulle expresse du Pape. La Bulle et les ordonnances sont notoires, et quoyqu'ils cachent le trafic qu'ils font d'eau-de-vie, M. de la Salle prétend qu'il ne l'est pas moins; qu'outre la notoriété il en a des preuves certaines, et qu'il les a surpris dans ce trafic, et qu'ils luy ont tendu des pièges pour l'y surprendre. . . . Ils ont chassé leur valet Robert à cause qu'il révéla qu'ils en traitaient jour et nuit."— *Ibid.* The writer says that he makes this last statement, not on the authority of La Salle, but on that of a memoir made at the time when the intendant, Talon, with whom he elsewhere says that he was well acquainted, returned to France. A great number of particulars are added respecting the Jesuit trade in furs.

[2] Albanel was prominent among the Jesuit explorers at this time. He is best known by his journey up the Saguenay to Hudson's Bay in 1672.

[3] "Pour vous parler franchement, ils [les Jésuites] songent autant à la conversion du Castor qu'à celle des âmes."— *Lettre de Frontenac à Colbert, 2 Nov., 1672.*

In his despatch of the next year, he says that the Jesuits ought to content themselves with instructing the Indians in their old missions, instead of neglecting them to make new ones in countries where there are "more beaver-skins to gain than souls to save."

[4] These forts were built by them, and were necessary to the security of their missions.

since no more beaver were left in his country, the missionaries were gone also. The Jesuits, pursues the memoir, will have no priests but themselves in their missions, and call them all Jansenists, not excepting the priests of St. Sulpice.

The bishop is next accused of harshness and intolerance, as well as of growing rich by tithes, and even by trade, in which it is affirmed he has a covert interest.[1] It is added that there exists in Quebec, under the auspices of the Jesuits, an association called the Sainte Famille, of which Madame Bourdon[2] is superior. They meet in the cathedral every Thursday, with closed doors, where they relate to each other—as they are bound by a vow to do—all they have learned, whether good or evil, concerning other people, during the week. It is a sort of female inquisition, for the benefit of the Jesuits, the secrets of whose friends, it is said, are kept, while no such discretion is observed with regard to persons not of their party.[3]

---

[1] François Xavier de Laval-Montmorency, first bishop of Quebec, was a prelate of austere character. His memory is cherished in Canada by adherents of the Jesuits and all ultramontane Catholics.

[2] This Madame Bourdon was the widow of Bourdon, the engineer (see The Jesuits in North America, p. 608). If we may credit the letters of Marie de l'Incarnation, she had married him from a religious motive, in order to charge herself with the care of his motherless children; stipulating in advance that he should live with her, not as a husband, but as a brother. As may be imagined, she was regarded as a most devout and saint-like person.

[3] "Il y a dans Québec une congrégation de femmes et de filles qu'ils [*les Jésuites*] appellent la sainte famille, dans laquelle on fait vœu sur les Saints Evangiles de dire tout ce qu'on sait de bien et de mal des personnes qu'on connoist. La Supérieure de cette compagnie s'appelle Madame Bourdon; une M*de.* Daillebout est, je crois, l'assistante et une M*de.* Charron, la Trésorière. La compagnie s'assemble tous les Jeudis dans la Cathédrale, à porte fermée, et là elles se disent les unes aux autres tout ce qu'elles ont appris. C'est une espèce d'Inquisition contre toutes les personnes qui ne sont pas unies avec les Jésuites. Ces personnes sont accusées de tenir secret ce qu'elles apprennent de mal des personnes de leur party et de n'avoir pas la mesme discretion pour les autres."—*Mémoire sur Mr de la Salle.*

The Madame Daillebout mentioned above was a devotee like Madame Bourdon, and, in one respect, her history was similar. See The Jesuits in North America, p. 585.

The association of the Sainte Famille was founded by the Jesuit Chaumonot at Montreal in 1663. Laval, Bishop of Quebec, afterwards encouraged its establishment at that place; and, as Chaumonot himself writes, caused it to be attached to the cathedral. *Vie de Chaumonot*, 83. For its establishment at Montreal, Faillon, *Vie de Mlle Mance*, I. 233.

Here follow a series of statements, which it is needless to repeat, as they do not concern La Salle. They relate to abuse of the confessional, hostility to other priests, hostility to civil authorities, and over-hasty baptisms, in regard to which La Salle is reported to have made a comparison, unfavorable to the Jesuits, between them and the Récollets and Sulpitians.

We now come to the second part of the memoir, entitled "History of Monsieur de la Salle." After stating that he left France at the age of twenty-one or twenty-two, with the purpose of attempting some new discovery, it makes the statements repeated in a former chapter, concerning his discovery of the Ohio, the Illinois, and possibly the Mississippi. It then mentions the building of Fort Frontenac, and says that one object of it was to prevent the Jesuits from becoming undisputed masters of the fur-trade.[1] Three years ago, it pursues, La Salle came to France, and obtained a grant of the fort; and it proceeds to give examples of the means used by the party opposed to him to injure his good name, and bring him within reach of the law. Once, when he was at Quebec, the farmer of the king's revenue, one of the richest men in the place, was extremely urgent in his proffers of hospitality, and at length, though he knew La Salle but slightly, persuaded him to lodge in his house. He had been here but a few days when his host's wife began to enact the part of the wife of Potiphar, and this with so much vivacity, that on one occasion La Salle was forced to take an abrupt leave, in order to avoid an infringement of the laws of hospitality. As he opened the door, he found the husband on the watch, and saw that it was a plot to entrap him.[2]

Another attack, of a different character, though in the same direction, was soon after made. The remittances which La Salle received from the various members and connections of

_____

"Ils [*les Jésuites*] ont tous une si grande envie de savoir tout ce qui se fait dans les familles qu'ils ont des Inspecteurs à gages dans la Ville, qui leur rapportent tout ce qui se fait dans les maisons," etc., etc. — *Lettre de Frontenac au Ministre, 13 Nov., 1673.*

[1] Mention has been made (p. 780, *note*) of the report set on foot by the Jesuit Dablon, to prevent the building of the fort.

[2] This story is told at considerable length, and the advances of the lady particularly described.

his family were sent through the hands of his brother, Abbé Cavelier, from whom his enemies were, therefore, very eager to alienate him. To this end, a report was made to reach the priest's ears, that La Salle had seduced a young woman, with whom he was living, in an open and scandalous manner, at Fort Frontenac. The effect of this device exceeded the wishes of its contrivers; for the priest, aghast at what he had heard, set out for the fort, to administer his fraternal rebuke; but, on arriving, in place of the expected abomination, found his brother, assisted by two Récollet friars, ruling with edifying propriety over a most exemplary household.

Thus far the memoir. From passages in some of La Salle's letters, it may be gathered that Abbé Cavelier gave him at times no little annoyance. In his double character of priest and elder brother, he seems to have constituted himself the counsellor, monitor, and guide of a man, who, though many years his junior, was in all respects incomparably superior to him, as the sequel will show. This must have been almost insufferable to a nature like that of La Salle, who, nevertheless, was forced to arm himself with patience, since his brother held the purse-strings. On one occasion, his forbearance was put to a severe proof, when, wishing to marry a damsel of good connections in the colony, Abbé Cavelier saw fit, for some reason, to interfere, and prevented the alliance.[1]

To resume the memoir. It declares that the Jesuits procured an ordinance from the Supreme Council, prohibiting traders from going into the Indian country, in order that they, the Jesuits, being already established there in their missions, might carry on trade without competition. But La Salle induced a good number of the Iroquois to settle around his fort; thus bringing the trade to his own door, without breaking the ordinance. These Iroquois, he is farther reported to have said, were very fond of him, and aided him in rebuilding the fort with cut stone. The Jesuits told the Iroquois on the south side of the lake, where they were established as missionaries, that La Salle was strengthening his defences, with the view of making war on them. They and the intendant, who was their creature, endeavored to embroil the Iroquois with the French, in order to ruin La Salle; writing to him at the

[1] Letter of La Salle, in possession of M. Margry.

same time that he was the bulwark of the country, and that he ought to be always on his guard. They also tried to persuade Frontenac that it was necessary to raise men and prepare for war. La Salle suspected them, and, seeing that the Iroquois, in consequence of their intrigues, were in an excited state, he induced the governor to come to Fort Frontenac, to pacify them. He accordingly did so; and a council was held, which ended in a complete restoration of confidence on the part of the Iroquois.[1] At this council they accused the two Jesuits, Bruyas and Pierron,[2] of spreading reports that the French were preparing to attack them. La Salle thought that the object of the intrigue was to make the Iroquois jealous of him, and engage Frontenac in expenses which would offend the king. After La Salle and the governor had lost credit by the rupture, the Jesuits would come forward as pacificators, in the full assurance that they could restore quiet, and appear in the attitude of saviors of the colony.

La Salle, pursues his reporter, went on to say that about this time a quantity of hemlock and verdigris was given him in a salad; and that the guilty person was a man in his employ, named Nicolas Perrot, otherwise called Jolycœur, who confessed the crime.[3] The memoir adds that La Salle, who recovered from the effects of the poison, wholly exculpates the Jesuits.

[1] Louis XIV. alludes to this visit, in a letter to Frontenac, dated 28 April, 1677. "I cannot but approve," he writes, "of what you have done, in your voyage to Fort Frontenac, to reconcile the minds of the Five Iroquois Nations, and to clear yourself from the suspicions they had entertained, and from the motives that might induce them to make war." Frontenac's despatches of this year, as well as of the preceding and following years, are missing from the archives.

In a memoir written in November, 1680, La Salle alludes to "le désir que l'on avoit que Monseigneur le Comte de Frontenac fist la guerre aux Iroquois." See Thomassy, *Géologie Pratique de la Louisiane*, 203.

[2] Bruyas was about this time stationed among the Onondagas. Pierron was among the Senecas. He had lately removed to them from the Mohawk country. *Relation des Jésuites, 1673–79*, p. 140 (Shea). Bruyas was also for a long time among the Mohawks.

[3] This puts the character of Perrot in a new light; for it is not likely that any other can be meant than the famous *voyageur*. I have found no mention elsewhere of the synonyme of Jolycœur. Poisoning was the current crime of the day; and persons of the highest rank had repeatedly been charged with it. The following is the passage: —

This attempt, which was not, as we shall see, the only one of the kind made against La Salle, is alluded to by him, in a letter to a friend at Paris, written in Canada, when he was on the point of departure on his great expedition to descend the Mississippi. The following is an extract from it: —

"I hope to give myself the honor of sending you a more particular account of this enterprise when it shall have had the success which I hope for it; but I have need of a strong protection for its support. It traverses the commercial operations of certain persons, who will find it hard to endure it. They intended to make a new Paraguay in these parts, and the route which I close against them gave them facilities for an advantageous correspondence with Mexico. This check will infallibly be a mortification to them; and you know how they deal with whatever opposes them. *Nevertheless, I am bound to render them the justice to say that the poison which was given me was not at all of their instigation.* The person who was conscious of the guilt, believing that I was their enemy, because he saw that our sentiments were opposed, thought to exculpate himself by accusing them; and I confess that at the time I was not sorry to have this indication of their ill-will: but, having afterwards carefully examined the affair, I clearly discovered the falsity of the accusation which this rascal had made against them. I nevertheless pardoned him, in order not to give notoriety to the affair; as the mere suspicion might sully their reputation, to which I should scrupulously avoid doing the slightest injury, unless I thought it necessary to the good of the public, and unless the fact were fully proved. Therefore, Monsieur, if anybody shared the suspicion which I felt, oblige me by undeceiving him."[1]

"Quoiqu'il en soit, Mr de la Salle se sentit quelque temps après empoissonné d'une salade dans laquelle on avoit meslé du ciguë, qui est poison en ce pays là, et du verd de gris. Il en fut malade à l'extrémité, vomissant presque continuellement 40 ou 50 jours après, et il ne réchappa que par la force extrême de sa constitution. Celuy qui luy donna le poison fut un nommé Nicolas Perrot, autrement Jolycœur, l'un de ses domestiques. . . . Il pouvait faire mourir cet homme, qui a confessé son crime, mais il s'est contenté de l'enfermer les fers aux pieds."—*Histoire de Mr de la Salle.*

[1] The following words are underlined in the original: "*Je suis pourtant obligé de leur rendre une justice, que le poison qu'on m'avoit donné n'éstoit point de leur instigation.*"—*Lettre de La Salle au Prince de Conti, 31 Oct., 1678.*

This letter, so honorable to La Salle, explains the statement made in the memoir, that, notwithstanding his grounds of complaint against the Jesuits, he continued to live on terms of courtesy with them, entertained them at his fort, and occasionally corresponded with them. The writer asserts, however, that they intrigued with his men to induce them to desert; employing for this purpose a young man named Deslauriers, whom they sent to him with letters of recommendation. La Salle took him into his service; but he soon after escaped, with several other men, and took refuge in the Jesuit missions.[1] The object of the intrigue is said to have been the reduction of La Salle's garrison to a number less than that which he was bound to maintain, thus exposing him to a forfeiture of his title of possession.

He is also stated to have declared that Louis Joliet was an impostor,[2] and a *donné* of the Jesuits,—that is, a man who worked for them without pay; and, farther, that when he, La Salle, came to court to ask for privileges enabling him to pursue his discoveries, the Jesuits represented in advance to the minister Colbert that his head was turned, and that he was fit for nothing but a mad-house. It was only by the aid of influential friends that he was at length enabled to gain an audience.

Here ends this remarkable memoir, which, criticise it as we may, does not exaggerate the jealousies and enmities that beset the path of the discoverer.

---

[1] In a letter to the king, Frontenac mentions that several men who had been induced to desert from La Salle had gone to Albany, where the English had received them well.— *Lettre de Frontenac au Roy, 6 Nov., 1679.* The Jesuits had a mission in the neighboring tribe of the Mohawks and elsewhere in New York.

[2] This agrees with expressions used by La Salle in a memoir addressed by him to Frontenac in November, 1680. In this, he intimates his belief that Joliet went but little below the mouth of the Illinois, thus doing flagrant injustice to that brave explorer.

Chapter VIII

1677, 1678

THE GRAND ENTERPRISE

La Salle at Fort Frontenac • La Salle at Court • His Memorial •
Approval of the King • Money and Means • Henri de Tonty
• Return to Canada

"I^F," writes a friend of La Salle, "he had preferred gain to
glory, he had only to stay at his fort, where he was making
more than twenty-five thousand livres a year."[1] He loved solitude and he loved power; and at Fort Frontenac he had
both, so far as each consisted with the other. The nearest settlement was a week's journey distant, and he was master of
all around him. He had spared no pains to fulfil the conditions on which his wilderness seigniory had been granted, and
within two years he had demolished the original wooden fort,
replacing it by another much larger, enclosed on the land side
by ramparts and bastions of stone, and on the water side by
palisades. It contained a range of barracks of squared timber,
a guard-house, a lodging for officers, a forge, a well, a mill,
and a bakery. Nine small cannon were mounted on the walls.
Two officers and a surgeon, with ten or twelve soldiers, made
up the garrison; and three or four times that number of masons, laborers, and canoe-men were at one time maintained at
the place.

Along the shore south of the fort was a small village of
French families, to whom La Salle had granted farms, and,
farther on, a village of Iroquois, whom he had persuaded to
settle here. Near these villages were the house and chapel of
two Récollet friars, Luc Buisset and Louis Hennepin. More
than a hundred French acres of land had been cleared of
wood, and planted in part with crops; while cattle, fowls, and
swine had been brought up from Montreal. Four vessels, of
from twenty-five to forty tons, had been built for the lake and
the river; but canoes served best for ordinary uses, and La

[1] *Mémoire pour Monseigneur le Marquis de Seignelay sur les Descouvertes du
Sieur de la Salle, 1682.*

Salle's followers became so skilled in managing them that they were reputed the best canoe-men in America. Feudal lord of the forests around him, commander of a garrison raised and paid by himself, founder of the mission, and patron of the church, he reigned the autocrat of his lonely little empire.[1]

It was not solely or chiefly for commercial gain that La Salle had established Fort Frontenac. He regarded it as a first step towards greater things; and now, at length, his plans were ripe and his time was come. In the autumn of 1677, he left the fort in charge of his lieutenant, descended the St. Lawrence to Quebec, and sailed for France. He had the patronage of Frontenac and the help of strong friends in Paris. It is said, as we have seen already, that his enemies denounced him, in advance, as a madman; but a memorial of his, which his friends laid before the minister Colbert, found a favorable hearing. In it he set forth his plans, or a portion of them. He first recounted briefly the discoveries he had made, and then described the country he had seen south and west of the Great Lakes. "It is nearly all so beautiful and so fertile; so free from forests, and so full of meadows, brooks, and rivers; so abounding in fish, game, and venison, that one can find there in plenty, and with little trouble, all that is needful for the support of flourishing colonies. The soil will produce every thing that is raised in France. Flocks and herds can be left out at pasture all winter; and there are even native wild cattle, which, instead of hair, have a fine wool that may answer for making cloth and hats. Their hides are better than those of France, as appears by the sample which the Sieur de la Salle has brought with him. Hemp and cotton grow here naturally, and may be manufactured with good results; so there can be no doubt that colonies planted here would become very prosperous. They would be increased by a great number of west-

[1] *État de la dépense faite par M* de la Salle, Gouverneur du Fort Frontenac. Récit de Nicolas de la Salle. Reveue faite au Fort de Frontenac, 1677; Mémoire sur le Projet du Sieur de la Salle* (Margry, I. 329). Plan of Fort Frontenac, published by Faillon, from the original sent to France by Denonville in 1685. *Relation des Découvertes du Sieur de la Salle.* When Frontenac was at the fort in September, 1677, he found only four *habitants.* It appears, by the *Relation des Découvertes du Sieur de la Salle,* that, three or four years later, there were thirteen or fourteen families. La Salle spent 34,426 francs on the fort. *Mémoire au Roy, Papiers de Famille.*

ern Indians, who are in the main of a tractable and social disposition; and as they have the use neither of our weapons nor of our goods, and are not in intercourse with other Europeans, they will readily adapt themselves to us, and imitate our way of life, as soon as they taste the advantages of our friendship and of the commodities we bring them; insomuch that these countries will infallibly furnish, within a few years, a great many new subjects to the Church and the King.

"It was the knowledge of these things, joined to the poverty of Canada, its dense forests, its barren soil, its harsh climate, and the snow that covers the ground for half the year, that led the Sieur de la Salle to undertake the planting of colonies in these beautiful countries of the West."

Then he recounts the difficulties of the attempt: the vast distances, the rapids and cataracts that obstruct the way; the cost of men, provisions, and munitions; the danger from the Iroquois, and the rivalry of the English, who covet the western country, and would gladly seize it for themselves. "But this last reason," says the memorial, "only animates the Sieur de la Salle the more, and impels him to anticipate them by the promptness of his action."

He declares that it was for this that he had asked for the grant of Fort Frontenac; and he describes what he had done at that post, in order to make it a secure basis for his enterprise. He says that he has now overcome the chief difficulties in his way, and that he is ready to plant a new colony at the outlet of Lake Erie, of which the English, if not prevented, might easily take possession. Towards the accomplishment of his plans, he asks the confirmation of his title to Fort Frontenac, and the permission to establish at his own cost two other posts, with seigniorial rights over all lands which he may discover and colonize within twenty years, and the government of all the country in question. On his part, he proposes to renounce all share in the trade carried on between the tribes of the Upper Lakes and the people of Canada.

La Salle seems to have had an interview with the minister, in which the proposals of his memorial were somewhat modified. He soon received in reply the following patent from the king:

"Louis, by the grace of God King of France and Navarre,

to our dear and well-beloved Robert Cavelier, Sieur de la Salle, greeting. We have received with favor the very humble petition made us in your name, to permit you to labor at the discovery of the western parts of New France; and we have the more willingly entertained this proposal, since we have nothing more at heart than the exploration of this country, through which, to all appearance, a way may be found to Mexico. . . . For this and other causes thereunto moving us, we permit you by these presents, signed with our hand, to labor at the discovery of the western parts of our aforesaid country of New France; and, for the execution of this enterprise, to build forts at such places as you may think necessary, and enjoy possession thereof under the same clauses and conditions as of Fort Frontenac, conformably to our letters patent of May thirteenth, 1675, which, so far as needful, we confirm by these presents. And it is our will that they be executed according to their form and tenor: on condition, nevertheless, that you finish this enterprise within five years, failing which, these presents shall be void, and of no effect; that you carry on no trade with the savages called Ottawas, or with other tribes who bring their peltries to Montreal; and that you do the whole at your own cost and that of your associates, to whom we have granted the sole right of trade in buffalo-hides. And we direct the Sieur Count Frontenac, our governor and lieutenant-general, and also Duchesneau, intendant of justice, police, and finance, and the officers of the supreme council of the aforesaid country, to see to the execution of these presents; for such is our pleasure.

"Given at St. Germain en Laye, this 12th day of May, 1678, and of our reign the 35th year."

This patent grants both more and less than the memorial had asked. It authorizes La Salle to build and own, not two forts only, but as many as he may see fit, provided that he do so within five years; and it gives him, besides, the monopoly of buffalo-hides, for which at first he had not petitioned. Nothing is said of colonies. To discover the country, secure it by forts, and find, if possible, a way to Mexico, are the only objects set forth; for Louis XIV. always discountenanced settlement in the West, partly as tending to deplete Canada, and partly as removing his subjects too far from his paternal control. It was but the year before that he refused to Louis Joliet the permission to plant a trading station in the Valley of the Mississippi.[1] La Salle, however, still held to his plan of a commercial and industrial colony, and, in connection with it, to another purpose, of which his memorial had made no mention. This was the building of a vessel on some branch of the Mississippi, in order to sail down that river to its mouth, and open a route to commerce through the Gulf of Mexico. It is evident that this design was already formed; for he had no sooner received his patent, than he engaged ship-carpenters, and procured iron, cordage, and anchors, not for one vessel, but for two.

What he now most needed was money; and, having none of his own, he set himself to raising it from others. A notary named Simonnet lent him four thousand livres; an advocate named Raoul, twenty-four thousand; and one Dumont, six thousand. His cousin François Plet, a merchant of Rue St. Martin, lent him about eleven thousand, at the interest of forty per cent; and, when he returned to Canada, Frontenac found means to procure him another loan, of about fourteen thousand, secured by the mortgage of Fort Frontenac. But his chief helpers were his family, who became sharers in his undertaking. "His brothers and relations," says a memorial afterwards addressed by them to the king, "spared nothing to enable him to respond worthily to the royal goodness;" and the document adds that, before his allotted five years were ended, his discoveries had cost them more than five hundred thousand livres (francs).[2] La Salle himself believed, and made others believe, that there was more profit than risk in his schemes.

Lodged rather obscurely in Rue de la Truanderie, and of a nature reserved and shy, he nevertheless found countenance and support from personages no less exalted than Colbert, Seignelay, and the Prince de Conti. Others, too, in stations less conspicuous, warmly espoused his cause, and none more so than the learned Abbé Renaudot, who helped him with tongue and pen, and seems to have been instrumental in in-

[1] *Colbert à Duchesneau, 28 Avril, 1677.*

[2] *Mémoire au Roy, présenté sous la Régence; Obligation du Sieur de la Salle envers le Sieur Plet; Autres Emprunts de Cavelier de la Salle* (Margry, I. 423–432).

troducing to him a man who afterwards proved invaluable. This was Henri de Tonty, an Italian officer, a *protégé* of the Prince de Conti, who sent him to La Salle as a person suited to his purposes. Tonty had but one hand, the other having been blown off by a grenade in the Sicilian wars.[1] His father, who had been governor of Gaeta, but who had come to France in consequence of political disturbances in Naples, had earned no small reputation as a financier, and had invented the form of life insurance still called the Tontine. La Salle learned to know his new lieutenant on the voyage across the Atlantic; and, soon after reaching Canada, he wrote of him to his patron in the following terms: "His honorable character and his amiable disposition were well known to you; but perhaps you would not have thought him capable of doing things for which a strong constitution, an acquaintance with the country, and the use of both hands seemed absolutely necessary. Nevertheless, his energy and address make him equal to any thing; and now, at a season when everybody is in fear of the ice, he is setting out to begin a new fort, two hundred leagues from this place, and to which I have taken the liberty to give the name of Fort Conti. It is situated near that great cataract, more than a hundred and twenty *toises* in height, by which the lakes of higher elevation precipitate themselves into Lake Frontenac [*Ontario*]. From there one goes by water, five hundred leagues, to the place where Fort Dauphin is to be begun; from which it only remains to descend the great river of the Bay of St. Esprit, to reach the Gulf of Mexico."[2]

[1] Tonty, *Mémoire*, in Margry, *Relations et Mémoires inédits*, 5.

[2] *Lettre de La Salle, 31 Oct., 1678.* Fort Conti was to have been built on the site of the present Fort Niagara. The name of Lac de Conti was given by La Salle to Lake Erie. The fort mentioned as Fort Dauphin was built, as we shall see, on the Illinois, though under another name. La Salle, deceived by Spanish maps, thought that the Mississippi discharged itself into the Bay of St. Esprit (Mobile Bay).

Henri de Tonty signed his name in the Gallicized, and not in the original Italian form *Tonti*. He wore a hand of iron or some other metal, which was usually covered with a glove. La Potherie says that he once or twice used it to good purpose when the Indians became disorderly, in breaking the heads of the most contumacious or knocking out their teeth. Not knowing at the time the secret of the unusual efficacy of his blows, they regarded him as a "medicine" of the first order. La Potherie erroneously ascribes the loss of his hand to a sabre-cut received in a *sortie* at Messina.

Besides Tonty, La Salle found in France another ally, La Motte de Lussière, to whom he offered a share in the enterprise, and who joined him at Rochelle, the place of embarkation. Here vexatious delays occurred. Bellinzani, director of trade, who had formerly taken lessons in rascality in the service of Cardinal Mazarin, abused his official position to throw obstacles in the way of La Salle, in order to extort money from him; and he extorted, in fact, a considerable sum, which his victim afterwards reclaimed. It was not till the fourteenth of July that La Salle, with Tonty, La Motte, and thirty men, set sail for Canada, and two months more elapsed before he reached Quebec. Here, to increase his resources and strengthen his position, he seems to have made a league with several Canadian merchants, some of whom had before been his enemies, and were to be so again. Here, too, he found Father Louis Hennepin, who had come down from Fort Frontenac to meet him.[1]

[1] *La Motte de Lussière à* —, *sans date*; *Mémoire de la Salle sur les Extorsions commises par Bellinzani*; *Société formée par La Salle*; *Relation de Henri de Tonty, 1684* (Margry, I. 338, 573; II. 7, 25).

Chapter IX

1678–1679

LA SALLE AT NIAGARA

Father Louis Hennepin • His Past Life; his Character • Embarkation • Niagara Falls • Indian Jealousy • La Motte and the Senecas • A Disaster • La Salle and his Followers

---

HENNEPIN was all eagerness to join in the adventure; and, to his great satisfaction, La Salle gave him a letter from his Provincial, Father Le Fèvre, containing the coveted permission. Whereupon, to prepare himself, he went into retreat at the Récollet convent of Quebec, where he remained for a time in such prayer and meditation as his nature, the reverse of spiritual, would permit. Frontenac, always partial to his Order, then invited him to dine at the château; and, having visited the bishop and asked his blessing, he went down to the Lower Town and embarked. His vessel was a small birch canoe, paddled by two men. With sandalled feet, a coarse gray capote, and peaked hood, the cord of St. Francis about his waist, and a rosary and crucifix hanging at his side, the father set forth on his memorable journey. He carried with him the furniture of a portable altar, which, in time of need, he could strap on his back like a knapsack.

He slowly made his way up the St. Lawrence, stopping here and there, where a clearing and a few log houses marked the feeble beginning of a parish and a seigniory. The settlers, though good Catholics, were too few and too poor to support a priest, and hailed the arrival of the friar with delight. He said Mass, exhorted a little, as was his custom, and on one occasion baptized a child. At length, he reached Montreal, where the enemies of the enterprise enticed away his two canoe-men. He succeeded in finding two others, with whom he continued his voyage, passed the rapids of the upper St. Lawrence, and reached Fort Frontenac at eleven o'clock at night, of the second of November, where his brethren of the mission, Ribourde and Buisset, received him with open arms.[1] La Motte, with most of the men, appeared on the eighth; but La Salle and Tonty did not arrive till more than a month later. Meanwhile, in pursuance of his orders, fifteen men set out in canoes for Lake Michigan and the Illinois, to trade with the Indians and collect provisions, while La Motte embarked in a small vessel for Niagara, accompanied by Hennepin.[2]

This bold, hardy, and adventurous friar, the historian of the expedition, and a conspicuous actor in it, has unwittingly painted his own portrait with tolerable distinctness. "I always," he says, "felt a strong inclination to fly from the world and live according to the rules of a pure and severe virtue; and it was with this view that I entered the Order of St. Francis."[3] He then speaks of his zeal for the saving of souls, but admits that a passion for travel and a burning desire to visit strange lands had no small part in his inclination for the missions.[4] Being in a convent in Artois, his Superior sent him to Calais, at the season of the herring-fishery, to beg alms, after the practice of the Franciscans. Here and at Dunkirk, he made friends of the sailors, and was never tired of their stories. So insatiable, indeed, was his appetite for them, that "often," he says, "I hid myself behind tavern doors while the sailors were telling of their voyages. The tobacco smoke made me very sick at the stomach; but, notwithstanding, I listened attentively to all they said about their adventures at sea and their travels in distant countries. I could have passed whole days and nights in this way without eating."[5]

He presently set out on a roving mission through Holland; and he recounts various mishaps which befell him, "in consequence of my zeal in laboring for the saving of souls." "I was at the bloody fight of Seneff," he pursues, "where so many perished by fire and sword, and where I had abundance of work in comforting and consoling the poor wounded sol-

[1] Hennepin, *Description de la Louisiane* (1683), 19; Ibid., *Voyage Curieux* (1704), 66. Ribourde had lately arrived.

[2] *Lettre de La Motte de la Lussière, sans date*; *Relation de Henri de Tonty écrite de Québec, le 14 Novembre, 1684* (Margry, I. 573). This paper, apparently addressed to Abbé Renaudot, is entirely distinct from Tonty's memoir of 1693, addressed to the minister Ponchartrain.

[3] Hennepin, *Nouvelle Découverte* (1697), 8.

[4] Ibid., *Avant Propos*, 5.

[5] Ibid., *Voyage Curieux* (1704), 12.

diers. After undergoing great fatigues, and running extreme danger in the sieges of towns, in the trenches, and in battles, where I exposed myself freely for the salvation of others, while the soldiers were breathing nothing but blood and carnage, I found myself at last in a way of satisfying my old inclination for travel."[1]

He got leave from his superiors to go to Canada, the most adventurous of all the missions; and accordingly sailed in 1675, in the ship which carried La Salle, who had just obtained the grant of Fort Frontenac. In the course of the voyage, he took it upon him to reprove a party of girls who were amusing themselves and a circle of officers and other passengers by dancing on deck. La Salle, who was among the spectators, was annoyed at Hennepin's interference, and told him that he was behaving like a pedagogue. The friar retorted, by alluding—unconsciously, as he says—to the circumstance that La Salle was once a pedagogue himself, having, according to Hennepin, been for ten or twelve years teacher of a class in a Jesuit school. La Salle, he adds, turned pale with rage, and never forgave him to his dying day, but always maligned and persecuted him.[2]

On arriving in Canada, he was sent up to Fort Frontenac, as a missionary. That wild and remote post was greatly to his liking. He planted a gigantic cross, superintended the building of a chapel for himself and his colleague, Buisset, and instructed the Iroquois colonists of the place. He visited, too, the neighboring Indian settlements, paddling his canoe in summer, when the lake was open, and journeying in winter on snow-shoes, with a blanket slung at his back. His most noteworthy journey was one which he made in the winter,—apparently of 1677,—with a soldier of the fort. They crossed the eastern extremity of Lake Ontario on snow-shoes, and pushed southward through the forests, towards Onondaga; stopping at evening to dig away the snow, which was several feet deep, and collect wood for their fire, which they were forced to replenish repeatedly during the night, to keep them-

---

[1] Hennepin, *Voyage Curieux* (1704), 13.

[2] Ibid., *Avis au Lecteur*. He elsewhere represents himself as on excellent terms with La Salle; with whom, he says, he used to read histories of travels at Fort Frontenac, after which they discussed together their plans of discovery.

selves from freezing. At length, they reached the great Onondaga town, where the Indians were much amazed at their
hardihood. Thence they proceeded eastward to the Oneidas,
and afterwards to the Mohawks, who regaled them with small
frogs, pounded up with a porridge of Indian corn. Here Hennepin found the Jesuit, Bruyas, who permitted him to copy a
dictionary of the Mohawk language[1] which he had compiled;
and here he presently met three Dutchmen, who urged him
to visit the neighboring settlement of Orange, or Albany, an
invitation which he seems to have declined.[2]

They were pleased with him, he says, because he spoke
Dutch. Bidding them farewell, he tied on his snow-shoes
again, and returned with his companion to Fort Frontenac.
Thus he inured himself to the hardships of the woods, and
prepared for the execution of the grand plan of discovery
which he calls his own; "an enterprise," to borrow his own
words, "capable of terrifying anybody but me."[3] When the
later editions of his book appeared, doubts had been expressed of his veracity. "I here protest to you, before God,"
he writes, addressing the reader, "that my narrative is faithful
and sincere, and that you may believe every thing related in
it."[4] And yet, as we shall see, this reverend father was the
most impudent of liars; and the narrative of which he speaks
is a rare monument of brazen mendacity. Hennepin, however,
had seen and dared much: for among his many failings fear
had no part; and, where his vanity or his spite was not involved, he often told the truth. His books have their value,
with all their enormous fabrications.[5]

[1] This was the *Racines Agnières* of Bruyas. It was published by Mr. Shea in
1862. Hennepin seems to have studied it carefully; for, on several occasions,
he makes use of words evidently borrowed from it, putting them into the
mouths of Indians speaking a dialect different from that of the Agniers, or
Mohawks.

[2] Compare Brodhead in *Hist. Mag.*, X. 268.

[3] "Une entreprise capable d'épouvanter tout autre que moi."—Hennepin,
Voyage Curieux, Avant Propos (1704).

[4] "Je vous proteste ici devant Dieu, que ma Relation est fidèle et sincère,"
etc.—Ibid., *Avis au Lecteur*.

[5] The nature of these fabrications will be shown hereafter. They occur, not
in the early editions of Hennepin's narrative, which are comparatively truthful, but in the edition of 1697 and those which followed. La Salle was dead
at the time of their publication.

La Motte and Hennepin, with sixteen men, went on board the little vessel of ten tons, which lay at Fort Frontenac. The friar's two brethren, Buisset and Ribourde, threw their arms about his neck as they bade him farewell; while his Indian proselytes, learning whither he was bound, stood with their hands pressed upon their mouths, in amazement at the perils which awaited their ghostly instructor. La Salle, with the rest of the party, was to follow as soon as he could finish his preparations. It was a boisterous and gusty day, the eighteenth of November. The sails were spread; the shore receded,—the stone walls of the fort, the huge cross that the friar had reared, the wigwams, the settlers' cabins, the group of staring Indians on the strand. The lake was rough; and the men, crowded in so small a craft, grew nervous and uneasy. They hugged the northern shore, to escape the fury of the wind, which blew savagely from the north-east; while the long, gray sweep of naked forests on their right betokened that winter was fast closing in. On the twenty-sixth, they reached the neighborhood of the Indian town of Taiaiagon,[1] not far from Toronto; and ran their vessel, for safety, into the mouth of a river,—probably the Humber,—where the ice closed about her, and they were forced to cut her out with axes. On the fifth of December, they attempted to cross to the mouth of the Niagara; but darkness overtook them, and they spent a comfortless night, tossing on the troubled lake, five or six miles from shore. In the morning, they entered the mouth of the Niagara, and landed on the point at its eastern side, where now stand the historic ramparts of Fort Niagara. Here they found a small village of Senecas, attracted hither by the fisheries, who gazed with curious eyes at the vessel, and listened in wonder as the voyagers sang *Te Deum*, in gratitude for their safe arrival.

Hennepin, with several others, now ascended the river in a canoe to the foot of the mountain ridge of Lewiston, which, stretching on the right hand and on the left, forms the acclivity of a vast plateau, rent with the mighty chasm, along which, from this point to the cataract, seven miles above,

---

[1]This place is laid down on a manuscript map sent to France by the Intendant Duchesneau, and now preserved in the Archives de la Marine, and also on several other contemporary maps.

rush, with the fury of an Alpine torrent, the gathered waters of four inland oceans. To urge the canoe farther was impossible. He landed, with his companions, on the west bank, near the foot of that part of the ridge now called Queenstown Heights, climbed the steep ascent, and pushed through the wintry forest on a tour of exploration. On his left sank the cliffs, the furious river raging below; till at length, in primeval solitudes, unprofaned as yet by the pettiness of man, the imperial cataract burst upon his sight.[1]

The explorers passed three miles beyond it, and encamped for the night on the banks of Chippewa Creek, scraping away the snow, which was a foot deep, in order to kindle a fire. In the morning, they retraced their steps, startling a number of deer and wild turkeys on their way, and rejoined their companions at the mouth of the river.

La Motte now began the building of a fortified house, some two leagues above the mouth of the Niagara.[2] Hot water was used to soften the frozen ground; but frost was not the only obstacle. The Senecas of the neighboring village betrayed a sullen jealousy at a design which, indeed, boded them no good. Niagara was the key to the four great lakes

[1] Hennepin's account of the falls and river of Niagara—especially his second account, on his return from the West—is very minute, and on the whole very accurate. He indulges in gross exaggeration as to the height of the cataract, which, in the edition of 1683, he states at five hundred feet, and raises to six hundred in that of 1697. He also says that there was room for four carriages to pass abreast under the American Fall without being wet. This is, of course, an exaggeration at the best; but it is extremely probable that a great change has taken place since his time. He speaks of a small lateral fall at the west side of the Horse Shoe Fall which does not now exist. Table Rock, now destroyed, is distinctly figured in his picture. He says that he descended the cliffs on the west side to the foot of the cataract, but that no human being can get down on the east side.

The name of Niagara, written *Onguiaahra* by Lalemant in 1641, and *Ongiara* by Sanson, on his map of 1657, is used by Hennepin in its present form. His description of the falls is the earliest known to exist. They are clearly indicated on the map of Champlain, 1632. For early references to them, see The Jesuits in North America, 500. A brief but curious notice of them is given by Gendron, *Quelques Particularitez du Pays des Hurons, 1659.* The indefatigable Dr. O'Callaghan has discovered thirty-nine distinct forms of the name Niagara. *Index to Colonial Documents of New York,* 465. It is of Iroquois origin, and in the Mohawk dialect is pronounced Nyàgarah.

[2] Tonty, *Relation, 1684* (Margry, I. 573).

above; and whoever held possession of it could, in no small measure, control the fur-trade of the interior. Occupied by the French, it would, in time of peace, intercept the trade which the Iroquois carried on between the western Indians and the Dutch and English at Albany, and in time of war threaten them with serious danger. La Motte saw the necessity of conciliating these formidable neighbors, and, if possible, cajoling them to give their consent to the plan. La Salle, indeed, had instructed him to that effect. He resolved on a journey to the great village of the Senecas, and called on Hennepin, who was busied in building a bark chapel for himself, to accompany him. They accordingly set out with several men well armed and equipped, and bearing at their backs presents of very considerable value. The village was beyond the Genesee, south-east of the site of Rochester.[1] After a march of five days, they reached it on the last day of December. They were conducted to the lodge of the great chief, where they were beset by a staring crowd of women and children. Two Jesuits, Raffeix and Julien Garnier, were in the village; and their presence boded no good for the embassy. La Motte, who seems to have had little love for priests of any kind, was greatly annoyed at seeing them; and when the chiefs assembled to hear what he had to say, he insisted that the two fathers should leave the council-house. At this, Hennepin, out of respect for his cloth, thought it befitting that he should retire also. The chiefs, forty-two in number, squatted on the ground, arrayed in ceremonial robes of beaver, wolf, or black squirrel skin. "The senators of Venice," writes Hennepin, "do not look more grave or speak more deliberately than the counsellors of the Iroquois." La Motte's interpreter harangued the attentive conclave, placed gift after gift at their feet,—coats, scarlet cloth, hatchets, knives, and beads,—and used all his eloquence to persuade them that the building of a fort on the banks of the Niagara, and a vessel on Lake Erie, were measures vital to their interest. They gladly took the gifts, but answered the interpreter's speech with evasive generalities; and having been entertained with the burning of an

[1] Near the town of Victor. It is laid down on the map of Galinée, and other unpublished maps. Compare Marshall, *Historical Sketches of the Niagara Frontier*, 14.

Indian prisoner, the discomfited embassy returned, half-famished, to Niagara.

Meanwhile, La Salle and Tonty were on their way from Fort Frontenac, with men and supplies, to join La Motte and his advance party. They were in a small vessel, with a pilot either unskilful or treacherous. On Christmas eve, he was near wrecking them off the Bay of Quinté. On the next day, they crossed to the mouth of the Genesee; and La Salle, after some delay, proceeded to the neighboring town of the Senecas, where he appears to have arrived just after the departure of La Motte and Hennepin. He, too, called them to a council, and tried to soothe the extreme jealousy with which they regarded his proceedings. "I told them my plan," he says, "and gave the best pretexts I could, and I succeeded in my attempt."[1] More fortunate than La Motte, he persuaded them to consent to his carrying arms and ammunition by the Niagara portage, building a vessel above the cataract, and establishing a fortified warehouse at the mouth of the river.

This success was followed by a calamity. La Salle had gone up the Niagara, to find a suitable place for a ship-yard, when he learned that the pilot in charge of the vessel he had left had disobeyed his orders, and ended by wrecking it on the coast. Little was saved except the anchors and cables destined for the new vessel to be built above the cataract. This loss threw him into extreme perplexity, and, as Hennepin says, "would have made anybody but him give up the enterprise."[2] The whole party were now gathered at the palisaded house which La Motte had built, a little below the mountain ridge of Lewiston. They were a motley crew of French, Flemings, and Italians, all mutually jealous. La Salle's enemies had tampered with some of the men; and none of them seemed to have had much heart for the enterprise. The fidelity even of

---

[1] *Lettre de La Salle à un de ses associés* (Margry, II. 32).

[2] *Description de la Louisiane* (1683), 41. It is characteristic of Hennepin that, in the editions of his book published after La Salle's death, he substitutes, for "anybody but him," "anybody but those who had formed so generous a design," meaning to include himself, though he lost nothing by the disaster, and had not formed the design.

On these incidents, compare the two narratives of Tonty, of 1684 and 1693. The book bearing Tonty's name is a compilation full of errors. He disowned its authorship.

La Motte was doubtful. "He served me very ill," says La Salle, "and Messieurs de Tonty and de la Forest know that he did his best to debauch all my men."[1] His health soon failed under the hardships of these winter journeyings, and he returned to Fort Frontenac, half-blinded by an inflammation of the eyes.[2] La Salle, seldom happy in the choice of subordinates, had, perhaps, in all his company but one man whom he could fully trust, and this was Tonty. He and Hennepin were on indifferent terms. Men thrown together in a rugged enterprise like this quickly learn to know each other; and the vain and assuming friar was not likely to commend himself to La Salle's brave and loyal lieutenant. Hennepin says that it was La Salle's policy to govern through the dissensions of his followers; and, from whatever cause, it is certain that those beneath him were rarely in perfect harmony.

[1] *Lettre de La Salle, 22 Août, 1682* (Margry, II. 212).
[2] *Lettre de La Motte, sans date.*

Chapter X

1679

THE LAUNCH OF THE "GRIFFIN"

The Niagara Portage • A Vessel on the Stocks • Suffering and Discontent • La Salle's Winter Journey • The Vessel launched • Fresh Disasters

A MORE important work than that of the warehouse at the mouth of the river was now to be begun. This was the building of a vessel above the cataract. The small craft which had brought La Motte and Hennepin with their advance party had been hauled to the foot of the rapids at Lewiston, and drawn ashore with a capstan, to save her from the drifting ice. Her lading was taken out, and must now be carried beyond the cataract to the calm water above. The distance to the destined point was at least twelve miles, and the steep heights above Lewiston must first be climbed. This heavy task was accomplished on the twenty-second of January. The level of the plateau was reached, and the file of burdened men, some thirty in number, toiled slowly on its way over the snowy plains and through the gloomy forests of spruce and naked oak-trees; while Hennepin plodded through the drifts with his portable altar lashed fast to his back. They came at last to the mouth of a stream which entered the Niagara two leagues above the cataract, and which was undoubtedly that now called Cayuga Creek.[1]

[1] It has been a matter of debate on which side of the Niagara the first vessel on the Upper Lakes was built. A close study of Hennepin, and a careful examination of the localities, have convinced me that the spot was that indicated above. Hennepin repeatedly alludes to a large detached rock, rising out of the water at the foot of the rapids above Lewiston, on the west side of the river. This rock may still be seen, immediately under the western end of the Lewiston suspension-bridge. Persons living in the neighborhood remember that a ferry-boat used to pass between it and the cliffs of the western shore; but it has since been undermined by the current and has inclined in that direction, so that a considerable part of it is submerged, while the gravel and earth thrown down from the cliff during the building of the bridge has filled the intervening channel. Opposite to this rock, and on the east side of the river, says Hennepin, are three mountains, about two leagues below the cataract. *Nouveau Voyage* (1704), 462, 466. To these "three mountains," as

Trees were felled, the place cleared, and the master-carpenter set his ship-builders at work. Meanwhile, two Mohegan hunters, attached to the party, made bark wigwams to lodge the men. Hennepin had his chapel, apparently of the same material, where he placed his altar, and on Sundays and saints' days said mass, preached and exhorted; while some of the men, who knew the Gregorian chant, lent their aid at the service. When the carpenters were ready to lay the keel of the vessel, La Salle asked the friar to drive the first bolt; "but the modesty of my religious profession," he says, "compelled me to decline this honor."

Fortunately, it was the hunting-season of the Iroquois, and most of the Seneca warriors were in the forests south of Lake Erie; yet enough remained to cause serious uneasiness. They loitered sullenly about the place, expressing their displeasure at the proceedings of the French. One of them, pretending

---

well as to the rock, he frequently alludes. They are also spoken of by La Hontan, who clearly indicates their position. They consist in the three successive grades of the acclivity: first, that which rises from the level of the water, forming the steep and lofty river bank; next, an intermediate ascent, crowned by a sort of terrace, where the tired men could find a second resting-place and lay down their burdens, whence a third effort carried them with difficulty to the level top of the plateau. That this was the actual "portage" or carrying place of the travellers is shown by Hennepin (1704), 114, who describes the carrying of anchors and other heavy articles up these heights in August, 1679. La Hontan also passed the Falls by way of the "three mountains" eight years later. La Hontan (1703), 106. It is clear, then, that the portage was on the east side, whence it would be safe to conclude that the vessel was built on the same side. Hennepin says that she was built at the mouth of a stream (*rivière*) entering the Niagara two leagues above the Falls. Excepting one or two small brooks, there is no stream on the west side but Chippewa Creek, which Hennepin had visited and correctly placed at about a league from the cataract. His distances on the Niagara are usually correct. On the east side, there is a stream which perfectly answers the conditions. This is Cayuga Creek, two leagues above the Falls. Immediately in front of it is an island about a mile long, separated from the shore by a narrow and deep arm of the Niagara, into which Cayuga Creek discharges itself. The place is so obviously suited to building and launching a vessel that, in the early part of this century, the government of the United States chose it for the construction of a schooner to carry supplies to the garrisons of the Upper Lakes. The neighboring village now bears the name of La Salle.

In examining this and other localities on the Niagara, I have been greatly aided by my friend, O. H. Marshall, Esq., of Buffalo, who is unrivalled in his knowledge of the history and traditions of the Niagara frontier.

to be drunk, attacked the blacksmith and tried to kill him; but the Frenchman, brandishing a red-hot bar of iron, held him at bay till Hennepin ran to the rescue, when, as he declares, the severity of his rebuke caused the savage to desist.[1] The work of the ship-builders advanced rapidly; and when the Indian visitors beheld the vast ribs of the wooden monster, their jealousy was redoubled. A squaw told the French that they meant to burn the vessel on the stocks. All now stood anxiously on the watch. Cold, hunger, and discontent found imperfect antidotes in Tonty's energy and Hennepin's sermons.

La Salle was absent, and his lieutenant commanded in his place. Hennepin says that Tonty was jealous because he, the friar, kept a journal, and that he was forced to use all manner of just precautions to prevent the Italian from seizing it. The men, being half-starved, in consequence of the loss of their provisions on Lake Ontario, were restless and moody, and their discontent was fomented by one of their number, who had very probably been tampered with by La Salle's enemies.[2] The Senecas refused to supply them with corn, and the frequent exhortations of the Récollet father proved an insufficient substitute. In this extremity, the two Mohegans did excellent service; bringing deer and other game, which relieved the most pressing wants of the party, and went far to restore their cheerfulness.

La Salle, meanwhile, had gone down to the mouth of the river, with a sergeant and a number of men; and here, on the high point of land where Fort Niagara now stands, he marked out the foundations of two blockhouses.[3] Then, leaving his

[1] Hennepin (1704), 97. On a paper drawn up at the instance of the Intendant Duchesneau, the names of the greater number of La Salle's men are preserved. These agree with those given by Hennepin: thus, the master-carpenter, whom he calls Maitre Moyse, appears as Moïse Hillaret, and the blacksmith, whom he calls La Forge, is mentioned as —— (illegible) dit la Forge.

[2] "This bad man," says Hennepin, "would infallibly have debauched our workmen, if I had not reassured them by the exhortations which I made them on fête days and Sundays, after divine service" (1704), 98.

[3] *Lettre de La Salle, 22 Août, 1682* (Margry, II. 229); *Relation de Tonty, 1684* (Ibid., I. 577). He called this new post Fort Conti. It was burned some months after, by the carelessness of the sergeant in command, and was the first of a succession of forts on this historic spot.

men to build them, he set out on foot for Fort Frontenac, where the condition of his affairs demanded his presence, and where he hoped to procure supplies to replace those lost in the wreck of his vessel. It was February, and the distance was some two hundred and fifty miles, through the snow-encumbered forests of the Iroquois, and over the ice of Lake Ontario. Two men attended him, and a dog dragged his baggage on a sledge. For food, they had only a bag of parched corn, which failed them two days before they reached the fort; and they made the rest of the journey fasting.

During his absence, Tonty finished the vessel, which was of about forty-five tons burden.[1] As spring opened, she was ready for launching. The friar pronounced his blessing on her; the assembled company sang *Te Deum*; cannon were fired; and French and Indians, warmed alike by a generous gift of brandy, shouted and yelped in chorus as she glided into the Niagara. Her builders towed her out and anchored her in the stream, safe at last from incendiary hands; and then, swinging their hammocks under her deck, slept in peace, beyond reach of the tomahawk. The Indians gazed on her with amazement. Five small cannon looked out from her portholes; and on her prow was carved a portentous monster, the Griffin, whose name she bore, in honor of the armorial bearings of Frontenac. La Salle had often been heard to say that he would make the griffin fly above the crows, or, in other words, make Frontenac triumph over the Jesuits.

They now took her up the river, and made her fast below the swift current at Black Rock. Here they finished her equipment, and waited for La Salle's return; but the absent commander did not appear. The spring and more than half of the summer had passed before they saw him again. At length, early in August, he arrived at the mouth of the Niagara, bringing three more friars; for, though no friend of the Jesuits, he was zealous for the Faith, and was rarely without a missionary in his journeyings. Like Hennepin, the three friars were all Flemings. One of them, Melithon Watteau, was to remain at Niagara; the others, Zenobe Membré and Gabriel Ribourde, were to preach the Faith among the tribes of the

[1] Hennepin (1683), 46. In the edition of 1697, he says that it was of sixty tons. I prefer to follow the earlier and more trustworthy narrative.

West. Ribourde was a hale and cheerful old man of sixty-four. He went four times up and down the Lewiston heights, while the men were climbing the steep pathway with their loads. It required four of them, well stimulated with brandy, to carry up the principal anchor destined for the "Griffin."

La Salle brought a tale of disaster. His enemies, bent on ruining the enterprise, had given out that he was embarked on a harebrained venture, from which he would never return. His creditors, excited by rumors set afloat to that end, had seized on all his property in the settled parts of Canada, though his seigniory of Fort Frontenac alone would have more than sufficed to pay all his debts. There was no remedy. To defer the enterprise would have been to give his adversaries the triumph that they sought; and he hardened himself against the blow with his usual stoicism.[1]

[1] La Salle's embarrassment at this time was so great that he purposed to send Tonty up the lakes in the "Griffin," while he went back to the colony to look after his affairs; but suspecting that the pilot, who had already wrecked one of his vessels, was in the pay of his enemies, he resolved at last to take charge of the expedition himself, to prevent a second disaster. *Lettre de La Salle, 22 Août, 1682* (Margry, II. 214). Among the creditors who bore hard upon him were Migeon, Charon, Giton, and Peloquin, of Montreal, in whose name his furs at Fort Frontenac had been seized. The intendant also placed under seal all his furs at Quebec, among which is set down the not very precious item of two hundred and eighty-four skins of *enfants du diable*, or skunks.

Chapter XI

1679

LA SALLE ON THE UPPER LAKES

The Voyage of the "Griffin" • Detroit • A Storm • St. Ignace of Michillimackinac • Rivals and Enemies • Lake Michigan • Hardships • A Threatened Fight • Fort Miami • Tonty's Misfortunes • Forebodings

THE "Griffin" had lain moored by the shore, so near that Hennepin could preach on Sundays from the deck to the men encamped along the bank. She was now forced up against the current with tow-ropes and sails, till she reached the calm entrance of Lake Erie. On the seventh of August, La Salle and his followers embarked, sang *Te Deum*, and fired their cannon. A fresh breeze sprang up; and with swelling canvas the "Griffin" ploughed the virgin waves of Lake Erie, where sail was never seen before. For three days they held their course over these unknown waters, and on the fourth turned northward into the Strait of Detroit. Here, on the right hand and on the left, lay verdant prairies, dotted with groves and bordered with lofty forests. They saw walnut, chestnut, and wild plum trees, and oaks festooned with grape-vines; herds of deer, and flocks of swans and wild turkeys. The bulwarks of the "Griffin" were plentifully hung with game which the men killed on shore, and among the rest with a number of bears, much commended by Hennepin for their want of ferocity and the excellence of their flesh. "Those," he says, "who will one day have the happiness to possess this fertile and pleasant strait, will be very much obliged to those who have shown them the way." They crossed Lake St. Clair,[1] and still sailed northward against the current, till now, sparkling in the sun, Lake Huron spread before them like a sea.

For a time they bore on prosperously. Then the wind died to a calm, then freshened to a gale, then rose to a furious tempest; and the vessel tossed wildly among the short, steep,

[1] They named it Sainte Clair, of which the present name is a perversion.

perilous waves of the raging lake. Even La Salle called on his followers to commend themselves to Heaven. All fell to their prayers but the godless pilot, who was loud in complaint against his commander for having brought him, after the honor he had won on the ocean, to drown at last ignominiously in fresh water. The rest clamored to the saints. St. Anthony of Padua was promised a chapel to be built in his honor, if he would but save them from their jeopardy; while in the same breath La Salle and the friars declared him patron of their great enterprise.[1] The saint heard their prayers. The obedient winds were tamed; and the "Griffin" plunged on her way through foaming surges that still grew calmer as she advanced. Now the sun shone forth on woody islands, Bois Blanc and Mackinaw and the distant Manitoulins,—on the forest wastes of Michigan and the vast blue bosom of the angry lake; and now her port was won, and she found her rest behind the point of St. Ignace of Michillimackinac, floating in that tranquil cove where crystal waters cover but cannot hide the pebbly depths beneath. Before her rose the house and chapel of the Jesuits, enclosed with palisades; on the right, the Huron village, with its bark cabins and its fence of tall pickets; on the left, the square compact houses of the French traders; and, not far off, the clustered wigwams of an Ottawa village.[2] Here was a centre of the Jesuit missions, and a centre of the Indian trade; and here, under the shadow of the cross, was much sharp practice in the service of Mammon. Keen traders, with or without a license; and lawless *coureurs de bois*, whom a few years of forest life had weaned from civilization, made St. Ignace their resort; and here there were many of them when the "Griffin" came. They and their employers hated and feared La Salle, who, sustained as he was by the governor, might set at nought the prohibition of the king, debarring him from traffic with these tribes. Yet, while plotting against him, they took pains to allay his distrust by a show of welcome.

The "Griffin" fired her cannon, and the Indians yelped in wonder and amazement. The adventurers landed in state, and

[1] Hennepin (1683), 58.

[2] There is a rude plan of the establishment in La Hontan, though, in several editions, its value is destroyed by the reversal of the plate.

marched, under arms, to the bark chapel of the Ottawa village, where they heard mass. La Salle knelt before the altar, in a mantle of scarlet, bordered with gold. Soldiers, sailors, and artisans knelt around him,—black Jesuits, gray Récollets, swarthy *voyageurs*, and painted savages; a devout but motley concourse.

As they left the chapel, the Ottawa chiefs came to bid them welcome, and the Hurons saluted them with a volley of musketry. They saw the "Griffin" at her anchorage, surrounded by more than a hundred bark canoes, like a Triton among minnows. Yet it was with more wonder than good-will that the Indians of the mission gazed on the floating fort, for so they called the vessel. A deep jealousy of La Salle's designs had been infused into them. His own followers, too, had been tampered with. In the autumn before, it may be remembered, he had sent fifteen men up the lakes, to trade for him, with orders to go thence to the Illinois, and make preparation against his coming. Early in the summer, Tonty had been despatched in a canoe from Niagara, to look after them.[1] It was high time. Most of the men had been seduced from their duty, and had disobeyed their orders, squandered the goods intrusted to them, or used them in trading on their own account. La Salle found four of them at Michillimackinac. These he arrested, and sent Tonty to the Falls of Ste. Marie, where two others were captured, with their plunder. The rest were in the woods, and it was useless to pursue them.

Anxious and troubled as to the condition of his affairs in Canada, La Salle had meant, after seeing his party safe at Michillimackinac, to leave Tonty to conduct it to the Illinois, while he himself returned to the colony. But Tonty was still at Ste. Marie, and he had none to trust but himself. Therefore, he resolved at all risks to remain with his men; "for," he says, "I judged my presence absolutely necessary to retain such of them as were left me, and prevent them from being enticed away during the winter." Moreover, he thought that he had detected an intrigue of his enemies to hound on the Iroquois against the Illinois, in order to defeat his plan by involving him in the war.

---

[1] *Relation de Tonty, 1684; Ibid., 1693.* He was overtaken at the Detroit by the "Griffin."

Early in September, he set sail again, and, passing westward into Lake Michigan,[1] cast anchor near one of the islands at the entrance of Green Bay. Here, for once, he found a friend in the person of a Pottawattamie chief, who had been so wrought upon by the politic kindness of Frontenac that he declared himself ready to die for the children of Onontio.[2] Here, too, he found several of his advance party, who had remained faithful, and collected a large store of furs. It would have been better had they proved false, like the rest. La Salle, who asked counsel of no man, resolved, in spite of his followers, to send back the "Griffin," laden with these furs, and others collected on the way, to satisfy his creditors.[3] It was a rash resolution, for it involved trusting her to the pilot, who had already proved either incompetent or treacherous. She fired a parting shot, and on the eighteenth of September set sail for Niagara, with orders to return to the head of Lake Michigan as soon as she had discharged her cargo. La Salle, with the fourteen men who remained, in four canoes, deeply laden with a forge, tools, merchandise, and arms, put out from the island and resumed his voyage.

The parting was not auspicious. The lake, glassy and calm in the afternoon, was convulsed at night with a sudden storm, when the canoes were midway between the island and the main shore. It was with difficulty that they could keep together, the men shouting to each other through the darkness. Hennepin, who was in the smallest canoe, with a heavy load, and a carpenter for a companion, who was awkward at the paddle, found himself in jeopardy which demanded all his nerve. The voyagers thought themselves happy when they gained at last the shelter of a little sandy cove, where they

---

[1] Then usually known as Lac des Illinois, because it gave access to the country of the tribes so called. Three years before, Allouez gave it the name of Lac St. Joseph, by which it is often designated by the early writers. Membré, Douay, and others, call it Lac Dauphin.

[2] "The Great Mountain," the Iroquois name for the governor of Canada. It was borrowed by other tribes also.

[3] In the license of discovery granted to La Salle, he is expressly prohibited from trading with the Ottawas and others who brought furs to Montreal. This traffic on the lakes was, therefore, illicit. His enemy, the Intendant Duchesneau, afterwards used this against him. *Lettre de Duchesneau au Ministre, 10 Nov., 1680.*

dragged up their canoes, and made their cheerless bivouac in the drenched and dripping forest. Here they spent five days, living on pumpkins and Indian corn, the gift of their Potta-wattamie friends, and on a Canada porcupine, brought in by La Salle's Mohegan hunter. The gale raged meanwhile with relentless fury. They trembled when they thought of the "Griffin." When at length the tempest lulled, they re-em-barked, and steered southward, along the shore of Wisconsin; but again the storm fell upon them, and drove them, for safety, to a bare, rocky, islet. Here they made a fire of drift-wood, crouched around it, drew their blankets over their heads, and in this miserable plight, pelted with sleet and rain, remained for two days.

At length they were afloat again; but their prosperity was brief. On the twenty-eighth, a fierce squall drove them to a point of rocks, covered with bushes, where they consumed the little that remained of their provisions. On the first of October, they paddled about thirty miles, without food, when they came to a village of Pottawattamies, who ran down to the shore to help them to land; but La Salle, fearing that some of his men would steal the merchandise and desert to the Indians, insisted on going three leagues farther, to the great indignation of his followers. The lake, swept by an east-erly gale, was rolling its waves against the beach, like the ocean in a storm. In the attempt to land, La Salle's canoe was nearly swamped. He and his three canoe-men leaped into the water, and, in spite of the surf, which nearly drowned them, dragged their vessel ashore, with all its load. He then went to the rescue of Hennepin, who, with his awkward companion, was in woful need of succor. Father Gabriel, with his sixty-four years, was no match for the surf and the violent under-tow. Hennepin, finding himself safe, waded to his relief, and carried him ashore on his sturdy shoulders; while the old friar, though drenched to the skin, laughed gayly under his cowl, as his brother missionary staggered with him up the beach.[1]

When all were safe ashore, La Salle, who distrusted the In-dians they had passed, took post on a hill, and ordered his

[1] Hennepin (1683), 79.

followers to prepare their guns for action. Nevertheless, as they were starving, an effort must be risked to gain a supply of food; and he sent three men back to the village to purchase it. Well armed, but faint with toil and famine, they made their way through the stormy forest, bearing a pipe of peace, but, on arriving, saw that the scared inhabitants had fled. They found, however, a stock of corn, of which they took a portion, leaving goods in exchange, and then set out on their return.

Meanwhile, about twenty of the warriors, armed with bows and arrows, approached the camp of the French, to reconnoitre. La Salle went to meet them, with some of his men, opened a parley with them, and kept them seated at the foot of the hill till his three messengers returned, when, on seeing the peace-pipe, the warriors set up a cry of joy. In the morning, they brought more corn to the camp, with a supply of fresh venison, not a little cheering to the exhausted Frenchmen, who, in dread of treachery, had stood under arms all night.

This was no journey of pleasure. The lake was ruffled with almost ceaseless storms; clouds big with rain above; a turmoil of gray and gloomy waves beneath. Every night the canoes must be shouldered through the breakers and dragged up the steep banks, which, as they neared the site of Milwaukee, became almost insurmountable. The men paddled all day, with no other food than a handful of Indian corn. They were spent with toil, sick with the haws and wild berries which they ravenously devoured, and dejected at the prospect before them. Father Gabriel's good spirits began to fail. He fainted several times, from famine and fatigue, but was revived by a certain "confection of Hyacinth," administered by Hennepin, who had a small box of this precious specific.

At length, they descried, at a distance, on the stormy shore, two or three eagles among a busy congregation of crows or turkey buzzards. They paddled in all haste to the spot. The feasters took flight; and the starved travellers found the mangled body of a deer, lately killed by the wolves. This good luck proved the inauguration of plenty. As they approached the head of the lake, game grew abundant; and, with the aid of the Mohegan, there was no lack of bear's meat and venison. They found wild grapes, too, in the woods, and gathered them by cutting down the trees to which the vines clung.

While thus employed, they were startled by a sight often so fearful in the waste and the wilderness, the print of a human foot. It was clear that Indians were not far off. A strict watch was kept, not, as it proved, without cause; for that night, while the sentry thought of little but screening himself and his gun from the floods of rain, party of Outagamies crept under the bank, where they lurked for some time before he discovered them. Being challenged, they came forward, professing great friendship, and pretending to have mistaken the French for Iroquois. In the morning, however, there was an outcry from La Salle's servant, who declared that the visitors had stolen his coat from under the inverted canoe where he had placed it; while some of the carpenters also complained of being robbed. La Salle well knew that, if the theft were left unpunished, worse would come of it. First, he posted his men at the woody point of a peninsula, whose sandy neck was interposed between them and the main forest. Then he went forth, pistol in hand, met a young Outagami, seized him, and led him prisoner to his camp. This done, he again set out, and soon found an Outagami chief,—for the wigwams were not far distant,—to whom he told what he had done, adding that, unless the stolen goods were restored, the prisoner should be killed. The Indians were in perplexity, for they had cut the coat to pieces and divided it. In this dilemma, they resolved, being strong in numbers, to rescue their comrade by force. Accordingly, they came down to the edge of the forest, or posted themselves behind fallen trees on the banks, while La Salle's men in their stronghold braced their nerves for the fight. Here three Flemish friars, with their rosaries, and eleven Frenchmen, with their guns, confronted a hundred and twenty screeching Outagamies. Hennepin, who had seen service, and who had always an exhortation at his tongue's end, busied himself to inspire the rest with a courage equal to his own. Neither party, however, had an appetite for the fray. A parley ensued: full compensation was made for the stolen goods, and the aggrieved Frenchmen were farther propitiated with a gift of beaver-skins.

Their late enemies, now become friends, spent the next day in dances, feasts, and speeches. They entreated La Salle not to advance further, since the Illinois, through whose country he must pass, would be sure to kill him; for, added these friendly counsellors, they hated the French because they had been instigating the Iroquois to invade their country. Here was another subject of anxiety. La Salle was confirmed in his belief that his busy and unscrupulous enemies were intriguing for his destruction.

He pushed on, however, circling around the southern shore of Lake Michigan, till he reached the mouth of the St. Joseph, called by him the Miamis. Here Tonty was to have rejoined him, with twenty men, making his way from Michillimackinac, along the eastern shore of the lake; but the rendezvous was a solitude, Tonty was nowhere to be seen. It was the first of November. Winter was at hand, and the streams would soon be frozen. The men clamored to go forward, urging that they should starve if they could not reach the villages of the Illinois before the tribe scattered for the winter hunt. La Salle was inexorable. If they should all desert, he said, he, with his Mohegan hunter and the three friars, would still remain and wait for Tonty. The men grumbled, but obeyed; and, to divert their thoughts, he set them at building a fort of timber on a rising ground at the mouth of the river.

They had spent twenty days at this task, and their work was well advanced, when at length Tonty appeared. He brought with him only half of his men. Provisions had failed; and the rest of his party had been left thirty leagues behind, to sustain themselves by hunting. La Salle told him to return and hasten them forward. He set out with two men. A violent north wind arose. He tried to run his canoe ashore through the breakers. The two men could not manage their vessel, and he with his one hand could not help them. She swamped, rolling over in the surf. Guns, baggage, and provisions were lost; and the three voyagers returned to the Miamis, subsisting on acorns by the way. Happily, the men left behind, excepting two deserters, succeeded, a few days after, in rejoining the party.[1]

[1] Hennepin (1683), 112; *Relation de Tonty, 1693.*

Thus was one heavy load lifted from the heart of La Salle. But where was the "Griffin"? Time enough, and more than enough, had passed for her voyage to Niagara and back again. He scanned the dreary horizon with an anxious eye. No returning sail gladdened the watery solitude, and a dark foreboding gathered on his heart. Yet farther delay was impossible. He sent back two men to Michillimackinac to meet her, if she still existed, and pilot her to his new fort of the Miamis, and then prepared to ascend the river, whose weedy edges were already glassed with thin flakes of ice.[1]

[1] The official account of this journey is given at length in the *Relation des Découvertes et des Voyages du Sieur de la Salle, 1679–80–81.* This valuable document, compiled from letters and diaries of La Salle, early in the year 1682, was known to Hennepin, who evidently had a copy of it before him, when he wrote his book, in which he incorporated many passages from it.

Chapter XII

1679, 1680

LA SALLE ON THE ILLINOIS

*The St. Joseph • Adventure of La Salle • The Prairies • Famine
• The Great Town of the Illinois • Indians • Intrigues • Difficulties • Policy of La Salle • Desertion. • Another Attempt
to poison him*

O N the third of December, the party re-embarked, thirty-
three in all, in eight canoes,[1] and ascended the chill current of the St. Joseph, bordered with dreary meadows and
bare gray forests. When they approached the site of the present village of South Bend, they looked anxiously along the
shore on their right, to find the portage or path leading to
the head-quarters of the Illinois. The Mohegan was absent,
hunting; and, unaided by his practised eye, they passed the
path without seeing it. La Salle landed to search the woods.
Hours passed, and he did not return. Hennepin and Tonty
grew uneasy, disembarked, bivouacked, ordered guns to be
fired, and sent out men to scour the country. Night came, but
not their lost leader. Muffled in their blankets and powdered
by the thick-falling snowflakes, they sat ruefully speculating as
to what had befallen him; nor was it till four o'clock of the
next afternoon that they saw him approaching along the margin of the river. His face and hands were besmirched with
charcoal; and he was farther decorated with two opossums
which hung from his belt, and which he had killed with a
stick as they were swinging head downwards from the bough
of a tree, after the fashion of that singular beast. He had
missed his way in the forest, and had been forced to make a
wide circuit around the edge of a swamp; while the snow, of
which the air was full, added to his perplexities. Thus he
pushed on through the rest of the day and the greater part
of the night, till, about two o'clock in the morning, he
reached the river again, and fired his gun as a signal to his
party. Hearing no answering shot, he pursued his way

[1] *Lettre de Duchesneau à ——, 10 Nov., 1680.*

along the bank, when he presently saw the gleam of a fire among the dense thickets close at hand. Not doubting that he had found the bivouac of his party, he hastened to the spot. To his surprise, no human being was to be seen. Under a tree beside the fire was a heap of dry grass impressed with the form of a man who must have fled but a moment before, for his couch was still warm. It was no doubt an Indian, ambushed on the bank, watching to kill some passing enemy. La Salle called out in several Indian languages; but there was dead silence all around. He then, with admirable coolness, took possession of the quarters he had found, shouting to their invisible proprietor that he was about to sleep in his bed; piled a barricade of bushes around the spot, rekindled the dying fire, warmed his benumbed hands, stretched himself on the dried grass, and slept undisturbed till morning.

The Mohegan had rejoined the party before La Salle's return, and with his aid the portage was soon found. Here the party encamped. La Salle, who was excessively fatigued, occupied, together with Hennepin, a wigwam covered in the Indian manner with mats of reeds. The cold forced them to kindle a fire, which, before daybreak, set the mats in a blaze; and the two sleepers narrowly escaped being burned along with their hut.

In the morning, the party shouldered their canoes and baggage, and began their march for the sources of the river Illinois, some five miles distant. Around them stretched a desolate plain, half-covered with snow, and strewn with the skulls and bones of buffalo; while, on its farthest verge, they could see the lodges of the Miami Indians, who had made this place their abode. As they filed on their way, a man named Duplessis, bearing a grudge against La Salle, who walked just before him, raised his gun to shoot him through the back, but was prevented by one of his comrades. They soon reached a spot where the oozy, saturated soil quaked beneath their tread. All around were clumps of alder-bushes, tufts of rank grass, and pools of glistening water. In the midst, a dark and lazy current, which a tall man might bestride, crept twisting like a snake among the weeds and rushes. Here were the sources of the Kankakee, one of the heads of the Illinois.[1] They set their canoes on this thread of water, embarked their baggage and themselves, and pushed down the sluggish streamlet, looking, at a little distance, like men who sailed on land. Fed by an unceasing tribute of the spongy soil, it quickly widened to a river; and they floated on their way through a voiceless, lifeless solitude of dreary oak barrens, or boundless marshes overgrown with reeds. At night, they built their fire on ground made firm by frost, and bivouacked among the rushes. A few days brought them to a more favored region. On the right hand and on the left stretched the boundless prairie, dotted with leafless groves and bordered by gray wintry forests, scorched by the fires kindled in the dried grass by Indian hunters, and strewn with the carcasses and the bleached skulls of innumerable buffalo. The plains were scored with their pathways, and the muddy edges of the river were full of their hoofprints. Yet not one was to be seen. At night, the horizon glowed with distant fires; and by day the savage hunters could be descried at times roaming on the verge of the prairie. The men, discontented and half-starved, would have deserted to them had they dared. La Salle's Mohegan could kill no game except two lean deer, with a few wild geese and swans. At length, in their straits, they made a happy discovery. It was a buffalo bull, fast mired

---

[1] The Kankakee was called at this time the Theakiki, or Haukiki (Marest); a name which, as Charlevoix says, was afterwards corrupted by the French to Kiakiki, whence, probably, its present form. In La Salle's time, the name Theakiki was given to the river Illinois, through all its course. It was also called the Rivière Seignelay, the Rivière des Macopins, and the Rivière Divine, or Rivière de la Divine. The latter name, when Charlevoix visited the country in 1721, was confined to the northern branch. He gives an interesting and somewhat graphic account of the portage and the sources of the Kankakee, in his letter, dated *De la Source du Theakiki, ce dix-sept Septembre, 1721.*

Why the Illinois should ever have been called the Divine, it is not easy to see. The Memoirs of St. Simon suggest an explanation. Madame de Frontenac and her friend, Mademoiselle d'Outrelaise, he tells us, lived together in apartments at the Arsenal, where they held their *salon* and exercised a great power in society. They were called at court *les Divines*. St. Simon, V. 335 (Cheruel). In compliment to Frontenac, the river may have been named after his wife or her friend. The suggestion is due to M. Margry. I have seen a map by Raudin, Frontenac's engineer, on which the river is called "Rivière de la Divine ou l'Outrelaise."

in a slough. They killed him, lashed a cable about him, and then twelve men dragged out the shaggy monster, whose ponderous carcass demanded their utmost efforts.

The scene changed again as they descended. On either hand ran ranges of woody hills, following the course of the river; and when they mounted to their tops, they saw beyond them a rolling sea of dull green prairie, a boundless pasture of the buffalo and the deer, in our own day strangely transformed,—yellow in harvest time with ripened wheat, and dotted with the roofs of a hardy and valiant yeomanry.[1]

They passed the site of the future town of Ottawa, and saw on their right the high plateau of Buffalo Rock, long a favorite dwelling-place of Indians. A league below, the river glided among islands bordered with stately woods. Close on their left towered a lofty cliff,[2] crested with trees that overhung the rippling current; while before them spread the valley of the Illinois, in broad low meadows, bordered on the right by the graceful hills at whose foot now lies the village of Utica. A population far more numerous then tenanted the valley. Along the right bank of the river were clustered the lodges of a great Indian town. Hennepin counted four hundred and sixty of them.[3] In shape, they were somewhat like the arched

[1] The change is very recent. Within the memory of men not yet old, wolves and deer, besides wild swans, wild turkeys, cranes, and pelicans, abounded in this region. In 1840, a friend of mine shot a deer from the window of a farmhouse, near the present town of La Salle. Running wolves on horseback was his favorite amusement in this part of the country. The buffalo long ago disappeared; but the early settlers found frequent remains of them. Mr. James Clark, of Utica, Ill., told me that he once found a large quantity of their bones and skulls in one place, as if a herd had perished in the snow-drifts.

[2] "Starved Rock." It will hold, hereafter, a conspicuous place in the narrative.

[3] *La Louisiane*, 137. Allouez (*Relation, 1673–79*) found three hundred and fifty-one lodges. This was in 1677. The population of this town, which embraced five or six distinct tribes of the Illinois, was continually changing. In 1675, Marquette addressed here an auditory composed of five hundred chiefs and old men, and fifteen hundred young men, besides women and children. He estimates the number of fires at five or six hundred. *Voyages du Père Marquette*, 98 (Lenox). Membré, who was here in 1680, says that it then contained seven or eight thousand souls. Membré in Le Clerc, *Premier Établissement de la Foy*, II. 173. On the remarkable manuscript map of Franquelin, 1684, it is set down at twelve hundred warriors, or about six thousand souls. This was after the destructive inroad of the Iroquois. Some years later, Rasle

top of a baggage wagon. They were built of a framework of poles, covered with mats of rushes, closely interwoven; and each contained three or four fires, of which the greater part served for two families.

Here, then, was the town; but where were the inhabitants? All was silent as the desert. The lodges were empty, the fires dead, and the ashes cold. La Salle had expected this; for he knew that in the autumn the Illinois always left their towns for their winter hunting, and that the time of their return had not yet come. Yet he was not the less embarrassed, for he would fain have bought a supply of food to relieve his famished followers. Some of them, searching the deserted town, presently found the *caches*, or covered pits, in which the Indians hid their stock of corn. This was precious beyond measure in their eyes, and to touch it would be a deep offence. La Salle shrank from provoking their anger, which might prove the ruin of his plans; but his necessity overcame his prudence, and he took thirty *minots* of corn, hoping to appease the owners by presents. Thus provided, the party embarked again, and resumed their downward voyage.

On New Year's Day, 1680, they landed and heard Mass.

---

reported upwards of twenty-four hundred families. *Lettre à son Frère*, in *Lettres Édifiantes*.

At times, nearly the whole Illinois population was gathered here. At other times, the several tribes that composed it separated, some dwelling apart from the rest; so that at one period the Illinois formed eleven villages, while at others they were gathered into two, of which this was much the larger. The meadows around it were extensively cultivated, yielding large crops, chiefly of Indian corn. The lodges were built along the river bank, for a distance of a mile, and sometimes far more. In their shape, though not in their material, they resembled those of the Hurons. There were no palisades or embankments.

This neighborhood abounds in Indian relics. The village graveyard appears to have been on a rising ground, near the river, immediately in front of the town of Utica. This is the only part of the river bottom, from this point to the Mississippi, not liable to inundation in the spring floods. It now forms part of a farm occupied by a tenant of Mr. James Clark. Both Mr. Clark and his tenant informed me that every year great quantities of human bones and teeth were turned up here by the plough. Many implements of stone are also found, together with beads and other ornaments of Indian and European fabric.

Then Hennepin wished a happy new year to La Salle first, and afterwards to all the men, making them a speech, which, as he tells us, was "most touching."[1] He and his two brethren next embraced the whole company in turn, "in a manner," writes the father, "most tender and affectionate," exhorting them, at the same time, to patience, faith, and constancy. Four days after these solemnities, they reached the long expansion of the river, then called Pimitoui, and now known as Peoria Lake, and leisurely made their way downward to the site of the city of Peoria.[2] Here, as evening drew near, they saw a faint spire of smoke curling above the gray forest, betokening that Indians were at hand. La Salle, as we have seen, had been warned that these tribes had been taught to regard him as their enemy; and when, in the morning, he resumed his course, he was prepared alike for peace or war.

The shores now approached each other; and the Illinois was once more a river, bordered on either hand with overhanging woods.[3]

At nine o'clock, doubling a point, he saw about eighty Illinois wigwams, on both sides of the river. He instantly ordered the eight canoes to be ranged in line, abreast, across the stream; Tonty on the right, and he himself on the left. The men laid down their paddles and seized their weapons; while, in this warlike guise, the current bore them swiftly into the midst of the surprised and astounded savages. The camps were in a panic. Warriors whooped and howled; squaws and children screeched in chorus. Some snatched their bows and war-clubs; some ran in terror; and, in the midst of the hubbub, La Salle leaped ashore, followed by his men. None knew better how to deal with Indians; and he made no sign of friendship, knowing that it might be construed as a token of fear. His little knot of Frenchmen stood, gun in hand, pas-

---

[1] "Les paroles les plus touchantes."—*Hennepin* (1683), 139. The later editions add the modest qualification, "que je pus."

[2] Peoria was the name of one of the tribes of the Illinois. Hennepin's dates here do not exactly agree with those of La Salle (*Lettre du 29 Sept., 1680*), who says that they were at the Illinois village on the first of January, and at Peoria Lake on the fifth.

[3] At least, it is so now at this place. Perhaps, in La Salle's time, it was not wholly so; for there is evidence, in various parts of the West, that the forest has made considerable encroachments on the open country.

sive, yet prepared for battle. The Indians, on their part, rallying a little from their fright, made all haste to proffer peace. Two of their chiefs came forward, holding out the calumet; while another began a loud harangue, to check the young warriors who were aiming their arrows from the farther bank. La Salle, responding to these friendly overtures, displayed another calumet; while Hennepin caught several scared children and soothed them with winning blandishments.[1] The uproar was quelled; and the strangers were presently seated in the midst of the camp, beset by a throng of wild and swarthy figures.

Food was placed before them; and, as the Illinois code of courtesy enjoined, their entertainers conveyed the morsels with their own hands to the lips of these unenviable victims of their hospitality, while others rubbed their feet with bear's grease. La Salle, on his part, made them a gift of tobacco and hatchets; and, when he had escaped from their caresses, rose and harangued them. He told them that he had been forced to take corn from their granaries, lest his men should die of hunger; but he prayed them not to be offended, promising full restitution or ample payment. He had come, he said, to protect them against their enemies, and teach them to pray to the true God. As for the Iroquois, they were subjects of the Great King, and therefore brethren of the French; yet, nevertheless, should they begin a war and invade the country of the Illinois, he would stand by them, give them guns, and fight in their defence, if they would permit him to build a fort among them for the security of his men. It was, also, he added, his purpose to build a great wooden canoe, in which to descend the Mississippi to the sea, and then return, bringing them the goods of which they stood in need; but if they would not consent to his plans, and sell provisions to his men, he would pass on to the Osages, who would then reap all the benefits of intercourse with the French, while they were left destitute, at the mercy of the Iroquois.[2]

This threat had its effect, for it touched their deep-rooted jealousy of the Osages. They were lavish of promises, and feasts and dances consumed the day. Yet La Salle soon

[1] Hennepin (1683), 142.
[2] Ibid., 144–149. The later editions omit a part of the above.

learned that the intrigues of his enemies were still pursuing him. That evening, unknown to him, a stranger appeared in the Illinois camp. He was a Mascoutin chief, named Monso, attended by five or six Miamis, and bringing a gift of knives, hatchets, and kettles to the Illinois.[1] The chiefs assembled in a secret nocturnal session, where, smoking their pipes, they listened with open ears to the harangue of the envoys. Monso told them that he had come in behalf of certain Frenchmen, whom he named, to warn his hearers against the designs of La Salle, whom he denounced as a partisan and spy of the Iroquois, affirming that he was now on his way to stir up the tribes beyond the Mississippi to join in a war against the Illinois, who, thus assailed from the east and from the west, would be utterly destroyed. There was no hope for them, he added, but in checking the farther progress of La Salle, or, at least, retarding it, thus causing his men to desert him. Having thrown his firebrand, Monso and his party left the camp in haste, dreading to be confronted with the object of their aspersions.[2]

In the morning, La Salle saw a change in the behavior of his hosts. They looked on him askance, cold, sullen, and suspicious. There was one Omawha, a chief, whose favor he had won the day before by the politic gift of two hatchets and three knives, and who now came to him in secret to tell him what had taken place at the nocturnal council. La Salle at once saw in it a device of his enemies; and this belief was confirmed, when, in the afternoon, Nicanopé, brother of the head chief, sent to invite the Frenchmen to a feast. They repaired to his lodge; but before dinner was served,—that is to say, while the guests, white and red, were seated on mats,

---

[1] "Un sauvage, nommé Monso, qui veut dire Chevreuil."— *La Salle*. Probably Monso is a misprint for Mouso, as *mousoa* is Illinois for *chevreuil*, or deer.

[2] Hennepin (1683), 151, (1704), 205; Le Clerc, II. 157; *Mémoire du Voyage de M. de la Salle*. This is a paper appended to Frontenac's Letter to the Minister, 9 Nov., 1680. Hennepin prints a translation of it in the English edition of his later work. It charges the Jesuit Allouez with being at the bottom of the intrigue. Compare *Lettre de La Salle, 29 Sept., 1680* (Margry, II. 41), and *Mémoire de La Salle*, in Thomassy, *Géologie Pratique de la Louisiane*, 203.

The account of the affair of Monso, in the spurious work bearing Tonty's name, is mere romance.

each with his hunting-knife in his hand, and the wooden bowl before him, which was to receive his share of the bear's or buffalo's meat, or the corn boiled in fat, with which he was to be regaled; while such was the posture of the company, their host arose and began a long speech. He told the Frenchmen that he had invited them to his lodge less to refresh their bodies with good cheer than to cure their minds of the dangerous purpose which possessed them, of descending the Mississippi. Its shores, he said, were beset by savage tribes, against whose numbers and ferocity their valor would avail nothing: its waters were infested by serpents, alligators, and unnatural monsters; while the river itself, after raging among rocks and whirlpools, plunged headlong at last into a fathomless gulf, which would swallow them and their vessel for ever.

La Salle's men were, for the most part, raw hands, knowing nothing of the wilderness, and easily alarmed at its dangers; but there were two among them, old *coureurs de bois*, who unfortunately knew too much; for they understood the Indian orator, and explained his speech to the rest. As La Salle looked around on the circle of his followers, he read an augury of fresh trouble in their disturbed and rueful visages. He waited patiently, however, till the speaker had ended, and then answered him, through his interpreter, with great composure. First, he thanked him for the friendly warning which his affection had impelled him to utter; but, he continued, the greater the danger, the greater the honor; and, even if the danger were real, Frenchmen would never flinch from it. But were not the Illinois jealous? Had they not been deluded by lies? "We were not asleep, my brother, when Monso came to tell you, under cover of night, that we were spies of the Iroquois. The presents he gave you, that you might believe his falsehoods, are at this moment buried in the earth under this lodge. If he told the truth, why did he skulk away in the dark? Why did he not show himself by day? Do you not see that when we first came among you, and your camp was all in confusion, we could have killed you without needing help from the Iroquois? And now, while I am speaking, could we not put your old men to death, while your young warriors are all gone away to hunt? If we meant to make war on you,

we should need no help from the Iroquois, who have so often
felt the force of our arms. Look at what we have brought you.
It is not weapons to destroy you, but merchandise and tools,
for your good. If you still harbor evil thoughts of us, be frank
as we are, and speak them boldly. Go after this impostor,
Monso, and bring him back, that we may answer him, face to
face; for he never saw either us or the Iroquois, and what can
he know of the plots that he pretends to reveal?"[1] Nicanopé
had nothing to reply, and, grunting assent in the depths of
his throat, made a sign that the feast should proceed.

The French were lodged in huts, near the Indian camp;
and, fearing treachery, La Salle placed a guard at night. On
the morning after the feast, he came out into the frosty air,
and looked about him for the sentinels. Not one of them was
to be seen. Vexed and alarmed, he entered hut after hut, and
roused his drowsy followers. Six of the number, including
two of the best carpenters, were nowhere to be found. Discontented and mutinous from the first, and now terrified by
the fictions of Nicanopé, they had deserted, preferring the
hardships of the midwinter forest to the mysterious terrors of
the Mississippi. La Salle mustered the rest before him, and
inveighed sternly against the cowardice and baseness of those
who had thus abandoned him, regardless of his many favors.
If any here, he added, are afraid, let them but wait till the
spring, and they shall have free leave to return to Canada,
safely and without dishonor.[2]

This desertion cut him to the heart. It showed him that he
was leaning on a broken reed; and he felt that, on an enterprise full of doubt and peril, there were scarcely four men in
his party whom he could trust. Nor was desertion the worst
he had to fear; for here, as at Fort Frontenac, an attempt was
made to kill him. Tonty tells us that poison was placed in the
pot in which their food was cooked, and that La Salle was
saved by an antidote which some of his friends had given him
before he left France. This, it will be remembered, was an
epoch of poisoners. It was in the following month that the

---

[1] The above is a paraphrase, with some condensation, from Hennepin,
whose account is substantially identical with that of La Salle.

[2] Hennepin (1683), 162. *Déclaration faite par Moyse Hillaret, charpentier de
barque, cy devant au service du Sr de la Salle.*

notorious La Voisin was burned alive, at Paris, for practices to which many of the highest nobility were charged with being privy, not excepting some in whose veins ran the blood of the gorgeous spendthrift who ruled the destinies of France.[1]

In these early French enterprises in the West, it was to the last degree difficult to hold men to their duty. Once fairly in the wilderness, completely freed from the sharp restraints of authority in which they had passed their lives, a spirit of lawlessness broke out among them with a violence proportioned to the pressure which had hitherto controlled it. Discipline had no resources and no guarantee; while those outlaws of the forest, the *coureurs de bois*, were always before their eyes, a standing example of unbridled license. La Salle, eminently skilful in his dealings with Indians, was rarely so happy with his own countrymen; and yet the desertions from which he was continually suffering were due far more to the inevitable difficulty of his position than to any want of conduct on his part.

[1] The equally noted Brinvilliers was burned four years before. An account of both will be found in the Letters of Madame de Sévigné. The memoirs of the time abound in evidence of the frightful prevalence of these practices, and the commotion which they excited in all ranks of society.

Chapter XIII

1680

FORT CRÈVECŒUR

Building of the Fort • Loss of the "Griffin" • A Bold Resolution • Another Vessel • Hennepin sent to the Mississippi • Departure of La Salle

LA SALLE now resolved to leave the Indian camp, and fortify himself for the winter in a strong position, where his men would be less exposed to dangerous influence, and where he could hold his ground against an outbreak of the Illinois or an Iroquois invasion. At the middle of January, a thaw broke up the ice which had closed the river; and he set out in a canoe, with Hennepin, to visit the site he had chosen for his projected fort. It was half a league below the camp, on a low hill or knoll, two hundred yards from the southern bank. On either side was a deep ravine, and in front a marshy tract, overflowed at high water. Thither, then, the party was removed. They dug a ditch behind the hill, connecting the two ravines, and thus completely isolating it. The hill was nearly square in form. An embankment of earth was thrown up on every side: its declivities were sloped steeply down to the bottom of the ravines and the ditch, and further guarded by *chevaux-de-frise*; while a palisade, twenty-five feet high, was planted around the whole. The lodgings of the men, built of musket-proof timber, were at two of the angles; the house of the friars at the third; the forge and magazine at the fourth; and the tents of La Salle and Tonty in the area within.

Hennepin laments the failure of wine, which prevented him from saying Mass; but every morning and evening he summoned the men to his cabin, to listen to prayers and preaching, and on Sundays and fête days they chanted vespers. Father Zenobe usually spent the day in the Indian camp, striving, with very indifferent success, to win them to the Faith, and to overcome the disgust with which their manners and habits inspired him.

Such was the first civilized occupation of the region which

now forms the State of Illinois. La Salle christened his new fort Fort Crèvecœur. The name tells of disaster and suffering, but does no justice to the iron-hearted constancy of the sufferer. Up to this time, he had clung to the hope that his vessel, the "Griffin," might still be safe. Her safety was vital to his enterprise. She had on board articles of the last necessity to him, including the rigging and anchors of another vessel, which he was to build at Fort Crèvecœur, in order to descend the Mississippi, and sail thence to the West Indies. But now his last hope had well-nigh vanished. Past all reasonable doubt, the "Griffin" was lost; and in her loss he and all his plans seemed ruined alike.

Nothing, indeed, was ever heard of her. Indians, fur-traders, and even Jesuits, have been charged with contriving her destruction. Some say that the Ottawas boarded and burned her, after murdering those on board; others accuse the Pottawattamies; others affirm that her own crew scuttled and sunk her; others, again, that she foundered in a storm.[1] As for La Salle, the belief grew in him to a settled conviction that she had been treacherously sunk by the pilot and the sailors to whom he had intrusted her; and he thought he had found evidence that the authors of the crime, laden with the merchandise they had taken from her, had reached the Mississippi and ascended it, hoping to join Du Lhut, a famous chief of *coureurs de bois*, and enrich themselves by traffic with the northern tribes.[2]

But whether her lading was swallowed in the depths of the lake, or lost in the clutches of traitors, the evil was alike past

[1] Charlevoix, I. 459; La Potherie, II. 140; La Hontan, *Memoir on the Fur-Trade of Canada*. I am indebted for a copy of this paper to Winthrop Sargent, Esq., who purchased the original at the sale of the library of the poet Southey. Like Hennepin, La Hontan went over to the English; and this memoir is written in their interest.

[2] *Lettre de La Salle à La Barre, Chicagou, 4 Juin, 1683*. This is a long letter, addressed to the successor of Frontenac, in the government of Canada. La Salle says that a young Indian belonging to him told him that three years before he saw a white man, answering the description of the pilot, a prisoner among a tribe beyond the Mississippi. He had been captured with four others on that river, while making his way with canoes, laden with goods, towards the Sioux. His companions had been killed. Other circumstances, which La Salle details at great length, convinced him that the white prisoner was no other than the pilot of the "Griffin." The evidence, however, is not conclusive.

remedy. She was gone, it mattered little how. The main-stay of the enterprise was broken; yet its inflexible chief lost neither heart nor hope. One path, beset with hardships and terrors, still lay open to him. He might return on foot to Fort Frontenac, and bring thence the needful succors.

La Salle felt deeply the dangers of such a step. His men were uneasy, discontented, and terrified by the stories with which the jealous Illinois still constantly filled their ears, of the whirlpools and the monsters of the Mississippi. He dreaded lest, in his absence, they should follow the example of their comrades, and desert. In the midst of his anxieties, a lucky accident gave him the means of disabusing them. He was hunting, one day, near the fort, when he met a young Illinois, on his way home, half-starved, from a distant war excursion. He had been absent so long that he knew nothing of what had passed between his countrymen and the French. La Salle gave him a turkey he had shot, invited him to the fort, fed him, and made him presents. Having thus warmed his heart, he questioned him, with apparent carelessness, as to the countries he had visited, and especially as to the Mississippi, on which the young warrior, seeing no reason to disguise the truth, gave him all the information he required. La Salle now made him the present of a hatchet, to engage him to say nothing of what had passed, and, leaving him in excellent humor, repaired, with some of his followers, to the Illinois camp. Here he found the chiefs seated at a feast of bear's meat, and he took his place among them on a mat of rushes. After a pause, he charged them with having deceived him in regard to the Mississippi; adding that he knew the river perfectly, having been instructed concerning it by the Master of Life. He then described it to them with so much accuracy that his astonished hearers, conceiving that he owed his knowledge to "medicine," or sorcery, clapped their hands to their mouths, in sign of wonder, and confessed that all they had said was but an artifice, inspired by their earnest desire that he should remain among them.[1] On this, La Salle's men took

[1] *Relation des Découvertes et des Voyages du Sr de la Salle, Seigneur et Gouverneur du Fort de Frontenac, au delà des grands Lacs de la Nouvelle France, faits par ordre de Monseigneur Colbert, 1679, 80 et 81.* Hennepin gives a story which is not essentially different, except that he makes himself a conspicuous actor in it.

heart again; and their courage rose still more when, soon after, a band of Chickasa, Arkansas, and Osage warriors, from the Mississippi, came to the camp on a friendly visit, and assured the French, not only that the river was navigable to the sea, but that the tribes along its banks would give them a warm welcome.

La Salle had now good reason to hope that his followers would neither mutiny nor desert in his absence. One chief purpose of his intended journey was to procure the anchors, cables, and rigging of the vessel which he meant to build at Fort Crèvecœur, and he resolved to see her on the stocks before he set out. This was no easy matter, for the pit-sawyers had deserted. "Seeing," he writes, "that I should lose a year if I waited to get others from Montreal, I said one day, before my people, that I was so vexed to find that the absence of two sawyers would defeat my plans, and make all my trouble useless, that I was resolved to try to saw the planks myself, if I could find a single man who would help me with a will." Hereupon, two men stepped forward and promised to do their best. They were tolerably successful, and, the rest being roused to emulation, the work went on with such vigor that within six weeks the hull of the vessel was half finished. She was of forty tons burden, and was built with high bulwarks, to protect those on board from Indian arrows.

La Salle now bethought him that, in his absence, he might get from Hennepin service of more value than his sermons; and he requested him to descend the Illinois, and explore it to its mouth. The friar, though hardy and daring, would fain have excused himself, alleging a troublesome bodily infirmity; but his venerable colleague, Ribourde, himself too old for the journey, urged him to go, telling him that, if he died by the way, his apostolic labors would redound to the glory of God. Membré had been living for some time in the Indian camp, and was thoroughly out of humor with the objects of his missionary efforts, of whose obduracy and filth he bitterly complained. Hennepin proposed to take his place, while he should assume the Mississippi adventure; but this Membré declined, preferring to remain where he was. Hennepin now reluctantly accepted the proposed task. "Anybody but me," he says, with his usual modesty, "would have been very much frightened at the dangers of such a journey; and, in fact, if I had not placed all my trust in God, I should not have been the dupe of the Sieur de la Salle, who exposed my life rashly."[1]

On the last day of February, Hennepin's canoe lay at the water's edge; and the party gathered on the bank to bid him farewell. He had two companions, Michel Accau, and a man known as the Picard du Gay,[2] though his real name was Antoine Auguel. The canoe was well laden with gifts for the Indians,—tobacco, knives, beads, awls, and other goods, to a very considerable value, supplied at La Salle's cost; "and, in fact," observes Hennepin, "he is liberal enough towards his friends."[3]

The friar bade farewell to La Salle, and embraced all the rest in turn. Father Ribourde gave him his benediction. "Be of good courage and let your heart be comforted," said the excellent old missionary, as he spread his hands in benediction over the shaven crown of the reverend traveller. Du Gay and Accau plied their paddles; the canoe receded, and vanished at length behind the forest. We will follow Hennepin hereafter on his adventures, imaginary and real. Meanwhile, we will trace the footsteps of his chief, urging his way, in the storms of winter, through those vast and gloomy wilds,—those realms of famine, treachery, and death, that lay betwixt him and his far-distant goal of Fort Frontenac.

On the first of March,[4] before the frost was yet out of the ground, when the forest was still leafless, and the oozy prairies still patched with snow, a band of discontented men were again gathered on the shore for another leave-taking. Hard by, the unfinished ship lay on the stocks, white and fresh from the saw and axe, ceaselessly reminding them of the hardship and peril that was in store. Here you would have seen the

[1] All of the above is from Hennepin; and it seems to be marked by his characteristic egotism. It appears, from La Salle's letters, that Accau was the real chief of the party; that their orders were to explore, not only the Illinois, but also a part of the Mississippi; and that Hennepin volunteered to go with the others. Accau was chosen because he spoke several Indian languages.

[2] An eminent writer has mistaken "Picard" for a personal name. Du Gay was called "Le Picard," because he came from the province of Picardy.

[3] (1683), 188. This commendation is suppressed in the later editions.

[4] Tonty erroneously places their departure on the twenty-second.

calm, impenetrable face of La Salle, and with him the Mohegan hunter, who seems to have felt towards him that admiring attachment which he could always inspire in his Indian retainers. Besides the Mohegan, four Frenchmen were to accompany him: Hunaut, La Violette, Collin, and Dautray.[1] His parting with Tonty was an anxious one, for each well knew the risks that environed both. Embarking with his followers in two canoes, he made his way upward amid the drifting ice; while the faithful Italian, with two or three honest men and twelve or thirteen knaves, remained to hold Fort Crèvecœur in his absence.

[1] *Déclaration faite par Moyse Hillaret, charpentier de barque.*

Chapter XIV

HARDIHOOD OF
LA SALLE

*The Winter Journey • The Deserted Town • Starved Rock •
Lake Michigan • The Wilderness • War Parties
• La Salle's Men give out • Ill Tidings • Mutiny •
Chastisement of the Mutineers*

LA SALLE well knew what was before him, and nothing but necessity spurred him to this desperate journey. He says that he could trust nobody else to go in his stead, and that, unless the articles lost in the "Griffin" were replaced without delay, the expedition would be retarded a full year, and he and his associates consumed by its expenses. "Therefore," he writes to one of them, "though the thaws of approaching spring greatly increased the difficulty of the way, interrupted as it was everywhere by marshes and rivers, to say nothing of the length of the journey, which is about five hundred leagues in a direct line, and the danger of meeting Indians of four or five different nations, through whose country we were to pass, as well as an Iroquois army, which we knew was coming that way; though we must suffer all the time from hunger; sleep on the open ground, and often without food; watch by night and march by day, loaded with baggage, such as blanket, clothing, kettle, hatchet, gun, powder, lead, and skins to make moccasins; sometimes pushing through thickets, sometimes climbing rocks covered with ice and snow, sometimes wading whole days through marshes where the water was waist-deep or even more, at a season when the snow was not entirely melted,—though I knew all this, it did not prevent me from resolving to go on foot to Fort Frontenac, to learn for myself what had become of my vessel, and bring back the things we needed."[1]

The winter had been a severe one; and when, an hour after leaving the fort, he and his companions reached the still water

---

[1] *Lettre de La Salle à un de ses associés* (Thouret?), *29 Sept., 1680* (Margry, II. 50).

of Peoria Lake, they found it sheeted with ice from shore to shore. They carried their canoes up the bank, made two rude sledges, placed the light vessels upon them, and dragged them to the upper end of the lake, where they encamped. In the morning, they found the river still covered with ice, too weak to bear them and too strong to permit them to break a way for the canoes. They spent the whole day in carrying them through the woods, toiling knee-deep in saturated snow. Rain fell in floods, and they took shelter at night in a deserted Indian hut.

In the morning, the third of March, they dragged their canoes half a league farther; then launched them, and, breaking the ice with clubs and hatchets, forced their way slowly up the stream. Again their progress was barred, and again they took to the woods, toiling onward till a tempest of moist, half-liquid snow forced them to bivouac for the night. A sharp frost followed, and in the morning the white waste around them was glazed with a dazzling crust. Now, for the first time, they could use their snow-shoes. Bending to their work, dragging their canoes, which glided smoothly over the polished surface, they journeyed on hour after hour and league after league, till they reached at length the great town of the Illinois, still void of its inhabitants.[1]

It was a desolate and lonely scene: the river gliding dark and cold between its banks of rushes; the empty lodges, covered with crusted snow; the vast white meadows; the distant cliffs, bearded with shining icicles; and the hills wrapped in forests, which glittered from afar with the icy incrustations that cased each frozen twig. Yet there was life in the savage landscape. The men saw buffalo wading in the snow, and they killed one of them. More than this: they discovered the tracks of moccasins. They cut rushes by the edge of the river, piled them on the bank, and set them on fire, that the smoke might attract the eyes of savages roaming near.

On the following day, while the hunters were smoking the meat of the buffalo, La Salle went out to reconnoitre, and presently met three Indians, one of whom proved to be Chas-

---

[1] Membré says that he was in the town at the time; but this could hardly have been the case. He was, in all probability, among the Illinois, in their camp near Fort Crèvecœur.

sagoac, the principal chief of the Illinois.[1] La Salle brought them to his bivouac, feasted them, gave them a red blanket, a kettle, and some knives and hatchets, made friends with them, promised to restrain the Iroquois from attacking them, told them that he was on his way to the settlements to bring arms and ammunition to defend them against their enemies, and, as the result of these advances, gained from the chief a promise that he would send provisions to Tonty's party at Fort Crèvecœur.

After several days spent at the deserted town, La Salle prepared to resume his journey. Before his departure, his attention was attracted to the remarkable cliff of yellow sandstone, now called Starved Rock, a mile or more above the village,— a natural fortress, which a score of resolute white men might make good against a host of savages; and he soon afterwards sent Tonty an order to examine it, and make it his stronghold in case of need.[2]

On the fifteenth, the party set out again, carried their canoes along the bank of the river as far as the rapids above Ottawa; then launched them and pushed their way upward, battling with the floating ice, which, loosened by a warm rain, drove down the swollen current in sheets. On the eighteenth, they reached a point some miles below the site of Joliet, and here found the river once more completely closed. Despairing of farther progress by water, they hid their canoes on an island, and struck across the country for Lake Michigan.

It was the worst of all seasons for such a journey. The nights were cold, but the sun was warm at noon, and the half-thawed prairie was one vast tract of mud, water, and discolored, half-liquid snow. On the twenty-second, they crossed marshes and inundated meadows, wading to the knee, till at noon they were stopped by a river, perhaps the Calumet.

[1] The same whom Hennepin calls Chassagouasse. He was brother of the chief, Nicanopé, who, in his absence, had feasted the French on the day after the nocturnal council with Monso. Chassagoac was afterwards baptized by Membré or Ribourde, but soon relapsed into the superstitions of his people, and died, as the former tells us, "doubly a child of perdition." See Le Clerc, II. 181.

[2] Tonty, *Mémoire*. The order was sent by two Frenchmen, whom La Salle met on Lake Michigan.

They made a raft of hard-wood timber, for there was no other, and shoved themselves across. On the next day, they could see Lake Michigan dimly glimmering beyond the waste of woods; and, after crossing three swollen streams, they reached it at evening. On the twenty-fourth, they followed its shore, till, at nightfall, they arrived at the fort, which they had built in the autumn at the mouth of the St. Joseph. Here La Salle found Chapelle and Leblanc, the two men whom he had sent from hence to Michillimackinac, in search of the "Griffin."[1] They reported that they had made the circuit of the lake, and had neither seen her nor heard tidings of her. Assured of her fate, he ordered them to rejoin Tonty at Fort Crèvecœur; while he pushed onward with his party through the unknown wild of Southern Michigan.

"The rain," says La Salle, "which lasted all day, and the raft we were obliged to make to cross the river, stopped us till noon of the twenty-fifth, when we continued our march through the woods, which was so interlaced with thorns and brambles that in two days and a half our clothes were all torn and our faces so covered with blood that we hardly knew each other. On the twenty-eighth, we found the woods more open, and began to fare better, meeting a good deal of game, which after this rarely failed us; so that we no longer carried provisions with us, but made a meal of roast meat wherever we happened to kill a deer, bear, or turkey. These are the choicest feasts on a journey like this; and till now we had generally gone without them, so that we had often walked all day without breakfast.

"The Indians do not hunt in this region, which is debatable ground between five or six nations who are at war, and, being afraid of each other, do not venture into these parts, except to surprise each other, and always with the greatest precaution and all possible secrecy. The reports of our guns and the carcasses of the animals we killed soon led some of them to find our trail. In fact, on the evening of the twenty-eighth, having made our fire by the edge of a prairie, we were surrounded by them; but as the man on guard waked us, and we posted ourselves behind trees with our guns, these savages, who are called Wapoos, took us

[1] *Déclaration de Moyse Hillaret; Relation des Découvertes.*

for Iroquois, and thinking that there must be a great many of us, because we did not travel secretly, as they do when in small bands, they ran off without shooting their arrows, and gave the alarm to their comrades, so that we were two days without meeting anybody."

La Salle guessed the cause of their fright; and, in order to confirm their delusion, he drew with charcoal, on the trunks of trees from which he had stripped the bark, the usual marks of an Iroquois war-party, with signs for prisoners and for scalps, after the custom of those dreaded warriors. This ingenious artifice, as will soon appear, was near proving the destruction of the whole party. He also set fire to the dry grass of the prairies over which he and his men had just passed, thus destroying the traces of their passage. "We practised this device every night, and it answered very well so long as we were passing over an open country; but, on the thirtieth, we got into great marshes, flooded by the thaws, and were obliged to cross them in mud or water up to the waist; so that our tracks betrayed us to a band of Mascoutins, who were out after Iroquois. They followed us through these marshes during the three days we were crossing them; but we made no fire at night, contenting ourselves with taking off our wet clothes and wrapping ourselves in our blankets on some dry knoll, where we slept till morning. At last, on the night of the second of April, there came a hard frost, and our clothes, which were drenched when we took them off, froze stiff as sticks, so that we could not put them on in the morning without making a fire to thaw them. The fire betrayed us to the Indians, who were encamped across the marsh; and they ran towards us with loud cries, till they were stopped half way by a stream so deep that they could not get over, the ice which had formed in the night not being strong enough to bear them. We went to meet them, within gun-shot; and whether our fire-arms frightened them, or whether they thought us more numerous than we were, or whether they really meant us no harm, they called out, in the Illinois language, that they had taken us for Iroquois, but now saw that we were friends and brothers; whereupon, they went off as they came, and we kept on our way till the fourth, when two of my men fell ill and could not walk."

In this emergency, La Salle went in search of some water-course by which they might reach Lake Erie, and soon came upon a small river, which was probably the Huron. Here, while the sick men rested, their companions made a canoe. There were no birch-trees; and they were forced to use elm bark, which at that early season would not slip freely from the wood until they loosened it with hot water. Their canoe being made, they embarked in it, and for a time floated pros-perously down the stream, when at length the way was barred by a matted barricade of trees fallen across the water. The sick men could now walk again, and, pushing eastward through the forest, the party soon reached the banks of the Detroit.

La Salle directed two of the men to make a canoe, and go to Michillimackinac, the nearest harborage. With the remain-ing two, he crossed the Detroit on a raft, and, striking a di-rect line across the country, reached Lake Erie, not far from Point Pelée. Snow, sleet, and rain pelted them with little in-termission; and when, after a walk of about thirty miles, they gained the lake, the Mohegan and one of the Frenchmen were attacked with fever and spitting of blood. Only one man now remained in health. With his aid, La Salle made another canoe, and, embarking the invalids, pushed for Niagara. It was Easter Monday when they landed at a cabin of logs above the cataract, probably on the spot where the "Griffin" was built. Here several of La Salle's men had been left the year before, and here they still remained. They told him woful news. Not only had he lost the "Griffin," and her lading of ten thousand crowns in value, but a ship from France, freighted with his goods, valued at more than twenty-two thousand livres, had been totally wrecked at the mouth of the St. Lawrence; and, of twenty hired men on their way from Europe to join him, some had been detained by his enemy, the Intendant Duchesneau, while all but four of the remain-der, being told that he was dead, had found means to return home.

His three followers were all unfit for travel: he alone re-tained his strength and spirit. Taking with him three fresh men at Niagara, he resumed his journey, and on the sixth of May descried, looming through floods of rain, the familiar shores of his seigniory and the bastioned walls of Fort Frontenac. During sixty-five days, he had toiled almost incessantly, travelling, by the course he took, about a thousand miles through a country beset with every form of peril and obstruction; "the most arduous journey," says the chronicler, "ever made by Frenchmen in America." Such was Cavelier de la Salle. In him, an unconquerable mind held at its service a frame of iron, and tasked it to the utmost of its endurance. The pioneer of western pioneers was no rude son of toil, but a man of thought, trained amid arts and letters.[1]

He had reached his goal; but for him there was neither rest nor peace. Man and Nature seemed in arms against him. His agents had plundered him; his creditors had seized his property; and several of his canoes, richly laden, had been lost in the rapids of the St. Lawrence.[2] He hastened to Montreal, where his sudden advent caused great astonishment; and where, despite his crippled resources and damaged credit, he succeeded, within a week, in gaining the supplies which he required, and the needful succors for the forlorn band on the Illinois. He had returned to Fort Frontenac, and was on the point of embarking for their relief, when a blow fell upon him more disheartening than any that had preceded. On the twenty-second of July, two *voyageurs*, Messier and Laurent, came to him with a letter from Tonty, who wrote that soon after La Salle's departure nearly all the men had deserted, after destroying Fort Crèvecœur, plundering the magazine, and throwing into the river all the arms, goods, and stores which they could not carry off. The messengers who brought this letter were speedily followed by two of the *habitants* of Fort Frontenac, who had been trading on the lakes, and who, with a fidelity which the unhappy La Salle rarely knew how to inspire, had travelled day and night to bring him their tidings. They reported that they had met the deserters, and that, having been reinforced by recruits gained at Michillimackinac

---

[1] A Rocky Mountain trapper, being complimented on the hardihood of himself and his companions, once said to the writer, "That's so; but a gentleman of the right sort will stand hardship better than anybody else." The history of Arctic and African travel, and the military records of all time, are a standing evidence that a trained and developed mind is not the enemy, but the active and powerful ally, of constitutional hardihood. The culture that enervates instead of strengthening is always a false or a partial one.

[2] Zenobe Membré in Le Clerc, II. 202.

and Niagara, they now numbered twenty men.[1] They had destroyed the fort on the St. Joseph, seized a quantity of furs belonging to La Salle at Michillimackinac, and plundered the magazine at Niagara. Here they had separated, eight of them coasting the south side of Lake Ontario to find harborage at Albany, a common refuge at that time of this class of scoundrels; while the remaining twelve, in three canoes, made for Fort Frontenac, along the north shore, intending to kill La Salle, as the surest means of escaping punishment.

He lost no time in lamentation. Of the few men at his command, he chose nine of the trustiest, embarked with them in canoes, and went to meet the marauders. After passing the Bay of Quinté, he took his station, with five of his party, at a point of land suited to his purpose, and detached the remaining four to keep watch. In the morning, two canoes were discovered, approaching without suspicion, one of them far in advance of the other. As the foremost drew near, La Salle's canoe darted out from under the leafy shore; two of the men handling the paddles, while he, with the remaining two, levelled their guns at the deserters, and called on them to surrender. Astonished and dismayed, they yielded at once; while two more, who were in the second canoe, hastened to follow their example. La Salle now returned to the fort with his prisoners, placed them in custody, and again set forth. He met the third canoe upon the lake at about six o'clock in the evening. His men vainly plied their paddles in pursuit. The mutineers reached the shore, took post among rocks and trees, levelled their guns, and showed fight. Four of La Salle's men made a circuit to gain their rear and dislodge them, on which

[1] When La Salle was at Niagara, in April, he had ordered Dautray, the best of the men who had accompanied him from the Illinois, to return thither as soon as he was able. Four men from Niagara were to go with him, and he was to rejoin Tonty with such supplies as that post could furnish. Dautray set out accordingly, but was met on the lakes by the deserters, who told him that Tonty was dead, and seduced his men. *Relation des Découvertes*. Dautray himself seems to have remained true; at least, he was in La Salle's service immediately after, and was one of his most trusted followers. He was of good birth, being the son of Jean Bourdon, a conspicuous personage in the early period of the colony; and his name appears on official records as Jean Bourdon, Sieur d'Autray.

they stole back to their canoe, and tried to escape in the darkness. They were pursued, and summoned to yield; but they replied by aiming their guns at their pursuers, who instantly gave them a volley, killed two of them, and captured the remaining three. Like their companions, they were placed in custody at the fort, to await the arrival of Count Frontenac.[1]

[1] La Salle's long letter, written apparently to his associate, Thouret, and dated 29 Sept., 1680, is the chief authority for the above. The greater part of this letter is incorporated almost verbatim, in the official narrative called *Relation des Découvertes*. Hennepin, Membré, and Tonty also speak of the journey from Fort Crèvecœur. The death of the two mutineers was used by La Salle's enemies as the basis of a charge of murder.

Chapter XV

INDIAN CONQUERORS

*The Enterprise renewed • Attempt to rescue Tonty • Buffalo • A
Frightful Discovery • Iroquois Fury • The Ruined Town • A
Night of Horror • Traces of the Invaders • No News of Tonty*

AND now La Salle's work must be begun afresh. He had
staked all, and all had seemingly been lost. In stern, relentless effort, he had touched the limits of human endurance;
and the harvest of his toil was disappointment, disaster, and
impending ruin. The shattered fabric of his enterprise was
prostrate in the dust. His friends desponded; his foes were
blatant and exultant. Did he bend before the storm? No human eye could pierce the depths of his reserved and haughty
nature; but the surface was calm, and no sign betrayed a
shaken resolve or an altered purpose. Where weaker men
would have abandoned all in despairing apathy, he turned
anew to his work with the same vigor and the same apparent
confidence as if borne on the full tide of success.

His best hope was in Tonty. Could that brave and true-
hearted officer, and the three or four faithful men who had
remained with him, make good their foothold on the Illinois,
and save from destruction the vessel on the stocks, and the
forge and tools so laboriously carried thither, then a basis was
left on which the ruined enterprise might be built up once
more. There was no time to lose. Tonty must be succored
soon, or succor would come too late. La Salle had already
provided the necessary material, and a few days sufficed to
complete his preparations. On the tenth of August, he embarked again for the Illinois. With him went his lieutenant,
La Forest, who held of him in fief an island, then called Belle
Isle, opposite Fort Frontenac.[1] A surgeon, ship-carpenters,
joiners, masons, soldiers, *voyageurs*, and laborers completed
his company, twenty-five men in all, with every thing needful
for the outfit of the vessel.

[1] *Robert Cavelier, Sʳ de la Salle, à François Daupin, Sʳ de la Forest, 10 Juin,
1679.*

857

His route, though difficult, was not so long as that which he had followed the year before. He ascended the river Humber; crossed to Lake Simcoe, and thence descended the Severn to the Georgian Bay of Lake Huron; followed its eastern shore, coasted the Manitoulin Islands, and at length reached Michillimackinac. Here, as usual, all was hostile; and he had great difficulty in inducing the Indians, who had been excited against him, to sell him provisions. Anxious to reach his destination, he pushed forward with twelve men, leaving La Forest to bring on the rest. On the fourth of November,[1] he reached the ruined fort at the mouth of the St. Joseph, and left five of his party, with the heavy stores, to wait till La Forest should come up, while he himself hastened forward with six Frenchmen and an Indian. A deep anxiety possessed him. The rumor, current for months past, that the Iroquois, bent on destroying the Illinois, were on the point of invading their country, had constantly gained strength. Here was a new disaster, which, if realized, might involve him and his enterprise in irretrievable wreck.

He ascended the St. Joseph, crossed the portage to the Kankakee, and followed its course downward till it joined the northern branch of the Illinois. He had heard nothing of Tonty on the way, and neither here nor elsewhere could he discover the smallest sign of the passage of white men. His friend, therefore, if alive, was probably still at his post; and he pursued his course with a mind lightened, in some small measure, of its load of anxiety.

When last he had passed here, all was solitude; but now the scene was changed. The boundless waste was thronged with life. He beheld that wondrous spectacle, still to be seen at times on the plains of the remotest West, and the memory of which can quicken the pulse and stir the blood after the lapse of years. Far and near, the prairie was alive with buffalo; now like black specks dotting the distant swells; now trampling by in ponderous columns, or filing in long lines, morning, noon, and night, to drink at the river,—wading, plunging, and snorting in the water; climbing the muddy shores, and staring

---

[1] This date is from the *Relation*. Membré says the twenty-eighth; but he is wrong, by his own showing, as he says that the party reached the Illinois village on the first of December, which would be an impossibility.

with wild eyes at the passing canoes. It was an opportunity
not to be lost. The party landed, and encamped for a hunt.
Sometimes they hid under the shelving bank, and shot them
as they came to drink; sometimes, flat on their faces, they
dragged themselves through the long dead grass, till the savage bulls, guardians of the herd, ceased their grazing, raised
their huge heads, and glared through tangled hair at the dangerous intruders. The hunt was successful. In three days, the
hunters killed twelve buffalo, besides deer, geese, and swans.
They cut the meat into thin flakes, and dried it in the sun, or
in the smoke of their fires. The men were in high spirits; de-
lighting in the sport, and rejoicing in the prospect of relieving
Tonty and his hungry followers with a plentiful supply.

They embarked again, and soon approached the great town
of the Illinois. The buffalo were far behind; and once more
the canoes glided on their way through a voiceless solitude.
No hunters were seen; no saluting whoop greeted their ears.
They passed the cliff afterwards called the Rock of St. Louis,
where La Salle had ordered Tonty to build his stronghold;
but, as he scanned its lofty top, he saw no palisades, no
cabins, no sign of human hand, and still its primeval crest of
forests overhung the gliding river. Now the meadow opened
before them where the great town had stood. They gazed,
astonished and confounded: all was desolation. The town had
vanished, and the meadow was black with fire. They plied
their paddles, hastened to the spot, landed; and, as they
looked around, their cheeks grew white, and the blood was
frozen in their veins.

Before them lay a plain once swarming with wild human
life, and covered with Indian dwellings; now a waste of devastation and death, strewn with heaps of ashes, and bristling
with the charred poles and stakes which had formed the
framework of the lodges. At the points of most of them were
stuck human skulls, half picked by birds of prey.[1] Near at
hand was the burial-ground of the village. The travellers sickened with horror as they entered its revolting precincts.

[1] "Il ne restoit que quelques bouts de perches brulées qui montroient quelle
avoit été l'étendue du village, et sur la plupart desquelles il y avoit des têtes
de morts plantées et mangées des corbeaux."—*Relation des Découvertes du S*
de la Salle.

Wolves in multitudes fled at their approach; while clouds of crows or buzzards, rising from the hideous repast, wheeled above their heads, or settled on the naked branches of the neighboring forest. Every grave had been rifled, and the bodies flung down from the scaffolds where, after the Illinois custom, many of them had been placed. The field was strewn with broken bones and torn and mangled corpses. A hyena warfare had been waged against the dead. La Salle knew the handiwork of the Iroquois. The threatened blow had fallen, and the wolfish hordes of the five cantons had fleshed their rabid fangs in a new victim.[1]

Not far distant, the conquerors had made a rude fort of trunks, boughs, and roots of trees laid together to form a circular enclosure; and this, too, was garnished with skulls, stuck on the broken branches, and protruding sticks. The *caches*, or subterranean storehouses of the villagers, had been broken open, and the contents scattered. The cornfields were laid waste, and much of the corn thrown into heaps and half burned. As La Salle surveyed this scene of havoc, one thought engrossed him: where were Tonty and his men? He searched the Iroquois fort: there were abundant traces of its savage occupants, and, among them, a few fragments of French clothing. He examined the skulls; but the hair, portions of which clung to nearly all of them, was in every case that of an Indian. Evening came on before he had finished the search. The sun set, and the wilderness sank to its savage rest. Night and silence brooded over the waste, where, far as the raven could wing his flight, stretched the dark domain of solitude and horror.

---

[1] "Beaucoup de carcasses à demi rongées par les loups, les sépulchres démolis, les os tirés de leurs fosses et épars par la campagne; . . . enfin les loups et les corbeaux augmentoient encore par leurs hurlemens et par leurs cris l'horreur de ce spectacle."—*Relation des Découvertes du Sr de la Salle.*

The above may seem exaggerated; but it accords perfectly with what is well established concerning the ferocious character of the Iroquois, and the nature of their warfare. Many other tribes have frequently made war upon the dead. I have myself known an instance in which five corpses of Sioux Indians, placed in trees, after the practice of the Western bands of that people, were thrown down and kicked into fragments by a war party of the Crows, who then held the muzzles of their guns against the skulls, and blew them to pieces. This happened near the head of the Platte, in the summer of 1846. Yet the Crows are much less ferocious than were the Iroquois in La Salle's time.

Yet there was no silence at the spot where La Salle and his companions made their bivouac. The howling of the wolves filled the air with fierce and dreary dissonance. More dangerous foes were not far off, for before nightfall they had seen fresh Indian tracks; "but, as it was very cold," says La Salle, "this did not prevent us from making a fire and lying down by it, each of us keeping watch in turn. I spent the night in a distress which you can imagine better than I can write it; and I did not sleep a moment with trying to make up my mind as to what I ought to do. My ignorance as to the position of those I was looking after, and my uncertainty as to what would become of the men who were to follow me with La Forest, if they arrived at the ruined village and did not find me there, made me apprehend every sort of trouble and disaster. At last, I decided to keep on my way down the river, leaving some of my men behind in charge of the goods, which it was not only useless, but dangerous, to carry with me, because we should be forced to abandon them when the winter fairly set in, which would be very soon."

This resolution was due to a discovery he had made the evening before, which offered, as he thought, a possible clew to the fate of Tonty and the men with him. He thus describes it: "Near the garden of the Indians, which was on the meadows, a league from the village, and not far from the river, I found six pointed stakes, set in the ground and painted red. On each of them was the figure of a man with bandaged eyes, drawn in black. As the savages often set stakes of this sort where they have killed people, I thought, by their number and position, that, when the Iroquois came, the Illinois, finding our men alone in the hut near their garden, had either killed them or made them prisoners. And I was confirmed in this, because, seeing no signs of a battle, I supposed that, on hearing of the approach of the Iroquois, the old men and other non-combatants had fled, and that the young warriors had remained behind to cover their flight, and afterwards followed, taking the French with them; while the Iroquois, finding nobody to kill, had vented their fury on the corpses in the graveyard."

Uncertain as was the basis of this conjecture, and feeble as was the hope it afforded, it determined him to push forward, in order to learn more. When daylight returned, he told his purpose to his followers, and directed three of them to await his return near the ruined village. They were to hide themselves on an island, conceal their fire at night, make no smoke by day, fire no guns, and keep a close watch. Should the rest of the party arrive, they, too, were to wait with similar precautions. The baggage was placed in a hollow of the rocks, at a place difficult of access; and, these arrangements made, La Salle set out on his perilous journey with the four remaining men, Dautray, Hunaut, You, and the Indian. Each was armed with two guns, a pistol, and a sword; and a number of hatchets and other goods were placed in the canoe, as presents for Indians whom they might meet.

Several leagues below the village, they found, on their right hand, close to the river, a sort of island, made inaccessible by the marshes and water which surrounded it. Here the flying Illinois had sought refuge with their women and children, and the place was full of their deserted huts. On the left bank, exactly opposite, was an abandoned camp of the Iroquois. On the level meadow stood a hundred and thirteen huts, and on the forest trees which covered the hills behind were carved the totems, or insignia, of the chiefs, together with marks to show the number of followers which each had led to the war. La Salle counted five hundred and eighty-two warriors. He found marks, too, for the Illinois killed or captured, but none to indicate that any of the Frenchmen had shared their fate.

As they descended the river, they passed, on the same day, six abandoned camps of the Illinois, and opposite to each was a camp of the invaders. The former, it was clear, had retreated in a body; while the Iroquois had followed their march, day by day, along the other bank. La Salle and his men pushed rapidly onward, passed Peoria Lake, and soon reached Fort Crèvecœur, which they found, as they expected, demolished by the deserters. The vessel on the stocks was still left entire, though the Iroquois had found means to draw out the iron nails and spikes. On one of the planks were written the words: "*Nous sommes tous sauvages: ce 15—1680;*" the work, no doubt, of the knaves who had pillaged and destroyed the fort.

La Salle and his companions hastened on, and during the following day passed four opposing camps of the savage armies. The silence of death now reigned along the deserted river, whose lonely borders, wrapped deep in forests, seemed lifeless as the grave. As they drew near the mouth of the stream, they saw a meadow on their right, and, on its farthest verge, several human figures, erect, yet motionless. They landed, and cautiously examined the place. The long grass was trampled down, and all around were strewn the relics of the hideous orgies which formed the ordinary sequel of an Iroquois victory. The figures they had seen were the half-consumed bodies of women, still bound to the stakes where they had been tortured. Other sights there were, too revolting for record.[1] All the remains were those of women and children. The men, it seemed, had fled, and left them to their fate.

Here, again, La Salle sought long and anxiously, without finding the smallest sign that could indicate the presence of Frenchmen. Once more descending the river, they soon reached its mouth. Before them, a broad eddying current rolled swiftly on its way; and La Salle beheld the Mississippi, the object of his day-dreams, the destined avenue of his ambition and his hopes. It was no time for reflections. The moment was too engrossing, too heavily charged with anxieties and cares. From a rock on the shore, he saw a tree stretched forward above the stream; and, stripping off its bark to make it more conspicuous, he hung upon it a board on which he had drawn the figures of himself and his men, seated in their canoe, and bearing a pipe of peace. To this he tied a letter for Tonty, informing him that he had returned up the river to the ruined village.

His four men had behaved admirably throughout, and they now offered to continue the journey, if he saw fit, and follow him to the sea; but he thought it useless to go farther, and was unwilling to abandon the three men whom he had ordered to await his return. Accordingly, they retraced their

[1] "On ne sçauroit exprimer la rage de ces furieux ni les tourmens qu'ils avoient fait souffrir aux misérables Tamaroa [*a tribe of the Illinois*]. Il y en avoit encore dans des chaudières qu'ils avoient laissées pleines sur les feux, qui depuis s'étoient éteints," etc., etc.— *Relation des Découvertes.*

course, and, paddling at times both day and night, urged their canoe so swiftly that they reached the village in the incredibly short space of four days.[1]

The sky was clear, and, as night came on, the travellers saw a prodigious comet blazing above this scene of desolation. On that night, it was chilling with a superstitious awe the hamlets of New England and the gilded chambers of Versailles; but it is characteristic of La Salle, that, beset as he was with perils, and surrounded with ghastly images of death, he coolly notes down the phenomenon, not as a portentous messenger of war and woe, but rather as an object of scientific curiosity.[2]

He found his three men safely ensconced upon their island, where they were anxiously looking for his return. After collecting a store of half-burnt corn from the ravaged granaries of the Illinois, the whole party began to ascend the river, and, on the sixth of January, reached the junction of the Kankakee with the northern branch. On their way downward, they had descended the former stream. They now chose the latter, and soon discovered, by the margin of the water, a rude cabin of bark. La Salle landed, and examined the spot, when an object met his eye which cheered him with a bright gleam of hope. It was but a piece of wood; but the wood had been cut with a saw. Tonty and his party, then, had passed this way, escaping from the carnage behind them. Unhappily, they had left no token of their passage at the fork of the two streams; and thus La Salle, on his voyage downward, had believed them to be still on the river below.

With rekindled hope, the travellers pursued their journey,

[1] The distance is about two hundred and fifty miles. The letters of La Salle, as well as the official narrative compiled from them, say that they left the village on the second of December, and returned to it on the eleventh, having left the mouth of the river on the seventh.

[2] This was the "Great Comet of 1680." Dr. B. A. Gould writes me: "It appeared in December, 1680, and was visible until the latter part of February, 1681, being especially brilliant in January." It was said to be the largest ever seen. By observations upon it, Newton demonstrated the regular revolutions of comets around the sun. "No comet," it is said, "has threatened the earth with a nearer approach than that of 1680." *Winthrop on Comets, Lecture II.* p. 44. Increase Mather, in his *Discourse concerning Comets*, printed at Boston in 1683, says of this one: "Its appearance was very terrible, the Blaze ascended above 60 Degrees almost to its Zenith." Mather thought it fraught with terrific portent to the nations of the earth.

leaving their canoes, and making their way overland towards the fort on the St. Joseph.

"Snow fell in extraordinary quantities all day," writes La Salle, "and it kept on falling for nineteen days in succession, with cold so severe that I never knew so hard a winter, even in Canada. We were obliged to cross forty leagues of open country, where we could hardly find wood to warm ourselves at evening, and could get no bark whatever to make a hut, so that we had to spend the night exposed to the furious winds which blow over these plains. I never suffered so much from cold, or had more trouble in getting forward, for the snow was so light, resting suspended as it were among the tall grass, that we could not use snow-shoes. Sometimes it was waist deep; and, as I walked before my men, as usual, to encourage them by breaking the path, I often had much ado, though I am rather tall, to lift my legs above the drifts, through which I pushed by the weight of my body."

At length, they reached their goal, and found shelter and safety within the walls of Fort Miami. Here was the party left in charge of La Forest; but, to his surprise and grief, La Salle heard no tidings of Tonty. He found some amends for the disappointment in the fidelity and zeal of La Forest's men, who had restored the fort, cleared ground for planting, and even sawed the planks and timber for a new vessel on the lake.

And now, while La Salle rests at Fort Miami, let us trace the adventures which befell Tonty and his followers, after their chief's departure from Fort Crèvecœur.

Chapter XVI

1680

TONTY AND THE IROQUOIS

WHEN La Salle set out on his rugged journey to Fort Frontenac, he left, as we have seen, fifteen men at Fort Crèvecœur,—smiths, ship-carpenters, housewrights, and soldiers, besides his servant l'Espérance and the two friars Membré and Ribourde. Most of the men were ripe for mutiny. They had no interest in the enterprise, and no love for its chief. They were disgusted with the present, and terrified at the future. La Salle, too, was for the most part a stern commander, impenetrable and cold; and when he tried to soothe, conciliate, and encourage, his success rarely answered to the excellence of his rhetoric. He could always, however, inspire respect, if not love; but now the restraint of his presence was removed. He had not been long absent, when a firebrand was thrown into the midst of the discontented and restless crew.

It may be remembered that La Salle had met two of his men, La Chapelle and Leblanc, at his fort on the St. Joseph, and ordered them to rejoin Tonty. Unfortunately, they obeyed. On arriving, they told their comrades that the "Griffin" was lost, that Fort Frontenac was seized by the creditors of La Salle, that he was ruined past recovery, and that they, the men, would never receive their pay. Their wages were in arrears for more than two years; and, indeed, it would have been folly to pay them before their return to the settlements, as to do so would have been a temptation to desert. Now, however, the effect on their minds was still worse, believing, as many of them did, that they would never be paid at all.

La Chapelle and his companion had brought a letter from La Salle to Tonty, directing him to examine and fortify the cliff so often mentioned, which overhung the river above the great Illinois village. Tonty, accordingly, set out on his errand with some of the men. In his absence, the malcontents destroyed the fort, stole powder, lead, furs, and provisions, and deserted, after writing on the side of the unfinished vessel the words seen by La Salle, "*Nous sommes tous sauvages*."[1] The brave young Sieur de Boisrondet, and the servant l'Espérance, hastened to carry the news to Tonty, who at once despatched four of those with him, by two different routes, to inform La Salle of the disaster.[2] Besides the two just named, there now remained with him only one hired man and the Récollet friars. With this feeble band, he was left among a horde of treacherous savages, who had been taught to regard him as a secret enemy. Resolved, apparently, to disarm their jealousy by a show of confidence, he took up his abode in the midst of them, making his quarters in the great village, whither, as spring opened, its inhabitants returned, to the number, according to Membré, of seven or eight thousand. Hither he conveyed the forge and such tools as he could recover, and here he hoped to maintain himself till La Salle should reappear. The spring and the summer were past, and he looked anxiously for his coming, unconscious that a storm was gathering in the east, soon to burst with devastation over the fertile wilderness of the Illinois.

I have recounted the ferocious triumphs of the Iroquois in another volume.[3] Throughout a wide semicircle around their

---

[1] For the particulars of this desertion, Membré in Le Clerc, II. 171, *Relation des Découvertes*; Tonty, *Mémoire, 1684, 1693; Déclaration faite par devant le Sr Duchesneau, Intendant en Canada, par Moyse Hillaret, charpentier de barque cy-devant au service du Sr de la Salle, Aoust, 1680.*

Moyse Hillaret, the "Maitre Moyse" of Hennepin, was a ringleader of the deserters, and seems to have been one of those captured by La Salle near Fort Frontenac. Twelve days after, Hillaret was examined by La Salle's enemy, the intendant; and this paper is the formal statement made by him. It gives the names of most of the men, and furnishes incidental confirmation of many statements of Hennepin, Tonty, Membré, and the *Relation des Découvertes*. Hillaret, Leblanc, and Le Meilleur, the blacksmith nicknamed La Forge, went off together, and the rest seem to have followed afterwards. Hillaret does not admit that any goods were wantonly destroyed.

There is before me a schedule of the debts of La Salle, made after his death. It includes a claim of this man for wages to the amount of 2,500 livres.

[2] Two of the messengers, Laurent and Messier, arrived safely. The others seem to have deserted.

[3] The Jesuits in North America.

cantons, they had made the forest a solitude; destroyed the Hurons, exterminated the Neutrals and the Eries, reduced the formidable Andastes to helpless insignificance, swept the borders of the St. Lawrence with fire, spread terror and desolation among the Algonquins of Canada; and now, tired of peace, they were seeking, to borrow their own savage metaphor, new nations to devour. Yet it was not alone their homicidal fury that now impelled them to another war. Strange as it may seem, this war was in no small measure one of commercial advantage. They had long traded with the Dutch and English of New York, who gave them, in exchange for their furs, the guns, ammunition, knives, hatchets, kettles, beads, and brandy which had become indispensable to them. Game was scarce in their country. They must seek their beaver and other skins in the vacant territories of the tribes they had destroyed; but this did not content them. The French of Canada were seeking to secure a monopoly of the furs of the north and west; and, of late, the enterprises of La Salle on the tributaries of the Mississippi had especially roused the jealousy of the Iroquois, fomented, moreover, by Dutch and English traders.[1] These crafty savages would fain reduce all these regions to subjection, and draw thence an exhaustless supply of furs, to be bartered for English goods with the traders of Albany. They turned their eyes first towards the Illinois, the most important, as well as one of the most accessible, of the western Algonquin tribes; and among La Salle's enemies were some in whom jealousy of a hated rival could so far override all the best interests of the colony that they did not scruple to urge on the Iroquois to an invasion which they hoped would prove his ruin. The chiefs convened, war was decreed, the war-dance was danced, the war-song sung, and five hundred warriors began their march. In their path lay the town of the Miamis, neighbors and kindred of the Illinois. It was always their policy to divide and conquer; and these forest Machiavels had intrigued so well among the Miamis, working craftily on their jealousy, that they induced them to join in the invasion, though there is every

---

[1] Duchesneau, in *Paris Docs.*, IX. 163.

reason to believe that they had marked these infatuated allies as their next victims.[1]

Go to the banks of the Illinois where it flows by the village of Utica, and stand on the meadow that borders it on the north. In front glides the river, a musket-shot in width; and from the farther bank rises, with gradual slope, a range of wooded hills that hide from sight the vast prairie behind them. A mile or more on your left these gentle acclivities end abruptly in the lofty front of the great cliff, called by the French the Rock of St. Louis, looking boldly out from the forests that environ it; and, three miles distant on your right, you discern a gap in the steep bluffs that here bound the valley, marking the mouth of the river Vermilion, called Aramoni by the French.[2] Now stand in fancy on this same spot in the early autumn of the year 1680. You are in the midst of the great town of the Illinois,—hundreds of mat-covered lodges, and thousands of congregated savages. Enter one of their dwellings: they will not think you an intruder. Some friendly squaw will lay a mat for you by the fire; you may seat yourself upon it, smoke your pipe, and study the lodge and its inmates by the light that streams through the holes at the top. Three or four fires smoke and smoulder on the ground down the middle of the long arched structure; and, as to each fire there are two families, the place is somewhat crowded

[1] There had long been a rankling jealousy between the Miamis and the Illinois. According to Membré, La Salle's enemies had intrigued successfully among the former, as well as among the Iroquois, to induce them to take arms against the Illinois.

[2] The above is from notes made on the spot. The following is La Salle's description of the locality in the *Relation des Découvertes*, written in 1681: "La rive gauche de la rivière, du coté du sud, est occupée par un long rocher, fort étroit et escarpé presque partout, à la réserve d'un endroit de plus d'une lieue de longueur, situé vis-à-vis du village, ou le terrain, tout covert de beaux chênes, s'étend par une pente douce jusqu'au bord de la rivière. Au delà de cette hauteur est une vaste plaine, qui s'étend bien loin du coté du sud, et qui est traversée par la rivière Aramoni, dont les bords sont couverts d'une lisière de bois peu large."

The Aramoni is laid down on the great manuscript map of Franquelin, 1684, and on the map of Coronelli, 1688. It is, without doubt, the Big Vermilion. Aramoni is the Illinois word for red, or vermilion. Starved Rock, or the Rock of St. Louis, is the highest and steepest escarpment of the *long rocher* above mentioned.

when all are present. But now there is breathing room, for many are in the fields. A squaw sits weaving a mat of rushes; a warrior, naked except his moccasins, and tattooed with fantastic devices, binds a stone arrow-head to its shaft, with the fresh sinews of a buffalo. Some lie asleep, some sit staring in vacancy, some are eating, some are squatted in lazy chat around a fire. The smoke brings water to your eyes; the fleas annoy you; small unkempt children, naked as young puppies, crawl about your knees and will not be repelled. You have seen enough. You rise and go out again into the sunlight. It is, if not a peaceful, at least a languid scene. A few voices break the stillness, mingled with the joyous chirping of crickets from the grass. Young men lie flat on their faces, basking in the sun. A group of their elders are smoking around a buffalo-skin on which they have just been playing a game of chance with cherry-stones. A lover and his mistress, perhaps, sit together under a shed of bark, without uttering a word. Not far off is the graveyard, where lie the dead of the village, some buried in the earth, some wrapped in skins and laid aloft on scaffolds, above the reach of wolves. In the cornfields around, you see squaws at their labor, and children driving off intruding birds; and your eye ranges over the meadows beyond, spangled with the yellow blossoms of the resin-weed and the Rudbeckia, or over the bordering hills still green with the foliage of summer.[1]

[1] The Illinois were an aggregation of distinct though kindred tribes, the Kaskaskias, the Peorias, the Kahokias, the Tamaroas, the Moingona, and others. Their general character and habits were those of other Indian tribes; but they were reputed somewhat cowardly and slothful. In their manners, they were more licentious than many of their neighbors, and addicted to practices which are sometimes supposed to be the result of a perverted civilization. Young men enacting the part of women were frequently to be seen among them. These were held in great contempt. Some of the early travellers, both among the Illinois and among other tribes, where the same practice prevailed, mistook them for hermaphrodites. According to Charlevoix (*Journal Historique*, 303), this abuse was due in part to a superstition. The Miamis and Piankishaws were in close affinities of language and habits with the Illinois. All these tribes belonged to the great Algonquin family. The first impressions which the French received of them, as recorded in the *Relation* of 1671, were singularly favorable; but a closer acquaintance did not confirm them. The Illinois traded with the lake tribes, to whom they carried slaves taken in war, receiving in exchange guns, hatchets, and other French goods. Marquette in *Relation, 1670*, 91.

This, or something like it, one may safely affirm, was the aspect of the Illinois village at noon of the tenth of September.[1] In a hut apart from the rest, you would probably have found the Frenchmen. Among them was a man, not strong in person, and disabled, moreover, by the loss of a hand; yet, in this den of barbarism, betraying the language and bearing of one formed in the most polished civilization of Europe. This was Henri de Tonty. The others were young Boisrondet, the servant l'Espérance, and a Parisian youth named Étienne Renault. The friars, Membré and Ribourde, were not in the village, but at a hut a league distant, whither they had gone to make a "retreat," for prayer and meditation. Their missionary labors had not been fruitful. They had made no converts, and were in despair at the intractable character of the objects of their zeal. As for the other Frenchmen, time, doubtless, hung heavy on their hands; for nothing can surpass the vacant monotony of an Indian town when there is neither hunting, nor war, nor feasts, nor dances, nor gambling, to beguile the lagging hours.

Suddenly the village was wakened from its lethargy as by the crash of a thunderbolt. A Shawanoe, lately here on a visit, had left his Illinois friends to return home. He now reappeared, crossing the river in hot haste, with the announcement that he had met, on his way, an army of Iroquois approaching to attack them. All was panic and confusion. The lodges disgorged their frightened inmates; women and children screamed, startled warriors snatched their weapons. There were less than five hundred of them, for the greater part of the young men had gone to war. A crowd of excited savages thronged about Tonty and his Frenchmen, already objects of their suspicion, charging them, with furious gesticulation, with having stirred up their enemies to invade them. Tonty defended himself in broken Illinois, but the naked mob were but half convinced. They seized the forge and tools and flung them into the river, with all the goods that had been saved from the deserters; then, distrusting their power to defend themselves, they manned the wooden canoes which lay in multitudes by the bank, embarked their women and children, and paddled down the stream to that island of dry land

[1] This is Membré's date. The narratives differ as to the day, though all agree as to the month.

in the midst of marshes which La Salle afterwards found filled with their deserted huts. Sixty warriors remained here to guard them, and the rest returned to the village. All night long fires blazed along the shore. The excited warriors greased their bodies, painted their faces, befeathered their heads, sang their war-songs, danced, stamped, yelled, and brandished their hatchets, to work up their courage to face the crisis. The morning came, and with it came the Iroquois.

Young warriors had gone out as scouts, and now they returned. They had seen the enemy in the line of forest that bordered the river Aramoni, or Vermilion, and had stealthily reconnoitred them. They were very numerous,[1] and armed for the most part with guns, pistols, and swords. Some had bucklers of wood or raw hide, and some wore those corselets of tough twigs interwoven with cordage which their fathers had used when fire-arms were unknown. The scouts added more, for they declared that they had seen a Jesuit among the Iroquois; nay, that La Salle himself was there, whence it must follow that Tonty and his men were enemies and traitors. The supposed Jesuit was but an Iroquois chief arrayed in a black hat, doublet, and stockings; while another, equipped after a somewhat similar fashion, passed in the distance for La Salle. But the Illinois were furious. Tonty's life hung by a hair. A crowd of savages surrounded him, mad with rage and terror. He had come lately from Europe, and knew little of Indians; but, as the friar Membré says of him, "he was full of intelligence and courage," and, when they heard him declare that he and his Frenchmen would go with them to fight the Iroquois, their threats grew less clamorous and their eyes glittered with a less deadly lustre.

Whooping and screeching, they ran to their canoes, crossed the river, climbed the woody hill, and swarmed down upon the plain beyond. About a hundred of them had guns; the rest were armed with bows and arrows. They were now face to face with the enemy, who had emerged from the woods of the Vermilion, and were advancing on the open prairie. With unwonted spirit, for their repute as warriors was by no means

---

[1] The *Relation des Découvertes* says, five hundred Iroquois and one hundred Shawanoes. Membré says that the allies were Miamis. He is no doubt right, as the Miamis had promised their aid, and the Shawanoes were at peace with the Illinois. Tonty is silent on the point.

high, the Illinois began, after their fashion, to charge; that is, they leaped, yelled, and shot off bullets and arrows, advancing as they did so; while the Iroquois replied with gymnastics no less agile, and howlings no less terrific, mingled with the rapid clatter of their guns. Tonty saw that it would go hard with his allies. It was of the last moment to stop the fight, if possible. The Iroquois were, or professed to be, at peace with the French; and, taking counsel of his courage, he resolved on an attempt to mediate, which may well be called a desperate one. He laid aside his gun, took in his hand a wampum belt as a flag of truce, and walked forward to meet the savage multitude, attended by Boisrondet, another Frenchman, and a young Illinois who had the hardihood to accompany him. The guns of the Iroquois still flashed thick and fast. Some of them were aimed at him, on which he sent back the two Frenchmen and the Illinois, and advanced alone, holding out the wampum belt.[1] A moment more, and he was among the infuriated warriors. It was a frightful spectacle: the contorted forms, bounding, crouching, twisting, to deal or dodge the shot; the small keen eyes that shone like an angry snake's; the parted lips pealing their fiendish yells; the painted features writhing with fear and fury, and every passion of an Indian fight; man, wolf, and devil, all in one.[2] With his swarthy com-

[1] Membré says that he went with Tonty: "J'étois aussi à côté du Sieur de Tonty." This is an invention of the friar's vanity. "Les deux pères Récollets étoient alors dans une cabane à une lieue du village, où ils s'étoient retirés pour faire une espèce de retraite, et ils ne furent avertis de l'arrivée des Iroquois que dans le temps du combat."—*Relation des Découvertes*. "Je rencontrai en chemin les pères Gabriel et Zenobe Membré, qui cherchoient de mes nouvelles."—Tonty, *Mémoire, 1693*. This was on his return from the Iroquois. The *Relation* confirms the statement, as far as concerns Membré: "Il rencontra le Père Zenobe [*Membré*], qui venoit pour le secourir, aiant été averti du combat et de sa blessure."

The perverted *Dernières Découvertes*, published without authority, under Tonty's name, says that he was attended by a slave, whom the Illinois sent with him as interpreter. In his narrative of 1684, Tonty speaks of a Sokokis (Saco) Indian who was with the Iroquois, and who spoke French enough to serve as interpreter.

[2] Being once in an encampment of Sioux when a quarrel broke out, and the adverse factions raised the war-whoop and began to fire at each other, I had a good, though for the moment a rather dangerous, opportunity of seeing the demeanor of Indians at the beginning of a fight. The fray was quelled before much mischief was done, by the vigorous intervention of the elder warriors, who ran between the combatants.

plexion and his half-savage dress, they thought he was an Indian, and thronged about him, glaring murder. A young warrior stabbed at his heart with a knife, but the point glanced aside against a rib, inflicting only a deep gash. A chief called out that, as his ears were not pierced, he must be a Frenchman. On this, some of them tried to stop the bleeding, and led him to the rear, where an angry parley ensued, while the yells and firing still resounded in the front. Tonty, breathless, and bleeding at the mouth with the force of the blow he had received, found words to declare that the Illinois were under the protection of the king and the governor of Canada, and to demand that they should be left in peace.[1]

A young Iroquois snatched Tonty's hat, placed it on the end of his gun, and displayed it to the Illinois, who, thereupon, thinking he was killed, renewed the fight; and the firing in front clattered more angrily than before. A warrior ran in, crying out that the Iroquois were giving ground, and that there were Frenchmen among the Illinois, who fired at them. On this, the clamor around Tonty was redoubled. Some wished to kill him at once; others resisted. "I was never," he writes, "in such perplexity, for at that moment there was an Iroquois behind me, with a knife in his hand, lifting my hair as if he were going to scalp me. I thought it was all over with me, and that my best hope was that they would knock me in the head instead of burning me, as I believed they would do." In fact, a Seneca chief demanded that he should be burned; while an Onondaga chief, a friend of La Salle, was for setting him free. The dispute grew fierce and hot. Tonty told them that the Illinois were twelve hundred strong, and that sixty Frenchmen were at the village, ready to back them. This invention, though not fully believed, had no little effect. The friendly Onondaga carried his point; and the Iroquois, having failed to surprise their enemies, as they had hoped, now saw an opportunity to delude them by a truce. They sent back Tonty with a belt of peace: he held it aloft in sight of the Illinois; chiefs and old warriors ran to stop the fight; the yells

---

[1] "Je leur fis connoistre que les Islinois étoient sous la protection du roy de France et du gouverneur du pays, que j'estois surpris qu'ils voulussent rompre avec les François et qu'ils voulussent *attendre* [sic] à une paix."— Tonty, *Mémoire, 1693.*

and the firing ceased; and Tonty, like one waked from a hideous nightmare, dizzy, almost fainting with loss of blood,
staggered across the intervening prairie, to rejoin his friends.
He was met by the two friars, Ribourde and Membré, who,
in their secluded hut, a league from the village, had but lately
heard of what was passing, and who now, with benedictions
and thanksgiving, ran to embrace him as a man escaped from
the jaws of death.

The Illinois now withdrew, re-embarking in their canoes,
and crossing again to their lodges; but scarcely had they
reached them, when their enemies appeared at the edge of the
forest on the opposite bank. Many found means to cross, and,
under the pretext of seeking for provisions, began to hover in
bands about the skirts of the town, constantly increasing in
numbers. Had the Illinois dared to remain, a massacre would
doubtless have ensued; but they knew their foe too well, set
fire to their lodges, embarked in haste, and paddled down the
stream to rejoin their women and children at the sanctuary
among the morasses. The whole body of the Iroquois now
crossed the river, took possession of the abandoned town,
building for themselves a rude redoubt or fort of the trunks
of trees and of the posts and poles forming the framework of
the lodges which escaped the fire. Here they ensconced themselves, and finished the work of havoc at their leisure.

Tonty and his companions still occupied their hut; but the
Iroquois, becoming suspicious of them, forced them to remove to the fort, crowded as it was with the savage crew. On
the second day, there was an alarm. The Illinois appeared in
numbers on the low hills, half a mile behind the town; and
the Iroquois, who had felt their courage, and who had been
told by Tonty that they were twice as numerous as themselves, showed symptoms of no little uneasiness. They proposed that he should act as mediator, to which he gladly
assented, and crossed the meadow towards the Illinois, accompanied by Membré, and by an Iroquois who was sent as
a hostage. The Illinois hailed the overtures with delight, gave
the ambassadors some refreshment, which they sorely needed,
and sent back with them a young man of their nation as a
hostage on their part. This indiscreet youth nearly proved the
ruin of the negotiation; for he was no sooner among the Iro-

quois than he showed such an eagerness to close the treaty, made such promises, professed such gratitude, and betrayed so rashly the numerical weakness of the Illinois, that he revived all the insolence of the invaders. They turned furiously upon Tonty, and charged him with having robbed them of the glory and the spoils of victory. "Where are all your Illinois warriors, and where are the sixty Frenchmen that you said were among them?" It needed all Tonty's tact and coolness to extricate himself from this new danger.

The treaty was at length concluded; but scarcely was it made, when the Iroquois prepared to break it, and set about constructing canoes of elm-bark, in which to attack the Illinois women and children in their island sanctuary. Tonty warned his allies that the pretended peace was but a snare for their destruction. The Iroquois, on their part, grew hourly more jealous of him, and would certainly have killed him, had it not been their policy to keep the peace with Frontenac and the French.

Several days after, they summoned him and Membré to a council. Six packs of beaver-skins were brought in; and the savage orator presented them to Tonty in turn, explaining their meaning as he did so. The first two were to declare that the children of Count Frontenac, that is, the Illinois, should not be eaten; the next was a plaster to heal Tonty's wound; the next was oil wherewith to anoint him and Membré, that they might not be fatigued in travelling; the next proclaimed that the sun was bright; and the sixth and last required them to decamp and go home.[1] Tonty thanked them for their gifts, but demanded when they themselves meant to go and leave the Illinois in peace. At this, the conclave grew angry; and, despite their late pledge, some of them said that before they went they would eat Illinois flesh. Tonty instantly kicked away the packs of beaver-skins, the Indian symbol of the

[1] An Indian speech, it will be remembered, is without validity, if not confirmed by presents, each of which has its special interpretation. The meaning of the fifth pack of beaver, informing Tonty that the sun was bright, — "que le soleil étoit beau," that is, that the weather was favorable for travelling, — is curiously misconceived by the editor of the *Dernières Découvertes*, who improves upon his original by substituting the words "par le cinquième paquet *ils nous exhortoient à adorer le Soleil*."

scornful rejection of a proposal; telling them that, since they meant to eat the governor's children, he would have none of their presents. The chiefs, in a rage, rose and drove him from the lodge. The French withdrew to their hut, where they stood all night on the watch, expecting an attack, and resolved to sell their lives dearly. At daybreak, the chiefs ordered them to begone.

Tonty, with admirable fidelity and courage, had done all in the power of man to protect the allies of Canada against their ferocious assailants; and he thought it unwise to persist farther in a course which could lead to no good, and which would probably end in the destruction of the whole party. He embarked in a leaky canoe with Membré, Ribourde, Boisrondet, and the remaining two men, and began to ascend the river. After paddling about five leagues, they landed to dry their baggage and repair their crazy vessel; when Father Ribourde, breviary in hand, strolled across the sunny meadows for an hour of meditation among the neighboring groves. Evening approached, and he did not return. Tonty, with one of the men, went to look for him; and, following his tracks, presently discovered those of a band of Indians, who had apparently seized or murdered him. Still, they did not despair. They fired their guns to guide him, should he still be alive; built a huge fire by the bank, and then, crossing the river, lay watching it from the other side. At midnight, they saw the figure of a man hovering around the blaze; then many more appeared, but Ribourde was not among them. In truth, a band of Kickapoos, enemies of the Iroquois, about whose camp they had been prowling in quest of scalps, had met and wantonly murdered the inoffensive old man. They carried his scalp to their village, and danced around it in triumph, pretending to have taken it from an enemy. Thus, in his sixty-fifth year, the only heir of a wealthy Burgundian house perished under the war-clubs of the savages for whose salvation he had renounced station, ease, and affluence.[1]

Meanwhile, a hideous scene was enacted at the ruined vil-

[1] Tonty, *Mémoire*; Membré in Le Clerc, II. 191. Hennepin, who hated Tonty, unjustly charges him with having abandoned the search too soon, admitting, however, that it would have been useless to continue it. This part of his narrative is a perversion of Membré's account.

lage of the Illinois. Their savage foes, balked of a living prey, wreaked their fury on the dead. They dug up the graves; they threw down the scaffolds. Some of the bodies they burned; some they threw to the dogs; some, it is affirmed, they ate.[1] Placing the skulls on stakes as trophies, they turned to pursue the Illinois, who, when the French withdrew, had abandoned their asylum and retreated down the river. The Iroquois, still, it seems, in awe of them, followed them along the opposite bank, each night encamping face to face with them; and thus the adverse bands moved slowly southward, till they were near the mouth of the river. Hitherto, the compact array of the Illinois had held their enemies in check; but now, suffering from hunger, and lulled into security by the assurances of the Iroquois that their object was not to destroy them, but only to drive them from the country, they rashly separated into their several tribes. Some descended the Mississippi; some, more prudent, crossed to the western side. One of their principal tribes, the Tamaroas, more credulous than the rest, had the fatuity to remain near the mouth of the Illinois, where they were speedily assailed by all the force of the Iroquois. The men fled, and very few of them were killed; but the women and children were captured to the number, it is said, of seven hundred.[2] Then followed that scene of torture, of which, some two weeks later, La Salle saw the revolting traces.[3] Sated, at length, with horrors, the conquerors withdrew, leading with them a host of captives, and exulting in their triumphs over women, children, and the dead.

After the death of Father Ribourde, Tonty and his companions remained searching for him till noon of the next day,

---

[1] "Cependant les Iroquois, aussitôt après le départ du S⁻ de Tonty, exercèrent leur rage sur les corps morts des Ilinois, qu'ils déterrèrent ou abbattèrent de dessus les échafauds où les Ilinois les laissent longtemps exposés avant que de les mettre en terre. Ils en brûlèrent la plus grande partie, ils en mangèrent même quelques uns, et jettèrent le reste aux chiens. Ils plantèrent les têtes de ces cadavres à demi décharnés sur des pieux," etc.—*Relation des Découvertes*.

[2] *Relation des Découvertes*; Frontenac to the King, *N.Y. Col. Docs.*, IX. 147. A memoir of Duchesneau makes the number twelve hundred.

[3] "Ils [*les Illinois*] trouvèrent dans leur campement des carcasses de leurs enfans que ces anthropophages avoient mangez, ne voulant même d'autre nourriture que la chair de ces infortunez."—*La Potherie*, II. 145, 146. Compare *note, ante,* p. 863.

and then in despair of again seeing him, resumed their journey. They ascended the river, leaving no token of their passage at the junction of its northern and southern branches. For food, they gathered acorns and dug roots in the meadows. Their canoe proved utterly worthless; and, feeble as they were, they set out on foot for Lake Michigan. Boisrondet wandered off, and was lost. He had dropped the flint of his gun, and he had no bullets; but he cut a pewter porringer into slugs, with which he shot wild turkeys, by discharging his piece with a firebrand; and after several days he had the good fortune to rejoin the party. Their object was to reach the Pottawattamies of Green Bay. Had they aimed at Michillimackinac, they would have found an asylum with La Forest at the fort on the St. Joseph; but unhappily they passed westward of that post, and, by way of Chicago, followed the borders of Lake Michigan northward. The cold was intense; and it was no easy task to grub up wild onions from the frozen ground to save themselves from starving. Tonty fell ill of a fever and a swelling of the limbs, which disabled him from travelling, and hence ensued a long delay. At length, they neared Green Bay, where they would have starved, had they not gleaned a few ears of corn and frozen squashes in the fields of an empty Indian town.

This enabled them to reach the bay, and, having patched an old canoe which they had the good luck to find, they embarked in it; whereupon, says Tonty, "there rose a north-west wind, which lasted five days, with driving snow. We consumed all our food; and, not knowing what to do next, we resolved to go back to the deserted town, and die by a warm fire in one of the wigwams. On our way, we saw a smoke: but our joy was short; for, when we reached the fire, we found nobody there. We spent the night by it; and before morning the bay froze. We tried to break a way for our canoe through the ice, but could not; and therefore we determined to stay there another night, and make moccasins, in order to reach the town. We made some out of Father Gabriel's cloak. I was angry with Étienne Renault for not finishing his; but he excused himself on account of illness, because he had a great oppression of the stomach, caused by eating a piece of an Indian shield, of rawhide, which he could not digest. His delay proved our salvation; for the next day, December fourth, as I was urging him to finish the moccasins, and he was still excusing himself on the score of his malady, a party of Kiskakon Ottawas, who were on their way to the Potta-wattamies, saw the smoke of our fire, and came to us. We gave them such a welcome as was never seen before. They took us into their canoes, and carried us to an Indian village, only two leagues off. There we found five Frenchmen, who received us kindly, and all the Indians seemed to take pleasure in sending us food; so that, after thirty-four days of starva-tion, we found our famine turned to abundance."

This hospitable village belonged to the Pottawattamies, and was under the sway of the chief who had befriended La Salle the year before, and who was wont to say that he knew but three great captains in the world, — Frontenac, La Salle, and himself.[1]

[1] Membré in Le Clerc, II. 199. The other authorities for the foregoing chap-ter are the letters of La Salle, the *Relation des Découvertes*, in which portions of them are embodied, and the two narratives of Tonty, of 1684 and 1693. They all agree in essential points.

In his letters of this period, La Salle dwells at great length on the devices by which, as he believed, his enemies tried to ruin him and his enterprise. He is particularly severe against the Jesuit Allouez, whom he charges with intriguing "pour commencer la guerre entre les Iroquois et les Illinois par le moyen des Miamis qu'on engageoit dans cette négociation afin ou de me faire massacrer avec mes gens par quelqu'une de ces nations ou de me brouiller avec les Iroquois." — *Lettre (à Thouret?)*, *22 Août, 1682*. He gives in detail the circumstances on which this suspicion rests, but which are not convincing. He says, farther, that the Jesuits gave out that Tonty was dead, in order to discourage the men going to his relief, and that Allouez encouraged the de-serters, "leur servoit de conseil, bénit mesme leurs balles, et les asseura plu-sieurs fois que M. de Tonty auroit la teste cassée." He also affirms that great pains were taken to spread the report that he was himself dead. A Kiskakon Indian, he says, was sent to Tonty with a story to this effect; while a Huron named Scortas was sent to him (La Salle) with false news of the death of Tonty. The latter confirms this statement, and adds that the Illinois had been told "que M. de la Salle estoit venu en leur pays pour les donner à manger aux Iroquois."

THE ILLINOIS TOWN

The Site of the Great Illinois Town.—This has not till now been determined, though there have been various conjectures concerning it. From a study of the contemporary documents and maps, I became satisfied, first, that the branch of the river Illinois, called the "Big Vermilion," was the *Aramoni* of the French explorers; and, secondly, that the cliff called "Starved Rock" was that known to the French as *Le Rocher*, or the Rock of St. Louis. If I was right in this conclusion, then the position of the Great Village was established; for there is abundant proof that it was on the north side of the river, above the Aramoni, and below Le Rocher. I accordingly went to the village of Utica, which, as I judged by the map, was very near the point in question, and mounted to the top of one of the hills immediately behind it, whence I could see the valley of the Illinois for miles, bounded on the farther side by a range of hills, in some parts rocky and precipitous, and in others covered with forests. Far on the right was a gap in these hills, through which the Big Vermilion flowed to join the Illinois; and somewhat towards the left, at the distance of a mile and a half, was a huge cliff, rising perpendicularly from the opposite margin of the river. This I assumed to be *Le Rocher* of the French, though from where I stood I was unable to discern the distinctive features which I was prepared to find in it. In every other respect, the scene before me was precisely what I had expected to see. There was a meadow on the hither side of the river, on which stood a farm-house; and this, as it seemed to me, by its relations with surrounding objects, might be supposed to stand in the midst of the space once occupied by the Illinois town.

On the way down from the hill, I met Mr. James Clark, the principal inhabitant of Utica, and one of the earliest settlers of this region. I accosted him, told him my objects, and requested a half hour's conversation with him, at his leisure. He seemed interested in the inquiry, and said he would visit me early in the evening at the inn, where, accordingly, he soon appeared. The conversation took place in the porch, where a number of farmers and others were gathered. I asked Mr. Clark if any Indian remains were found in the neighborhood. "Yes," he replied, "plenty of them." I then inquired if there was any one spot where they were more numerous than elsewhere. "Yes," he answered again, pointing towards the farm-house on the meadow: "on my farm down yonder by the river, my tenant ploughs up teeth and bones by the peck every spring, besides arrow-heads, beads, stone hatchets, and other things of that sort." I replied that this was precisely what I had expected, as I had been led to believe that the principal town of the Illinois Indians once covered that very spot. "If," I added, "I am right in this belief, the great rock beyond the river is the one which the first explorers occupied as a fort; and I can describe it to you from their accounts of it, though I have never seen it, except from the top of the hill where the trees on and around it prevented me from seeing any part but the front." The men present now gathered around to listen. "The rock," I continued, "is nearly a hundred and fifty feet high, and rises directly from the water. The front and two sides are perpendicular and inaccessible; but there is one place where it is possible for a man to climb up, though with difficulty. The top is large enough and level enough for houses and fortifications." Here several of the men exclaimed: "That's just it." "You've hit it exactly." I then asked if there was any other rock on that side of the river which could answer to the description. They all agreed that there was no such rock on either side, along the whole length of the river. I then said: "If the Indian town was in the place where I suppose it to have been, I can tell you the nature of the country which lies behind the hills on the farther side of the river, though I know nothing about it, except what I have learned from writings nearly two centuries old. From the top of the hills, you look out upon a great prairie reaching as far as you can see, except that it is crossed by a belt of woods, following the course of a stream which enters the main river a few miles below." (See *ante*, p. 869, *note*.) "You are exactly right again," replied Mr. Clark, "we call that belt of timber the 'Vermilion Woods,' and the stream is the Big Vermilion." "Then," I said, "the Big Vermilion is the river which the French called the Aramoni; 'Starved Rock' is the same on which they built a fort called St. Louis, in the year 1682; and your farm is on the site of the great town of the Illinois."

I spent the next day in examining these localities, and was fully confirmed in my conclusions. Mr. Clark's tenant showed me the spot where the human bones were ploughed up. It was no doubt the graveyard violated by the Iroquois. The Illinois returned to the village after their defeat, and long continued to occupy it. The scattered bones were probably collected and restored to their place of burial.

Chapter XVII

1680

THE ADVENTURES OF HENNEPIN

Hennepin an Impostor • His Pretended Discovery • His Actual Discovery • Captured by the Sioux • The Upper Mississippi

---

IT was on the last day of the winter that preceded the invasion of the Iroquois that Father Hennepin, with his two companions, Accau and Du Gay, had set out from Fort Crèvecœur to explore the Illinois to its mouth. It appears from his own later statements, as well as from those of Tonty, that more than this was expected of him, and that La Salle had instructed him to explore, not alone the Illinois, but also the Upper Mississippi. That he actually did so, there is no reasonable doubt; and, could he have contented himself with telling the truth, his name would have stood high as a bold and vigorous discoverer. But his vicious attempts to malign his commander, and plunder him of his laurels, have wrapped his genuine merit in a cloud.

Hennepin's first book was published soon after his return from his travels, and while La Salle was still alive. In it, he relates the accomplishment of the instructions given him, without the smallest intimation that he did more.[1] Fourteen years after, when La Salle was dead, he published another edition of his travels,[2] in which he advanced a new and surprising pretension. Reasons connected with his personal safety, he declares, before compelled him to remain silent; but a time at length has come when the truth must be revealed. And he proceeds to affirm that, before ascending the Mississippi, he, with his two men, explored its whole course from the Illinois to the sea, thus anticipating the discovery which forms the crowning laurel of La Salle.

"I am resolved," he says, "to make known here to the whole world the mystery of this discovery, which I have hith-

---

[1] *Description de la Louisiane, nouvellement découverte*, Paris, 1683.

[2] *Nouvelle Découverte d'un très grand Pays situé dans l'Amérique*, Utrecht, 1697.

erto concealed, that I might not offend the Sieur de la Salle, who wished to keep all the glory and all the knowledge of it to himself. It is for this that he sacrificed many persons whose lives he exposed, to prevent them from making known what they had seen, and thereby crossing his secret plans. . . . I was certain that, if I went down the Mississippi, he would not fail to traduce me to my superiors for not taking the northern route, which I was to have followed in accordance with his desire and the plan we had made together. But I saw myself on the point of dying of hunger, and knew not what to do; because the two men who were with me threatened openly to leave me in the night, and carry off the canoe, and every thing in it, if I prevented them from going down the river to the nations below. Finding myself in this dilemma, I thought that I ought not to hesitate, and that I ought to prefer my own safety to the violent passion which possessed the Sieur de la Salle of enjoying alone the glory of this discovery. The two men, seeing that I had made up my mind to follow them, promised me entire fidelity; so, after we had shaken hands together as a mutual pledge, we set out on our voyage."[1]

He then proceeds to recount at length the particulars of his alleged exploration. The story was distrusted from the first.[2] Why had he not told it before? An excess of modesty, a lack of self-assertion, or a too sensitive reluctance to wound the susceptibilities of others, had never been found among his foibles. Yet some, perhaps, might have believed him, had he not, in the first edition of his book, gratuitously and distinctly declared that he did not make the voyage in question. "We had some designs," he says, "of going down the river Colbert [Mississippi] as far as its mouth; but the tribes that took us prisoners gave us no time to navigate this river both up and down."[3]

In declaring to the world the achievement which he had so long concealed and so explicitly denied, the worthy mission-

---

[1] *Nouvelle Découverte*, 248, 250, 251.

[2] See the preface of the Spanish translation by Don Sebastian Fernandez de Medrano, 1699, and also the letter of Gravier, dated 1701, in Shea's *Early Voyages on the Mississippi*. Barcia, Charlevoix, Kalm, and other early writers, put a low value on Hennepin's veracity.

[3] *Description de la Louisiane*, 218.

ary found himself in serious embarrassment. In his first book, he had stated that, on the twelfth of March, he left the mouth of the Illinois on his way northward, and that, on the eleventh of April, he was captured by the Sioux, near the mouth of the Wisconsin, five hundred miles above. This would give him only a month to make his alleged canoe-voyage from the Illinois to the Gulf of Mexico, and again upward to the place of his capture,—a distance of three thousand two hundred and sixty miles. With his means of transportation, three months would have been insufficient.[1] He saw the difficulty; but, on the other hand, he saw that he could not greatly change either date without confusing the parts of his narrative which preceded and which followed. In this perplexity, he chose a middle course, which only involved him in additional contradictions. Having, as he affirms, gone down to the Gulf and returned to the mouth of the Illinois, he set out thence to explore the river above; and he assigns the twenty-fourth of April as the date of this departure. This gives him forty-three days for his voyage to the mouth of the river and back. Looking farther, we find that, having left the Illinois on the twenty-fourth, he paddled his canoe two hundred leagues northward, and was then captured by the Sioux on the twelfth of the same month. In short, he ensnares himself in a hopeless confusion of dates.[2]

Here, one would think, is sufficient reason for rejecting his story; and yet the general truth of the descriptions, and a certain verisimilitude which marks it, might easily deceive a careless reader, and perplex a critical one. These, however, are

[1] La Salle, in the following year, with a far better equipment, was more than three months and a half in making the journey. A Mississippi trading-boat of the last generation, with sails and oars, ascending against the current, was thought to do remarkably well if it could make twenty miles a day. Hennepin, if we believe his own statements, must have ascended at an average rate of sixty miles, though his canoe was large and heavily laden.

[2] Hennepin here falls into gratuitous inconsistencies. In the edition of 1697, in order to gain a little time, he says that he left the Illinois on his voyage southward on the eighth of March, 1680; and yet, in the preceding chapter, he repeats the statement of the first edition, that he was detained at the Illinois by floating ice till the twelfth. Again, he says, in the first edition, that he was captured by the Sioux on the eleventh of April; and, in the edition of 1697, he changes this date to the twelfth, without gaining any advantage by doing so.

easily explained. Six years before Hennepin published his pretended discovery, his brother friar, Father Chrétien Le Clerc, published an account of the Récollet missions among the Indians, under the title of "Établissement de la Foi." This book, offensive to the Jesuits, is said to have been suppressed by order of government; but a few copies fortunately survive.[1] One of these is now before me. It contains the journal of Father Zenobe Membré, on his descent of the Mississippi in 1681, in company with La Salle. The slightest comparison of his narrative with that of Hennepin is sufficient to show that the latter framed his own story out of incidents and descriptions furnished by his brother missionary, often using his very words, and sometimes copying entire pages, with no other alterations than such as were necessary to make himself, instead of La Salle and his companions, the hero of the exploit. The records of literary piracy may be searched in vain for an act of depredation more recklessly impudent.[2]

Such being the case, what faith can we put in the rest of Hennepin's story? Fortunately, there are tests by which the earlier parts of his book can be tried; and, on the whole, they square exceedingly well with contemporary records of un-

[1] Le Clerc's book had been made the text of an attack on the Jesuits. See *Reflexions sur un Livre intitulé Premier Établissement de la Foi.* This piece is printed in the *Morale Pratique des Jésuites.*

[2] Hennepin may have copied from the unpublished journal of Membré, which the latter had placed in the hands of his Superior, or he may have compiled from Le Clerc's book, relying on the suppression of the edition to prevent detection. He certainly saw and used it; for he elsewhere borrows the exact words of the editor. He is so careless that he steals from Membré passages which he might easily have written for himself; as, for example, a description of the opossum and another of the cougar, animals with which he was acquainted. Compare the following pages of the *Nouvelle Découverte* with the corresponding pages of Le Clerc: Hennepin, 252, Le Clerc, II. 217; H. 253, Le C. II. 218; H. 257, Le C. II. 221; H. 259, Le C. II. 224; H. 262, Le C. II. 226; H. 265, Le C. II. 229; H. 267, Le C. II. 233; H. 270, Le C. II. 235; H. 280, Le C. II. 240; H. 295, Le C. II. 249; H. 296, Le C. II. 250; H. 297, Le C. II. 253; H. 299, Le C. II. 254; H. 301, Le C. II. 257. Some of these parallel passages will be found in Sparks's *Life of La Salle*, where this remarkable fraud was first fully exposed. In Shea's *Discovery of the Mississippi*, there is an excellent critical examination of Hennepin's works. His plagiarisms from Le Clerc are not confined to the passages cited above; for, in his later editions, he stole largely from other parts of the suppressed *Établissement de la Foi.*

doubted authenticity. Bating his exaggerations respecting the Falls of Niagara, his local descriptions, and even his estimates of distance, are generally accurate. He constantly, it is true, magnifies his own acts, and thrusts himself forward as one of the chiefs of an enterprise, to the costs of which he had contributed nothing, and to which he was merely an appendage; and yet, till he reaches the Mississippi, there can be no doubt that in the main he tells the truth. As for his ascent of that river to the country of the Sioux, the general statement is fully confirmed by La Salle, Tonty, and other contemporary writers.[1] For the details of the journey, we must rest on Hennepin alone, whose account of the country, and of the peculiar traits of its Indian occupants, afford, as far as they go, good evidence of truth. Indeed, this part of his narrative could only have been written by one well versed in the savage life of this north-western region.[2] Trusting, then, to his own guidance in

[1] It is certain that persons having the best means of information believed at the time in Hennepin's story of his journeys on the Upper Mississippi. The compiler of the *Relation des Découvertes*, who was in close relations with La Salle and those who acted with him, does not intimate a doubt of the truth of the report which Hennepin on his return gave to the Provincial Commissary of his Order, and which is in substance the same which he published two years later. The *Relation*, it is to be observed, was written only a few months after the return of Hennepin, and embodies the pith of his narrative of the Upper Mississippi, no part of which had then been published.

[2] In this connection, it is well to examine the various Sioux words which Hennepin uses incidentally, and which he must have acquired by personal intercourse with the tribe, as no Frenchman then understood the language. These words, as far as my information reaches, are in every instance correct. Thus, he says that the Sioux called his breviary a "bad spirit," — *Ouackanché*. *Wakanshe*, or *Wakanshecha*, would express the same meaning in modern English spelling. He says elsewhere that they called the guns of his companions *Manzaouackanché*, which he translates, "iron possessed with a bad spirit." The western Sioux to this day call a gun *Manzawakan*, "metal possessed with a spirit." *Chonga* (*shonka*), "a dog," *Ouasi* (*wahsee*), "a pine-tree," *Chinnen* (*shinnan*), "a robe," or "garment," and other words, are given correctly, with their interpretations. The word *Louis*, affirmed by Hennepin to mean "the sun," seems at first sight a wilful inaccuracy, as this is not the word used in general by the Sioux. The Yankton band of this people, however, call the sun *oouee*, which, it is evident, represents the French pronunciation of *Louis*, omitting the initial letter. This Hennepin would be apt enough to supply, thereby conferring a compliment alike on himself, Louis Hennepin, and on the king, Louis XIV., who, to the indignation of his brother monarchs, had chosen the sun as his emblem.

the absence of better, let us follow in the wake of his adventurous canoe.

It was laden deeply with goods belonging to La Salle, and meant by him as presents to Indians on the way, though the travellers, it appears, proposed to use them in trading on their own account. The friar was still wrapped in his gray capote and hood, shod with sandals, and decorated with the cord of St. Francis. As for his two companions, Accau[1] and Du Gay, it is tolerably clear that the former was the real leader of the party, though Hennepin, after his custom, thrusts himself into the foremost place. Both were somewhat above the station of ordinary hired hands; and Du Gay had an uncle who was an ecclesiastic of good credit at Amiens, his native place.

In the forests that overhung the river, the buds were feebly swelling with advancing spring. There was game enough. They killed buffalo, deer, beavers, wild turkeys, and now and then a bear swimming in the river. With these, and the fish which they caught in abundance, they fared sumptuously, though it was the season of Lent. They were exemplary, however, at their devotions. Hennepin said prayers at morning and night, and the *angelus* at noon, adding a petition to St. Anthony of Padua, that he would save them from the peril that beset their way. In truth, there was a lion in the path. The ferocious character of the Sioux, or Dacotah, who occupied the region of the Upper Mississippi, was already known to the French; and Hennepin, with excellent reason, prayed that it might be his fortune to meet them, not by night, but by day.

On the eleventh or twelfth of April, they stopped in the afternoon to repair their canoe; and Hennepin busied himself in daubing it with pitch, while the others cooked a turkey. Suddenly, a fleet of Sioux canoes swept into sight, bearing a

---

Various trivial incidents touched upon by Hennepin, while recounting his life among the Sioux, seem to me to afford a strong presumption of an actual experience. I speak on this point with the more confidence, as the Indians in whose lodges I was once domesticated for several weeks belonged to a western band of the same people.

[1] Called Ako by Hennepin. In contemporary documents, it is written Accau, Acau, D'Accau, Dacau, Dacan, and D'Accault.

war-party of a hundred and twenty naked savages, who, on seeing the travellers, raised a hideous clamor; and, some leaping ashore and others into the water, they surrounded the astonished Frenchmen in an instant.[1] Hennepin held out the peace-pipe; but one of them snatched it from him. Next, he hastened to proffer a gift of Martinique tobacco, which was better received. Some of the old warriors repeated the name *Miamiha*, giving him to understand that they were a war-party, on the way to attack the Miamis; on which, Hennepin, with the help of signs and of marks which he drew on the sand with a stick, explained that the Miamis had gone across the Mississippi, beyond their reach. Hereupon, he says that three or four old men placed their hands on his head, and began a dismal wailing; while he with his handkerchief wiped away their tears, in order to evince sympathy with their affliction, from whatever cause arising. Notwithstanding this demonstration of tenderness, they refused to smoke with him in his peace-pipe, and forced him and his companions to embark, and paddle across the river; while they all followed behind, uttering yells and howlings which froze the missionary's blood.

On reaching the farther side, they made their camp-fires, and allowed their prisoners to do the same. Accau and Du Gay slung their kettle; while Hennepin, to propitiate the Sioux, carried to them two turkeys, of which there were several in the canoe. The warriors had seated themselves in a ring, to debate on the fate of the Frenchmen; and two chiefs presently explained to the friar, by significant signs, that it had been resolved that his head should be split with a war-club. This produced the effect which was no doubt intended. Hennepin ran to the canoe, and quickly returned with one of the men, both loaded with presents, which he threw into the midst of the assembly; and then, bowing his head, offered them at the same time a hatchet with which to kill him, if they wished to do so. His gifts and his submission seemed to appease them. They gave him and his companions a dish of beaver's flesh; but, to his great concern, they returned his

[1] The edition of 1683 says that there were thirty-three canoes: that of 1697 raises the number to fifty. The number of Indians is the same in both. The later narrative is more in detail than the former.

peace-pipe, an act which he interpreted as a sign of danger. That night, the Frenchmen slept little, expecting to be murdered before morning. There was, in fact, a great division of opinion among the Sioux. Some were for killing them and taking their goods; while others, eager above all things that French traders should come among them with the knives, hatchets, and guns of which they had heard the value, contended that it would be impolitic to discourage the trade by putting to death its pioneers.

Scarcely had morning dawned on the anxious captives, when a young chief, naked, and painted from head to foot, appeared before them, and asked for the pipe, which the friar gladly gave him. He filled it, smoked it, made the warriors do the same, and, having given this hopeful pledge of amity, told the Frenchmen that, since the Miamis were out of reach, the war-party would return home, and that they must accompany them. To this Hennepin gladly agreed, having, as he declares, his great work of exploration so much at heart that he rejoiced in the prospect of achieving it even in their company.

He soon, however, had a foretaste of the affliction in store for him; for, when he opened his breviary and began to mutter his morning devotion, his new companions gathered about him with faces that betrayed their superstitious terror, and gave him to understand that his book was a bad spirit with which he must hold no more converse. They thought, indeed, that he was muttering a charm for their destruction. Accau and Du Gay, conscious of the danger, begged the friar to dispense with his devotions, lest he and they alike should be tomahawked; but Hennepin says that his sense of duty rose superior to his fears, and that he was resolved to repeat his office at all hazards, though not until he had asked pardon of his two friends for thus imperilling their lives. Fortunately, he presently discovered a device by which his devotion and his prudence were completely reconciled. He ceased the muttering which had alarmed the Indians, and, with the breviary open on his knees, sang the service in loud and cheerful tones. As this had no savor of sorcery, and as they now imagined that the book was teaching its owner to sing for their amusement, they conceived a favorable opinion of both alike.

These Sioux, it may be observed, were the ancestors of

those who committed the horrible but not unprovoked massacres of 1863, in the valley of the St. Peter. Hennepin complains bitterly of their treatment of him, which, however, seems to have been tolerably good. Afraid that he would lag behind, as his canoe was heavy and slow,[1] they placed several warriors in it, to aid him and his men in paddling. They kept on their way from morning till night, building huts for their bivouac when it rained, and sleeping on the open ground when the weather was fair, which, says Hennepin, "gave us a good opportunity to contemplate the moon and stars." The three Frenchmen took the precaution of sleeping at the side of the young chief who had been the first to smoke the peace-pipe, and who seemed inclined to befriend them; but there was another chief, one Aquipaguetin, a crafty old savage, who, having lost a son in war with the Miamis, was angry that the party had abandoned their expedition, and thus deprived him of his revenge. He therefore kept up a dismal lament through half the night; while other old men, crouching over Hennepin as he lay trying to sleep, stroked him with their hands, and uttered wailings so lugubrious that he was forced to the belief that he had been doomed to death, and that they were charitably bemoaning his fate.[2]

One night, the captives were, for some reason, unable to bivouac near their protector, and were forced to make their fire at the end of the camp. Here they were soon beset by a crowd of Indians, who told them that Aquipaguetin had at length resolved to tomahawk them. The malcontents were gathered in a knot at a little distance, and Hennepin hastened to appease them by another gift of knives and tobacco. This was but one of the devices of the old chief to deprive them of their goods without robbing them outright. He had with him the bones of a deceased relative, which he was carrying home wrapped in skins prepared with smoke after the Indian

---

[1] And yet it had, by his account, made a distance of thirteen hundred and eighty miles from the mouth of the Mississippi upward in twenty-four days.

[2] This weeping and wailing over Hennepin once seemed to me an anomaly in his account of Sioux manners, as I am not aware that such practices are to be found among them at present. They are mentioned, however, by other early writers. Le Sueur, who was among them in 1699–1700, was wept over no less than Hennepin. See the abstract of his journal in La Harpe.

fashion, and gayly decorated with bands of dyed porcupine quills. He would summon his warriors, and, placing these relics in the midst of the assembly, call on all present to smoke in their honor; after which, Hennepin was required to offer a more substantial tribute in the shape of cloth, beads, hatchets, tobacco, and the like, to be laid upon the bundle of bones. The gifts thus acquired were then, in the name of the deceased, distributed among the persons present.

On one occasion, Aquipaguetin killed a bear, and invited the chiefs and warriors to feast upon it. They accordingly assembled on a prairie, west of the river, where, after the banquet, they danced a "medicine-dance." They were all painted from head to foot, with their hair oiled, garnished with red and white feathers, and powdered with the down of birds. In this guise, they set their arms akimbo, and fell to stamping with such fury that the hard prairie was dented with the prints of their moccasins; while the chief's son, crying at the top of his throat, gave to each in turn the pipe of war. Meanwhile, the chief himself, singing in a loud and rueful voice, placed his hands on the heads of the three Frenchmen, and from time to time interrupted his music to utter a vehement harangue. Hennepin could not understand the words, but his heart sank as the conviction grew strong within him that these ceremonies tended to his destruction. It seems, however, that, after all the chief's efforts, his party was in the minority, the greater part being adverse to either killing or robbing the three strangers.

Every morning, at daybreak, an old warrior shouted the signal of departure; and the recumbent savages leaped up, manned their birchen fleet, and piled their paddles against the current, often without waiting to break their fast. Sometimes they stopped for a buffalo-hunt on the neighboring prairies; and there was no lack of provisions. They passed Lake Pepin, which Hennepin called the Lake of Tears, by reason of the howlings and lamentations here uttered over him by Aquipaguetin; and, nineteen days after his capture, landed near the site of St. Paul. The father's sorrows now began in earnest. The Indians broke his canoe to pieces, having first hidden their own among the alder-bushes. As they belonged to different bands and different villages, their mutual jealousy now overcame all their prudence; and each proceeded to claim his share of the captives and the booty. Happily, they made an amicable distribution, or it would have fared ill with the three Frenchmen; and each taking his share, not forgetting the priestly vestments of Hennepin, the splendor of which they could not sufficiently admire, they set out across the country for their villages, which lay towards the north, in the neighborhood of Lake Buade, now called Mille Lac.

Being, says Hennepin, exceedingly tall and active, they walked at a prodigious speed, insomuch that no European could long keep pace with them. Though the month of May had begun, there were frosts at night; and the marshes and ponds were glazed with ice, which cut the missionary's legs as he waded through. They swam the larger streams, and Hennepin nearly perished with cold as he emerged from the icy current. His two companions, who were smaller than he, and who could not swim, were carried over on the backs of the Indians. They showed, however, no little endurance; and he declares that he should have dropped by the way, but for their support. Seeing him disposed to lag, the Indians, to spur him on, set fire to the dry grass behind him, and then, taking him by the hands, ran forward with him to escape the flames. To add to his misery, he was nearly famished, as they gave him only a small piece of smoked meat once a day, though it does not appear that they themselves fared better. On the fifth day, being by this time in extremity, he saw a crowd of squaws and children approaching over the prairie, and presently descried the bark lodges of an Indian town. The goal was reached. He was among the homes of the Sioux.

Chapter XVIII

1680, 1681

HENNEPIN AMONG THE SIOUX

Signs of Danger • Adoption • Hennepin and his Indian Relatives
• The Hunting Party • The Sioux Camp • Falls of St. Anthony •
A Vagabond Friar • His Adventures on the Mississippi • Greysolon
Du Lhut • Return to Civilization

As Hennepin entered the village, he beheld a sight which caused him to invoke St. Anthony of Padua. In front of the lodges were certain stakes, to which were attached bundles of straw, intended, as he supposed, for burning him and his friends alive. His concern was redoubled when he saw the condition of the Picard Du Gay, whose hair and face had been painted with divers colors, and whose head was decorated with a tuft of white feathers. In this guise, he was entering the village, followed by a crowd of Sioux, who compelled him to sing and keep time to his own music by rattling a dried gourd containing a number of pebbles. The omens, indeed, were exceedingly threatening; for treatment like this was usually followed by the speedy immolation of the captive. Hennepin ascribes it to the effect of his invocations, that, being led into one of the lodges, among a throng of staring squaws and children, he and his companions were seated on the ground, and presented with large dishes of birch bark, containing a mess of wild rice boiled with dried whortleberries; a repast which he declares to have been the best that had fallen to his lot since the day of his captivity.[1]

[1] The Sioux, or Dacotah, as they call themselves, were a numerous people, separated into three great divisions, which were again subdivided into bands. Those among whom Hennepin was a prisoner belonged to the division known as the Issanti, Issanyati, or, as he writes it, Issati, of which the principal band was the Meddewakantonwan. The other great divisions, the Yanktons and the Tintonwans, or Tetons, lived west of the Mississippi, extending beyond the Missouri, and ranging as far as the Rocky Mountains. The Issanti cultivated the soil; but the extreme western bands subsisted on the buffalo alone. The former had two kinds of dwelling,—the *teepee*, or skin lodge, and

894

This soothed his fears: but, as he allayed his famished appetite, he listened with anxious interest to the vehement jargon of the chiefs and warriors, who were disputing among themselves to whom the three captives should respectively belong; for it seems that, as far as related to them, the question of distribution had not yet been definitely settled. The debate ended in the assigning of Hennepin to his old enemy Aquipaguetin, who, however, far from persisting in his evil designs, adopted him on the spot as his son. The three companions must now part company. Du Gay, not yet quite reassured of his safety, hastened to confess himself to Hennepin; but Accau proved refractory, and refused the offices of religion, which did not prevent the friar from embracing them both, as he says, with an extreme tenderness. Tired as he was, he was forced to set out with his self-styled father to his village, which was fortunately not far off. An unpleasant walk of a few miles through woods and marshes brought them to the borders of a sheet of water, apparently Lake Buade, where five of Aquipaguetin's wives received the party

---

the bark lodge. The teepee, which was used by all the Sioux, consists of a covering of dressed buffalo hide, stretched on a conical stack of poles. The bark lodge was peculiar to the Eastern Sioux; and examples of it might be seen, until within a few years, among the bands on the St. Peter's. In its general character, it was like the Huron and Iroquois houses, but was inferior in construction. It had a ridge roof, framed of poles, extending from the posts which formed the sides; and the whole was covered with elm-bark. The lodges in the villages to which Hennepin was conducted were probably of this kind.

The name Sioux is an abbreviation of *Nadouessioux*, an Ojibwa word, meaning *enemies*. The Ojibwas used it to designate this people, and occasionally also the Iroquois, being at deadly war with both.

Rev. Stephen R. Riggs, for many years a missionary among the Issanti Sioux, says that this division consists of four distinct bands. They ceded all their lands east of the Mississippi to the United States in 1837, and lived on the St. Peter's till driven thence in consequence of the massacres of 1862, 1863. The Yankton Sioux consist of two bands, which are again subdivided. The Assiniboins, or Hohays, are an offshoot from the Yanktons, with whom they are now at war. The Tintonwan or Teton Sioux, forming the most western division, and the largest, comprise seven bands, and are among the bravest and fiercest tenants of the prairie.

The earliest French writers estimate the total number of the Sioux at forty thousand; but this is little better than conjecture. Mr. Riggs, in 1852, placed it at about twenty-five thousand.

in three canoes, and ferried them to an island on which the village stood.

At the entrance of the chief's lodge, Hennepin was met by a decrepit old Indian, withered with age, who offered him the peace-pipe, and placed him on a bear-skin which was spread by the fire. Here, to relieve his fatigue,—for he was well-nigh spent,—a small boy anointed his limbs with the fat of a wild-cat, supposed to be sovereign in these cases by reason of the great agility of that animal. His new father gave him a bark platter of fish, covered him with a buffalo-robe, and showed him six or seven of his wives, who were thenceforth, he was told, to regard him as a son. The chief's household was numerous; and his allies and relatives formed a considerable clan, of which the missionary found himself an involuntary member. He was scandalized when he saw one of his adopted brothers carrying on his back the bones of a deceased friend, wrapped in the chasuble of brocade which they had taken with other vestments from his box.

Seeing their new relative so enfeebled that he could scarcely stand, the Indians made for him one of their sweating baths,[1] where they immersed him in steam three times a week; a process from which he thinks he derived great benefit. His strength gradually returned, in spite of his meagre fare; for there was a dearth of food, and the squaws were less attentive to his wants than to those of their children. They respected him, however, as a person endowed with occult powers, and stood in no little awe of a pocket compass which he had with him, as well as of a small metal pot with feet moulded after the face of a lion. This last seemed in their eyes a "medicine" of the most formidable nature, and they would not touch it without first wrapping it in a beaver-skin. For the rest, Hennepin made himself useful in various ways. He shaved the heads of the children, as was the custom of the tribe; bled certain asthmatic persons; and dosed others with orvietan, the famous panacea of his time, of which he had brought with

[1] These baths consist of a small hut, covered closely with buffalo-skins, into which the patient and his friends enter, carefully closing every aperture. A pile of heated stones is placed in the middle, and water is poured upon them, raising a dense vapor. They are still (1868) in use among the Sioux and some other tribes.

him a good supply. With respect to his missionary functions, he seems to have given himself little trouble, unless his attempt to make a Sioux vocabulary is to be regarded as preparatory to a future apostleship. "I could gain nothing over them," he says, "in the way of their salvation, by reason of their natural stupidity." Nevertheless, on one occasion, he baptized a sick child, naming it Antoinette in honor of St. Anthony of Padua. It seemed to revive after the rite, but soon relapsed and presently died, "which," he writes, "gave me great joy and satisfaction." In this, he was like the Jesuits, who could find nothing but consolation in the death of a newly baptized infant, since it was thus assured of a paradise which, had it lived, it would probably have forfeited by sharing in the superstitions of its parents.

With respect to Hennepin and his Indian father, there seems to have been little love on either side; but Ouasicoudé, the principal chief of the Sioux of this region, was the fast friend of the three white men. He was angry that they had been robbed, which he had been unable to prevent, as the Sioux had no laws, and their chiefs little power; but he spoke his mind freely, and told Aquipaguetin and the rest, in full council, that they were like a dog who steals a piece of meat from a dish, and runs away with it. When Hennepin complained of hunger, the Indians had always promised him that early in the summer he should go with them on a buffalo hunt, and have food in abundance. The time at length came, and the inhabitants of all the neighboring villages prepared for departure. To each band was assigned its special hunting-ground, and he was expected to accompany his Indian father. To this he demurred; for he feared lest Aquipaguetin, angry at the words of the great chief, might take this opportunity to revenge the insult put upon him. He therefore gave out that he expected a party of "spirits," that is to say, Frenchmen, to meet him at the mouth of the Wisconsin, bringing a supply of goods for the Indians; and he declares that La Salle had in fact promised to send traders to that place. Be this as it may, the Indians believed him; and, true or false, the assertion, as will be seen, answered the purpose for which it was made.

The Indians set out in a body to the number of two

hundred and fifty warriors, with their women and children. The three Frenchmen, who, though in different villages, had occasionally met during the two months of their captivity, were all of the party. They descended Rum River, which forms the outlet of Mille Lac, and which is called the St. Francis by Hennepin. None of the Indians had offered to give him passage; and, fearing lest he should be abandoned, he stood on the bank, hailing the passing canoes and begging to be taken in. Accau and Du Gay presently appeared, paddling a small canoe which the Indians had given them; but they would not listen to the missionary's call, and Accau, who had no love for him, cried out that he had paddled him long enough already. Two Indians, however, took pity on him, and brought him to the place of encampment, where Du Gay tried to excuse himself for his conduct, but Accau was sullen and kept aloof.

After reaching the Mississippi, the whole party encamped together opposite to the mouth of Rum River, pitching their tents of skin, or building their bark huts, on the slope of a hill by the side of the water. It was a wild scene, this camp of savages among whom as yet no traders had come and no handiwork of civilization had found its way; the tall warriors, some nearly naked, some wrapped in buffalo-robes, and some in shirts of dressed deer-skin fringed with hair and embroidered with dyed porcupine quills, war-clubs of stone in their hands, and quivers at their backs filled with stone-headed arrows; the squaws, cutting smoke-dried meat with knives of flint, and boiling it in rude earthen pots of their own making, driving away, meanwhile, with shrill cries, the troops of lean dogs, which disputed the meal with a crew of hungry children. The whole camp, indeed, was threatened with starvation. The three white men could get no food but unripe berries, from the effects of which Hennepin thinks they might all have died, but for timely doses of his orvietan.

Being tired of the Indians, he became anxious to set out for the Wisconsin to find the party of Frenchmen, real or imaginary, who were to meet him at that place. That he was permitted to do so was due to the influence of the great chief Ouasicoudé, who always befriended him, and who had soundly berated his two companions for refusing him a seat in their canoe. Du Gay wished to go with him; but Accau, who liked the Indian life as much as he disliked Hennepin, preferred to remain with the hunters. A small birch canoe was given to the two adventurers, together with an earthen pot; and they had also between them a gun, a knife, and a robe of beaver-skin. Thus equipped, they began their journey, and soon approached the Falls of St. Anthony, so named by Hennepin in honor of the inevitable St. Anthony of Padua.[1] As they were carrying their canoe by the cataract, they saw five or six Indians, who had gone before, and one of whom had climbed into an oak-tree beside the principal fall, whence in a loud and lamentable voice he was haranguing the spirit of the waters, as a sacrifice to whom he had just hung a robe of beaver-skin among the branches.[2] Their attention was soon engrossed by another object. Looking over the edge of the cliff which overhung the river below the falls, Hennepin saw a snake, which, as he avers, was six feet long,[3] writhing upward towards the holes of the swallows in the face of the precipice, in order to devour their young. He pointed him out to Du Gay, and they pelted him with

[1] Hennepin's notice of the Falls of St. Anthony, though brief, is sufficiently accurate. He says, in his first edition, that they are forty or fifty feet high, but adds ten feet more in the edition of 1697. In 1821, according to Schoolcraft, the perpendicular fall measured forty feet. Great changes, however, have taken place here, and are still in progress. The rock is a very soft, friable sandstone, overlaid by a stratum of limestone; and it is crumbling with such rapidity under the action of the water that the cataract will soon be little more than a rapid. Other changes equally disastrous, in an artistic point of view, are going on even more quickly. Beside the falls stands a city, which, by an ingenious combination of the Greek and Sioux languages, has received the name of Minneapolis, or City of the Waters, and which, in 1867, contained ten thousand inhabitants, two national banks, and an opera-house; while its rival city of St. Anthony, immediately opposite, boasted a gigantic water-cure and a State university. In short, the great natural beauty of the place is utterly spoiled.

[2] Oanktayhee, the principal deity of the Sioux, was supposed to live under these falls, though he manifested himself in the form of a buffalo. It was he who created the earth, like the Algonquin Manabozho, from mud brought to him in the paws of a musk-rat. Carver, in 1766, saw an Indian throw every thing he had about him into the cataract as an offering to this deity.

[3] In the edition of 1683. In that of 1697, he has grown to seven or eight feet. The bank-swallows still make their nests in these cliffs, boring easily into the soft sandstone.

stones, till he fell into the river, but not before his contortions and the darting of his forked tongue had so affected the Picard's imagination that he was haunted that night with a terrific incubus.

They paddled sixty leagues down the river in the heats of July, and killed no large game but a single deer, the meat of which soon spoiled. Their main resource was the turtles, whose shyness and watchfulness caused them frequent disappointments and many involuntary fasts. They once captured one of more than common size; and, as they were endeavoring to cut off his head, he was near avenging himself by snapping off Hennepin's finger. There was a herd of buffalo in sight on the neighboring prairie; and Du Gay went with his gun in pursuit of them, leaving the turtle in Hennepin's custody. Scarcely was he gone when the friar, raising his eyes, saw that their canoe, which they had left at the edge of the water, had floated out into the current. Hastily turning the turtle on his back, he covered him with his habit of St. Francis, on which, for greater security, he laid a number of stones, and then, being a good swimmer, struck out in pursuit of the canoe, which he at length overtook. Finding that it would overset if he tried to climb into it, he pushed it before him to the shore, and then paddled towards the place, at some distance above, where he had left the turtle. He had no sooner reached it than he heard a strange sound, and beheld a long file of buffalo—bulls, cows, and calves—entering the water not far off, to cross to the western bank. Having no gun, as became his apostolic vocation, he shouted to Du Gay, who presently appeared, running in all haste, and they both paddled in pursuit of the game. Du Gay aimed at a young cow, and shot her in the head. She fell in shallow water near an island, where some of the herd had landed; and, being unable to drag her out, they waded into the water and butchered her where she lay. It was forty-eight hours since they had tasted food. Hennepin made a fire, while Du Gay cut up the meat. They feasted so bountifully that they both fell ill, and were forced to remain two days on the island, taking doses of orvietan, before they were able to resume their journey.

Apparently they were not sufficiently versed in woodcraft

to smoke the meat of the cow; and the hot sun soon robbed them of it. They had a few fish-hooks, but were not always successful in the use of them. On one occasion, being nearly famished, they set their line, and lay watching it, uttering prayers in turn. Suddenly, there was a great turmoil in the water. Du Gay ran to the line, and, with the help of Hennepin, drew in two large cat-fish.[1] The eagles, or fish-hawks, now and then dropped a newly caught fish, of which they gladly took possession; and once they found a purveyor in an otter which they saw by the bank, devouring some object of an appearance so wonderful that Du Gay cried out that he had a devil between his paws. They scared him from his prey, which proved to be a spade-fish, or, as Hennepin correctly describes it, a species of sturgeon, with a bony projection from his snout in the shape of a paddle. They broke their fast upon him, undeterred by this eccentric appendage.

If Hennepin had had an eye for scenery, he would have found in these his vagabond rovings wherewith to console himself in some measure for his frequent fasts. The young Mississippi, fresh from its northern springs, unstained as yet by unhallowed union with the riotous Missouri, flowed calmly on its way amid strange and unique beauties; a wilderness, clothed with velvet grass; forest-shadowed valleys; lofty heights, whose smooth slopes seemed levelled with the scythe; domes and pinnacles, ramparts and ruined towers, the work of no human hand. The canoe of the voyagers, borne on the tranquil current, glided in the shade of gray crags festooned with honeysuckles; by trees mantled with wild grape-vines, dells bright with the flowers of the white euphorbia, the blue gentian, and the purple balm; and matted forests, where the red squirrels leaped and chattered. They passed the great cliff whence the Indian maiden threw herself in her despair;[2] and Lake Pepin lay before them, slumbering in the

---

[1] Hennepin speaks of their size with astonishment, and says that the two together would weigh twenty-five pounds. Cat-fish have been taken in the Mississippi, weighing more than a hundred and fifty pounds.

[2] The "Lover's Leap," or "Maiden's Rock," from which a Sioux girl, Winona, or the "Eldest Born," is said to have thrown herself in the despair of disappointed affection. The story, which seems founded in truth, will be found, not without embellishments, in Mrs. Eastman's *Legends of the Sioux*.

July sun; the far-reaching sheets of sparkling water, the
woody slopes, the tower-like crags, the grassy heights basking
in sunlight or shadowed by the passing cloud; all the fair outline of its graceful scenery, the finished and polished master-
work of Nature. And when at evening they made their
bivouac fire, and drew up their canoe, while dim, sultry
clouds veiled the west, and the flashes of the silent heat-light-
ning gleamed on the leaden water, they could listen, as they
smoked their pipes, to the mournful cry of the whippoorwills
and the quavering scream of the owls.

Other thoughts than the study of the picturesque occupied
the mind of Hennepin, when one day he saw his Indian father, Aquipaguetin, whom he had supposed five hundred
miles distant, descending the river with ten warriors in canoes. He was eager to be the first to meet the traders, who,
as Hennepin had given out, were to come with their goods
to the mouth of the Wisconsin. The two travellers trembled
for the consequences of this encounter; but the chief, after a
short colloquy, passed on his way. In three days, he returned
in ill-humor, having found no traders at the appointed spot.
The Picard was absent at the time, looking for game, and
Hennepin was sitting under the shade of his blanket, which
he had stretched on forked sticks to protect him from the sun,
when he saw his adopted father approaching with a threatening look and a war-club in his hand. He attempted no violence, however, but suffered his wrath to exhale in a severe
scolding, after which he resumed his course up the river with
his warriors.

If Hennepin, as he avers, really expected a party of traders
at the Wisconsin, the course he now took is sufficiently ex-
plicable. If he did not expect them, his obvious course was to
rejoin Tonty on the Illinois, for which he seems to have had
no inclination; or to return to Canada by way of the Wisconsin, an attempt which involved the risk of starvation, as the
two travellers had but ten charges of powder left. Assuming,
then, his hope of the traders to have been real, he and Du
Gay resolved, in the mean time, to join a large body of Sioux
hunters, who, as Aquipaguetin had told them, were on a
stream which he calls Bull River, now the Chippeway, entering the Mississippi near Lake Pepin. By so doing, they would

gain a supply of food, and save themselves from the danger of encountering parties of roving warriors.

They found this band, among whom was their companion Accau, and followed them on a grand hunt along the borders of the Mississippi. Du Gay was separated for a time from Hennepin, who was placed in a canoe with a withered squaw more than eighty years old. In spite of her age, she handled her paddle with great address, and used it vigorously, as occasion required, to repress the gambols of three children, who, to Hennepin's annoyance, occupied the middle of the canoe. The hunt was successful. The Sioux warriors, active as deer, chased the buffalo on foot with their stone-headed arrows, on the plains behind the heights that bordered the river; while the old men stood sentinels at the top, watching for the approach of enemies. One day an alarm was given. The warriors rushed towards the supposed point of danger, but found nothing more formidable than two squaws of their own nation, who brought strange news. A war-party of Sioux, they said, had gone towards Lake Superior, and had met by the way five "Spirits;" that is to say, five Europeans. Hennepin was full of curiosity to learn who the strangers might be; and they, on their part, were said to have shown great anxiety to know the nationality of the three white men who, as they were told, were on the river. The hunt was over; and the hunters, with Hennepin and his companion, were on their way northward to their towns, when they met the five "Spirits" at some distance below the Falls of St. Anthony. They proved to be Daniel Greysolon du Lhut with four well-armed Frenchmen.

This bold and enterprising man, stigmatized by the Intendant Duchesneau as a leader of *coureurs de bois*, was a cousin of Tonty, born at Lyons. He belonged to that caste of the lesser nobles, whose name was legion, and whose admirable military qualities shone forth so conspicuously in the wars of Louis XIV. Though his enterprises were independent of those of La Salle, they were at this time carried on in connection with Count Frontenac and certain merchants in his interest, of whom Du Lhut's uncle, Patron, was one; while Louvigny, his brother-in-law, was in alliance with the governor, and was an officer of his guard. Here, then, was a kind of family league, countenanced by Frontenac, and acting conjointly with him, in order, if the angry letters of the intendant are to be believed, to reap a clandestine profit under the shadow of the governor's authority, and in violation of the royal ordinances. The rudest part of the work fell to the share of Du Lhut, who, with a persistent hardihood, not surpassed, perhaps, even by La Salle, was continually in the forest, in the Indian towns, or in remote wilderness outposts planted by himself, exploring, trading, fighting, ruling lawless savages, and whites scarcely less ungovernable, and on one or more occasions varying his life by crossing the ocean, to gain interviews with the colonial minister Seignelay, amid the splendid vanities of Versailles. Strange to say, this man of hardy enterprise was a martyr to the gout, which for more than a quarter of a century grievously tormented him; though for a time he thought himself cured by the intercession of the Iroquois saint, Catharine Tegahkouita, to whom he had made a vow to that end. He was, without doubt, an habitual breaker of the royal ordinances regulating the fur-trade; yet his services were great to the colony and to the crown, and his name deserves a place of honor among the pioneers of American civilization.[1]

[1] The facts concerning Du Lhut have been gleaned from a variety of contemporary documents, chiefly the letters of his enemy, Duschesneau, who always puts him in the worst light, especially in his despatch to Seignelay of 10 Nov., 1679, where he charges both him and the governor with carrying on an illicit trade with the English of New York. Du Lhut himself, in a memoir dated 1685 (see Harrisse, *Bibliographie*, 176), strongly denies these charges. Du Lhut built a trading fort on Lake Superior, called Cananistigoyan (La Hontan), or Kamalastigouia (Perrot). It was on the north side, at the mouth of a river entering Thunder Bay, where Fort William now stands. In 1684, he caused two Indians, who had murdered several Frenchmen on Lake Superior, to be shot. He displayed in this affair great courage and coolness, undaunted by the crowd of excited savages who surrounded him and his little band of Frenchmen. The long letter, in which he recounts the capture and execution of the murderers, is before me. Duschesneau makes his conduct on this occasion the ground of a charge of rashness. In 1686, Denonville, then governor of the colony, ordered him to fortify the Detroit; that is, the strait between Lakes Erie and Huron. He went thither with fifty men and built a palisade fort, which he occupied for some time. In 1687, he, together with Tonty and Durantaye, joined Denonville against the Senecas, with a body of Indians from the Upper Lakes. In 1689, during the panic that followed the Iroquois invasion of Montreal, Du Lhut, with twenty-eight Canadians, attacked

When Hennepin met him, he had been about two years in the wilderness. In September, 1678, he left Quebec, for the purpose of exploring the region of the Upper Mississippi, and establishing relations of friendship with the Sioux and their kindred, the Assiniboins. In the summer of 1679, he visited three large towns of the eastern division of the Sioux, including those visited by Hennepin in the following year, and planted the king's arms in all of them. Early in the autumn, he was at the head of Lake Superior, holding a council with the Assiniboins and the lake tribes, and inducing them to live at peace with the Sioux. In all this, he acted in a public capacity, under the authority of the governor; but it is not to be supposed that he forgot his own interests or those of his associates. The intendant angrily complains that he aided and abetted the *coureurs de bois* in their lawless courses, and sent down in their canoes great quantities of beaver-skins consigned to the merchants in league with him, under cover of whose names the governor reaped his share of the profits.

In June, 1680, while Hennepin was in the Sioux villages, Du Lhut set out from the head of Lake Superior, with two

---

twenty-two Iroquois in canoes, received their fire without returning it, bore down upon them, killed eighteen of them, and captured three, only one escaping. In 1695, he was in command at Fort Frontenac. In 1697, he succeeded to the command of a company of infantry, but was suffering wretchedly from the gout at Fort Frontenac. In 1710, Vaudreuil, in a despatch to the minister, Ponchartrain, announced his death as occurring in the previous winter, and added the brief comment, "c'était un très-honnête homme." Other contemporaries speak to the same effect. "M^r· Dulhut, Gentilhomme Lionnois, qui a beaucoup de mérite et de capacité."— *La Hontan*, I. 103 (1703). "Le Sieur du Lut, homme d'esprit et d'expérience."— *Le Clerc*, II. 137. Charlevoix calls him "one of the bravest officers the king has ever had in this colony." His name is variously spelled Du Luc, Du Lud, Du Lude, Du Lut, Du Luth, Du Lhut. For an account of the Iroquois virgin, Tegahkouita, whose intercession is said to have cured him of the gout, see Charlevoix, I. 572.

On a contemporary manuscript map by the Jesuit Raffeix, representing the routes of Marquette, La Salle, and Du Lhut, are the following words, referring to the last-named discoverer, and interesting in connection with Hennepin's statements: "M^r· du Lude le premier a esté chez les Sioux en 1678, et a esté proche la source du Mississippi, et ensuite vint retirer le P. Louis [*Hennepin*] qui avoit esté fait prisonnier chez les Sioux." Du Lhut here appears as the deliverer of Hennepin. One of his men was named Pepin; hence, no doubt, the name of Lake Pepin.

canoes, four Frenchmen, and an Indian, to continue his explorations.[1] He ascended a river, apparently the Burnt Wood, and reached from thence a branch of the Mississippi which seems to have been the St. Croix. It was now that, to his surprise, he learned that there were three Europeans on the main river below; and, fearing that they might be Englishmen or Spaniards, encroaching on the territories of the king, he eagerly pressed forward to solve his doubts. When he saw Hennepin, his mind was set at rest; and the travellers met with mutual cordiality. They followed the Indians to their villages of Mille Lac, where Hennepin had now no reason to complain of their treatment of him. The Sioux gave him and Du Lhut a grand feast of honor, at which were seated a hundred and twenty naked guests; and the great chief Ouasi-coudé, with his own hands, placed before Hennepin a bark dish containing a mess of smoked meat and wild rice.

Autumn had come, and the travellers bethought them of going home. The Sioux, consoled by their promises to return with goods for trade, did not oppose their departure; and they set out together, eight white men in all. As they passed St. Anthony's Falls, two of the men stole two buffalo-robes which were hung on trees as offerings to the spirit of the cataract. When Du Lhut heard of it, he was very angry, telling the men that they had endangered the lives of the whole party. Hennepin admitted that, in the view of human prudence, he was right, but urged that the act was good and praiseworthy, inasmuch as the offerings were made to a false god; while the men, on their part, proved mutinous, declaring that they wanted the robes and meant to keep them. The travellers continued their journey in great ill-humor, but were presently soothed by the excellent hunting which they found on the way. As they approached the Wisconsin, they stopped to dry the meat of the buffalo they had killed, when to their amazement they saw a war-party of Sioux approaching in a fleet of canoes. Hennepin represents himself as showing on this occasion an extraordinary courage, going to meet the Indians with a peace-pipe, and instructing Du Lhut, who knew more of these matters than he, how he ought to behave. The

---

[1] *Memoir on the French Dominion in Canada, N. Y. Col. Docs.*, IX. 781.

Sioux proved not unfriendly, and said nothing of the theft of the buffalo-robes. They soon went on their way to attack the Illinois and Missouris, leaving the Frenchmen to ascend the Wisconsin unmolested.

After various adventures, they reached the station of the Jesuits at Green Bay; but its existence is wholly ignored by Hennepin, whose zeal for his own Order will not permit him to allude to this establishment of the rival missionaries.[1] He is equally reticent with regard to the Jesuit mission at Michil-limackinac, where the party soon after arrived, and where they spent the winter. The only intimation which he gives of its existence consists in the mention of the Jesuit Pierson, who was a Fleming like himself, and who often skated with him on the frozen lake, or kept him company in fishing through a hole in the ice.[2] When the spring opened, Henne-pin descended Lake Huron, followed the Detroit to Lake Erie, and proceeded thence to Niagara. Here he spent some time in making a fresh examination of the cataract, and then resumed his voyage on Lake Ontario. He stopped, however, at the great town of the Senecas, near the Genesee, where, with his usual spirit of meddling, he took upon him the func-tions of the civil and military authorities, convoked the chiefs to a council, and urged them to set at liberty certain Ottawa prisoners whom they had captured in violation of treaties. Having settled this affair to his satisfaction, he went to Fort Frontenac, where his brother missionary, Buisset, received him with a welcome rendered the warmer by a story which had reached him that the Indians had hanged Hennepin with his own cord of St. Francis.

From Fort Frontenac he went to Montreal; and leaving his two men on a neighboring island, that they might escape the payment of duties on a quantity of furs which they had with them, he paddled alone towards the town. Count Frontenac

[1] On the other hand, he sets down on his map of 1683 a mission of the Récollets at a point north of the farthest sources of the Mississippi, to which no white man had ever penetrated.

[2] He says that Pierson had come among the Indians to learn their language; that he "retained the frankness and rectitude of our country," and "a dispo-sition always on the side of candor and sincerity. In a word, he seemed to me to be all that a Christian ought to be" (1697), 433.

chanced to be here, and, looking from the window of a house near the river, he saw, approaching in a canoe, a Récollet father, whose appearance indicated the extremity of hard service; for his face was worn and sunburnt, and his tattered habit of St. Francis was abundantly patched with scraps of buffalo-skin. When at length he recognized the long-lost Hennepin, he received him, as the father writes, "with all the tenderness which a missionary could expect from a person of his rank and quality." He kept him for twelve days in his own house, and listened with interest to such of his adventures as the friar saw fit to divulge.

And here we bid farewell to Father Hennepin. "Providence," he writes, "preserved my life that I might make known my great discoveries to the world." He soon after went to Europe, where the story of his travels found a host of readers, but where he died at last in a deserved obscurity.[1]

---

[1] Since the two preceding chapters were written, the letters of La Salle have been brought to light by the researches of M. Margry. They confirm, in nearly all points, the conclusions given above; though, as before observed (*note*, p. 846), they show misstatements, on the part of Hennepin, concerning his position at the outset of the expedition. La Salle writes: "J'ay fait remonter le fleuve Colbert, nommé par les Iroquois Gastacha, par les Outaouais Mississipy, par un canot conduit par deux de mes gens, l'un nommé Michel Accault et l'autre Picard, auxquels le R. P. Hennepin se joignit pour ne perdre pas l'occasion de prescher l'Évangile aux peuples qui habitent dessus et qui n'en avoient jamais oui parler." In the same letter, he recounts their voyage on the Upper Mississippi, and their capture by the Sioux, in accordance with the story of Hennepin himself. Hennepin's assertion, that La Salle had promised to send a number of men to meet him at the mouth of the Wisconsin, turns out to be true. "Estans tous revenus en chasse avec les Nadouessioux [*Sioux*] vers Ouisconsing [*Wisconsin*], le R. P. Louis Hempin [*Hennepin*] et Picard prirent résolution de venir jusqu'à l'emboucheure de la rivière où j'avois promis d'envoyer de mes nouvelles, comme j'avois fait par six hommes que les Jésuistes desbauchèrent en leur disant que le R. P. Louis et ses compagnons de voyage avoient esté tuez."

It is clear that La Salle understood Hennepin; for, after speaking of his journey, he adds: "J'ai cru qu'il estoit à propos de vous faire le narré des aventures de ce canot parce que je ne doute pas qu'on en parle; et si vous souhaitez en conférer avec le P. Louis Hempin, Récollect, qui est repassé en France, il faut un peu le connoistre, car il ne manquera pas d'exagérer toutes choses, c'est son caractère, et à moy mesme il m'a escrit comme s'il eust esté tout près d'estre bruslé, quoiqu'il n'en ait pas esté seulement en danger; mais il croit qu'il luy est honorable de le faire de la sorte, et *il parle plus conformé-*

ment à ce qu'il veut qu'à ce qu'il scait." — *Lettre de La Salle, 22 Août, 1682 (1681?)* (Margry, II. 259).

On his return to France, Hennepin got hold of the manuscript *Relation des Découvertes*, compiled for the government from La Salle's letters, and, as already observed, made very free use of it in the first edition of his book, printed in 1683. In 1699, he wished to return to Canada; but, in a letter of that year, Louis XIV. orders the governor to seize him, should he appear, and send him prisoner to Rochefort. This seems to have been in consequence of his renouncing the service of the French crown, and dedicating his edition of 1697 to William III. of England.

More than twenty editions of Hennepin's travels appeared, in French, English, Dutch, German, Italian, and Spanish. Most of them include the mendacious narrative of the pretended descent of the Mississippi. For a list of them, see *Hist. Mag.*, I. 346; II. 24.

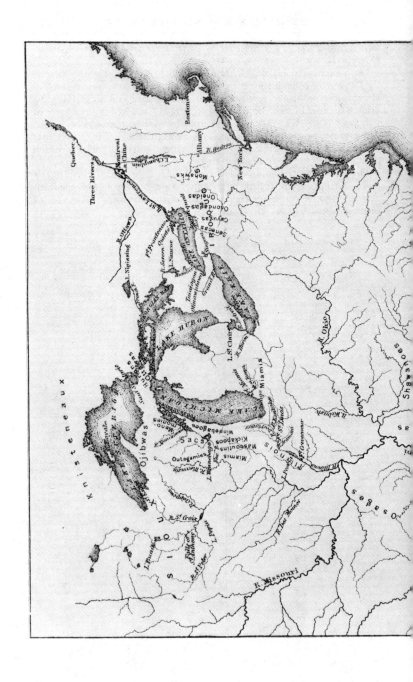

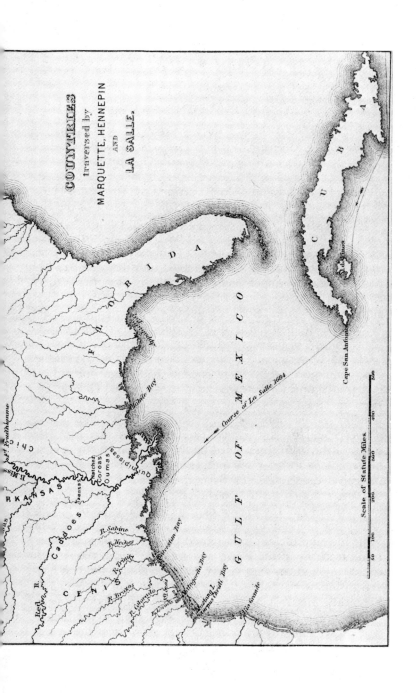

COUNTRIES
traversed by
MARQUETTE, HENNEPIN
AND
LA SALLE.

F L O R I D A

C U B A

C. de Cruz

Cape San Antonio

G U L F   O F   M E X I C O

Course of La Salle 1684

Mobile Bay

Sessidiquino

Natchez
Coroas
Youmas
Tænsas

R K A N S A S

C H I C

R. Miss.

Ft Prudhomme

Caddoes

Red R.

C E N I S

R. Sabine
R. Neches
R. Trinity
R. Brazos
R. Colorado

Galveston Bay

R. S. Antonio
R. del Norte
San Bernard
L. Bay
Corpus Christi Bay

Rio Grande

Scale of Statute Miles

50   100   200   300   400   500

Chapter XIX

1681

LA SALLE BEGINS ANEW

His Constancy • His Plans • His Savage Allies • He becomes Snow-blind • Negotiations • Grand Council • La Salle's Oratory • Meeting with Tonty • Preparation • Departure

---

IN tracing the adventures of Tonty and the rovings of Hennepin, we have lost sight of La Salle, the pivot of the enterprise. Returning from the desolation and horror in the valley of the Illinois, he had spent the winter at Fort Miami, on the St. Joseph, by the borders of Lake Michigan. Here he might have brooded on the redoubled ruin that had befallen him: the desponding friends, the exulting foes; the wasted energies, the crushing load of debt, the stormy past, the black and lowering future. But his mind was of a different temper. He had no thought but to grapple with adversity, and out of the fragments of his ruin to build up the fabric of success.

He would not recoil; but he modified his plans to meet the new contingency. His white enemies had found, or rather, perhaps, had made, a savage ally in the Iroquois. Their incursions must be stopped, or his enterprise would come to nought; and he thought he saw the means by which this new danger could be converted into a source of strength. The tribes of the West, threatened by the common enemy, might be taught to forget their mutual animosities, and join in a defensive league, with La Salle at its head. They might be colonized around his fort in the valley of the Illinois, where, in the shadow of the French flag, and with the aid of French allies, they could hold the Iroquois in check, and acquire in some measure the arts of a settled life. The Franciscan friars could teach them the Faith; and La Salle and his associates could supply them with goods, in exchange for the vast harvest of furs which their hunters could gather in these boundless wilds. Meanwhile, he would seek out the mouth of the Mississippi; and the furs gathered at his colony in the Illinois would then find a ready passage to the markets of the world. Thus might this ancient slaughter-field of warring savages be redeemed to civilization and Christianity; and a stable settlement, half-feudal, half-commercial, grow up in the heart of the western wilderness. This plan was but a part of the original scheme of his enterprise, adapted to new and unexpected circumstances; and he now set himself to its execution with his usual vigor, joined to an address that, when dealing with Indians, never failed him.

There were allies close at hand. Near Fort Miami were the huts of twenty-five or thirty savages, exiles from their homes, and strangers in this western world. Several of the English colonies, from Virginia to Maine, had of late years been harassed by Indian wars; and the Puritans of New England, above all, had been scourged by the deadly outbreak of King Philip's war. Those engaged in it had paid a bitter price for their brief triumphs. A band of refugees, chiefly Abenakis and Mohegans, driven from their native seats, had roamed into these distant wilds, and were wintering in the friendly neighborhood of the French. La Salle soon won them over to his interests. One of their number was the Mohegan hunter, who for two years had faithfully followed his fortunes, and who had been four years in the West. He is described as a prudent and discreet young man, in whom La Salle had great confidence, and who could make himself understood in several western languages, belonging, like his own, to the great Algonquin tongue. This devoted henchman proved an efficient mediator with his countrymen. The New-England Indians, with one voice, promised to follow La Salle, asking no recompense but to call him their chief, and yield to him the love and admiration which he rarely failed to command from this hero-worshipping race.

New allies soon appeared. A Shawanoe chief from the valley of the Ohio, whose following embraced a hundred and fifty warriors, came to ask the protection of the French against the all-destroying Iroquois. "The Shawanoes are too distant," was La Salle's reply; "but let them come to me at the Illinois, and they shall be safe." The chief promised to join him in the autumn, at Fort Miami, with all his band. But, more important than all, the consent and co-operation of the Illinois must be gained; and the Miamis, their neighbors, and of late their enemies, must be taught the folly of their league with the Iroquois, and the necessity of joining in the new confederation. Of late, they had been made to see the perfidy of their dangerous allies. A band of the Iroquois, returning from the slaughter of the Tamaroa Illinois, had met and murdered a band of Miamis on the Ohio, and had not only refused satisfaction, but had entrenched themselves in three rude forts of trees and brushwood in the heart of the Miami country. The moment was favorable for negotiating; but, first, La Salle wished to open a communication with the Illinois, some of whom had begun to return to the country they had abandoned. With this view, and also, it seems, to procure provisions, he set out on the first of March, with his lieutenant, La Forest, and fifteen men.

The country was sheeted in snow, and the party journeyed on snow-shoes; but, when they reached the open prairies, the white expanse glared in the sun with so dazzling a brightness that La Salle and several of the men became snow-blind. They stopped and encamped under the edge of a forest; and here La Salle remained in darkness for three days, suffering extreme pain. Meanwhile, he sent forward La Forest, and most of the men, keeping with him his old attendant Hunaut. Going out in quest of pine-leaves,—a decoction of which was supposed to be useful in cases of snow-blindness,—this man discovered the fresh tracks of Indians, followed them, and found a camp of Outagamies, or Foxes, from the neighborhood of Green Bay. From them he heard welcome news. They told him that Tonty was safe among the Pottawattamies, and that Hennepin had passed through their country on his return from among the Sioux.[1]

A thaw took place; the snow melted rapidly; the rivers were opened; the blind men began to recover; and, launching the canoes which they had dragged after them, the party pursued their way by water. They soon met a band of Illinois. La Salle gave them presents, condoled with them on their losses, and urged them to make peace and alliance with the Miamis. Thus, he said, they could set the Iroquois at defiance; for he himself, with his Frenchmen and his Indian friends, would make his abode among them, supply them with goods, and

---

[1] *Relation des Découvertes.* Compare *Lettre de La Salle* (Margry, II. 144).

aid them to defend themselves. They listened, well pleased, promised to carry his message to their countrymen, and furnished him with a large supply of corn.[1] Meanwhile, he had rejoined La Forest, whom he now sent to Michillimackinac to await Tonty, and tell him to remain there till he, La Salle, should arrive.

Having thus accomplished the objects of his journey, he returned to Fort Miami, whence he soon after ascended the St. Joseph to the village of the Miami Indians, on the portage, at the head of the Kankakee. Here he found unwelcome guests. These were three Iroquois warriors, who had been for some time in the place, and who, as he was told, had demeaned themselves with the insolence of conquerors, and spoken of the French with the utmost contempt. He hastened to confront them, rebuked and menaced them, and told them that now, when he was present, they dared not repeat the calumnies which they had uttered in his absence. They stood abashed and confounded, and during the following night secretly left the town and fled. The effect was prodigious on the minds of the Miamis, when they saw that La Salle, backed by ten Frenchmen, could command from their arrogant visitors a respect which they, with their hundreds of warriors, had wholly failed to inspire. Here, at the outset, was an augury full of promise for the approaching negotiations.

There were other strangers in the town,—a band of eastern Indians, more numerous than those who had wintered at the fort. The greater number were from Rhode Island, including, probably, some of King Philip's warriors; others were from New York, and others again from Virginia. La Salle called them to a council, promised them a new home in the West, under the protection of the Great King, with rich lands, an abundance of game, and French traders to supply them with the goods which they had once received from the English. Let them but help him to make peace between the Miamis and the Illinois, and he would insure for them a future of prosperity and safety. They listened with open ears, and promised their aid in the work of peace.

On the next morning, the Miamis were called to a grand

[1] This seems to have been taken from the secret repositories, or *caches*, of the ruined town of the Illinois.

council. It was held in the lodge of their chief, from which the mats were removed, that the crowd without might hear what was said. La Salle rose and harangued the concourse. Few men were so skilled in the arts of forest rhetoric and diplomacy. After the Indian mode, he was, to follow his chroniclers, "the greatest orator in North America."[1] He began with a gift of tobacco, to clear the brains of his auditory; next, for he had brought a canoe-load of presents to support his eloquence, he gave them cloth to cover their dead, coats to dress them, hatchets to build a grand scaffold in their honor, and beads, bells, and trinkets of all sorts, to decorate their relatives at a grand funeral feast. All this was mere metaphor. The living, while appropriating the gifts to their own use, were pleased at the compliment offered to their dead; and their delight redoubled as the orator proceeded. One of their great chiefs had lately been killed; and La Salle, after a eulogy of the departed, declared that he would now raise him to life again; that is, that he would assume his name and give support to his squaws and children. This flattering announcement drew forth an outburst of applause; and when, to confirm his words, his attendants placed before them a huge pile of coats, shirts, and hunting-knives, the whole assembly exploded in yelps of admiration.

Now came the climax of the harangue, introduced by a farther present of six guns.

"He who is my master, and the master of all this country, is a mighty chief, feared by the whole world; but he loves peace, and the words of his lips are for good alone. He is called the King of France, and he is the mightiest among the chiefs beyond the great water. His goodness reaches even to your dead, and his subjects come among you to raise them up to life. But it is his will to preserve the life he has given: it is his will that you should obey his laws, and make no war without the leave of Onontio, who commands in his name at Quebec, and who loves all the nations alike, because such is the will of the Great King. You ought, then, to live at peace with your neighbors, and above all with the Illinois. You have had causes of quarrel with them; but their defeat has avenged

[1] "En ce genre, il étoit le plus grand orateur de l'Amérique Septentrionale." — *Relation des Découvertes.*

you. Though they are still strong, they wish to make peace with you. Be content with the glory of having obliged them to ask for it. You have an interest in preserving them; since, if the Iroquois destroy them, they will next destroy you. Let us all obey the Great King, and live together in peace, under his protection. Be of my mind, and use these guns that I have given you, not to make war, but only to hunt and to defend yourselves."[1]

So saying, he gave two belts of wampum to confirm his words; and the assembly dissolved. On the following day, the chiefs again convoked it, and made their reply in form. It was all that La Salle could have wished. "The Illinois is our brother, because he is the son of our Father, the Great King." "We make you the master of our beaver and our lands, of our minds and our bodies." "We cannot wonder that our brothers from the East wish to live with you. We should have wished so too, if we had known what a blessing it is to be the children of the Great King." The rest of this auspicious day was passed in feasts and dances, in which La Salle and his Frenchmen all bore part. His new scheme was hopefully begun. It remained to achieve the enterprise, twice defeated, of the discovery of the mouth of the Mississippi, that vital condition of his triumph, without which all other success was meaningless and vain.

To this end, he must return to Canada, appease his creditors, and collect his scattered resources. Towards the end of May, he set out in canoes from Fort Miami, and reached Michillimackinac after a prosperous voyage. Here, to his great joy, he found Tonty and Zenobe Membré, who had lately arrived from Green Bay. The meeting was one at which even his stoic nature must have melted. Each had for the other a tale of disaster; but, when La Salle recounted the long succession of his reverses, it was with the tranquil tone and cheerful look of one who relates the incidents of an ordinary journey. Membré looked on him with admiration. "Any one else," he says, "would have thrown up his hand and abandoned the enterprise; but, far from this, with a firmness and constancy

[1] Translated from the *Relation*, where these councils are reported at great length.

that never had its equal, I saw him more resolved than ever to continue his work and push forward his discovery."[1]

Without loss of time, they embarked together for Fort Frontenac, paddled their canoes a thousand miles, and safely reached their destination. Here, in this third beginning of his enterprise, La Salle found himself beset with embarrassments. Not only was he burdened with the fruitless costs of his two former efforts, but the heavy debts which he had incurred in building and maintaining Fort Frontenac had not been wholly paid. The fort and the seigniory were already deeply mortgaged; yet, through the influence of Count Frontenac, the assistance of his secretary, Barrois, a consummate man of business, and the support of a wealthy relative, he found means to appease his creditors and even to gain fresh advances. To this end, however, he was forced to part with a portion of his monopolies. Having first made his will at Montreal, in favor of a cousin who had befriended him,[2] he mustered his men, and once more set forth, resolved to trust no more to agents, but to lead on his followers, in a united body, under his own personal command.[3]

At the beginning of autumn, he was at Toronto, where the long and difficult portage to Lake Simcoe detained him a fortnight. He spent a part of it in writing an account of what had lately occurred to a correspondent in France, and he closes his letter thus: "This is all I can tell you this year. I have a hundred things to write, but you could not believe how hard it is to do it among Indians. The canoes and their

---

[1] Membré in Le Clerc, II. 208. Tonty, in his memoir of 1693, speaks of the joy of La Salle at the meeting. The *Relation*, usually very accurate, says, erroneously, that Tonty had gone to Fort Frontenac. La Forest had gone thither, not long before La Salle's arrival.

[2] *Copie du testament du deffunt S' de la Salle, 11 Août, 1681.* The relative was François Plet, to whom he was deeply in debt.

[3] "On apprendra à la fin de cette année, 1682, le succès de la découverte qu'il étoit résolu d'achever, au plus tard le printemps dernier, ou de périr en y travaillant. Tant de traverses et de malheurs toujours arrivés en son absence l'ont fait résoudre à ne se fier plus à personne et à conduire lui-même tout son monde, tout son équipage, et toute son entreprise, de laquelle il espéroit une heureuse conclusion."

The above is a part of the closing paragraph of the *Relation des Découvertes*, so often cited.

lading must be got over the portage, and I must speak to them continually, and bear all their importunity, or else they will do nothing I want. I hope to write more at leisure next year, and tell you the end of this business, which I hope will turn out well: for I have M. de Tonty, who is full of zeal; thirty Frenchmen, all good men, without reckoning such as I cannot trust; and more than a hundred Indians, some of them Shawanoes, and others from New England, all of whom know how to use guns."

It was October before he reached Lake Huron. Day after day, and week after week, the heavy-laden canoes crept on along the lonely wilderness shores, by the monotonous ranks of bristling moss-bearded firs; lake and forest, forest and lake; a dreary scene haunted with yet more dreary memories,— disasters, sorrows, and deferred hopes; time, strength, and wealth spent in vain; a ruinous past and a doubtful future; slander, obloquy, and hate. With unmoved heart, the patient voyager held his course, and drew up his canoes at last on the beach at Fort Miami.

Chapter XX

1681–1682

SUCCESS OF LA SALLE

*His Followers • The Chicago Portage • Descent of the Mississippi •
The Lost Hunter • The Arkansas • The Taensas • The Natchez •
Hostility • The Mouth of the Mississippi • Louis XIV. proclaimed
Sovereign of the Great West*

THE season was far advanced. On the bare limbs of the
forest hung a few withered remnants of its gay autumnal
livery; and the smoke crept upward through the sullen November air from the squalid wigwams of La Salle's Abenaki
and Mohegan allies. These, his new friends, were savages
whose midnight yells had startled the border hamlets of New
England; who had danced around Puritan scalps, and whom
Puritan imaginations painted as incarnate fiends. La Salle
chose eighteen of them, whom he added to the twenty-three
Frenchmen who remained with him, some of the rest having
deserted and others lagged behind. The Indians insisted on
taking their squaws with them. These were ten in number,
besides three children; and thus the expedition included fifty-
four persons, of whom some were useless, and others a
burden.

On the 21st of December, Tonty and Membré set out from
Fort Miami with some of the party in six canoes, and crossed
to the little river Chicago.[1] La Salle, with the rest of the men,

[1] La Salle, *Relation de la Découverte, 1682,* in Thomassy, *Géologie Pratique de
la Louisiane,* 9; *Lettre du Père Zenobe Membré, 3 Juin, 1682; Ibid., 14 Août, 1682;*
Membré in Le Clerc, II. 214; Tonty, *1684, 1693; Procès Verbal de la Prise de
Possession de la Louisiane; Feuilles détachées d'une Lettre de La Salle* (Margry,
II. 164); *Récit de Nicolas de la Salle* (Ibid., I. 547).

The narrative ascribed to Membré and published by Le Clerc is based on
the document preserved in the Archives Scientifiques de la Marine, entitled
*Relation de la Découverte de l'Embouchure de la Rivière Mississippi faite par le
Sieur de la Salle, l'année passée, 1682.* The writer of the narrative has used it
very freely, copying the greater part verbatim, with occasional additions of a
kind which seem to indicate that he had taken part in the expedition. The
Relation de la Découverte, though written in the third person, is the official
report of the discovery made by La Salle, or perhaps for him by Membré.

joined them a few days later. It was the dead of winter, and the streams were frozen. They made sledges, placed on them the canoes, the baggage, and a disabled Frenchman; crossed from the Chicago to the northern branch of the Illinois, and filed in a long procession down its frozen course. They reached the site of the great Illinois village, found it tenant-less, and continued their journey, still dragging their canoes, till at length they reached open water below Lake Peoria.

La Salle had abandoned for a time his original plan of building a vessel for the navigation of the Mississippi. Bitter experience had taught him the difficulty of the attempt, and he resolved to trust to his canoes alone. They embarked again, floating prosperously down between the leafless forests that flanked the tranquil river; till, on the sixth of February, they issued upon the majestic bosom of the Mississippi. Here, for the time, their progress was stopped; for the river was full of floating ice. La Salle's Indians, too, had lagged behind; but, within a week, all had arrived, the navigation was once more free, and they resumed their course. Towards evening, they saw on their right the mouth of a great river; and the clear current was invaded by the headlong torrent of the Missouri, opaque with mud. They built their camp-fires in the neigh-boring forest; and at daylight, embarking anew on the dark and mighty stream, drifted swiftly down towards unknown destinies. They passed a deserted town of the Tamaroas; saw, three days after, the mouth of the Ohio;[1] and, gliding by the wastes of bordering swamp, landed on the twenty-fourth of February near the Third Chickasaw Bluffs.[2] They encamped, and the hunters went out for game. All returned, excepting Pierre Prudhomme; and, as the others had seen fresh tracks of Indians, La Salle feared that he was killed. While some of his followers built a small stockade fort on a high bluff[3] by the river, others ranged the woods in pursuit of the missing

[1] Called by Membré the Ouabache (Wabash).

[2] La Salle, *Relation de la Découverte de l'Embouchure, etc.*; Thomassy, 10. Membré gives the same date; but the *Procès Verbal* makes it the twenty-sixth.

[3] Gravier, in his letter of 16 Feb., 1701, says that he encamped near a "great bluff of stone, called Fort Prudhomme, because M. de la Salle, going on his discovery, entrenched himself here with his party, fearing that Prudhomme, who had lost himself in the woods, had been killed by the Indians, and that he himself would be attacked."

hunter. After six days of ceaseless and fruitless search, they met two Chickasaw Indians in the forest; and, through them, La Salle sent presents and peace-messages to that warlike people, whose villages were a few days' journey distant. Several days later, Prudhomme was found, and brought in to the camp, half-dead. He had lost his way while hunting; and, to console him for his woes, La Salle christened the newly built fort with his name, and left him, with a few others, in charge of it.

Again they embarked; and, with every stage of their adventurous progress, the mystery of this vast New World was more and more unveiled. More and more they entered the realms of spring. The hazy sunlight, the warm and drowsy air, the tender foliage, the opening flowers, betokened the reviving life of Nature. For several days more they followed the writhings of the great river, on its tortuous course through wastes of swamp and canebrake, till on the thirteenth of March[1] they found themselves wrapped in a thick fog. Neither shore was visible; but they heard on the right the booming of an Indian drum and the shrill outcries of the war-dance. La Salle at once crossed to the opposite side, where, in less than an hour, his men threw up a rude fort of felled trees. Meanwhile, the fog cleared; and, from the farther bank, the astonished Indians saw the strange visitors at their work. Some of the French advanced to the edge of the water, and beckoned them to come over. Several of them approached, in a wooden canoe, to within the distance of a gun-shot. La Salle displayed the calumet, and sent a Frenchman to meet them. He was well received; and, the friendly mood of the Indians being now apparent, the whole party crossed the river.

On landing, they found themselves at a town of the Kappa band of the Arkansas, a people dwelling near the mouth of the river which bears their name. "The whole village," writes Membré to his superior, "came down to the shore to meet us, except the women, who had run off. I cannot tell you the civility and kindness we received from these barbarians, who brought us poles to make huts, supplied us with firewood during the three days we were among them, and took turns in feasting us. But, my Reverend Father, this gives no idea of

[1] La Salle, *Relation*; Thomassy, II.

the good qualities of these savages, who are gay, civil, and free-hearted. The young men, though the most alert and spir-ited we had seen, are nevertheless so modest that not one of them would take the liberty to enter our hut, but all stood quietly at the door. They are so well formed that we were in admiration at their beauty. We did not lose the value of a pin while we were among them."

Various were the dances and ceremonies with which they entertained the strangers, who, on their part, responded with a solemnity which their hosts would have liked less, if they had understood it better. La Salle and Tonty, at the head of their followers, marched to the open area in the midst of the village. Here, to the admiration of the gazing crowd of war-riors, women, and children, a cross was raised bearing the arms of France. Membré, in canonicals, sang a hymn; the men shouted *Vive le Roi*; and La Salle, in the king's name, took formal possession of the country.[1] The friar, not, he flatters himself, without success, labored to expound by signs the mysteries of the Faith; while La Salle, by methods equally satisfactory, drew from the chief an acknowledgment of fealty to Louis XIV.[2]

After touching at several other towns of this people, the voyagers resumed their course, guided by two of the Arkan-sas; passed the sites, since become historic, of Vicksburg and Grand Gulf; and, about three hundred miles below the Ar-kansas, stopped by the edge of a swamp on the western side of the river.[3] Here, as their two guides told them, was the path to the great town of the Taensas. Tonty and Membré

[1] *Procès Verbal de la Prise de Possession du Pays des Arkansas, 14 Mars, 1682.*

[2] The nation of the Akanseas, Alkansas, or Arkansas, dwelt on the west bank of the Mississippi, near the mouth of the Arkansas. They were divided into four tribes, living for the most part in separate villages. Those first vis-ited by La Salle were the Kappas, or Quapaws, a remnant of whom still subsists. The others were the Topingas, or Tongengas; the Torimans; and the Osotouoy, or Sauthouis. According to Charlevoix, who saw them in 1721, they were regarded as the tallest and best-formed Indians in America, and were known as *les Beaux Hommes*. Gravier says that they once lived on the Ohio.

[3] In Tensas County, Louisiana. Tonty's estimates of distance are here much too low. They seem to be founded on observations of latitude, without reck-oning the windings of the river. It may interest sportsmen to know that the party killed several large alligators, on their way. Membré is much astonished that such monsters should be born of eggs, like chickens.

were sent to visit it. They and their men shouldered their birch canoe through the swamp, and launched it on a lake which had once formed a portion of the channel of the river. In two hours, they reached the town; and Tonty gazed at it with astonishment. He had seen nothing like it in America: large square dwellings, built of sun-baked mud mixed with straw, arched over with a dome-shaped roof of canes, and placed in regular order around an open area. Two of them were larger and better than the rest. One was the lodge of the chief; the other was the temple, or house of the sun. They entered the former, and found a single room, forty feet square, where, in the dim light,—for there was no opening but the door,—the chief sat awaiting them on a sort of bedstead, three of his wives at his side, while sixty old men, wrapped in white cloaks woven of mulberry-bark, formed his divan. When he spoke, his wives howled to do him honor; and the assembled councillors listened with the reverence due to a potentate for whom, at his death, a hundred victims were to be sacrificed. He received the visitors graciously, and joyfully accepted the gifts which Tonty laid before him.[1] This interview over, the Frenchmen repaired to the temple, wherein were kept the bones of the departed chiefs. In construction, it was much like the royal dwelling. Over it were rude wooden figures, representing three eagles turned towards the east. A strong mud wall surrounded it, planted with stakes, on which were stuck the skulls of enemies sacrificed to the Sun; while before the door was a block of wood, on which lay a large shell surrounded with the braided hair of the victims. The interior was rude as a barn, dimly lighted from the doorway, and full of smoke. There was a structure in the middle which Membré thinks was a kind of altar; and before it burned a perpetual fire, fed with three logs laid end to end, and watched by two old men devoted to this sacred office. There was a mysterious recess, too, which the strangers were forbidden to explore, but which, as Tonty was told, contained the riches of the nation, consisting of pearls from the

[1] Tonty, *1684*, *1693*. In the spurious narrative, published in Tonty's name, the account is embellished and exaggerated. Compare Membré in Le Clerc, II. 227. La Salle's statements in the *Relation* of 1682 (Thomassy, 12) sustain those of Tonty.

Gulf, and trinkets obtained, probably through other tribes, from the Spaniards and other Europeans.

The chief condescended to visit La Salle at his camp; a favor which he would by no means have granted, had the visitors been Indians. A master of ceremonies and six attendants preceded him, to clear the path and prepare the place of meeting. When all was ready, he was seen advancing, clothed in a white robe, and preceded by two men bearing white fans, while a third displayed a disk of burnished copper, doubtless to represent the Sun, his ancestor, or, as others will have it, his elder brother. His aspect was marvellously grave, and he and La Salle met with gestures of ceremonious courtesy. The interview was very friendly; and the chief returned well pleased with the gifts which his entertainer bestowed on him, and which, indeed, had been the principal motive of his visit.

On the next morning, as they descended the river, they saw a wooden canoe full of Indians; and Tonty gave chase. He had nearly overtaken it, when more than a hundred men appeared suddenly on the shore, with bows bent to defend their countrymen. La Salle called out to Tonty to withdraw. He obeyed; and the whole party encamped on the opposite bank. Tonty offered to cross the river with a peace-pipe, and set out accordingly with a small party of men. When he landed, the Indians made signs of friendship by joining their hands,—a proceeding by which Tonty, having but one hand, was somewhat embarrassed; but he directed his men to respond in his stead. La Salle and Membré now joined him, and went with the Indians to their village, three leagues distant. Here they spent the night. "The Sieur de la Salle," writes Membré, "whose very air, engaging manners, tact, and address attract love and respect alike, produced such an effect on the hearts of these people that they did not know how to treat us well enough."[1]

The Indians of this village were the Natchez; and their chief was brother of the great chief, or Sun, of the whole nation. His town was several leagues distant, near the site of the city of Natchez; and thither the French repaired to visit him. They saw what they had already seen among the Taen-

[1] Membré in Le Clerc, II. 232.

sas,— a religious and political despotism, a privileged caste descended from the sun, a temple, and a sacred fire.[1] La Salle planted a large cross, with the arms of France attached, in the midst of the town; while the inhabitants looked on with a satisfaction which they would hardly have displayed, had they understood the meaning of the act.

The French next visited the Coroas, at their village, two leagues below; and here they found a reception no less auspicious. On the thirty-first of March, as they approached Red River, they passed in the fog a town of the Oumas; and, three days later, discovered a party of fishermen, in wooden canoes, among the canes along the margin of the water. They fled at sight of the Frenchmen. La Salle sent men to reconnoitre, who, as they struggled through the marsh, were greeted with a shower of arrows; while, from the neighboring village of the Quinipissas,[2] invisible behind the canebrake, they heard the sound of an Indian drum and the whoops of the mustering warriors. La Salle, anxious to keep the peace with all the tribes along the river, recalled his men, and pursued his voyage. A few leagues below, they saw a cluster of Indian lodges on the left bank, apparently void of inhabitants. They landed,

[1] The Natchez and the Taensas, whose habits and customs were similar, did not, in their social organization, differ radically from other Indians. The same principle of clanship, or *totemship*, so widely spread, existed in full force among them, combined with their religious ideas, and developed into forms of which no other example, equally distinct, is to be found. (For Indian clanship, see The Jesuits in North America, *Introduction*.) Among the Natchez and Taensas, the principal clan formed a ruling caste; and its chiefs had the attributes of demi-gods. As descent was through the female, the chief's son never succeeded him, but the son of one of his sisters; and as she, by the usual totemic law, was forced to marry in another clan,— that is, to marry a common mortal,— her husband, though the destined father of a demi-god, was treated by her as little better than a slave. She might kill him, if he proved unfaithful; but he was forced to submit to her infidelities in silence.

The customs of the Natchez have been described by Du Pratz, Le Petit, Penicaut, and others. Charlevoix visited their temple in 1721, and found it in a somewhat shabby condition. At this time, the Taensas were extinct. In 1729, the Natchez, enraged by the arbitrary conduct of a French commandant, massacred the neighboring settlers, and were in consequence expelled from their country, and nearly destroyed. A few still survive, incorporated with the Creeks; but they have lost their peculiar customs.

[2] In St. Charles County, on the left bank, not far above New Orleans.

and found three of them filled with corpses. It was a village of the Tangibao, sacked by their enemies only a few days before.[1]

And now they neared their journey's end. On the sixth of April, the river divided itself into three broad channels. La Salle followed that of the west, and D'Autray that of the east; while Tonty took the middle passage. As he drifted down the turbid current, between the low and marshy shores, the brackish water changed to brine, and the breeze grew fresh with the salt breath of the sea. Then the broad bosom of the great Gulf opened on his sight, tossing its restless billows, limitless, voiceless, lonely as when born of chaos, without a sail, without a sign of life.

La Salle, in a canoe, coasted the marshy borders of the sea; and then the reunited parties assembled on a spot of dry ground, a short distance above the mouth of the river. Here a column was made ready, bearing the arms of France, and inscribed with the words, —

LOUIS LE GRAND, ROY DE FRANCE ET DE NAVARRE, RÈGNE; LE NEUVIÈME AVRIL, 1682.

The Frenchmen were mustered under arms; and, while the New England Indians and their squaws looked on in wondering silence, they chanted the *Te Deum*, the *Exaudiat*, and the *Domine salvum fac Regem*. Then, amid volleys of musketry and shouts of *Vive le Roi*, La Salle planted the column in its place, and, standing near it, proclaimed in a loud voice, —

"In the name of the most high, mighty, invincible, and victorious Prince, Louis the Great, by the grace of God King of France and of Navarre, Fourteenth of that name, I, this ninth day of April, one thousand six hundred and eighty-two, in virtue of the commission of his Majesty, which I hold in my hand, and which may be seen by all whom it may concern, have taken, and do now take, in the name of his Majesty and of his successors to the crown, possession of this country of Louisiana, the seas, harbors, ports, bays, adjacent straits, and all the nations, peoples, provinces, cities, towns, villages, mines, minerals, fisheries, streams, and rivers, within the ex-

---

[1] Hennepin uses this incident, as well as most of those which have preceded it, in making up the story of his pretended voyage to the Gulf.

tent of the said Louisiana, from the mouth of the great river
St. Louis, otherwise called the Ohio, . . . as also along the
river Colbert, or Mississippi, and the rivers which discharge
themselves thereinto, from its source beyond the country of
the Nadouessioux . . . as far as its mouth at the sea, or Gulf
of Mexico, and also to the mouth of the River of Palms, upon
the assurance we have had from the natives of these countries,
that we are the first Europeans who have descended or ascended the said river Colbert; hereby protesting against all
who may hereafter undertake to invade any or all of these
aforesaid countries, peoples, or lands, to the prejudice of the
rights of his Majesty, acquired by the consent of the nations
dwelling herein. Of which, and of all else that is needful, I
hereby take to witness those who hear me, and demand an
act of the notary here present."[1]

Shouts of *Vive le Roi* and volleys of musketry responded to
his words. Then a cross was planted beside the column, and
a leaden plate buried near it, bearing the arms of France, with
a Latin inscription, *Ludovicus Magnus regnat*. The weather-
beaten voyagers joined their voices in the grand hymn of the
Vexilla Regis: —

> "The banners of Heaven's King advance,
> The mystery of the Cross shines forth;"

and renewed shouts of *Vive le Roi* closed the ceremony.

On that day, the realm of France received on parchment a
stupendous accession. The fertile plains of Texas; the vast

---

[1] In the passages omitted above, for the sake of brevity, the Ohio is mentioned as being called also the *Olighin-* (Alleghany) *Sipou*, and *Chukagoua*;
and La Salle declares that he takes possession of the country with the consent
of the nations dwelling in it, of whom he names the Chaouanons (Shawanoes), Kious, or Nadouessious (Sioux), Chikachas (Chickasaws), Motan-
tees(?), Illinois, Mitchigamias, Arkansas, Natchez, and Koroas. This alleged
consent is, of course, mere farce. If there could be any doubt as to the meaning of the words of La Salle, as recorded in the *Procès Verbal de la Prise de
Possession de la Louisiane*, it would be set at rest by Le Clerc, who says: "Le
Sieur de la Salle prit au nom de sa Majesté possession de ce fleuve, *de toutes
les rivières qui y entrent, et de tous les pays qu'elles arrosent*." These words are
borrowed from the report of La Salle (see Thomassy, 14). A copy of the
original *Procès Verbal* is before me. It bears the name of Jacques de la Métairie, Notary of Fort Frontenac, who was one of the party.

basin of the Mississippi, from its frozen northern springs to the sultry borders of the Gulf; from the woody ridges of the Alleghanies to the bare peaks of the Rocky Mountains,—a region of savannahs and forests, sun-cracked deserts, and grassy prairies, watered by a thousand rivers, ranged by a thousand warlike tribes, passed beneath the sceptre of the Sultan of Versailles; and all by virtue of a feeble human voice, inaudible at half a mile.

Chapter XXI
1682, 1683
ST. LOUIS OF THE ILLINOIS

*Louisiana • Illness of La Salle • His Colony on the Illinois • Fort
St. Louis • Recall of Frontenac • Le Febvre de la Barre • Critical
Position of La Salle • Hostility of the New Governor • Triumph of
the Adverse Faction • La Salle sails for France*

LOUISIANA was the name bestowed by La Salle on the new domain of the French crown. The rule of the Bourbons in the West is a memory of the past, but the name of the Great King still survives in a narrow corner of their lost empire. The Louisiana of to-day is but a single State of the American republic. The Louisiana of La Salle stretched from the Alleghanies to the Rocky Mountains; from the Rio Grande and the Gulf to the farthest springs of the Missouri.[1]

La Salle had written his name in history; but his hard-earned success was but the prelude of a harder task. Herculean labors lay before him, if he would realize the schemes with which his brain was pregnant. Bent on accomplishing them, he retraced his course, and urged his canoes upward against the muddy current. The party were famished. They had little to subsist on but the flesh of alligators. When they reached the Quinipissas, who had proved hostile on their way down, they resolved to risk an interview with them, in the hope of obtaining food. The treacherous savages dissembled, brought them corn, and on the following night made an attack upon them, but met with a bloody repulse. They next revisited the Coroas, and found an unfavorable change in their disposition towards them. They feasted them, indeed,

[1] The boundaries are laid down on the great map of Franquelin, made in 1684, and preserved in the Dépôt des Cartes of the Marine. The line runs along the south shore of Lake Erie, and thence follows the heads of the streams flowing into Lake Michigan. It then turns north-west, and is lost in the vast unknown of the now British Territories. On the south, it is drawn by the heads of the streams flowing into the Gulf, as far west as Mobile, after which it follows the shore of the Gulf to a little south of the Rio Grande; then runs west, north-west, and finally north, along the range of the Rocky Mountains.

but during the repast surrounded them with an overwhelming force of warriors. The French, however, kept so well on their guard, that their entertainers dared not make an attack, and suffered them to depart unmolested.[1]

And now, in a career of unwonted success and anticipated triumph, La Salle was arrested by a foe against which the boldest heart avails nothing. As he ascended the Mississippi, he was seized by a dangerous illness. Unable to proceed, he sent forward Tonty to Michillimackinac, whence, after despatching news of their discovery to Canada, he was to return to the Illinois. La Salle himself lay helpless at Fort Prudhomme, the palisade work which his men had built at the Chickasaw Bluffs on their way down. Father Zenobe Membré attended him; and, at the end of July, he was once more in a condition to advance by slow movements towards Fort Miami, which he reached in about a month.

In September, he rejoined Tonty at Michillimackinac, and in the following month wrote to a friend in France: "Though my discovery is made, and I have descended the Mississippi to the Gulf of Mexico, I cannot send you this year either an account of my journey or a map. On the way back, I was attacked by a deadly disease which kept me in danger of my life for forty days, and left me so weak that I could think of nothing for four months after. I have hardly strength enough now to write my letters, and the season is so far advanced that I cannot detain a single day this canoe which I send expressly to carry them. If I had not feared being forced to winter on the way, I should have tried to get to Quebec to meet the new governor, if it is true that we are to have one; but, in my present condition, this would be an act of suicide on account of the bad nourishment I should have all winter, in case the snow and ice stopped me on the way. Besides, my presence is absolutely necessary in the place to which I am going. I pray you, my dear sir, to give me once more all the help you can. I have great enemies, who have succeeded in all they have undertaken. I do not pretend to resist them, but only to justify myself, so that I can pursue by sea the plans I have begun here by land."

[1] Tonty, *1684, 1693*.

This was what he had proposed to himself from the first; that is, to abandon the difficult access through Canada, beset with enemies, and open a way to his western domain through the Gulf and the Mississippi. This was the aim of all his toilsome explorations. Could he have accomplished his first intention of building a vessel on the Illinois and descending in her to the Gulf, he would have been able to defray in good measure the costs of the enterprise by means of the furs and buffalo-hides collected on the way and carried in her to France. With a fleet of canoes, this was impossible; and there was nothing to offset the enormous outlay which he and his associates had made. He meant, as we have seen, to found on the banks of the Illinois a colony of French and Indians to answer the double purpose of a bulwark against the Iroquois and a place of storage for the furs of all the western tribes; and he hoped in the following year to secure an outlet for this colony and for all the trade of the valley of the Mississippi, by occupying the mouth of that river with a fort and another colony. This, too, was an essential part of his original design.

But for his illness, he would have gone to France to provide for its execution. Meanwhile, he ordered Tonty to collect as many men as possible, and begin the projected colony on the banks of the Illinois. A report soon after reached him that those pests of the wilderness, the Iroquois, were about to renew their attacks on the western tribes. This would be fatal to his plans; and, following Tonty to the Illinois, he rejoined him near the site of the great town.

The cliff called "Starved Rock," now pointed out to travellers as the chief natural curiosity of the region, rises, steep on three sides as a castle wall, to the height of a hundred and twenty-five feet above the river. In front, it overhangs the water that washes its base; its western brow looks down on the tops of the forest trees below; and on the east lies a wide gorge or ravine, choked with the mingled foliage of oaks, walnuts, and elms; while in its rocky depths a little brook creeps down to mingle with the river. From the trunk of the stunted cedar that leans forward from the brink, you may drop a plummet into the river below, where the cat-fish and the turtles may plainly be seen gliding over the wrinkled sands of the clear and shallow current. The cliff is accessible only from behind, where a man may climb up, not without difficulty, by a steep and narrow passage. The top is about an acre in extent. Here, in the month of December, La Salle and Tonty began to entrench themselves. They cut away the forest that crowned the rock, built storehouses and dwellings of its remains, dragged timber up the rugged pathway, and encircled the summit with a palisade.[1]

Thus the winter passed, and meanwhile the work of negotiation went prosperously on. The minds of the Indians had been already prepared. In La Salle they saw their champion against the Iroquois, the standing terror of all this region. They gathered around his stronghold like the timorous peas-

[1] "Starved Rock" perfectly answers, in every respect, to the indications of the contemporary maps and documents concerning "Le Rocher," the site of La Salle's fort of St. Louis. It is laid down on several contemporary maps, besides the great map of La Salle's discoveries, made in 1684. They all place it on the south side of the river; whereas Buffalo Rock, three miles above, which has been supposed to be the site of the fort, is on the north. The latter is crowned by a plateau of great extent, is but sixty feet high, is accessible at many points, and would require a large force to defend it; whereas La Salle chose "Le Rocher," because a few men could hold it against a multitude. Charlevoix, in 1721, describes both rocks, and says that the top of Buffalo Rock had been occupied by the Miami village, so that it was known as *Le Fort des Miamis*. This is confirmed by Joutel, who found the Miamis here in 1687. Charlevoix then speaks of "Le Rocher," calling it by that name; says that it is about a league below, on the left or south side, forming a sheer cliff, very high, and looking like a fortress on the border of the river. He saw remains of palisades at the top, which, he thinks, were made by the Illinois (*Journal Historique*, Let. XXVII.), though his countrymen had occupied it only three years before. "The French reside on the rock (Le Rocher), which is very lofty and impregnable."— *Memoir on Western Indians*, 1718, in N. Y. *Col. Docs.*, IX. 890. St. Cosme, passing this way in 1699, mentions it as "Le Vieux Fort," and says that it is "a rock about a hundred feet high at the edge of the river, where M. de la Salle built a fort, since abandoned."— *Journal de St. Cosme*. Joutel, who was here in 1687, says, "Fort St. Louis is on a steep rock, about two hundred feet high, with the river running at its base." He adds that its only defences were palisades. The true height, as stated above, is about a hundred and twenty-five feet.

A traditional interest also attaches to this rock. It is said that, in the Indian wars that followed the assassination of Pontiac, a few years after the cession of Canada, a party of Illinois, assailed by the Pottawattamies, here took refuge, defying attack. At length, they were all destroyed by starvation, and hence the name of "Starved Rock."

For other proofs concerning this locality, see *ante*, p. 881.

antry of the middle ages around the rock-built castle of their
feudal lord. From the wooden ramparts of St. Louis,—for so
he named his fort,—high and inaccessible as an eagle's nest,
a strange scene lay before his eye. The broad, flat valley of the
Illinois was spread beneath him like a map, bounded in the
distance by its low wall of woody hills. The river wound at
his feet in devious channels among islands bordered with
lofty trees; then, far on the left, flowed calmly westward
through the vast meadows, till its glimmering blue ribbon
was lost in hazy distance.

There had been a time, and that not remote, when these
fair meadows were a waste of death and desolation, scathed
with fire, and strewn with the ghastly relics of an Iroquois
victory. Now all was changed. La Salle looked down from his
rock on a concourse of wild human life. Lodges of bark and
rushes, or cabins of logs, were clustered on the open plain or
along the edges of the bordering forests. Squaws labored,
warriors lounged in the sun, naked children whooped and
gambolled on the grass. Beyond the river, a mile and a half
on the left, the banks were studded once more with the
lodges of the Illinois, who, to the number of six thousand,
had returned, since their defeat, to this their favorite dwelling-place. Scattered along the valley, among the adjacent hills,
or over the neighboring prairie, were the cantonments of a
half-score of other tribes, and fragments of tribes, gathered
under the protecting ægis of the French: Shawanoes from the
Ohio, Abenakis from Maine, Miamis from the sources of the
Kankakee, with others whose barbarous names are hardly
worth the record.[1] Nor were these La Salle's only dependants.
By the terms of his patent, he held seigniorial rights over this

[1] This singular extemporized colony of La Salle, on the banks of the Illinois, is laid down in detail on the great map of La Salle's discoveries, by Jean
Baptiste Franquelin, finished in 1684. There can be no doubt that this part of
the work is composed from authentic data. La Salle himself, besides others
of his party, came down from the Illinois in the autumn of 1683, and undoubtedly supplied the young engineer with materials. The various Indian
villages, or cantonments, are all indicated, with the number of warriors belonging to each, the aggregate corresponding very nearly with that of La
Salle's report to the minister. The Illinois, properly so called, are set down at
1,200 warriors; the Miamis, at 1,300; the Shawanoes, at 200; the Ouiatenons
(Weas), at 500; the Peanqhichia (Piankishaw) band, at 150; the Pepikokia, at

wild domain; and he now began to grant it out in parcels to his followers. These, however, were as yet but a score; a lawless band, trained in forest license, and marrying, as their detractors affirm, a new squaw every day in the week. This was after their lord's departure, for his presence imposed a check on these eccentricities.

La Salle, in a memoir addressed to the Minister of the Marine, reports the total number of the Indians around Fort St. Louis at about four thousand warriors, or twenty thousand souls. His diplomacy had been crowned with a marvellous

---

160; the Kilatica, at 300; and the Ouabona, at 70; in all, 3,880 warriors. A few others, probably Abenakis, lived in the fort.

The Fort St. Louis is placed, on the map, at the exact site of Starved Rock, and the Illinois village at the place where, as already mentioned (see p. 881), Indian remains in great quantities are yearly ploughed up. The Shawanoe camp, or village, is placed on the south side of the river, behind the fort. The country is here hilly, broken, and now, as in La Salle's time, covered with wood, which, however, soon ends in the open prairie. A short time since, the remains of a low, irregular earthwork of considerable extent were discovered at the intersection of two ravines, about twenty-four hundred feet behind, or south of, Starved Rock. The earthwork follows the line of the ravines on two sides. On the east, there is an opening, or gateway, leading to the adjacent prairie. The work is very irregular in form, and shows no trace of the civilized engineer. In the stump of an oak-tree upon it, Dr. Paul counted a hundred and sixty rings of annual growth. The village of the Shawanoes (Chaouenons), on Franquelin's map, corresponds with the position of this earthwork. I am indebted to the kindness of Dr. John Paul, and Colonel D. F. Hitt, the proprietor of Starved Rock, for a plan of these curious remains and a survey of the neighboring district. I must also express my obligations to Mr. W. E. Bowman, photographer at Ottawa, for views of Starved Rock and other features of the neighboring scenery.

An interesting relic of the early explorers of this region was found a few years ago at Ottawa, six miles above Starved Rock, in the shape of a small iron gun, buried several feet deep in the drift of the river. It consists of a welded tube of iron, about an inch and a half in calibre, strengthened by a series of thick iron rings, cooled on, after the most ancient as well as the most recent method of making cannon. It is about fourteen inches long, the part near the muzzle having been burst off. The construction is very rude. Small field-pieces, on a similar principle, were used in the fourteenth century. Several of them may be seen at the Musée d'Artillerie at Paris. In the time of Louis XIV., the art of casting cannon was carried to a high degree of perfection. The gun in question may have been made by a French blacksmith on the spot. A far less probable supposition is, that it is a relic of some unrecorded visit of the Spaniards; but the pattern of the piece would have been antiquated, even in the time of De Soto.

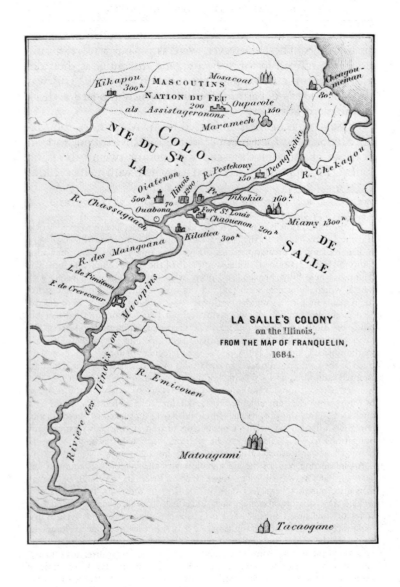

LA SALLE'S COLONY
on the Illinois,
FROM THE MAP OF FRANQUELIN,
1684.

success, for which his thanks were due, first to the Iroquois, and the universal terror they inspired; next, to his own address and unwearied energy. His colony had sprung up, as it were, in a night; but might not a night suffice to disperse it?

The conditions of maintaining it were twofold: first, he must give efficient aid to his savage colonists against the Iroquois; secondly, he must supply them with French goods in exchange for their furs. The men, arms, and ammunition for their defence, and the goods for trading with them, must be brought from Canada, until a better and surer avenue of supply could be provided through the entrepôt which he meant to establish at the mouth of the Mississippi. Canada was full of his enemies; but, as long as Count Frontenac was in power, he was sure of support. Count Frontenac was in power no longer. He had been recalled to France through the intrigues of the party adverse to La Salle; and Le Febvre de la Barre reigned in his stead.

La Barre was an old naval officer of rank, advanced to a post for which he proved himself notably unfit. If he was without the arbitrary passions which had been the chief occasion of the recall of his predecessor, he was no less without his energies and his talents. He showed a weakness and an avarice for which his age may have been in some measure answerable. He was no whit less unscrupulous than his predecessor in his secret violation of the royal ordinances regulating the fur-trade, which it was his duty to enforce. Like Frontenac, he took advantage of his position to carry on an illicit traffic with the Indians; but it was with different associates. The late governor's friends were the new governor's enemies; and La Salle, armed with his monopolies, was the object of his especial jealousy.[1]

Meanwhile, La Salle, buried in the western wilderness, remained for the time ignorant of La Barre's disposition to-

---

[1] The royal instructions to La Barre, on his assuming the government, dated at Versailles, 10 May, 1682, require him to give no farther permission to make journeys of discovery towards the Sioux and the Mississippi, as his Majesty thinks his subjects better employed in cultivating the land. The letter adds, however, that La Salle is to be allowed to continue his discoveries, if they appear to be useful. The same instructions are repeated in a letter of the Minister of the Marine to the new intendant of Canada, De Meules.

wards him, and made an effort to secure his good-will and countenance. He wrote to him from his rock of St. Louis, early in the spring of 1683, expressing the hope that he should have from him the same support as from Count Frontenac; "although," he says, "my enemies will try to influence you against me." His attachment to Frontenac, he pursues, has been the cause of all the late governor's enemies turning against him. He then recounts his voyage down the Mississippi; says that, with twenty-two Frenchmen, he caused all the tribes along the river to ask for peace; and speaks of his right under the royal patent to build forts anywhere along his route, and grant out lands around them, as at Fort Frontenac.

"My losses in my enterprises," he continues, "have exceeded forty thousand crowns. I am now going four hundred leagues south-south-west of this place, to induce the Chickasaws to follow the Shawanoes, and other tribes, and settle, like them, at St. Louis. It remained only to settle French colonists here, and this I have already done. I hope you will not detain them as *coureurs de bois*, when they come down to Montreal to make necessary purchases. I am aware that I have no right to trade with the tribes who descend to Montreal, and I shall not permit such trade to my men; nor have I ever issued licenses to that effect, as my enemies say that I have done."[1]

Again, on the fourth of June following, he writes to La Barre, from the Chicago portage, complaining that some of his colonists, going to Montreal for necessary supplies, have been detained by his enemies, and begging that they may be allowed to return, that his enterprise may not be ruined. "The Iroquois," he pursues, "are again invading the country. Last year, the Miamis were so alarmed by them that they abandoned their town and fled; but at my return they came back, and have been induced to settle with the Illinois at my fort of St. Louis. The Iroquois have lately murdered some families of their nation, and they are all in terror again. I am afraid they will take flight, and so prevent the Missouris and neighboring tribes from coming to settle at St. Louis, as they are about to do.

"Some of the Hurons and French tell the Miamis that I am

[1] *Lettre de La Salle à La Barre, Fort St. Louis, 2 Avril, 1683*. The above is condensed from passages in the original.

keeping them here for the Iroquois to destroy. I pray that you will let me hear from you, that I may give these people some assurances of protection before they are destroyed in my sight. Do not suffer my men who have come down to the settlements to be longer prevented from returning. There is great need here of reinforcements. The Iroquois, as I have said, have lately entered the country; and a great terror prevails. I have postponed going to Michillimackinac, because, if the Iroquois strike any blow in my absence, the Miamis will think that I am in league with them; whereas, if I and the French stay among them, they will regard us as protectors. But, Monsieur, it is in vain that we risk our lives here, and that I exhaust my means in order to fulfil the intentions of his Majesty, if all my measures are crossed in the settlements below, and if those who go down to bring munitions, without which we cannot defend ourselves, are detained under pretexts trumped up for the occasion. If I am prevented from bringing up men and supplies, as I am allowed to do by the permit of Count Frontenac, then my patent from the king is useless. It would be very hard for us, after having done what was required, even before the time prescribed, and after suffering severe losses, to have our efforts frustrated by obstacles got up designedly.

"I trust that, as it lies with you alone to prevent or to permit the return of the men whom I have sent down, you will not so act as to thwart my plans. A part of the goods which I have sent by them belong not to me, but to the Sieur de Tonty, and are a part of his pay. Others are to buy munitions indispensable for our defence. Do not let my creditors seize them. It is for their advantage that my fort, full as it is of goods, should be held against the enemy. I have only twenty men, with scarcely a hundred pounds of powder; and I cannot long hold the country without more. The Illinois are very capricious and uncertain. . . . If I had men enough to send out to reconnoitre the enemy, I would have done so before this; but I have not enough. I trust you will put it in my power to obtain more, that this important colony may be saved."[1]

[1] *Lettre de La Salle à La Barre, Portage de Chicagou, 4 Juin, 1683.* The substance of the letter is given above, in a condensed form. A passage is omitted,

While La Salle was thus writing to La Barre, La Barre was writing to Seignelay, the Marine and Colonial Minister, decrying his correspondent's discoveries, and pretending to doubt their reality. "The Iroquois," he adds, "have sworn his [La Salle's] death. The imprudence of this man is about to involve the colony in war."[1] And again he writes, in the following spring, to say that La Salle was with a score of vagabonds at Green Bay, where he set himself up as a king, pillaged his countrymen, and put them to ransom, exposed the tribes of the West to the incursions of the Iroquois, and all under pretence of a patent from his Majesty, the provisions of which he grossly abused; but, as his privileges would expire on the twelfth of May ensuing, he would then be forced to come to Quebec, where his creditors, to whom he owed more than thirty thousand crowns, were anxiously awaiting him.[2]

Finally, when La Barre received the two letters from La Salle, of which the substance is given above, he sent copies of them to the Minister Seignelay, with the following comment: "By the copies of the Sieur de la Salle's letters, you will perceive that his head is turned, and that he has been bold enough to give you intelligence of a false discovery, and that, instead of returning to the colony to learn what the king wishes him to do, he does not come near me, but keeps in the backwoods, five hundred leagues off, with the idea of attracting the inhabitants to him, and building up an imaginary kingdom for himself, by debauching all the bankrupts and idlers of this country. If you will look at the two letters I had from him, you can judge the character of this personage better than I can. Affairs with the Iroquois are in such a state that I cannot allow him to muster all their enemies together and put himself at their head. All the men who brought me

---

in which La Salle expresses his belief that his vessel, the "Griffin," had been destroyed, not by Indians, but by the pilot, who, as he thinks, had been induced to sink her, and then, with some of the crew, attempted to join Du Lhut with their plunder, but were captured by Indians on the Mississippi.

[1] *Lettre de La Barre au Ministre, 14 Nov., 1682.*

[2] *Lettre de La Barre au Ministre, 30 Avril, 1683.* La Salle had spent the winter, not at Green Bay, as this slanderous letter declares, but in the Illinois country.

news from him have abandoned him, and say not a word about returning, *but sell the furs they have brought as if they were their own*; so that he cannot hold his ground much longer."[1] Such calumnies had their effect. The enemies of La Salle had already gained the ear of the king; and he had written in August, from Fontainebleau, to his new governor of Canada: "I am convinced, like you, that the discovery of the Sieur de la Salle is very useless, and that such enterprises ought to be prevented in future, as they tend only to debauch the inhabitants by the hope of gain, and to diminish the revenue from beaver-skins."[2]

In order to understand the posture of affairs at this time, it must be remembered that Dutch and English traders of New York were urging on the Iroquois to attack the western tribes, with the object of gaining, through their conquest, the control of the fur-trade of the interior, and diverting it from Montreal to Albany. The scheme was full of danger to Canada, which the loss of the trade would have ruined. La Barre and his associates were greatly alarmed at it. Its complete success would have been fatal to their hopes of profit; but they nevertheless wished it such a measure of success as would ruin their rival, La Salle. Hence, no little satisfaction mingled with their anxiety, when they heard that the Iroquois were again threatening to invade the Miamis and the Illinois; and thus La Barre, whose duty it was strenuously to oppose the intrigue of the English, and use every effort to quiet the ferocious bands whom they were hounding against the Indian allies of the French, was, in fact, but half-hearted in the work. He cut off La Salle from all supplies; detained the men whom he sent for succor; and, at a conference with the Iroquois, told them that they were welcome to plunder and kill him.[3]

The old governor, and the unscrupulous ring with which he was associated, now took a step to which he was doubtless

---

[1] *Lettre de La Barre au Ministre, 4 Nov., 1683.*

[2] *Lettre du Roy à La Barre, 5 Août, 1683.*

[3] *Mémoire pour rendre compte à Monseigneur le Marquis de Seignelay de l'État où le Sieur de Lasalle a laissé le Fort Frontenac pendant le temps de sa découverte.* On La Barre's conduct, see Count Frontenac and New France under Louis XIV. chap. v.

emboldened by the tone of the king's letter, in condemnation of La Salle's enterprise. He resolved to seize Fort Frontenac, the property of La Salle, under the pretext that the latter had not fulfilled the conditions of the grant, and had not maintained a sufficient garrison.[1] Two of his associates, La Chesnaye and Le Ber, armed with an order from him, went up and took possession, despite the remonstrances of La Salle's creditors and mortgagees; lived on La Salle's stores, sold for their own profit, and (it is said) that of La Barre, the provisions sent by the king, and turned in the cattle to pasture on the growing crops. La Forest, La Salle's lieutenant, was told that he might retain the command of the fort, if he would join the associates; but he refused, and sailed in the autumn for France.[2]

Meanwhile, La Salle remained at the Illinois in extreme embarrassment, cut off from supplies, robbed of his men who had gone to seek them, and disabled from fulfilling the pledges he had given to the surrounding Indians. Such was his position, when reports came to Fort St. Louis that the Iroquois were at hand. The Indian hamlets were wild with terror, beseeching him for succor which he had no power to give. Happily, the report proved false. No Iroquois appeared; the threatened attack was postponed, and the summer passed away in peace. But La Salle's position, with the governor his declared enemy, was intolerable and untenable; and there was no resource but in the protection of the court. Early in the autumn, he left Tonty in command of the rock, bade farewell to his savage retainers, and descended to Quebec, intending to sail for France.

On his way, he met the Chevalier de Baugis, an officer of

---

[1] La Salle, when at Mackinaw, on his way to Quebec, in 1682, had been recalled to the Illinois, as we have seen, by a threatened Iroquois invasion. There is before me a copy of a letter which he then wrote to Count Frontenac, begging him to send up more soldiers to the fort, at his (La Salle's) expense. Frontenac, being about to sail for France, gave this letter to his newly arrived successor, La Barre, who, far from complying with the request, withdrew La Salle's soldiers already at the fort, and then made its defenceless state a pretext for seizing it. This statement is made in the memoir, addressed to Seignelay, before cited.

[2] These are the statements of the memorial, addressed in La Salle's behalf, to the minister, Seignelay.

the king's dragoons, commissioned by La Barre to take possession of Fort St. Louis, and bearing letters from the governor, ordering La Salle to come to Quebec; a superfluous command as he was then on his way thither. He smothered his wrath, and wrote to Tonty to receive De Baugis well. The chevalier and his party proceeded to the Illinois, and took possession of the fort; De Baugis commanding for the governor, while Tonty remained as representative of La Salle. The two officers could not live in harmony; but, with the return of spring, each found himself in sore need of aid from the other. Towards the end of March, the Iroquois attacked their citadel, and besieged it for six days, but at length withdrew, discomfited, carrying with them a number of Indian prisoners, most of whom escaped from their clutches.[1]

Meanwhile, La Salle had sailed for France.

[1] Tonty, *1684, 1693*; *Lettre de La Barre au Ministre, 5 Juin, 1684*; *Ibid., 9 Juillet, 1684*.

Chapter XXII

1680–1683

LA SALLE PAINTED BY HIMSELF

Difficulty of knowing him • His Detractors • His Letters • Vexations of his Position • His Unfitness for Trade • Risks of Correspondence • His Reported Marriage • Alleged Ostentation • Motives of Action • Charges of Harshness • Intrigues against him • Unpopular Manners • A Strange Confession • His Strength and his Weakness • Contrasts of his Character

WE have seen La Salle in his acts. While he crosses the sea, let us look at him in himself. Few men knew him, even of those who saw him most. Reserved and self-contained as he was, with little vivacity or gayety or love of pleasure, he was a sealed book to those about him. His daring energy and endurance were patent to all; but the motive forces that urged him, and the influences that wrought beneath the surface of his character, were hidden where few eyes could pierce. His enemies were free to make their own interpretations, and they did not fail to use the opportunity.

The interests arrayed against him were incessantly at work. His men were persuaded to desert and rob him; the Iroquois were told that he was arming the western tribes against them; the western tribes were told that he was betraying them to the Iroquois; his proceedings were denounced to the court; and continual efforts were made to alienate his associates. They, on their part, sore as they were from disappointment and loss, were in a mood to listen to the aspersions cast upon him; and they pestered him with letters, asking questions, demanding explanations, and dunning him for money. It is through his answers that we are best able to judge him; and at times, by those touches of nature which make the whole world kin, they teach us to know him and to feel for him.

The main charges against him were that he was a crackbrained schemer, that he was harsh to his men, that he traded where he had no right to trade, and that his discoveries were nothing but a pretence for making money. No accusations appear that touch his integrity or his honor.

It was hard to convince those who were always losing by him. A remittance of good dividends would have been his best answer, and would have made any other answer needless; but, instead of bills of exchange, he had nothing to give but excuses and explanations. In the autumn of 1680, he wrote to an associate who had demanded the long deferred profits: "I have had many misfortunes in the last two years. In the autumn of '78, I lost a vessel by the fault of the pilot; in the next summer, the deserters I told you about robbed me of eight or ten thousand livres' worth of goods. In the autumn of '79, I lost a vessel worth more than ten thousand crowns; in the next spring, five or six rascals stole the value of five or six thousand livres in goods and beaver-skins, at the Illinois, when I was absent. Two other men of mine, carrying furs worth four or five thousand livres, were killed or drowned in the St. Lawrence, and the furs were lost. Another robbed me of three thousand livres in beaver-skins stored at Michilli-mackinac. This last spring, I lost about seventeen hundred livres' worth of goods by the upsetting of a canoe. Last winter, the fort and buildings at Niagara were burned by the fault of the commander; and, in the spring, the deserters, who passed that way, seized a part of the property that remained, and escaped to New York. All this does not discourage me in the least, and will only defer for a year or two the returns of profit which you ask for this year. These losses are no more my fault than the loss of the ship 'St. Joseph' was yours. I cannot be everywhere, and cannot help making use of the people of the country."

He begs his correspondent to send out an agent of his own. "He need not be very *savant*, but he must be faithful, patient of labor, and fond neither of gambling, women, nor good cheer; for he will find none of these with me. Trusting in what he will write you, you may close your ears to what priests and Jesuits tell you.

"After having put matters in good trim for trade, I mean to withdraw, though I think it will be very profitable; for I am disgusted to find that I must always be making excuses, which is a part I cannot play successfully. I am utterly tired of this business; for I see that it is not enough to put property and life in constant peril, but that it requires more pains to answer envy and detraction than to overcome the difficulties inseparable from my undertaking."

And he makes a variety of proposals, by which he hopes to get rid of a part of his responsibility to his correspondent. He begs him again to send out a confidential agent, saying that for his part he does not want to have any account to render, except that which he owes to the court, of his discoveries. He adds, strangely enough for a man burdened with such liabilities, "I have neither the habit nor the inclination to keep books, nor have I anybody with me who knows how." He says to another correspondent, "I think, like you, that partnerships in business are dangerous, on account of the little practice I have in these matters." It is not surprising that he wanted to leave his associates to manage business for themselves: "You know that this trade is good; and, with a trusty agent to conduct it for you, you run no risk. As for me, I will keep the charge of the forts, the command of posts and of men, the management of Indians and Frenchmen, and the establishment of the colony, which will remain my property, leaving your agent and mine to look after our interests, and drawing my half without having any hand in what belongs to you."

La Salle was a very indifferent trader; and his heart was not in the commercial part of his enterprise. He aimed at achievement, and thirsted after greatness. His ambition was to found another France in the West; and, if he meant to govern it also,—as without doubt he did,—it is not a matter of wonder or of blame. His misfortune was that, in the pursuit of a great design, he was drawn into complications of business, with which he was ill fitted to grapple. He had not the instinct of the successful merchant. He dared too much, and often dared unwisely; attempted more than he could grasp; and forgot, in his sanguine anticipations, to reckon with enormous and incalculable risks.

Except in the narrative parts, his letters are rambling and unconnected, which is natural enough, written, as they were, at odd moments, by camp-fires and among Indians. The style is crude; and, being well aware of this, he disliked writing, especially as the risk was extreme that his letters would miss their destination. "There is too little good faith in this country, and too many people on the watch, for me to trust anybody with what I wish to send you. Even sealed letters are not too safe. Not only are they liable to be lost or stopped by the way, but even such as escape the curiosity of spies lie at Montreal, waiting a long time to be forwarded."

Again, he writes: "I cannot pardon myself for the stoppage of my letters, though I made every effort to make them reach you. I wrote to you in '79 (in August), and sent my letters to M. de la Forest, who gave them in good faith to my brother. I don't know what he has done with them. I wrote you another, by the vessel that was lost last year. I sent two canoes, by two different routes; but the wind and the rain were so furious that they wintered on the way, and I found my letters at the fort on my return. I now send you one of them, which I wrote last year to M. Thouret, in which you will find a full account of what passed, from the time when we left the outlet of Lake Erie down to the sixteenth of August, 1680. What preceded was told at full length in the letters my brother has seen fit to intercept."

This brother was the Sulpitian priest, Jean Cavelier, who had been persuaded that La Salle's enterprise would be ruinous, and therefore set himself, sometimes to stop it altogether, and sometimes to manage it in his own way. "His conduct towards me," says La Salle, "has always been so strange, through the small love he bears me, that it was clear gain for me when he went away; since, while he stayed, he did nothing but cross all my plans, which I was forced to change every moment to suit his caprice."

There was one point on which the interference of his brother and of his correspondents was peculiarly annoying. They thought it for their interest that he should remain a single man; whereas, it seems that his devotion to his purpose was not so engrossing as to exclude more tender subjects.

"I am told that you have been uneasy about my pretended marriage. I had not thought about it at that time; and I shall not make any engagement of the sort, till I have given you reason to be satisfied with me. It is a little extraordinary that I must render account of a matter which is free to all the world.

"In fine, Monsieur, it is only as an earnest of something

more substantial that I write to you so much at length. I do not doubt that you will hereafter change the ideas about me which some persons wish to give you, and that you will be relieved of the anxiety which all that has happened reasonably causes you. I have written this letter at more than twenty different times; and I am more than a hundred and fifty leagues from where I began it. I have still two hundred more to get over, before reaching the Illinois. I am taking with me twenty-five men to the relief of the six or seven who remain with the Sieur de Tonty."

This was the journey which ended in that scene of horror at the ruined town of the Illinois.

To the same correspondent, pressing him for dividends, he says: "You repeat continually that you will not be satisfied unless I make you large returns of profit. Though I have reason to thank you for what you have done for this enterprise, it seems to me that I have done still more, since I have put every thing at stake; and it would be hard to reproach me either with foolish outlays or with the ostentation which is falsely imputed to me. Let my accusers explain what they mean. Since I have been in this country, I have had neither servants nor clothes nor fare which did not savor more of meanness than of ostentation; and the moment I see that there is any thing with which either you or the court find fault, I assure you that I will give it up: for the life I am leading has no other attraction for me than that of honor; and the more danger and difficulty there is in undertakings of this sort, the more worthy of honor I think they are."

His career attests the sincerity of these words. They are a momentary betrayal of the deep enthusiasm of character which may be read in his life, but to which he rarely allowed the faintest expression.

"Above all," he continues, "if you want me to keep on, do not compel me to reply to all the questions and fancies of priests and Jesuits. They have more leisure than I; and I am not subtle enough to anticipate all their empty stories. I could easily give you the information you ask; but I have a right to expect that you will not believe all you hear, nor require me to prove to you that I am not a madman. That is the first point to which you should have attended, before having business with me; and, in our long acquaintance, either you must have found me out, or else I must have had long intervals of sanity."

To another correspondent, he defends himself against the charge of harshness to his men: "The facility I am said to want is out of place with this sort of people, who are libertines, for the most part; and to indulge them means to tolerate blasphemy, drunkenness, lewdness, and a license incompatible with any kind of order. It will not be found that I have in any case whatever treated any man harshly, except for blasphemies and other such crimes, openly committed. These I cannot tolerate: first, because such compliance would give grounds for another accusation, much more just; secondly, because, if I allowed such disorders to become habitual, it would be hard to keep the men in subordination and obedience, as regards executing the work I am commissioned to do; thirdly, because the debaucheries, too common with this rabble, are the source of endless delays and frequent thieving; and, finally, because I am a Christian, and do not want to bear the burden of their crimes.

"What is said about my servants has not even a show of truth; for I use no servants here, and all my men are on the same footing. I grant that, as those who have lived with me are steadier and give me no reason to complain of their behavior, I treat them as gently as I should treat the others, if they resembled them; and, as those who were formerly my servants are the only ones I can trust, I speak more openly to them than to the rest, who are generally spies of my enemies. The twenty-two men who deserted and robbed me are not to be believed on their word, deserters and thieves as they are. They are ready enough to find some pretext for their crime; and it needs as unjust a judge as the intendant to prompt such rascals to enter complaints against a person to whom he had given a warrant to arrest them. But, to show the falsity of these charges, Martin Chartier, who was one of those who excited the rest to do as they did, was never with me at all; and the rest had made their plot before seeing me." And he proceeds to relate, in great detail, a variety of circumstances to prove that his men had been instigated first to desert, and then to slander him;

adding, "Those who remain with me are the first I had, and they have not left me for six years."

"I have a hundred other proofs of the bad counsel given to these deserters, and will produce them when wanted; but as they themselves are the only witnesses of the severity they complain of, while the witnesses of their crimes are unimpeachable, why am I refused the justice I demand, and why is their secret escape connived at?

"I do not know what you mean by having popular manners. There is nothing special in my food, clothing, or lodging, which are all the same for me as for my men. How can it be that I do not talk with them? I have no other company. M. de Tonty has often found fault with me, because I stopped too often to talk with them. You do not know the men one must employ here, when you exhort me to make merry with them. They are incapable of that; for they are never pleased, unless one gives free rein to their drunkenness and other vices. If that is what you call having popular manners, neither honor nor inclination would let me stoop to gain their favor in a way so disreputable; and, besides, the consequences would be dangerous, and they would have the same contempt for me that they have for all who treat them in this fashion.

"You write me that even my friends say that I am not a man of popular manners. I do not know what friends they are. I know of none in this country. To all appearance, they are enemies, more subtle and secret than the rest. I make no exceptions; for I know that those who seem to give me support do not do it out of love for me, but because they are in some sort bound in honor, and that in their hearts they think I have dealt ill with them. M. Plet will tell you what he has heard about it himself, and the reasons they have to give.[1] I have seen it for a long time; and these secret stabs they give me show it very plainly. After that, it is not surprising that I open my mind to nobody, and distrust everybody. I have reasons that I cannot write.

[1] His cousin, François Plet, was in Canada in 1680, where, with La Salle's approval, he carried on the trade of Fort Frontenac, in order to indemnify himself for money advanced. La Salle always speaks of him with esteem and gratitude.

"For the rest, Monsieur, pray be well assured that the information you are so good as to give me is received with a gratitude equal to the genuine friendship from which it proceeds; and, however unjust are the charges made against me, I should be much more unjust myself, if I did not feel that I have as much reason to thank you for telling me of them as I have to complain of others for inventing them.

"As for what you say about my look and manner, I myself confess that you are not far from right. But *naturam expellas*; and, if I am wanting in expansiveness and show of feeling towards those with whom I associate, *it is only through a timidity which is natural to me, and which has made me leave various employments, where, without it, I could have succeeded.* But, as I judged myself ill-fitted for them on account of this defect, I have chosen a life more suited to my solitary disposition; which, nevertheless, does not make me harsh to my people, though, joined to a life among savages, it makes me, perhaps, less polished and complaisant than the atmosphere of Paris requires. I well believe that there is self-love in this; and that, knowing how little I am accustomed to a more polite life, the fear of making mistakes makes me more reserved than I like to be. So I rarely expose myself to conversation with those in whose company I am afraid of making blunders, and can hardly help making them. Abbé Renaudot knows with what repugnance I had the honor to appear before Monseigneur de Conti; and sometimes it took me a week to make up my mind to go to the audience, that is, when I had time to think about myself, and was not driven by pressing business. It is much the same with letters, which I never write except when pushed to it, and for the same reason. It is a defect of which I shall never rid myself as long as I live, often as it spites me against myself, and often as I quarrel with myself about it."

Here is a strange confession for a man like La Salle. Without doubt, the timidity of which he accuses himself had some of its roots in pride; but not the less was his pride vexed and humbled by it. It is surprising that, being what he was, he could have brought himself to such an avowal under any circumstances or any pressure of distress. Shyness; a morbid fear of committing himself; an incapacity to express, and much more to simulate feeling,—a trait sometimes seen in those with whom feeling is most deep,—are strange ingredients in the character of a man who had grappled so dauntlessly with life on its harshest and rudest side. They were deplorable defects for one in his position. He lacked that sympathetic power, the inestimable gift of the true leader of men, in which lies the difference between a willing and a constrained obedience. This solitary being, hiding his shyness under a cold reserve, could rouse no enthusiasm in his followers. He lived in the purpose which he had made a part of himself, nursed his plans in secret, and seldom asked or accepted advice. He trusted himself, and learned more and more to trust no others. One may fairly infer that distrust was natural to him; but the inference may possibly be wrong. Bitter experience had schooled him to it; for he lived among snares, pitfalls, and intriguing enemies. He began to doubt even the associates who, under representations he had made them in perfect good faith, had staked their money on his enterprise, and lost it, or were likely to lose it. They pursued him with advice and complaint, and half-believed that he was what his maligners called him, a visionary or a madman. It galled him that they had suffered for their trust in him, and that they had repented their trust. His lonely and shadowed nature needed the mellowing sunshine of success, and his whole life was a fight with adversity.

All that appears to the eye is his intrepid conflict with obstacles without, but this, perhaps, was no more arduous than the invisible and silent strife of a nature at war with itself; the pride, aspiration, and bold energy that lay at the base of his character battling against the superficial weakness that mortified and angered him. In such a man, the effect of such an infirmity is to concentrate and intensify the force within. In one form or another, discordant natures are common enough; but very rarely is the antagonism so irreconcilable as in him. And the greater the antagonism, the greater the pain. There are those in whom the sort of timidity from which he suffered is matched with no quality that strongly revolts against it. These gentle natures may at least have peace, but for him there was no peace.

Cavelier de La Salle stands in history like a statue cast in iron; but his own unwilling pen betrays the man, and reveals in the stern, sad figure an object of human interest and pity.[1]

[1] The following is the character of La Salle, as drawn by his friend, Abbé Bernou, in a memorial to the minister Seignelay: "Il est irréprochable dans ses mœurs, réglé dans sa conduite, et qui veut de l'ordre parmy ses gens. Il est savant, judicieux, politique, vigilant, infatigable, sobre, et intrépide. Il entend suffisament l'architecture civile, militaire, et navale, ainsy que l'agriculture; il parle ou entend quatre ou cinq langues des Sauvages, et a beaucoup de facilité pour apprendre les autres. Il sçait toutes leurs manières et obtient d'eux tout ce qu'il veut par son adresse, par son éloquence, et parce qu'il est beaucoup estimé d'eux. Dans ses voyages il ne fait pas meilleure chère que le moindre de ses gens et se donne plus de peine que pas un pour les encourager, et il y a lieu de croire qu'avec la protection de Monseigneur il fondera des colonies plus considérables que toutes celles que les François ont établies jusqu'à présent."—*Mémoire pour Monseigneur le Marquis de Seignelay, 1682* (Margry, II. 277).

The extracts given in the foregoing chapter are from La Salle's long letters of 29 Sept., 1680, and 22 Aug., 1682 (1681?). Both are printed in the second volume of the Margry collection, and the originals of both are in the Bibliothèque Nationale. The latter seems to have been written to La Salle's friend, Abbé Bernou; and the former, to a certain M. Thouret.

Chapter XXIII

1684

A NEW ENTERPRISE

La Salle at Court • His Proposals • Occupation of Louisiana •
Invasion of Mexico • Royal Favor • Preparation • A Divided
Command • Beaujeu and La Salle • Mental Condition of La Salle
• His Farewell to his Mother

WHEN La Salle reached Paris, he went to his old lodgings in Rue de la Truanderie, and, it is likely enough, thought for an instant of the adventures and vicissitudes he had passed since he occupied them before. Another ordeal awaited him. He must confront, not painted savages, with tomahawk and knife, but, what he shrank from more, the courtly throngs that still live and move in the pages of Sévigné and Saint-Simon.

The news of his discovery and the rumor of his schemes were the talk of a moment among the courtiers, and then were forgotten. It was not so with their master. La Salle's friends and patrons did not fail him. A student and a recluse in his youth, and a backwoodsman in his manhood, he had what was to him the formidable honor of an interview with royalty itself, and stood with such philosophy as he could command before the gilded arm-chair, where, majestic and awful, the power of France sat embodied. The king listened to all he said; but the results of the interview were kept so secret that it was rumored in the ante-chambers that his proposals had been rejected.[1]

On the contrary, they had met with more than favor. The moment was opportune for La Salle. The king had long been irritated against the Spaniards, because they not only excluded his subjects from their American ports, but forbade them to enter the Gulf of Mexico. Certain Frenchmen who had sailed on this forbidden sea had been seized and imprisoned, and more recently a small vessel of the royal navy had been captured for the same offence. This had drawn from the king a

[1] *Lettres de l'Abbé Tronson, 8 Avril, 10 Avril, 1684* (Margry, II. 354).

declaration that every sea should be free to all his subjects; and Count d'Estrées was sent with a squadron to the Gulf, to exact satisfaction of the Spaniards, or fight them if they refused it.[1] This was in time of peace. War had since arisen between the two crowns, and brought with it the opportunity of settling the question for ever. In order to do so, the minister Seignelay, like his father Colbert, proposed to establish a French port on the Gulf, as a permanent menace to the Spaniards and a basis of future conquest. It was in view of this plan that La Salle's past enterprises had been favored; and the proposals he now made were in perfect accord with it.

These proposals were set forth in two memorials. The first of them states that the late Monseigneur Colbert deemed it important for the service of his Majesty to discover a port in the Gulf of Mexico; that to this end the memorialist, La Salle, made five journeys of upwards of five thousand leagues, in great part on foot; and traversed more than six hundred leagues of unknown country, among savages and cannibals, at the cost of a hundred and fifty thousand francs. He now proposes to return by way of the Gulf of Mexico and the mouth of the Mississippi to the countries he has discovered, whence great benefits may be expected: first, the cause of God may be advanced by the preaching of the gospel to many Indian tribes; and, secondly, great conquests may be effected for the glory of the king, by the seizure of provinces rich in silver mines, and defended only by a few indolent and effeminate Spaniards. The Sieur de la Salle, pursues the memorial, binds himself to be ready for the accomplishment of this enterprise within one year after his arrival on the spot; and he asks for this purpose only one vessel and two hundred men, with their arms, munitions, pay, and maintenance. When Monseigneur shall direct him, he will give the details of what he proposes. The memorial then describes the boundless extent, the fertility and resources of the country watered by the river Colbert, or Mississippi; the necessity of guarding it against foreigners, who will be eager to seize it now that La Salle's discovery has made it known, and the ease with which it may be defended by one or two forts at a proper distance above its mouth,

[1] *Lettres du Roy et du Ministre sur la Navigation du Golfe du Mexique, 1669–1682* (Margry, III. 3–14).

which would form the key to an interior region eight hundred leagues in extent. "Should foreigners anticipate us," he adds, "they will complete the ruin of New France, which they already hem in by their establishments of Virginia, Pennsylvania, New England, and Hudson's Bay."[1]

The second memorial is more explicit. The place, it says, which the Sieur de la Salle proposes to fortify, is on the river Colbert, or Mississippi, sixty leagues above its mouth, where the soil is very fertile, the climate very mild, and whence we, the French, may control the continent; since, the river being narrow, we could defend ourselves by means of fire-ships against a hostile fleet, while the position is excellent both for attacking an enemy or retreating in case of need. The neighboring Indians detest the Spaniards, but love the French, having been won over by the kindness of the Sieur de la Salle. We could form of them an army of more than fifteen thousand savages, who, supported by the French and Abenakis, followers of the Sieur de la Salle, could easily subdue the province of New Biscay (the most northern province of Mexico), where there are but four hundred Spaniards, more fit to work the mines than to fight. On the north of New Biscay lie vast forests, extending to the river Seignelay[2] (Red River), which is but forty or fifty leagues from the Spanish province. This river affords the means of attacking it to great advantage.

In view of these facts, pursues the memorial, the Sieur de la Salle offers, if the war with Spain continues, to undertake this conquest with two hundred men from France. He will take on his way fifty buccaneers at St. Domingo, and direct the four thousand Indian warriors at Fort St. Louis of the Illinois to descend the river and join him. He will separate his force into three divisions, and attack at the same time the centre and the two extremities of the province. To accomplish this great design, he asks only for a vessel of thirty guns, a few cannon for the forts, and power to raise in France two hundred such men as he shall think fit, to be armed, paid, and maintained six months at the king's charge. And the Sieur de

---

[1] *Mémoire du Sr de la Salle, pour rendre compte à Monseigneur de Seignelay de la découverte qu'il a faite par l'ordre de sa Majesté.*

[2] This name, also given to the Illinois, is used to designate Red River on the map of Franquelin, where the forests above mentioned are represented.

la Salle binds himself, if the execution of this plan is prevented for more than three years, by peace with Spain, to refund to his Majesty all the costs of the enterprise, on pain of forfeiting the government of the ports he will have established.[1]

Such, in brief, was the substance of this singular proposition. And, first, it is to be observed that it is based on a geographical blunder, the nature of which is explained by the map of La Salle's discoveries made in this very year. Here the river Seignelay, or Red River, is represented as running parallel to the northern border of Mexico, and at no great distance from it; the region now called Texas being almost entirely suppressed. According to the map, New Biscay might be reached from this river in a few days; and, after crossing the intervening forests, the coveted mines of Ste. Barbe, or Santa Barbara, would be within striking distance.[2] That La Salle believed in the possibility of invading the Spanish province of New Biscay from Red River there can be no doubt; neither can it reasonably be doubted that he hoped at some future day to make the attempt; and yet it is incredible that a man in his sober senses could have proposed this scheme with the intention of attempting to execute it at the time and in the manner which he indicates.[3] This memorial bears some

[1] *Mémoire du Sr de la Salle sur l'Entreprise qu'il a proposé à Monseigneur le Marquis de Seignelay sur une des provinces de Mexique.*

[2] Both the memorial and the map represent the banks of Red River as inhabited by Indians, called Terliquiquimechi, and known to the Spaniards as *Indios bravos*, or *Indios de guerra*. The Spaniards, it is added, were in great fear of them, as they made frequent inroads into Mexico. La Salle's Mexican geography was, in all respects, confused and erroneous; nor was Seignelay better informed. Indeed, Spanish jealousy placed correct information beyond their reach.

[3] While the plan, as proposed in the memorial, was clearly impracticable, the subsequent experience of the French in Texas tended to prove that the tribes of that region could be used with advantage in attacking the Spaniards of Mexico, and that an inroad on a comparatively small scale might have been successfully made with their help. In 1689, Tonty actually made the attempt, as we shall see, but failed, from the desertion of his men. In 1697, the Sieur de Louvigny wrote to the Minister of the Marine, asking to complete La Salle's discoveries, and invade Mexico from Texas. *Lettre de M. de Louvigny, 14 Oct., 1697*. In an unpublished memoir of the year 1700, the seizure of the Mexican mines is given as one of the motives of the colonization of Louisiana.

indications of being drawn up in order to produce a certain effect on the minds of the king and the minister. La Salle's immediate necessity was to obtain from them the means for establishing a fort and a colony within the mouth of the Mississippi. This was essential to his own plans; nor did he in the least exaggerate the value of such an establishment to the French nation, and the importance of anticipating other powers in the possession of it. But he thought that he needed a more glittering lure to attract the eyes of Louis and Seignelay; and thus, it may be, he held before them, in a definite and tangible form, the project of Spanish conquest which had haunted his imagination from youth, trusting that the speedy conclusion of peace, which actually took place, would absolve him from the immediate execution of the scheme, and give him time, with the means placed at his disposal, to mature his plans and prepare for eventual action. Such a procedure may be charged with indirectness; but there is a different explanation, which we shall suggest hereafter, and which implies no such reproach.[1]

Even with this madcap enterprise lopped off La Salle's scheme of Mississippi trade and colonization, perfectly sound in itself, was too vast for an individual; above all, for one crippled and crushed with debt. While he grasped one link of the great chain, another, no less essential, escaped from his hand; while he built up a colony on the Mississippi, it was

---

[1] Another scheme, with similar aims, but much more practicable, was at this very time before the court. Count Peñalossa, a Spanish creole, born in Peru, had been governor of New Mexico, where he fell into a dispute with the Inquisition, which involved him in the loss of property, and for a time of liberty. Failing to obtain redress in Spain, he renounced his allegiance in disgust, and sought refuge in France, where, in 1682, he first proposed to the king the establishment of a colony of French buccaneers at the mouth of Rio Bravo, on the Gulf of Mexico. In January, 1684, after the war had broken out, he proposed to attack the Spanish town of Panuco, with twelve hundred buccaneers from St. Domingo; then march into the interior, seize the mines, conquer Durango, and occupy New Mexico. It was proposed to combine his plan with that of La Salle; but the latter, who had an interview with him, expressed distrust, and showed characteristic reluctance to accept a colleague. It is extremely probable, however, that his knowledge of Peñalossa's original proposal had some influence in stimulating him to lay before the court proposals of his own, equally attractive. Peace was concluded before the plans of the Spanish adventurer could be carried into effect.

reasonably certain that evil would befall his distant colony of the Illinois.

The glittering project which he now unfolded found favor in the eyes of the king and the minister; for both were in the flush of an unparalleled success, and looked in the future, as in the past, for nothing but triumphs. They granted more than the petitioner asked, as indeed they well might, if they expected the accomplishment of all that he proposed to attempt. La Forest, La Salle's lieutenant, ejected from Fort Frontenac by La Barre, was now at Paris; and he was despatched to Canada, empowered to reoccupy, in La Salle's name, both Fort Frontenac and Fort St. Louis of the Illinois. The king himself wrote to La Barre in a strain that must have sent a cold thrill through the veins of that official. "I hear," he says, "that you have taken possession of Fort Frontenac, the property of the Sieur de la Salle, driven away his men, suffered his land to run to waste, and even told the Iroquois that they might seize him as an enemy of the colony." He adds, that, if this is true, La Barre must make reparation for the wrong, and place all La Salle's property, as well as his men, in the hands of the Sieur de la Forest, "as I am satisfied that Fort Frontenac was not abandoned, as you wrote to me that it had been."[1] Four days later, he wrote to the intendant of Canada, Meules, to the effect that the bearer, La Forest, is to suffer no impediment, and that La Barre is to surrender to him without reserve all that belongs to La Salle.[2] Armed with this letter, La Forest sailed for Canada.[3]

A chief object of his mission, as it was represented to Seignelay, was, not only to save the colony at the Illinois

---

[1] *Lettre du Roy à La Barre, Versailles, 10 Avril, 1684.*

[2] *Lettre du Roy à De Meules, Versailles, 14 Avril, 1684.* Seignelay wrote to De Meules to the same effect.

[3] On La Forest's mission,— *Mémoire pour representer à Monseigneur le Marquis de Seignelay la nécessité d'envoyer le Sr de la Forest en diligence à la Nouvelle France; Lettre du Roy à La Barre, 14 Avril, 1684; Ibid., 31 Oct., 1684.*

There is before me a promissory note of La Salle to La Forest, of 5,200 livres, dated at Rochelle, 17 July, 1684. This seems to be pay due to La Forest, who had served as La Salle's officer for nine years. A memorandum is attached, signed by La Salle, to the effect that it is his wish that La Forest reimburse himself, "*par préférence*," out of any property of his (La Salle's) in France or Canada.

from being broken up by La Barre, but also to collect La Salle's scattered followers, muster the savage warriors around the rock of St. Louis, and lead the whole down the Mississippi, to co-operate in the attack on New Biscay. If La Salle meant that La Forest should seriously attempt to execute such a scheme, then the charges of his enemies that his brain was turned were better founded than he would have us think.[1]

He had asked for two vessels,[2] and four were given to him. Agents were sent to Rochelle and Rochefort to gather recruits. A hundred soldiers were enrolled, besides mechanics and laborers; and thirty volunteers, including gentlemen and burghers of condition, joined the expedition. And, as the plan was one no less of colonization than of war, several families embarked for the new land of promise, as well as a number of girls, lured by the prospect of almost certain matrimony. Nor were missionaries wanting. Among them was La Salle's brother, Cavelier, and two other priests of St. Sulpice. Three Récollets were added: Zenobe Membré, who was then in France, Anastase Douay, and Maxime Le Clerc. The principal vessel was the "Joly," belonging to the royal navy, and carrying thirty-six guns. Another armed vessel, of six guns, was added, together with a store-ship and a ketch.

La Salle had asked for sole command of the expedition, with a subaltern officer, and one or two pilots to sail the vessels as he should direct. Instead of complying, Seignelay gave the command of the vessels to Beaujeu, a captain of the royal navy, whose authority was restricted to their management at sea, while La Salle was to prescribe the route they were to take, and have entire control of the troops and colonists on

---

[1] The attitude of La Salle, in this matter, is incomprehensible. In July, La Forest was at Rochefort, complaining because La Salle had ordered him to stay in garrison at Fort Frontenac. *Beaujeu à Villermont, 10 July, 1684.* This means an abandonment of the scheme of leading the warriors at the rock of St. Louis down the Mississippi; but, in the next month, La Salle writes to Seignelay that he is afraid La Barre will use the Iroquois war as a pretext to prevent La Forest from making his journey (to the Illinois), and that in this case he will himself try to go up the Mississippi, and meet the Illinois warriors; so that, in five or six months from the date of the letter, the minister will hear of his departure to attack the Spaniards. *La Salle à Seignelay, Août, 1684.* Either this is sheer folly, or else it is meant to delude the minister.

[2] *Mémoire de ce qui aura esté accordé au Sieur de la Salle.*

land.[1] This arrangement displeased both parties. Beaujeu, an old and experienced officer, was galled that a civilian should be set over him, and he, too, a burgher lately ennobled; nor was La Salle the man to soothe his ruffled spirit. Detesting a divided command, cold, reserved, and impenetrable, he would have tried the patience of a less excitable colleague. Beaujeu, on his part, though set to a task which he disliked, seems to have meant to do his duty, and to have been willing at the outset to make the relations between himself and his unwelcome associate as agreeable as possible. Unluckily, La Salle discovered that the wife of Beaujeu was devoted to the Jesuits. We have seen the extreme distrust with which he regarded these guides of his youth, and he seems now to have fancied that Beaujeu was their secret ally. Possibly, he suspected that information of his movements would be given to the Spaniards; more probably, he had undefined fears of adverse machinations. Granting that such existed, it was not his interest to stimulate them by needlessly exasperating the naval commander. His deportment, however, was not conciliating; and Beaujeu, prepared to dislike him, presently lost temper. While the vessels still lay at Rochelle; while all was bustle and preparation; while stores, arms, and munitions were embarking; while boys and vagabonds were enlisting as soldiers for the expedition, Beaujeu was venting his disgust in long letters to the minister.

"You have ordered me, Monseigneur, to give all possible aid to this undertaking, and I shall do so to the best of my power; but permit me to take great credit to myself, for I find it very hard to submit to the orders of the Sieur de la Salle, whom I believe to be a man of merit, but who has no experience of war except with savages, and who has no rank, while I have been captain of a ship thirteen years, and have served thirty by sea and land. Besides, Monseigneur, he has told me that, in case of his death, you have directed that the Sieur de Tonty shall succeed him. This, indeed, is very hard; for, though I am not acquainted with that country, I should be very dull, if, being on the spot, I did not know, at the end of a month, as much of it as they do. I beg, Monseigneur, that

[1] *Lettre du Roy à La Salle, 12 Avril, 1684; Mémoire pour servir d'Instruction au Sieur de Beaujeu, 14 Avril, 1684.*

I may at least share the command with them; and that, as regards war, nothing may be done without my knowledge and concurrence; for, as to their commerce, I neither intend nor desire to know any thing about it."

Seignelay answered by a rebuff, and told him to make no trouble about the command. This increased his irritation, and he wrote: "In my last letter, Monseigneur, I represented to you the hardship of compelling me to obey M. de la Salle, who has no rank, and *never commanded anybody but school-boys*; and I begged you at least to divide the command between us. I now, Monseigneur, take the liberty to say that I will obey without repugnance, if you order me to do so, having reflected that there can be no competition between the said Sieur de la Salle and me.

"Thus far, he has not told me his plan; and he changes his mind every moment. He is a man so suspicious, and so afraid that one will penetrate his secrets, that I dare not ask him any thing. He says that M. de Parassy, commissary's clerk, with whom he has often quarrelled, is paid by his enemies to defeat his undertaking; and many other things with which I will not trouble you."

"He pretends that I am only to command the sailors, and have no authority over the volunteer officers and the hundred soldiers who are to take passage in the 'Joly;' and that they are not to recognize or obey me in any way during the voyage."

"He has covered the decks with boxes and chests of such prodigious size that neither the cannon nor the capstan can be worked."

La Salle drew up a long list of articles, defining the respective rights and functions of himself and Beaujeu, to whom he presented it for signature. Beaujeu demurred at certain military honors demanded by La Salle, saying that, if a marshal of France should come on board his ship, he would have none left to offer him. The point was referred to the naval intendant; and, the articles of the treaty having been slightly modified, Beaujeu set his name to it. "By this," he says, "you can judge better of the character of M. de la Salle than by all I can say. He is a man who wants smoke [form and ceremony]. I will give him his fill of it, and, perhaps, more than he likes.

"I am bound to an unknown country, to seek what is about as hard to find as the philosopher's stone. It vexes me, Monseigneur, that you should have been involved in a business the success of which is very uncertain. M. de la Salle begins to doubt it himself."

While Beaujeu wrote thus to the minister, he was also writing to Cabart de Villermont, one of his friends at Paris, with whom La Salle was also on friendly terms. These letters are lively and entertaining, and by no means suggestive of any secret conspiracy. He might, it is true, have been more reserved in his communications; but he betrays no confidence, for none was placed in him. It is the familiar correspondence of an irritable but not ill-natured veteran, who is placed in an annoying position, and thinks he is making the best of it.

La Salle thought that the minister had been too free in communicating the secrets of the expedition to the naval intendant at Rochefort, and through him to Beaujeu. It is hard to see how Beaujeu was to blame for this; but La Salle nevertheless fell into a dispute with him. "He could hardly keep his temper, and used expressions which obliged me to tell him that I cared very little about his affairs, and that the king himself would not speak as he did. He retracted, made excuses, and we parted good friends."

"I do not like his suspiciousness. I think him a good, honest Norman; but Normans are out of fashion. It is one thing to-day, another to-morrow. It seems to me that he is not so sure about his undertaking as he was at Paris. This morning, he came to see me, and told me he had changed his mind, and meant to give a new turn to the business, and go to another coast. He gave very poor reasons, to which I assented, to avoid a quarrel. I thought, by what he said, that he wanted to find a scapegoat to bear the blame, in case his plan does not succeed as he hopes. For the rest, I think him a brave man, and a true; and I am persuaded that, if this business fails, it will be because he does not know enough, and will not trust us of the profession. As for me, I shall do my best to help him, as I have told you before; and I am delighted to have him keep his secret, so that I shall not have to answer for the result. Pray do not show my letters, for fear of committing me with him. He is too suspicious already, and never was Norman so Norman as he, which is a great hinderance to business."

Beaujeu came from the same province, and calls himself jocularly *un bon gros Normand*. His good-nature, however, rapidly gave way as time went on. "Yesterday," he writes, "this Monsieur told me that he meant to go to the Gulf of Mexico. A little while ago, as I said before, he talked about going to Canada. I see nothing certain in it. It is not that I do not believe that all he says is true; but not being of the profession, and not liking to betray his ignorance, he is puzzled what to do.

"I shall go straight forward, without regarding a thousand whims and *bagatelles*. His continual suspicion would drive anybody mad except a Norman like me; but I shall humor him, as I have always done, even to sailing my ship on dry land, if he likes."

A few days later, there was an open quarrel. "M. de la Salle came to me, and said, rather haughtily and in a tone of command, that I must put provisions for three months more on board my vessel. I told him it was impossible, as she had more lading already than anybody ever dared to put in her before. He would not hear reason, but got angry and abused me in good French, and found fault with me because the vessel would not hold his three months' provisions. He said I ought to have told him of it before. 'And how would you have me tell you,' said I, 'when you never tell me what you mean to do?' We had still another quarrel. He asked me where his officers should take their meals. I told him that they might take them where he pleased; for I gave myself no trouble in the matter, having no orders. He answered that they should not mess on bacon, while the rest ate fowls and mutton. I said that, if he would send fowls and mutton on board, his people should eat them; but, as for bacon, I had often ate it myself. At this, he went off and complained to M. Dugué that I refused to embark his provisions, and told him that he must live on bacon. I excused him as not knowing how to behave himself, having spent his life among school-boy brats and savages. Nevertheless, I offered to him, his brother, and two of his friends, seats at my table and the same fare as myself. He answered my civility by an impertinence, saying that he distrusted people who offered so much and seemed so obliging. I could not help telling him that I saw he was brought up in the provinces."

This was touching La Salle on a sensitive point. Beaujeu continues: "In fact, you knew him better than I; for I always took him for a gentleman (*honnête homme*). I see now that he is any thing but that. Pray set Abbé Renaudot and M. Morel right about this man, and tell them he is not what they take him for. Adieu. It has struck twelve: the postman is just going."

Bad as was the state of things, it soon grew worse. Renaudot wrote to La Salle that Beaujeu was writing to Villermont every thing that happened, and that Villermont showed the letters to all his acquaintance. Villermont was a relative of the Jesuit Beschefer; and this was sufficient to suggest some secret machination to the mind of La Salle. Villermont's fault, however, seems to have been simple indiscretion, for which Beaujeu took him sharply to task. "I asked you to burn my letters; and I cannot help saying that I am angry with you, not because you make known my secrets, but because you show letters scrawled in haste, and sent off without being even read over. M. de la Salle not having told me his secret, though M. de Seignelay ordered him to tell me, I am not obliged to keep it, and have as good a right as anybody to make my conjectures on what I read about it in the *Gazette de Hollande*. Let Abbé Renaudot glorify M. de la Salle as much as he likes, and make him a Cortez, a Pizarro, or an Almagro: that is nothing to me; but do not let him speak of me as an obstacle in his hero's way. Let him understand that I know how to execute the orders of the court as well as he."

"You ask how I get on with M. de la Salle. Don't you know that this man is impenetrable, and that there is no knowing what he thinks of one? He told a person of note whom I will not name that he had suspicions about our correspondence, as well as about Madame de Beaujeu's devotion to the Jesuits. His distrust is incredible. If he sees one of his people speak to the rest, he suspects something, and is gruff with them. He told me himself that he wanted to get rid of M. de Tonty, who is in America."

La Salle's claim to exclusive command of the soldiers on board the "Joly" was a source of endless trouble. Beaujeu declared that he would not set sail till officers, soldiers, and volunteers had all sworn to obey him when at sea, at which La Salle had the indiscretion to say, "If I am not master of my soldiers, how can I make him [Beaujeu] do his duty in case he does not want to do it?"

Beaujeu says that this affair made a great noise among the officers at Rochefort, and adds: "*There are very few people who do not think that his brain is touched.* I have spoken to some who have known him twenty years. They all say that he was always rather visionary."

It is difficult not to suspect that the current belief at Rochefort had some foundation; and that the deadly strain of extreme hardship, prolonged anxiety, and alternation of disaster and success, joined to the fever which nearly killed him, had unsettled his judgment and given a morbid development to his natural defects. His universal suspicion, which included even the stanch and faithful Henri de Tonty; his needless provocation of persons whose good-will was necessary to him; his doubts whether he should sail for the Gulf or for Canada, when to sail to Canada would have been to renounce, or expose to almost certain defeat, an enterprise long cherished and definitely planned,—all point to one conclusion. It may be thought that his doubts were feigned, in order to hide his destination to the last moment; but, if so, he attempted to blind not only his ill wishers, but his mother, whom he also left in uncertainty as to his route.

Unless we assume that his scheme of invading Mexico was thrown out as a bait to the king, it is hard to reconcile it with the supposition of mental soundness. To base so critical an attempt on a geographical conjecture, which rested on the slightest possible information, and was, in fact, a total error; to postpone the perfectly sound plan of securing the mouth of the Mississippi, to a wild project of leading fifteen thousand savages for an unknown distance, through an unknown country, to attack an unknown enemy, was something more than Quixotic daring. The king and the minister saw nothing impracticable in it, for they did not know the country or its inhabitants. They saw no insuperable difficulty in mustering and keeping together fifteen thousand of the most wayward and unstable savages on earth, split into a score and more of tribes, some hostile to each other and some to the French; nor in the problem of feeding such a mob, on a march of hundreds of miles; nor in the plan of drawing four thousand of them from the Illinois, nearly two thousand miles distant, though some of these intended allies had no canoes or other means of transportation, and though, travelling in such numbers, they would infallibly starve on the way to the rendezvous. It is difficult not to see in all this the chimera of an overwrought brain, no longer able to distinguish between the possible and the impossible.

Preparation dragged slowly on; the season was growing late; the king grew impatient, and found fault with the naval intendant. Meanwhile, the various members of the expedition had all gathered at Rochelle. Joutel, a fellow-townsman of La Salle, returning to his native Rouen, after sixteen years in the army, found all astir with the new project. His father had been gardener to Henri Cavelier, La Salle's uncle; and, being of an adventurous spirit, he volunteered for the enterprise, of which he was to become the historian. With La Salle's brother, the priest, and two of his nephews, one of whom was a boy of fourteen, Joutel set out for Rochelle, where all were to embark together for their promised land.[1]

La Salle wrote a parting letter to his mother at Rouen:—

"ROCHELLE, 18 July, 1684.

"MADAME MY MOST HONORED MOTHER,—

"At last, after having waited a long time for a favorable wind, and having had a great many difficulties to overcome, we are setting sail with four vessels, and nearly four hundred men on board. Everybody is well, including little Colin and my nephew. We all have good hope of a happy success. We are not going by way of Canada, but by the Gulf of Mexico. I passionately wish, and so do we all, that the success of this voyage may contribute to your repose

---

[1] Joutel, *Journal Historique*, 12.

and comfort. Assuredly, I shall spare no effort that it may; and I beg you, on your part, to preserve yourself for the love of us.

"You need not be troubled by the news from Canada, which are nothing but the continuation of the artifices of my enemies. I hope to be as successful against them as I have been thus far, and to embrace you a year hence with all the pleasure that the most grateful of children can feel with so good a mother as you have always been. Pray let this hope, which shall not disappoint you, support you through whatever trials may happen, and be sure that you will always find me with a heart full of the feelings which are due to you. Madame my Most Honored Mother, from your most humble and most obedient servant and son,

"DE LA SALLE.

"My brother, my nephews, and all the others, greet you, and take their leave of you."

This memorable last farewell has lain for two hundred years among the family papers of the Caveliers.[1]

[1] The letters of Beaujeu to Seignelay and to Cabart de Villermont, with most of the other papers on which this chapter rests, will be found in Margry, II. 354–471. This indefatigable investigator has also brought to light a number of letters from a brother officer of Beaujeu, Machaut-Rougemont, written at Rochefort, just after the departure of the expedition from Rochelle, and giving some idea of the views there entertained concerning it. He says: "L'on ne peut pas faire plus d'extravagances que le Sieur de la Salle n'en a fait sur toutes ses prétentions de commandement. Je plains beaucoup le pauvre Beaujeu d'avoir affaire à une humeur si saturnienne. . . . Je le croy beaucoup visionnaire . . . Beaujeu a une sotte commission."

Chapter XXIV

1684, 1685

THE VOYAGE

Disputes with Beaujeu • St. Domingo • La Salle attacked with Fever • His Desperate Condition • The Gulf of Mexico • A Vain Search and a Fatal Error

THE four ships sailed from Rochelle on the twenty-fourth of July. Four days after, the "Joly" broke her bowsprit, by design as La Salle fancied. They all put back to Rochefort, where the mischief was quickly repaired; and they put to sea again. La Salle, and the chief persons of the expedition, with a crowd of soldiers, artisans, and women, the destined mothers of Louisiana, were all on board the "Joly." Beaujeu wished to touch at Madeira, to replenish his water-casks. La Salle refused, lest by doing so the secret of the enterprise might reach the Spaniards. One Paget, a Huguenot, took up the word in support of Beaujeu. La Salle told him that the affair was none of his; and, as Paget persisted with increased warmth and freedom, he demanded of Beaujeu if it was with his consent that a man of no rank spoke to him in that manner. Beaujeu sustained the Huguenot. "That is enough," returned La Salle, and withdrew into his cabin.[1]

This was not the first misunderstanding; nor was it the last. There was incessant chafing between the two commanders; and the sailors of the "Joly" were soon of one mind with their captain. When the ship crossed the tropic, they made ready a tub on deck to baptize the passengers, after the villanous practice of the time; but La Salle refused to permit it, at which they were highly exasperated, having promised themselves a bountiful ransom, in money or liquor, from their victims. "Assuredly," says Joutel, "they would gladly have killed us all."

When, after a wretched voyage of two months, the ships reached St. Domingo, a fresh dispute occurred. It had been

[1] *Lettre (sans nom d'auteur) écrite de St. Domingue, 14 Nov., 1684* (Margry, II. 492); *Mémoire autographe de l'Abbé Jean Cavelier sur le Voyage de 1684.* Compare Joutel.

resolved at a council of officers to stop at Port de Paix; but Beaujeu, on pretext of a fair wind, ran by that place in the night, and cast anchor at Petit Goave, on the other side of the island. La Salle was extremely vexed; for he expected to meet at Port de Paix the Marquis de Saint-Laurent, lieutenant-general of the islands, Bégon, the intendant, and De Cussy, governor of La Tortue, who had orders to supply him with provisions and give him all possible aid.

The "Joly" was alone: the other vessels had lagged behind. She had more than fifty sick men on board, and La Salle was of the number. He sent a messenger to Saint-Laurent, Bégon, and Cussy, begging them to come to him; ordered Joutel to get the sick ashore, suffocating as they were in the hot and crowded ship; and caused the soldiers to be landed on a small island in the harbor. Scarcely had the voyagers sung *Te Deum* for their safe arrival, when two of the lagging vessels appeared, bringing tidings that the third, the ketch "St. François," had been taken by Spanish buccaneers. She was laden with provisions, tools, and other necessaries for the colony; and the loss was irreparable. Beaujeu was answerable for it; for, had he anchored at Port de Paix, it would not have occurred. The lieutenant-general, with Bégon and Cussy, who presently arrived, plainly spoke their minds to him.[1]

La Salle's illness increased. "I was walking with him one day," writes Joutel, "when he was seized of a sudden with such a weakness that he could not stand, and was obliged to lie down on the ground. When he was a little better, I led him to a chamber of a house that the brothers Duhaut had hired. Here we put him to bed, and in the morning he was attacked by a violent fever."[2] "It was so violent that," says another of his shipmates, "his imagination pictured to him things equally terrible and amazing."[3] He lay delirious in the wretched garret, attended by his brother, and one or two others who stood faithful to him. A goldsmith of the neighborhood, moved at his deplorable condition, offered the use of his house; and Abbé Cavelier had him removed thither. But

---

[1] *Mémoire de MM. de Saint-Laurens et Bégon* (Margry, II. 499); Joutel, *Journal Historique*, 28.

[2] *Relation de Henri Joutel* (Margry, III. 98).

[3] *Lettre (sans nom d'auteur), 14 Nov., 1684* (Margry, II. 496).

there was a tavern hard by, and the patient was tormented with daily and nightly riot. At the height of the fever, a party of Beaujeu's sailors spent a night in singing and dancing before the house; and says Cavelier, "The more we begged them to be quiet, the more noise they made." La Salle lost reason and well-nigh life; but at length his mind resumed its balance, and the violence of the disease abated. A friendly Capucin friar offered him the shelter of his roof; and two of his men supported him thither on foot, giddy with exhaustion and hot with fever. Here he found repose, and was slowly recovering, when some of his attendants rashly told him the loss of the ketch "St. François;" and the consequence was a critical return of the disease.[1]

There was no one to fill his place. Beaujeu would not; Cavelier could not. Joutel, the gardener's son, was apparently the most trusty man of the company; but the expedition was virtually without a head. The men roamed on shore, and plunged into every excess of debauchery, contracting diseases which eventually killed them.

Beaujeu, in the extremity of ill-humor, resumed his correspondence with Seignelay. "But for the illness of the Sieur de la Salle," he writes, "I could not venture to report to you the progress of our voyage, as I am charged only with the navigation, and he with the secrets; but as his malady has deprived him of the use of his faculties, both of body and mind, I have thought myself obliged to acquaint you with what is passing, and of the condition in which we are."

He then declares that the ships freighted by La Salle were so slow that the "Joly" had continually been forced to wait for them, thus doubling the length of the voyage; that he had not had water enough for the passengers, as La Salle had not told him that there were to be any such till the day they came on board; that great numbers were sick, and that he had told La Salle there would be trouble if he filled all the space between decks with his goods, and forced the soldiers and sailors to sleep on deck; that he had told him he would get no provisions at St. Domingo, but that he insisted on stopping; that it had always been so; that whatever he proposed La

[1] The above particulars are from the memoir of La Salle's brother, Abbé Cavelier, already cited.

Salle would refuse, alleging orders from the king; "and now," pursues the ruffled commander, "everybody is ill; and he himself has a violent fever, as dangerous, the surgeon tells me, to the mind as to the body."

The rest of the letter is in the same strain. He says that, a day or two after La Salle's illness began, his brother Cavelier came to ask him to take charge of his affairs, but that he did not wish to meddle with them, especially as nobody knows any thing about them, and as La Salle has sold some of the ammunition and provisions; that Cavelier tells him that he thinks his brother keeps no accounts, wishing to hide his affairs from everybody; that he learns from buccaneers that the entrance of the Mississippi is very shallow and difficult, and that this is the worst season for navigating the Gulf; that the Spaniards have in these seas six vessels of from thirty to sixty guns each, besides row-galleys; but that he is not afraid, and will perish, or bring back an account of the Mississippi. "Nevertheless," he adds, "if the Sieur de la Salle dies, I shall pursue a course different from that which he has marked out; for I do not approve his plans."

"If," he continues, "you permit me to speak my mind, M. de la Salle ought to have been satisfied with discovering his river, without undertaking to conduct three vessels with troops two thousand leagues through so many different climates, and across seas entirely unknown to him. I grant that he is a man of knowledge, that he has reading, and even some tincture of navigation; but there is so much difference between theory and practice, that a man who has only the former will always be at fault. There is also a great difference between conducting canoes on lakes and along a river, and navigating ships with troops on distant oceans."[1]

While Beaujeu was complaining of La Salle, his followers were deserting him. It was necessary to send them on board ship, and keep them there; for there were French buccaneers at Petit Goave, who painted the promised land in such dismal colors that many of the adventurers completely lost heart. Some, too, were dying. "The air of this place is bad," says Joutel; "so are

---

[1] *Lettre de Beaujeu au Ministre, 20 Oct., 1684.*

the fruits; and there are plenty of women worse than either."[1]

It was near the end of November before La Salle could resume the voyage. He was told that Beaujeu had said that he would not wait longer for the store-ship "Aimable," and that she might follow as she could.[2] Moreover, La Salle was on ill terms with Aigron, her captain, who had declared that he would have nothing more to do with him.[3] Fearing, therefore, that some mishap might befall her, he resolved to embark in her himself, with his brother Cavelier, Membré, Douay, and others, the trustiest of his followers. On the twenty-fifth, they set sail; the "Joly" and the little frigate "Belle" following. They coasted the shore of Cuba, and landed at the Isle of Pines, where La Salle shot an alligator, which the soldiers ate; and the hunters brought in a wild pig, half of which he sent to Beaujeu. Then they advanced to Cape St. Antoine, where bad weather and contrary winds long detained them. A load of cares oppressed the mind of La Salle, pale and haggard with recent illness, wrapped within his own thoughts, and seeking sympathy from none.

At length, they entered the Gulf of Mexico, that forbidden sea, whence, by a Spanish decree, dating from the reign of Philip II., all foreigners were excluded on pain of extermination.[4] Not a man on board knew the secrets of its perilous navigation. Cautiously feeling their way, they held a northwesterly course, till on the twenty-eighth of December a sailor at the mast-head of the "Aimable" saw land. La Salle and all the pilots had been led to form an exaggerated idea of the force of the easterly currents; and they therefore supposed themselves near the Bay of Appalache, when, in fact, they were much farther westward.

On New Year's Day, they anchored three leagues from the shore. La Salle, with the engineer Minet, went to explore it, and found nothing but a vast marshy plain, studded with clumps of rushes. Two days after there was a thick fog, and, when at length it cleared, the "Joly" was nowhere to be seen.

[1] *Relation de Henri Joutel* (Margry, III. 105).

[2] *Mémoire autographe de l'Abbé Jean Cavelier.*

[3] *Lettre de Beaujeu au Ministre, 20 Oct., 1684.*

[4] *Letter of Don Luis de Onis to the Secretary of State* (American State Papers, XII. 27–31).

La Salle, in the "Aimable," followed closely by the little frigate "Belle," stood westward along the coast. When at the mouth of the Mississippi, in 1682, he had taken its latitude, but unhappily could not determine its longitude; and now every eye on board was strained to detect in the monotonous lines of the low shore some tokens of the great river. In fact, they had already passed it. On the sixth of January, a wide opening was descried between two low points of land; and the adjacent sea was discolored with mud. "La Salle," writes his brother Cavelier, "has always thought that this was the Mississippi." To all appearance, it was the entrance of Galveston Bay.[1] But why did he not examine it? Joutel says that his attempts to do so were frustrated by the objections of the pilot of the "Aimable," to which, with a facility very unusual with him, he suffered himself to yield. Cavelier declares, on the other hand, that he would not enter the opening because he was afraid of missing the "Joly." But he might have entered with one of his two vessels, while the other watched outside for the absent ship. From whatever cause, he lay here five or six days, waiting in vain for Beaujeu;[2] till, at last, thinking that he must have passed westward, he resolved to follow. The "Aimable" and the "Belle" again spread their sails, and coasted the shores of Texas. Joutel, with a boat's crew, tried to land, but the sand-bars and breakers repelled him. A party of Indians swam out through the surf, and were taken on board; but La Salle could learn nothing from them, as their language was unknown to him. Again, Joutel tried to land, and again the breakers repelled him. He approached as near as he dared, and saw vast plains and a dim expanse of forest; buffalo running with their heavy gallop along the shore, and deer grazing on the marshy meadows.

Soon after, he succeeded in landing at a point somewhere between Matagorda Island and Corpus Christi Bay. The aspect of the country was not cheering, with its barren plains, its reedy marshes, its interminable oyster-beds, and broad flats of mud bare at low tide. Joutel and his men sought in vain

---

[1] "La hauteur nous a fait remarquer . . . que ce que nous avions vu le sixième janvier estoit en effet la principale entrée de la rivière que nous cherchions."— *Lettre de La Salle au Ministre, 4 Mars, 1685.*

[2] *Mémoire autographe de l'Abbé Cavelier.*

for fresh water; and, after shooting some geese and ducks, returned to the "Aimable." Nothing had been seen of Beaujeu and the "Joly;" the coast was trending southward; and La Salle, convinced that he must have passed the missing ship, turned to retrace his course. He had sailed but a few miles, when the wind failed, a fog covered the sea, and he was forced to anchor opposite one of the openings into the lagoons north of Mustang Island. At length, on the nineteenth, there came a faint breeze: the mists rolled away before it, and to his great joy he saw the "Joly" approaching.

"His joy," says Joutel, "was short." Beaujeu's lieutenant, Aire, came on board to charge him with having caused the separation, and La Salle retorted by throwing the blame on Beaujeu. Then came a debate as to their position. The priest Esmanville was present, and reports that La Salle seemed greatly perplexed. He had more cause for perplexity than he knew; for, in his ignorance of the longitude of the Mississippi, he had sailed more than four hundred miles beyond it.

Of this, he had not the faintest suspicion. In full sight from his ship lay a reach of those vast lagoons, which, separated from the sea by narrow strips of land, line this coast with little interruption from Galveston Bay to the Rio Grande. The idea took possession of him that the Mississippi discharged itself into these lagoons, and thence made its way to the sea through the various openings he had seen along the coast, chief among which was that he had discovered on the sixth, about fifty leagues from the place where he now was.[1]

---

[1] "Depuis que nous avions quitté cette rivière qu'il croyoit infailliblement estre le fleuve Colbert [*Mississippi*] nous avions fait environ 45 lieues ou 50 au plus."—Cavelier, *Mémoire*. This, taken in connection with the statement of La Salle, that this "principale entrée de la rivière que nous cherchions" was twenty-five or thirty leagues north-east from the entrance of the Bay of St. Louis (Matagorda Bay), shows that it can have been no other than the entrance of Galveston Bay, mistaken by him for the chief outlet of the Mississippi. It is evident that he imagined Galveston Bay to form a part of the chain of lagoons from which it is, in fact, separated. He speaks of these lagoons as "une espèce de baye fort longue et fort large, *dans laquelle le fleuve Colbert se décharge.*" He adds that, on his descent to the mouth of the river in 1682, he had been deceived in supposing that this expanse of salt water, where no shore was in sight, was the open sea. *Lettre de La Salle au Ministre, 4 Mars, 1685.* Galveston Bay and the mouth of the Mississippi differ little in latitude, though separated by about five and a half degrees of longitude.

Yet he was full of doubt as to what he should do. Four days after rejoining Beaujeu, he wrote him the strange request to land the troops, that he "might fulfil his commission;" that is, that he might set out against the Spaniards.[1] More than a week passed, a gale had set in, and nothing was done. Then La Salle wrote again, intimating some doubt as to whether he was really at one of the mouths of the Mississippi, and saying that, being sure that he had passed the principal mouth, he was determined to go back to look for it.[2] Meanwhile, Beaujeu was in a state of great irritation. The weather was stormy, and the coast was dangerous. Supplies were scanty; and La Salle's soldiers, still crowded in the "Joly," were consuming the provisions of the ship. Beaujeu gave vent to his annoyance, and La Salle retorted in the same strain.

According to Joutel, he urged the naval commander to sail back in search of the river; and Beaujeu refused, unless La Salle should give the soldiers provisions. La Salle, he adds, offered to supply them with rations for fifteen days; and Beaujeu declared this insufficient. There is reason, however, to believe that the request was neither made by the one nor refused by the other so positively as here appears.

[1] *Lettre de La Salle à Beaujeu, 23 Jan., 1685* (Margry, II. 526).
[2] This letter is dated, "De l'emboucheure d'une rivière que *je crois estre* une des descharges du Mississipy" (Margry, II. 528).

Chapter XXV

1685

LA SALLE IN TEXAS

*A Party of Exploration • Wreck of the "Aimable" • Landing of
the Colonists • A Forlorn Position • Indian Neighbors • Friendly
Advances of Beaujeu • His Departure • A Fatal Discovery*

IMPATIENCE to rid himself of his colleague and command
alone no doubt had its influence on the judgment of La
Salle. He presently declared that he would land the soldiers,
and send them along shore till they came to the principal outlet of the river. On this, the engineer Minet took up the
word, expressed his doubts as to whether the Mississippi discharged itself into the lagoons at all, represented that, even if
it did, the soldiers would be exposed to great risks, and gave
as his opinion that all should reimbark and continue the
search in company. The advice was good, but La Salle resented it as coming from one in whom he recognized no right
to give it. "He treated me," complains the engineer, "as if I
were the meanest of mankind."[1]

He persisted in his purpose, and sent Joutel and Moranget
with a party of soldiers to explore the coast. They made their
way north-eastward along the shore of Matagorda Island till
they were stopped on the third day by what Joutel calls a
river, but which was in fact the entrance of Matagorda Bay.
Here they encamped, and tried to make a raft of driftwood.
"The difficulty was," says Joutel, "our great number of men,
and the few of them who were fit for any thing except eating.
As I said before, they had all been caught by force or surprise,
so that our company was like Noah's ark, which contained
animals of all sorts." Before their raft was finished, they descried to their great joy the ships which had followed them
along the coast.[2]

La Salle landed, and announced that here was the western

---

[1] *Relation de Minet; Lettre de Minet à Seignelay, 6 July, 1685* (Margry, II. 591,
602).

[2] Joutel, *Journal Historique*, 68; *Relation* (Margry, III. 143–146). Compare
Journal d'Esmanville (Margry, II. 510).

mouth of the Mississippi, and the place to which the king had
sent him. He said further that he would land all his men, and
bring the "Aimable" and the "Belle" to the safe harborage
within. Beaujeu remonstrated, alleging the shallowness of the
water and the force of the currents; but his remonstrance was
vain.[1]

The Bay of St. Louis, now Matagorda Bay, forms a broad
and sheltered harbor, accessible from the sea by a narrow passage, obstructed by sand-bars and by the small island now
called Pelican Island. Boats were sent to sound and buoy out
the channel, and this was successfully accomplished on the
sixteenth of February. The "Aimable" was ordered to enter;
and, on the twentieth, she weighed anchor. La Salle was on
shore watching her. A party of men, at a little distance, were
cutting down a tree to make a canoe. Suddenly, some of them
ran towards him with terrified faces, crying out that they had
been set upon by a troop of Indians, who had seized their
companions and carried them off. La Salle ordered those
about him to take their arms, and at once set out in pursuit.
He overtook the Indians, and opened a parley with them;
but, when he wished to reclaim his men, he discovered that
they had been led away during the conference to the Indian
camp, a league and a half distant. Among them was one of
his lieutenants, the young Marquis de la Sablonnière. He was
deeply vexed, for the moment was critical; but the men must
be recovered, and he led his followers in haste towards the
camp. Yet he could not refrain from turning a moment to
watch the "Aimable," as she neared the shoals; and he remarked with deep anxiety to Joutel, who was with him, that
if she held that course she would soon be aground.

They hurried on till they saw the Indian huts. About fifty
of them, oven-shaped, and covered with mats and hides, were
clustered on a rising ground, with their inmates gathered
among and around them. As the French entered the camp,
there was the report of a cannon from the seaward. The startled savages dropped flat with terror. A different fear seized
La Salle, for he knew that the shot was a signal of disaster.
Looking back, he saw the "Aimable" furling her sails, and his

[1] *Relation de Minet* (Margry, II. 591).

heart sank with the conviction that she had struck upon the reef. Smothering his distress,—she was laden with all the stores of the colony,—he pressed forward among the filthy wigwams, whose astonished inmates swarmed about the band of armed strangers, staring between curiosity and fear. La Salle knew those with whom he was dealing, and, without ceremony, entered the chief's lodge with his followers. The crowd closed around them, naked men and half-naked women, described by Joutel as of singular ugliness. They gave buffalo meat and dried porpoise to the unexpected guests, but La Salle, racked with anxiety, hastened to close the interview; and, having without difficulty recovered the kidnapped men, he returned to the beach, leaving with the Indians, as usual, an impression of good-will and respect.

When he reached the shore, he saw his worst fears realized. The "Aimable" lay careened over on the reef, hopelessly aground. Little remained but to endure the calamity with firmness, and to save, as far as might be, the vessel's cargo. This was no easy task. The boat which hung at her stern had been stove in,—it is said, by design. Beaujeu sent a boat from the "Joly," and one or more Indian pirogues were procured. La Salle urged on his men with stern and patient energy; a quantity of gunpowder and flour was safely landed; but now the wind blew fresh from the sea, the waves began to rise, a storm came on, the vessel, rocking to and fro on the sand-bar, opened along her side, the ravenous waves were strewn with her treasures; and, when the confusion was at its height, a troop of Indians came down to the shore, greedy for plunder. The drum was beat; the men were called to arms; La Salle set his trustiest followers to guard the gunpowder, in fear, not of the Indians alone, but of his own countrymen. On that lamentable night, the sentinels walked their rounds through the dreary bivouac among the casks, bales, and boxes which the sea had yielded up; and here, too, their fate-hunted chief held his drearier vigil, encompassed with treachery, darkness, and the storm.

Not only La Salle, but Joutel and others of his party, believed that the wreck of the "Aimable" was intentional. Aigron, who commanded her, had disobeyed orders and disregarded signals. Though he had been directed to tow the vessel through the channel, he went in under sail; and, though little else was saved from the wreck, his personal property, including even some preserved fruits, was all landed safely. He had long been on ill terms with La Salle.[1]

All La Salle's company were now encamped on the sands at the left side of the inlet where the "Aimable" was wrecked.[2] "They were all," says the engineer Minet, "sick with nausea and dysentery. Five or six died every day, in consequence of brackish water and bad food. There was no grass, but plenty of rushes and plenty of oysters. There was nothing to make ovens, so that they had to eat flour saved from the wreck, boiled into messes of porridge with this brackish water. Along the shore were quantities of uprooted trees and rotten logs, thrown up by the sea and the lagoon." Of these, and fragments of the wreck, they made a sort of rampart to protect their camp; and here, among tents and hovels, bales, boxes, casks, spars, dismounted cannon, and pens for fowls and swine, were gathered the dejected men and homesick women who were to seize New Biscay, and hold for France a region large as half Europe. The Spaniards, whom they were to conquer, were they knew not where. They knew not where they were themselves; and, for the fifteen thousand Indian allies who were to have joined them, they found two hundred squalid savages, more like enemies than friends.

In fact, it was soon made plain that these their neighbors wished them no good. A few days after the wreck, the prairie was seen on fire. As the smoke and flame rolled towards them before the wind, La Salle caused all the grass about the camp

[1] *Procès Verbal du Sieur de la Salle sur le Naufrage de la Flûte l'Aimable; Lettre de La Salle à Seignelay, 4 Mars, 1685; Lettre de Beaujeu à Seignelay, sans date.* Beaujeu did his best to save the cargo. The loss included nearly all the provisions, 60 barrels of wine, 4 cannon, 1,620 balls, 400 grenades, 4,000 pounds of iron, 5,000 pounds of lead, most of the tools, a forge, a mill, cordage, boxes of arms, nearly all the medicines, and most of the baggage of the soldiers and colonists. Aigron returned to France in the "Joly," and was thrown into prison, "comme il paroist clairement que cet accident est arrivé par sa faute."— *Seignelay au Sieur Arnoul, 22 Juillet, 1685* (Margry, II. 604).

[2] A map, entitled *Entrée du Lac où on a laissé le Sr de la Salle*, made by the engineer Minet, and preserved in the Archives de la Marine, represents the entrance of Matagorda Bay, the camp of La Salle on the left, Indian camps on the borders of the bay, the "Belle" at anchor within, the "Aimable" stranded at the entrance, and the "Joly" anchored in the open sea.

to be cut and carried away, and especially around the spot where the powder was placed. The danger was averted; but it soon became known that the Indians had stolen a number of blankets and other articles, and carried them to their wigwams. Unwilling to leave his camp, La Salle sent his nephew Moranget and several other volunteers, with a party of men, to reclaim them. They went up the bay in a boat, landed at the Indian camp, and, with more mettle than discretion, marched into it, sword in hand. The Indians ran off, and the rash adventurers seized upon several canoes as an equivalent for the stolen goods. Not knowing how to manage them, they made slow progress on their way back, and were overtaken by night before reaching the French camp. They landed, made a fire, placed a sentinel, and lay down on the dry grass to sleep. The sentinel followed their example, when suddenly they were awakened by the war-whoop and a shower of arrows. Two volunteers, Oris and Desloges, were killed on the spot; a third, named Gayen, was severely wounded; and young Moranget received an arrow through the arm. He leaped up and fired his gun at the vociferous but invisible foe. Others of the party did the same, and the Indians fled.

It was about this time that Beaujeu prepared to return to France. He had accomplished his mission, and landed his passengers at what La Salle assured him to be one of the mouths of the Mississippi. His ship was in danger on this exposed and perilous coast, and he was anxious to find shelter. For some time past, his relations with La Salle had been amicable, and it was agreed between them that Beaujeu should stop at Galveston Bay, the supposed chief mouth of the Mississippi; or, failing to find harborage here, that he should proceed to Mobile Bay, and wait there till April, to hear from his colleague. Two days before the wreck of the "Aimable," he wrote to La Salle: "I wish with all my heart that you would have more confidence in me. For my part, I will always make the first advances; and I will follow your counsel whenever I can do so without risking my ship. I will come back to this place, if you want to know the results of the voyage I am going to make. If you wish, I will go to Martinique for provisions and reinforcements. In fine, there is nothing I am not ready to do: you have only to speak."

La Salle had begged him to send ashore a number of cannon and a quantity of iron, stowed in the "Joly," for the use of the colony; and Beaujeu replies: "I wish very much that I could give you your iron, but it is impossible except in a harbor; for it is on my ballast, and under your cannon, my spare anchors, and all my stowage. It would take three days to get it out, which cannot be done in this place, where the sea runs like mountains when the slightest wind blows outside. I would rather come back to give it to you, in case you do not send the 'Belle' to Baye du St. Esprit [Mobile Bay] to get it. . . . I beg you once more to consider the offer I make you to go to Martinique to get provisions for your people. I will ask the intendant for them in your name; and, if they are refused, I will take them on my own account."[1]

To this La Salle immediately replied: "I received with singular pleasure the letter you took the trouble to write me; for I found in it extraordinary proofs of kindness in the interest you take in the success of an affair which I have the more at heart, as it involves the glory of the king and the honor of Monseigneur de Seignelay. I have done my part towards a perfect understanding between us, and have never been wanting in confidence; but, even if I could be so, the offers you make are so obliging that they would inspire complete trust." He nevertheless declines them; assuring Beaujeu at the same time that he has reached the place he sought, and is in a fair way of success, if he can but have the cannon, cannon-balls, and iron stowed on board the "Joly."[2]

Directly after he writes again, "I cannot help conjuring you once more to try to give us the iron." Beaujeu replies: "To show you how ardently I wish to contribute to the success of your undertaking, I have ordered your iron to be got out, in spite of my officers and sailors, who tell me that I endanger my ship by moving every thing in the depth of the hold on a coast like this, where the seas are like mountains. I hesitated to disturb my stowage, not so much to save trouble as because no ballast is to be got hereabout; and I have therefore had six cannon, from my lower deck battery, let down into the hold to take the place of the iron." And he again urges

[1] *Lettre de Beaujeu à La Salle, 18 Fév., 1685* (Margry, II. 542).
[2] *Lettre de La Salle à Beaujeu, 18 Fév., 1685* (Margry, II. 546).

La Salle to accept his offer to bring provisions to the colonists from Martinique.

On the next day, the "Aimable" was wrecked. Beaujeu remained a fortnight longer on the coast, and then told La Salle that, being out of wood, water, and other necessaries, he must go to Mobile Bay to get them. Nevertheless, he lingered a week more, repeated his offer to bring supplies from Martinique, which La Salle again refused, and at last set sail on the twelfth of March, after a leave-taking which was courteous on both sides.[1]

La Salle and his colonists were left alone. Several of them had lost heart, and embarked for home with Beaujeu. Among these was Minet, the engineer, who had fallen out with La Salle, and who, when he reached France, was imprisoned for deserting him. Even his brother, the priest Jean Cavelier had a mind to abandon the enterprise, but was persuaded at last to remain, along with his nephew, the hot-headed Moranget, and the younger Cavelier, a mere school-boy. The two Récollet friars, Zenobe Membré and Anastase Douay, the trusty Joutel, a man of sense and observation, and the Marquis de la Sablonnière, a debauched noble whose patrimony was his sword, were now the chief persons of the forlorn company. The rest were soldiers, raw and undisciplined, and artisans, most of whom knew nothing of their vocation. Add to these the miserable families and the infatuated young women who had come to tempt fortune in the swamps and cane-brakes of the Mississippi.

La Salle set out to explore the neighborhood. Joutel remained in command of the so-called fort. He was beset with wily enemies, and often at night the Indians would crawl in the grass around his feeble stockade, howling like wolves; but a few shots would put them to flight. A strict guard was kept; and a wooden horse was set in the enclosure, to punish the sentinel who should sleep at his post. They stood in daily fear of a more formidable foe, and once they saw a sail, which they doubted not was Spanish; but she happily passed without discovering them. They hunted on the prairies, and speared fish in the neighboring pools. On Easter Day, the

[1] The whole of this correspondence between Beaujeu and La Salle will be found in Margry, II.

Sieur le Gros, one of the chief men of the company, went out after the service to shoot snipes; but, as he walked barefoot through the marsh, a snake bit him, and he soon after died. Two men deserted, to starve on the prairie, or to become savages among savages. Others tried to escape, but were caught; and one of them was hung. A knot of desperadoes conspired to kill Joutel; but one of them betrayed the secret, and the plot was crushed.

La Salle returned from his exploration, but his return brought no cheer. He had been forced to renounce the illusion to which he had clung so long, and was convinced at last that he was not at the mouth of the Mississippi. The wreck of the "Aimable" itself was not pregnant with consequences so disastrous.

NOTE.—The conduct of Beaujeu, hitherto judged chiefly by the printed narrative of Joutel, is set in a new and more favorable light by his correspondence with La Salle. Whatever may have been their mutual irritation, it is clear that the naval commander was anxious to discharge his duty in a manner to satisfy Seignelay, and that he may be wholly acquitted of any sinister design. When he left La Salle on the twelfth of March, he meant to sail in search of the Bay of Mobile (Baye du St. Esprit), partly because he hoped to find it a safe harbor, where he could get La Salle's cannon out of the hold and find ballast to take their place, and partly to get a supply of wood and water, of which he was in extreme need. He told La Salle that he would wait there till the middle of April, in order that he (La Salle) might send the "Belle" to receive the cannon; but on this point there was no definite agreement between them. Beaujeu was ignorant of the position of the bay, which he thought much nearer than it actually was. After trying two days to reach it, the strong head-winds and the discontent of his crew induced him to bear away for Cuba; and, after an encounter with pirates and various adventures, he reached France about the first of July. He was coldly received by Seignelay, who wrote to the intendant at Rochelle: "His Majesty has seen what you wrote about the idea of the Sieur de Beaujeu, that the Sieur de la Salle is not at the mouth of the Mississippi. He seems to found this belief on such weak conjectures that no great attention need be given to his account, especially as *this man* has been prejudiced from the first against La Salle's enterprise." *Lettre de Seignelay à Arnoul, 22 Juillet, 1685* (Margry, II. 604). The minister at the same time warns Beaujeu to say nothing in disparagement of the enterprise, under pain of the king's displeasure.

The narrative of the engineer, Minet, sufficiently explains a curious map, made by him, as he says, not on the spot, but on the voyage homeward, and still preserved in the Archives Scientifiques de la Marine. This map includes two distinct sketches of the mouth of the Mississippi. The first, which corresponds to that made by Franquelin in 1684, is entitled "Embouchure de la Rivière comme M. de la Salle la marque dans sa Carte." The second bears the words, "Costes et Lacs par la Hauteur de sa Rivière, comme nous les avons trouvés." These "Costes et Lacs" are a rude representation of the lagoons of Matagorda Bay and its neighborhood, into which the Mississippi is made to discharge, in accordance with the belief of La Salle. A portion of the coast-line is drawn from actual, though superficial, observation. The rest is merely conjectural.

Chapter XXVI

1685–1687

ST. LOUIS OF TEXAS

The Fort • Misery and Dejection • Energy of La Salle • His Journey of Exploration • Adventures and Accidents • The Buffalo • Duhaut • Indian Massacre • Return of La Salle • A New Calamity • A Desperate Resolution • Departure for Canada • Wreck of the "Belle" • Marriage • Sedition • Adventures of La Salle's Party • The Cenis • The Camanches • The Only Hope • The Last Farewell

O F what avail to plant a colony by the mouth of a petty Texan river? The Mississippi was the life of the enterprise, the condition of its growth and of its existence. Without it, all was futile and meaningless; a folly and a ruin. Cost what it might, the Mississippi must be found.

But the demands of the hour were imperative. The hapless colony, cast ashore like a wreck on the sands of Matagorda Bay, must gather up its shattered resources, and recruit its exhausted strength, before it essayed anew its pilgrimage to the "fatal river." La Salle during his explorations had found a spot which he thought well fitted for a temporary establishment. It was on the river which he named the La Vache,[1] now the Lavaca, which enters the head of Matagorda Bay; and thither he ordered all the women and children, and most of the men, to remove; while the rest, thirty in number, remained with Joutel at the fort near the mouth of the bay. Here they spent their time in hunting, fishing, and squaring the logs of drift-wood which the sea washed up in abundance, and which La Salle proposed to use in building his new station on the Lavaca. Thus the time passed till mid-summer, when Joutel received orders to abandon his post, and rejoin the main body of the colonists. To this end, the little frigate "Belle" was sent down the bay. She was a gift from the king to La Salle, who had brought her safely over the bar, and regarded her as a mainstay of his hopes. She now took on

[1] Called by Joutel Rivière aux Bœufs.

board the stores and some of the men, while Joutel with the
rest followed along shore to the post on the Lavaca. Here he
found a state of things that was far from cheering. Crops had
been sown, but the drought and the cattle had nearly destroyed them. The colonists were lodged under tents and hovels; and the only solid structure was a small square enclosure
of pickets, in which the gunpowder and the brandy were
stored. The site was good, a rising ground by the river; but
there was no wood within the distance of a league, and no
horses or oxen to drag it. Their work must be done by men.
Some felled and squared the timber; and others dragged it by
main force over the matted grass of the prairie, under the
scorching Texan sun. The gun-carriages served to make the
task somewhat easier; yet the strongest men soon gave out
under it. Joutel went down to the first fort, made a raft and
brought up the timber collected there, which proved a most
seasonable and useful supply. Palisades and buildings began
to rise. The men labored without spirit, yet strenuously; for
they labored under the eye of La Salle. The carpenters
brought from Rochelle proved worthless; and he himself
made the plans of the work, marked out the tenons and mor-
tises, and directed the whole.[1]

Death, meanwhile, made withering havoc among his followers; and under the sheds and hovels that shielded them
from the sun lay a score of wretches slowly wasting away with
the diseases contracted at St. Domingo. Of the soldiers en-
listed for the expedition by La Salle's agents, many are affirmed to have spent their lives in begging at the church doors
of Rochefort, and were consequently incapable of discipline.
It was impossible to prevent either them or the sailors from
devouring persimmons and other wild fruits to a destructive
excess. Nearly all fell ill; and, before the summer had passed,
the graveyard had more than thirty tenants.[2] The bearing of
La Salle did not aid to raise the drooping spirits of his followers. The results of the enterprise had been far different from
his hopes; and, after a season of flattering promise, he had

[1] Joutel, *Journal Historique*, 108; *Relation* (Margry, III. 174); *Procès Verbal
fait au poste de St. Louis, le 18 Avril, 1686.*

[2] Joutel, *Journal Historique*, 109. Le Clerc, who was not present, says a
hundred.

entered again on those dark and obstructed paths which seemed his destined way of life. The present was beset with trouble; the future, thick with storms. The consciousness quickened his energies; but it made him stern, harsh, and often unjust to those beneath him.

Joutel was returning to camp one afternoon with the master-carpenter, when they saw game; and the carpenter went after it. He was never seen again. Perhaps he was lost on the prairie, perhaps killed by Indians. He knew little of his trade, but they nevertheless had need of him. Le Gros, a man of character and intelligence, suffered more and more from the bite of the snake received in the marsh on Easter Day. The injured limb was amputated, and he died. La Salle's brother, the priest, lay ill; and several others among the chief persons of the colony were in the same condition.

Meanwhile, the work was urged on. A large building was finished, constructed of timber, roofed with boards and raw hides, and divided into apartments for lodging and other uses. La Salle gave the new establishment his favorite name of Fort St. Louis, and the neighboring bay was also christened after the royal saint.[1] The scene was not without its charms. Towards the south-east stretched the bay with its bordering meadows; and on the north-east the Lavaca ran along the base of green declivities. Around, far and near, rolled a sea of prairie, with distant forests, dim in the summer haze. At times, it was dotted with the browsing buffalo, not yet scared from their wonted pastures; and the grassy swells were spangled with the flowers for which Texas is renowned, and which now form the gay ornaments of our gardens.

And now, the needful work accomplished, and the colony in some measure housed and fortified, its indefatigable chief prepared to renew his quest of the "fatal river," as Joutel repeatedly calls it. Before his departure, he made some preliminary explorations, in the course of which, according to the report of his brother the priest, he found evidence that the

---

[1] The Bay of St. Louis, St. Bernard's Bay, or Matagorda Bay,—for it has borne all these names,—was also called Espiritu Santo Bay by the Spaniards, in common with several other bays in the Gulf of Mexico. An adjoining bay still retains the name.

Spaniards had long before had a transient establishment at a spot about fifteen leagues from Fort St. Louis.[1]

It was the last day of October when La Salle set out on his great journey of exploration. His brother Cavelier, who had now recovered, accompanied him with fifty men; and five cannon-shot from the fort saluted them as they departed. They were lightly equipped; but some of them wore corselets made of staves, to ward off arrows. Descending the Lavaca, they pursued their course eastward on foot along the margin of the bay, while Joutel remained in command of the fort. It was two leagues above the mouth of the river; and in it were thirty-four persons, including three Récollet friars, a number of women and girls from Paris, and two young orphan daughters of one Talon, a Canadian, who had lately died. Their live-stock consisted of some hogs and a litter of eight pigs, which, as Joutel does not forget to inform us, passed their time in wallowing in the ditch of the palisade; a cock and hen, with a young family; and a pair of goats, which, in a temporary dearth of fresh meat, were sacrificed to the needs of the invalid Abbé Cavelier. Joutel suffered no man to lie idle. The blacksmith, having no anvil, was supplied with a cannon as a substitute. Lodgings were built for the women and girls, and separate lodgings for the men. A small chapel was afterwards added, and the whole was fenced with a palisade. At the four corners of the house were mounted eight pieces of cannon, which, in the absence of balls, were loaded

[1] Cavelier, in his report to the minister, says: "We reached a large village, enclosed with a kind of wall made of clay and sand, and fortified with little towers at intervals, where we found the arms of Spain engraved on a plate of copper, with the date of 1588, attached to a stake. The inhabitants gave us a kind welcome, and showed us some hammers and an anvil, two small pieces of iron cannon, a small brass culverin, some pike-heads, some old sword-blades, and some books of Spanish comedy; and thence they guided us to a little hamlet of fishermen, about two leagues distant, where they showed us a second stake, also with the arms of Spain, and a few old chimneys. All this convinced us that the Spaniards had formerly been here."—Cavelier, *Relation du Voyage que mon frère entreprit pour découvrir l'embouchure du fleuve de Missisipy*. The above is translated from the original draft of Cavelier, which is in my possession. It was addressed to the colonial minister, after the death of La Salle. The statement concerning the Spaniards needs confirmation.

with bags of bullets.[1] Between the palisades and the stream lay a narrow strip of marsh, the haunt of countless birds; and at a little distance it deepened into pools full of fish. All the surrounding prairies swarmed with game,—buffalo, deer, hares, turkeys, ducks, geese, swans, plover, snipe, and grouse. The river supplied the colonists with turtles, and the bay with oysters. Of these last, they often found more than they wanted; for when, in their excursions, they shoved their log canoes into the water, wading shoeless through the deep, tenacious mud, the sharp shells would cut their feet like knives; "and what was worse," says Joutel, "the salt water came into the gashes, and made them smart atrociously."

He sometimes amused himself with shooting alligators. "I never spared them when I met them near the house. One day I killed an extremely large one, which was nearly four feet and a half in girth, and about twenty feet long." He describes with accuracy that curious native of the south-western plains, the "horned frog," which, deceived by its uninviting appearance, he erroneously supposed to be venomous. "We had some of our animals bitten by snakes; among the others, a bitch that had belonged to the deceased Sieur le Gros. She was bitten in the jaw when she was with me as I was fishing by the shore of the bay. I gave her a little theriac [*an antidote then in vogue*], which cured her, as it did one of our sows, which came home one day with her head so swelled that she could hardly hold it up. Thinking it must be some snake that had bitten her, I gave her a dose of the theriac mixed with meal and water." The patient began to mend at once. "I killed a good many rattlesnakes by means of the aforesaid bitch, for, when she saw one, she would bark around him, sometimes for a half hour together, till I took my gun and shot him. I often found them in the bushes, making a noise with their tails. When I had killed them, our hogs ate them." He devotes many pages to the plants and animals of the neighborhood, most of which may easily be recognized from his description.

With the buffalo, which he calls "our daily bread," his experiences were many and strange. Being, like the rest of the

[1] Compare Joutel with the Spanish account in *Carta en que se da noticia de un viaje hecho à la Bahia de Espíritu Santo y de la poblacion que tenian ahi los Franceses; Coleccion de Varios Documentos*, 25.

party, a novice in the art of shooting them, he met with many disappointments. Once, having mounted to the roof of the large house in the fort, he saw a dark moving object on a swell of the prairie three miles off; and, rightly thinking that it was a herd of buffalo, he set out with six or seven men to try to kill some of them. After a while, he discovered two bulls lying in a hollow; and, signing to the rest of his party to keep quiet, he made his approach, gun in hand. The bulls presently jumped up, and stared through their manes at the intruder. Joutel fired. It was a close shot; but the bulls merely shook their shaggy heads, wheeled about, and galloped heavily away. The same luck attended him the next day. "We saw plenty of buffalo. I approached several bands of them, and fired again and again, but could not make one of them fall." He had not yet learned that a buffalo rarely falls at once, unless hit in the spine. He continues: "I was not discouraged; and after approaching several more bands,—which was hard work, because I had to crawl on the ground, so as not to be seen,—I found myself in a herd of five or six thousand, but, to my great vexation, I could not bring one of them down. They all ran off to the right and left. It was near night, and I had killed nothing. Though I was very tired, I tried again, approached another band, and fired a number of shots, but not a buffalo would fall. The skin was off my knees with crawling. At last, as I was going back to rejoin our men, I saw a buffalo lying on the ground. I went towards it, and saw that it was dead. I examined it, and found that the bullet had gone in near the shoulder. Then I found others dead like the first. I beckoned the men to come on, and we set to work to cut up the meat; a task which was new to us all." It would be impossible to write a more true and characteristic sketch of the experience of a novice in shooting buffalo on foot. A few days after, he went out again, with Father Anastase Douay, approached a bull, fired, and broke his shoulder. The bull hobbled off on three legs. Douay ran in his cassock to head him back, while Joutel reloaded his gun; upon which, the enraged beast butted at the missionary, and knocked him down. He very narrowly escaped with his life. "There was another missionary," pursues Joutel, "named Father Maxime Le Clerc, who was very well fitted for such an undertaking as ours, because he was equal to any thing, even to butchering a buffalo; and, as I said before that every one of us must lend a hand, because we were too few for anybody to be waited upon, I made the women, girls, and children do their part, as well as him; for, as they all wanted to eat, it was fair that they all should work." He had a scaffolding built near the fort, and set them to smoking buffalo meat, against a day of scarcity.[1]

Thus the time passed till the middle of January; when, late one evening, as all were gathered in the principal building, conversing perhaps, or smoking, or playing at cards, or dozing by the fire in homesick dreams of France, a man on guard came in to report that he had heard a voice from the river. They all went down to the bank, and descried a man in a canoe, who called out, "Dominic!" This was the name of the younger of the two brothers Duhaut, who was one of Joutel's followers. As the canoe approached, they recognized the elder, who had gone with La Salle on his journey of discovery, and who was perhaps the greatest villain of the company. Joutel was much perplexed. La Salle had ordered him to admit nobody into the fort without a pass and a watchword. Duhaut, when questioned, said that he had none, but told at the same time so plausible a story that Joutel no longer hesitated to receive him. As La Salle and his men were pursuing their march along the prairie, Duhaut, who was in the rear, had stopped to mend his moccasins, and, when he tried to overtake the party, had lost his way, mistaking a buffalo-path for the trail of his companions. At night, he fired his gun as a signal, but there was no answering shot. Seeing no hope of rejoining them, he turned back for the fort, found one of the canoes which La Salle had hidden at the shore, paddled by night and lay close by day, shot turkeys, deer, and buffalo for food, and, having no knife, cut the meat with a sharp flint, till after a month of excessive hardship he reached his destination. As the inmates of Fort St. Louis gathered about the weather-beaten wanderer, he told them dreary tidings. The pilot of the "Belle," such was his story, had gone with five men to sound along the shore, by order of La Salle, who was

[1] For the above incidents of life at Fort St. Louis, see Joutel, *Relation* (Margry, III. 185–218, *passim*). The printed condensation of the narrative omits most of these particulars.

then encamped in the neighborhood with his party of explorers. The boat's crew, being overtaken by the night, had rashly bivouacked on the beach, without setting a guard; and, as they slept, a band of Indians had rushed in upon them, and butchered them all. La Salle, alarmed by their long absence, had searched along the shore, and at length found their bodies scattered about the sands and half-devoured by wolves.[1] Well would it have been, if Duhaut had shared their fate.

Weeks and months dragged on, when, at the end of March, Joutel, chancing to mount on the roof of one of the buildings, saw seven or eight men approaching over the prairie. He went out to meet them with an equal number, well armed; and, as he drew near, recognized, with mixed joy and anxiety, La Salle and some of those who had gone with him. His brother Cavelier was at his side, with his cassock so tattered that, says Joutel, "there was hardly a piece left large enough to wrap a farthing's worth of salt. He had an old cap on his head, having lost his hat by the way. The rest were in no better plight, for their shirts were all in rags. Some of them carried loads of meat, because M. de la Salle was afraid that we might not have killed any buffalo. We met with great joy and many embraces. After our greetings were over, M. de la Salle, seeing Duhaut, asked me in an angry tone how it was that I had received this man who had abandoned him. I told him how it had happened, and repeated Duhaut's story. Duhaut defended himself, and M. de la Salle's anger was soon over. We went into the house, and refreshed ourselves with some bread and brandy, as there was no wine left."[2]

La Salle and his companions told their story. They had wandered on through various savage tribes, with whom they had more than one encounter, scattering them like chaff by the terror of their fire-arms. At length, they found a more

[1] Joutel, *Relation* (Margry, III. 206). Compare Le Clerc, II. 296. Cavelier, always disposed to exaggerate, says that ten men were killed. La Salle had previously had encounters with the Indians, and punished them severely for the trouble they had given his men. Le Clerc says of the principal fight, "Several Indians were wounded, a few were killed, and others made prisoners; one of whom, a girl of three or four years, was baptized, and died a few days after, as the first-fruit of this mission, and a sure conquest sent to Heaven."

[2] Joutel, *Relation* (Margry, III. 219).

friendly band, and learned much touching the Spaniards, who, they were told, were universally hated by the tribes of that country. It would be easy, said their informants, to gather a host of warriors and lead them over the Rio Grande; but La Salle was in no condition for attempting conquests, and the tribes in whose alliance he had trusted had, a few days before, been at blows with him. The invasion of New Biscay must be postponed to a more propitious day. Still advancing, he came to a large river, which he at first mistook for the Mississippi; and, building a fort of palisades, he left here several of his men.[1] The fate of these unfortunates does not appear. He now retraced his steps towards Fort St. Louis, and, as he approached it, detached some of his men to look for his vessel, the "Belle," for whose safety, since the loss of her pilot, he had become very anxious.

On the next day, these men appeared at the fort, with downcast looks. They had not found the "Belle" at the place where she had been ordered to remain, nor were any tidings to be heard of her. From that hour, the conviction that she was lost possessed the mind of La Salle.

Surrounded as he was, and had always been, with traitors, the belief now possessed him that her crew had abandoned the colony, and made sail for the West Indies or for France. The loss was incalculable. He had relied on this vessel to transport the colonists to the Mississippi, as soon as its exact position could be ascertained; and, thinking her a safer place of deposit than the fort, he had put on board of her all his papers and personal baggage, besides a great quantity of stores, ammunition, and tools.[2] In truth, she was of the last necessity to the unhappy exiles, and their only resource for escape from a position which was fast becoming desperate.

La Salle, as his brother tells us, fell dangerously ill; the fatigues of his journey, joined to the effects upon his mind of this last disaster, having overcome his strength, though not

[1] Cavelier says that he actually reached the Mississippi; but, on the one hand, the abbé did not know whether the river in question was the Mississippi or not; and, on the other, he is somewhat inclined to mendacity. Le Clerc says that La Salle thought he had found the river. According to the *Procès Verbal* of 18 April, 1686, "il y arriva le 13 Février." Joutel says that La Salle told him "qu'il n'avoit point trouvé sa rivière."

[2] *Procès Verbal fait au poste de St. Louis, le 18 Avril, 1686.*

his fortitude. "In truth," writes the priest, "after the loss of the vessel which deprived us of our only means of returning to France, we had no resource but in the firm guidance of my brother, whose death each of us would have regarded as his own."[1]

La Salle no sooner recovered than he embraced a resolution which could be the offspring only of a desperate necessity. He determined to make his way by the Mississippi and the Illinois to Canada, whence he might bring succor to the colonists, and send a report of their condition to France. The attempt was beset with uncertainties and dangers. The Mississippi was first to be found, then followed through all the perilous monotony of its interminable windings to a goal which was to be but the starting-point of a new and not less arduous journey. Cavelier, his brother, Moranget, his nephew, the friar Anastase Douay, and others to the number of twenty, were chosen to accompany him. Every corner of the magazine was ransacked for an outfit. Joutel generously gave up the better part of his wardrobe to La Salle and his two relatives. Duhaut, who had saved his baggage from the wreck of the "Aimable," was required to contribute to the necessities of the party; and the scantily furnished chests of those who had died were used to supply the wants of the living. Each man labored with needle and awl to patch his failing garments, or supply their place with buffalo or deer skins. On the twenty-second of April, after Mass and prayers in the chapel, they issued from the gate, each bearing his pack and his weapons, some with kettles slung at their backs, some with axes, some with gifts for Indians. In this guise, they held their way in silence across the prairie; while anxious eyes followed them from the palisades of St. Louis, whose inmates, not excepting Joutel himself, seem to have been ignorant of the extent and difficulty of the undertaking.[2]

"On May Day," he writes, "at about two in the afternoon,

[1] Cavelier, *Relation du Voyage pour découvrir l'Embouchure du Fleuve de Missisipy.*

[2] Joutel, *Journal Historique*, 140; Anastase Douay in Le Clerc, II. 303; Cavelier, *Relation*. The date is from Douay. It does not appear, from his narrative, that they meant to go further than the Illinois. Cavelier says that, after resting here, they were to go to Canada. Joutel supposed that they would go only to the Illinois. La Salle seems to have been even more reticent than usual.

as I was walking near the house, I heard a voice from the river below, crying out several times, *Qui vive?* Knowing that the Sieur Barbier had gone that way with two canoes to hunt buffalo, I thought that it might be one of these canoes coming back with meat, and did not think much of the matter till I heard the same voice again. I answered, *Versailles*, which was the password I had given the Sieur Barbier, in case he should come back in the night. But, as I was going towards the bank, I heard other voices which I had not heard for a long time. I recognized among the rest that of M. Chefdeville, which made me fear that some disaster had happened. I ran down to the bank, and my first greeting was to ask what had become of the "Belle." They answered that she was wrecked on the other side of the bay, and that all on board were drowned except the six who were in the canoe; namely, the Sieur Chefdeville, the Marquis de la Sablonnière, the man named Teissier, a soldier, a girl, and a little boy."[1]

From the young priest Chefdeville, Joutel learned the particulars of the disaster. Water had failed on board the "Belle;" a boat's crew of five men had gone in quest of it; the wind rose, their boat was swamped, and they were all drowned. Those who remained had now no means of going ashore; but, if they had no water, they had wine and brandy in abundance, and Teissier, the master of the vessel, was drunk every day. After a while, they left their moorings, and tried to reach the fort; but they were few, weak, and unskilful. A violent north wind drove them on a sand-bar. Some of them were drowned in trying to reach land on a raft. Others were more successful; and, after a long delay, they found a stranded canoe, in which they made their way to St. Louis, bringing with them some of La Salle's papers and baggage saved from the wreck.

These multiplied disasters bore hard on the spirits of the colonists; and Joutel, like a good commander as he was, spared no pains to cheer them. "We did what we could to amuse ourselves and drive away care. I encouraged our people to dance and sing in the evenings; for, when M. de la Salle was among us, pleasure was often banished. Now there is no

[1] Joutel, *Relation* (Margry, III. 226).

use in being melancholy on such occasions. It is true that M. de la Salle had no great cause for merry-making, after all his losses and disappointments; but his troubles made others suffer also. Though he had ordered me to allow to each person only a certain quantity of meat at every meal, I observed this rule only when meat was rare. The air here is very keen, and one has a great appetite. One must eat and act, if he wants good health and spirits. I speak from experience; for once, when I had ague chills, and was obliged to keep the house with nothing to do, I was dreary and downhearted. On the contrary, if I was busy with hunting or any thing else, I was not so dull by half. So I tried to keep the people as busy as possible. I set them to making a small cellar to keep meat fresh in hot weather; but, when M. de la Salle came back, he said it was too small. As he always wanted to do every thing on a grand scale, he prepared to make a large one, and marked out the plan." This plan of the large cellar, like more important undertakings of its unhappy projector, proved too extensive for execution, the colonists being engrossed by the daily care of keeping themselves alive.

A gleam of hilarity shot for an instant out of the clouds. The young Canadian, Barbier, usually conducted the hunting-parties; and some of the women and girls often went out with them, to aid in cutting up the meat. Barbier became enamoured of one of the girls; and, as his devotion to her was the subject of comment, he asked Joutel for leave to marry her. The commandant, after due counsel with the priests and friars, vouchsafed his consent, and the rite was duly solemnized; whereupon, fired by the example, the Marquis de la Sablonnière begged leave to marry another of the girls. Joutel, the gardener's son, concerned that a marquis should so abase himself, and anxious at the same time for the morals of the fort, which La Salle had especially commended to his care, not only flatly refused, but, in the plenitude of his authority, forbade the lovers all farther intercourse.

Father Zenobe Membré, Superior of the mission, gave unwilling occasion for further merriment. These worthy friars were singularly unhappy in their dealings with the buffalo, one of which, it may be remembered, had already knocked down Father Anastase. Undeterred by his example, Father

Zenobe one day went out with the hunters, carrying a gun like the rest. Joutel shot a buffalo, which was making off, badly wounded, when a second shot stopped it, and it presently lay down. The father superior thought it was dead; and, without heeding the warning shout of Joutel, he approached, and pushed it with the butt of his gun. The bull sprang up with an effort of expiring fury, and, in the words of Joutel, "trampled on the father, took the skin off his face in several places, and broke his gun, so that he could hardly manage to get away, and remained in an almost helpless state for more than three months. Bad as the accident was, he was laughed at nevertheless for his rashness."

The mishaps of the friars did not end here. Father Maxime Le Clerc was set upon by a boar belonging to the colony. "I do not know," says Joutel, "what spite the beast had against him, whether for a beating or some other offence; but, however this may be, I saw the father running and crying for help, and the boar running after him. I went to the rescue, but could not come up in time. The father stooped as he ran, to gather up his cassock from about his legs; and the boar, which ran faster than he, struck him in the arm with his tusks, so that some of the nerves were torn. Thus, all three of our good Récollet fathers were near being the victims of animals."[1]

In spite of his efforts to encourage them, the followers of Joutel were fast losing heart. Father Maxime Le Clerc kept a journal, in which he set down various charges against La Salle. Joutel got possession of the paper, and burned it on the urgent entreaty of the friars, who dreaded what might ensue, should the absent commander become aware of the aspersions cast upon him. The elder Duhaut fomented the rising discontent of the colonists, played the demagogue, told them that La Salle would never return, and tried to make himself their leader. Joutel detected the mischief, and, with a lenity which he afterwards deeply regretted, contented himself with a rebuke to the offender, and words of reproof and encouragement to the dejected band.

He had caused the grass to be cut near the fort, so as to

---

[1] Joutel, *Relation* (Margry, III. 244, 246).

form a sort of playground; and here, one evening, he and some of the party were trying to amuse themselves, when they heard shouts from beyond the river, and Joutel recognized the voice of La Salle. Hastening to meet him in a wooden canoe, he brought him and his party to the fort. Twenty men had gone out with him, and eight had returned. Of the rest, four had deserted, one had been lost, one had been devoured by an alligator; and the rest, giving out on the march, had probably perished in attempting to regain the fort. The travellers told of a rich country, a wild and beautiful landscape,—woods, rivers, groves, and prairies; but all availed nothing, and the acquisition of five horses was but an indifferent return for the loss of twelve men.

After leaving the fort, they had journeyed towards the north-east, over plains green as an emerald with the young verdure of April, till at length they saw, far as the eye could reach, the boundless prairie alive with herds of buffalo. The animals were in one of their tame or stupid moods; and they killed nine or ten of them without the least difficulty, drying the best parts of the meat. They crossed the Colorado on a raft, and reached the banks of another river, where one of the party, named Hiens, a German of Würtemberg, and an old buccaneer, was mired and nearly suffocated in a mud-hole. Unfortunately, as will soon appear, he managed to crawl out; and, to console him, the river was christened with his name. The party made a bridge of felled trees, on which they crossed in safety. La Salle now changed their course, and journeyed eastward, when the travellers soon found themselves in the midst of a numerous Indian population, where they were feasted and caressed without measure. At another village, they were less fortunate. The inhabitants were friendly by day and hostile by night. They came to attack the French in their camp, but withdrew, daunted by the menacing voice of La Salle, who had heard them approaching through the cane-brake.

La Salle's favorite Shawanoe hunter, Nika, who had followed him from Canada to France, and from France to Texas, was bitten by a rattlesnake; and, though he recovered, the accident detained the party for several days. At length, they resumed their journey, but were stopped by a river, called by

Douay "La Rivière des Malheurs." La Salle and Cavelier, with a few others, tried to cross on a raft, which, as it reached the channel, was caught by a current of marvellous swiftness. Douay and Moranget, watching the transit from the edge of the cane-brake, beheld their commander swept down the stream, and vanishing, as it were, in an instant. All that day they remained with their companions on the bank, lamenting in despair for the loss of their guardian angel, for so Douay calls La Salle.[1] It was fast growing dark, when, to their unspeakable relief, they saw him advancing with his party along the opposite bank, having succeeded, after great exertion, in guiding the raft to land. How to rejoin him was now the question. Douay and his companions, who had tasted no food that day, broke their fast on two young eagles which they knocked out of their nest, and then spent the night in rueful consultation as to the means of crossing the river. In the morning, they waded into the marsh, the friar with his breviary in his hood, to keep it dry, and hacked among the canes till they had gathered enough to make another raft; on which, profiting by La Salle's experience, they safely crossed, and rejoined him.

Next, they became entangled in a cane-brake, where La Salle, as usual with him in such cases, took the lead, a hatchet in each hand, and hewed out a path for his followers. They soon reached the villages of the Cenis Indians, on and near the river Trinity, a tribe then powerful, but long since extinct. Nothing could surpass the friendliness of their welcome. The chiefs came to meet them, bearing the calumet, and followed by warriors in shirts of embroidered deer-skin. Then the whole village swarmed out like bees, gathering around the visitors with offerings of food and all that was precious in their eyes. La Salle was lodged with the great chief; but he compelled his men to encamp at a distance, lest the ardor of their gallantry might give occasion of offence. The lodges of the Cenis, forty or fifty feet high, and covered with a thatch of meadow-grass, looked like huge bee-hives. Each held several families, whose fire was in the middle, and their beds

[1] "Ce fût une desolation extrême pour nous tous qui desesperions de revoir jamais nostre Ange tutélaire, le Sieur de la Salle. . . . Tout le jour se passa en pleurs et en larmes."—Douay in Le Clerc, II. 315.

around the circumference. The spoil of the Spaniards was to be seen on all sides: silver lamps and spoons, swords, old muskets, money, clothing, and a bull of the Pope dispensing the Spanish colonists of new Mexico from fasting during summer.[1] These treasures, as well as their numerous horses, were obtained by the Cenis from their neighbors and allies, the Camanches, that fierce prairie banditti who then, as now, scourged the Mexican border with their bloody forays. A party of these wild horsemen was in the village. Douay was edified at seeing them make the sign of the cross in imitation of the neophytes of one of the Spanish missions. They enacted, too, the ceremony of the Mass; and one of them, in his rude way, drew a sketch of a picture he had seen in some church which he had pillaged, wherein the friar plainly recognized the Virgin weeping at the foot of the cross. They invited the French to join them on a raid into New Mexico; and they spoke with contempt, as their tribesmen will speak to this day, of the Spanish creoles, saying that it would be easy to conquer a nation of cowards who make people walk before them with fans to cool them in hot weather.[2]

Soon after leaving the Cenis villages, both La Salle and his nephew, Moranget, were attacked by fever. This caused a delay of more than two months, during which the party seem to have remained encamped on the Neches, or possibly the Sabine. When at length the invalids had recovered sufficient strength to travel, the stock of ammunition was nearly spent, some of the men had deserted, and the condition of the travellers was such that there seemed no alternative but to return to Fort St. Louis. This they accordingly did, greatly aided in their march by the horses bought from the Cenis, and suffering no very serious accident by the way, excepting the loss of La Salle's servant, Dumesnil, who was seized by an alligator while attempting to cross the Colorado.

The temporary excitement caused among the colonists by their return soon gave place to a dejection bordering on despair. "This pleasant land," writes Cavelier, "seemed to us an abode of weariness and a perpetual prison." Flattering themselves with the delusion, common to exiles of every kind, that

[1] Douay in Le Clerc, II. 321; Cavelier, *Relation*.
[2] Douay in Le Clerc, II. 324, 325.

they were objects of solicitude at home, they watched daily, with straining eyes, for an approaching sail. Ships, indeed, had ranged the coast to seek them, but with no friendly intent. Their thoughts dwelt, with unspeakable yearning, on the France they had left behind, which, to their longing fancy, was pictured as an unattainable Eden. Well might they despond; for of a hundred and eighty colonists, besides the crew of the "Belle," less than forty-five remained. The weary precincts of Fort St. Louis, with its fence of rigid palisades, its area of trampled earth, its buildings of weather-stained timber, and its well-peopled graveyard without, were hateful to their sight. La Salle had a heavy task to save them from despair. His composure, his unfailing equanimity, his words of encouragement and cheer, were the breath of life to this forlorn company; for, though he could not impart to minds of less adamantine temper the audacity of hope with which he still clung to the final accomplishment of his purposes, the contagion of his hardihood touched, nevertheless, the drooping spirits of his followers.[1]

The journey to Canada was clearly their only hope; and, after a brief rest, La Salle prepared to renew the attempt. He proposed that Joutel should this time be of the party; and should proceed from Quebec to France, with his brother Cavelier, to solicit succors for the colony, while he himself returned to Texas. A new obstacle was presently interposed. La Salle, whose constitution seems to have suffered from his long course of hardships, was attacked in November with hernia. Joutel offered to conduct the party in his stead; but La Salle replied that his own presence was indispensable at the Illinois. He had the good fortune to recover, within four or five weeks, sufficiently to undertake the journey; and all in the fort busied themselves in preparing an outfit. In such straits were they for clothing, that the sails of the "Belle" were cut up to

[1] "L'égalité d'humeur du Chef rassuroit tout le monde; et il trouvoit des resources à tout par son esprit qui relevoit les espérances les plus abatues." —Joutel, *Journal Historique*, 152.

"Il seroit difficile de trouver dans l'Histoire un courage plus intrepide et plus invincible que celuy du Sieur de la Salle dans les évenemens contraires; il ne fût jamais abatu, et il espéroit toujours avec le secours du Ciel de venir à bout de son entreprise malgré tous les obstacles qui se présentoient." —Douay in Le Clerc, II. 327.

make coats for the adventurers. Christmas came, and was solemnly observed. There was a midnight Mass in the chapel, where Membré, Cavelier, Douay, and their priestly brethren, stood before the altar, in vestments strangely contrasting with the rude temple and the ruder garb of the worshippers. And as Membré elevated the consecrated wafer, and the lamps burned dim through the clouds of incense, the kneeling group drew from the daily miracle such consolation as true Catholics alone can know. When Twelfth Night came, all gathered in the hall, and cried, after the jovial old custom, *"The King drinks,"* with hearts, perhaps, as cheerless as their cups, which were filled with cold water.

On the morrow, the band of adventurers mustered for the fatal journey.[1] The five horses, bought by La Salle of the Indians, stood in the area of the fort, packed for the march; and here was gathered the wretched remnant of the colony, those who were to go and those who were to stay behind. These latter were about twenty in all: Barbier, who was to command in the place of Joutel; Sablonnière, who, despite his title of Marquis, was held in great contempt;[2] the friars, Membré and Le Clerc,[3] and the priest, Chefdeville, besides a surgeon, soldiers, laborers, seven women and girls, and several children, doomed, in this deadly exile, to wait the issues of the journey, and the possible arrival of a tardy succor. La Salle had made them a last address, delivered, we are told, with that winning air which, though alien from his usual bearing, seems to have been at times a natural expression of this unhappy man.[4] It was a bitter parting, one of sighs, tears,

[1] I follow Douay's date, who makes the day of departure the seventh of January, or the day after Twelfth Night. Joutel thinks it was the twelfth of January, but professes uncertainty as to all his dates at this time, as he lost his notes.

[2] He had to be kept on short allowance, because he was in the habit of bargaining away every thing given to him. He had squandered the little that belonged to him at St. Domingo, in amusements "indignes de sa naissance," and in consequence was suffering from diseases which disabled him from walking. *Procès Verbal, 18 Avril, 1686.*

[3] Maxime le Clerc was a relative of the author of *L'Établissement de la Foi.*

[4] "Il fit une Harangue pleine d'éloquence et de cet air engageant qui luy estoit si naturel: toute la petite Colonie y estoit presente et en fût touchée jusques aux larmes, persuadée de la nécessité de son voyage et de la droiture de ses intentions."—Douay in Le Clerc, II. 330.

and embracings; the farewell of those on whose souls had sunk a heavy boding that they would never meet again.[1] Equipped and weaponed for the journey, the adventurers filed from the gate, crossed the river, and held their slow march over the prairies beyond, till intervening woods and hills shut Fort St. Louis for ever from their sight.

[1] "Nous nous separâmes les uns des autres, d'une manière si tendre et si triste qu'il sembloit que nous avions tous le secret pressentiment que nous ne nous reverrions jamais."—Joutel, *Journal Historique*, 158.

Chapter XXVII
1687
ASSASSINATION OF LA SALLE

*His Followers • Prairie Travelling • A Hunters' Quarrel •
The Murder of Moranget • The Conspiracy • Death of
La Salle • His Character*

THE travellers were crossing a marshy prairie towards a distant belt of woods, that followed the course of a little river. They led with them their five horses, laden with their scanty baggage, and, with what was of no less importance, their stock of presents for Indians. Some wore the remains of the clothing they had worn from France, eked out with deerskins, dressed in the Indian manner; and some had coats of old sail-cloth. Here was La Salle, in whom one would have known, at a glance, the chief of the party; and the priest, Cavelier, who seems to have shared not one of the high traits of his younger brother. Here, too, were their nephews, Moranget and the boy Cavelier, now about seventeen years old; the trusty soldier Joutel; and the friar Anastase Douay. Duhaut followed, a man of respectable birth and education; and Liotot, the surgeon of the party. At home, they might perhaps have lived and died with a fair repute; but the wilderness is a rude touchstone, which often reveals traits that would have lain buried and unsuspected in civilized life. The German Hiens, the ex-buccaneer, was also of the number. He had probably sailed with an English crew; for he was sometimes known as *Gemme Anglais*, or "English Jem."[1] The Sieur de Marle; Teissier, a pilot; l'Archevêque, a servant of Duhaut; and others, to the number in all of seventeen,—made up the party; to which is to be added Nika, La Salle's Shawanoe hunter, who, as well as another Indian, had twice crossed the ocean with him, and still followed his fortunes with an admiring though undemonstrative fidelity.

They passed the prairie, and neared the forest. Here they

---

[1] Tonty also speaks of him as "un flibustier anglois." In another document, he is called "James."

saw buffalo; and the hunters approached, and killed several of them. Then they traversed the woods; found and forded the shallow and rushy stream, and pushed through the forest beyond, till they again reached the open prairie. Heavy clouds gathered over them, and it rained all night; but they sheltered themselves under the fresh hides of the buffalo they had killed.

It is impossible, as it would be needless, to follow the detail of their daily march.[1] It was such an one, though with unwonted hardship, as is familiar to the memory of many a prairie traveller of our own time. They suffered greatly from the want of shoes, and found for a while no better substitute than a casing of raw buffalo-hide, which they were forced to keep always wet, as, when dry, it hardened about the foot like iron. At length, they bought dressed deer-skin from the Indians, of which they made tolerable moccasins. The rivers, streams, and gullies filled with water were without number; and, to cross them, they made a boat of bull-hide, like the "bull boat" still used on the Upper Missouri. This did good service, as, with the help of their horses, they could carry it with them. Two or three men could cross in it at once, and the horses swam after them like dogs. Sometimes they traversed the sunny prairie; sometimes dived into the dark recesses of the forest, where the buffalo, descending daily from their pastures in long files to drink at the river, often made a broad and easy path for the travellers. When foul weather arrested them, they built huts of bark and long meadow-grass; and, safely sheltered, lounged away the day, while their horses, picketed near by, stood steaming in the rain. At night, they usually set a rude stockade about their camp; and here, by the grassy border of a brook, or at the edge of a grove where a spring bubbled up through the sands, they lay asleep around the embers of their fire, while the man on guard listened to the deep

[1] Of the three narratives of this journey, those of Joutel, Cavelier, and Anastase Douay, the first is by far the best. That of Cavelier seems the work of a man of confused brain and indifferent memory. Some of his statements are irreconcilable with those of Joutel and Douay; and known facts of his history justify the suspicion of a wilful inaccuracy. Joutel's account is of a very different character, and seems to be the work of an honest and intelligent man. Douay's account is brief; but it agrees with that of Joutel, in most essential points.

breathing of the slumbering horses, and the howling of the wolves that saluted the rising moon as it flooded the waste of prairie with pale mystic radiance.

They met Indians almost daily: sometimes a band of hunters, mounted or on foot, chasing buffalo on the plains; sometimes a party of fishermen: sometimes a winter camp, on the slope of a hill or under the sheltering border of a forest. They held intercourse with them in the distance by signs; often they disarmed their distrust, and attracted them into their camp; and often they visited them in their lodges, where, seated on buffalo-robes, they smoked with their entertainers, passing the pipe from hand to hand, after the custom still in use among the prairie tribes. Cavelier says that they once saw a band of a hundred and fifty mounted Indians attacking a herd of buffalo with lances pointed with sharpened bone. The old priest was delighted with the sport, which he pronounces "the most diverting thing in the world." On another occasion, when the party were encamped near the village of a tribe which Cavelier calls Sassory, he saw them catch an alligator about twelve feet long, which they proceeded to torture as if he were a human enemy, first putting out his eyes, and then leading him to the neighboring prairie, where, having confined him by a number of stakes, they spent the entire day in tormenting him.[1]

Holding a northerly course, the travellers crossed the Brazos, and reached the waters of the Trinity. The weather was unfavorable, and on one occasion they encamped in the rain during four or five days together. It was not an harmonious company. La Salle's cold and haughty reserve had returned, at least for those of his followers to whom he was not partial. Duhaut and the surgeon Liotot, both of whom were men of some property, had a large pecuniary stake in the enterprise, and were disappointed and incensed at its ruinous result. They had a quarrel with young Moranget, whose hot and hasty temper was as little fitted to conciliate as was the harsh reserve of his uncle. Already at Fort St. Louis, Duhaut had intrigued among the men; and the mild admonition of Joutel had not, it seems, sufficed to divert him from his sinsister

[1] Cavelier, *Relation*.

purposes. Liotot, it is said, had secretly sworn vengeance against La Salle, whom he charged with having caused the death of his brother, or, as some will have it, his nephew. On one of the former journeys, this young man's strength had failed; and, La Salle having ordered him to return to the fort, he had been killed by Indians on the way.

The party moved again as the weather improved, and on the fifteenth of March encamped within a few miles of a spot which La Salle had passed on his preceding journey, and where he had left a quantity of Indian corn and beans in *cache*; that is to say, hidden in the ground or in a hollow tree. As provisions were falling short, he sent a party from the camp to find it. These men were Duhaut, Liotot,[1] Hiens the buccaneer, Teissier, l'Archevêque, Nika the hunter, and La Salle's servant, Saget. They opened the *cache*, and found the contents spoiled; but, as they returned from their bootless errand, they saw buffalo; and Nika shot two of them. They now encamped on the spot, and sent the servant to inform La Salle, in order that he might send horses to bring in the meat. Accordingly, on the next day, he directed Moranget and De Marle, with the necessary horses, to go with Saget to the hunters' camp. When they arrived, they found that Duhaut and his companions had already cut up the meat, and laid it upon scaffolds for smoking, though it was not yet so dry as, it seems, this process required. Duhaut and the others had also put by, for themselves, the marrow-bones and certain portions of the meat, to which, by woodland custom, they had a perfect right. Moranget, whose rashness and violence had once before caused a fatal catastrophe, fell into a most unreasonable fit of rage, berated and menaced Duhaut and his party, and ended by seizing upon the whole of the meat, including the reserved portions. This added fuel to the fire of Duhaut's old grudge against Moranget and his uncle. There is reason to think that he had harbored deadly designs, the execution of which was only hastened by the present outbreak. The surgeon also bore hatred against Moranget, whom he had nursed with constant attention when wounded by an Indian arrow, and who had since repaid him with abuse.

[1] Called Lanquetot by Tonty.

These two now took counsel apart with Hiens, Teissier, and l'Archevêque; and it was resolved to kill Moranget that night. Nika, La Salle's devoted follower, and Saget, his faithful servant, must die with him. All of the five were of one mind, except the pilot Teissier, who neither aided nor opposed the plot.

Night came; the woods grew dark; the evening meal was finished, and the evening pipes were smoked. The order of the guard was arranged; and, doubtless by design, the first hour of the night was assigned to Moranget, the second to Saget, and the third to Nika. Gun in hand, each stood watch in turn over the silent but not sleeping forms around him, till, his time expiring, he called the man who was to relieve him, wrapped himself in his blanket, and was soon buried in a slumber that was to be his last. Now the assassins rose. Duhaut and Hiens stood with their guns cocked, ready to shoot down any one of the destined victims who should resist or fly. The surgeon, with an axe, stole towards the three sleepers, and struck a rapid blow at each in turn. Saget and Nika died with little movement; but Moranget started spasmodically into a sitting posture, gasping and unable to speak; and the murderers compelled De Marle, who was not in their plot, to compromise himself by despatching him.

The floodgates of murder were open, and the torrent must have its way. Vengeance and safety alike demanded the death of La Salle. Hiens, or "English Jem," alone seems to have hesitated; for he was one of those to whom that stern commander had always been partial. Meanwhile, the intended victim was still at his camp, about six miles distant. It is easy to picture, with sufficient accuracy, the features of the scene,— the sheds of bark and branches, beneath which, among blankets and buffalo-robes, camp-utensils, pack-saddles, rude harness, guns, powder-horns, and bullet-pouches, the men lounged away the hour, sleeping or smoking, or talking among themselves; the blackened kettles that hung from tripods of poles over the fires; the Indians strolling about the place or lying, like dogs in the sun, with eyes half-shut, yet all observant; and, in the neighboring meadow, the horses grazing under the eye of a watchman.

It was the eighteenth of March. Moranget and his companions had been expected to return the night before; but the whole day passed, and they did not appear. La Salle became very anxious. He resolved to go and look for them; but, not well knowing the way, he told the Indians who were about the camp that he would give them a hatchet, if they would guide him. One of them accepted the offer; and La Salle prepared to set out in the morning, at the same time directing Joutel to be ready to go with him. Joutel says: "That evening, while we were talking about what could have happened to the absent men, he seemed to have a presentiment of what was to take place. He asked me if I had heard of any machinations against them, or if I had noticed any bad design on the part of Duhaut and the rest. I answered that I had heard nothing, except that they sometimes complained of being found fault with so often; and that this was all I knew, besides which, as they were persuaded that I was in his interest, they would not have told me of any bad design they might have. We were very uneasy all the rest of the evening."

In the morning, La Salle set out with his Indian guide. He had changed his mind with regard to Joutel, whom he now directed to remain in charge of the camp and to keep a careful watch. He told the friar Anastase Douay to come with him instead of Joutel, whose gun, which was the best in the party, he borrowed for the occasion, as well as his pistol. The three proceeded on their way, La Salle, the friar, and the Indian. "All the way," writes the friar, "he spoke to me of nothing but matters of piety, grace, and predestination; enlarging on the debt he owed to God, who had saved him from so many perils during more than twenty years of travel in America. Suddenly, I saw him overwhelmed with a profound sadness, for which he himself could not account. He was so much moved that I scarcely knew him." He soon recovered his usual calmness; and they walked on till they approached the camp of Duhaut, which was on the farther side of a small river. Looking about him with the eye of a woodsman, La Salle saw two eagles circling in the air nearly over him, as if attracted by carcasses of beasts or men. He fired his gun and his pistol, as a summons to any of his followers who might be within hearing. The shots reached the ears of the conspirators. Rightly conjecturing by whom they were fired, several of them, led by Duhaut, crossed the river at a little distance above, where trees or other intervening objects hid them from sight. Duhaut and the surgeon crouched like Indians in the long, dry, reed-like grass of the last summer's growth, while l'Archevêque stood in sight near the bank. La Salle, continuing to advance, soon saw him, and, calling to him, demanded where was Moranget. The man, without lifting his hat, or any show of respect, replied in an agitated and broken voice, but with a tone of studied insolence, that Moranget was strolling about somewhere. La Salle rebuked and menaced him. He rejoined with increased insolence, drawing back, as he spoke, towards the ambuscade, while the incensed commander advanced to chastise him. At that moment, a shot was fired from the grass, instantly followed by another; and, pierced through the brain, La Salle dropped dead.

The friar at his side stood terror-stricken, unable to advance or to fly; when Duhaut, rising from the ambuscade, called out to him to take courage, for he had nothing to fear. The murderers now came forward, and with wild looks gathered about their victim. "There thou liest, great Bashaw! There thou liest!"[1] exclaimed the surgeon Liotot, in base exultation over the unconscious corpse. With mockery and insult, they stripped it naked, dragged it into the bushes, and left it there, a prey to the buzzards and the wolves.

Thus in the vigor of his manhood, at the age of forty-three, died Robert Cavelier de la Salle, "one of the greatest men," writes Tonty, "of this age;" without question one of the most remarkable explorers whose names live in history. His faithful officer Joutel thus sketches his portrait: "His firmness, his courage, his great knowledge of the arts and sciences, which made him equal to every undertaking, and his untiring energy, which enabled him to surmount every obstacle, would have won at last a glorious success for his grand enterprise, had not all his fine qualities been counterbalanced by a haughtiness of manner which often made him insupportable, and by a harshness towards those under his command, which drew upon him an implacable hatred, and was at last the cause of his death."[2]

[1] "Te voilà grand Bacha, te voilà!"—Joutel, *Journal Historique*, 203.
[2] *Journal Historique*, 203.

The enthusiasm of the disinterested and chivalrous Champlain was not the enthusiasm of La Salle; nor had he any part in the self-devoted zeal of the early Jesuit explorers. He belonged not to the age of the knight-errant and the saint, but to the modern world of practical study and practical action. He was the hero, not of a principle nor of a faith, but simply of a fixed idea and a determined purpose. As often happens with concentred and energetic natures, his purpose was to him a passion and an inspiration; and he clung to it with a certain fanaticism of devotion. It was the offspring of an ambition vast and comprehensive, yet acting in the interest both of France and of civilization.

Serious in all things, incapable of the lighter pleasures, incapable of repose, finding no joy but in the pursuit of great designs, too shy for society and too reserved for popularity, often unsympathetic and always seeming so, smothering emotions which he could not utter, schooled to universal distrust, stern to his followers and pitiless to himself, bearing the brunt of every hardship and every danger, demanding of others an equal constancy joined to an implicit deference, heeding no counsel but his own, attempting the impossible and grasping at what was too vast to hold,—he contained in his own complex and painful nature the chief springs of his triumphs, his failures, and his death.

It is easy to reckon up his defects, but it is not easy to hide from sight the Roman virtues that redeemed them. Beset by a throng of enemies, he stands, like the King of Israel, head and shoulders above them all. He was a tower of adamant, against whose impregnable front hardship and danger, the rage of man and of the elements, the southern sun, the northern blast, fatigue, famine, and disease, delay, disappointment, and deferred hope emptied their quivers in vain. That very pride which, Coriolanus-like, declared itself most sternly in the thickest press of foes, has in it something to challenge admiration. Never, under the impenetrable mail of paladin or crusader, beat a heart of more intrepid mettle than within the stoic panoply that armed the breast of La Salle. To estimate aright the marvels of his patient fortitude, one must follow on his track through the vast scene of his interminable journeyings, those thousands of weary miles of forest, marsh, and river, where, again and again, in the bitterness of baffled striving, the untiring pilgrim pushed onward towards the goal which he was never to attain. America owes him an enduring memory; for, in this masculine figure, she sees the pioneer who guided her to the possession of her richest heritage.[1]

[1] On the assassination of La Salle, the evidence is fourfold: 1. The narrative of Douay, who was with him at the time. 2. That of Joutel, who learned the facts, immediately after they took place, from Douay and others, and who parted from La Salle an hour or more before his death. 3. A document preserved in the Archives de la Marine, entitled *"Relation de la Mort du Sr de la Salle, suivant le rapport d'un nommé Couture à qui M. Cavelier l'apprit en passant au pays des Akansa, avec toutes les circonstances que le dit Couture a apprises d'un François que M. Cavelier avoit laissé aux dits pays des Akansa, crainte qu'il ne gardât pas le secret."* 4. The authentic memoir of Tonty, of which a copy from the original is before me, and which has recently been printed by Margry.

The narrative of Cavelier unfortunately fails us several weeks before the death of his brother, the remainder being lost. On a study of these various documents, it is impossible to resist the conclusion that neither Cavelier nor Douay always wrote honestly. Joutel, on the contrary, gives the impression of sense, intelligence, and candor throughout. Charlevoix, who knew him long after, says that he was "un fort honnête homme, et le seul de la troupe de M. de la Salle, sur qui ce célèbre voyageur pût compter." Tonty derived his information from the survivors of La Salle's party. Couture, whose statements are embodied in the *Relation de la Mort de M. de la Salle*, was one of Tonty's men, who, as will be seen hereafter, were left by him at the mouth of the Arkansas, and to whom Cavelier told the story of his brother's death. Couture also repeats the statements of one of La Salle's followers, undoubtedly a Parisian boy, named Barthelemy, who was violently prejudiced against his chief, whom he slanders to the utmost of his skill, saying that he was so enraged at his failures that he did not approach the sacraments for two years; that he nearly starved his brother Cavelier, allowing him only a handful of meal a day; that he killed with his own hand "quantité de personnes," who did not work to his liking; and that he killed the sick in their beds, without mercy, under the pretence that they were counterfeiting sickness, in order to escape work. These assertions certainly have no other foundation than the undeniable rigor of La Salle's command. Douay says that he confessed and made his devotions on the morning of his death, while Cavelier always speaks of him as the hope and the staff of the colony.

Douay declares that La Salle lived an hour after the fatal shot; that he gave him absolution, buried his body, and planted a cross on his grave. At the time, he told Joutel a different story; and the latter, with the best means of learning the facts, explicitly denies the friar's printed statement. Couture, on the authority of Cavelier himself, also says that neither he nor Douay was permitted to take any step for burying the body. Tonty says that Cavelier begged leave to do so, but was refused. Douay, unwilling to place upon record facts from which the inference might easily be drawn that he had been terrified from discharging his duty, no doubt invented the story of the burial, as well as that of the edifying behavior of Moranget, after he had been struck in the head with an axe.

The locality of La Salle's assassination is sufficiently clear, from a comparison of the several narratives; and it is also indicated on a contemporary manuscript map, made on the return of the survivors of the party to France. The scene of the catastrophe is here placed on a southern branch of the Trinity.

La Salle's debts, at the time of his death, according to a schedule presented in 1701 to Champigny, intendant of Canada, amounted to 106,831 livres, without reckoning interest. This cannot be meant to include all, as items are given which raise the amount much higher. In 1678 and 1679 alone, he contracted debts to the amount of 97,184 livres, of which 46,000 were furnished by Branssac, fiscal attorney of the Seminary of Montreal. This was to be paid in beaver-skins. Frontenac, at the same time, became his surety for 13,623 livres. In 1684, he borrowed 34,825 livres from the Sieur Pen, at Paris. These sums do not include the losses incurred by his family, which, in the memorial presented by them to the king, are set down at 500,000 livres for the expeditions between 1678 and 1683, and 300,000 livres for the fatal Texan expedition of 1684. These last figures are certainly exaggerated.

Chapter XXVIII

1687, 1688

THE INNOCENT AND THE GUILTY

Triumph of the Murderers • Danger of Joutel • Joutel among the Cenis • White Savages • Insolence of Duhaut and his Accomplices • Murder of Duhaut and Liotot • Hiens, the Buccaneer • Joutel and his Party • Their Escape • They reach the Arkansas • Bravery and Devotion of Tonty • The Fugitives reach the Illinois • Unworthy Conduct of Cavelier • He and his Companions return to France

---

FATHER ANASTASE DOUAY returned to the camp, and, aghast with grief and terror, rushed into the hut of Cavelier. "My poor brother is dead!" cried the priest, instantly divining the catastrophe from the horror-stricken face of the messenger. Close behind came the murderers, Duhaut at their head. Cavelier, his young nephew, and Douay himself, all fell on their knees, expecting instant death. The priest begged piteously for half an hour to prepare for his end; but terror and submission sufficed, and no more blood was shed. The camp yielded without resistance; and Duhaut was lord of all. In truth, there were none to oppose him; for, except the assassins themselves, the party was now reduced to six persons: Joutel, Douay, the elder Cavelier, his young nephew, and two other boys, the orphan Talon and a lad called Barthelemy.

Joutel, for the moment, was absent; and l'Archevêque, who had a kindness for him, went quietly to seek him. He found him on a hillock, making a fire of dried grass, in order that the smoke might guide La Salle on his return, and watching the horses grazing in the meadow below. "I was very much surprised," writes Joutel, "when I saw him approaching. When he came up to me, he seemed all in confusion, or, rather, out of his wits. He began with saying that there was very bad news. I asked what it was. He answered that the Sieur de la Salle was dead, and also his nephew the Sieur de Moranget, his Indian hunter, and his servant. I was petrified, and did not know what to say; for I saw that they had been murdered. The man added that, at first, the murderers had sworn to kill me too. I easily believed it, for I had always been in the interest of M. de la Salle, and had commanded in his place; and it is hard to please everybody, or prevent some from being dissatisfied. I was greatly perplexed as to what I ought to do, and whether I had not better escape to the woods, whithersoever God should guide me; but, by bad or good luck, I had no gun and only one pistol, without balls or powder except what was in my powder-horn. To whatever side I turned, my life was in great peril. It is true that l'Archevêque assured me that they had changed their minds, and had agreed to murder nobody else, unless they met with resistance. So, being in no condition, as I just said, to go far, having neither arms nor powder, I abandoned myself to Providence, and went back to the camp, where I found that these wretched murderers had seized every thing belonging to M. de la Salle, and even my personal effects. They had also taken possession of all the arms. The first words that Duhaut said to me were, that each should command in turn, to which I made no answer. I saw M. Cavelier praying in a corner, and Father Anastase in another. He did not dare to speak to me, nor did I dare to go towards him till I had seen the designs of the assassins. They were in furious excitement, but, nevertheless, very uneasy and embarrassed. I was some time without speaking, and, as it were, without moving, for fear of giving umbrage to our enemies.

"They had cooked some meat, and, when it was suppertime, they distributed it as they saw fit, saying that formerly their share had been served out to them, but that it was they who would serve it out in future. They, no doubt, wanted me to say something that would give them a chance to make a noise; but I managed always to keep my mouth closed. When night came and it was time to stand guard, they were in perplexity, as they could not do it alone; therefore, they said to M. Cavelier, Father Anastase, me, and the others who were not in the plot with them, that all we had to do was to stand guard as usual; that there was no use in thinking about what had happened, that what was done was done; that they had been driven to it by despair, and that they were sorry for it, and meant no more harm to anybody. M. Cavelier took up the word, and told them that when they killed M. de la Salle they killed themselves, for there was nobody but him who could get us out of this country. At last, after a good deal of talk on both sides, they gave us our arms. So we stood guard; during which, M. Cavelier told me how they had come to the camp, entered his hut like so many madmen, and seized every thing in it."

Joutel, Douay, and the two Caveliers spent a sleepless night, consulting as to what they should do. They mutually pledged themselves to stand by each other to the last, and to escape as soon as they could from the company of the assassins. In the morning, Duhaut and his accomplices, after much discussion, resolved to go to the Cenis villages; and, accordingly, the whole party broke up their camp, packed their horses, and began their march. They went five leagues, and encamped at the edge of a grove. On the following day, they advanced again till noon, when heavy rains began, and they were forced to stop by the banks of a river. "We passed the night and the next day there," says Joutel; "and during that time my mind was possessed with dark thoughts. It was hard to prevent ourselves from being in constant fear among such men, and we could not look at them without horror. When I thought of the cruel deeds they had committed, and the danger we were in from them, I longed to revenge the evil they had done us. This would have been easy while they were asleep, but M. Cavelier dissuaded us, saying that we ought to leave vengeance to God, and that he himself had more to revenge than we, having lost his brother and his nephew."

The comic alternated with the tragic. On the twenty-third, they reached the bank of a river too deep to ford. Those who knew how to swim crossed without difficulty, but Joutel, Cavelier, and Douay were not of the number. Accordingly, they launched a log of light, dry wood, embraced it with one arm, and struck out for the other bank with their legs and the arm that was left free. But the friar became frightened. "He only clung fast to the aforesaid log," says Joutel, "and did nothing to help us forward. While I was trying to swim, my body being stretched at full length, I hit him in the belly with my feet; on which he thought it was all over with him, and, I can answer for it, he invoked St. Francis with might and main. I could not help laughing, though I was myself in danger of drowning." Some Indians who had joined the party swam to the rescue, and pushed the log across.

The path to the Cenis villages was exceedingly faint, and but for the Indians they would have lost the way. They crossed the main stream of the Trinity in a boat of raw hides, and then, being short of provisions, held a council to determine what they should do. It was resolved that Joutel, with Hiens, Liotot, and Teissier, should go in advance to the villages and buy a supply of corn. Thus, Joutel found himself doomed to the company of three villains, who, he strongly suspected, were contriving an opportunity to kill him; but, as he had no choice, he dissembled his doubts, and set out with his sinister companions; Duhaut having first supplied him with goods for the intended barter.

They rode over hills and plains till night, encamped, supped on a wild turkey, and continued their journey till the afternoon of the next day, when they saw three men approaching on horseback, one of whom, to Joutel's alarm, was dressed like a Spaniard. He proved, however, to be a Cenis Indian, like the others. The three turned their horses' heads, and accompanied the Frenchmen on their way. At length, they neared the Indian town, which, with its large thatched lodges, looked like a cluster of gigantic haystacks. Their approach had been made known, and they were received in solemn state. Twelve of the elders came to meet them in their dress of ceremony, each with his face daubed red or black, and his head adorned with painted plumes. From their shoulders hung deer-skins wrought with gay colors. Some carried war-clubs; some, bows and arrows; some, the blades of Spanish rapiers, attached to wooden handles decorated with hawk's bells and bunches of feathers. They stopped before the honored guests, and, raising their hands aloft, uttered howls so extraordinary that Joutel could hardly preserve the gravity which the occasion demanded. Having next embraced the Frenchmen, the elders conducted them into the village, attended by a crowd of warriors and young men; ushered them into their town-hall, a large lodge, devoted to councils, feasts, dances, and other public assemblies; seated them on mats, and squatted in a ring around them. Here they were regaled with sagamite or Indian porridge, corn-cake, beans, bread made of the meal of parched corn, and another kind of bread made of the kernels of nuts and the seed of sunflowers. Then the pipe was lighted, and all smoked together. The four Frenchmen proposed to open a traffic for provisions, and their entertainers grunted assent.

Joutel found a Frenchman in the village. He was a young man from Provence, who had deserted from La Salle on his last journey, and was now, to all appearance, a savage like his adopted countrymen, being naked like them, and affecting to have forgotten his native language. He was very friendly, however, and invited the visitors to a neighboring village, where he lived, and where, as he told them, they would find a better supply of corn. They accordingly set out with him, escorted by a crowd of Indians. They saw lodges and clusters of lodges scattered along their path at intervals, each with its field of corn, beans, and pumpkins, rudely cultivated with a wooden hoe. Reaching their destination, which was four or five leagues distant, they were greeted with the same honors as at the first village; and, the ceremonial of welcome over, were lodged in the abode of the savage Frenchman. It is not to be supposed, however, that he and his squaws, of whom he had a considerable number, dwelt here alone; for these lodges of the Cenis often contained eight or ten families. They were made by firmly planting in a circle tall, straight, young trees, such as grew in the swamps. The tops were then bent inward and lashed together; great numbers of cross-pieces were bound on, and the frame thus constructed was thickly covered with thatch, a hole being left at the top for the escape of the smoke. The inmates were ranged around the circumference of the structure, each family in a kind of stall, open in front, but separated from those adjoining it by partitions of mats. Here they placed their beds of cane, their painted robes of buffalo and deer-skin, their cooking utensils of pottery, and other household goods; and here, too, the head of the family hung his bow, quiver, lance, and shield. There was nothing in common but the fire, which burned in the middle of the lodge, and was never suffered to go out. These dwellings were of great size, and Joutel declares that he has seen some of them sixty feet in diameter.[1]

[1] The lodges of the Florida Indians were somewhat similar. The winter lodges of the now nearly extinct Mandans, though not so high in proportion

It was in one of the largest that the four travellers were now lodged. A place was assigned them where to bestow their baggage; and they took possession of their quarters amid the silent stares of the whole community. They asked their renegade countryman, the Provençal, if they were safe. He replied that they were; but this did not wholly reassure them, and they spent a somewhat wakeful night. In the morning, they opened their budgets, and began a brisk trade in knives, awls, beads, and other trinkets, which they exchanged for corn and beans. Before evening, they had acquired a considerable stock; and Joutel's three companions declared their intention of returning with it to the camp, leaving him to continue the trade. They went, accordingly, in the morning; and Joutel was left alone. On the one hand, he was glad to be rid of them; on the other, he found his position among the Cenis very irksome, and, as he thought, insecure. Besides the Provençal, who had gone with Liotot and his companions, there were two other French deserters among this tribe, and Joutel was very desirous to see them, hoping that they could tell him the way to the Mississippi; for he was resolved to escape, at the first opportunity, from the company of Duhaut and his accomplices. He, therefore, made the present of a knife to a young Indian, whom he sent to find the two Frenchmen, and invite them to come to the village. Meanwhile, he continued his barter, but under many difficulties; for he could only explain himself by signs, and his customers, though friendly by day, pilfered his goods by night. This, joined to the fears and troubles which burdened his mind, almost deprived him of sleep, and, as he confesses, greatly depressed his spirits. Indeed, he had little cause for cheerfulness, in the past, present, or future. An old Indian, one of the patriarchs of the tribe, observing his dejection, and anxious

---

to their width, and built of more solid materials, as the rigor of a northern climate requires, bear a general resemblance to those of the Cenis.

The Cenis tattooed their faces and some parts of their bodies, by pricking powdered charcoal into the skin. The women tattooed the breasts; and this practice was general among them, notwithstanding the pain of the operation, as it was thought very ornamental. Their dress consisted of a sort of frock, or wrapper of skin, from the waist to the knees. The men, in summer, wore nothing but the waist-cloth.

to relieve it, one evening brought him a young wife, saying that he made him a present of her. She seated herself at his side; "but," says Joutel, "as my head was full of other cares and anxieties, I said nothing to the poor girl. She waited for a little time; and then, finding that I did not speak a word, she went away."[1]

Late one night, he lay between sleeping and waking on the buffalo-robe that covered his bed of canes. All around the great lodge, its inmates were buried in sleep; and the fire that still burned in the midst cast ghostly gleams on the trophies of savage chivalry, the treasured scalp-locks, the spear and war-club, and shield of whitened bull-hide, that hung by each warrior's resting-place. Such was the weird scene that lingered on the dreamy eyes of Joutel, as he closed them at last in a troubled sleep. The sound of a footstep soon wakened him; and, turning, he saw at his side the figure of a naked savage, armed with a bow and arrows. Joutel spoke, but received no answer. Not knowing what to think, he reached out his hand for his pistols; on which the intruder withdrew, and seated himself by the fire. Thither Joutel followed; and, as the light fell on his features, he looked at him closely. His face was tattooed, after the Cenis fashion, in lines drawn from the top of the forehead and converging to the chin; and his body was decorated with similar embellishments. Suddenly, this supposed Indian rose, and threw his arms around Joutel's neck, making himself known, at the same time, as one of the Frenchmen who had deserted from La Salle and taken refuge among the Cenis. He was a Breton sailor named Ruter. His companion, named Grollet, also a sailor, had been afraid to come to the village, lest he should meet La Salle. Ruter expressed surprise and regret when he heard of the death of his late commander. He had deserted him but a few months before. That brief interval had sufficed to transform him into a savage; and both he and his companion found their present reckless and ungoverned way of life greatly to their liking. He could tell nothing of the Mississippi; and on the next day he went home, carrying with him a present of beads for his wives, of which last he had made a large collection.

[1] *Journal Historique*, 237.

In a few days, he reappeared, bringing Grollet with him. Each wore a bunch of turkey-feathers dangling from his head, and each had wrapped his naked body in a blanket. Three men soon after arrived from Duhaut's camp, commissioned to receive the corn which Joutel had purchased. They told him that Duhaut and Liotot, the tyrants of the party, had resolved to return to Fort St. Louis, and build a vessel to escape to the West Indies; "a visionary scheme," writes Joutel, "for our carpenters were all dead; and, even if they had been alive, they were so ignorant, that they would not have known how to go about the work; besides, we had no tools for it. Nevertheless, I was obliged to obey, and set out for the camp with the provisions."

On arriving, he found a wretched state of affairs. Douay and the two Caveliers, who had been treated by Duhaut with great harshness and contempt, had been told to make their mess apart; and Joutel now joined them. This separation restored them their freedom of speech, of which they had hitherto been deprived; but it subjected them to incessant hunger, as they were allowed only food enough to keep them from famishing. Douay says that quarrels were rife among the assassins themselves, the malcontents being headed by Hiens, who was enraged that Duhaut and Liotot should have engrossed all the plunder. Joutel was helpless, for he had none to back him but two priests and a boy.

He and his companions talked of nothing around their solitary camp-fire but the means of escaping from the villanous company into which they were thrown. They saw no resource but to find the Mississippi, and thus make their way to Canada, a prodigious undertaking in their forlorn condition; nor was there any probability that the assassins would permit them to go. These, on their part, were beset with difficulties. They could not return to civilization without manifest peril of a halter; and their only safety was to turn buccaneers or savages. Duhaut, however, still held to his plan of going back to Fort St. Louis; and Joutel and his companions, who, with good reason, stood in daily fear of him, devised among themselves a simple artifice to escape from his company. The elder Cavelier was to tell him that they were too fatigued for the journey, and wished to stay among the Cenis; and to beg him to allow them a portion of the goods, for which Cavelier was to give his note of hand. The old priest, whom a sacrifice of truth, even on less important occasions, cost no great effort, accordingly opened the negotiation; and to his own astonishment, and that of his companions, gained the assent of Duhaut. Their joy, however, was short; for Ruter, the French savage, to whom Joutel had betrayed his intention, when inquiring the way to the Mississippi, told it to Duhaut, who on this changed front, and made the ominous declaration that he and his men would also go to Canada. Joutel and his companions were now filled with alarm; for there was no likelihood that the assassins would permit them, the witnesses of their crime, to reach the settlements alive. In the midst of their trouble, the sky was cleared as by the crash of a thunderbolt.

Hiens and several others had gone, some time before, to the Cenis villages to purchase horses; and here they had been detained by the charms of the Indian women. During their stay, Hiens heard of Duhaut's new plan of going to Canada by the Mississippi; and he declared to those with him that he would not consent. On a morning early in May, he appeared at Duhaut's camp, with Ruter and Grollet, the French savages, and about twenty Indians. Duhaut and Liotot, it is said, were passing the time by practising with bows and arrows in front of their hut. One of them called to Hiens, "Good-morning;" but the buccaneer returned a sullen answer. He then accosted Duhaut, telling him that he had no mind to go up the Mississippi with him, and demanding a share of the goods. Duhaut replied that the goods were his own, since La Salle had owed him money. "So you will not give them to me?" returned Hiens. "No," was the answer. "You are a wretch!" exclaimed Hiens. "You killed my master."[1] And, drawing a pistol from his belt, he fired at Duhaut, who staggered three or four paces, and fell dead. Almost at the same instant, Ruter fired his gun at Liotot, shot three balls into his body, and stretched him on the ground mortally wounded.

[1] "Tu es un misérable. Tu as tué mon maistre."—Tonty, *Mémoire*. Tonty derived his information from some of those present. Douay and Joutel have each left an account of this murder. They agree in essential points; though Douay says that, when it took place, Duhaut had moved his camp beyond the Cenis villages, which is contrary to Joutel's statement.

Douay and the two Caveliers stood in extreme terror, thinking that their turn was to come next. Joutel, no less alarmed, snatched his gun to defend himself; but Hiens called to him to fear nothing, declaring that what he had done was only to avenge the death of La Salle, to which, nevertheless, he had been privy, though not an active sharer in the crime. Liotot lived long enough to make his confession, after which Ruter killed him by exploding a pistol loaded with a blank charge of powder against his head. Duhaut's myrmidon, l'Archevêque, was absent, hunting, and Hiens was for killing him on his return; but the two priests and Joutel succeeded in dissuading him.

The Indian spectators beheld these murders with undisguised amazement, and almost with horror. What manner of men were these who had pierced the secret places of the wilderness to riot in mutual slaughter? Their fiercest warriors might learn a lesson in ferocity from these heralds of civilization. Joutel and his companions, who could not dispense with the aid of the Cenis, were obliged to explain away, as they best might, the atrocity of what they had witnessed.[1]

Hiens, and others of the French, had before promised to join the Cenis on an expedition against a neighboring tribe with whom they were at war; and the whole party having removed to the Indian village, the warriors and their allies prepared to depart. Six Frenchmen went with Hiens; and the rest, including Joutel, Douay, and the Caveliers, remained behind, in the lodge where Joutel had been domesticated, and where none were now left but women, children, and old men. Here they remained a week or more, watched closely by the Cenis, who would not let them leave the village; when news at length arrived of a great victory, and the warriors soon after returned with forty-eight scalps. It was the French guns that won the battle, but not the less did they glory in their prowess; and several days were spent in ceremonies and feasts of triumph.[2]

When all this hubbub of rejoicing had subsided, Joutel and his companions broke to Hiens their plan of attempting to

[1] Joutel, *Relation* (Margry, III. 371).

[2] These are described by Joutel. Like nearly all the early observers of Indian manners, he speaks of the practice of cannibalism.

reach home by way of the Mississippi. As they had expected, he opposed it vehemently, declaring that, for his own part, he would not run such a risk of losing his head; but at length he consented to their departure, on condition that the elder Cavelier should give him a certificate of his entire innocence of the murder of La Salle, which the priest did not hesitate to do. For the rest, Hiens treated his departing fellow-travellers with the generosity of a successful freebooter; for he gave them a good share of the plunder he had won by his late crime, supplying them with hatchets, knives, beads, and other articles of trade, besides several horses. Meanwhile, adds Joutel, "we had the mortification and chagrin of seeing this scoundrel walking about the camp in a scarlet coat laced with gold which had belonged to the late Monsieur de la Salle, and which he had seized upon, as also upon all the rest of his property." A well-aimed shot would have avenged the wrong, but Joutel was clearly a mild and moderate person; and the elder Cavelier had constantly opposed all plans of violence. Therefore, they stifled their emotions, and armed themselves with patience.

Joutel's party consisted, besides himself, of the Caveliers, uncle and nephew, Anastase Douay, De Marle, Teissier, and a young Parisian named Barthelemy. Teissier, an accomplice in the murders of Moranget and La Salle, had obtained a pardon, in form, from the elder Cavelier. They had six horses and three Cenis guides. Hiens embraced them at parting, as did the ruffians who remained with him. Their course was north-east, towards the mouth of the Arkansas, a distant goal, the way to which was beset with so many dangers that their chance of reaching it seemed small. It was early in June, and the forests and prairies were green with the verdure of opening summer. They soon reached the Assonis, a tribe near the Sabine, who received them well, and gave them guides to the nations dwelling towards Red River. On the twenty-third, they approached a village, the inhabitants of which, regarding them as curiosities of the first order, came out in a body to see them; and, eager to do them honor, required them to mount on their backs, and thus make their entrance in procession. Joutel, being large and heavy, weighed down his bearer, insomuch that two of his countrymen were forced to sustain him, one on each side. On arriving, an old chief washed their faces with warm water from an earthen pan, and then invited them to mount on a scaffold of canes, where they sat in the hot sun listening to four successive speeches of welcome, of which they understood not a word.[1]

At the village of another tribe, farther on their way, they met with a welcome still more oppressive. Cavelier, the unworthy successor of his brother, being represented as the chief of the party, became the principal victim of their attentions. They danced the calumet before him; while an Indian, taking him, with an air of great respect, by the shoulders, as he sat, shook him in cadence with the thumping of the drum. They then placed two girls close beside him, as his wives; while, at the same time, an old chief tied a painted feather in his hair. These proceedings so scandalized him that, pretending to be ill, he broke off the ceremony; but they continued to sing all night, with so much zeal that several of them were reduced to a state of complete exhaustion.

At length, after a journey of about two months, during which they lost one of their number,—De Marle, accidentally drowned while bathing,—the travellers approached the river Arkansas, at a point not far above its junction with the Mississippi. Led by their Indian guides, they traversed a rich district of plains and woods, and stood at length on the borders of the stream. Nestled beneath the forests of the farther shore, they saw the lodges of a large Indian town; and here, as they gazed across the broad current, they presently descried an object which nerved their spent limbs, and thrilled their homesick hearts with joy. It was a tall, wooden cross; and near it was a small house, built evidently by Christian hands. With one accord, they fell on their knees, and raised their hands to Heaven in thanksgiving. Two men, in European dress, issued from the door of the house, and fired their guns to salute the excited travellers, who, on their part, replied with a volley. Canoes put out from the farther shore, and ferried them to

---

[1] These Indians were a portion of the Cadodaquis, or Caddoes, then living on Red River. The travellers afterwards visited other villages of the same people. Tonty was here two years afterwards, and mentions the curious custom of washing the faces of guests.

the town, where they were welcomed by Couture and De Launay, two followers of Henri de Tonty.[1]

That brave, loyal, and generous man, always vigilant and always active, beloved and feared alike by white men and by red,[2] had been ejected, as we have seen, by the agent of the governor, La Barre, from the command of Fort St. Louis of the Illinois. An order from the king had reinstated him; and he no sooner heard the news of La Salle's landing on the shores of the Gulf, and of the disastrous beginnings of his colony,[3] than he prepared, on his own responsiblity and at his own cost, to go to his assistance. He collected twenty-five Frenchmen and eleven Indians, and set out from his fortified rock on the thirteenth of February, 1686;[4] descended the Mississippi, and reached its mouth in Holy Week. All was solitude, a voiceless desolation of river, marsh, and sea. He despatched canoes to the east and to the west, searching the coast for some thirty leagues on either side. Finding no trace of his friend, who at that moment was ranging the prairies of Texas, in no less fruitless search of his "fatal river," Tonty wrote for him a letter, which he left in the charge of an Indian chief, who preserved it with reverential care, and gave it, fourteen years after, to Iberville, the founder of Louisiana.[5] Deeply disappointed at his failure, Tonty retraced his

[1] Joutel, *Journal Historique*, 298.

[2] *Journal de St. Cosme, 1699*. This journal has been printed by Mr. Shea, from the copy in my possession. St. Cosme, who knew Tonty well, speaks of him in the warmest terms of praise.

[3] In the autumn of 1685, Tonty made a journey from the Illinois to Michillimackinac, to seek news of La Salle. He there learned, by a letter of the new governor, Denonville, just arrived from France, of the landing of La Salle, and the loss of the "Aimable," as recounted by Beaujeu, on his return. He immediately went back on foot to Fort St. Louis of the Illinois, and prepared to descend the Mississippi; "dans l'espérance de lui donner secours." *Lettre de Tonty au Ministre, 24 Aoust, 1686*; *Ibid. à Cabart de Villermont, même date*; *Mémoire de Tonty*; *Procès Verbal de Tonty, 13 Avril, 1686*.

[4] The date is from the *Procès Verbal*. In the *Mémoire*, hastily written, long after, he falls into errors of date.

[5] Iberville sent it to France, and Charlevoix gives a portion of it. *Histoire de la Nouvelle France*, II. 259. Singularly enough, the date, as printed by him, is erroneous, being 20 April, 1685, instead of 1686. There is no doubt whatever, from its relations with concurrent events, that this journey was in the latter year.

course, and ascended the Mississippi to the villages of the Arkansas, where some of his men volunteered to remain. He
left six of them; and of this number were Couture and De
Launay.[1]

Cavelier and his companions, followed by a crowd of Indians, some carrying their baggage, some struggling for a
view of the white strangers, entered the log cabin of their two
hosts. Rude as it was, they found in it an earnest of peace and
safety, and a foretaste of home. Couture and De Launay were
moved even to tears by the story of their disasters, and of the
catastrophe that crowned them. La Salle's death was carefully
concealed from the Indians, many of whom had seen him on
his descent of the Mississippi, and who regarded him with
prodigious respect. They lavished all their hospitality on his
followers; feasted them on corn-bread, dried buffalo meat,
and watermelons, and danced the calumet before them, the
most august of all their ceremonies. On this occasion, Cavelier's patience failed him again; and pretending, as before, to
be ill, he called on his nephew to take his place. There were
solemn dances, too, in which the warriors—some bedaubed
with white clay, some with red, and some with both; some
wearing feathers, and some the horns of buffalo; some naked,
and some in painted shirts of deer-skin, fringed with scalp-
locks, insomuch, says Joutel, that they looked like a troop of
devils—leaped, stamped, and howled from sunset till dawn.
All this was partly to do the travellers honor, and partly to
extort presents. They made objections, however, when asked
to furnish guides; and it was only by dint of great offers that
four were at length procured. With these, the travellers resumed their journey in a wooden canoe, about the first of
August,[2] descended the Arkansas, and soon reached the dark
and inexorable river, so long the object of their search, rolling, like a destiny through its realms of solitude and shade.

[1] Tonty, *Mémoire*; Ibid., *Lettre à Monseigneur de Ponchartrain, 1690*; Joutel,
Journal Historique, 301.

[2] Joutel says that the Parisian boy, Barthelemy, was left behind. It was this
youth who afterwards uttered the ridiculous defamation of La Salle mentioned in a preceding note. The account of the death of La Salle, taken from
the lips of Couture, was received by him from Cavelier and his companions,
during their stay at the Arkansas. Couture was by trade a carpenter, and was
a native of Rouen.

They launched their canoe on its turbid bosom, plied their oars against the current, and slowly won their way upward, following the writhings of this watery monster through canebrake, swamp, and fen. It was a hard and toilsome journey, under the sweltering sun of August; now on the water, now knee-deep in mud, dragging their canoe through the unwholesome jungle. On the nineteenth, they passed the mouth of the Ohio; and their Indian guides made it an offering of buffalo meat. On the first of September, they passed the Missouri, and soon after saw Marquette's pictured rock, and the line of craggy heights on the east shore, marked on old French maps as "the Ruined Castles." Then, with a sense of relief, they turned from the great river into the peaceful current of the Illinois. They were eleven days in ascending it, in their large and heavy wooden canoe, when at length, on the afternoon of the fourteenth of September, they saw, towering above the forest and the river, the cliff crowned with the palisades of Fort St. Louis of the Illinois. As they drew near, a troop of Indians, headed by a Frenchman, descended from the rock, and fired their guns to salute them. They landed, and followed the forest path that led towards the fort, when they were met by Boisrondet, Tonty's comrade in the Iroquois war, and two other Frenchmen, who no sooner saw them than they called out, demanding where was La Salle. Cavelier, fearing lest he and his party would lose the advantage they might derive from his character of representative of his brother, was determined to conceal his death; and Joutel, as he himself confesses, took part in the deceit. Substituting equivocation for falsehood, they replied that La Salle had been with them nearly as far as the Cenis villages, and that, when they parted, he was in good health. This, so far as they were concerned, was, literally speaking, true; but Douay and Teissier, the one a witness and the other a sharer in his death, could not have said so much without a square falsehood, and therefore evaded the inquiry.

Threading the forest path, and circling to the rear of the rock, they climbed the rugged height, and reached the top. Here they saw an area, encircled by the palisades that fenced the brink of the cliff, and by several dwellings, a store-house, and a chapel. There were Indian lodges too; for some of the red allies of the French made their abode with them.[1] Tonty was absent, fighting the Iroquois; but his lieutenant, Bellefontaine, received the travellers, and his little garrison of bushrangers greeted them with a salute of musketry, mingled with the whooping of the Indians. A *Te Deum* followed at the chapel; "and, with all our hearts," says Joutel, "we gave thanks to God, who had preserved and guided us." At length, the tired travellers were among countrymen and friends. Bellefontaine found a room for the two priests; while Joutel, Teissier, and young Cavelier were lodged in the storehouse.

The Jesuit Allouez was lying ill at the fort; and Joutel, Cavelier, and Douay went to visit him. He showed great anxiety when told that La Salle was alive, and on his way to the Illinois; asked many questions, and could not hide his agitation. When, some time after, he had partially recovered, he left St. Louis, as if to shun a meeting with the object of his alarm.[2]

---

[1] The condition of Fort St. Louis, at this time, may be gathered from several passages of Joutel. The houses, he says, were built at the brink of the cliff, forming, with the palisades, the circle of defence. The Indians lived in the area.

[2] Joutel adds that this was occasioned by "une espèce de conspiration qu'on a voulu faire contre les interests de Monsieur de la Salle."—*Journal Historique*, 350.

"Ce Père appréhendoit que le dit sieur ne l'y recontrast, . . . suivant ce que j'en ai pu apprendre, les Pères avoient avancé plusieurs choses pour contrebarrer l'entreprise et avoient voulu détacher plusieurs nations de Sauvages, lesquelles s'estoient données à M. de la Salle. Ils avoient esté mesme jusques à vouloir destruire le fort Saint-Louis, en ayant construit un à Chicago, où ils avoient attiré une partie des Sauvages, ne pouvant en quelque façon s'emparer du dit fort. Pour conclure, le bon Père, ayant eu peur d'y estre trouvé, aima mieux se précautionner en prenant le devant. . . . Quoyque M. Cavelier eust dit au Père qu'il pouvoit rester, il partit quelques sept ou huit jours avant nous."—*Relation* (Margry, III. 500).

La Salle always saw the influence of the Jesuits in the disasters that befell him. His repeated assertion, that they wished to establish themselves in the valley of the Mississippi, receives confirmation from a document entitled *Mémoire sur la proposition à faire par les R. Pères Jésuites pour la découverte des environs de la rivière du Mississipi et pour voir si elle est navigable jusqu'à la mer.* It is a memorandum of propositions to be made to the minister Seignelay, and was apparently put forward as a feeler, before making the propositions in form. It was written after the return of Beaujeu to France, and before La Salle's death became known. It intimates that the Jesuits were entitled to

Once before, in 1679, Allouez had fled from the Illinois on hearing of the approach of La Salle.

The season was late, and they were eager to hasten forward that they might reach Quebec in time to return to France in the autumn ships. There was not a day to lose. They bade farewell to Bellefontaine, from whom, as from all others, they had concealed the death of La Salle, and made their way across the country to Chicago. Here they were detained a week by a storm; and, when at length they embarked in a canoe furnished by Bellefontaine, the tempest soon forced them to put back. On this, they abandoned their design, and returned to Fort St. Louis, to the astonishment of its inmates.

It was October when they arrived; and, meanwhile, Tonty had returned from the Iroquois war, where he had borne a conspicuous part in the famous attack on the Senecas, by the Marquis de Denonville.[1] He listened with deep interest to the mournful story of his guests. Cavelier knew him well. He knew, so far as he was capable of knowing, his generous and disinterested character, his long and faithful attachment to La Salle, and the invaluable services he had rendered him. Tonty had every claim on his confidence and affection. Yet he did not hesitate to practise on him the same deceit which he had practised on Bellefontaine. He told him that he had left his brother in good health on the Gulf of Mexico, and drew upon him, in La Salle's name, for an amount stated by Joutel at about four thousand livres, in furs, besides a canoe and a

---

precedence in the valley of the Mississippi, as having first explored it. It affirms that *La Salle had made a blunder, and landed his colony, not at the mouth of the river, but at another place*; and it asks permission to continue the work in which he has failed. To this end, it petitions for means to build a vessel at St. Louis of the Illinois, together with canoes, arms, tents, tools, provisions, and merchandise for the Indians; and it also asks for La Salle's maps and papers, and for those of Beaujeu. On their part, it pursues, the Jesuits will engage to make a complete survey of the river, and return an exact account of its inhabitants, its plants, and its other productions.

[1]Tonty, Du Lhut, and Durantaye came to the aid of Denonville with a hundred and eighty Frenchmen, chiefly *coureurs de bois*, and four hundred Indians from the upper country. Their services were highly appreciated; and Tonty especially is mentioned in the despatches of Denonville with great praise.

quantity of other goods, all of which were delivered to him by the unsuspecting victim.[1]

This was at the end of the winter, when the old priest and his companions had been living for months on Tonty's hospitality. They set out for Canada on the twenty-first of March, reached Chicago on the twenty-ninth, and thence proceeded to Michillimackinac. Here Cavelier sold some of Tonty's furs to a merchant, who gave him in payment a draft on Montreal, thus putting him in funds for his voyage home. The party continued their journey in canoes by way of French River and the Ottawa, and safely reached Montreal on the seventeenth of July. Here they procured the clothing of which they were wofully in need, and then descended the river to Quebec, where they took lodging, some with the Récollet friars, and some with the priests of the Seminary, in order to escape the questions of the curious. At the end of August, they embarked for France, and early in October arrived safely at Rochelle. None of the party were men of especial energy or force of character; and yet, under the spur of a dire necessity, they had achieved one of the most adventurous journeys on record.

Now, at length, they disburdened themselves of their gloomy secret; but the sole result seems to have been an order from the king for the arrest of the murderers, should they

---

[1] "Monsieur Tonty, croyant M. de la Salle vivant, ne fit pas de difficulté de luy donner pour environ quatre mille liv. de pelleterie, de castors, loutres, un canot, et autres effets."—Joutel, *Journal Historique*, 349.

Tonty himself does not make the amount so great: "Sur ce qu'ils m'assuroient qu'il étoit resté au Golfe de Mexique en bonne santé, je les reçus comme si ç'avoit esté lui mesme et luy prestay [*à Cavalier*] plus de 700 francs."—Tonty, *Mémoire*.

Cavelier must have known that La Salle was insolvent. Tonty had long served without pay. Douay says that he made the stay of the party at the fort very agreeable, and speaks of him, with some apparent compunction, as "ce brave gentilhomme, toujours inséparablement attaché aux intérêts du Sieur de la Salle, dont nous luy avons caché la déplorable destinée."

Couture, from the Arkansas, brought word to Tonty, several months after, of La Salle's death, adding that Cavelier had concealed it, with no other purpose than that of gaining money or supplies from him (Tonty), in his brother's name. Cavelier had a letter from La Salle, desiring Tonty to give him supplies, and pay him 2,652 livres in beaver. If Cavelier is to be believed, this beaver belonged to La Salle.

appear in Canada.[1] Joutel was disappointed. It had been his hope throughout that the king would send a ship to the relief of the wretched band at Fort St. Louis of Texas. But Louis XIV. hardened his heart and left them to their fate.

[1] *Lettre du Roy à Denonville, 1 Mai, 1689.* Joutel must have been a young man, at the time of the Mississippi expedition; for Charlevoix saw him at Rouen, thirty-five years after. He speaks of him with emphatic praise; but it must be admitted that his connivance in the deception practised by Cavelier on Tonty leaves a shade on his character, as well as on that of Douay. In other respects, every thing that appears concerning him is highly favorable, which is not the case with Douay, who, on one or two occasions, makes wilful misstatements.

Douay says that the elder Cavelier made a report of the expedition to the minister Seignelay. This report remained unknown in an English collection of autographs and old manuscripts, whence I obtained it by purchase, in 1854, both the buyer and seller being at the time ignorant of its exact character. It proved, on examination, to be a portion of the first draft of Cavelier's report to Seignelay. It consists of twenty-six small folio pages, closely written in a clear hand, though in a few places obscured by the fading of the ink, as well as by occasional erasures and interlineations of the writer. It is, as already stated, confused and unsatisfactory in its statements; and all the latter part has been lost. On reaching France, he had the impudence to tell Abbé Tronson, Superior of St. Sulpice, "qu'il avait laissé M. de la Salle dans un très-beau pays avec M. de Chefdeville en bonne santé."—*Lettre de Tronson à Mad. Fauvel-Cavelier, 29 Nov., 1688.*

Cavelier addressed to the king a memorial on the importance of keeping possession of the Illinois. It closes with an earnest petition for money, in compensation for his losses, as, according to his own statement, he was completely *épuisé.* It is affirmed in a memorial of the heirs of his cousin, François Plet, that he concealed the death of La Salle some time after his return to France, in order to get possession of property which would otherwise have been seized by the creditors of the deceased. The prudent abbé died rich and very old, at the house of a relative, having inherited a large estate after his return from America. Apparently, this did not satisfy him; for there is before me the copy of a petition, written about 1717, in which he asks, jointly with one of his nephews, to be given possession of the seigniorial property held by La Salle in America. The petition was refused.

Young Cavelier, La Salle's nephew, died some years after, an officer in a regiment. He has been erroneously supposed to be the same with one De la Salle, whose name is appended to a letter giving an account of Louisiana, and dated at Toulon, 3 Sept., 1698. This person was the son of a naval official at Toulon, and was not related to the Caveliers.

Chapter XXIX

1688–1689

FATE OF THE TEXAN COLONY

Tonty attempts to rescue the Colonists • His Difficulties and Hardships • Spanish Hostility • Expedition of Alonzo de Leon • He reaches Fort St. Louis • A Scene of Havoc • Destruction of the French • The End

---

H ENRI DE TONTY, on his rock of St. Louis, was visited in September by Couture, and two Indians from the Arkansas. Then, for the first time, he heard with grief and indignation of the death of La Salle, and the deceit practised by Cavelier. The chief whom he had served so well was beyond his help; but might not the unhappy colonists left on the shores of Texas still be rescued from destruction? Couture had confirmed what Cavelier and his party had already told him, that the tribes south of the Arkansas were eager to join the French in an invasion of northern Mexico; and he soon after received from the governor, Denonville, a letter informing him that war had again been declared against Spain. As bold and enterprising as La Salle himself, he resolved on an effort to learn the condition of the few Frenchmen left on the borders of the Gulf, relieve their necessities, and, should it prove practicable, make them the nucleus of a war-party to cross the Rio Grande, and add a new province to the domain of France. It was the revival, on a small scale, of La Salle's scheme of Mexican invasion; and there is no doubt that, with a score of French musketeers, he could have gathered a formidable party of savage allies from the tribes of Red River, the Sabine, and the Trinity. This daring adventure and the rescue of his suffering countrymen divided his thoughts, and he prepared at once to execute the double purpose.[1]

He left Fort St. Louis of the Illinois early in December, in a pirogue, or wooden canoe, with five Frenchmen, a Shawanoe warrior, and two Indian slaves; and, after a long and painful journey, reached the villages of the Caddoes on Red

[1] Tonty, *Mémoire.*

River on the twenty-eighth of March. Here he was told that Hiens and his companions were at a village eighty leagues distant; and thither he was preparing to go in search of them, when all his men, excepting the Shawanoe and one Frenchman, declared themselves disgusted with the journey, and refused to follow him. Persuasion was useless, and there was no means of enforcing obedience. He found himself abandoned; but he still pushed on, with the two who remained faithful. A few days after, they lost nearly all their ammunition in crossing a river. Undeterred by this accident, Tonty made his way to the village where Hiens and those who had remained with him were said to be; but no trace of them appeared, and the demeanor of the Indians, when he inquired for them, convinced him that they had been put to death. He charged them with having killed the Frenchmen, whereupon the women of the village raised a wail of lamentation; "and I saw," he says, "that what I had said to them was true." They refused to give him guides; and this, with the loss of his ammunition, compelled him to forego his purpose of making his way to the colonists on the Bay of St. Louis. With bitter disappointment, he and his two companions retraced their course, and at length approached Red River. Here they found the whole country flooded. Sometimes they waded to the knees, sometimes to the neck, sometimes pushed their slow way on rafts. Night and day it rained without ceasing. They slept on logs placed side by side to raise them above the mud and water, and fought their way with hatchets through the inundated canebrakes. They found no game but a bear, which had taken refuge on an island in the flood; and they were forced to eat their dogs. "I never in my life," writes Tonty, "suffered so much." In judging these intrepid exertions, it is to be remembered that he was not, at least in appearance, of a robust constitution, and that he had but one hand. They reached the Mississippi on the eleventh of July, and the Arkansas villages on the thirty-first. Here Tonty was detained by an attack of fever. He resumed his journey when it began to abate, and reached his fort of the Illinois in September.[1]

While the king of France abandoned the exiles of Texas to

[1] Two causes have contributed to detract, most unjustly, from Tonty's reputation: the publication, under his name, but without his authority, of a

their fate, a power dark, ruthless, and terrible, was hovering around the feeble colony on the Bay of St. Louis, searching with pitiless eye to discover and tear out that dying germ of civilization from the bosom of the wilderness in whose savage immensity it lay hidden. Spain claimed the Gulf of Mexico and all its coasts as her own of unanswerable right, and the viceroys of Mexico were strenuous to enforce her claim. The

---

perverted account of the enterprises in which he took part; and the confounding him with his brother, Alphonse de Tonty, who long commanded at Detroit, where charges of peculation were brought against him. There are very few names in French-American history mentioned with such unanimity of praise as that of Henri de Tonty. Hennepin finds some fault with him; but his censure is commendation. The despatches of the governor, Denonville, speak in strong terms of his services in the Iroquois war, praise his character, and declare that he is fit for any bold enterprise, adding that he deserves reward from the king. The missionary, St. Cosme, who travelled under his escort in 1699, says of him: "He is beloved by all the *voyageurs*." . . . "It was with deep regret that we parted from him: . . . he is the man who best knows the country; . . . he is loved and feared everywhere. . . . Your grace will, I doubt not, take pleasure in acknowledging the obligations we owe him."

Tonty held the commission of captain; but, by a memoir which he addressed to Ponchartrain in 1690, it appears that he had never received any pay. Count Frontenac certifies the truth of the statement, and adds a recommendation of the writer. In consequence, probably, of this, the proprietorship of Fort St. Louis of the Illinois was granted in the same year to Tonty, jointly with La Forest, formerly La Salle's lieutenant. Here they carried on a trade in furs. In 1699, a royal declaration was launched against the *coureurs de bois*; but an express provision was added in favor of Tonty and La Forest, who were empowered to send up the country yearly two canoes, with twelve men, for the maintenance of this fort. With such a limitation, this fort and the trade carried on at it must have been very small. In 1702, we find a royal order, to the effect that La Forest is henceforth to reside in Canada, and Tonty on the Mississippi; and that the establishment at the Illinois is to be discontinued. In the same year, Tonty joined D'Iberville in Lower Louisiana, and was sent by that officer from Mobile to secure the Chickasaws in the French interest. His subsequent career and the time of his death do not appear. He seems never to have received the reward which his great merit deserved. Those intimate with the late lamented Dr. Sparks will remember his often-expressed wish that justice should be done to the memory of Tonty.

Fort St. Louis of the Illinois was afterwards reoccupied by the French. In 1718, a number of them, chiefly traders, were living here; but, three years later, it was again deserted, and Charlevoix, passing the spot, saw only the remains of its palisades.

capture of one of La Salle's four vessels at St. Domingo had made known his designs, and, in the course of the three succeeding years, no less than four expeditions were sent out from Vera Cruz to find and destroy him. They scoured the whole extent of the coast, and found the wrecks of the "Aimable" and the "Belle;" but the colony of St. Louis,[1] inland and secluded, escaped their search. For a time, the jealousy of the Spaniards was lulled to sleep. They rested in the assurance that the intruders had perished, when fresh advices from the frontier province of New Leon caused the Viceroy, Galve, to order a strong force, under Alonzo de Leon, to march from Coahuila, and cross the Rio Grande. Guided by a French prisoner, probably one of the deserters from La Salle, they pushed their way across wild and arid plains, rivers, prairies, and forests, till at length they approached the Bay of St. Louis, and descried, far off, the harboring-place of the French.[2] As they drew near, no banner was displayed, no sentry challenged; and the silence of death reigned over the shattered palisades and neglected dwellings. The Spaniards spurred their reluctant horses through the gateway, and a scene of desolation met their sight. No living thing was stirring. Doors were torn from their hinges; broken boxes, staved barrels, and rusty kettles, mingled with a great number of stocks of arquebuses and muskets, were scattered about in confusion. Here, too, trampled in mud and soaked with rain, they saw more than two hundred books, many of which still retained the traces of costly bindings. On the adjacent prairie lay three dead bodies, one of which, from fragments of dress still clinging to the wasted remains, they saw to be that of a woman. It was in vain to question the imperturbable savages, who, wrapped to the throat in their buffalo-robes, stood gazing on the scene with looks of wooden immobility. Two

[1] Fort St. Louis of Texas is not to be confounded with Fort St. Louis of the Illinois.

[2] After crossing the Del Norte, they crossed in turn the Upper Nueces, the Hondo (Rio Frio), the De Leon (San Antonio), and the Guadalupe, and then, turning southward, descended to the Bay of St. Bernard. . . . Manuscript map of "Route que firent les Espagnols, pour venir enlever les Français restez à la Baye St. Bernard ou St. Louis, après la perte du vaisseau de Mr de la Salle, en 1689." Margry's collection.

strangers, however, at length arrived.[1] Their faces were smeared with paint, and they were wrapped in buffalo-robes like the rest; yet these seeming Indians were L'Archevêque, the tool of La Salle's murderer, Duhaut, and Grollet, the companion of the white savage, Ruter. The Spanish commander, learning that these two men were in the district of the tribe called Texas,[2] had sent to invite them to his camp under a pledge of good treatment; and they had resolved to trust Spanish clemency rather than endure longer a life that had become intolerable. From them, the Spaniards learned nearly all that is known of the fate of Barbier, Zenobe Membré, and their companions. Three months before, a large band of Indians had approached the fort, the inmates of which had suffered severely from the ravages of the small-pox. From fear of treachery, they refused to admit their visitors, but received them at a cabin without the palisades. Here the French began a trade with them; when suddenly a band of warriors, yelling the war-whoop, rushed from an ambuscade under the bank of the river, and butchered the greater number. The children of one Talon, together with an Italian and a young man from Paris, named Breman, were saved by the Indian women, who carried them off on their backs. L'Archevêque and Grollet, who, with others of their stamp, were domesticated in the Indian villages, came to the scene of slaughter, and, as they affirmed, buried fourteen dead bodies.[3]

[1] May 1st. The Spaniards reached the fort April 22d.

[2] This is the first instance in which the name occurs. In a letter written by a member of De Leon's party, the Texan Indians are mentioned several times. See *Coleccion de Varios Documentos*, 25. They are described as an agricultural tribe, and were, to all appearance, identical with the Cenis. The name Tejas, or Texas, was first applied as a local designation to a spot on the river Neches, in the Cenis territory, whence it extended to the whole country. See Yoakum, *History of Texas*, 52.

[3] *Derrotero de la Jornada que hizo el General Alonso de Leon para el descubrimiento de la Bahia del Espíritu Santo, y poblacion de Franceses. Ano de 1689*. This is the official journal of the expedition, signed by Alonzo de Leon. I am indebted to Colonel Thomas Aspinwall for the opportunity of examining it. The name of Espiritu Santo was, as before mentioned, given by the Spaniards to St. Louis, and Matagorda Bay, as well as to two other bays of the Gulf of Mexico.

Carta en que se da noticia de un viaje hecho à la Bahia de Espíritu Santo y de la poblacion que tenian ahi los Franceses. Coleccion de Varios Documentos para la Historia de la Florida, 25.

L'Archevêque and Grollet were sent to Spain, where, in spite of the pledge given them, they were thrown into prison, with the intention of sending them back to labor in the mines. The Indians, some time after De Leon's expedition, gave up their captives to the Spaniards. The Italian was imprisoned at Vera Cruz. Breman's fate is unknown. Pierre and Jean Baptiste Talon, who were now old enough to bear arms, were enrolled in the Spanish navy, and, being captured in 1696 by a French ship of war, regained their liberty; while their younger brothers and their sister were carried to Spain by the Viceroy.[1] With respect to the ruffian companions of Hiens, the conviction of Tonty that they had been put to death by the Indians may have been well founded; but the buccaneer himself is said to have been killed in a quarrel with his accomplice, Ruter, the white savage; and thus in ignominy and darkness died the last embers of the doomed colony of La Salle.

Here ends the wild and mournful story of the explorers of the Mississippi. Of all their toil and sacrifice, no fruit re-

---

This is a letter from a person accompanying the expedition of De Leon. It is dated May 18, 1689, and agrees closely with the journal cited above, though evidently by another hand. Compare Barcia, *Ensayo Cronológico*, 294. Barcia's story has been doubted; but these authentic documents prove the correctness of his principal statements, though on minor points he seems to have indulged his fancy.

The viceroy of New Spain, in a report to the king, 1690, says that, in order to keep the Texas and other Indians of that region in obedience to his Majesty, he has resolved to establish eight missions among them. He adds that he has appointed, as governor, or commander, in that province, Don Domingo Teran de los Rios, who will make a thorough exploration of it, carry out what De Leon has begun, prevent the farther intrusion of foreigners like La Salle, and go in pursuit of the remnant of the French, who are said still to remain among the tribes of Red River. I owe this document to the kindness of Mr. Buckingham Smith.

[1] *Mémoire sur lequel on a interrogé les deux Canadiens [Pierre et Jean Baptiste Talon] qui sont soldats dans la Compagnie de Feuguerolles. A Brest, 14 Février, 1698.*

Interrogations faites à Pierre et Jean Baptiste Talon à leur arrivée de la Vera-crux. This paper, which differs in some of its details from the preceding, was sent by D'Iberville, the founder of Louisiana, to Abbé Cavelier. Appended to it is a letter from D'Iberville, written in May, 1704, in which he confirms the chief statements of the Talons, by information obtained by him from a Spanish officer at Pensacola.

mained but a great geographical discovery, and a grand type of incarnate energy and will. Where La Salle had ploughed, others were to sow the seed; and on the path which the un-despairing Norman had hewn out, the Canadian D'Iberville was to win for France a vast though a transient dominion.

APPENDIX

I

EARLY UNPUBLISHED MAPS OF THE MISSISSIPPI AND THE GREAT LAKES

Most of the maps described below are to be found in the Dépôt des Cartes de la Marine et des Colonies, at Paris. Taken together, they exhibit the progress of western discovery, and illustrate the records of the explorers.

THE MAP OF GALINÉE, 1670

THIS map has a double title: *Carte du Canada et des Terres découuertes vers le lac Derié*, and *Carte du Lac Ontario et des habitations qui l'enuironnent ensemble le pays que Messrs. Dolier et Galinée, missionnaires du seminaire de St. Sulpice, ont parcouru*. It professes to represent only the country actually visited by the two missionaries. Beginning with Montreal, it gives the course of the Upper St. Lawrence and the shores of Lake Ontario, the river Niagara, the north shore of Lake Erie, the Strait of Detroit, and the eastern and northern shores of Lake Huron. Galinée did not know the existence of the peninsula of Michigan, and merges Lakes Huron and Michigan into one, under the name of "Michigané, ou Mer Douce des Hurons." He was also entirely ignorant of the south shore of Lake Erie. He represents the outlet of Lake Superior as far as the Saut Ste. Marie, and lays down the river Ottawa in great detail, having descended it on his return. The Falls of the Genesee are indicated, as also the Falls of Niagara, with the inscription, "Sault qui tombe au rapport des sauvages de plus de 200 pieds de haut." Had the Jesuits been disposed to aid him, they could have given him much additional information, and corrected his most serious errors; as, for example, the omission of the peninsula of Michigan. The first attempt to map out the Great Lakes was that of Champlain, in 1632. This of Galinée may be called the second.

The map of Lake Superior, published in the Jesuit Relation of 1670, 1671, was made at about the same time with Galinée's map. Lake Superior is here styled "Lac Tracy, ou Supérieur." Though not so exact as it has been represented, this map indicates that the Jesuits had explored every part of this fresh-water ocean, and that they had a thorough knowledge of the straits connecting the three Upper Lakes, and of the adjacent bays, inlets, and shores. The peninsula of Michigan, ignored by Galinée, is represented in its proper place.

Three years or more after Galinée made the map mentioned above, another, indicating a greatly increased knowledge of the country, was made by some person whose name does not appear. This map, which is somewhat more than four feet long and about two feet and a half wide, has no title. All the Great Lakes, through their entire extent, are laid down on it with considerable accuracy. Lake Ontario is called "Lac Ontario, ou de Frontenac." Fort Frontenac is indicated, as well as the Iroquois colonies of the north shore. Niagara is "Chute haute de 120 toises par où le Lac Erié tombe dans le Lac Frontenac." Lake Erie is "Lac Teiocha-rontiong, dit communément Lac Erié." Lake St. Clair is "Tsiketo, ou Lac de la Chaudière." Lake Huron is "Lac Huron, ou Mer Douce des Hurons." Lake Superior is "Lac Supérieur." Lake Michigan is "Lac Mitchiganong, ou des Illinois." On Lake Michigan, immediately opposite the site of Chicago, are written the words, of which the following is the literal translation: "The largest vessels can come to this place from the outlet of Lake Erie, where it discharges into Lake Frontenac [Ontario]; and from this marsh into which they can enter, there is only a distance of a thousand paces to the River La Divine [Des Plaines], which can lead them to the River Colbert [Mississippi], and thence to the Gulf of Mexico." This map was evidently made after that voyage of La Salle in which he discovered the Illinois, or at least the Des Plaines branch of it. The Ohio is laid down with the inscription, "River Ohio, so called by the Iroquois on account of its beauty, which the Sieur de la Salle descended." (*Ante*, p. 743, *note.*)

We now come to the map of Marquette, which is a rude sketch of a portion of Lakes Superior and Michigan, and of the route pursued by him and Joliet up the Fox River of Green Bay, down the Wisconsin, and thence down the Mississippi as far as the Arkansas. The river Illinois is also laid down, as it was by this course that he returned to Lake Michigan after his memorable voyage. He gives no name to the Wisconsin. The Mississippi is called "Rivière de la Concep-

tion;" the Missouri, the Pekitanoui; and the Ohio, the Ouabouskiaou, though La Salle, its discoverer, had previously
given it its present name, borrowed from the Iroquois. The
Illinois is nameless, like the Wisconsin. At the mouth of a
river, perhaps the Des Moines, Marquette places the three villages of the Peoria Indians visited by him. These, with the
Kaskaskias, Maroas, and others, on the map, were merely sub-
tribes of the aggregation of savages, known as the Illinois. On
or near the Missouri, he places the Ouchage (Osages), the
Oumessourit (Missouris), the Kansa (Kanzas), the Paniassa
(Pawnees), the Maha (Omahas), and the Pahoutet (Pah-
Utahs?). The names of many other tribes, "esloignées dans les
terres," are also given along the course of the Arkansas, a river
which is nameless on the map. Most of these tribes are now
indistinguishable. This map has recently been engraved and
published.

Not long after Marquette's return from the Mississippi, another map was made by the Jesuits, with the following title:
*Carte de la nouvelle decouverte que les peres Iesuites ont fait en
l'année 1672, et continuée par le P. Iacques Marquette de la
mesme Compagnie accompagné de quelques françois en l'année
1673, qu'on pourra nommer en françois la Manitoumie.*
This title is very elaborately decorated with figures drawn
with a pen, and representing Jesuits instructing Indians. The
map is the same published by Thevenot, not without considerable variations, in 1681. It represents the Mississippi from a
little above the Wisconsin to the Gulf of Mexico, the part
below the Arkansas being drawn from conjecture. The river
is named "Mitchisipi, ou grande Rivière." The Wisconsin, the
Illinois, the Ohio, the Des Moines (?), the Missouri, and the
Arkansas, are all represented, but in a very rude manner. Marquette's route, in going and returning, is marked by lines; but
the return route is incorrect. The whole map is so crude and
careless, and based on information so inexact, that it is of
little interest.

The Jesuits made also another map, without title, of the
four Upper Lakes and the Mississippi to a little below the
Arkansas. The Mississippi is called "Riuuiere Colbert." The
map is remarkable as including the earliest representation of
the Upper Mississippi, based, perhaps, on the reports of In-

dians. The Falls of St. Anthony are indicated by the word "Saut." It is possible that the map may be of later date than at first appears, and that it may have been drawn in the interval between the return of Hennepin from the Upper Mississippi and that of La Salle from his discovery of the mouth of the river. The various temporary and permanent stations of the Jesuits are marked by crosses.

Of far greater interest is the small map of Louis Joliet, made and presented to Count Frontenac after the discoverer's return from the Mississippi. It is entitled *Carte de la de-couuerte du Sr Jolliet ou l'on voit La Communication du fleuue St. Laurens auec les lacs frontenac, Erié, Lac des Hurons et Ilinois.* Then succeeds the following, written in the same antiquated French, as if it were a part of the title: "Lake Frontenac [Ontario] is separated by a fall of half a league from Lake Erié, from which one enters that of the Hurons, and by the same navigation, into that of the Illinois [Michigan], from the head of which one crosses to the Divine River [Rivière Divine; *i.e.*, the Des Plaines branch of the river Illinois], by a portage of a thousand paces. This river falls into the river Colbert [Mississippi], which discharges itself into the Gulf of Mexico." A part of this map is based on the Jesuit map of Lake Superior, the legends being here for the most part identical, though the shape of the lake is better given by Joliet. The Mississippi, or "Riuiere Colbert," is made to flow from three lakes in latitude 47°, and it ends in latitude 37°, a little below the mouth of the Ohio, the rest being apparently cut off to make room for Joliet's letter to Frontenac (*ante*, p. 772), which is written on the lower part of the map. The valley of the Mississippi is called on the map "Colbertie, ou Amerique Occidentale." The Missouri is represented without name, and against it is a legend, of which the following is the literal translation: "By one of these great rivers which come from the west and discharge themselves into the river Colbert, one will find a way to enter the Vermilion Sea (Gulf of California). I have seen a village which was not more than twenty days' journey by land from a nation which has commerce with those of California. If I had come two days sooner, I should have spoken with those who had come from thence, and had brought four hatchets as a present." The Ohio has no name, but a legend over it states that La Salle had descended it. (See *ante,* p. 743, *note.*)

Joliet, at about the same time, made another map, larger than that just mentioned, but not essentially different. The letter to Frontenac is written upon both. There is a third map, of which the following is the title: *Carte generalle de la France septentrionale contenant la descouuerte du pays des Illinois, faite par le Sr Jolliet.* This map, which is inscribed with a dedication by the Intendant Duchesneau to the minister Colbert, was made some time after the voyage of Joliet and Marquette. It is an elaborate piece of work, but very inaccurate. It represents the continent from Hudson's Strait to Mexico and California, with the whole of the Atlantic and a part of the Pacific coast. An open sea is made to extend from Hudson's Strait westward to the Pacific. The St. Lawrence and all the Great Lakes are laid down with tolerable correctness, as also is the Gulf of Mexico. The Mississippi, called "Messasipi," flows into the Gulf, from which it extends northward nearly to the "Mer du Nord." Along its course, above the Wisconsin, which is called "Miskous," is a long list of Indian tribes, most of which cannot now be recognized, though several are clearly sub-tribes of the Sioux. The Ohio is called "Ouaboustikou." The whole map is decorated with numerous figures of animals, natives of the country, or supposed to be so. Among them are camels, ostriches, and a giraffe, which are placed on the plains west of the Mississippi. But the most curious figure is that which represents one of the monsters seen by Joliet and Marquette, painted on a rock by the Indians. It corresponds with Marquette's description (*ante,* p. 767). This map, which is an early effort of the engineer Franquelin, does more credit to his skill as a designer than to his geographical knowledge, which appears in some respects behind his time.

Carte de l'Amérique Septentrionale depuis l'embouchure de la Rivière St. Laurens jusques au Sein Mexique. On this curious little map, the Mississippi is called "Riuiere Buade" (the family name of Frontenac); and the neighboring country is "La Frontenacie." The Illinois is "Riuiere de la Diuine ou Loutrelaise," and the Arkansas is "Riuiere Bazire." The Mississippi is made to head in three lakes, and to discharge itself into

"B. du S. Esprit" (Mobile Bay). Some of the legends and the orthography of various Indian names are clearly borrowed from Marquette. This map appears to be the work of Raudin, Frontenac's engineer. I owe a tracing of it to the kindness of Henry Harrisse, Esq.

Carte des Parties les plus occidentales du Canada, par le Père Pierre Raffeix, S.J. This rude map shows the course of Du Lhut from the head of Lake Superior to the Mississippi, and partly confirms the story of Hennepin, who, Raffeix says in a note, was rescued by Du Lhut. The course of Joliet and Marquette is given, with the legend "Voyage et première découverte du Mississipy faite par le P. Marquette et M.ʳ· Joliet en 1672." The route of La Salle in 1679, 1680, is also laid down.

In the Dépôt des Cartes de la Marine is another map of the Upper Mississippi, which seems to have been made by or for Du Lhut. Lac Buade, the "Issatis," the "Tintons," the "Houelbatons," the "Poualacs," and other tribes of this region, appear upon it. This is the map numbered 208 in the *Cartographie* of Harrisse.

Another map deserving mention is a large and fine one, entitled *Carte de l'Amerique Septentrionale et partie de la Meridionale . . . avec les nouvelles decouvertes de la Riviere Missisipi, ou Colbert.* It appears to have been made in 1682 or 1683, before the descent of La Salle to the mouth of the Mississippi was known to the maker, who seems to have been Franquelin. The lower Mississippi is omitted, but its upper portions are elaborately laid down; and the name *La Louisiane* appears in large gold letters along its west side. The Falls of St. Anthony are shown, and above them is written "Armes du Roy gravées sur cet arbre l'an 1679." This refers to the *acte de prise de possession* of Du Lhut in July of that year, and this part of the map seems made from data supplied by him.

We now come to the great map of Franquelin, the most remarkable of all the early maps of the interior of North America, though hitherto completely ignored by both American and Canadian writers. It is entitled *Carte de la Louisiane ou des Voyages du S.ʳ· de la Salle et des pays qu'il a découverts depuis la Nouvelle France jusqu'au Golfe Mexique les années 1679, 80, 81, et 82, par Jean Baptiste Louis Franquelin. l'an 1684. Paris.* Franquelin was a young engineer, who held the post of hydrographer to the king, at Quebec, in which Joliet succeeded him. Several of his maps are preserved, including one made in 1681, in which he lays down the course of the Mississippi,—the lower part from conjecture,—making it discharge itself into Mobile Bay. It appears from a letter of the Governor, La Barre, that Franquelin was at Quebec in 1683, engaged on a map which was probably that of which the title is given above, though, had La Barre known that it was to be called a map of the journeys of his victim La Salle, he would have been more sparing of his praises. "He" (Franquelin), writes the governor, "is as skilful as any in France, but extremely poor and in need of a little aid from his Majesty as an Engineer: he is at work on a very correct map of the country, which I shall send you next year in his name; meanwhile, I shall support him with some little assistance."—*Colonial Documents of New York*, IX. 205.

The map is very elaborately executed, and is six feet long and four and a half wide. It exhibits the political divisions of the continent, as the French then understood them; that is to say, all the regions drained by streams flowing into the St. Lawrence and the Mississippi are claimed as belonging to France, and this vast domain is separated into two grand divisions, La Nouvelle France and La Louisiane. The boundary line of the former, New France, is drawn from the Penobscot to the southern extremity of Lake Champlain, and thence to the Mohawk, which it crosses a little above Schenectady, in order to make French subjects of the Mohawk Indians. Thence it passes by the sources of the Susquehanna and the Alleghany, along the southern shore of Lake Erie, across Southern Michigan, and by the head of Lake Michigan, whence it sweeps north-westward to the sources of the Mississippi. Louisiana includes the entire valley of the Mississippi and the Ohio, besides the whole of Texas. The Spanish province of Florida comprises the peninsula and the country east of the Bay of Mobile, drained by streams flowing into the Gulf; while Carolina, Virginia, and the other English provinces, form a narrow strip between the Alleghanies and the Atlantic.

The Mississippi is called "Missisipi, ou Rivière Colbert;" the Missouri, "Grande Rivière des Emissourittes, ou Missourits;" the Illinois, "Rivière des Ilinois, ou Macopins;" the Ohio, which La Salle had before called by its present name, "Fleuve St. Louis, ou Chucagoa, ou Casquinampogamou;" one of its principal branches is "Ohio, ou Olighin" (Alleghany); the Arkansas, "Rivière des Acansea;" the Red River, "Rivière Seignelay," a name which had once been given to the Illinois. Many smaller streams are designated by names which have been entirely forgotten.

The nomenclature differs materially from that of Coronelli's map, published four years later. Here the whole of the French territory is laid down as "Canada, ou La Nouvelle France," of which "La Louisiane" forms an integral part. The map of Homannus, like that of Franquelin, makes two distinct provinces, of which one is styled "Canada" and the other "La Louisiane," the latter including Michigan and the greater part of New York. Franquelin gives the shape of Hudson's Bay, and of all the Great Lakes, with remarkable accuracy. He makes the Mississippi bend much too far to the West. The peculiar sinuosities of its course are indicated; and some of its bends, as, for example, that at New Orleans, are easily recognized. Its mouths are represented with great minuteness; and it may be inferred from the map that, since La Salle's time, they have advanced considerably into the sea.

Perhaps the most interesting feature in Franquelin's map is his sketch of La Salle's evanescent colony on the Illinois, engraved for this volume. He reproduced the map in 1688, for presentation to the king, with the title *Carte de l'Amérique Septentrionale, depuis le 25 jusqu'au 65 degré de latitude et environ 140 et 235 degrés de longitude, etc.* In this map, Franquelin corrects various errors in that which preceded. One of these corrections consists in the removal of a branch of the river Illinois which he had marked on his first map,—as will be seen by referring to the portion of it in this book,—but which does not in fact exist. On this second map, La Salle's colony appears in much diminished proportions, his Indian settlements having in good measure dispersed.

Two later maps of New France and Louisiana, both bearing Franquelin's name, are preserved in the Dépôt des Cartes de la Marine, as well as a number of smaller maps and sketches, also by him. They all have more or less of the features of the great map of 1684, which surpasses them all in interest and completeness.

The remarkable manuscript map of the Upper Mississippi by Le Sueur belongs to a period later than the close of this narrative.

These various maps, joined to contemporary documents, show that the Valley of the Mississippi received, at an early date, the several names of Manitoumie, Frontenacie, Colbertie, and La Louisiane. This last name, which it long retained, is due to La Salle. The first use of it which I have observed is in a conveyance of the Island of Belleisle, made by him to his lieutenant, La Forest, in 1679.

II

THE ELDORADO OF MATHIEU SÂGEAN

FATHER HENNEPIN had among his contemporaries two rivals in the fabrication of new discoveries. The first was the noted La Hontan, whose book, like his own, had a wide circulation and proved a great success. La Hontan had seen much, and portions of his story have a substantial value; but his account of his pretended voyage up the "Long River" is a sheer fabrication. His "Long River" corresponds in position with the St. Peter, but it corresponds in nothing else; and the populous nations whom he found on it—the Eokoros, the Esanapes, and the Gnacsitares, no less than their neighbors the Mozeemlek and the Tahuglauk—are as real as the nations visited by Captain Gulliver. But La Hontan did not, like Hennepin, add slander and plagiarism to mendacity, or seek to appropriate to himself the credit of genuine discoveries made by others.

Mathieu Sâgean is a personage less known than Hennepin or La Hontan; for, though he surpassed them both in fertility of invention, he was illiterate, and never made a book. In 1701, being then a soldier in a company of marines at Brest, he revealed a secret which he declared that he had locked within his breast for twenty years, having been unwilling to impart it to the Dutch and English, in whose service he had been during the whole period. His story was written down from his dictation, and sent to the minister Ponchartrain. It is preserved in the Bibliothèque Nationale, and in 1863 it was printed by Mr. Shea.

He was born, he declares, at La Chine in Canada, and engaged in the service of La Salle about twenty years before the revelation of his secret; that is, in 1681. Hence, he would have been, at the utmost, only fourteen years old, as La Chine did not exist before 1667. He was with La Salle at the building of Fort St. Louis of the Illinois, and was left here as one of a hundred men under command of Tonty. Tonty, it is to be observed, had but a small fraction of this number; and Sâgean describes the fort in a manner which shows that he never saw it. Being desirous of making some new discovery, he obtained leave from Tonty, and set out with eleven other Frenchmen and two Mohegan Indians. They ascended the Mississippi a hundred and fifty leagues, carried their canoes by a cataract, went forty leagues farther, and stopped a month to hunt. While thus employed, they found another river, fourteen leagues distant, flowing south-south-west. They carried their canoes thither, meeting on the way many lions, leopards, and tigers, which did them no harm; then they embarked, paddled a hundred and fifty leagues farther, and found themselves in the midst of the great nation of the Acanibas, dwelling in many fortified towns, and governed by King Hagaren, who claimed descent from Montezuma. The king, like his subjects, was clothed with the skins of men. Nevertheless, he and they were civilized and polished in their manners. They worshipped certain frightful idols of gold in the royal palace. One of them represented the ancestor of their monarch armed with lance, bow, and quiver, and in the act of mounting his horse; while in his mouth he held a jewel as large as a goose's egg, which shone like fire, and which, in the opinion of Sâgean, was a carbuncle. Another of these images was that of a woman mounted on a golden unicorn, with a horn more than a fathom long. After passing, pursues the story, between these idols, which stand on platforms of gold, each thirty feet square, one enters a magnificent vestibule, conducting to the apartment of the king. At the four corners of this vestibule are stationed bands of music, which, to the taste of Sâgean, was of very poor quality. The palace is of vast extent, and the private apartment of the king is twenty-eight or thirty feet square; the walls, to the height of eighteen feet, being of bricks of solid gold, and the pavement of the same. Here the king dwells alone, served only by his wives, of whom he takes a new one every day. The Frenchmen alone had the privilege of entering, and were graciously received.

These people carry on a great trade in gold with a nation, believed by Sâgean to be the Japanese, as the journey to them lasts six months. He saw the departure of one of the caravans, which consisted of more than three thousand oxen, laden with gold, and an equal number of horsemen, armed with lances, bows, and daggers. They receive iron and steel in exchange for their gold. The king has an army of a hundred thousand men, of whom three-fourths are cavalry. They have golden trumpets, with which they make very indifferent music; and also golden drums, which, as well as the drummer, are carried on the backs of oxen. The troops are practised once a week in shooting at a target with arrows; and the king rewards the victor with one of his wives, or with some honorable employment.

These people are of a dark complexion and hideous to look upon, because their faces are made long and narrow by pressing their heads between two boards in infancy. The women, however, are as fair as in Europe; though, in common with the men, their ears are enormously large. All persons of distinction among the Acanibas wear their finger-nails very long. They are polygamists, and each man takes as many wives as he wants. They are of a joyous disposition, moderate drinkers, but great smokers. They entertained Sâgean and his followers during five months with the fat of the land; and any woman who refused a Frenchman was ordered to be killed. Six girls were put to death with daggers for this breach of hospitality. The king, being anxious to retain his visitors in his service, offered Sâgean one of his daughters, aged fourteen years, in marriage; and, when he saw him resolved to depart, promised to keep her for him till he should return.

The climate is delightful, and summer reigns throughout the year. The plains are full of birds and animals of all kinds, among which are many parrots and monkeys, besides the wild cattle, with humps like camels, which these people use as beasts of burden.

King Hagaren would not let the Frenchmen go till they had sworn by the sky, which is the customary oath of the Acanibas, that they would return in thirty-six moons, and bring him a supply of beads and other trinkets from Canada. As gold was to be had for the asking, each of the eleven Frenchmen took away with him sixty small bars, weighing about four pounds each. The king ordered two hundred horsemen to escort them, and carry the gold to their canoes; which they did, and then bade them farewell with terrific howlings, meant, doubtless, to do them honor.

After many adventures, wherein nearly all his companions came to a bloody end, Sâgean, and the few others who survived, had the ill luck to be captured by English pirates, at the mouth of the St. Lawrence. He spent many years among them in the East and West Indies, but would not reveal the secret of his Eldorado to these heretical foreigners.

Such was the story, which so far imposed on the credulity of the Minister Ponchartrain as to persuade him that the matter was worth serious examination. Accordingly, Sâgean was sent to Louisiana, then in its earliest infancy as a French colony. Here he met various persons who had known him in Canada, who denied that he had ever been on the Mississippi, and contradicted his account of his parentage. Nevertheless, he held fast to his story, and declared that the gold mines of the Acanibas could be reached without difficulty by the river Missouri. But Sauvolle and Bienville, chiefs of the colony, were obstinate in their unbelief; and Sâgean and his King Hagaren lapsed alike into oblivion.

THE OLD RÉGIME
IN CANADA

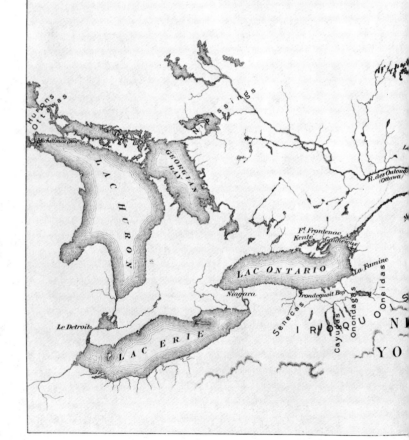

CANADA

AND ADJACENT COUNTRIES

towards the close

OF THE

17TH CENTURY.

Hurons
Ottawas

Michilimacinac

NIP ssings

GEORGIAN BAY

LAC HURON

R. des Outoua
(Ottawa)

Fᵗ Frontenac,
Kente   Gandeiques

LAC ONTARIO   La Famine

Niagara

Trondequoit Bay

Le Detroit

LAC ERIE

Senecas   IRO Q U   O Oneidas

Cayugas   Onondagas

NI

YO

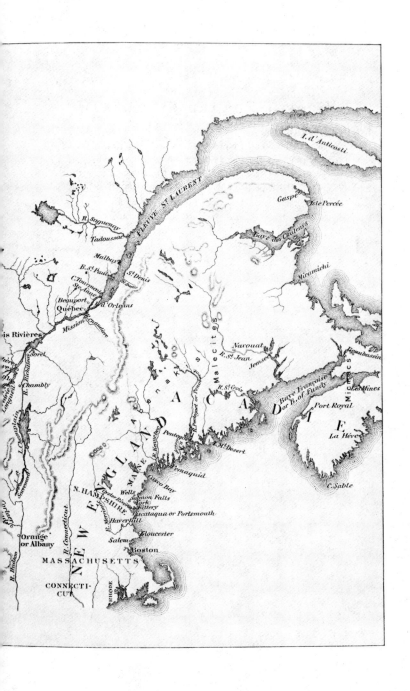

I. d'Anticosti

FLEUVE St LAURENT

Gaspé
Este Percée

R. Saguenay
Tadoussac

Baye des Chaleurs

Malbay

B. St Paul
St Denis

C. Tourmente
Ste Anne
Beauport
Québec
I. d'Orléans

Miramichi

Mission
Chaudier

is Rivières
Sorel

Navouat
Jemser

Pigaubassin

R. St Jean

R. Chambly

R. St Goir

Les Mines

Chambly

Baye Françoise
or B. of Fundy

Port Royal

L. Champlain

Penteg

La Hève

R. St Sevame

Casco Bay

Mt Desert

Pemaquid

Orange
or Albany

N. HAMPSHIRE

R. Hudson

Salmon Falls
York
Kittery
Pascataqua or Portsmouth

Oyster River
Wells

Haverhill

Gloucester

Salem

Boston

MASSACHUSETTS

R. Connecticut

C. Sable

CONNECTI-
CUT

RHODE

Contents

Prefatory Note
TO REVISED EDITION

WHEN this book was written, I was unable to gain access to certain indispensable papers relating to the rival claimants to Acadia, La Tour and D'Aunay, and therefore deferred all attempts to treat that subject. The papers having at length come to hand, the missing chapters are supplied in the present edition, which also contains some additional matter of less prominence.

The title of "The Old Régime in Canada" is derived from the third and principal of the three sections into which the book is divided.

June 16, 1893

Preface

"THE physiognomy of a government," says De Tocqueville, "can best be judged in its colonies, for there its characteristic traits usually appear larger and more distinct. When I wish to judge of the spirit and the faults of the administration of Louis XIV., I must go to Canada. Its deformity is there seen as through a microscope."

The monarchical administration of France, at the height of its power and at the moment of its supreme triumph, stretched an arm across the Atlantic and grasped the North American continent. This volume attempts to show by what methods it strove to make good its hold, why it achieved a certain kind of success, and why it failed at last. The political system which has fallen, and the antagonistic system which has prevailed, seem, at first sight, to offer nothing but contrasts; yet out of the tomb of Canadian absolutism come voices not without suggestion even to us. Extremes meet, and Autocracy and Democracy often touch hands, at least in their vices.

The means of knowing the Canada of the past are ample. The pen was always busy in this outpost of the old monarchy. The king and the minister demanded to know every thing; and officials of high and low degree, soldiers and civilians, friends and foes, poured letters, despatches, and memorials, on both sides of every question, into the lap of government. These masses of paper have in the main survived the perils of revolutions and the incendiary torch of the Commune. Add to them the voluminous records of the Superior Council of Quebec, and numerous other documents preserved in the civil and ecclesiastical depositories of Canada.

The governments of New York and of Canada have caused a large part of the papers in the French archives, relating to their early history, to be copied and brought to America, and valuable contributions of material from the same quarter have been made by the State of Massachusetts and by private Canadian investigators. Nevertheless, a great deal has still remained in France, uncopied and unexplored. In the course of several visits to that country, I have availed myself of these supplementary papers, as well as of those which had before been copied, sparing neither time nor pains to explore every part of the field. With the help of a system of classified notes, I have collated the evidence of the various writers, and set down without reserve all the results of the examination, whether favorable or unfavorable. Some of them are of a character which I regret, since they cannot be agreeable to persons for whom I have a very cordial regard. The conclusions drawn from the facts may be matter of opinion, but it will be remembered that the facts themselves can be overthrown only by overthrowing the evidence on which they rest, or bringing forward counter-evidence of equal or greater strength; and neither task will be found an easy one.[1]

I have received most valuable aid in my inquiries from the great knowledge and experience of M. Pierre Margry, Chief of the Archives of the Marine and Colonies at Paris. I beg also warmly to acknowledge the kind offices of Abbé Henri Raymond Casgrain and Grand Vicar Cazeau, of Quebec, together with those of James Le Moine, Esq., M. Eugène Taché, Hon. P. J. O. Chauveau, and other eminent Canadians, and Henry Harrisse, Esq.

The few extracts from original documents, which are printed in the appendix, may serve as samples of the material out of which the work has been constructed. In some instances their testimony might be multiplied twenty-fold. When the place of deposit of the documents cited in the margin is not otherwise indicated, they will, in nearly all cases, be found in the Archives of the Marine and Colonies.

In the present book we examine the political and social machine; in the next volume of the series we shall see this machine in action.

BOSTON, *July 1, 1874*

---

[1] Those who wish to see the subject from a point of view opposite to mine cannot do better than consult the work of the Jesuit Charlevoix, with the excellent annotation of Mr. Shea. (History and General Description of New France, by the Rev. P. F. X. de Charlevoix, S.J., translated with notes by John Gilmary Shea. 6 vols. New York: 1866–1872.)

THE FEUDAL CHIEFS OF ACADIA

Chapter I

1497–1643

LA TOUR AND D'AUNAY

The Acadian Quarrel • Biencourt • Claude and Charles de la Tour • Sir William Alexander • Claude de Razilly • Charles de Menou d'Aunay Charnisay • Cape Sable • Port Royal • The Heretics of Boston and Plymouth • Madame de la Tour • War and Litigation • La Tour worsted • He asks Help from the Boston Puritans

WITH the opening of the seventeenth century began that contest for the ownership of North America which was to remain undecided for a century and a half. England claimed the continent through the discovery by the Cabots in 1497 and 1498, and France claimed it through the voyage of Verrazzano in 1524. Each resented the claim of the other, and each snatched such fragments of the prize as she could reach, and kept them if she could. In 1604 Henry IV. of France gave to De Monts all America from the 40th to the 46th degree of north latitude, including the sites of Philadelphia on one hand, and Montreal on the other;[1] while, eight years after, Louis XIII. gave to Madame de Guercheville and the Jesuits the whole continent from Florida to the St. Lawrence, that is, the whole of the future British colonies. Again, in 1621, James I. of England made over a part of this generous domain to a subject of his own, Sir William Alexander, to whom he gave, under the name of Nova Scotia, the peninsula which is now so called, together with a vast adjacent wilderness, to be held forever as a fief of the Scottish Crown.[2] Sir William, not yet satisfied, soon got an additional grant of the "River and Gulf of Canada," along with a belt of land three hundred miles wide, reaching across the continent.[3] Thus the king of France gave to Frenchmen the sites of Boston, New York, and Washington, and the king of England gave to a Scotch-

[1] See *Pioneers of France in the New World*, 184.

[2] *Charter of New Scotland in favour of Sir William Alexander*.

[3] *Charter of the Country and Lordship of Canada in America*, 2 Feb., 1628–9, in *Publications of the Prince Society, 1873*.

man the sites of Quebec and Montreal. But while the seeds of international war were thus sown broadcast over the continent, an obscure corner of the vast regions in dispute became the scene of an intestine strife like the bloody conflicts of two feudal chiefs in the depths of the middle ages.

After the lawless inroads of Argall, the French, with young Biencourt at their head, still kept a feeble hold on Acadia. After the death of his father, Poutrincourt, Biencourt took his name, by which thenceforth he is usually known. In his distress he lived much like an Indian, roaming the woods with a few followers, and subsisting on fish, game, roots, and lichens. He seems, however, to have found means to build a small fort among the rocks and fogs of Cape Sable. He named it Fort Loméron, and here he appears to have maintained himself for a time by fishing and the fur trade.

Many years before, a French boy of fourteen years, Charles Saint Etienne de la Tour, was brought to Acadia by his father, Claude de la Tour, where he became attached to the service of Biencourt (Poutrincourt), and, as he himself says, served as his ensign and lieutenant. He says, further, that Biencourt on his death left him all his property in Acadia. It was thus, it seems, that La Tour became owner of Fort Loméron and its dependencies at Cape Sable, whereupon he begged the king to give him help against his enemies, especially the English, who, as he thought, meant to seize the country. And he begged also for a commission to command in Acadia for his Majesty.[1]

In fact, Sir William Alexander soon tried to dispossess him and seize his fort. Charles de la Tour's father had been captured at sea by the privateer Kirke, and carried to England. Here, being a widower, he married a lady of honor of the queen, and, being a Protestant, renounced his French allegiance.

Alexander made him a baronet of Nova Scotia, a new title which King James had authorized Sir William to confer on persons of consideration aiding him in his work of colonizing Acadia. Alexander now fitted out two ships, with which he sent the elder La Tour to Cape Sable. On arriving, the father,

[1] *La Tour au Roy, 25 July, 1627.*

says the story, made the most brilliant offers to his son if he would give up Fort Loméron to the English, to which young La Tour is reported to have answered in a burst of patriotism, that he would take no favors except from his sovereign, the king of France. On this, the English are said to have attacked the fort, and to have been beaten off. As the elder La Tour could not keep his promise to deliver the place to the English, they would have no more to do with him, on which his dutiful son offered him an asylum under condition that he should never enter the fort. A house was built for him outside the ramparts, and here the trader, Nicolas Denys, found him in 1635. It is Denys who tells the above story,[1] which he probably got from the younger La Tour, and which, as he tells it, is inconsistent with the known character of its pretended hero, who was no model of loyalty to his king, being a chameleon whose principles took the color of his interests. Denys says, further, that the elder La Tour had been invested with the Order of the Garter, and that the same dignity was offered to his son; which is absurd. The truth is, that Sir William Alexander, thinking that the two La Tours might be useful to him, made them both baronets of Nova Scotia.[2]

Young La Tour, while begging Louis XIII. for a commission to command in Acadia, got from Sir William Alexander not only the title of Baronet, but also a large grant of land at and near Cape Sable, to be held as a fief of the Scottish Crown.[3] Again, he got from the French king a grant of land on the river St. John, and, to make assurance doubly sure, got leave from Sir William Alexander to occupy it.[4] This he soon did, and built a fort near the mouth of the river, not far from the present city of St. John.

Meanwhile the French had made a lodgment on the rock of Quebec, and not many years after, all North America from Florida to the Arctic circle, and from Newfoundland to the

[1] Denys, *Description géographique et historique*.

[2] *Grant from Sir William Alexander to Sir Claude de St. Etienne (de la Tour), 30 Nov., 1629. Ibid. to Charles de St. Etienne, Esq., Seigneur de St. Denniscourt and Baigneux, 12 May, 1630.* Hazard, *State Papers*, I. 294, 298. The names of both father and son appear on the list of baronets of Nova Scotia.

[3] *Patent from Sir William Alexander to Claude and Charles de la Tour, 30 April, 1630.*

[4] Williamson, *History of Maine*, I. 246.

springs of the St. Lawrence, was given by King Louis to the Company of New France, with Richelieu at its head.[1] Sir William Alexander, jealous of this powerful rivalry, caused a private expedition to be fitted out under the brothers Kirke. It succeeded, and the French settlements in Acadia and Canada were transferred by conquest to England. England soon gave them back by the treaty of St. Germain,[2] and Claude de Razilly, a knight of Malta, was charged to take possession of them in the name of King Louis.[3] Full powers were given him over the restored domains, together with grants of Acadian lands for himself.[4]

Razilly reached Port Royal in August, 1632, with three hundred men, and the Scotch colony planted there by Alexander gave up the place in obedience to an order from the king of England. Unfortunately for Charles de la Tour, Razilly brought with him an officer destined to become La Tour's worst enemy. This was Charles de Menou d'Aunay Charnisay, a gentleman of birth and character, who acted as his commander's man of trust, and who, in Razilly's name, presently took possession of such other feeble English and Scotch settlements as had been begun by Alexander or the people of New England along the coasts of Nova Scotia and Maine. This placed the French Crown and the Company of New France in sole possession for a time of the region then called Acadia.

When Acadia was restored to France, La Tour's English title to his lands at Cape Sable became worthless. He hastened to Paris to fortify his position, and, suppressing his dallyings with England and Sir William Alexander, he succeeded not only in getting an extensive grant of lands at Cape Sable, but also the title of lieutenant-general for the king in Fort Loméron and its dependencies,[5] and commander at Cape Sable for the Company of New France.

[1] See *Pioneers of France*, 313.

[2] *Traité de St. Germain en Laye, 29* Mars, *1632, Article 3*. For reasons of the restitution, see *Pioneers of France*, 323, 324.

[3] *Convention avec le Sieur de Razilly pour aller reçevoir la Restitution du Port Royal,* etc., *27 Mars, 1632. Commission du Sieur de Razilly, 10 May, 1632.*

[4] *Concession de la rivière et baye Saincte Croix à M. de Razilly, 29 May, 1632.*

[5] *Revocation de la Commission du Sieur Charles de Saint Etienne, Sieur de la Tour, 23 Fév., 1641.*

Razilly, who represented the king in Acadia, died in 1635, and left his authority to D'Aunay Charnisay, his relative and second in command. D'Aunay made his headquarters at Port Royal, and nobody disputed his authority except La Tour, who pretended to be independent of him in virtue of his commission from the Crown and his grant from the Company. Hence rose dissensions that grew at last into war.

The two rivals differed widely in position and qualities. Charles de Menou, Seigneur d'Aunay Charnisay, came of an old and distinguished family of Touraine,[1] and he prided himself above all things on his character of *gentilhomme français*. Charles Saint Etienne de la Tour was of less conspicuous lineage.[2] In fact, his father, Claude de la Tour, is said by his enemies to have been at one time so reduced in circumstances that he carried on the trade of a mason in Rue St. Germain at Paris. The son, however, is called *gentilhomme d'une naissance distinguée*, both in papers of the court and in a legal document drawn up in the interest of his children. As he came to Acadia when a boy he could have had little education, and both he and D'Aunay carried on trade, which in France would have derogated from their claims as gentlemen, though in America the fur trade was not held inconsistent with *noblesse*.

Of La Tour's little kingdom at Cape Sable, with its rocks, fogs, and breakers, its seal-haunted islets and iron-bound shores guarded by Fort Loméron, we have but dim and uncertain glimpses. After the death of Biencourt, La Tour is said to have roamed the woods with eighteen or twenty men, "living a vagabond life with no exercise of religion."[3] He himself

[1] The modern representative of this family, Comte Jules de Menou, is the author of a remarkable manuscript book, written from family papers and official documents, and entitled *L'Acadie colonisée par Charles de Menou d'Aunay Charnisay*. I have followed Comte de Menou's spelling of the name. It is often written D'Aulnay, and by New England writers D'Aulney. The manuscript just mentioned is in my possession. Comte de Menou is also the author of a printed work called *Preuves de l'Histoire de la Maison de Menou*.

[2] The true surname of La Tour's family, which belonged to the neighborhood of Evreux, in Normandy, was Turgis. The designation of La Tour was probably derived from the name of some family estate, after a custom common in France under the old régime. The Turgis's arms were "d'or au chevron de sable, accompagné de trois palmes de même."

[3] Menou, *L'Acadie colonisée par Charles de Menou d'Aunay Charnisay.*

admits that he was forced to live like the Indians, as did Bien-court before him.[1] Better times had come, and he was now commander of Fort Loméron, or, as he called it, Fort La Tour, with a few Frenchmen and abundance of Micmac In-dians. His next neighbor was the adventurer Nicolas Denys, who with a view to the timber trade had settled himself with twelve men on a small river a few leagues distant. Here Ra-zilly had once made him a visit, and was entertained under a tent of boughs with a sylvan feast of wild pigeons, brant, teal, woodcock, snipe, and larks, cheered by profuse white wine and claret, and followed by a dessert of wild raspberries.[2]

On the other side of the Acadian peninsula D'Aunay reigned at Port Royal like a feudal lord, which in fact he was. Denys, who did not like him, says that he wanted only to rule, and treated his settlers like slaves; but this, even if true at the time, did not always remain so. D'Aunay went to France in 1641, and brought out, at his own charge, twenty families to people his seigniory.[3] He had already brought out a wife, having espoused Jeanne Molin or Motin, daughter of the Seigneur de Courcelles. What with old settlers and new, about forty families were gathered at Port Royal and on the river Annapolis, and over these D'Aunay ruled like a feudal Robinson Crusoe.[4] He gave each colonist a farm charged with a perpetual rent of one sou an arpent, or French acre. The houses of the settlers were log cabins, and the manor-house of their lord was a larger building of the same kind. The most pressing need was of defence, and D'Aunay lost no time in repairing and reconstructing the old fort on the point between Allen's River and the Annapolis. He helped his ten-ants at their work, and his confessor describes him as return-ing to his rough manor-house on a wet day, drenched with rain and bespattered with mud, but in perfect good humor, after helping some of the inhabitants to mark out a field. The confessor declares that during the eleven months of his ac-quaintance with him he never heard him speak ill of anybody whatever, a statement which must probably be taken with al-

[1] *La Tour au Roy, 25 Juillet, 1627.*
[2] Denys, *Description géographique et historique.*
[3] Rameau, *Une Colonie féodale en Amérique*, I. 93 (ed. 1889).
[4] *Ibid.*, I. 96, 97.

lowance. Yet this proud scion of a noble stock seems to have given himself with good grace to the rough labors of the frontiersman, while Father Ignace, the Capuchin friar, praises him for the merit, transcendent in clerical eyes, of constant attendance at mass and frequent confession.[1]

With his neighbors, the Micmac Indians, he was on the best of terms. He supplied their needs, and they brought him the furs that enabled him in some measure to bear the heavy charges of an establishment that could not for many years be self-supporting. In a single year the Indians are said to have brought three thousand moose skins to Port Royal, besides beaver and other valuable furs. Yet, from a commercial point of view, D'Aunay did not prosper. He had sold or mortgaged his estates in France, borrowed large sums, built ships, bought cannon, levied soldiers, and brought over immigrants. He is reported to have had three hundred fighting men at his principal station, and sixty cannon mounted on his ships and forts; for besides Port Royal he had two or three smaller establishments.[2]

Port Royal was a scene for an artist, with its fort, its soldiers in breastplate and morion, armed with pike, halberd, or matchlock, its manor-house of logs, and its seminary of like construction, its twelve Capuchin friars, with cowled heads, sandalled feet, and the cord of Saint Francis; the birch canoes of Micmac and Abenaki Indians lying along the strand, and their feathered and painted owners lounging about the place or dozing around their wigwam fires. It was mediævalism married to primeval savagery. The friars were supported by a fund supplied by Richelieu, and their chief business was to convert the Indians into vassals of France, the Church, and the Chevalier d'Aunay. Hard by was a wooden chapel, where the seignior knelt in dutiful observance of every rite, and where, under a stone chiselled with his ancient scutcheon, one of his children lay buried. In the fort he had not forgotten to provide a dungeon for his enemies.

[1] *Lettre du Père Ignace de Paris, Capuchin, 6 Aoust, 1653.*

[2] *Certificat à l'égard de M. d'Aunay Charnisay, signé Michel Boudrot, Lieutenant Général en l'Acadie, et autres, anciens habitans au pays, 5 Oct., 1687. Lettre du Roy de gouverneur et lieutenant général es costes de l'Acadie pour Charles de Menou, Sieur d'Aulnay Charnisay, Fév., 1647.*

The worst of these was Charles de la Tour. Before the time of Razilly and his successor, D'Aunay, La Tour had felt himself the chief man in Acadia; but now he was confronted by a rival higher in rank, superior in resources and court influence, proud, ambitious, and masterful.[1] He was bitterly jealous of D'Aunay, and, to strengthen himself against so formidable a neighbor, he got from the Company of New France the grant of a tract of land at the mouth of the river St. John, where he built a fort and called it after his own name, though it was better known as Fort St. Jean.[2] Thither he removed from his old post at Cape Sable, and Fort St. Jean now became his chief station. It confronted its rival, Port Royal, across the intervening Bay of Fundy.

Now began a bitter feud between the two chiefs, each claiming lands occupied by the other. The Court interposed to settle the dispute, but in its ignorance of Acadian geography its definitions were so obscure that the question was more embroiled than ever.[3]

While the domestic feud of the rivals was gathering to a head, foreign heretics had fastened their clutches on various parts of the Atlantic coast which France and the Church claimed as their own. English heretics had made lodgment in Virginia, and Dutch heretics at the mouth of the Hudson, while other sectaries of the most malignant type had kennelled among the sands and pine trees of Plymouth, and others still, slightly different, but equally venomous, had ensconced themselves on or near the small peninsula of Shawmut, at the head of La Grande Baye, or the Bay of Massachusetts. As it was not easy to dislodge them, the French dissembled for the present, yielded to the logic of events, and bided their time. But the interlopers soon began to swarm

---

[1] Besides succeeding to the authority of Razilly, D'Aunay had bought of his heirs their land claims in Acadia. *Arrêts du Conseil, 9 Mars, 1642.*

[2] *Concession de la Compagnie de la Nouvelle France à Charles de Saint-Etienne, Sieur de la Tour, Lieutenant Général de l'Acadie, du Fort de la Tour, dans la Rivière de St. Jean, du 15 Janvier, 1635,* in *Mémoires des Commissaires,* V. 118 (ed. 1756, 12mo).

[3] *Louis XIII à d'Aunay, 10 Fév., 1638.* This seems to be the occasion of Charlevoix's inexact assertion that Acadia was divided into three governments, under D'Aunay, La Tour, and Nicolas Denys, respectively. The title of Denys, such as it was, had no existence till 1654.

northward and invade the soil of Acadia, sacred to God and the king. Small parties from Plymouth built trading-houses at Machias and at what is now Castine, on the Penobscot. As they were competitors in trade, no less than foes of God and King Louis, and as they were too few to resist, both La Tour and D'Aunay resolved to expel them; and in 1633 La Tour attacked the Plymouth trading-house at Machias, killed two of the five men he found there, carried off the other three, and seized all the goods.[1] Two years later D'Aunay attacked the Plymouth trading station at Penobscot, the Pentegoet of the French, and took it in the name of King Louis. That he might not appear in the part of a pirate, he set a price on the goods of the traders and then, having seized them, gave in return his promise to pay at some convenient time if the owners would come to him for the money.

He had called on La Tour to help him in this raid against Penobscot, but La Tour, unwilling to recognize his right to command, had refused. He had hoped that D'Aunay, becoming disgusted with his Acadian venture, which promised neither honor nor profit, would give it up, go back to France, and stay there. About the year 1638 D'Aunay did in fact go to France, but not to stay, for in due time he reappeared, bringing with him his bride, Jeanne Motin, who had had the courage to share his fortunes, and whom he now installed at Port Royal, a sure sign, as his rival thought, that he meant to make his home there. Disappointed and angry, La Tour now lost patience, went to Port Royal, and tried to stir D'Aunay's soldiers to mutiny; then set on his Indian friends to attack a boat in which was one of D'Aunay's soldiers and a Capuchin friar, the soldier being killed, though the friar escaped.[2] This was the beginning of a quarrel waged partly at Port Royal and St. Jean, and partly before the admiralty court of Guienne and the royal council, partly with bullets and cannon shot, and partly with edicts, decrees, and *procès verbaux*. As D'Aunay had taken a wife, so too would La Tour, and he charged his agent Desjardins to bring him one from France. The agent acquitted himself of his delicate mission, and shipped to Acadia one Marie Jacquelin, daughter of a barber of Mans, if we

[1] Hubbard, *History of New-England*, 163.
[2] Menou, *L'Acadie colonisée par Charles de Menou d'Aunay*.

may believe the questionable evidence of his rival. Be this as it may, Marie Jacquelin proved a prodigy of mettle and energy, espoused her husband's cause with passionate vehemence, and backed his quarrel like the intrepid Amazon she was. She joined La Tour at Fort St. Jean, and proved the most strenuous of allies.

About this time D'Aunay heard that the English of Plymouth meant to try to recover Penobscot from his hands. On this he sent nine soldiers thither with provisions and munitions. La Tour seized them on the way, carried them to Fort St. Jean, and, according to his enemies, treated them like slaves. D'Aunay heard nothing of this till four months after, when, being told of it by Indians, he sailed in person to Penobscot with two small vessels, reinforced the place, and was on his way back to Port Royal when La Tour met him with two armed pinnaces. A fight took place and one of D'Aunay's vessels was dismasted. He fought so well, however, that Captain Jamin, his enemy's chief officer, was killed, and the rest, including La Tour, his new wife, and his agent Desjardins were forced to surrender, and were carried prisoners to Port Royal.

At the request of the Capuchin friars D'Aunay set them all at liberty, after compelling La Tour to sign a promise to keep the peace in future.[1] Both parties now laid their cases before the French courts, and, whether from the justice of his cause or from superior influence, D'Aunay prevailed. La Tour's commission was revoked, and he was ordered to report himself in France to receive the king's commands. Trusting to his remoteness from the seat of power, and knowing that the king was often ill served and worse informed, he did not obey, but remained in Acadia exercising his authority as before. D'Aunay's father, from his house in Rue St. Germain, watched over his son's interests, and took care that La Tour's conduct should not be unknown at court. A decree was thereupon issued directing D'Aunay to seize his rival's forts in the name of the king, and place them in charge of trusty persons. The order was precise, but D'Aunay had not at the time force enough to execute it, and the frugal king sent him only six

---

[1] Menou, *L'Acadie colonisée par Charles de Menou d'Aunay.*

soldiers. Hence he could only show the royal order to La Tour and offer him a passage to France on one of his vessels if he had the discretion to obey. La Tour refused, on which D'Aunay returned to France to report his rival's contumacy. At about the same time La Tour's French agent sent him a vessel with succors. The king ordered it to be seized; but the order came too late, for the vessel had already sailed from Rochelle bound to Fort St. Jean.

When D'Aunay reported the audacious conduct of his enemy, the royal council ordered that the offender should be brought prisoner to France,[1] and D'Aunay, as the king's lieutenant-general in Acadia, was again required to execute the decree.[2] La Tour was now in the position of a rebel, and all legality was on the side of his enemy, who represented royalty itself.

D'Aunay sailed at once for Acadia, and in August, 1642, anchored at the mouth of the St. John, before La Tour's fort, and sent three gentlemen in a boat to read to its owner the decree of the council and the order of the king. La Tour snatched the papers, crushed them between his hands, abused the envoys roundly, put them and their four sailors into prison, and kept them there above a year.[3]

His position was now desperate, for he had placed himself in open revolt. Alarmed for the consequences, he turned for help to the heretics of Boston. True Catholics detested them as foes of God and man, but La Tour was neither true Catholic nor true Protestant, and would join hands with anybody who could serve his turn. Twice before he had made advances to the Boston malignants, and sent to them first one Rochet, and then one Lestang, with proposals of trade and alliance. The envoys were treated with courtesy, but could get no promise of active aid.[4]

La Tour's agent, Desjardins, had sent him from Rochelle a ship, called the St. Clement, manned by a hundred and forty Huguenots, laden with stores and munitions, and commanded by Captain Mouron. In due time La Tour at his Fort

[1] *Arrêt du Conseil, 21 Fév., 1642.*
[2] Menou, *L'Acadie colonisée.*
[3] Menou, *L'Acadie colonisée.* Moreau, *Histoire de l'Acadie,* 169, 170.
[4] Hubbard, *History of New England,* chap. liv. Winthrop, II. 42, 88.

St. Jean heard that the St. Clement lay off the mouth of the river, unable to get in because D'Aunay blockaded the entrance with two armed ships and a pinnace. On this he resolved to appeal in person to the heretics. He ran the blockade in a small boat under cover of night, and, accompanied by his wife, boarded the St. Clement and sailed for Boston.[1]

[1] Menou, *L'Acadie colonisée*.

Chapter II

1643–1645

LA TOUR AND THE PURITANS

La Tour at Boston • His Meeting with Winthrop • Boston in 1643
• Training Day • An Alarm • La Tour's Bargain • Doubts and
Disputes • The Allies sail • La Tour and Endicott • D'Aunay's
Overture to the Puritans • Marie's Mission

O N the 12th of June, 1643, the people of the infant town of Boston saw with some misgiving a French ship entering their harbor. It chanced that the wife of Captain Edward Gibbons, with her children, was on her way in a boat to a farm belonging to her husband on an island in the harbor. One of La Tour's party, who had before made a visit to Boston, and had been the guest of Gibbons, recognized his former hostess, and he, with La Tour and a few sailors, cast off from the ship and went to speak to her in a boat that was towed at the stern of the St. Clement. Mrs. Gibbons, seeing herself chased by a crew of outlandish foreigners, took refuge on the island where Fort Winthrop was afterwards built, which was then known as the "Governor's Garden," as it had an orchard, a vineyard, and "many other conveniences."[1] The islands in the harbor, most of which were at that time well wooded, seem to have been favorite places of cultivation, as sheep and cattle were there safe from those pests of the mainland, the wolves. La Tour, no doubt to the dismay of Mrs. Gibbons and her children, landed after them, and was presently met by the governor himself, who, with his wife, two sons, and a daughter-in-law, had apparently rowed over to their garden for the unwonted recreation of an afternoon's outing.[2] La Tour made himself known to the governor, and, after mutual civilities, told him that a ship bringing supplies from France had been stopped by his enemy, D'Aunay, and that he had come to ask for help to raise the blockade and bring her to his fort. Winthrop replied that, before answer-

[1] Wood, *New England's Prospect*, Part I. chap. x.
[2] Winthrop II. 197.

ing, he must consult the magistrates. As Mrs. Gibbons and her children were anxious to get home, the governor sent them to town in his own boat, promising to follow with his party in that of La Tour, who had placed it at his disposal. Meanwhile, the people of Boston had heard of what was taking place, and were in some anxiety, since, in a truly British distrust of all Frenchmen, they feared lest their governor might be kidnapped and held for ransom. Some of them accordingly took arms, and came in three boats to the rescue. In fact, remarks Winthrop, "if La Tour had been ill-minded towards us, he had such an opportunity as we hope neither he nor any other shall ever have the like again."[1] The castle, or fort, which was on another island hard by, was defenceless, its feeble garrison having been lately withdrawn, and its cannon might easily have been turned on the town.

Boston, now in its thirteenth year, was a straggling village, with houses principally of boards or logs, gathered about a plain wooden meeting-house which formed the heart or vital organ of the place. The rough peninsula on which the infant settlement stood was almost void of trees, and was crowned by a hill split into three summits, whence the name of Tremont, or Trimount, still retained by a street of the present city. Beyond the narrow neck of the peninsula were several smaller villages with outlying farms; but the mainland was for the most part a primeval forest, possessed by its original owners, wolves, bears, and rattlesnakes. These last undesirable neighbors made their favorite haunt on a high rocky hill, called Rattlesnake Hill, not far inland, where, down to the present generation, they were often seen, and where good specimens may occasionally be found to this day.[2]

Far worse than wolves or rattlesnakes were the Pequot Indians, a warlike race who had boasted that they would wipe the whites from the face of the earth, but who, by hard marching and fighting, had lately been brought to reason.

Worse than wolves, rattlesnakes, and Indians together were

---

[1] *Ibid.*

[2] Blue Hill in Milton. "Up into the country is a high hill which is called rattlesnake hill, where there is great store of these poysonous creatures." (Wood, *New England's Prospect.*) "They [the wolves] be the greatest inconveniency the country hath." (*Ibid.*)

the theological quarrels that threatened to kill the colony in its infancy. Children are taught that the Puritans came to New England in search of religious liberty. The liberty they sought was for themselves alone. It was the liberty to worship in their own way, and to prevent all others from doing the like. They imagined that they held a monopoly of religious truth, and were bound in conscience to defend it against all comers. Their mission was to build up a western Canaan, ruled by the law of God, to keep it pure from error, and, if need were, purge it of heresy by persecution; to which ends they set up one of the most detestable theocracies on record. Church and state were joined in one. Church members alone had the right to vote. There was no choice but to remain politically a cipher, or embrace, or pretend to embrace, the extremest dogmas of Calvin. Never was such a premium offered to cant and hypocrisy; yet in the early days hypocrisy was rare, so intense and pervading was the faith of the founders of New England.

It was in the churches themselves, the appointed sentinels and defenders of orthodoxy, that heresy lifted its head and threatened the state with disruption. Where minds different in complexion and character were continually busied with subtle questions of theology, unity of opinion could not be long maintained; and innovation found a champion in one Mrs. Hutchinson, a woman of great controversial ability and inexhaustible fluency of tongue. Persons of a mystical turn of mind, or a natural inclination to contrariety, were drawn to her preachings, and the church of Boston, with three or four exceptions, went over to her in a body. "Sanctification," "justification," "revelations," the "covenant of grace," and the "covenant of works," mixed in furious battle with all the subtleties, sophistries, and venom of theological war, while the ghastly spectre of Antinomianism hovered over the fray, carrying terror to the souls of the faithful. The embers of the strife still burned hot when La Tour appeared to bring another firebrand.

As a "papist" or "idolater," though a mild one, he was sorely prejudiced in Puritan eyes, while his plundering of the Plymouth trading-house some years before, and killing two of its five tenants, did not tend to produce impressions in his favor; but it being explained that all five were drunk, and had begun the fray by firing on the French, the ire against him cooled a little. Landing with Winthrop, he was received under the hospitable roof of Captain Gibbons, whose wife had recovered from her fright at his approach. He went to church on Sunday, and the gravity of his demeanor gave great satisfaction, a solemn carriage being of itself a virtue in Puritan eyes. Hence he was well treated, and his men were permitted to come ashore daily in small numbers. The stated training day of the Boston militia fell in the next week, and La Tour asked leave to exercise his soldiers with the rest. This was granted, and, escorted by the Boston trained band, about forty of them marched to the muster field, which was probably the Common, a large tract of pasture land in which was a marshy pool, the former home of a colony of frogs, perhaps not quite exterminated by the sticks and stones of Puritan boys. This pool, cleaned, paved, and curbed with granite, preserves to this day the memory of its ancient inhabitants, and is still the Frog Pond, though bereft of frogs.

The Boston trained band, in steel caps and buff coats, went through its exercise, and the visitors, we are told, expressed high approval. When the drill was finished, the Boston officers invited La Tour's officers to dine, while his rank and file were entertained in like manner by the Puritan soldiers. There were more exercises in the afternoon, and this time it was the turn of the French, who, says Winthrop, "were very expert in all their postures and motions." A certain "judicious minister," in dread of popish conspiracies, was troubled in spirit at this martial display, and prophesied that "store of blood would be spilled in Boston," a prediction that was not fulfilled, although an incident took place which startled some of the spectators. The Frenchmen suddenly made a sham charge, sword in hand, which the women took for a real one. The alarm was soon over; and as this demonstration ended the performance, La Tour asked leave of the governor to withdraw his men to their ship. The leave being granted, they fired a salute and marched to the wharf where their boat lay, escorted, as before, by the Boston trained band. During the whole of La Tour's visit he and Winthrop went amicably to church together every Sunday, the governor being attended, on these and all other occasions while the strangers were in town, by a guard of honor of musketeers and halberd men. La Tour and his chief officers had their lodging and meals in the houses of the principal townsmen, and all seemed harmony and good will.

La Tour, meanwhile, had laid his request before the magistrates, and produced among other papers the commission to Mouron, captain of his ship, dated in the last April, and signed and sealed by the vice-admiral of France, authorizing Mouron to bring supplies to La Tour, whom the paper styled lieutenant-general for the king in Acadia; La Tour also showed a letter, genuine or forged, from the agent of the Company of New France, addressed to him as lieutenant-general, and warning him to beware of D'Aunay: from all which the Boston magistrates inferred that their petitioner was on good terms with the French government,[1] notwithstanding a letter sent them by D'Aunay the year before, assuring them that La Tour was a proclaimed rebel, which in fact he was. Throughout this affair one is perplexed by the French official papers, whose entanglements and contradictions in regard to the Acadian rivals are past unravelling.

La Tour asked only for such help as would enable him to bring his own ship to his own fort, and, as his papers seemed to prove that he was a recognized officer of his king, Winthrop and the magistrates thought that they might permit him to hire such ships and men as were disposed to join him.

La Tour had tried to pass himself as a Protestant, but his professions were distrusted, notwithstanding the patience with which he had listened to the long-winded sermons of the Reverend John Cotton. As to his wife, however, there appears to have been but one opinion. She was approved as a sound Protestant "of excellent virtues;" and her denunciations of D'Aunay no doubt fortified the prejudice which was already strong against him for his seizure of the Plymouth trading-house at Penobscot, and for his aggressive and masterful character, which made him an inconvenient neighbor.

With the permission of the governor and the approval of

[1] Count Jules de Menou, in his remarkable manuscript book now before me, expresses his belief that the commission of the vice-admiral was genuine, but that the letter of the agent of the Company was a fabrication.

most of the magistrates, La Tour now made a bargain with
his host, Captain Gibbons, and a merchant named Thomas
Hawkins. They agreed to furnish him with four vessels; to
arm each of these with from four to fourteen small cannon,
and man them with a certain number of sailors, La Tour himself completing the crews with Englishmen hired at his own
charge. Hawkins was to command the whole. The four vessels were to escort La Tour and his ship, the St. Clement, to
the mouth of the St. John, in spite of D'Aunay and all other
opponents. The agreement ran for two months, and La Tour
was to pay £250 sterling a month for the use of the four ships,
and mortgage to Gibbons and Hawkins his fort and all his
Acadian property as security. Winthrop would give no commissions to Hawkins or any others engaged in the expedition,
and they were all forbidden to fight except in self-defence; but
the agreement contained the significant clause that all plunder
was to be equally divided according to rule in such enterprises. Hence it seems clear that the contractors had an eye to
booty; yet no means were used to hold them to their good
behavior.

Now rose a brisk dispute, and the conduct of Winthrop
was sharply criticised. Letters poured in upon him concerning
"great dangers," "sin upon the conscience," and the like. He
himself was clearly in doubt as to the course he was taking,
and he soon called another meeting of magistrates, in which
the inevitable clergy were invited to join; and they all fell to
discussing the matter anew. As every man of them had studied the Bible daily from childhood up, texts were the chief
weapons of the debate. Doubts were advanced as to whether
Christians could lawfully help idolaters, and Jehoshaphat,
Ahab, and Josias were brought forward as cases in point.
Then Solomon was cited to the effect that "he that meddleth
with the strife that belongs not to him takes a dog by the
ear;" to which it was answered that the quarrel did belong to
us, seeing that Providence now offered us the means to
weaken our enemy, D'Aunay, without much expense or trouble to ourselves. Besides, we ought to help a neighbor in distress, seeing that Joshua helped the Gibeonites, and
Jehoshaphat helped Jehoram against Moab with the approval
of Elisha. The opposing party argued that "by aiding papists

we advance and strengthen popery;" to which it was replied that the opposite effect might follow, since the grateful papist, touched by our charity, might be won to the true faith and turned from his idols.

Then the debate continued on the more worldly grounds of expediency and statecraft, and at last Winthrop's action was approved by the majority. Still, there were many doubters, and the governor was severely blamed. John Endicott wrote to him that La Tour was not to be trusted, and that he and D'Aunay had better be left to fight it out between them, since if we help the former to put down his enemy he will be a bad neighbor to us.

Presently came a joint letter from several chief men of the colony, Saltonstall, Bradstreet, Nathaniel Ward, John Norton, and others, saying in substance: We fear international law has been ill observed; the merits of the case are not clear; we are not called upon in charity to help La Tour (see 2 Chronicles xix. 2, and Proverbs xxvi. 17); this quarrel is for England and France, and not for us; if D'Aunay is not completely put down, we shall have endless trouble; and "he that loses his life in an unnecessary quarrel dies the devil's martyr."

This letter, known as the "Ipswich letter," touched Winthrop to the quick. He thought that it trenched on his official dignity, and the asperity of his answer betrays his sensitiveness. He calls the remonstrance "an act of an exorbitant nature," and says that it "blows a trumpet to division and dissension." "If my neighbor is in trouble," he goes on to say, "I must help him;" he maintains that "there is great difference between giving permission to hire to guard or transport, and giving commission to fight," and he adds the usual Bible text, "The fear of man bringeth a snare; but whoso putteth his trust in the Lord shall be safe."[1]

In spite of Winthrop's reply, the Ipswich letter had great effect, and he and the Boston magistrates were much blamed, especially in the country towns. The governor was too candid not to admit that he had been in fault, though he limits his

[1] Winthrop's *Answer to the Ipswich Letter about La Tour* (no date), in *Hutchinson Papers*, 122. Bradstreet writes to him on the 21st of June, "Our ayding of Latour was very grievous to many hereabouts, the design being feared to be unwarrantable by dyvers."

self-accusation to three points: first, that he had given La Tour an answer too hastily; next, that he had not sufficiently consulted the elders or ministers; and lastly, that he had not opened the discussion with prayer.

The upshot was that La Tour and his allies sailed on the 14th of July. D'Aunay's three vessels fled before them to Port Royal. La Tour tried to persuade his Puritan friends to join him in an attack; but Hawkins, the English commander, would give no order to that effect, on which about thirty of the Boston men volunteered for the adventure. D'Aunay's followers had ensconced themselves in a fortified mill, whence they were driven with some loss. After burning the mill and robbing a pinnace loaded with furs, the Puritans returned home, having broken their orders and compromised their colony.

In the next summer, La Tour, expecting a serious attack from D'Aunay, who had lately been to France, and was said to be on his way back with large reinforcements, turned again to Massachusetts for help. The governor this time was John Endicott, of Salem. To Salem the suppliant repaired, and as Endicott spoke French the conference was easy. The rugged bigot had before expressed his disapproval of "having anything to do with these idolatrous French;" but, according to Hubbard, he was so moved with compassion at the woful tale of his visitor that he called a meeting of magistrates and ministers to consider if anything could be done for him. The magistrates had by this time learned caution, and the meeting would do nothing but write a letter to D'Aunay, demanding satisfaction for his seizure of Penobscot and other aggressions, and declaring that the men who escorted La Tour to his fort in the last summer had no commission from Massachusetts, yet that if they had wronged him he should have justice, though if he seized any New England trading vessels they would hold him answerable. In short, La Tour's petition was not granted.

D'Aunay, when in France, had pursued his litigation against his rival, and the royal council had ordered that the contumacious La Tour should be seized, his goods confiscated, and he himself brought home a prisoner; which decree D'Aunay was empowered to execute, if he could. He had returned to Acadia the accredited agent of the royal will. It was reported at Boston that a Biscayan pirate had sunk his ship on the way; but the wish was father to the thought, and the report proved false. D'Aunay arrived safely, and was justly incensed at the support given by the Puritans in the last year to his enemy. But he too had strong reasons for wishing to be on good terms with his heretic neighbors. King Louis, moreover, had charged him not to offend them, since, when they helped La Tour, they had done so in the belief that he was commissioned as lieutenant-general for the king, and therefore they should be held blameless.

Hence D'Aunay made overtures of peace and friendship to the Boston Puritans. Early in October, 1644, they were visited by one Monsieur Marie, "supposed," says the chronicle, "to be a friar, but habited like a gentleman." He was probably one of the Capuchins who formed an important part of D'Aunay's establishment at Port Royal. The governor and magistrates received him with due consideration; and along with credentials from D'Aunay he showed them papers under the great seal of France, wherein the decree of the royal council was set forth in full, La Tour condemned as a rebel and traitor, and orders given to arrest both him and his wife. Henceforth there was no room to doubt which of the rival chiefs had the king and the law on his side. The envoy, while complaining of the aid given to La Tour, offered terms of peace to the governor and magistrates, who replied to his complaints with their usual subterfuge, that they had given no commission to those who had aided La Tour, declaring at the same time that they could make no treaty without the concurrence of the commissioners of the United Colonies. They then desired Marie to set down his proposals in writing, on which he went to the house of one Mr. Fowle, where he lodged, and drew up in French his plan for a treaty, adding the proposal that the Bostonians should join D'Aunay against La Tour. Then he came back to the place of meeting and discussed the subject for half a day, sometimes in Latin with the magistrates, and sometimes in French with the governor, that old soldier being probably ill versed in the classic tongues. In vain they all urged that D'Aunay should come to terms with La Tour. Marie replied, that if La Tour would give himself up his life would be spared, but that if he were caught he would lose his head as a traitor; adding that his wife was worse than he, being the mainspring of his rebellion. Endicott and the magistrates refused active alliance; but the talk ended in a provisional treaty of peace, duly drawn up in Latin, Marie keeping one copy and the governor the other. The agreement needed ratification by the commissioners of the United Colonies on one part, and by D'Aunay on the other. What is most curious in the affair is the attitude of Massachusetts, which from first to last figures as an independent state, with no reference to the king under whose charter it was building up its theocratic republic, and consulting none but the infant confederacy of the New England colonies, of which it was itself the head. As the commissioners of the confederacy were not then in session, Endicott and the magistrates took the matter provisionally into their own hands.

Marie had made good despatch, for he reached Boston on a Friday and left it on the next Tuesday, having finished his business in about three days, or rather two, as one of the three was "the Sabbath." He expressed surprise and gratification at the attention and courtesy with which he had been treated. His hosts supplied him with horses, and some of them accompanied him to Salem, where he had left his vessel, and whence he sailed for Port Royal, well pleased.

Just before he came to Boston, that town had received a visit from Madame de la Tour, who, soon after her husband's successful negotiation with Winthrop in the past year, had sailed for France in the ship St. Clement. She had labored strenuously in La Tour's cause; but the influence of D'Aunay's partisans was far too strong, and, being charged with complicity in her husband's misconduct, she was forbidden to leave France on pain of death. She set the royal command at naught, escaped to England, took passage in a ship bound for America, and after long delay landed at Boston. The English shipmaster had bargained to carry her to her husband at Fort St. Jean; but he broke his bond, and was sentenced by the Massachusetts courts to pay her £2,000 as damages. She was permitted to hire three armed vessels then lying in the harbor, to convey her to Fort St. Jean, where she arrived safely and rejoined La Tour.

Meanwhile, D'Aunay was hovering off the coast, armed with the final and conclusive decree of the royal council, which placed both husband and wife under the ban, and enjoined him to execute its sentence. But a resort to force was costly and of doubtful result, and D'Aunay resolved again to try the effect of persuasion. Approaching the mouth of the St. John, he sent to the fort two boats, commanded by his lieutenant, who carried letters from his chief promising to La Tour's men pardon for their past conduct and payment of all wages due them if they would return to their duty. An adherent of D'Aunay declares that they received these advances with insults and curses. It was a little before this time that Madame de la Tour arrived from Boston. The same writer says that she fell into a transport of fury, "behaved like one possessed with a devil," and heaped contempt on the Catholic faith in the presence of her husband, who approved everything she did; and he further affirms that she so berated and reviled the Récollet friars in the fort that they refused to stay, and set out for Port Royal in the depth of winter, taking with them eight soldiers of the fort who were too good Catholics to remain in such a nest of heresy and rebellion. They were permitted to go, and provided with an old pinnace and two barrels of Indian corn, with which, unfortunately for La Tour, they safely reached their destination.

On her arrival from Boston, Madame de la Tour had given her husband a piece of politic advice. Her enemies say that she had some time before renounced her faith to gain the favor of the Puritans; but there is reason to believe that she had been a Huguenot from the first. She now advised La Tour to go to Boston, declare himself a Protestant, ask for a minister to preach to his men, and promise that, if the Bostonians would help him to master D'Aunay and conquer Acadia, he would share the conquest with them. La Tour admired the sagacious counsels of his wife, and sailed for Boston to put them in practice just before the friars and the eight deserters sailed for Port Royal, thus leaving their departure unopposed.

At Port Royal both friars and deserters found a warm welcome. D'Aunay paid the eight soldiers their long arrears of wages, and lodged the friars in the seminary with his Capuchins. Then he questioned them, and was well rewarded. They told him that La Tour had gone to Boston, leaving his wife with only forty-five men to defend the fort. Here was a golden opportunity. D'Aunay called his officers to council. All were of one mind. He mustered every man about Port Royal and embarked them in the armed ship of three hundred tons that had brought him from France; he then crossed the Bay of Fundy with all his force, anchored in a small harbor a league from Fort St. Jean, and sent the Récollet Père André to try to seduce more of La Tour's men, an attempt which proved a failure. D'Aunay lay two months at his anchorage, during which time another ship and a pinnace joined him from Port Royal. Then he resolved to make an attack. Meanwhile, La Tour had persuaded a Boston merchant to send one Grafton to Fort St. Jean in a small vessel loaded with provisions, and bringing also a letter to Madame de la Tour containing a promise from her husband that he would join her in a month. When the Boston vessel appeared at the mouth of the St. John, D'Aunay seized it, placed Grafton and the few men with him on an island, and finally supplied them with a leaky sail-boat to make their way home as they best could.

D'Aunay now landed two cannon to batter Fort St. Jean on the land side, and on the 17th of April, having brought his largest ship within pistol-shot of the water rampart, he summoned the garrison to surrender.[1] They answered with a volley of cannon-shot, then hung out a red flag, and, according

[1] The site of Fort St. Jean, or Fort La Tour, has been matter of question. At Carleton, opposite the present city of St. John, are the remains of an earthen fort, by some supposed to be that of La Tour, but which is no doubt of later date, as the place was occupied by a succession of forts down to the Seven Years' War. On the other hand, it has been assumed that Fort La Tour was at Jemsec, which is about seventy miles up the river. Now, in the second mortgage deed of Fort La Tour to Major Gibbons, May 10, 1645, the fort is described as "*situé près de l'embouchure de la rivière de St. Jean.*" Moreover, there is a cataract just above the mouth of the river, which, though submerged at high tide, cannot be passed by heavy ships at any time; and as D'Aunay brought his largest ship of war to within pistol-shot of the fort, it must have been below the cataract. Mr. W. F. Ganong, after careful examination, is convinced that Fort La Tour was at Portland Point, on the east side of the St. John, at its mouth. See his paper on the subject in *Transactions of the Royal Society of Canada*, 1891.

to D'Aunay's reporter, shouted "a thousand insults and blasphemies"![1] Towards evening a breach was made in the wall, and D'Aunay ordered a general assault. Animated by their intrepid mistress, the defenders fought with desperation, and killed or wounded many of the assailants, not without severe loss on their own side. Numbers prevailed at last; all resistance was overcome; the survivors of the garrison were made prisoners, and the fort was pillaged. Madame de la Tour, her maid, and another woman, who were all of their sex in the place, were among the captives; also Madame de la Tour's son, a mere child. D'Aunay pardoned some of his prisoners, but hanged the greater part, "to serve as an example to posterity," says his reporter. Nicolas Denys declares that he compelled Madame de la Tour to witness the execution with a halter about her neck; but the more trustworthy accounts say nothing of this alleged outrage. On the next day, the 18th of April, the bodies of the dead were decently buried, an inventory was made of the contents of the fort, and D'Aunay set his men to repair it for his own use. These labors occupied three weeks or more, during a part of which Madame de la Tour was left at liberty, till, being detected in an attempt to correspond with her husband by means of an Indian, she was put into confinement; on which, according to D'Aunay's reporter, "she fell ill with spite and rage," and died within three weeks, after, as he tells us, renouncing her heresy in the chapel of the fort.

[1] See *Procès Verbal d'André Certain*, in Appendix A.

Chapter III

1645–1710

THE VICTOR VANQUISHED

*D'Aunay's Envoys to the Puritans • Their Reception at Boston •
Winthrop and his "papist" Guests • Reconciliation • Treaty • Be-
havior of La Tour • Royal Favors to D'Aunay • His Hopes • His
Death • His Character • Conduct of the Court towards him •
Intrigues of La Tour • Madame d'Aunay • La Tour marries her
• Children of D'Aunay • Descendants of La Tour*

Having triumphed over his rival, D'Aunay was left free
to settle his accounts with the Massachusetts Puritans,
who had offended him anew by sending provisions to Fort
St. Jean, having always insisted that they were free to trade
with either party. They, on their side, were no less indignant
with him for his seizure of Grafton's vessel and harsh treatment of him and his men.

After some preliminary negotiation and some rather sharp
correspondence, D'Aunay, in September, 1646, sent a pinnace
to Boston, bearing his former envoy, Marie, accompanied by
his own secretary and by one Monsieur Louis.

It was Sunday, the Puritan Sabbath, when the three envoys
arrived; and the pious inhabitants were preparing for the afternoon sermon. Marie and his two colleagues were met at
the wharf by two militia officers and conducted through the
silent and dreary streets to the house of Captain, now Major,
Gibbons, who seems to have taken upon himself in an especial manner the office of entertaining strangers of consequence.

All was done with much civility, but no ceremony, for the
Lord's day must be kept inviolate. Winthrop, who had again
been chosen governor, now sent an officer, with a guard of
musketeers, to invite the envoys to his own house. Here he
regaled them with wine and sweetmeats, and then informed
them of "our manner that all men either come to our publick
meetings or keep themselves quiet in their houses."[1] He then

[1]Winthrop, II. 273, 275.

laid before them such books in Latin and French as he had, and told them that they were free to walk in his garden. Though the diversion offered was no doubt of the dullest, since the literary resources of the colony then included little besides arid theology, and the walk in the garden promised but moderate delights among the bitter pot herbs provided against days of fasting, the victims resigned themselves with good grace, and, as the governor tells us, "gave no offence." Sunset came at last and set the captives free.

On Monday both sides fell to business. The envoys showed their credentials, but, as the commissioners of the United Colonies were not yet in session, nothing conclusive could be done till Tuesday. Then, all being assembled, each party made its complaints of the conduct of the other, and a long discussion followed. Meals were provided for the three visitors at the "ordinary," or inn, where the magistrates dined during the sessions of the General Court. The governor, as their host, always sat with them at the board and strained his Latin to do honor to his guests. They, on their part, that courtesies should be evenly divided, went every morning at eight o'clock to the governor's house, whence he accompanied them to the place of meeting, and at night he, or some of the commissioners in his stead, attended them to their lodging at the house of Major Gibbons.

Serious questions were raised on both sides; but as both wanted peace, explanations were mutually made and accepted. The chief difficulty lay in the undeniable fact that, in escorting La Tour to his fort in 1643, the Massachusetts volunteers had chased D'Aunay to Port Royal, killed some of his men, burned his mill, and robbed his pinnace, for which wrongs the envoys demanded heavy damages. It was true that the governor and magistrates had forbidden acts of aggression on the part of the volunteers; but on the other hand they had had reason to believe that their prohibition would be disregarded, and had taken no measures to enforce it. The envoys clearly had good ground of complaint; and here, says Winthrop, "they did stick two days." At last they yielded so far as to declare that what D'Aunay wanted was not so much compensation in money as satisfaction to his honor by an acknowledgment of their fault on the part of the Massachusetts authorities; and they further declared that he would accept a moderate present in token of such acknowledgment. The difficulty now was to find such a present. The representatives of Massachusetts presently bethought themselves of a "very fair new sedan" which the viceroy of Mexico had sent to his sister, and which had been captured in the West Indies by one Captain Cromwell, a corsair, who gave it to "our governor." Winthrop, to whom it was entirely useless, gladly parted with it in such a cause, and the sedan, being graciously accepted, ended the discussion.[1] The treaty was signed in duplicate by the commissioners of the United Colonies and the envoys of D'Aunay, and peace was at last concluded.

The conference had been conducted with much courtesy on both sides. One small cloud appeared, but soon passed away. The French envoys displayed the *fleur-de-lys* at the masthead of their pinnace as she lay in the harbor. The townsmen were incensed, and Monsieur Marie was told that to fly foreign colors in Boston harbor was not according to custom. He insisted for a time, but at length ordered the offending flag to be lowered.

On the 28th of September the envoys bade farewell to Winthrop, who had accompanied them to their pinnace with a guard of honor. Five cannon saluted them from Boston, five from "the Castle," and three from Charlestown. A supply of mutton and a keg of sherry were sent on board their vessel, and then, after firing an answering salute from their swivels, they stood down the bay till their sails disappeared among the islands.

La Tour had now no more to hope from his late supporters. He had lost his fort, and, what was worse, he had lost his indomitable wife. Throughout the winter that followed his disaster he had been entertained by Samuel Maverick, at his house on Noddle's Island. In the spring he begged hard for further help, and, as he begged in vain, he sailed for Newfoundland to make the same petition to Sir David Kirke, who then governed that island. Kirke refused, but lent him a pinnace and sent him back to Boston. Here some merchants had the good nature or folly to intrust him with goods for the

[1] Winthrop, II. 274.

Indian trade, to the amount of four hundred pounds. Thus equipped, he sailed for Acadia in Kirke's pinnace, manned with his own followers and five New England men. On reaching Cape Sable he conspired with the master of the pinnace and his own men to sieze the vessel and set the New England sailors ashore, which was done, La Tour, it is said, shooting one of them in the face with a pistol. It was winter, and the outcasts roamed along the shore for a fortnight, half frozen and half starved, till they were met by Micmac Indians, who gave them food and a boat, in which, by rare good fortune, they reached Boston, where their story convinced the most infatuated that they had harbored a knave. "Whereby," solemnly observes the pious but much mortified Winthrop, who had been La Tour's best friend, "it appeared (as the Scripture saith) that there is no confidence in an unfaithful or carnal man."[1]

When the capture of Fort St. Jean was known at court the young king was well pleased, and promised to send D'Aunay the gift of a ship;[2] but he forgot to keep his word, and requited his faithful subject with the less costly reward of praises and honors. After a preamble reciting his merits, and especially his "care, courage, and valor" in "taking by our express order and reducing again under our authority the fort on the St. John which La Tour had rebelliously occupied with the aid of foreign sectaries," the king confirms D'Aunay's authority in Acadia, and extends it on paper from the St. Lawrence to Virginia, empowering him to keep for himself such parts of this broad domain as he might want, and grant out the rest to others, who were to hold of him as vassals. He could build forts and cities, at his own expense; command by land and sea, make war or peace within the limits of his grant, appoint officers of government, justice, and police, and, in short, exercise sovereign power with the simple reservation of homage to the king, and a tenth part of all gold, silver, and copper to the royal treasury. A full monopoly of the fur trade throughout his dominion was conferred on him, and any infringement of it was to be punished by confiscation of ships and goods, and thirty thousand livres of damages. On his part

[1] Winthrop, II. 266.
[2] *Le Roy à M. d'Aunay Charnisay, 28 Sept., 1645.*

he was enjoined to "establish the name, power, and authority of the king, subject the nations to his rule, and teach them the knowledge of the true God and the light of the Christian faith."[1] Acadia, in short, was made an hereditary fief, and D'Aunay and his heirs became lords of a domain as large as a European kingdom.

D'Aunay had spent his substance in the task of civilizing a wilderness.[2] The king had not helped him; and though he belonged to a caste which held commerce in contempt, he must be a fur trader or a bankrupt. La Tour's Fort St. Jean was a better trading station than Port Royal, and it had wofully abridged D'Aunay's profits. Hence an ignoble competition in beaver-skins had greatly embittered their quarrel. All this was over; Fort St. Jean, the best trading stand in Acadia, was now in its conqueror's hands, and his monopoly was no longer a mere name, but a reality.

Everything promised a thriving trade and a growing colony, when the scene was suddenly changed. On the 24th of May, 1650, a dark and stormy day, D'Aunay and his valet were in a birch canoe in the basin of Port Royal, not far from the mouth of the Annapolis. Perhaps neither master nor man was skilled in the management of the treacherous craft that bore them. The canoe overset. D'Aunay and the valet clung to it and got astride of it, one at each end. There they sat, sunk to the shoulders, the canoe though under water having buoyancy enough to keep them from sinking further. So they remained an hour and a half, and at the end of that time D'Aunay was dead, not from drowning but from cold, for the water still retained the chill of winter. The valet remained alive, and in this condition they were found by Indians and brought to the north shore of the Annapolis, whither Father Ignace, the superior of the Capuchins, went to find the body of his patron, brought it to the fort, and buried it in the

---

[1] *Lettre du Roy de Gouverneur et Lieutenant Général es costes de l'Acadie pour Charles de Menou d'Aulnay Charnisay, Fév., 1647. Lettre de la Reyne régente au même, 13 Avril, 1647.*

[2] His heirs estimated his outlays for the colony at 800,000 livres. *Mémoire des filles du feu Seigneur d'Aulnay Charnisay, 1686. Placet de Joseph de Menou d'Aunay Charnisay, fils ainé du feu Charles de Menou d'Aunay Charnisay, 1658.*

chapel, in presence of his wife and all the soldiers and inhabitants.[1]

The Father Superior highly praises the dead chief, and is astonished that the earth does not gape and devour the slanderers who say that he died in desperation, as one abandoned of God. He admits that, in former times, cavillers might have found wherewith to accuse him, but declares that before his death he had amended all his faults. This is the testimony of a Capuchin, whose fraternity he had always favored. The Récollets, on the other hand, whose patron was La Tour, complained that D'Aunay had ill-used them, and demanded redress.[2]

He seems to have been a favorable example of his class, loyal to his faith and his king, tempering pride with courtesy, and generally true to his cherished ideal of the *gentilhomme Français*. In his qualities, as in his birth, he was far above his rival, and his death was the ruin of the only French colony in Acadia that deserved the name.

At the news of his enemy's fate a new hope possessed La Tour. He still had agents in France interested to serve him, while the father of D'Aunay, who acted as his attorney, was feeble with age, and his children were too young to defend their interests.

There is an extraordinary document, bearing date February, 1651, or less than a year after D'Aunay's death. It is a complete reversal of the decree of 1647 in his favor. La Tour suddenly appears as the favorite of royalty, and all the graces before lavished on his enemy are now heaped upon him. The lately proscribed "rebel and traitor" is confirmed as governor and lieutenant-general in New France. His services to God and the king are rehearsed "as of our certain knowledge," and he is praised with the same emphasis used towards D'Aunay in the decree of 1647, and almost in the same words. The paper goes on to say that he, La Tour, would have converted the Indians and conquered Acadia for the king if D'Aunay had not prevented him.[3]

---

[1] *Lettre du Rev. P. Ignace, Capucin, 6 Aoust, 1653.*

[2] Papers to this effect are among the many pieces cited in the *Arrêt du Conseil d'État à l'égard du Seigneur de la Tour, 6 Mars, 1644.*

[3] *Confirmation de Gouverneur et Lieutenant Général pour le Roy de la Nouvelle France, à la Coste de l'Acadie, au Sr. Charles de St. Étienne, Chevalier de la*

Unless this document is a fabrication in the interest of La Tour, as there is some reason to believe, it suggests strange reflections on colonial administration during the minority of Louis XIV. Genuine or not, La Tour profited by it, and after a visit to France, which proved a successful and fruitful one, he returned to Acadia with revived hopes. The widow of D'Aunay had eight children, all minors, and their grand-father, the octogenarian René de Menou, had been appointed their guardian. He sent an incompetent and faithless person to Port Royal to fulfil the wardship of which he was no longer capable.

The unfortunate widow and her children needed better help. D'Aunay had employed as his agent one Le Borgne, a merchant of Rochelle, who now succeeded in getting the old man under his influence and inducing him to sign an ac-knowledgment, said to be false, that D'Aunay's heirs owed him 260,000 livres.[1] Le Borgne next came to Port Royal to push his schemes, and here he inveigled or frightened the widow into signing a paper to the effect that she and her children owed him 205,286 livres. It was fortunate for his un-scrupulous plans that he had to do with the soft and tractable Madame d'Aunay, and not with the high-spirited and intelli-gent amazon, Madame La Tour. Le Borgne now seized on Port Royal as security for the alleged debts, while La Tour on his return from his visit to France induced the perplexed and helpless widow to restore to him Fort St. Jean, con-quered by her late husband. Madame d'Aunay, beset with in-sidious enemies, saw herself and her children in danger of total ruin. She applied to the Duc de Vendôme, grand mas-ter, chief, and superintendent of navigation, and offered to share all her Acadian claims with him if he would help her in her distress; but, from the first, Vendôme looked more to his own interests than to hers. La Tour was not satisfied with her

---

Tour, 27 Fév., 1651. A copy of this strange paper is before me. Comte de Menou, and, after him, his follower, Moreau, doubt the genuineness of the document, which, however, is alluded to without suspicion in the legal paper entitled *Mémoire* in re *Charles de St. Étienne, Seigneur de la Tour* (fils) *et ses frères et sœurs,* 1700. This *Mémoire* is in the interest of the heirs of La Tour, and is to be judged accordingly.

[1] *Mémoire* in re *Charles de St. Étienne,* (fils de la Tour,) etc.

concessions to him, and perplexing questions rose between them touching land claims and the fur trade. To end these troubles she took a desperate step, and on the 24th of February, 1653, married her tormentor, the foe of her late husband, who had now been dead not quite three years.[1] Her chief thought seems to have been for her children whose rights are guarded, though to little purpose, in the marriage contract. She and La Tour took up their abode at Fort St. Jean. Of the children of her first marriage four were boys and four were girls. They were ruined at last by the harpies leagued to plunder them, and sought refuge in France, where the boys were all killed in the wars of Louis XIV., and at least three of the girls became nuns.[2]

Now follow complicated disputes, without dignity or interest, and turning chiefly on the fur trade. Le Borgne and his son, in virtue of their claims on the estate of D'Aunay, which were sustained by the French courts, got a lion's share of Acadia; a part fell also to La Tour and his children by his new wife, while Nicolas Denys kept a feeble hold on the shore of the Gulf of St. Lawrence as far north as Cape Rosiers.

War again broke out between France and England, and, in 1654, Major Robert Sedgwick of Charlestown, Massachusetts, who had served in the civil war as a major-general of Cromwell, led a small New England force to Acadia under a commission from the Protector, captured Fort St. Jean, Port Royal, and all the other French stations, and conquered the colony for England. It was restored to France by the treaty of Breda, and captured again in 1690 by Sir William Phips. The treaty of Ryswick again restored it to France, till, in 1710, it was finally seized for England by General Nicholson.

When, after Sedgwick's expedition, the English were in possession of Acadia, La Tour, not for the first time, tried to fortify his claims by a British title, and, jointly with Thomas Temple and William Crown, obtained a grant of the colony from Cromwell, though he soon after sold his share to his copartner, Temple. He seems to have died in 1666.[3] Descen-

---

[1] Rameau, I. 120. Menou and Moreau think that this marriage took place two or three years later.

[2] Menou, *L'Acadie colonisée.*

[3] Rameau, I. 122.

dants of his were living in Acadia in 1830, and some may probably still be found there. As for D'Aunay, no trace of his blood is left in the land where he gave wealth and life for France and the Church.

CANADA A MISSION

Chapter IV

1653–1658

THE JESUITS AT ONONDAGA

*The Iroquois War • Father Poncet • His Adventures • Jesuit Bold-
ness • Le Moyne's Mission • Chaumonot and Dablon • Iroquois
Ferocity • The Mohawk Kidnappers • Critical Position • The Colony of Onondaga • Speech of Chaumonot • Omens of Destruction
• Device of the Jesuits • The Medicine Feast • The Escape*

IN the summer of 1653, all Canada turned to fasting and penance, processions, vows, and supplications. The saints and
the Virgin were beset with unceasing prayer. The wretched
little colony was like some puny garrison, starving and sick,
compassed with inveterate foes, supplies cut off, and succor
hopeless.

At Montreal, the advance guard of the settlements, a sort
of Castle Dangerous, held by about fifty Frenchmen, and said
by a pious writer of the day to exist only by a continuous
miracle, some two hundred Iroquois fell upon twenty-six
Frenchmen. The Christians were outmatched, eight to one;
but, says the chronicle, the Queen of Heaven was on their
side, and the Son of Mary refuses nothing to his holy
mother.[1] Through her intercession, the Iroquois shot so
wildly that at their first fire every bullet missed its mark, and
they met with a bloody defeat. The palisaded settlement of
Three Rivers, though in a position less exposed than that of
Montreal, was in no less jeopardy. A noted war-chief of the
Mohawk Iroquois had been captured here the year before,
and put to death; and his tribe swarmed out, like a nest of
angry hornets, to revenge him. Not content with defeating
and killing the commandant, Du Plessis Bochart, they encamped during winter in the neighboring forest, watching for
an opportunity to surprise the place. Hunger drove them off,
but they returned in spring, infesting every field and pathway;
till, at length, some six hundred of their warriors landed in
secret and lay hidden in the depths of the woods, silently bid-

[1] Le Mercier, *Relation, 1653,* 3.

ing their time. Having failed, however, in an artifice designed to lure the French out of their defences, they showed themselves on all sides, plundering, burning, and destroying, up to the palisades of the fort.[1]

Of the three settlements which, with their feeble dependencies, then comprised the whole of Canada, Quebec was least exposed to Indian attacks, being partially covered by Montreal and Three Rivers. Nevertheless, there was no safety this year, even under the cannon of Fort St. Louis. At Cap Rouge, a few miles above, the Jesuit Poncet saw a poor woman who had a patch of corn beside her cabin, but could find nobody to harvest it. The father went to seek aid, met one Mathurin Franchetot, whom he persuaded to undertake the charitable task, and was returning with him, when they both fell into an ambuscade of Iroquois, who seized them and dragged them off. Thirty-two men embarked in canoes at Quebec to follow the retreating savages and rescue the prisoners. Pushing rapidly up the St. Lawrence, they approached Three Rivers, found it beset by the Mohawks, and bravely threw themselves into it, to the great joy of its defenders and discouragement of the assailants.

Meanwhile, the intercession of the Virgin wrought new marvels at Montreal, and a bright ray of hope beamed forth from the darkness and the storm to cheer the hearts of her votaries. It was on the 26th of June that sixty of the Onondaga Iroquois appeared in sight of the fort, shouting from a distance that they came on an errand of peace, and asking safe-conduct for some of their number. Guns, scalping-knives, tomahawks, were all laid aside; and, with a confidence truly astonishing, a deputation of chiefs, naked and defenceless, came into the midst of those whom they had betrayed so often. The French had a mind to seize them, and pay them in kind for past treachery; but they refrained, seeing in this wondrous change of heart the manifest hand of Heaven. Nevertheless, it can be explained without a miracle. The Iroquois, or, at least, the western nations of their league, had just be-

---

[1] So bent were they on taking the place, that they brought their families, in order to make a permanent settlement. — Marie de l'Incarnation, *Lettre du 6 Sept.*, *1653*.

come involved in war with their neighbors the Eries,[1] and "one war at a time" was the sage maxim of their policy.

All was smiles and blandishment in the fort at Montreal; presents were exchanged, and the deputies departed, bearing home golden reports of the French. An Oneida deputation soon followed; but the enraged Mohawks still infested Montreal and beleaguered Three Rivers, till one of their principal chiefs and four of their best warriors were captured by a party of Christian Hurons. Then, seeing themselves abandoned by the other nations of the league and left to wage the war alone, they, too, made overtures of peace.

A grand council was held at Quebec. Speeches were made, and wampum-belts exchanged. The Iroquois left some of their chief men as pledges of sincerity, and two young soldiers offered themselves as reciprocal pledges on the part of the French. The war was over; at least Canada had found a moment to take breath for the next struggle. The fur trade was restored again, with promise of plenty; for the beaver, profiting by the quarrels of their human foes, had of late greatly multiplied. It was a change from death to life; for Canada lived on the beaver, and, robbed of this, her only sustenance, had been dying slowly since the strife began.[2]

"Yesterday," writes Father Le Mercier, "all was dejection and gloom; to-day, all is smiles and gayety. On Wednesday, massacre, burning, and pillage; on Thursday, gifts and visits, as among friends. If the Iroquois have their hidden designs, so, too, has God.

"On the day of the Visitation of the Holy Virgin, the chief, Aontarisati,[3] so regretted by the Iroquois, was taken prisoner by our Indians, instructed by our fathers, and baptized; and, on the same day, being put to death, he ascended to heaven.

---

[1] See *Jesuits in North America*, 705. The Iroquois, it will be remembered, consisted of five "nations," or tribes,—the Mohawks, Oneidas, Onondagas, Cayugas, and Senecas. For an account of them, see the work just cited, Introduction.

[2] According to Le Mercier, beaver to the value of from 200,000 to 300,000 livres was yearly brought down to the colony before the destruction of the Hurons (1649–50). Three years later, not one beaver skin was brought to Montreal during a twelvemonth, and Three Rivers and Quebec had barely enough to pay for keeping the fortifications in repair.

[3] The chief whose death had so enraged the Mohawks.

I doubt not that he thanked the Virgin for his misfortune and the blessing that followed, and that he prayed to God for his countrymen.

"The people of Montreal made a solemn vow to celebrate publicly the *fête* of this mother of all blessings; whereupon the Iroquois came to ask for peace.

"It was on the day of the Assumption of this Queen of angels and of men that the Hurons took at Montreal that other famous Iroquois chief, whose capture caused the Mohawks to seek our alliance.

"On the day when the Church honors the Nativity of the Holy Virgin, the Iroquois granted Father Poncet his life; and he, or rather the Holy Virgin and the holy angels, labored so well in the work of peace, that on St. Michael's Day it was resolved in a council of the elders that the father should be conducted to Quebec, and a lasting treaty made with the French."[1]

Happy as was this consummation, Father Poncet's path to it had been a thorny one. He has left us his own rueful story, written in obedience to the command of his superior. He and his companion in misery had been hurried through the forests, from Cap Rouge on the St. Lawrence to the Indian towns on the Mohawk. He tells us how he slept among dank weeds, dropping with the cold dew; how frightful colics assailed him as he waded waist-deep through a mountain stream; how one of his feet was blistered and one of his legs benumbed; how an Indian snatched away his reliquary and lost the precious contents. "I had," he says, "a picture of Saint Ignatius with our Lord bearing the cross, and another of Our Lady of Pity surrounded by the five wounds of her Son. They were my joy and my consolation; but I hid them in a bush, lest the Indians should laugh at them." He kept, however, a little image of the crown of thorns, in which he found great comfort, as well as in communion with his patron saints, Saint Raphael, Saint Martha, and Saint Joseph. On one occasion he asked these celestial friends for something to soothe his thirst, and for a bowl of broth to revive his strength. Scarcely had he framed the petition when an Indian gave him

[1] *Relation*, 1653, 18.

some wild plums; and in the evening, as he lay fainting on the ground, another brought him the coveted broth. Weary and forlorn, he reached at last the lower Mohawk town, where, after being stripped, and, with his companion, forced to run the gauntlet, he was placed on a scaffold of bark, surrounded by a crowd of grinning and mocking savages. As it began to rain, they took him into one of their lodges, and amused themselves by making him dance, sing, and perform various fantastic tricks for their amusement. He seems to have done his best to please them; "but," adds the chronicler, "I will say in passing, that as he did not succeed to their liking in these buffooneries (*singeries*), they would have put him to death, if a young Huron prisoner had not offered himself to sing, dance, and make wry faces in place of the father, who had never learned the trade."

Having sufficiently amused themselves, they left him for a time in peace; when an old one-eyed Indian approached, took his hands, examined them, selected the left forefinger, and calling a child four or five years old, gave him a knife, and told him to cut it off, which the imp proceeded to do, his victim meanwhile singing the *Vexilla Regis*. After this preliminary, they would have burned him, like Franchetot, his unfortunate companion, had not a squaw happily adopted him in place, as he says, of a deceased brother. He was installed at once in the lodge of his new relatives, where, bereft of every rag of Christian clothing, and attired in leggins, moccasins, and a greasy shirt, the astonished father saw himself transformed into an Iroquois. But his deliverance was at hand. A special agreement providing for it had formed a part of the treaty concluded at Quebec; and he now learned that he was to be restored to his countrymen. After a march of almost intolerable hardship, he saw himself once more among Christians; Heaven, as he modestly thinks, having found him unworthy of martyrdom.

"At last," he writes, "we reached Montreal on the 21st of October, the nine weeks of my captivity being accomplished, in honor of Saint Michael and all the holy angels. On the 6th of November the Iroquois who conducted me made their presents to confirm the peace; and thus, on a Sunday evening, eighty-and-one days after my capture,—that is to say, nine times nine days,—this great business of the peace was happily concluded, the holy angels showing by this number nine, which is specially dedicated to them, the part they bore in this holy work."[1] This incessant supernaturalism is the key to the early history of New France.

Peace was made; but would peace endure? There was little chance of it, and this for several reasons. First, the native fickleness of the Iroquois, who, astute and politic to a surprising degree, were in certain respects, like all savages, mere grown-up children. Next, their total want of control over their fierce and capricious young warriors, any one of whom could break the peace with impunity whenever he saw fit; and, above all, the strong probability that the Iroquois had made peace in order, under cover of it, to butcher or kidnap the unhappy remnant of the Hurons who were living, under French protection, on the island of Orleans, immediately below Quebec. I have already told the story of the destruction of this people and of the Jesuit missions established among them.[2] The conquerors were eager to complete their bloody triumph by seizing upon the refugees of Orleans, killing the elders, and strengthening their own tribes by the adoption of the women, children, and youths. The Mohawks and the Onondagas were competitors for the prize. Each coveted the Huron colony, and each was jealous lest his rival should pounce upon it first.

When the Mohawks brought home Poncet, they covertly gave wampum-belts to the Huron chiefs, and invited them to remove to their villages. It was the wolf's invitation to the lamb. The Hurons, aghast with terror, went secretly to the Jesuits, and told them that demons had whispered in their ears an invitation to destruction. So helpless were both the Hurons and their French supporters, that they saw no recourse but dissimulation. The Hurons promised to go, and only sought excuses to gain time.

The Onondagas had a deeper plan. Their towns were already full of Huron captives, former converts of the Jesuits, cherishing their memory and constantly repeating their

[1] Poncet in *Relation, 1653*, 17. On Poncet's captivity see also *Morale Pratique des Jésuites*, vol. xxxiv. (4to) chap. xii.
[2] *Jesuits in North America*.

praises. Hence their tyrants conceived the idea that by planting at Onondaga a colony of Frenchmen under the direction of these beloved fathers, the Hurons of Orleans, disarmed of suspicion, might readily be led to join them. Other motives, as we shall see, tended to the same end, and the Onondaga deputies begged, or rather demanded, that a colony of Frenchmen should be sent among them.

Here was a dilemma. Was not this, like the Mohawk invitation to the Hurons, an invitation to butchery? On the other hand, to refuse would probably kindle the war afresh. The Jesuits had long nursed a project bold to temerity. Their great Huron mission was ruined; but might not another be built up among the authors of this ruin, and the Iroquois themselves, tamed by the power of the Faith, be annexed to the kingdoms of Heaven and of France? Thus would peace be restored to Canada, a barrier of fire opposed to the Dutch and English heretics, and the power of the Jesuits vastly increased. Yet the time was hardly ripe for such an attempt. Before thrusting a head into the tiger's jaws, it would be well to try the effect of thrusting in a hand. They resolved to compromise with the danger, and before risking a colony at Onondaga to send thither an envoy who could soothe the Indians, confirm them in pacific designs, and pave the way for more decisive steps. The choice fell on Father Simon Le Moyne.

The errand was mainly a political one; and this sagacious and able priest, versed in Indian languages and customs, was well suited to do it. "On the second day of the month of July, the festival of the Visitation of the Most Holy Virgin, ever favorable to our enterprises, Father Simon Le Moyne set out from Quebec for the country of the Onondaga Iroquois." In these words does Father Le Mercier chronicle the departure of his brother Jesuit. Scarcely was he gone when a band of Mohawks, under a redoubtable half-breed known as the Flemish Bastard, arrived at Quebec; and, when they heard that the envoy was to go to the Onondagas without visiting their tribe, they took the imagined slight in high dudgeon, displaying such jealousy and ire that a letter was sent after Le Moyne, directing him to proceed to the Mohawk towns before his return. But he was already beyond reach, and the angry Mohawks were left to digest their wrath.

At Montreal, Le Moyne took a canoe, a young Frenchman, and two or three Indians, and began the tumultuous journey of the Upper St. Lawrence. Nature, or habit, had taught him to love the wilderness life. He and his companions had struggled all day against the surges of La Chine, and were bivouacked at evening by the Lake of St. Louis, when a cloud of mosquitoes fell upon them, followed by a shower of warm rain. The father, stretched under a tree, seems clearly to have enjoyed himself. "It is a pleasure," he writes, "the sweetest and most innocent imaginable, to have no other shelter than trees planted by Nature since the creation of the world." Sometimes, during their journey, this primitive tent proved insufficient, and they would build a bark hut or find a partial shelter under their inverted canoe. Now they glided smoothly over the sunny bosom of the calm and smiling river, and now strained every nerve to fight their slow way against the rapids, dragging their canoe upward in the shallow water by the shore, as one leads an unwilling horse by the bridle, or shouldering it and bearing it through the forest to the smoother current above. Game abounded; and they saw great herds of elk quietly defiling between the water and the woods, with little heed of men, who in that perilous region found employment enough in hunting one another.

At the entrance of Lake Ontario they met a party of Iroquois fishermen, who proved friendly, and guided them on their way. Ascending the Onondaga, they neared their destination; and now all misgivings as to their reception at the Iroquois capital were dispelled. The inhabitants came to meet them, bringing roasting ears of the young maize and bread made of its pulp, than which they knew no luxury more exquisite. Their faces beamed welcome. Le Moyne was astonished. "I never," he says, "saw the like among Indians before." They were flattered by his visit, and, for the moment, were glad to see him. They hoped for great advantages from the residence of Frenchmen among them; and, having the Erie war on their hands, they wished for peace with Canada. "One would call me brother," writes Le Moyne; "another, uncle; another, cousin. I never had so many relations."

He was overjoyed to find that many of the Huron converts, who had long been captives at Onondaga, had not forgotten the teachings of their Jesuit instructors. Such influence as they had with their conquerors was sure to be exerted in behalf of the French. Deputies of the Senecas, Cayugas, and Oneidas at length arrived, and, on the 10th of August, the criers passed through the town, summoning all to hear the words of Onontio. The naked dignitaries, sitting, squatting, or lying at full length, thronged the smoky hall of council. The father knelt and prayed in a loud voice, invoking the aid of Heaven, cursing the demons who are spirits of discord, and calling on the tutelar angels of the country to open the ears of his listeners. Then he opened his packet of presents and began his speech. "I was full two hours," he says, "in making it, speaking in the tone of a chief, and walking to and fro, after their fashion, like an actor on a theatre." Not only did he imitate the prolonged accents of the Iroquois orators, but he adopted and improved their figures of speech, and addressed them in turn by their respective tribes, bands, and families, calling their men of note by name, as if he had been born among them. They were delighted; and their ejaculations of approval— *hoh-hoh-hoh*—came thick and fast at every pause of his harangue. Especially were they pleased with the eighth, ninth, tenth, and eleventh presents, whereby the reverend speaker gave to the four upper nations of the league four hatchets to strike their new enemies, the Eries; while by another present he metaphorically daubed their faces with the war-paint. However it may have suited the character of a Christian priest to hound on these savage hordes to a war of extermination which they had themselves provoked, it is certain that, as a politician, Le Moyne did wisely; since in the war with the Eries lay the best hope of peace for the French.

The reply of the Indian orator was friendly to overflowing. He prayed his French brethren to choose a spot on the lake of Onondaga, where they might dwell in the country of the Iroquois, as they dwelt already in their hearts. Le Moyne promised, and made two presents to confirm the pledge. Then, his mission fulfilled, he set out on his return, attended by a troop of Indians. As he approached the lake, his escort showed him a large spring of water, possessed, as they told him, by a bad spirit. Le Moyne tasted it, then boiled a little of it, and produced a quantity of excellent salt. He had discovered the famous salt-springs of Onondaga. Fishing and hunting, the party pursued their way till, at noon of the 7th of September, Le Moyne reached Montreal.[1]

When he reached Quebec, his tidings cheered for a while the anxious hearts of its tenants; but an unwonted incident soon told them how hollow was the ground beneath their feet. Le Moyne, accompanied by two Onondagas and several Hurons and Algonquins, was returning to Montreal, when he and his companions were set upon by a war-party of Mohawks. The Hurons and Algonquins were killed. One of the Onondagas shared their fate, and the other, with Le Moyne himself, was seized and bound fast. The captive Onondaga, however, was so loud in his threats and denunciations, that the Mohawks released both him and the Jesuit.[2] Here was a foreshadowing of civil war, Mohawk against Onondaga, Iroquois against Iroquois. The quarrel was patched up, but fresh provocations were imminent.

The Mohawks took no part in the Erie war, and hence their hands were free to fight the French and the tribes allied with them. Reckless of their promises, they began a series of butcheries, fell upon the French at Isle aux Oies, killed a lay brother of the Jesuits at Sillery, and attacked Montreal. Here, being roughly handled, they came for a time to their senses, and offered terms, promising to spare the French, but declaring that they would still wage war against the Hurons and Algonquins. These were allies whom the French were pledged to protect; but so helpless was the colony, that the insolent and humiliating proffer was accepted, and another peace ensued, as hollow as the last. The indefatigable Le Moyne was sent to the Mohawk towns to confirm it, "so far," says the chronicle, "as it is possible to confirm a peace made by infidels backed by heretics."[3] The Mohawks received him with great rejoicing; yet his life was not safe for a moment. A warrior, feigning madness, raved through the town with uplifted hatchet, howling for his blood; but the saints watched over

---

[1] *Journal du Père Le Moine, Relation, 1654*, chaps. vi. vii.

[2] Compare *Relation*, 1654, 33, and *Lettre de Marie de l'Incarnation, 18 Octobre, 1654.*

[3] *Copie de Deux Lettres envoyées de la Nouvelle France au Père Procureur des Missions de la Compagnie de Jésus.*

him and balked the machinations of hell. He came off alive and returned to Montreal, spent with famine and fatigue.

Meanwhile a deputation of eighteen Onondaga chiefs arrived at Quebec. There was a grand council. The Onondagas demanded a colony of Frenchmen to dwell among them. Lauson, the governor, dared neither to consent nor to refuse. A middle course was chosen, and two Jesuits, Chaumonot and Dablon, were sent, like Le Moyne, partly to gain time, partly to reconnoitre, and partly to confirm the Onondagas in such good intentions as they might entertain. Chaumonot was a veteran of the Huron mission, who, miraculously as he himself supposed, had acquired a great fluency in the Huron tongue, which is closely allied to that of the Iroquois. Dablon, a new-comer, spoke, as yet, no Indian.

Their voyage up the St. Lawrence was enlivened by an extraordinary bear-hunt, and by the antics of one of their Indian attendants, who, having dreamed that he had swallowed a frog, roused the whole camp by the gymnastics with which he tried to rid himself of the intruder. On approaching Onondaga, they were met by a chief who sang a song of welcome, a part of which he seasoned with touches of humor, apostrophizing the fish in the river Onondaga, naming each sort, great or small, and calling on them in turn to come into the nets of the Frenchmen and sacrifice life cheerfully for their behoof. Hereupon there was much laughter among the Indian auditors. An unwonted cleanliness reigned in the town; the streets had been cleared of refuse, and the arched roofs of the long houses of bark were covered with red-skinned children staring at the entry of the "black robes." Crowds followed behind, and all was jubilation. The dignitaries of the tribe met them on the way, and greeted them with a speech of welcome. A feast of bear's meat awaited them; but, unhappily, it was Friday, and the fathers were forced to abstain.

"On Monday, the 15th of November, at nine in the morning, after having secretly sent to Paradise a dying infant by the waters of baptism, all the elders and the people having assembled, we opened the council by public prayer." Thus writes Father Dablon. His colleague, Chaumonot, a Frenchman bred in Italy, now rose, with a long belt of wampum in his hand, and proceeded to make so effective a display of his rhetorical gifts that the Indians were lost in admiration, and their orators put to the blush by his improvements on their own metaphors. "If he had spoken all day," said the delighted auditors, "we should not have had enough of it." "The Dutch," added others, "have neither brains nor tongues; they never tell us about Paradise and Hell; on the contrary, they lead us into bad ways."

On the next day the chiefs returned their answer. The council opened with a song or chant, which was divided into six parts, and which, according to Dablon, was exceedingly well sung. The burden of the fifth part was as follows: —

"Farewell war; farewell tomahawk; we have been fools till now; henceforth we will be brothers; yes, we will be brothers."

Then came four presents, the third of which enraptured the fathers. It was a belt of seven thousand beads of wampum. "But this," says Dablon, "was as nothing to the words that accompanied it." "It is the gift of the faith," said the orator; "it is to tell you that we are believers; it is to beg you not to tire of instructing us; have patience, seeing that we are so dull in learning prayer; push it into our heads and our hearts." Then he led Chaumonot into the midst of the assembly, clasped him in his arms, tied the belt about his waist, and protested, with a suspicious redundancy of words, that as he clasped the father, so would he clasp the faith.

What had wrought this sudden change of heart? The eagerness of the Onondagas that the French should settle among them, had, no doubt, a large share in it. For the rest, the two Jesuits saw abundant signs of the fierce, uncertain nature of those with whom they were dealing. Erie prisoners were brought in and tortured before their eyes, one of them being a young stoic of about ten years, who endured his fate without a single outcry. Huron women and children, taken in war and adopted by their captors, were killed on the slightest provocation, and sometimes from mere caprice. For several days the whole town was in an uproar with the crazy follies of the "dream feast,"[1] and one of the Fathers nearly lost his life in this Indian Bedlam.

[1] See *Jesuits in North America*, 447.

One point was clear; the French must make a settlement at Onondaga, and that speedily, or, despite their professions of brotherhood, the Onondagas would make war. Their attitude became menacing; from urgency they passed to threats; and the two priests felt that the critical posture of affairs must at once be reported at Quebec. But here a difficulty arose. It was the beaver-hunting season; and, eager as were the Indians for a French colony, not one of them would offer to conduct the Jesuits to Quebec in order to fetch one. It was not until nine masses had been said to Saint John the Baptist, that a number of Indians consented to forego their hunting, and escort Father Dablon home.[1] Chaumonot remained at Onondaga, to watch his dangerous hosts and soothe their rising jealousies.

It was the 2d of March when Dablon began his journey. His constitution must have been of iron, or he would have succumbed to the appalling hardships of the way. It was neither winter nor spring. The lakes and streams were not yet open, but the half-thawed ice gave way beneath the foot. One of the Indians fell through and was drowned. Swamp and forest were clogged with sodden snow, and ceaseless rains drenched them as they toiled on, knee-deep in slush. Happily, the St. Lawrence was open. They found an old wooden canoe by the shore, embarked, and reached Montreal after a journey of four weeks.

Dablon descended to Quebec. There was long and anxious counsel in the chambers of Fort St. Louis. The Jesuits had information that, if the demands of the Onondagas were rejected, they would join the Mohawks to destroy Canada. But why were they so eager for a colony of Frenchmen? Did they want them as hostages, that they might attack the Hurons and Algonquins without risk of French interference; or would they masacre them, and then, like tigers mad with the taste of blood, turn upon the helpless settlements of the St. Lawrence? An abyss yawned on either hand. Lauson, the governor, was in an agony of indecision, but at length declared for the lesser and remoter peril, and gave his voice for the colony. The Jesuits were of the same mind, though it was they, and not he, who must bear the brunt of danger. "The blood of

[1] De Quen, *Relation*, 1656, 35. Chaumonot, in his Autobiography, ascribes the miracle to the intercession of the deceased Brébeuf.

the martyrs is the seed of the Church," said one of them, "and, if we die by the fires of the Iroquois, we shall have won eternal life by snatching souls from the fires of Hell."

Preparation was begun at once. The expense fell on the Jesuits, and the outfit is said to have cost them seven thousand livres,—a heavy sum for Canada at that day. A pious gentleman, Zachary Du Puys, major of the fort of Quebec, joined the expedition with ten soldiers; and between thirty and forty other Frenchmen also enrolled themselves, impelled by devotion or destitution. Four Jesuits, Le Mercier, the superior, with Dablon, Ménard, and Frémin, besides two lay brothers of the order, formed, as it were, the pivot of the enterprise. The governor made them the grant of a hundred square leagues of land in the heart of the Iroquois country,—a preposterous act, which, had the Iroquois known it, would have rekindled the war; but Lauson had a mania for land-grants, and was himself the proprietor of vast domains which he could have occupied only at the cost of his scalp.

Embarked in two large boats and followed by twelve canoes filled with Hurons, Onondagas, and a few Senecas lately arrived, they set out on the 17th of May "to attack the demons," as Le Mercier writes, "in their very stronghold." With shouts, tears, and benedictions, priests, soldiers, and inhabitants waved farewell from the strand. They passed the bare steeps of Cape Diamond and the mission-house nestled beneath the heights of Sillery, and vanished from the anxious eyes that watched the last gleam of their receding oars.[1]

Meanwhile three hundred Mohawk warriors had taken the war-path, bent on killing or kidnapping the Hurons of Orleans. When they heard of the departure of the colonists for Onondaga, their rage was unbounded; for not only were they full of jealousy towards their Onondaga confederates, but they had hitherto derived great profit from the control which their local position gave them over the traffic between this tribe and the Dutch of the Hudson, upon whom the Onondagas, in common with all the upper Iroquois, had been dependent for their guns, hatchets, scalping-knives, beads, blankets, and brandy. These supplies would now be furnished

[1] Marie de l'Incarnation, *Lettres*, *1656*. Le Mercier, *Relation*, *1657*, chap. iv. Chaulmer, *Nouveau Monde*, II. 265, 322, 319.

by the French, and the Mohawk speculators saw their occupation gone. Nevertheless, they had just made peace with the French, and, for the moment, were not quite in the mood to break it. To wreak their spite, they took a middle course, crouched in ambush among the bushes at Point St. Croix, ten or twelve leagues above Quebec, allowed the boats bearing the French to pass unmolested, and fired a volley at the canoes in the rear, filled with Onondagas, Senecas, and Hurons. Then they fell upon them with a yell, and, after wounding a lay brother of the Jesuits who was among them, flogged and bound such of the Indians as they could seize. The astonished Onondagas protested and threatened; whereupon the Mohawks feigned great surprise, declared that they had mistaken them for Hurons, called them brothers, and suffered the whole party to escape without further injury.[1]

The three hundred maurauders now paddled their large canoes of elm-bark stealthily down the current, passed Quebec undiscovered in the dark night of the 19th of May, landed in early morning on the island of Orleans, and ambushed themselves to surprise the Hurons as they came to labor in their cornfields. They were tolerably successful, killed six, and captured more than eighty, the rest taking refuge in their fort, where the Mohawks dared not attack them.

At noon, the French on the rock of Quebec saw forty canoes approaching from the island of Orleans, and defiling, with insolent parade, in front of the town, all crowded with the Mohawks and their prisoners, among whom were a great number of Huron girls. Their captors, as they passed, forced them to sing and dance. The Hurons were the allies, or rather the wards of the French, who were in every way pledged to protect them. Yet the cannon of Fort St. Louis were silent, and the crowd stood gaping in bewilderment and fright. Had an attack been made, nothing but a complete success and the capture of many prisoners to serve as hostages could have prevented the enraged Mohawks from taking their revenge on the Onondaga colonists. The emergency demanded a prompt and clear-sighted soldier. The governor, Lauson, was a gray-haired civilian, who, however enterprising as a speculator in

---

[1] Compare Marie de l'Incarnation, *Lettre 14 Août, 1656,* Le Jeune, *Relation, 1657,* 9.

wild lands, was in no way matched to the desperate crisis of the hour. Some of the Mohawks landed above and below the town, and plundered the houses from which the scared inhabitants had fled. Not a soldier stirred and not a gun was fired. The French, bullied by a horde of naked savages, became an object of contempt to their own allies.

The Mohawks carried their prisoners home, burned six of them, and adopted or rather enslaved the rest.[1]

Meanwhile the Onondaga colonists pursued their perilous way. At Montreal they exchanged their heavy boats for canoes, and resumed their journey with a flotilla of twenty of these sylvan vessels. A few days after, the Indians of the party had the satisfaction of pillaging a small band of Mohawk hunters, in vicarious reprisal for their own wrongs. On the 26th of June, as they neared Lake Ontario, they heard a loud and lamentable voice from the edge of the forest; whereupon, having beaten their drum to show that they were Frenchmen, they beheld a spectral figure, lean and covered with scars, which proved to be a pious Huron, one Joachim Ondakout, captured by the Mohawks in their descent on the island of Orleans, five or six weeks before. They had carried him to their village and begun to torture him; after which they tied him fast and lay down to sleep, thinking to resume their pleasure on the morrow. His cuts and burns being only on the surface, he had the good fortune to free himself from his bonds, and, naked as he was, to escape to the woods. He held his course north-westward, through regions even now a wilderness, gathered wild strawberries to sustain life, and, in fifteen days, reached the St. Lawrence, nearly dead with exhaustion. The Frenchmen gave him food and a canoe, and the living skeleton paddled with a light heart for Quebec.

The colonists themselves soon began to suffer from hunger. Their fishing failed on Lake Ontario, and they were forced to content themselves with cranberries of the last year, gathered in the meadows. Of their Indians, all but five deserted them. The Father Superior fell ill, and when they reached the mouth of the Oswego many of the starving Frenchmen had completely lost heart. Weary and faint, they dragged their canoes

[1] See authorities just cited, and Perrot, *Mœurs des Sauvages*, 106.

up the rapids, when suddenly they were cheered by the sight of a stranger canoe swiftly descending the current. The Onondagas, aware of their approach, had sent it to meet them, laden with Indian corn and fresh salmon. Two more canoes followed, freighted like the first; and now all was abundance till they reached their journey's end, the Lake of Onondaga. It lay before them in the July sun, a glittering mirror, framed in forest verdure.

They knew that Chaumonot with a crowd of Indians was awaiting them at a spot on the margin of the water, which he and Dablon had chosen as the site of their settlement. Landing on the strand, they fired, to give notice of their approach, five small cannon which they had brought in their canoes. Waves, woods, and hills resounded with the thunder of their miniature artillery. Then re-embarking, they advanced in order, four canoes abreast, towards the destined spot. In front floated their banner of white silk, embroidered in large letters with the name of Jesus. Here were Du Puys and his soldiers, with the picturesque uniforms and quaint weapons of their time; Le Mercier and his Jesuits in robes of black; hunters and bush-rangers; Indians painted and feathered for a festal day. As they neared the place where a spring bubbling from the hillside is still known as the "Jesuits' Well," they saw the edge of the forest dark with the muster of savages whose yells of welcome answered the salvo of their guns. Happily for them, a flood of summer rain saved them from the harangues of the Onondaga orators, and forced white men and red alike to seek such shelter as they could find. Their hosts, with hospitable intent, would fain have sung and danced all night; but the Frenchmen pleaded fatigue, and the courteous savages, squatting around their tents, chanted in monotonous tones to lull them to sleep. In the morning they woke refreshed, sang *Te Deum*, reared an altar, and, with a solemn mass, took possession of the country in the name of Jesus.[1]

Three things, which they saw or heard of in their new home, excited their astonishment. The first was the vast flight of wild pigeons which in spring darkened the air around the Lake of Onondaga; the second was the salt springs of Salina;

[1] Le Mercier, *Relation, 1657,* 14.

the third was the rattlesnakes, which Le Mercier describes with excellent precision, adding that, as he learns from the Indians, their tails are good for toothache and their flesh for fever. These reptiles, for reasons best known to themselves, haunted the neighborhood of the salt-springs, but did not intrude their presence into the abode of the French.

On the 17th of July, Le Mercier and Chaumonot, escorted by a file of soldiers, set out for Onondaga, scarcely five leagues distant. They followed the Indian trail, under the leafy arches of the woods, by hill and hollow, still swamp and gurgling brook, till through the opening foliage they saw the Iroquois capital, compassed with cornfields and girt with its rugged palisade. As the Jesuits, like black spectres, issued from the shadows of the forest, followed by the plumed soldiers with shouldered arquebuses, the red-skinned population swarmed out like bees, and they defiled to the town through gazing and admiring throngs. All conspired to welcome them. Feast followed feast throughout the afternoon, till, what with harangues and songs, bear's meat, beaver-tails, and venison, beans, corn, and grease, they were wellnigh killed with kindness. "If, after this, they murder us," writes Le Mercier, "it will be from fickleness, not premeditated treachery." But the Jesuits, it seems, had not sounded the depths of Iroquois dissimulation.[1]

There was one exception to the real or pretended joy. Some Mohawks were in the town, and their orator was insolent and sarcastic; but the ready tongue of Chaumonot turned the laugh against him and put him to shame.

Here burned the council fire of the Iroquois, and at this very time the deputies of the five tribes were assembling. The session opened on the 24th. In the great council house, on the earthen floor and the broad platforms beneath the smoke-begrimed concave of the bark roof, stood, sat, or squatted, the wisdom and valor of the confederacy; Mohawks, Oneidas, Onondagas, Cayugas, and Senecas; sachems, counsellors, or-

---

[1] The Jesuits were afterwards told by Hurons, captive among the Mohawks and the Onondagas, that, from the first, it was intended to massacre the French as soon as their presence had attracted the remnant of the Hurons of Orleans into the power of the Onondagas. *Lettre du P. Ragueneau au R. P. Provincial, 31 Août, 1658.*

ators, warriors fresh from Erie victories; tall, stalwart figures, limbed like Grecian statues.

The pressing business of the council over, it was Chaumonot's turn to speak. But, first, all the Frenchmen, kneeling in a row, with clasped hands, sang the *Veni Creator*, amid the silent admiration of the auditors. Then Chaumonot rose, with an immense wampum-belt in his hand.

"It is not trade that brings us here. Do you think that your beaver skins can pay us for all our toils and dangers? Keep them, if you like; or, if any fall into our hands, we shall use them only for your service. We seek not the things that perish. It is for the Faith that we have left our homes to live in your hovels of bark, and eat food which the beasts of our country would scarcely touch. We are the messengers whom God has sent to tell you that his Son became a man for the love of you; that this man, the Son of God, is the prince and master of men; that he has prepared in heaven eternal joys for those who obey him, and kindled the fires of hell for those who will not receive his word. If you reject it, whoever you are,—Onondaga, Seneca, Mohawk, Cayuga, or Oneida,— know that Jesus Christ, who inspires my heart and my voice, will plunge you one day into hell. Avert this ruin; be not the authors of your own destruction; accept the truth; listen to the voice of the Omnipotent."

Such, in brief, was the pith of the father's exhortation. As he spoke Indian like a native, and as his voice and gestures answered to his words, we may believe what Le Mercier tells us, that his hearers listened with mingled wonder, admiration, and terror. The work was well begun. The Jesuits struck while the iron was hot, built a small chapel for the mass, installed themselves in the town, and preached and catechised from morning till night.

The Frenchmen at the lake were not idle. The chosen site of their settlement was the crown of a hill commanding a broad view of waters and forests. The axemen fell to their work, and a ghastly wound soon gaped in the green bosom of the woodland. Here, among the stumps and prostrate trees of the unsightly clearing, the blacksmith built his forge, saw and hammer plied their trade; palisades were shaped and beams squared, in spite of heat, mosquitoes, and fever. At one time twenty men were ill, and lay gasping under a wretched shed of bark; but they all recovered, and the work went on till at length a capacious house, large enough to hold the whole colony, rose above the ruin of the forest. A palisade was set around it, and the Mission of Saint Mary of Gannentaa[1] was begun.

France and the Faith were intrenched on the Lake of Onondaga. How long would they remain there? The future alone could tell. The mission, it must not be forgotten, had a double scope, half ecclesiastical, half political. The Jesuits had essayed a fearful task,—to convert the Iroquois to God and to the king, thwart the Dutch heretics of the Hudson, save souls from hell, avert ruin from Canada, and thus raise their order to a place of honor and influence both hard earned and well earned. The mission at Lake Onondaga was but a base of operations. Long before they were lodged and fortified here, Chaumonot and Ménard set out for the Cayugas, whence the former proceeded to the Senecas, the most numerous and powerful of the five confederate nations; and in the following spring another mission was begun among the Oneidas. Their reception was not unfriendly; but such was the reticence and dissimulation of these inscrutable savages, that it was impossible to foretell results. The women proved, as might be expected, far more impressible than the men; and in them the fathers placed great hope; since in this, the most savage people of the continent, women held a degree of political influence never perhaps equalled in any civilized nation.[2]

[1] Gannentaa or Ganuntaah is still the Iroquois name for Lake Onondaga. According to Morgan, it means "Material for Council Fire."

[2] Women, among the Iroquois, had a council of their own, which, according to Lafitau, who knew this people well, had the initiative in discussion, subjects presented by them being settled in the council of chiefs and elders. In this latter council the women had an orator, often of their own sex, to represent them. The matrons had a leading voice in determining the succession of chiefs. There were also female chiefs, one of whom, with her attendants, came to Quebec with an embassy in 1655 (Marie de l'Incarnation). In the torture of prisoners, great deference was paid to the judgment of the women, who, says Champlain, were thought more skilful and subtle than the men.

The learned Lafitau, whose book appeared in 1724, dwells at length on the resemblance of the Iroquois to the ancient Lycians, among whom, according

But while infants were baptized and squaws converted, the crosses of the mission were many and great. The devil bestirred himself with more than his ordinary activity; "for," as one of the fathers writes, "when in sundry nations of the earth men are rising up in strife against us (the Jesuits), then how much more the demons, on whom we continually wage war!" It was these infernal sprites, as the priests believed, who engendered suspicions and calumnies in the dark and superstitious minds of the Iroquois, and prompted them in dreams to destroy the apostles of the faith. Whether the foe was of earth or hell, the Jesuits were like those who tread the lava-crust that palpitates with the throes of the coming eruption, while the molten death beneath their feet glares white-hot through a thousand crevices. Yet, with a sublime enthusiasm and a glorious constancy, they toiled and they hoped, though the skies around were black with portent.

In the year in which the colony at Onondaga was begun, the Mohawks murdered the Jesuit Garreau, on his way up the Ottawa. In the following spring, a hundred Mohawk warriors came to Quebec, to carry more of the Hurons into slavery, though the remnant of that unhappy people, since the catastrophe of the last year, had sought safety in a palisaded camp within the limits of the French town, and immediately under the ramparts of Fort St. Louis. Here, one might think, they would have been safe; but Charny, son and successor of Lauson, seems to have been even more imbecile than his father, and listened meekly to the threats of the insolent strangers who told him that unless he abandoned the Hurons to their mercy, both they and the French should feel the weight of Mohawk tomahawks. They demanded further, that the French should give them boats to carry their prisoners; but, as there were none at hand, this last humiliation was spared. The Mohawks were forced to make canoes, in which they carried off as many as possible of their victims.

When the Onondagas learned this last exploit of their ri-

---

to Grecian writers, women were in the ascendant. "Gynecocracy, or the rule of women," continues Lafitau, "which was the foundation of the Lycian government, was probably common in early times to nearly all the barbarous people of Greece." *Mœurs des Sauvages*, I. 460 (ed. in 4to)

vals, their jealousy knew no bounds, and a troop of them descended to Quebec to claim their share in the human plunder. Deserted by the French, the despairing Hurons abandoned themselves to their fate, and about fifty of those whom the Mohawks had left obeyed the behest of their tyrants and embarked for Onondaga. They reached Montreal in July, and thence proceeded towards their destination in company with the Onondaga warriors. The Jesuit Ragueneau, bound also for Onondaga, joined them. Five leagues above Montreal, the warriors left him behind; but he found an old canoe on the bank, in which, after abandoning most of his baggage, he contrived to follow with two or three Frenchmen who were with him. There was a rumor that a hundred Mohawk warriors were lying in wait among the Thousand Islands, to plunder the Onondagas of their Huron prisoners. It proved a false report. A speedier catastrophe awaited these unfortunates.

Towards evening on the 3d of August, after the party had landed to encamp, an Onondaga chief made advances to a Christian Huron girl, as he had already done at every encampment since leaving Montreal. Being repulsed for the fourth time, he split her head with his tomahawk. It was the beginning of a massacre. The Onondagas rose upon their prisoners, killed seven men, all Christians, before the eyes of the horrified Jesuit, and plundered the rest of all they had. When Ragueneau protested, they told him with insolent mockery that they were acting by direction of the governor and the superior of the Jesuits. The priest himself was secretly warned that he was to be killed during the night; and he was surprised in the morning to find himself alive.[1] On reaching Onondaga, some of the Christian captives were burned, including several women and their infant children.[2]

The confederacy was a hornet's nest, buzzing with preparation, and fast pouring out its wrathful swarms. The indomitable Le Moyne had gone again to the Mohawks, whence he wrote that two hundred of them had taken the war-path against the Algonquins of Canada; and, a little later, that all were gone but women, children, and old men. A great war-party of twelve hundred Iroquois from all the five cantons

---

[1] *Lettre de Ragueneau au R. P. Provincial, 9 Août, 1657 (Rel., 1657).*

[2] *Ibid., 21 Août, 1658 (Rel., 1658).*

was to advance into Canada in the direction of the Ottawa. The settlements on the St. Lawrence were infested with prowling warriors, who killed the Indian allies of the French, and plundered the French themselves, whom they treated with an insufferable insolence; for they felt themselves masters of the situation, and knew that the Onondaga colony was in their power. Near Montreal they killed three Frenchmen. "They approach like foxes," writes a Jesuit, "attack like lions, and disappear like birds." Charny, fortunately, had resigned the government in despair, in order to turn priest, and the brave soldier Aillebout had taken his place. He caused twelve of the Iroquois to be seized and held as hostages. This seemed to increase their fury. An embassy came to Quebec and demanded the release of the hostages, but were met with a sharp reproof and a flat refusal.

At the mission on Lake Onondaga the crisis was drawing near. The unbridled young warriors, whose capricious lawlessness often set at naught the monitions of their crafty elders, killed wantonly at various times thirteen Christian Hurons, captives at Onondaga. Ominous reports reached the ears of the colonists. They heard of a secret council at which their death was decreed. Again, they heard that they were to be surprised and captured, that the Iroquois in force were then to descend upon Canada, lay waste the outlying settlements, and torture them, the colonists, in sight of their countrymen, by which they hoped to extort what terms they pleased. At length, a dying Onondaga, recently converted and baptized, confirmed the rumors, and revealed the whole plot.

It was to take effect before the spring opened; but the hostages in the hands of Aillebout embarrassed the conspirators and caused delay. Messengers were sent in haste to call in the priests from the detached missions, and all the colonists, fifty-three in number, were soon gathered at their fortified house on the lake. Their situation was frightful. Fate hung over them by a hair, and escape seemed hopeless. Of Du Puys's ten soldiers, nine wished to desert, but the attempt would have been fatal. A throng of Onondaga warriors were day and night on the watch, bivouacked around the house. Some of them had built their huts of bark before the gate, and here, with calm, impassive faces, they lounged and smoked their pipes; or, wrapped in their blankets, strolled about the yards and outhouses, attentive to all that passed. Their behavior was very friendly. The Jesuits, themselves adepts in dissimulation, were amazed at the depth of their duplicity; for the conviction had been forced upon them that some of the chiefs had nursed their treachery from the first. In this extremity Du Puys and the Jesuits showed an admirable coolness, and among them devised a plan of escape, critical and full of doubt, but not devoid of hope.

First, they must provide means of transportation; next, they must contrive to use them undiscovered. They had eight canoes, all of which combined would not hold half their company. Over the mission-house was a large loft or garret, and here the carpenters were secretly set at work to construct two large and light flat-boats, each capable of carrying fifteen men. The task was soon finished. The most difficult part of their plan remained.

There was a beastly superstition prevalent among the Hurons, the Iroquois, and other tribes. It consisted of a "medicine" or mystic feast, in which it was essential that the guests should devour every thing set before them, however inordinate in quantity, unless absolved from duty by the person in whose behalf the solemnity was ordained; he, on his part, taking no share in the banquet. So grave was the obligation, and so strenuously did the guests fulfil it, that even their ostrich digestion was sometimes ruined past redemption by the excess of this benevolent gluttony. These *festins à manger tout* had been frequently denounced as diabolical by the Jesuits, during their mission among the Hurons; but now, with a pliancy of conscience as excusable in this case as in any other, they resolved to set aside their scruples, although, judged from their point of view, they were exceedingly well founded.

Among the French was a young man who had been adopted by an Iroquois chief, and who spoke the language fluently. He now told his Indian father that it had been revealed to him in a dream that he would soon die unless the spirits were appeased by one of these magic feasts. Dreams were the oracles of the Iroquois, and woe to those who slighted them. A day was named for the sacred festivity. The fathers killed their hogs to meet the occasion, and, that nothing might be wanting, they ransacked their stores for all that might give piquancy to the entertainment. It took place in the evening of the 20th of March, apparently in a large enclosure outside the palisade surrounding the mission-house. Here, while blazing fires or glaring pine-knots shed their glow on the wild assemblage, Frenchmen and Iroquois joined in the dance, or vied with each other in games of agility and skill. The politic fathers offered prizes to the winners, and the Indians entered with zest into the sport, the better, perhaps, to hide their treachery and hoodwink their intended victims; for they little suspected that a subtlety, deeper this time than their own, was at work to countermine them. Here, too, were the French musicians; and drum, trumpet, and cymbal lent their clangor to the din of shouts and laughter. Thus the evening wore on, till at length the serious labors of the feast began. The kettles were brought in, and their steaming contents ladled into the wooden bowls which each provident guest had brought with him. Seated gravely in a ring, they fell to their work. It was a point of high conscience not to flinch from duty on these solemn occasions; and though they might burn the young man to-morrow, they would gorge themselves like vultures in his behoof to-day.

Meantime, while the musicians strained their lungs and their arms to drown all other sounds, a band of anxious Frenchmen, in the darkness of the cloudy night, with cautious tread and bated breath, carried the boats from the rear of the mission-house down to the border of the lake. It was near eleven o'clock. The miserable guests were choking with repletion. They prayed the young Frenchman to dispense them from further surfeit. "Will you suffer me to die?" he asked, in piteous tones. They bent to their task again, but Nature soon reached her utmost limit; and they sat helpless as a conventicle of gorged turkey-buzzards, without the power possessed by those unseemly birds to rid themselves of the burden. "That will do," said the young man; "you have eaten enough; my life is saved. Now you can sleep till we come in the morning to waken you for prayers."[1] And one of his companions played soft airs on a violin to lull them to repose. Soon all

[1] *Lettre de Marie de l'Incarnation à son fils, 4 Octobre, 1658.*

were asleep, or in a lethargy akin to sleep. The few remaining Frenchmen now silently withdrew and cautiously descended to the shore, where their comrades, already embarked, lay on their oars anxiously awaiting them. Snow was falling fast as they pushed out upon the murky waters. The ice of the winter had broken up, but recent frosts had glazed the surface with a thin crust. The two boats led the way, and the canoes followed in their wake, while men in the bows of the foremost boat broke the ice with clubs as they advanced. They reached the outlet and rowed swiftly down the dark current of the Oswego. When day broke, Lake Onondaga was far behind, and around them was the leafless, lifeless forest.

When the Indians woke in the morning, dull and stupefied from their nightmare slumbers, they were astonished at the silence that reigned in the mission-house. They looked through the palisade. Nothing was stirring but a bevy of hens clucking and scratching in the snow, and one or two dogs imprisoned in the house and barking to be set free. The Indians waited for some time, then climbed the palisade, burst in the doors, and found the house empty. Their amazement was unbounded. How, without canoes, could the French have escaped by water? and how else could they escape? The snow which had fallen during the night completely hid their footsteps. A superstitious awe seized the Iroquois. They thought that the "black-robes" and their flock had flown off through the air.

Meanwhile the fugitives pushed their flight with the energy of terror, passed in safety the rapids of the Oswego, crossed Lake Ontario, and descended the St. Lawrence with the loss of three men drowned in the rapids. On the 3d of April they reached Montreal, and on the 23d arrived at Quebec. They had saved their lives; but the mission of Onondaga was a miserable failure.[1]

---

[1] On the Onondaga mission, the authorities are Marie de l'Incarnation, *Lettres Historiques*, and *Relations des Jésuites*, *1657* and *1658*, where the story is told at length, accompanied with several interesting letters and journals. Chaumonot, in his *Autobiographie*, speaks only of the Seneca mission, and refers to the *Relations* for the rest. Dollier de Casson, in his *Histoire du Montréal*, mentions the arrival of the fugitives at that place, the sight of which, he adds complacently, cured them of their fright. The *Journal des Supérieurs*

des Jésuites chronicles with its usual brevity the ruin of the mission and the return of the party to Quebec.

The contemporary Jesuits, in their account, say nothing of the superstitious character of the feast. It is Marie de l'Incarnation who lets out the secret. The later Jesuit Charlevoix, much to his credit, repeats the story without reserve.

Since the above chapter was written the remarkable narratives of Pierre Esprit Radisson have been rescued from the obscurity where they have lain for more than two centuries. Radisson, a native of St. Malo, was a member of the colony at Onondaga; but having passed into the service of England, he wrote in a language which, for want of a fitter name, may be called English. He does not say that the feast was of the kind known as *festin à manger tout*, though he asserts that one of the priests pretended to have broken his arm, and that the Indians believed that the "feasting was to be done for the safe recovery of the ffather's health." Like the other writers, he says that the feasters gorged themselves like wolves and became completely helpless, "making strange kinds of faces that turned their eyes up and downe," till, when almost bursting, they were forced to cry *Skenon*, which according to Radisson means *enough*. Radisson adds that it was proposed that the French, "being three and fifty in number, while the Iroquois were but 100 beasts not able to budge," should fall upon the impotent savages and kill them all, but that the Jesuits would not consent. His account of the embarkation and escape of the colonists agrees with that of the other writers. See *Second Voyage made in the Upper Country of the Iroquoits*, in *Publications of the Prince Society*, 1885.

The Sulpitian Allet, in the *Morale Pratique des Jésuites*, says that the French placed effigies of soldiers in the fort to deceive the Indians.

Chapter V

THE HOLY WARS OF MONTREAL

Dauversière • Mance and Bourgeoys • Miracle • A Pious Defaulter • Jesuit and Sulpitian • Montreal in 1659 • The Hospital Nuns • The Nuns and the Iroquois • More Miracles • The Murdered Priests • Brigeac and Closse • Soldiers of the Holy Family

---

O N the 2d of July, 1659, the ship "St. André" lay in the harbor of Rochelle, crowded with passengers for Canada. She had served two years as a hospital for marines, and was infected with a contagious fever. Including the crew, some two hundred persons were on board, more than half of whom were bound for Montreal. Most of these were sturdy laborers, artisans, peasants, and soldiers, together with a troop of young women, their present or future partners; a portion of the company set down on the old record as "sixty virtuous men and thirty-two pious girls." There were two priests also, Vignal and Le Maître, both destined to a speedy death at the hands of the Iroquois. But the most conspicuous among these passengers for Montreal were two groups of women in the habit of nuns, under the direction of Marguerite Bourgeoys and Jeanne Mance. Marguerite Bourgeoys, whose kind, womanly face bespoke her fitness for the task, was foundress of the school for female children at Montreal; her companion, a tall, austere figure, worn with suffering and care, was directress of the hospital. Both had returned to France for aid, and were now on their way back, each with three recruits, three being the mystic number, as a type of the Holy Family, to whose worship they were especially devoted.

Amid the bustle of departure, the shouts of sailors, the rattling of cordage, the flapping of sails, the tears and the embracings, an elderly man, with heavy plebeian features, sallow with disease, and in a sober, half-clerical dress, approached Mademoiselle Mance and her three nuns, and, turning his eyes to heaven, spread his hands over them in benediction. It was Le Royer de la Dauversière, founder of the sisterhood of

St. Joseph, to which the three nuns belonged. "Now, O Lord," he exclaimed, with the look of one whose mission on earth is fulfilled, "permit thou thy servant to depart in peace!"

Sister Maillet, who had charge of the meagre treasury of the community, thought that something more than a blessing was due from him; and asked where she should apply for payment of the interest of the twenty thousand livres which Mademoiselle Mance had placed in his hands for investment. Dauversière changed countenance, and replied, with a troubled voice: "My daughter, God will provide for you. Place your trust in Him."[1] He was bankrupt, and had used the money of the sisterhood to pay a debt of his own, leaving the nuns penniless.

I have related in another place[2] how an association of devotees, inspired, as they supposed, from heaven, had undertaken to found a religious colony at Montreal in honor of the Holy Family. The essentials of the proposed establishment were to be a seminary of priests dedicated to the Virgin, a hospital to Saint Joseph, and a school to the Infant Jesus; while a settlement was to be formed around them simply for their defence and maintenance. This pious purpose had in part been accomplished. It was seventeen years since Mademoiselle Mance had begun her labors in honor of Saint Joseph. Marguerite Bourgeoys had entered upon hers more recently; yet even then the attempt was premature, for she found no white children to teach. In time, however, this want was supplied, and she opened her school in a stable, which answered to the stable of Bethlehem, lodging with her pupils in the loft, and instructing them in Roman Catholic Christianity, with such rudiments of mundane knowledge as she and her advisers thought fit to impart.

Mademoiselle Mance found no lack of hospital work, for blood and blows were rife at Montreal, where the woods were full of Iroquois, and not a moment was without its peril. Though years began to tell upon her, she toiled patiently at her dreary task, till, in the winter of 1657, she fell on the ice of the St. Lawrence, broke her right arm, and dislocated the

[1] Faillon, *Vie de M'lle Mance*, I. 172. This volume is illustrated with a portrait of Dauversière.

[2] *The Jesuits in North America*.

wrist. Bonchard, the surgeon of Montreal, set the broken bones, but did not discover the dislocation. The arm in consequence became totally useless, and her health wasted away under incessant and violent pain. Maisonneuve, the civil and military chief of the settlement, advised her to go to France for assistance in the work to which she was no longer equal; and Marguerite Bourgeoys, whose pupils, white and red, had greatly multiplied, resolved to go with her for a similar object. They set out in September, 1658, landed at Rochelle, and went thence to Paris. Here they repaired to the seminary of St. Sulpice; for the priests of this community were joined with them in the work at Montreal, of which they were afterwards to become the feudal proprietors.

Now ensued a wonderful event, if we may trust the evidence of sundry devout persons. Olier, the founder of St. Sulpice, had lately died, and the two pilgrims would fain pay their homage to his heart, which the priests of his community kept as a precious relic, enclosed in a leaden box. The box was brought, when the thought inspired Mademoiselle Mance to try its miraculous efficacy and invoke the intercession of the departed founder. She did so, touching her disabled arm gently with the leaden casket. Instantly a grateful warmth pervaded the shrivelled limb, and from that hour its use was restored. It is true that the Jesuits ventured to doubt the Sulpitian miracle, and even to ridicule it; but the Sulpitians will show to this day the attestation of Mademoiselle Mance herself, written with the fingers once paralyzed and powerless.[1] Nevertheless, the cure was not so thorough as to permit her again to take charge of her patients.

Her next care was to visit Madame de Bullion, a devout lady of great wealth, who was usually designated at Montreal as "the unknown benefactress," because, though her charities were the mainstay of the feeble colony, and though the source from which they proceeded was well known, she affected, in the interest of humility, the greatest secrecy, and required those who profited by her gifts to pretend ignorance whence they came. Overflowing with zeal for the pious enterprise, she received her visitor with enthusiasm, lent an open ear to her

---

[1] For an account of this miracle, written in perfect good faith and supported by various attestations, see Faillon, *Vie de M'lle Mance*, chap. iv.

recital, responded graciously to her appeal for aid, and paid over to her the sum, munificent at that day, of twenty-two thousand francs. Thus far successful, Mademoiselle Mance repaired to the town of La Flèche to visit Le Royer de la Dauversière.

It was this wretched fanatic who, through visions and revelations, had first conceived the plan of a hospital in honor of Saint Joseph at Montreal.[1] He had found in Mademoiselle Mance a zealous and efficient pioneer; but the execution of his scheme required a community of hospital nuns, and therefore he had labored for the last eighteen years to form one at La Flèche, meaning to despatch its members in due time to Canada. The time at length was come. Three of the nuns were chosen, Sisters Brésoles, Macé, and Maillet, and sent under the escort of certain pious gentlemen to Rochelle. Their exit from La Flèche was not without its difficulties. Dauversière was in ill odor, not only from the multiplicity of his debts, but because, in his character of agent of the association of Montreal, he had at various times sent thither those whom his biographer describes as "the most virtuous girls to be found at La Flèche," intoxicating them with religious excitement, and shipping them for the New World against the will of their parents. It was noised through the town that he had kidnapped and sold them; and now the report spread abroad that he was about to crown his iniquity by luring away three young nuns. A mob gathered at the convent gate, and the escort were forced to draw their swords to open a way for the terrified sisters.

Of the twenty-two thousand francs which she had received, Mademoiselle Mance kept two thousand for immediate needs, and confided the rest to the hands of Dauversière, who, hard pressed by his creditors, used it to pay one of his debts; and then, to his horror, found himself unable to replace it. Racked by the gout and tormented by remorse, he betook himself to his bed in a state of body and mind truly pitiable. One of the miracles, so frequent in the early annals of Montreal, was vouchsafed in answer to his prayer, and he was enabled to journey to Rochelle and bid farewell to his nuns. It was but

[1] See *The Jesuits in North America*.

a brief respite; he returned home to become the prey of a host of maladies, and to die at last a lingering and painful death.

While Mademoiselle Mance was gaining recruits in La Flèche, Marguerite Bourgeoys was no less successful in her native town of Troyes, and she rejoined her companions at Rochelle, accompanied by Sisters Châtel, Crolo, and Raisin, her destined assistants in the school at Montreal. Meanwhile, the Sulpitians and others interested in the pious enterprise, had spared no effort to gather men to strengthen the colony, and young women to serve as their wives; and all were now mustered at Rochelle, waiting for embarkation. Their waiting was a long one. Laval, bishop at Quebec, was allied to the Jesuits, and looked on the colonists of Montreal with more than coldness. Sulpitian writers say that his agents used every effort to discourage them, and that certain persons at Rochelle told the master of the ship in which the emigrants were to sail that they were not to be trusted to pay their passage-money. Hereupon ensued a delay of more than two months before means could be found to quiet the scruples of the prudent commander. At length the anchor was weighed, and the dreary voyage begun.

The woe-begone company, crowded in the filthy and infected ship, were tossed for two months more on the relentless sea, buffeted by repeated storms and wasted by a contagious fever, which attacked nearly all of them and reduced Mademoiselle Mance to extremity. Eight or ten died and were dropped overboard, after a prayer from the two priests. At length land hove in sight; the piny odors of the forest regaled their languid senses as they sailed up the broad estuary of the St. Lawrence and anchored under the rock of Quebec.

High aloft, on the brink of the cliff, they saw the *fleur-de-lis* waving above the fort of St. Louis, and, beyond, the cross on the tower of the cathedral traced against the sky; the houses of the merchants on the strand below, and boats and canoes drawn up along the bank. The bishop and the Jesuits greeted them as co-workers in a holy cause, with an unction not wholly sincere. Though a unit against heresy, the pious founders of New France were far from unity among themselves. To the thinking of the Jesuits, Montreal was a government within a government, a wheel within a wheel. This rival Sulpitian settlement was, in their eyes, an element of disorganization adverse to the disciplined harmony of the Canadian Chruch, which they would fain have seen, with its focus at Quebec, radiating light unrefracted to the uttermost parts of the colony. That is to say, they wished to control it unchecked, through their ally, the bishop.

The emigrants, then, were received with a studious courtesy, which veiled but thinly a stiff and persistent opposition. The bishop and the Jesuits were especially anxious to prevent the La Flèche nuns from establishing themselves at Montreal, where they would form a separate community, under Sulpitian influence; and, in place of the newly arrived sisters, they wished to substitute nuns from the Hôtel Dieu of Quebec, who would be under their own control. That which most strikes the non-Catholic reader throughout this affair is the constant reticence and dissimulation practised, not only between Jesuits and Montrealists, but among the Montrealists themselves. Their self-devotion, great as it was, was fairly matched by their disingenuousness.[1]

All difficulties being overcome, the Montrealists embarked in boats and ascended the St. Lawrence, leaving Quebec infected with the contagion they had brought. The journey now made in a single night cost them fifteen days of hardship and danger. At length they reached their new home. The little settlement lay before them, still gasping betwixt life and death, in a puny, precarious infancy. Some forty small, compact houses were ranged parallel to the river, chiefly along the line of what is now St. Paul's Street. On the left there was a fort, and on a rising ground at the right a massive windmill of stone, enclosed with a wall or palisade pierced for musketry, and answering the purpose of a redoubt or blockhouse.[2] Fields, studded with charred and blackened stumps, between which crops were growing, stretched away to the

---

[1] See, for example, chapter iv. of Faillon's Life of Mademoiselle Mance. The evidence is unanswerable, the writer being the partisan and admirer of most of those whose *pieuse tromperie*, to use the expression of Dollier de Casson, he describes in apparent unconsciousness that anybody will see reason to cavil at it.

[2] *Lettre du Vicomte d'Argenson, Gouverneur du Canada, 4 Août, 1659*, MS.

edges of the bordering forest; and the green, shaggy back of the mountain towered over all.

There were at this time a hundred and sixty men at Montreal, about fifty of whom had families, or at least wives. They greeted the new-comers with a welcome which, this time, was as sincere as it was warm, and bestirred themselves with alacrity to provide them with shelter for the winter. As for the three nuns from La Flèche, a chamber was hastily made for them over two low rooms which had served as Mademoiselle Mance's hospital. This chamber was twenty-five feet square, with four cells for the nuns, and a closet for stores and clothing, which for the present was empty, as they had landed in such destitution that they were forced to sell all their scanty equipment to gain the bare necessaries of existence. Little could be hoped from the colonists, who were scarcely less destitute than they. Such was their poverty,—thanks to Dauversière's breach of trust,—that when their clothes were worn out, they were unable to replace them, and were forced to patch them with such material as came to hand. Maisonneuve, the governor, and the pious Madame d'Aillebout, being once on a visit to the hospital, amused themselves with trying to guess of what stuff the habits of the nuns had originally been made, and were unable to agree on the point in question.[1]

Their chamber, which they occupied for many years, being hastily built of ill-seasoned planks, let in the piercing cold of the Canadian winter through countless cracks and chinks; and the driving snow sifted through in such quantities that they were sometimes obliged, the morning after a storm, to remove it with shovels. Their food would freeze on the table before them, and their coarse brown bread had to be thawed on the hearth before they could cut it. These women had been nurtured in ease, if not in luxury. One of them, Judith de Brésoles, had in her youth, by advice of her confessor, run away from parents who were devoted to her, and immured herself in a convent, leaving them in agonies of doubt as to her fate. She now acted as superior of the little community. One of her nuns records of her that she had a fervent devotion for the Infant Jesus; and that, along with many more

---

[1] *Annales des Hospitalières de Villemarie, par la Sœur Morin*, a contemporary record, from which Faillon gives long extracts.

spiritual graces, he inspired her with so transcendent a skill in cookery, that "with a small piece of lean pork and a few herbs she could make soup of a marvellous relish."[1] Sister Macé was charged with the care of the pigs and hens, to whose wants she attended in person, though she, too, had been delicately bred. In course of time, the sisterhood was increased by additions from without; though more than twenty girls who entered the hospital as novices recoiled from the hardship, and took husbands in the colony. Among a few who took the vows, Sister Jumeau should not pass unnoticed. Such was her humility, that, though of a good family and unable to divest herself of the marks of good breeding, she pretended to be the daughter of a poor peasant, and persisted in repeating the pious falsehood till the merchant Le Ber told her flatly that he did not believe her.

The sisters had great need of a man to do the heavy work of the house and garden, but found no means of hiring one, when an incident, in which they saw a special providence, excellently supplied the want. There was a poor colonist named Jouaneaux to whom a piece of land had been given at some distance from the settlement. Had he built a cabin upon it, his scalp would soon have paid the forfeit; but, being bold and hardy, he devised a plan by which he might hope to sleep in safety without abandoning the farm which was his only possession. Among the stumps of his clearing there was one hollow with age. Under this he dug a sort of cave, the entrance of which was a small hole carefully hidden by brushwood. The hollow stump was easily converted into a chimney; and by creeping into his burrow at night, or when he saw signs of danger, he escaped for some time the notice of the Iroquois. But, though he could dispense with a house, he needed a barn for his hay and corn; and while he was building one, he fell from the ridge of the roof and was seriously hurt. He was carried to the Hôtel Dieu, where the nuns showed him every attention, until, after a long confinement, he at last recovered. Being of a grateful nature and enthusiastically devout, he was so touched by the kindness of his benefactors, and so moved by the spectacle of their piety, that

[1] "C'était par son recours à l'Enfant Jésus qu'elle trouvait tous ces secrets et d'autres semblables," writes in our own day the excellent annalist, Faillon.

he conceived the wish of devoting his life to their service. To this end a contract was drawn up, by which he pledged himself to work for them as long as strength remained; and they, on their part, agreed to maintain him in sickness or old age.

This stout-hearted retainer proved invaluable; though, had a guard of soldiers been added, it would have been no more than the case demanded. Montreal was not palisaded, and at first the hospital was as much exposed as the rest. The Iroquois would skulk at night among the houses, like wolves in a camp of sleeping travellers on the prairies; though the human foe was, of the two, incomparably the bolder, fiercer, and more bloodthirsty. More than once one of these prowling savages was known to have crouched all night in a rank growth of wild mustard in the garden of the nuns, vainly hoping that one of them would come out within reach of his tomahawk. During summer, a month rarely passed without a fight, sometimes within sight of their windows. A burst of yells from the ambushed marksmen, followed by a clatter of musketry, would announce the opening of the fray, and promise the nuns an addition to their list of patients. On these occasions they bore themselves according to their several natures. Sister Morin, who had joined their number three years after their arrival, relates that Sister Brésoles and she used to run to the belfry and ring the tocsin to call the inhabitants together. "From our high station," she writes, "we could sometimes see the combat, which terrified us extremely, so that we came down again as soon as we could, trembling with fright, and thinking that our last hour was come. When the tocsin sounded, my Sister Maillet would become faint with excess of fear; and my Sister Macé, as long as the alarm continued, would remain speechless, in a state pitiable to see. They would both get into a corner of the rood-loft, before the Holy Sacrament, so as to be prepared for death; or else go into their cells. As soon as I heard that the Iroquois were gone, I went to tell them, which comforted them and seemed to restore them to life. My Sister Brésoles was stronger and more courageous; her terror, which she could not help, did not prevent her from attending the sick and receiving the dead and wounded who were brought in."

The priests of St. Sulpice, who had assumed the entire spiritual charge of the settlement, and who were soon to assume its entire temporal charge also, had for some years no other lodging than a room at the hospital, adjoining those of the patients. They caused the building to be fortified with palisades, and the houses of some of the chief inhabitants were placed near it, for mutual defence. They also built two fortified houses, called Ste. Marie and St. Gabriel, at the two extremities of the settlement, and lodged in them a considerable number of armed men, whom they employed in clearing and cultivating the surrounding lands, the property of their community. All other outlying houses were also pierced with loopholes, and fortified as well as the slender means of their owners would permit. The laborers always carried their guns to the field, and often had need to use them. A few incidents will show the state of Montreal and the character of its tenants.

In the autumn of 1657 there was a truce with the Iroquois, under cover of which three or four of them came to the settlement. Nicolas Godé and Jean Saint-Père were on the roof of their house, laying thatch; when one of the visitors aimed his arquebuse at Saint-Père, and brought him to the ground like a wild turkey from a tree. Now ensued a prodigy; for the assassins, having cut off his head and carried it home to their village, were amazed to hear it speak to them in good Iroquois, scold them for their perfidy, and threaten them with the vengeance of Heaven; and they continued to hear its voice of admonition even after scalping it and throwing away the skull.[1] This story, circulated at Montreal on the alleged authority of the Indians themselves, found believers among the most intelligent men of the colony.

Another miracle, which occurred several years later, deserves to be recorded. Le Maître, one of the two priests who had sailed from France with Mademoiselle Mance and her nuns, being one day at the fortified house of St. Gabriel, went out with the laborers, in order to watch while they were at their work. In view of a possible enemy, he had girded himself with an earthly sword; but seeing no sign of danger, he presently took out his breviary, and, while reciting his office

---

[1] Dollier de Casson, *Histoire du Montréal, 1657, 1658.*

with eyes bent on the page, walked into an ambuscade of Iroquois, who rose before him with a yell.

He shouted to the laborers, and, drawing his sword, faced the whole savage crew, in order, probably, to give the men time to snatch their guns. Afraid to approach, the Iroquois fired and killed him; then rushed upon the working party, who escaped into the house, after losing several of their number. The victors cut off the head of the heroic priest, and tied it in a white handkerchief which they took from a pocket of his cassock. It is said that on reaching their villages they were astonished to find the handkerchief without the slightest stain of blood, but stamped indelibly with the features of its late owner, so plainly marked that none who had known him could fail to recognize them.[1] This not very original miracle, though it found eager credence at Montreal, was received coolly, like other Montreal miracles, at Quebec; and Sulpitian writers complain that the bishop, in a long letter which he wrote to the Pope, made no mention of it whatever.

Le Maître, on the voyage to Canada, had been accompanied by another priest, Guillaume de Vignal, who met a fate more deplorable than that of his companion, though unattended by any recorded miracle. Le Maître had been killed in August. In the October following, Vignal went with thirteen men, in a flat-boat and several canoes, to Isle à la Pierre, nearly opposite Montreal, to get stone for the seminary which the priests had recently begun to build. With him was a pious and valiant gentleman named Claude de Brigeac, who, though but thirty years of age, had come as a soldier to Montreal, in the hope of dying in defence of the true church, and thus reaping the reward of a martyr. Vignal and three or four men had scarcely landed when they were set upon by a large band of Iroquois who lay among the bushes waiting to receive them. The rest of the party, who were still in their boats, with a cowardice rare at Montreal, thought only of saving themselves. Claude de Brigeac alone leaped ashore and ran to aid his comrades. Vignal was soon mortally wounded.

---

[1] This story is told by Sister Morin, Marguerite Bourgeoys, and Dollier de Casson, on the authority of one Lavigne, then a prisoner among the Iroquois, who declared that he had seen the handkerchief in the hands of the returning warriors.

Brigeac shot the chief dead with his arquebuse, and then, pistol in hand, held the whole troop for an instant at bay; but his arm was shattered by a gun-shot, and he was seized, along with Vignal, René Cuillérier, and Jacques Dufresne. Crossing to the main shore, immediately opposite Montreal, the Iroquois made, after their custom, a small fort of logs and branches, in which they ensconced themselves, and then began to dress the wounds of their prisoners. Seeing that Vignal was unable to make the journey to their villages, they killed him, divided his flesh, and roasted it for food.

Brigeac and his fellows in misfortune spent a woful night in this den of wolves; and in the morning their captors, having breakfasted on the remains of Vignal, took up their homeward march, dragging the Frenchmen with them. On reaching Oneida, Brigeac was tortured to death with the customary atrocities. Cuillérier, who was present, declared that they could wring from him no cry of pain, but that throughout he ceased not to pray for their conversion. The witness himself expected the same fate, but an old squaw happily adopted him, and thus saved his life. He eventually escaped to Albany, and returned to Canada by the circuitous but comparatively safe route of New York and Boston.

In the following winter, Montreal suffered an irreparable loss in the death of the brave Major Closse, a man whose intrepid coolness was never known to fail in the direst emergency. Going to the aid of a party of laborers attacked by the Iroquois, he was met by a crowd of savages, eager to kill or capture him. His servant ran off. He snapped a pistol at the foremost assailant, but it missed fire. His remaining pistol served him no better, and he was instantly shot down. "He died," writes Dollier de Casson, "like a brave soldier of Christ and the king." Some of his friends once remonstrating with him on the temerity with which he exposed his life, he replied, "Messieurs, I came here only to die in the service of God; and if I thought I could not die here, I would leave this country to fight the Turks, that I might not be deprived of such a glory."[1]

The fortified house of Ste. Marie, belonging to the priests

[1] Dollier de Casson, *Histoire du Montréal, 1661, 1662.*

of St. Sulpice, was the scene of several hot and bloody fights. Here, too, occurred the following nocturnal adventure. A man named Lavigne, who had lately returned from captivity among the Iroquois, chancing to rise at night and look out of the window, saw by the bright moonlight a number of naked warriors stealthily gliding round a corner and crouching near the door, in order to kill the first Frenchman who should go out in the morning. He silently woke his comrades; and, having the rest of the night for consultation, they arranged their plan so well, that some of them, sallying from the rear of the house, came cautiously round upon the Iroquois, placed them between two fires, and captured them all.

The summer of 1661 was marked by a series of calamities scarcely paralleled even in the annals of this disastrous epoch. Early in February, thirteen colonists were surprised and captured; next came a fight between a large band of laborers and two hundred and sixty Iroquois; in the following month, ten more Frenchmen were killed or taken; and thenceforth, till winter closed, the settlement had scarcely a breathing space. "These hobgoblins," writes the author of the *Relation* of this year, "sometimes appeared at the edge of the woods, assailing us with abuse; sometimes they glided stealthily into the midst of the fields, to surprise the men at work; sometimes they approached the houses, harassing us without ceasing, and, like importunate harpies or birds of prey, swooping down on us whenever they could take us unawares."[1]

Speaking of the disasters of this year, the soldier-priest, Dollier de Casson, writes: "God, who afflicts the body only for the good of the soul, made a marvellous use of these calamities and terrors to hold the people firm in their duty towards Heaven. Vice was then almost unknown here, and in the midst of war religion flourished on all sides in a manner very different from what we now see in time of peace."[2]

The war was, in fact, a war of religion. The small redoubts of logs, scattered about the skirts of the settlement to serve as points of defence in case of attack, bore the names of saints, to whose care they were commended. There was one placed under a higher protection and called the *Redoubt of the Infant*

[1] Le Jeune, *Relation, 1661,* p. 3 (ed. 1858).
[2] *Histoire du Montréal, 1660, 1661.*

Jesus. Chomedey de Maisonneuve, the pious and valiant governor of Montreal, to whom its successful defence is largely due, resolved, in view of the increasing fury and persistency of the Iroquois attacks, to form among the inhabitants a military fraternity, to be called "Soldiers of the Holy Family of Jesus, Mary, and Joseph;" and to this end he issued a proclamation, of which the following is the characteristic beginning: —

"We, Paul de Chomedey, governor of the island of Montreal and lands thereon dependent, on information given us from divers quarters that the Iroquois have formed the design of seizing upon this settlement by surprise or force, have thought it our duty, seeing that this island is the property of the Holy Virgin,[1] to invite and exhort those zealous for her service to unite together by squads, each of seven persons; and after choosing a corporal by a plurality of voices, to report themselves to us for enrolment in our garrison, and, in this capacity, to obey our orders, to the end that the country may be saved."

Twenty squads, numbering in all one hundred and forty men, whose names, appended to the proclamation, may still be seen on the ancient records of Montreal, answered the appeal and enrolled themselves in the holy cause.

The whole settlement was in a state of religious exaltation. As the Iroquois were regarded as actual myrmidons of Satan in his malign warfare against Mary and her divine Son, those who died in fighting them were held to merit the reward of martyrs, assured of a seat in paradise.

And now it remains to record one of the most heroic feats of arms ever achieved on this continent. That it may be rated as it merits, it will be well to glance for a moment at the condition of Canada, under the portentous cloud of war which constantly overshadowed it.[2]

---

[1] This is no figure of speech. The Associates of Montreal, after receiving a grant of the island from Jean de Lauson, placed it under the protection of the Virgin, and formally declared her to be the proprietor of it from that day forth for ever.

[2] In all that relates to Montreal, I cannot be sufficiently grateful to the Abbé Faillon, the indefatigable, patient, conscientious chronicler of its early history; an ardent and prejudiced Sulpitian, a priest who three centuries ago would have passed for credulous, and, withal, a kind-hearted and estimable

man. His numerous books on his favorite theme, with the vast and heterogeneous mass of facts which they embody, are invaluable, provided their partisan character be well kept in mind. His recent death leaves his principal work unfinished. His *Histoire de la Colonie Française en Canada*—it might more fitly be called *Histoire du Montréal*—is unhappily little more than half complete.

Chapter VI

THE HEROES OF THE LONG SAUT

Suffering and Terror • François Hertel • The Captive Wolf • The threatened Invasion • Daulac des Ormeaux • The Adventurers at the Long Saut • The Attack • A Desperate Defence • A Final Assault • The Fort taken

---

CANADA had writhed for twenty years, with little respite, under the scourge of Iroquois war. During a great part of this dark period the entire French population was less than three thousand. What, then, saved them from destruction? In the first place, the settlements were grouped around three fortified posts, Quebec, Three Rivers, and Montreal, which in time of danger gave asylum to the fugitive inhabitants. Again, their assailants were continually distracted by other wars, and never, except at a few spasmodic intervals, were fully in earnest to destroy the French colony. Canada was indispensable to them. The four upper nations of the league soon became dependent on her for supplies; and all the nations alike appear, at a very early period, to have conceived the policy on which they afterwards distinctly acted, of balancing the rival settlements of the Hudson and the St. Lawrence, the one against the other. They would torture, but not kill. It was but rarely that, in fits of fury, they struck their hatchets at the brain; and thus the bleeding and gasping colony lingered on in torment.

The seneschal of New France, son of the governor Lauson, was surprised and killed on the island of Orleans, along with seven companions. About the same time, the same fate befell the son of Godefroy, one of the chief inhabitants of Quebec. Outside the fortifications there was no safety for a moment. A universal terror seized the people. A comet appeared above Quebec, and they saw in it a herald of destruction. Their excited imaginations turned natural phenomena into portents and prodigies. A blazing canoe sailed across the sky; confused cries and lamentations were heard in the air; and a voice of thunder sounded from mid-heaven.[1] The Jesuits despaired for their scattered and persecuted flocks. "Everywhere," writes their superior, "we see infants to be saved for heaven, sick and dying to be baptized, adults to be instructed, but everywhere we see the Iroquois. They haunt us like persecuting goblins. They kill our new-made Christians in our arms. If they meet us on the river, they kill us. If they find us in the huts of our Indians, they burn us and them together."[2] And he appeals urgently for troops to destroy them, as a holy work inspired by God, and needful for his service.

Canada was still a mission, and the influence of the church was paramount and pervading. At Quebec, as at Montreal, the war with the Iroquois was regarded as a war with the hosts of Satan. Of the settlers' cabins scattered along the shores above and below Quebec, many were provided with small iron cannon, made probably by blacksmiths in the colony; but they had also other protectors. In each was an image of the Virgin or some patron saint, and every morning the pious settler knelt before the shrine to beg the protection of a celestial hand in his perilous labors of the forest or the farm.

When, in the summer of 1658, the young Vicomte d'Argenson came to assume the thankless task of governing the colony, the Iroquois war was at its height. On the day after his arrival, he was washing his hands before seating himself at dinner in the hall of the Château St. Louis, when cries of alarm were heard, and he was told that the Iroquois were close at hand. In fact, they were so near that their warwhoops and the screams of their victims could plainly be heard. Argenson left his guests, and, with such a following as he could muster at the moment, hastened to the rescue; but the assailants were too nimble for him. The forests, which grew at that time around Quebec, favored them both in attack and in retreat. After a year or two of experience, he wrote urgently to the court for troops. He adds that, what with the demands of the harvest, and the unmilitary character of many of the settlers, the colony could not furnish more than a hundred men for offensive operations. A vigorous aggressive war, he insists, is absolutely necessary, and this not

[1] Marie de l'Incarnation, *Lettre, Sept.*, *1661*.

[2] *Relation, 1660* (anonymous), 3.

only to save the colony, but to save the only true faith; "for," to borrow his own words, "it is this colony alone which has the honor to be in the communion of the Holy Church. Everywhere else reigns the doctrine of England or Holland, to which I can give no other name, because there are as many creeds as there are subjects who embrace them. They do not care in the least whether the Iroquois and the other savages of this country have or have not a knowledge of the true God, or else they are so malicious as to inject the venom of their errors into souls incapable of distinguishing the truth of the gospel from the falsehoods of heresy; and hence it is plain that religion has its sole support in the French colony, and that, if this colony is in danger, religion is equally in danger."[1]

Among the most interesting memorials of the time are two letters, written by François Hertel, a youth of eighteen, captured at Three Rivers, and carried to the Mohawk towns in the summer of 1661. He belonged to one of the best families of Canada, and was the favorite child of his mother, to whom the second of the two letters is addressed. The first is to the Jesuit Le Moyne, who had gone to Onondaga, in July of that year, to effect the release of French prisoners in accordance with the terms of a truce.[2] Both letters were written on birch bark:—

MY REVEREND FATHER:—The very day when you left Three Rivers I was captured, at about three in the afternoon, by four Iroquois of the Mohawk tribe. I would not have been taken alive, if, to my sorrow, I had not feared that I was not in a fit state to die. If you came here, my Father, I could have the happiness of confessing to you; and I do not think they would do you any harm; and I think that I could return home with you. I pray you to pity my poor mother, who is in great trouble. You know, my Father, how fond she is of me. I have heard from a Frenchman, who was taken at Three Rivers on the 1st of August, that she is well, and comforts herself with the hope that I shall see you. There are three of us Frenchmen alive here. I

[1] *Papiers d'Argenson; Mémoire sur le sujet de la guerre des Iroquois, 1659* (1660?). MS.

[2] *Journal des Jésuites*, 300.

commend myself to your good prayers, and particularly to the Holy Sacrifice of the Mass. I pray you, my Father, to say a mass for me. I pray you give my dutiful love to my poor mother, and console her, if it pleases you.

My Father, I beg your blessing on the hand that writes to you, which has one of the fingers burned in the bowl of an Indian pipe, to satisfy the Majesty of God which I have offended. The thumb of the other hand is cut off; but do not tell my mother of it.

My Father, I pray you to honor me with a word from your hand in reply, and tell me if you shall come here before winter.

> Your most humble and most obedient servant,
> FRANÇOIS HERTEL.

The following is the letter to his mother, sent probably, with the other, to the charge of Le Moyne: —

> MY MOST DEAR AND HONORED MOTHER: — I know very well that my capture must have distressed you very much. I ask you to forgive my disobedience. It is my sins that have placed me where I am. I owe my life to your prayers, and those of M. de Saint-Quentin, and of my sisters. I hope to see you again before winter. I pray you to tell the good brethren of Notre Dame to pray to God and the Holy Virgin for me, my dear mother, and for you and all my sisters.
>
> Your poor
> FANCHON.

This, no doubt, was the name by which she had called him familiarly when a child. And who was this "Fanchon," this devout and tender son of a fond mother? New England can answer to her cost. When, twenty-nine years later, a band of French and Indians issued from the forest and fell upon the fort and settlement of Salmon Falls, it was François Hertel who led the attack; and when the retiring victors were hard pressed by an overwhelming force, it was he who, sword in hand, held the pursuers in check at the bridge of Wooster River, and covered the retreat of his men. He was ennobled for his services, and died at the age of eighty, the founder of one of the most distinguished families of Canada.[1] To the New England of old he was the abhorred chief of Popish malignants and murdering savages. The New England of to-day will be more just to the brave defender of his country and his faith.

In May, 1660, a party of French Algonquins captured a Wolf, or Mohegan, Indian, naturalized among the Iroquois, brought him to Quebec, and burned him there with their usual atrocity of torture. A modern Catholic writer says that the Jesuits could not save him; but this is not so. Their influence over the consciences of the colonists was at that time unbounded, and their direct political power was very great. A protest on their part, and that of the newly arrived bishop, who was in their interest, could not have failed of effect. The truth was, they did not care to prevent the torture of prisoners of war, not solely out of that spirit of compliance with the savage humor of Indian allies which stains so often the pages of French American history, but also, and perhaps chiefly, from motives purely religious. Torture, in their eyes, seems to have been a blessing in disguise. They thought it good for the soul, and in case of obduracy the surest way of salvation. "We have very rarely indeed," writes one of them, "seen the burning of an Iroquois without feeling sure that he was on the path to Paradise; and we never knew one of them to be surely on the path to Paradise without seeing him pass through this fiery punishment."[2] So they let the Wolf burn; but first, having instructed him after their fashion, they baptized him, and his savage soul flew to heaven out of the fire. "Is it not," pursues the same writer, "a marvel to see a wolf changed at one stroke into a lamb, and enter into the fold of Christ, which he came to ravage?"

Before he died he requited their spiritual cares with a startling secret. He told them that eight hundred Iroquois warriors were encamped below Montreal; that four hundred more, who had wintered on the Ottawa, were on

[1] His letters of nobility, dated 1716, will be found in Daniel's *Histoire des Grandes Familles Françaises du Canada*, 404.

[2] *Relation, 1660*, 31.

the point of joining them; and that the united force would swoop upon Quebec, kill the governor, lay waste the town, and then attack Three Rivers and Montreal.[1] This time, at least, the Iroquois were in deadly earnest. Quebec was wild with terror. The Ursulines and the nuns of the Hôtel Dieu took refuge in the strong and extensive building which the Jesuits had just finished, opposite the Parish Church. Its walls and palisades made it easy of defence; and in its yards and court were lodged the terrified Hurons, as well as the fugitive inhabitants of the neighboring settlements. Others found asylum in the fort, and others in the convent of the Ursulines, which, in place of nuns, was occupied by twenty-four soldiers, who fortified it with redoubts, and barricaded the doors and windows. Similar measures of defence were taken at the Hôtel Dieu, and the streets of the Lower Town were strongly barricaded. Everybody was in arms, and the *Qui vive* of the sentries and patrols resounded all night.[2]

Several days passed, and no Iroquois appeared. The refugees took heart, and began to return to their deserted farms and dwellings. Among the rest was a family consisting of an old woman, her daughter, her son-in-law, and four small children, living near St. Anne, some twenty miles below Quebec. On reaching home the old woman and the man went to their work in the fields, while the mother and children remained in the house. Here they were pounced upon and captured by eight renegade Hurons, Iroquois by adoption, who placed them in their large canoe, and paddled up the river with their prize. It was Saturday, a day dedicated to the Virgin; and the captive mother prayed to her for aid, "feeling," writes a Jesuit, "a full conviction that, in passing before Quebec on a Saturday, she would be delivered by the power of this Queen of Heaven." In fact, as the marauders and their captives glided in the darkness of night by Point Levi, under the shadow of the shore, they were greeted with a volley of musketry

[1] Marie de l'Incarnation, *Lettre, 25 Juin, 1660.*
[2] On this alarm at Quebec compare Marie de l'Incarnation, *25 Juin, 1660; Relation, 1660,* 5; Juchereau, *Histoire de l'Hôtel-Dieu de Québec,* 125; and *Journal des Jésuites,* 282.

from the bushes, and a band of French and Algonquins dashed into the water to seize them. Five of the eight were taken, and the rest shot or drowned. The governor had heard of the descent at St. Anne, and despatched a party to lie in ambush for the authors of it. The Jesuits, it is needless to say, saw a miracle in the result. The Virgin had answered the prayer of her votary. "Though it is true," observes the father who records the marvel, "that, in the volley, she received a mortal wound." The same shot struck the infant in her arms. The prisoners were taken to Quebec, where four of them were tortured with even more ferocity than had been shown in the case of the unfortunate Wolf.[1] Being questioned, they confirmed his story, and expressed great surprise that the Iroquois had not come, adding that they must have stopped to attack Montreal or Three Rivers. Again all was terror, and again days passed and no enemy appeared. Had the dying converts, so charitably despatched to heaven through fire, sought an unhallowed consolation in scaring the abettors of their torture with a lie? Not at all. Bating a slight exaggeration, they had told the truth. Where, then, were the Iroquois? As one small point of steel disarms the lightning of its terrors, so did the heroism of a few intrepid youths divert this storm of war and save Canada from a possible ruin.

In the preceding April, before the designs of the Iroquois were known, a young officer named Daulac, commandant of the garrison of Montreal, asked leave of Maisonneuve, the governor, to lead a party of volunteers against the enemy. His plan was bold to desperation. It was known that Iroquois warriors in great numbers had wintered among the forests of the Ottawa. Daulac proposed to waylay them

[1] The torturers were Christian Algonquins, converts of the Jesuits. Chaumonot, who was present to give spiritual aid to the sufferers, describes the scene with horrible minuteness. "I could not," he says, "deliver them from their torments." Perhaps not: but it is certain that the Jesuits as a body, with or without the bishop, could have prevented the atrocity, had they seen fit. They sometimes taught their converts to pray for their enemies. It would have been well had they taught them not to torture them. I can recall but one instance in which they did so. The prayers for enemies were always for a spiritual, not a temporal good. The fathers held the body in slight account and cared little what happened to it.

on their descent of the river, and fight them without regard to disparity of force. The settlers of Montreal had hitherto acted solely on the defensive, for their numbers had been too small for aggressive war. Of late their strength had been somewhat increased, and Maisonneuve, judging that a display of enterprise and boldness might act as a check on the audacity of the enemy, at length gave his consent.

Adam Daulac, or Dollard, Sieur des Ormeaux, was a young man of good family, who had come to the colony three years before, at the age of twenty-two. He had held some military command in France, though in what rank does not appear. It was said that he had been involved in some affair which made him anxious to wipe out the memory of the past by a noteworthy exploit; and he had been busy for some time among the young men of Montreal, inviting them to join him in the enterprise he meditated. Sixteen of them caught his spirit, struck hands with him, and pledged their word. They bound themselves by oath to accept no quarter; and, having gained Maisonneuve's consent, they made their wills, confessed, and received the sacraments. As they knelt for the last time before the altar in the chapel of the Hôtel Dieu, that sturdy little population of pious Indian-fighters gazed on them with enthusiasm, not unmixed with an envy which had in it nothing ignoble. Some of the chief men of Montreal, with the brave Charles Le Moyne at their head, begged them to wait till the spring sowing was over, that they might join them; but Daulac refused. He was jealous of the glory and the danger, and he wished to command, which he could not have done had Le Moyne been present.

The spirit of the enterprise was purely mediæval. The enthusiasm of honor, the enthusiasm of adventure, and the enthusiasm of faith, were its motive forces. Daulac was a knight of the early crusades among the forests and savages of the New World. Yet the incidents of this exotic heroism are definite and clear as a tale of yesterday. The names, ages, and occupations of the seventeen young men may still be read on the ancient register of the parish of Montreal; and the notarial acts of that year, preserved in the records of the city, contain minute accounts of such property as each of them possessed. The three eldest were of twenty-eight, thirty, and thirty-one years respectively. The age of the rest varied from twenty-one to twenty-seven. They were of various callings,—soldiers, armorers, locksmiths, lime-burners, or settlers without trades. The greater number had come to the colony as part of the reinforcement brought by Maisonneuve in 1653.

After a solemn farewell they embarked in several canoes well supplied with arms and ammunition. They were very indifferent canoe-men; and it is said that they lost a week in vain attempts to pass the swift current of St. Anne, at the head of the island of Montreal. At length they were more successful, and entering the mouth of the Ottawa, crossed the Lake of Two Mountains, and slowly advanced against the current.

Meanwhile, forty warriors of that remnant of the Hurons who, in spite of Iroquois persecutions, still lingered at Quebec, had set out on a war-party, led by the brave and wily Etienne Annahotaha, their most noted chief. They stopped by the way at Three Rivers, where they found a band of Christian Algonquins under a chief named Mituvemeg. Annahotaha challenged him to a trial of courage, and it was agreed that they should meet at Montreal, where they were likely to find a speedy opportunity of putting their mettle to the test. Thither, accordingly, they repaired, the Algonquin with three followers, and the Huron with thirty-nine.

It was not long before they learned the departure of Daulac and his companions. "For," observes the honest Dollier de Casson, "the principal fault of our Frenchmen is to talk too much." The wish seized them to share the adventure, and to that end the Huron chief asked the governor for a letter to Daulac, to serve as credentials. Maisonneuve hesitated. His faith in Huron valor was not great, and he feared the proposed alliance. Nevertheless, he at length yielded so far as to give Annahotaha a letter in which Daulac was told to accept or reject the proffered reinforcement as he should see fit. The Hurons and Algonquins now embarked and paddled in pursuit of the seventeen Frenchmen.

They meanwhile had passed with difficulty the swift cur-

rent at Carillon, and about the first of May reached the foot
of the more formidable rapid called the Long Saut, where
a tumult of waters, foaming among ledges and boulders,
barred the onward way. It was needless to go farther. The
Iroquois were sure to pass the Saut, and could be fought
here as well as elsewhere. Just below the rapid, where the
forest sloped gently to the shore, among the bushes and
stumps of the rough clearing made in constructing it, stood
a palisade fort, the work of an Algonquin war-party in the
past autumn. It was a mere enclosure of trunks of small
trees planted in a circle, and was already ruinous. Such as
it was, the Frenchmen took possession of it. Their first
care, one would think, should have been to repair and
strengthen it; but this they seem not to have done: possibly, in the exaltation of their minds, they scorned such precaution. They made their fires, and slung their kettles on
the neighboring shore; and here they were soon joined by
the Hurons and Algonquins. Daulac, it seems, made no objection to their company, and they all bivouacked together.
Morning and noon and night they prayed in three different
tongues; and when at sunset the long reach of forests on
the farther shore basked peacefully in the level rays, the rapids joined their hoarse music to the notes of their evening
hymn.

In a day or two their scouts came in with tidings that
two Iroquois canoes were coming down the Saut. Daulac
had time to set his men in ambush among the bushes at a
point where he thought the strangers likely to land. He
judged aright. The canoes, bearing five Iroquois, approached, and were met by a volley fired with such precip-
itation that one or more of them escaped the shot, fled into
the forest, and told their mischance to their main body,
two hundred in number, on the river above. A fleet of canoes suddenly appeared, bounding down the rapids, filled
with warriors eager for revenge. The allies had barely time
to escape to their fort, leaving their kettles still slung over
the fires. The Iroquois made a hasty and desultory attack,
and were quickly repulsed. They next opened a parley, hoping, no doubt, to gain some advantage by surprise. Failing
in this, they set themselves, after their custom on such oc-

casions, to building a rude fort of their own in the neighboring forest.

This gave the French a breathing-time, and they used
it for strengthening their defences. Being provided with
tools, they planted a row of stakes within their palisade, to
form a double fence, and filled the intervening space with
earth and stones to the height of a man, leaving some
twenty loopholes, at each of which three marksmen were
stationed. Their work was still unfinished when the Iroquois were upon them again. They had broken to pieces
the birch canoes of the French and their allies, and, kindling the bark, rushed up to pile it blazing against the palisade; but so brisk and steady a fire met them that they
recoiled and at last gave way. They came on again, and
again were driven back, leaving many of their number on
the ground, among them the principal chief of the Senecas.
Some of the French dashed out, and, covered by the fire of
their comrades, hacked off his head, and stuck it on the
palisade, while the Iroquois howled in a frenzy of helpless
rage. They tried another attack, and were beaten off a third
time.

This dashed their spirits, and they sent a canoe to call to
their aid five hundred of their warriors who were mustered
near the mouth of the Richelieu. These were the allies
whom, but for this untoward check, they were on their way
to join for a combined attack on Quebec, Three Rivers, and
Montreal. It was maddening to see their grand project
thwarted by a few French and Indians ensconced in a paltry
redoubt, scarcely better than a cattle-pen; but they were
forced to digest the affront as best they might.

Meanwhile, crouched behind trees and logs, they beset
the fort, harassing its defenders day and night with a spat-
tering fire and a constant menace of attack. Thus five days
passed. Hunger, thirst, and want of sleep wrought fatally
on the strength of the French and their allies, who, pent up
together in their narrow prison, fought and prayed by
turns. Deprived as they were of water, they could not swallow the crushed Indian corn, or "hominy," which was their
only food. Some of them, under cover of a brisk fire, ran
down to the river and filled such small vessels as they had;

but this pittance only tantalized their thirst. They dug a hole in the fort, and were rewarded at last by a little muddy water oozing through the clay.

Among the assailants were a number of Hurons, adopted by the Iroquois and fighting on their side. These renegades now shouted to their countrymen in the fort, telling them that a fresh army was close at hand; that they would soon be attacked by seven or eight hundred warriors; and that their only hope was in joining the Iroquois, who would receive them as friends. Annahotaha's followers, half dead with thirst and famine, listened to their seducers, took the bait, and, one, two, or three at a time, climbed the palisade and ran over to the enemy, amid the hootings and execrations of those whom they deserted. Their chief stood firm; and when he saw his nephew, La Mouche, join the other fugitives, he fired his pistol at him in a rage. The four Algonquins, who had no mercy to hope for, stood fast, with the courage of despair.

On the fifth day an uproar of unearthly yells from seven hundred savage throats, mingled with a clattering salute of musketry, told the Frenchmen that the expected reinforcement had come; and soon, in the forest and on the clearing, a crowd of warriors mustered for the attack. Knowing from the Huron deserters the weakness of their enemy, they had no doubt of an easy victory. They advanced cautiously, as was usual with the Iroquois before their blood was up, screeching, leaping from side to side, and firing as they came on; but the French were at their posts, and every loophole darted its tongue of fire. Besides muskets, they had heavy musketoons of large calibre, which, scattering scraps of lead and iron among the throng of savages, often maimed several of them at one discharge. The Iroquois, astonished at the persistent vigor of the defence, fell back discomfited. The fire of the French, who were themselves completely under cover, had told upon them with deadly effect. Three days more wore away in a series of futile attacks, made with little concert or vigor; and during all this time Daulac and his men, reeling with exhaustion, fought and prayed as before, sure of a martyr's reward.

The uncertain, vacillating temper common to all Indians

now began to declare itself. Some of the Iroquois were for going home. Others revolted at the thought, and declared that it would be an eternal disgrace to lose so many men at the hands of so paltry an enemy, and yet fail to take revenge. It was resolved to make a general assault, and volunteers were called for to lead the attack. After the custom on such occasions, bundles of small sticks were thrown upon the ground, and those picked them up who dared, thus accepting the gage of battle, and enrolling themselves in the forlorn hope. No precaution was neglected. Large and heavy shields four or five feet high were made by lashing together three split logs with the aid of cross-bars. Covering themselves with these mantelets, the chosen band advanced, followed by the motley throng of warriors. In spite of a brisk fire, they reached the palisade, and, crouching below the range of shot, hewed furiously with their hatchets to cut their way through. The rest followed close, and swarmed like angry hornets around the little fort, hacking and tearing to get in.

Daulac had crammed a large musketoon with powder, and plugged up the muzzle. Lighting the fuse inserted in it, he tried to throw it over the barrier, to burst like a grenade among the crowd of savages without; but it struck the ragged top of one of the palisades, fell back among the Frenchmen and exploded, killing and wounding several of them, and nearly blinding others. In the confusion that followed, the Iroquois got possession of the loopholes, and, thrusting in their guns, fired on those within. In a moment more they had torn a breach in the palisade; but, nerved with the energy of desperation, Daulac and his followers sprang to defend it. Another breach was made, and then another. Daulac was struck dead, but the survivors kept up the fight. With a sword or a hatchet in one hand and a knife in the other, they threw themselves against the throng of enemies, striking and stabbing with the fury of madmen; till the Iroquois, despairing of taking them alive, fired volley after volley and shot them down. All was over, and a burst of triumphant yells proclaimed the dear-bought victory.

Searching the pile of corpses, the victors found four Frenchmen still breathing. Three had scarcely a spark of life, and, as no time was to be lost, they burned them on the spot. The fourth, less fortunate, seemed likely to survive, and they reserved him for future torments. As for the Huron deserters, their cowardice profited them little. The Iroquois, regardless of their promises, fell upon them, burned some at once, and carried the rest to their villages for a similar fate. Five of the number had the good fortune to escape, and it was from them, aided by admissions made long afterwards by the Iroquois themselves, that the French of Canada derived all their knowledge of this glorious disaster.[1]

[1] When the fugitive Hurons reached Montreal, they were unwilling to confess their desertion of the French, and declared that they and some others of their people, to the number of fourteen, had stood by them to the last. This was the story told by one of them to the Jesuit Chaumonot, and by him communicated in a letter to his friends at Quebec. The substance of this letter is given by Marie de l'Incarnation, in her letter to her son of June 25, 1660. The Jesuit *Relation* of this year gives another long account of the affair, also derived from the Huron deserters, who this time only pretended that ten of their number remained with the French. They afterwards admitted that all had deserted but Annahotaha, as appears from the account drawn up by Dollier de Casson, in his *Histoire du Montréal*. Another contemporary, Belmont, who heard the story from an Iroquois, makes the same statement. All these writers, though two of them were not friendly to Montreal, agree that Daulac and his followers saved Canada from a disastrous invasion. The governor, Argenson, in a letter written on the fourth of July following, and in his *Mémoire sur le sujet de la guerre des Iroquois*, expresses the same conviction. Before me is an extract, copied from the *Petit Registre de la Cure de Montréal*, giving the names and ages of Daulac's men.

Radisson, the famous *voyageur*, says that, on his way down the Ottawa from Lake Superior, he passed the Long Saut eight days after the destruction of Daulac and his party; and he gives an account of the fight that answers on the whole to those of the other writers. He adds, however, that the Hurons remained outside the fort, which was too small to hold them, and that only the 17 Frenchmen and 4 Algonquins, or 21 in all, were under cover. He also says that the reinforcement which joined the 200 Iroquois who began the attack consisted of "550 Iroquois of the lower nation" (Mohawks) "and 50 Orijonot" (Oneidas?), making with the original assailants 800 in all. *Publications of the Prince Society*, 1885, p. 233. Radisson, whose narratives were not written till some years after the events that they record, forgets the date of the fight at the Long Saut, which would appear from him to have happened three years after it really took place.

Abbé Faillon took extreme pains to collect the evidence touching Daulac's heroism, and, though Radisson's writings were unknown to him, his narrative should be consulted by those interested in the subject. See his anonymous *Histoire de la Colonie Française au Canada*, II. chap. xv.

To the colony it proved a salvation. The Iroquois had had fighting enough. If seventeen Frenchmen, four Algonquins, and one Huron, behind a picket fence, could hold seven hundred warriors at bay so long, what might they expect from many such, fighting behind walls of stone? For that year they thought no more of capturing Quebec and Montreal, but went home dejected and amazed, to howl over their losses, and nurse their dashed courage for a day of vengeance.

Chapter VII

THE DISPUTED BISHOPRIC

Domestic Strife • Jesuit and Sulpitian • Abbé Queylus • François de Laval • The Zealots of Caen • Gallican and Ultramontane • The Rival Claimants • Storm at Quebec • Laval Triumphant

---

CANADA, gasping under the Iroquois tomahawk, might, one would suppose, have thought her cup of tribulation full, and, sated with inevitable woe, have sought consolation from the wrath without in a holy calm within. Not so, however; for while the heathen raged at the door, discord rioted at the hearthstone. Her domestic quarrels were wonderful in number, diversity, and bitterness. There was the standing quarrel of Montreal and Quebec, the quarrels of priests with each other, of priests with the governor, and of the governor with the intendant, besides ceaseless wranglings of rival traders and rival peculators.

Some of these disputes were local and of no special significance; while others are very interesting, because, on a remote and obscure theatre, they represent, sometimes in striking forms, the contending passions and principles of a most important epoch of history. To begin with one which even to this day has left a root of bitterness behind it.

The association of pious enthusiasts who had founded Montreal[1] was reduced in 1657 to a remnant of five or six persons, whose ebbing zeal and overtaxed purses were no longer equal to the devout but arduous enterprise. They begged the priests of the Seminary of St. Sulpice to take it off their hands. The priests consented; and, though the conveyance of the island of Montreal to these its new proprietors did not take effect till some years later, four of the Sulpitian fathers, Queylus, Souart, Galinée, and Allet, came out to the colony and took it in charge. Thus far Canada had had no bishop, and the Sulpitians now aspired to give it one from their own brotherhood. Many years before, when the Recollets had a

[1] See *Jesuits in North America*, chap. xv.

foothold in the colony, they too, or at least some of them, had cherished the hope of giving Canada a bishop of their own.[1] As for the Jesuits, who for nearly thirty years had of themselves constituted the Canadian church, they had been content thus far to dispense with a bishop; for, having no rivals in the field, they had felt no need of episcopal support.

The Sulpitians put forward Queylus as their candidate for the new bishopric. The assembly of French clergy approved, and Cardinal Mazarin himself seemed to sanction, the nomination. The Jesuits saw that their time of action was come. It was they who had borne the heat and burden of the day, the toils, privations, and martyrdoms, while as yet the Sulpitians had done nothing and endured nothing. If any body of ecclesiastics was to have the nomination of a bishop, it clearly belonged to them, the Jesuits. Their might, too, matched their right. They were strong at court; Mazarin withdrew his assent, and the Jesuits were invited to name a bishop to their liking.

Meanwhile the Sulpitians, despairing of the bishopric, had sought their solace elsewhere. Ships bound for Canada had usually sailed from ports within the jurisdiction of the Archbishop of Rouen, and the departing missionaries had received their ecclesiastical powers from him, till he had learned to regard Canada as an outlying section of his diocese. Not unwilling to assert his claims, he now made Queylus his vicar-general for all Canada, thus clothing him with episcopal powers, and placing him over the heads of the Jesuits. Queylus, in effect, though not in name, a bishop, left his companion Souart in the spiritual charge of Montreal, came down to Quebec, announced his new dignity, and assumed the curacy of the parish. The Jesuits received him at first with their usual urbanity, an exercise of self-control rendered more easy by their knowledge that one more potent than Queylus would soon arrive to supplant him.[2]

---

[1] *Mémoire qui faict pour l'affaire des P. P. Recollects de la prouince de St. Denys ditte de Paris touchant le droict qu'ils ont depuis l'an 1615, d'aller en Quanada soubs l'authorité de Sa Maiesté, etc.,* 1637.

[2] A detailed account of the experiences of Queylus at Quebec, immediately after his arrival, as related by himself, will be found in a memoir by the Sulpitian Allet, in *Morale Pratique des Jésuites,* XXXIV. chap. xii. In chapter ten of the same volume the writer says that he visited Queylus at Mont St.

The vicar of the Archbishop of Rouen was a man of many virtues, devoted to good works, as he understood them; rich, for the Sulpitians were under no vow of poverty; generous in alms-giving, busy, indefatigable, overflowing with zeal, vivacious in temperament and excitable in temper, impatient of opposition, and, as it seems, incapable, like his destined rival, of seeing any way of doing good but his own. Though the Jesuits were outwardly courteous, their partisans would not listen to the new curé's sermons, or listened only to find fault, and germs of discord grew vigorously in the parish of Quebec. Prudence was not among the virtues of Queylus. He launched two sermons against the Jesuits, in which he likened himself to Christ and them to the Pharisees. "Who," he supposed them to say, "is this Jesus, so beloved of the people, who comes to cast discredit on us, who for thirty or forty years have governed church and state here, with none to dispute us?"[1] He denounced such of his hearers as came to pick flaws in his discourse, and told them it would be better for their souls if they lay in bed at home, sick of a "good quartan fever." His ire was greatly kindled by a letter of the Jesuit Pijart, which fell into his hands through a female adherent, the pious Madame d'Aillebout, and in which that father declared that he, Queylus, was waging war on him and his brethren more savagely than the Iroquois.[2] "He was as crazy at sight of a Jesuit," writes an adverse biographer, "as a mad dog at sight of water."[3] He cooled, however, on being shown certain papers which proved that his position was neither so strong nor so secure as he had supposed; and the governor, Argenson, at length persuaded him to retire to Montreal.[4]

The queen mother, Anne of Austria, always inclined to the Jesuits, had invited Father Le Jeune, who was then in France,

---

Valérien, after his return from Canada. "Il me prit à part; nous nous promenâmes assez longtemps dans le jardin et il m'ouvrit son cœur sur la conduite des Jésuites dans le Canada et partout ailleurs. Messieurs de St. Sulpice savent bien ce qu'il m'en a pu dire, et je suis assuré qu'ils ne diront pas que je l'ai dû prendre pour des mensonges."

[1] *Journal des Jésuites*, Oct., 1657.
[2] *Journal des Jésuites*, Oct., 1657.
[3] Viger, *Notice Historique sur l'Abbé de Queylus*.
[4] *Papiers d'Argenson*.

to make choice of a bishop for Canada. It was not an easy task. No Jesuit was eligible, for the sage policy of Loyola had excluded members of the order from the bishopric. The signs of the times portended trouble for the Canadian church, and there was need of a bishop who would assert her claims and fight her battles. Such a man could not be made an instrument of the Jesuits; therefore there was double need that he should be one with them in sympathy and purpose. They made a sagacious choice. Le Jeune presented to the queen mother the name of François Xavier de Laval-Montmorency, Abbé de Montigny.

Laval, for by this name he was thenceforth known, belonged to one of the proudest families of Europe, and, churchman as he was, there is much in his career to remind us that in his veins ran the blood of the stern Constable of France, Anne de Montmorency. Nevertheless, his thoughts from childhood had turned towards the church, or, as his biographers will have it, all his aspirations were heavenward. He received the tonsure at the age of nine. The Jesuit Bagot confirmed and moulded his youthful predilections; and, at a later period, he was one of a band of young zealots, formed under the auspices of Bernières de Louvigni, royal treasurer at Caen, who, though a layman, was reputed almost a saint. It was Bernières who had borne the chief part in the pious fraud of the pretended marriage through which Madame de la Peltrie escaped from her father's roof to become foundress of the Ursulines of Quebec.[1] He had since renounced the world, and dwelt at Caen, in a house attached to an Ursuline convent, and known as the Hermitage. Here he lived like a monk, in the midst of a community of young priests and devotees, who looked to him as their spiritual director, and whom he trained in the maxims and practices of the most extravagant, or, as his admirers say, the most sublime ultramontane piety.[2]

The conflict between the Jesuits and the Jansenists was then at its height. The Jansenist doctrines of election and salvation by grace, which sapped the power of the priesthood and impugned the authority of the Pope himself in his capacity of

[1] See Jesuits in North America, chap. xiv.

[2] La Tour, *Vie de Laval*, gives his maxims at length.

holder of the keys of heaven, were to the Jesuits an abomination; while the rigid morals of the Jansenists stood in stern
contrast to the pliancy of Jesuit casuistry. Bernières and his
disciples were zealous, not to say fanatical, partisans of the
Jesuits. There is a long account of the "Hermitage" and its
inmates from the pen of the famous Jansenist, Nicole; an opponent, it is true, but one whose qualities of mind and character give weight to his testimony.[1]

"In this famous Hermitage," says Nicole, "the late Sieur de
Bernières brought up a number of young men, to whom he
taught a sort of sublime and transcendental devotion called
passive prayer, because in it the mind does not act at all, but
merely receives the divine operation; and this devotion is the
source of all those visions and revelations in which the Hermitage is so prolific." In short, he and his disciples were mystics of the most exalted type. Nicole pursues: "After having
thus subtilized their minds, and almost sublimed them into
vapor, he rendered them capable of detecting Jansenists under
any disguise, insomuch that some of his followers said that
they knew them by the scent, as dogs know their game; but
the aforesaid Sieur de Bernières denied that they had so subtile a sense of smell, and said that the mark by which he detected Jansenists was their disapproval of his teachings or
their opposition to the Jesuits."

The zealous band at the Hermitage was aided in its efforts
to extirpate error by a sort of external association in the city
of Caen, consisting of merchants, priests, officers, petty nobles, and others, all inspired and guided by Bernières. They
met every week at the Hermitage, or at the houses of each
other. Similar associations existed in other cities of France,
besides a fraternity in the Rue St. Dominique at Paris, which
was formed by the Jesuit Bagot, and seems to have been the
parent, in a certain sense, of the others. They all acted together when any important object was in view.

Bernières and his disciples felt that God had chosen them
not only to watch over doctrine and discipline in convents
and in families, but also to supply the prevalent deficiency of

---

[1] *Mémoire pour faire connoistre l'esprit et la conduite de la Compagnie établie
en la ville de Caen, appellée l'Hermitage* (Bibliothèque Nationale, Imprimés
Partie Réservée). Written in 1660.

zeal in bishops and other dignitaries of the church. They kept, too, a constant eye on the humbler clergy, and whenever a new preacher appeared in Caen, two of their number were deputed to hear his sermon and report upon it. If he chanced to let fall a word concerning the grace of God, they denounced him for Jansenistic heresy. Such commotion was once raised in Caen by charges of sedition and Jansenism, brought by the Hermitage against priests and laymen hitherto without attaint, that the Bishop of Bayeux thought it necessary to interpose; but even he was forced to pause, daunted by the insinuations of Bernières that he was in secret sympathy with the obnoxious doctrines.

Thus the Hermitage and its affiliated societies constituted themselves a sort of inquisition in the interest of the Jesuits; "for what," asks Nicole, "might not be expected from persons of weak minds and atrabilious dispositions, dried up by constant fasts, vigils, and other austerities, besides meditations of three or four hours a day, and told continually that the church is in imminent danger of ruin through the machinations of the Jansenists, who are represented to them as persons who wish to break up the foundations of the Christian faith and subvert the mystery of the Incarnation; who believe neither in transubstantiation, the invocation of saints, nor indulgences; who wish to abolish the sacrifice of the Mass and the sacrament of Penitence, oppose the worship of the Holy Virgin, deny free-will and substitute predestination in its place, and, in fine, conspire to overthrow the authority of the Supreme Pontiff."

Among other anecdotes, Nicole tells the following: One of the young zealots of the Hermitage took it into his head that all Caen was full of Jansenists, and that the curés of the place were in league with them. He inoculated four others with this notion, and they resolved to warn the people of their danger. They accordingly made the tour of the streets, without hats or collars, and with coats unbuttoned, though it was a cold winter day, stopping every moment to proclaim in a loud voice that all the curés, excepting two, whom they named, were abettors of the Jansenists. A mob was soon following at their heels, and there was great excitement. The magistrates chanced to be in session, and, hearing of the disturbance, they

sent constables to arrest the authors of it. Being brought to
the bar of justice and questioned by the judge, they answered
that they were doing the work of God, and were ready to die
in the cause; that Caen was full of Jansenists, and that the
curés had declared in their favor, inasmuch as they denied any
knowledge of their existence. Four of the five were locked up
for a few days, tried, and sentenced to a fine of a hundred
livres, with a promise of further punishment should they
again disturb the peace.[1]

The fifth, being pronounced out of his wits by the physicians, was sent home to his mother, at a village near Argentan, where two or three of his fellow zealots presently joined
him. Among them, they persuaded his mother, who had hitherto been devoted to household cares, to exchange them for
a life of mystical devotion. "These three or four persons," says
Nicole, "attracted others as imbecile as themselves." Among
these recruits were a number of women, and several priests.
After various acts of fanaticism, "two or three days before last
Pentecost," proceeds the narrator, "they all set out, men and
women, for Argentan. The priests had drawn the skirts of
their cassocks over their heads, and tied them about their
necks with twisted straw. Some of the women had their heads
bare, and their hair streaming loose over their shoulders.
They picked up filth on the road, and rubbed their faces with
it, and the most zealous ate it, saying that it was necessary to
mortify the taste. Some held stones in their hands, which they
knocked together to draw the attention of the passers-by.
They had a leader, whom they were bound to obey; and
when this leader saw any mud-hole particularly deep and
dirty, he commanded some of the party to roll themselves in
it, which they did forthwith.[2]

"After this fashion, they entered the town of Argentan, and

---

[1] Nicole is not the only authority for this story. It is also told by a very
different writer. See *Notice Historique de l'Abbaye de Ste. Claire d'Argentan*,
124.

[2] These proceedings were probably intended to produce the result which
was the constant object of the mystics of the Hermitage; namely, the "annihilation of self," with a view to a perfect union with God. To become despised of men was an important, if not an essential, step in this mystical
suicide.

marched, two by two, through all the streets, crying with a loud voice that the Faith was perishing, and that whoever wished to save it must quit the country and go with them to Canada, whither they were soon to repair. It is said that they still hold this purpose, and that their leaders declare it revealed to them that they will find a vessel ready at the first port to which Providence directs them. The reason why they choose Canada for an asylum is, that Monsieur de Montigny (*Laval*), Bishop of Petræa, who lived at the Hermitage a long time, where he was instructed in mystical theology by Monsieur de Bernières, exercises episcopal functions there; and that the Jesuits, who are their oracles, reign in that country."

This adventure, like the other, ended in a collision with the police. "The priests," adds Nicole, "were arrested, and are now waiting trial, and the rest were treated as mad, and sent back with shame and confusion to the places whence they had come."

Though these pranks took place after Laval had left the Hermitage, they serve to characterize the school in which he was formed; or, more justly speaking, to show its most extravagant side. That others did not share the views of the celebrated Jansenist, may be gathered from the following passage of the funeral oration pronounced over the body of Laval half a century later:—

"The humble abbé was next transported into the terrestrial paradise of Monsieur de Bernières. It is thus that I call, as it is fitting to call it, that famous Hermitage of Caen, where the seraphic author of the 'Christian Interior' (*Bernières*) transformed into angels all those who had the happiness to be the companions of his solitude and of his spiritual exercises. It was there that, during four years, the fervent abbé drank the living and abounding waters of grace which have since flowed so benignly over this land of Canada. In this celestial abode his ordinary occupations were prayer, mortification, instruction of the poor, and spiritual readings or conferences; his recreations were to labor in the hospitals, wait upon the sick and poor, make their beds, dress their wounds, and aid them in their most repulsive needs."[1]

[1] *Eloge funèbre de Messire François Xavier de Laval-Montmorency, par Messire de la Colombière, Vicaire Général.*

In truth, Laval's zeal was boundless, and the exploits of self-humiliation recorded of him were unspeakably revolting.[1] Bernières himself regarded him as a light by which to guide his own steps in ways of holiness. He made journeys on foot about the country, disguised, penniless, begging from door to door, and courting scorn and opprobrium, "in order," says his biographer, "that he might suffer for the love of God." Yet, though living at this time in a state of habitual religious exaltation, he was by nature no mere dreamer; and in whatever heights his spirit might wander, his feet were always planted on the solid earth. His flaming zeal had for its servants a hard, practical nature, perfectly fitted for the battle of life, a narrow intellect, a stiff and persistent will, and, as his enemies thought, the love of domination native to his blood.

Two great parties divided the Catholics of France,—the Gallican or national party, and the ultramontane or papal party. The first, resting on the Scriptural injunction to give tribute to Cæsar, held that to the king, the Lord's anointed, belonged the temporal, and to the church the spiritual power. It held also that the laws and customs of the church of France could not be broken at the bidding of the Pope.[2] The ultramontane party, on the other hand, maintained that the Pope, Christ's vicegerent on earth, was supreme over earthly rulers, and should of right hold jurisdiction over the clergy of all Christendom, with powers of appointment and removal. Hence they claimed for him the right of nominating bishops in France. This had anciently been exercised by assemblies of the French clergy, but in the reign of Francis I. the king and the Pope had combined to wrest it from them by the Concordat of Bologna. Under this compact, which was still in force, the Pope appointed French bishops on the nomination of the king, a plan which displeased the Gallicans, and did not satisfy the ultramontanes.

The Jesuits, then as now, were the most forcible exponents of ultramontane principles. The church to rule the world; the

---

[1] See La Tour, *Vie de Laval*, Liv. I. Some of them were closely akin to that of the fanatics mentioned above, who ate "immondices d'animaux" to mortify the taste.

[2] See the famous *Quatre Articles* of 1682, in which the liberties of the Gallican Church are asserted.

Pope to rule the church; the Jesuits to rule the Pope: such was and is the simple programme of the Order of Jesus, and to it they have held fast, except on a few rare occasions of misunderstanding with the Vicegerent of Christ.[1] In the question of papal supremacy, as in most things else, Laval was of one mind with them.

Those versed in such histories will not be surprised to learn that, when he received the royal nomination, humility would not permit him to accept it; nor that, being urged, he at length bowed in resignation, still protesting his unworthiness. Nevertheless, the royal nomination did not take effect. The ultramontanes outflanked both the king and the Gallicans, and by adroit strategy made the new prelate completely a creature of the papacy. Instead of appointing him Bishop of Quebec, in accordance with the royal initiative, the Pope made him his vicar apostolic for Canada, thus evading the king's nomination, and affirming that Canada, a country of infidel savages, was excluded from the concordat, and under his (the Pope's) jurisdiction pure and simple. The Gallicans were enraged. The Archbishop of Rouen vainly opposed, and the parliaments of Rouen and of Paris vainly protested. The papal party prevailed. The king, or rather Mazarin, gave his consent, subject to certain conditions, the chief of which was an oath of allegiance; and Laval, grand vicar apostolic, decorated with the title of Bishop of Petræa, sailed for his wilderness diocese in the spring of 1659.[2] He was but thirty-six years of age, but even when a boy he could scarcely have seemed young.

Queylus, for a time, seemed to accept the situation, and tacitly admit the claim of Laval as his ecclesiastical superior; but, stimulated by a letter from the Archbishop of Rouen, he soon threw himself into an attitude of opposition,[3] in which the popularity which his generosity to the poor had won for him gave him an advantage very annoying to his adversary.

---

[1] For example, not long after this time, the Jesuits, having a dispute with Innocent XI., threw themselves into the party of opposition.

[2] Compare La Tour, *Vie de Laval*, with the long statement in Faillon, *Colonie Française*, II. 315–335. Faillon gives various documents in full, including the royal letter of nomination and those in which the King gives a reluctant consent to the appointment of the vicar apostolic.

[3] *Journal des Jésuites, Sept., 1657.*

The quarrel, it will be seen, was three-sided,—Gallican against ultramontane, Sulpitian against Jesuit, Montreal against Quebec. To Montreal the recalcitrant abbé, after a brief visit to Quebec, had again retired; but even here, girt with his Sulpitian brethren and compassed with partisans, the arm of the vicar apostolic was long enough to reach him.

By temperament and conviction Laval hated a divided authority, and the very shadow of a schism was an abomination in his sight. The young king, who, though abundantly jealous of his royal power, was forced to conciliate the papal party, had sent instructions to Argenson, the governor, to support Laval, and prevent divisions in the Canadian church.[1] These instructions served as the pretext of a procedure sufficiently summary. A squad of soldiers, commanded, it is said, by the governor himself, went up to Montreal, brought the indignant Queylus to Quebec, and shipped him thence for France.[2] By these means, writes Father Lalemant, order reigned for a season in the church.

It was but for a season. Queylus was not a man to bide his defeat in tranquillity, nor were his brother Sulpitians disposed to silent acquiescence. Laval, on his part, was not a man of half measures. He had an agent in France, and partisans strong at court. Fearing, to borrow the words of a Catholic writer, that the return of Queylus to Canada would prove "injurious to the glory of God," he bestirred himself to prevent it. The young king, then at Aix, on his famous journey to the frontiers of Spain to marry the Infanta, was induced to write to Queylus, ordering him to remain in France.[3] Queylus, however, repaired to Rome; but even against this movement provision had been made: accusations of Jansenism had gone before him, and he met a cold welcome. Nevertheless, as he had powerful friends near the Pope, he succeeded in removing these adverse impressions, and even in obtaining certain bulls relating to the establishment of the parish of Montreal, and favorable to the Sulpitians. Provided with these, he set at nought the king's letter, embarked under an

---

[1] *Lettre du Roi à d'Argenson, 14 Mai, 1659.*

[2] Belmont, *Histoire du Canada, A.D. 1659.* Memoir by Abbé d'Allet, in *Morale Pratique des Jésuites,* XXXIV. 725.

[3] *Lettre du Roi à Queylus, 27 Feb., 1660.*

assumed name, and sailed to Quebec, where he made his appearance on the 3d of August, 1661,[1] to the extreme wrath of Laval.

A ferment ensued. Laval's partisans charged the Sulpitians with Jansenism and opposition to the will of the Pope. A preacher more zealous than the rest denounced them as priests of Antichrist; and as to the bulls in their favor, it was affirmed that Queylus had obtained them by fraud from the Holy Father. Laval at once issued a mandate forbidding him to proceed to Montreal till ships should arrive with instructions from the King.[2] At the same time he demanded of the governor that he should interpose the civil power to prevent Queylus from leaving Quebec.[3] As Argenson, who wished to act as peacemaker between the belligerent fathers, did not at once take the sharp measures required of him, Laval renewed his demand on the next day, calling on him, in the name of God and the king, to compel Queylus to yield the obedience due to him, the vicar apostolic.[4] At the same time he sent another to the offending abbé, threatening to suspend him from priestly functions if he persisted in his rebellion.[5]

The incorrigible Queylus, who seems to have lived for some months in a simmer of continual indignation, set at nought the vicar apostolic as he had set at nought the king, took a boat that very night, and set out for Montreal under cover of darkness. Great was the ire of Laval when he heard the news in the morning. He despatched a letter after him, declaring him suspended *ipso facto*, if he did not instantly return and make his submission.[6] This letter, like the rest, failed of the desired effect; but the governor, who had received a second mandate from the king to support Laval and prevent a schism,[7] now reluctantly interposed the secular arm, and Queylus was again compelled to return to France.[8]

[1] *Journal des Jésuites, Août, 1661.*
[2] *Lettre de Laval à Queylus, 4 Août, 1661.*
[3] *Lettre de Laval à d'Argenson, Ibid.*
[4] *Lettre de Laval à d'Argenson, 5 Août, 1661.*
[5] *Lettre de Laval à Queylus, Ibid.*
[6] *Ibid, 6 Août, 1661.*
[7] *Lettre du Roi à d'Argenson, 13 Mai, 1660.*
[8] For the governor's attitude in this affair, consult the *Papiers d'Argenson*, containing his despatches.

His expulsion was a Sulpitian defeat. Laval, always zealous for unity and centralization, had some time before taken steps to repress what he regarded as a tendency to independence at Montreal. In the preceding year he had written to the Pope: "There are some secular priests (*Sulpitians*) at Montreal, whom the Abbé de Queylus brought out with him in 1657, and I have named for the functions of curé the one among them whom I thought the least disobedient." The bulls which Queylus had obtained from Rome related to this very curacy, and greatly disturbed the mind of the vicar apostolic. He accordingly wrote again to the Pope: "I pray your Holiness to let me know your will concerning the jurisdiction of the Archbishop of Rouen. M. l'Abbé de Queylus, who has come out this year as vicar of this archbishop, has tried to deceive us by surreptitious letters, and has obeyed neither our prayers nor our repeated commands to desist. But he has received orders from the king to return immediately to France, to render an account of his disobedience, and he has been compelled by the governor to conform to the will of his Majesty. What I now fear is that, on his return to France, by using every kind of means, employing new artifices, and falsely representing our affairs, he may obtain from the court of Rome powers which may disturb the peace of our church; for the priests whom he brought with him from France, and who live at Montreal, are animated with the same spirit of disobedience and division; and I fear, with good reason, that all belonging to the seminary of St. Sulpice, who may come hereafter to join them, will be of the same disposition. If what is said is true, that by means of fraudulent letters the right of patronage of the pretended parish of Montreal has been granted to the superior of this seminary, and the right of appointment to the Archbishop of Rouen, then is altar reared against altar in our church of Canada; for the clergy of Montreal will always stand in opposition to me, the vicar apostolic, and to my successors."[1]

These dismal forebodings were never realized. The Holy See annulled the obnoxious bulls; the Archbishop of Rouen renounced his claims, and Queylus found his position untenable.

[1] *Lettre de Laval au Pape, 22 Oct., 1661*. Printed by Faillon, from the original in the archives of the Propaganda.

Seven years later, when Laval was on a visit to France, a reconciliation was brought about between them. The former vicar of the Archbishop of Rouen made his submission to the vicar of the Pope, and returned to Canada as a missionary. Laval's triumph was complete, to the joy of the Jesuits, silent, if not idle, spectators of the tedious and complex quarrel.

WE are touching delicate ground. To many excellent Catholics of our own day Laval is an object of veneration. The Catholic university of Quebec glories in bearing his name, and certain modern ecclesiastical writers rarely mention him in terms less reverent than "the virtuous prelate," or "the holy prelate." Nor are some of his contemporaries less emphatic in eulogy. Mother Juchereau de Saint-Denis, Superior of the Hôtel Dieu, wrote immediately after his death: "He began in his tenderest years the study of perfection, and we have reason to think that he reached it, since every virtue which Saint Paul demands in a bishop was seen and admired in him;" and on his first arrival in Canada, Mother Marie de l'Incarnation, Superior of the Ursulines, wrote to her son that the choice of such a prelate was not of man, but of God. "I will not," she adds, "say that he is a saint, but I may say with truth that he lives like a saint and an apostle." And she describes his austerity of life; how he had but two servants, a gardener—whom he lent on occasion to his needy neighbors—and a valet; how he lived in a small hired house, saying that he would not have one of his own if he could build it for only five sous; and how, in his table, furniture, and bed, he showed the spirit of poverty, even, as she thinks, to excess. His servant, a lay brother named Houssart, testified, after his death, that he slept on a hard bed, and would not suffer it to be changed even when it became full of fleas; and, what is more to the purpose, that he gave fifteen hundred or two thousand francs to the poor every year.[1] Houssart also gives the following specimen of his austerities: "I have seen him

---

[1] *Lettre du Frère Houssart, ancien serviteur de M̃g̃'r de Laval à M. Tremblay, 1 Sept., 1708.* This letter is printed, though with one or two important omissions, in the *Abeille*, Vol. I. (Quebec, 1848.)

keep cooked meat five, six, seven, or eight days in the heat of summer, and when it was all mouldy and wormy he washed it in warm water and ate it, and told me that it was very good." The old servant was so impressed by these and other proofs of his master's sanctity, that "I determined," he says, "to keep every thing I could that had belonged to his holy person, and after his death to soak bits of linen in his blood when his body was opened, and take a few bones and carti- lages from his breast, cut off his hair, and keep his clothes, and such things, to serve as most precious relics." These pious cares were not in vain, for the relics proved greatly in demand.

Several portraits of Laval are extant. A drooping nose of portentous size; a well-formed forehead; a brow strongly arched; a bright, clear eye; scanty hair, half hidden by a black skullcap; thin lips, compressed and rigid, betraying a spirit not easy to move or convince; features of that indescribable cast which marks the priestly type: such is Laval, as he looks grimly down on us from the dingy canvas of two centuries ago.

He is one of those concerning whom Protestants and Cath- olics, at least ultramontane Catholics, will never agree in judg- ment. The task of eulogizing him may safely be left to those of his own way of thinking. It is for us to regard him from the standpoint of secular history. And, first, let us credit him with sincerity. He believed firmly that the princes and rulers of this world ought to be subject to guidance and control at the hands of the Pope, the vicar of Christ on earth. But he himself was the Pope's vicar, and, so far as the bounds of Canada extended, the Holy Father had clothed him with his own authority. The glory of God demanded that this author- ity should suffer no abatement, and he, Laval, would be guilty before Heaven if he did not uphold the supremacy of the church over the powers both of earth and of hell.

Of the faults which he owed to nature, the principal seems to have been an arbitrary and domineering temper. He was one of those who by nature lean always to the side of author- ity; and in the English Revolution he would inevitably have stood for the Stuarts; or, in the American Revolution, for the Crown. But being above all things a Catholic and a priest, he was drawn by a constitutional necessity to the ultramontane party, or the party of centralization. He fought lustily, in his way, against the natural man; and humility was the virtue to the culture of which he gave his chief attention, but soil and climate were not favorable. His life was one long assertion of the authority of the church, and this authority was lodged in himself. In his stubborn fight for ecclesiastical ascendancy, he was aided by the impulses of a nature that loved to rule, and could not endure to yield. His principles and his instinct of domination were acting in perfect unison, and his conscience was the handmaid of his fault. Austerities and mortifications, playing at beggar, sleeping in beds full of fleas, or performing prodigies of gratuitous dirtiness in hospitals, however fatal to self-respect, could avail little against influences working so powerfully and so insidiously to stimulate the most subtle of human vices. The history of the Roman church is full of Lavals.

The Jesuits, adepts in human nature, had made a sagacious choice when they put forward this conscientious, zealous, dogged, and pugnacious priest to fight their battles. Nor were they ill pleased that, for the present, he was not Bishop of Canada, but only vicar apostolic; for, such being the case, they could have him recalled if, on trial, they did not like him, while an unacceptable bishop would be an evil past remedy.

Canada was entering a state of transition. Hitherto ecclesiastical influence had been all in all. The Jesuits, by far the most educated and able body of men in the colony, had controlled it, not alone in things spiritual, but virtually in things temporal also; and the governor may be said to have been little else than a chief of police, under the direction of the missionaries. The early governors were themselves deeply imbued with the missionary spirit. Champlain was earnest above all things for converting the Indians; Montmagny was half-monk, for he was a Knight of Malta; Aillebout was so insanely pious, that he lived with his wife like monk and nun. A change was at hand. From a mission and a trading station, Canada was soon to become, in the true sense, a colony; and civil government had begun to assert itself on the banks of the St. Lawrence. The epoch of the martyrs and apostles was passing away, and the man of the sword and the man of the gown—the soldier and the legist—were threatening to supplant the paternal sway of priests; or, as Laval might have said, the hosts of this world were beleaguering the sanctuary, and he was called of Heaven to defend it. His true antagonist, though three thousand miles away, was the great minister Colbert, as purely a statesman as the vicar apostolic was purely a priest. Laval, no doubt, could see behind the statesman's back another adversary, the devil.

Argenson was governor when the crozier and the sword began to clash, which is merely another way of saying that he was governor when Laval arrived. He seems to have been a man of education, moderation, and sense, and he was also an earnest Catholic; but if Laval had his duties to God, so had Argenson his duties to the king, of whose authority he was the representative and guardian. If the first collisions seem trivial, they were no less the symptoms of a grave antagonism. Argenson could have purchased peace only by becoming an agent of the church.

The vicar apostolic, or, as he was usually styled, the bishop, being, it may be remembered, titular Bishop of Petræa in Arabia, presently fell into a quarrel with the governor touching the relative position of their seats in church,—a point which, by the way, was a subject of contention for many years, and under several successive governors. This time the case was referred to the ex-governor, Aillebout, and a temporary settlement took place.[1] A few weeks after, on the fête of Saint Francis Xavier, when the Jesuits were accustomed to ask the dignitaries of the colony to dine in their refectory after mass, a fresh difficulty arose,—Should the governor or the bishop have the higher seat at table? The question defied solution; so the fathers invited neither of them.[2]

Again, on Christmas, at the midnight mass, the deacon offered incense to the bishop, and then, in obedience to an order from him, sent a subordinate to offer it to the governor, instead of offering it himself. Laval further insisted that the priests of the choir should receive incense before the governor received it. Argenson resisted, and a bitter quarrel ensued.[3]

[1] Lalemant, in *Journal des Jésuites*, Sept., 1659.
[2] *Ibid.*, Dec., 1659.
[3] *Ibid.*; *Lettre d'Argenson à MM. de la Compagnie de St. Sulpice.*

The late governor, Aillebout, had been church-warden *ex officio*;[1] and in this pious community the office was esteemed as an addition to his honors. Argenson had thus far held the same position; but Laval declared that he should hold it no longer. Argenson, to whom the bishop had not spoken on the subject, came soon after to a meeting of the wardens, and, being challenged, denied Laval's right to dismiss him. A dispute ensued, in which the bishop, according to his Jesuit friends, used language not very respectful to the representative of royalty.[2]

On occasion of the "solemn catechism," the bishop insisted that the children should salute him before saluting the governor. Argenson hearing of this, declined to come. A compromise was contrived. It was agreed that when the rival dignitaries entered, the children should be busied in some manual exercise which should prevent their saluting either. Nevertheless, two boys, "enticed and set on by their parents," saluted the governor first, to the great indignation of Laval. They were whipped on the next day for breach of orders.[3]

Next there was a sharp quarrel about a sentence pronounced by Laval against a heretic, to which the governor, good Catholic as he was, took exception.[4] Palm Sunday came, and there could be no procession and no distribution of branches, because the governor and the bishop could not agree on points of precedence.[5] On the day of the Fête Dieu, however, there was a grand procession, which stopped from time to time at temporary altars, or *reposoirs*, placed at intervals along its course. One of these was in the fort, where the soldiers were drawn up, waiting the arrival of the procession. Laval demanded that they should take off their hats. Argenson assented, and the soldiers stood uncovered. Laval now insisted that they should kneel. The governor replied that it was their duty as soldiers to stand; whereupon the bishop

---

[1] *Livre des Délibérations de la Fabrique de Québec.*
[2] *Journal des Jésuites*, Nov., 1660.
[3] *Ibid.*, Feb., 1661.
[4] *Ibid.*
[5] *Ibid.*, Avril, 1661.

refused to stop at the altar, and ordered the procession to move on.[1]

The above incidents are set down in the private journal of the superior of the Jesuits, which was not meant for the public eye. The bishop, it will be seen, was, by the showing of his friends, in most cases the aggressor. The disputes in question, though of a nature to provoke a smile on irreverent lips, were by no means so puerile as they appear. It is difficult in a modern democratic society to conceive the substantial importance of the signs and symbols of dignity and authority, at a time and among a people where they were adjusted with the most scrupulous precision, and accepted by all classes as exponents of relative degrees in the social and political scale. Whether the bishop or the governor should sit in the higher seat at table thus became a political question, for it defined to the popular understanding the position of church and state in their relations to government.

Hence it is not surprising to find a memorial, drawn up apparently by Argenson, and addressed to the council of state, asking for instructions when and how a governor—lieutenant-general for the king—ought to receive incense, holy water, and consecrated bread; whether the said bread should be offered him with sound of drum and fife; what should be the position of his seat at church; and what place he should hold in various religious ceremonies; whether in feasts, assemblies, ceremonies, and councils of *a purely civil character*, he or the bishop was to hold the first place; and, finally, if the bishop could excommunicate the inhabitants or others for acts of a civil and political character, when the said acts were pronounced lawful by the governor.

The reply to the memorial denies to the bishop the power of excommunication in civil matters, assigns to him the second place in meetings and ceremonies of a civil character, and is very reticent as to the rest.[2]

Argenson had a brother, a counsellor of state, and a fast friend of the Jesuits. Laval was in correspondence with him, and, apparently sure of sympathy, wrote to him touching his relations with the governor. "Your brother," he begins, "re-

[1] *Ibid., Juin, 1661.*
[2] *Advis et Résolutions demandés sur la Nouvelle France.*

ceived me on my arrival with extraordinary kindness;" but he
proceeds to say that, perceiving with sorrow that he entertained a groundless distrust of those good servants of God,
the Jesuit fathers, he, the bishop, thought it his duty to give
him in private a candid warning which ought to have done
good, but which, to his surprise, the governor had taken
amiss, and had conceived, in consequence, a prejudice against
his monitor.[1]

Argenson, on his part, writes to the same brother, at about
the same time. "The Bishop of Petræa is so stiff in opinion,
and so often transported by his zeal beyond the rights of his
position, that he makes no difficulty in encroaching on the
functions of others; and this with so much heat that he will
listen to nobody. A few days ago he carried off a servant girl
of one of the inhabitants here, and placed her by his own
authority in the Ursuline convent, on the sole pretext that he
wanted to have her instructed, thus depriving her master of
her services, though he had been at great expense in bringing
her from France. This inhabitant is M. Denis, who, not
knowing who had carried her off, came to me with a petition
to get her out of the convent. I kept the petition three days
without answering it, to prevent the affair from being noised
abroad. The Reverend Father Lalemant, with whom I communicated on the subject, and who greatly blamed the Bishop
of Petræa, did all in his power to have the girl given up quietly, but without the least success, so that I was forced to
answer the petition, and permit M. Denis to take his servant
wherever he should find her; and, if I had not used means to
bring about an accommodation, and if M. Denis, on the refusal which was made him to give her up, had brought the
matter into court, I should have been compelled to take measures which would have caused great scandal, and all from the
self-will of the Bishop of Petræa, who says that *a bishop can
do what he likes*, and threatens nothing but excommunication."[2]

In another letter he speaks in the same strain of this redundancy of zeal on the part of the bishop, which often, he says,

[1] *Lettre de Laval à M. d'Argenson, frère du Gouverneur, 20 Oct., 1659.*

[2] "—Qui dict *quun Evesque peult ce qu'il veult* et ne menace que dexcommunication." *Lettre d'Argenson à son Frère, 1659.*

takes the shape of obstinacy and encroachment on the rights of others. "It is greatly to be wished," he observes, "that the Bishop of Petræa would give his confidence to the Reverend Father Lalemant instead of Father Ragueneau;"[1] and he praises Lalemant as a person of excellent sense. "It would be well," he adds, "if the rest of their community were of the same mind; for in that case they would not mix themselves up with various matters in the way they do, and would leave the government to those to whom God has given it in charge."[2]

One of Laval's modern admirers, the worthy Abbé Ferland, after confessing that his zeal may now and then have savored of excess, adds in his defence, that a vigorous hand was needed to compel the infant colony to enter "the good path;" meaning, of course, the straitest path of Roman Catholic orthodoxy. We may hereafter see more of this stringent system of colonial education, its success, and the results that followed.

[1] *Ibid., 21 Oct., 1659.*
[2] *Ibid., 7 July, 1660.*

LAVAL AND AVAUGOUR

*Reception of Argenson • His Difficulties • His Recall • Dubois
d'Avaugour • The Brandy Quarrel • Distress of Laval •
Portents • The Earthquake*

WHEN Argenson arrived to assume the government, a
curious greeting had awaited him. The Jesuits asked
him to dine; vespers followed the repast; and then they conducted him into a hall, where the boys of their school—disguised, one as the Genius of New France, one as the Genius
of the Forest, and others as Indians of various friendly
tribes—made him speeches by turn, in prose and verse. First,
Pierre du Quet, who played the Genius of New France, presented his Indian retinue to the governor, in a complimentary
harangue. Then four other boys, personating French colonists, made him four flattering addresses, in French verse.
Charles Denis, dressed as a Huron, followed, bewailing the
ruin of his people, and appealing to Argenson for aid. Jean
François Bourdon, in the character of an Algonquin, next
advanced on the platform, boasted his courage, and declared
that he was ashamed to cry like the Huron. The Genius of
the Forest now appeared, with a retinue of wild Indians from
the interior, who, being unable to speak French, addressed
the governor in their native tongues, which the Genius proceeded to interpret. Two other boys, in the character of prisoners just escaped from the Iroquois, then came forward,
imploring aid in piteous accents; and, in conclusion, the
whole troop of Indians, from far and near, laid their bows
and arrows at the feet of Argenson, and hailed him as their
chief.[1]

Besides these mock Indians, a crowd of genuine savages

[1] *La Reception de Monseigneur le Vicomte d'Argenson par toutes les nations du
pais de Canada à son entrée au gouvernement de la Nouvelle France; à Quebecq
au College de la Compagnie de Jésus, le 28 de Juillet de l'année 1658.* The speeches,
in French and Indian, are here given *verbatim*, with the names of all the boys
who took part in the ceremony.

had gathered at Quebec to greet the new "Ononthio." On the next day—at his own cost, as he writes to a friend—he gave them a feast, consisting of "seven large kettles full of Indian corn, peas, prunes, sturgeons, eels, and fat, which they devoured, having first sung me a song, after their fashion."[1]

These festivities over, he entered on the serious business of his government, and soon learned that his path was a thorny one. He could find, he says, but a hundred men to resist the twenty-four hundred warriors of the Iroquois;[2] and he begs the proprietary company which he represented to send him a hundred more, who could serve as soldiers or laborers, according to the occasion.

The company turned a deaf ear to his appeals. They had lost money in Canada, and were grievously out of humor with it. In their view, the first duty of a governor was to collect their debts, which, for more reasons than one, was no easy task. While they did nothing to aid the colony in its distress, they beset Argenson with demands for the thousand pounds of beaver-skins, which the inhabitants had agreed to send them every year, in return for the privilege of the fur trade, a privilege which the Iroquois war made for the present worthless. The perplexed governor vents his feelings in sarcasm. "They (*the company*) take no pains to learn the truth; and, when they hear of settlers carried off and burned by the Iroquois, they will think it a punishment for not settling old debts, and paying over the beaver-skins."[3] "I wish," he adds, "they would send somebody to look after their affairs here. I would gladly give him the same lodging and entertainment as my own."

Another matter gave him great annoyance. This was the virtual independence of Montreal; and here, if nowhere else, he and the bishop were of the same mind. On one occasion he made a visit to the place in question, where he expected to be received as governor-general; but the local governor, Maisonneuve, declined, or at least postponed, to take his orders and give him the keys of the fort. Argenson accordingly speaks of Montreal as "a place which makes so much noise,

[1] *Papiers d'Argenson. Kebec, 5 Sept., 1658.*

[2] *Mémoire sur le subject* (sic) *de la Guerre des Iroquois, 1659.*

[3] *Papiers d'Argenson, 21 Oct., 1659.*

but which is of such small account."[1] He adds that, besides wanting to be independent, the Montrealists want to monopolize the fur trade, which would cause civil war; and that the king ought to interpose to correct their obstinacy.

In another letter he complains of Aillebout, who had preceded him in the government, though himself a Montrealist. Argenson says that, on going out to fight the Iroquois, he left Aillebout at Quebec, to act as his lieutenant; that, instead of doing so, he had assumed to govern in his own right; that he had taken possession of his absent superior's furniture, drawn his pay, and in other respects behaved as if he never expected to see him again. "When I returned," continues the governor, "I made him director in the council, without pay, as there was none to give him. It was this, I think, that made him remove to Montreal, for which I do not care, provided the glory of our Master suffer no prejudice thereby."[2]

These extracts may, perhaps, give an unjust impression of Argenson, who, from the general tenor of his letters, appears to have been a temperate and reasonable person. His patience and his nervous system seem, however, to have been taxed to the utmost. His pay could not support him. "The costs of living here are horrible," he writes. "I have only two thousand crowns a year for all my expenses, and I have already been forced to run into debt to the company to an equal amount."[3] Part of his scanty income was derived from a fishery of eels, on which sundry persons had encroached, to his great detriment.[4] "I see no reason," he adds, "for staying here any longer. When I came to this country, I hoped to enjoy a little repose, but I am doubly deprived of it; on one hand by enemies without, and incessant petty disputes within; and, on the other, by the difficulty I find in subsisting. The profits of the fur trade have been so reduced that all the inhabitants are in the greatest poverty. They are all insolvent, and cannot pay the merchants their advances."

His disgust at length reached a crisis. "I am resolved to stay

[1] Ibid., 4 Août, 1659.
[2] Ibid. Double de la lettre escripte par le Vaisseau du Gaigneur, parti le 6 Septembre (1658).
[3] Ibid. Lettre à M. de Morangi, 5 Sept., 1658.
[4] Délibérations de la Compagnie de la Nouvelle France.

here no longer, but to go home next year. My horror of dissension, and the manifest certainty of becoming involved in disputes with certain persons with whom I am unwilling to quarrel, oblige me to anticipate these troubles, and seek some way of living in peace. These excessive fatigues are far too much for my strength. I am writing to Monsieur the President, and to the gentlemen of the Company of New France, to choose some other man for this government."[1] And again, "if you take any interest in this country, see that the person chosen to command here has, besides the true piety necessary to a Christian in every condition of life, great firmness of character and strong bodily health. I assure you that without these qualities he cannot succeed. Besides, it is absolutely necessary that he should be a man of property and of some rank, so that he will not be despised for humble birth, or suspected of coming here to make his fortune; for in that case he can do no good whatever."[2]

His constant friction with the head of the church distressed the pious governor, and made his recall doubly a relief. According to a contemporary writer, Laval was the means of delivering him from the burden of government, having written to the President Lamoignon to urge his removal.[3] Be this as it may, it is certain that the bishop was not sorry to be rid of him.

The Baron Dubois d'Avaugour arrived to take his place. He was an old soldier of forty years' service,[4] blunt, imperative, and sometimes obstinate to perverseness; but full of energy, and of a probity which even his enemies confessed. "He served a long time in Germany while you were there," writes the minister Colbert to the Marquis de Tracy, "and you must have known his talents, as well as his *bizarre* and somewhat impracticable temper." On landing, he would have no reception, being, as Father Lalemant observes, "an enemy of all ceremony." He went, however, to see the Jesuits, and "took

[1] *Papiers d' Argenson. Lettre à son Frère, 1659.*

[2] *Ibid. Lettre (à son Frère?), 4 Nov., 1660.* The originals of Argenson's letters were destroyed in the burning of the library of the Louvre by the Commune.

[3] Lachenaye, *Mémoire sur le Canada.*

[4] Avaugour, *Mémoire, 4 Août, 1663.*

a morsel of food in our refectory."[1] Laval was prepared to receive him with all solemnity at the church; but the governor would not go. He soon set out on a tour of observation as far as Montreal, whence he returned delighted with the country, and immediately wrote to Colbert in high praise of it, observing that the St. Lawrence was the most beautiful river he had ever seen.[2]

It was clear from the first that, while he had a prepossession against the bishop, he wished to be on good terms with the Jesuits. He began by placing some of them on the council; but they and Laval were too closely united; and if Avaugour thought to separate them, he signally failed. A few months only had elapsed when we find it noted in Father Lalemant's private journal that the governor had dissolved the council and appointed a new one, and that other "changes and troubles" had befallen. The inevitable quarrel had broken out; it was a complex one, but the chief occasion of dispute was fortunate for the ecclesiastics, since it placed them, to a certain degree, morally in the right.

The question at issue was not new. It had agitated the colony for years, and had been the spring of some of Argenson's many troubles. Nor did it cease with Avaugour, for we shall trace its course hereafter, tumultuous as a tornado. It was simply the temperance question; not as regards the colonists, though here, too, there was great room for reform, but as regards the Indians.

Their inordinate passion for brandy had long been the source of excessive disorders. They drank expressly to get drunk, and when drunk they were like wild beasts. Crime and violence of all sorts ensued; the priests saw their teachings despised and their flocks ruined. On the other hand, the sale of brandy was a chief source of profit, direct or indirect, to all those interested in the fur trade, including the principal persons of the colony. In Argenson's time, Laval launched an excommunication against those engaged in the abhorred traffic; for nothing less than total prohibition would content the clerical party, and besides the spiritual penalty, they demanded the punishment of death against the contumacious

[1] Lalemant, *Journal des Jésuites, Sept., 1661.*
[2] *Lettre d'Avaugour au Ministre, 1661.*

offender. Death, in fact, was decreed. Such was the posture of affairs when Avaugour arrived; and, willing as he was to conciliate the Jesuits, he permitted the decree to take effect, although, it seems, with great repugnance. A few weeks after his arrival, two men were shot and one whipped, for selling brandy to Indians.[1] An extreme though partially suppressed excitement shook the entire settlement, for most of the colonists were, in one degree or another, implicated in the offence thus punished. An explosion soon followed; and the occasion of it was the humanity or good-nature of the Jesuit Lalemant.

A woman had been condemned to imprisonment for the same cause, and Lalemant, moved by compassion, came to the governor to intercede for her. Avaugour could no longer contain himself, and answered the reverend petitioner with characteristic bluntness. "You and your brethren were the first to cry out against the trade, and now you want to save the traders from punishment. I will no longer be the sport of your contradictions. Since it is not a crime for this woman, it shall not be a crime for anybody."[2] And in this posture he stood fast, with an inflexible stubbornness.

Henceforth there was full license to liquor dealers. A violent reaction ensued against the past restriction, and brandy flowed freely among French and Indians alike. The ungodly drank to spite the priests and revenge themselves for the "constraint of consciences," of which they loudly complained. The utmost confusion followed, and the principles on which the pious colony was built seemed upheaved from the foundation. Laval was distracted with grief and anger. He outpoured himself from the pulpit in threats of divine wrath, and launched fresh excommunications against the offenders; but such was the popular fury, that he was forced to yield and revoke them.[3]

Disorder grew from bad to worse. "Men gave no heed to bishop, preacher, or confessor," writes Father Charlevoix. "The French have despised the remonstrances of our prelate,

[1] *Journal des Jésuites, Oct., 1661.*
[2] La Tour, *Vie de Laval*, Liv. V.
[3] *Journal des Jésuites, Feb., 1662.* The sentence of excommunication is printed in the Appendix to the *Esquisse de la Vie de Laval*. It bears date February 24. It was on this very day that he was forced to revoke it.

because they are supported by the civil power," says the superior of the Ursulines. "He is almost dead with grief, and pines away before our eyes."

Laval could bear it no longer, but sailed for France, to lay his complaints before the court, and urge the removal of Avaugour. He had, besides, two other important objects, as will appear hereafter. His absence brought no improvement. Summer and autumn passed, and the commotion did not abate. Winter was drawing to a close, when, at length, outraged Heaven interposed an awful warning to the guilty colony.

Scarcely had the bishop left his flock when the skies grew portentous with signs of the chastisement to come. "We beheld," gravely writes Father Lalemant, "blazing serpents which flew through the air, borne on wings of fire. We beheld above Quebec a great globe of flame, which lighted up the night, and threw out sparks on all sides. This same meteor appeared above Montreal, where it seemed to issue from the bosom of the moon, with a noise as loud as cannon or thunder, and after sailing three leagues through the air it disappeared behind the mountain whereof this island bears the name."[1]

Still greater marvels followed. First, a Christian Algonquin squaw, described as "innocent, simple, and sincere," being seated erect in bed, wide awake, by the side of her husband, in the night between the fourth and fifth of February, distinctly heard a voice saying, "Strange things will happen today; the earth will quake!" In great alarm she whispered the prodigy to her husband, who told her that she lied. This silenced her for a time; but when, the next morning, she went into the forest with her hatchet to cut a faggot of wood, the same dread voice resounded through the solitude, and sent her back in terror to her hut.[2]

These things were as nothing compared with the marvel that befell a nun of the hospital, Mother Catherine de Saint-Augustin, who died five years later, in the odor of sanctity. On the night of the fourth of February, 1663, she beheld in the spirit four furious demons at the four corners of Quebec,

[1] Lalemant, *Relation, 1663*, 2.
[2] *Ibid.*, 6.

shaking it with a violence which plainly showed their purpose
of reducing it to ruins; "and this they would have done," says
the story, "if a personage of admirable beauty and ravishing
majesty [*Christ*], whom she saw in the midst of them, and
who, from time to time, gave rein to their fury, had not restrained them when they were on the point of accomplishing
their wicked design." She also heard the conversation of these
demons, to the effect that people were now well frightened,
and many would be converted; but this would not last long,
and they, the demons, would have them in time. "Let us keep
on shaking," they cried, encouraging each other, "and do our
best to upset every thing."[1]

Now, to pass from visions to facts: "At half-past five
o'clock on the morning of the fifth," writes Father Lalemant,
"a great roaring sound was heard at the same time through
the whole extent of Canada. This sound, which produced an
effect as if the houses were on fire, brought everybody out of
doors; but instead of seeing smoke and flame, they were
amazed to behold the walls shaking, and all the stones moving as if they would drop from their places. The houses
seemed to bend first to one side and then to the other. Bells
sounded of themselves; beams, joists, and planks cracked; the
ground heaved, making the pickets of the palisades dance in
a way that would have seemed incredible had we not seen it
in divers places.

"Everybody was in the streets; animals ran wildly about;
children cried; men and women, seized with fright, knew not
where to take refuge, expecting every moment to be buried
under the ruins of the houses, or swallowed up in some abyss
opening under their feet. Some, on their knees in the snow,
cried for mercy, and others passed the night in prayer; for the
earthquake continued without ceasing, with a motion much
like that of a ship at sea, insomuch that sundry persons felt
the same qualms of stomach which they would feel on the
water. In the forests the commotion was far greater. The trees
struck one against the other as if there were a battle between
them; and you would have said that not only their branches,

[1] Ragueneau, *Vie de Catherine de St. Augustin*, Liv. IV. chap. i. The same
story is told by Juchereau, Lalemant, and Marie de l'Incarnation, to whom
Charlevoix erroneously ascribes the vision, as does also the Abbé La Tour.

but even their trunks started out of their places and leaped on each other with such noise and confusion that the Indians said that the whole forest was drunk."

Mary of the Incarnation gives a similar account, as does also Frances Juchereau de Saint-Ignace; and these contemporary records are sustained to some extent by the evidence of geology.[1] A remarkable effect was produced on the St. Lawrence, which was so charged with mud and clay that for many weeks the water was unfit to drink. Considerable hills and large tracts of forest slid from their places, some into the river, and some into adjacent valleys. A number of men in a boat near Tadoussac stared aghast at a large hill covered with trees, which sank into the water before their eyes; streams were turned from their courses; water-falls were levelled; springs were dried up in some places, while in others new springs appeared. Nevertheless, the accounts that have come down to us seem a little exaggerated, and sometimes ludicrously so; as when, for example, Mother Mary of the Incarnation tells us of a man who ran all night to escape from a fissure in the earth which opened behind him and chased him as he fled.

It is perhaps needless to say that "spectres and phantoms of fire, bearing torches in their hands," took part in the convulsion. "The fiery figure of a man vomiting flames" also appeared in the air, with many other apparitions too numerous to mention. It is recorded that three young men were on their way through the forest to sell brandy to the Indians, when one of them, a little in advance of the rest, was met by a hideous spectre which nearly killed him with fright. He had scarcely strength enough to rejoin his companions, who, seeing his terror, began to laugh at him. One of them, however, presently came to his senses, and said: "This is no laughing matter; we are going to sell liquor to the Indians against

---

[1] Professor Sterry Hunt, whose intimate knowledge of Canadian geology is well known, tells me that the shores of the St. Lawrence are to a great extent formed of beds of gravel and clay resting on inclined strata of rock, so that earth-slides would be the necessary result of any convulsion like that of 1663. He adds that the evidence that such slides have taken place on a great scale is very distinct at various points along the river, especially at Les Eboulemens, on the north shore.

the prohibitions of the church, and perhaps God means to punish our disobedience." On this they all turned back. That night they had scarcely lain down to sleep when the earthquake roused them, and they ran out of their hut just in time to escape being swallowed up along with it.[1]

With every allowance, it is clear that the convulsion must have been a severe one, and it is remarkable that in all Canada not a life was lost. The writers of the day see in this a proof that God meant to reclaim the guilty and not destroy them. At Quebec there was for the time an intense revival of religion. The end of the world was thought to be at hand, and everybody made ready for the last judgment. Repentant throngs beset confessionals and altars; enemies were reconciled; fasts, prayers, and penances filled the whole season of Lent. Yet, as we shall see, the devil could still find wherewith to console himself.

It was midsummer before the shocks wholly ceased and the earth resumed her wonted calm. An extreme drought was followed by floods of rain, and then Nature began her sure work of reparation. It was about this time that the thorn which had plagued the church was at length plucked out. Avaugour was summoned home. He took his recall with magnanimity, and on his way wrote at Gaspé a memorial to Colbert, in which he commends New France to the attention of the king. "The St. Lawrence," he says, "is the entrance to what may be made the greatest state in the world;" and, in his purely military way, he recounts the means of realizing this grand possibility. Three thousand soldiers should be sent to the colony, to be discharged and turned into settlers after three years of service. During these three years they may make Quebec an impregnable fortress, subdue the Iroquois, build a strong fort on the river where the Dutch have a miserable wooden redoubt, called Fort Orange [*Albany*], and finally open a way by that river to the sea. Thus the heretics will be driven out, and the king will be master of America, at a total cost of about four hundred thousand francs yearly for ten years. He closes his

[1] Marie de l'Incarnation, *Lettre du 20 Août, 1663*. It appears from Morton, Josselyn, and other writers, that the earthquake extended to New England and New Netherlands, producing similar effects on the imagination of the people.

memorial by a short allusion to the charges against him, and to his forty years of faithful service; and concludes, speaking of the authors of his recall, Laval and the Jesuits: "By reason of the respect I owe their cloth, I will rest content, monseigneur, with assuring you that I have not only served the king with fidelity, but also, by the grace of God, with very good success, considering the means at my disposal."[1] He had, in truth, borne himself as a brave and experienced soldier; and he soon after died a soldier's death, while defending the fortress of Zrin, in Croatia, against the Turks.[2]

[1] Avaugour, *Mémoire, Gaspé, 4 Août, 1663.*

[2] *Lettre de Colbert au Marquis de Tracy, 1664. Mémoire du Roy, pour servir d'instruction au Sieur Talon.*

Chapter X

LAVAL AND DUMESNIL

Péronne Dumesnil • The Old Council • Alleged Murder • The New Council • Bourdon and Villeray • Strong Measures • Escape of Dumesnil • Views of Colbert

---

THOUGH the proposals of Avaugour's memorial were not adopted, it seems to have produced a strong impression at court. For this impression the minds of the king and his minister had already been prepared. Two years before, the inhabitants of Canada had sent one of their number, Pierre Boucher, to represent their many grievances and ask for aid.[1] Boucher had had an audience of the young king, who listened with interest to his statements; and when in the following year he returned to Quebec, he was accompanied by an officer named Dumont, who had under his command a hundred soldiers for the colony, and was commissioned to report its condition and resources.[2] The movement seemed to betoken that the government was wakening at last from its long inaction.

Meanwhile the Company of New France, feudal lord of Canada, had also shown signs of returning life. Its whole history had been one of mishap, followed by discouragement and apathy; and it is difficult to say whether its ownership of Canada had been more hurtful to itself or to the colony. At the eleventh hour it sent out an agent invested with powers of controller-general, intendant, and supreme judge, to inquire into the state of its affairs. This agent, Péronne Dumesnil, arrived early in the autumn of 1660, and set himself with great vigor to his work. He was an advocate of the Parliament of Paris, an active, aggressive, and tenacious person, of a temper well fitted to rip up an old abuse or probe a delinquency to the bottom. His proceedings quickly raised a storm at Quebec.

---

[1] To promote the objects of his mission, Boucher wrote a little book, *Histoire Véritable et Naturelle des Mœurs et Productions du Pays de la Nouvelle France*. He dedicates it to Colbert.

[2] A long journal of Dumont is printed anonymously in the *Relation* of 1663.

It may be remembered that, many years before, the company had ceded its monopoly of the fur trade to the inhabitants of the colony, in consideration of that annual payment in beaver-skins which had been so tardily and so rarely made. The direction of the trade had at that time been placed in the hands of a council composed of the governor, the superior of the Jesuits, and several other members. Various changes had since taken place, and the trade was now controlled by another council, established without the consent of the company,[1] and composed of the principal persons in the colony. The members of this council, with certain prominent merchants in league with them, engrossed all the trade, so that the inhabitants at large profited nothing by the right which the company had ceded;[2] and as the councillors controlled not only the trade but all the financial affairs of Canada, while the remoteness of their scene of operations made it difficult to supervise them, they were able, with little risk, to pursue their own profit, to the detriment both of the company and the colony. They and their allies formed a petty trading oligarchy, as pernicious to the prosperity of Canada as the Iroquois war itself.

The company, always anxious for its beaver-skins, made several attempts to control the proceedings of the councillors and call them to account, but with little success, till the vigorous Dumesnil undertook the task, when, to their wrath and consternation, they and their friends found themselves attacked by wholesale accusations of fraud and embezzlement. That these charges were exaggerated there can be little doubt; that they were unfounded is incredible, in view of the effect they produced.

The councillors refused to acknowledge Dumesnil's powers as controller, intendant, and judge, and declared his proceedings null. He retorted by charging them with usurpation. The excitement increased, and Dumesnil's life was threatened.

He had two sons in the colony. One of them, Péronne de Mazé, was secretary to Avaugour, then on his way up the St. Lawrence to assume the government. The other, Péronne des

---

[1] *Registres du Conseil du Roy; Reponse à la requeste presentée au Roy.*

[2] *Arrêt du Conseil d'Etat, 7 Mars, 1657.* Also *Papiers d'Argenson,* and *Extrait des Registres de Conseil d'Etat, 15 Mars, 1656.*

Touches, was with his father at Quebec. Towards the end of August this young man was attacked in the street in broad daylight, and received a kick which proved fatal. He was carried to his father's house, where he died on the twenty-ninth. Dumesnil charges four persons, all of whom were among those into whose affairs he had been prying, with having taken part in the outrage; but it is very uncertain who was the immediate cause of Des Touches's death. Dumesnil, himself the supreme judicial officer of the colony, made complaint to the judge in ordinary of the company; but he says that justice was refused, the complaint suppressed by authority, his allegations torn in pieces, and the whole affair hushed.[1]

At the time of the murder, Dumesnil was confined to his house by illness. An attempt was made to rouse the mob against him, by reports that he had come to the colony for the purpose of laying taxes; but he sent for some of the excited inhabitants, and succeeded in convincing them that he was their champion rather than their enemy. Some Indians in the neighborhood were also instigated to kill him, and he was forced to conciliate them by presents.

He soon renewed his attacks, and in his quality of intendant called on the councillors and their allies to render their accounts, and settle the long arrears of debt due to the company. They set his demands at naught. The war continued month after month. It is more than likely that when in the spring of 1662 Avaugour dissolved and reconstructed the council, his action had reference to these disputes; and it is clear that when in the following August Laval sailed for France, one of his objects was to restore the tranquillity which Dumesnil's proceedings had disturbed. There was great need; for, what with these proceedings and the quarrel about brandy, Quebec was a little hell of discord, the earthquake not having as yet frightened it into propriety.

[1] Dumesnil, *Mémoire*. Under date August 31 the *Journal des Jésuites* makes this brief and guarded mention of the affair: "Le fils de Mons. du Mesnil . . . fut enterré le mesme iour, tué d'vn coup de pié par N." Who is meant by N. it is difficult to say. The register of the parish church records the burial as follows: —

"L'an 1661. Le 30 Aoust a esté enterré au Cemetiere de Quebec Michel peronne dit Sr. des Touches fils de Mr. du Mesnil decedé le Jour precedent a sa Maison."

The bishop's success at court was triumphant. Not only did he procure the removal of Avaugour, but he was invited to choose a new governor to replace him.[1] This was not all; for he succeeded in effecting a complete change in the government of the colony. The Company of New France was called upon to resign its claims;[2] and, by a royal edict of April, 1663, all power, legislative, judicial, and executive, was vested in a council composed of the governor whom Laval had chosen, of Laval himself, and of five councillors, an attorney-general, and a secretary, to be chosen by Laval and the governor jointly.[3] Bearing with them blank commissions to be filled with the names of the new functionaries, Laval and his governor sailed for Quebec, where they landed on the fifteenth of September. With them came one Gaudais-Dupont, a royal commissioner instructed to inquire into the state of the colony.

No sooner had they arrived than Laval and Mézy, the new governor, proceeded to construct the new council. Mézy knew nobody in the colony, and was, at this time, completely under Laval's influence. The nominations, therefore, were virtually made by the bishop alone, in whose hands, and not in those of the governor, the blank commissions had been placed.[4] Thus for the moment he had complete control of the government; that is to say, the church was mistress of the civil power.

Laval formed his council as follows: Jean Bourdon for attorney-general; Rouer de Villeray, Juchereau de la Ferté, Ruette d'Auteuil, Le Gardeur de Tilly, and Matthieu Damours for councillors; and Peuvret de Mesnu for secretary. The royal commissioner, Gaudais, also took a prominent place at the board.[5] This functionary was on the point of marrying his niece to a son of Robert Giffard, who had a strong

[1] La Tour, *Vie de Laval*, Liv. V.

[2] See the deliberations and acts to this end in *Edits et Ordonnances concernant le Canada*, I. 30–32.

[3] *Edit de Création du Conseil Supérieur de Quebec*.

[4] *Commission actroyée au Sieur Gaudais. Mémoire pour servir d'Instruction au Sieur Gaudais*. A sequel to these instructions, marked *secret*, shows that, notwithstanding Laval's extraordinary success in attaining his objects, he and the Jesuits were somewhat distrusted. Gaudais is directed to make, with great discretion and caution, careful inquiry into the bishop's conduct, and with equal secrecy to ascertain why the Jesuits had asked for Avaugour's recall.

[5] As substitute for the *intendant*, an officer who had been appointed but who had not arrived.

interest in suppressing Dumesnil's accusations.[1] Dumesnil had laid his statements before the commissioner, who quickly rejected them, and took part with the accused.

Of those appointed to the new council, their enemy Dumesnil says that they were "incapable persons," and their associate Gaudais, in defending them against worse charges, declares that they were "unlettered, of little experience, and nearly all unable to deal with affairs of importance." This was, perhaps, unavoidable; for, except among the ecclesiastics, education was then scarcely known in Canada. But if Laval may be excused for putting incompetent men in office, nothing can excuse him for making men charged with gross public offences the prosecutors and judges in their own cause; and his course in doing so gives color to the assertion of Dumesnil, that he made up the council expressly to shield the accused and smother the accusation.[2]

The two persons under the heaviest charges received the two most important appointments: Bourdon, attorney-general, and Villeray, keeper of the seals. La Ferté was also one of the accused.[3] Of Villeray, the governor Argenson had written in 1659: "Some of his qualities are good enough, but

[1] Dumesnil here makes one of the few mistakes I have been able to detect in his long memorials. He says that the name of the niece of Gaudais was *Marie Nau*. It was, in fact, *Michelle-Therese Nau*, who married Joseph, son of Robert Giffard, on the 22d of October, 1663. Dumesnil had forgotten the bride's first name. The elder Giffard was surety for Repentigny, whom Dumesnil charged with liabilities to the company, amounting to 644,700 livres. Giffard was also father-in-law of Juchereau de la Ferté, one of the accused.

[2] Dumesnil goes further than this, for he plainly intimates that the removing from power of the company, to whom the accused were responsible, and the placing in power of a council formed of the accused themselves, was a device contrived from the first by Laval and the Jesuits, to get their friends out of trouble.

[3] Bourdon is charged with not having accounted for an immense quantity of beaver-skins which had passed through his hands during twelve years or more, and which are valued at more than 300,000 livres. Other charges are made against him in connection with large sums borrowed in Lauson's time on account of the colony. In a memorial addressed to the king in council, Dumesnil says that, in 1662, Bourdon, according to his own accounts, had in his hands 37,516 livres belonging to the company, which he still retained.

Villeray's liabilities arose out of the unsettled accounts of his father-in-law, Charles Sevestre, and are set down at more than 600,000 livres. La Ferté's are of a smaller amount. Others of the council were indirectly involved in the charges.

confidence cannot be placed in him, on account of his insta-
bility."[1] In the same year, he had been ordered to France, "to
purge himself of sundry crimes wherewith he stands
charged."[2] He was not yet free of suspicion, having returned
to Canada under an order to make up and render his accounts, which he had not yet done. Dumesnil says that he
first came to the colony in 1651, as valet of the governor Lauson, who had taken him from the jail at Rochelle, where he
was imprisoned for a debt of seventy-one francs, "as appears
by the record of the jail of date July eleventh in that year."
From this modest beginning he became in time the richest
man in Canada.[3] He was strong in orthodoxy, and an ardent
supporter of the bishop and the Jesuits. He is alternately
praised and blamed, according to the partisan leanings of the
writer.

Bourdon, though of humble origin, was, perhaps, the most
intelligent man in the council. He was chiefly known as an
engineer, but he had also been a baker, a painter, a syndic of
the inhabitants, chief gunner at the fort, and collector of customs for the company. Whether guilty of embezzlement or
not, he was a zealous devotee, and would probably have died
for his creed. Like Villeray, he was one of Laval's stanchest
supporters, while the rest of the council were also sound in
doctrine and sure in allegiance.

In virtue of their new dignity, the accused now claimed
exemption from accountability; but this was not all. The
abandonment of Canada by the company, in leaving Dumesnil without support, and depriving him of official character,
had made his charges far less dangerous. Nevertheless, it was
thought best to suppress them altogether, and the first act of
the new government was to this end.

On the twentieth of September, the second day after the
establishment of the council, Bourdon, in his character of
attorney-general, rose and demanded that the papers of Jean
Péronne Dumesnil should be seized and sequestered. The
council consented, and, to complete the scandal, Villeray was
commissioned to make the seizure in the presence of Bour-

[1] *Lettre d' Argenson, 20 Nov., 1659.*
[2] *Edit du Roy, 13 Mai, 1659.*
[3] *Lettre de Colbert à Frontenac, 17 Mai, 1674.*

don. To color the proceeding, it was alleged that Dumesnil had obtained certain papers unlawfully from the *greffe* or record office. "As he was thought," says Gaudais, "to be a violent man," Bourdon and Villeray took with them ten soldiers well armed, together with a locksmith and the secretary of the council. Thus prepared for every contingency, they set out on their errand, and appeared suddenly at Dumesnil's house between seven and eight o'clock in the evening. "The aforesaid Sieur Dumesnil," further says Gaudais, "did not refute the opinion entertained of his violence; for he made a great noise, shouted *robbers!* and tried to rouse the neighborhood, outrageously abusing the aforesaid Sieur de Villeray and the attorney-general, in great contempt of the authority of the council, which he even refused to recognize."

They tried to silence him by threats, but without effect; upon which they seized him and held him fast in a chair; "me," writes the wrathful Dumesnil, "who had lately been their judge." The soldiers stood over him and stopped his mouth while the others broke open and ransacked his cabinet, drawers, and chest, from which they took all his papers, refusing to give him an inventory, or to permit any witness to enter the house. Some of these papers were private; among the rest were, he says, the charges and specifications, nearly finished, for the trial of Bourdon and Villeray, together with the proofs of their "peculations, extortions, and malversations." The papers were enclosed under seal, and deposited in a neighboring house, whence they were afterwards removed to the council-chamber, and Dumesnil never saw them again. It may well be believed that this, the inaugural act of the new council, was not allowed to appear on its records.[1]

On the twenty-first, Villeray made a formal report of the seizure to his colleagues; upon which, "by reason of the insults, violences, and irreverences therein set forth against the aforesaid Sieur de Villeray, commissioner, as also against the authority of the council," it was ordered that the offending Dumesnil should be put under arrest; but Gaudais, as he declares, prevented the order from being carried into effect.

Dumesnil, who says that during the scene at his house he

---

[1] The above is drawn from the two memorials of Gaudais and of Dumesnil. They do not contradict each other as to the essential facts.

had expected to be murdered like his son, now, though unsupported and alone, returned to the attack, demanded his
papers, and was so loud in threats of complaint to the king
that the council were seriously alarmed. They again decreed
his arrest and imprisonment; but resolved to keep the decree
secret till the morning of the day when the last of the returning ships was to sail for France. In this ship Dumesnil had
taken his passage, and they proposed to arrest him unexpect-
edly on the point of embarkation, that he might have no time
to prepare and despatch a memorial to the court. Thus a full
year must elapse before his complaints could reach the minister, and seven or eight months more before a reply could be
returned to Canada. During this long delay the affair would
have time to cool. Dumesnil received a secret warning of this
plan, and accordingly went on board another vessel, which
was to sail immediately. The council caused the six cannon of
the battery in the Lower Town to be pointed at her, and
threatened to sink her if she left the harbor; but she disregarded them, and proceeded on her way.

On reaching France, Dumesnil contrived to draw the attention of the minister Colbert to his accusations, and to the
treatment they had brought upon him. On this Colbert demanded of Gaudais, who had also returned in one of the autumn ships, why he had not reported these matters to him.
Gaudais made a lame attempt to explain his silence, gave his
statement of the seizure of the papers, answered in vague
terms some of Dumesnil's charges against the Canadian financiers, and said that he had nothing to do with the rest. In
the following spring Colbert wrote as follows to his relative
Terron, intendant of marine: —

"I do not know what report M. Gaudais has made to you,
but family interests and the connections which he has at Quebec should cause him to be a little distrusted. On his arrival
in that country, having constituted himself chief of the council, he despoiled an agent of the Company of Canada of all
his papers, in a manner very violent and extraordinary, and
this proceeding leaves no doubt whatever that these papers
contained matters the knowledge of which it was wished absolutely to suppress. I think it will be very proper that you
should be informed of the statements made by this agent, in

order that, through him, an exact knowledge may be acquired of every thing that has taken place in the management of affairs."[1]

Whether Terron pursued the inquiry does not appear. Meanwhile new quarrels had arisen at Quebec, and the questions of the past were obscured in the dust of fresh commotions. Nothing is more noticeable in the whole history of Canada, after it came under the direct control of the Crown, than the helpless manner in which this absolute government was forced to overlook and ignore the disobedience and rascality of its functionaries in this distant transatlantic dependency.

As regards Dumesnil's charges, the truth seems to be, that the financial managers of the colony, being ignorant and unpractised, had kept imperfect and confused accounts, which they themselves could not always unravel; and that some, if not all of them, had made illicit profits under cover of this confusion. That their stealings approached the enormous sum at which Dumesnil places them is not to be believed. But, even on the grossly improbable assumption of their entire innocence, there can be no apology for the means, subversive of all justice, by which Laval enabled his partisans and supporters to extricate themselves from embarrassment.

[1] *Lettre de Colbert à Terron, Rochelle, 8 Fev., 1664.* "Il a spolié un agent de la Compagnie de Canada de tous ses papiers d'une manière fort violente et extraordinaire, et ce procédé ne laisse point à douter que dans ces papiers il n'y eût des choses dont on a voulu absolument supprimer la connaissance." Colbert seems to have received an exaggerated impression of the part borne by Gaudais in the seizure of the papers.

NOTE.—Dumesnil's principal memorial, preserved in the archives of the Marine and Colonies, is entitled *Mémoire concernant les Affaires du Canada, qui montre et fait voir que sous prétexte de la Gloire de Dieu, d'Instruction des Sauvages, de servir le Roy et de faire la nouvelle Colonie, il a été pris et diverti trois millions de livres ou environ.* It forms in the copy before me thirty-eight pages of manuscript, and bears no address; but seems meant for Colbert, or the council of state. There is a second memorial, which is little else than an abridgment of the first. A third, bearing the address *Au Roy et à nos Seigneurs du Conseil (d'Etat)*, and signed *Péronne Dumesnil*, is a petition for the payment of 10,132 livres due to him by the company for his services in Canada, "ou il a perdu son fils assassiné par les comptables du dit pays, qui n'ont voulu rendre compte au dit suppliant, Intendant, et ont pillé sa maison, ses meubles et papiers le 20 du mois de Septembre dernier, dont il y a acte."

Gaudais, in compliance with the demands of Colbert, gives his statement in a long memorial, *Le Sieur Gaudais Dupont à Monseigneur de Colbert, 1664.*

Dumesnil, in his principal memorial, gives a list of the alleged defaulters, with the special charges against each, and the amounts for which he reckons them liable. The accusations cover a period of ten or twelve years, and sometimes more. Some of them are curiously suggestive of more recent "rings." Thus Jean Gloria makes a charge of thirty-one hundred livres (francs) for fireworks to celebrate the king's marriage, when the actual cost is said to have been about forty livres. Others are alleged to have embezzled the funds of the company, under cover of pretended payments to imaginary creditors; and Argenson himself is said to have eked out his miserable salary by drawing on the company for the pay of soldiers who did not exist.

The records of the Council preserve a guarded silence about this affair. I find, however, under date 20 Sept., 1663, "Pouvoir à M. de Villeray de faire recherche dans la maison *d'un nommé du Mesnil* des papiers appartenants au Conseil concernant Sa Majesté;" and under date 18 March, 1664, "Ordre pour l'ouverture du coffre contenant les papiers de Dumesnil," and also an "Ordre pour mettre l'Inventaire des biens du Sr. Dumesnil entre les mains du Sr. Fillion."

Chapter XI

LAVAL AND MÉZY

*The Bishop's Choice • A Military Zealot • Hopeful Beginnings •
Signs of Storm • The Quarrel • Distress of Mézy • He Refuses to
Yield • His Defeat and Death*

WE have seen that Laval, when at court, had been invited
to choose a governor to his liking. He soon made his
selection. There was a pious officer, Saffray de Mézy, major
of the town and citadel of Caen, whom he had well known
during his long stay with Bernières at the Hermitage. Mézy
was the principal member of the company of devotees formed
at Caen under the influence of Bernières and his disciples. In
his youth he had been headstrong and dissolute. Worse still,
he had been, it is said, a Huguenot; but both in life and doctrine his conversion had been complete, and the fervid mysticism of Bernières acting on his vehement nature had
transformed him into a red-hot zealot. Towards the hermits
and their chief he showed a docility in strange contrast with
his past history, and followed their inspirations with an ardor
which sometimes overleaped its mark.

Thus a Jacobin monk, a doctor of divinity, once came to
preach at the church of St. Paul at Caen; on which, according
to their custom, the brotherhood of the Hermitage sent two
persons to make report concerning his orthodoxy. Mézy and
another military zealot, "who," says the narrator, "hardly
know how to read, and assuredly do not know their catechism," were deputed to hear his first sermon; wherein this
Jacobin, having spoken of the necessity of the grace of Jesus
Christ in order to the doing of good deeds, these two wise-
acres thought that he was preaching Jansenism; and thereupon, after the sermon, the Sieur de Mézy went to the proc-
tor of the ecclesiastical court and denounced him."[1]

His zeal, though but moderately tempered with knowl-

---

[1] Nicole, *Mémoire pour faire connoistre l'esprit et la conduite de la Compagnie
appellée l'Hermitage.*

edge, sometimes proved more useful than on this occasion. The Jacobin convent at Caen was divided against itself. Some of the monks had embraced the doctrines taught by Bernières, while the rest held dogmas which he declared to be contrary to those of the Jesuits, and therefore heterodox. A prior was to be elected, and, with the help of Bernières, his partisans gained the victory, choosing one Father Louis, through whom the Hermitage gained a complete control in the convent. But the adverse party presently resisted, and complained to the provincial of their order, who came to Caen to close the dispute by deposing Father Louis. Hearing of his approach, Bernières asked aid from his military disciple, and De Mézy sent him a squad of soldiers, who guarded the convent doors and barred out the provincial.[1]

Among the merits of Mézy, his humility and charity were especially admired; and the people of Caen had more than once seen the town major staggering across the street with a beggar mounted on his back, whom he was bearing dry-shod through the mud in the exercise of those virtues.[2] In this he imitated his master Bernières, of whom similar acts are recorded.[3] However dramatic in manifestation, his devotion was not only sincere but intense. Laval imagined that he knew him well. Above all others, Mézy was the man of his choice; and so eagerly did he plead for him, that the king himself paid certain debts which the pious major had contracted, and thus left him free to sail for Canada.

His deportment on the voyage was edifying, and the first days of his accession were passed in harmony. He permitted Laval to form the new council, and supplied the soldiers for the seizure of Dumesnil's papers. A question arose concerning Montreal, a subject on which the governors and the bishop rarely differed in opinion. The present instance was no exception to the rule. Mézy removed Maisonneuve, the local governor, and immediately replaced him; the effect being, that whereas he had before derived his authority from the seigniors of the island, he now derived it from the governor-

[1] *Ibid.*

[2] Juchereau, *Histoire de l'Hôtel-Dieu*, 149.

[3] See the laudatory notice of Bernières de Louvigny in the *Nouvelle Biographie Universelle*.

general. It was a movement in the interest of centralized power, and as such was cordially approved by Laval.

The first indication to the bishop and the Jesuits that the new governor was not likely to prove in their hands as clay in the hands of the potter, is said to have been given on occasion of an interview with an embassy of Iroquois chiefs, to whom Mézy, aware of their duplicity, spoke with a decision and haughtiness that awed the savages and astonished the ecclesiastics.

He seems to have been one of those natures that run with an engrossing vehemence along any channel into which they may have been turned. At the Hermitage he was all devotee; but climate and conditions had changed, and he or his symptoms changed with them. He found himself raised suddenly to a post of command, or one which was meant to be such. The town major of Caen was set to rule over a region far larger than France. The royal authority was trusted to his keeping, and his honor and duty forbade him to break the trust. But when he found that those who had procured for him his new dignities had done so that he might be an instrument of their will, his ancient pride started again into life, and his headstrong temper broke out like a long-smothered fire. Laval stood aghast at the transformation. His lamb had turned wolf.

What especially stirred the governor's dudgeon was the conduct of Bourdon, Villeray, and Auteuil, those faithful allies whom Laval had placed on the council, and who, as Mézy soon found, were wholly in the bishop's interest. On the 13th of February he sent his friend Angoville, major of the fort, to Laval, with a written declaration to the effect that he had ordered them to absent themselves from the council, because, having been appointed "on the persuasion of the aforesaid Bishop of Petræa, who knew them to be wholly his creatures, they wish to make themselves masters in the aforesaid council, and have acted in divers ways against the interests of the king and the public for the promotion of personal and private ends, and have formed and fomented cabals, contrary to their duty and their oath of fidelity to his aforesaid Majesty."[1] He

[1] *Ordre de M. de Mézy de faire sommation à l'Evêque de Petrée, 13 Fev., 1664. Notification du dit Ordre, même date.* (Registre du Conseil Supérieur.)

further declares that advantage had been taken of the facility of his disposition and his ignorance of the country to surprise him into assenting to their nomination; and he asks the bishop to acquiesce in their expulsion, and join him in calling an assembly of the people to choose others in their place. Laval refused; on which Mézy caused his declaration to be placarded about Quebec and proclaimed by sound of drum.

The proposal of a public election, contrary as it was to the spirit of the government, opposed to the edict establishing the council, and utterly odious to the young autocrat who ruled over France, gave Laval a great advantage. "I reply," he wrote, "to the request which Monsieur the Governor makes me to consent to the interdiction of the persons named in his declaration, and proceed to the choice of other councillors or officers by an assembly of the people, that neither my conscience nor my honor, nor the respect and obedience which I owe to the will and commands of the king, nor my fidelity and affection to his service, will by any means permit me to do so."[1]

Mézy was dealing with an adversary armed with redoubtable weapons. It was intimated to him that the sacraments would be refused, and the churches closed against him. This threw him into an agony of doubt and perturbation; for the emotional religion which had become a part of his nature, though overborne by gusts of passionate irritation, was still full of life within him. Tossing between the old feeling and the new, he took a course which reveals the trouble and confusion of his mind. He threw himself for counsel and comfort on the Jesuits, though he knew them to be one with Laval against him, and though, under cover of denouncing sin in general, they had lashed him sharply in their sermons. There is something pathetic in the appeal he makes them. For the glory of God and the service of the king, he had come, he says, on Laval's solicitation, to seek salvation in Canada; and being under obligation to the bishop, who had recommended him to the king, he felt bound to show proofs of his gratitude on every occasion. Yet neither gratitude to a benefactor nor the respect due to his character and person should be permit-

[1] *Réponse de l'Evêque de Petrée, 16 Fev., 1664.*

ted to interfere with duty to the king, "since neither conscience nor honor permit us to neglect the requirements of
our office and betray the interests of his Majesty, after receiving orders from his lips, and making oath of fidelity between
his hands." He proceeds to say that, having discovered practices of which he felt obliged to prevent the continuance, he
had made a declaration expelling the offenders from office;
that the bishop and all the ecclesiastics had taken this declaration as an offence; that, regardless of the king's service, they
had denounced him as a calumniator, an unjust judge, without gratitude, and perverted in conscience; and that one of
the chief among them had come to warn him that the sacraments would be refused and the churches closed against him.
"This," writes the unhappy governor, "has agitated our soul
with scruples; and we have none from whom to seek light
save those who are our declared opponents, pronouncing
judgment on us without knowledge of cause. Yet as our salvation and the duty we owe the king are the things most
important to us on earth, and as we hold them to be inseparable the one from the other; and as nothing is so certain as
death, and nothing so uncertain as the hour thereof; and as
there is no time to inform his Majesty of what is passing and
to receive his commands; and as our soul, though conscious
of innocence, is always in fear,—we feel obliged, despite their
opposition, to have recourse to the reverend father casuists of
the House of Jesus, to tell us in conscience what we can do
for the fulfilment of our duty at once to God and to the
king."[1]

The Jesuits gave him little comfort. Lalemant, their superior, replied by advising him to follow the directions of his
confessor, a Jesuit, so far as the question concerned spiritual
matters, adding that in temporal matters he had no advice to
give.[2] The distinction was illusory. The quarrel turned wholly
on temporal matters, but it was a quarrel with a bishop. To
separate in such a case the spiritual obligation from the temporal was beyond the skill of Mézy, nor would the confessor
have helped him.

[1] *Mézy aux PP. Jésuites, Fait au Château de Quebec ce dernier jour de Fevrier,
1664.*

[2] *Lettre du P.H. Lalemant à Mr. le Gouverneur.*

Perplexed and troubled as he was, he would not reinstate
Bourdon and the two councillors. The people began to
clamor at the interruption of justice, for which they blamed
Laval, whom a recent imposition of tithes had made unpopular. Mézy thereupon issued a proclamation, in which, after
mentioning his opponents as the most subtle and artful persons in Canada, he declares that, in consequence of petitions
sent him from Quebec and the neighboring settlements, he
had called the people to the council chamber, and by their
advice had appointed the Sieur de Chartier as attorney-general in place of Bourdon.[1]

Bourdon replied by a violent appeal from the governor to
the remaining members of the council,[2] on which Mézy declared him excluded from all public functions whatever, till
the king's pleasure should be known.[3] Thus church and state
still frowned on each other, and new disputes soon arose to
widen the breach between them. On the first establishment of
the council, an order had been passed for the election of a
mayor and two aldermen (échevins) for Quebec, which it was
proposed to erect into a city, though it had only seventy
houses and less than a thousand inhabitants. Repentigny was
chosen mayor, and Madry and Charron aldermen; but the
choice was not agreeable to the bishop, and the three functionaries declined to act, influence having probably been
brought to bear on them to that end. The council now resolved that a mayor was needless, and the people were permitted to choose a syndic in his stead. These municipal
elections were always so controlled by the authorities that the
element of liberty which they seemed to represent was little
but a mockery. On the present occasion, after an unaccountable delay of ten months, twenty-two persons cast their votes
in presence of the council, and the choice fell on Charron.
The real question was whether the new syndic should belong
to the governor or to the bishop. Charron leaned to the governor's party. The ecclesiastics insisted that the people were
dissatisfied, and a new election was ordered, but the voters
did not come. The governor now sent messages to such of

[1] *Declaration du Sieur de Mézy, 10 Mars, 1664.*

[2] *Bourdon au Conseil, 13 Mars, 1664.*

[3] *Ordre du Gouverneur, 13 Mars, 1664.*

the inhabitants as he knew to be in his interest, who gathered in the council chamber, voted under his eye, and again chose a syndic agreeable to him. Laval's party protested in vain.[1]

The councillors held office for a year, and the year had now expired. The governor and the bishop, it will be remembered, had a joint power of appointment; but agreement between them was impossible. Laval was for replacing his partisans, Bourdon, Villeray, Auteuil, and La Ferté. Mézy refused; and on the eighteenth of September he reconstructed the council by his sole authority, retaining of the old councillors only Amours and Tilly, and replacing the rest by Denis, La Tesserie, and Péronne de Mazé, the surviving son of Dumesnil. Again Laval protested; but Mézy proclaimed his choice by sound of drum, and caused placards to be posted, full, according to Father Lalemant, of abuse against the bishop. On this he was excluded from confession and absolution. He complained loudly; "but our reply was," says the father, "that God knew every thing."[2]

This unanswerable but somewhat irrelevant response failed to satisfy him, and it was possibly on this occasion that an incident occurred which is recounted by the bishop's eulogist, La Tour. He says that Mézy, with some unknown design, appeared before the church at the head of a band of soldiers, while Laval was saying mass. The service over, the bishop presented himself at the door, on which, to the governor's confusion, all the soldiers respectfully saluted him.[3] The story may have some foundation, but it is not supported by contemporary evidence.

On the Sunday after Mézy's *coup d'état*, the pulpits resounded with denunciations. The people listened, doubtless, with becoming respect; but their sympathies were with the governor; and he, on his part, had made appeals to them at more than one crisis of the quarrel. He now fell into another indiscretion. He banished Bourdon and Villeray, and ordered them home to France.

They carried with them the instruments of their revenge,

---

[1] *Registre du Conseil Supérieur.*

[2] *Journal des Jésuites, Oct., 1664.*

[3] La Tour, *Vie de Laval*, Liv. VII. It is charitable to ascribe this writer's many errors to carelessness.

the accusations of Laval and the Jesuits against the author of their woes. Of these accusations one alone would have sufficed. Mézy had appealed to the people. It is true that he did so from no love of popular liberty, but simply to make head against an opponent; yet the act alone was enough, and he received a peremptory recall. Again Laval had triumphed. He had made one governor and unmade two, if not three. The modest Levite, as one of his biographers calls him in his earlier days, had become the foremost power in Canada.

Laval had a threefold strength at court; his high birth, his reputed sanctity, and the support of the Jesuits. This was not all, for the permanency of his position in the colony gave him another advantage. The governors were named for three years, and could be recalled at any time; but the vicar apostolic owed his appointment to the Pope, and the Pope alone could revoke it. Thus he was beyond reach of the royal authority, and the court was in a certain sense obliged to conciliate him. As for Mézy, a man of no rank or influence, he could expect no mercy. Yet, though irritable and violent, he seems to have tried conscientiously to reconcile conflicting duties, or what he regarded as such. The governors and intendants, his successors, received, during many years, secret instructions from the court to watch Laval, and cautiously prevent him from assuming powers which did not belong to him. It is likely that similar instructions had been given to Mézy,[1] and that the attempt to fulfil them had aided to embroil him with one who was probably the last man on earth with whom he would willingly have quarrelled.

An inquiry was ordered into his conduct; but a voice more potent than the voice of the king had called him to another tribunal. A disease, the result perhaps of mental agitation, seized upon him and soon brought him to extremity. As he lay gasping between life and death, fear and horror took possession of his soul. Hell yawned before his fevered vision, peopled with phantoms which long and lonely meditations, after the discipline of Loyola, made real and palpable to his

[1] The royal commissioner, Gaudais, who came to Canada with Mézy, had, as before mentioned, orders to inquire with great secrecy into the conduct of Laval. The intendant, Talon, who followed immediately after, had similar instructions.

thought. He smelt the fumes of infernal brimstone, and heard the howlings of the damned. He saw the frown of the angry Judge, and the fiery swords of avenging angels, hurling wretches like himself, writhing in anguish and despair, into the gulf of unutterable woe. He listened to the ghostly counsellors who besieged his bed, bowed his head in penitence, made his peace with the church, asked pardon of Laval, confessed to him, and received absolution at his hands; and his late adversaries, now benign and bland, soothed him with promises of pardon, and hopes of eternal bliss.

Before he died, he wrote to the Marquis de Tracy, newly appointed viceroy, a letter which indicates that even in his penitence he could not feel himself wholly in the wrong.[1] He also left a will in which the pathetic and the quaint are curiously mingled. After praying his patron, Saint Augustine, with Saint John, Saint Peter, and all the other saints, to intercede for the pardon of his sins, he directs that his body shall be buried in the cemetery of the poor at the hospital, as being unworthy of more honored sepulture. He then makes various legacies of piety and charity. Other bequests follow, one of which is to his friend Major Angoville, to whom he leaves two hundred francs, his coat of English cloth, his camlet mantle, a pair of new shoes, eight shirts with sleeve buttons, his sword and belt, and a new blanket for the major's servant. Felix Aubert is to have fifty francs, with a gray jacket, a small coat of gray serge, "which," says the testator, "has been worn for a while," and a pair of long white stockings. And in a codicil he farther leaves to Angoville his best black coat, in order that he may wear mourning for him.[2]

His earthly troubles closed on the night of the sixth of May. He went to his rest among the paupers; and the priests, serenely triumphant, sang requiems over his grave.

[1] *Lettre de Mézy au Marquis de Tracy, 26 Avril, 1665.*

[2] *Testament du Sieur de Mézy.* This will, as well as the letter, is engrossed in the registers of the council.

NOTE.—Mézy sent home charges against the bishop and the Jesuits which seem to have existed in Charlevoix's time, but for which, as well as for those made by Laval, I have sought in vain.

The substance of these mutual accusations is given thus by the minister Colbert, in a memorial addressed to the Marquis de Tracy, in 1665: "Les Jésuites l'accusent d'avarice et de violences; et lui qu'ils voulaient entre-prendre sur l'autorité qui lui a été commise par le Roy, en sorte que n'ayant que de leurs créatures dans le Conseil Souverain, toutes les résolutions s'y prenaient selon leurs sentiments."

The papers cited are drawn partly from the *Registres du Conseil Supérieur*, still preserved at Quebec, and partly from the Archives of the Marine and Colonies. Laval's admirer, the abbé La Tour, in his eagerness to justify the bishop, says that the quarrel arose from a dispute about precedence between Mézy and the intendant, and from the ill-humor of the governor because the intendant shared the profits of his office. The truth is, that there was no intendant in Canada during the term of Mézy's government. One Robert had been appointed to the office, but he never came to the colony. The commissioner Gaudais, during the two or three months of his stay at Que-bec, took the intendant's place at the council-board; but harmony between Laval and Mézy was unbroken till after his departure. Other writers say that the dispute arose from the old question about brandy. Towards the end of the quarrel there was some disorder from this source, but even then the brandy question was subordinate to other subjects of strife.

Chapter XII

1662–1680

LAVAL AND THE SEMINARY

Laval's Visit to Court • The Seminary • Zeal of the Bishop • His Eulogists • Church and State • Attitude of Laval

---

THAT memorable journey of Laval to court, which caused the dissolution of the Company of New France, the establishment of the Supreme Council, the recall of Avaugour, and the appointment of Mézy, had yet other objects and other results. Laval, vicar apostolic and titular bishop of Petræa, wished to become in title, as in fact, bishop of Quebec. Thus he would gain an increase of dignity and authority, necessary, as he thought, in his conflicts with the civil power; "for," he wrote to the cardinals of the Propaganda, "I have learned from long experience how little security my character of vicar apostolic gives me against those charged with political affairs: I mean the officers of the Crown, perpetual rivals and contemners of the authority of the church."[1]

This reason was for the Pope and the cardinals. It may well be believed that he held a different language to the king. To him he urged that the bishopric was needed to enforce order, suppress sin, and crush heresy. Both Louis XIV. and the queen mother favored his wishes;[2] but difficulties arose and interminable disputes ensued on the question, whether the proposed bishopric should depend immediately on the Pope or on the Archbishop of Rouen. It was a revival of the old quarrel of Gallican and ultramontane. Laval, weary of hope deferred, at length declared that he would leave the colony if he could not be its bishop in title; and in 1674, after eleven years of delay, the king yielded to the Pope's demands, and the vicar apostolic became first bishop of Quebec.

If Laval had to wait for his mitre, he found no delay and no difficulty in attaining another object no less dear to him.

[1] For a long extract from this letter, copied from the original in the archives of the Propaganda at Rome, see Faillon, *Colonie Française*, III. 432.

[2] *Anne d'Autriche à Laval, 23 Avril, 1662; Louis XIV. au Pape, 28 Jan., 1664; Louis XIV. au Duc de Créquy, Ambassadeur à Rome, 28 June, 1664.*

He wished to provide priests for Canada, drawn from the Canadian population, fed with sound and wholesome doctrine, reared under his eye, and moulded by his hand. To this end he proposed to establish a seminary at Quebec. The plan found favor with the pious king, and a decree signed by his hand sanctioned and confirmed it. The new seminary was to be a corporation of priests under a superior chosen by the bishop; and, besides its functions of instruction, it was vested with distinct and extraordinary powers. Laval, an organizer and a disciplinarian by nature and training, would fain subject the priests of his diocese to a control as complete as that of monks in a convent. In France, the curé or parish priest was, with rare exceptions, a fixture in his parish, whence he could be removed only for grave reasons, and through prescribed forms of procedure. Hence he was to a certain degree independent of the bishop. Laval, on the contrary, demanded that the Canadian curé should be removable at his will, and thus placed in the position of a missionary, to come and go at the order of his superior. In fact, the Canadian parishes were for a long time so widely scattered, so feeble in population, and so miserably poor, that, besides the disciplinary advantages of this plan, its adoption was at first almost a matter of necessity. It added greatly to the power of the church; and, as the colony increased, the king and the minister conceived an increasing distrust of it. Instructions for the "fixation" of the curés were repeatedly sent to the colony, and the bishop, while professing to obey, repeatedly evaded them. Various fluctuations and changes took place; but Laval had built on strong foundations, and at this day the system of removable curés prevails in most of the Canadian parishes.[1]

Thus he formed his clergy into a family with himself at its head. His seminary, the mother who had reared them, was further charged to maintain them, nurse them in sickness, and support them in old age. Under her maternal roof the tired priest found repose among his brethren; and thither every

[1] On the establishment of the seminary, *Mandement de l'Evêque de Petrée, pour l'Etablissement du Séminaire de Québec; Approbation du Roy* (*Edits et Ordonnances*, I. 33, 35); La Tour, *Vie de Laval*, Liv. VI.; *Esquisse de la Vie de Laval*, Appendix. Various papers bearing on the subject are printed in the Canadian *Abeille*, from originals in the archives of the seminary.

year he repaired from the charge of his flock in the wilderness, to freshen his devotion and animate his zeal by a season of meditation and prayer.

The difficult task remained to provide the necessary funds. Laval imposed a tithe of one-thirteenth on all products of the soil, or, as afterwards settled, on grains alone. This tithe was paid to the seminary, and by the seminary to the priests. The people, unused to such a burden, clamored and resisted; and Mézy, in his disputes with the bishop, had taken advantage of their discontent. It became necessary to reduce the tithe to a twenty-sixth, which, as there was little or no money among the inhabitants, was paid in kind. Nevertheless, the scattered and impoverished settlers grudged even this contribution to the support of a priest whom many of them rarely saw, and the collection of it became a matter of the greatest difficulty and uncertainty. How the king came to the rescue, we shall hereafter see.

Besides the great seminary where young men were trained for the priesthood, there was the lesser seminary where boys were educated in the hope that they would one day take orders. This school began in 1668, with eight French and six Indian pupils, in the old house of Madame Couillard; but so far as the Indians were concerned it was a failure. Sooner or later they all ran wild in the woods, carrying with them as fruits of their studies a sufficiency of prayers, offices, and chants learned by rote, along with a feeble smattering of Latin and rhetoric, which they soon dropped by the way. There was also a sort of farm-school attached to the seminary, for the training of a humbler class of pupils. It was established at the parish of St. Joachim, below Quebec, where the children of artisans and peasants were taught farming and various mechanical arts, and thoroughly grounded in the doctrine and discipline of the church.[1] The Great and Lesser Seminary still subsist, and form one of the most important Roman Catholic institutions on this continent. To them has recently been added the Laval University, resting on the same foundation, and supported by the same funds.

[1] *Annales du Petit Séminaire de Quebec*, see *Abeille*, Vol. I.; *Notice Historique sur le Petit Séminaire de Quebec, Ibid.*, Vol. II; *Notice Historique sur la Paroisse de St. Joachim, Ibid.*, Vol. I. The *Abeille* is a journal published by the seminary.

Whence were these funds derived? Laval, in order to imitate the poverty of the apostles, had divested himself of his
property before he came to Canada; otherwise there is little
doubt that in the fulness of his zeal he would have devoted it
to his favorite object. But if he had no property he had influence, and his family had both influence and wealth. He acquired vast grants of land in the best parts of Canada. Some
of these he sold or exchanged; others he retained till the year
1680, when he gave them, with nearly all else that he then
possessed, to his seminary at Quebec. The lands with which
he thus endowed it included the seigniories of the Petite Nation, the island of Jesus, and Beaupré. The last is of great
extent, and at the present day of immense value. Beginning a few
miles below Quebec, it borders the St. Lawrence for a distance
of sixteen leagues, and is six leagues in depth, measured from the
river. From these sources the seminary still draws an abundant
revenue, though its seigniorial rights were commuted on the
recent extinction of the feudal tenure in Canada.

Well did Laval deserve that his name should live in that of
the university which a century and a half after his death owed
its existence to his bounty. This father of the Canadian
church, who has left so deep an impress on one of the communities which form the vast population of North America,
belonged to a type of character to which an even justice is
rarely done. With the exception of the Canadian Garneau, a
liberal Catholic, those who have treated of him, have seen
him through a medium intensely Romanist, coloring, hiding,
and exaggerating by turns both his actions and the traits of
his character. Tried by the Romanist standard, his merits were
great; though the extraordinary influence which he exercised
in the affairs of the colony were, as already observed, by no
means due to his spiritual graces alone. To a saint sprung
from the *haute noblesse*, Earth and Heaven were alike propitious. When the vicar-general Colombière pronounced his funeral eulogy in the sounding periods of Bossuet, he did not
fail to exhibit him on the ancestral pedestal where his virtues
would shine with redoubled lustre. "The exploits of the heroes of the House of Montmorency," exclaims the reverend
orator, "form one of the fairest chapters in the annals of Old
France; the heroic acts of charity, humility, and faith,

achieved by a Montmorency, form one of the fairest in the annals of New France. The combats, victories, and conquests of the Montmorency in Europe would fill whole volumes; and so, too, would the triumphs won by a Montmorency, in America, over sin, passion, and the devil." Then he crowns the high-born prelate with a halo of fourfold saintship. "It was with good reason that Providence permitted him to be called Francis: for the virtues of all the saints of that name were combined in him; the zeal of Saint Francis Xavier, the charity of Saint Francis of Sales, the poverty of Saint Francis of Assissi, the self-mortification of Saint Francis Borgia; but poverty was the mistress of his heart, and he loved her with incontrollable transports."

The stories which Colombière proceeds to tell of Laval's asceticism are confirmed by other evidence, and are, no doubt, true. Nor is there any reasonable doubt that, had the bishop stood in the place of Brébeuf or Charles Lalemant, he would have suffered torture and death like them. But it was his lot to strive, not against infidel savages, but against countrymen and Catholics, who had no disposition to burn him, and would rather have done him reverence than wrong.

To comprehend his actions and motives, it is necessary to know his ideas in regard to the relations of church and state. They were those of the extreme ultramontanes, which a recent Jesuit preacher has expressed with tolerable distinctness. In a sermon uttered in the Church of Notre Dame, at Montreal, on the first of November, 1872, he thus announced them. "The supremacy and infallibility of the Pope; the independence and liberty of the church; *the subordination and submission of the state to the church*; in case of conflict between them, the church to decide, the state to submit: for whoever follows and defends these principles, life and a blessing; for whoever rejects and combats them, death and a curse."[1]

These were the principles which Laval and the Jesuits

---

[1] This sermon was preached by Father Braun, S.J., on occasion of the "Golden Wedding," or fiftieth anniversary, of Bishop Bourget of Montreal. A large body of the Canadian clergy were present, some of whom thought his expressions too emphatic. A translation by another Jesuit is published in the "Montreal Weekly Herald" of Nov. 2, 1872; and the above extract is copied *verbatim*.

strove to make good. Christ was to rule in Canada through his deputy the bishop, and God's law was to triumph over the laws of man. As in the halcyon days of Champlain and Montmagny, the governor was to be the right hand of the church, to wield the earthly sword at her bidding, and the council was to be the agent of her high behests.

France was drifting toward the triumph of the *parti dévot*, the sinister reign of petticoat and cassock, the era of Maintenon and Tellier, and the fatal atrocities of the dragonnades. Yet the advancing tide of priestly domination did not flow smoothly. The unparalleled prestige which surrounded the throne of the young king, joined to his quarrels with the Pope and divisions in the church itself, disturbed, though they could not check its progress. In Canada it was otherwise. The colony had been ruled by priests from the beginning, and it only remained to continue in her future the law of her past. She was the fold of Christ; the wolf of civil government was among the flock, and Laval and the Jesuits, watchful shepherds, were doing their best to chain and muzzle him.

According to Argenson, Laval had said, "A bishop can do what he likes;" and his action answered reasonably well to his words. He thought himself above human law. In vindicating the assumed rights of the church, he invaded the rights of others, and used means from which a healthy conscience would have shrunk. All his thoughts and sympathies had run from childhood in ecclesiastical channels, and he cared for nothing outside the church. Prayer, meditation, and asceticism had leavened and moulded him. During four years he had been steeped in the mysticism of the Hermitage, which had for its aim the annihilation of self, and through self-annihilation the absorption into God.[1] He had passed from a life of visions to a life of action. Earnest to fanaticism, he saw but one great object, the glory of God on earth. He was penetrated by the poisonous casuistry of the Jesuits, based on the assumption that all means are permitted when the end is the service of God; and as Laval, in his own opinion, was always doing the service of God, while his opponents were always doing that of the devil, he enjoyed, in the use of means, a latitude of which we have seen him avail himself.

[1] See the maxims of Bernières published by La Tour.

THE COLONY AND THE KING

Chapter XIII

1661–1665

ROYAL INTERVENTION

Fontainebleau • Louis XIV. • Colbert • The Company of the West • Evil Omens • Action of the King • Tracy, Courcelle, and Talon • The Regiment of Carignan-Salières • Tracy at Quebec • Miracles • A Holy War

---

LEAVE Canada behind; cross the sea, and stand, on an evening in June, by the edge of the forest of Fontainebleau. Beyond the broad gardens, above the long ranges of moonlit trees, rise the walls and pinnacles of the vast chateau; a shrine of history, the gorgeous monument of lines of vanished kings, haunted with memories of Capet, Valois, and Bourbon.

There was little thought of the past at Fontainebleau in June, 1661. The present was too dazzling and too intoxicating; the future, too radiant with hope and promise. It was the morning of a new reign; the sun of Louis XIV. was rising in splendor, and the rank and beauty of France were gathered to pay it homage. A youthful court, a youthful king; a pomp and magnificence such as Europe had never seen; a delirium of ambition, pleasure, and love,—wrought in many a young heart an enchantment destined to be cruelly broken. Even cold courtiers felt the fascination of the scene, and tell us of the music at evening by the borders of the lake; of the gay groups that strolled under the shadowing trees, floated in gilded barges on the still water, or moved slowly in open carriages around its borders. Here was Anne of Austria, the king's mother, and Marie Thérèse, his tender and jealous queen; his brother, the Duke of Orleans, with his bride of sixteen, Henriette of England; and his favorite, that vicious butterfly of the court, the Count de Guiche. Here, too, were the humbled chiefs of the civil war, Beaufort and Condé, obsequious before their triumphant master. Louis XIV., the centre of all eyes, in the flush of health and vigor, and the pride of new-fledged royalty, stood, as he still stands on the canvas of Philippe de Champagne, attired in a splendor which would have been effeminate but for the stately port of the youth who wore it.[1]

Fortune had been strangely bountiful to him. The nations of Europe, exhausted by wars and dissensions, looked upon him with respect and fear. Among weak and weary neighbors, he alone was strong. The death of Mazarin had released him from tutelage; feudalism in the person of Condé was abject before him; he had reduced his parliaments to submission; and, in the arrest of the ambitious prodigal Fouquet, he was preparing a crushing blow to the financial corruption which had devoured France.

Nature had formed him to act the part of king. Even his critics and enemies praise the grace and majesty of his presence, and he impressed his courtiers with an admiration which seems to have been to an astonishing degree genuine. He carried airs of royalty even into his pleasures; and, while his example corrupted all France, he proceeded to the apartments of Montespan or Fontanges with the majestic gravity of Olympian Jove. He was a devout observer of the forms of religion; and, as the buoyancy of youth passed away, his zeal was stimulated by a profound fear of the devil. Mazarin had reared him in ignorance; but his faculties were excellent in their way, and, in a private station, would have made him an efficient man of business. The vivacity of his passions, and his inordinate love of pleasure, were joined to a persistent will and a rare power of labor. The vigorous mediocrity of his understanding delighted in grappling with details. His astonished courtiers saw him take on himself the burden of administration, and work at it without relenting for more than half a century. Great as was his energy, his pride was far greater. As king by divine right, he felt himself raised immeasurably above the highest of his subjects; but, while vindicating with unparalleled haughtiness his claims to supreme authority, he was, at the outset, filled with a sense of the duties of his high place, and fired by an ambition to make his reign beneficent to France as well as glorious to himself.

Above all rulers of modern times, he was the embodiment

---

[1] On the visit of the court at Fontainebleau in the summer of 1661, see *Mémoires de Madame de Motteville*, *Mémoires de Madame de La Fayette*, *Mémoires de l'Abbé de Choisy*, and Walckenaer, *Mémoires sur Madame de Sevigné*.

of the monarchical idea. The famous words ascribed to him, "I am the state," were probably never uttered; but they perfectly express his spirit. "It is God's will," he wrote in 1666, "that whoever is born a subject should not reason, but obey;"[1] and those around him were of his mind. "The state is in the king," said Bossuet, the great mouthpiece of monarchy; "the will of the people is merged in his will. Oh kings, put forth your power boldly, for it is divine and salutary to human kind."[2]

For a few brief years, his reign was indeed salutary to France. His judgment of men, when not obscured by his pride and his passion for flattery, was good; and he had at his service the generals and statesmen formed in the freer and bolder epoch that had ended with his accession. Among them was Jean Baptiste Colbert, formerly the intendant of Mazarin's household, a man whose energies matched his talents, and who had preserved his rectitude in the midst of corruption. It was a hard task that Colbert imposed on his proud and violent nature to serve the imperious king, morbidly jealous of his authority, and resolved to accept no initiative but his own. He must counsel while seeming to receive counsel, and lead while seeming to follow. The new minister bent himself to the task, and the nation reaped the profit. A vast system of reform was set in action amid the outcries of nobles, financiers, churchmen, and all who profited by abuses. The methods of this reform were trenchant and sometimes violent, and its principles were not always in accord with those of modern economic science; but the good that resulted was incalculable. The burdens of the laboring classes were lightened, the public revenues increased, and the wholesale plunder of the public money arrested with a strong hand. Laws were reformed and codified; feudal tyranny, which still subsisted in many quarters, was repressed; agriculture and productive industry of all kinds were encouraged, roads and canals opened, trade stimulated, a commercial marine created, and a powerful navy formed as if by magic.[3]

---

[1] *Œuvres de Louis XIV.*, II. 283.

[2] Bossuet, *Politique tirée de l'Ecriture sainte*, 370 (1843).

[3] On Colbert, see Clément, *Histoire de Colbert*. Clément, *Lettres et Mémoires de Colbert*; Chéruel, *Administration monarchique en France*, II. chap. vi.; Henri Martin, *Histoire de France*, XIII., etc.

It is in his commercial, industrial, and colonial policy that the profound defects of the great minister's system are most apparent. It was a system of authority, monopoly, and exclusion, in which the government, and not the individual, acted always the foremost part. Upright, incorruptible, ardent for the public good, inflexible, arrogant, and domineering, he sought to drive France into paths of prosperity, and create colonies by the energy of an imperial will. He feared, and with reason, that the want of enterprise and capital among the merchants would prevent the broad and immediate results at which he aimed; and, to secure these results, he established a series of great trading corporations, in which the principles of privilege and exclusion were pushed to their utmost limits. Prominent among them was the Company of the West. The king signed the edict creating it on the 24th of May, 1664. Any person in the kingdom or out of it might become a partner by subscribing, within a certain time, not less than three thousand francs. France was a mere patch on the map, compared to the vast domains of the new association. Western Africa from Cape Verd to the Cape of Good Hope, South America between the Amazon and the Orinoco, Cayenne, the Antilles, and all New France, from Hudson's Bay to Virginia and Florida were bestowed on it for ever, to be held of the Crown on the simple condition of faith and homage. As, according to the edict, the glory of God was the chief object in view, the company was required to supply its possessions with a sufficient number of priests, and diligently to exclude all teachers of false doctrine. It was empowered to build forts and war-ships, cast cannon, wage war, make peace, establish courts, appoint judges, and otherwise to act as sovereign within its own domains. A monopoly of trade was granted it for forty years.[1] Sugar from the Antilles, and furs from Canada, were the chief source of expected profit; and Africa was to supply the slaves to raise the sugar. Scarcely was the grand machine set in motion, when its directors betrayed a narrowness and blindness of policy which boded the enterprise no good. Canada was a chief sufferer. Once more, bound hand and foot, she was handed over to a selfish league of merchants; monopoly in trade, monopoly in religion, monopoly

[1] *Edit d'Etablissement de la Compagnie des Indes Occidentales.*

in government. Nobody but the company had a right to
bring her the necessaries of life; and nobody but the company
had a right to exercise the traffic which alone could give her
the means of paying for these necessaries. Moreover, the supplies which it brought were insufficient, and the prices which
it demanded were exorbitant. It was throttling its wretched
victim. The Canadian merchants remonstrated.[1] It was clear
that, if the colony was to live, the system must be changed;
and a change was accordingly ordered. The company gave up
its monopoly of the fur trade, but reserved the right to levy a
duty of one-fourth of the beaver-skins, and one-tenth of the
moose-skins: and it also reserved the entire trade of Tadoussac; that is to say, the trade of all the tribes between the lower
St. Lawrence and Hudson's Bay. It retained besides the exclusive right of transporting furs in its own ships, thus controlling the commerce of Canada, and discouraging, or rather
extinguishing, the enterprise of Canadian merchants. On its
part, it was required to pay governors, judges, and all the
colonial officials out of the duties which it levied.[2]

Yet the king had the prosperity of Canada at heart; and he
proceeded to show his interest in her after a manner hardly
consistent with his late action in handing her over to a mercenary guardian. In fact, he acted as if she had still remained
under his paternal care. He had just conferred the right of
naming a governor and intendant upon the new company;
but he now assumed it himself, the company, with a just
sense of its own unfitness, readily consenting to this suspen-
sion of one of its most important privileges. Daniel de Rémy,
Sieur de Courcelle, was appointed governor, and Jean Baptiste Talon intendant.[3] The nature of this duplicate govern-

[1] *Lettre du Conseil Souverain à Colbert, 1668.*

[2] *Arrêt du Conseil du Roy qui accorde à la Compagnie le quart des castors, le
dixième des orignaux et la traite de Tadoussac: Instruction à Monseigneur de
Tracy et à Messieurs le Gouverneur et l'Intendant.*

This company prospered as little as the rest of Colbert's trading companies. Within ten years it lost 3,523,000 livres, besides blighting the colonies
placed under its control. *Recherches sur les Finances*, cited by Clément, *Histoire
de Colbert.*

[3] *Commission de Lieutenant Général en Canada, etc., pour M. de Courcelle, 23
Mars, 1665; Commission d'Intendant de la Justice, Police, et Finances en Canada,
etc., pour M. Talon, 23 Mars, 1665.*

ment will appear hereafter. But, before appointing rulers for Canada, the king had appointed a representative of the Crown for all his American domains. The Maréchal d'Estrades had for some time held the title of viceroy for America; and, as he could not fulfil the duties of that office, being at the time ambassador in Holland, the Marquis de Tracy was sent in his place, with the title of lieutenant-general.[1]

Canada at this time was an object of very considerable attention at court, and especially in what was known as the *parti dévot*. The *Relations* of the Jesuits, appealing equally to the spirit of religion and the spirit of romantic adventure, had, for more than a quarter of a century, been the favorite reading of the devout, and the visit of Laval at court had greatly stimulated the interest they had kindled. The letters of Argenson, and especially of Avaugour, had shown the vast political possibilities of the young colony, and opened a vista of future glories alike for church and for king.

So, when Tracy set sail he found no lack of followers. A throng of young nobles embarked with him, eager to explore the marvels and mysteries of the western world. The king gave him two hundred soldiers of the regiment of Carignan-Salières, and promised that a thousand more should follow. After spending more than a year in the West Indies, where, as Mother Mary of the Incarnation expresses it, "he performed marvels and reduced everybody to obedience," he at length sailed up the St. Lawrence, and, on the thirtieth of June, 1665, anchored in the basin of Quebec. The broad, white standard, blazoned with the arms of France, proclaimed the representative of royalty; and Point Levi and Cape Diamond and the distant Cape Tourmente roared back the sound of the saluting cannon. All Quebec was on the ramparts or at the landing-place, and all eyes were strained at the two vessels as they slowly emptied their crowded decks into the boats alongside. The boats at length drew near, and the lieutenant-general and his suite landed on the quay with a pomp such as Quebec had never seen before.

Tracy was a veteran of sixty-two, portly and tall, "one of the largest men I ever saw," writes Mother Mary; but he was

[1] *Commission de Lieutenant Général de l'Amérique Méridionale et Septentrionale pour M. Prouville de Tracy, 19 Nov., 1663.*

sallow with disease, for fever had seized him, and it had fared
ill with him on the long voyage. The Chevalier de Chaumont
walked at his side, and young nobles surrounded him, gorgeous in lace and ribbons and majestic in leonine wigs.
Twenty-four guards in the king's livery led the way, followed
by four pages and six valets;[1] and thus, while the Frenchmen
shouted and the Indians stared, the august procession
threaded the streets of the Lower Town, and climbed the
steep pathway that scaled the cliffs above. Breathing hard,
they reached the top, passed on the left the dilapidated walls
of the fort and the shed of mingled wood and masonry which
then bore the name of the Castle of St. Louis; passed on the
right the old house of Couillard and the site of Laval's new
seminary, and soon reached the square betwixt the Jesuit college and the cathedral. The bells were ringing in a phrensy of
welcome. Laval in pontificals, surrounded by priests and Jesuits, stood waiting to receive the deputy of the king; and, as
he greeted Tracy and offered him the holy water, he looked
with anxious curiosity to see what manner of man he was.
The signs were auspicious. The deportment of the lieutenant-
general left nothing to desire. A *prie-dieu* had been placed for
him. He declined it. They offered him a cushion, but he
would not have it; and, fevered as he was, he knelt on the
bare pavement with a devotion that edified every beholder.
Te Deum was sung, and a day of rejoicing followed.

There was good cause. Canada, it was plain, was not to be
wholly abandoned to a trading company. Louis XIV. was resolved that a new France should be added to the old. Soldiers,
settlers, horses, sheep, cattle, young women for wives, were
all sent out in abundance by his paternal benignity. Before
the season was over, about two thousand persons had landed
at Quebec at the royal charge. "At length," writes Mother
Juchereau, "our joy was completed by the arrival of two vessels with Monsieur de Courcelle, our governor; Monsieur
Talon, our intendant, and the last companies of the regiment
of Carignan." More state and splendor, more young nobles,
more guards and valets: for Courcelle, too, says the same
chronicler, "had a superb train; and Monsieur Talon, who

[1] Juchereau says that this was his constant attendance when he went
abroad.

naturally loves glory, forgot nothing which could do honor to the king." Thus a sunbeam from the court fell for a moment on the rock of Quebec. Yet all was not sunshine; for the voyage had been a tedious one, and disease had broken out in the ships. That which bore Talon had been a hundred and seventeen days at sea,[1] and others were hardly more fortunate. The hospital was crowded with the sick; so, too, were the church and the neighboring houses; and the nuns were so spent with their labors that seven of them were brought to the point of death. The priests were busied in converting the Huguenots, a number of whom were detected among the soldiers and emigrants. One of them proved refractory, declaring with oaths that he would never renounce his faith. Falling dangerously ill, he was carried to the hospital, where Mother Catherine de Saint-Augustin bethought her of a plan of conversion. She ground to powder a small piece of a bone of Father Brébeuf, the Jesuit martyr, and secretly mixed the sacred dust with the patient's gruel; whereupon, says Mother Juchereau, "this intractable man forthwith became gentle as an angel, begged to be instructed, embraced the faith, and abjured his errors publicly with an admirable fervor."[2]

Two or three years before, the church of Quebec had received as a gift from the Pope, the bodies or bones of two saints; Saint Flavian and Saint Félicité. They were enclosed in four large coffers or reliquaries, and a grand procession was now ordered in their honor. Tracy, Courcelle, Talon, and the agent of the company, bore the canopy of the Host. Then came the four coffers on four decorated litters, carried by the principal ecclesiastics. Laval followed in pontificals. Forty-seven priests, and a long file of officers, nobles, soldiers, and inhabitants, followed the precious relics amid the sound of music and the roar of cannon.[3]

"It is a ravishing thing," says Mother Mary, "to see how marvellously exact is Monsieur de Tracy, at all these holy ceremonies, where he is always the first to come, for he would not lose a single moment of them. He has been seen in

[1] *Talon au ministre, 4 Oct., 1665.*

[2] Le Mercier tells the same story in the *Relation* of 1665.

[3] Compare Marie de l'Incarnation, *Lettre, 16 Oct., 1666*, with La Tour, *Vie de Laval*, chap. x.

church for six hours together, without once going out." But while the lieutenant-general thus edified the colony, he betrayed no lack of qualities equally needful in his position. In Canada, as in the West Indies, he showed both vigor and conduct. First of all, he had been ordered to subdue or destroy the Iroquois, and the regiment of Carignan-Salières was the weapon placed in his hands for this end. Four companies of this corps had arrived early in the season, four more came with Tracy, more yet with Salières, their colonel, and now the number was complete. As with slouched hat and plume, bandoleer, and shouldered firelock, these bronzed veterans of the Turkish wars marched at the tap of drum through the narrow street, or mounted the rugged way that led up to the fort, the inhabitants gazed with a sense of profound relief. Tame Indians from the neighboring missions, wild Indians from the woods, stared in silent wonder at their new defenders. Their numbers, their discipline, their uniform, and their martial bearing, filled the savage beholders with admiration.

Carignan-Salières was the first regiment of regular troops ever sent to America by the French government. It was raised in Savoy by the Prince of Carignan in 1644, but was soon employed in the service of France; where, in 1652, it took a conspicuous part, on the side of the king, in the battle with Condé and the Fronde at the Porte St. Antoine. After the peace of the Pyrenees, the Prince of Carignan, unable to support the regiment, gave it to the king, and it was, for the first time, incorporated into the French armies. In 1664, it distinguished itself, as part of the allied force of France, in the Austrian war against the Turks. In the next year it was ordered to America, along with the fragment of a regiment formed of Germans, the whole being placed under the command of Colonel de Salières. Hence its double name.[1]

[1] For a long notice of the regiment of Carignan-Salières (Lorraine), see Susane, *Ancienne Infanterie Française*, V. 236. The portion of it which returned to France from Canada formed a nucleus for the reconstruction of the regiment, which, under the name of the regiment of Lorraine, did not cease to exist as a separate organization till 1794. When it came to Canada it consisted, says Susane, of about a thousand men, besides about two hundred of the other regiment incorporated with it. Compare *Mémoire du Roy pour servir d'instruction au Sieur Talon*, which corresponds very nearly with Susane's statement.

Fifteen heretics were discovered in its ranks, and quickly converted.[1] Then the new crusade was preached; the crusade against the Iroquois, enemies of God and tools of the devil. The soldiers and the people were filled with a zeal half warlike and half religious. "They are made to understand," writes Mother Mary, "that this is a holy war, all for the glory of God and the salvation of souls. The fathers are doing wonders in inspiring them with true sentiments of piety and devotion. Fully five hundred soldiers have taken the scapulary of the Holy Virgin. It is we (*the Ursulines*), who make them; it is a real pleasure to do such work;" and she proceeds to relate a "*beau miracle*," by which God made known his satisfaction at the fervor of his military servants.

The secular motives for the war were in themselves strong enough; for the growth of the colony absolutely demanded the cessation of Iroquois raids, and the French had begun to learn the lesson that, in the case of hostile Indians, no good can come of attempts to conciliate, unless respect is first imposed by a sufficient castigation. It is true that the writers of the time paint Iroquois hostilities in their worst colors. In the innumerable letters which Mother Mary of the Incarnation sent home every autumn, by the returning ships, she spared no means to gain the sympathy and aid of the devout; and, with similar motives, the Jesuits in their printed *Relations*, took care to extenuate nothing of the miseries which the pious colony endured. Avaugour, too, in urging the sending out of a strong force to fortify and hold the country, had advised that, in order to furnish a pretext and disarm the jealousy of the English and Dutch, exaggerated accounts should be given of danger from the side of the savage confederates. Yet, with every allowance, these dangers and sufferings were sufficiently great.

The three upper nations of the Iroquois were comparatively pacific; but the two lower nations, the Mohawks and Oneidas, were persistently hostile; making inroads into the colony by way of Lake Champlain and the Richelieu, murdering and

---

[1] Besides these, there was Berthier, a captain. "Voilà" writes Talon to the king, "le 16me converti; ainsi votre Majesté moissonne déjà à pleines mains de la gloire pour Dieu, et pour elle bien de la renommée dans toute l'étendue de la Chrétienté." *Lettre du 7 Oct., 1665.*

scalping, and then vanishing like ghosts. Tracy's first step was to send a strong detachment to the Richelieu to build a picket fort below the rapids of Chambly, which take their name from that of the officer in command. An officer named Sorel soon afterwards built a second fort on the site of the abandoned palisade work built by Montmagny, at the mouth of the river, where the town of Sorel now stands; and Salières, colonel of the regiment, added a third fort, two or three leagues above Chambly.[1] These forts could not wholly bar the passage against the nimble and wily warriors who might pass them in the night, shouldering their canoes through the woods. A blow, direct and hard, was needed, and Tracy prepared to strike it.

Late in the season an embassy from the three upper nations — the Onondagas, Cayugas, and Senecas — arrived at Quebec, led by Garacontié, a famous chief whom the Jesuits had won over, and who proved ever after a staunch friend of the French. They brought back the brave Charles Le Moyne of Montreal, whom they had captured some three months before, and now restored as a peace-offering, taking credit to themselves that "not even one of his nails had been torn out, nor any part of his body burnt."[2] Garacontié made a peace speech, which, as rendered by the Jesuits, was an admirable specimen of Iroquois eloquence; but, while joining hands with him and his companions, the French still urged on their preparations to chastise the contumacious Mohawks.

[1] See the map in the *Relation* of 1665. The accompanying text of the *Relation* is incorrect.

[2] *Explanation of the eleven Presents of the Iroquois Ambassadors*, N. Y. *Colonial Docs.*, IX. 37.

Chapter XIV

1666, 1667

THE MOHAWKS CHASTISED

Courcelle's March • His Failure and Return • Courcelle and the Jesuits • Mohawk Treachery • Tracy's Expedition • Burning of the Mohawk Towns • French and English • Dollier de Casson at St. Anne • Peace • The Jesuits and the Iroquois

THE GOVERNOR, Courcelle, says Father Le Mercier, "breathed nothing but war," and was bent on immediate action. He was for the present subordinate to Tracy, who, however, forebore to cool his ardor, and allowed him to proceed. The result was an enterprise bold to rashness. Courcelle, with about five hundred men, prepared to march in the depth of a Canadian winter to the Mohawk towns, a distance estimated at three hundred leagues. Those who knew the country, vainly urged the risks and difficulties of the attempt. The adventurous governor held fast to his purpose, and only waited till the St. Lawrence should be well frozen. Early in January, it was a solid floor; and on the ninth the march began. Officers and men stopped at Sillery, and knelt in the little mission chapel before the shrine of Saint Michael, to ask the protection and aid of the warlike archangel; then they resumed their course, and, with their snow-shoes tied at their backs, walked with difficulty and toil over the bare and slippery ice. A keen wind swept the river, and the fierce cold gnawed them to the bone. Ears, noses, fingers, hands, and knees were frozen; some fell in torpor, and were dragged on by their comrades to the shivering bivouac. When, after a march of ninety miles, they reached Three Rivers, a considerable number were disabled, and had to be left behind; but others joined them from the garrison, and they set out again. Ascending the Richelieu, and passing the new forts at Sorel and Chambly, they reached at the end of the month the third fort, called Ste. Thérèse. On the thirtieth they left it, and continued their march up the frozen stream. About two hundred of them were Canadians, and of these seventy were old Indian-fighters from Montreal, versed in woodcraft, seasoned to the climate, and trained among dangers and alarms. Courcelle quickly learned their value, and his "Blue Coats," as he called them, were always placed in the van.[1] Here, wrapped in their coarse blue capotes, with blankets and provisions strapped at their backs, they strode along on snow-shoes, which recent storms had made indispensable. The regulars followed as they could. They were not yet the tough and experienced woodsmen that they and their descendants afterwards became; and their snow-shoes embarrassed them, burdened as they were with the heavy loads which all carried alike, from Courcelle to the lowest private.

Lake Champlain lay glaring in the winter sun, a sheet of spotless snow; and the wavy ridges of the Adirondacks bordered the dazzling landscape with the cold gray of their denuded forests. The long procession of weary men crept slowly on under the lee of the shore; and when night came they bivouacked by squads among the trees, dug away the snow with their snow-shoes, piled it in a bank around them, built their fire in the middle, and crouched about it on beds of spruce or hemlock;[2] while, as they lay close packed for mutual warmth, the winter sky arched them like a vault of burnished steel, sparkling with the cold diamond lustre of its myriads of stars. This arctic serenity of the elements was varied at times by heavy snow-storms; and, before they reached their journey's end, the earth and the ice were buried to the unusual depth of four feet. From Lake Champlain they passed to Lake George,[3] and the frigid glories of its snow-wrapped mountains; thence crossed to the Hudson, and groped their way through the woods in search of the Mohawk towns. They soon went astray; for thirty Algonquins, whom they had taken as guides, had found the means of a grand debauch at Fort Ste. Thérèse, drunk themselves into helplessness, and lingered behind. Thus Courcelle and his men mistook the path, and, marching by way of Saratoga

---

[1] Dollier de Casson, *Histoire du Montréal*, A.D. 1665, 1666.

[2] One of the men, telling the story of their sufferings to Daniel Gookin, of Massachusetts, indicated this as their mode of encamping. See Mass. Hist. Coll., first series, I. 161.

[3] *Carte des grands lacs, Ontario et autres . . . et des pays traversez par MM. de Tracy et Courcelle pour aller attaquer les agniés (Mohawks)*, 1666.

Lake and Long Lake,[1] found themselves, on Saturday the twentieth of February, close to the little Dutch hamlet of Corlaer or Schenectady. Here the chief man in authority told them that most of the Mohawks and Oneidas had gone to war with another tribe. They, however, caught a few stragglers, and had a smart skirmish with a party of warriors, losing an officer and several men. Half frozen and half starved, they encamped in the neighboring woods, where, on Sunday, three envoys appeared from Albany, to demand why they had invaded the territories of his Royal Highness the Duke of York. It was now that they learned for the first time that the New Netherlands had passed into English hands, a change which boded no good to Canada. The envoys seemed to take their explanations in good part, made them a present of wine and provisions, and allowed them to buy further supplies from the Dutch of Schenectady. They even invited them to enter the village, but Courcelle declined, partly because the place could not hold them all, and partly because he feared that his men, once seated in a chimney-corner, could never be induced to leave it.

Their position was cheerless enough; for the vast beds of snow around them were soaking slowly under a sullen rain, and there was danger that the lakes might thaw and cut off their retreat. "Ye Mohaukes," says the old English report of the affair, "were all gone to their Castles with resolution to fight it out against the french, who, being refresht and supplyed wth the aforesaid provisions, made a shew of marching towards the Mohaukes Castles, but with faces about, and great sylence and dilligence, return'd towards Cannada." "Surely," observes the narrator, "so bould and hardy an attempt hath not hapned in any age."[2] The end hardly answered to the beginning. The retreat, which began on Sunday night, was rather precipitate. The Mohawks hovered about their rear, and took a few prisoners; but famine and cold proved more deadly foes, and sixty men perished before they reached the shelter of Fort Ste. Thérèse. On the eighth of March,

[1] *Ibid.*

[2] *A Relation of the Govern^r. of Cannada, his March with 600 Volunteirs into ye Territoryes of His Royall Highnesse the Duke of Yorke in America.* See Doc. Hist. N. Y. I. 71.

Courcelle came to the neighboring fort of St. Louis or Chambly. Here he found the Jesuit Albanel acting as chaplain; and, being in great ill humor, he charged him with causing the failure of the expedition by detaining the Algonquin guides. This singular notion took such possession of him, that, when a few days after he met the Jesuit Frémin at Three Rivers, he embraced him ironically, saying, at the same time, "My father, I am the unluckiest gentleman in the world; and you, and the rest of you, are the cause of it."[1] The pious Tracy, and the prudent Talon, tried to disarm his suspicions, and with such success that he gave up an intention he had entertained of discarding his Jesuit confessor, and forgot or forgave the imagined wrong.

Unfortunate as this expedition was, it produced a strong effect on the Iroquois by convincing them that their forest homes were no safe asylum from French attacks. In May, the Senecas sent an embassy of peace; and the other nations, including the Mohawks, soon followed. Tracy, on his part, sent the Jesuit Bêchefer to learn on the spot the real temper of the savages, and ascertain whether peace could safely be made with them. The Jesuit was scarcely gone when news came that a party of officers hunting near the outlet of Lake Champlain had been set upon by the Mohawks, and that seven of them had been captured or killed. Among the captured was Leroles, a cousin of Tracy, and among the killed was a young gentleman named Chasy, his nephew.

On this the Jesuit envoy was recalled; twenty-four Iroquois deputies were seized and imprisoned; and Sorel, captain in the regiment of Carignan, was sent with three hundred men to chastise the perfidious Mohawks. If, as it seems, he was expected to attack their fortified towns or "castles," as the English call them, his force was too small. This time, however, there was no fighting. At two days from his journey's end, Sorel met the famous chief called the Flemish Bastard, bringing back Leroles and his fellow-captives, and charged, as he alleged, to offer full satisfaction for the murder of Chasy. Sorel believed him, retraced his course, and with the Bastard in his train returned to Quebec.

[1] *Journal des Jésuites, Mars, 1666.*

Quebec was full of Iroquois deputies, all bent on peace or pretending to be so. On the last day of August, there was a grand council in the garden of the Jesuits. Some days later, Tracy invited the Flemish Bastard and a Mohawk chief named Agariata to his table, when allusion was made to the murder of Chasy. On this the Mohawk, stretching out his arm, exclaimed in a braggart tone, "This is the hand that split the head of that young man." The indignation of the company may be imagined. Tracy told his insolent guest that he should never kill anybody else; and he was led out and hanged in presence of the Bastard.[1] There was no more talk of peace. Tracy prepared to march in person against the Mohawks with all the force of Canada.

On the day of the Exaltation of the Cross, "for whose glory," says the chronicler, "this expedition is undertaken," Tracy and Courcelle left Quebec with thirteen hundred men. They crossed Lake Champlain, and launched their boats again on the waters of St. Sacrament, now Lake George. It was the first of the warlike pageants that have made that fair scene historic. October had begun, and the romantic wilds breathed the buoyant life of the most inspiring of American seasons, when the blue-jay screams from the woods; the wild duck splashes along the lake; and the echoes of distant mountains prolong the quavering cry of the loon; when weather-stained rocks are plumed with the fiery crimson of the sumac, the claret hues of young oaks, the amber and scarlet of the maple, and the sober purple of the ash; or when gleams of sunlight, shot aslant through the rents of cool autumnal clouds, chase fitfully along the glowing sides of painted mountains. Amid this gorgeous euthanasia of the dying season, the three hundred boats and canoes trailed in long procession up the lake, threaded the labyrinth of the Narrows, that sylvan fairy-land of tufted islets and quiet waters, and landed at length where Fort William Henry was afterwards built.[2]

---

[1] This story rests chiefly on the authority of Nicolas Perrot, *Mœurs des Sauvages*, 113. La Potherie also tells it, with the addition of the chief's name. Colden follows him. The *Journal des Jésuites* mentions that the chief who led the murderers of Chasy arrived at Quebec on the sixth of September. Marie de l'Incarnation mentions the hanging of an Iroquois at Quebec, late in the autumn, for violating the peace.

[2] *Carte . . . des pays traversez par MM. de Tracy et Courcelles, etc.*

About a hundred miles of forests, swamps, rivers, and mountains, still lay between them and the Mohawk towns. There seems to have been an Indian path; for this was the ordinary route of the Mohawk and Oneida war-parties: but the path was narrow, broken, full of gullies and pitfalls, crossed by streams, and in one place interrupted by a lake which they passed on rafts. A hundred and ten "Blue Coats," of Montreal, led the way, under Charles Le Moyne. Repentigny commanded the levies from Quebec. In all there were six hundred Canadians; six hundred regulars; and a hundred Indians from the missions, who ranged the woods in front, flank, and rear, like hounds on the scent. Red or white, Canadians or regulars, all were full of zeal. "It seems to them," writes Mother Mary, "that they are going to lay siege to Paradise, and win it and enter in, because they are fighting for religion and the faith."[1] Their ardor was rudely tried. Officers as well as men carried loads at their backs, whence ensued a large blister on the shoulders of the Chevalier de Chaumont, in no way used to such burdens. Tracy, old, heavy, and infirm, was inopportunely seized with the gout. A Swiss soldier tried to carry him on his shoulders across a rapid stream; but midway his strength failed, and he was barely able to deposit his ponderous load on a rock. A Huron came to his aid, and bore Tracy safely to the farther bank. Courcelle was attacked with cramps, and had to be carried for a time like his commander. Provisions gave out, and men and officers grew faint with hunger. The Montreal soldiers had for chaplain a sturdy priest, Dollier de Casson, as large as Tracy and far stronger; for the incredible story is told of him that, when in good condition, he could hold two men seated on his extended hands.[2] Now, however, he was equal to no such exploit, being not only deprived of food, but also of sleep, by the necessity of listening at night to the confessions of his pious flock; and his shoes, too, had failed him, nothing remaining but the upper leather, which gave him little comfort among the sharp stones. He bore up manfully, being by nature brave

---

[1] Marie de l'Incarnation, *Lettre du 16 Oct., 1666.*

[2] Grandet, *Notice manuscrite sur Dollier de Casson*, extract given by J. Viger in appendix to *Histoire du Montréal* (Montreal, 1868).

and light-hearted; and, when a servant of the Jesuits fell into
the water, he threw off his cassock and leaped after him. His
strength gave out, and the man was drowned; but a grateful
Jesuit led him aside and requited his efforts with a morsel of
bread.[1] A wood of chestnut-trees full of nuts at length stayed
the hunger of the famished troops.

It was Saint Theresa's day when they approached the lower
Mohawk town. A storm of wind and rain set in; but, anxious
to surprise the enemy, they pushed on all night amid the
moan and roar of the forest; over slippery logs, tangled roots,
and oozy mosses; under dripping boughs and through saturated bushes. This time there was no want of good guides;
and when in the morning they issued from the forest, they
saw, amid its cornfields, the palisades of the Indian stronghold. They had two small pieces of cannon brought from the
lake by relays of men, but they did not stop to use them.
Their twenty drums beat the charge, and they advanced to
seize the place by *coup-de-main*. Luckily for them, a panic had
seized the Indians. Not that they were taken by surprise, for
they had discovered the approaching French, and, two days
before, had sent away their women and children in preparation for a desperate fight; but the din of the drums, which
they took for so many devils in the French service; and the
armed men advancing from the rocks and thickets in files that
seemed interminable,—so wrought on the scared imagination
of the warriors that they fled in terror to their next town, a
short distance above. Tracy lost no time, but hastened in pursuit. A few Mohawks were seen on the hills, yelling and firing
too far for effect. Repentigny, at the risk of his scalp, climbed
a neighboring height, and looked down on the little army,
which seemed so numerous as it passed beneath, "that,"
writes the superior of the Ursulines, "he told me that he
thought the good angels must have joined with it; whereat
he stood amazed."

The second town or fort was taken as easily as the first; so,
too, were the third and the fourth. The Indians yelled, and
fled without killing a man; and still the troops pursued, following the broad trail which led from town to town along

[1] Dollier de Casson, *Histoire de Montréal*, A.D. 1665, 1666.

the valley of the Mohawk. It was late in the afternoon when the fourth town was entered,[1] and Tracy thought that his work was done; but an Algonquin squaw who had followed her husband to the war, and who had once been a prisoner among the Mohawks, told him that there was still another above. The sun was near its setting, and the men were tired with their pitiless marching; but again the order was given to advance. The eager squaw showed the way, holding a pistol in one hand and leading Courcelle with the other; and they soon came in sight of Andaraqué, the largest and strongest of the Mohawk forts. The drums beat with fury, and the troops prepared to attack, but there were none to oppose them. The scouts sent forward, reported that the warriors had fled. The last of the savage strongholds was in the hands of the French.

"God has done for us," says Mother Mary, "what he did in ancient days for his chosen people, striking terror into our enemies, insomuch that we were victors without a blow. Certain it is that there is miracle in all this; for, if the Iroquois had stood fast, they would have given us a great deal of trouble and caused our army great loss, seeing how they were fortified and armed, and how haughty and bold they are."

The French were astonished as they looked about them. These Iroquois forts were very different from those that Jogues had seen here twenty years before, or from that which in earlier times set Champlain and his Hurons at defiance. The Mohawks had had counsel and aid from their Dutch friends, and adapted their savage defences to the rules of European art. Andaraqué was a quadrangle formed of a triple palisade, twenty feet high, and flanked by four bastions. Large vessels of bark filled with water were placed on the platforms of the palisade for defence against fire. The dwellings which these fortifications enclosed were in many cases built of wood, though the form and arrangement of the primitive bark lodge of the Iroquois seems to have been preserved. Some of the wooden houses were a hundred and twenty feet

[1] Marie de l'Incarnation says that there were four towns in all. I follow the *Acte de prise de possession*, made on the spot. Five are here mentioned.

long, with fires for eight or nine families. Here and in subterranean *caches* was stored a prodigious quantity of Indian-corn and other provisions; and all the dwellings were supplied with carpenters' tools, domestic utensils, and many other appliances of comfort.

The only living things in Andaraqué, when the French entered, were two old women, a small boy, and a decrepit old man, who, being frightened by the noise of the drums, had hidden himself under a canoe. From them the victors learned that the Mohawks, retreating from the other towns, had gathered here, resolved to fight to the last; but at sight of the troops their courage failed, and the chief was first to run, crying out, "Let us save ourselves, brothers; the whole world is coming against us."

A cross was planted, and at its side the royal arms. The troops were drawn up in battle array, when Jean Baptiste du Bois, an officer deputed by Tracy, advancing sword in hand to the front, proclaimed in a loud voice that he took possession in the name of the king of all the country of the Mohawks; and the troops shouted three times, *Vive le Roi*.[1]

That night a mighty bonfire illumined the Mohawk forests; and the scared savages from their hiding-places among the rocks saw their palisades, their dwellings, their stores of food, and all their possessions, turned to cinders and ashes. The two old squaws captured in the town, threw themselves in despair into the flames of their blazing homes. When morning came, there was nothing left of Andaraqué but smouldering embers, rolling their pale smoke against the painted background of the October woods. *Te Deum* was sung and mass said; and then the victors began their backward march, burning, as they went, all the remaining forts, with all their hoarded stores of corn, except such as they needed for themselves. If they had failed to destroy their enemies in battle, they hoped that winter and famine would do the work of shot and steel.

While there was distress among the Mohawks, there was trouble among their English neighbors, who claimed as their own the country which Tracy had invaded. The English authorities were the more disquieted, because they feared that

---

[1] *Acte de prise de possession, 17 Oct., 1666.*

the lately conquered Dutch might join hands with the French against them. When Nicolls, governor of New York, heard of Tracy's advance, he wrote to the governors of the New England colonies, begging them to join him against the French invaders, and urging that, if Tracy's force were destroyed or captured, the conquest of Canada would be an easy task. There was war at the time between the two crowns; and the British court had already entertained this project of conquest, and sent orders to its colonies to that effect. But the New England governors, ill prepared for war, and fearing that their Indian neighbors, who were enemies of the Mohawks, might take part with the French, hesitated to act, and the affair ended in a correspondence, civil if not sincere, between Nicolls and Tracy.[1] The treaty of Bréda, in the following year, secured peace for a time between the rival colonies.

The return of Tracy was less fortunate than his advance. The rivers, swollen by autumn rains, were difficult to pass; and in crossing Lake Champlain two canoes were overset in a storm, and eight men were drowned. From St. Anne, a new fort built early in the summer on Isle La Motte, near the northern end of the lake, he sent news of his success to Quebec, where there was great rejoicing and a solemn thanksgiving. Signs and prodigies had not been wanting to attest the interest of the upper and nether powers in the crusade against the myrmidons of hell. At one of the forts on the Richelieu, "the soldiers," says Mother Mary, "were near dying of fright. They saw a great fiery cavern in the sky, and from this cavern came plaintive voices mixed with frightful howlings. Perhaps it was the demons, enraged because we had depopulated a country where they had been masters so long, and had said mass and sung the praises of God in a place where there had never before been any thing but foulness and abomination."

Tracy had at first meant to abandon Fort St. Anne; but he changed his mind after returning to Quebec. Meanwhile the season had grown so late that there was no time to send proper supplies to the garrison. Winter closed, and the place was not only ill provisioned, but was left without a priest.

---

[1] See the correspondence in *N. Y. Col. Docs.*, III. 118–156. Compare *Hutchinson Collection*, 407, and *Mass. Hist. Coll.*, XVIII. 102.

Tracy wrote to the superior of the Sulpitians at Montreal to send one without delay; but the request was more easily made than fulfilled, for he forgot to order an escort, and the way was long and dangerous. The stout-hearted Dollier de Casson was told, however, to hold himself ready to go at the first opportunity. His recent campaigning had left him in no condition for braving fresh hardships, for he was nearly disabled by a swelling on one of his knees. By way of cure he resolved to try a severe bleeding, and the Sangrado of Montreal did his work so thoroughly that his patient fainted under his hands. As he returned to consciousness, he became aware that two soldiers had entered the room. They told him that they were going in the morning to Chambly, which was on the way to St. Anne; and they invited him to go with them. "Wait till the day after to-morrow," replied the priest, "and I will try." The delay was obtained; and, on the day fixed, the party set out by the forest path to Chambly, a distance of about four leagues. When they reached it, Dollier de Casson was nearly spent, but he concealed his plight from the commanding officer, and begged an escort to St. Anne, some twenty leagues farther. As the officer would not give him one, he threatened to go alone, on which ten men and an ensign were at last ordered to conduct him. Thus attended, he resumed his journey after a day's rest. One of the soldiers fell through the ice, and none of his comrades dared help him. Dollier de Casson, making the sign of the cross, went to his aid, and, more successful than on the former occasion, caught him and pulled him out. The snow was deep; and the priest, having arrived in the preceding summer, had never before worn snow-shoes, while a sack of clothing, and his portable chapel which he carried at his back, joined to the pain of his knee and the effects of his late bleeding, made the march a purgatory.

He was sorely needed at Fort St. Anne. There was pestilence in the garrison. Two men had just died without absolution, while more were at the point of death, and praying for a priest. Thus it happened that when the sentinel descried far off, on the ice of Lake Champlain, a squad of soldiers approaching, and among them a black cassock, every officer and man not sick, or on duty, came out with one accord to meet the new-comer. They overwhelmed him with welcome and with thanks. One took his sack, another his portable chapel, and they led him in triumph to the fort. First he made a short prayer, then went his rounds among the sick, and then came to refresh himself with the officers. Here was La Motte de la Lucière, the commandant; La Durantaye, a name destined to be famous in Canadian annals; and a number of young subalterns. The scene was no strange one to Dollier de Casson, for he had been an officer of cavalry in his time, and fought under Turenne;[1] a good soldier, without doubt, at the mess table or in the field, and none the worse a priest that he had once followed the wars. He was of a lively humor, given to jests and mirth; as pleasant a father as ever said *Benedicite*. The soldier and the gentleman still lived under the cassock of the priest. He was greatly respected and beloved; and his influence as a peace-maker, which he often had occasion to exercise, is said to have been remarkable. When the time demanded it, he could use arguments more cogent than those of moral suasion. Once, in a camp of Algonquins, when, as he was kneeling in prayer, an insolent savage came to interrupt him, the father, without rising, knocked the intruder flat by a blow of his fist, and the other Indians, far from being displeased, were filled with admiration at the exploit.[2]

His cheery temper now stood him in good stead; for there was dreary work before him, and he was not the man to flinch from it. The garrison of St. Anne had nothing to live on but salt pork and half-spoiled flour. Their hogshead of vinegar had sprung a leak, and the contents had all oozed out. They had rejoiced in the supposed possession of a reasonable stock of brandy; but they soon discovered that the sailors, on the voyage from France, had emptied the casks and filled them again with salt-water. The scurvy broke out with fury. In a short time, forty out of the sixty men became victims of the loathsome malady. Day or night, Dollier de Casson and Forestier, the equally devoted young surgeon, had no rest. The surgeon's strength failed, and the priest was himself slightly

---

[1] Grandet, *Notice manuscrite sur Dollier de Casson*, extracts from copy in possession of the late Jacques Viger.

[2] *Ibid.*, cited by Faillon, *Colonie Française*, III. 395, 396.

attacked with the disease. Eleven men died; and others languished for want of help, for their comrades shrank from entering the infected dens where they lay. In their extremity some of them devised an ingenious expedient. Though they had nothing to bequeath, they made wills in which they left imaginary sums of money to those who had befriended them, and thenceforth they found no lack of nursing.

In the intervals of his labors, Dollier de Casson would run to and fro for warmth and exercise on a certain track of beaten snow, between two of the bastions, reciting his breviary as he went, so that those who saw him might have thought him out of his wits. One day La Motte called out to him as he was thus engaged, "Eh, Monsieur le curé, if the Iroquois should come, you must defend that bastion. My men are all deserting me, and going over to you and the doctor." To which the father replied, "Get me some litters with wheels, and I will bring them out to man my bastion. They are brave enough now; no fear of their running away." With banter like this, they sought to beguile their miseries; and thus the winter wore on at Fort St. Anne.[1]

Early in spring they saw a troop of Iroquois approaching, and prepared as well as they could to make fight; but the strangers proved to be ambassadors of peace. The destruction of the Mohawk towns had produced a deep effect, not on that nation alone, but also on the other four members of the league. They were disposed to confirm the promises of peace which they had already made; and Tracy had spurred their good intentions by sending them a message that, unless they quickly presented themselves at Quebec, he would hang all the chiefs whom he had kept prisoners after discovering their treachery in the preceding summer. The threat had its effect: deputies of the Oneidas, Onondagas, Cayugas, and Senecas presently arrived in a temper of befitting humility. The Mohawks were at first afraid to come: but in April they sent the Flemish Bastard with overtures of peace; and in July, a large

---

[1] The above curious incidents are told by Dollier de Casson, in his *Histoire du Montréal*, preserved in manuscript in the Mazarin Library at Paris. He gives no hint that the person in question was himself, but speaks of him as *un ecclésiastique*. His identity is, however, made certain by internal evidence, by a passage in the *Notice* of Grandet, and by other contemporary allusions.

deputation of their chiefs appeared at Quebec. They and the rest left some of their families as hostages, and promised that, if any of their people should kill a Frenchman, they would give them up to be hanged.[1]

They begged, too, for blacksmiths, surgeons, and Jesuits to live among them. The presence of the Jesuits in their town was in many ways an advantage to them; while to the colony it was of the greatest importance. Not only was conversion to the church justly regarded as the best means of attaching the Indians to the French, and alienating them from the English; but the Jesuits living in the midst of them could influence even those whom they could not convert, soothe rising jealousies, counteract English intrigues, and keep the rulers of the colony informed of all that was passing in the Iroquois towns. Thus, half Christian missionaries, half political agents, the Jesuits prepared to resume the hazardous mission of the Iroquois. Frémin and Pierron were ordered to the Mohawks, Bruyas to the Oneidas, and three others were named for the remaining three nations of the league. The troops had made the peace; the Jesuits were the rivets to hold it fast; and peace endured without absolute rupture for nearly twenty years. Of all the French expeditions against the Iroquois, that of Tracy was the most productive of good.

NOTE.—On Tracy's expedition against the Mohawks compare Faillon, *Histoire de la Colonie Française au Canada*, III.

[1] *Lettre du Père Jean Pierron, de la Compagnie de Jésus, escripte de la Motte (Fort Ste. Anne) sur le lac Champlain, le 12me d'aoust, 1667.*

Chapter XV

1665–1672

PATERNAL GOVERNMENT

Talon • Restriction and Monopoly • Views of Colbert • Political Galvanism • A Father of the People

---

TRACY'S work was done, and he left Canada with the glittering *noblesse* in his train. Courcelle and Talon remained to rule alone; and now the great experiment was begun. Paternal royalty would try its hand at building up a colony, and Talon was its chosen agent. His appearance did him no justice. The regular contour of his oval face, about which fell to his shoulders a cataract of curls, natural or supposititious; the smooth lines of his well-formed features, brows delicately arched, and a mouth more suggestive of feminine sensibility than of masculine force,—would certainly have misled the disciple of Lavater.[1] Yet there was no want of manhood in him. He was most happily chosen for the task placed in his hands, and from first to last approved himself a vigorous executive officer. He was a true disciple of Colbert, formed in his school and animated by his spirit.

Being on the spot, he was better able than his master to judge the working of the new order of things. With regard to the company, he writes that it will profit by impoverishing the colony; that its monopolies dishearten the people and paralyze enterprise; that it is thwarting the intentions of the king, who wishes trade to be encouraged; and that, if its exclusive privileges are maintained, Canada in ten years will be less populous than now.[2] But Colbert clung to his plan, though he wrote in reply that to satisfy the colonists he had persuaded the company to forego the monopolies for a year.[3] As this proved insufficient, the company was at length forced to give up permanently its right of exclusive trade, still exacting its share of beaver and moose skins. This was its chief source

---

[1] His portrait is at the Hôtel Dieu of Quebec. An engraving from it will be found in the third volume of Shea's Charlevoix.

[2] *Talon à Colbert, 4 Oct., 1665.*

[3] *Colbert à Talon, 5 Avril, 1666.*

of profit; it begrudged every sou deducted from it for charges of government, and the king was constantly obliged to do at his own cost that which the company should have done. In one point it showed a ceaseless activity; and this was the levying of duties, in which it was never known to fail.

Trade, even after its exercise was permitted, was continually vexed by the hand of authority. One of Tracy's first measures had been to issue a decree reducing the price of wheat one half. The council took up the work of regulation, and fixed the price of all imported goods in three several tariffs,—one for Quebec, one for Three Rivers, and one for Montreal.[1] It may well be believed that there was in Canada little capital and little enterprise. Industrially and commercially, the colony was almost dead. Talon set himself to galvanize it; and, if one man could have supplied the intelligence and energy of a whole community, the results would have been triumphant.

He had received elaborate instructions, and they indicate an ardent wish for the prosperity of Canada. Colbert had written to him that the true means to strengthen the colony was to "cause justice to reign, establish a good police, protect the inhabitants, discipline them against enemies, and procure for them peace, repose, and plenty."[2] "And as," the minister further says, "the king regards his Canadian subjects, from the highest to the lowest, almost as his own children, and wishes them to enjoy equally with the people of France the mildness and happiness of his reign, the Sieur Talon will study to solace them in all things and encourage them to trade and industry. And, seeing that nothing can better promote this end than entering into the details of their households and of all their little affairs, it will not be amiss that he visit all their settlements one after the other in order to learn their true condition, provide as much as possible for their wants, and, performing the duty of a good head of a family, put them in the way of making some profit." The intendant was also told to encourage fathers to inspire their children with piety, together with "profound love and respect for the royal person of his Majesty."[3]

[1] Tariff of Prices, in *N. Y. Colonial Docs.* IX. 36.
[2] *Colbert à Talon, 5 Avril, 1666.*
[3] *Instruction au Sieur Talon, 27 Mars, 1665.*

Talon entered on his work with admirable zeal. Sometimes he used authority, sometimes persuasion, sometimes promises of reward. Sometimes, again, he tried the force of example. Thus he built a ship to show the people how to do it, and rouse them to imitation.[1] Three or four years later, the experiment was repeated. This time it was at the cost of the king, who applied the sum of forty thousand livres[2] to the double purpose of promoting the art of ship-building, and saving the colonists from vagrant habits by giving them employment. Talon wrote that three hundred and fifty men had been supplied that summer with work at the charge of government.[3]

He despatched two engineers to search for coal, lead, iron, copper, and other minerals. Important discoveries of iron were made; but three generations were destined to pass before the mines were successfully worked.[4] The copper of Lake Superior raised the intendant's hopes for a time, but he was soon forced to the conclusion that it was too remote to be of practical value. He labored vigorously to develop arts and manufactures; made a barrel of tar, and sent it to the king as a specimen; caused some of the colonists to make cloth of the wool of the sheep which the king had sent out; encouraged others to establish a tannery, and also a factory of hats and of shoes. The Sieur Follin was induced by the grant of a monopoly to begin the making of soap and potash.[5] The people were ordered to grow hemp,[6] and urged to gather the nettles of the country as material for cordage; and the Ursulines were supplied with flax and wool, in order that they might teach girls to weave and spin.

Talon was especially anxious to establish trade between Canada and the West Indies; and, to make a beginning, he freighted the vessel he had built with salted cod, salmon, eels, pease, fish-oil, staves, and planks, and sent her thither to exchange her cargo for sugar, which she was in turn to

[1] *Talon à Colbert, Oct., 1667; Colbert à Talon, 20 Fev., 1668.*

[2] *Dépêche de Colbert, 11 Fev., 1671.*

[3] *Talon à Colbert, 2 Nov., 1671.*

[4] Charlevoix speaks of these mines as having been forgotten for seventy years, and rediscovered in his time. After passing through various hands, they were finally worked on the king's account.

[5] *Régistre du Conseil Souverain.*

[6] Marie de l'Incarnation, *Choix des Lettres de,* 371.

exchange in France for goods suited for the Canadian market.[1] Another favorite object with him was the fishery of seals and white porpoises for the sake of their oil; and some of the chief merchants were urged to undertake it, as well as the establishment of stationary cod-fisheries along the Lower St. Lawrence. But, with every encouragement, many years passed before this valuable industry was placed on a firm basis.

Talon saw with concern the huge consumption of wine and brandy among the settlers, costing them, as he wrote to Colbert, a hundred thousand livres a year; and, to keep this money in the colony, he declared his intention of building a brewery. The minister approved the plan, not only on economic grounds, but because "the vice of drunkenness would thereafter cause no more scandal by reason of the cold nature of beer, the vapors whereof rarely deprive men of the use of judgment."[2] The brewery was accordingly built, to the great satisfaction of the poorer colonists.

Nor did the active intendant fail to acquit himself of the duty of domiciliary visits, enjoined upon him by the royal instructions; a point on which he was of one mind with his superiors, for he writes that "those charged in this country with his Majesty's affairs are under a strict obligation to enter into the detail of families."[3] Accordingly we learn from Mother Juchereau, that "he studied with the affection of a father how to succor the poor and cause the colony to grow; entered into the minutest particulars; visited the houses of the inhabitants, and caused them to visit him; learned what crops each one was raising; taught those who had wheat to sell it at a profit, helped those who had none, and encouraged everybody." And Dollier de Casson represents him as visiting in turn every house at Montreal, and giving aid from the king to such as needed it.[4] Horses, cattle, sheep, and other domestic animals, were sent out at the royal charge in considerable numbers, and distributed gratuitously, with an order that none of the young should be killed till the country was sufficiently stocked. Large quantities of goods were also sent from

[1] Le Mercier, *Rel. 1667*, 3; *Dépêches de Talon*.
[2] *Colbert à Talon, 20 Fev., 1668*.
[3] *Mémoire de 1667*.
[4] *Histoire du Montréal, A.D. 1666, 1667*.

the same high quarter. Some of these were distributed as gifts, and the rest bartered for corn to supply the troops. As the intendant perceived that the farmers lost much time in coming from their distant clearings to buy necessaries at Quebec, he caused his agents to furnish them with the king's goods at their own houses, to the great annoyance of the merchants of Quebec, who complained that their accustomed trade was thus forestalled.[1]

These were not the only cares which occupied the mind of Talon. He tried to open a road across the country to Acadia, an almost impossible task, in which he and his successors completely failed. Under his auspices, Albanel penetrated to Hudson's Bay, and Saint Lusson took possession in the king's name of the country of the Upper Lakes. It was Talon, in short, who prepared the way for the remarkable series of explorations described in another work.[2] Again and again he urged upon Colbert and the king a measure from which, had it taken effect, momentous consequences must have sprung. This was the purchase or seizure of New York, involving the isolation of New England, the subjection of the Iroquois, and the undisputed control of half the continent.

Great as were his opportunities of abusing his trust, it does not appear that he took advantage of them. He held lands and houses in Canada,[3] owned the brewery which he had established, and embarked in various enterprises of productive industry; but, so far as I can discover, he is nowhere accused of making illicit gains, and there is reason to believe that he acquitted himself of his charge with entire fidelity.[4] His health failed in 1668, and for this and other causes he asked for his recall. Colbert granted it with strong expressions of regret; and when, two years later, he resumed the intendancy, the colony seems to have welcomed his return.

[1] *Talon à Colbert, 10 Nov., 1670.*

[2] *La Salle and the Discovery of the Great West.*

[3] In 1682, the Intendant Meules, in a despatch to the minister, makes a statement of Talon's property in Quebec. The chief items are the brewery and a house of some value on the descent of Mountain Street. He owned, also, the valuable seigniory, afterwards barony, Des Islets, in the immediate neighborhood.

[4] Some imputations against him, not of much weight, are, however, made in a memorial of Aubert de la Chesnaye, a merchant of Quebec.

Chapter XVI

1661–1673

MARRIAGE AND POPULATION

Shipment of Emigrants • *Soldier Settlers* • *Importation of Wives* •
Wedlock • *Summary Methods* • *The Mothers of Canada* • *Boun-
ties on Marriage* • *Celibacy Punished* • *Bounties on
Children* • *Results*

THE peopling of Canada was due in the main to the king.
Before the accession of Louis XIV. the entire population,
priests, nuns, traders, and settlers, did not exceed twenty-five
hundred;[1] but scarcely had he reached his majority when the
shipment of men to the colony was systematically begun.
Even in Argenson's time, loads of emigrants sent out by the
Crown were landed every year at Quebec. The Sulpitians of
Montreal also brought over colonists to people their seigniorial estate; the same was true on a small scale of one or two
other proprietors, and once at least the company sent a considerable number: yet the government was the chief agent of
emigration. Colbert did the work, and the king paid for it.

In 1661, Laval wrote to the cardinals of the Propaganda,
that during the past two years the king had spent two
hundred thousand livres on the colony; that, since 1659, he
had sent out three hundred men a year; and that he had
promised to send an equal number every summer during ten
years.[2] These men were sent by squads in merchant-ships,
each one of which was required to carry a certain number. In
many instances, emigrants were bound on their arrival to enter into the service of colonists already established. In this
case the employer paid them wages, and after a term of three
years they became settlers themselves.[3]

The destined emigrants were collected by agents in the
provinces, conducted to Dieppe or Rochelle, and thence em-

---

[1] Le Clerc, *Etablissement de la Foy*, II. 4.

[2] *Lettre de Laval envoyée à Rome, 21 Oct., 1661* (extract in Faillon from Archives of the Propaganda).

[3] Marie de l'Incarnation, *18 Août, 1664*. These *engagés* were sometimes also
brought over by private persons.

barked. At first men were sent from Rochelle itself, and its neighborhood; but Laval remonstrated, declaring that he wanted none from that ancient stronghold of heresy.[1] The people of Rochelle, indeed, found no favor in Canada. Another writer describes them as "persons of little conscience, and almost no religion," adding that the Normans, Percherons, Picards, and peasants of the neighborhood of Paris, are docile, industrious, and far more pious. "It is important," he concludes, "in beginning a new colony, to sow good seed."[2] It was, accordingly, from the north-western provinces that most of the emigrants were drawn.[3] They seem in the main to have been a decent peasantry, though writers who, from their position, should have been well informed, have denounced them in unmeasured terms.[4] Some of them could read and write, and some brought with them a little money.

Talon was constantly begging for more men, till Louis XIV. at length took alarm. Colbert replied to the over-zealous intendant, that the king did not think it expedient to depopulate France, in order to people Canada; that he wanted men for his armies; and that the colony must rely chiefly on increase from

[1] *Colbert à Laval, 18 Mars, 1664.*

[2] *Mémoire de 1664* (anonymous).

[3] See a paper by Garneau in *Le National* of Quebec, 28 October, 1856, embodying the results of research among the papers of the early notaries of Quebec. The chief emigration was from Paris, Normandy, Poitou, Pays d'Aunis, Brittany, and Picardy. Nearly all those from Paris were sent by the king from houses of charity.

[4] "Une foule d'aventuriers, ramassés au hazard en France, presque tous de la lie du peuple, la plupart oberés de dettes ou chargés de crimes." etc. La Tour, *Vie de Laval*, Liv. IV. "Le vice a obligé la plupart de chercher ce pays comme un asile pour se mettre à couvert de leurs crimes," Meules, *Depêche de 1682*. Meules was intendant in that year. Marie de l'Incarnation, after speaking of the emigrants as of a very mixed character, says that it would have been far better to send a few who were good Christians, rather than so many who give so much trouble. *Lettre du — Oct., 1669.*

Le Clerc, on the other hand, is emphatic in praise, calling the early colonists, "très honnêtes gens, ayant de la probité, de la droiture, et de la religion. . . . L'on a examiné et choisi les habitants, et renvoyé en France les personnes vicieuses." If, he adds, any such were left "ils effacaient glorieusement par leur pénitence les taches de leur première condition." Charlevoix is almost as strong in praise as La Tour in censure. Both of them wrote in the next century. We shall have means hereafter of judging between these conflicting statements.

within. Still the shipments did not cease; and, even while tempering the ardor of his agent, the king gave another proof
how much he had the growth of Canada at heart.[1]

The regiment of Carignan-Salières had been ordered home,
with the exception of four companies kept in garrison,[2] and a
considerable number discharged in order to become settlers.
Of those who returned, six companies were, a year or two
later, sent back, discharged in their turn, and converted into
colonists. Neither men nor officers were positively constrained to remain in Canada; but the officers were told that
if they wished to please his Majesty this was the way to do
so; and both they and the men were stimulated by promises
and rewards. Fifteen hundred livres were given to La Motte,
because he had married in the country and meant to remain
there. Six thousand livres were assigned to other officers, because they had followed, or were about to follow, La Motte's
example; and twelve thousand were set apart to be distributed
to the soldiers under similar conditions.[3] Each soldier who
consented to remain and settle was promised a grant of land
and a hundred livres in money; or, if he preferred it, fifty
livres with provisions for a year. This military colonization
had a strong and lasting influence on the character of the Canadian people.

But if the colony was to grow from within, the new settlers
must have wives. For some years past, the Sulpitians had sent
out young women for the supply of Montreal; and the king,
on a larger scale, continued the benevolent work. Girls for the
colony were taken from the hospitals of Paris and of Lyons,
which were not so much hospitals for the sick as houses of
refuge for the poor. Mother Mary writes in 1665 that a
hundred had come that summer, and were nearly all provided
with husbands, and that two hundred more were to come
next year. The case was urgent, for the demand was great.

[1] The king had sent out more emigrants than he had promised, to judge
from the census reports during the years 1666, 1667, and 1668. The total population for those years is 3418, 4312, and 5870, respectively. A small part of
this growth may be set down to emigration not under government auspices,
and a large part to natural increase, which was enormous at this time, from
causes which will soon appear.

[2] *Colbert à Talon, 20 Fev., 1668.*

[3] *Ibid.*

Complaints, however, were soon heard that women from cities made indifferent partners; and peasant girls, healthy, strong, and accustomed to field work, were demanded in their place. Peasant girls were therefore sent, but this was not all. Officers as well as men wanted wives; and Talon asked for a consignment of young ladies. His request was promptly answered. In 1667, he writes: "They send us eighty-four girls from Dieppe and twenty-five from Rochelle; among them are fifteen or twenty of pretty good birth; several of them are really *demoiselles*, and tolerably well brought up." They complained of neglect and hardship during the voyage. "I shall do what I can to soothe their discontent," adds the intendant; "for if they write to their correspondents at home how ill they have been treated it would be an obstacle to your plan of sending us next year a number of select young ladies."[1]

Three years later we find him asking for three or four more in behalf of certain bachelor officers. The response surpassed his utmost wishes; and he wrote again: "It is not expedient to send more *demoiselles*. I have had this year fifteen of them, instead of the four I asked for."[2]

As regards peasant girls, the supply rarely equalled the demand. Count Frontenac, Courcelle's successor, complained of the scarcity: "If a hundred and fifty girls and as many servants," he says, "had been sent out this year, they would all have found husbands and masters within a month."[3]

The character of these candidates for matrimony has not escaped the pen of slander. The caustic La Hontan, writing fifteen or twenty years after, draws the following sketch of the mothers of Canada: "After the regiment of Carignan was disbanded, ships were sent out freighted with girls of indifferent virtue, under the direction of a few pious old duennas, who divided them into three classes. These vestals were, so to

---

[1] "Des demoiselles bien choisies." *Talon à Colbert, 27 Oct., 1667.*

[2] *Ibid., 2 Nov., 1671.*

[3] *Frontenac à Colbert, 2 Nov., 1672.* This year only eleven girls had been sent. The scarcity was due to the indiscretion of Talon, who had written to the minister that, as many of the old settlers had daughters just becoming marriageable, it would be well, in order that they might find husbands, to send no more girls from France at present.

The next year, 1673, the king writes that, though he is involved in a great war, which needs all his resources, he has nevertheless sent sixty more girls.

speak, piled one on the other in three different halls, where
the bridegrooms chose their brides as a butcher chooses his
sheep out of the midst of the flock. There was wherewith to
content the most fantastical in these three harems; for here
were to be seen the tall and the short, the blond and the
brown, the plump and the lean; everybody, in short, found a
shoe to fit him. At the end of a fortnight not one was left. I
am told that the plumpest were taken first, because it was
thought that, being less active, they were more likely to keep
at home, and that they could resist the winter cold better.
Those who wanted a wife applied to the directresses, to
whom they were obliged to make known their possessions
and means of livelihood before taking from one of the three
classes the girl whom they found most to their liking. The
marriage was concluded forthwith, with the help of a priest
and a notary, and the next day the governor-general caused
the couple to be presented with an ox, a cow, a pair of swine,
a pair of fowls, two barrels of salted meat, and eleven crowns
in money."[1]

As regards the character of the girls, there can be no doubt
that this amusing sketch is, in the main, maliciously untrue.
Since the colony began, it had been the practice to send back
to France women of the class alluded to by La Hontan, as
soon as they became notorious.[2] Those who were not taken
from institutions of charity usually belonged to the families
of peasants overburdened with children, and glad to find the
chance of establishing them.[3] How some of them were obtained appears from a letter of Colbert to Harlay, Archbishop
of Rouen. "As, in the parishes about Rouen," he writes, "fifty
or sixty girls might be found who would be very glad to go
to Canada to be married, I beg you to employ your credit
and authority with the curés of thirty or forty of these par-

---

[1]La Hontan, *Nouveaux Voyages*, I. 11 (1709). In some of the other editions,
the same account is given in different words, equally lively and scandalous.

[2]This is the statement of Boucher, a good authority. A case of the sort in
1658 is mentioned in the correspondence of Argenson. Boucher says further,
that an assurance of good character was required from the relations or friends
of the girl who wished to embark. This refers to a period anterior to 1663,
when Boucher wrote his book. Colbert evidently cared for no qualification
except the capacity of maternity.

[3]*Témoignage de la Mère du Plessis de Sainte-Hélène* (extract in Faillon).

ishes, to try to find in each of them one or two girls disposed to go voluntarily for the sake of a settlement in life."[1]

Mistakes nevertheless occurred. "Along with the honest people," complains Mother Mary, "comes a great deal of *canaille* of both sexes, who cause a great deal of scandal."[2] After some of the young women had been married at Quebec, it was found that they had husbands at home. The priests became cautious in tying the matrimonial knot, and Colbert thereupon ordered that each girl should provide herself with a certificate from the curé or magistrate of her parish to the effect that she was free to marry. Nor was the practical intendant unmindful of other precautions to smooth the path to the desired goal. "The girls destined for this country," he writes, "besides being strong and healthy, ought to be entirely free from any natural blemish or any thing personally repulsive."[3]

Thus qualified canonically and physically, the annual consignment of young women was shipped to Quebec, in charge of a matron employed and paid by the king. Her task was not an easy one, for the troop under her care was apt to consist of what Mother Mary in a moment of unwonted levity calls "mixed goods."[4] On one occasion the office was undertaken

[1] *Colbert à l'Archevêque de Rouen, 27 Fev., 1670.*
That they were not always destitute may be gathered from a passage in one of Talon's letters. "Entre les filles qu'on fait passer ici il y en a qui ont de légitimes et considérables prétentions aux successions de leurs parents, même entre celles qui sont tirées de l'Hôpital Général." The General Hospital of Paris had recently been established (1656) as a house of refuge for the "Bohemians," or vagrants of Paris. The royal edict creating it says that "les pauvres mendiants et invalides des deux sexes y seraient enfermés pour estre employés aux manufactures et aultres travaux selon leur pouvoir." They were gathered by force in the streets by a body of special police, called "Archers de l'Hôpital." They resisted at first, and serious riots ensued. In 1662, the General Hospital of Paris contained 6262 paupers. See Clément, *Histoire de Colbert*, 113. Mother de Sainte-Hélène says that the girls sent from this asylum had been there from childhood in charge of nuns.

[2] "Beaucoup de canaille de l'un et l'autre sexe qui causent beaucoup de scandale." *Lettre du — Oct., 1669.*

[3] *Talon à Colbert, 10 Nov., 1670.*

[4] "Une marchandise mêlée." *Lettre du — Oct., 1668.* In that year, 1668, the king spent 40,000 livres in the shipment of men and girls. In 1669, a hundred and fifty girls were sent; in 1670, a hundred and sixty-five; and Talon asks for a hundred and fifty or two hundred more to supply the soldiers who had got ready their houses and clearings, and were now prepared to marry. The total number of girls sent from 1665 to 1673, inclusive, was about a thousand.

by the pious widow of Jean Bourdon. Her flock of a hundred and fifty girls, says Mother Mary, "gave her no little trouble on the voyage; for they are of all sorts, and some of them are very rude and hard to manage." Madame Bourdon was not daunted. She not only saw her charge distributed and married, but she continued to receive and care for the subsequent ship-loads as they arrived summer after summer. She was indeed chief among the pious duennas of whom La Hontan irreverently speaks. Marguerite Bourgeoys did the same good offices for the young women sent to Montreal. Here the "king's girls," as they were called, were all lodged together in a house to which the suitors repaired to make their selection. "I was obliged to live there myself," writes the excellent nun, "because families were to be formed;"[1] that is to say, because it was she who superintended these extemporized unions. Meanwhile she taught the girls their catechism, and, more fortunate than Madame Bourdon, inspired them with a confidence and affection which they retained long after.

At Quebec, where the matrimonial market was on a larger scale, a more ample bazaar was needed. That the girls were assorted into three classes, each penned up for selection in a separate hall, is a statement probable enough in itself, but resting on no better authority than that of La Hontan. Be this as it may, they were submitted together to the inspection of the suitor; and the awkward young peasant or the rugged soldier of Carignan was required to choose a bride without delay from among the anxious candidates. They, on their part, were permitted to reject any applicant who displeased them, and the first question, we are told, which most of them asked was whether the suitor had a house and a farm.

Great as was the call for wives, it was thought prudent to stimulate it. The new settler was at once enticed and driven into wedlock. Bounties were offered on early marriages. Twenty livres were given to each youth who married before the age of twenty, and to each girl who married before the age of sixteen.[2] This, which was called the "king's gift," was exclusive of the dowry given by him to every girl brought over by his orders. The dowry varied greatly in form and

[1] Extract in Faillon, *Colonie Française*, III. 214.
[2] *Arrêt du Conseil d'Etat du Roy* (see *Edits et Ordonnances*, I. 67).

value; but, according to Mother Mary, it was sometimes a
house with provisions for eight months. More often it was
fifty livres in household supplies, besides a barrel or two of
salted meat. The royal solicitude extended also to the children
of colonists already established. "I pray you," writes Colbert
to Talon, "to commend it to the consideration of the whole
people, that their prosperity, their subsistence, and all that is
dear to them, depend on a general resolution, never to be
departed from, to marry youths at eighteen or nineteen years
and girls at fourteen or fifteen; since abundance can never
come to them except through the abundance of men."[1] This
counsel was followed by appropriate action. Any father of a
family who, without showing good cause, neglected to marry
his children when they had reached the ages of twenty and
sixteen was fined;[2] and each father thus delinquent was required to present himself every six months to the local authorities to declare what reason, if any, he had for such delay.[3]
Orders were issued, a little before the arrival of the yearly
ships from France, that all single men should marry within a
fortnight after the landing of the prospective brides. No
mercy was shown to the obdurate bachelor. Talon issued an
order forbidding unmarried men to hunt, fish, trade with the
Indians, or go into the woods under any pretence whatsoever.[4] In short, they were made as miserable as possible. Colbert goes further. He writes to the intendant, "those who may

[1] *Colbert à Talon, 20 Fev., 1668.*
[2] *Arrêts du Conseil d'Etat, 1669* (cited by Faillon); *Arrêt du Conseil d'Etat,
1670* (see *Edits et Ordonnances*, I. 67); *Ordonnance du Roy, 5 Avril, 1669*. See
Clément, *Instructions, etc., de Colbert*, III. 2me Partie, 657.
[3] *Registre du Conseil Souverain.*
[4] *Talon au Ministre, 10 Oct., 1670.* Colbert highly approves this order. Faillon
found a case of its enforcement among the ancient records of Montreal. In
December, 1670, François Le Noir, an inhabitant of La Chine, was summoned before the judge, because, though a single man, he had traded with
Indians at his own house. He confessed the fact, but protested that he would
marry within three weeks after the arrival of the vessels from France, or,
failing to do so, that he would give a hundred and fifty livres to the church
of Montreal, and an equal sum to the hospital. On this condition he was
allowed to trade, but was still forbidden to go into the woods. The next year
he kept his word, and married Marie Magdeleine Charbonnier, late of Paris.

The prohibition to go into the woods was probably intended to prevent
the bachelor from finding a temporary Indian substitute for a French wife.

seem to have absolutely renounced marriage should be made to bear additional burdens, and be excluded from all honors: it would be well even to add some marks of infamy."[1] The success of these measures was complete. "No sooner," says Mother Mary, "have the vessels arrived than the young men go to get wives; and, by reason of the great number they are married by thirties at a time." Throughout the length and breadth of Canada, Hymen, if not Cupid, was whipped into a frenzy of activity. Dollier de Casson tells us of a widow who was married afresh before her late husband was buried.[2]

Nor was the fatherly care of the king confined to the humbler classes of his colonists. He wished to form a Canadian *noblesse*, to which end early marriages were thought needful among officers and others of the better sort. The progress of such marriages was carefully watched and reported by the intendant. We have seen the reward bestowed upon La Motte for taking to himself a wife, and the money set apart for the brother officers who imitated him. In his despatch of October, 1667, the intendant announces that two captains are already married to two damsels of the country; that a lieutenant has espoused a daughter of the governor of Three Rivers; and that "four ensigns are in treaty with their mistresses, and are already half engaged."[3] The paternal care of government, one would think, could scarcely go further.

It did, however, go further. Bounties were offered on children. The king, in council, passed a decree "that in future all inhabitants of the said country of Canada who shall have living children to the number of ten, born in lawful wedlock, not being priests, monks, or nuns, shall each be paid out of the moneys sent by his Majesty to the said country a pension of three hundred livres a year, and those who shall have

---

[1] "Il serait à propos de leur augmenter les charges, de les priver de tous honneurs, même d'y ajouter quelque marque d'infamie." *Lettre du 20 Fev., 1668.*

[2] *Histoire du Montréal,* A.D. *1671, 1672.*

[3] "Quatre enseignes sont en pourparler avec leurs maîtresses et sont déjà à demi engagés." *Dépêche du 27 Oct., 1667.* The lieutenant was René Gaultier de Varennes, who on the 26th September, 1667, married Marie Bochart, daughter of the governor of Three Rivers, *aged twelve years.* One of the children of this marriage was Varennes de la Vérendrye, whose son discovered the Rocky Mountains.

twelve children, a pension of four hundred livres; and that, to this effect, they shall be required to declare the number of their children every year in the months of June or July to the intendant of justice, police, and finance, established in the said country, who, having verified the same, shall order the payment of said pensions, one-half in cash, and the other half at the end of each year."[1] This was applicable to all. Colbert had before offered a reward, intended specially for the better class, of twelve hundred livres to those who had fifteen children, and eight hundred to those who had ten.

These wise encouragements, as the worthy Faillon calls them, were crowned with the desired result. A despatch of Talon in 1670 informs the minister that most of the young women sent out last summer are pregnant already, and in 1671 he announces that from six hundred to seven hundred children have been born in the colony during the year; a prodigious number in view of the small population. The climate was supposed to be particularly favorable to the health of women, which is somewhat surprising in view of recent American experience. "The first reflection I have to make," says Dollier de Casson, "is on the advantage that women have in this place (*Montreal*) over men, for though the cold is very wholesome to both sexes, it is incomparably more so to the female, who is almost immortal here." Her fecundity matched her longevity, and was the admiration of Talon and his successors, accustomed as they were to the scanty families of France.

Why with this great natural increase joined to an immigration which, though greatly diminishing, did not entirely cease, was there not a corresponding increase in the population of the colony? Why, more than half a century after the king took Canada in charge, did the census show a total of less than twenty-five thousand souls? The reasons will appear hereafter.

---

[1] *Edits et Ordonnances*, I. 67. It was thought at this time that the Indians, mingled with the French, might become a valuable part of the population. The reproductive qualities of Indian women, therefore, became an object of Talon's attention, and he reports that they impair their fertility by nursing their children longer than is necessary; "but," he adds, "this obstacle to the speedy building up of the colony can be overcome by a police regulation." *Mémoire sur l'Etat Présent du Canada*, 1667.

It is a peculiarity of Canadian immigration, at this its most flourishing epoch, that it was mainly an immigration of single men and single women. The cases in which entire families came over were comparatively few.[1] The new settler was found by the king; sent over by the king; and supplied by the king with a wife, a farm, and sometimes with a house. Well did Louis XIV. earn the title of Father of New France. But the royal zeal was spasmodic. The king was diverted to other cares, and soon after the outbreak of the Dutch war in 1672 the regular despatch of emigrants to Canada wellnigh ceased; though the practice of disbanding soldiers in the colony, giving them lands, and turning them into settlers, was continued in some degree, even to the last.

[1] The principal emigration of families seems to have been in 1669 when, at the urgency of Talon, then in France, a considerable number were sent out. In the earlier period the emigration of families was, relatively, much greater. Thus, in 1634, the physician Giffard brought over seven to people his seigniory of Beauport. Before 1663, when the king took the colony in hand, the emigrants were for the most part apprenticed laborers.

The zeal with which the king entered into the work of stocking his colony is shown by numberless passages in his letters, and those of his minister. "The end and the rule of all your conduct," says Colbert to the intendant Bouteroue, "should be the increase of the colony; and on this point you should never be satisfied, but labor without ceasing to find every imaginable expedient for preserving the inhabitants, attracting new ones, and multiplying them by marriage." *Instruction pour M. Bouteroue, 1668.*

Chapter XVII

THE NEW HOME

Military Frontier • The Canadian Settler • Seignior and Vassal •
Example of Talon • Plan of Settlement • Aspect of Canada •
Quebec • The River Settlements • Montreal • The Pioneers

WE have seen the settler landed and married; let us follow him to his new home. At the end of Talon's administration, the head of the colony, that is to say the island
of Montreal and the borders of the Richelieu, was the seat of
a peculiar colonization, the chief object of which was to protect the rest of Canada against Iroquois incursions. The lands
along the Richelieu, from its mouth to a point above Chambly, were divided in large seigniorial grants among several officers of the regiment of Carignan, who in their turn granted
out the land to the soldiers, reserving a sufficient portion as
their own. The officer thus became a kind of feudal chief, and
the whole settlement a permanent military cantonment admirably suited to the object in view. The disbanded soldier was
practically a soldier still, but he was also a farmer and a land-
holder.

Talon had recommended this plan as being in accordance
with the example of the Romans. "The practice of that politic
and martial people," he wrote, "may, in my opinion, be wisely adopted in a country a thousand leagues distant from its
monarch. And as the peace and harmony of peoples depend
above all things on their fidelity to their sovereign, our first
kings, better statesmen than is commonly supposed, introduced into newly conquered countries men of war, of approved trust, in order at once to hold the inhabitants to their
duty within, and repel the enemy from without."[1]

The troops were accordingly discharged, and settled not
alone on the Richelieu, but also along the St. Lawrence, between Lake St. Peter and Montreal, as well as at some other
points. The Sulpitians, feudal owners of Montreal, adopted a

[1] *Projets de Réglemens, 1667* (see *Edits et Ordonnances,* II. 29).

similar policy, and surrounded their island with a border of fiefs large and small, granted partly to officers and partly to humbler settlers, bold, hardy, and practised in bush-fighting. Thus a line of sentinels was posted around their entire shore, ready to give the alarm whenever an enemy appeared. About Quebec the settlements, covered as they were by those above, were for the most part of a more pacific character.

To return to the Richelieu. The towns and villages which have since grown upon its banks and along the adjacent shores of the St. Lawrence owe their names to these officers of Carignan, ancient lords of the soil: Sorel, Chambly, Saint Ours, Contrecœur, Varennes, Verchères. Yet let it not be supposed that villages sprang up at once. The military seignior, valiant and poor as Walter the Penniless, was in no condition to work such magic. His personal possessions usually consisted of little but his sword and the money which the king had paid him for marrying a wife. A domain varying from half a league to six leagues in front on the river, and from half a league to two leagues in depth, had been freely given him. When he had distributed a part of it in allotments to the soldiers, a variety of tasks awaited him: to clear and cultivate his land; to build his seigniorial mansion, often a log hut; to build a fort; to build a chapel; and to build a mill. To do all this at once was impossible. Chambly, the chief proprietor on the Richelieu, was better able than the others to meet the exigency. He built himself a good house, where, with cattle and sheep furnished by the king, he lived in reasonable comfort.[1] The king's fort, close at hand, spared him and his tenants the necessity of building one for themselves, and furnished, no doubt, a mill, a chapel, and a chaplain. His brother officers, Sorel excepted, were less fortunate. They and their tenants were forced to provide defence as well as shelter. Their houses were all built together, and surrounded by a palisade, so as to form a little fortified village. The ever-active benevolence of the king had aided them in the task, for the soldiers were still maintained by him while clearing the lands and building the houses destined to be their own; nor was it till this work was done that the provident government des-

[1] *Frontenac au Ministre, 2 Nov., 1672.* Marie de l'Incarnation speaks of these officers on the Richelieu as *très honnêtes gens.*

patched them to Quebec with orders to bring back wives. The settler, thus lodged and wedded, was required on his part to aid in clearing lands for those who should come after him.[1]

It was chiefly in the more exposed parts of the colony, that the houses were gathered together in palisaded villages, thus forcing the settler to walk or paddle some distance to his farm. He naturally preferred to build when he could on the front of his farm itself, near the river, which supplied the place of a road. As the grants of land were very narrow, his house was not far from that of his next neighbor, and thus a line of dwellings was ranged along the shore, forming what in local language was called a *côte*, a use of the word peculiar to Canada, where it still prevails.

The impoverished seignior rarely built a chapel. Most of the early Canadian churches were built with funds furnished by the seminaries of Quebec or of Montreal, aided by contributions of material and labor from the parishioners.[2] Meanwhile mass was said in some house of the neighborhood by a missionary priest, paddling his canoe from village to village, or from *côte* to *côte*.

The mill was an object of the last importance. It was built of stone and pierced with loopholes, to serve as a blockhouse in case of attack. The great mill at Montreal was one of the chief defences of the place. It was at once the duty and the right of the seignior to supply his tenants, or rather vassals, with this essential requisite, and they on their part were required to grind their grain at his mill, leaving the fourteenth part in payment. But for many years there was not a seigniory in Canada, where this fraction would pay the wages of a miller; and, except the ecclesiastical corporations, there were few seigniors who could pay the cost of building. The first

---

[1]"Sa Majesté semble prétendre faire la dépense entière pour former le commencement des habitations par l'abattis du bois, la culture et semence de deux arpens de terre, l'avance de quelques farines aux familles venantes," etc., etc. *Projets de Réglemens, 1667.* This applied to civil and military settlers alike. The established settler was allowed four years to clear two arpents of land for a new-comer. The soldiers were maintained by the king during a year, while preparing their farms and houses. Talon asks that two years more be given them. *Talon au Roy, 10 Nov., 1670.*

[2]La Tour, *Vie de Laval*, chap. x.

settlers were usually forced to grind for themselves after the tedious fashion of the Indians.

Talon, in his capacity of counsellor, friend, and father to all Canada, arranged the new settlements near Quebec in the manner which he judged best, and which he meant to serve as an example to the rest of the colony. It was his aim to concentrate population around this point, so that, should an enemy appear, the sound of a cannon-shot from the Château St. Louis might summon a numerous body of defenders to this the common point of rendezvous.[1] He bought a tract of land near Quebec, laid it out, and settled it as a model seigniory, hoping, as he says, to kindle a spirit of emulation among the new-made seigniors to whom he had granted lands from the king. He also laid out at the royal cost three villages in the immediate neighborhood, planning them with great care, and peopling them partly with families newly arrived, partly with soldiers, and partly with old settlers, in order that the new-comers might take lessons from the experience of these veterans. That each village might be complete in itself, he furnished it as well as he could with the needful carpenter, mason, blacksmith, and shoemaker. These inland villages, called respectively Bourg Royal, Bourg la Reine, and Bourg Talon, did not prove very thrifty.[2] Wherever the settlers were allowed to choose for themselves, they ranged their dwellings along the watercourses. With the exception of Talon's villages, one could have seen nearly every house in Canada, by paddling a canoe up the St. Lawrence and the Richelieu. The settlements formed long thin lines on the edges of the rivers; a convenient arrangement, but one very unfavorable to defence, to ecclesiastical control, and to strong government. The king soon discovered this; and repeated orders were sent to concentrate the inhabitants and form Canada into villages, instead of *côtes*. To do so would have involved a general revocation of grants and abandonment of houses and clearings, a measure too arbitrary and too wasteful, even for Louis XIV., and one extremely difficult to

[1] *Projets de Réglemens, 1667.*

[2] In 1672, the king, as a mark of honor, attached these villages to Talon's seigniory. Documents on Seigniorial Tenure.

enforce. Canada persisted in attenuating herself, and the royal will was foiled.

As you ascended the St. Lawrence, the first harboring place of civilization was Tadoussac, at the mouth of the Saguenay, where the company had its trading station, where its agents ruled supreme, and where, in early summer, all was alive with canoes and wigwams, and troops of Montagnais savages, bringing their furs to market. Leave Tadoussac behind, and, embarked in a sail-boat or a canoe, follow the northern coast. Far on the left, twenty miles away, the southern shore lies pale and dim, and mountain ranges wave their faint outline along the sky. You pass the beetling rocks of Mal Bay, a solitude but for the bark hut of some wandering Indian beneath the cliff; the Eboulements with their wild romantic gorge, and foaming waterfalls; and the Bay of St. Paul with its broad valley and its woody mountains, rich with hidden stores of iron. Vast piles of savage verdure border the mighty stream, till at length the mountain of Cape Tourmente upheaves its huge bulk from the bosom of the water, shadowed by lowering clouds, and dark with forests. Just beyond, begin the settlements of Laval's vast seigniory of Beaupré, which had not been forgotten in the distribution of emigrants, and which, in 1667, contained more inhabitants than Quebec itself.[1] The ribbon of rich meadow land that borders that beautiful shore, was yellow with wheat in harvest time, and on the woody slopes behind, the frequent clearings and the solid little dwellings of logs continued for a long distance to relieve the sameness of the forest. After passing the cataract of Montmorenci, there was another settlement, much smaller, at Beauport, the seigniory of the ex-physician Giffard, one of the earliest proprietors in Canada. The neighboring shores of the island of Orleans were also edged with houses and clearings. The promontory of Quebec now towered full in sight, crowned with church, fort, chateau, convents, and seminary. There was little else on the rock. Priests, nuns, government

---

[1] The census of 1667 gives to Quebec only 448 souls; Côte de Beaupré, 656; Beauport, 123; Island of Orleans, 529; other settlements included under the government of Quebec, 1,011; Côte de Lauzon (south shore), 113; Trois Rivières and its dependencies, 666; Montreal, 766. Both Beaupré and Isle d'Orleans belonged at this time to the bishop.

officials, and soldiers, were the denizens of the Upper Town; while commerce and the trades were cabined along the strand beneath.[1] From the gallery of the chateau, you might toss a pebble far down on their shingled roofs. In the midst of them was the magazine of the company, with its two round towers and two projecting wings. It was here that all the beaver-skins of the colony were collected, assorted, and shipped for France. The so-called chateau St. Louis was an indifferent wooden structure planted on a site truly superb; above the Lower Town, above the river, above the ships, gazing abroad on a majestic panorama of waters, forests, and mountains.[2] Behind it was the area of the fort, of which it formed one side. The governor lived in the chateau, and soldiers were on guard night and day in the fort. At some little distance was the convent of the Ursulines, ugly but substantial,[3] where Mother Mary of the Incarnation ruled her pupils and her nuns; and a little further on, towards the right, was the Hôtel Dieu. Between them were the massive buildings of the Jesuits, then as now facing the principal square. At one side was their church, newly finished; and opposite, across the square, stood and still stands the great church of Notre Dame. Behind the church was Laval's seminary, with the extensive enclosures belonging to it. The *sénéchaussée* or court-house, the tavern of one Jacques Boisdon on the square near the church, and a few houses along the line of what is now St. Louis Street, comprised nearly all the civil part of the Upper Town. The ecclesiastical buildings were of stone, and the church of Notre Dame and the Jesuit College were marvels of size and solidity in view of the poverty and weakness of the colony.[4]

[1] According to Juchereau, there were seventy houses at Quebec about the time of Tracy's arrival.

[2] In 1660, an exact inventory was taken of the contents of the fort and chateau; a beggarly account of rubbish. The chateau was then a long low building roofed with shingles.

[3] There is an engraving of it in Abbé Casgrain's interesting *Vie de Marie de l'Incarnation*. It was burned in 1686.

[4] The first stone of Notre Dame de Quebec was laid in September, 1647, and the first mass was said in it on the 24th of December, 1650. The side walls still remain as part of the present structure. The Jesuit college was also begun in 1647. The walls and roof were finished in 1649. The church connected with it, since destroyed, was begun in 1666. *Journal des Jésuites.*

Proceeding upward along the north shore of the St. Lawrence, one found a cluster of houses at Cap Rouge, and, further on, the frequent rude beginnings of a seigniory. The settlements thickened on approaching Three Rivers, a fur-trading hamlet enclosed with a square palisade. Above this place, a line of incipient seigniories bordered the river, most of them granted to officers: Laubia, a captain; Labadie, a sergeant; Moras, an ensign; Berthier, a captain; Raudin, an ensign; La Valterie, a lieutenant.[1] Under their auspices, settlers, military and civilian, were ranging themselves along the shore, and ugly gaps in the forest thickly set with stumps bore witness to their toils. These settlements rapidly extended, till in a few years a chain of houses and clearings reached with little interruption from Quebec to Montreal. Such was the fruit of Tracy's chastisement of the Mohawks, and the influx of immigrants that followed.

As you approached Montreal, the fortified mill built by the Sulpitians at Point aux Trembles towered above the woods; and soon after the newly built chapel of the Infant Jesus. More settlements followed, till at length the great fortified mill of Montreal rose in sight; then the long row of compact wooden houses, the Hôtel Dieu, and the rough masonry of the seminary of St. Sulpice. Beyond the town, the clearings continued at intervals till you reached Lake St. Louis, where young Cavelier de la Salle had laid out his seigniory of La Chine, and abandoned it to begin his hard career of western exploration. Above the island of Montreal, the wilderness was broken only by a solitary trading station on the neighboring Isle Pérot.

Now cross Lake St. Louis, shoot the rapids of La Chine, and follow the southern shore downward. Here the seigniories of Longueuil, Boucherville, Varennes, Verchères, and Contrecœur were already begun. From the fort of Sorel one could visit the military seigniories along the Richelieu or descend towards Quebec, passing on the way those of Lussaudière, Becancour, Lotbinière, and others still in a shapeless infancy. Even far below Quebec, at St. Anne de la Pocatière,

---

[1]Documents on the Seigniorial Tenure; Abstracts of Titles. Most of these grants, like those on the Richelieu, were made by Talon in 1672; but the land had, in many cases, been occupied and cleared in anticipation of the title.

River Ouelle, and other points, cabins and clearings greeted the eye of the passing canoeman.

For a year or two, the settler's initiation was a rough one; but when he had a few acres under tillage he could support himself and his family on the produce, aided by hunting, if he knew how to use a gun, and by the bountiful profusion of eels which the St. Lawrence never failed to yield in their season, and which, smoked or salted, supplied his larder for months. In winter he hewed timber, sawed planks, or split shingles for the market of Quebec, obtaining in return such necessaries as he required. With thrift and hard work he was sure of comfort at last; but the former habits of the military settlers and of many of the others were not favorable to a routine of dogged industry. The sameness and solitude of their new life often became insufferable; nor, married as they had been, was the domestic hearth likely to supply much consolation. Yet, thrifty or not, they multiplied apace. "A poor man," says Mother Mary, "will have eight children and more, who run about in winter with bare heads and bare feet, and a little jacket on their backs, live on nothing but bread and eels, and on that grow fat and stout." With such treatment the weaker sort died; but the strong survived, and out of this rugged nursing sprang the hardy Canadian race of bush-rangers and bush-fighters.

Chapter XVIII

1663–1763

CANADIAN FEUDALISM

Transplantation of Feudalism • Precautions • Faith and Homage • The Seignior • The Censitaire • Royal Intervention • The Gentilhomme • Canadian Noblesse

---

C ANADIAN society was beginning to form itself, and at its base was the feudal tenure. European feudalism was the indigenous and natural growth of political and social conditions which preceded it. Canadian feudalism was an offshoot of the feudalism of France, modified by the lapse of centuries, and further modified by the royal will.

In France, as in the rest of Europe, the system had lost its vitality. The warrior-nobles who placed Hugh Capet on the throne, and began the feudal monarchy, formed an aristocratic republic, and the king was one of their number, whom they chose to be their chief. But, through the struggles and vicissitudes of many succeeding reigns, royalty had waxed and oligarchy had waned. The fact had changed and the theory had changed with it. The king, once powerless among a host of turbulent nobles, was now a king indeed. Once a chief, because his equals had made him so, he was now the anointed of the Lord. This triumph of royalty had culminated in Louis XIV. The stormy energies and bold individualism of the old feudal nobles had ceased to exist. They who had held his predecessors in awe had become his obsequious servants. He no longer feared his nobles; he prized them as gorgeous decorations of his court, and satellites of his royal person.

It was Richelieu who first planted feudalism in Canada.[1] The king would preserve it there, because with its teeth drawn he was fond of it, and because, as the feudal tenure prevailed in Old France, it was natural that it should prevail also in the New. But he continued as Richelieu had begun, and moulded it to the form that pleased him. Nothing was left which could threaten his absolute and undivided authority over the colony. In France, a multitude of privileges and

[1] By the charter of the Company of the Hundred Associates, 1627.

prescriptions still clung, despite its fall, about the ancient ruling class. Few of these were allowed to cross the Atlantic, while the old, lingering abuses, which had made the system odious, were at the same time lopped away. Thus retrenched, Canadian feudalism was made to serve a double end; to produce a faint and harmless reflection of French aristocracy, and simply and practically to supply agencies for distributing land among the settlers.

The nature of the precautions which it was held to require appear in the plan of administration which Talon and Tracy laid before the minister. They urge that, in view of the distance from France, special care ought to be taken to prevent changes and revolutions, aristocratic or otherwise, in the colony, whereby in time sovereign jurisdictions might grow up, as formerly occurred in various parts of France.[1] And, in respect to grants already made, an inquiry was ordered, to ascertain "if seigniors in distributing lands to their vassals have exacted any conditions injurious to the rights of the Crown and the subjection due solely to the king." In the same view the seignior was denied any voice whatever in the direction of government; and it is scarcely necessary to say that the essential feature of feudalism in the day of its vitality, the requirement of military service by the lord from the vassal, was utterly unknown in Canada. The royal governor called out the militia whenever he saw fit, and set over it what officers he pleased.

The seignior was usually the immediate vassal of the Crown, from which he had received his land gratuitously. In a few cases, he made grants to other seigniors inferior in the feudal scale, and they, his vassals, granted in turn to their vassals, the *habitants* or cultivators of the soil.[2] Sometimes the

---

[1] *Projet de Réglement fait par MM. de Tracy et Talon pour la justice et la distribution des terres du Canada, Jan. 24, 1667.*

[2] Most of the seigniories of Canada were simple fiefs; but there were some exceptions. In 1671, the king, as a mark of honor to Talon, erected his seigniory Des Islets into a barony; and it was soon afterwards made an earldom, *comté*. In 1676, the seigniory of St. Laurent, on the island of Orleans, once the property of Laval, and then belonging to François Berthelot, councillor of the king, was erected into an earldom. In 1681, the seigniory of Portneuf, belonging to Réné Robineau, chevalier, was made a barony. In 1700, three seigniories on the south side of the St. Lawrence were united into the barony of Longueuil. See Papers on the Feudal Tenure in Canada, Abstract of Titles.

habitant held directly of the Crown, in which case there was no step between the highest and lowest degrees of the feudal scale. The seignior held by the tenure of faith and homage, the *habitant* by the inferior tenure *en censive*. Faith and homage were rendered to the Crown or other feudal superior whenever the seigniory changed hands, or, in the case of seigniories held by corporations, after long stated intervals. The following is an example, drawn from the early days of the colony, of the performance of this ceremony by the owner of a fief to the seignior who had granted it to him. It is that of Jean Guion, vassal of Giffard, seignior of Beauport. The act recounts how, in presence of a notary, Guion presented himself at the principal door of the manor-house of Beauport; how, having knocked, one Boullé, farmer of Giffard, opened the door, and in reply to Guion's question if the seignior was at home, replied that he was not, but that he, Boullé, was empowered to receive acknowledgments of faith and homage from the vassals in his name. "After the which reply," proceeds the act, "the said Guion, being at the principal door, placed himself on his knees on the ground, with head bare, and without sword or spurs, and said three times these words: 'Monsieur de Beauport, Monsieur de Beauport, Monsieur de Beauport, I bring you the faith and homage which I am bound to bring you on account of my fief Du Buisson, which I hold as a man of faith of your seigniory of Beauport, declaring that I offer to pay my seigniorial and feudal dues in their season, and demanding of you to accept me in faith and homage as aforesaid.' "[1]

The following instance is the more common one of a seignior holding directly of the Crown. It is widely separated from the first in point of time, having occurred a year after the army of Wolfe entered Quebec. Philippe Noël had lately died, and Jean Noël, his son, inherited his seigniory of Tilly and Bonsecours. To make the title good, faith and homage must be renewed. Jean Noël was under the bitter necessity of rendering this duty to General Murray, governor for the king of Great Britain. The form is the same as in the case of

[1]Ferland, *Notes sur les Registres de Notre Dame de Québec*, 65. This was a *fief en roture*, as distinguished from a *fief noble*, to which judicial powers and other privileges were attached.

Guion, more than a century before. Noël repairs to the Government House at Quebec, and knocks at the door. A servant opens it. Noël asks if the governor is there. The servant replies that he is. Murray, informed of the visitor's object, comes to the door, and Noël then and there, "without sword or spurs, with bare head, and one knee on the ground," repeats the acknowledgment of faith and homage for his seigniory. He was compelled, however, to add a detested innovation, the oath of fidelity to his Britannic Majesty, coupled with a pledge to keep his vassals in obedience to the new sovereign.[1]

The seignior was a proprietor holding that relation to the feudal superior which, in its pristine character, has been truly described as servile in form, proud and bold in spirit. But in Canada this bold spirit was very far from being strengthened by the changes which the policy of the Crown had introduced into the system. The reservation of mines and minerals, oaks for the royal navy, roadways, and a site, if needed, for royal forts and magazines, had in it nothing extraordinary. The great difference between the position of the Canadian seignior and that of the vassal proprietor of the Middle Ages lay in the extent and nature of the control which the Crown and its officers held over him. A decree of the king, an edict of the council, or an ordinance of the intendant, might at any moment change old conditions, impose new ones, interfere between the lord of the manor and his grantees, and modify or annul his bargains, past or present. He was never sure whether or not the government would let him alone; and against its most arbitrary intervention he had no remedy.

One condition was imposed on him which may be said to form the distinctive feature of Canadian feudalism; that of clearing his land within a limited time on pain of forfeiting it. The object was the excellent one of preventing the lands of the colony from lying waste. As the seignior was often the penniless owner of a domain three or four leagues wide and proportionably deep, he could not clear it all himself, and was therefore under the necessity of placing the greater part in the hands of those who could. But he was forbidden to sell any

[1] See the act in *Observations de Sir L. H. Lafontaine, Bart., sur la Tenure Seigneuriale*, 217, note.

part of it which he had not cleared. He must grant it without price, on condition of a small perpetual rent; and this brings us to the cultivator of the soil, the *censitaire*, the broad base of the feudal pyramid.[1]

The tenure *en censive* by which the *censitaire* held of the seignior consisted in the obligation to make annual payments in money, produce, or both. In Canada these payments, known as *cens et rente*, were strangely diverse in amount and kind; but, in all the early period of the colony, they were almost ludicrously small. A common charge at Montreal was half a sou and half a pint of wheat for each arpent. The rate usually fluctuated in the early times between half a sou and two sous, so that a farm of a hundred and sixty arpents would pay from four to sixteen francs, of which a part would be in money and the rest in live capons, wheat, eggs, or all three together, in pursuance of contracts as amusing in their precision as they are bewildering in their variety. Live capons, estimated at twenty sous each, though sometimes not worth ten, form a conspicuous feature in these agreements, so that on pay-day the seignior's barnyard presented an animated scene. Later in the history of the colony grants were at somewhat higher rates. Payment was commonly made on St. Martin's day, when there was a general muster of tenants at the seigniorial mansion, with a prodigious consumption of tobacco and a corresponding retail of neighborhood gossip, joined to the outcries of the captive fowls

---

[1] The greater part of the grants made by the old Company of New France were resumed by the Crown for neglect to occupy and improve the land, which was granted out anew under the administration of Talon. The most remarkable of these forfeited grants is that of the vast domain of La Citière, large enough for a kingdom. Lauson, afterwards governor, had obtained it from the company, but had failed to improve it. Two or three sub-grants which he had made from it were held valid; the rest was reunited to the royal domain. On repeated occasions at later dates, negligent seigniors were threatened with the loss of half or the whole of their land, and various cases are recorded in which the threat took effect. In 1741, an ordinance of the governor and intendant reunited to the royal domain seventeen seigniories at one stroke; but the former owners were told that if within a year they cleared and settled a reasonable part of the forfeited estates, the titles should be restored to them. *Edits et Ordonnances*, II. 555. In the case of the *habitant* or *censitaire* forfeitures for neglect to improve the land and live on it are very numerous.

bundled together for delivery, with legs tied, but throats at full liberty.

A more considerable but a very uncertain source of income to the seignior were the *lods et ventes*, or mutation fines. The land of the *censitaire* passed freely to his heirs; but if he sold it, a twelfth part of the purchase-money must be paid to the seignior. The seignior, on his part, was equally liable to pay a mutation fine to his feudal superior if he sold his seigniory; and for him the amount was larger, being a *quint*, or a fifth of the price received, of which, however, the greater part was deducted for immediate payment. This heavy charge, constituting, as it did, a tax on all improvements, was a principal cause of the abolition of the feudal tenure in 1854.

The obligation of clearing his land and living on it was laid on seignior and *censitaire* alike; but the latter was under a variety of other obligations to the former, partly imposed by custom and partly established by agreement when the grant was made. To grind his grain at the seignior's mill, bake his bread in the seignior's oven, work for him one or more days in the year, and give him one fish in every eleven, for the privilege of fishing in the river before his farm; these were the most annoying of the conditions to which the *censitaire* was liable. Few of them were enforced with much regularity. That of baking in the seignior's oven was rarely carried into effect, though occasionally used for purposes of extortion. It is here that the royal government appears in its true character, so far as concerns its relations with Canada, that of a well-meaning despotism. It continually intervened between *censitaire* and seignior, on the principle that "as his Majesty gives the land for nothing, he can make what conditions he pleases, and change them when he pleases."[1] These interventions were usually favorable to the *censitaire*. On one occasion an intendant reported to the minister, that in his opinion all rents ought to be reduced to one sou and one live capon for every arpent of front, equal in most cases to forty superficial arpents.[2] Every thing, he remarks, ought to be brought down

[1] This doctrine is laid down in a letter of the Marquis de Beauharnois, governor, to the minister, 1734.

[2] *Lettre de Raudot, père, au Ministre, 10 Nov., 1707.*

to the level of the first grants "made in days of innocence," a happy period which he does not attempt to define. The minister replies that the diversity of the rent is, in fact, vexatious, and that, for his part, he is disposed to abolish it altogether.[1] Neither he nor the intendant gives the slightest hint of any compensation to the seignior. Though these radical measures were not executed, many changes were decreed from time to time in the relations between seignior and *censitaire*, sometimes as a simple act of sovereign power, and sometimes on the ground that the grants had been made with conditions not recognized by the *Coutume de Paris*. This was the code of law assigned to Canada; but most of the contracts between seignior and *censitaire* had been agreed upon in good faith by men who knew as much of the *Coutume de Paris* as of the Capitularies of Charlemagne, and their conditions had remained in force unchallenged for generations. These interventions of government sometimes contradicted each other, and often proved a dead letter. They are more or less active through the whole period of the French rule.

The seignior had judicial powers, which, however, were carefully curbed and controlled. His jurisdiction, when exercised at all, extended in most cases only to trivial causes. He very rarely had a prison, and seems never to have abused it. The dignity of a seigniorial gallows with *high justice* or jurisdiction over heinous offences was granted only in three or four instances.[2]

Four arpents in front by forty in depth were the ordinary dimensions of a grant *en censive*. These ribbons of land, nearly a mile and a half long, with one end on the river and the other on the uplands behind, usually combined the advantages of meadows for cultivation, and forests for timber and firewood. So long as the *censitaire* brought in on St. Martin's day his yearly capons and his yearly handful of copper, his title against the seignior was perfect. There are farms in Canada which have passed from father to son for two hundred years. The condition of the cultivator was incomparably bet-

---

[1] *Lettre de Ponchartrain à Raudot, père, 13 Juin, 1708.*

[2] Baronies and *comtés* were empowered to set up gallows and pillories, to which the arms of the owner were affixed. See, for example, the edict creating the Barony des Islets.

ter than that of the French peasant, crushed by taxes, and oppressed by feudal burdens far heavier than those of Canada. In fact, the Canadian settler scorned the name of peasant, and then, as now, was always called the *habitant*. The government held him in wardship, watched over him, interfered with him, but did not oppress him or allow others to oppress him. Canada was not governed to the profit of a class, and if the king wished to create a Canadian *noblesse* he took care that it should not bear hard on the country.[1]

Under a genuine feudalism, the ownership of land conferred nobility; but all this was changed. The king and not the soil was now the parent of honor. France swarmed with landless nobles, while *roturier* land-holders grew daily more numerous. In Canada half the seigniories were in *roturier* or plebeian hands, and in course of time some of them came into possession of persons on very humble degrees of the social scale. A seigniory could be bought and sold, and a trader or a thrifty *habitant* might, and often did become the buyer.[2] If the Canadian noble was always a seignior, it is far from being true that the Canadian seignior was always a noble.

In France, it will be remembered, nobility did not in itself imply a title. Besides its titled leaders, it had its rank and file, numerous enough to form a considerable army. Under the later Bourbons, the penniless young nobles were, in fact, enrolled into regiments, turbulent, difficult to control, obeying officers of high rank, but scorning all others, and conspicuous by a fiery and impetuous valor which on more than one occasion turned the tide of victory. The *gentilhomme*, or untitled

[1] On the seignorial tenure, I have examined the whole of the mass of papers printed at the time when the question of its abolition was under discussion. A great deal of legal research and learning was then devoted to the subject. The argument of Mr. Dunkin in behalf of the seigniors, and the observations of Judge Lafontaine, are especially instructive, as is also the collected correspondence of the governors and intendants with the central government on matters relating to the seigniorial system.

[2] In 1712, the engineer Catalogne made a very long and elaborate report on the condition of Canada, with a full account of all the seigniorial estates. Of ninety-one seigniories, fiefs, and baronies, described by him, ten belonged to merchants, twelve to husbandmen, and two to masters of small river craft. The rest belonged to religious corporations, members of the council, judges, officials of the Crown, widows, and discharged officers or their sons.

noble, had a distinctive character of his own, gallant, punctilious, vain; skilled in social and sometimes in literary and artistic accomplishments, but usually ignorant of most things except the handling of his rapier. Yet there were striking exceptions; and to say of him, as has been said, that "he knew nothing but how to get himself killed," is hardly just to a body which has produced some of the best writers and thinkers of France.

Sometimes the origin of his nobility was lost in the mists of time; sometimes he owed it to a patent from the king. In either case, the line of demarcation between him and the classes below him was perfectly distinct; and in this lies an essential difference between the French *noblesse* and the English gentry, a class not separated from others by a definite barrier. The French *noblesse*, unlike the English gentry, constituted a caste.

The *gentilhomme* had no vocation for emigrating. He liked the army and he liked the court. If he could not be of it, it was something to live in its shadow. The life of a backwoods settler had no charm for him. He was not used to labor; and he could not trade, at least in retail, without becoming liable to forfeit his nobility. When Talon came to Canada, there were but four noble families in the colony.[1] Young nobles in abundance came out with Tracy; but they went home with him. Where, then, should be found the material of a Canadian *noblesse*? First, in the regiment of Carignan, of which most of the officers were *gentilshommes*; secondly, in the issue of patents of nobility to a few of the more prominent colonists. Tracy asked for four such patents; Talon asked for five more;[2] and such requests were repeated at intervals by succeeding governors and intendants, in behalf of those who had gained their favor by merit or otherwise. Money smoothed the path to advancement, so far had *noblesse* already fallen from its old estate. Thus Jacques Le Ber, the merchant, who

[1] Talon, *Mémoire sur l'Etat présent du Canada, 1667*. The families of Repentigny, Tilly, Poterie, and Aillebout appear to be meant.
[2] Tracy's request was in behalf of Bourdon, Boucher, Auteuil, and Juchereau. Talon's was in behalf of Godefroy, Le Moyne, Denis, Amiot, and Couillard.

had long kept a shop at Montreal, got himself made a gentleman for six thousand livres.[1]

All Canada soon became infatuated with *noblesse*; and country and town, merchant and seignior, vied with each other for the quality of *gentilhomme*. If they could not get it, they often pretended to have it, and aped its ways with the zeal of Monsieur Jourdain himself. "Everybody here," writes the intendant Meules, "calls himself *Esquire*, and ends with thinking himself a gentleman." Successive intendants repeat this complaint. The case was worst with *roturiers* who had acquired seigniories. Thus Noel Langlois was a good carpenter till he became owner of a seigniory, on which he grew lazy and affected to play the gentleman. The real *gentilshommes*, as well as the spurious, had their full share of official stricture. The governor Denonville speaks of them thus: "Several of them have come out this year with their wives, who are very much cast down; but they play the fine lady, nevertheless. I had much rather see good peasants; it would be a pleasure to me to give aid to such, knowing, as I should, that within two years their families would have the means of living at ease; for it is certain that a peasant who can and will work is well off in this country, while our nobles with nothing to do can never be any thing but beggars. Still they ought not to be driven off or abandoned. The question is how to maintain them."[2]

The intendant Duchesneau writes to the same effect: "Many of our *gentilshommes*, officers, and other owners of seigniories, lead what in France is called the life of a country gentleman, and spend most of their time in hunting and fishing. As their requirements in food and clothing are greater than those of the simple *habitants*, and as they do not devote themselves to improving their land, they mix themselves up in trade, run in debt on all hands, incite their young *habitants* to range the woods, and send their own children there to trade for furs in the Indian villages and in the depths of the forest, in spite of the prohibition of his Majesty. Yet, with all this, they are in miserable poverty."[3]

[1] Faillon, *Vie de Mademoiselle Le Ber*, 325.
[2] *Lettre de Denonville au Ministre, 10 Nov., 1686.*
[3] *Lettre de Duchesneau au Ministre, 10 Nov., 1679.*

Their condition, indeed, was often deplorable. "It is piti-ful," says the intendant Champigny, "to see their children, of which they have great numbers, passing all summer with nothing on them but a shirt, and their wives and daughters working in the fields."[1] In another letter he asks aid from the king for Repentigny with his thirteen children, and for Tilly with his fifteen. "We must give them some corn at once," he says, "or they will starve."[2] These were two of the original four noble families of Canada. The family of Aillebout, an-other of the four, is described as equally destitute. "Pride and sloth," says the same intendant, "are the great faults of the people of Canada, and especially of the nobles and those who pretend to be such. I pray you grant no more letters of no-bility, unless you want to multiply beggars."[3] The governor Denonville is still more emphatic: "Above all things, mon-seigneur, permit me to say that the nobles of this new country are every thing that is most beggarly, and that to increase their number is to increase the number of do-nothings. A new country requires hard workers, who will handle the axe and mattock. The sons of our councillors are no more indus-trious than the nobles; and their only resource is to take to the woods, trade a little with the Indians, and, for the most part, fall into the disorders of which I have had the honor to inform you. I shall use all possible means to induce them to engage in regular commerce; but as our nobles and council-lors are all very poor and weighed down with debt, they could not get credit for a single crown piece."[4] "Two days ago," he writes in another letter, "Monsieur de Saint-Ours, a gentleman of Dauphiny, came to me to ask leave to go back to France in search of bread. He says that he will put his ten children into the charge of any who will give them a living, and that he himself will go into the army again. His wife and he are in despair; and yet they do what they can. I have seen two of his girls reaping grain and holding the plough. Other families are in the same condition. They come to me with

---

[1] *Lettre de Champigny au Ministre, 26 Août, 1687.*
[2] *Ibid., 6 Nov., 1687.*
[3] *Mémoire instructif sur le Canada, joint à la lettre de M. de Champigny du 10 May, 1691.*
[4] *Lettre de Denonville au Ministre, 13 Nov., 1685.*

tears in their eyes. All our married officers are beggars; and I entreat you to send them aid. There is need that the king should provide support for their children, or else they will be tempted to go over to the English."[1] Again he writes that the sons of the councillor D'Amours have been arrested as *coureurs de bois*, or outlaws in the bush; and that if the minister does not do something to help them, there is danger that all the sons of the *noblesse*, real or pretended, will turn bandits, since they have no other means of living.

The king, dispenser of charity for all Canada, came promptly to the rescue. He granted an alms of a hundred crowns to each family, coupled with a warning to the recipients of his bounty that "their misery proceeds from their ambition to live as persons of quality and without labor."[2] At the same time, the minister announced that no more letters of nobility would be granted in Canada; adding, "to relieve the country of some of the children of those who are really noble, I send you (*the governor*) six commissions of *Gardes de la Marine*, and recommend you to take care not to give them to any who are not actually *gentilshommes*." The *Garde de la Marine* answered to the midshipman of the English or American service. As the six commissions could bring little relief to the crowd of needy youths, it was further ordained that sons of nobles or persons living as such should be enrolled into companies at eight sous a day for those who should best conduct themselves, and six sous a day for the others. Nobles in Canada were also permitted to trade, even at retail, without derogating from their rank.[3]

They had already assumed this right, without waiting for the royal license; but thus far it had profited them little. The *gentilhomme* was not a good shopkeeper, nor, as a rule, was the shopkeeper's vocation very lucrative in Canada. The domestic trade of the colony was small; and all trade was exposed to such vicissitudes from the intervention of intendants, ministers, and councils, that at one time it was

---

[1] *Ibid.*, *10 Nov., 1686*. (Condensed in the translation.)
[2] Abstract of Denonville's Letters, and of the Minister's Answers, in *N.Y. Colonial Docs.*, IX. 317, 318.
[3] *Letter de Meules au Ministre, 1685*.

almost banished. At best, it was carried on under conditions auspicious to a favored few and withering to the rest. Even when most willing to work, the position of the *gentilhomme* was a painful one. Unless he could gain a post under the Crown, which was rarely the case, he was as complete a political cipher as the meanest *habitant*. His rents were practically nothing, and he had no capital to improve his seigniorial estate. By a peasant's work he could gain a peasant's living, and this was all. The prospect was not inspiring. His long initiation of misery was the natural result of his position and surroundings; and it is no matter of wonder that he threw himself into the only field of action which in time of peace was open to him. It was trade, but trade seasoned by adventure and ennobled by danger; defiant of edict and ordinance, outlawed, conducted in arms among forests and savages,— in short, it was the Western fur trade. The tyro was likely to fail in it at first, but time and experience formed him to the work. On the Great Lakes, in the wastes of the Northwest, on the Mississippi and the plains beyond, we find the roving *gentilhomme*, chief of a gang of bush-rangers, often his own *habitants*; sometimes proscribed by the government, sometimes leagued in contraband traffic with its highest officials, a hardy vidette of civilization, tracing unknown streams, piercing unknown forests, trading, fighting, negotiating, and building forts. Again we find him on the shores of Acadia or Maine, surrounded by Indian retainers, a menace and a terror to the neighboring English colonist. Saint-Castin, Du Lhut, La Durantaye, La Salle, La Motte-Cadillac, Iberville, Bienville, La Vérendrye, are names that stand conspicuous on the page of half-savage romance that refreshes the hard and practical annals of American colonization. But a more substantial debt is due to their memory. It was they, and such as they, who discovered the Ohio, explored the Mississippi to its mouth, discovered the Rocky Mountains, and founded Detroit, St. Louis, and New Orleans.

Even in his earliest day, the *gentilhomme* was not always in the evil plight where we have found him. There were a few exceptions to the general misery, and the chief among them is that of the Le Moynes of Montreal. Charles Le Moyne, son of an innkeeper of Dieppe and founder of a family the most truly eminent in Canada, was a man of sterling qualities who had been long enough in the colony to learn how to live there.[1] Others learned the same lesson at a later day, adapted themselves to soil and situation, took root, grew, and became more Canadian than French. As population increased, their seigniories began to yield appreciable returns, and their reserved domains became worth cultivating. A future dawned upon them; they saw in hope their names, their seigniorial estates, their manor-houses, their tenantry, passing to their children and their children's children. The beggared noble of the early time became a sturdy country gentleman; poor, but not wretched; ignorant of books, except possibly a few scraps of rusty Latin picked up in a Jesuit school; hardy as the hardiest woodsman, yet never forgetting his quality of *gentilhomme*; scrupulously wearing its badge, the sword, and copying as well as he could the fashions of the court, which glowed on his vision across the sea in all the effulgence of Versailles, and beamed with reflected ray from the chateau of Quebec. He was at home among his tenants, at home among the Indians, and never more at home than when, a gun in his hand and a crucifix on his breast, he took the war-path with a crew of painted savages and Frenchmen almost as wild, and pounced like a lynx from the forest on some lonely farm or outlying hamlet of New England. How New England hated him, let her records tell. The reddest blood streaks on her old annals mark the track of the Canadian *gentilhomme*.

[1]Berthelot, proprietor of the *comté* of St. Laurent, and Robineau, of the barony of Portneuf, may also be mentioned as exceptionally prosperous. Of the younger Charles Le Moyne, afterwards Baron de Longueuil, Frontenac the governor says, "son fort et sa maison nous donnent une idée des chateaux de France fortifiez." His fort was of stone and flanked with four towers. It was nearly opposite Montreal, on the south shore.

Chapter XIX

THE RULERS OF CANADA

Nature of the Government • The Governor • The Council Courts and Judges • The Intendant • His Grievances • Strong Government • Sedition and Blasphemy • Royal Bounty • Defects and Abuses

---

THE government of Canada was formed in its chief features after the government of a French province. Throughout France the past and the present stood side by side. The kingdom had a double administration; or rather, the shadow of the old administration and the substance of the new. The government of provinces had long been held by the high nobles, often kindred to the Crown; and hence, in former times, great perils had arisen, amounting during the civil wars to the danger of dismemberment. The high nobles were still governors of provinces; but here, as elsewhere, they had ceased to be dangerous. Titles, honors, and ceremonial they had in abundance; but they were deprived of real power. Close beside them was the royal intendant, an obscure figure, lost amid the vainglories of the feudal sunset, but in the name of the king holding the reins of government; a check and a spy on his gorgeous colleague. He was the king's agent: of modest birth, springing from the legal class; owing his present to the king, and dependent on him for his future; learned in the law and trained to administration. It was by such instruments that the powerful centralization of the monarchy enforced itself throughout the kingdom, and, penetrating beneath the crust of old prescriptions, supplanted without seeming to supplant them. The courtier noble looked down in the pride of rank on the busy man in black at his side; but this man in black, with the troop of officials at his beck, controlled finance, the royal courts, public works, and all the administrative business of the province.

The governor-general and the intendant of Canada answered to those of a French province. The governor, excepting in the earliest period of the colony, was a military noble;

in most cases bearing a title and sometimes of high rank. The intendant, as in France, was usually drawn from the *gens de robe*, or legal class.[1] The mutual relations of the two officers were modified by the circumstances about them. The governor was superior in rank to the intendant; he commanded the troops, conducted relations with foreign colonies and Indian tribes, and took precedence on all occasions of ceremony. Unlike a provincial governor in France, he had great and substantial power. The king and the minister, his sole masters, were a thousand leagues distant, and he controlled the whole military force. If he abused his position, there was no remedy but in appeal to the court, which alone could hold him in check. There were local governors at Montreal and Three Rivers; but their power was carefully curbed, and they were forbidden to fine or imprison any person without authority from Quebec.[2]

The intendant was virtually a spy on the governor-general, of whose proceedings and of every thing else that took place he was required to make report. Every year he wrote to the minister of state, one, two, three, or four letters, often forty or fifty pages long, filled with the secrets of the colony, political and personal, great and small, set forth with a minuteness often interesting, often instructive, and often excessively tedious.[3] The governor, too, wrote letters of pitiless length; and each of the colleagues was jealous of the letters of the other. In truth, their relations to each other were so critical, and perfect harmony so rare, that they might almost be described as natural enemies. The court, it is certain, did not desire their perfect accord; nor, on the other hand, did it wish them to quarrel: it aimed to keep them on such terms that, without

[1] The governor was styled in his commission, *Gouverneur et Lieutenant-Général en Canada, Acadie, Isle de Terreneuve, et autres pays de la France Septentrionale*; and the intendant, *Intendant de la Justice, Police, et Finances en Canada, Acadie, Terreneuve, et autres pays de la France Septentrionale.*

[2] The Sulpitian seigniors of Montreal claimed the right of appointing their own local governor. This was denied by the court, and the excellent Sulpitian governor, Maisonneuve, was removed by De Tracy, to die in patient obscurity at Paris. Some concessions were afterwards made in favor of the Sulpitian claims.

[3] I have carefully read about two thousand pages of these letters.

deranging the machinery of administration, each should be a check on the other.[1]

The governor, the intendant, and the supreme council or court, were absolute masters of Canada under the pleasure of the king. Legislative, judicial, and executive power, all centred in them. We have seen already the very unpromising beginnings of the supreme council. It had consisted at first of the governor, the bishop, and five councillors chosen by them. The intendant was soon added to form the ruling triumvirate; but the appointment of the councillors, the occasion of so many quarrels, was afterwards exercised by the king himself.[2] Even the name of the council underwent a change in the interest of his autocracy, and he commanded that it should no longer be called the *Supreme*, but only the *Superior* Council. The same change had just been imposed on all the high tribunals of France.[3] Under the shadow of the *fleur-de-lis*, the king alone was to be supreme.

In 1675, the number of councillors was increased to seven, and in 1703 it was again increased to twelve; but the character of the council or court remained the same. It issued decrees for the civil, commercial, and financial government of the colony, and gave judgment in civil and criminal causes according to the royal ordinances and the *Coutume de Paris*. It exercised also the function of registration borrowed from the parliament of Paris. That body, it will be remembered, had no analogy whatever with the English parliament. Its ordinary functions were not legislative, but judicial; and it was composed of judges hereditary under certain conditions. Nevertheless, it had long acted as a check on the royal power through its right of registration. No royal edict had the force of law till entered upon its books, and this custom had so

[1] The governor and intendant made frequent appeals to the court to settle questions arising between them. Several of these appeals are preserved. The king wrote replies on the margin of the paper, but they were usually too curt and general to satisfy either party.

[2] *Déclaration du Roi du 16me Juin, 1703.* Appointments were made by the king many years earlier. As they were always made on the recommendation of the governor and intendant, the practical effect of the change was merely to exclude the bishop from a share in them. The West India Company made the nominations during the ten years of its ascendancy.

[3] Cheruel, *Administration Monarchique en France*, II. 100.

deep a root in the monarchical constitution of France, that even Louis XIV., in the flush of his power, did not attempt to abolish it. He did better; he ordered his decrees to be registered, and the humbled parliament submissively obeyed. In like manner all edicts, ordinances, or declarations relating to Canada were entered on the registers of the superior council at Quebec. The order of registration was commonly affixed to the edict or other mandate, and nobody dreamed of disobeying it.[1]

The council or court had its attorney-general, who heard complaints and brought them before the tribunal if he thought necessary; its secretary, who kept its registers, and its *huissiers* or attendant officers. It sat once a week; and, though it was the highest court of appeal, it exercised at first original jurisdiction in very trivial cases.[2] It was empowered to establish subordinate courts or judges throughout the colony. Besides these there was a judge appointed by the king for each of the three districts into which Canada was divided, those of Quebec, Three Rivers, and Montreal. To each of the three royal judges were joined a clerk and an attorney-general under the supervision and control of the attorney-general of the superior court, to which tribunal appeal lay from all the subordinate jurisdictions. The jurisdiction of the seigniors within their own limits has already been mentioned. They were entitled by the terms of their grants to the exercise of "high, middle, and low justice;" but most of them were practically restricted to the last of the three, that is, to petty disputes between the *habitants*, involving not more than sixty sous, or offences for which the fine did not exceed ten sous.[3] Thus limited, their judgments were often useful in saving time, trouble, and money to the disputants. The corporate seigniors of Montreal long continued to hold a feudal court in form, with attorney-general, clerk, and *huissier*; but very few other

[1] Many general edicts relating to the whole kingdom are also registered on the books of the council, but the practice in this respect was by no means uniform.

[2] See the *Registres du Conseil Supérieur*, preserved at Quebec. Between 1663 and 1673 are a multitude of judgments on matters great and small; from murder, rape, and infanticide, down to petty nuisances, misbehavior of servants, and disputes about the price of a sow.

[3] Doutre et Lareau, *Histoire du Droit Canadien*, 135.

seigniors were in a condition to imitate them. Added to all these tribunals was the bishop's court at Quebec to try causes held to be within the province of the church.

The office of judge in Canada was no sinecure. The people were of a litigious disposition, partly from their Norman blood, partly perhaps from the idleness of the long and tedious winter, which gave full leisure for gossip and quarrel, and partly from the very imperfect manner in which titles had been drawn and the boundaries of grants marked out, whence ensued disputes without end between neighbor and neighbor.

"I will not say," writes the satirical La Hontan, "that Justice is more chaste and disinterested here than in France; but, at least, if she is sold, she is sold cheaper. We do not pass through the clutches of advocates, the talons of attorneys, and the claws of clerks. These vermin do not infest Canada yet. Everybody pleads his own cause. Our Themis is prompt, and she does not bristle with fees, costs, and charges. The judges have only four hundred francs a year, a great temptation to look for law in the bottom of the suitor's purse. Four hundred francs! Not enough to buy a cap and gown, so these gentry never wear them."[1]

Thus far La Hontan. Now let us hear the king himself. "The greatest disorder which has hitherto existed in Canada," writes Louis XIV. to the intendant Meules, "has come from the small degree of liberty which the officers of justice have had in the discharge of their duties, by reason of the violence to which they have been subjected, and the part they have been obliged to take in the continual quarrels between the governor and the intendant; insomuch that justice having been administered by cabal and animosity, the inhabitants have hitherto been far from the tranquillity and repose which cannot be found in a place where everybody is compelled to take side with one party or another."[2]

Nevertheless, on ordinary local questions between the *habitants*, justice seems to have been administered on the whole fairly; and judges of all grades often interposed in their personal capacity to bring parties to an agreement without a

[1]La Hontan, I. 21 (ed. 1705). In some editions, the above is expressed in different language.

[2]*Instruction du Roy pour le Sieur de Meules, 1682.*

trial. From head to foot, the government kept its attitude of paternity.

Beyond and above all the regular tribunals, beyond and above the council itself, was the independent jurisdiction lodged in the person of the king's man, the intendant. His commission empowered him, if he saw fit, to call any cause whatever before himself for judgment; and he judged exclusively the cases which concerned the king, and those involving the relations of seignior and vassal.[1] He appointed subordinate judges, from whom there was appeal to him; but from his decisions, as well as from those of the superior council, there was no appeal but to the king in his council of state.

On any Monday morning one would have found the superior council in session in the antechamber of the governor's apartment, at the Château St. Louis. The members sat at a round table. At the head was the governor, with the bishop on his right, and the intendant on his left. The councillors sat in the order of their appointment, and the attorney-general also had his place at the board. As La Hontan says, they were not in judicial robes, but in their ordinary dress, and all but the bishop wore swords.[2] The want of the cap and gown greatly disturbed the intendant Meules, and he begs the minister to consider how important it is that the councillors, in order to inspire respect, should appear in public in long black robes, which on occasions of ceremony they should exchange for robes of red. He thinks that the principal persons of the colony would thus be induced to train up their children to so enviable a dignity; "and," he concludes, "as none of the councillors can afford to buy red robes, I hope that the king will vouchsafe to send out nine such. As for the black robes, they can furnish those themselves."[3] The king did not respond, and the nine robes never arrived.

The official dignity of the council was sometimes exposed to trials against which even red gowns might have proved an insufficient protection. The same intendant urges that the tribunal ought to be provided immediately with a house of its own. "It is not decent," he says, "that it should sit in the

---

[1] See the commissions of various intendants, in *Edits et Ordonnances*, III.

[2] Compare La Poterie, I. 260, and La Tour, *Vie de Laval*, Liv. VII.

[3] *Meules au Ministre, 28 Sept., 1685.*

governor's antechamber any longer. His guards and valets make such a noise, that we cannot hear each other speak. I have continually to tell them to keep quiet, which causes them to make a thousand jokes at the councillors as they pass in and out."[1] As the governor and the council were often on ill terms, the official head of the colony could not always be trusted to keep his attendants on their good behavior. The minister listened to the complaint of Meules, and adopted his suggestion that the government should buy the old brewery of Talon, a large structure of mingled timber and masonry on the banks of the St. Charles. It was at an easy distance from the chateau; passing the Hôtel Dieu and descending the rock, one reached it by a walk of a few minutes. It was accordingly repaired, partly rebuilt, and fitted up to serve the double purpose of a lodging for the intendant and a court-house. Henceforth the transformed brewery was known as the Palace of the Intendant, or the Palace of Justice; and here the council and inferior courts long continued to hold their sessions.

Some of these inferior courts appear to have needed a lodging quite as much as the council. The watchful Meules informs the minister that the royal judge for the district of Quebec was accustomed in winter, with a view to saving fuel, to hear causes and pronounce judgment by his own fireside, in the midst of his children, whose gambols disturbed the even distribution of justice.[2]

The superior council was not a very harmonious body. As its three chiefs, the man of the sword, the man of the church, and the man of the law, were often at variance, the councillors attached themselves to one party or the other, and hot disputes sometimes ensued. The intendant, though but third in rank, presided at the sessions, took votes, pronounced judgment, signed papers, and called special meetings. This matter of the presidency was for some time a source of contention between him and the governor, till the question was set at rest by a decree of the king.

The intendants in their reports to the minister do not paint the council in flattering colors. One of them complains that the councillors, being busy with their farms, neglect their of-

[1] *Ibid., 12 Nov., 1684.*
[2] *Ibid.*

ficial duties. Another says that they are all more or less in trade. A third calls them uneducated persons of slight account, allied to the chief families and chief merchants in Canada, in whose interest they make laws; and he adds that, as a year and a half or even two years usually elapse before the answer to a complaint is received from France, they take advantage of this long interval to the injury of the king's service.[1] These and other similar charges betray the continual friction between the several branches of the government.

The councillors were rarely changed, and they usually held office for life. In a few cases the king granted to the son of a councillor yet living the right of succeeding his father when the charge should become vacant.[2] It was a post of honor and not of profit, at least of direct profit. The salaries were very small, and coupled with a prohibition to receive fees.

Judging solely by the terms of his commission, the intendant was the ruling power in the colony. He controlled all expenditure of public money, and not only presided at the council but was clothed in his own person with independent legislative as well as judicial power. He was authorized to issue ordinances having the force of law whenever he thought necessary, and, in the words of his commission, "to order every thing as he shall see just and proper."[3] He was directed to be present at councils of war, though war was the special province of his colleague, and to protect soldiers and all others from official extortion and abuse; that is, to protect them from the governor. Yet there were practical difficulties in the way of his apparent power. The king, his master, was far away; but official jealousy was busy around him, and his patience was sometimes put to the proof. Thus the royal judge of Quebec had fallen into irregularities. "I can do nothing with him," writes the intendant; "he keeps on good terms with the governor and council and sets me at naught." The governor had, as he thought, treated him amiss. "You have

---

[1] *Ibid.*, *12 Nov.*, *1684.*

[2] A son of Amours was named in his father's lifetime to succeed him, as was also a son of the attorney-general Auteuil. There are several other cases. A son of Tilly, to whom the right of succeeding his father had been granted, asks leave to sell it to the merchant La Chesnaye.

[3] Commissions of Bouteroue, Duchesneau, Meules, etc.

told me," he writes to the minister, "to bear every thing from him and report to you;" and he proceeds to recount his grievances. Again, "the attorney-general is bold to insolence, and needs to be repressed. The king's interposition is necessary." He modestly adds that the intendant is the only man in Canada whom his Majesty can trust, and that he ought to have more power.[1]

These were far from being his only troubles. The enormous powers with which his commission clothed him were sometimes retrenched by contradictory instructions from the king;[2] for this government, not of laws but of arbitrary will, is marked by frequent inconsistencies. When he quarrelled with the governor, and the governor chanced to have strong friends at court, his position became truly pitiable. He was berated as an imperious master berates an offending servant. "Your last letter is full of nothing but complaints." "You have exceeded your authority." "Study to know yourself and to understand clearly the difference there is between a governor and an intendant." "Since you fail to comprehend the difference between you and the officer who represents the king's person, you are in danger of being often condemned, or rather of being recalled, for his Majesty cannot endure so many petty complaints, founded on nothing but a certain *quasi* equality between the governor and you, which you assume, but which does not exist." "Meddle with nothing beyond your functions." "Take good care to tell me nothing but the truth." "You ask too many favors for your adherents." "You must not spend more than you have authority to spend, or it will be taken out of your pay." In short, there are several letters from the minister Colbert to his colonial man-of-all-work, which, from beginning to end, are one continued scold.[3]

The luckless intendant was liable to be held to account for

[1] *Meules au Ministre, 12 Nov., 1684.*

[2] Thus, Meules is flatly forbidden to compel litigants to bring causes before him (*Instruction pour le Sieur de Meules, 1682*), and this prohibition is nearly of the same date with the commission in which the power to do so is expressly given him.

[3] The above examples are all taken from the letters of Colbert to the intendant Duchesneau. It is an extreme case, but other intendants are occasionally treated with scarcely more ceremony.

the action of natural laws. "If the population does not increase in proportion to the pains I take," writes the king to Duchesneau, "you are to lay the blame on yourself for not having executed my principal order (*to promote marriages*) and for having failed in the principal object for which I sent you to Canada."[1]

A great number of ordinances of intendants are preserved. They were usually read to the people at the doors of churches after mass, or sometimes by the curé from his pulpit. They relate to a great variety of subjects,—regulation of inns and markets, poaching, preservation of game, sale of brandy, rent of pews, stray hogs, mad dogs, tithes, matrimonial quarrels, fast driving, wards and guardians, weights and measures, nuisances, value of coinage, trespass on lands, building churches, observance of Sunday, preservation of timber, seignior and vassal, settlement of boundaries, and many other matters. If a curé with some of his parishioners reported that his church or his house needed repair or rebuilding, the intendant issued an ordinance requiring all the inhabitants of the parish, "both those who have consented and those who have not consented," to contribute materials and labor, on pain of fine or other penalty.[2] The militia captain of the *côte* was to direct the work and see that each parishioner did his due part, which was determined by the extent of his farm; so, too, if the *grand voyer*, an officer charged with the superintendence of highways, reported that a new road was wanted or that an old one needed mending, an ordinance of the intendant set the whole neighborhood at work upon it, directed, as in the other case, by the captain of militia. If children were left fatherless, the intendant ordered the curé of the parish to assemble their relations or friends for the choice of a guardian. If a *censitaire* did not clear his land and live on it, the intendant took it from him and gave it back to the seignior.[3]

Chimney-sweeping having been neglected at Quebec, the intendant commands all householders promptly to do their

[1] *Le Roi à Duchesneau, 11 Juin, 1680.*

[2] See, among many examples, the ordinance of 24th December, 1715. *Edits et Ordonnances*, II. 443.

[3] Compare the numerous ordinances printed in the second and third volumes of *Edits et Ordonnances*.

duty in this respect, and at the same time fixes the pay of the sweep at six sous a chimney. Another order forbids quarrelling in church. Another assigns pews in due order of precedence to the seignior, the captain of militia, and the wardens. The intendant Raudot, who seems to have been inspired even more than the others with the spirit of paternal intervention, issued a mandate to the effect that, whereas the people of Montreal raise too many horses, which prevents them from raising cattle and sheep, "being therein ignorant of their true interest. . . . Now, therefore, we command that each inhabitant of the *côtes* of this government shall hereafter own no more than two horses or mares and one foal; the same to take effect after the sowing-season of the ensuing year, 1710, giving them time to rid themselves of their horses in excess of said number, after which they will be required to kill any of such excess that may remain in their possession."[1] Many other ordinances, if not equally preposterous, are equally stringent; such, for example, as that of the intendant Bigot, in which, with a view of promoting agriculture, and protecting the morals of the farmers by saving them from the temptations of cities, he proclaims to them: "We prohibit and forbid you to remove to this town (*Quebec*) under any pretext whatever, without our permission in writing, on pain of being expelled and sent back to your farms, your furniture and goods confiscated, and a fine of fifty livres laid on you for the benefit of the hospitals. And, furthermore, we forbid all inhabitants of the city to let houses or rooms to persons coming from the country, on pain of a fine of a hundred livres, also applicable to the hospitals."[2] At about the same time a royal edict, designed to prevent the undue subdivision of farms, forbade the country people, except such as were authorized to live in villages, to build a house or barn on any piece of land less than one and a half arpents wide and thirty arpents long;[3] while a subsequent ordinance of the intendant commands the immediate demolition of certain houses built in contravention of the edict.[4]

[1] *Edits et Ordonnances*, II. 273.
[2] *Ibid.*, II. 399.
[3] *Ibid.*, I. 585.
[4] *Ibid.*, II. 400.

The spirit of absolutism is everywhere apparent. "It is of very great consequence," writes the intendant Meules, "that the people should not be left at liberty to speak their minds."[1]

Hence public meetings were jealously restricted. Even those held by parishioners under the eye of the curé to estimate the cost of a new church seem to have required a special license from the intendant. During a number of years a meeting of the principal inhabitants of Quebec was called in spring and autumn by the council to discuss the price and quality of bread, the supply of firewood, and other similar matters. The council commissioned two of its members to preside at these meetings, and on hearing their report took what action it thought best. Thus, after the meeting held in February, 1686, it issued a decree, in which, after a long and formal preamble, it solemnly ordained, "that besides white-bread and light brown-bread, all bakers shall hereafter make dark brown-bread whenever the same shall be required."[2] Such assemblies, so controlled, could scarcely, one would think, wound the tenderest susceptibilities of authority; yet there was evident distrust of them, and after a few years this modest shred of self-government is seen no more. The syndic, too, that functionary whom the people of the towns were at first allowed to choose, under the eye of the authorities, was conjured out of existence by a word from the king. Seignior, *censitaire*, and citizen were prostrate alike in flat subjection to the royal will. They were not free even to go home to France. No inhabitant of Canada, man or woman, could do so without leave; and several intendants express their belief that without this precaution there would soon be a falling off in the population.

In 1671 the council issued a curious decree. One Paul Dupuy had been heard to say that there is nothing like righting one's self, and that when the English cut off the head of Charles I. they did a good thing, with other discourse to the like effect. The council declared him guilty of speaking ill of royalty in the person of the king of England, and uttering words tending to sedition. He was condemned to be dragged from prison by the public executioner, and led in his shirt,

[1] "Il ne laisse pas d'être de très grande conséquence de ne pas laisser la liberté au peuple de dire son sentiment." — *Meules au Ministre, 1685.*

[2] *Edits et Ordonnances*, II. 112.

with a rope about his neck, and a torch in his hand, to the gate of the Château St. Louis, there to beg pardon of the king; thence to the pillory of the Lower Town to be branded with a *fleur-de-lis* on the cheek, and set in the stocks for half an hour; then to be led back to prison, and put in irons "till the information against him shall be completed."[1]

If irreverence to royalty was thus rigorously chastised, irreverence to God was threatened with still sharper penalties. Louis XIV., ever haunted with the fear of the devil, sought protection against him by his famous edict against swearing, duly registered on the books of the council at Quebec. "It is our will and pleasure," says this pious mandate, "that all persons convicted of profane swearing or blaspheming the name of God, the most Holy Virgin, his mother, or the saints, be condemned for the first offence to a pecuniary fine according to their possessions and the greatness and enormity of the oath and blasphemy; and if those thus punished repeat the said oaths, then for the second, third, and fourth time they shall be condemned to a double, triple, and quadruple fine; and for the fifth time, they shall be set in the pillory on Sunday or other festival days, there to remain from eight in the morning till one in the afternoon, exposed to all sorts of opprobrium and abuse, and be condemned besides to a heavy fine; and for the sixth time, they shall be led to the pillory, and there have the upper lip cut with a hot iron; and for the seventh time, they shall be led to the pillory and have the lower lip cut; and if, by reason of obstinacy and inveterate bad habit, they continue after all these punishments to utter the said oaths and blasphemies, it is our will and command that they have the tongue completely cut out, so that thereafter they cannot utter them again."[2] All those who should hear anybody swear were further required to report the fact to the nearest judge within twenty-four hours, on pain of fine.

This is far from being the only instance in which the temporal power lends aid to the spiritual. Among other cases, the following is worth mentioning: Louis Gaboury, an inhabitant

[1] *Jugements et Délibérations du Conseil Supérieur.*

[2] *Edit du Roy contre les Jureurs et Blasphémateurs, du 30me Juillet, 1666.* See *Edits et Ordonnances*, I. 62.

of the island of Orleans, charged˙ with eating meat in Lent without asking leave of the priest, was condemned by the local judge to be tied three hours to a stake in public, and then led to the door of the chapel, there on his knees, with head bare and hands clasped, to ask pardon of God and the king. The culprit appealed to the council, which revoked the sentence and imposed only a fine.[1]

The due subordination of households had its share of attention. Servants who deserted their masters were to be set in the pillory for the first offence, and whipped and branded for the second; while any person harboring them was to pay a fine of twenty francs.[2] On the other hand, nobody was allowed to employ a servant without a license.[3]

In case of heinous charges, torture of the accused was permitted under the French law; and it was sometimes practised in Canada. Condemned murderers and felons were occasionally tortured before being strangled; and the dead body, enclosed in a kind of iron cage, was left hanging for months at the top of Cape Diamond, a terror to children and a warning to evil-doers. Yet, on the whole, Canadian justice, tried by the standard of the time, was neither vindictive nor cruel.

In reading the voluminous correspondence of governors and intendants, the minister and the king, nothing is more apparent than the interest with which, in the early part of his reign, Louis XIV. regarded his colony. One of the faults of his rule is the excess of his benevolence; for not only did he give money to support parish priests, build churches, and aid the seminary, the Ursulines, the missions, and the hospitals; but he established a fund destined, among other objects, to relieve indigent persons, subsidized nearly every branch of trade and industry, and in other instances did for the colonists what they would far better have learned to do for themselves.

Meanwhile the officers of government were far from suffering from an excess of royal beneficence. La Hontan says that the local governor of Three Rivers would die of hunger if, besides his pay, he did not gain something by trade with the Indians; and that Perrot, local governor of Montreal, with

[1] Doutre et Lareau, *Histoire du Droit Canadien*, 163.
[2] *Réglement de Police, 1676.*
[3] *Edits et Ordonnances*, II. 53.

one thousand crowns of salary, traded to such purpose that in a few years he made fifty thousand crowns. This trade, it may be observed, was in violation of the royal edicts. The pay of the governor-general varied from time to time. When La Poterie wrote it was twelve thousand francs a year, besides three thousand which he received in his capacity of local governor of Quebec.[1] This would hardly tempt a Frenchman of rank to expatriate himself; and yet some, at least, of the governors came out to the colony for the express purpose of mending their fortunes; indeed, the higher nobility could scarcely, in time of peace, have other motives for going there. The court and the army were their element, and to be elsewhere was banishment. We shall see hereafter by what means they sought compensation for their exile in Canadian forests. Loud complaints sometimes found their way to Versailles. A memorial addressed to the regent duke of Orleans, immediately after the king's death, declares that the ministers of state, who have been the real managers of the colony, have made their creatures and relations governors and intendants, and set them free from all responsibility. High colonial officers, pursues the writer, come home rich, while the colony languishes almost to perishing.[2] As for lesser offices, they were multiplied to satisfy needy retainers, till lean and starving Canada was covered with official leeches, sucking, in famished desperation, at her bloodless veins.

The whole system of administration centred in the king, who, to borrow the formula of his edicts, "in the fulness of our power and our certain knowledge," was supposed to direct the whole machine, from its highest functions to its pet-

---

[1]In 1674, the governor-general received 20,718 francs, out of which he was to pay 8,718 to his guard of twenty men and officers. *Ordonnance du Roy, 1675.* Yet in 1677, in the *Etat de la Dépense que le Roy veut et ordonne estre faite,* etc., the total pay of the governor-general is set down at 3,000 francs, and so also in 1681, 1682, and 1687. The local governor of Montreal was to have 1,800 francs, and the governor of Three Rivers 1,200. It is clear, however, that this *Etat de dépense* is not complete, as there is no provision for the intendant. The first councillor received 500 francs, and the rest 300 francs each, equal in Canadian money to 400. An ordinance of 1676 gives the intendant 12,000 francs. It is tolerably clear that the provision of 3,000 francs for the governor-general was meant only to apply to his capacity of local governor of Quebec.

[2]*Mémoire addressé au Régent, 1715.*

tiest intervention in private affairs. That this theory, like all extreme theories of government, was an illusion, is no fault of Louis XIV. Hard-working monarch as he was, he spared no pains to guide his distant colony in the paths of prosperity. The prolix letters of governors and intendants were carefully studied; and many of the replies, signed by the royal hand, enter into details of surprising minuteness. That the king himself wrote these letters is incredible; but in the early part of his reign he certainly directed and controlled them. At a later time, when more absorbing interests engrossed him, he could no longer study in person the long-winded despatches of his Canadian officers. They were usually addressed to the minister of state, who caused abstracts to be made from them, for the king's use, and perhaps for his own.[1] The minister or the minister's secretary could suppress or color as he or those who influenced him saw fit.

In the latter half of his too long reign, when cares, calamities, and humiliations were thickening around the king, another influence was added to make the theoretical supremacy of his royal will more than ever a mockery. That prince of annalists, Saint-Simon, has painted Louis XIV. ruling his realm from the bedchamber of Madame de Maintenon; seated with his minister at a small table beside the fire, the king in an arm-chair, the minister on a stool with his bag of papers on a second stool near him. In another arm-chair, at another table, on the other side of the fire, sat the sedate favorite, busy to all appearance with a book or a piece of tapestry, but listening to every thing that passed. "She rarely spoke," says Saint-Simon, "except when the king asked her opinion, which he often did; and then she answered with great deliberation and gravity. She never or very rarely showed a partiality for any measure, still less for any person; but she had an understanding with the minister, who never dared do otherwise than she wished. Whenever any favor or appointment was in question, the business was settled between them beforehand. She would send to the minister that she wanted to speak to him, and he did not dare bring the matter on the carpet till he had received her orders." Saint-Simon next recounts the

[1] Many of these abstracts are still preserved in the Archives of the Marine and Colonies.

subtle methods by which Maintenon and the minister, her tool, beguiled the king to do their will, while never doubting that he was doing his own. "He thought," concludes the annalist, "that it was he alone who disposed of all appointments; while in reality he disposed of very few indeed, except on the rare occasions when he had taken a fancy to somebody, or when somebody whom he wanted to favor had spoken to him in behalf of somebody else."[1]

Add to all this the rarity of communication with the distant colony. The ships from France arrived at Quebec in July, August, or September, and returned in November. The machine of Canadian government, wound up once a year, was expected to run unaided at least a twelvemonth. Indeed, it was often left to itself for two years, such was sometimes the tardiness of the overburdened government in answering the despatches of its colonial agents. It is no matter of surprise that a writer well versed in its affairs calls Canada the "country of abuses."[2]

[1]*Mémoires du Duc de Saint-Simon*, XIII. 38, 39 (Cheruel, 1857). Saint-Simon, notwithstanding the independence of his character, and his violent prejudices, held a high position at court; and his acute and careful observation, joined to his familiar acquaintance with ministers and other functionaries, both in and out of office, gives a rare value to his matchless portraitures, and makes him indispensable to the annalist of his time.

[2]*Etat présent du Canada*, *1758*.

Chapter XX

1663–1763

TRADE AND INDUSTRY

*Trade in Fetters • The Huguenot Merchants • Royal Patronage •
The Fisheries • Cries for Help • Agriculture • Manufactures •
Arts of Ornament • Finance • Card Money • Repudiation • Im-
posts • The Beaver Trade • The Fair at Montreal • Contraband
Trade • A Fatal System • Trouble and Change • The Coureurs
de Bois • The Forest • Letter of Carheil*

WE have seen the head of the colony, its guiding intellect and will: it remains to observe its organs of nutrition. Whatever they might have been under a different treatment, they were perverted and enfeebled by the regimen to which they were subjected.

The spirit of restriction and monopoly had ruled from the beginning. The old governor Lauson, seignior for a while of a great part of the colony, held that Montreal had no right to trade directly with France, but must draw all her supplies from Quebec;[1] and this preposterous claim was revived in the time of Mézy. The successive companies to whose hands the colony was consigned had a baneful effect on individual enterprise. In 1674, the charter of the West India Company was revoked, and trade was declared open to all subjects of the king; yet commerce was still condemned to wear the ball and chain. New restrictions were imposed, meant for good, but resulting in evil. Merchants not resident in the colony were forbidden all trade, direct or indirect, with the Indians.[2] They were also forbidden to sell any goods at retail except in August, September, and October;[3] to trade anywhere in Canada above Quebec; and to sell clothing or domestic articles ready made. This last restriction was designed to develop colonial industry. No person, resident or not, could trade with the English colonies, or go thither without a special passport, and

[1]Faillon, *Colonie Française*, II. 244.
[2]*Réglement de Police, 1676*, Art. xl.
[3]*Edits et Ord.*, II. 100.

rigid examination by the military authorities.[1] Foreign trade of any kind was stiffly prohibited. In 1719, after a new company had engrossed the beaver trade, its agents were empowered to enter all houses in Canada, whether ecclesiastical or secular, and search them for foreign goods, which when found were publicly burned.[2] In the next year, the royal council ordered that vessels engaged in foreign trade should be captured by force of arms, like pirates, and confiscated along with their cargoes;[3] while anybody having an article of foreign manufacture in his possession was subjected to a heavy fine.[4]

Attempts were made to fix the exact amount of profit which merchants from France should be allowed to make in the colony. One of the first acts of the superior council was to order them to bring their invoices immediately before that body, which thereupon affixed prices to each article. The merchant who sold and the purchaser who bought above this tariff were alike condemned to heavy penalties; and so, too, was the merchant who chose to keep his goods rather than sell them at the price ordained.[5] Resident merchants, on the other hand, were favored to the utmost. They could sell at what price they saw fit; and, according to La Hontan, they made great profit by the sale of laces, ribbons, watches, jewels, and similar superfluities to the poor but extravagant colonists.

A considerable number of the non-resident merchants were Huguenots, for most of the importations were from the old Huguenot city of Rochelle. No favor was shown them; they were held under rigid restraint, and forbidden to exercise their religion, or to remain in the colony during winter without special license.[6] This sometimes bore very hard upon them. The governor Denonville, an ardent Catholic, states the case of one Bernon, who had done great service to the colony, and whom La Hontan mentions as the principal French

---

[1] *Edits et Ord.*, I. 489.
[2] *Ibid.*, I. 402.
[3] *Ibid.*, I. 425.
[4] *Ibid.*, I. 505.
[5] *Ibid.*, II. 17, 19.
[6] *Réglement de Police, 1676.* Art. xxxvii.

merchant in the Canadian trade. "It is a pity," says Denonville, "that he cannot be converted. As he is a Huguenot, the bishop wants me to order him home this autumn, which I have done, though he carries on a large business, and a great deal of money remains due to him here."[1]

For a long time the ships from France went home empty, except a favored few which carried furs, or occasionally a load of dried pease or of timber. Payment was made in money when there was any in Canada, or in bills of exchange. The colony, drawing every thing from France, and returning little besides beaver skins, remained under a load of debt. French merchants were discouraged, and shipments from France languished. As for the trade with the West Indies, which Talon had tried by precept and example to build up, the intendant reports in 1680 that it had nearly ceased; though six years later it grew again to the modest proportions of three vessels loaded with wheat.[2]

The besetting evil of trade and industry in Canada was the habit they contracted, and were encouraged to contract, of depending on the direct aid of government. Not a new enterprise was set on foot without a petition to the king to lend a helping hand. Sometimes the petition was sent through the governor, sometimes through the intendant; and it was rarely refused. Denonville writes that the merchants of Quebec, by a combined effort, had sent a vessel of sixty tons to France with colonial produce; and he asks that the royal commissaries at Rochefort be instructed to buy the whole cargo, in order to encourage so deserving an enterprise. One Hazeur set up a saw-mill, at Mal Bay. Finding a large stock of planks and timber on his hands, he begs the king to send two vessels to carry them to France; and the king accordingly did so. A similar request was made in behalf of another saw-mill at St. Paul's Bay. Denonville announces that one Riverin wishes to embark in the whale and cod fishery, and that though strong in zeal he is weak in resources. The minister replies, that he is to be encouraged, and that his Majesty will favorably con-

---

[1] *Denonville au Ministre, 1685.*

[2] *Ibid., 1686.* The year before, about 18,000 *minots* of grain were sent hither. In 1736, the shipments reached 80,000 *minots.*

sider his enterprise.[1] Various gifts were soon after made him. He now took to himself a partner, the Sieur Chalons; whereupon the governor writes to ask the minister's protection for them. "The Basques," he says, "formerly carried on this fishery, but some monopoly or other put a stop to it." The remedy he proposes is homœopathic. He asks another monopoly for the two partners. Louis Joliet, the discoverer of the Mississippi, made a fishing station on the island of Anticosti; and he begs help from the king, on the ground that his fishery will furnish a good and useful employment to young men. The Sieur Vitry wished to begin a fishery of white porpoises, and he begs the king to give him two thousand pounds of cod-line and two thousand pounds of one and two inch rope. His request was granted, on which he asked for five hundred livres. The money was given him, and the next year he asked to have the gift renewed.[2]

The king was very anxious to develop the fisheries of the colony. "His Majesty," writes the minister, "wishes you to induce the inhabitants to unite with the merchants for this object, and to incite them by all sorts of means to overcome their natural laziness, since there is no other way of saving them from the misery in which they now are."[3] "I wish," says the zealous Denonville, "that fisheries could be well established to give employment to our young men, and prevent

[1] The interest felt by the king in these matters is shown in a letter signed by his hand in which he enters with considerable detail into the plans of Riverin. *Le Roy à Denonville et Champigny, 1 Mai, 1689.* He afterwards ordered boats, harpooners, and cordage to be sent him, for which he was to pay at his convenience. Four years later, he complains that, though Riverin had been often helped, his fisheries were of slight account. "Let him take care," pursues the king, "that he does not use his enterprises as a pretext to obtain favors." *Mémoire du Roy à Frontenac et Champigny, 1693.*

[2] All the above examples are drawn from the correspondence of the governor and intendant with the minister, between 1680 and 1699, together with a memorial of Hazeur and another of Riverin, addressed to the minister.

Vitry's porpoise-fishing appears to have ended in failure. In 1707 the intendant Raudot granted the porpoise fishery of the seigniory of Rivière Ouelle to six of the *habitans*. This fishery is carried on here successfully at the present day. A very interesting account of it was published in the *Opinion Publique*, 1873, by my friend Abbé Casgrain, whose family residence is the seigniorial mansion of Rivière Ouelle.

[3] *Mémoire pour Denonville et Champigny, 8 Mars, 1688.*

them from running wild in the woods;" and he adds mournfully, "they (*the fisheries*) are enriching Boston at our expense." "They are our true mines," urges the intendant Meules; "but the English of Boston have got possession of those of Acadia, which belong to us; and we ought to prevent it." It was not prevented; and the Canadian fisheries, like other branches of Canadian industry, remained in a state of almost hopeless languor.[1]

The government applied various stimulants. One of these, proposed by the intendant Duchesneau, is characteristic. He advises the formation of a company which should have the exclusive right of exporting fish; but which on its part should be required to take, at a fixed price, all that the inhabitants should bring them. This notable plan did not find favor with the king.[2] It was practised, however, in the case of beaver skins, and also in that of wood-ashes. The farmers of the revenue were required to take this last commodity at a fixed price, on their own risk, and in any quantity offered. They remonstrated, saying that it was unsalable; adding that, if the inhabitants would but take the trouble to turn it into potash, it might be possible to find a market for it. The king released them entirely, coupling his order to that effect with a eulogy of free trade.[3]

In all departments of industry, the appeals for help are endless. Governors and intendants are so many sturdy beggars for the languishing colony. "Send us money to build storehouses, to which the *habitants* can bring their produce and receive goods from the government in exchange." "Send us a teacher to make sailors of our young men: it is a pity the colony

---

[1] The Canadian fisheries must not be confounded with the French fisheries of Newfoundland, which were prosperous, but were carried on wholly from French ports.

In a memorial addressed by the partners Chalons and Riverin to the minister Seignelay, they say: "Baston (*Boston*) et toute sa colonie nous donne un exemple qui fait honte à nostre nation, puisqu'elle s'augmente tous les jours par cette pesche (*de la morue*) qu'elle fait la plus grande partie sur nos costes pendant que les François ne s'occupent à rien." Meules urges that the king should undertake the fishing business himself, since his subjects cannot or will not.

[2] *Ministre à Duchesneau, 15 Mai, 1678.*

[3] *Le Roy à Duchesneau, 11 Juin, 1680.*

should remain in such a state for want of instruction for youth."[1] "We want a surgeon: there is none in Canada who can set a bone."[2] "Send us some tilers, brick-makers, and potters."[3] "Send us iron-workers to work our mines."[4] "It is to be wished that his Majesty would send us all sorts of artisans, especially potters and glass-workers."[5] "Our Canadians need aid and instruction in their fisheries; they need pilots."[6]

In 1688, the intendant reported that Canada was entirely without either pilots or sailors; and, as late as 1712, the engineer Catalogne informed the government that, though the St. Lawrence was dangerous, a pilot was rarely to be had. "There ought to be trade with the West Indies and other places," urges another writer. "Everybody says it is best, but nobody will undertake it. Our merchants are too poor, or else are engrossed by the fur trade."[7]

The languor of commerce made agriculture languish. "It is of no use now," writes Meules, in 1682, "to raise any crops except what each family wants for itself." In vain the government sent out seeds for distribution. In vain intendants lectured the farmers, and lavished well-meant advice. Tillage remained careless and slovenly. "If," says the all-observing Catalogne, "the soil were not better cultivated in Europe than here, three-fourths of the people would starve." He complains that the festivals of the church are so numerous that not ninety working days are left during the whole working season. The people, he says, ought to be compelled to build granaries to store their crops, instead of selling them in autumn for almost nothing, and every *habitant* should be required to keep two or three sheep. The intendant Champigny calls for seed of hemp and flax, and promises to visit the farms, and show the people the lands best suited for their culture. He thinks that favors should be granted to those who raise hemp and flax as well as to those who marry. Denonville

[1] *Mémoire à Monseigneur le Marquis de Seignelay, présenté par les Sieurs Chalons et Riverin, 1686.*

[2] *Champigny au Ministre, 1688.*

[3] *Ibid.*

[4] *Denonville au Ministre, 1686.*

[5] *Mémoire de Catalogne, 1712.*

[6] *Denonville au Ministre, 1686.*

[7] *Mémoire de Chalons et Riverin présenté au Marquis de Seignelay.*

is of opinion thàt each *habitant* should be compelled to raise a little hemp every year, and that the king should then buy it of him at a high price.[1] It will be well, he says, to make use of severity, while, at the same time, holding out a hope of gain; and he begs that weavers be sent out to teach the women and girls, who spend the winter in idleness, how to weave and spin. Weaving and spinning, however, as well as the culture of hemp and flax, were neglected till 1705, when the loss of a ship laden with goods for the colony gave the spur to home industry; and Madame de Repentigny set the example of making a kind of coarse blanket of nettle and linden bark.[2]

The jealousy of colonial manufactures shown by England appears but rarely in the relations of France with Canada. According to its light, the French government usually did its best to stimulate Canadian industry, with what results we have just seen. There was afterwards some improvement. In 1714, the intendant Bégon reported that coarse fabrics of wool and linen were made; that the sisters of the congregation wove cloth for their own habits as good as the same stuffs in France; that black cloth was made for priests, and blue cloth for the pupils of the colleges. The inhabitants, he says, have been taught these arts by necessity. They were naturally adroit at handiwork of all kinds; and during the last half century of the French rule, when the population had settled into comparative stability, many of the mechanic arts were practised with success, notwithstanding the assertion of the Abbé La Tour that every thing but bread and meat had still to be brought from France. This change may be said to date from the peace of Utrecht, or a few years before it. At that time, one Duplessis had a new vessel on the stocks. Catalogne, who states the fact, calls it the beginning of ship-building in Canada, evidently ignorant that Talon had made a fruitless beginning more than forty years before.

Of the arts of ornament not much could have been expected; but, strangely enough, they were in somewhat better condition than the useful arts. The nuns of the Hôtel-Dieu made artificial flowers for altars and shrines, under the direc-

[1] *Denonville au Ministre, 13 Nov., 1685.*
[2] *Beauharnois et Raudot au Ministre, 1705.*

tion of Mother Juchereau;[1] and the boys of the seminary were taught to make carvings in wood for the decoration of churches.[2] Pierre, son of the merchant Le Ber, had a turn for painting, and made religious pictures, described as very indifferent.[3] His sister Jeanne, an enthusiastic devotee, made embroideries for vestments and altars, and her work was much admired.

The colonial finances were not prosperous. In the absence of coin, beaver-skins long served as currency. In 1669, the council declared wheat a legal tender, at four francs the *minot* or three French bushels;[4] and, five years later, all creditors were ordered to receive moose-skins in payment at the market rate.[5] Coin would not remain in the colony. If the company or the king sent any thither, it went back in the returning ships. The government devised a remedy. A coinage was ordered for Canada one-fourth less in value than that of France. Thus the Canadian livre or franc was worth, in reality, fifteen sous instead of twenty.[6] This shallow expedient produced only a nominal rise of prices, and coin fled the colony as before. Trade was carried on for a time by means of negotiable notes, payable in furs, goods, or farm produce. In 1685, the intendant Meules issued a card currency. He had no money to pay the soldiers, "and not knowing," he informs the minister, "to what saint to make my vows, the idea occurred to me of putting in circulation notes made of cards, each cut into four pieces; and I have issued an ordinance commanding the inhabitants to receive them in payment."[7] The cards were common playing cards, and each piece was stamped with a *fleur-de-lis* and a crown, and signed by the governor, the intendant, and the clerk of the treasury at Quebec.[8] The example of Meules found ready imitation. Governors and intendants made card money whenever they saw fit; and, being worthless everywhere but in Canada, it showed no dis-

[1] Juchereau, *Hist. de l'Hôtel-Dieu*, 244.
[2] *Abeille*, II. 13.
[3] Faillon, *Vie de Mlle. Le Ber*, 331.
[4] *Edits et Ord.*, II. 47.
[5] *Ibid.*, II. 55.
[6] This device was of very early date. See Boucher, *Hist. Véritable*, chap. xiv.
[7] *Meules au Ministre, 24 Sept., 1685.*
[8] *Mémoire addressé au Régent, 1715.*

position to escape the colony. It was declared convertible not into coin, but into bills of exchange; and this conversion could only take place at brief specified periods. "The currency used in Canada," says a writer in the last years of the French rule, "has no value as a representative of money. It is the sign of a sign."[1] It was card representing paper, and this paper was very often dishonored. In 1714, the amount of card rubbish had risen to two million livres. Confidence was lost, and trade was half dead. The minister Ponchartrain came to the rescue, and promised to redeem it at half its nominal value. The holders preferred to lose half rather than the whole, and accepted the terms. A few of the cards were redeemed at the rate named; then the government broke faith, and payment ceased. "This afflicting news," says a writer of the time, "was brought out by the vessel which sailed from France last July."

In 1717, the government made another proposal, and the cards were converted into bills of exchange. At the same time a new issue was made, which it was declared should be the last.[2] This issue was promptly redeemed, but twelve years later another followed it. In the interval, a certain quantity of coin circulated in the colony; but it underwent fluctuations through the intervention of government; and, within eight years, at least four edicts were issued affecting its value.[3] Then came more promises to pay, till, in the last bitter years of its existence, the colony floundered in drifts of worthless paper.

One characteristic grievance was added to the countless woes of Canadian commerce. The government was so jealous of popular meetings of all kinds, that for a long time it forbade merchants to meet together for discussing their affairs; and, it was not till 1717 that the establishment of a *bourse* or exchange was permitted at Quebec and Montreal.[4]

In respect of taxation, Canada, as compared with France, had no reason to complain. If the king permitted governors and intendants to make card money, he permitted nobody to impose taxes but himself. The Canadians paid no direct civil tax, except in a few instances where temporary and local as-

[1] *Considérations sur l'Etat du Canada, 1758.*
[2] *Edits et Ord.*, I. 370.
[3] *Ibid.*, 400, 432, 436, 484.
[4] Doutre et Lareau, *Hist. du Droit Canadien*, 254.

sessments were ordered for special objects. It was the fur trade on which the chief burden fell. One-fourth of the beaver-skins, and one-tenth of the moose-hides, belonged to the king; and wine, brandy, and tobacco contributed a duty of ten per cent. During a long course of years, these were the only imposts. The king, also, retained the exclusive right of the fur trade at Tadoussac. A vast tract of wilderness extending from St. Paul's Bay to a point eighty leagues down the St. Lawrence, and stretching indefinitely northward towards Hudson's Bay, formed a sort of royal preserve, whence every settler was rigidly excluded. The farmers of the revenue had their trading-houses at Tadoussac, whither the northern tribes, until war, pestilence, and brandy consumed them, brought every summer a large quantity of furs.

When, in 1674, the West India Company, to whom these imposts had been granted, was extinguished, the king resumed possession of them. The various duties, along with the trade of Tadoussac, were now farmed out to one Oudiette and his associates, who paid the Crown three hundred and fifty thousand livres for their privilege.[1]

We come now to a trade far more important than all the rest together, one which absorbed the enterprise of the colony, drained the life-sap from other branches of commerce, and, even more than a vicious system of government, kept them in a state of chronic debility,—the hardy, adventurous, lawless, fascinating fur trade. In the eighteenth century, Canada exported a moderate quantity of timber, wheat, the herb called ginseng, and a few other commodities; but from first to last she lived chiefly on beaver-skins. The government tried without ceasing to control and regulate this traffic; but it never succeeded. It aimed, above all things, to bring the trade home to the colonists, to prevent them from going to the

---

[1] The annual return to the king from the *ferme du Canada* was, for some years, 119,000 francs (livres). Out of this were paid from 35,000 to 40,000 francs a year for "ordinary charges." The governor, intendant, and all troops except the small garrisons of Quebec, Montreal, and Three Rivers, were paid from other sources. There was a time when the balance must have been in the king's favor; but profit soon changed to loss, owing partly to wars, partly to the confusion into which the beaver trade soon fell. "His Majesty," writes the minister to the governor in 1698, "may soon grow tired of a colony which, far from yielding him any profit, costs him immense sums every year."

Indians, and induce the Indians to come to them. To this end
a great annual fair was established by order of the king at
Montreal. Thither every summer a host of savages came down
from the lakes in their bark canoes. A place was assigned them
at a little distance from the town. They landed, drew up their
canoes in a line on the bank, took out their packs of beaver-
skins, set up their wigwams, slung their kettles, and encamped
for the night. On the next day, there was a grand council on
the common, between St. Paul Street and the river. Speeches
of compliment were made amid a solemn smoking of pipes.
The governor-general was usually present, seated in an arm-
chair, while the visitors formed a ring about him, ranged in
the order of their tribes. On the next day the trade began in
the same place. Merchants of high and low degree brought
up their goods from Quebec, and every inhabitant of Montreal, of any substance, sought a share in the profit. Their
booths were set along the palisades of the town, and each had
an interpreter, to whom he usually promised a certain portion
of his gains. The scene abounded in those contrasts—not always edifying, but always picturesque—which mark the
whole course of French Canadian history. Here was a throng
of Indians armed with bows and arrows, war-clubs, or the
cheap guns of the trade; some of them completely naked except for the feathers on their heads and the paint on their
faces; French bush-rangers tricked out with savage finery;
merchants and *habitants* in their coarse and plain attire, and
the grave priests of St. Sulpice robed in black. Order and sobriety were their watchwords, but the wild gathering was beyond their control. The prohibition to sell brandy could
rarely be enforced; and the fair ended at times in a pandemonium of drunken frenzy. The rapacity of trade, and the
license of savages and *coureurs de bois*, had completely transformed the pious settlement.

A similar fair was established at Three Rivers, for the Algonquin tribes north of that place. These yearly markets did
not fully answer the desired object. There was a constant tendency among the inhabitants of Canada to form settlements
above Montreal, in order to intercept the Indians on their
way down, drench them with brandy, and get their furs from
them at low rates in advance of the fair. Such settlements

were forbidden, but not prevented. The audacious "squatter" defied edict and ordinance and the fury of drunken savages, and boldly planted himself in the path of the descending trade. Nor is this a matter of surprise; for he was usually the secret agent of some high colonial officer, an intendant, the local governor, or the governor-general, who often used his power to enforce the law against others, and to violate it himself.

This was not all; for the more youthful and vigorous part of the male population soon began to escape into the woods, and trade with the Indians far beyond the limits of the remotest settlements. Here, too, many of them were in league with the authorities, who denounced the abuse while secretly favoring the portion of it in which they themselves were interested. The home government, unable to prevent the evil, tried to regulate it. Licenses were issued for the forest trade.[1] Their number was limited to twenty-five, and the privileges which they conferred varied at different periods. In La Hontan's time, each license authorized the departure of two canoes loaded with goods. One canoe only was afterwards allowed, bearing three men with about four hundred pounds of freight. The licenses were sometimes sold for the profit of government, but many were given to widows of officers and other needy persons, to the hospitals, or to favorites and retainers of the governor. Those who could not themselves use them sold them to merchants or *voyageurs*, at a price varying from a thousand to eighteen hundred francs. They were valid for a year and a half; and each canoeman had a share in the profits, which, if no accident happened, were very large. The license system was several times suppressed and renewed again; but, like the fair at Montreal, it failed completely to answer its purpose, and restrain the young men of Canada from a general exodus into the wilderness.[2]

The most characteristic features of the Canadian fur trade still remain to be seen. Oudiette and his associates were not only charged with collecting the revenue, but were also vested

[1] *Ordres du Roy au sujet de la Traite du Canada, 1681.*

[2] Before me is one of these licenses, signed by the governor Denonville. A condition of carrying no brandy is appended to it.

with an exclusive right of transporting all the beaver-skins of the colony to France. On their part they were compelled to receive all beaver-skins brought to their magazines; and, after deducting the fourth belonging to the king, to pay for the rest at a fixed price. This price was graduated to the different qualities of the fur; but the average cost to the collectors was a little more than three francs a pound. The inhabitants could barter their furs with merchants; but the merchants must bring them all to the magazines of Oudiette, who paid in receipts convertible into bills of exchange. He soon found himself burdened with such a mass of beaver-skins, that the market was completely glutted. The French hatters refused to take them all; and for the part which they consented to take, they paid chiefly in hats, which Oudiette was not allowed to sell in France, but only in the French West Indies, where few people wanted them. An unlucky fashion of small hats diminished the consumption of fur and increased his embarrassments, as did also a practice common among the hatters of mixing rabbit fur with the beaver. In his extremity he bethought him of setting up a hat factory for himself under the name of a certain licensed hatter, thinking thereby to alarm his customers into buying his stock.[1] The other hatters rose in wrath and petitioned the minister. The new factory was suppressed, and Oudiette soon became bankrupt. Another company of farmers of the revenue took his place with similar results. The action of the law of supply and demand was completely arrested by the peremptory edict which, with a view to the prosperity of the colony and the profit of the king, required the company to take every beaver-skin offered.

All Canada, thinking itself sure of its price, rushed into the beaver trade, and the accumulation of unsalable furs became more and more suffocating. The farmers of the revenue could not meet their engagements. Their bills of exchange were unpaid, and Canada was filled with distress and consternation. In 1700, a change of system was ordered. The monopoly of exporting beaver was placed in the hands of a company formed of the chief inhabitants of Canada. Some of them hes-

[1] *Mémoire touchant le Commerce du Canada, 1687.*

itated to take the risk; but the government was not to be trifled with, and the minister, Ponchartrain, wrote in terms so peremptory, and so menacing to the recusants, that, in the words of a writer of the time, he "shut everybody's mouth." About a hundred and fifty merchants accordingly subscribed to the stock of the new company, and immediately petitioned the king for a ship and a loan of seven hundred thousand francs. They were required to take off the hands of the farmers of the revenue an accumulation of more than six hundred thousand pounds of beaver, for which, however, they were to pay but half its usual price. The market of France absolutely refused it, and the directors of the new company saw no better course than to burn three-fourths of the troublesome and perishable commodity; nor was this the first resort to this strange expedient. One cannot repress a feeling of indignation at the fate of the interesting and unfortunate animals uselessly sacrificed to a false economic system. In order to rid themselves of what remained, the directors begged the king to issue a decree, requiring all hatters to put at least three ounces of genuine beaver-fur into each hat.

All was in vain. The affairs of the company fell into a confusion which was aggravated by the bad faith of some of its chief members. In 1707, it was succeeded by another company, to whose magazines every *habitant* or merchant was ordered to bring every beaver-skin in his possession within forty-eight hours; and the company, like its predecessors, was required to receive it, and pay for it in written promises. Again the market was overwhelmed with a surfeit of beaver. Again the bills of exchange were unpaid, and all was confusion and distress. Among the memorials and petitions to which this state of things gave birth, there is one conspicuous by the presence of good sense and the absence of self-interest. The writer proposes that there should be no more monopoly, but that everybody should be free to buy beaver-skins and send them to France, subject only to a moderate duty of entry. The proposal was not accepted. In 1721, the monopoly of exporting beaver-skins was given to the new West India Company; but this time it was provided that the government should direct from time to time, according to the capacities of the market, the quantity of furs which the company should be forced to receive.[1]

Out of the beaver trade rose a huge evil, baneful to the growth and the morals of Canada. All that was most active and vigorous in the colony took to the woods, and escaped from the control of intendants, councils, and priests, to the savage freedom of the wilderness. Not only were the possible profits great; but, in the pursuit of them, there was a fascinating element of adventure and danger. The bush-rangers or *coureurs de bois* were to the king an object of horror. They defeated his plans for the increase of the population, and shocked his native instinct of discipline and order. Edict after edict was directed against them; and more than once the colony presented the extraordinary spectacle of the greater part of its young men turned into forest outlaws. But severity was dangerous. The offenders might be driven over to the English, or converted into a lawless banditti, renegades of civilization and the faith. Therefore, clemency alternated with rigor, and declarations of amnesty with edicts of proscription. Neither threats nor blandishments were of much avail. We hear of seigniories abandoned; farms turning again into forests; wives and children left in destitution. The exodus of the *coureurs de bois* would take, at times, the character of an organized movement. The famous Du Lhut is said to have made a general combination of the young men of Canada to follow him into the woods. Their plan was to be absent four years, in order that the edicts against them might have time to relent. The intendant Duchesneau reported that eight hundred men out of a population of less than ten thousand souls had vanished from sight in the immensity of a boundless wilderness. Whereupon the king ordered that any person going into the woods without a license should be whipped

[1]On the fur trade the documents consulted are very numerous. The following are the most important: *Mémoire sur ce qui concerne le Commerce du Castor et ses dépendances, 1715*; *Mémoire concernant le Commerce de Traite entre les François et les Sauvages, 1691*; *Mémoire sur le Canada addressé au Régent, 1715*; *Mémoire sur les Affaires de Canada dans leur Estat présent, 1696*; *Mémoire des Négotiants de la Rochelle qui font Commerce en Canada sur la Proposition de ne plus recevoir les Castors et d'engager les Habitants à la Culture des Terres et Pesche de la Molue, 1696*; *Mémoire du Sr. Riverin sur la Traite et la Ferme du Castor, 1696*; *Mémoire touchant le Commerce du Canada, 1687*, etc.

and branded for the first offence, and sent for life to the gal-leys for the second.[1] The order was more easily given than enforced. "I must not conceal from you, monseigneur," again writes Duchesneau, "that the disobedience of the *coureurs de bois* has reached such a point that everybody boldly contra-venes the king's interdictions; that there is no longer any con-cealment; and that parties are collected with astonishing insolence to go and trade in the Indian country. I have done all in my power to prevent this evil, which may cause the ruin of the colony. I have enacted ordinances against the *coureurs de bois*; against the merchants who furnish them with goods; against the gentlemen and others who harbor them, and even against those who have any knowledge of them, and will not inform the local judges. All has been in vain; inasmuch as some of the most considerable families are interested with them, and the governor lets them go on and even shares their profits."[2] "You are aware, monseigneur," writes Denonville, some years later, "that the *coureurs de bois* are a great evil, but you are not aware how great this evil is. It deprives the coun-try of its effective men; makes them indocile, debauched, and incapable of discipline, and turns them into pretended nobles, wearing the sword and decked out with lace, both they and their relations, who all affect to be gentlemen and ladies. As for cultivating the soil, they will not hear of it. This, along with the scattered condition of the settlements, causes their children to be as unruly as Indians, being brought up in the same manner. Not that there are not some very good people here, but they are in a minority."[3] In another despatch he enlarges on their vagabond and lawless ways, their indiffer-ence to marriage, and the mischief caused by their example; describes how, on their return from the woods, they swagger like lords, spend all their gains in dress and drunken revelry, and despise the peasants, whose daughters they will not deign to marry, though they are peasants themselves.

It was a curious scene when a party of *coureurs de bois* re-turned from their rovings. Montreal was their harboring

[1] *Le Roy à Frontenac, 30 Avril, 1681.* On another occasion, it was ordered that any person thus offending should suffer death.
[2] *N. Y. Colonial Docs.*, IX. 131.
[3] Denonville, *Mémoire sur l'Estat des Affaires de la Nouvelle France.*

place, and they conducted themselves much like the crew of a man-of-war paid off after a long voyage. As long as their beaver-skins lasted, they set no bounds to their riot. Every house in the place, we are told, was turned into a drinking shop. The new-comers were bedizened with a strange mixture of French and Indian finery; while some of them, with instincts more thoroughly savage, stalked about the streets as naked as a Pottawattamie or a Sioux. The clamor of tongues was prodigious, and gambling and drinking filled the day and the night. When at last they were sober again, they sought absolution for their sins; nor could the priests venture to bear too hard on their unruly penitents, lest they should break wholly with the church and dispense thenceforth with her sacraments.

Under such leaders as Du Lhut, the *coureurs de bois* built forts of palisades at various points throughout the West and Northwest. They had a post of this sort at Detroit some time before its permanent settlement, as well as others on Lake Superior and in the valley of the Mississippi. They occupied them as long as it suited their purposes, and then abandoned them to the next comer. Michillimackinac was, however, their chief resort; and thence they would set out, two or three together, to roam for hundreds of miles through the endless meshwork of interlocking lakes and rivers which seams the northern wilderness.

No wonder that a year or two of bush-ranging spoiled them for civilization. Though not a very valuable member of society, and though a thorn in the side of princes and rulers, the *coureur de bois* had his uses, at least from an artistic point of view; and his strange figure, sometimes brutally savage, but oftener marked with the lines of a dare-devil courage, and a reckless, thoughtless gayety, will always be joined to the memories of that grand world of woods which the nineteenth century is fast civilizing out of existence. At least, he is picturesque, and with his red-skin companion serves to animate forest scenery. Perhaps he could sometimes feel, without knowing that he felt them, the charms of the savage nature that had adopted him. Rude as he was, her voice may not always have been meaningless for one who knew her haunts so well; deep recesses where, veiled in foliage, some wild shy

rivulet steals with timid music through breathless caves of verdure; gulfs where feathered crags rise like castle walls, where
the noonday sun pierces with keen rays athwart the torrent,
and the mossed arms of fallen pines cast wavering shadows
on the illumined foam; pools of liquid crystal turned emerald
in the reflected green of impending woods; rocks on whose
rugged front the gleam of sunlit waters dances in quivering
light; ancient trees hurled headlong by the storm to dam the
raging stream with their forlorn and savage ruin; or the stern
depths of immemorial forests, dim and silent as a cavern, columned with innumerable trunks, each like an Atlas upholding
its world of leaves, and sweating perpetual moisture down its
dark and channelled rind; some strong in youth, some grisly
with decrepit age, nightmares of strange distortion, gnarled
and knotted with wens and goitres; roots intertwined beneath
like serpents petrified in an agony of contorted strife; green
and glistening mosses carpeting the rough ground, mantling
the rocks, turning pulpy stumps to mounds of verdure, and
swathing fallen trunks as bent in the impotence of rottenness,
they lie outstretched over knoll and hollow, like mouldering
reptiles of the primeval world, while around, and on and
through them, springs the young growth that battens on their
decay,—the forest devouring its own dead. Or, to turn from
its funereal shade to the light and life of the open woodland,
the sheen of sparkling lakes, and mountains basking in the
glory of the summer noon, flecked by the shadows of passing
clouds that sail on snowy wings across the transparent azure.[1]

Yet it would be false coloring to paint the half-savage *coureur de bois* as a romantic lover of nature. He liked the woods
because they emancipated him from restraint. He liked the
lounging ease of the camp-fire, and the license of Indian villages. His life has a dark and ugly side, which is nowhere
drawn more strongly than in a letter written by the Jesuit
Carheil to the intendant Champigny. It was at a time when

---

[1]An adverse French critic gives as his opinion that the sketch of the primeval wilderness on the preceding page is drawn from fancy, and not from
observation. It is, however, copied in every particular, without exception,
from a virgin forest in a deep moist valley by the upper waters of the little
river Pemigewasset in northern New Hampshire, where I spent a summer
afternoon a few days before the passage was written.

some of the outlying forest posts, originally either missions or transient stations of *coureurs de bois*, had received regular garrisons. Carheil writes from Michillimackinac, and describes the state of things around him like one whom long familiarity with them had stripped of every illusion.[1]

But here, for the present, we pause; for the father touches on other matters than the *coureurs de bois*, and we reserve him and his letter for the next chapter.

[1] See the letter in Appendix I.

Chapter XXI

THE MISSIONS—THE BRANDY QUESTION

The Jesuits and the Iroquois • Mission Villages • Michillimackinac • Father Carheil • Temperance • Brandy and the Indians • Strong Measures • Disputes • License and Prohibition • Views of the King • Trade and the Jesuits

FOR a year or two after De Tracy had chastised the Mohawks, and humbled the other Iroquois nations, all was rose color on the side of that dreaded confederacy. The Jesuits, defiant as usual of hardship and death, had begun their ruined missions anew. Bruyas took the Mission of the Martyrs among the Mohawks; Milet, that of Saint Francis Xavier, among the Oneidas; Lamberville, that of Saint John the Baptist among the Onondagas; Carheil, that of Saint Joseph among the Cayugas; and Raffeix and Julien Garnier shared between them the three missions of the Senecas. The Iroquois, after their punishment, were in a frame of mind so hopeful, that the fathers imagined for a moment that they were all on the point of accepting the faith. This was a consummation earnestly to be wished, not only from a religious, but also from a political point of view. The complete conversion of the Iroquois meant their estrangement from the heretic English and Dutch, and their firm alliance with the French. It meant safety for Canada, and it ensured for her the fur trade of the interior freed from English rivalry. Hence the importance of these missions, and hence their double character. While the Jesuit toiled to convert his savage hosts, he watched them at the same time with the eye of a shrewd political agent; reported at Quebec the result of his observations, and by every means in his power sought to alienate them from England, and attach them to France.

Their simple conversion, by placing them wholly under his influence, would have outweighed in political value all other agencies combined; but the flattering hopes of the earlier years soon vanished. Some petty successes against other tribes so elated the Iroquois, that they ceased to care for French alliance or French priests. Then a few petty reverses would dash their spirits, and dispose them again to listen to Jesuit counsels. Every success of a war-party was a loss to the faith, and every reverse was a gain. Meanwhile a more repulsive or a more critical existence than that of a Jesuit father in an Iroquois town is scarcely conceivable. The torture of prisoners turned into a horrible festivity for the whole tribe; foul and crazy orgies in which, as the priest thought, the powers of darkness took a special delight; drunken riots, the work of Dutch brandy, when he was forced to seek refuge from death in his chapel,—a sanctuary which superstitious fear withheld the Indians from violating; these, and a thousand disgusts and miseries, filled the record of his days, and he bore them all in patience. Not only were the early Canadian Jesuits men of an intense religious zeal, but they were also men who lived not for themselves but for their order. Their faults were many and great, but the grandeur of their self-devotion towers conspicuous over all.

At Caughnawaga, near Montreal, may still be seen the remnants of a mission of converted Iroquois, whom the Jesuits induced to leave the temptations of their native towns and settle here, under the wing of the church. They served as a bulwark against the English, and sometimes did good service in time of war. At Sillery, near Quebec, a band of Abenaquis, escaping from the neighborhood of the English towards the close of Philip's War, formed another mission of similar character. The Sulpitians had a third at the foot of the mountain of Montreal, where two massive stone towers of the fortified Indian town are standing to this day. All these converted savages, as well as those of Lorette and other missions far and near, were used as allies in war, and launched in scalping parties against the border settlements of New England.

Not only the Sulpitians, but also the seminary priests of Quebec, the Recollets, and even the Capuchins, had missions more or less important, and more or less permanent; but the Jesuits stood always in the van of religious and political propagandism; and all the forest tribes felt their influence, from Acadia and Maine to the plains beyond the Mississippi. Next in importance to their Iroquois missions were those among the Algonquins of the northern lakes. Here was the grand domain of the beaver trade; and the chief woes of the missionary sprang not from the Indians, but from his own countrymen. Beaver-skins had produced an effect akin to that of gold in our own day, and the deepest recesses of the wilderness were invaded by eager seekers after gain. The focus of the evil was at Father Marquette's old mission of Michillimackinac. First, year after year came a riotous invasion of *coureurs de bois*, and then a garrison followed to crown the mischief. Discipline was very weak at these advanced posts, and, to eke out their pay, the soldiers were allowed to trade; brandy, whether permitted or interdicted, being the chief article of barter. Father Etienne Carheil was driven almost to despair; and he wrote to the intendant, his fast friend and former pupil, the long letter already mentioned. "Our missions," he says, "are reduced to such extremity that we can no longer maintain them against the infinity of disorder, brutality, violence, injustice, impiety, impurity, insolence, scorn, and insult, which the deplorable and infamous traffic in brandy has spread universally among the Indians of these parts. . . . In the despair in which we are plunged, nothing remains for us but to abandon them to the brandy sellers as a domain of drunkenness and debauchery."

He complains bitterly of the officers in command of the fort, who, he says, far from repressing disorders, encourage them by their example, and are even worse than their subordinates, "insomuch that all our Indian villages are so many taverns for drunkenness and Sodoms for iniquity, which we shall be forced to leave to the just wrath and vengeance of God." He insists that the garrisons are entirely useless, as they have only four occupations: first, to keep open liquor shops for crowds of drunken Indians; secondly, to roam from place to place, carrying goods and brandy under the orders of the commandant, who shares their profits; thirdly, to gamble day and night; fourthly, to "turn the fort into a place which I am ashamed to call by its right name;" and he describes, with a curious amplitude of detail, the swarms of Indian girls who are hired to make it their resort. "Such, monseigneur, are the only employments of the soldiers maintained here so many years. If this can be called doing the king service, I admit that such service is done for him here now, and has always been done for him here; but I never saw any other done in my life." He further declares that the commandants oppose and malign the missionaries, while of the presents which the king sends up the country for distribution to the Indians, they, the Indians, get nothing but a little tobacco, and the officer keeps the rest for himself.[1]

From the misconduct of officers and soldiers, he passes to that of the *coureurs de bois* and licensed traders; and here he is equally severe. He dilates on the evils which result from permitting the colonists to go to the Indians instead of requiring the Indians to come to the settlements. "It serves only to rob the country of all its young men, weaken families, deprive wives of their husbands, sisters of their brothers, and parents of their children; expose the voyagers to a hundred dangers of body and soul; involve them in a multitude of expenses, some necessary, some useless, and some criminal; accustom them to do no work, and at last disgust them with it for ever; make them live in constant idleness, unfit them completely for any trade, and render them useless to themselves, their families, and the public. But it is less as regards the body than as regards the soul, that this traffic of the French among the savages is infinitely hurtful. It carries them far away from churches, separates them from priests and nuns, and severs them from all instruction, all exercise of religion, and all spiritual aid. It sends them into places wild and almost inaccessible, through a thousand perils by land and water, to carry on by base, abject, and shameful means a trade which would much better be carried on at Montreal."

But in the complete transfer of the trade to Montreal, he sees insuperable difficulties, and he proceeds to suggest, as the last and best resort, that garrisons and officers should be withdrawn, and licenses abolished; that discreet and virtuous persons should be chosen to take charge of all the trade of the

[1] Of the officers in command at Michillimackinac while Carheil was there, he partially excepts La Durantaye from his strictures, but bears very hard on La Motte-Cadillac, who hated the Jesuits and was hated by them in turn. La Motte, on his part, writes that "the missionaries wish to be masters wherever they are, and cannot tolerate anybody above themselves." *N. Y. Colonial Docs.*, IX. 587. For much more emphatic expressions of his views concerning them, see two letters from him, translated in Sheldon's *Early History of Michigan*.

upper country; that these persons should be in perfect sympathy and correspondence with the Jesuits; and that the trade should be carried on at the missions of the Jesuits and in their presence.[1]

This letter brings us again face to face with the brandy question, of which we have seen something already in the quarrel between Avaugour and the bishop. In the summer of 1648, there was held at the mission of Sillery a temperance meeting; the first in all probability on this continent. The drum beat after mass, and the Indians gathered at the summons. Then an Algonquin chief, a zealous convert of the Jesuits, proclaimed to the crowd a late edict of the governor imposing penalties for drunkenness, and, in his own name and that of the other chiefs, exhorted them to abstinence, declaring that all drunkards should be handed over to the French for punishment. Father Jerome Lalemant looked on delighted. "It was," he says, "the finest public act of jurisdiction exercised among the Indians since I have been in this country. From the beginning of the world they have all thought themselves as great lords, the one as the other, and never before submitted to their chiefs any further than they chose to do so."[2]

There was great need of reform; for a demon of drunkenness seemed to possess these unhappy tribes. Nevertheless, with all their rage for brandy, they sometimes showed in regard to it a self-control quite admirable in its way. When at a fair, a council, or a friendly visit, their entertainers regaled them with rations of the coveted liquor, so prudently measured out that they could not be the worse for it, they would unite their several portions in a common stock, which they would then divide among a few of their number, thus enabling them to attain that complete intoxication which, in their view, was the true end of all drinking. The objects of this singular benevolence were expected to requite it in kind on some future occasion.

A drunken Indian with weapons within reach, was very dangerous, and all prudent persons kept out of his way. This

---

[1] *Lettre du Père Etienne Carheil de la Compagnie de Jésus à l'Intendant Champigny, Michillimackinac, 30 Août, 1702 (Archives Nationales)*, Appendix I.
[2] Lalemant, *Rel., 1648*, p. 43.

greatly pleased him; for, seeing everybody run before him, he fancied himself a great chief, and howled and swung his tomahawk with redoubled fury. If, as often happened, he maimed or murdered some wretch not nimble enough to escape, his countrymen absolved him from all guilt, and blamed only the brandy. Hence, if an Indian wished to take a safe revenge on some personal enemy, he would pretend to be drunk; and, not only murders but other crimes were often committed by false claimants to the bacchanalian privilege.

In the eyes of the missionaries, brandy was a fiend with all crimes and miseries in his train; and, in fact, nothing earthly could better deserve the epithet infernal than an Indian town in the height of a drunken debauch. The orgies never ceased till the bottom of the barrel was reached. Then came repentance, despair, wailing, and bitter invective against the white men, the cause of all the woe. In the name of the public good, of humanity, and above all of religion, the bishop and the Jesuits denounced the fatal traffic.

Their case was a strong one; but so was the case of their opponents. There was real and imminent danger that the thirsty savages, if refused brandy by the French, would seek it from the Dutch and English of New York. It was the most potent lure and the most killing bait. Wherever it was found, thither the Indians and their beaver-skins were sure to go, and the interests of the fur trade, vital to the colony, were bound up with it. Nor was this all, for the merchants and the civil powers insisted that religion and the saving of souls were bound up with it no less; since, to repel the Indians from the Catholic French, and attract them to the heretic English, was to turn them from ways of grace to ways of perdition.[1] The argument, no doubt, was dashed largely with hypocrisy in those who used it; but it was one which the priests were greatly perplexed to answer.

In former days, when Canada was not yet transformed from a mission to a colony, the Jesuits entered with a high hand on the work of reform. It fared hard with the culprit caught in the act of selling brandy to Indians. They led him,

---

[1] "Ce commerce est absolument nécessaire pour attirer les sauvages dans les colonies françoises, et par ce moyen leur donner les premières teintures de la foy." *Mémoire de Colbert, joint à sa lettre à Duchesneau du 24 Mai, 1678.*

after the sermon, to the door of the church; where, kneeling on the pavement, partially stript and bearing in his hand the penitential torch, he underwent a vigorous flagellation, laid on by Father Le Mercier himself, after the fashion formerly practised in the case of refractory school-boys.[1] Bishop Laval not only discharged against the offenders volleys of wholesale excommunication, but he made of the offence a "reserved case;" that is, a case in which the power of granting absolution was reserved to himself alone. This produced great commotion, and a violent conflict between religious scruples and a passion for gain. The bishop and the Jesuits stood inflexible; while their opponents added bitterness to the quarrel by charging them with permitting certain favored persons to sell brandy, unpunished, and even covertly selling it themselves.[2]

Appeal was made to the king, who, with his Jesuit confessor, guardian of his conscience on one side, and Colbert, guardian of his worldly interests on the other, stood in some perplexity. The case was referred to the fathers of the Sorbonne, and they, after solemn discussion, pronounced the selling of brandy to Indians a mortal sin.[3] It was next referred to an assembly of the chief merchants and inhabitants of Canada, held under the eye of the governor, intendant, and council, in the Château St. Louis. Each was directed to state his

---

[1] *Mémoire de Dumesnil, 1671.*

[2] *Lettre de Charles Aubert de la Chesnaye, 24 Oct., 1693.* After speaking of the excessive rigor of the bishop, he adds: "L'on dit, et il est vrai, que dans ces temps si fâcheux, sous prétexte de pauvreté dans les familles, certaines gens avoient permission d'en traiter, je crois toujours avec la réserve de ne pas enivrer." Dumesnil, *Mémoire de 1671,* says that Laval excommunicated all brandy-sellers, "à l'exception, néanmoins, de quelques particuliers qu'il vou-lait favoriser." He says further that the bishop and the Jesuit Ragueneau had a clerk whom they employed at 500 francs a year to trade with the Indians, paying them in liquors for their furs; and that for a time the ecclesiastics had this trade to themselves, their severities having deterred most others from venturing into it. La Salle, *Mémoire de 1678,* declares that, "Ils (*les Jésuites*) refusent l'absolution à ceux qui ne veulent pas promettre de n'en plus vendre, et s'ils meurent en cet état, ils les privent de la sépulture ecclésiastique: au contraire, ils se permettent à eux mesmes sans aucune difficulté ce mesme trafic, quoyque toute sorte de trafic soit interdite à tous les ecclésiastiques par les ordonnances du Roy et par une bulle expresse du Pape." I give these assertions as I find them, and for what they are worth.

[3] *Délibération de la Sorbonne sur la Traite des Boissons, 8 Mars, 1675.*

views in writing. The great majority were for unrestricted trade in brandy; a few were for a limited and guarded trade; and two or three declared for prohibition.[1] Decrees of prohibition were passed from time to time, but they were unavailing. They were revoked, renewed, and revoked again. They were, in fact, worse than useless; for their chief effect was to turn traders and *coureurs de bois* into troops of audacious contrabandists. Attempts were made to limit the brandy trade to the settlements, and exclude it from the forest country, where its regulation was impossible; but these attempts, like the others, were of little avail. It is worthy of notice that, when brandy was forbidden everywhere else, it was permitted in the trade of Tadoussac, carried on for the profit of government.[2]

In spite of the Sorbonne, in spite of Père La Chaise, and of the Archbishop of Paris, whom he also consulted, the king was never at heart a prohibitionist.[3] His Canadian revenue was drawn from the fur trade; and the singular argument of the partisans of brandy, that its attractions were needed to keep the Indians from contact with heresy, served admirably to salve his conscience. Bigot as he was, he distrusted the Bishop of Quebec, the great champion of the anti-liquor movement. His own letters, as well as those of his minister, prove that he saw or thought that he saw motives for the crusade very different from those inscribed on its banners. He wrote to Saint-Vallier, Laval's successor in the bishopric, that the brandy trade was very useful to the kingdom of France; that it should be regulated, but not prevented; that the consciences of his subjects must not be disturbed by denunciations of it as a sin; and that "it is well that you (*the bishop*) should take care that the zeal of the ecclesiastics is not excited by personal interests and passions."[4] Perhaps he alludes to the spirit of encroachment and domination which he and his min-

---

[1] *Procès-verbal de l'Assemblée tenue au Château de St. Louis de Québec, le 26 Oct., 1676, et jours suivants.*

[2] *Lettre de Charles Aubert de la Chesnaye, 24 Oct., 1693.* In the course of the quarrel a severe law passed by the General Court of Massachusetts against the sale of liquors to Indians was several times urged as an example to be imitated. A copy of it was sent to the minister, and is still preserved in the Archives of the Marine and Colonies.

[3] See, among other evidence, *Mémoire sur la Traite des Boissons, 1678.*

[4] *Le Roy à Saint-Vallier, 7 Avril, 1691.*

ister in secret instructions to their officers often impute to the bishop and the clergy, or perhaps he may have in mind other accusations which had reached him from time to time during many years, and of which the following from the pen of the most noted of Canadian governors will serve as an example. Count Frontenac declares that the Jesuits greatly exaggerate the disorders caused by brandy, and that they easily convince persons "who do not know the interested motives which have led them to harp continually on this string for more than forty years. . . . They have long wished to have the fur trade entirely to themselves, and to keep out of sight the trade which they have always carried on in the woods, and which they are carrying on there now."[1]

TRADE OF THE JESUITS.—As I have observed in a former volume, the charge against the Jesuits of trading in beaver-skins dates from the beginning of the colony. In the private journal of Father Jerome Lalemant, their superior, occurs the following curious passage, under date of November, 1645: "*Pour la traite des castors*. Le 15 de Nov. le bruit estant qu'on s'en alloit icy publier la defense qui auoit esté publiée aux Trois Riuieres que pas vn n'eut à traiter auec les sauuages, le P. Vimont demanda à Mons. des Chastelets commis general si nous serions de pire condition soubs eux que soubs Messieurs de la Compagnie. La conclusion fut que non et *que cela iroit pour nous à l'ordinaire, mais que nous le fissions doucement*." *Journal des Jésuites*. Two years after, on the request of Lalemant, the governor Montmagny, and his destined successor Aillebout, gave the Jesuits a certificate to the effect that "les pères de la compagnie de Jésus sont innocents de la calomnie qui leur a été imputée, et *ce qu'ils en ont fait a été pour le bien de la communauté et pour un bon sujet*." This leaves it to be inferred that they actually traded, though with good intentions. In 1664, in reply to similar "calumnies," the Jesuits made by proxy a declaration before the council, stating, "que les dits Révérends Pères Jésuites n'ont fait jamais aucune profession de vendre et n'ont jamais rien vendu, *mais seulement que les marchandises qu'ils donnent aux particuliers ne sont que pour avoir leurs nécessités*." This is an admission in a thin disguise. The word *nécessités* is of very elastic interpretation. In a memoir of Talon, 1667, he mentions, "la traite de pelleteries qu'on assure qu'ils (*les Jésuites*) font aux Outaouacks et au Cap de la Madeleine; ce que je ne sais pas de science certaine."

That which Talon did not know with certainty is made reasonably clear for us by a line in the private journal of Father Le Mercier, who writes under date of 17 August, 1665, "Le Père Frémin remonte supérieur au Cap de la Magdeleine, ou le temporel est en bon estat. *Comme il est delivré de tout soin d'aucune traite*, il doit s'appliquer à l'instruction tant des Montagnets que des Algonquins." Father Charles Albanel was charged, under Frémin, with the

[1] *Frontenac au Ministre, 29 Oct., 1676.*

affairs of the mission, including doubtless the temporal interests, to the prosperity of which Father Le Mercier alludes, and the cares of trade from which Father Frémin was delivered. Cavelier de la Salle declared in 1678, "Le père Arbanelle (*Albanel*) jésuite a traité au Cap (*de la Madeleine*) pour 700 pistoles de peaux d'orignaux et de castors; luy mesme me l'a dit en 1667. Il vend le pain, le vin, le bled, le lard, et il tient magazin au Cap aussi bien que le frère Joseph à Québec. Ce frère gagne 500 pour 100 sur tous les peuples. Ils (*les Jésuites*) ont bâti leur collège en partie de leur traite et en partie de l'emprunt." La Salle further says that Frémin, being reported to have made enormous profits, "ce père répondit au gouverneur (*qui lui en avait fait des plaintes*) par un billet que luy a conservé, que c'estoit une calomnie que ce grand gain prétendu; puisque tout ce qui se passoit par ses mains ne pouvoit produire par an que quatre mille de revenant bon, tous frais faits, sans comprendre les gages des domestiques." La Salle gives also many other particulars, especially relating to Michillimackinac, where, as he says, the Jesuits had a large stock of beaver-skins. According to Peronne Dumesnil, *Mémoire de 1671*, the Jesuits had at that time more than 20,000 francs a year, partly from trade and partly from charitable contributions of their friends in France.

The king repeatedly forbade the Jesuits and other ecclesiastics in Canada to carry on trade. On one occasion he threatened strong measures should they continue to disobey him. *Le Roi à Frontenac, 28 Avril, 1677*. In the same year the minister wrote to the intendant Duchesneau: "Vous ne sauriez apporter trop de precautions pour abolir entièrement la coustume que les Ecclesiastiques seculiers et reguliers avaient pris de traitter ou de faire traitter leurs valets," *18 Avril, 1677*.

The Jesuits entered also into other branches of trade and industry with a vigor and address which the inhabitants of Canada might have emulated with advantage. They were successful fishers of eels. In 1646, their eel-pots at Sillery are said to have yielded no less than forty thousand eels, some of which they sold at the modest price of thirty sous a hundred. Ferland, *Notes sur les Registres de N. D. de Québec*, 82. The members of the order were exempted from payment of duties, and in 1674 they were specially empowered to construct mills, including sugar-mills, and keep slaves, apprentices, and hired servants. *Droits Canadien*, 180.

Chapter XXII

1663–1763

PRIESTS AND PEOPLE

Church and State • The Bishop and the King • The King and the Curés • The New Bishop • The Canadian Curé • Ecclesiastical Rule • Saint-Vallier and Denonville • Clerical Rigor • Jesuit and Sulpitian • Courcelle and Châtelain • The Recollets • Heresy and Witchcraft • Canadian Nuns • Jeanne Le Ber • Education • The Seminary • Saint Joachim • Miracles of Saint Anne • Canadian Schools

WHEN Laval and the Jesuits procured the recall of Mézy, they achieved a seeming triumph; yet it was but a defeat in disguise. While ordering home the obnoxious governor, the king and Colbert made a practical assertion of their power too strong to be resisted. A vice-regal officer, a governor, an intendant, and a regiment of soldiers, were silent but convincing proofs that the mission days of Canada were over, and the dream of a theocracy dispelled for ever. The ecclesiastics read the signs of the times, and for a while seemed to accept the situation.

The king on his part, in vindicating the civil power, had shown a studious regard to the sensibilities of the bishop and his allies. The lieutenant-general Tracy, a zealous devotee, and the intendant Talon, who at least professed to be one, were not men to offend the clerical party needlessly. In the choice of Courcelle, the governor, a little less caution had been shown. His chief business was to fight the Iroquois, for which he was well fitted, but he presently showed signs of a willingness to fight the Jesuits also. The colonists liked him for his lively and impulsive speech; but the priests were of a different mind, and so, too, was his colleague Talon, a prudent person who studied the amenities of life and knew how to pursue his ends with temper and moderation. On the subject of the clergy he and the governor substantially agreed, but the ebullitions of the one and the smooth discretion of the other were mutually repugnant to both. Talon complained of his colleague's impetuosity; and Colbert directed him to use his best efforts to keep Courcelle within bounds and prevent him from publicly finding fault with the bishop and the Jesuits.[1] Next we find the minister writing to Courcelle himself to soothe his ruffled temper, and enjoining him to act discreetly, "because," said Colbert, "as the colony grows the king's authority will grow with it, and the authority of the priests will be brought back in time within lawful bounds."[2]

Meanwhile, Talon had been ordered to observe carefully the conduct of the bishop and the Jesuits, "who," says the minister, "have hitherto nominated governors for the king, and used every means to procure the recall of those chosen without their participation;[3] filled offices with their adherents, and tolerated no secular priests except those of one mind with them."[4] Talon, therefore, under the veil of a reverent courtesy, sharply watched them. They paid courtesy with courtesy, and the intendant wrote home to his master that he saw nothing amiss in them. He quickly changed his mind. "I should have had less trouble and more praise," he writes in the next year, "if I had been willing to leave the power of the church where I found it."[5] "It is easy," he says again, "to incur the ill-will of the Jesuits if one does not accept all their opinions and abandon one's self to their direction even in temporal matters; for their encroachments extend to affairs of police, which concern only the civil magistrate;" and he recommends that one or two of them be sent home as disturbers of the peace.[6] They, on their part, changed attitude towards both him and the governor. One of them, Father Bardy, less discreet than the rest, is said to have preached a sermon against them at Quebec, in which he likened them to a pair of toadstools springing up in a night, adding that a good remedy would soon be found, and that Courcelle would have to run home like other governors before him.[7]

Tracy escaped clerical attacks. He was extremely careful not

[1] *Colbert à Talon, 20 Fev., 1668.*
[2] *Colbert à Courcelle, 19 Mai, 1669.*
[3] *Instruction au Sieur Talon.*
[4] *Mémoire pour M. de Tracy.*
[5] *Talon au Ministre, 13 Nov., 1666.*
[6] Talon, *Mémoire de 1667.*
[7] La Salle, *Mémoire de 1678.* This sermon was preached on the 12th of March, 1667.

to provoke them; and one of his first acts was to restore to the council the bishop's adherents, whom Mézy had expelled.[1] And if, on the one hand, he was too pious to quarrel with the bishop, so, on the other, the bishop was too prudent to invite collision with a man of his rank and influence.

After all, the dispute between the civil and ecclesiastical powers was not fundamental. Each had need of the other. Both rested on authority, and they differed only as to the boundary lines of their respective shares in it. Yet the dispute of boundaries was a serious one, and it remained a source of bitterness for many years. The king, though rigidly Catholic, was not yet sunk in the slough of bigotry into which Maintenon and the Jesuits succeeded at last in plunging him. He had conceived a distrust of Laval, and his jealousy of his royal authority disposed him to listen to the anti-clerical counsels of his minister. How needful they both thought it to prune the exuberant growth of clerical power, and how cautiously they set themselves to do so, their letters attest again and again. "The bishop," writes Colbert, "assumes a domination far beyond that of other bishops throughout the Christian world, and particularly in the kingdom of France."[2] "It is the will of his Majesty that you confine him and the Jesuits within just bounds, and let none of them overstep these bounds in any manner whatsoever. Consider this as a matter of the greatest importance, and one to which you cannot give too much attention."[3] "But," the prudent minister elsewhere writes, "it is of the greatest consequence that the bishop and the Jesuits do not perceive that the intendant blames their conduct."[4]

It was to the same intendant that Colbert wrote, "it is necessary to diminish as much as possible the excessive number of priests, monks, and nuns, in Canada." Yet in the very next year, and on the advice of Talon, he himself sent four more to the colony. His motive was plain. He meant that they

[1] A curious account of his relations with Laval is given in a letter of La Motte-Cadillac, 28 September, 1694.

[2] *Colbert à Duchesneau, 1 Mai, 1677.*

[3] *Ibid., 28 Avril, 1677.*

[4] *Instruction pour M. Bouteroue, 1668.*

should serve as a counterpoise to the Jesuits.[1] They were mendicant friars, belonging to the branch of the Franciscans
known as the Recollets; and they were supposed to be free
from the ambition for the aggrandizement of their order
which was imputed, and with reason, to the Jesuits. Whether
the Recollets were free from it or not, no danger was to be
feared from them; for Laval and the Jesuits were sure to oppose them, and they would need the support of the government too much to set themselves in opposition to it. "The
more Recollets we have," says Talon, "the better will the too
firmly rooted authority of the others be balanced."[2]

While Louis XIV. tried to confine the priests to their ecclesiastical functions, he was at the same time, whether from
religion, policy, or both combined, very liberal to the Canadian church, of which, indeed, he was the main-stay. In the
yearly estimate of "ordinary charges" of the colony, the
church holds the most prominent place; and the appropria-
tions for religious purposes often exceed all the rest together.
Thus, in 1667, out of a total of 36,360 francs, 28,000 are assigned to church uses.[3] The amount fluctuated, but was always relatively large. The Canadian curés were paid in great
part by the king, who for many years gave eight thousand
francs annually towards their support. Such was the poverty
of the country that, though in 1685 there were only twenty-
five curés,[4] each costing about five hundred francs a year, the
tithes utterly failed to meet the expense. As late as 1700, the
intendant declared that Canada without the king's help could
not maintain more than eight or nine curés. Louis XIV.
winced under these steady demands, and reminded the bishop
that more than four thousand curés in France lived on less

[1] *Mémoire succinct des principaux points des intentions du Roy sur le pays de
Canada, 18 Mai, 1669.*
[2] *Talon au Ministre, 10 Oct., 1670.*
[3] Of this, 6,000 francs were given to the Jesuits, 6,000 to the Ursulines,
9,000 to the cathedral, 4,000 to the seminary, and 3,000 to the Hôtel-Dieu.
Etat de dépense, etc., 1677. The rest went to pay civil officers and garrisons. In
1682, the amount for church uses was only 12,000 francs. In 1687 it was 13,500.
In 1689, it rose to 34,000, including Acadia.
[4] Increased soon after to thirty-six by Saint-Vallier, Laval's successor.

than two hundred francs a year.[1] "You say," he wrote to the intendant, "that it is impossible for a Canadian curé to live on five hundred francs. Then you must do the impossible to accomplish my intentions, which are always that the curés should live on the tithes alone."[2] Yet the head of the church still begged for money, and the king still paid it. "We are in the midst of a costly war," wrote the minister to the bishop, "yet in consequence of your urgency the gifts to ecclesiastics will be continued as before."[3] And they did continue. More than half a century later, the king was still making them, and during the last years of the colony he gave twenty thousand francs annually to support Canadian curés.[4]

The maintenance of curés was but a part of his bounty. He endowed the bishopric with the revenues of two French abbeys, to which he afterwards added a third. The vast tracts of land which Laval had acquired were freed from feudal burdens, and emigrants were sent to them by the government in such numbers that, in 1667, the bishop's seigniory of Beaupré and Orleans contained more than a fourth of the entire population of Canada.[5] He had emerged from his condition of apostolic poverty to find himself the richest land-owner in the colony.

If by favors like these the king expected to lead the ecclesiastics into compliance with his wishes, he was doomed to disappointment. The system of movable curés, by which the bishop like a military chief could compel each member of his clerical army to come and go at his bidding, was from the first repugnant to Louis XIV. On the other hand, the bishop clung to it with his usual tenacity. Colbert denounced it as contrary to the laws of the kingdom.[6] "His Majesty has reason to believe," he writes, "that the chief source of the difficulty

---

[1] *Mémoire à Duchesneau, 15 Mai, 1678; Le Roy à Duchesneau, 11 Juin, 1680.*

[2] *Le Roy à Duchesneau, 30 Avril, 1681.*

[3] *Le Ministre à l'Evêque, 8 Mai, 1694.*

[4] Bougainville, *Mémoire, 1757.*

[5] Entire population, 4,312; Beaupré and Orleans, 1,185. *Recensement de 1667.* Laval, it will be remembered, afterwards gave his lands to the seminary of Quebec. He previously exchanged the island of Orleans with the Sieur Berthelot for the island of Jesus. Berthelot gave him a large sum of money in addition.

[6] *Le Ministre à Duchesneau, 15 Mai, 1678.*

which the bishop makes on this point is his wish to preserve a greater authority over the curés."[1] The inflexible prelate, whose heart was bound up in the system he had established, opposed evasion and delay to each expression of the royal will; and even a royal edict failed to produce the desired effect. In the height of the dispute, Laval went to court, and, on the ground of failing health, asked for a successor in the bishopric. The king readily granted his prayer. The successor was appointed; but when Laval prepared to embark again for Canada, he was given to understand that he was to remain in France. In vain he promised to make no trouble;[2] and it was not till after an absence of four years that he was permitted to return, no longer as its chief, to his beloved Canadian church.[3]

Meanwhile Saint-Vallier, the new bishop, had raised a new tempest. He attacked that organization of the seminary of Quebec by which Laval had endeavored to unite the secular priests of Canada into an attached and obedient family, with the bishop as its head and the seminary as its home, a plan of which the system of movable curés was an essential part. The Canadian priests, devoted to Laval, met the innovations of Saint-Vallier with an opposition which seemed only to confirm his purpose. Laval, old and worn with toil and asceticism, was driven almost to despair. The seminary of Quebec was the cherished work of his life, and, to his thinking, the citadel of the Canadian church; and now he beheld it battered and breached before his eyes. His successor, in fact, was trying to place the church of Canada on the footing of the church of France. The conflict lasted for years, with the rancor that marks the quarrels of non-combatants of both sexes. "He" (*Saint-Vallier*), says one of his opponents, "has made himself contemptible to almost everybody, and particularly odious to the priests born in Canada; for there is

[1] *Instruction à M. de Meules, 1682.*

[2] *Laval au Père la Chaise, 1687.* This forms part of a curious correspondence printed in the *Foyer Canadien* for 1866, from originals in the Archevêché of Quebec.

[3] From a *mémoire* of 18 Feb., 1685 (*Archives de Versailles*) it is plain that the court, in giving a successor to Laval, thought that it had ended the vexed question of movable curés.

between them and him a mutual antipathy difficult to overcome."[1] He is described by the same writer as a person "without reflection and judgment, extreme in all things, secret and artful, passionate when opposed, and a flatterer when he wishes to gain his point." This amiable critic adds that Saint-Vallier believes a bishop to be inspired, in virtue of his office, with a wisdom that needs no human aid, and that whatever thought comes to him in prayer is a divine inspiration to be carried into effect at all costs and in spite of all opposition.

The new bishop, notwithstanding the tempest he had raised, did not fully accomplish that establishment of the curés in their respective parishes which the king and the minister so much desired. The Canadian curé was more a missionary than a parish priest; and nature as well as Bishop Laval threw difficulties in the way of settling him quietly over his charge.

On the Lower St. Lawrence, where it widens to an estuary, six leagues across, a ship from France, the last of the season, holds her way for Quebec, laden with stores and clothing, household utensils, goods for Indian trade, the newest court fashions, wine, brandy, tobacco, and the king's orders from Versailles. Swelling her patched and dingy sails, she glides through the wildness and the solitude where there is nothing but her to remind you of the great troubled world behind and the little troubled world before. On the far verge of the ocean-like river, clouds and mountains mingle in dim confusion; fresh gusts from the north dash waves against the ledges, sweep through the quivering spires of stiff and stunted fir-trees, and ruffle the feathers of the crow, perched on the dead bough after his feast of mussels among the sea-weed. You are not so solitary as you think. A small birch canoe rounds the point of rocks, and it bears two men; one in an old black cassock, and the other in a buckskin coat; both working hard at the paddle to keep their slender craft off the shingle and the breakers. The man in the cassock is Father Morel, aged forty-eight, the oldest country curé in Canada, most of his brethren being in the vigor of youth as they had

[1] The above is from an anonymous paper, written apparently in 1695, and entitled *Mémoire pour le Canada*.

need to be. His parochial charge embraces a string of incipient parishes extending along the south shore from Rivière du Loup to Rivière du Sud, a distance reckoned at twenty-seven leagues, and his parishioners number in all three hundred and twenty-eight souls. He has administered spiritual consolation to the one inhabitant of Kamouraska; visited the eight families of La Bouteillerie and the five families of La Combe; and now he is on his way to the seigniory of St. Denis with its two houses and eleven souls.[1]

The father lands where a shattered eel-pot high and dry on the pebbles betrays the neighborhood of man. His servant shoulders his portable chapel, and follows him through the belt of firs, and the taller woods beyond, till the sunlight of a desolate clearing shines upon them. Charred trunks and limbs encumber the ground; dead trees, branchless, barkless, pierced by the woodpeckers, in part black with fire, in part bleached by sun and frost, tower ghastly and weird above the labyrinth of forest ruins, through which the priest and his follower wind their way, the cat-bird mewing, and the blue-jay screaming as they pass. Now the golden-rod and the aster, harbingers of autumn, fringe with purple and yellow the edge of the older clearing, where wheat and maize, the settler's meagre harvest, are growing among the stumps.

Wild-looking women, with sunburnt faces and neglected hair, run from their work to meet the curé; a man or two follow with soberer steps and less exuberant zeal; while half-savage children, the *coureurs de bois* of the future, bareheaded, barefooted, and half-clad, come to wonder and stare. To set up his altar in a room of the rugged log cabin, say mass, hear confessions, impose penance, grant absolution, repeat the office of the dead over a grave made weeks before, baptize, perhaps, the last infant; marry, possibly, some pair who may or may not have waited for his coming; catechize as well as time and circumstance would allow the shy but turbulent brood of some former wedlock: such was the work of the parish priest in the remoter districts. It was seldom that his charge was

---

[1] These particulars are from the *Plan général de l'estat présent des missions du Canada, fait en l'année, 1683*. It is a list and description of the parishes with the names and ages of the curés, and other details. See *Abeille*, I. This paper was drawn up by order of Laval.

quite so scattered, and so far extended as that of Father Morel; but there were fifteen or twenty others whose labors were
like in kind, and in some cases no less arduous. All summer
they paddled their canoes from settlement to settlement; and
in winter they toiled on snow-shoes over the drifts; while the
servant carried the portable chapel on his back, or dragged it
on a sledge. Once, at least, in the year, the curé paid his visit
to Quebec, where, under the maternal roof of the seminary,
he made his retreat of meditation and prayer, and then returned to his work. He rarely had a house of his own, but
boarded in that of the seignior or one of the *habitants*. Many
parishes or aggregations of parishes had no other church than
a room fitted up for the purpose in the house of some pious
settler. In the larger settlements, there were churches and
chapels of wood, thatched with straw, often ruinous, poor to
the last degree, without ornaments, and sometimes without
the sacred vessels necessary for the service.[1] In 1683, there
were but seven stone churches in all the colony. The population was so thin and scattered that many of the settlers heard
mass only three or four times a year, and some of them not
so often. The sick frequently died without absolution, and
infants without baptism.

The splendid self-devotion of the early Jesuit missions has
its record; so, too, have the unseemly bickerings of bishops
and governors: but the patient toils of the missionary curé
rest in the obscurity where the best of human virtues are buried from age to age. What we find set down concerning him
is, that Louis XIV. was unable to see why he should not live
on two hundred francs a year as well as a village curé by the
banks of the Garonne. The king did not know that his cassock
and all his clothing cost him twice as much and lasted half as
long; that he must have a canoe and a man to paddle it; and
that when on his annual visit the seminary paid him five or
six hundred francs, partly in clothes, partly in stores, and
partly in money, the end of the year found him as poor as
before except only in his conscience.

The Canadian priests held the manners of the colony under
a rule as rigid as that of the Puritan churches of New En-

[1] Saint-Vallier, *Estat présent de l'Eglise et de la Colonie Française*, 22 (ed.
1856).

gland, but with the difference that in Canada a large part of the population was restive under their control, while some of the civil authorities, often with the governor at their head, supported the opposition. This was due, partly to an excess of clerical severity, and partly to the continued friction between the secular and ecclesiastical powers. It sometimes happened, however, that a new governor arrived, so pious that the clerical party felt that they could rely on him. Of these rare instances the principal is that of Denonville, who, with a wife as pious as himself, and a young daughter, landed at Quebec, in 1685. On this, Bishop Saint-Vallier, anxious to turn his good dispositions to the best account, addressed to him a series of suggestions or rather directions for the guidance of his conduct, with a view to the spiritual profit of those over whom he was appointed to rule. The document was put on file, and the following are some of the points in it. It is divided into five different heads: "Touching feasts," "touching balls and dances," "touching comedies and other declamations," "touching dress," "touching irreverence in church." The governor and madame his wife are desired to accept no invitations to suppers, that is to say late dinners, as tending to nocturnal hours and dangerous pastimes; and they are further enjoined to express dissatisfaction, and refuse to come again, should any entertainment offered them be too sumptuous. "Although," continues the bishop under the second head of his address, "balls and dances are not sinful in their nature, nevertheless they are so dangerous by reason of the circumstances that attend them, and the evil results that almost inevitably follow, that, in the opinion of Saint Francis of Sales, it should be said of them as physicians say of mushrooms, that at best they are good for nothing;" and, after enlarging on their perils, he declares it to be of great importance to the glory of God and the sanctification of the colony, that the governor and his wife neither give such entertainments nor countenance them by their presence. "Nevertheless," adds the mentor, "since the youth and vivacity of mademoiselle their daughter requires some diversion, it is permitted to relent somewhat, and indulge her in a little moderate and proper dancing, provided that it be solely with persons of her own sex, and in the presence of madame her mother; but by no means in the presence of men or youths, since it is this mingling of sexes which causes the disorders that spring from balls and dances." Private theatricals in any form are next interdicted to the young lady. The bishop then passes to the subject of her dress, and exposes the abuses against which she is to be guarded. "The luxury of dress," he says, "appears in the rich and dazzling fabrics wherein the women and girls of Canada attire themselves, and which are far beyond their condition and their means; in the excess of ornaments which they put on; in the extraordinary head-dresses which they affect, their heads being uncovered and full of strange trinkets; and in the immodest curls so expressly forbidden in the epistles of Saint Peter and Saint Paul, as well as by all the fathers and doctors of the church, and which God has often severely punished, as may be seen by the example of the unhappy Pretextata, a lady of high quality, who, as we learn from Saint Jerome, who knew her, had her hands withered, and died suddenly five months after, and was pre-cipitated into hell, as God had threatened her by an angel; because, by order of her husband, she had curled the hair of her niece, and attired her after a worldly fashion."[1]

Whether the Marquis and Marchioness Denonville profited by so apt and terrible a warning, or whether their patience and good-nature survived the episcopal onslaught, does not appear on record. The subject of feminine apparel received great attention, both from Saint-Vallier and his predecessor, each of whom issued a number of pastoral mandates concern-ing it. Their severest denunciations were aimed at low-necked dresses, which they regarded as favorite devices of the enemy for the snaring of souls; and they also used strong language against certain knots of ribbons called *fontanges*, with which

[1] "Témoin entr'autres l'exemple de la malheureuse Prétextate, dame de grande condition, laquelle au rapport de S. Jérôme, dont elle étoit connue, eut les mains desséchées et cinq mois après mourut subitement et fut préci-pitée en enfer, ainsi que Dieu l'en avoit menacée par un Ange pour avoir par le commandement de son mari frisé et habillé mondainement sa nièce." *Di-vers points à représenter à Mr. le Gouverneur et à Madame la Gouvernante, signé Jean, évesque de Québec. (Registre de l'Evêché de Québec.)* The bishop on an-other occasion holds up the sad fate of Pretextata as a warning to Canadian mothers; but in the present case he slightly changes the incidents to make the story more applicable to the governor and his wife.

the belles of Quebec adorned their heads. Laval launches strenuous invectives against "the luxury and vanity of women and girls, who, forgetting the promises of their baptism, decorate themselves with the pomp of Satan, whom they have so solemnly renounced; and, in their wish to please the eyes of men, make themselves the instruments and the captives of the fiend."[1]

In the journal of the superior of the Jesuits we find, under date of February 4, 1667, a record of the first ball in Canada, along with the pious wish, "God grant that nothing further come of it." Nevertheless more balls were not long in following; and, worse yet, sundry comedies were enacted under no less distinguished patronage than that of Frontenac, the governor. Laval denounced them vigorously, the Jesuit Dablon attacked them in a violent sermon; and such excitement followed that the affair was brought before the royal council, which declined to interfere.[2] This flurry, however, was nothing to the storm raised ten or twelve years later by other dramatic aggressions, an account of which will appear in the sequel of this volume.

The morals of families were watched with unrelenting vigilance. Frontenac writes in a mood unusually temperate, "they (*the priests*) are full of virtue and piety, and if their zeal were less vehement and more moderate they would perhaps succeed better in their efforts for the conversion of souls; but they often use means so extraordinary, and in France so unusual, that they repel most people instead of persuading them. I sometimes tell them my views frankly and as gently as I can, as I know the murmurs that their conduct excites, and often receive complaints of the constraint under which they place consciences. This is above all the case with the ecclesiastics at Montreal, where there is a curé from Franche Comté who wants to establish a

[1] *Mandement contre le luxe et la vanité des femmes et des filles, 1682.* (*Registres de l'Evêché de Québec.*) A still more vigorous denunciation is contained in *Ordonnance contre les vices de luxe et d'impureté, 1690.* This was followed in the next year by a stringent list of rules called *Réglement pour la conduite des fidèles de ce diocèse.*

[2] *Arrêts du 24 et 28 juin par lesquels cette affaire (des comédies) est renvoyés à Sa Majesté, 1681.* (?) (*Registre du Conseil Souverain.*)

sort of inquisition worse than that of Spain, and all out of an excess of zeal."[1]

It was this curé, no doubt, of whom La Hontan complains. That unsanctified young officer was quartered at Montreal, in the house of one of the inhabitants. "During a part of the winter I was hunting with the Algonquins; the rest of it I spent here very disagreeably. One can neither go on a pleasure party, nor play a game of cards, nor visit the ladies, without the curé knowing it and preaching about it publicly from his pulpit. The priests excommunicate masqueraders, and even go in search of them to pull off their masks and overwhelm them with abuse. They watch more closely over the women and girls than their husbands and fathers. They prohibit and burn all books but books of devotion. I cannot think of this tyranny without cursing the indiscreet zeal of the curé of this town. He came to the house where I lived, and, finding some books on my table, presently pounced on the romance of Petronius, which I valued more than my life because it was not mutilated. He tore out almost all the leaves, so that if my host had not restrained me when I came in and saw the miserable wreck, I should have run after this rampant shepherd and torn out every hair of his beard."[2]

La Motte-Cadillac, the founder of Detroit, seems to have had equal difficulty in keeping his temper. "Neither men of honor nor men of parts are endured in Canada; nobody can live here but simpletons and slaves of the ecclesiastical domination. The count (*Frontenac*) would not have so many troublesome affairs on his hands if he had not abolished a Jericho in the shape of a house built by messieurs of the seminary of Montreal, to shut up, as they said, girls who caused scandal; if he had allowed them to take officers and soldiers to go into houses at midnight and carry off women from their husbands and whip them till the blood flowed because they had been at a ball or worn a mask; if he had said nothing against the curés who went the rounds with the soldiers and compelled women and girls to shut themselves up in their houses at nine

---

[1] *Frontenac au Ministre*, 20 Oct., *1691*.

[2] La Hontan, I. 60 (ed. 1709). Other editions contain the same story in different words.

o'clock of summer evenings; if he had forbidden the wearing of lace, and made no objection to the refusal of the communion to women of quality because they wore a *fontange*; if he had not opposed excommunications flung about without sense or reason; if, I say, the count had been of this way of thinking he would have stood as a nonpareil, and have been put very soon on the list of saints, for saint-making is cheap in this country."[1]

While the Sulpitians were thus rigorous at Montreal, the bishop and his Jesuit allies were scarcely less so at Quebec. There was little good-will between them and the Sulpitians, and some of the sharpest charges against the followers of Loyola are brought by their brother priests at Montreal. The Sulpitian Allet writes: "The Jesuits hold such domination over the people of this country that they go into the houses and see every thing that passes there. They then tell what they have learned to each other at their meetings, and on this information they govern their policy. The Jesuit, Father Ragueneau, used to go every day down to the Lower Town, where the merchants live, to find out all that was going on in their families; and he often made people get up from table to confess to him." Allet goes on to say that Father Châtelain also went continually to the Lower Town with the same object, and that some of the inhabitants complained of him to Courcelle, the governor. One day Courcelle saw the Jesuit, who was old and somewhat infirm, slowly walking by the Château, cane in hand, on his usual errand, on which he sent a sergeant after him to request that he would not go so often to the Lower Town, as the people were annoyed by the frequency of his visits. The father replied in wrath, "Go and tell Monsieur de Courcelle that I have been there ever since he was governor, and that I shall go there after he has ceased to be governor;" and he kept on his way as before. Courcelle reported his answer to the superior, Le Mercier, and demanded to have him sent home as a punishment; but the superior effected a compromise. On the following Thursday, after mass in the cathedral, he invited Courcelle into the sacristy, where Father Châtelain was awaiting them; and here, at Le

---

[1] *La Motte-Cadillac à* ———, *28 Sept., 1694.*

Mercier's order, the old priest begged pardon of the offended governor on his knees.[1]

The Jesuits derived great power from the confessional; and, if their accusers are to be believed, they employed unusual means to make it effective. Cavelier de la Salle says: "They will confess nobody till he tells his name, and no servant till he tells the name of his master. When a crime is confessed, they insist on knowing the name of the accomplice, as well as all the circumstances, with the greatest particularity. Father Châtelain especially never fails to do this. They enter as it were by force into the secrets of families, and thus make themselves formidable; for what cannot be done by a clever man devoted to his work, who knows all the secrets of every family; above all when he permits himself to tell them when it is for his interest to do so?"[2]

The association of women and girls known as the Congregation of the Holy Family, which was formed under Jesuit auspices, and which met every Thursday with closed doors in the cathedral, is said to have been very useful to the fathers in their social investigations.[3] The members are affirmed to have been under a vow to tell each other every good or evil deed they knew of every person of their acquaintance; so that this pious gossip became a copious source of information to those in a position to draw upon it. In Talon's time the Congregation of the Holy Family caused such commotion in Quebec that he asked the council to appoint a commission to inquire into its proceedings. He was touching dangerous ground. The affair was presently hushed, and the application cancelled on the register of the council.[4]

The Jesuits had long exercised solely the function of confessors in the colony, and a number of curious anecdotes are on record showing the reluctance with which they admitted

[1] *Mémoire d'Allet*. The author was at one time secretary to Abbé Quélus. The paper is printed in the *Morale pratique des Jésuites*. The above is one of many curious statements which it contains.

[2] La Salle, *Mémoire, 1678*.

[3] See Discovery of the Great West, 795.

[4] *Représentation faite au conseil au sujet de certaines assemblées de femmes ou filles sous le nom de la Sainte Famille, 1667.* (*Registre du Conseil Souverain.*) The paper is cancelled by lines drawn over it; and the following minute, duly attested, is appended to it: "Rayé du consentement de M. Talon."

the secular priests, and above all the Recollets, to share in it. The Recollets, of whom a considerable number had arrived from time to time, were on excellent terms with the civil powers, and were popular with the colonists; but with the bishop and the Jesuits they were not in favor, and one or two sharp collisions took place. The bishop was naturally annoyed when, while he was trying to persuade the king that a curé needed at least six hundred francs a year, these mendicant friars came forward with an offer to serve the parishes for nothing; nor was he, it is likely, better pleased when, having asked the hospital nuns eight hundred francs annually for two masses a day in their chapel, the Recollets underbid him, and offered to say the masses for three hundred.[1] They, on their part, complain bitterly of the bishop, who, they say, would gladly have ordered them out of the colony, but being unable to do this, tried to shut them up in their convent, and prevent them from officiating as priests among the people. "We have as little liberty," says the Recollet writer, "as if we were in a country of heretics." He adds that the inhabitants ask earnestly for the ministrations of the friars, but that the bishop replies with invectives and calumnies against the order, and that when the Recollets absolve a penitent he often annuls the absolution.[2]

In one respect this Canadian church militant achieved a complete success. Heresy was scoured out of the colony. When Maintenon and her ghostly prompters overcame the better nature of the king, and wrought on his bigotry and his vanity to launch him into the dragonnades; when violence and lust bore the crucifix into thousands of Huguenot homes, and the land reeked with nameless infamies; when churches rang with *Te Deums*, and the heart of France withered in anguish; when, in short, this hideous triumph of the faith was won, the royal tool of priestly ferocity sent orders that heresy

[1] "Mon dit sieur l'evesque leur fait payer (*aux hospitalières*) 800*l*. par an pour deux messes qu'il leur fait dire par ses Séminaristes que les Récollets leurs voisins leur offrent pour 300*l*." *La Barre au Ministre, 1682.*

[2] *Mémoire instructif contenant la conduite des PP. Récollets de Paris en leurs missions de Canada, 1684.* This paper, of which only a fragment is preserved, was written in connection with a dispute of the Recollets with the bishop who opposed their attempt to establish a church in Quebec.

should be treated in Canada as it had been treated in France.[1] The orders were needless. The pious Denonville replies, "Praised be God, there is not a heretic here." He adds that a few abjured last year, and that he should be very glad if the king would make them a present. The Jesuits, he further says, go every day on board the ships in the harbor to look after the new converts from France.[2] Now and then at a later day a real or suspected Jansenist found his way to Canada, and sometimes an *esprit fort*, like La Hontan, came over with the troops; but on the whole a community more free from positive heterodoxy perhaps never existed on earth. This exemption cost no bloodshed. What it did cost we may better judge hereafter.

If Canada escaped the dragonnades, so also she escaped another infliction from which a neighboring colony suffered deplorably. Her peace was never much troubled by witches. They were held to exist, it is true; but they wrought no panic. Mother Mary of the Incarnation reports on one occasion the discovery of a magician in the person of a converted Huguenot miller who, being refused in marriage by a girl of Quebec, bewitched her, and filled the house where she lived with demons, which the bishop tried in vain to exorcise. The miller was thrown into prison, and the girl sent to the Hôtel-Dieu, where not a demon dared enter. The infernal crew took their revenge by creating a severe influenza among the citizens.[3]

If there are no Canadian names on the calendar of saints, it is not because in by-ways and obscure places Canada had not virtues worthy of canonization. Not alone her male martyrs and female devotees, whose merits have found a chronicle and a recognition; not the fantastic devotion of Madame d'Aillebout, who, lest she should not suffer enough, took to herself a vicious and refractory servant girl, as an exercise of patience; and not certainly the mediæval pietism of Jeanne Le Ber, the venerated recluse of Montreal. There are others quite as wor-

---

[1] *Mémoire du Roy à Denonville, 31 Mai, 1686.* The king here orders the imprisonment of heretics who refuse to abjure, or the quartering of soldiers on them. What this meant the history of the dragonnades will show.

[2] *Denonville au Ministre, 10 Nov., 1686.*

[3] Marie de l'Incarnation, *Lettre de —Sept., 1661.*

thy of honor, whose names have died from memory. It is difficult to conceive a self-abnegation more complete than that of the hospital nuns of Quebec and Montreal. In the almost total absence of trained and skilled physicians, the burden of the sick and wounded fell upon them. Of the two communities, that of Montreal was the more wretchedly destitute, while that of Quebec was exposed, perhaps, to greater dangers. Nearly every ship from France brought some form of infection, and all infection found its way to the Hôtel-Dieu of Quebec. The nuns died, but they never complained. Removed from the arena of ecclesiastical strife, too busy for the morbidness of the cloister, too much absorbed in practical benevolence to become the prey of illusions, they and their sister community were models of that benign and tender charity of which the Roman Catholic Church is so rich in examples. Nor should the Ursulines and the nuns of the Congregation be forgotten among those who, in another field of labor, have toiled patiently according to their light.

Mademoiselle Jeanne Le Ber belonged to none of these sisterhoods. She was the favorite daughter of the chief merchant of Montreal, the same who, with the help of his money, got himself ennobled. She seems to have been a girl of a fine and sensitive nature; ardent, affectionate, and extremely susceptible to religious impressions. Religion at last gained absolute sway over her. Nothing could appease her longings or content the demands of her excited conscience but an entire consecration of herself to heaven. Constituted as she was, the resolution must have cost her an agony of mental conflict. Her story is a strange, and, as many will think, a very sad one. She renounced her suitors, and wished to renounce her inheritance; but her spiritual directors, too far-sighted to permit such a sacrifice, persuaded her to hold fast to her claims, and content herself with what they called "poverty of heart." Her mother died, and her father, left with a family of young children, greatly needed her help; but she refused to leave her chamber where she had immured herself. Here she remained ten years, seeing nobody but her confessor and the girl who brought her food. Once only she emerged, and this was when her brother lay dead in the adjacent room, killed in a fight with the English. She suddenly appeared before her astonished sisters, stood for a moment in silent prayer by the body, and then vanished without uttering a word. "Such," says her modern biographer, "was the sublimity of her virtue and the grandeur of her soul." Not content with this domestic seclusion, she caused a cell to be made behind the altar in the newly built church of the Congregation, and here we will permit ourselves to cast a stolen glance at her through the narrow opening through which food was passed in to her. Her bed, a pile of straw which she never moved, lest it should become too soft, was so placed that her head could touch the partition, that alone separated it from the Host on the altar. Here she lay wrapped in a garment of coarse gray serge, worn, tattered, and unwashed. An old blanket, a stool, a spinning-wheel, a belt and shirt of haircloth, a scourge, and a pair of shoes made by herself of the husks of Indian-corn, appear to have formed the sum of her furniture and her wardrobe. Her employments were spinning and working embroidery for churches. She remained in this voluntary prison about twenty years; and the nun who brought her food testifies that she never omitted a mortification or a prayer, though commonly in a state of profound depression, and what her biographer calls "complete spiritual aridity."

When her mother died, she had refused to see her; and, long after, no prayer of her dying father could draw her from her cell. "In the person of this modest virgin," writes her reverend eulogist, "we see, with astonishment, the love of God triumphant over earthly affection for parents, and a complete victory of faith over reason and of grace over nature."

In 1711, Canada was threatened with an attack by the English; and she gave the nuns of the Congregation an image of the Virgin on which she had written a prayer to protect their granary from the invaders. Other persons, anxious for a similar protection, sent her images to write upon; but she declined the request. One of the disappointed applicants then stole the inscribed image from the granary of the Congregation, intending to place it on his own when the danger drew near. The English, however, did not come, their fleet having suffered a ruinous shipwreck ascribed to the prayers of Jeanne Le Ber. "It was," writes the Sulpitian Belmont, "the greatest miracle that ever happened since the days of Moses." Nor was

this the only miracle of which she was the occasion. She herself declared that once when she had broken her spinning-
wheel, an angel came and mended it for her. Angels also assisted in her embroidery, "no doubt," says Mother Juchereau,
"taking great pleasure in the society of this angelic creature."
In the church where she had secluded herself, an image of the
Virgin continued after her death to heal the lame and cure
the sick.[1]

Though she rarely permitted herself to speak, yet some
oracular utterance of the sainted recluse would now and then
escape to the outer world. One of these was to the effect that
teaching poor girls to read, unless they wanted to be nuns,
was robbing them of their time. Nor was she far wrong, for
in Canada there was very little to read except formulas of devotion and lives of saints. The dangerous innovation of a
printing-press had not invaded the colony,[2] and the first Canadian newspaper dates from the British conquest.

All education was controlled by priests or nuns. The ablest
teachers in Canada were the Jesuits. Their college of Quebec
was three years older than Harvard. We hear at an early date
of public disputations by the pupils, after the pattern of those
tournaments of barren logic which preceded the reign of inductive reason in Europe, and of which the archetype is to be
found in the scholastic duels of the Sorbonne. The boys were
sometimes permitted to act certain approved dramatic pieces
of a religious character, like the *Sage Visionnaire*. On one occasion they were allowed to play the Cid of Corneille, which,
though remarkable as a literary work, contained nothing
threatening to orthodoxy. They were taught a little Latin, a
little rhetoric, and a little logic; but against all that might
rouse the faculties to independent action, the Canadian
schools prudently closed their doors. There was then no rival
population, of a different origin and a different faith, to compel competition in the race of intelligence and knowledge.
The church stood sole mistress of the field. Under the old

---

[1] Faillon, *L'Héroine chrétienne du Canada, ou Vie de Mlle. Le Ber*. This is a
most elaborate and eulogistic life of the recluse. A shorter account of her will
be found in Juchereau, *Hôtel-Dieu*. She died in 1714, at the age of fifty-two.

[2] A printing-press was afterwards brought to Canada, but was soon sent
back again.

régime the real object of education in Canada was a religious and, in far less degree, a political one. The true purpose of the schools was: first, to make priests; and, secondly, to make obedient servants of the church and the king. All the rest was extraneous and of slight account. In regard to this matter, the king and the bishop were of one mind. "As I have been informed," Louis XIV. writes to Laval, "of your continued care to hold the people in their duty towards God and towards me by the good education you give or cause to be given to the young, I write this letter to express my satisfaction with conduct so salutary, and to exhort you to persevere in it."[1]

The bishop did not fail to persevere. The school for boys attached to his seminary became the most important educational institution in Canada. It was regulated by thirty-four rules, "in honor of the thirty-four years which Jesus lived on earth." The qualities commended to the boys as those which they should labor diligently to acquire were, "humility, obedience, purity, meekness, modesty, simplicity, chastity, charity, and an ardent love of Jesus and his Holy Mother."[2] Here is a goodly roll of Christian virtues. What is chiefly noticeable in it is, that truth is allowed no place. That manly but unaccommodating virtue was not, it seems, thought important in forming the mind of youth. Humility and obedience lead the list, for in unquestioning submission to the spiritual director lay the guaranty of all other merits.

We have seen already that, besides this seminary for boys, Laval established another for educating the humbler colonists. It was a sort of farm-school, though besides farming various mechanical trades were also taught in it. It was well adapted to the wants of a great majority of Canadians, whose tendencies were any thing but bookish; but here, as elsewhere, the real object was religious. It enabled the church to extend her influence over classes which the ordinary schools could not reach. Besides manual training, the pupils were taught to read and write; and for a time a certain number of them received some instruction in Latin. When, in 1686, Saint-Vallier visited the school, he found in all thirty-one boys under the charge of two priests; but the number was afterwards greatly re-

[1] *Le Roy à Laval, 9 Avril, 1667* (extract in Faillon).
[2] *Ancien réglement du Petit Séminaire de Québec,* see *Abeille,* VIII., no. 32.

duced, and the place served, as it still serves, chiefly as a retreat during vacations for the priests and pupils of the seminary of Quebec. A spot better suited for such a purpose cannot be conceived.

From the vast meadows of the parish of St. Joachim, that here border the St. Lawrence, there rises like an island a low flat hill, hedged round with forests like the tonsured head of a monk. It was here that Laval planted his school. Across the meadows, a mile or more distant, towers the mountain promontory of Cape Tourmente. You may climb its woody steeps, and from the top, waist-deep in blueberry-bushes, survey, from Kamouraska to Quebec, the grand Canadian world outstretched below; or mount the neighboring heights of St. Anne, where, athwart the gaunt arms of ancient pines, the river lies shimmering in summer haze, the cottages of the *habitants* are strung like beads of a rosary along the meadows of Beaupré, the shores of Orleans bask in warm light, and far on the horizon the rock of Quebec rests like a faint gray cloud; or traverse the forest till the roar of the torrent guides you to the rocky solitude where it holds its savage revels. High on the cliffs above, young birch-trees stand smiling in the morning sun; while in the abyss beneath the snowy waters plunge from depth to depth, and, half way down, the slender harebell hangs from its mossy nook, quivering in the steady thunder of the cataract. Game on the river; trout in lakes, brooks, and pools; wild fruits and flowers on meadows and mountains,—a thousand resources of honest and wholesome recreation here wait the student emancipated from books, but not parted for a moment from the pious influence that hangs about the old walls embosomed in the woods of St. Joachim. Around on plains and hills stand the dwellings of a peaceful peasantry, as different from the restless population of the neighboring states as the denizens of some Norman or Breton village.

Above all, do not fail to make your pilgrimage to the shrine of St. Anne. You may see her chapel four or five miles away, nestled under the heights of the Petit Cap. Here, when Aillebout was governor, he began with his own hands the pious work, and a *habitant* of Beaupré, Louis Guimont, sorely afflicted with rheumatism, came grinning with pain to lay three stones in the foundation, in honor probably of Saint Anne, Saint Joachim, and their daughter, the Virgin. Instantly he was cured. It was but the beginning of a long course of miracles continued more than two centuries, and continuing still. Their fame spread far and wide. The devotion to Saint Anne became a distinguishing feature of Canadian Catholicity, till at the present day at least thirteen parishes bear her name. But of all her shrines none can match the fame of St. Anne du Petit Cap. Crowds flocked thither on the week of her festival, and marvellous cures were wrought unceasingly, as the sticks and crutches hanging on the walls and columns still attest. Sometimes the whole shore was covered with the wigwams of Indian converts who had paddled their birch canoes from the farthest wilds of Canada. The more fervent among them would crawl on their knees from the shore to the altar. And, in our own day, every summer a far greater concourse of pilgrims, not in paint and feathers, but in cloth and millinery, and not in canoes, but in steamboats, bring their offerings and their vows to the "Bonne Sainte Anne."[1]

To return to Laval's industrial school. Judging from repeated complaints of governors and intendants of the dearth of skilled workmen, the priests in charge of it were more successful in making good Catholics than in making good masons, carpenters, blacksmiths, and weavers; and the number of pupils, even if well trained, was at no time sufficient to meet the wants of the colony;[2] for, though the Canadians showed an aptitude for mechanical trades, they preferred above all things the savage liberty of the backwoods.

The education of girls was in the hands of the Ursulines and the nuns of the Congregation, of whom the former, besides careful instruction in religious duties, taught their pupils

[1] For an interesting account of the shrine at the Petit Cap, see Casgrain, *Le Pélérinage de la Bonne Sainte Anne*, a little manual of devotion printed at Quebec. I chanced to visit the old chapel in 1871, during a meeting of the parish to consider the question of reconstructing it, as it was in a ruinous state. Passing that way again two years after, I found the old chapel still standing, and a new one, much larger, half finished.

[2] Most of them were moreover retained, after leaving the school, by the seminary, as servants, farmers, or vassals. La Tour, *Vie de Laval*, Liv. VI.

"all that a girl ought to know."[1] This meant exceedingly little besides the manual arts suited to their sex; and, in the case of the nuns of the Congregation, who taught girls of the poorer class, it meant still less. It was on nuns as well as on priests that the charge fell, not only of spiritual and mental, but also of industrial, training. Thus we find the king giving to a sisterhood of Montreal a thousand francs to buy wool, and a thousand more for teaching girls to knit.[2] The king also maintained a teacher of navigation and surveying at Quebec on the modest salary of four hundred francs.

During the eighteenth century, some improvement is perceptible in the mental state of the population. As it became more numerous and more stable, it also became less ignorant; and the Canadian *habitant*, towards the end of the French rule, was probably better taught, so far as concerned religion, than the mass of French peasants. Yet secular instruction was still extremely meagre, even in the *noblesse*. "In spite of this defective education," says the famous navigator, Bougainville, who knew the colony well in its last years, "the Canadians are naturally intelligent. They do not know how to write, but they speak with ease and with an accent as good as the Parisian."[3] He means, of course, the better class. "Even the children of officers and gentlemen," says another writer, "scarcely know how to read and write; they are ignorant of the first elements of geography and history."[4] And evidence like this might be extended.

When France was heaving with the throes that prepared the Revolution; when new hopes, new dreams, new thoughts,—good and evil, false and true,—tossed the troubled waters of French society, Canada caught something of its social corruption, but not the faintest impulsion of its roused mental life. The torrent surged on its way; while, in the deep nook beside it, the sticks and dry leaves floated their

---

[1] A lire, à écrire, les prières, les mœurs chrétiennes, et tout ce qu'une fille doit savoir. Marie de l'Incarnation, *Lettre du 9 Août, 1668.*

[2] *Denonville au Ministre, 13 Nov., 1685.*

[3] Bougainville, *Mémoire de 1757* (see Margry, *Relations inédites*).

[4] *Mémoire de 1736; Détail de toute la Colonie* (published by Hist. Soc. of Quebec).

usual round, and the unruffled pool slept in the placidity of intellectual torpor.[1]

[1]Several Frenchmen of a certain intellectual eminence made their abode in Canada from time to time. The chief among them are the Jesuit Lafitau, author of *Mœurs des Sauvages Américains*; the Jesuit Charlevoix, traveller and historian; the physician Sarrazin; and the Marquis de la Galisonnière, the most enlightened of the French governors of Canada. Sarrazin, a naturalist as well as a physician, has left his name to the botanical genus *Sarracenia*, of which the curious American species, *S. purpurea*, the "pitcher-plant," was described by him. His position in the colony was singular and characteristic. He got little or no pay from his patients; and, though at one time the only genuine physician in Canada (*Callières et Beauharnois au Ministre, 3 Nov., 1702*), he was dependent on the king for support. In 1699, we find him thanking his Majesty for 300 francs a year, and asking at the same time for more, as he has nothing else to live on. (*Callières et Champigny au Ministre, 20 Oct., 1699.*) Two years later the governor writes that, as he serves almost everybody without fees, he ought to have another 300 francs. (*Ibid., 5 Oct., 1701.*) The additional 300 francs was given him; but, finding it insufficient, he wanted to leave the colony. "He is too useful," writes the governor again: "we cannot let him go." His yearly pittance of 600 francs, French money, was at one time re-enforced by his salary as member of the Superior Council. He died at Quebec in 1734.

Chapter XXIII

1640–1763

MORALS AND MANNERS

Social Influence of the Troops • A Petty Tyrant • Brawls • Violence and Outlawry • State of the Population • Views of Denonville • Brandy • Beggary • The Past and the Present • Inns • State of Quebec • Fires • The Country Parishes • Slavery • Views of La Hontan • Of Hocquart • Of Bougainville • Of Kalm • Of Charlevoix

---

THE mission period of Canada, or the period anterior to the year 1663, when the king took the colony in charge, has a character of its own. The whole population did not exceed that of a large French village. Its extreme poverty, the constant danger that surrounded it, and, above all, the contagious zeal of the missionaries, saved it from many vices, and inspired it with an extraordinary religious fervor. Without doubt an ideal picture has been drawn of this early epoch. Trade as well as propagandism was the business of the colony, and the colonists were far from being all in a state of grace; yet it is certain that zeal was higher, devotion more constant, and popular morals more pure, than at any later period of the French rule.

The intervention of the king wrought a change. The annual shipments of emigrants made by him were, in the most favorable view, of a very mixed character, and the portion which Mother Mary calls *canaille* was but too conspicuous. Along with them came a regiment of soldiers fresh from the license of camps and the excitements of Turkish wars, accustomed to obey their officers and to obey nothing else, and more ready to wear the scapulary of the Virgin in campaigns against the Mohawks than to square their lives by the rules of Christian ethics. "Our good king," writes Sister Morin, of Montreal, "has sent troops to defend us from the Iroquois, and the soldiers and officers have ruined the Lord's vineyard, and planted wickedness and sin and crime in our soil of Canada."[1]

---

[1] *Annales de l'Hôtel-Dieu St. Joseph*, cited by Faillon.

Few, indeed, among the officers followed the example of one
of their number, Paul Dupuy, who, in his settlement of Isle
aux Oies, below Quebec, lived, it is said, like a saint, and on
Sundays and fête days exhorted his servants and *habitants*
with such unction that their eyes filled with tears.[1] Nor, let us
hope, were there many imitators of Major La Fredière, who,
with a company of the regiment, was sent to garrison Montreal, where he ruled with absolute sway over settlers and soldiers alike. His countenance naturally repulsive was made
more so by the loss of an eye; yet he was irrepressible in
gallantry, and women and girls fled in terror from the military
Polyphemus. The men, too, feared and hated him, not without reason. One morning a settler named Demers was hoeing
his field, when he saw a sportsman gun in hand striding
through his half-grown wheat. "Steady there, steady," he
shouted in a tone of remonstrance; but the sportsman gave
no heed. "Why do you spoil a poor man's wheat?" cried the
outraged cultivator. "If I knew who you were, I would go
and complain of you." "Whom would you complain to?" demanded the sportsman, who then proceeded to walk back
into the middle of the wheat, and called out to Demers, "You
are a rascal, and I'll thrash you." "Look at home for rascals,"
retorted Demers, "and keep your thrashing for your dogs."
The sportsman came towards him in a rage to execute his
threat. Demers picked up his gun, which, after the custom of
the time, he had brought to the field with him, and, advancing to meet his adversary, recognized La Fredière, the commandant. On this he ran off. La Fredière sent soldiers to
arrest him, threw him into prison, put him in irons, and the
next day mounted him on the wooden horse, with a weight
of sixty pounds tied to each foot. He repeated the torture a
day or two after, and then let his victim go, saying, "If I could
have caught you when I was in your wheat, I would have
beaten you well."

The commandant next turned his quarters into a dram-
shop for Indians, to whom he sold brandy in large quantities,
but so diluted that his customers, finding themselves partially
defrauded of their right of intoxication, complained griev-

[1] Juchereau, *Hôtel-Dieu de Québec*, 511.

ously. About this time the intendant Talon made one of his domiciliary visits to Montreal, and when, in his character of father of the people, he inquired if they had any complaints to make, every tongue was loud in accusation against La Fredière. Talon caused full depositions to be made out from the statements of Demers and other witnesses. Copies were deposited in the hands of the notary, and it is from these that the above story is drawn. The tyrant was removed, and ordered home to France.[1]

Many other officers embarked in the profitable trade of selling brandy to Indians, and several garrison posts became centres of disorder. Others, of the regiment became notorious brawlers. A lieutenant of the garrison of Montreal named Carion, and an ensign named Morel, had for some reason conceived a violent grudge against another ensign named Lormeau. On Pentecost day, just after vespers, Lormeau was walking by the river with his wife. They had passed the common and the seminary wall, and were in front of the house of the younger Charles Le Moyne, when they saw Carion coming towards them. He stopped before Lormeau, looked him full in the face, and exclaimed, "Coward." "Coward yourself," returned Lormeau; "take yourself off." Carion drew his sword, and Lormeau followed his example. They exchanged a few passes; then closed, and fell to the ground grappled together. Lormeau's wig fell off; and Carion, getting the uppermost, hammered his bare head with the hilt of his sword. Lormeau's wife, in a frenzy of terror, screamed *murder*. One of the neighbors, Monsieur Belêtre, was at table with Charles Le Moyne and a Rochelle merchant named Baston. He ran out with his two guests, and they tried to separate the combatants, who still lay on the ground foaming like a pair of enraged bull-dogs. All their efforts were useless. "Very well," said Le Moyne in disgust, "if you won't let go, then kill each other if you like." A former military servant of Carion now ran up, and began to brandish his sword in behalf of his late master. Carion's comrade, Morel, also arrived, and, regardless of the angry protest of Le Moyne, stabbed repeatedly at Lor-

[1] *Information contre La Fredière*. See Faillon, *Colonie Française*, III. 386. The dialogue, as here given from the depositions, is translated as closely as possible.

meau as he lay. Lormeau had received two or three wounds in the hand and arm with which he parried the thrusts, and was besides severely mauled by the sword-hilt of Carion, when two Sulpitian priests, drawn by the noise, appeared on the scene. One was Frémont, the curé; the other was Dollier de Casson. That herculean father, whose past soldier life had made him at home in a fray, and who cared nothing for drawn swords, set himself at once to restore peace, upon which, whether from the strength of his arm, or the mere effect of his presence, the two champions released their gripe on each other's throats, rose, sheathed their weapons, and left the field.[1]

Montreal, a frontier town at the head of the colony, was the natural resort of desperadoes, offering, as we have seen, a singular contrast between the rigor of its clerical seigniors and the riotous license of the lawless crew which infested it. Dollier de Casson tells the story of an outlaw who broke prison ten or twelve times, and whom no walls, locks, or fetters could hold. "A few months ago," he says, "he was caught again, and put into the keeping of six or seven men, each with a good gun. They stacked their arms to play a game of cards, which their prisoner saw fit to interrupt to play a game of his own. He made a jump at the guns, took them under his arm like so many feathers, aimed at these fellows with one of them, swearing that he would kill the first who came near him, and so, falling back step by step, at last bade them good-by, and carried off all their guns. Since then he has not been caught, and is roaming the woods. Very likely he will become chief of our banditti, and make great trouble in the country when it pleases him to come back from the Dutch settlements, whither they say he is gone along with another rascal, and a French woman so depraved that she is said to have given or sold two of her children to the Indians."[2]

When the governor, La Barre, visited Montreal, he found there some two hundred reprobates gambling, drinking, and stealing. If hard pressed by justice, they had only to cross the

[1] *Requête de Lormeau à M. d'Aillebout. Dépositions de MM. de Longueuil (Le Moyne), de Baston, de Belêtre, et autres.* Cited by Faillon, *Colonie Française,* III. 393.

[2] Dollier de Casson, *Histoire de Montréal, 1671–72.*

river and place themselves beyond the seigniorial jurisdiction. The military settlements of the Richelieu were in a condition somewhat similar, and La Barre complains of a prevailing spirit of disobedience and lawlessness.[1] The most orderly and thrifty part of Canada appears to have been at this time the côte of Beaupré, belonging to the seminary of Quebec. Here the settlers had religious instruction from their curés, and industrial instruction also if they wanted it. Domestic spinning and weaving were practised at Beaupré sooner than in any other part of the colony.

When it is remembered that a population which in La Barre's time did not exceed ten thousand, and which forty years later did not much exceed twice that number, was scattered along both sides of a great river for three hundred miles or more; that a large part of this population was in isolated groups of two, three, five, ten, or twenty houses at the edge of a savage wilderness; that between them there was little communication except by canoes; that the settlers were disbanded soldiers, or others whose lives had been equally adverse to habits of reflection or self-control; that they rarely saw a priest, and that a government omnipotent in name had not arms long enough to reach them,—we may listen without surprise to the lamentations of order-loving officials over the unruly condition of a great part of the colony. One accuses the seigniors, who, he says, being often of low extraction, cannot keep their vassals in order.[2] Another dwells sorrowfully on the "terrible dispersion" of the settlements where the inhabitants "live in a savage independence." But it is better that each should speak for himself, and among the rest let us hear the pious Denonville.

"This, monseigneur, seems to me the place for rendering you an account of the disorders which prevail not only in the woods, but also in the settlements. They arise from the idleness of young persons, and the great liberty which fathers, mothers, and guardians have for a long time given them, or allowed them to assume, of going into the forest under pretence of hunting or trading. This has come to such a pass, that, from the moment a boy can carry a gun, the father can-

[1] *La Barre au Ministre, 4 Nov., 1683.*
[2] Catalogne, *Mémoire addressé au Ministre, 1712.*

not restrain him and dares not offend him. You can judge the mischief that follows. These disorders are always greatest in the families of those who are *gentilshommes*, or who through laziness or vanity pass themselves off as such. Having no resource but hunting, they must spend their lives in the woods, where they have no curés to trouble them, and no fathers or guardians to constrain them. I think, monseigneur, that martial law would suit their case better than any judicial sentence.

"Monsieur de la Barre suppressed a certain order of knighthood which had sprung up here, but he did not abolish the usages belonging to it. It was thought a fine thing and a good joke to go about naked and tricked out like Indians, not only on carnival days, but on all other days of feasting and debauchery. These practices tend to encourage the disposition of our young men to live like savages, frequent their company, and be for ever unruly and lawless like them. I cannot tell you, monseigneur, how attractive this Indian life is to all our youth. It consists in doing nothing, caring for nothing, following every inclination, and getting out of the way of all correction." He goes on to say that the mission villages governed by the Jesuits and Sulpitians are models of good order, and that drunkards are never seen there except when they come from the neighboring French settlements; but that the other Indians who roam at large about the colony, do prodigious mischief, because the children of the seigniors not only copy their way of life, but also run off with their women into the woods.[1]

"Nothing," he continues, "can be finer or better conceived than the regulations framed for the government of this country; but nothing, I assure you, is so ill observed as regards both the fur trade and the general discipline of the colony. One great evil is the infinite number of drinking-shops, which makes it almost impossible to remedy the disorders resulting from them. All the rascals and idlers of the country are attracted into this business of tavern-keeping. They never

[1] Raudot, who was intendant early in the eighteenth century, is a little less gloomy in his coloring, but says that Canadian children were without discipline or education, had no respect for parents or curés, and owned no superiors. This, he thinks, is owing to "la folle tendresse des parents qui les empêche de les corriger et de leur former le caractère qu'ils ont dur et féroce."

dream of tilling the soil; but, on the contrary, they deter the other inhabitants from it, and end with ruining them. I know seigniories where there are but twenty houses, and more than half of them dram shops. At Three Rivers there are twenty-five houses, and liquor may be had at eighteen or twenty of them. Villemarie (*Montreal*) and Quebec are on the same footing."

The governor next dwells on the necessity of finding occupation for children and youths, a matter which he regards as of the last importance. "It is sad to see the ignorance of the population at a distance from the abodes of the curés, who are put to the greatest trouble to remedy the evil by travelling from place to place through the parishes in their charge."[1]

La Barre, Champigny, and Duchesneau write in a similar strain. Bishop Saint-Vallier, in an epistolary journal which he printed of a tour through the colony made on his first arrival, gives a favorable account of the disposition of the people, especially as regards religion. He afterwards changed his views. An abstract made from his letters for the use of the king states that he "represents, like M. Denonville, that the Canadian youth are for the most part wholly demoralized."[2]

"The bishop was very sorry," says a correspondent of the minister at Quebec, "to have so much exaggerated in the letter he printed at Paris the morality of the people here."[3] He preached a sermon on the sins of the inhabitants and issued a pastoral mandate, in which he says, "Before we knew our flock we thought that the English and the Iroquois were the only wolves we had to fear; but God having opened our eyes to the disorders of this diocese, and made us feel more than ever the weight of our charge, we are forced to confess that our most dangerous foes are drunkenness, luxury, impurity, and slander."[4]

Drunkenness was at this time the most destructive vice in the colony. One writer declares that most of the Canadians drink so much brandy in the morning, that they are unfit for

[1] *Denonville au Ministre, 13 Nov. 1685.*
[2] *N. Y. Colonial Documents*, IX. 278.
[3] *Ibid.*, IX. 388.
[4] *Ordonnance contre les vices de l'ivrognerie, luxe, et impureté, 31 Oct., 1690.*

work all day.[1] Another says that a canoe-man when he is tired will lift a keg of brandy to his lips and drink the raw liquor from the bung-hole, after which, having spoiled his appetite, he goes to bed supperless; and that, what with drink and hardship, he is an old man at forty. Nevertheless the race did not deteriorate. The prevalence of early marriages, and the birth of numerous offspring before the vigor of the father had been wasted, ensured the strength and hardihood which characterized the Canadians. As Denonville describes them so they long remained. "The Canadians are tall, well-made, and well set on their legs (*bien plantés sur leurs jambes*), robust, vigorous, and accustomed in time of need to live on little. They have intelligence and vivacity, but are wayward, light-minded, and inclined to debauchery."

As the population increased, as the rage for bush-ranging began to abate, and, above all, as the curés multiplied, a change took place for the better. More churches were built, the charge of each priest was reduced within reasonable bounds, and a greater proportion of the inhabitants remained on their farms. They were better watched, controlled, and taught, by the church. The ecclesiastical power, wherever it had a hold, was exercised, as we have seen, with an undue rigor, yet it was the chief guardian of good morals; and the colony grew more orderly and more temperate as the church gathered more and more of its wild and wandering flock fairly within its fold. In this, however, its success was but relative. It is true that in 1715 a well-informed writer says that the people were "perfectly instructed in religion;"[2] but at that time the statement was only partially true.

During the seventeenth century, and some time after its close, Canada swarmed with beggars, a singular feature in a new country where a good farm could be had for the asking. In countries intensely Roman Catholic begging is not regarded as an unmixed evil, being supposed to promote two cardinal virtues,—charity in the giver and humility in the receiver. The Canadian officials nevertheless tried to restrain it. Vagabonds of both sexes were ordered to leave Quebec, and nobody was allowed to beg without a certificate of poverty

[1] *N.Y. Colonial Documents*, IX. 398.
[2] *Mémoire adressé au Regent.*

from the curé or the local judge.[1] These orders were not always observed. Bishop Saint-Vallier writes that he is overwhelmed by beggars,[2] and the intendant echoes his complaint. Almshouses were established at Montreal, Three Rivers, and Quebec;[3] and when Saint-Vallier founded the General Hospital, its chief purpose was to serve, not as a hospital in the ordinary sense of the word, but as a house of refuge, after the plan of the General Hospital of Paris.[4] Appeal, as usual, was made to the king. Denonville asks his aid for two destitute families, and says that many others need it. Louis XIV. did not fail to respond, and from time to time he sent considerable sums for the relief of the Canadian poor.[5]

Denonville says, "The principal reason of the poverty of this country is the idleness and bad conduct of most of the people. The greater part of the women, including all the *demoiselles*, are very lazy."[6] Meules proposes as a remedy that the king should establish a general workshop in the colony, and pay the workmen himself during the first five or six years.[7] "The persons here," he says, "who have wished to make a figure are nearly all so overwhelmed with debt that they may be considered as in the last necessity."[8] He adds that many of the people go half-naked even in winter. "The merchants of this country," says the intendant Duchesneau, "are all plunged in poverty, except five or six at the most; it is the same with the artisans, except a small number, because the vanity of the women and the debauchery of the men consume all their gains. As for such of the laboring class as apply themselves steadily to cultivating the soil, they not only live very

[1] *Réglement de Police, 1676.*

[2] *N.Y. Colonial Documents*, IX. 279.

[3] *Edits et Ordonnances*, II. 119.

[4] On the General Hospital of Quebec, see Juchereau, 355. In 1692, the minister writes to Frontenac and Champigny that they should consider well whether this house of refuge will not "augmenter la fainéantise parmi les habitans," by giving them a sure support in poverty.

[5] As late as 1701, six thousand livres were granted. *Callières au Ministre, 4 Nov., 1701.*

[6] *Denonville et Champigny au Ministre, 6 Nov., 1687.*

[7] *Meules au Ministre, 12 Nov., 1682.*

[8] Meules, *Mémoire touchant le Canada et l'Acadie, 1684.*

well, but are incomparably better off than the better sort of peasants in France."[1]

All the writers lament the extravagant habits of the people; and even La Hontan joins hands with the priests in wishing that the supply of ribbons, laces, brocades, jewelry, and the like, might be cut off by act of law. Mother Juchereau tells us that, when the English invasion was impending, the belles of Canada were scared for a while into modesty in order to gain the favor of heaven; but, as may be imagined, the effect was short, and Father La Tour declares that in his time all the fashions except *rouge* came over regularly in the annual ships.

The manners of the mission period, on the other hand, were extremely simple. The old governor, Lauzon, lived on pease and bacon like a laborer, and kept no man-servant. He was regarded, it is true, as a miser, and held in slight account.[2] Magdeleine Bochart, sister of the governor of Three Rivers, brought her husband two hundred francs in money, four sheets, two table-cloths, six napkins of linen and hemp, a mattress, a blanket, two dishes, six spoons and six tin plates, a pot and a kettle, a table and two benches, a kneading-trough, a chest with lock and key, a cow, and a pair of hogs.[3] But the Bocharts were a family of distinction, and the bride's dowry answered to her station. By another marriage contract, at about the same time, the parents of the bride, being of humble degree, bind themselves to present the bridegroom with a barrel of bacon, deliverable on the arrival of the ships from France.[4]

Some curious traits of this early day appear in the license of Jean Boisdon as innkeeper. He is required to establish himself on the great square of Quebec, close to the church, so that the parishioners may conveniently warm and refresh themselves between the services; but he is forbidden to entertain anybody during high mass, sermon, catechism, or vespers.[5] Matters soon changed; Jean Boisdon lost his

---

[1] *Duchesneau au Ministre, 10 Nov., 1679.*

[2] *Mémoire d'Aubert de la Chesnaye, 1676.*

[3] *Contrat de marriage,* cited by Ferland, *Notes,* 73.

[4] *Contrat de marriage,* cited by Benjamin Sulte in *Revue Canadienne,* IX. 111.

[5] *Acte officielle, 1648,* cited by Ferland, *Cours d'Histoire du Canada,* I. 365.

monopoly, and inns sprang up on all hands. They did not want for patrons, and we find some of their proprietors mentioned as among the few thriving men in Canada. Talon tried to regulate them, and, among other rules, ordained that no innkeeper should furnish food or drink to any hired laborer whatever, or to any person residing in the place where his inn was situated. An innkeeper of Montreal was fined for allowing the syndic of the town to dine under his roof.[1]

One gets glimpses of the pristine state of Quebec through the early police regulations. Each inhabitant was required to make a gutter along the middle of the street before his house, and also to remove refuse and throw it into the river. All dogs, without exception, were ordered home at nine o'clock. On Tuesdays and Fridays there was a market in the public square, whither the neighboring *habitants*, male and female, brought their produce for sale, as they still continue to do. Smoking in the street was forbidden, as a precaution against fire; householders were required to provide themselves with ladders, and when the fire alarm was rung all able-bodied persons were obliged to run to the scene of danger with buckets or kettles full of water.[2] This did not prevent the Lower Town from burning to the ground in 1682. It was soon rebuilt, but a repetition of the catastrophe seemed very likely. "This place," says Denonville, "is in a fearful state as regards fire; for the houses are crowded together out of all reason, and so surrounded with piles of cord-wood that it is pitiful to see."[3] Add to this the stores of hay for the cows kept by many of the inhabitants for the benefit of their swarming progeny. The houses were at this time low, compact buildings, with gables of masonry, as required by law; but many had wooden fronts, and all had roofs covered with cedar shingles. The anxious governor begs that, as the town has not a *sou* of revenue, his Majesty will be pleased to make it the gift of two hundred crowns' worth of leather fire-buckets.[4] Six or seven years after, certain citizens were authorized by the council to import from France, at their own cost, "a pump

[1] Faillon, *Colonie Française*, III. 405.
[2] *Réglement de Police, 1672. Ibid., 1676.*
[3] *Denonville au Ministre, 20 Août, 1685.*
[4] *Ibid.*

after the Dutch fashion, for throwing water on houses in case of fire."[1] How a fire was managed at Quebec appears from a letter of the engineer, Vasseur, describing the burning of Laval's seminary in 1701. Vasseur was then at Quebec, directing the new fortifications. On a Monday in November, all the pupils of the seminary and most of the priests went, according to their weekly custom, to recreate themselves at a house and garden at St. Michel, a short distance from town. The few priests who remained went after dinner to say vespers at the church. Only one, Father Petit, was left in the seminary, and he presently repaired to the great hall to rekindle the fire in the stove and warm the place against the return of his brethren. His success surpassed his wishes. A firebrand snapped out in his absence and set the pine floor in a blaze. Father Boucher, curé of Point Levi, chanced to come in, and was half choked by the smoke. He cried *fire!* the servants ran for water; but the flames soon mastered them; they screamed the alarm, and the bells began to ring. Vasseur was dining with the intendant at his palace by the St. Charles, when he heard a frightened voice crying out, "Monsieur, you are wanted; you are wanted." He sprang from table, saw the smoke rolling in volumes from the top of the rock, ran up the steep ascent, reached the seminary, and found an excited crowd making a prodigious outcry. He shouted for carpenters. Four men came to him, and he set them at work with such tools as they had to tear away planks and beams, and prevent the fire from spreading to the adjacent parts of the building; but, when he went to find others to help them, they ran off. He set new men in their place, and these too ran off the moment his back was turned. A cry was raised that the building was to be blown up, on which the crowd scattered for their lives. Vasseur now gave up the seminary for lost, and thought only of cutting off the fire from the rear of the church, which was not far distant. In this he succeeded, by tearing down an intervening wing or gallery. The walls of the burning building were of massive stone, and by seven o'clock the fire had spent itself. We hear nothing of the Dutch pump, nor does it appear that the soldiers of the garrison made any

[1] *Réglement de 1691*, extract in Ferland.

effort to keep order. Under cover of the confusion, property was stolen from the seminary to the amount of about two thousand livres, which is remarkable, considering the religious character of the building, and the supposed piety of the people. "There were more than three hundred persons at the fire," says Vasseur; "but thirty picked men would have been worth more than the whole of them."[1]

August, September, and October were the busy months at Quebec. Then the ships from France discharged their lading, the shops and warehouses of the Lower Town were filled with goods, and the *habitants* came to town to make their purchases. When the frosts began, the vessels sailed away, the harbor was deserted, the streets were silent again, and like ants or squirrels the people set at work to lay in their winter stores. Fathers of families packed their cellars with beets, carrots, potatoes, and cabbages; and, at the end of autumn, with meat, fowls, game, fish, and eels, all frozen to stony hardness. Most of the shops closed, and the long season of leisure and amusement began. New Year's day brought visits and mutual gifts. Thence till Lent dinner parties were frequent, sometimes familiar and sometimes ceremonious. The governor's little court at the chateau was a standing example to all the aspiring spirits of Quebec, and forms and orders of precedence were in some houses punctiliously observed. There were dinners to the military and civic dignitaries and their wives, and others, quite distinct, to prominent citizens. The wives and daughters of the burghers of Quebec are said to have been superior in manners to women of the corresponding class in France. "They have wit," says La Potherie, "delicacy, good voices, and a great fondness for dancing. They are discreet, and not much given to flirting; but when they undertake to catch a lover it is not easy for him to escape the bands of Hymen."[2]

So much for the town. In the country parishes, there was the same autumnal stowing away of frozen vegetables, meat, fish, and eels, and unfortunately the same surfeit of leisure through five months of the year. During the seventeenth cen-

[1] *Vasseur au Ministre, 24 Nov., 1701.* Like Denonville before him, he urges the need of fire-buckets.
[2] La Potherie, I. 279.

tury, many of the people were so poor that women were forced to keep at home from sheer want of winter clothing. Nothing, however, could prevent their running from house to house to exchange gossip with the neighbors, who all knew each other, and, having nothing else to do, discussed each other's affairs with an industry which often bred bitter quarrels. At a later period, a more general introduction of family weaving and spinning served at once to furnish clothing and to promote domestic peace.

The most important persons in a parish were the curé, the seignior, and the militia captain. The seignior had his bench of honor in the church. Immediately behind it was the bench of the militia captain, whose duty it was to drill the able-bodied men of the neighborhood, direct road-making and other public works, and serve as deputy to the intendant, whose ordinances he was required to enforce. Next in honor came the local judge, if any there was, and the church-wardens.

The existence of slavery in Canada dates from the end of the seventeenth century. In 1688, the attorney-general made a visit to Paris, and urged upon the king the expediency of importing negroes from the West Indies as a remedy for the scarcity and dearness of labor. The king consented, but advised caution, on the ground that the rigor of the climate would make the venture a critical one.[1] A number of slaves were brought into the colony; but the system never flourished, the climate and other circumstances being hostile to it. Many of the colonists, especially at Detroit and other outlying posts, owned slaves of a remote Indian tribe, the Pawnees. The fact is remarkable, since it would be difficult to find another of the wild tribes of the continent capable of subjection to domestic servitude. The Pawnee slaves were captives taken in war and sold at low prices to the Canadians. Their market value was much impaired by their propensity to run off.

It is curious to observe the views of the Canadians taken at different times by different writers. La Hontan says, "They are vigorous, enterprising, and indefatigable, and need nothing but education. They are presumptuous and full of self-

---

[1] *Instruction au Sr. de Frontenac, 1689.* On Canadian slavery, see a long paper, *l'Esclavage en Canada*, published by the Historical Society of Montreal.

conceit, regard themselves as above all the nations of the earth, and, unfortunately, have not the veneration for their parents that they ought to have. The women are generally pretty; few of them are brunettes; many of them are discreet, and a good number are lazy. They are fond to the last degree of dress and show, and each tries to outdo the rest in the art of catching a husband."[1]

Fifty years later, the intendant Hocquart writes, "The Canadians are fond of distinctions and attentions, plume themselves on their courage, and are extremely sensitive to slights or the smallest corrections. They are self-interested, vindictive, prone to drunkenness, use a great deal of brandy, and pass for not being at all truthful. This portrait is true of many of them, particularly the country people: those of the towns are less vicious. They are all attached to religion, and criminals are rare. They are volatile, and think too well of themselves, which prevents their succeeding as they might in farming and trade. They have not the rude and rustic air of our French peasants. If they are put on their honor and governed with justice, they are tractable enough; but their natural disposition is indocile."[2]

The navigator Bougainville, in the last years of the French rule, describes the Canadian *habitant* as essentially superior to the French peasant, and adds, "He is loud, boastful, mendacious, obliging, civil, and honest; indefatigable in hunting, travelling, and bush-ranging, but lazy in tilling the soil."[3]

The Swedish botanist, Kalm, an excellent observer, was in Canada a few years before Bougainville, and sketches from life the following traits of Canadian manners. The language is that of the old English translation. "The men here (*at Montreal*) are extremely civil, and take their hats off to every person indifferently whom they meet in the streets. The women in general are handsome; they are well bred and virtuous, with an innocent and becoming freedom. They dress out very fine on Sundays, and though on the other days they do not take much pains with the other parts of their dress, yet they are very fond of adorning their heads, the hair of which is

[1]La Hontan, II. 81 (ed. 1709).
[2]*Mémoire de 1736.*
[3]*Mémoire de 1757,* printed in Margry, *Relations Inédites.*

always curled and powdered and ornamented with glittering bodkins and aigrettes. They are not averse to taking part in all the business of housekeeping, and I have with pleasure seen the daughters of the better sort of people, and of the governor (*of Montreal*) himself, not too finely dressed, and going into kitchens and cellars to look that every thing be done as it ought. What I have mentioned above of their dressing their heads too assiduously is the case with all the ladies throughout Canada. Their hair is always curled even when they are at home in a dirty jacket, and short coarse petticoat that does not reach to the middle of their legs. On those days when they pay or receive visits they dress so gayly that one is almost induced to think their parents possess the greatest honors in the state. They are no less attentive to have the newest fashions, and they laugh at each other when they are not dressed to each other's fancy. One of the first questions they propose to a stranger is, whether he is married; the next, how he likes the ladies of the country, and whether he thinks them handsomer than those of his own country; and the third, whether he will take one home with him. The behavior of the ladies seemed to me somewhat too free at Quebec, and of a more becoming modesty at Montreal. Those of Quebec are not very industrious. The young ladies, especially those of a higher rank, get up at seven and dress till nine, drinking their coffee at the same time. When they are dressed, they place themselves near a window that opens into the street, take up some needlework and sew a stitch now and then, but turn their eyes into the street most of the time. When a young fellow comes in, whether they are acquainted with him or not, they immediately lay aside their work, sit down by him, and begin to chat, laugh, joke, and invent *double-entendres*, and this is reckoned being very witty. In this manner they frequently pass the whole day, leaving their mothers to do the business of the house. They are likewise cheerful and content, and nobody can say that they want either wit or charms. Their fault is that they think too well of themselves. However, the daughters of people of all ranks without exception go to market and carry home what they have bought. The girls at Montreal are very much displeased that those at Quebec get husbands sooner than they. The reason of this is that many young gentlemen who come over from France with the ships are captivated by the ladies at Quebec and marry them; but, as these gentlemen seldom go up to Montreal, the girls there are not often so happy as those of the former place."[1]

Long before Kalm's visit, the Jesuit Charlevoix, a traveller and a man of the world, wrote thus of Quebec in a letter to the Duchesse de Lesdiguières: "There is a select little society here which wants nothing to make it agreeable. In the *salons* of the wives of the governor and of the intendant, one finds circles as brilliant as in other countries." These circles were formed partly of the principal inhabitants, but chiefly of military officers and government officials, with their families. Charlevoix continues, "Everybody does his part to make the time pass pleasantly, with games and parties of pleasure; drives and canoe excursions in summer, sleighing and skating in winter. There is a great deal of hunting and shooting, for many Canadian gentlemen are almost destitute of any other means of living at their ease. The news of the day amounts to very little indeed, as the country furnishes scarcely any, while that from Europe comes all at once. Science and the fine arts have their turn, and conversation does not fail. The Canadians breathe from their birth an air of liberty, which makes them very pleasant in the intercourse of life, and our language is nowhere more purely spoken. One finds here no rich persons whatever, and this is a great pity; for the Canadians like to get the credit of their money, and scarcely anybody amuses himself with hoarding it. They say it is very different with our neighbors the English, and one who knew the two colonies only by the way of living, acting, and speaking of the colonists would not hesitate to judge ours the more flourishing. In New England and the other British colonies, there reigns an opulence by which the people seem not to know how to profit; while in New France poverty is hidden under an air of ease which appears entirely natural. The English colonist keeps as much and spends as little as possible: the French colonist enjoys what he has got, and often makes a display of what he has not got. The one labors for his heirs: the other leaves them to get on as they can, like himself. I could push

---

[1]Kalm, *Travels into North America*, translated into English by John Reinold Forster (London, 1771), 56, 282, etc.

the comparison farther; but I must close here: the king's ship is about to sail, and the merchant vessels are getting ready to follow. In three days perhaps, not one will be left in the harbor."[1]

And now we, too, will leave Canada. Winter draws near, and the first patch of snow lies gleaming on the distant mountain of Cape Tourmente. The sun has set in chill autumnal beauty, and the sharp spires of fir-trees on the heights of Sillery stand stiff and black against the pure cold amber of the fading west. The ship sails in the morning; and, before the old towers of Rochelle rise in sight, there will be time to smoke many a pipe, and ponder what we have seen on the banks of the St. Lawrence.

[1] Charlevoix, *Journal Historique*, 80 (ed. 1744).

Chapter XXIV
1663–1763
CANADIAN ABSOLUTISM

Formation of Canadian Character • The Rival Colonies • England and France • New England • Characteristics of Race • Military Qualities • The Church • The English Conquest

---

NOT institutions alone, but geographical position, climate, and many other conditions unite to form the educational influences that, acting through successive generations, shape the character of nations and communities.

It is easy to see the nature of the education, past and present, which wrought on the Canadians and made them what they were. An ignorant population, sprung from a brave and active race, but trained to subjection and dependence through centuries of feudal and monarchical despotism, was planted in the wilderness by the hand of authority, and told to grow and flourish. Artificial stimulants were applied, but freedom was withheld. Perpetual intervention of government, regulations, restrictions, encouragements sometimes more mischievous than restrictions, a constant uncertainty what the authorities would do next, the fate of each man resting less with himself than with another, volition enfeebled, self-reliance paralyzed,—the condition, in short, of a child held always under the rule of a father, in the main well-meaning and kind, sometimes generous, sometimes neglectful, often capricious, and rarely very wise,—such were the influences under which Canada grew up. If she had prospered, it would have been sheer miracle. A man, to be a man, must feel that he holds his fate, in some good measure, in his own hands.

But this was not all. Against absolute authority there was a counter influence, rudely and wildly antagonistic. Canada was at the very portal of the great interior wilderness. The St. Lawrence and the Lakes were the highway to that domain of savage freedom; and thither the disfranchised, half-starved seignior, and the discouraged *habitant* who could find no market for his produce, naturally enough betook themselves. Their lesson of savagery was well learned, and for many a year a boundless license and a stiff-handed authority battled for the control of Canada. Nor, to the last, were church and state fairly masters of the field. The French rule was drawing towards its close when the intendant complained that though twenty-eight companies of regular troops were quartered in the colony, there were not soldiers enough to keep the people in order.[1] One cannot but remember that in a neighboring colony, far more populous, perfect order prevailed, with no other guardians than a few constables chosen by the people themselves.

Whence arose this difference, and other differences equally striking, between the rival colonies? It is easy to ascribe them to a difference of political and religious institutions; but the explanation does not cover the ground. The institutions of New England were utterly inapplicable to the population of New France, and the attempt to apply them would have wrought nothing but mischief. There are no political panaceas, except in the imagination of political quacks. To each degree and each variety of public development there are corresponding institutions, best answering the public needs; and what is meat to one is poison to another. Freedom is for those who are fit for it. The rest will lose it, or turn it to corruption. Church and state were right in exercising authority over a people which had not learned the first rudiments of self-government. Their fault was not that they exercised authority, but that they exercised too much of it, and, instead of weaning the child to go alone, kept him in perpetual leading-strings, making him, if possible, more and more dependent, and less and less fit for freedom.

In the building up of colonies, England succeeded and France failed. The cause lies chiefly in the vast advantage drawn by England from the historical training of her people in habits of reflection, forecast, industry, and self-reliance,— a training which enabled them to adopt and maintain an invigorating system of self-rule, totally inapplicable to their rivals.

The New England colonists were far less fugitives from oppression than voluntary exiles seeking the realization of an

[1] *Mémoire de 1736* (printed by the Historical Society of Quebec).

idea. They were neither peasants nor soldiers, but a substantial Puritan yeomanry, led by Puritan gentlemen and divines in thorough sympathy with them. They were neither sent out by the king, governed by him, nor helped by him. They grew up in utter neglect, and continued neglect was the only boon they asked. Till their increasing strength roused the jealousy of the Crown, they were virtually independent; a republic, but by no means a democracy. They chose their governor and all their rulers from among themselves, made their own government and paid for it, supported their own clergy, defended themselves, and educated themselves. Under the hard and repellent surface of New England society lay the true foundations of a stable freedom,—conscience, reflection, faith, patience, and public spirit. The cement of common interests, hopes, and duties compacted the whole people like a rock of conglomerate; while the people of New France remained in a state of political segregation, like a basket of pebbles held together by the enclosure that surrounds them.

It may be that the difference of historical antecedents would alone explain the difference of character between the rival colonies; but there are deeper causes, the influence of which went far to determine the antecedents themselves. The Germanic race, and especially the Anglo-Saxon branch of it, is peculiarly masculine, and, therefore, peculiarly fitted for self-government. It submits its action habitually to the guidance of reason, and has the judicial faculty of seeing both sides of a question. The French Celt is cast in a different mould. He sees the end distinctly, and reasons about it with an admirable clearness; but his own impulses and passions continually turn him away from it. Opposition excites him; he is impatient of delay, is impelled always to extremes, and does not readily sacrifice a present inclination to an ultimate good. He delights in abstractions and generalizations, cuts loose from unpleasing facts, and roams through an ocean of desires and theories.

While New England prospered and Canada did not prosper, the French system had at least one great advantage. It favored military efficiency. The Canadian population sprang in great part from soldiers, and was to the last systematically reinforced by disbanded soldiers. Its chief occupation was a continual training for forest war; it had little or nothing to lose, and little to do but fight and range the woods. This was not all. The Canadian government was essentially military. At its head was a soldier nobleman, often an old and able commander, and those beneath him caught his spirit and emulated his example. In spite of its political nothingness, in spite of poverty and hardship, and in spite even of trade, the upper stratum of Canadian society was animated by the pride and fire of that gallant *noblesse* which held war as its only worthy calling, and prized honor more than life. As for the *habitant*, the forest, lake, and river were his true school; and here, at least, he was an apt scholar. A skilful woodsman, a bold and adroit canoe-man, a willing fighter in time of need, often serving without pay, and receiving from government only his provisions and his canoe, he was more than ready at any time for any hardy enterprise; and in the forest warfare of skirmish and surprise there were few to match him. An absolute government used him at will, and experienced leaders guided his rugged valor to the best account.

The New England man was precisely the same material with that of which Cromwell formed his invincible "Ironsides;" but he had very little forest experience. His geographical position cut him off completely from the great wilderness of the interior. The sea was his field of action. Without the aid of government, and in spite of its restrictions, he built up a prosperous commerce, and enriched himself by distant fisheries, neglected by the rivals before whose doors they lay. He knew every ocean from Greenland to Cape Horn, and the whales of the north and of the south had no more dangerous foe. But he was too busy to fight without good cause, and when he turned his hand to soldiering it was only to meet some pressing need of the hour. The New England troops in the early wars were bands of raw fishermen and farmers, led by civilians decorated with military titles, and subject to the slow and uncertain action of legislative bodies. The officers had not learned to command, nor the men to obey. The remarkable exploit of the capture of Louisbourg, the strongest fortress in America, was the result of mere audacity and hardihood, backed by the rarest good luck.

One great fact stands out conspicuous in Canadian history,—the Church of Rome. More even than the royal power she shaped the character and the destinies of the colony. She was its nurse and almost its mother; and, wayward and headstrong as it was, it never broke the ties of faith that held it to her. It was these ties which, in the absence of political franchises, formed under the old régime the only vital coherence in the population. The royal government was transient; the church was permanent. The English conquest shattered the whole apparatus of civil administration at a blow, but it left her untouched. Governors, intendants, councils, and commandants, all were gone; the principal seigniors fled the colony; and a people who had never learned to control themselves or help themselves were suddenly left to their own devices. Confusion, if not anarchy, would have followed but for the parish priests, who in a character of double paternity, half spiritual and half temporal, became more than ever the guardians of order throughout Canada.

This English conquest was the grand crisis of Canadian history. It was the beginning of a new life. With England came Protestantism, and the Canadian church grew purer and better in the presence of an adverse faith. Material growth, an increased mental activity, an education real though fenced and guarded, a warm and genuine patriotism, all date from the peace of 1763. England imposed by the sword on reluctant Canada the boon of rational and ordered liberty. Through centuries of striving she had advanced from stage to stage of progress, deliberate and calm, never breaking with her past, but making each fresh gain the base of a new success, enlarging popular liberties while bating nothing of that height and force of individual development which is the brain and heart of civilization; and now, through a hard-earned victory, she taught the conquered colony to share the blessings she had won. A happier calamity never befell a people than the conquest of Canada by the British arms.

APPENDIX

I

A. La Tour and D'Aunay

[*Literatim.*]

Collection de M. Margry

L'an mil six cent quarante quatre le vint cinq jour d'octobre deux mois après la signification faits de l'arrest du conseil en date du 5 mai de la mesme année au Sieur de la Tour et à tous ceux qui estoient avec luy dans le fort de la Rivière St. Jean par la Montjoie le 15 8bre 1644 Mr Charles de Menou chevalier Seigneur d'Aunay Charnisay, gouverneur et Lieutenant général pour le Roy dans toute l'Etendue descostes d'Acadie pais de la Nouvelle France, veu le refus du d. de la Tour et l'obstination dans laquelle estoient ses gens, equipa de rechef deux de ses chaloupes pour tenter par les voies de douceur de ramener ces esprits rebelles à l'obeissance qu'ils doivent à sa Majeste pour lequel effet mon dit Sieur deputa un lieutenant de son vaisseau pour commander une d'icelles et son sergent pour l'autre auec commandement de sa part d'aller à la riviere St. Jean faire tout effort pour adroitement remonter quelqu'uns de ces esprits rebelles, les emboucher et leur donner lettres pour leur camarade signés de mon dit Sieur avec assurance d'abolition de leurs crimes et payements de leurs gages s'ils se rangeoient à leur devoir de veritables sujets, leur devant montrer comme les arrets du conseil obligeoient mon dit Sieur à pareils traitemens. Ce qu'ayant fidellement executé ils ne receurent pour toute reponse qu'injures et imprecations de ces malheureux et huit jours après la femme du dit Sieur de la Tour arrivant à la riviere de St. Jean conduite par un vaisseau anglois obligea son mary d'aller à Boston vers les Anglois se declarer de leur religion, comme elle venoit de faire et leur demander un ministre pour son habitation et par là obliger tout le corps des Anglois à les maintenir dans leurs biens avec offre qu'ils partageroient toute la coste d'Acadie après qu'ils s'en seroient rendus maistres: Et le 28 de Janvier 1645 la dite dame parla si insolemment aux réverends peres Recollects qui pour lors estoient dans son habitation que fai-

sant la Démoniaque et mepris scandaleux de la religion Catholique, apostolique et Romaine son mary présent, qui
adhéroit à toutes ses actions, ils furent contraints de sortir et
chercher moyen de se retirer quoyque dans ces contrées
l'Hiver soit très rigoureux, ce que le dit Sieur de la Tour et sa
femme leur octroierent avec dérision et injures leur donnant
pour cet effet une vieille pinasse qui couloid quasy bas d'eau
avec deux bariques de bled d'Inde pour toutes vitailles, ce qui
sera justifié par une attestation de ceux mesmes qui estoient
dans le service du Sr de la Tour et sa femme et une lettre d'un
des susdits pères Recollects superieur dans le d. lieu et huit
ou neuf des gens du d. Sr de la Tour counaissant le deplorable
estat de cette habitation ed la formelle rebellion du S^r de la
Tour sa femme et du reste de leurs camarades contre le devoir
qu'ils doivent à dieu et au Roy se retirérent semblablement et
accompagnerent les dits reverends pères Recollects, lesquels
avec beaucoup de perils se vinrent rendre dans le Port Royal
demeure ordinaire du Sr. d'Aunay, lequel après avoir esté
imbu de tout ce que dessus les receut tous humainement en-
voiant les deux religieux Recollects dans la maison des Reverends peres Capucins missionaires qui les receurent avec tant
d'affection et les firent tant de charité et saints offices qu'ils en
demeurent tous confus aussy bien que les huid personnes qui
les accompagnoient voyant le favorable accueil que leur fit
mon dit Sieur qui ne se contenta pas de les loger et nourrir
comme les siens propres mais les paya leurs gages que le dit
La Tour de tant d'années qu'ils l'avoient servy leur avoid re-
fusé. Ce qui est prouvé par une reconnoissance de ces mesmes
personnes pour les sommes qui leur ont esté mises entre les
mains, signée de leurs mains. Ce régalement ayant esté donné
comme dessus est dit, Mon dit sieur s'informant plus parti-
culierement de l'estat au quel estoient ces miserables esprits,
l'obstination du reste de ceux qui estoient demeurez avec le
dit la Tour, et qu'il estoit party pour aller vers les Anglois
dans Boston pour tascher de renvoyer comme jà cy dessus est
dit le traitté de paix fait avec les dits Anglois et le sieur Marie
confident de Mon d. Sieur D'Aunay et engager par mesme
moyen quelque marchand pour amener quelques vitailles dans
la riviere de Saint Jean dans la quelle il n'avoit laissé que quarante cinq personnes, ce que mon dit sieur considerant fit as-

semblées de tous les officiers qui pour lors estoient auprès de sa personne, où il fut conclud de prendre cette occasion aux cheveux. Et quoyque ne le peut quasy permettre et qu'il falloit risquer pour une affaire de telle consequence, ce qui obligea mon dit sieur de monter le plus grand de ses navires du port de trois cents tonneaux, equipé en guerre, pour se mettre en garde à l'entrée de la Rivière St. Jean afin de surprendre le dit La Tour avec une partie de son monde, qui pensoit à la faveur de la rigueur de l'Hiver faire son voyage sans qu'il en fust aucune nouvelle, ce que mon dit sieur ayant executé et pris rade à une lieue du fort de la Rivière St. Jean assisté d'un religieux Capucin missionnaire et des deux susdits Recollects, envoya de rechef vers la dite femme La Tour et tous ceux qui pour lors estoient avec elle le Révérend Père André Recollect par une de ses chaloupes, le quel se promettoit d'attirer peut-estre quelquuns à resipiscence, leur faisant connoitre le bon accueil que luy et leurs camarades avoient receu de mon dit Sieur, ce qui ne reussit non plus que les autres fois du passé. Deux mois s'écoulèrent dans semblable attente, après quoy mon dit Sieur prid resolution de battre le fer pendant qu'il estoit chaud, voyant un de ses navires aussy equipé en guerre qui l'estoit venu trouver du Port Royal selon qu'il l'avoit ainsy ordonné accompagné d'une pinasse aussi chargée de monde et après avoir reallié de toutes ses Habitations les personnes capables de porter mousquets, il fit descendre une bonne partie de ses hommes à terre ed mettre deux pièces de canon avec ordre de les mettre promptement en batterie le plus proche du fort de la Rivière de St. Jean qu'ils pourroient avec assurance qu'aussytost qu'ils avoient effectué son commandement ils approcheroient ce navire à la portée du pistolet, afin que sans donner jour aux assiegés de se reconnoistre on pust faire un tonnerre et par mer et par terre, donner à mesme temps qu'il y auroit breche faite, pendant l'exécution de ces ordres un petit navire Anglois se présenta pour entrer dans la dite rivière chargé de vitailles et munitions de guerre, dans lequel il y avoit un des domestiques du d. La Tour qui estoit chargé de Lettres de son maistre pour la ditte dame sa femme qui l'assuroit dans un mois ou deux venir la trouver en meilleur estat et posture qu'il pourroit. Le dit domestique avoit outre plus une lettre du gouverneur de la grande baye des anglois addressante à la dite dame par laquelle il l'exhortoit à faire son profit des instructions qu'elle avoit recues pendant sa residence. Le dit navire fut pris et arresté par mon dit Sieur et l'equipage renvoyé au lieu d'où il estoit party, avec une chaloupe que mon dit sieur leur donna pour cet effet, lequel estant une fois de retour fit rapport à Messieurs les magistrats du gouvernement des Anglois que leur navire avoid esté pris en negotiant avec les francois et que le traité de paix quils avoient fait avec le Sieur Marie nestoit gardé avec mil autres plaintes dont ils vouloient couvrir le sujet de leur voyage, ce qui obligea ces Messieurs de deputer un exprès vers mon dit Sieur pour luy demander raison du bien pris par luy sur un de leurs marchands contre les articles de paix que le Sieur Marie, confident, leur avoit laissé signer de sa part—À quoy mon dit Sieur leur fit response et déclara à leur député la fourbe de leur dit marchand, le quel par un désir de lucre abusoit de leur commission et au lieu d'aller négotiant dans les Habitations des véritables François, Il alloit rompant par luy mesmes ce traité de paix passé entre ses magistrats et le Sieur Marie, confident, portant ainsi frauduleusement des munitions de vivres et de guerre pour maintenir des rebelles dans leur desobeissance et contre le devoir qu'il doivent à leur prince naturel. Toutes les quelles raisons payerent entièrement et le député et Messieurs les Magistrats de la Grande Baie le susdit député estant party et mon dit Sieur D'Aunay ayant recue nouvelle que la batterie estoit en estat et ses gens qui estoient à terre disposés à faire ce quil leur ordonneroit, se resolut de haster le pas et avant que le d. Sieur De la Tour en eust le vent faire tout son effort, ce qui luy arriva si Heureusement qu'après avoir encore une fois sommé ces malheureux, lesquels lui envoierent pour response une vollée de canon à balle, aborant le pavillon rouge sur leurs bastions avec mil injures et blasphemes et avoir fait battre le dit fort de la Rivière de St Jean tant par terre que par son grand navire, qu'il avoit emmené à portée de pistolet d'iceluy ce qui rasa une partie de leur parapets il s'en rendit maistre par un assaut général qu'il fit donner sur le soir de la mesme Journée le Lendemain Pasques ce qui fut accompagné d'une si grande benediction de Dieu, que quoyque la perte des Hommes que mon dit sieur a fait soit grande elle eut esté encore plus sanglante. Une partie des assiegéz furent tuez dans la chaleur du combat et l'autre fait prisonniers entre autres la femme du dit La Tour, son fils et sa fille de Chambre et une autre femme qui est tout cequ'il y avoit dans le dit fort de sexe feminin toutes lesquelles ne recurent aucun tort ny à leur Honneur ny à leurs personnes. Une partie des prisonniers recut grace de mon dit Sieur et le reste des plus seditieux fut pendu et etranglé pour servir de memoire et d'exemple, à la postérité d'une si obstinée rébellion ce qui est prouvé par l'attestation qu'en ont rendue et signée une bonne partie de ceux qui ont recue la vie et pareille gratification. Le Lendemain 18 Avril 1645 mon dit sieur fit inhumer tous les morts tant de part que d'autre avec la distinction pour tant requise en telle rencontre du party faisant prier Dieu et faire un service solemnel à tous ceux que deux révérends pères Capucins missionnaires qui avoient esté presens à tout jugement estre deu, ce qui est prouvé aussi bien que tout ce que dessus par une attestation authentique des mesmes susd. révérends pères Capucins missionnaires après quoy mon dit Sieur fit travailler pour combler les travaux de dehors faits par les assiegeans et reparer ceux de la place mettre ordre aux deffauts d'icelle par luy reconnus et faire inventaire de tout ce qui se trouva de reste dans icelle après le pillage fait par les compagnons que mon dit sieur leur avoit donné et faire ensuite renvituailler le dit lieu de toutes choses necessaires pour la conservation d'iceluy et enfin poser une personne capable et fidele pour le service du Roi ce que dura l'espace de trois semaines ou un mois pendant le quel la femme du dit La Tour qui estoit dans le Commencement en Liberté fut resserrée par une Lettre qu'on trouva qu'elle ecrivoit à son mary et pratique qu'elle faisoit de lui faire tenir par le moyen des Sauvages afin de la pouvoir par la première occasion envoyer en France à nos Seigneurs du Conseil en bonne sauve garde, ce qui l'alarma de telle sorte que de depit et de rage elle tomba malade et nonobstant tous les bons traitemens et Charités que L'on exerça en son endroit mourut le 15 Juin après avoir abjuré publiquement dans la chapelle du mesme fort L'Heresie qu'elle avoit professée parmy les Anglois àla grande Baye. Ce qui est justifié par l'attestation désjà cy dessus alleguée des deux réverends pères Capucins Missionaires.

Le présent procés verbal a esté fait par nous, André Certain prevost et garde du Scel Royal de La Coste d'Acadie pays de la Nouvelle france à la requeste de Monsieur d'Aunay Charnisay Gouverneur et Lieutenant general pour le Roy en toute l'Etendue de la Coste d'Acadie pays de la Nouvelle France le 10e jour de may 1645 et rendu et dès le mesme jour et an que dessus pour lui servir et valoir aussi que de raison. Le tout en présence de tesmoins et principaux chefs des Francois qui sont dans la dite coste signé Longvilliers Poincy, Bernard Marot, Dubreuil Vismes, Javille, Jean Laurent, Henry Dansmartin, Barthelemy Aubert, Leclerc et Certain prevost et Garde du Sceau Royal.

II

B. *The Hermitage of Caen*

MÉMOIRE POUR FAIRE CONNOISTRE L'ESPRIT ET LA CON-
DUITE DE LA COMPAGNIE ESTABLIE EN LA VILLE DE CAEN,
APPELÉE L'HERMITAGE

(Extrait.)[1] *Bibliothèque Nationale*

C'est en ce fameux Hermitage que le dit feu Sieur de Bernières a eslevé plusieurs jeunes gens auxquels il enseignoit une
espèce d'oraison sublime et transcendante que l'on appelle
l'oraison purement passive, parceque l'esprit n'y agit point,
mais reçoit seulement la divine opération; c'est cette espèce
d'oraison qui est la source de tant de visions et de révélations,
dont l'Hermitage est si fécond; et après qu'il leur avoit subti-
lizé et presque fait évaporer l'esprit par cette oraison rafinée,
il les rendoit capables de reconnoistre les Jansenistes les plus
cachéz; en sorte que quelques uns de ces disciples ont dit
qu'ils le connoissoient au flairer, comme les chiens font leur
gibier, pour ensuite leur faire la chasse, néantmoins le dit
Sieur de Bernières disoit qu'il n'avoit pas l'odorat si subtil,
mais que la marque à laquelle il connoissoit les Jansénistes
estoit quand on improuvoit sa conduite ou que l'on estoit
opposé aux Jésuites . . . . Au commencement les personnes
de cette compagnie ne se mesloient que de l'assistance des
pauvres, mais depuis que le feu Sieur de Bernières qui estoit
un simple laïque, qui n'avoit point d'estude, s'en estant rendu
le maistre, il persuada a ceux qui en sont qu'elle n'estoit pas
seulement establie pour prendre soin des pauvres, mais de
toutes les autres bonnes œuvres, publiques ou particulières,
qui regardent la Piété et la Religion et que Dieu les avoit
suscitez, principalement pour suppléér aux défauts et négli-
gences des Prélats, des Pasteurs, des Magistrats, des Juges et
autres Supérieurs Ecclésiastiques et Politiques qui faute de
s'appliquer assez aux devoirs de leurs charges, obmettent dans
les occasions beaucoup de bien qu'ils pourroient procurer, et

---

[1] This *mémoire* forms 116 pages in the copy in my possession.

négligent de résister à beaucoup de maux, d'abus et d'erreurs qu'ils pourroient empêcher; et que pour remédier à ces manquements, il estoit expédient que Dieu suscitat plusieurs gens de bien de toutes sortes de conditions qui s'unissent ensemble pour travailler à l'avancement du bien qui se peut faire en chaque profession, et pour extirper les erreurs, les abus et les vices qui s'y glissent souvent, par la négligence ou connivence mesme de ceux qui sont le plus obligez par leur ministère d'y donner ordre.

Et c'est dans cette pensée que ces messieurs croyent avoir droit à se mesler de toutes choses, de s'ingérer de toutes les actions un peu éclatantes qui regardent la Religion, de s'ingérer en censeurs publics, pour corriger et controller tout ce qui leur deplaist, d'entrer et de pénétrer dans les secrets des maisons et des familles particulières, comme aussi dans la conduite des communautez Religieuses pour y gouverner toutes choses à leur gré; et bien que ces messieurs soient fort ignorans, bien qu'ils n'ayent aucune experience des affaires et qu'ils passent dans le jugement de tous ceux qui les connoissent pour personnes qui n'ont qu'un Zèle impetueux et violent, sans lumières et sans discrétion, neantmoins ils présument avoir assez de capacité pour réformer la vie, les mœurs, les sentimens et la doctrine de tous les autres. Et ce qu'il y a de plus fascheux et de plus dangereux en cela, c'est que si on ne défère aveuglément à tous leurs sentimens, si on improuve leur conduite et si l'on oppose la moindre résistance à leurs entreprises, quoyqu'injustes et violentes, ils unissent toutes leurs forces pour les faire réussir et pour cet effet ils réclament les secours de tous ceux qui leur sont unis, à Paris, à Rouen et ailleurs, pour décrier, pour diffamer et pour perdre ceux qui leur résistent et qui veulent s'opposer au cours de leurs violences et de leurs injustice, de sorte qu'on peut assurer avec vérité que cette compagnie a dégénéré en une cabale et en une faction dangereuse et pernicieuse, tant à l'Eglise qu'à la Patrie, estant certain que depuis peu d'années ils ont excité beaucoup de troubles et de divisions dans toute la ville de Caen, et notamment dans le clergé et mesme en plusieurs autres lieux de la Basse-Normandie ainsi qu'il paroistra par les articles suivants de ce mémoire.

Il est arrivé quelques fois qu'ayant eu de faux avis que

des maris maltroitoient leurs femmes ou que des femmes n'estoient pas fidèles à leurs maris ou que des filles ne se gouvernoient pas bien, ils se sont ingérez sur le rapport qui en estoit fait en leur assemblée de chercher les moyens de remédier à ces maux, et ils en ont choisi de si impertinents et de si indiscrets que cela a esté capable de causer bien du désordre et de la division dans les familles et dans toute la ville; car souvent voulant empescher une légère faute, on en fait naistre de grands scandales, lorsque l'on agit par emportement plustost que par prudence.

Ce n'est pas seulement dans les familles particulières qu'ils s'introduisent pour en fureter les secrets, pour en connoitre les défauts et pour en usurper la direction et le gouvernement, mais encore dans les maisons Religieuses, dont les unes se sont soumises à leur domination, comme les Ursulines de Caen, les moynes de l'Abbaye d'Ardenne de l'ordre de Premontré, proche de cette ville et depuis peu les filles de Sainte-Marie; et les autres leur ayant tesmoigné quelque résistance, ils ont employé toute leur industrie pour en venir à bout; et où l'artifice a manqué, ils y ont adjouté les violences et les menaces. . . . .

Mais il ne faut point chercher de marques plus visibles de la persévérance, pour mieux dire du progrès de ces faux ermites dans leurs emportemens que ce qu'ont fait cet hiver passé cinq jeunes hommes nourris en l'Hermitage et élevés sous la direction et discipline du feu Sieur de Bernières. On leur avoit si bien imprimé dans l'esprit que tout estoit rempli de Jansénistes dans la ville de Caen, et que les curez en estoient les fauteurs et protecteurs, qu'un d'entre eux s'imagina que Dieu l'inspiroit fortement advertir le peuple de Caen que les curez estoient des fauteurs d'Hérétiques et par conséquent des excomuniez; et ayant persuadé à ses compagnons d'annoncer publiquement à toute la ville ce crime prétendu des Curez d'une manière qui touchast le peuple et qui fut capable de l'exciter contre ces Pasteurs, ils résolurent de faire cette publication le mercredi quatrième du mois de Febvrier dernier, et jugèrent que pour se disposer à exécuter dignement ce que Dieu leur avoit inspiré, il falloit faire ensemble une communion extraordinaire, immédiatement avant que de l'entreprendre. Ils assistèrent donc pour cet effet et dans la pa-

roisse de Saint-Ouen à la messe d'un prestre qu'on dit estre
de leur cabale, et communièrent tous cinq de sa main; et après
leur communion, le plus zélé mit bas son pourpoint et le
laissa avec son chapeau dans l'Eglise; et accompagné des
quatre autres qui le suivoient sans chapeaux, sans colets et le
pourpoint deboutonné, non-obstant la rigueur extrème du
froid; ils marchèrent en cet équipage par toute la ville, annon-
çant à haute voix que les curez de Caen à l'exception de deux
qu'ils nommoient étoient fauteurs de Jansénistes et excom-
muniez, parce qu'ils avoient signé un acte devant l'official de
Caen, où ils attestent qu'ils ne connoissent point de Jansenistes dans la dite ville et répétoient cet advertissement de dix
pas en dix pas, ce qui emeut toute la ville et attira à leur suite
une grande multitude de populace qui se persuadant que ces
gens estoient envoyés de Dieu pour leur donner cet advertissement, témoignoient desja de l'emotion contre les curez.
Mais les magistrats qui estoient alors au siège en ayant esté
advertis, ils envoyèrent leurs huissiers pour les arrester et les
emmener, et ayant esté interrogez par le juge sur le sujet d'une
action si extraordinaire, ils respondirent hardiment qu'ils l'a-
voient entreprise pour le service de Dieu et qu'ils estoient
prests de souffrir la mort pour soustenir la vérité de ce qu'ils
annonçoient, qu'ils avoient connoissance certaine qu'il y avoit
grand nombre de Jansénistes en la ville de Caen, et que les
curez s'en estoient declarez les fauteurs, par la déclaration
qu'ils avoient donnée qu'ils n'en connoissoient point; ensuitte
de quoy quatre d'entre eux furent renvoyez en prison et le
cinquième fut mis entre les mains de ses parents sur une attestation que donnèrent les médecins qu'il estoit hypocon-
driaque et peu de jours après le lieutenant criminel ayant in-
struit le procez, les quatre prisonniers furent condamnez à
cent livres d'amende; il leur fut deffendu et à tous autres de
s'assembler ni d'exciter aucun scandale, il fut ordonné qu'ils
seroient mis entre les mains de leur parents pour s'en
charger et en faire bonne et seure garde, avec deffense de les
laisser entrer dans la ville et aux fauxbourgs, sur peines au
cas appartenantes. . . .

Car de quelles entreprises ne sont pas capables des personnes d'esprit faible et d'humeur atrabilaire que d'ailleurs on
a desséchées par des jeûnes, des veilles et d'autres austéritez

continuelles et par des méditations de trois ou quatre heures par jour, lorsque l'on ne les entretient presque d'autre chose, si non que leur Religion et l'Eglise sont en un très grand danger de se perdre, par la faction et la conspiration des Jansénistes lesquels on leur représente dans les livres, dans les sermons et dans les conférences, comme des gens qui veulent renverser les fondements de la Religion et de la Piété Chrestienne, qui veulent détruire le mystère de l'Incarnation, qui ne croyent point à la Transubstantation ni l'Invocation des Saints, ne les Indulgences, qui veulent abolir le sacrifice de la messe et le sacrement de la Pénitence, qui combatent la dévotion et la culte de la Sainte-Vierge, qui nient le franc arbitre et qui substituent en sa place le destin et la fatalité des Turcs, et enfin qui machinent la ruine de l'authorité des Souverains Pontifes. Qu'y a-t-il de plus aisé que d'animer les esprits imbéciles d'eux mesmes et prévenus de ces fausses imaginations contre des Evesques, des Docteurs, des Curez, et contre d'autres personnes très vertueuses et très catholiques, lorsqu'on leur fait croire que toutes ces personnes conspirent à establir une hérésie abominable!

C. Laval and Argenson

LETTRE DE L'EVESQUE DE PETRÉE A M. D'ARGENSON, FRÈRE DU GOUVERNEUR

(Extrait.) Papiers d'Argenson

Jai reçeu dans mon entrée dans le pays de Monsieur votre frère toutes les marques d'une bienveillance extraordinaire; iay fait mon possible pour la recongnoistre et luy ay rendu tous les respects que je dois à une personne de sa vertu et de son mérite joint à la qualité qu'il porte; comme son plus véritable amy et fidelle serviteur iay cru estre obligé de luy donner un advis important pour le bien de l'Eglise et qui luy devoit estre utile s'il l'eust pris dans la mesme disposition que ie suis asseuré que vous l'auries reçeu; cestoit seul à seul à cœur ouvert avec marques assez évidentes que ce que ie luy disois estoit vray veu qu'il estoit fondé sur des sentimens que i'avois veu

moy mesme paroistre en diverses assemblées publiques; cependant il ne fist que trop congnoistre qu'il ne trouvoit auqunnement bon que ie luy donnaisses cet advertissement et
me voullut faire embrasser le party de ceux qui avaient tout
subject de se plaindre de son procédé envers eux, mais que je
ne pretendois auqunnement justifier n'en ayant auqunne
plainte de leur part pour luy faire et d'ailleurs estans asses
desintéressés; vous pouvez bien iuger quels sont ceux dont ie
veux parler sans vous les nommer puisque vous mesme qui
avez une affection sincère et bien réglée pour ces dignes ouvriers évangéliques m'avez avoué que vous aviez doulleur de
le voir partir dans les sentiments où il estoit à leur esgard sans
beaucoup de fondement du moins suffisamment recongneu
pour lors; ce que ie luy dis avoir sceu de vous pour ne rien
omettre de ce que je me persuadois qui estoit capable de lui
faire avouer une vérité qui nestoit que trop apparente, ce qui
devoit un peu le calmer son esprit sembla l'aigrir et se fascha
de ce que vous m'aviez faict de cette ouverture, ie ne scais
depuis ce qu'il a pensé de moy, mais il semble que je luy sois
suspect et qu'il aye crû que i'embrasse la cause de ces bons
serviteurs de Dieu à son preiudice, mais ie puis bien asseurer
qu'ils n'ont pour luy que des sentimens de respect et que la
plus forte passion que iaye est de le voir dans une parfaite
union et intelligence avec eux.

QUEBEC CE 20 OCTOBRE 1659

LETTRE DE M. D'ARGENSON, 1660

(Extrait.) Papiers d'Argenson

Monsieur de Petrée a une telle adherence à ses sentiments
et un zèle qui le porte souvent hors du droict de sa charge
qu'il ne faict aucune difficulté d'empieter sur le pouvoir des
aultres et avec tant de chaleur qu'il n'écoute personne. Il en-
leva ces jours derniers une fille servente d'un habitant d'icy, et
la mit de son autorité dans les Hursulines sur le seul prétexte
qu'il vouloit la faire instruire, et par là il priva cet habitant du
service qu'il prétendoit de sa servente qui luy avoit faict beaucoup de dépense a amener de France. Cet habitant est M.
Denis lequel ne cognoissant pas qui l'avoit soubstret me présenta requeste pour l'avoir Je gardé [*sic*] la requeste sans la

répondre trois jours pour empescher l'éclat de cette affaire. Le R. P. Lalement avec lequel j'en communiqué et lequel blasma fort le procedé de M.ᵉ de Petrée s'employa de tout son pouvoir pour la faire rendre sans bruit et n'y gaigna rien, si bien que je fus obligé de repondre la requeste et de permettre à cet habitant de reprendre sa servente où il la trouveroit, et si je n'eusse insinué soubs main d'accommoder cette affaire et que l'habitant a qui on refusa de la rendre l'eut poursuivi en justice j'eusse esté obligé de la luy rendre et de pousser tout avec beaucoup de scandal et cela (*à cause de*) la volonté de M.ᵉ de Petrée qui dict *qu'un evesque peult ce qu'il veult, et ne menace que dexcommunication.*

Lettre de M. d'Argenson

(*Extraits.*) *Papiers d'Argenson*

Kebec le 7 Juillet, 1660

M.ᵉ de Petrée a faist naistre cette contestation et ie puis dire auec verité que son zêle en plusieurs rencontres approche fort d'une grande atache à son sentiment et d'empietement sur la charge des aultres comme vous le verrez par un billet icy joint. . . . De toutes ces contestations que j'ay eu auec M.ᵉ de Petrée j'ay tousjours faist le R. P. Lalemand médiateur; c'est une personne d'un si grand merite et d'un sens si achevé que ie pense qu'on ne peult rien y adjouter; il seroit bien à souhaiter que touts ceux de sa maison suivissent ses sentiments; ils ne se mesleroient pas de censurer plusieurs choses comme ils font et laisseroient le gouvernement des affaires a ceux que Dieu a ordonné pour cela.

D. *Péronne Dumesnil*

Le Sieur Gaudais du Pont à Monseigneur de Colbert. 1664

(*Extrait.*) *Archives de la Marine*

Quelque 7 ou 8 jours après l'etablissement du Conseil Souverain, en consequence des lettres patentes de Sa majesté, le

Procureur Général du dit Conseil jugeant qu'il était de sa charge de reprendre les (*papiers*) de cette plainte pour ne pas laisser un tel attentat impuni, fit sa requête verbale au dit Conseil tendante à ce qu'il lui fut donné commission pour informer contre le dit Sieur Du Mesnil; et que si le dit Sieur Du Mesnil, avait avis de la dite commission qu'il ne manquerait pas de détourner ces dits papiers, demandant qu'il lui fut permis de saisir et de sequestrer ici et apposer le sceau au coffre ou armoire en laquelle se trouveraient les dits papiers, et pour ce faire qu'il plut au dit Conseil nommer tel Commissaire qu'il jugerait à propos. Le dit Conseil entérinant la requête du dit Procureur Général, nomma le Sieur de Villeray, pour, en la presence du dit Procureur Général et assistance de son Greffier vaquer à la dite information, &c.

Et d'autant que le dit Sieur Du Mesnil était estimé homme violent et qu'il pourrait faire quelque boutade, pour donner main forte à la justice, Mr. le Gouverneur fut prié par les dits Conseillers de faire escorter le dit Sieur Commissaire par quelque nombre de soldats.

Le dit Sieur de Villeray assisté, comme dit est pour l'execution de sa commission, se transporta au logis du dit Sieur Du Mesnil, laissant à quartier l'escorte de soldats pour s'en servir en cas de besoin.

Le dit Sieur Du Mesnil ne trompa pas l'opinion que l'on avait eue de sa violence, fit grand bruit, cria aux voleurs, voulant emouvoir son voisinage, outrageant d'injures les dits Sieurs de Villeray et Procureur Général au grand mépris de l'autorité du Conseil, refusant même de le reconnaître. Ce qui n'empêcha pas le dit Sieur de Villeray d'exécuter sa commission de saisir les papiers du dit Sieur Du Mesnil, qui en donna la clef, y fit apposer le sceau et icelui sequestrer es mains d'un voisin du dit Sieur Du Mesnil et de son consentement.

Le lendemain le dit Sieur de Villeray rapporta son procès verbal au dit conseil, attesté du dit Procureur Général, et signé du Greffier du dit Conseil et sur les injures, violences et irrévérences y contenues tant contre le dit Sieur Commissaire que l'autorité du Conseil, fit decerner un décret de prise de corps contre le dit Sieur Du Mesnil, dont j'empêchai l'exécution.

Memoire de Dumesnil concernant les affaires du Canada

(Extrait.) Archives de la Marine

10 Septembre, 1671

Les dits Sieurs de Mésy, Gouverneur, de Pétrée, Evêque, et Dupont Gaudais, arrivés au dit Quebec le 16ᵉ jour de Septembre 1663, furent le lendemain salués et visités par le dit Du Mesnil précédent juge, lequel par devoir et civilité leur dit par forme d'avis que par des arrêts du conseil du Roi, qu'il leur représenta en date du 27 Mars 1647 et 13 Mai 1659 tous les commis et receveurs des dits deniers publics étaient exclus de toutes charges publiques, jusqu'à ce qu'ils eussent rendu et assuré leurs comptes, et le nommé Villeray chassé du conseil de la traite pour y avoir entré par voies et moyens illicites; et ordonné qu'il viendrait en France pour le purger de ses crimes; ce qu'il n'a pas fait, et pour nommer les autres commis, receveurs, auxquels il aurait commencé à faire le procès pendant qu'il était juge.

Nonobstant lesquels dires, actes et arrêts représentés, les dits Sieurs de Mésy, Evêque de Pétrée, et Dupont Gaudais, n'ont délaissé de prendre et admettre avec eux au dit Conseil Souverain les dits comptables; lesquels par ce moyen se prétendent à couvert et exempts de rendre les dits comptes. Le dit établissement de conseil fait et arrêté par les dits Commissaires le 18 du mois de Septembre, deux jours après leur arrivée; et pour Procureur Général prennent un nommé Jean Bourdon, boulanger et cannonier au fort et aussi comptable de 8 à 900,000 livres, comme il sera montré et qu'il a prêté son nom.

Le 20 du mois de Septembre, deux jours après l'établissement du dit conseil, les dits Villeray soi-disant conseiller et commissaire et Bourdon, Procureur Général accompagnés de deux sergents, d'un serrurier et de dix soldats du fort, bien armés vont en la maison du dit Du Mesnil, Intendant et Contrôleur Général, et peu auparavant leur juge souverain, sur les 7 a 8 heures du soir pour piller sa maison; ce qu'ils firent; ayant fait rompre la porte de son cabinet, ses armoires et un coffret; pris et emporté ce qu'ils ont trouvé dedans et notamment tous ses papiers dans lesquels étaient leurs procès presque faits, et les preuves de leurs péculats, concussions et malversations, sans aucun inventaire ni forme de justice, étant le dit Du Mesnil, lors des dites violences, tenu et arrêté sur un siége et rudement traité par les soldats jusques à l'empêcher d'appeler du secours et des témoins pour voir ce qui se passait en sa maison et comme il était lié et arrêté.

Cette action violente ainsi faite et le dit Du Mesnil se voyant délivré du massacre de sa personne dont il était menacé, et d'être assassiné comme son fils s'en va trouver le dit Sieur Dupont Gaudais prenant qualité d'Intendant pour lui en faire plainte, qu'il ne voulut entendre, disant que c'était de son ordonnance et du dit Conseil que la dite action et prise de papiers avait été faite; à quoi le dit Du Mesnil repartit qu'il s'en plaindrait au Roi, et lui en demanderait justice, ce qui obligea le dit Dupont Gaudais de dire au dit Du Mesnil qu'il donnât sa requête; ce qui fut fait, et sur laquelle fut par le dit Conseil ordonné le 22 du dit mois de Septembre, deux jours après cette violence que le dit Dupont Gaudais serait commissaire pour vérifier les faits d'icelle requête; ce que poursuivant le dit Du Mesnil, il eut ordre verbal du dit Sr. Gaudais de mettre au Greffe ses causes et moyens de récusation, de nullité de prise à partie et de demandes; ce que le dit Du Mesnil fit comme appert par l'acte signé du Greffier du dit Conseil du 28 du dit mois de Septembre sur lesquelles récusations, prises à partie et demandes, le dit Conseil n'a rien voulu ordonner, comme appert par autre acte du dit Greffier du 21 Octobre ensuivant, jour ordonné pour l'embarquement et départ des vaisseaux du dit Quebec pour retourner en France.

Mais au lieu de statuer et ordonner sur les faits, moyens et conclusions du dit Du Mesnil, le dit Conseil sans plainte, sans partie et sans information a dressé emprisonnement du dit Du Mesnil et caché le décret sans le mettre au Greffe dans l'intention de le faire paraître et executer du même temps que le dit Du Mesnil se voudrait embarquer pour revenir en France, afin qu'il n'eût pas le temps de donner avis des violences qu'on lui faisait: de quoi averti il s'embarqua quelques jours auparavant les autres et fut reçu par le Capitaine Gardeur dans son navire, nonobstant les défenses qui lui en avaient été faites par le dit nouveau Conseil et que six pièces de canon de la plate forme d'en bas fussent pointées contre son navire pour le faire obéir à leurs ordonnances.

Tous ces massacres, assassins et pillages n'ont été faits au dit Du Mesnil, Intendant, par les dits comptables, ordonnateurs et preneurs de bien public et leurs parents et alliés que pour tâcher à couvrir et s'exempter de compter, payer et rendre ce qu'ils ont pillé, savoir. . . . .

E. *Laval and Mésy*

ORDRE DE M.^R DE MÉSY DE FAIRE SOMMATION A L'EVÊQUE DE PÉTRÉE

(Extrait.) Registre du Conseil Supérieur

13 FEVRIER, 1664

Le Sieur d'Angoville, Major de la Garnison entretenue par le Roi dans le Fort de St Louis à Québec pays de la Nouvelle France, est commandé par nous Sieur de Mésy, Lieutenant Général et Gouverneur pour Sa Majesté dans toute l'étendue du dit pays, aller dire et avertir Monsieur l'Evêque de Pétrée étant présentement dans la chambre qui servait ci-devant aux Assemblées du Conseil au dit pays, que les Sieurs nommés pour Conseillers et le Sieur Bourdon pour Procureur du Roi au dit conseil à la persuasion du dit Sieur de Pétrée qui les connaissait entièrement ses créatures s'étant voulu rendre les maîtres declarés et portés en diverses manières dans le dit Conseil contre les Intérêts du Roi et du public pour appuyer et autoriser les intérêts d'autrui en particulier, il leur a été commandé par notre ordre pour la conservation des intérêts du Roi en ce pays, de s'absenter du dit Conseil jusqu'à ce que à notre diligence par le retour des premiers vaisseaux qui viendront, Sa Majesté ait été informée de leur conduite, et qu'ils se soient justifiés des cabales qu'ils ont formées, fomentées et entretenues contre leur devoir et le serment de fidélité qu'ils étaient obligés de garder à Sa dite Majesté.

Priant le dit Sieur Evêque acquiescer à la dite interdiction pour le bien du service du Roi, et vouloir procéder par l'avis d'une Assemblée publique à nouvelle nomination des Conseillers en la place des dits Sieurs Interdits pour pouvoir rendre la justice aux peuples et habitants de ce pays, Déclarant que nous Sieur de Mésy ne pouvons en nommer aucun de notre part en la façon en laquelle nous avons été surpris par notre facilité lors de la première nomination manque d'une parfaite connaissance, et que s'il est fait quelque chose au préjudice de cet avertissement par aucun des dits Conseillers interdits, ils seront traités comme désobeissants, fomenteurs de rebellions et contraires au repos public.

(Signé)   "MÉSY"

RÉPONSE DE L'EVEQUE DE PÉTRÉE

Registre du Conseil Supérieur

16 FEV. 1664

Laissant à part les paroles offensives et accusations injurieuses qui me regardent dans l'affiche mise au son du tambour le treizième de ce mois de Fevrier, au poteau public, dont je prétends me justifier devant Sa Majesté je réponds à la prière que Monsieur le Gouverneur m'y fait d'agréer l'interdiction des personnes qui y sont comprises, et de vouloir procéder à la nomination d'autres Conseillers ou Officiers et ce par l'avis d'une assemblée publique, que ni ma conscience ni mon honneur, ni le respect et obéissance que je dois aux volontés et commandements du Roi, ni la fidélité et l'affection que je dois à son service ne me le permettent aucunement jusques à ce que dans un jugement légitime les desnommés dans la susdite affiche soient convaincus des crimes dont on les y accuse.

A Quebec ce seizième Février mil-six-cent-soixante-quatre.

(Signé)   "FRANÇOIS," EVÊQUE DE QUEBEC

Enrégistré à la requête de Mgr. l'Evêque de Pétrée ce 16 Fevrier 1664 par moi Secrétaire au Conseil Souverain soussigné.

(Signé)   PEUVRET, Secret^re,
avec paraphe

Lettre de Mésy aux Jésuites

(Extrait.) Collection de l'Abbé Ferland

Comme ainsi soit que la gloire de Dieu, le service du Roi et le service du public nous aient engagés de venir en ce pays pour y rencontrer notre salut par la sollicitation de M. l'Evêque de Pétrée qui nous a fait agréer au Roi pour avoir l'honneur d'être son Lieutenant Gonéral et Gouverneur de toute la Nouvelle France, représenter sa personne dans le Conseil Souverain qu'il a établi dans ce dit pays pour exercer la justice, police et finance, ce qui nous tient lieu d'obligation vers mon dit Sieur l'Evêque pour lui donner des marques de reconnaissance en toutes rencontres. A quoi nous sommes aussi obligés par son mérite particulier et par le respect qui est dû à son caractère, mais que ne doit entrer en nulle consideration pour le regard du service et de la fidélité que nous sommes obligé de rendre à S. M.; n'étant pas ni de notre conscience ni de notre honneur d'avoir accepté la commission dont il nous a honoré, pour n'en pas faire le deub de notre charge et de trahir les intérêts de Sa dite Majesté; lui en ayant fait le serment de fidélité entre ses mains et d'en avoir reçu le commandement par sa bouche. Pourquoi ayant rencontré plusieurs pratiques que nous avons cru en conscience par devoir être obligé d'en empêcher la suite, nous aurions fait publier notre déclaration du 13ᵉ jour de Février dernier, et ne l'ayant pu faire faire sans y intéresser le Sʳ Evêque, notre dite déclaration nous fait passer dans son esprit et de tous Messieurs les Ecclésiastiques qui considèrent ce point d'une prétendue offense sans avoir égard aucunement aux intérêts du Roy pour un calomniateur, mauvais juge, un ingrat et conscience erronnée et plusieurs autres termes injurieux qui se publient journellement contre l'autorité du Roy, en faisant un point de réprobation de la dite prétendue offense, un des principaux nous étant venu avertir que l'on nous pourrait faire fermer la porte des Eglises et nous empêcher de recevoir les Sᵗˢ Sacrements, si nous ne réparions la dite prétendue offense, ce qui nous donne un scrupule en l'âme; et de plus ne pouvant nous adresser pour nous en éclaircir qu'à des personnes qui se déclarent nos parties et qui jugent du fait sans en savoir la cause; mais n'y ayant rien de si important au monde que le salut et la fidélité que nous devons garder pour les intérêts du Roi que nous tenons inséparables l'un de l'autre, et reconnaissant qu'il n'y a rien de si certain que la mort et rien de si inconnu que l'heure, et que le temps est long pour informer Sa Majesté de ce qui se passe, pour en recevoir ses ordres, et qu'en attendant, une âme est toujours dans la crainte quoiqu'elle se connaisse dans l'innocence, nous sommes obligé avoir néanmoins recours aux Révérends Pères Casuistes de la maison de Jesus pour nous dire en leur conscience ce que nous pouvons pour la décharge de la nôtre et pour garder la fidélité que nous devons avoir pour le service du Roi, les priant qu'ils aient agréable signer ce qu'ils jugeront au bas de cet écrit, afin de nous servir de garantie vers sa Majesté.

Fait au Château de Quebec, ce dernier jour de Février, 1664.

"MÉSY"

III

F. *Marriage and Population*
LETTRE DE COLBERT A TALON
(Extrait.) Archives de la Marine

PARIS, 20 FEVRIER, 1668

Sa Majesté a fait une gratification de 1500 livres à Mr de Lamotte, 1er Capitaine au Régiment de Carignan-Salières, tant en considération du service qu'il rend en Canada, de la construction des forts et de ses expéditions qui ont été faites contre les Iroquois, que du mariage qu'il a contracté dans le pays, et de la résolution qu'il a prise de s'y habituer. Elle a ordonné de plus la somme de 6000 livres pour être distribuées aux officiers des mêmes troupes, ou qui s'y sont dejà mariés ou qui s'y marieront afin de leur donner des moyens de s'établir et de mieux s'affermir dans la pensée ou ils sont de ne pas revenir en France. Elle fait un autre fond de 12,000 livres pour être distribué aux soldats qui resteront aux pays et qui s'y marieront, autres que ceux des quatre compagnies qu'elle y laisse, ces derniers étant entretenus par le paiement de leur solde . . . . 1200 livres pour celui des meilleurs habitants qui a 15 enfants, et 800 livres pour l'autre qui en a dix. Elle a aussi gratifié M. l'Evêque de Pétrée d'une somme de 6000 livres pour continuer à l'assister pour soutenir sa dignité, fournir aux besoins de son Eglise et de son séminaire, et enfin 40,000 livres pour être employées à la levée de 150 hommes et de 50 filles depuis 16 jusqu'a 30 ans et non au dela; outre 235 que la Compagnie y fait passer cette année, et qui devaient y être passées l'année dernière; 12 Cavales, 2 étalons, 2 gros ânes de Mirbelais et 50 brebis; à quoi l'on travaille dans les provinces du royaume, et l'on n'oublie rien pour l'embarquement partant de la Rochelle vers la fin du mois prochain.

. . . . Je vous prie de bien faire considérér à tout le pays que leur bien, leur subsistance, et tout ce qui peut les regarder de plus près dépend d'une résolution publique à laquelle il ne soit jamais contrevenu de marier les garçons à 18 ou 19 ans, et les filles à 14 ou 15 ans; que les oppositions de n'avoir pas suffisamment pour vivre doivent être rejetées, parceque dans ces pays et le Canada premièrement où tout le monde travaille, il se produit pour tous la subsistance et que l'abondance ne peut jamais leur venir que par l'abondance des hommes. . . . . Il serait bon de rendre les charges et servitudes doubles à l'égard des garçons qui ne se marieraient point à cet âge . . . . et à l'egard de ceux qui sembleraient avoir absolument renoncé au mariage, il serait à propos de leur augmenter les charges, de les priver de tous honneurs, même d'y ajouter quelque marque d'infamie.

. . . . Bien que le Royaume de France soit autant peuplé qu'aucun pays du monde, il est certain qu'il serait difficile d'entretenir de grandes armées et de faire passer en même temps de grandes Colonies dans les pays éloignés. . . . . Il faut donc se réduire à tirer seulement chaque année avec précaution un nombre d'habitants de l'un et de l'autre sexe, pour les envoyer au Canada, et fonder principalement l'augmentation de la colonie sur l'augmentation des mariages, à mesure que le nombre des colons augmentera.

Lettre de Talon a Colbert

(Extrait.) Archives de la Marine

10 Novembre, 1670

. . . . De toutes les filles venues cette année au nombre de 165, il n'en reste pas 30 a marier. Après que les soldats venus cette année auront travaillé à faire une habitation, ils se porteront au mariage; pour quoi il serait bon qu'il plût à Sa Majesté d'envoyer encore 150 à 200 filles.

. . . . Il serait bon de recommander que les filles destinées à ce pays ne soient nullement disgrâciées de la nature, qu'elles n'aient rien de rebuttant à l'extérieur; qu'elles soient saines et fortes pour le travail de campagne, ou dumoins qu'elles aient quelqu'industrie pour les ouvrages de main.

. . . . Trois ou quatre filles de naissance et distinguées par la qualité serviraient peut-être utilement à lier par le mariage des officiers qui ne tiennent au pays que par les appointements et l'emolument de leurs terres, et qui par la disproportion des conditions ne s'engagent pas davantage. Si le Roi fait passer d'autres filles ou femmes veuves de l'Ancienne à la Nouvelle-France, il est bon de les faire accompagner d'un certificat de leur Curé ou du juge du lieu qui fasse connaître qu'elles sont libres et en état d'être mariées, sans quoi les Ecclésiastiques d'ici font difficulté de leur conférer ce sacrement; à la vérité ce n'est pas sans raison, 2 ou 3 doubles mariages s'étant reconnus ici; on pourrait prendre la même précaution pour les hommes veufs.

LETTRE DE TALON A COLBERT

(Extrait.) Archives de la Marine

2 NOVEMBRE, 1671

. . . . Le nombre des enfants nés cette année est de 6 à 700. . . . . J'estime qu'il n'est plus nécessaire de faire passer des demoiselles, en ayant reçu cette année quinze ainsi qualifiées au lieu de quatre que je demandais pour faire des alliances avec les officiers ou les principaux habitants d'ici. . . . .

G. Chateau St. Louis

This structure, destined to be famous in Canadian history, was originally built by Samuel de Champlain. The cellar still remains, under the wooden platform of the present Durham Terrace. Behind the château was the area of the fort, now an open square. In the most famous epoch of its history, the time of Frontenac, the château was old and dilapidated, and the fort was in a sad condition. "The walls are all down," writes Frontenac in 1681; "there are neither gates nor guardhouse; the whole place is open." On this the new intendant, Meules, was ordered to report what repairs were needed. Meanwhile La Barre had come to replace Frontenac, whose complaints he repeats. He says that the wall is in ruin for a distance of a hundred and eighty *toises*. "The workmen ask 6000 francs to repair it. I could get it done in France for 2000. The cost frightens me. I have done nothing." (*La Barre au Ministre, 1682.*) Meules, however, received orders to do what was necessary; and, two years later, he reports that he has rebuilt the wall, repaired the fort, and erected a building, intended at first for the council, within the area. This building stood near the entrance of the present St. Louis Street, and was enclosed by an extension of the fort wall.

Denonville next appears on the scene, with his usual disposition to fault-finding. The so-called château, he says (1685) is built of wood, "and is dry as a match. There is a place where with a bundle of straw it could be set on fire at any time; . . . some of the gates will not close; there is no watch-tower, and no place to shoot from." (*Denonville au Ministre, 20 Août, 1685.*)

When Frontenac resumed the government, he was much disturbed at the condition of the château, and begged for slate to cover the roof, as the rain was coming in everywhere. At the same time the intendant, Champigny, reports it to be rotten and ruinous. This was in the year made famous by the English attack, and the dramatic scene in the hall of the old building when Frontenac defied the envoy of Admiral Phipps, whose fleet lay in the river below. In the next summer, 1691, Frontenac again asks for slate to cover the roof, and for 15,000 or 20,000 francs to repair his mansion. In the next year the king promises to send him 12,000 francs, in instalments. Frontenac acknowledges the favor; and says that he will erect a new building, and try in the mean time not to be buried under the old one, as he expects to be every time the wind blows hard. (*Frontenac au Ministre, 15 Sept., 1692.*) A misunderstanding with the intendant, who had control of the money, interrupted the work. Frontenac writes the next year that he had been obliged to send for carpenters, during the night, to prop up the château, lest he should be crushed under the ruins. The wall of the fort was however strengthened, and partly rebuilt to the height of sixteen feet, at a cost of 13,629 francs. It was a time of war, and a fresh attack was expected from the English. (*Frontenac et Champigny au Ministre, 4 Nov., 1693.*) In the year 1854, the workmen employed in demolishing a part of this wall, adjoining the garden of the château, found a copper plate bearing an inscription in Latin as follows: "In the year of Redemption 1693, under the reign of the most august, most invincible, and most Christian King of France, Louis the Great, fourteenth of that name, the most excellent Louis de Buade, Count of Frontenac, governor for the second time of all New France, seeing that the rebellious inhabitants of New England, who three years ago were repulsed, routed, and completely vanquished by him when they besieged this town of Quebec, are threatening to renew the siege this very year, has caused to be built, at the expense of the king, this citadel, with the fortifications adjoining thereto, for the defence of the country, for the security of the people, and for confounding yet again that nation perfidious alike towards its God and its lawful king. And he [*Frontenac*] has placed here this first stone."

A year later, the rebuilding of the château was begun in earnest. Frontenac says that nothing but a miracle has saved him from being buried under its ruins; that he has pulled every thing down, and begun again from the foundation, but that the money has given out. (*Frontenac au Ministre, 4 Nov., 1694.*) Accordingly, he and the intendant sold six licenses for the fur trade; but at a rate unusually low, for they brought only 4,400 francs. The king, hearing of this, sent 6,000 more. Frontenac is profuse in thanks; and at the same time begs for another 6000 francs, "to complete a work which is the ornament and beauty of the city" (1696). The minister sent 8,000 more, which was soon gone; and Frontenac drew on the royal treasurer for 5,047 in addition. The intendant complains of his extravagance, and says that he will have nothing but perfection; and that, besides the château, he has insisted on building two guard-houses, with Mansard roofs, at the two sides of the gate. "I must do as he says," adds the intendant, "or there will be a quarrel." (*Champigny au Ministre, 13 Oct., 1697.*) In a letter written two days after, Frontenac speaks with great complacency of his château, and asks for another 6,000 francs to finish it. As the case was urgent, he sold six more licenses, at 1,000 francs each; but he died too soon to see the completion of his favorite work (1698). The new château was not finished before 1700, and even then it had no cistern. In a pen-sketch of Quebec on a manuscript map of 1699, preserved in the Dépôt des Cartes de la Marine, the new château is distinctly represented. In front is a gallery or balcony, resting on a wall and buttresses at the edge of the cliff. Above the gallery is a range of high windows along the face of the building, and over these a range of small windows and a

Mansard roof. In the middle is a porch opening on the gallery; and on the left extends a battery, on the ground now occupied by a garden along the brink of the cliff. A watercolor sketch of the château taken in 1804, from the land-side, by William Morrison, Jr., is in my possession. The building appears to have been completely remodelled in the interval. It is two stories in height; the Mansard roof is gone, and a row of attic windows surmounts the second story. In 1809 it was again remodelled, at a cost of ten thousand pounds sterling. A third story was added; and the building, resting on the buttresses which still remain under the balustrade of Durham Terrace, had an imposing effect when seen from the river. It was destroyed by fire in 1834.

H. Trade and Industry
Lettre de Denonville au Ministre
(Extrait.) Archives de la Marine

A Quebec le 13 Novembre, 1685

. . J'ai remarqué, Monseigneur que les femmes et filles, y sont assez paresseuses par le manque de menus ouvrages à se donner, il y a un peu trop de luxe dans la pauvreté génerale des demoiselles ou soi disantes; les menus ouvrages de capots et de chemises de traite les occupent un peu, pendant l'hiver, et leur font gagner quelque chose, mais cela ne dure pas, l'endroit de pauvreté de ce pays, est le manque de toilles et de serges ou draps, cependant c'est ici le pays du monde le plus propre à faire des chanvres, et du fil, et par consequent de la toille, si on s'en voulait donner la peine. Mr. Talon s'y est donné du soin pour cela, aussi y a-t-il une côte qui est celle de Beaupré, ou on en fait, mais ce n'est que chez quelques habitans. J'ai fort exhorté la dessus tous les peuples d'y travailler, pour y réussir, il faut y apporter de la sévérité et de l'utilité si il y a moyen, ce dernier avec le temps et l'industrie arrivera, et le premier de ma part ne manquera pas, je n'ai pu avoir d'autre raison, pourquoi on ne faisait point de chanvres, si ce n'est que l'on n'avait pas assez de temps, à cause que les saisons de labourer, semer et recueillir sont trop courtes, car en ce pays le bled ne se sème qu'en Avril et May. Si le Roy voulait acheter les chanvres un peu plus cher jusques à ce que l'on fut en train, cela pourait les animer, avec un ordre à chacun d'en fournir une certaine quantité on pourra les faire agir, si outre cela on avait quelques ouvriers tisserands à distribuer par paroisses, et qui ne fussent à la charge du peuple que pour leurs nourritures, ce serait un moyen pour faire apprendre aux enfants. Les Curés nous rendraient compte du nombre de ceux qui apprendraient à préparer la chanvre et fillasse, et à faire de la toille; avant que d'en venir là il faudrait montrer à filer aux filles et aux femmes, car il y en a très peu, qui sachent tenir le fuseau, c'est en cela que les filles de la congrégation de Montréal feront merveilles. Il nous est venu de la part de Mr. Arnoul deux bariques de graine de chanvre que je ferai distribuer et dont je me ferai rendre compte.

Je croyais, Monseigneur, une ordonnance necessaire encore à faire pour engager chaque habitant à avoir deux ou trois brebis, n'y en ayant pas suffisament dans le pays.

. . . . Il n'est pas possible qu'on ne puisse faire une verrerie en ce pays, la plus grande affaire sont les ouvriers qui enchérissent tout car l'on donne ordinairement et communément à chaque ouvrier par jour quarante sols nouris, cinquante sols et un écu, et tous ces maraux n'en sont pas plus riches car ils mettent tout à boire.

Signé: Le M^{QUIS} de Denonville

Mémoire a Monseigneur le Marquis de Seignelay, sur l'établissement du commerce en Canada, présenté par les Sieurs Chalons et Riverin

(Extrait.) Archives de la Marine

(Joint à la lettre du Sieur de Riverin, du 7 Fevrier, 1686.)

. . . . En effet si cette colonie n'a pas avancé depuis le temps de son établissement, c'est que les habitants qui la composent ou par leur négligence ou par leur peu d'expérience dans les affaires, ou enfin par leur impuissance ne se sont pas mis en estat de se servir des avantages qu'elle renferme en elle-mesme, et des moyens qu'elle leur fournit pour un commerce solide et considerable.

Car il ne faut pas regarder la traitte des pelleteries à laquelle seule on s'est attaché jusqu'à présent et qui finira avec le temps par la destruction des bestes, comme un moyen propre à son avancement, au contraire l'expérience a fait connoistre qu'elle rend les habitans fainéans et vagabonds, qu'elle les détourne de la culture des terres, de la pesche, de la navigation et des autres entreprises.

Mémoire du Sieur de Catalogne, Ingénieur, sur les plans des habitations et Seigneuries des Gouvernemens de Quebec, de Montréal et des Trois-Rivières

(Extrait.[1]) Archives de la Marine

7 Novembre, 1712

Observations sur l'établissement.—Que par rapport à la grande étendue qu'on a donnée à l'établissement, il n'y a pas le quart des ouvriers qu'il faudroit pour bien étendre et cultiver les terres.

Que les laboureurs ne se donnent pas assez de soin pour cultiver les terres, étant certain que la semence d'un minot de blé, semé sur de la terre cultivée comme en France, produira plus que deux autres comme on sème en Canada.

Que comme les saisons sont trop courtes et souvent très mauvaises, il serait à souhaiter que l'Eglise permit les travaux indispensables, que les fêtes d'été obligent de chômer, étant très vrai que depuis le mois de Mai que les semences commencent jusques à la fin de Septembre, il n'y a pas 90 journées de travail, par rapport aux fêtes et au mauvais temps. C'est pourtant dans cette espace que roule la solidité de cet établissement. Il faudrait assujetir les habitans négligens à travailler à la culture des terres, en les privant des voyages qui les dispensent de travailler, et cela parce qu'un voyage de deux ou trois mois leur produit 30 ou 40 escus en perdant la saison du travail à la terre, qui les fait demeurer en friche.

Les obliger de semer quantité de chanvre et lin qui vient en ce pays plus gros qu'en Europe. Ils s'en relâchent parceque, disent-ils, il y a trop de peine et de soins à le mettre en œuvre. Il est vrai qu'il y a peu de gens qui s'entendent et qui le font payer bien cher.

[1] This *mémoire* is 70 pages in length.

Assujetir les habitans à nourrir et à élever des bêtes à cornes, au lieu du grand nombre de chevaux qui ruinent le Pacage et qui entrainent les habitans à des grosses dépenses, tant que pour leurs équipages qui sont fort chers que par la grande quantité de fourages et de grains qu'il faut pendant 7 ou 8 mois de l'année, étant très vrai que l'entretien d'un cheval coûte autant que deux bœufs.

Obliger les Seigneurs pour faciliter l'établissement de leurs Seigneuries de donner suffisamment des terres pour commencer à un prix modique et à construire des moulins et les commodités publiques; plusieurs consomment le tiers de leur temps à aller faires leur farines à 15 ou 20 lieues, et que les Seigneurs, dès que les Seigneuries sont établies, concèdent des terres sans que les tenanciers soient obligés de payer des rentes qu'après 6 ans que les terres soient en valeur.

Ordonner au grand voyer de donner son application à faire établir les chemins et ponts nécessaires au public, qui est une nécessité fort essentielle.

Obliger les habitans ou ceux qui sont en état, de faire des greniers pourque chacun fût en état de conserver du grain pour deux années; cela fait une fois, l'abondance se trouvera toujours au Canada au lieu que la plupart, faute de cette commodité, en manquent très souvent, étant obligé de le vendre à vil prix.

Châtier sévérement tous ceux qui sont convaincus de fraude, mauvaise foi et imposture, qui est un mal qui commence à être bien en racine et qui indubitablement le privera de tout commerce, les marchands des îles et de Plaisance s'en étant déja plaints.

Que comme il n'y a pas de notaires dans tous les lieux, que les conventions et les marchés faits en présence de deux témoins vaudront pendant un temps fixé.

Il serait à souhaiter que S. M. voulût établir dans chaque ville des conseils à juger sans frais sur le fait du commerce et des affaires qui n'entrent pas dans la coutume. Ces sortes de procédures aussi bien que les autres, ne prennent aucune fin que lorsque les parties n'ont plus d'argent pour plaider, qui est la ruine des familles.

Engager un certain nombre de gens du pays a étudier le pilotage, même les officiers des troupes, particulièrement du fleuve St. Laurent qui est très dangereux, la plupart du temps ne se trouvant pas un seul pilote en Canada, et cependant on commence à donner dans la construction; le capitaine du Port et M. Duplessis ayant mis un vaisseau de 3 à 400 tonneaux sur les chantiers.

Congédier de temps en temps des soldats en leur permettant de se marier, après qu'ils auront un établissement.

Il s'est établi une coutume dans ce pays autorisée par le magistrat, qui même ne me parait pas naturelle, de laisser des bestiaux à l'abandon qui la plupart gâtent les grains et les prairies, n'y ayant presque point de terres closes qui causent des contestes et de la mesintelligence entre les voisins; pour obvier à cela il faudrait qu'il y eut des gardiens pour chaque nature d'animaux pour les mener dans les communes, car tel qui n'a pas un pouce de terre, envoie ses animaux paître sur les terres de ses voisins, en disant que l'abandon est donné; Si S. M. voulait couper la racine à une pépinière de procès et de mésintelligence entre les Seigneurs et habitans, il serait à souhaiter qu'elle voulut donner une ordonnance tendante à ce que les Seigneuries et autres concessions demeureraient dans les limites qu'elles se trouvent à présent, sans avoir égard aux titres portés dans les contrats, pour la quantité et les rumbs de vent qui y sont annoncés, étant à remarquer que les anciens Seigneurs et habitans se sont établis de bonne foi, que les terres ont été limitées par des arpenteurs peu intelligens, et aujourd'hui que la chicane est en vogue, chacun veut suivre les termes de son contrat qui tendent la plupart à l'impossible. Mr. Raudot a donnè une ordonnance à ce sujet pour l'île de Montréal seulement.

Comme la plupart des rues de Quebec et de Montréal sont souvent impraticables, tant par les rochers que par les bourbiers, s'il plaisait à S. M. d'ordonner que les deniers qui proviennent des amendes et certaines confiscations seraient employés à les mettre en état.

Que la subordination du vassal à son Seigneur n'est point objet à   . Cette erreur vient qu'il a été accordé des Seigneuries à des roturiers qui n'ont pas su maintenir le droit que la raison leur donne à l'égard de leur co-sujets, même les officiers de milice qui leur sont dépendants, n'ont la plupart aucun égard pour leur superiorité et veulent dans les occasions passer pour indépendants.

Il serait à souhaiter que S. M. voulût envoyer dans ce pays toute sorte d'artisans, particulièrement des ouvriers en cordages et filages, des potiers et un verrier, et ils trouveraient à s'occuper. Si S. M. voulait faire envoyer en marchandises une partie des appointemens de Messrs. les officiers, cela leur adoucirait la dureté qu'eux seuls trouvent dans le pays, par la grande cherté des marchandises causée par le mauvais retour de la monnaie de cartes qui fait acheter 3 et 4 pour 100.

Veu: VAUDREUIL.

Veu: BÉGON.   CATALOGNE

I. Letter of Father Carheil

LETTRE DU PÈRE ETIENNE DE CARHEIL, DE LA COMPAGNIE DE JÉSUS, A L'INTENDANT DE CHAMPIGNY

(Extrait.[1]) Archives Nationales

A MICHILIMAKINA, LE 30 D'AOUST, 1702

. . . . Nos Missions sont réduites à une telle extrémité, que nous ne pouvons plus les soutenir contre une multitude infinie de désordres, de brutalitez, de violences, d'injustices, d'impietez, d'impudicitez, d'insolences, de mépris, d'insultes que l'infâme et funeste traitte d'eau-de-vie y cause universellement dans toutes les nations d'icy haut, où l'on vient la faire, allant de villages en villages et courant les lacs avec une quantité prodigieuse de barils, sans garder aucune mesure. Si Sa Majesté avoit veu une seule fois ce qui se passe et icy et à Montréal, dans tous les temps qu'on y fait cette malheureuse traitte, je suis sur qu'elle ne balanceroit pas un moment, dès la premiere vue, à la déffendre pour jamais sous les plus rigoureuses peines.

Dans le désespoir où nous sommes, il ne nous reste point d'autre party à prendre que celui de quitter nos Missions et de les abandonner aux traittants d'eau-de-vie, pour y établir le domaine de leur traitte, de l'ivrognerie et de l'impureté. C'est ce que nous allons proposer à nos supérieurs en Canada et en France, y étant contraints par l'état d'inutilité et d'impuissance

[1]This letter is 45 pages long.

de faire aucun fruit où l'on nous a réduits par la permission de cette déplorable traitte, permission que l'on n'a obtenue de Sa Majesté que sous un pretexte aparent de raisons que l'on scait être fausses, permission qu'elle n'accorderoit point, si ceux auxquels elle se raporte de la vérité la lui fesoient connoistre comme ils la connoissent eux-mêmes et tout le Canada avec eux, permission enfin qui est le plus grand mal et le principe de tous les maux qui arrivent présentement au pays, et surtout des naufrages dont on n'entendoit point encore parler ici et que nous apprenons arriver maintenant presque touttes les années ou dans la venue ou dans le retour de nos vaisseaux en France, par une juste punition de Dieu qui fait périr par l'eau ce que l'on avoit mal acquis par l'eau-de-vie, ou qui entend empêcher le transport pour prévenir le mauvais usage qu'on en feroit. Si cette permission n'est révoquée par une déffense contraire, nous n'aurons plus que faire de demeurer dans aucune de nos Missions d'icy haut, pour y perdre le reste de notre vie, et touttes nos peines dans une pure inutilité sous l'empire d'une continuelle ivrognerie et d'une impureté universelle qu'on ne permet pas moins aux traitteurs d'eau-de-vie que la traitte même dont elle est l'accompagnement et la suite. Si Sa Majesté veut sauver nos missions et soutenir l'établissement de la Religion, comme nous ne doutons point qu'elle le veuille, nous la suplions très-humblement de croire, ce qui est très véritable, qu'il n'y a point d'autre moyen de le pouvoir faire que d'abolir les deux infâmes commerces qui les ont réduites à la nécessité prochaine de périr et qui ne tarderont pas à achever de les perdre, s'ils ne sont au plus tost abolis par ses ordres et mis hors d'état d'être rétablis. Le premier est le commerce de l'eau-de-vie; le second est le commerce des femmes sauvages avec les François, qui sont tous deux aussy publics l'un que l'autre, sans que nous puissions y remédier, pour n'estre pas appuyez des commandans qui, bien loin de les vouloir empêcher par les remontrances que nous leur faisons, les exercent eux-mêmes avec plus de liberté que leurs inférieurs, et les autorisent tellement par leur exemple qu'en le regardant on s'en fait une permission générale et une assurance d'impunité qui les rend communs à tout ce qui vient icy de François en traitte, de sorte que tous les villages de nos Sauvages ne sont plus que des cabarets pour l'ivrognerie et des Sodomes pour l'impureté, d'où il faut que nous nous retirions, les abandonnant à la juste colère de Dieu et à ses vengeances.

Vous voyez par là que, de quelque manière qu'on établisse le commerce François avec les Sauvages, si l'on veut nous retenir parmi eux, nous y conserver et nous y soutenir en qualité de missionnaires dans le libre exercice de nos fonctions avec espérance d'y faire du fruit, il faut nous délivrer des commandans et de leurs garnisons qui, bien loin d'estre nécessaires, sont au contraire si pernicieuses que nous pouvons dire avec vérité qu'elles sont le plus grand mal de nos missions, ne servant qu'à nuire à la traitte ordinaire des voyageurs et à l'avancement de la Foy. Depuis qu'elles sont venues icy haut, nous n'y avons plus veu que corruption universelle qu'elles ont répandues par leur vie scandaleuse dans tous les esprits de ces nations qui en sont présentement infectées. Tout le service prétendu qu'on veut faire croire au Roy qu'elles rendent se réduit à quatre principales occupations dont nous vous prions instamment de vouloir bien informer le Roy.

La première est de tenir un cabaret public d'eau-de-vie où ils la traittent continuellement aux Sauvages qui ne cessent point de s'enyvrer, quelques opositions que nous y puissions faire. C'est en vain que nous leur parlons pour les arrêter; nous n'y gagnons rien que d'être accusez de nous oposer nous-mêmes au Service du Roy en voulant empêcher une traitte qui leur est permise.

La seconde occupation des soldats est d'estre envoyez d'un poste à l'autre par les Commandans, pour y porter leurs marchandises et leur eau-de-vie, après s'être accommodés ensemble, sans que les uns et les autres ayent d'autre soin que celuy de s'entr'ayder mutuellement dans leur commerce, et afin que cela s'exécute plus facilement des deux costez comme ils le souhaitent, ils faut que les commandans se ferment les yeux pour user de connivence et ne voir aucun des désordres de leur soldats, quelques visibles, publics et scandaleux qu'ils soient, et il faut réciproquement que les soldats, outre qu'ils traittent leurs propres marchandises, se fassent encore les traitteurs de celles de leurs Commandans qui souvent même les obligent d'en acheter d'eux pour leur permettre d'aller où ils veulent.

Leur troisième occupation est de faire de leur fort un lieu que j'ay honte d'apeler par son nom, où les femmes ont apris que leurs corps pouvoient tenir lieu de marchandises et qu'elles seroient mieux reçues que le castor, de sorte que c'est présentement le commerce le plus ordinaire, le plus continuel et le plus en vogue. Quelques efforts que puissent faire tous les missionnaires pour décrier et pour l'abolir, au lieu de diminuer, il augmente et se multiplie tous les jours de plus en plus; tous les soldats tiennent table ouverte à touttes les femmes de leur connaissance dans leur maison; depuis le matin jusqu'au soir, elles y passent les journées entières, les unes après les autres, assises à leur feu et souvent sur leur lit dans des entretiens et des actions propre de leur commerce qui ne s'achève ordinairement que la nuit, la foule étant trop grande pendant la journée pour qu'ils puissent l'achever, quoyque souvent aussy ils s'entrelaissent une maison vide de monde pour n'en pas différer l'achêvement jusqu'à la nuit.

La quatrième occupation des soldats est celle du jeu qui a lieu dans les tems où les traitteurs se rassemblent; il y va quelquefois à un tel point que n'étans pas contens d'y passer le jour, ils y passent encore la nuit entière, et il n'arrive même que trop souvent dans l'ardeur de l'aplication qu'ils ne se souviement pas, ou s'ils s'en souviennent, qu'ils méprisent de garder les postes. Mais ce qui augmente en cela leur désordre, c'est qu'un attachement si opiniâtre au jeu n'est presque jamais sans une ivrognerie commune à tous les joueurs, et que l'ivrognerie est presque toujours suivie de querelles qui s'excitent entre eux lesquelles venant à paroître publiquement aux yeux des Sauvages, causent parmi eux trois grands scandales: le premier de les voir ivres, le second de les voir s'entrebatre avec fureur les uns contre les autres jusqu'à prendre des fusils en main pour s'entretuer, le troisième de voir que les Missionnaires n'y peuvent apporter aucun remède.

Voila, Monseigneur, les quatre seules ocupations des garnisons que l'on a tenues ici pendant tant d'années. Si ces sortes d'ocupations peuvent s'apeler le service du Roy, j'avoue qu'elles luy ont actuellement et toujours rendu quelqu'un de ces quatre services, mais je n'en ai point veu d'autres que ces quatre-là; et par conséquent, si on ne juge pas que ce soit là des services nécessaires au Roy, il n'y a point eu jusqu'à présent de nécessité de les tenir icy, et après leur rapel, il n'y en aura point de les y rétablir.

Cependant comme cette nécessité prétendue des Garnisons est l'unique pretexte que l'on prend pour y envoyer des Commandans, nous vous prions, Monseigneur, d'être bien persuadé de la fausseté de ce prétexte, afin que, sous ces spécieuses aparences du service du Roy, on ne se fasse pas une obligation d'en envoyer, puisque les Commandans ne viennent icy que pour y faire la traitte de concert avec leurs soldats sans se mettre en peine de tout le reste. Ils n'ont de liaison avec les Missionnaires que par les endroits où ils les croient utiles pour leur temporel, et hors de là ils leur sont contraires dès qu'ils veulent s'opposer au désordre qui, ne s'accordant ny avec le service de Dieu ny avec le service du Roy, ne laisse pas d'être avantageux à leur commerce, au quel il n'est rien qu'ils ne sacrifient. C'est là l'unique cause qui a mis le déréglement dans nos Missions, et qui les a tellement désolées par l'ascendant que les Commandans ont pris sur les Missionnaires en s'attirant toute l'autorité soit à l'égard des François, soit à l'égard des Sauvages, que nous n'avons pas d'autre pouvoir que celui d'y travailler inutilement sous leur domination qui s'est élevée jusqu'à nous pour nous faire des crimes civils et des accusations prétendues juridiques des propres fonctions de notre état et de notre devoir, comme l'a toujours fait Monsieur de la Motte qui ne voulait pas même que nous nous servissions du mot de désordre et qui intente en effet procez au père Pinet pour s'en être servi.

. . . . Vous voyez, Monseigneur, que je me suis beaucoup étendu sur les articles des Commandans et des garnisons pour vous faire comprendre que c'est là qu'est venu tout le malheur de nos Missions. Ce sont les Commandans, ce sont les garnisons, qui, se joignant avec les traitteurs d'eau-de-vie les ont entièrement désolées par l'ivrognerie et par une impudicité presque universelle que l'on y a établie par une continuelle impunité de l'une et de l'autre, que les puissances civiles ne tolèrent pas seulement, mais qu'elles permettent, puisque les pouvant empêcher, elles ne les empêchent pas. Je ne crains donc point de vous déclarer que si l'on remet icy haut dans nos missions des Commandans traitteurs et des garnisons de soldats traitteurs, nous ne doutons point que nous ne soyons contraints de les quitter, n'y pouvant rien faire pour le salut des âmes. C'est à vous d'informer Sa Majesté de l'extrémité où l'on nous réduit et de luy demander pour nous notre délivrance, afin que nous puissions travailler à l'etablissement de la Religion sans ces empêchemens qui l'ont arrêté jusqu'à présent.

J. The Government and the Clergy

MÉMOIRE DE TALON SUR L'ETAT PRÉSENT DU CANADA,
1667

(Extrait.) Archives de la Marine

. . . L'Ecclésiastique est composé d'un Evesque, ayant le tiltre de Pétrée, In partibus infidelium, et se servant du caractère et de l'autorité de Vicaire Apostolique.

Il a soubs [*sous*] luy neuf Prestres, et plusieurs clercs qui vivent en communauté quand ils sont près de lui dans son Séminaire, et séparément à la campagne quand ils y sont envoyez par voye de mission pour desservir les cures qui ne sont pas encore fondées. Il y a pareillement les Pères de la Compagnie de Jésus, au nombre de trente-cinq, la pluspart desquels sont employez aux Missions étrangères: ouvrage digne de leur zèle et de leur piété s'il est exempt du meslange de l'intérest dont on les dit susceptibles, par la traitte des pelleteries qu'on assure qu'ils font aux 8ta8aks [*Outaouaks*], et au Cap de la Magdelaine; ce que je ne sçay pas de science certaine.

La vie de ces Ecclésiastiques, par tout ce qui paroist au dehors, est fort réglée, et peut servir de bon exemple et d'un bon modèle aux séculiers qui la peuvent imiter; mais comme ceux qui composent cette Colonie ne sont pas tous d'esgale force, ny de vertu pareille, ou n'ont pas tous les mesmes dispositions au bien, quelques-uns tombent aysément dans leur disgrâce pour ne pas se conformer à leur manière de vivre, ne pas suivre tous leurs sentimens, et ne s'abandonner pas à leur conduite qu'ils estendent jusques sur le temporel, empiétant mesme sur la police extérieure qui regarde le seul magistrat.

On a lieu de soupconner que la pratique dans laquelle ils sont, qui n'est pas bien conforme à celle des Ecclésiastiques de l'Ancienne France, a pour but de partager l'autorité temporelle qui, jusques au temps de l'arrivée des troupes du Roy en Canada, résidoit principalement en leur personnes.

À ce mal qui va jusques a géhenner [*gêner*] et contraindre les consciences, et par là desgoûter les colons les plus attachez au pays, on peut donner pour remède l'ordre de balancer avec adresse et modération cette autorité par celle qui réside ez [*dans les*] personnes envoyées par Sa Majesté pour le Gouvernement: ce qui a desjà été pratiqué; de permettre de renvoyer un ou deux Ecclésiastiques de ceux qui reconnoissent moins cette autorité temporelle, et qui troublent le plus par leur conduite le repos de la Colonie, et introduire quatre Ecclésiastiques entre les séculiers ou les réguliers, les faisant bien autoriser pour l'administration des Sacremens, sans qu'ils puissent estre inquiétez: autrement ils deviendroient inutiles au pays, parce que s'ils ne se conformoient pas à la pratique de ceux qui y sont aujourd'huy M. l'Evesque leur deffendroit d'administrer les Sacremens.

Pour estre mieux informé de cette conduite des consciences, on peut entendre Monsieur Dubois, Aumosnier au régiment de Carignan, qui a ouy plusieurs Confessions en secret, et à la desrobée, et Monsieur de Bretonvilliers sur ce qu'il a appris par les Ecclésiastiques de son Séminaire establi à Mont-Réal.

LETTRE DU MINISTRE A MR. TALON, 20 FEVRIER, 1668

(Extrait.) Archives de la Marine

. . . Il faut que l'application d'un Gouverneur et d'un Intendant aide a adoucir le mal, et non à l'effet que le Gouverneur ne se porte à aucune extrémité, contre les Sieurs Evêque et les P. P. Jésuites, quand bien même ils auraient abusé du pouvoir que leur habit et le respect qu'on a naturellement pour la religion leur donne. En se contentant par des conférences particulières de resserrer ce pouvoir, autant que se pourra, dans les bornes d'une légitime autorité et espérant que, quand le pays sera plus peuplé, qui est la seule et unique chose que doit convier le dit Sr. Gouverneur et Intendant à y donner leurs soins quand à présent, l'autorité Royale qui sera la plus reconnue des peuples prévaudra sur l'autre et la contiendra dans de justes limites.

. . . Je ne m'explique point avec vous sur ce sujet, parceque je sais qu'à part ses bonnes qualités il [*M. de Courcelle*] a usé d'emportement dont il est bon qu'il se corrige. Insinuez lui aussi honnêtement les sentiments qu'il doit avoir et ce que je viens de vous dire au sujet du Sieur de Ressan, et qu'il ne doit jamais blâmer la conduite de l'Evêque de Pétrée ni des Jésuites en public, étant assez d'en user avec eux avec grande circonspection, se contentant seulement lorsqu'ils entreprendront trop de leur faire connaître et d'en envoyer des mémoires, afin que je confère avec leurs Supérieurs de ces entreprises et en cas qu'ils en fassent qu'on puisse les interdire.

INSTRUCTION POUR M. DE BOUTEROUE, 1668

(Extrait.) Archives de la Marine

Il faut empescher autant qu'il se pourra la trop grande quantité des prestres, religieux, et religieuses . . . s'entremettre quelquefois et dans les occasions pour les porter à adoucir cette trop grande séverité, estant très-important que lesdits evesque et Jésuites ne s'aperçoivent jamais qu'il veuille blasmer leur conduite.

Signé   COLBERT

For the instructions on this subject, more precise and emphatic than the above, given by the king to Talon in 1665, see N.Y. Colonial Docs., IX. 24.

LETTRE DE COLBERT A DUCHESNEAU, 15 AVRIL, 1676

(Extrait.) Archives de la Marine

Eviter les contestations . . . sans toutefois préjudicier aux précautions qui sont à prendre et aux mesures à garder pour empescher que la puissance ecclésiastique n'entreprenne rien sur la temporelle, à quoy les ecclésiastiques sont assez portés.

LETTRE DU MINISTRE A DUCHESNEAU, LE 28 AVRIL, 1677

(Extrait.) Archives de la Marine

. . . Je vous dirai premièrement que Sa Majesté est bien persuadée de la piété de tous les Ecclésiastiques et de leurs bonnes intentions pour le succez du sujet de leurs missions, mais Sa Majesté veut que vous preniez garde qu'ils n'entreprennent rien tant sur son authorité Royalle que sur la justice et police du pays et que vous les resserriez précisement dans les bornes de l'authorité que les Ecclésiastiques ont dans le Royaume, sans souffrir qu'ils les passent en quelque sorte et manière que ce soit, et cette maxime généralle vous doit servir pour toutes les difficultez de cette nature qui pourront survenir; mais pour parvenir à ce point il seroit nécessaire que vous-mesme vous travailliassiez à vous rendre habil sur ces matières en lisant les autheurs qui en ont traitté, observer tout ce qui se passe et à envoyer tous les ans des mémoires sur les difficultez que vous aurez et auxquelles vous n'aurez pas pu remédier; considerez cette matière comme très importante et à laquelle vous ne sçauriez donner trop d'application.

LETTRE DU MINISTRE A DUCHESNEAU, LE PREMIER MAY, 1677

(Extrait.) Archives de la Marine

. . Je suis encore obligé de vous dire que l'on voit clairement qu'encore que le dit Sieur Evesque soit un homme de bien et qu'il fasse fort bien son devoir, il ne laisse pas d'affecter une domination qui passe de beaucoup au delà des bornes que les Evesques ont dans tout le monde chrestien et particulièrement dans le Royaume et ainsy vous devez vous appliquer à bien connoistre et à sçavoir le plus parfaitement que vous pourrez l'estendue du pouvoir des Evesques et les remèdes que l'authorité Royalle a apporté pour en empescher l'abus et leur trop grande domination, afin que vous puissiez de concert avec Monsieur le Comte de Frontenac dans les occasions importantes y apporter les mesmes remèdes, en quoy vous devez toujours agir avec beaucoup de modération et de retenue. . . . Comme je vois que Monsieur l'Evesque de Quebec, ainsi que je viens de vous dire affecte une authorité un peu trop indépendante de l'authorité Royalle et que par cette raison il seroit peut-estre bon qu'il n'eust pas de seance dans le conseil, vous devez bien examiner toutes les occasions et tous les moyens que l'on pourrait pratiquer, pour luy donner à luy-mesme l'envie de n'y plus venir; mais vous devez en cela vous conduire avec beaucoup de retenue, et bien prendre garde que qui ce soit ne descouvre ce que je vous escris sur ce point.

Mémoire du Roi aux Sieurs de Frontenac et de Champigny, Année 1692

(Extrait.) Archives de la Marine

. . . Sa Majesté veut aussy qu'ils [*Frontenac et Champigny*] assistent de leur authorité les Jesuites et les Récolets et tous autres Ecclésiastiques sans néantmoins souffrir qu'ils portent l'authorité ecclésiastique plus loin qu'elle ne doit s'entendre. Elle ne veut pas qu'ils se dispensent de faire doucement et avec toute la discrétion possible des remonstrances au dit Sieur Evesque dans les occasions où ils reconnoistront que les Ecclésiastiques agissent par un zèle immodéré ou par d'autres passions, afin de l'engager à y remédier et à faire tout ce qui dépend avec lui pour procurer le repos des consciences. Les dits Sieurs de Frontenac et de Champigny doivent se tenir en cela dans les voyes de la seule excitation et informer sa Majesté de tout ce qui se passera à cet égard.

Lettre de Monsieur de la Mothe Cadillac

(Extrait.) Archives de la Marine

28 Septembre, 1694

. . . . La chose ne se passa pas ainsi qu'il l'a raconté dans cet article et le suivant; ceux qui savent l'histoire de ce temps là en parlent autrement et voicy le fait: Monsieur de Laval fit diverses tentatives à peu près comme celles qu'on void aujourd'huy dont le but a toujours été de prévaloir sur l'autorité du gouvernement; Monsieur de Tracy pour lors Vice-roy de ce pays, voyait tranquillement le désir de cette élévation, et comme c'estoit un homme dévot, il ne jugea pas à propos de prêter le colet à cette cohorte Ecclésiastique, dont la puissance étoit redoutable. Monsieur Talon dans cette conjoncture fit paroître une plus forte résolution et risqua pour l'intérest du Roy de perdre son crédit et sa fortune; il vid qu'il falloit étouffer cet orage dans son berceau et enfin par ses remontrances et par ses soins, il fit donner un arrêt favorable et tel qu'il se l'étoit proposé. Monsieur de Laval voyant alors qu'on l'avoit rengainé et qu'on l'avoit coupé à demi-vent, il creut suivant la politique de l'Eglise qu'il falloit attendre un temps plus favorable; ayant donc mis armes bas, on tacha de rajuster les affaires par l'entremise même de Monsieur de Tracy qui obtint de Monsieur Talon au jour de sa réconciliation que l'arrêt en question seroit rayé et batonné, non pas pour le désaprouver ou pour l'avoir trouvé contraire à toute bonne justice, comme le veut persuader le procureur général; mais afin que Monsieur de Laval ne fut pas reprochable de ses écarts et de ses injustes pretentions; ce fut une foiblesse à Monsieur Talon de s'être laissé vaincre par de telles soumissions.

. . . . Il faut être ici pour voir les menées qui se font tous les jours pour renverser le plan et les projets d'un Gouverneur. Il faut une tête aussi ferme et aussi plombée que celle de Monsieur le Comte pour se soutenir contres les ambusches que partout on lui dresse; s'il veut la paix cela suffit pour qu'on s'y oppose et qu'on crie que tout est perdu; s'il veut faire la guerre, on lui expose la ruine de la collonie. Il n'auroit pas tant d'affaires sur les bras, s'il n'avoit pas aboli un Hiericho qui etait une maison que Messieurs du Séminaire de Montreal avoient fait bâtir pour renfermer, disoient-ils, les filles de mauvaise vie. S'il avoit voulu leur permettre de prendre des soldats et leur donner des officiers pour aller dans les maisons arracher des femmes à minuit et couchées avec leurs maris, pour avoir été au bal ou en masque et les faire fesser jusques au sang dans ce Hiericho; s'il n'avait rien dit encore contre des Curés qui faisoient la ronde avec des soldats et qui obligeoient en esté les filles et les femmes à se renfermer à neuf heures chez elles, s'il avoit voulu déffendre de porter de la dentelle, s'il n'avoit rien dit sur ce qu'on refusoit la communion à des femmes de qualité pour avoir une fontange, s'il ne s'opposoit point encore aux excommunications qu'on jette à tort et à travers, aux scandales qui s'en suivent, s'il ne faisoit les officiers que par la voye des communautés, s'il vouloit déffendre le vin et l'eau de vie aux sauvages, s'il ne disoit mot sur le sujet des cures fixes et droits de patronage, si Monsieur le Comte estoit de ces avis-là, ce seroit assurément un homme sans pareil et il seroit bientôt sur la liste des plus grands saints, car on les canonise dans ce pais à bon marché.

K. *Canadian Curés—Education—Discipline*

Lettre du Marquis de Denonville au Ministre

(Extrait.) Archives de la Marine

A Quebec 15 Novembre, 1685

. . . Vous me permettrez, Monseigneur, de vous demander la grâce de faire quelques réflections sur les moyens d'occuper la jeunesse du pays, dans son bas âge, et dans l'âge le plus avancé, que je vous rende compte de mes pensées la dessus, puisque c'est une des choses la plus essentielle de la colonie.

Pour y parvenir, Monseigneur, le premier moyen à mon gré, est de multiplier le nombre des Curés, et de les rendre plus fixes et résidentaires, Mr. notre Evêque en est si convaincu par la connaissance qu'il a prise de son diocèse dans ses visites, et dans le voyage que nous avons fait ensemble, qu'il n'a point de plus grand empressement que de pouvoir contribuer à cet établissement qui serait un moyen sur, pour faire des écoles, auxquelles les curés s'occuperaient et ainsi accoutumeraient les enfans de bonne heure à s'assugétir et à s'occuper: Mais, Monseigneur, pour faire cet établissement utilement, il faudrait multiplier le nombre des curés jusques au nombre de cinquante et un. Le mémoire que je vous en envoye, vous fera assez bien voir, que si on les étend davantage et qu'il faille que les curés passent et repassent la rivière, comme ils font à présent pour faire leurs fonctions, ils employent avec bien du travail tout le temps qu'ils pourraient donner à instruire la jeunesse, si leurs cures étaient moins étendues. Outre cela, Monseigneur, à l'entrée et à la sortie de l'hiver, il y a prés de deux mois que l'on ne saurait passer la rivière, qui en bien des endroits a une lieue de largeur, et beaucoup plus en d'autres. Si bien que dans ces temps il faut que les malades demeurent sans aucun secours spirituel.

C'est une pitié, Monseigneur, que de voir l'ignorance dans laquelle les peuples éloignés du séjour des Curés vivent en ce pays, et les peines que les missionnaires et Curés se donnent pour y remédier en parcourant leurs cures, sur le pied qu'elles sont selon le mémoire que je vous en envoye. Vous y verrez, Monseigneur, le chemin qu'il leur faut faire pour visiter leur paroisses dans les rigueurs de l'hiver.

Puisque j'ai entamé l'affaire des Curés vous me permettrez d'achever de vous dire que pour la subsistance d'un curé selon les connaissances que j'ai pu prendre du pays, depuis que j'y suis, selon le prix des denrées, on ne saurait donner moins à un curé pour sa subsistance que quatre cent livres, monoye de France, attendu qu'il ne faut pas compter sur aucun revenant bon du dedans de l'Eglise. Il est bien vrai qu'il y a quelques cures qui sont mieux peuplées dont les dismes sont assez raisonables pour pouvoir suffir à leur entretien, mais il y en a très peu sur ce pied là.

J'ai trouvé ici dans le Séminaire de l'Evêché, le commencement de deux établissements qui seraient admirables pour la Colonie, si on lés pouvait augmenter, ce sont, Monseigneur, deux maisons où l'on retire des enfans pour les instruire, dans l'une on y met ceux auxquels on trouve de la disposition pour les lettres, auxquelles on s'attache de les former pour l'Eglise, qui dans la suite peuvent rendre plus de service que les prêtres Français étants plus faits que les autres aux fatigues et aux manieres du pays.

Dans l'autre maison on y met ceux qui ne sont propres que pour être artisans, et à ceux là on apprends des métiers. Je croirais que ce serait là un moyen admirable pour commencer un établissement de manufactures, qui sont absolument nécessaires pour le secours de ce pays.

Mr. notre Evêque est charmé de ces établissements, et voudrait bien être en état de les soutenir et augmenter. Mais comme tout cela ne se peut faire sans dépense tant pour l'augmentation du nombre des Curés que pour cette espèce de manufacture, et qu'il conviendrait d'en faire de grandes, pour y réussir, je ne vois qu'un moyen assuré pour cela, qui serait que le Roy voulut bien donner une grosse abbaye à Mr. notre Evêque sans l'attacher à l'Evêché, comme il n'a l'esprit et le cœur occupés que des soins de faire du bien aux pauvres et augmenter la foi et le salut des âmes, il est certain que Sa Majesté, aurait le plaisir de voir employer le revenu de ce bénéfice en bonnes et saintes œuvres, qui feraient merveille pour le bien de la colonie son soutien et son augmentation.

J'ai trouvé à Villemarie en l'isle de Montreal, un établissement de sœurs de la congrégation, sous la conduite de la sœur Bourgeois, qui fait de grands biens à toute la colonie, elles furent brulées l'an passé où elles perdirent tout; il seroit fort nécessaire qu'elles se rétablissent, elles n'ont pas le premier sol, j'y ai trouvé un autre établissement de filles de la providence qui travaillent ensemble, elles pourront commencer quelque manfacture de ce côté là, si vous avez la bonté de continuer la gratification de mil livres pour les laines, et mil livres pour apprendre à tricoter. Il y a encore un troisième établissement pour faire des maîtres d'écoles.

Il faut revenir s'il vous plait, Monseigneur, à voir ce qui se peut faire pour dissipliner les grands garçons, et pour donner de l'occupation aux enfans des gentilshommes et autres soidisans et vivans comme tels.

Avant tout, Monseigneur, vous me permettrez de vous dire que la noblesse de ce pays nouveau, est tout ce qu'il y a de plus gueux et que d'en augmenter le nombre est augmenter le nombre des fainéants. Un pays neuf demande des gens laborieux et industrieux, et qui mettent la main à la hache et à la pioche. Les enfans de nos conseillers ne sont pas plus laborieux, et n'ont de ressource que les bois, où ils font quelque traite, et la plupart font tous les désordres dont j'ai eu l'honneur de vous entretenir, je ne m'oublierai en rien de ce qu'il y aurait à faire pour les engager à entrer dans le commerce, mais comme nos nobles et conseillers sont tous fort pauvres et accablés de debtes, ils ne sauraient trouver de crédit pour un écu.

Le seul moyen qui me parait le plus assuré pour discipliner cette jeunesse serait que le Roy voulut bien entretenir en ce pays, quelques compagnies, dont on donnerait le commandement a gens d'authorité et de bonnes mœurs et appliqués, comme à Mr. le Chevalier de Caillière, à Mr. de Varénes, Gouverneur des trois Rivières, ou au Sr. Prévot, Major de Quebec, avec des Lieutenants du pays que l'on choisirait, lesquels ne devraient point avoir peine d'obeir, à ceux auxquels naturellement ils doivent obéir.

Chronology

1844   Elected Phi Beta Kappa, graduates from Harvard, and en-
              ters Harvard Law School.

1845   Publishes in *Knickerbocker, or New-York Monthly Magazine*
              five sketches about his early vacation excursions. Conducts
              research on Pontiac in New York, Pennsylvania, and
              Michigan.

1846   Graduates from Harvard Law School in January, resisting
              severe visual disability by having his sister read law books
              to him. Travels to New York and Pennsylvania for re-
              search on Pontiac's conspiracy, but by late March he is
              alarmingly overwrought. Goes then with his cousin
              Quincy Shaw, via St. Louis and the site of Pontiac's assas-
              sination, to the California and Oregon Trail and Fort Lar-
              amie. Hunts buffalo. Lives among the Sioux for several
              weeks. Joins their summer hunt for buffalo and their prep-
              arations for war, although he is weakened by dysentery
              and his nervous disorder. Breaks down completely soon
              after his return to New England. While convalescing at a
              clinic on Staten Island, New York, dictates *The Oregon
              Trail* to a member of his family or to a paid secretary.

1847   Publishes "The Oregon Trail. Or a Summer's Journey
              Out of Bounds" serially in *Knickerbocker*, the first install-
              ment signed "A Bostonian," the others under his own
              name, Francis Parkman, Jr.

1848   Begins work on *The Conspiracy of Pontiac,* first of a series
              of volumes on Anglo-French wars in North America. Ner-
              vous ailment persists; symptoms include feeling of ner-
              vous exhaustion and an inability to bear sunlight, to write
              with eyes open, or to concentrate on any intellectual sub-
              ject for more than a few minutes at a time. He follows the
              historian William H. Prescott's method: has documents
              read aloud to him and writes his notes and drafts of the
              manuscript in a box fitted with wire grids that guide his
              hand.

1849   Publishes *The California and Oregon Trail* ("California"
              added by publisher to exploit gold-rush fever), subse-
              quently issued as *The Oregon Trail.*

1850   Marries Catherine Scollay Bigelow, daughter of well-known Boston doctor. Three children: Grace Parkman Coffin (1851-1928), Francis Parkman III (1854-1857), Katherine Parkman Coolidge (1858-1900).

1851   Publishes *The History of the Conspiracy of Pontiac* (2 volumes). Permanently hampered by ailing knee joint.

1852   Publishes admiring essay on James Fenimore Cooper's life (1789–1851) and works, in *North American Review*.

1853–56   Illness forces him to abandon historical work. Begins novel for diversion and takes up study of horticulture.

1856   Publishes *Vassall Morton*, his partly autobiographical and only novel, emphasizing the protagonist's endurance through extreme physical and emotional hardship. Visits Montreal, Ottawa, and Quebec (October–November).

1857   His son, Francis, dies.

1858   His wife dies. His nervous illness worsens; he feels as if "a steel band is tightening around his head." Consults doctors in Paris, one of whom predicts he will go mad.

1859   Returns to Boston via Nice and Genoa and lives with mother and two sisters. His daughters live with his sister-in-law. Joins Massachusetts Horticultural Society and begins to spend summers at Jamaica Pond, where he pursues his horticultural avocation.

1862–63   Enters into business partnership to sell flowers, but firm dissolves within a year. Aroused by Civil War crisis and chagrined that poor health disqualifies him for service. Writes series of letters to Boston *Daily Advertiser* on decline of political leadership.

1865   Publication of *Pioneers of France in the New World*, a popular work, establishes his reputation as a historian. Travels to Richmond to collect Confederate papers for Boston Athenaeum.

1866   Publishes *The Book of Roses*, starts life-long correspondence with Abbé Henri-Raymond Casgrain of Canada, and begins series of Canadian visits for historical research.

1867   Travels for five weeks through Iowa, Illinois, Missouri,
            and Minnesota, gathering material on discovery of the
            Mississippi. *The Jesuits in North America in the Seventeenth
            Century* published.

1868   Elected to Board of Overseers at Harvard. In Paris (No-
            vember) to recover from illness. Consults material on Old
            Northwest and colonial New York, assisted by govern-
            ment archivist, Pierre Margry.

1869   Leaves Paris (March) for Boston. *The Discovery of the Great
            West* published.

1870   Publishes enlarged edition of *Pontiac* as *The Conspiracy of
            Pontiac and the Indian War after the Conquest of Canada*.
            Explores Mt. Desert, Maine. Publishes reminiscence of his
            stay (1844) at convent of Passionist Fathers in Rome.

1871   First meeting with Abbé Casgrain when Casgrain comes
            to Boston. Parkman makes brief visit to Nova Scotia and
            New Brunswick. Accepts professorship in horticulture at
            Bussey Institute (Harvard) but resigns in less than a year.
            After his mother dies, he shares Chestnut Street house
            with sister, Lizzie, for the rest of his life.

1872   In Europe (July–October) and sees Pierre Margry in
            Paris. Revises *The Oregon Trail*.

1873   Visits Canada for several weeks (August) to increase his
            knowledge of French-Canadians. Sees Casgrain. Elected
            to Saturday Club, which was founded by Emerson before
            the Civil War.

1874   *The Old Régime in Canada* published. Howells' review in-
            troduces Parkman to wider public in America and En-
            gland. Visits Quebec (July).

1875   Elected to the Harvard Corporation.

1876   Reviews first volume of Pierre Margry, *Découvertes et Établissements des Français dans l'Ouest et dans le Sud de l'Amérique Septentrionale (1614–1754), Mémoires et Documents originaux*, in *The Nation*. By persuading the U.S. Congress to subsidize this edition, Parkman gains access to materials he was not allowed to see when composing *The Discovery of the Great West*. Produces a new flower, *lilium Parkmanii*, and is elected to the Royal Historical Society in London. Visits Lake Champlain and Ottawa (August–September).

1877   Publishes *Count Frontenac and New France under Louis XIV*.

1878   Articles on suffrage and democracy (1878–1880) answered by feminists and liberals. Laval University's proposal to award Parkman honorary degree blocked by Catholic opposition offended by his anti-clericalism. Visits Lake George, Fort Ticonderoga, Quebec (November).

1879   Publishes *La Salle and the Discovery of the Great West*, an enlarged and revised edition of *The Discovery of the Great West* (1869), based on documents in Margry's collection. Awarded honorary degree from McGill University. Examines Louisbourg fortress in Quebec (August). *North American Review* publishes his "The Woman Question," which argues against women's suffrage.

1880   Helps to found St. Botolph Club in Boston.

1884   Publishes *Montcalm and Wolfe* ahead of its chronological place in *France and England in North America* because it has always been the most important part of the history for him and he wants to be sure to complete it before he dies.

1885   Travels through Florida to study the scenes of action described in *Pioneers of France*, places he had not been able to visit while writing *Pioneers* during the Civil War. Publishes revised edition of *Pioneers*, with new descriptions of Florida and some revisions of the section on Champlain. Awarded LL.D. by Williams College.

1887   Publishes *Some of the Reasons Against Woman Suffrage*. Travels to Europe for the last time.

1889   Awarded LL.D. by Harvard.

1890   Publishes *Our Common Schools* to defend the public schools against what he considers dangerous competition from parochial schools.

1892   Publishes *A Half-Century of Conflict*, the last two volumes of his *France and England in North America*.

1893   In June completes a new section to be added to the beginning of *The Old Régime in Canada* because he has gained access to documents that were unavailable when he published the first edition. Dies November 8, 1893, at Jamaica Pond, Boston. His *Journals* and *Letters* were published in 1947 and 1960, respectively.

Note on the Texts

This volume reprints the first four parts of Francis Parkman's seven-part history, *France and England in North America*; the remaining three parts are reprinted in the companion volume. Parkman published these seven works separately, under their individual titles, between 1865 and 1892. He referred to these separate titles as "parts" of a single enterprise, and he wrote, "Each work is designed to be a unit in itself, independently of the rest; but the whole, taken as a series, will form a connected history of France in the New World." The four parts (or works) that make up this volume—*Pioneers of France in the New World*, *The Jesuits in North America in the Seventeenth Century*, *La Salle and the Discovery of the Great West*, and *The Old Régime in Canada*—went through many reprintings during Parkman's lifetime. His publishers, Little, Brown & Co., referred to these issues as "editions," but, with two notable exceptions, they were reprinted from the original stereotype plates.

Parkman first conceived the idea of a comprehensive history of France and England in North America while an undergraduate at Harvard in the 1840s; and as early as 1851, when he published *The Conspiracy of Pontiac*, he tried out a version of the entire narrative, from the earliest explorations through the Indian wars of the mid-1760s. He spent the following forty years gathering the materials for his study, and he traveled widely in both Europe and North America to collect manuscripts, consult archives, and visit sites described in his history. This accumulation of data became a vital part of his project, and although his ill-health and the weakness of his eyes forced him to employ assistants to read aloud from his sources and to write from his dictation, he took great pains to insure the accuracy of his work. With the aid of readers, he corrected his own proofs and dictated changes directly to the printers.

He revised only three of the seven parts of *France and England in North America*, and the changes made in each of these volumes were designed to incorporate new material that had been originally unavailable. To approximate Parkman's own conception of *France and England in North America*, therefore, this volume reprints the first revised edition (1885) of *Pioneers of France in the New World* (first published 1865), the first edition (1867) of *The Jesuits in North America in the Seventeenth Century*, and the first revised editions (1879 and 1893, respectively) of *La Salle and the Discovery of the Great West* (first published in 1869 as *The Discovery of the Great West*) and *The Old Régime in Canada* (first published 1874). The text of *France and England in North America* in the edition of Parkman's *Complete Works* (1897–98) was prepared after his death and without his supervision. Collation has shown that, though the text is based on the same earlier editions chosen for inclusion here, unauthorized changes were introduced editorially in diction, orthography, and punctuation.

Pioneers of France was the first of the series to appear (in 1865), and it went through twenty-three reprintings before a new edition, completely reset, was published in 1885. Parkman added in this revised edition extensive descriptions of the natural settings in Florida, which the Civil War had prevented him from visiting twenty years earlier. He also revised his account of Champlain's Canadian explorations, correcting geographical errors and making minor changes in the prose. It is this twenty-fifth "edition," or the first revised edition, that is reprinted here.

Parkman's revisions of *The Jesuits in North America*, on the other hand, were virtually insignificant. For example, he subsequently qualified a generalization about American Indian families, changing "The child belongs to the clan" to "The child belongs, in most cases, to the clan." This volume reprints the first edition, and cites the later changes in the Notes.

When Parkman wrote the original version of the third part of his series (initially titled *The Discovery of the Great West*), his access to certain documentary evidence of central importance was blocked by the protectiveness and hard bargaining of the French archivist and scholar Pierre Margry. Parkman negotiated for years with Margry and political acquaintances in the United States to arrange the publication of Margry's seventeenth-century documents. Finally the United States

Congress, persuaded of the importance of the documents, granted money to subsidize Margry's edition and Parkman was at last allowed to see the sequestered evidence. The completely revised and reset edition of this third part of his history (retitled *La Salle and the Discovery of the Great West*), published just ten years after the first edition, uses the new material to justify the addition of La Salle's name to the title. Structural and stylistic revisions mark this version as the one Parkman wished to stand in his seven-part history, and it is the one reprinted here.

Parkman's revisions of *The Old Régime in Canada* consisted almost exclusively of additions. In his "Prefatory Note to the Revised Edition," dated June 18, 1893, he noted that he had been unable to study "certain indispensable papers" while preparing the first edition of 1874, and that he had now added a whole new section, "The Feudal Chiefs of Acadia," based on his belated receipt of those documents. For this new edition he also revised and enlarged some footnotes to take account of other new information, and he emended the table of contents and the index to reflect the added sections. The text for the body of the history, however, was printed from the plates of the original edition, with the new introductory section and the revised notes added. The three chapters that comprise "The Feudal Chiefs of Acadia" were first published in two installments in *The Atlantic Monthly* in January and February of 1893. This volume reprints the 1894 book edition rather than the periodical versions, assuming that the few changes in the new chapters were made by Parkman before he wrote the new preface, only five months before his death.

The standards for American English continue to fluctuate and in some ways were conspicuously different in earlier periods from what they are now. In nineteenth-century writings, for example, a word might be spelled in more than one way, even in the same work, and such variations might be carried into print. Commas were sometimes used expressively to suggest the movements of voice, and capitals were sometimes meant to give significances to a word beyond those it might have in its uncapitalized form. Since modernization would remove such effects, this volume has preserved the spelling, punctuation, capitalization, and wording of those first or first revised editions, which, of the available texts, appear most faithful to Parkman's intentions. It has also retained the original tables of contents despite their inconsistencies with the chapter headings found in the body of the text. The present volume represents the *texts* of these editions; it does not attempt to reproduce the features of their typographic design—such as the display capitalization of chapter openings.

Some changes, however, have been made. Parkman's references to page numbers have been changed to conform to the pages in these volumes, and his four indexes have been combined to make up a single one here. Obvious typographical errors have been corrected, and they are here listed: 61.34, as as; 143.34-35, Brebeuf; 159.4, Hochelega; 250.2, Lawrence.; 265.39, canibalism; 418.35, Iamais; 420.33, ceinture; 427.35, p.   ; 473.16, gain; 520.24, Enfin; 653.33 cœur.; 656.34, Algonquin; 659.11, "Apprenez; 659.12, Dieu."; 659.12, "Jamais,"; 659.12, "ne; 659.13, péchés."; 680.41, Ragueneau; 788.37, S˙; 796.8, Salle"; 883.34, *Paris*; 883.35, *Utrecht*; 890.34, reconciled; 956.5, Bay.[1]; 1000.21, him; 1000.40, *Douay in Le Clerc*; 1002.41, *Douay in Le Clerc*; 1003.42, *Douay in Le Clerc*; 1072.6, Argall; 1145.30, down; 1147.28, martys; 1234.37, captain; 1276.22, "Monsieur; 1276.28, aforesaid."; 1341.17, wierd; 1380.37, Louisburg.

Notes

In the notes below, the numbers refer to page and line of the present volume (the line count includes chapter headings). No note is made for material included in a standard desk-reference book. Notes printed at the foot of pages within the text are by the author.

PIONEERS OF FRANCE IN THE NEW WORLD

23.23   Mr. Bancroft] The United States historian, George Bancroft (1800–91), not H. H. Bancroft, who later sponsored histories of the peoples on the Pacific Coast of North and South America.

36.1   Crichton of France] An allusion to "the Admirable Crichton," the Scottish prodigy James Crichton (1560?–82), who was said to be extraordinarily versatile in letters, athletics, and military arts.

42.37   Marot] Clement Marot (1496–1544) was a French Lutheran poet who had to flee his country several times because of Catholic persecution. His translation of the Psalms was written during two years of relatively quiet service in the royal court (1537–39) and published in 1539.

59.29   the Bartrams] John Bartram and his son William were American botanists and naturalists. William's *Travels Through North and South Carolina, Georgia, East and West Florida . . .* was published in Philadelphia in 1791.

64.5–23   The wilderness . . . nature.] This description of the landscape was strengthened and revised after Parkman visited Florida in 1885, and the note at the end of the paragraph, "the universal tragedy of nature," did not appear in the first edition.

99.39–40   I . . . features.] Here again Parkman refers to his journey to Florida in 1885, after the first edition of *Pioneers* had been published.

108.11–12   and now . . . Seville,] Added in the edition of 1885.

153.10   Bayard] Pierre Terrail, Chevalier de Bayard (1473?–1524), the *"Chevalier sans peur et sans reproche."*

THE JESUITS IN NORTH AMERICA IN THE SEVENTEENTH CENTURY

371.9   The child . . . clan] Later Parkman qualified this statement: "The child belongs, in most cases, to the clan . . ."

371.24–25   with . . . it] Later Parkman qualified this statement: "with the rule of descent usually belonging to it . . ."

531.6   Simeon Stylites]   St. Simeon Stylites (390?–459) lived for thirty
years on a column sixty feet high, receiving from his disciples food and other
necessities, and counseling pilgrims who came to him for spiritual advice.

565.33   the evening mass]   Later Parkman revised this statement: "the
early mass . . ."

630.37   *Collection of Papers*, 166.]   Later Parkman changed the page number to 240.

LA SALLE AND THE DISCOVERY OF THE GREAT WEST

786.2   King Stork]   In the fable *The Frogs Desiring a King*, Jupiter first
gives the frogs a log, but they complain of its inactivity. Jupiter responds by
sending them a stork, which devours them.

797.22   wishing to marry]   That is, La Salle wished to marry.

THE OLD RÉGIME IN CANADA

1165.34–36   *Mémoire . . . 1637*.]   The 1894 edition erroneously repeated
the notes on page 1167. The correct notes are restored, here and at 1164.36,
according to the 1874 first edition.

1325.25–26   the close of Philip's War,]   That is, 1676.

1401.8   *Mésy*]   Parkman spells the name "Mézy" in the text.

LIBRARY OF CONGRESS CATALOGING IN PUBLICATION DATA

PARKMAN, FRANCIS, 1823–1893.
    France and England in North America.

    (The Library of America)
    Edited by David Levin.
    Includes bibliographical references and indexes.
    Contents: v.1.   Pioneers of France in the New World. The Jesuits in
North America in the seventeenth century. La Salle and the discovery of the
Great West. The old régime in Canada—v.2.   Count Frontenac and New
France under Louis XIV. A half-century of conflict. Montcalm and Wolfe.
    1. Canada—History—To 1763 (New France)   I. Levin, David,
1924–   .   II. Title.   III. Series: Library of America.
    F1030.P24   1983   971.01   82-18658
    ISBN 0-940450-10-0 (v.1)   AACR2
    ISBN 0-940450-11-9 (v.2)

Index

Abenakis, the, 913, 920, 934; form a part of La Salle's colony on the Illinois, 935 *note*.

Abenakis Indians, the adventure of Biencourt with the, 217, 218.

Abenaquis, where found, 347; ask for a missionary, 623.

Abraham, Plains of, whence the name, 633 *note*.

Absolutism in Canada, 1377–78.

Acadia, De Monts's scheme to colonize, 184; derivation of the name, 184 *note;* granted Madame de Guercheville, 221; the ruin of, 232–40; its conquest, and transfer, 1074; captured by England, and restored by treaty to France, 1103; Talon attempts to open communication with, 1254.

Acanibas, the, a tribe of Indians in the story of Sâgean, 1052–54.

Acau, 888 *note*. See *Accau*.

Accau, Michel, accompanies Hennepin on his trip to the Mississippi, 846, 883; the real leader of the party, 846 *note*, 888; various ways of spelling the name, 888 *note;* his life with the Sioux, 889–99; is again joined by Hennepin, 903.

Accault, Michel, 908 *note*. See *Accau*.

Adieu à la France, 196.

Adirondack Mountains, 255.

Adoption of prisoners as members of the tribe, 383, 556, 615, 696, 710.

Adventures and sufferings of an Algonquin woman, 615–17; of another, 617–19.

Agariata, Mohawk chief, hanged by Tracy, 1240 and *note*.

Agnier, a name for the Mohawks, 368 *note*.

Agniers, the, 811 *note*.

Agriculture, unprosperous state of, 1310.

Aigron, commander of the "Aimable," 973, 979; imprisoned in France, 980 *note*.

Aiguillon, Duchess d', founds a Hôtel-Dieu at Quebec, 527.

Aillebout, governor of Quebec, seizes Iroquois hostages, 1129; "insanely pious," 1180; removes to Montreal, 1188.

Aillebout, Madame d', mentioned, 1140, 1166; fantastic devotion of, 1350.

"Aimable," the, 973–75, 978; wreck of, 978–80; her cargo, 980 *note*.

Aire, lieutenant of Beaujeu, 975.

Akanseas, the, 923 *note*. See *Arkansas*.

Ako, 888 *note*. See *Accau*.

Alabama, State of, 29.

Albanel, a Jesuit explorer, 794.

Albanel, Jesuit, chaplain at Fort Chambly, 1239; explores to Hudson's Bay, 1254.

Albany, formerly Rensselaerswyck, its condition in 1643, 560.

Albany, 811, 855.

Alexander, Sir William, his attempts to colonize Acadia, 316; mentioned, 323; gift of land in America to, 1071; fails in an attack upon Fort Loméron, 1073; success of his expedition against French settlers at Acadia, 1074.

Alexander the Sixth, Pope, 155, 283.

Algonquin family, the, tribes of, 870 *note*.

Algonquin Indians, the, 183, 250 *note;* at Tadoussac, 243; a war feast at Quebec, 251; led by Champlain against the Iroquois, 252; their bad faith to him, 253; their encampment, 253, 255; their oracle, 254; their route towards the enemy, 256; meet the Iroquois, 257; the fight with the Iroquois, 258–59; their victory, 259; their retreat, 259; their settlement on the Ottawa, 275 *note;* on Lake Huron, 290 *note;* involved in a fight concerning an Iroquois prisoner, 303.

Algonquins, a comprehensive term, 345; regions occupied by them in 1535, 345–46; the designation, how ap-

Indies, the wealth of, 150.

Industrial School, the, established by Laval, 1354.

Industries, Canadian, 1311.

"Infernal Wolf," the, 481; a name for the Devil, *ib. note.*

Influence of the missions salutary, 622.

Initiatory fast for obtaining a guardian manitou, 386.

Inns, peculiar regulations touching, 1368.

Instructions for the missionaries to the Hurons, 439.

Intendant of Canada, rank and duties of, 1289, 1293; presides in the superior council, 1294; the ruling power

87; the power invested in him, 87; proposes to extend his dominion from Newfoundland to the South Sea, 88; his despatches to the King, 87, 88 *note;* his plans of settling the New World, 87–88; his fleet, 88; who comprised his company, 88; sails from Cadiz, 89; at the Canaries, 89; extract from his letter, 88–89 *note;* overtaken by a storm, 89; reaches Dominica, 90; some of his men desert, 90; arrival at Porto Rico, 90; quoted, 91; becalmed in the Bahama Channel, 91; invokes heavenly aid on his attack, 91; lands at Florida, 92; descries Ribaut's ships, 92; interviews the Frenchmen, 92, 93 *note;* attacks their ships, 93; founds St. Augustine, 94; escapes the attack of the French through divine interposition, 98; resolves to attack Fort Caroline, 98; marches with five hundred men, 99–101; attacks the fort, 101; his massacre of the Frenchmen, 102–03; his humanity to women and children, 103; ignominious treatment of his prisoners, 104; returns to St. Augustine, 106; his piety, 106; goes to reconnoitre, 107; marches to Matanzas Inlet, 108; the King's indorsement of his atrocities, 108, 119 *note;* interview with the Frenchmen, 108–10; the French surrender to him, 110; butchery of the French heretics, 111; quoted, concerning the massacre, 111–12; meets Ribaut at Anastasia Island, 113; interview with Ribaut, 113, 114; butchery of Ribaut and his party, 114; quoted concerning death of Ribaut, 115; his return to St. Augustine, 117; his deeds applauded, 117; his despatch to the King, 117; returns to Spain, 123; strengthens Fort Caroline, 127; his inscription over the massacred Frenchmen, 135; returns to America and rebuilds San Mateo, 138; summoned home, 138; death of, 138, 138 *note;* crushed French Protestantism in America, 139; quoted, 175.

Menomonies, the, 748; their place of abode, 750; meet Saint-Lusson at the Saut, 756; visited by Marquette and Joliet, 762.

Menou, Count Jules de, 1087 *note.*

Mercœur, Duc de, 180.

"Mer Douce," (Lake Huron), 290.

Mesnu, Peuvret de, secretary of Laval's council, 1200.

Messier, 867 *note.*

Messina, 806 *note.*

Messou. See *Manabozho.*

Mestigoit, an Indian hunter, 417, 418, 422, 425; his skill and courage, 429; helps Le Jeune to reach Quebec, *ib.*

Métairie, Jacques de la, 928 *note.*

Meules, proposes a remedy to suppress mendicity, 1367.

Meules. See *De Meules.*

Mexican fabrics found in Indian cemeteries, 455 *note.*

Mexico, conquest of, by Cortés, 26; mentioned, 30, 227, 804; La Salle's knowledge about it erroneous, 957 *note;* seizure of the mines a motive for colonization of Louisiana, 957 *note.*

Mexico, Gulf of, 742, 754, 764, 771, 929, 930, 958 *note;* claimed by Spain, 754, 954, 973, 1036; reached by La Salle, 927; forbidden to the French, 954.

Mézy, Saffray, Sieur de, appointed governor of Canada at Laval's request, 1200; under Laval's influence, 1200; sketch of, 1207; his piety and humility, 1208; change in his character, 1209; his quarrel with Laval, 1210; threatened with the wrath of the church, 1210; appeals to the Jesuits, 1210, 1211; removes Attorney-General Bourdon from office, 1212; reconstructs the council, 1213; banishes Bourdon and Villeray to France, 1213; is himself recalled, 1214; his death, 1214–15; his will, 1215; charges against Laval, 1216 *note.*

Miami, Fort, its situation, 912.

Miami or Miamis River, 743 *note,* 829.

Miamiha, its signification, 889.

Miamis, the, cannibalism among them, 362; their place of abode, 750; visited by Dablon, 751; remove to the banks

*This book is set in 10 point Linotron Galliard, a face
designed for photocomposition by Matthew Carter and based
on the sixteenth-century face Granjon. The paper is Olin
Nyalite and conforms to guidelines adopted by the Committee
on Book Longevity of the Council on Library Resources.
The binding material is Brillianta, a 100% rayon cloth
made by Van Heek-Scholco Textielfabrieken, Holland.
Composition by Haddon Craftsmen, Inc. and
The Clarinda Company. Printing and binding by R. R. Donnelley & Sons Company.
Designed by Bruce Campbell.*

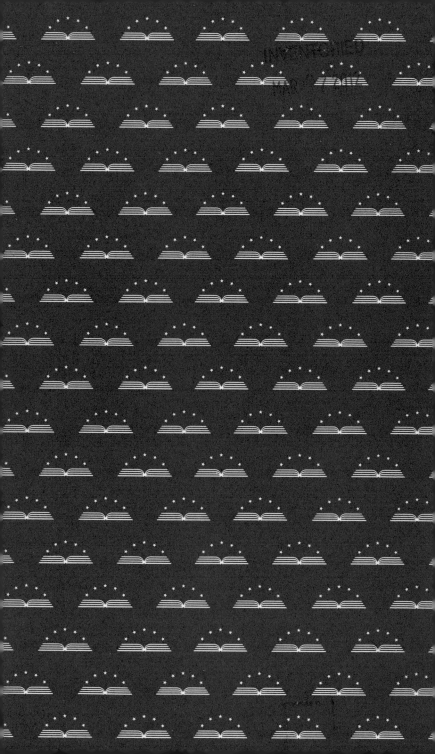